NUMBERS

THE PREACHER'S OUTLINE & SERMON BIBLE®

NUMBERS

THE PREACHER'S OUTLINE & SERMON BIBLE®

OLD TESTAMENT

NEW INTERNATIONAL VERSION

Leadership Ministries Worldwide
Chattanooga, TN

THE PREACHER'S OUTLINE & SERMON BIBLE® - NUMBERS
NEW INTERNATIONAL VERSION
Copyright © 2009 by
ALPHA-OMEGA MINISTRIES, INC.

All Rights Reserved

The Holy Bible, New International Version
Copyright © 1973, 1978, 1984 by International Bible Society
Used by permission of Zondervan Bible Publishers

All other Bible study aids,
references, indexes, reference materials
Copyright © 1991 by Alpha-Omega Ministries, Inc.

All rights reserved. No part of this publication may be reproduced, stored in a retrieval system, or transmitted in any form or by any means—electronic, mechanical, photo-copy, recording, or otherwise—without the prior permission of the copyright owners.

Previous Editions of **The Preacher's Outline & Sermon Bible®**,
New International Version NT   Copyright © 1998
King James Version   Copyright © 1991, 1996, 2000
by Alpha-Omega Ministries, Inc.

Please address all requests for information or permission to:
Leadership Ministries Worldwide
PO Box 21310
Chattanooga, TN 37424-0310
Ph.# (423) 855-2181   FAX (423) 855-8616   E-Mail info@outlinebible.org
http://www.outlinebible.org

Library of Congress Catalog Card Number: 00133499
International Standard Book Number: 978-1-57407-120-7

Printed in the United States of America

2   3   4   5   6   16   17   18   19   20

LEADERSHIP MINISTRIES WORLDWIDE

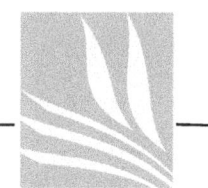

DEDICATED

To all the men and women of the world who preach and teach the Gospel of
our Lord Jesus Christ and
to the Mercy and Grace of God

- Demonstrated to us in Christ Jesus our Lord.

  In him we have redemption through his blood, the forgiveness of sins, in accordance with the riches of God's grace. (Ep.1:7)

- Out of the mercy and grace of God, His Word has flowed. Let every person know that God will have mercy upon him, forgiving and using him to fulfill His glorious plan of salvation.

  For God so loved the world that he gave his one and only Son, that whoever believes in him shall not perish but have eternal life. For God did not send his Son into the world to condemn the world, but to save the world through him. (Jn.3:16-17)

  This is good, and pleases God our Savior, who wants all men to be saved and to come to a knowledge of the truth. (1 Ti.2:3-4)

The Preacher's Outline & Sermon Bible®

is written for God's servants to use in their study, teaching, and preaching of God's Holy Word…

- to share the Word of God with the world.
- to help believers, both ministers and laypersons, in their understanding, preaching, and teaching of God's Word.
- to do everything we possibly can to lead men, women, boys, and girls to give their hearts and lives to Jesus Christ and to secure the eternal life that He offers.
- to do all we can to minister to the needy of the world.
- to give Jesus Christ His proper place, the place the Word gives Him. Therefore, no work of Leadership Ministries Worldwide—no Outline Bible Resources—will ever be personalized.

ACKNOWLEDGMENTS AND BIBLIOGRAPHY

Every child of God is precious to the LORD and deeply loved. And every child as a servant of the LORD touches the lives of those who come in contact with him or his ministry. The writing ministries of the following servants have touched this work, and we are grateful that God brought their writings our way. We hereby acknowledge their ministry to us, being fully aware that there are so many others down through the years whose writings have touched our lives and who deserve mention, but whose names have faded from our memory. May our wonderful LORD continue to bless the ministries of these dear servants—and the ministries of us all—as we diligently labor to reach the world for Christ and to meet the desperate needs of those who suffer so much.

THE REFERENCE WORKS

Archer, Gleason L. Jr. *A Survey of Old Testament Introduction*. Chicago, IL: Moody Bible Institute of Chicago, 1974.

Atlas of the World. Hammond Concise Edition. Maplewood, NJ: Hammond Incorporated, 1993.

Baker's Dictionary of Theology. Everett F. Harrison, Editor-in-Chief. Grand Rapids, MI: Baker Book House, 1960.

Barker, William P. *Everyone in the Bible*. Westwood, NJ: Fleming H. Revell Co., 1966.

Brown, Francis. *The New Brown-Driver-Briggs-Gesenius Hebrew-English Lexicon*. Peabody, MA: Hendrickson Publishers, 1979.

Cruden's Complete Concordance of the Old & New Testament. Philadelphia, PA: The John C. Winston Co., 1930.

Dake, Finis Jennings. *Dake's Annotated Reference Bible, The Holy Bible*. Lawrenceville, GA: Dake Bible Sales, Inc., 1963.

Elwell, Walter A., Editor. *The Evangelical Dictionary of Theology*. Grand Rapids, MI: Baker Book House, 1984.

Funk & Wagnalls Standard Desk Dictionary. Lippincott & Crowell, Publishers, 1980, Vol.2.

Geisler, Norman. *A Popular Survey of the Old Testament*. Grand Rapids, MI: Baker Book House, 1977.

Good News Bible. Old Testament: © American Bible Society, 1976. New Testament: © American Bible Society, 1966, 1971, 1976. Collins World.

Good, Joseph. *Rosh HaShanah and the Messianic Kingdom to Come*. Pt. Arthur, TX: Hatikva Ministries, 1989.

Harrison, Roland Kenneth. *Introduction to the Old Testament*. Grand Rapids, MI: Eerdmans Publishing Company, 1969.

Josephus, Flavius. *Complete Works*. Grand Rapids, MI: Kregel Publications, 1981.

Kelley, Page H. *Exodus: Called for Redemptive Mission. January Bible Study*. Nashville, TN: Convention Press, 1977.

Kohlenberger, John R. III. *The Interlinear NIV Hebrew-English Old Testament*. Grand Rapids, MI: Zondervan Publishing House, 1987.

Kouffman, Donald T. *The Dictionary of Religious Terms*. Westwood, NJ: Fleming H. Revell Co., 1967.

Life Application® Bible. Wheaton, IL: Tyndale House Publishers, Inc., 1991.

Life Application® Study Bible. New International Version. Tyndale House Publishers, Inc.: Wheaton, IL 1991 and Zondervan Publishing House: Grand Rapids, MI, 1984.

Lindsell, Harold and Woodbridge, Charles J. *A Handbook of Christian Truth*. Westwood, NJ: Fleming H. Revell Company, A Division of Baker Book House, 1953.

Lipis, Joan R. *Celebrate Passover Haggadah*. San Francisco, CA: Purple Pomegranate Productions, 1993.

Living Quotations for Christians. Edited by Sherwood Eliot Wirt and Kersten Beckstrom. New York, NY: Harper & Row, Publishers, 1974.

Lockyer, Herbert. *All the Books and Chapters of the Bible*. Grand Rapids, MI: Zondervan Publishing House, 1966.

———. *All the Men of the Bible*. Grand Rapids, MI: Zondervan Publishing House, 1958.

———. *All the Miracles of the Bible*. Grand Rapids, MI: Zondervan Publishing House, 1961.

———. *All the Parables of the Bible*. Grand Rapids, MI: Zondervan Publishing House, 1963.

———. *The Women of the Bible*. Grand Rapids, MI: Zondervan Publishing House, 1967.

Martin, Alfred. *Survey of the Scriptures, Part I, II, III*. Chicago, IL: Moody Bible Institute of Chicago, 1961.

McDowell, Josh. *Evidence That Demands a Verdict*, Vol.1. San Bernardino, CA: Here's Life Publishers, Inc., 1979.

Miller, Madeleine S. & J. Lane. *Harper's Bible Dictionary*. New York, NY: Harper & Row Publishers, 1961.

Nave, Orville J. *Nave's Topical Bible*. Nashville, TN: The Southwestern Company. Copyright © by J.B. Henderson, 1921.

New American Standard Bible, Reference Edition. La Habra, CA: The Lockman Foundation, 1975.

New American Standard Bible, Updated Edition. La Habra, CA: The Lockman Foundation, 1995.

Acknowledgments and Bibliography

The Reference Works
(continued)

New Bible Dictionary, 3rd Edition. Leicester, England: Universities & Colleges Christian Fellowship, 1996.

New International Version Study Bible. Grand Rapids, MI: Zondervan Bible Publishers, 1985.

New Living Translation, Holy Bible. Wheaton, IL: Tyndale House Publishers, Inc., 1996.

NIV Exhaustive Concordance. Grand Rapids, MI: Zondervan Corporation, 1990.

Orr, William. *How We May Know That God Is*. Wheaton, IL: Van Kampen Press, n.d.

Owens, John Joseph. *Analytical Key to the Old Testament*, Vols.1, 2, 3. Grand Rapids, MI: Baker Book House, 1989.

Payne, J. Barton. *Encyclopedia of Biblical Prophecy*. New York, NY: Harper & Row, Publishers, 1973.

Pilgrim Edition, Holy Bible. New York, NY: Oxford University Press, 1952.

Ridout, Samuel. *Lectures on the Tabernacle*. New York, NY: Loizeaux Brothers, Inc., 1914.

Roget's 21st Century Thesaurus, Edited by Barbara Ann Kipfer. New York, NY: Dell Publishing, 1992.

Rosen, Ceil and Moishe. *Christ in the Passover*. Chicago, IL: Moody Press, 1978.

Slemming, C.W. *Made According To Pattern*. Fort Washington, PA: Christian Literature Crusade, 1983.

Smith, William. *Smith's Bible Dictionary*. Peabody, MA: Hendrickson Publishers, n.d.

Soltau, Henry W. *The Holy Vessels and Furniture of the Tabernacle*. Grand Rapids, MI: Kregel Publications, 1971.

———. *The Tabernacle the Priesthood and the Offerings*. Grand Rapids, MI: Kregel Publications, 1972.

Stone, Nathan J. *Names of God*. Chicago, IL: Moody Press, 1944.

Strong, James. *Strong's Exhaustive Concordance of the Bible*. Nashville, TN: Thomas Nelson, Inc., 1990.

———. *The Tabernacle of Israel*. Grand Rapids, MI: Kregel Publications, 1987.

The Amplified Bible. Scripture taken from THE AMPLIFIED BIBLE, Old Testament copyright © 1965, 1987 by the Zondervan Corporation. The Amplified New Testament copyright © 1958, 1987 by The Lockman Foundation. Used by permission.

The Hebrew-Greek Key Study Bible, New International Version. Spiros Zodhiates, Th.D., Executive Editor. Chattanooga, TN: AMG Publishers, 1996.

The Holy Bible in Four Translations. Minneapolis, MN: Worldwide Publications. Copyright © The Iversen-Norman Associates: New York, NY, 1972.

The Interlinear Bible, Vol.1, 2, & 3, Translated by Jay P. Green, Sr. Grand Rapids, MI: Baker Book House Company, 1976.

The International Standard Bible Encyclopaedia, Edited by James Orr. Grand Rapids, MI: Eerdmans Publishing Company, 1939.

The NASB Greek/Hebrew Dictionary and Concordance. La Habra, CA: The Lockman Foundation, 1988.

The New Compact Bible Dictionary, Edited by T. Alton Bryant. Grand Rapids, MI: Zondervan Publishing House, 1967. Used by permission of Zondervan Publishing House.

The New Scofield Reference Bible, Edited by C.I. Scofield. New York, NY: Oxford University Press, 1967.

The New Thompson Chain Reference Bible. Indianapolis, IN: B.B. Kirkbride Bible Co., Inc., 1964.

The Open Bible. Nashville, TN: Thomas Nelson Publishers, 1975.

The Quest Study Bible. New International Version. Grand Rapids, MI: Zondervan Publishing House, 1994.

The Zondervan Pictorial Encyclopedia of the Bible, Vol.1. Merrill C. Tenney, Editor. Grand Rapids, MI: Zondervan Publishing House, 1982.

Theological Wordbook of the Old Testament, Edited by R. Laird Harris. Chicago, IL: Moody Bible Institute of Chicago, 1980.

Unger, Merrill F. & William White, Jr. *Nelson's Expository Dictionary of the Old Testament*. Nashville, TN: Thomas Nelson Publishers, 1980.

Vine, W.E., Merrill F. Unger, William White, Jr. *Vine's Complete Expository Dictionary of Old and New Testament Words*. Nashville, TN: Thomas Nelson Publishers, 1985.

Webster's Seventh New Collegiate Dictionary. Springfield, MA: G. & C. Merriam Company, Publishers, 1971.

Wilson, William. *Wilson's Old Testament Word Studies*. McLean, VA: MacDonald Publishing Company, n.d.

Wood, Leon. *A Survey of Israel's History*. Grand Rapids, MI: Zondervan Publishing House, 1982.

Young, Edward J. *An Introduction to the Old Testament*. Grand Rapids, MI: Eerdmans Publishing Company, 1964.

Young, Robert. *Young's Analytical Concordance to the Bible*. Grand Rapids, MI: Eerdmans Publishing Company, n.d.

Zehr, Paul M. *Glimpses of the Tabernacle*. Lancaster, PA: Mennonite Information Center, 1976.

Acknowledgments and Bibliography

The Commentaries

Ashley, Timothy R. *The Book of Numbers*. "The New International Commentary on the Old Testament." Grand Rapids, MI: Eerdmans Publishing Co., 1993.

Barclay, William. *The Old Law & The New Law*. Edinburgh, Scotland: The Saint Andrew Press, 1972.

Barnes' Notes, Exodus to Esther. F.C. Cook, Editor. Grand Rapids, MI: Baker Book House, n.d.

Briscoe, Stuart. *The Ten Commandments*. Wheaton, IL: Harold Shaw Publishers, 1986.

Burroughs, P.E., D.D. *Old Testament Studies*. Nashville, TN: Sunday School Board, Southern Baptist Convention, 1915.

Bush, George. *Numbers*. Minneapolis, MN: Klock & Klock Christian Publishers, Inc., 1981.

Gill, John. *Gill's Commentary*, Vol.1. Grand Rapids, MI: Baker Book House, 1980.

Henry, Matthew. *Matthew Henry's Commentary*, 6 Volumes. Old Tappan, NJ: Fleming H. Revell Co., n.d.

Heslop, William G. *Nuggets from Numbers*. Grand Rapids, MI: Kregel Publications, 1975.

Jones, Kenneth E. *The Book of Numbers*. "Shield Bible Study Series." Grand Rapids, MI: Baker Book House, 1972.

Keil-Delitzsch. *Commentary on the Old Testament*, Vol.1. Grand Rapids, MI: Eerdmans Publishing Company, n.d.

Mackintosh, C.H. *Notes on Numbers*. Neptune, NJ: Loizeaux Brothers, 1965.

Maclaren, Alexander. *Expositions of Holy Scripture*, 11 Vols. Grand Rapids, MI: Eerdmans Publishing Company, 1952-59.

McGee, J. Vernon. *Thru The Bible*, Vol.1. Nashville, TN: Thomas Nelson Publishers, 1981.

Noordtzij, A. *Bible Student's Commentary, Numbers*. Grand Rapids, MI: Zondervan Publishing House, 1983.

Olford, Stephen. *The Tabernacle, Camping With God*. Neptune, NJ: Loizeaux Brothers, 1971.

Philips, James. *The Preacher's Commentary on Numbers*. Nashville, TN: Word Publishing, 1987, 2003.

Pink, Arthur W. *The Ten Commandments*. Grand Rapids, MI: Baker Books, 1994.

Poole, Matthew. *Matthew Poole's Commentary on the Holy Bible*. Peabody, MA: Hendrickson Publishers, n.d.

Saphir, Adolph. *Christ and Israel*. Grand Rapids, MI: Kregel Publications, n.d.

Spurgeon, C.H. *Spurgeon's Sermon Notes. Genesis to Malachi*. Westwood, NJ: Fleming H. Revell Co., n.d.

Strauss, Lehman. *Devotional Studies in Galatians & Ephesians*. Neptune, NJ: Loizeaux Brothers, 1957.

The Biblical Illustrator, Leviticus—Numbers. Edited by Exell, Joseph S. Grand Rapids, MI: Baker Book House, 1966.

The Complete Biblical Library: The Old Testament. Volume 3: Study Bible, Leviticus–Numbers. Springfield, MO: World Library Press, Inc., 1995.

The Expositor's Bible Commentary, Vol.2. Gaebelein, Frank E., Editor. Grand Rapids, MI: Zondervan Publishing House, 1990.

The Interpreter's Bible, 12 Vols. New York, NY: Abingdon Press, 1956.

The Pulpit Commentary. 23 Volumes. Edited by H.D.M. Spence & Joseph S. Exell. Grand Rapids, MI: Eerdmans Publishing Company, 1950.

Thomas, W.H. Griffith. *Through the Pentateuch Chapter by Chapter*. Grand Rapids, MI: Eerdmans Publishing Company, 1957.

Von Rad, Gerhard. *Deuteronomy*. Germany: SCM Press Ltd, 1966. USA Rights by The Westminster Press: Philadelphia, PA.

Wiersbe, Warren W. *Be Obedient*. Wheaton, IL: Victor Books, 1991.

Wuest, Kenneth S. *Ephesians and Colossians*. "Word Studies in the Greek New Testament," Vol.1. Grand Rapids, MI: Eerdmans Publishing Co., 1966.

Youngblood, Ronald F. *Exodus*. Chicago, IL: Moody Press, 1983.

ABBREVIATIONS

&	=	and		O.T.	=	Old Testament
bc.	=	because		p./pp.	=	page/pages
concl.	=	conclusion		pt.	=	point
cp.	=	compare		quest.	=	question
ct.	=	contrast		rel.	=	religion
e.g.	=	for example		rgt.	=	righteousness
f.	=	following		thru	=	through
illust.	=	illustration		v./vv.	=	verse/verses
N.T.	=	New Testament		vs.	=	versus

THE BOOKS OF THE OLD TESTAMENT

Book	Abbreviation	Chapters	Book	Abbreviation	Chapters
GENESIS	Gen. or Ge.	50	Ecclesiastes	Eccl. or Ec.	12
Exodus	Ex.	40	The Song of Solomon	S. of Sol. or Song	8
Leviticus	Lev. or Le.	27	Isaiah	Is.	66
Numbers	Num. or Nu.	36	Jeremiah	Jer. or Je.	52
Deuteronomy	Dt. or De.	34	Lamentations	Lam.	5
Joshua	Josh. or Jos.	24	Ezekiel	Ezk. or Eze.	48
Judges	Judg. or Jud.	21	Daniel	Dan. or Da.	12
Ruth	Ruth or Ru.	4	Hosea	Hos. or Ho.	14
1 Samuel	1 Sam. or 1 S.	31	Joel	Joel	3
2 Samuel	2 Sam. or 2 S.	24	Amos	Amos or Am.	9
1 Kings	1 Ki. or 1 K.	22	Obadiah	Obad. or Ob.	1
2 Kings	2 Ki. or 2 K.	25	Jonah	Jon. or Jona.	4
1 Chronicles	1 Chron. or 1 Chr.	29	Micah	Mic. or Mi.	7
2 Chronicles	2 Chron. or 2 Chr.	36	Nahum	Nah. or Na.	3
Ezra	Ezra or Ezr.	10	Habakkuk	Hab.	3
Nehemiah	Neh. or Ne.	13	Zephaniah	Zeph. or Zep.	3
Esther	Est.	10	Haggai	Hag.	2
Job	Job or Jb.	42	Zechariah	Zech. or Zec.	14
Psalms	Ps.	150	Malachi	Mal.	4
Proverbs	Pr.	31			

THE BOOKS OF THE NEW TESTAMENT

Book	Abbreviation	Chapters	Book	Abbreviation	Chapters
MATTHEW	Mt.	28	1 Timothy	1 Tim. or 1 Ti.	6
Mark	Mk.	16	2 Timothy	2 Tim. or 2 Ti.	4
Luke	Lk. or Lu.	24	Titus	Tit.	3
John	Jn.	21	Philemon	Phile. or Phm.	1
The Acts	Acts or Ac.	28	Hebrews	Heb. or He.	13
Romans	Ro.	16	James	Jas. or Js.	5
1 Corinthians	1 Cor. or 1 Co.	16	1 Peter	1 Pt. or 1 Pe.	5
2 Corinthians	2 Cor. or 2 Co.	13	2 Peter	2 Pt. or 2 Pe.	3
Galatians	Gal. or Ga.	6	1 John	1 Jn.	5
Ephesians	Eph. or Ep.	6	2 John	2 Jn.	1
Philippians	Ph.	4	3 John	3 Jn.	1
Colossians	Col.	4	Jude	Jude	1
1 Thessalonians	1 Th.	5	Revelation	Rev. or Re.	22
2 Thessalonians	2 Th.	3			

HOW TO USE
The Preacher's Outline & Sermon Bible®

Follow these easy steps to gain maximum benefit from The POSB.

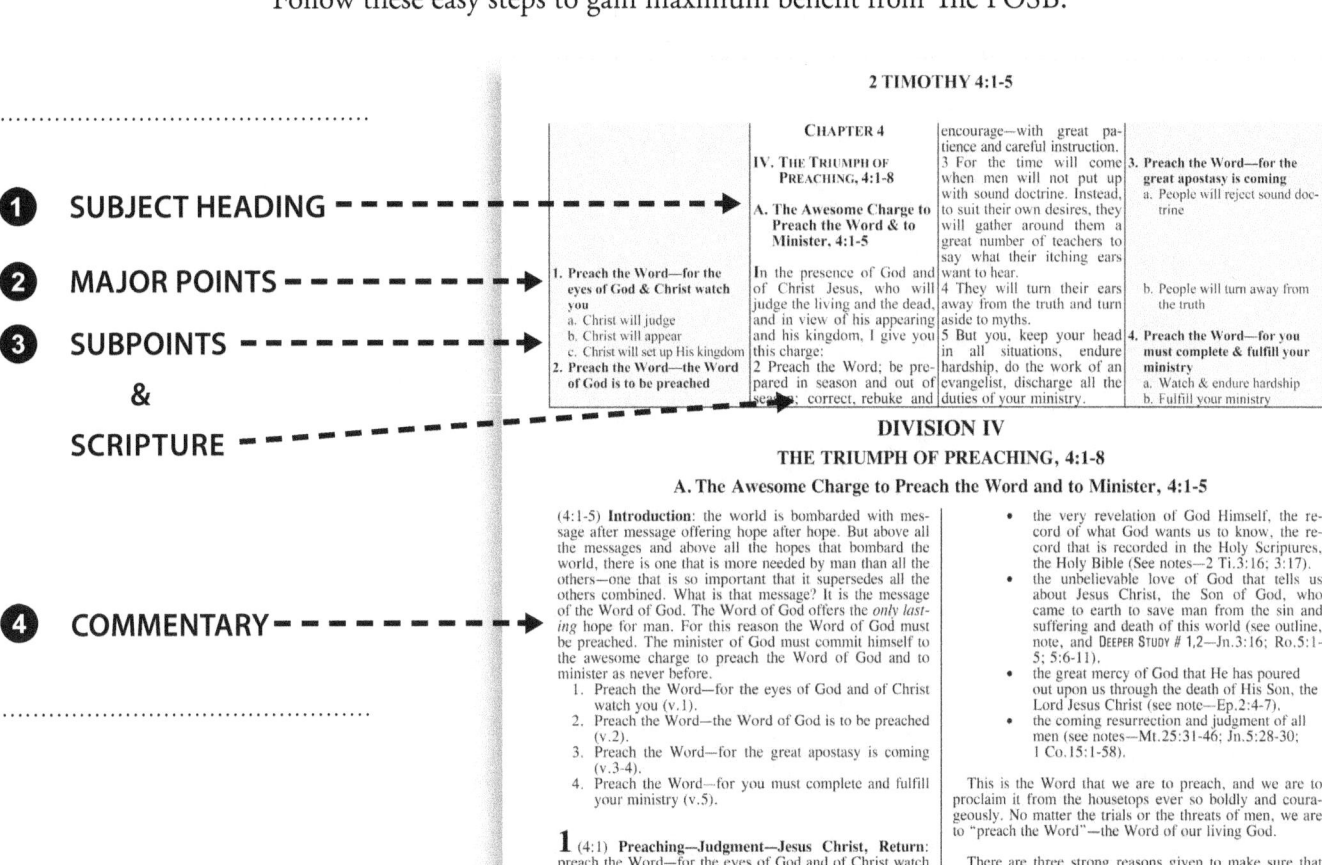

❶ Glance at the **Subject Heading**. Think about it for a moment.

❷ Glance at the **Subject Heading** again, and then the **Major Points** (1, 2, 3, etc.). Do this several times, reviewing them together while quickly grasping the overall subject.

❸ Glance at **both** the **Major Points** and **Subpoints** together while reading the **Scripture**. Do this slower than Step 2. Note how these points sit directly beside the related verse and simply restate what the Scripture is saying—in Outline form.

❹ Next read the **Commentary**. Note that the *Major Point Numbers* in the Outline match those in the Commentary. When applicable, a small raised number (**DS1, DS2, etc.**) at the end of a Subject Heading or Outline Point directs you to a related **Deeper Study** in the Commentary (not shown here).

Finally, read the **Thoughts** and **Support Scripture** (not shown).

As you read and re-read, pray that the Holy Spirit will bring to your attention exactly what you should preach and teach. May God bless you richly as you study and teach His Word.

The POSB contains everything you need for sermon preparation:

1. **The Subject Heading** describes the overall theme of the passage and is located directly above the Scripture (keyed *alphabetically*).

2. **Major Points** are keyed with an outline *number* guiding you to related commentary. Note that the Commentary includes *"Thoughts"* (life application) and abundant Supporting Scriptures.

3. **Subpoints** explain and clarify the Scripture as needed.

4. **Commentary** is fully researched and developed for every point.
   - **Thoughts (in bold)** help apply the Scripture to real life.
   - **Deeper Studies** provide in-depth discussions of key words or phrases.

Woe to me if I do not preach the gospel!
(1 Co.9:16)

TABLE OF CONTENTS
NUMBERS

	PAGE
INTRODUCTION TO NUMBERS	1
GENERAL OUTLINE OF NUMBERS	11
DIVISION I. THE PREPARATION FOR THE MARCH TO THE PROMISED LAND, 1:1–10:36	13
DIVISION II. THE TRAGIC, DEVASTATING FAILURE OF ISRAEL: WHY PEOPLE FORFEIT THEIR RIGHT TO ENTER THE PROMISED LAND, 11:1–14:45	103
DIVISION III. THE FORTY LONG YEARS OF WILDERNESS WANDERINGS: A PICTURE OF THE BELIEVER'S PILGRIMAGE THROUGH THIS WORLD AS HE PREPARES TO ENTER THE PROMISED LAND, 15:1–25:18	132
DIVISION IV. THE PREPARATION FOR THE MARCH INTO THE PROMISED LAND, 26:1–36:13	241
PRACTICAL BIBLE HELPS AND RESOURCES	327
CHART 1: THE TABERNACLE IN THE WILDERNESS	329
CHART 2: THE TABERNACLE INTERIOR	330
CHART 3: THE ENCAMPMENT OF THE TRIBES	331
CHART 4: THE MARCHING POSITIONS OF THE TRIBES	331
MAP 1: THE DESERT OR WILDERNESS WANDERINGS OF ISRAEL	332
MAP 2: THE BORDERS OF THE PROMISED LAND OF CANAAN AND THE MISSION OF THE TWELVE SPIES	333
TYPES, SYMBOLS, AND PICTURES	
➢ Alphabetical Outline	334
➢ Chronological Outline	339
OUTLINE & SUBJECT INDEX	343

THE FOURTH BOOK OF MOSES, CALLED
NUMBERS

AUTHOR: Moses, the great lawgiver and prophet of God. Moses was the great leader who led the Israelites from Egyptian slavery and through the wilderness wanderings. The evidence is strong, very strong, that Moses is the author.

1. The book of *Numbers* itself claims to have been written by Moses.

> The LORD spoke to Moses in the Tent of Meeting in the Desert of Sinai on the first day of the second month of the second year after the Israelites came out of Egypt. He said (Nu. 1:1).
>
> Here are the stages in the journey of the Israelites when they came out of Egypt by divisions under the leadership of Moses and Aaron. At the LORD's command Moses recorded the stages in their journey. This is their journey by stages (Nu. 33:1-2).

2. Jesus Christ Himself implied that Moses was the author by stating that it was Moses who had actually lifted up the snake in the desert.

> Just as Moses lifted up the snake in the desert, so the Son of Man must be lifted up (Jn.3:14; see Nu.21:9).
>
> So Moses made a bronze snake and put it up on a pole. Then when anyone was bitten by a snake and looked at the bronze snake, he lived (Nu.21:9).

3. The New Testament mentions several events in *Numbers* that associate them with Moses.

> I have indeed seen the oppression of my people in Egypt. I have heard their groaning and have come down to set them free. Now come, I will send you back to Egypt.' "This is the same Moses whom they had rejected with the words, 'Who made you ruler and judge?' He was sent to be their ruler and deliverer by God himself, through the angel who appeared to him in the bush. He led them out of Egypt and did wonders and miraculous signs in Egypt, at the Red Sea and for forty years in the desert (Ac.7:34-36).
>
> For I do not want you to be ignorant of the fact, brothers, that our forefathers were all under the cloud and that they all passed through the sea. They were all baptized into Moses in the cloud and in the sea. They all ate the same spiritual food and drank the same spiritual drink; for they drank from the spiritual rock that accompanied them, and that rock was Christ. Nevertheless, God was not pleased with most of them; their bodies were scattered over the desert (1 Co.10:1-5).
>
> Moses was faithful as a servant in all God's house, testifying to what would be said in the future. But Christ is faithful as a son over God's house. And we are his house, if we hold on to our courage and the hope of which we boast. So, as the Holy Spirit says: "Today, if you hear his voice, do not harden your hearts as you did in the rebellion, during the time of testing in the desert, where your fathers tested and tried me and for forty years saw what I did (He.3:5-9).

4. Without exception, the Old Testament always refers to Moses as the author of the Pentateuch, the first five books of the Bible (Ex.17:14; 24:4; 34:27; Nu.33:1-2; Jos.1:7-8; 8:31-32; 1 K.2:3; 8:9, 53; 2 K.10:31; 14:6; Ezr.6:18; Ne.13:1; Da.9:11-13; Mal.4:4).

5. Without exception, the New Testament always refers to Moses as the author of the Pentateuch, which includes *Numbers* (Mt.8:4; 19:7-8; 23:2; Mk.1:44; 7:10; 10:3-4; 12:19, 26; Lu.5:14; 16:29-31; 20:37; 24:27, 44; Jn.1:17; 3:14; 5:45-46; 6:32; 7:19, 22-23; Ac.3:22; 13:39; 15:1, 5, 21; 26:22; 28:23; Ro.10:5, 19; 1 Co.9:9; 2 Co.3:15).

For several centuries now there has been a popular theory surrounding the Bible that is called *the documentary hypothesis*. This theory says there are four major sources for the Pentateuch, each of which was written sometime between 900–400 B.C. These sources are said to be...

- *J* (for Jehovah or Yahweh). This represents the writer or source that used the Hebrew name *Jehovah* or *Yahweh* for God throughout the Pentateuch.
- *E* (for Elohim). This represents the writer or source that used the Hebrew name *Elohim* for God.
- *D* (for Deuteronomist). This represents the writer or source that recorded the different accounts of the law throughout the Pentateuch.
- *P* (for Priestly). This represents the writer or source that recorded the information dealing with the *priests*.

The first person to suggest the theory of *the documentary hypothesis* was a French physician, Jean Astruc, in 1752. Note that he was a physician, not a theologian. The theory was later picked up by the German historian and Biblical writer, J.G. Eichhorn in 1787. However, *the documentary hypothesis* was not thoroughly developed and popularized until Julius Wellhausen who lived from 1844-1918 (Victor Hamilton. *The Book of Genesis*, Chapters 1–17, p.13).

The Expositor's Bible Commentary has an excellent statement in answer to the critics of the Mosaic authorship:

> *Many of the arguments given by [critical] scholars may be countered by evidence from within the Bible and from what we now know concerning patterns of writing in the ancient world that run directly counter to the basic postulates of standard critical theory. But the most telling distinction between non-evangelical scholars and evangelical scholars is one's starting point. When a person begins with the...divine inspiration of Scripture and...inerrancy, then the dates of Scripture are read quite differently than if one does not begin with a belief in the inspiration, authority, and inerrancy of Scripture....*
>
> *We may conclude...that the essential content of the book did come from Moses, the servant of the LORD. His name is repeatedly in the book; he is the principal human protagonist in the book; and he is the one with the training, opportunity, motivation, and opportunity to produce the book. It is almost axiomatic to observe that God brings good out of even*

INTRODUCTION TO NUMBERS

the most grim, the most dismal situations. We may reckon that one of the good things that came out of the ghastly waste of life and energy of the condemned, rebellious first generation of the Hebrew people was the opportunity the desert experience afforded Moses, prince and prophet of God, to write the books that are associated so strongly with his name.

If Moses was the principal writer of the Book of Numbers, then we may assert that he would have written these accounts over a lengthy period that included the stay of Israel in the Desert of Sinai as well as on their encampments en route to the plains of Moab. Much of the unevenness of style may be occasioned by the periodic nature of the writing. But the unity of the book overrides its uneven style. The Book of Numbers may be regarded as The Memoirs of Moses in the Desert Years.[1]

DATE: Moses obviously wrote *Numbers* sometime between 1445-1406 B.C., perhaps closer to 1406 B.C. This much is known: *Numbers* covers thirty-eight of the forty years of wilderness wanderings. The history of *Numbers* picks up in the 13th month after the exodus from Egyptian slavery and ends with the forty years of wandering. Therefore, the book could not have been completed until after Israel's wanderings in the desert. (See *Introduction, Date—Genesis, Volume 1 or 2* for more discussion.) However, the book was completed sometime before Moses died (De. 31:24).

TO WHOM WRITTEN: the people of Israel and all people in general. However it is important to note this fact: there are at least two groups of believers seen in the book of *Numbers*. The first group is the first generation of believers who were delivered from Egyptian slavery by the miraculous power of God. But this group of believers failed God miserably. They became gripped with a spirit of unbelief and rebellion, complaining and grumbling against God and His dear servant Moses. As a result, they were condemned to die in the desert wilderness. They were barred from the promised land and never allowed to enter it.

The other group seen in the book of *Numbers* is the second generation of believers, the sons and daughters of the first generation. When the first generation rebelled against God, God did not hold the children accountable, not any child twenty years old or younger. God had condemned the first generation to wander about in the desert wilderness until the last adult had died. The forty years of wilderness wanderings were used by God to discipline and strengthen the children, teaching them not to follow after their parents in unbelief and rebellion. The children were taught the great hope of the promised land, to diligently seek after the inheritance promised by God. The events covered in the great book of *Numbers* stood as a strong warning to the second generation of believers, a warning not to imitate their parents in unbelief and rebellion. The great book of *Numbers* also stands as a strong warning to every believer of every generation, a warning not to follow in the steps of unbelief and rebellion against God.

PURPOSE: three purposes are seen in the great book of *Numbers*.

1. The *Historical Purpose*: to give a permanent record of Israel's *Wilderness Wanderings*, of the people's journey from Mt. Sinai to the border of the promised land of Canaan. This period of history covered about 38½ years of the 40 year period known as the *wilderness wanderings*. It was during this period that the first generation of believers died out under the judgment of God. But of paramount importance is this fact: it was during the *wilderness wanderings* that God took the children—the second generation of believers—and trained them. God prepared them—toughened, strengthened, and disciplined them—to conquer and inherit the promised land.

2. The *Doctrinal or Spiritual Purpose*: several doctrinal or spiritual lessons are clearly seen as the great Book of *Numbers* is studied.

   a. We learn more and more about endurance and hope, about how to grow in endurance and hope as we march to the promised land of God.

> For everything that was written in the past was written to teach us, so that through endurance and the encouragement of the Scriptures we might have hope (Ro.15:4).

   b. We learn that we must not lust nor set our hearts on evil things as the Israelites did.

> Now these things occurred as examples to keep us from setting our hearts on evil things as they did (1 Co.10:6).

   c. We learn that any of us can fall into unbelief and rebellion, complaining and grumbling. Even Moses did (Nu.20:1-13). This stands as a clear warning to us all: we can arouse God's judgment to strike out against us, just as it did against Moses and the Israelites.

> Do not be idolaters, as some of them were; as it is written: "The people sat down to eat and drink and got up to indulge in pagan revelry." We should not commit sexual immorality, as some of them did--and in one day twenty-three thousand of them died. We should not test the Lord, as some of them did—and were killed by snakes. And do not grumble, as some of them did—and were killed by the destroying angel. These things happened to them as examples and were written down as warnings for us, on whom the fulfillment of the ages has come (1 Co.10:7-11).
>
> So, as the Holy Spirit says: "Today, if you hear his voice, do not harden your hearts as you did in the rebellion, during the time of testing in the desert, where your fathers tested and tried me and for forty years saw what I did. That is why I was angry with that generation, and I said, 'Their hearts are always going astray, and they have not known my ways.' So I declared on oath in my anger, 'They shall never enter my rest.'" See to it, brothers, that none of you has a sinful, unbelieving heart that turns away from the living God (He.3:7-12).
>
> As has just been said: "Today, if you hear his voice, do not harden your hearts as you did in the rebellion." Who were they who heard and rebelled? Were they not all

---

[1] *The Expositor's Bible Commentary*, Vol.2. Frank E. Gaebelein, Editor. (Grand Rapids, MI: Zondervan Publishing House, 1990), pp.665, 668.

INTRODUCTION TO NUMBERS

those Moses led out of Egypt? And with whom was he angry for forty years? Was it not with those who sinned, whose bodies fell in the desert? And to whom did God swear that they would never enter his rest if not to those who disobeyed? So we see that they were not able to enter, because of their unbelief. Therefore, since the promise of entering his rest still stands, let us be careful that none of you be found to have fallen short of it (He.3:15-4:1).

(See Introduction, *Special Features—Numbers* for other doctrinal and spiritual lessons, especially points 1, 3, 7, 11, 12, 13, 14, 15, 16, 17, 18, 19, 21, 23.)

3. The *Christological or Christ-Centered Purpose*: the great book of *Numbers* points to Jesus Christ.
   a. Jesus Christ is the fulfillment of the atoning sacrifice. (See outline and notes—Nu.6:13-20; 7:10-88; 9:1-14; 21:4-20; 15:1-29; 19:1-22; 21:1-35; 28:1-29:40.)

   The next day John saw Jesus coming toward him and said, "Look, the Lamb of God, who takes away the sin of the world! (Jn.1:29).
   When Christ came as high priest of the good things that are already here, he went through the greater and more perfect tabernacle that is not man-made, that is to say, not a part of this creation. He did not enter by means of the blood of goats and calves; but he entered the Most Holy Place once for all by his own blood, having obtained eternal redemption. The blood of goats and bulls and the ashes of a heifer sprinkled on those who are ceremonially unclean sanctify them so that they are outwardly clean. How much more, then, will the blood of Christ, who through the eternal Spirit offered himself unblemished to God, cleanse our consciences from acts that lead to death, so that we may serve the living God! (He.9:11-14).

   b. Jesus Christ is the Light of the world as symbolized by the Lampstand. (See outline and notes—Nu.8:1-4.)

   In him was life, and that life was the light of men (Jn.1:4).
   When Jesus spoke again to the people, he said, "I am the light of the world. Whoever follows me will never walk in darkness, but will have the light of life." (Jn.8:12).
   I have come into the world as a light, so that no one who believes in me should stay in darkness (Jn.12:46).

   c. Jesus Christ is the coming Deliverer—the great Star and Scepter—who will conquer all enemies and rule over them, sitting upon the very throne of David and of God Himself. (See outline and notes—Nu.24:17-19.)

   "I have told you these things, so that in me you may have peace. In this world you will have trouble. But take heart! I have overcome the world." (Jn.16:33).
   For as in Adam all die, so in Christ all will be made alive. But each in his own turn: Christ, the firstfruits; then, when he comes, those who belong to him. Then the end will come, when he hands over the kingdom to God the Father after he has destroyed all dominion, authority and power (1 Co.15:22-24).
   To him who overcomes, I will give the right to sit with me on my throne, just as I overcame and sat down with my Father on his throne (Re.3:21).
   Of the increase of his government and peace there will be no end. He will reign on David's throne and over his kingdom, establishing and upholding it with justice and righteousness from that time on and forever. The zeal of the LORD Almighty will accomplish this (Is.9:7; see Is.53:12).
   "The days are coming," declares the LORD, "when I will raise up to David a righteous Branch, a King who will reign wisely and do what is just and right in the land (Je.23:5; see Da.7:14).

SPECIAL FEATURES:

1. *Numbers* is "A Great Book That Focuses upon the Promised Land of God." What is *the promised land* of God? What is the inheritance God promised to Abraham and his descendants (believers)? What does Scripture say? Because of the importance of the promised land in *Numbers*, the subject is being mentioned here as point 1 of the *Special Features*. But because of the length of the point, it is actually being discussed in point 26 of the *Special Features*.

2. *Numbers* is "The Great Book on the Believer's Pilgrimage." As the believer marches through this life, he encounters trial after trial and temptation after temptation. Life is full of pitfalls and enemies that oppose his reaching the promised land of God. *Numbers* takes the pilgrimage of Israel and pictures the believer's pilgrimage through life as he faces trials and temptations, pitfalls, and enemies. The subject of the entire book is the pilgrimage of the Israelites as they march to the promised land of God. The very subjects of the outlines of *Numbers* clearly show this.

3. *Numbers* is "A Great Book on the History of Salvation." Through trial after trial, this book shows how God saves His people and leads them to the promised land of God.

4. *Numbers* is "A Great Book That Covers the Only Acceptable Approach and Worship of God." There is a right way and a wrong way to approach and worship God. This is stressed time and again: the only acceptable way to approach and worship God is through the atoning sacrifice, a symbol of God's dear Son, the Lord Jesus Christ. (See outline and notes—Nu.6:22-27; 7:10-88; 8:1-4; 9:1-14; 15:1-16; 19:1-22; 28:1-29:40.)

5. *Numbers* is "The Great Book That Distinguishes—Covers the Differences—Between the Priests and the Levites." (See outline and notes—Nu.1:47-54; 3:1-51; 8:5-26; 18:1-32; 26:57-62.)

6. *Numbers* is "The Great Book of Census Records." All together, six census polls were taken:
   ⇒ There were two major census polls taken of the nation as a whole (see outline and notes—Nu.1:1-2:34; 26:1-56).

INTRODUCTION TO NUMBERS

⇒ There were three census polls taken of the Levites (see outline and notes—Nu.3:1-39; 4:21-49; 26:57-62).

⇒ There was one census taken of the firstborn sons of the nation (see outline and note—Nu.3:40-51).

7. *Numbers* is "A Great Book on the Preparation for the March to the Promised Land of God: A Symbol of Heaven and of Spiritual Conquest and Rest." (See outline and notes—Nu.1:1-10:36; 26:1-36:13.)

8. *Numbers* is "The Great Book That Covers the Tragic, Devastating Failure of Israel: The Book that Shows Why People Forfeit Their Right to Enter the Promised Land of God." (See outline and notes—Nu.11:1-14:45.)

9. *Numbers* is "The Great Book That Covers the Long, Difficult *Wilderness Wanderings* of Israel." This is a picture of the *Believer's Pilgrimage* through this world as he prepares to enter the promised land of God. (See outline and notes—Nu.1:1-36:13.)

10. *Numbers* is "The Great Book That Covers the Interesting Story of Balaam, his Donkey, and his Encounters with God." (See outline and notes—Nu. 22:1-25:18.)

11. *Numbers* is "A Great Book That Covers the Very Heart of the Nazarite Vow." The Nazarite vow was a very special provision for the person who longed to draw closer to God. (See outline and notes—Nu. 6:1-27.)

12. *Numbers* is "The Great Book on Holiness." It demonstrates the utter necessity to live a holy life—a righteous life, a life totally set apart to God. Every chapter either stresses or illustrates the obligation of the believer to live a holy life, a life totally set apart to God.

13. *Numbers* is "A Great Book of Types, Symbols, and Pictures of God's Dear Son, the Lord Jesus Christ." (See chart on Types, Symbols, and Pictures.) A large number of types are clearly seen, focusing upon such major subjects as these:

⇒ The atoning sacrifice of Jesus Christ as the Savior of the world (see outline and notes—Nu.6:13-20; 7:10-88; 9:1-14; 21:4-20; 15:1-29; 19:1-22; 21:1-35; 28:1-29:40).

⇒ The symbol of Christ, the Light of the world (see outline and notes—Nu.8:1-4).

⇒ The symbol of Christ as the Coming Deliverer—the great Star and Scepter—who will conquer all enemies and rule over them (see outline and notes—Nu.24:17-19).

14. *Numbers* is "A Book That Reveals the Chilling Reality of God's Justice and Judgment." God chastises and disciplines believers when they sin. Moreover, He condemns and executes judgment upon evil unbelievers who rebel and sin beyond repentance. (See outline and notes—Nu.11:1-14:45; 16:1-50; 20:7-13; 21:1-35; 25:1-18.)

15. *Numbers* is "A Great Book That Demonstrates the Awesome Importance of Intercessory Prayer." Time and again the great prayer warrior Moses is seen interceding for God's mercy in times of terrible stress, and God is seen intervening. God saved His people because of prayer. The lesson is forceful: God hears the desperate cry of those who cry out to Him. Intercession works. (See outline and notes—Nu.21:4-20, esp. 7; 11:1-3; 11:4-35; 12:13-16; 13:1-14:45,, esp. 10-25; 16:1-50, esp. 1-15; 20:2-6; 21:4-20, esp. 7; 27:14-17.)

16. *Numbers* is "The Great Book That Demonstrates the Breathtaking Guidance of God." God guides His people day by day. To teach this wonderful truth, God gave Israel the *pillar of cloud* or the *fiery cloud* by day and by night. This was a cloud that symbolized God's presence. The cloud hung right above the Tabernacle. At night it glowed like fire so the people could see and have a continued, unbroken assurance of God's presence. God guided His people by moving the cloud when it was time for the Israelites to march and by stopping the cloud over a particular spot when it was time for the people to set up camp. (See outline and notes—Nu.8:15-23; 10:11-12; 10:33-34; see 11:25; 12:5, 10, 14:14; 16:42.)

17. *Numbers* is "The Great Book That Reveals the Amazing Mercy and Grace of God." Time and again, God had mercy and showered His grace upon His people despite their terrible unbelief and disobedience. He chastised them in order to correct them and to keep them from damaging themselves beyond repair. But in every case, He had mercy and bestowed His grace upon them. He gave them another chance. This He did until they went beyond repentance and repair, went to a point when they would never turn to follow Him wholeheartedly. Up to this point, God had mercy upon them. *Numbers* is the great book revealing the mercy and grace of God. (Every chapter and every event reveals the mercy and grace of God, but special occasions would be these: Nu. 11:1-14:45; 16:1-50; 17:11-13; 19;1-22; 20:2-13; 21:4-9; 21:33-35; 22:1-25:18; 27:12-25; 28:1-29:40; 31:1-54; 33:1-56; 34:1-29; 35:1-34.)

18. *Numbers* is "The Great Book That Stresses the Word of God." "The LORD spoke" is used over 150 times in twenty-plus ways throughout the book. This fact points strongly to the inspiration of *Numbers*, that the great book is "God-inspired" (2 Ti.3:16).

19. *Numbers* is "A Great Book That Shows the Absolute Necessity of Obedience." Disobedience results in judgment. This great book exposes the disobedient heart and behavior of Israel and the judgment that fell upon them. This alone shows the great importance of obedience. But more than this, the positive message of obedience is magnificently demonstrated in the life of Moses and even in the behavior of the Israelites when they were faithful. Practically every page of *Numbers* stresses obedience. The fact that the people obeyed "just as the LORD commanded" is stated over thirty times.

20. *Numbers* is "A Great Book That Unfolds the History of Redemption." Every page stresses this one glorious fact: God saves and delivers His people day by day as they march to the promised land of God. He strengthens His dear people to conquer all the trials and enemies of life. He gives them whatever provisions are necessary to reach the destination of the promised land. It is His redemptive power—His salvation and deliverance—that assures the believer's inheritance, the inheritance of heaven, of living eternally with God in the new heavens and earth.

21. *Numbers* is "One of the Great Books Written as a Strong Warning to People."

> **For everything that was written in the past was written to teach us, so that through endurance and the encouragement of the Scriptures we might have hope (Ro. 15:4).**
>
> **Now these things occurred as examples to keep us from setting our hearts on evil things as they did (1 Co. 10:6).**
>
> **These things happened to them as examples and were written down as warnings for us, on whom the fulfillment of the ages has come (1 Co. 10:11).**

22. *Numbers* is "The Great Book That Reveals the Overwhelming Patience of God." God is patient, long-suffering. Patience is one of the basic traits of God's character, and He

INTRODUCTION TO NUMBERS

demonstrated His patience time and again with His erring people. There is a verse in *Numbers* that describes God's patience in descriptive terms. In fact, the verse describes the full nature of God that comes into play when dealing with us:

> 'The LORD is slow to anger, abounding in love and forgiving sin and rebellion. Yet he does not leave the guilty unpunished; he punishes the children for the sin of the fathers to the third and fourth generation.' (Nu. 14:18. See *Special Features*, pt.17—*Introduction to Numbers* for more discussion.)

23. *Numbers* is "The Great Book with an Uninspiring Title." The English name comes from the Greek title of the book (Arithmoi). This title was obviously given to the book because of the census records found throughout (Chapters 1-4, 26). "In the wilderness" is the Hebrew title given to the book, being taken from Chapter 1:5. *Numbers* sounds more like a math book than a spiritual book. Nevertheless, *Numbers* is a very spiritual book, one of the *greatest spiritual books* ever written. It is the history of the believer's pilgrimage upon earth as he marches to the promised land of God and of heaven. Just glance at the major subjects covered by this great book:

24. *Numbers* is "The Great Book That Exposes the Terrible Evil of Unbelief and Rebellion, of Complaining and Grumbling." This was the constant sin of Israel, the sin that led to their tragic, devastating judgment. They were barred from ever entering the promised land of God. They never received their inheritance because of the sins of unbelief and rebellion against God. Even Moses himself lost the right to enter the promised land. Neither he nor the first generation of believers ever knew the spiritual rest and the conquering power of God over the enemies of the promised land. (See outline and notes—Nu.11:1–14:45; 16:1-50; 20:2-13; 21:4-20; 25:1-18; 32:1-42; 33:5-49.)

    I. THE PREPARATION FOR THE MARCH TO THE PROMISED LAND, 1:1–10:36
    II. THE TRAGIC, DEVASTATING FAILURE OF ISRAEL: WHY PEOPLE FORFEIT THEIR RIGHT TO ENTER THE PROMISED LAND, 11:1–14:45
    III. THE FORTY LONG YEARS OF WILDERNESS WANDERINGS: A PICTURE OF THE BELIEVER'S PILGRIMAGE THROUGH THIS WORLD AS HE PREPARES TO ENTER THE PROMISED LAND, 15:1–25:18
    IV. THE PREPARATION FOR THE MARCH TO ENTER THE PROMISED LAND, 26:1–36:13

25. *Numbers* is "A Great Book of Instructive and Practical Laws." Note these subjects:
⇒ The Basic Laws That Keep God's People United and Pure: How God's People Must Live Pure Lives, 5:1-31
⇒ The Special Provision Instituted for Drawing Closer to God—the Nazarite Vow and the Special Benediction of God upon His People: The Importance and Seriousness of Vows, 6:1-27
⇒ Event 1—God Gave Various Laws to Help Govern His People: Being Reassured and Prepared for the Promised Land, 15:1-41
⇒ Event 4—God Spelled Out the Service of the Priests and Levites: The Duties, Support, and Tithing of God's Ministers, 18:1-32
⇒ Event 5—God Gave the Law to Govern the Offering of the Red Heifer and the Cleansing Water: A Symbol of Christ, His Sacrifice and Cleansing Power, 19:1-22
⇒ The Basic Law that Gave Women an Inheritance in the Promised Land: Five Women of Enormous Courage, Faith, and Hope, 27:1-11
⇒ The Offerings and Sacrifices Commanded by the LORD: The Picture of Man's Need to Continually Approach and Worship God through the Atonement Secured by the Sacrifice (a Symbol of God's Dear Son, the Lord Jesus Christ), 28:1–29:40
⇒ The Laws that Govern Vows: The Obligation to Keep Vows and to Consider Others in Making Vows, 30:1-16
⇒ The Women Who Inherited Property: A Picture of Strong Faith in the Promised Land—a Symbol of Spiritual Conquest and Rest and of Heaven, 37:1-13

26. *Numbers* is "A Great Book That Focuses upon the Promised Land of God." What is *the promised land* of God? What is the inheritance God promised to Abraham and his descendants (believers)? What does Scripture say? As stated earlier, because of the importance of the promised land in *Numbers*, the subject was mentioned as point 1 of the *Special Features*. But because of the length of the point, it is actually being discussed here in point 26.

Scripture teaches that God promised to give Abraham and his descendants the *promised land* of Canaan (Ge.12:1). God actually promised land to Abraham. But note:

⇒ The land was only promised: it lay out in the future; it was not to be immediately possessed. The land was just what believers have called it for centuries, *the promised land*. It was to be the great hope of Abraham. This is the reason the land of Canaan is referred to as *the promised land*.

All Abraham had to go on was the promise of God, on what God had said. Abraham had to step out in faith and believe God's Word—His promise—about *the promised land*. Note several facts about this great promise to Abraham.

    a. *The promised land* definitely refers to Palestine, the land of Israel. This is clearly stated by God time and again.
      1) Note God's promise to Abraham.

> Abram traveled through the land as far as the site of the great tree of Moreh at Shechem. At that time the Canaanites were in the land. The LORD appeared to Abram and said, "To your offspring I will give this land." So he built an altar there to the LORD, who had appeared to him (Ge. 12:6-7).
>
> The LORD said to Abram after Lot had parted from him, "Lift up your eyes from where you are and look north and south, east and west. All the land that you see I will give to you and your offspring forever….Go, walk through the length and breadth of the land, for I am giving it to you." (Ge. 13:14-15, 17).
>
> He also said to him, "I am the LORD, who brought you out of Ur of the Chaldeans to give you this land to

INTRODUCTION TO NUMBERS

take possession of it."...On that day the LORD made a covenant with Abram and said, "To your descendants I give this land, from the river of Egypt to the great river, the Euphrates—the land of the Kenites, Kenizzites, Kadmonites, Hittites, Perizzites, Rephaites, Amorites, Canaanites, Girgashites and Jebusites." (Ge. 15:7, 18-21).

The whole land of Canaan, where you are now an alien, I will give as an everlasting possession to you and your descendants after you; and I will be their God." (Ge. 17:8).

2) Note God's promise to Abraham's son, Isaac.

Stay in this land for a while, and I will be with you and will bless you. For to you and your descendants I will give all these lands and will confirm the oath I swore to your father Abraham (Ge. 26:3).

3) Note God's promise to Abraham's grandson, Jacob.

There above it stood the LORD, and he said: "I am the LORD, the God of your father Abraham and the God of Isaac. I will give you and your descendants the land on which you are lying (Ge. 28:13).

The land I gave to Abraham and Isaac I also give to you, and I will give this land to your descendants after you." (Ge. 35:12).

b. *The promised land* definitely refers to heaven. The promised land of Canaan is a symbol (a type, a picture, an illustration) of heaven, of God's promise to the believer that he will inherit heaven, the new heavens and earth. Note two facts:
1) God's promised land refers to *the whole world*. It is *the whole world* that Abraham and believers are to *inherit*.

It was not through law that Abraham and his offspring received the promise that he would be heir of the world, but through the righteousness that comes by faith (Ro. 4:13).

The inheritance of the whole world could only refer to the *new heavens and earth*—the new universe—that God is going to recreate in the end time. It could not refer to a corruptible universe that is deteriorating, wasting away, and running down, that would eventually cease to exist millions of years from now—cease to exist just by the natural process of time. (See outlines and notes—2 Pe.3:1-18 for more discussion.)

But the day of the Lord will come like a thief. The heavens will disappear with a roar; the elements will be destroyed by fire, and the earth and everything in it will be laid bare. Since everything will be destroyed in this way, what kind of people ought you to be? You ought to live holy and godly lives as you look forward to the day of God and speed its coming. That day will bring about the destruction of the heavens by fire, and the elements will melt in the heat. But in keeping with his promise we are looking forward to a new heaven and a new earth, the home of righteousness (2 Pe. 3:10-13).

Then I saw a new heaven and a new earth, for the first heaven and the first earth had passed away, and there was no longer any sea. I saw the Holy City, the new Jerusalem, coming down out of heaven from God, prepared as a bride beautifully dressed for her husband. And I heard a loud voice from the throne saying, "Now the dwelling of God is with men, and he will live with them. They will be his people, and God himself will be with them and be their God. He will wipe every tear from their eyes. There will be no more death or mourning or crying or pain, for the old order of things has passed away." (Re. 21:1-4).

In the beginning you laid the foundations of the earth, and the heavens are the work of your hands. They will perish, but you remain; they will all wear out like a garment. Like clothing you will change them and they will be discarded. But you remain the same, and your years will never end (Ps. 102:25-27).

All the stars of the heavens will be dissolved and the sky rolled up like a scroll; all the starry host will fall like withered leaves from the vine, like shriveled figs from the fig tree (Is. 34:4).

Lift up your eyes to the heavens, look at the earth beneath; the heavens will vanish like smoke, the earth will wear out like a garment and its inhabitants die like flies. But my salvation will last forever, my righteousness will never fail (Is. 51:6).

"Behold, I will create new heavens and a new earth. The former things will not be remembered, nor will they come to mind (Is. 65:17).

"As the new heavens and the new earth that I make will endure before me," declares the LORD, "so will your name and descendants endure (Is. 66:22).

2) God's promised land refers to *a heavenly country* and *a heavenly city*. It is a heavenly home—a heavenly country and city that are eternal—that Abraham and believers are to inherit. Note how clearly Scripture states this:

By faith Abraham, when called to go to a place he would later receive as his inheritance, obeyed and went, even though he did not know where he was going. By faith he made his home in the promised land like a stranger in a foreign country; he lived in tents, as did Isaac and Jacob, who were heirs with him of the same promise. For he was looking forward to the city with foundations, whose architect and builder is God....All these people were still living by faith when they died. They did not receive the things promised; they only saw them and welcomed them from a distance. And they admitted that they were aliens and strangers on earth. People who say such things show that they are looking for a country of their own. If they had been thinking of the country they had left, they would have had opportunity to return. Instead, they were longing for a better country--a heavenly one. Therefore God is not ashamed to be called their God, for he has prepared a city for them (He. 11:8-10, 13-16).

But you have come to Mount Zion, to the heavenly Jerusalem, the city of the living God. You have come to thousands upon thousands of angels in joyful assembly (He. 12:22).

For here we do not have an enduring city [a perfect heavenly city], but we are looking for the city that is to come (He. 13:14).

I saw the Holy City, the new Jerusalem, coming down out of heaven from God, prepared as a bride beautifully dressed for her husband. And I heard a loud voice from the throne saying, "Now the dwelling of God is with men, and he will live with them. They will be his people, and God himself will be with them and be their God. He will wipe every tear from their eyes. There will be no more death or mourning or crying or pain, for the old order of things has passed away." (Re. 21:2-4).

And he carried me away in the Spirit to a mountain great and high, and showed me the Holy City, Jerusalem, coming down out of heaven from God (Re. 21:10).

c. *The promised land* represented many things to Abraham.
  1) The promised land was the assurance of *a personal inheritance*: the possession of a new country, of his own property with all its good land, wealth, and rights. Abraham believed that he would live in a new city within his own land and country—all given by God Himself. And the land was to be forever, for it was promised by the eternal God Himself.

  Note this, for it is important: Abraham's hope was for a permanent, eternal city and country. True, he was physically journeying all throughout the promised land of Canaan, believing that God was going to give him and his seed (descendents) the land of Canaan. But while he was journeying, his hope was for the permanent, eternal city and country of God. Abraham knew that God's promised land referred to the heavenly as well as to the earthly land. Note how clearly Scripture states this:

⇒ All the land that you see I will give to you and your offspring forever (Ge. 13:15).

God's promise included the eternal, permanent possession of the promised land, and Abraham knew this.

⇒ By faith he made his home in the promised land like a stranger in a foreign country; he lived in tents, as did Isaac and Jacob, who were heirs with him of the same promise. For he was looking forward to the city with foundations, whose architect and builder is God (He. 11:9-10).

This refers to the heavenly Jerusalem, the capital of the new heavens and earth (see He.12:22; 13:14. See pt.2 above. Also see note—Re.21:2.)

⇒ All these people were still living by faith when they died. They did not receive the things promised; they only saw them and welcomed them from a distance. And they admitted that they were aliens and strangers on earth. People who say such things show that they are looking for a country of their own. If they had been thinking of the country they had left, they would have had opportunity to return. Instead, they were longing for a better country—a heavenly one. Therefore God is not ashamed to be called their God, for he has prepared a city for them (He. 11:13-16).

Note v.15: it clearly states that Abraham's mind was on the heavenly and eternal country. If it had not been, he would have returned to his former home. He would have never wandered about, suffering the hardships he bore.

Thought 1. Note how the promise given to Abraham parallels the promise given to the believer. Abraham was to inherit *the promised land* if he turned away from the world and followed God. We are to inherit *the promised land of heaven* if we turn away from the world and follow God. *The promised land* is a symbol, a type, a picture of heaven.
(1) The promise given to Abraham.

The whole land of Canaan, where you are now an alien, I will give as an everlasting possession to you and your descendants after you; and I will be their God" (Ge. 17:8).

Introduction to Numbers

(2) The promise given to the believer.

> In my Father's house are many rooms; if it were not so, I would have told you. I am going there to prepare a place for you. And if I go and prepare a place for you, I will come back and take you to be with me that you also may be where I am (Jn. 14:2-3).
>
> Now we know that if the earthly tent we live in is destroyed, we have a building from God, an eternal house in heaven, not built by human hands (2 Co. 5:1).
>
> But our citizenship is in heaven. And we eagerly await a Savior from there, the Lord Jesus Christ, who, by the power that enables him to bring everything under his control, will transform our lowly bodies so that they will be like his glorious body (Ph. 3:20-21).
>
> By faith Abraham, when called to go to a place he would later receive as his inheritance, obeyed and went, even though he did not know where he was going. By faith he made his home in the promised land like a stranger in a foreign country; he lived in tents, as did Isaac and Jacob, who were heirs with him of the same promise. For he was looking forward to the city with foundations, whose architect and builder is God (He. 11:8-10).
>
> All these people were still living by faith when they died. They did not receive the things promised; they only saw them and welcomed them from a distance. And they admitted that they were aliens and strangers on earth. People who say such things show that they are looking for a country of their own. If they had been thinking of the country they had left, they would have had opportunity to return. Instead, they were longing for a better country—a heavenly one. Therefore God is not ashamed to be called their God, for he has prepared a city for them (He. 11:13-16).
>
> Praise be to the God and Father of our Lord Jesus Christ! In his great mercy he has given us new birth into a living hope through the resurrection of Jesus Christ from the dead, and into an inheritance that can never perish, spoil or fade--kept in heaven for you, who through faith are shielded by God's power until the coming of the salvation that is ready to be revealed in the last time (1 Pe. 1:3-5).
>
> "Blessed are those who wash their robes, that they may have the right to the tree of life and may go through the gates into the city [New Jerusalem]" (Re. 22:14).

2) The promised land was the assurance of *conquest and rest, of spiritual victory and spiritual rest*. The promised land was to bring a God-given peace and security, freedom and liberty, deliverance and salvation to Abraham. The promised land meant victory and rest to Abraham, a God-given victory and rest...
- from having to wander about
- from never being settled
- from restlessness
- from being exposed to all kinds of trials, dangers, threats, attacks, slavery, and bondage that comes from having no settled home within this world, from having no place that is given and protected by God Himself

To Abraham, the promised land was the assurance of victory and rest, the conquest and triumph over all enemies, a victory and rest that was to be given by God Himself.

Thought 1. Note how the spiritual victory and rest promised to Abraham represents the spiritual rest promised to the believer (see note—He.4:1 for more discussion).

(1) The promise given to Abraham.

> "I will make you into a great nation and I will bless you; I will make your name great, and you will be a blessing. I will bless those who bless you, and whoever curses you I will curse; and all peoples on earth will be blessed through you." (Ge. 12:2-3).
>
> After this, the word of the LORD came to Abram in a vision: "Do not be afraid, Abram. I am your shield, your very great reward." (Ge. 15:1).
>
> I will surely bless you and make your descendants as numerous as the stars in the sky and as the sand on the seashore. Your descendants will take possession of the cities of their enemies, and through your offspring all nations on earth will be blessed, because you have obeyed me." (Ge. 22:17-18).

(2) The promise given to the believer.

> Take my yoke upon you and learn from me, for I am gentle and humble in heart, and you will find rest for your souls (Mt. 11:29).
>
> Then I heard a voice from heaven say, "Write: Blessed are the dead who die in the Lord from now on." "Yes," says the Spirit, "they will rest from their labor, for their deeds will follow them." (Re. 14:13).
>
> Therefore, since the promise of entering his rest still stands, let us be careful that none of you be found to have fallen short of it. For

we also have had the gospel preached to us, just as they did; but the message they heard was of no value to them, because those who heard did not combine it with faith. Now we who have believed enter that rest, just as God has said, "So I declared on oath in my anger, 'They shall never enter my rest.'" And yet his work has been finished since the creation of the world (He. 4:1-3).

Let us, therefore, make every effort to enter that rest, so that no one will fall by following their example of disobedience (He. 4:11).

The LORD replied, "My Presence will go with you, and I will give you rest." (Ex. 33:14).

I said, "Oh, that I had the wings of a dove! I would fly away and be at rest (Ps. 55:6).

Be at rest once more, O my soul, for the LORD has been good to you (Ps. 116:7).

To whom he said, "This is the resting place, let the weary rest"; and, "This is the place of repose"—but they would not listen (Is. 28:12).

3) The promised land was the assurance of *God's own presence*, that is, of God's love, care, provision, and protection. Abraham was bound to know this: if God was going to give him the promised land, then God must love and care for him. God would therefore provide and protect him no matter what lay ahead. God—His strong presence—would be with him through all the trials and struggles of life.

Thought 1. Abraham's assurance of God's presence symbolizes the believer's experience. The believer can be assured of God's presence: of God's love, care, provision, and protection.

(1) The promise given to Abraham.

The whole land of Canaan, where you are now an alien, I will give as an everlasting possession to you and your descendants after you; and I will be their God." (Ge. 17:8).

I am with you and will watch over you wherever you go, and I will bring you back to this land. I will not leave you until I have done what I have promised you." (Ge. 28:15).

(2) The promise given to the believer.

When you go to war against your enemies and see horses and chariots and an army greater than yours, do not be afraid of them, because the LORD your God, who brought you up out of Egypt, will be with you (De. 20:1).

When you pass through the waters, I will be with you; and when you pass through the rivers, they will not sweep over you. When you walk through the fire, you will not be burned; the flames will not set you ablaze (Is. 43:2).

But seek first his kingdom and his righteousness, and all these things will be given to you as well (Mt. 6:33).

And teaching them to obey everything I have commanded you. And surely I am with you always, to the very end of the age." (Mt. 28:20).

Keep your lives free from the love of money and be content with what you have, because God has said, "Never will I leave you; never will I forsake you." (He. 13:5).

OUTLINE OF NUMBERS

THE PREACHER'S OUTLINE AND SERMON BIBLE® is unique. It differs from all other Study Bibles and Sermon Resource Materials in that every Passage and Subject is outlined right beside the Scripture. When you choose any *Subject* below and turn to the reference, you have not only the Scripture, but also an outline of the Scripture and Subject *already prepared for you—verse by verse.*

For a quick example, choose one of the subjects below and turn over to the Scripture; you will find this to be a marvelous help for more *organized* and *streamlined* study.

In addition, every point of the Scripture and Subject is *fully developed in a Commentary with supporting Scripture* at the end of each point. Again, this arrangement makes sermon preparation much simpler and more efficient.

Note something else: The Subjects of *Numbers* have titles that are both Biblical and *practical*. The practical titles are often more appealing to people. This *benefit* is clearly seen for use on billboards, bulletins, church newsletters, etc.

A suggestion: for the *quickest* overview of *Numbers*, first read all the Division titles (I, II, III, etc.), then come back and read the individual outline titles.

OUTLINE OF NUMBERS

PART I: THE FIRST GENERATION OF ISRAELITES OR BELIEVERS

I. **THE PREPARATION FOR THE MARCH TO THE PROMISED LAND, 1:1–10:36**

   A. The Organization of Israel—the First Census: Mobilizing God's People for the March to the Promised Land, 1:1–2:34
   B. The Organization of the Priests, the Levites, and the Firstborn—the Second and Third Census Records: Called to Be Assistants, 3:1-51
   C. The Organization of the Mature Levites and Their Duties—the Fourth Census: Knowing One's Job and Doing It, 4:1-49
   D. The Basic Laws That Keep God's People United and Pure: God's People Must Live Pure Lives, 5:1-31
   E. The Special Provision Instituted for Drawing Closer to God—the Nazarite Vow and the Special Benediction of God: The Importance and Seriousness of Vows, 6:1-27
   F. The Spontaneous Offerings at the Dedication of the Tabernacle: Supporting God's Work and Approaching Him Exactly as He Says, 7:1-89
   G. The Placement of the Lampstand and the Setting Apart of the Levites to Serve God: Standing Forth as Lights and Servants of God, 8:1-26
   H. The Three Special Provisions of God: God's Great Deliverance, His Guidance, and His Call to Arise and Follow Him, 9:1–10:10
   I. The Great March to the Promised Land Finally Begins: A Picture of the Believer Finally Beginning His March to the Promised Land of Heaven, 10:11-36

II. **THE TRAGIC, DEVASTATING FAILURE OF ISRAEL: WHY PEOPLE FORFEIT THEIR RIGHT TO ENTER THE PROMISED LAND, 11:1–14:45**

   A. The First Tragic Failure Seen in the People: Distrusting God—Complaining and Grumbling, Craving and Lusting, 11:1-35
   B. The Second Tragic Failure Seen in Two Leaders, Miriam and Aaron: Distrusting God—Criticizing and Questioning the Call of God's Servant, 12:1-16
   C. The Final Tragic Failure That Dooms the People—the Twelve Spies and Their Mixed Report: Distrusting God—Being Negative, Fearful, and Defeated, Disbelieving and Rebelling against God, 13:1–14:45

III. **THE FORTY LONG YEARS OF WILDERNESS WANDERINGS: A PICTURE OF THE BELIEVER'S PILGRIMAGE THROUGH THIS WORLD AS HE PREPARES TO ENTER THE PROMISED LAND, 15:1–25:18**

   A. Event 1—God Gave Various Laws to Help Govern His People: Being Reassured and Prepared for the Promised Land, 15:1-41
   B. Event 2—A Dangerous Rebellion by Korah and His Allies: God Judges All Grumbling and Unbelief, All Rebellion and Unauthorized Approaches, 16:1-50
   C. Event 3—The Budding of Aaron's Staff: The Test to Vindicate God's Priest and His Ministry (a Symbol of Christ or of the Minister), 17:1-13
   D. Event 4—God Spelled Out the Service of the Priests and Levites: The Duties, Support, and Tithing of God's Ministers, 18:1-32
   E. Event 5—God Gave the Law to Govern the Offering of the Red Heifer and the Cleansing Water: A Symbol of Christ, His Sacrifice and Cleansing Power, 19:1-22
   F. Event 6—the Last Year of Israel in the Wilderness: Five Sad Events, 20:1-29
   G. Event 7—the First Military Victories and the Bronze Snake: A Picture of Desperate Vows, of Christ the Savior, and of God's Protection and Victory, 21:1-35
   H. Event 8—the Story of Balaam, His Donkey, and His Three Encounters with God: A Picture of the Unseen, Unknown Attempts by the Powers of Darkness to Defeat God's People, 22:1-41
   I. Event 9—the Story of Balaam and the Seven Startling Oracles or Prophecies Pronounced by Him: The Blessings of God and a Glimpse into the Future, 23:1–24:25
   J. Event 10: The Ultimate Rebellion of God's People and the End of the Forty Years of Wilderness Wanderings: Apostasy—Turning to Worldliness, to the Worship of Sex and Other Gods, 25:1-18

PART II: THE SECOND GENERATION OF ISRAELITES OR BELIEVERS

IV. THE PREPARATION FOR THE MARCH INTO THE PROMISED LAND, 26:1–36:13

A. The Organization of the Second Generation—the Second Nationwide Census: Mobilizing God's People to Enter and Inherit the Promised Land, 26:1-65
B. The Basic Law That Gave Women an Inheritance in the Promised Land: Five Women of Enormous Courage, Faith, and Hope, 27:1-11
C. The Appointment of Joshua As the Successor to Moses: A Strong Picture of God Preparing the Believer for Death, 27:12-23
D. The Offerings and Sacrifices Commanded by the LORD: A Picture of Man's Need to Continually Approach and Worship God Through the Atonement Secured by the Sacrifice (a Symbol of God's Dear Son, the Lord Jesus Christ), 28:1–29:40
E. The Laws That Govern Vows: The Obligation to Keep Vows and to Consider Others in Making Vows, 30:1-16
F. The Conquest of the Most Dangerous and Threatening Enemies, the Midianites: A Picture of Conquering the Seductive, Immoral Enemies of the World, 31:1-54
G. The Settlement East of the Jordan River: A Picture of Compromise, Selfishness, Covetousness, Disloyalty, and Half-Hearted Commitment, 32:1-42
H. The Review of the Wilderness Wanderings and a Strong Charge to Take Possession of the Promised Land: A Picture of God's Faithfulness and Man's Failure, 33:1-56
I. The Boundaries of Canaan, the Promised Land: The Great Gift and Assurance of God—His People Will Inherit the Promised Land, 34:1-29
J. The Inheritance of the Levites and the Cities of Refuge: The Provision of God for His Ministers and for All Who Need Refuge from the Storms and Threats of Life, 35:1-34
K. The Women Who Inherited Property: A Picture of Strong Faith in the Promised Land of God, 36:1-13

DIVISION I

THE PREPARATION FOR THE MARCH TO THE PROMISED LAND, 1:1–10:36

(1:1-10:36) **DIVISION OVERVIEW—Wilderness Wanderings, Overview of—Israel, Wilderness Wanderings of—Numbers, Book of, Title**: *Numbers*—what an unappealing, uninteresting title. *Numbers* sounds more like a math book than a spiritual journey. Yet, this is exactly what this great book is: one of the greatest spiritual journeys ever taken by a body of believers.

Numbers is the spiritual journey (pilgrimage) of Israel as they marched to the promised land of God. There are actually two generations of Israelites dealt with throughout this journey. The first generation of Israelites were those who had been delivered from the slavery of Egypt (a symbol of the world). To these believers God gave the great principles necessary for inheriting the promised land of God—if they would just follow God with their whole hearts. (See outline and note—Ex. 19:5-9; DEEPER STUDY # 1—Ex. 19:5-6 for more discussion.)

The first generation is seen preparing and beginning their journey to the promised land with great excitement and joy. But they soon develop a terrible spirit of unbelief and rebellion, complaining and grumbling. Consequently, the judgment of God falls. They are condemned to wander about in the desert for forty long, exhausting years, wander about until they all die (all except Joshua and Caleb). They are barred from the promised land, never to receive the glorious inheritance promised by God.

The second generation of Israelites were the sons and daughters of the parents who had sinned so terribly. Only the adults twenty years old or older were judged and condemned to die in the desert wilderness. All the children were spared. It was these—the second generation of believers—whom God prepared to enter the promised land. He used the forty years of wilderness wanderings to teach, strengthen, discipline, and toughen the children so they would be spiritually prepared to enter the promised land and claim the glorious inheritance promised by God. Their history is covered in the last ten chapters (26:1-35:13).

The history of the first generation is vividly pictured in the first twenty-five chapters (1:1-25:18). The great book of *Numbers* opens with the first generation preparing for their march to the promised land. Excitement and joy—a sense of adventure, anticipation, and hope—flood their hearts. They are about to embark on the most wonderful journey of their lives, to receive the glorious inheritance of the promised land of God Himself.

THE PREPARATION FOR THE MARCH TO THE PROMISED LAND, 1:1–10:36

A. The Organization of Israel—the First Census: Mobilizing God's People for the March to the Promised Land, 1:1-2:34

B. The Organization of the Priests, the Levites, and the Firstborn—the Second and Third Census Records: Called to Be Assistants, 3:1-51

C. The Organization of the Mature Levites and Their Duties—the Fourth Census: Knowing One's Job and Doing It, 4:1-49

D. The Basic Laws That Keep God's People United and Pure: God's People Must Live Pure Lives, 5:1-31

E. The Special Provision Instituted for Drawing Closer to God—the Nazarite Vow and the Special Benediction of God: The Importance and Seriousness of Vows, 6:1-27

F. The Spontaneous Offerings at the Dedication of the Tabernacle: Supporting God's Work and Approaching Him Exactly as He Says, 7:1-89

DIVISION I
1:1–10:36

G. The Placement of the Lampstand and the Setting Apart of the Levites to Serve God: Standing Forth As Lights and Servants of God, 8:1-26

H. The Three Special Provisions of God: Acknowledging God's Great Deliverance, His Guidance, and His Call to Arise and Follow Him, 9:1–10:10

I. The Great March to the Promised Land Finally Begins: A Picture of the Believer Finally Beginning His March to the Promised Land of Heaven, 10:11-36

THE BOOK OF NUMBERS

I. THE PREPARATION FOR THE MARCH TO THE PROMISED LAND, 1:1–10:36

A. The Organization of Israel—the First Census: Mobilizing God's People for the March to the Promised Land, 1:1–2:34

1. The strong emphasis: "The Lord spoke"—guided, directed His people
   a. Spoke in the Tent of Meeting
   b. Spoke in the desert wilderness
   c. Spoke 13 months after the deliverance from Egyptian slavery
2. The military census: The people of God must prepare for warfare
   a. To take a census of all Iraelites: Listing every man by name
   b. To identify all men able to serve in the army—20 years old & above
3. The selection of leaders: Some must be willing to serve as leaders
   a. Tribe of Reuben: Elizur
   b. Tribe of Simeon: Shelumiel
   c. Tribe of Judah: Nahshon
   d. Tribe of Issachar: Nethanel
   e. Tribe of Zebulun: Eliab
   f. Tribe from Joseph
      1) Tribe of Ephraim: Elishama
      2) Tribe of Manasseh: Gamaliel
   g. Tribe of Benjamin: Abidan
   h. Tribe of Dan: Ahiezer
   i. Tribe of Asher: Pagiel
   j. Tribe of Gad: Eliasaph
   k. Tribe of Naphtali: Ahira
   l. These were the tribal leaders, the chiefs or heads of the clans of Israel
4. The results of the census:

CHAPTER 1

The LORD spoke to Moses in the Tent of Meeting in the Desert of Sinai on the first day of the second month of the second year after the Israelites came out of Egypt. He said:

2 "Take a census of the whole Israelite community by their clans and families, listing every man by name, one by one.

3 You and Aaron are to number by their divisions all the men in Israel twenty years old or more who are able to serve in the army.

4 One man from each tribe, each the head of his family, is to help you.

5 These are the names of the men who are to assist you: from Reuben, Elizur son of Shedeur;

6 From Simeon, Shelumiel son of Zurishaddai;

7 From Judah, Nahshon son of Amminadab;

8 From Issachar, Nethanel son of Zuar;

9 From Zebulun, Eliab son of Helon;

10 From the sons of Joseph: from Ephraim, Elishama son of Ammihud; from Manasseh, Gamaliel son of Pedahzur;

11 From Benjamin, Abidan son of Gideoni;

12 From Dan, Ahiezer son of Ammishaddai;

13 From Asher, Pagiel son of Ocran;

14 From Gad, Eliasaph son of Deuel;

15 From Naphtali, Ahira son of Enan."

16 These were the men appointed from the community, the leaders of their ancestral tribes. They were the heads of the clans of Israel.

17 Moses and Aaron took these men whose names had been given,

18 And they called the whole community together on the first day of the second month. The people indicated their ancestry by their clans and families, and the men twenty years old or more were listed by name, one by one,

19 As the LORD commanded Moses. And so he counted them in the Desert of Sinai:

20 From the descendants of Reuben the firstborn son of Israel: All the men twenty years old or more who were able to serve in the army were listed by name, one by one, according to the records of their clans and families.

21 The number from the tribe of Reuben was 46,500.

22 From the descendants of Simeon: All the men twenty years old or more who were able to serve in the army were counted and listed by name, one by one, according to the records of their clans and families.

23 The number from the tribe of Simeon was 59,300.

24 From the descendants of Gad: All the men twenty years old or more who were able to serve in the army were listed by name, according to the records of their clans and families.

25 The number from the tribe of Gad was 45,650.

26 From the descendants of Judah: All the men twenty years old or more who were able to serve in the army were listed by name, according to the records of their clans and families.

27 The number from the tribe of Judah was 74,600.

28 From the descendants of Issachar: All the men twenty years old or more who were able to serve in the army were listed by name, according to the records of their clans and families.

29 The number from the tribe of Issachar was 54,400.

30 From the descendants of Zebulun: All the men twenty years old or more who were able to serve in the army were listed by name, according to the records of their clans and

---

Every believer must believe God & serve in the army of God

a. The leaders compiling the census
   1) All men 20 years old or older were listed by name, one by one

   2) The census was taken just as the Lord commanded in the Desert of Sinai

b. The number of men from each tribe who were able to serve in the army
   1) The tribe of Reuben: 46,500

   2) The tribe of Simeon: 59,300

   3) The tribe of Gad: 45,650

   4) The tribe of Judah: 74,600

   5) The tribe of Issachar: 54,400

   6) The tribe of Zebulun: 57,400

NUMBERS 1:1–2:34

7) The tribe of Ephraim: 40,500	families. 31 The number from the tribe of Zebulun was 57,400. 32 From the sons of Joseph: From the descendants of Ephraim: All the men twenty years old or more who were able to serve in the army were listed by name, according to the records of their clans and families. 33 The number from the tribe of Ephraim was 40,500.	46 The total number was 603,550. 47 The families of the tribe of Levi, however, were not counted along with the others. 48 The LORD had said to Moses: 49 "You must not count the tribe of Levi or include them in the census of the other Israelites.	3) The total number: 603,550 **5. The setting apart of the Levites to the sacred task of the Tabernacle: Some must serve God in special ministries** a. They were excluded from the military

8) The tribe of Manasseh: 32,200	34 From the descendants of Manasseh: All the men twenty years old or more who were able to serve in the army were listed by name, according to the records of their clans and families.
	35 The number from the tribe of Manasseh was 32,200.
		50 Instead, appoint the Levites to be in charge of the tabernacle of the Testimony—over all its furnishings and everything belonging to it. They are to carry the tabernacle and all its furnishings; they are to take care of it and encamp around it.	b. They were placed in charge of the Tabernacle
			  1) In charge of materials & furnishings
			  2) In charge of transporting it

9) The tribe of Benjamin: 35,400	36 From the descendants of Benjamin: All the men twenty years old or more who were able to serve in the army were listed by name, according to the records of their clans and families. 37 The number from the tribe of Benjamin was 35,400.	51 Whenever the tabernacle is to move, the Levites are to take it down, and whenever the tabernacle is to be set up, the Levites shall do it. Anyone else who goes near it shall be put to death. 52 The Israelites are to set up their tents by divisions, each man in his own camp under his own standard.	3) In charge of taking it down & erecting it c. They were in charge of protecting the Tabernacle: To execute anyone who went near, profaned, or plundered it (a symbol of the church) d. They were to camp around the Tabernacle 1) To set their tents by divisions with each man under his own standard
10) The tribe of Dan: 62,700	38 From the descendants of Dan: All the men twenty years old or more who were able to serve in the army were listed by name, according to the records of their clans and families. 39 The number from the tribe of Dan was 62,700.	53 The Levites, however, are to set up their tents around the tabernacle of the Testimony so that wrath will not fall on the Israelite community. The Levites are to be responsible for the care of the tabernacle of the Testimony."	2) The purpose: • To prevent God's wrath from falling upon the people due to their neglect of the Tabernacle & their allowing it to be abused or robbed
11) The tribe of Asher: 41,500	40 From the descendants of Asher: All the men twenty years old or more who were able to serve in the army were listed by name, according to the records of their clans and families. 41 The number from the tribe of Asher was 41,500.	54 The Israelites did all this just as the LORD commanded Moses. **CHAPTER 2** The LORD said to Moses and Aaron:	• To teach people to approach God with fear & reverence
12) The tribe of Naphtali: 53,400	42 From the descendants of Naphtali: All the men twenty years old or more who were able to serve in the army were listed by name, according to the records of their clans and families. 43 The number from the tribe of Naphtali was 53,400.	2 "The Israelites are to camp around the Tent of Meeting some distance from it, each man under his standard with the banners of his family." 3 On the east, toward the sunrise, the divisions of the camp of Judah are to encamp under their standard. The leader of the people of Judah is Nahshon son of Amminadab.	**6. The placement of the Tabernacle in the center of the camp: All must know that God dwells in the midst of His people & guides them as they march to the promised land** **7. The placement of the tribes around the Tabernacle, each man under his banner: Each believer must take his place under the standard of Christ & stand fast under the banner of God's family**

c. The accuracy & total of the men
  1) The men were counted by Moses & Aaron & the twelve leaders of Israel
  2) The men were counted by families
	44 These were the men counted by Moses and Aaron and the twelve leaders of Israel, each one representing his family.
	45 All the Israelites twenty years old or more who were able to serve in Israel's army were counted according to their families.
		4 His division numbers 74,600.
		5 The tribe of Issachar will camp next to them. The leader of the people of Issachar is Nethanel son of Zuar.
			a. On the east:
			  1) The division of Judah
			    • The leader: Nahshon
			    • Division number: 74,600
			  2) The division of Issachar
			    • The leader: Nethanel

NUMBERS 1:1–2:34

- Division number: 54,400
3) The division of Zebulun
  - The leader: Eliab

- Division number: 57,400
4) The total of the three divisions: 186,400
5) The marching position: In the forefront—to lead the way

b. On the south
  1) The division of Reuben
    - The leader: Elizur

  - Division number: 46,500
  2) The division of Simeon
    - The leader: Shelumiel

  - Division number 59,300
  3) The division of Gad
    - The leader: Eliasaph

  - Division number: 45,650
  4) The total of three divisions: 151,450
  5) The marching position: Second in line

c. In the center: The Tabernacle & the Levites—marched in the same order as they camped

d. On the west
  1) The division of Ephraim
    - The leader: Elishama

  - Division number: 40,500
  2) The division of Manasseh
    - The leader: Gamaliel

6 His division numbers 54,400.
7 The tribe of Zebulun will be next. The leader of the people of Zebulun is Eliab son of Helon.
8 His division numbers 57,400.
9 All the men assigned to the camp of Judah, according to their divisions, number 186,400. They will set out first.
10 On the south will be the divisions of the camp of Reuben under their standard. The leader of the people of Reuben is Elizur son of Shedeur.
11 His division numbers 46,500.
12 The tribe of Simeon will camp next to them. The leader of the people of Simeon is Shelumiel son of Zurishaddai.
13 His division numbers 59,300.
14 The tribe of Gad will be next. The leader of the people of Gad is Eliasaph son of Deuel.
15 His division numbers 45,650.
16 All the men assigned to the camp of Reuben, according to their divisions, number 151,450. They will set out second.
17 Then the Tent of Meeting and the camp of the Levites will set out in the middle of the camps. They will set out in the same order as they encamp, each in his own place under his standard.
18 On the west will be the divisions of the camp of Ephraim under their standard. The leader of the people of Ephraim is Elishama son of Ammihud.
19 His division numbers 40,500.
20 The tribe of Manasseh will be next to them. The leader of the people of Manasseh is Gamaliel son of Pedahzur.
21 His division numbers 32,200.
22 The tribe of Benjamin will be next. The leader of the people of Benjamin is Abidan son of Gideoni.
23 His division numbers 35,400.
24 All the men assigned to the camp of Ephraim, according to their divisions, number 108,100. They will set out third.
25 On the north will be the divisions of the camp of Dan, under their standard. The leader of the people of Dan is Ahiezer son of Ammishaddai.
26 His division numbers 62,700.
27 The tribe of Asher will camp next to them. The leader of the people of Asher is Pagiel son of Ocran.
28 His division numbers 41,500.
29 The tribe of Naphtali will be next. The leader of the people of Naphtali is Ahira son of Enan.
30 His division numbers 53,400.
31 All the men assigned to the camp of Dan number 157,600. They will set out last, under their standards.
32 These are the Israelites, counted according to their families. All those in the camps, by their divisions, number 603,550.
33 The Levites, however, were not counted along with the other Israelites, as the LORD commanded Moses.
34 So the Israelites did everything the LORD commanded Moses; that is the way they encamped under their standards, and that is the way they set out, each with his clan and family.

- Division number: 32,200
3) The division of Benjamin
  - The leader: Abidan

- Division number: 35,400
4) The total of the these divisions: 108,100
5) The marching position: Third in line

e. On the north
  1) The division of Dan
    - The leader: Ahiezer

  - Division number: 62,700
  2) The division of Asher
    - The leader: Pagiel

  - Division number: 41,500
  3) The division of Naphtali
    - The leader: Ahira

  - Division number: 53,400
  4) The total of the three divisions: 157,600
  5) The marching position: Fourth in line

f. The accuracy & total of the men
  1) The way they were counted: By families
  2) The total numbered: 603,550
  3) The Levites were not counted

8. **The obedience of God's people: Every believer must do everything God commands**
  a. They camped as God commanded
  b. They marched as God commanded

DIVISION I

THE PREPARATION FOR THE MARCH TO THE PROMISED LAND, 1:1–10:36

A. The Organization of Israel—the First Census: Mobilizing God's People for the March to the Promised Land, 1:1–2:34

(1:1-2:34) **Introduction—Promised Land—Enemies, of Believers, List of—Pitfalls, List of—Believers, Need of, Other Believers—Mobilization, of Believers—Believers, Described As, Army—Enemies, of Life—Enemies, Victory Over**: the promised land is the great hope of the believer. As the believer marches through this world, he is to

NUMBERS 1:1–2:34

be ever pressing on to the promised land of God. What is the promised land? What is the great hope God has given to the believer? The promised land means at least two things:

⇒ First, the promised land means conquest and rest. It means conquering all the enemies, trials, and temptations of this life. It also means spiritual rest, learning to rest in God—to be free from all the guilt and anxiety, loneliness and emptiness, sin and shame of this world. As stated, the promised land means conquest and rest. It means being victorious over all the enemies of life and possessing spiritual rest, the rest of God Himself (see *Special Features*, pt.26—Introduction to *Numbers* for more discussion).

⇒ Second, the promised land means heaven itself, living forever in the eternal presence of God—in the new heavens and earth (2 Pe. 3:10-13; Re. 21:1-4; Is. 65:17; 66:22).

Throughout life, the believer is to stay focused upon the promised land of heaven. He is to march forth day by day, keeping his eyes focused upon the great hope God has given. But as he marches, he must realize one fact: he cannot march alone. He does not live in a vacuum. He is not alone on the earth. He needs to walk side by side with other believers. Mobilization is needed. Believers must be mobilized as they walk together throughout this life.

Life is filled with pitfalls and enemies, enemies that will attack and destroy us unless we are mobilized, prepared to conquer them. What pitfalls and what enemies? There are pitfalls such as...

- greed
- covetousness
- materialism
- humanism
- pornography
- lust
- illicit sex
- lying
- stealing
- cheating
- anger
- malice
- idolatry
- unbelief
- murmuring
- complaining
- gluttony

There are enemies such as...
- those who ridicule and persecute
- those who oppose and create problems
- those who hate and despise
- those who abuse and assault
- those who are lawless and violent
- those who are murderers and war-mongers
- those who are selfish and hoarding
- those who are mean-spirited and spiteful
- those who are wicked and evil
- those who seek to destroy

The list could go on and on. The pitfalls and enemies against the believer are innumerable. This is the reason the believer must stand with other believers, mobilized together with them as they all march to the promised land of heaven. The believer can never stand alone and be victorious. He can never triumph over the pitfalls and enemies of this life alone. He must stand with other believers, stand in the church of the living God, stand mobilized with God's people to march forth to the promised land of God, heaven itself.

This is the subject of this passage. It shows how God mobilized His people (the Israelites) to march forth to the promised land. By mobilizing them, God gave us a picture of the church. He has shown us how to mobilize the church—all believers together—in order to be victorious over the pitfalls and enemies of this life. He has shown us how to mobilize as we march together—side by side—to the promised land of God. Note the outline points, how God tells us to mobilize: *The Organization of Israel—the First Census: Mobilizing God's People for the March to the Promised Land*, 1:1-2:34.

1. The strong emphasis: "The LORD spoke"—guided, directed His people (statement used over 150 times in 20 plus ways) (1:1).
2. The military census: the people of God must prepare for warfare (1:2-3).
3. The selection of leaders: some must be willing to serve as leaders (1:4-16).
4. The results of the census: every believer must believe God and serve in the army of God (1:17-46).
5. The setting apart of the Levites to the sacred task of the Tabernacle: some must serve God in special ministries (1:47-54).
6. The placement of the Tabernacle in the center of the camp: all must know that God dwells in the midst of His people and guides them as they march to the promised land (2:1-2).
7. The placement of the tribes around the Tabernacle, each man under his banner: each believer must take his place under the standard of Christ and stand fast under the banner of God's family (2:2-33).
8. The obedience of God's people: every believer must do everything God commands (2:34).

1 (1:1) **Word of God, Purpose—Guidance, of God—Leadership, of God**: there was the strong emphasis, "The LORD spoke" to His people. That is, He gave instructions, guided and directed His people as they marched to the promised land of God. This statement, "The LORD spoke," is used over 150 times in twenty plus ways in the Book of Numbers alone. This fact points strongly to the inspiration of Numbers, that the book is "God-breathed" (2 Ti. 3:16). God guided His people by speaking to Moses and by having Moses declare His Word to the people.

God is the Great Communicator. God communicates with His people in the same way that men communicate with men, by word of mouth. As stated, God spoke to Moses, and Moses declared God's Word to the people. God's Word—His speaking to men—is one of the great proofs that He is the living and true God. Other gods are mute, silent—never speaking directly to men. They are false gods. Note where and when God spoke.

a. God spoke to Moses in the Tent of Meeting. This refers to "the tabernacle" (v.51) or to "the tabernacle of the Testimony" (vv.50, 53). The Tabernacle was the worship center of that day (see *Exodus*, Chapters 25-40 for more discussion). The meaning of the word *tabernacle* (miskan) means dwelling. It was the very dwelling place of God Himself, a symbol of His very presence. It was, therefore, only natural that God would meet Moses and speak with him in the Tabernacle or Tent of Meeting.

b. God spoke with Moses in the desert or wilderness. The Israelites were still camped at the foot of Mt. Sinai. It was while the people were in the wilderness that God confronted and spoke with Moses.

c. God spoke thirteen months after the deliverance of His people from Egyptian slavery. Note this: God's people had been camped at the foot of Mt. Sinai for thirteen months (Ex. 19:1). During the thirteen months—just a little more than one year—God had given His people the law, led them to construct the Tabernacle, and formed them into a great nation of people. Only one thing remained to be done before they could begin their march to the promised land: they must be mobilized and organized into a great army of people for God. Remember, the population of the Israelites was over two to three million at this time. They could not march and survive through the desert wilderness as vagabonds, as a loosely knit, drifting group of people with little bands of people wandering off, moving about as they wished. Organization and mobilization were necessary. This was the reason God was now meeting with Moses, to give him guidance and direction in mobilizing the people.

Thought 1. God speaks to us. He guides and directs us day by day. God loves us and wants us to conquer all the pitfalls and enemies of this life. As we march toward the promised land of heaven:
- God will meet and speak with us *in the church*.
- God will meet and speak with us *in the desert or wilderness*.

No matter where we are, God will meet and speak with us. We simply have to be available, as Moses was. We need to get alone in the church or out in the desert or wilderness to seek the face of God. We need to ask God to meet and speak with us, to guide and direct us. When we seek God, He meets and speaks to us.

> "So I say to you: Ask and it will be given to you; seek and you will find; knock and the door will be opened to you." (Lu. 11:9)
>
> If you remain in me and my words remain in you, ask whatever you wish, and it will be given you. (Jn. 15:7)
>
> But when he, the Spirit of truth, comes, he will guide you into all truth. He will not speak on his own; he will speak only what he hears, and he will tell you what is yet to come. (Jn. 16:13)
>
> All Scripture is God-breathed and is useful for teaching, rebuking, correcting and training in righteousness. (2 Ti. 3:16)
>
> For this God is our God for ever and ever; he will be our guide even to the end. (Ps. 48:14)
>
> You guide me with your counsel, and afterward you will take me into glory. (Ps. 73:24)
>
> He will call upon me, and I will answer him; I will be with him in trouble, I will deliver him and honor him. (Ps. 91:15)
>
> Whether you turn to the right or to the left, your ears will hear a voice behind you, saying, "This is the way; walk in it." (Is. 30:21)
>
> Then you will call, and the LORD will answer; you will cry for help, and he will say: Here am I. If you do away with the yoke of oppression, with the pointing finger and malicious talk... (Is. 58:9)
>
> Before they call I will answer; while they are still speaking I will hear. (Is. 65:24)
>
> 'Call to me and I will answer you and tell you great and unsearchable things you do not know.' (Je. 33:3)

2 (1:2-3) **Israel, Census of—Military, Census of—Warfare, Spiritual—Spiritual Warfare—Census, of Israel**: there was the military census. The people of God had to be prepared for warfare as they marched to the promised land.

They were to take a census of all Israelites. Note that every man was to be listed by name, one by one. Every man twenty years old or older was to be identified and mobilized to serve in the army. No person was allowed to opt out, not if he was physically fit and able. To refuse to serve in God's army was a great sin, bringing severe judgment (Nu. 14:1f; De. 20:3-4). Every able-bodied man had to serve and was expected to fight against the enemies of God's people.

Thought 1. Believers must be prepared for warfare as they march to the promised land. Why? Because we are in a spiritual warfare. We do not wrestle against flesh and blood, but against principalities and powers and spiritual wickedness in high places.

The spiritual pitfalls and enemies of life seek to captivate and destroy every one of us. We must, therefore, be mobilized and prepared for warfare. How can we be prepared? By putting on the whole armor of God. This is exactly what God declares in His holy Word.

> Finally, be strong in the Lord and in his mighty power. Put on the full armor of God so that you can take your stand against the devil's schemes. For our struggle is not against flesh and blood, but against the rulers, against the authorities, against the powers of this dark world and against the spiritual forces of evil in the heavenly realms. Therefore put on the full armor of God, so that when the day of evil comes, you may be able to stand your ground, and after you have done everything, to stand. Stand firm then, with the belt of truth buckled around your waist, with the breastplate of righteousness in place, and with your feet fitted with the readiness that comes from the gospel of peace. In addition to all this, take up the shield of faith, with which you can extinguish all the flaming arrows of the evil one. Take the helmet of salvation and the sword of the Spirit, which is the word of God. And pray in the Spirit on all occasions with all kinds of prayers and requests. With this in mind, be alert and always keep on praying for all the saints. (Ep. 6:10-18)
>
> The weapons we fight with are not the weapons of the world. On the contrary, they have divine power to demolish strongholds. (2 Co. 10:4)
>
> Timothy, my son, I give you this instruction in keeping with the prophecies once made about you, so that by following them you may fight the good fight. (1 Ti. 1:18)
>
> Fight the good fight of the faith. Take hold of the eternal life to which you were called when you made your good confession in the presence of many witnesses. (1 Ti. 6:12)
>
> Endure hardship with us like a good soldier of Christ Jesus. No one serving as a soldier gets involved in civilian affairs—he wants to please his commanding officer. (2 Ti. 2:3-4)

3 (1:4-16) **Leaders, Appointment of—Leadership, Appointment of—Leaders, Willingness to Serve—Church, Leadership of—Church, Need of**: there was the selection of leaders. Some of the people had to be willing to serve as leaders.

God told Moses to select one man from each tribe to help him in taking the census (v.4). These men were to be the leaders of each tribe, men who were to serve as the assistants to Moses. They were his partners in the ministry of mobilizing the people. The point to see is their willingness to serve. They were willing to serve both as the leaders of the tribes and in this particular ministry of mobilizing the people.

> **Thought 1.** Some people must step forth as leaders. Leaders are desperately needed as God's people march to the promised land of heaven. Leaders are needed to guide God's people, to protect them from the pitfalls and enemies of this life. The church of God needs leaders, people who step forth and proclaim loudly and clearly, "I will help. I will accept the position. I will take the leadership role. I will give guidance to those who need direction."
>
> > "Therefore go and make disciples of all nations, baptizing them in the name of the Father and of the Son and of the Holy Spirit, and teaching them to obey everything I have commanded you. And surely I am with you always, to the very end of the age." (Mt. 28:19-20)
> >
> > "My food," said Jesus, "is to do the will of him who sent me and to finish his work." (Jn. 4:34)
> >
> > Now get up and stand on your feet. I have appeared to you to appoint you as a servant and as a witness of what you have seen of me and what I will show you. (Ac. 26:16)
> >
> > For we are God's fellow workers; you are God's field, God's building. (1 Co. 3:9)
> >
> > So do not be ashamed to testify about our Lord, or ashamed of me his prisoner. But join with me in suffering for the gospel, by the power of God. (2 Ti. 1:8)
> >
> > And the things you have heard me say in the presence of many witnesses entrust to reliable men who will also be qualified to teach others. Endure hardship with us like a good soldier of Christ Jesus. (2 Ti. 2:2-3)
> >
> > Then I heard the voice of the LORD saying, "Whom shall I send? And who will go for us?" And I said, "Here am I. Send me!" (Is. 6:8)

4 (1:17-46) **Census, of Israel—Israel, Census of—Service, Duty of—Ministry, Duty of—Army, of God—Military, of God**: there were the results of the census. Every believer was to believe God and serve in the army of God.

Note that the number of men able to fight were listed tribe by tribe. As stated, every man was to be listed in a register by name, identifying him as a legitimate member of his particular tribe (v.2). A record of each individual was to be very important when they reached the promised land. Each tribe was to receive so much of the promised land as an inheritance from God. And within each tribe, every individual family was to receive a certain inheritance. It was critical, therefore, to know one's lineage or ancestry, that one belonged to a particular tribe. Every person had to be registered, had to have his name written in the book of God's people in order to receive his share of the promised land.

Note the total number of men twenty years old and older: 603,550 (v.46). No doubt, this meant a population of two to four million, depending upon how many children were figured for each family. What a strong declaration of God's faithfulness! He was fulfilling His promise to Abraham...

- that He would bless Abraham with a great nation of people
- that He would send through the descendants of Abraham the promised seed of the Messiah, the Savior of the world
- that He would use Abraham's descendants to bless the world—to be His people, His missionary force and witnesses upon the earth (see outline and notes—Ge. 12:1-3)

Note that the census was begun on the very day that God commanded it to be taken (vv.1, 18). A deep sense of God's faithfulness to His people is immediately seen by glancing at the total number of fighting men within each tribe (twenty years old or older). Note the following chart:

⇒	Reuben	*46,500*
⇒	Simeon	*59,300*
⇒	Gad	*45,650*
⇒	Judah	*74,600*
⇒	Issachar	*54,400*
⇒	Zebulun	*57,400*
⇒	Ephraim	*40,500*
⇒	Manasseh	*32,200*
⇒	Benjamin	*35,400*
⇒	Dan	*62,700*
⇒	Asher	*41,500*
⇒	Naphtali	*53,400*
	TOTAL:	*603,550*

> **Thought 1.** There are three strong lessons in this passage:
> (1) Every believer must believe God. He must be registered in the Book of Life and claim God and the family of God as his lineage and ancestry. He will never reach the promised land of God unless he believes God. God keeps a register, a Book of Life, in which the name of every true believer is written.
>
> > However, do not rejoice that the spirits submit to you, but rejoice that your names are written in heaven. (Lu. 10:20)
> >
> > He who overcomes will, like them, be dressed in white. I will never blot out his name from the book of life, but will acknowledge his name before my Father and his angels. (Re. 3:5)
> >
> > And I saw the dead, great and small, standing before the throne, and books were opened. Another book was opened, which is the book of life. The dead were judged according to what they had done as recorded in the books. (Re. 20:12)

Nothing impure will ever enter it, nor will anyone who does what is shameful or deceitful, but only those whose names are written in the Lamb's book of life. (Re. 21:27)

And if anyone takes words away from this book of prophecy, God will take away from him his share in the tree of life and in the holy city, which are described in this book. (Re. 22:19)

But now, please forgive their sin—but if not, then blot me out of the book you have written. The LORD replied to Moses, "Whoever has sinned against me I will blot out of my book." (Ex. 32:32-33)

The LORD will write in the register of the peoples: "This one was born in Zion." Selah (Ps. 87:6)

Those who are left in Zion, who remain in Jerusalem, will be called holy, all who are recorded among the living in Jerusalem. (Is. 4:3)

At that time Michael, the great prince who protects your people, will arise. There will be a time of distress such as has not happened from the beginning of nations until then. But at that time your people—everyone whose name is found written in the book—will be delivered. (Da. 12:1)

Then those who feared the LORD talked with each other, and the LORD listened and heard. A scroll of remembrance was written in his presence concerning those who feared the LORD and honored his name. (Mal. 3:16)

(2) Every believer must serve in the army of God. He must demonstrate that he truly believes in God by fighting against the enemies of life and the enemies of God. He must be in a constant battle against the evil and lawlessness of this world, against the greed and lust of the wicked.

The night is nearly over; the day is almost here. So let us put aside the deeds of darkness and put on the armor of light. (Ro. 13:12)

For our struggle is not against flesh and blood, but against the rulers, against the authorities, against the powers of this dark world and against the spiritual forces of evil in the heavenly realms. (Ep. 6:12)

But since we belong to the day, let us be self-controlled, putting on faith and love as a breastplate, and the hope of salvation as a helmet. (1 Th. 5:8)

Fight the good fight of the faith. Take hold of the eternal life to which you were called when you made your good confession in the presence of many witnesses. (1 Ti. 6:12)

And the things you have heard me say in the presence of many witnesses entrust to reliable men who will also be qualified to teach others. Endure hardship with us like a good soldier of Christ Jesus. (2 Ti. 2:2-3)

Be self-controlled and alert. Your enemy the devil prowls around like a roaring lion looking for someone to devour. (1 Pe. 5:8)

(3) God is faithful. He fulfills His promises to His people.

God, who has called you into fellowship with his Son Jesus Christ our Lord, is faithful. (1 Co. 1:9)

God did this so that, by two unchangeable things in which it is impossible for God to lie, we who have fled to take hold of the hope offered to us may be greatly encouraged. (He. 6:18)

So then, those who suffer according to God's will should commit themselves to their faithful Creator and continue to do good. (1 Pe. 4:19)

Know therefore that the LORD your God is God; he is the faithful God, keeping his covenant of love to a thousand generations of those who love him and keep his commands. (De. 7:9)

Praise be to the LORD, who has given rest to his people Israel just as he promised. Not one word has failed of all the good promises he gave through his servant Moses. (1 K. 8:56)

Your love, O LORD, reaches to the heavens, your faithfulness to the skies. (Ps. 36:5)

5 (1:47-54) **Levites, Duty of—Tabernacle, Protection of—Laymen, Duties of—Church, Duties of Laymen Within**: there was the setting apart of the Levites to the sacred task of the Tabernacle. Some of God's people had to serve God in special ministries. The Levites were appointed for the spiritual service of the Tabernacle, as helpers or assistants to the priests.

a. The Levites were excluded from the military (v.49). Why? Because they were the ones in charge of the spiritual service of the Tabernacle. They were not, therefore, included in the military census just taken.

b. The Levites were placed in charge of the Tabernacle itself. They were in charge of all the materials and furnishings and everything else that belonged to the Tabernacle. Moreover, they were in charge of taking the Tabernacle down, transporting it, and erecting it at the new campsites.

c. The Levites were in charge of protecting the Tabernacle (v.51). They were to execute any unauthorized person who went near the Tabernacle, any who profaned or plundered it.

d. The Levites were to camp around the Tabernacle (vv.52-53). They were the protectors of the Tabernacle; therefore, they had to camp close by to keep it from being plundered, robbed, abused, or profaned. There were certain preparations that had to be made for a person to approach the Tabernacle. The Levites had to make sure that no one approached it unprepared. It was their duty to keep God's wrath from falling upon the people because of some neglect or because someone came unprepared. It was their duty to teach the people to approach God with fear and reverence. *The Expositor's Bible Commentary* makes the point that God's presence was both a blessing and a curse:

⇒ a blessing for all those who approached God with reverence and respect

⇒ a curse for all those who approached God without respect or reverence[1]

---

[1] *The Expositor's Bible Commentary*, Vol.2. Frank E. Gaebelein, Editor, p.711.

Thought 1. The Levites were appointed to a very special ministry among God's people. There are always special ministries, special needs that must be met. The church needs people to step forth and accept the challenge of these special ministries.

Just think of the needs existing within every community of the world...
- the needs of the orphans, widows, and widowers
- the needs of the prisoners, broken-hearted, and backslidden
- the needs of the diseased, suffering, and hospitalized
- the needs of the hungry, thirsty, and poor
- the needs of the empty, lonely, and purposeless
- the needs of the lost, dying, and doomed

Some people need to step forth and accept the challenge. Dedication and commitment are needed. The special needs of the world must be met.

> "The Spirit of the Lord is on me, because he has anointed me to preach good news to the poor. He has sent me to proclaim freedom for the prisoners and recovery of sight for the blind, to release the oppressed." (Lu. 4:18)
> And if anyone gives even a cup of cold water to one of these little ones because he is my disciple, I tell you the truth, he will certainly not lose his reward. (Mt. 10:42)
> Just as the Son of Man did not come to be served, but to serve, and to give his life as a ransom for many. (Mt. 20:28)
> Then the King will say to those on his right, 'Come, you who are blessed by my Father; take your inheritance, the kingdom prepared for you since the creation of the world. For I was hungry and you gave me something to eat, I was thirsty and you gave me something to drink, I was a stranger and you invited me in, I needed clothes and you clothed me, I was sick and you looked after me, I was in prison and you came to visit me.' (Mt. 25:34-36)
> Not so with you. Instead, whoever wants to become great among you must be your servant, and whoever wants to be first must be slave of all. (Mk. 10:43-44)
> Now that I, your Lord and Teacher, have washed your feet, you also should wash one another's feet. (Jn. 13:14)
> Again Jesus said, "Simon son of John, do you truly love me?" He answered, "Yes, Lord, you know that I love you." Jesus said, "Take care of my sheep." (Jn. 21:16)
> Carry each other's burdens, and in this way you will fulfill the law of Christ. (Ga. 6:2)
> Therefore, as we have opportunity, let us do good to all people, especially to those who belong to the family of believers. (Ga. 6:10)
> Serve wholeheartedly, as if you were serving the Lord, not men. (Ep. 6:7)
> Command those who are rich in this present world not to be arrogant nor to put their hope in wealth, which is so uncertain, but to put their hope in God, who richly provides us with everything for our enjoyment. Command them to do good, to be rich in good deeds, and to be generous and willing to share. (1 Ti. 6:17-18)

6 (2:1-2) **Tabernacle, Placement of—Guidance, of God—Promised Land**: there was the placement of the Tabernacle in the center of the camp. The people were to know one supreme fact: God dwells in the midst of His people and guides them as they march to the promised land. (Pictures of *The Tabernacle, The Encampment of the Tribes*, and *The Marching Positions of the Tribes* are being placed at the end of ch.2, pp.28-30.)

The relationship of God to His people is the stress here. The Tabernacle sat right in the middle of the camp with all the tribes placed equally around it. The picture was that of a square formation: three tribes were placed on each of the four sides of the Tabernacle, some distance from it. The point is this: the presence of God—the Tabernacle—sat right in the midst of His people. God was equally present to help any and all. He was equally present to guide any and all. One person could reach God as easily as the next person. God was available, right in the midst of His people. And He would be available until they reached the promised land. This was to be His permanent position: the Tabernacle was always to sit in the midst of the people.

Thought 1. God dwells in the midst of His people; He dwells in the midst of the church. He is always available to help and guide His people. This is the strong declaration of Scripture.

(1) God guides His people.

> To shine on those living in darkness and in the shadow of death, to guide our feet into the path of peace. (Lu. 1:79)
> But when he, the Spirit of truth, comes, he will guide you into all truth. He will not speak on his own; he will speak only what he hears, and he will tell you what is yet to come. (Jn. 16:13)
> He makes me lie down in green pastures, he leads me beside quiet waters. (Ps. 23:2)
> He guides the humble in what is right and teaches them his way. (Ps. 25:9)
> For this God is our God for ever and ever; he will be our guide even to the end. (Ps. 48:14)
> You guide me with your counsel, and afterward you will take me into glory. (Ps. 73:24)
> Whether you turn to the right or to the left, your ears will hear a voice behind you, saying, "This is the way; walk in it." (Is. 30:21)
> I will lead the blind by ways they have not known, along unfamiliar paths I will guide them; I will turn the darkness into light before them and make the rough places smooth. These are the things I will do; I will not forsake them. (Is. 42:16)

(2) God is our helper.

> So we say with confidence, "The Lord is my helper; I will not be afraid. What can man do to me?" (He. 13:6)
> "I am with you and will watch over you wherever you go, and I will bring you back

to this land. I will not leave you until I have done what I have promised you." (Ge. 28:15)

The LORD replied, "My Presence will go with you, and I will give you rest." (Ex. 33:14)

The LORD is my strength and my shield; my heart trusts in him, and I am helped. My heart leaps for joy and I will give thanks to him in song. (Ps. 28:7)

For the LORD loves the just and will not forsake his faithful ones. They will be protected forever, but the offspring of the wicked will be cut off. (Ps. 37:28)

Yet I am poor and needy; may the LORD think of me. You are my help and my deliverer; O my God, do not delay. (Ps. 40:17)

Have mercy on me, O God, have mercy on me, for in you my soul takes refuge. I will take refuge in the shadow of your wings until the disaster has passed. (Ps. 57:1)

So do not fear, for I am with you; do not be dismayed, for I am your God. I will strengthen you and help you; I will uphold you with my righteous right hand. (Is. 41:10)

When you pass through the waters, I will be with you; and when you pass through the rivers, they will not sweep over you. When you walk through the fire, you will not be burned; the flames will not set you ablaze. (Is. 43:2)

Even to your old age and gray hairs I am he, I am he who will sustain you. I have made you and I will carry you; I will sustain you and I will rescue you. (Is. 46:4)

Thought 2. One thing makes the church advance: giving God and His Word the prominent place in the midst of His people. The church has to listen to God—pay attention to His Word—in order to be guided and blessed by God. God guides and blesses only those who listen to Him, only those who follow His instructions and walk in the direction He points. The church that follows God's Word...

- is the church that marches forth like a mighty army, victorious and triumphant over the enemies of the world
- is the conquering church that conquers all the pitfalls and enemies of the world

You are already clean because of the word I have spoken to you. (Jn. 15:3)

Sanctify them by the truth; your word is truth. (Jn. 17:17)

But these are written that you may believe that Jesus is the Christ, the Son of God, and that by believing you may have life in his name. (Jn. 20:31)

I am not ashamed of the gospel, because it is the power of God for the salvation of everyone who believes: first for the Jew, then for the Gentile. (Ro. 1:16)

All Scripture is God-breathed and is useful for teaching, rebuking, correcting and training in righteousness. (2 Ti. 3:16)

For the word of God is living and active. Sharper than any double-edged sword, it penetrates even to dividing soul and spirit, joints and marrow; it judges the thoughts and attitudes of the heart. (He. 4:12)

Like newborn babies, crave pure spiritual milk, so that by it you may grow up in your salvation. (1 Pe. 2:2)

How can a young man keep his way pure? By living according to your word. (Ps. 119:9)

Your word is a lamp to my feet and a light for my path. (Ps. 119:105)

The unfolding of your words gives light; it gives understanding to the simple. (Ps. 119:130)

For these commands are a lamp, this teaching is a light, and the corrections of discipline are the way to life. (Pr. 6:23)

"Is not my word like fire," declares the LORD, "and like a hammer that breaks a rock in pieces?" (Je. 23:29)

7 (2:2-33) **Tabernacle, Placement of—Standing Fast—Perseverance—Family of God—Church—Relationships—God, Presence of**: there was placement of the tribes around the Tabernacle, each man under his banner. The lesson of this point is striking: each believer must take his place under the standard of Christ and stand fast under the banner of God's family. (See pictures of *The Encampment of the Tribes* and *The Tabernacle* at the end of ch.2, pp.28-30.)

The people of God were to camp around the Tabernacle in a square formation. They were also to march in the same formation, a formation that placed the Tabernacle in the very middle of God's people. Everyone had to know his or her relationship to the others. Each individual had to know his place within the tribe, and each tribe had to know its place in relationship to the other tribes. But most important, everyone had to know his or her place in relation to the Tabernacle, the symbol of God's very presence. The presence of God was the focus:

⇒ It was He who was going to lead His people to the promised land.
⇒ It was He who was going to give them the strength to conquer the pitfalls and enemies along the way.
⇒ It was He who was going to give them the help and guidance they needed.

Therefore, each individual had to know—beyond any question—his relationship to God. He had to know where he stood among God's people; he had to know under what banner he was to march. Note: this is exactly what Scripture says: each man was to stand under his standard with the banners of the tribe waving in the wind (v.2). Note the word *host* or *division* (saba) running throughout this passage (vv.4, 6, 8, etc.). The word means unit, troop, band, host, division, or army. The idea is that of a military camp or a pilgrim camp. God's people can be pictured either as an army or as pilgrims. They are pilgrims or an army marching to the promised land of God.

Note that God's people were to camp some distance away from the Tabernacle. Scripture says elsewhere that the tribes were to be one thousand yards from the Tabernacle (Jos. 3:4). The Levites were to camp between the secular tribes and the Tabernacle in order to protect the abuse of God's presence (vv.3, 23, 29, 35).

Thought 1. Two descriptive pictures of believers are seen in this point.

(1) Believers are like pilgrims walking through the desert and wilderness of this world. They are marching to the promised land of heaven.

> All these people were still living by faith when they died. They did not receive the things promised; they only saw them and welcomed them from a distance. And they admitted that they were aliens and strangers on earth. (He. 11:13)
>
> Let us, then, go to him outside the camp, bearing the disgrace he bore. For here we do not have an enduring city, but we are looking for the city that is to come. (He. 13:13-14)
>
> Dear friends, I urge you, as aliens and strangers in the world, to abstain from sinful desires, which war against your soul. (1 Pe. 2:11)
>
> And Jacob said to Pharaoh, "The years of my pilgrimage are a hundred and thirty. My years have been few and difficult, and they do not equal the years of the pilgrimage of my fathers." (Ge. 47:9)
>
> I also established my covenant with them to give them the land of Canaan, where they lived as aliens. (Ex. 6:4)
>
> We are aliens and strangers in your sight, as were all our forefathers. Our days on earth are like a shadow, without hope. (1 Chr. 29:15)
>
> "Hear my prayer, O LORD, listen to my cry for help; be not deaf to my weeping. For I dwell with you as an alien, a stranger, as all my fathers were. Look away from me, that I may rejoice again before I depart and am no more." (Ps. 39:12-13)

(2) Believers are like soldiers in the desert and wilderness of this world. They are soldiers marching forth to conquer all the pitfalls and enemies of this world, marching forth to the promised land of God.

> For our struggle is not against flesh and blood, but against the rulers, against the authorities, against the powers of this dark world and against the spiritual forces of evil in the heavenly realms. Therefore put on the full armor of God, so that when the day of evil comes, you may be able to stand your ground, and after you have done everything, to stand. (Ep. 6:12-13)
>
> In truthful speech and in the power of God; with weapons of righteousness in the right hand and in the left. (2 Co. 6:7)
>
> The weapons we fight with are not the weapons of the world. On the contrary, they have divine power to demolish strongholds. (2 Co. 10:4)
>
> Take the helmet of salvation and the sword of the Spirit, which is the word of God. (Ep. 6:17)
>
> But since we belong to the day, let us be self-controlled, putting on faith and love as a breastplate, and the hope of salvation as a helmet. (1 Th. 5:8)
>
> Fight the good fight of the faith. Take hold of the eternal life to which you were called when you made your good confession in the presence of many witnesses. (1 Ti. 6:12)
>
> Endure hardship with us like a good soldier of Christ Jesus. No one serving as a soldier gets involved in civilian affairs—he wants to please his commanding officer. (2 Ti. 2:3-4)
>
> For the word of God is living and active. Sharper than any double-edged sword, it penetrates even to dividing soul and spirit, joints and marrow; it judges the thoughts and attitudes of the heart. (He. 4:12)
>
> They overcame him by the blood of the Lamb and by the word of their testimony; they did not love their lives so much as to shrink from death. (Re. 12:11)

Thought 2. Every believer has his appointed place in the army of God. Each believer is related to other believers, and all believers are related to Christ. We are the family of God, standing under the great standard of Christ and the great banner of God. Following Him, we must proclaim our loyalty to Him, giving strong testimony to His great salvation.

(1) Every believer has his own place under the great standard of Christ and banner of God.

> You did not choose me, but I chose you and appointed you to go and bear fruit—fruit that will last. Then the Father will give you whatever you ask in my name. (Jn. 15:16)
>
> Just as each of us has one body with many members, and these members do not all have the same function, so in Christ we who are many form one body, and each member belongs to all the others. (Ro. 12:4-5)
>
> Each one should remain in the situation which he was in when God called him. (1 Co. 7:20)
>
> Now you are the body of Christ, and each one of you is a part of it. (1 Co. 12:27)
>
> "You are my witnesses," declares the LORD, "and my servant whom I have chosen, so that you may know and believe me and understand that I am he. Before me no god was formed, nor will there be one after me." (Is. 43:10)

(2) We are to proclaim the standard of Christ and the banner of God—bear strong witness and testimony for Him.

> "Therefore go and make disciples of all nations, baptizing them in the name of the Father and of the Son and of the Holy Spirit, and teaching them to obey everything I have commanded you. And surely I am with you always, to the very end of the age." (Mt. 28:19-20)
>
> "But you will receive power when the Holy Spirit comes on you; and you will be my witnesses in Jerusalem, and in all Judea and Samaria, and to the ends of the earth." (Ac. 1:8)
>
> "For we cannot help speaking about what we have seen and heard." (Ac. 4:20)

"Go, stand in the temple courts," he said, "and tell the people the full message of this new life." (Ac. 5:20)

It is written: "I believed; therefore I have spoken." With that same spirit of faith we also believe and therefore speak. (2 Co. 4:13)

So do not be ashamed to testify about our Lord, or ashamed of me his prisoner. But join with me in suffering for the gospel, by the power of God. (2 Ti. 1:8)

But in your hearts set apart Christ as Lord. Always be prepared to give an answer to everyone who asks you to give the reason for the hope that you have. But do this with gentleness and respect. (1 Pe. 3:15)

Thought 3. The Tabernacle was placed right in the middle of God's people for one reason and one reason only: so that God could dwell with His people and guide them as they marched to the promised land. So it is with us.

(1) Jesus Christ became flesh and dwelt among us.

The Word became flesh and made his dwelling among us. We have seen his glory, the glory of the One and Only, who came from the Father, full of grace and truth. (Jn. 1:14)

(2) The Spirit of God dwells within the church.

Don't you know that you yourselves are God's temple and that God's Spirit lives in you? (1 Co. 3:16)

The body is a unit, though it is made up of many parts; and though all its parts are many, they form one body. So it is with Christ. For we were all baptized by one Spirit into one body—whether Jews or Greeks, slave or free—and we were all given the one Spirit to drink. Now the body is not made up of one part but of many. If the foot should say, "Because I am not a hand, I do not belong to the body," it would not for that reason cease to be part of the body. And if the ear should say, "Because I am not an eye, I do not belong to the body," it would not for that reason cease to be part of the body. If the whole body were an eye, where would the sense of hearing be? If the whole body were an ear, where would the sense of smell be? But in fact God has arranged the parts in the body, every one of them, just as he wanted them to be. (1 Co. 12:12-18)

(3) The Spirit of God dwells within the body of every individual believer.

Do you not know that your body is a temple of the Holy Spirit, who is in you, whom you have received from God? You are not your own; you were bought at a price. Therefore honor God with your body. (1 Co. 6:19-20)

And I will ask the Father, and he will give you another Counselor to be with you forever—the Spirit of truth. The world cannot accept him, because it neither sees him nor knows him. But you know him, for he lives with you and will be in you. (Jn. 14:16-17)

You, however, are controlled not by the sinful nature but by the Spirit, if the Spirit of God lives in you. And if anyone does not have the Spirit of Christ, he does not belong to Christ. (Ro. 8:9)

Guard the good deposit that was entrusted to you—guard it with the help of the Holy Spirit who lives in us. (2 Ti. 1:14)

As for you, the anointing you received from him remains in you, and you do not need anyone to teach you. But as his anointing teaches you about all things and as that anointing is real, not counterfeit—just as it has taught you, remain in him. (1 Jn. 2:27)

8 (2:34) **Obedience—Commandments, of God**: there was the obedience of God's people. They did everything that God commanded. They camped exactly as God commanded, and they marched exactly as God commanded.

Thought 1. God's people must obey God and do exactly what He says. There must be absolute compliance in following God, in obeying His Word. The individual believer must obey God, and the church as a whole must obey God. When the believer and the church are obedient—when they obey God exactly as He says—then they will walk triumphantly over the pitfalls and enemies of this life. They will be mobilized, ready to fight the good fight of faith. They will be victorious as they march to the promised land of heaven.

"Not everyone who says to me, 'Lord, Lord,' will enter the kingdom of heaven, but only he who does the will of my Father who is in heaven." (Mt. 7:21)

Jesus replied, "If anyone loves me, he will obey my teaching. My Father will love him, and we will come to him and make our home with him." (Jn. 14:23)

If you obey my commands, you will remain in my love, just as I have obeyed my Father's commands and remain in his love. (Jn. 15:10)

You are my friends if you do what I command. (Jn. 15:14)

Blessed are those who wash their robes, that they may have the right to the tree of life and may go through the gates into the city. (Re. 22:14)

The LORD your God commands you this day to follow these decrees and laws; carefully observe them with all your heart and with all your soul. (De. 26:16)

Do not let this Book of the Law depart from your mouth; meditate on it day and night, so that you may be careful to do everything written in it. Then you will be prosperous and successful. (Jos. 1:8)

(See pp.28-30 for pictures of *The Tabernacle, The Encampment of the Tribes,* and *The Marching Positions of the Tribes.*)

NUMBERS 1:1–2:34

TYPES, SYMBOLS, AND PICTURES
(Numbers 1:1–2:34)

Historical Term	Type or Picture (Scriptural Basis for Each)	Life Application for Today's Believer	Biblical Application
The Promised Land Nu.1:1-2:34; 5:1-31; 34:1-15	*The promised land definitely refers to Palestine, the land of Canaan or of Israel. But the promised land also refers to heaven. The promised land of Canaan is a symbol (a type, a picture, an illustration) of heaven, of God's promise to the believer that he will inherit heaven, the new heavens and earth. The promised land represented many things to Abraham.* 1. *The promised land was the assurance of a personal inheritance: the possession of a new country, of his own property with all its good land, wealth, and rights. Abraham believed that he would live in a new city within his own land and country—all given by God Himself. And the land was to be forever, for it was promised by the eternal God Himself.* 2. *The promised land was the assurance of conquest and rest, of spiritual victory and spiritual rest. The promised land was to bring a God-given peace and security, freedom and liberty, deliverance and salvation to Abraham.* 3. *The promised land was the assurance of God's own presence, that is, of God's love, care, provision, and protection. Abraham was bound to know this: if God was going to give him the promised land, then God must love and care for him. God would therefore provide and protect him no matter what lay ahead. God—His strong presence—would be with him through all the trials and struggles of life.* **Not one of you will enter the land I swore with uplifted hand to make your home, except Caleb son of Jephunneh and Joshua son of Nun. (Nu.14:30)**	It is the obedient who will receive the inheritance of God, the promised land that flows with milk and honey. The obedient person is the person who lives a life of separation, a life that is entirely different from the immoral and lawless people of the earth.	*But seek first his kingdom and his righteousness, and all these things will be given to you as well (Mt.6:33).* *And teaching them to obey everything I have commanded you. And surely I am with you always, to the very end of the age" (Mt. 28:20).* *"Be careful, or your hearts will be weighed down with dissipation, drunkenness and the anxieties of life, and that day will close on you unexpectedly like a trap (Lu. 21:34).* *With many other words he warned them; and he pleaded with them, "Save yourselves from this corrupt generation" (Ac. 2:40).* *"Therefore, I urge you, brothers, in view of God's mercy, to offer your bodies as living sacrifices, holy and pleasing to God—this is your spiritual act of worship. Do not conform any longer to the pattern of this world, but be transformed by the renewing of your mind. Then you will be able to test and approve what God's will is—his good, pleasing and perfect will" (Ro.12:1-2).* *Therefore come out from them and be separate, says the Lord. Touch no unclean thing, and I will receive you." (2 Co. 6:17).* *Have nothing to do with the fruitless deeds of darkness, but rather expose them (Ep. 5:11).*

NUMBERS 1:1–2:34

Historical Term	Type or Picture (Scriptural Basis for Each)	Life Application for Today's Believer	Biblical Application
The Tabernacle Nu.1:47-54; 4:1-20 (See also Le.17:3-9)	*The Tabernacle symbolizes or pictures three major things:* *1. The Tabernacle symbolizes or pictures the ministry of Jesus Christ. The materials used to construct the Tabernacle are pictures of God's redemption in Jesus Christ. The various furnishings show God's great plan of salvation for the repentant sinner. (See all notes—Ex.25:1-9; 10-22; 23-30; 31-40; 27:1-21; 30:1-10.)* *2. The Tabernacle symbolizes or pictures the ministry of the church. The Tabernacle was a worship center in which God dwelt, and the Tabernacle stood as a witness to the world. So does the church.* *3. The Tabernacle symbolizes or pictures the Christian believer, the person who truly follows God. The Tabernacle was the dwelling place for God's presence upon earth, standing as a strong witness to the LORD.* **Instead, appoint the Levites to be in charge of the tabernacle of the Testimony—over all its furnishings and everything belonging to it. They are to carry the tabernacle and all its furnishings; they are to take care of it and encamp around it (Nu.1:50).**	1. The Tabernacle of Moses reveals every aspect of Jesus Christ and His work as the Word who became flesh and dwelt ("tabernacled") among us (John 1:14; see note—He.9:1-14). 2. God's presence and witness dwell within the church in two ways: ⇒ God's Spirit dwells within believers. ⇒ God's Spirit dwells among—within the very presence of—believers when two or three of them gather together. 3. The believer—his body—is the very temple of God, the sanctuary and dwelling place for the presence and witness of God upon earth.	*For where two or three come together in my name, there am I with them." (Mt. 18:20).* *I in them and you in me. May they be brought to complete unity to let the world know that you sent me and have loved them even as you have loved me (Jn. 17:23; see also 1 Co. 6:19-20; 2 Co. 6:16; Ga. 2:20; Col. 1:27).* *Don't you know that you yourselves [plural, referring to the church, the body or assembly of believers] are God's temple and that God's Spirit lives in you? (1 Co. 3:16).* *Do you not know that your body is a temple of the Holy Spirit, who is in you, whom you have received from God? You are not your own; you were bought at a price. Therefore honor God with your body (1 Co. 6:19-20).* *And in him you too are being built together to become a dwelling in which God lives by his Spirit (Ep. 2:22).* *For you died, and your life is now hidden with Christ in God (Col. 3:3).*

The Tabernacle in the Wilderness

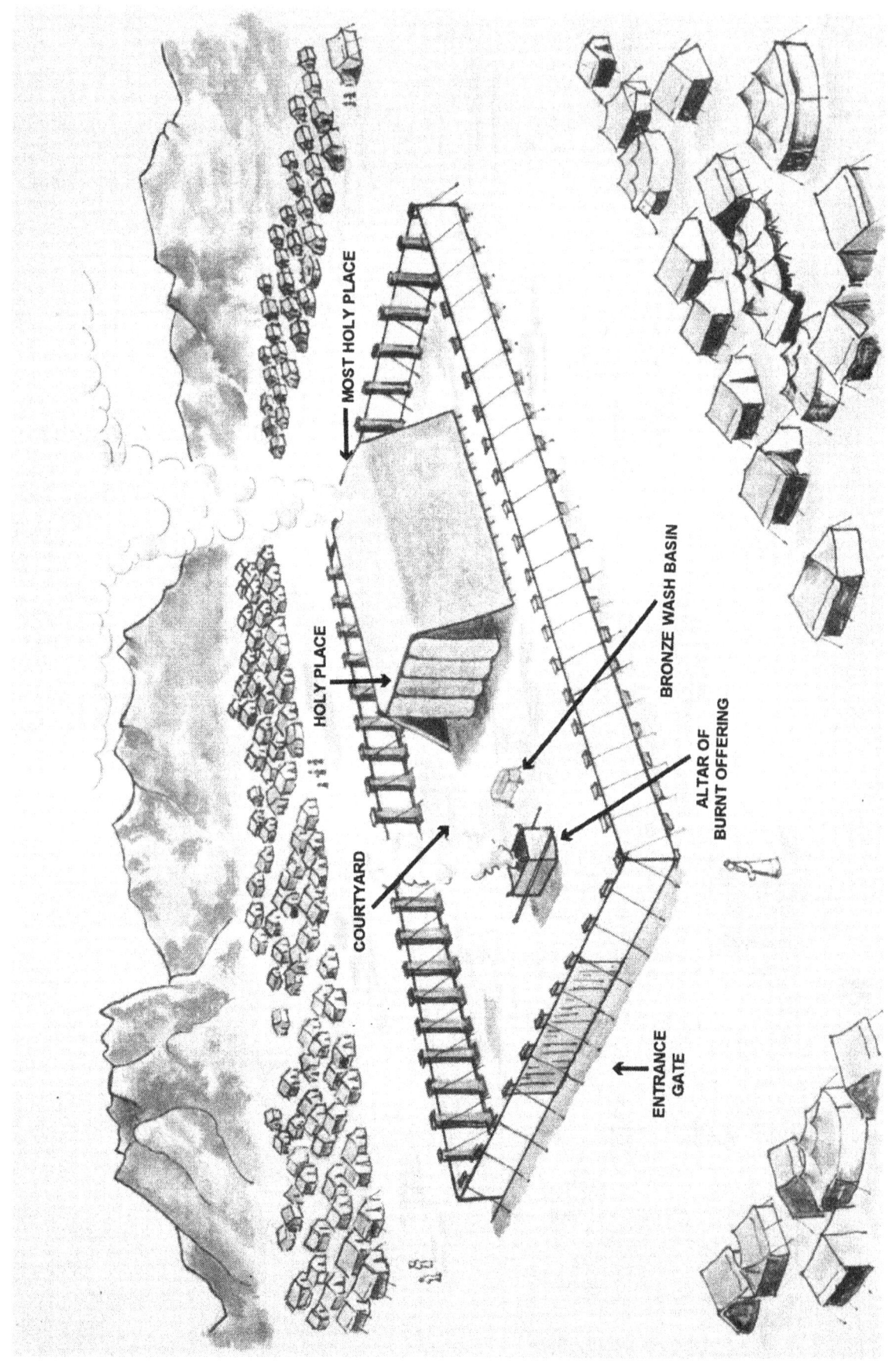

THE TABERNACLE (INTERIOR)

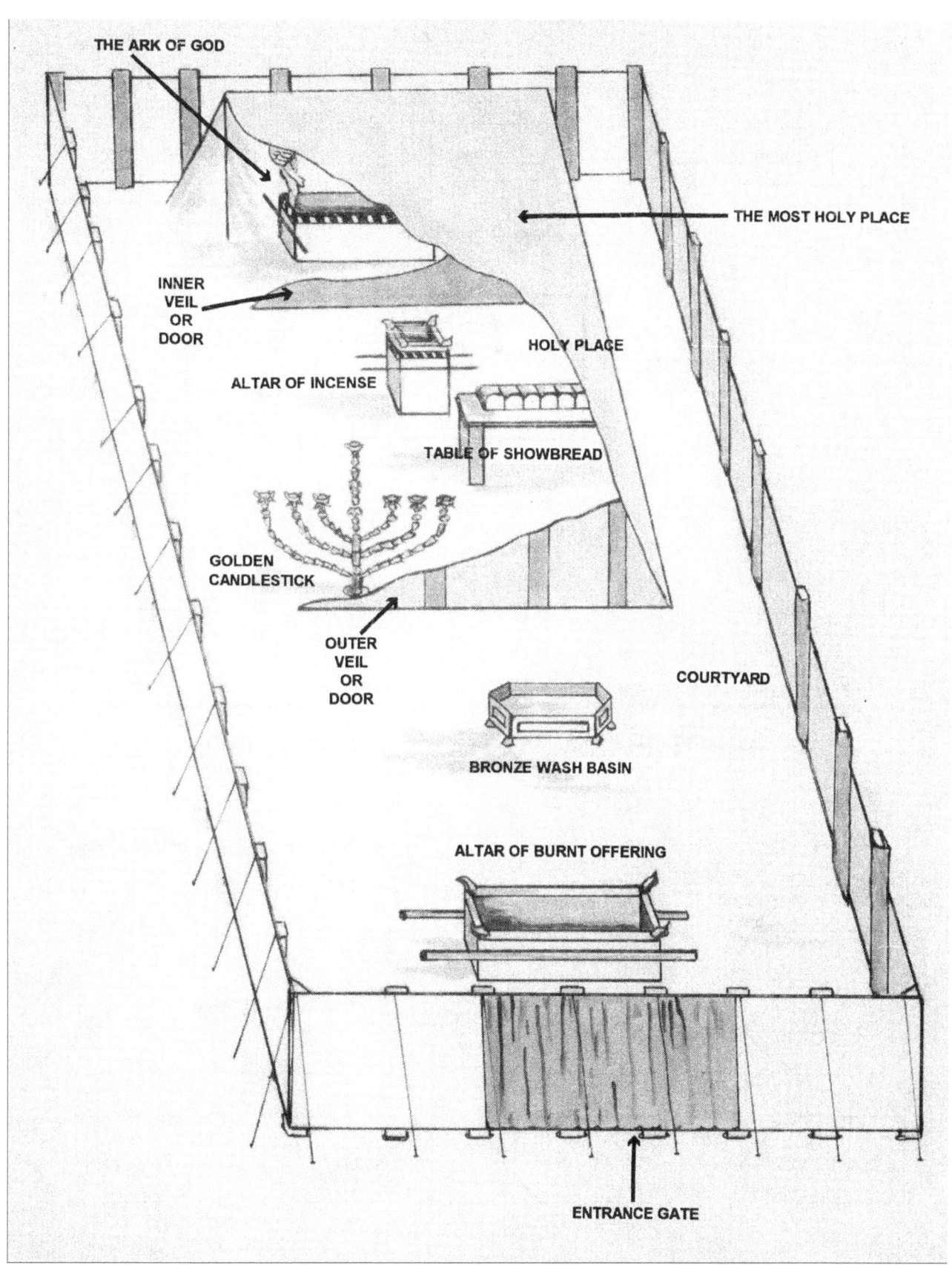

THE ENCAMPMENT OF THE TRIBES

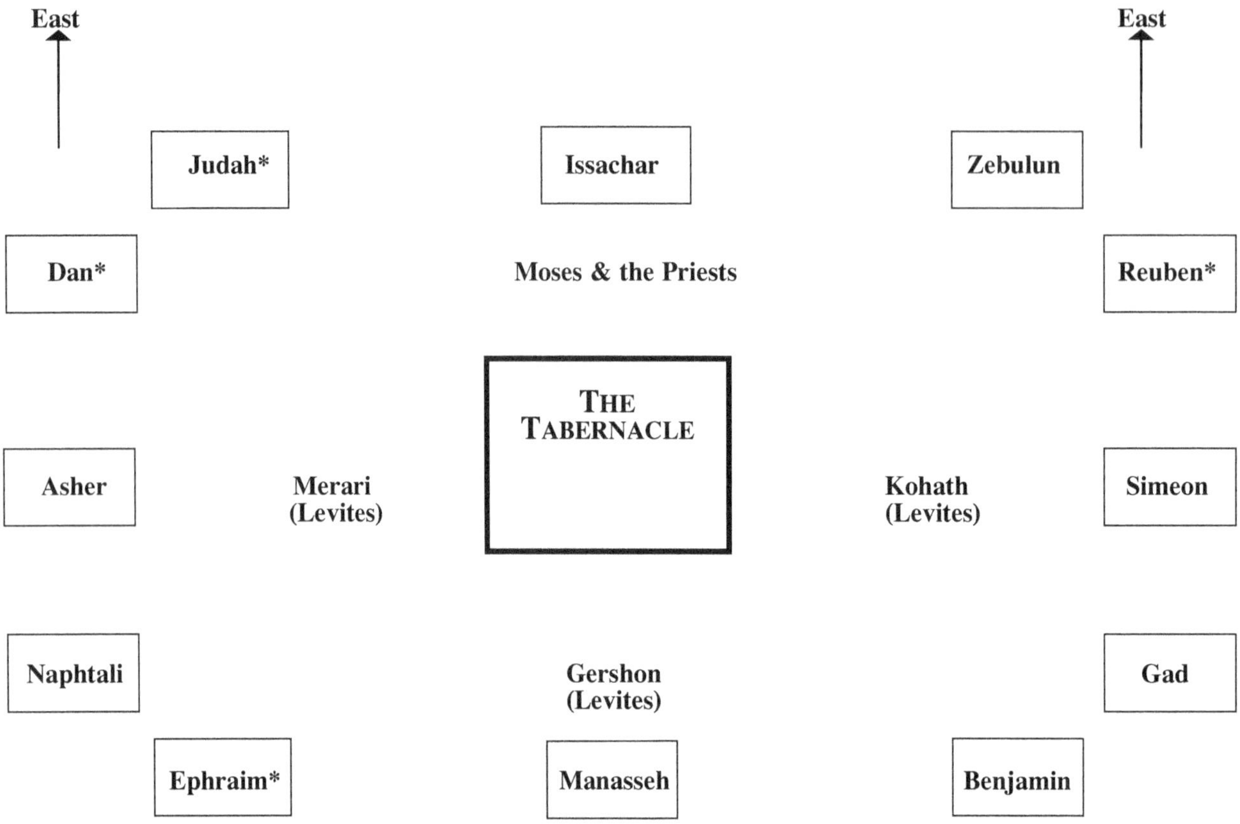

East
East
Judah*
Issachar
Zebulun
Dan*
Moses & the Priests
Reuben*
THE TABERNACLE
Asher
Merari (Levites)
Kohath (Levites)
Simeon
Naphtali
Gershon (Levites)
Gad
Ephraim*
Manasseh
Benjamin

(* *The leading tribe of the group*)

THE MARCHING POSITIONS OF THE TRIBES[2]

DAN
EPHRAIM
REUBEN
JUDAH
ASHER
Kohathites carry the Tabernacle furnishings
MANASSEH
Gershonites & Merarites carry the Tabernacle
SIMEON
Levites carry the ark
ISSACHAR
NAPHTALI
BENJAMIN
GAD
ZEBULUN

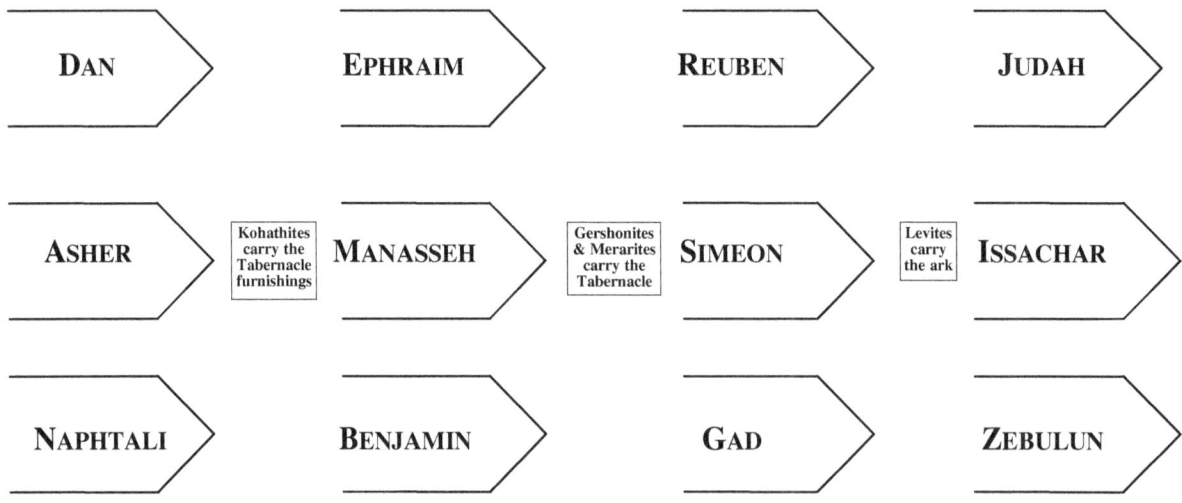

2 The idea for the Marching Positions of the Tribes is taken from the *New International Version Study Bible.* (Grand Rapids, MI: Zondervan Bible Publishers, 1985), p.192.

NUMBERS 3:1-51

CHAPTER 3

B. The Organization of the Priests, the Levites, & the Firstborn—the Second & Third Census Records: Called to Be Assistants, 3:1-51

1. The family line of Aaron & Moses: Some are anointed & ordained to serve God

   a. The four sons of Aaron—Nadab (the firstborn), Abihu, Eleazar, & Ithamar—were anointed & ordained to serve as priests
   b. The two oldest sons (Nadab & Abihu) had been struck dead by the LORD (Le. 10:1-2)
      1) Had offered unauthorized fire: Approached God in a wrong way
      2) Had left no sons to continue their names among the priests
   c. The two youngest sons served as priests

2. The appointment of the Levites: Some are set apart to be assistants

   a. Called to be the assistants to the High Priest, Aaron (a symbol of Christ)
      1) To take care of all the work of the Tabernacle itself
      2) To take care of all the furnishings of the Tabernacle
      3) To be totally given over to assist the High Priest
      4) To protect the sanctity of the sanctuary: Guard it against the abuse of intruders
   b. Called by God to a very special position: To become the substitute, the replacement for the firstborn sons—to be given to the service of God instead of the firstborn sons
      1) The special position: "The Levites are mine"
      2) The authority of the call
         • The historical fact: God had set apart the firstborn to serve Him since Egypt (Ex. 13:2f; 22:29; 34:19f)
         • The sovereignty of God

3. The census, placement, & duties of the Levites: A picture of doing one's job well

   a. The LORD's charge to Moses
      1) To count every male one month old or older
      2) The picture of total obedience: Moses did exactly what God commanded
   b. The overall view of the Levites
      1) The three sons of Levi: Gershon, Kohath, & Merari
      2) The Gershonite clans: Libni & Shimei
      3) The Kohathite clans: Amram, Izhar, Hebron, & Uzziel
      4) The Merarite clans: Mahli & Mushi
   c. The detailed look at the Gershonites
      1) The clans: Libnites & Shimeites
      2) Their census number: 7,500
      3) Their camp: To the west behind the Tabernacle
      4) Their leader: Eliasaph, son of Lael
      5) Their duties: To take care of the tent of the Tabernacle, its coverings & curtains
         • The entrance curtain
         • The courtyard curtains
         • The entrance curtain to the courtyard
         • The ropes & all else related to the coverings & curtains
   d. The detailed look at the Kohathites
      1) Their clans: Amramites, Izhorites, Hebronites, Uzzielites
      2) Their census number: 8,600
      3) Their overall responsibility: The care of the sanctuary
      4) Their camp: The south side of the Tabernacle
      5) Their leader: Elizaphan, son of Uzziel
      6) Their duties: To take

This is the account of the family of Aaron and Moses at the time the LORD talked with Moses on Mount Sinai. 2 The names of the sons of Aaron were Nadab the firstborn and Abihu, Eleazar and Ithamar. 3 Those were the names of Aaron's sons, the anointed priests, who were ordained to serve as priests. 4 Nadab and Abihu, however, fell dead before the LORD when they made an offering with unauthorized fire before him in the Desert of Sinai. They had no sons; so only Eleazar and Ithamar served as priests during the lifetime of their father Aaron.

5 The LORD said to Moses, 6 "Bring the tribe of Levi and present them to Aaron the priest to assist him. 7 They are to perform duties for him and for the whole community at the Tent of Meeting by doing the work of the tabernacle. 8 They are to take care of all the furnishings of the Tent of Meeting, fulfilling the obligations of the Israelites by doing the work of the tabernacle. 9 Give the Levites to Aaron and his sons; they are the Israelites who are to be given wholly to him. 10 Appoint Aaron and his sons to serve as priests; anyone else who approaches the sanctuary must be put to death."

11 The LORD also said to Moses, 12 "I have taken the Levites from among the Israelites in place of the first male offspring of every Israelite woman. The Levites are mine, 13 For all the firstborn are mine. When I struck down all the firstborn in Egypt, I set apart for myself every firstborn in Israel, whether man or animal. They are to be mine. I am the LORD."

14 The LORD said to Moses in the Desert of Sinai, 15 "Count the Levites by their families and clans. Count every male a month old or more."

16 So Moses counted them, as he was commanded by the word of the LORD.

17 These were the names of the sons of Levi: Gershon, Kohath and Merari.

18 These were the names of the Gershonite clans: Libni and Shimei.

19 The Kohathite clans: Amram, Izhar, Hebron and Uzziel.

20 The Merarite clans: Mahli and Mushi. These were the Levite clans, according to their families.

21 To Gershon belonged the clans of the Libnites and Shimeites; these were the Gershonite clans.

22 The number of all the males a month old or more who were counted was 7,500. 23 The Gershonite clans were to camp on the west, behind the tabernacle. 24 The leader of the families of the Gershonites was Eliasaph son of Lael. 25 At the Tent of Meeting the Gershonites were responsible for the care of the tabernacle and tent, its coverings, the curtain at the entrance to the Tent of Meeting, 26 The curtains of the courtyard, the curtain at the entrance to the courtyard surrounding the tabernacle and altar, and the ropes—and everything related to their use.

27 To Kohath belonged the clans of the Amramites, Izharites, Hebronites and Uzzielites; these were the Kohathite clans. 28 The number of all the males a month old or more was 8,600. The Kohathites were responsible for the care of the sanctuary. 29 The Kohathite clans were to camp on the south side of the tabernacle. 30 The leader of the families of the Kohathite clans was Elizaphan son of Uzziel. 31 They were responsible for

NUMBERS 3:1-51

Outline	Scripture	Outline

care of...
• The Ark, the table, & the lampstand
• the altars & utensils
• the inner curtain & all else related to their use
7) The chief administrator over all the Levites was given special oversight over the sanctuary & the Kohathites: Eleazar, son of Aaron
e. The detailed look at the Merarites
  1) Their clans: The Mahlites & the Mushites
  2) Their census number: 6,200
 	
  3) Their leader: Zuriel, son of Abihail
  4) Their camp: The north side of the Tabernacle
  5) Their duties: To take care of...
• The supporting frames of the Tabernacle, crossbars, posts, bases, & all else related to their use
• The posts of the courtyard with their bases, pegs, & ropes
f. The detailed look at Moses & Aaron
  1) Their camp: To the east toward the sunrise, in front of the Tabernacle
  2) Their duties: Had overall responsibility for the sanctuary—in behalf of the people
  3) The warning: Anyone other than a priest or Levite who approached the sanctuary was to be executed
g. The total number of Levites one month old or older: 22,000
	the care of the ark, the table, the lampstand, the altars, the articles of the sanctuary used in ministering, the curtain, and everything related to their use.
	32 The chief leader of the Levites was Eleazar son of Aaron, the priest. He was appointed over those who were responsible for the care of the sanctuary.
	33 To Merari belonged the clans of the Mahlites and the Mushites; these were the Merarite clans.
	34 The number of all the males a month old or more who were counted was 6,200.
	35 The leader of the families of the Merarite clans was Zuriel son of Abihail; they were to camp on the north side of the tabernacle.
	36 The Merarites were appointed to take care of the frames of the tabernacle, its crossbars, posts, bases, all its equipment, and everything related to their use,
	37 As well as the posts of the surrounding courtyard with their bases, tent pegs and ropes.
	38 Moses and Aaron and his sons were to camp to the east of the tabernacle, toward the sunrise, in front of the Tent of Meeting. They were responsible for the care of the sanctuary on behalf of the Israelites. Anyone else who approached the sanctuary was to be put to death.
	39 The total number of Levites counted at the LORD's command by Moses and Aaron according to their clans, including every male a month old or more, was 22,000.
	40 The LORD said to Moses, "Count all the firstborn Israelite males who are a month old or more and make a list of their names.
	41 Take the Levites for me in place of all the firstborn of the Israelites, and the livestock of the Levites in place of all the firstborn of the livestock of the Israelites. I am the LORD."
	42 So Moses counted all the firstborn of the Israelites, as the LORD commanded him.
	43 The total number of firstborn males a month old or more, listed by name, was 22,273.
	44 The LORD also said to Moses,
	45 "Take the Levites in place of all the firstborn of Israel, and the livestock of the Levites in place of their livestock. The Levites are to be mine. I am the LORD.
	46 To redeem the 273 firstborn Israelites who exceed the number of the Levites,
	47 Collect five shekels for each one, according to the sanctuary shekel, which weighs twenty gerahs.
	48 Give the money for the redemption of the additional Israelites to Aaron and his sons."
	49 So Moses collected the redemption money from those who exceeded the number redeemed by the Levites.
	50 From the firstborn of the Israelites he collected silver weighing 1,365 shekels, according to the sanctuary shekel.
	51 Moses gave the redemption money to Aaron and his sons, as he was commanded by the word of the LORD.
		4. The census of the firstborn & their replacement by the Levites: A picture of redemption
		a. The LORD's charge: To count all the firstborn sons in Israel: One month old or older
		  1) To substitute the Levites for all the firstborn of Israel, to replace them as the servants of God
		  2) To substitute the livestock of the Levites for the firstborn livestock of Israel (to be used in the sacrifices)
		b. The strict obedience of Moses
		c. The number of firstborn sons one month old or older: 22,273
		
		d. The special charge
		  1) To substitute the Levites for the firstborn Israelites: The Levites were thereafter to be the LORD's, His servants
		
		  2) To redeem the 273, pay the price for the firstborn sons who exceeded the number of Levites
		• To collect five pieces of silver for each one
		
		• To give the redemption money to the priests (Aaron & his sons)
		
		  3) The obedience of Moses: He collected the redemption money
		
		• He collected 1,365 shekels (about 34 pounds of silver)
		
		• He gave the money to the priests, Aaron & his sons
		• He was careful to obey God—totally

DIVISION I

THE PREPARATION FOR THE MARCH TO THE PROMISED LAND, 1:1–10:36

B. The Organization of the Priests, the Levites, and the Firstborn—the Second and Third Census Records: Called to Be Assistants, 3:1-51

(3:1-51) **Introduction—Ministry, Work of—Assistants, Needed—Ministers, Needed—Work, of the Ministry**: the magnitude of the ministry is overwhelming. No matter the size of the church, the work never is done. There are always people to see, places to go, and work to be done. There are always people who need encouragement, counseling, visiting, and a closer walk with the LORD—some help in some way. Beyond this, there is the task of constantly reaching out to the lost who do not know Christ. Then there is the regular and ongoing administrative care

NUMBERS 3:1-51

of the church, looking after the buildings, grounds, purchasing, and finances. Moreover, the minister has to live in God's Word—reading and studying—always preparing to preach and teach. This is an endless task that demands a great deal of time every day if anointed messages and lessons are to be used by God to bless His people. On and on the list could go, for the task of the church and of God's minister never ends.

This fact tells us something: there is a need for assistants. The minister and the church need helpers, a large number of helpers to minister to people within the church and to reach out to the lost of the world—carrying out all the functions of the church. God expects every church and every minister to get the job done. But the task cannot be done without assistants stepping forth and committing themselves to the ministry.

This is the subject of this particular Scripture: "Called to be assistants." God was mobilizing His people for the march to the promised land.

⇒ In chapters 1 and 2, the people of God were counted and organized into military divisions. The people of God were mobilized into a great army and given a banner or standard to identify their tribes, the great family to which they belonged. They were then arranged around the Tabernacle and given their permanent positions for camping and marching. The people of God—each person—knew his place within the army of God, knew exactly where he was to march and what he was to do—all except the Levites.

⇒ Now, in chapter 3, the Levites were to be counted and organized by their tribes and assigned their tasks. The Levites had been set apart to the service of God. Consequently, they were not counted with the secular tribes or army divisions.

The Levites would not be fighting in the wars; they would be carrying on the ministry of the Tabernacle for God and His people. The Levites were called to be the assistants to the priests.

This is the subject of this great passage: *The Organization of the Priests, the Levites, and the Firstborn—the Second and Third Census Records: Called to Be Assistants,* 3:1-51.

1. The family line of Aaron and Moses: some are anointed and ordained to serve God (vv.1-4).
2. The appointment of the Levites: some are set apart to be assistants (vv.5-13).
3. The census, placement, and duties of the Levites: a picture of doing one's job well (vv.14-39).
4. The census of the firstborn and their replacement by the Levites: a picture of redemption (vv.40-51).

1 (3:1-4) **Ministers, Called—Ministers, Warning to—Warning, to Ministers—Anointing, of Ministers—Ordination, of Ministers—Aaron, Sons of**: there was the family line of Aaron and Moses. Aaron and his sons were anointed and ordained to serve God. Note that the family line of Moses was not given. The focus was upon Aaron and his sons who were to serve as priests.

a. The four sons of Aaron were Nadab (the firstborn), Abihu, Eleazar, and Ithamar (v.1). All four sons were anointed and ordained to serve as priests, the ministers of God to His people (v.3). The anointing and consecration set them apart from the secular world. They were to have a very special commitment to God. They were appointed to be the official teachers of God's people. But more than this, God ordained the priests to be a type, a picture of the coming Savior and Messiah of the world. The people of that day did not know this: nevertheless, the New Testament clearly states this fact (He. 2:17; 4:14-15; 5:5; 6:20; 7:26; 8:1). Moreover, the work of the priests clearly shows this. As Gordon Wenham points out, the priests were the only ones who "had the right to handle the blood, to touch the altar, and to enter the tent of Meeting."[1] This clearly symbolizes what Jesus Christ Himself did:

⇒ Christ is the only who had the right to handle
⇒ the sacrificial blood. In fact, He Himself was the sacrifice who shed His blood for the sins of the world.
⇒ Christ alone has the right to touch the altar: no other person—no other sacrifice lying upon the altar—could please God other than the perfect person and sacrifice, Christ Himself.
⇒ Christ alone has the right to enter the tent of meeting, the inner sanctuary of God: no other person is acceptable other than the perfect, sinless Son of God.

In addition to all this, the priests were ordained to be the official mediators standing between God and the people. They were to represent God before the people and represent the people before God. Again, the priests were a symbol, a picture of Christ who stands before God as our Mediator (1 Ti. 2:5; He. 8:6; 9:15, 24; 12:24; 1 Jn. 2:1).

The point is this: the priests were set apart from the secular world. They were no longer ordinary: they stood before God in a very special position, appointed to a very special ministry. They were appointed to the service of God, appointed to minister to the people of God. They were to be a testimony to the world—a testimony that God is holy and can be approached only through the sacrifice with no defect (a symbol of Christ). This they were to proclaim both to God's people and to the pagan nations that surrounded them.

b. Note that the two oldest sons of Aaron, Nadab and Abihu, had been struck dead by the LORD (Le.10:1-2). These two priests—and keep in mind that they were *ordained priests*—offered unauthorized fire before the LORD. What does this mean? Briefly stated, they approached God in a wrong way, contrary to His direct command. They offered a false worship to God: a self-made worship, a worship created in their own minds, a worship of self-righteousness. There is also the possibility that the two priests went into the Most Holy Place; and no person was allowed to enter this hallowed, holy room except the High Priest, and he only once a year. Then there is the possibility that the two priests entered the Tabernacle while drunk or intoxicated (see outline and notes—Le. 10:1-2; 10:4-11 for more discussion). No matter the case, because of their terrible sin, God struck them dead. Obviously, a lightning bolt of fire from God's glory shot out and burned them. They died before the LORD (see outline and note—Le. 10:1-2 for more discussion).

Note the other terrible tragedy mentioned about these two priests: they had no sons. There was no one to continue their names among the priests. When they died, their family name or line died. Their story ended.

c. The two youngest sons were the only sons who served as priests during Aaron's lifetime (v.4). This is significant: at this particular time in the history of Israel, there were only three priests ministering to God's people.

---

1 Gordon J. Wenham. *The Book of Numbers.* "The New International Commentary on the Old Testament." (Grand Rapids, MI: Eerdmans Publishing Co., 1979), p.69.

NUMBERS 3:1-51

An impossible task: serving a population of two to four million. They needed help—desperately. They needed assistants, a large body of laypersons who would step forth and accept the challenge, appointed by God to help in the ministry.

Thought 1. Some persons are anointed and ordained to serve God: the ministers who fill the pulpits of the world. They break the bread of life to us and minister to our needs. But note: they cannot do the task alone. The magnitude of the ministry is too overwhelming. There is simply too much to be done. They need help: they need assistants who will stand in the gap with them.

> You did not choose me, but I chose you and appointed you to go and bear fruit—fruit that will last. Then the Father will give you whatever you ask in my name. (Jn. 15:16)
> But the Lord said to Ananias, "Go! This man is my chosen instrument to carry my name before the Gentiles and their kings and before the people of Israel." (Ac.9:15)
> Then Barnabas went to Tarsus to look for Saul, and when he found him, he brought him to Antioch. So for a whole year Barnabas and Saul met with the church and taught great numbers of people. The disciples were called Christians first at Antioch. (Ac. 11:25-26)
> 'Now get up and stand on your feet. I have appeared to you to appoint you as a servant and as a witness of what you have seen of me and what I will show you.' (Ac. 26:16)
> He has made us competent as ministers of a new covenant—not of the letter but of the Spirit; for the letter kills, but the Spirit gives life. (2 Co. 3:6)
> Therefore, since through God's mercy we have this ministry, we do not lose heart. (2 Co. 4:1)
> All this is from God, who reconciled us to himself through Christ and gave us the ministry of reconciliation. (2 Co. 5:18)
> I became a servant of this gospel by the gift of God's grace given me through the working of his power. (Ep. 3:7)
> If you continue in your faith, established and firm, not moved from the hope held out in the gospel. This is the gospel that you heard and that has been proclaimed to every creature under heaven, and of which I, Paul, have become a servant. (Col. 1:23)
> I thank Christ Jesus our Lord, who has given me strength, that he considered me faithful, appointing me to his service. (1 Ti. 1:12)
> And of this gospel I was appointed a herald and an apostle and a teacher. (2 Ti. 1:11)
> So Elijah went from there and found Elisha son of Shaphat. He was plowing with twelve yoke of oxen, and he himself was driving the twelfth pair. Elijah went up to him and threw his cloak around him. (1 K. 19:19)
> Then I heard the voice of the Lord saying, "Whom shall I send? And who will go for us?" And I said, "Here am I. Send me!" (Is. 6:8)

Thought 2. The two priests, Nadab and Abihu, stand as a stark warning to the ministers of God. The work of the ministry is serious business, and the task of the minister is of critical importance. Human life and destiny are at stake; consequently, the responsibility of the minister is enormously heavy. God holds the minister accountable for the souls and lives of people—all because the fruitfulness of life and the eternal fate of people lie in his hands. Therefore, the minister must make absolutely sure that he approaches God exactly as God says:
⇒ not in a worship created by his own mind
⇒ not in self-righteousness
⇒ not in a self-made worship
⇒ not in laziness
⇒ not abusing authority
⇒ not with disrespect and irreverence
⇒ not in drunkenness and intoxication
⇒ not having been a glutton
⇒ not having stolen
⇒ not with greed
⇒ not living in lust and immorality

The minister of God must approach God exactly as God says: he must demonstrate that he reveres the holy presence of God by approaching God through God's son, the Lord Jesus Christ. Moreover, he must teach people to approach God exactly as God dictates, through the Lord Jesus Christ. And he must teach people to respect and revere the holy presence of God. Again, this passage stands as a stark warning to the ministers of God. In the words of *The Expositor's Bible Commentary*:

> *The deaths of Aaron's newly consecrated sons should warn God's ministers of the awesome seriousness of their task....seemingly the most common reports of failure we hear of God's ministers in our day are of their malfeasance, indolence, greed, lust, and abuse of power. Tragically the lessons of the past are forgotten with frightful ease. The spiritual descendants of Nadab and Abihu continue to occupy the ranks of the 'ministers' of God.*[2]

2 (3:5-13) **Assistants—Laymen, Calling of—Call, of Laypersons—Levites, Calling of—Levites, Duty of**: there was the appointment of the Levites. They were set apart to be assistants to the priests.

a. The Levites were called to be assistants to the High Priest, Aaron, and to the other priests. Keep in mind that the priests were a symbol of Christ. This particular Scripture makes a clear distinction between the priests and their assistants. The priests were the anointed, ordained ministers of God, ultimately responsible for the people and for the Tabernacle of God (a symbol of the church). The Levites were laypersons called by God to step forth and serve as assistants to the priests. They were called out of the secular world just as the priests had been to give full time to the service of God. But their call and work was to be

---

[2] *The Expositor's Bible Commentary,* Vol.2. Frank E. Gaebelein, Editor, p.721.

helpers, assistants to the priests. Their ministry was distinct, set apart from the secular world, but it was to be under the supervision of the priests. Note exactly what their work was:

1) They were to take care of all the work of the Tabernacle itself (v.7). They performed whatever duties the priests and the worshippers needed.
2) They were to take care of all the furnishings of the Tabernacle (v.8). This, of course, included day-to-day care and maintenance, but it also included the moving of the Tabernacle from campsite to campsite. They were responsible for taking it apart, packing, transporting, and erecting the Tabernacle as God's people marched to the promised land (Nu. 1:50-51).
3) They were to be totally given over to assist the High Priest and the other priests (v.9). Note how the privilege of their call was stressed: among all the people of God, they were the ones chosen to serve as assistants to God.
4) They were to protect the sanctity of the sanctuary, to guard it against the abuse of intruders and robbers (v.10; see Nu. 1:51). Note the words *anyone else* (zar): the phrase means unauthorized, illegitimate, a person outside the family, a foreigner. Simply stated, the Levites were to keep any unauthorized person away from the Tabernacle. If a person did not belong at the Tabernacle, he was to be kept away. The Levites even had the right to execute an intruder.

b. The Levites were called by God to a very special position, a very meaningful position. Note this: they became the substitute, the replacement for the firstborn sons. They were to be given to the service of God *instead of* the firstborn sons. Note how meaningful this was to God: "the Levites are mine." They were His because all the firstborn had been His. Ever since the deliverance from Egypt, the firstborn had been appointed to serve God within each family. The firstborn son was also responsible for the service of God among the people of God. When God executed judgment upon Egypt by striking down the firstborn son, He laid claim to the firstborn sons of Israel. He had delivered the firstborn sons of Israel from judgment; therefore, He had the right to lay claim to their lives. After Egypt, they were appointed to serve God as the servants of his ministry. They were to take care of God's people, to be His ministers among the people. In the firstborn son, each family had a picture or symbol of the great salvation of God when He delivered them from the slavery of Egypt (a symbol of the world).

But now, the Levites were being set apart as the substitute, the replacement for the firstborn sons. Note the stress upon the sovereignty of God: they are to be His. "I am the LORD." God is sovereign; therefore, He has the right to replace the firstborn with the Levites. He has the right to call whom He wills to serve His people.

Thought 1. The need is great. At every turn of life people are crying for help. All over the world people are crying:

⇒ the orphans ⇒ the poor
⇒ the widows ⇒ the empty
⇒ the widowers ⇒ the lonely
⇒ the prisoners ⇒ the purposeless
⇒ the brokenhearted ⇒ the dying
⇒ the backslidden ⇒ the sick
⇒ the suffering ⇒ the hospitalized
⇒ the hungry ⇒ the lost
⇒ the thirsty ⇒ the doomed

The list of people crying for help and needing help is beyond imagination. The ministers of God—most of them—are doing everything they can. But they need help. They need men and women who will step forth and be assistants, helpers in the ministry. The person called must step forth and accept the call, not reject it.

"What do you think? There was a man who had two sons. He went to the first and said, 'Son, go and work today in the vineyard.' 'I will not,' he answered, but later he changed his mind and went. Then the father went to the other son and said the same thing. He answered, 'I will, sir,' but he did not go." (Mt. 21:28-30)

"The man with the two talents also came. 'Master,' he said, 'you entrusted me with two talents; see, I have gained two more.' His master replied, 'Well done, good and faithful servant! You have been faithful with a few things; I will put you in charge of many things. Come and share your master's happiness!'" (Mt. 25:22-23)

He went to him and bandaged his wounds, pouring on oil and wine. Then he put the man on his own donkey, took him to an inn and took care of him. (Lu. 10:34)

From everyone who has been given much, much will be demanded; and from the one who has been entrusted with much, much more will be asked. (Lu. 12:48)

Therefore, I urge you, brothers, in view of God's mercy, to offer your bodies as living sacrifices, holy and pleasing to God—this is your spiritual act of worship. (Ro. 12:1)

Therefore, my dear brothers, stand firm. Let nothing move you. Always give yourselves fully to the work of the Lord, because you know that your labor in the Lord is not in vain. (1 Co. 15:58)

Yes, and I ask you, loyal yokefellow, help these women who have contended at my side in the cause of the gospel, along with Clement and the rest of my fellow workers, whose names are in the book of life. (Ph. 4:3)

If anyone speaks, he should do it as one speaking the very words of God. If anyone serves, he should do it with the strength God provides, so that in all things God may be praised through Jesus Christ. To him be the glory and the power for ever and ever. Amen. (1 Pe. 4:11)

Then Moses said, "You have been set apart to the LORD today, for you were against your own sons and brothers, and he has blessed you this day." (Ex. 32:29)

I was eyes to the blind and feet to the lame. (Jb. 29:15)

My son, give me your heart and let your eyes keep to my ways. (Pr. 23:26)

She opens her arms to the poor and extends her hands to the needy. (Pr. 31:20)

Then I heard the voice of the Lord saying, "Whom shall I send? And who will go for us?" And I said, "Here am I. Send me!" (Is. 6:8)

NUMBERS 3:1-51

The Sovereign LORD has given me an instructed tongue, to know the word that sustains the weary. He wakens me morning by morning, wakens my ear to listen like one being taught. (Is. 50:4)

'But now be strong, O Zerubbabel,' declares the LORD. 'Be strong, O Joshua son of Jehozadak, the high priest. Be strong, all you people of the land,' declares the LORD, 'and work. For I am with you,' declares the LORD Almighty. (Hag. 2:4)

3 (3:14-39) **Census, of Levites—Levites, Census of—Levites, Duties of—Levites, Placement of—Assistants, Duties of—Ministers, Assistants to**: there were the census, placement, and duties of the Levites. This is a picture of knowing one's job and doing it well. The Levites needed to be numbered just as the other tribes of God's people were. Just how many men were available for God's service needed to be known. They were to be ministers of God's people, scattered out among them (Nu. 35:1-8). Therefore, the leadership had to know how many Levites were available for the ministry.

a. The LORD charged Moses to count every male Levite who was one month old or older (v.15). Note the total, explicit obedience of Moses: he did exactly what God commanded (v.16). He took a census of the Levites in order to find out how many were available for the ministry.

b. The overall view of the Levites includes just three sons of Levi: Gershon, Kohath, and Merari (vv.17-20).

c. The detailed look at the Gershonites is clearly seen in the Scripture and outline (vv.21-26). The Gershonites were responsible for taking care of the tent of the Tabernacle: its covers and curtains (vv.25-26). There were three curtains that served as entrances to the Tabernacle: a curtain covering the entrance to the court (vv.26; 4:26); a second curtain at the entrance to the tent itself (vv.25, 31, 4:25); and a third curtain that set apart the Most Holy Place from everything else within the Tabernacle (vv.4-5).

d. A detailed look at the Kohathites is also clearly seen in the Scripture and outline (vv.27-32). Note that Eleazar was the chief supervisor for the Gershonites (v.32). Most likely this was because the Gershonites were in charge of the ark and the other major furnishings of the Tabernacle.

e. A detailed look at the Merarites is also clearly seen in the Scripture and outline (vv.33-37).

f. Note the detailed look at Moses and Aaron (vv.38-39). Moses and Aaron camped in the most honored location, east of the Tabernacle, facing the sun. The morning sun would rise and shine on the entrance to the Tabernacle, symbolizing the life-giving light of God that shone upon His people.[3] Moses and Aaron camped at this honored location because of their responsibility to work in and around the Tabernacle.

Note that the total number of Levites one month old or older was 22,000 (v.39). This means that the number of adults available for service was a very small number.

Thought 1. Every Levite had his place of service; he had a particular job to do for God and for His people. His duties were spelled out in detail. So it should be with every assistant, every helper in the service of God. He should be assigned particular duties to perform for God. Once assigned, the assistant must fulfill his ministry. He must do the work, do it faithfully and well—do it with all his heart and mind.

"My food," said Jesus, "is to do the will of him who sent me and to finish his work." (Jn. 4:34)

I have brought you glory on earth by completing the work you gave me to do. (Jn. 17:4)

However, I consider my life worth nothing to me, if only I may finish the race and complete the task the Lord Jesus has given me—the task of testifying to the gospel of God's grace. (Ac. 20:24)

Therefore, my dear brothers, stand firm. Let nothing move you. Always give yourselves fully to the work of the Lord, because you know that your labor in the Lord is not in vain. (1 Co. 15:58)

Serve wholeheartedly, as if you were serving the Lord, not men. (Ep. 6:7)

And whatever you do, whether in word or deed, do it all in the name of the Lord Jesus, giving thanks to God the Father through him. (Col. 3:17)

Whatever you do, work at it with all your heart, as working for the Lord, not for men. (Col. 3:23)

For I am already being poured out like a drink offering, and the time has come for my departure. I have fought the good fight, I have finished the race, I have kept the faith. (2 Ti. 4:6-7)

Therefore, since we are receiving a kingdom that cannot be shaken, let us be thankful, and so worship God acceptably with reverence and awe. (He. 12:28)

Serve the LORD with fear and rejoice with trembling. (Ps. 2:11)

4 (3:40-51) **Firstborn, Census of—Census, of the Firstborn—Redemption, Picture of**: there was the census of the firstborn and their replacement by the Levites. Note: this is a picture of redemption. Remember that the Levites were to become the substitute, the replacement for the firstborn sons (Nu.3:11-13). The Levites were counted by God as a redemption for the firstborn of the Israelites. Throughout history, God had accepted the firstborn of animals to be sacrificed to Him, but He had never approved the sacrifice of persons as an offering. Something else was always substituted for a person. In the present Scripture, a Levite was substituted for the firstborn son as an offering to the service of God. Note that the firstborn of livestock was also included in the substitutionary arrangement. A Levite was substituted for the firstborn, and a Levite's livestock was substituted for the firstborn livestock.[4]

a. Note the LORD's charge: to count all the firstborn sons in Israel one month old or older (vv.40-41). Remember, the firstborn had been responsible for the spiritual welfare of God's people (vv.11-13). Now the Levites were to replace the firstborn as the servants of God. As pointed out above, the livestock of the Levites was also to be substituted for the livestock of the firstborn. This meant that the livestock of the Levites was to be used in the sacrifices offered up to God.

---

[3] *The Expositor's Bible Commentary*, Vol.2. Frank E. Gaebelein, Editor, p.727.

[4] *Ibid.*, pp.728-729.

b. Note the strict obedience of Moses: he took a census of all the firstborn sons in Israel, one month old or older.

c. The number of firstborn sons—one month old or older—was 22,273. Note that there were 273 more firstborn sons than there were Levites (22,000).

d. Now comes the special charge from the LORD to Moses: he was to substitute the Levites for the firstborn Israelites. The Levites thereafter were to be the LORD's, His servants (vv.44-51).

But what about the 273 firstborn sons who exceeded the number of Levites (vv.46-47)? They had to be redeemed; that is, the ransom price had to be paid for them. The price of redemption was five pieces of silver for each one. Note that the ransom price was to be given to the priest for the service of God (v.48).

Again, the obedience of Moses was stressed. He collected the ransom money for each person. He collected about 34 pounds of silver and gave the money to the priest for the service of God. Note the reemphasis: he was careful to obey God—totally (v.51).

Thought 1. This is clearly a picture of redemption. The Levites were servants of God who redeemed the firstborn sons of Israel. As such, they are pictures of the Lord Jesus Christ who paid the redemption price for His people. But note: Jesus Christ did not pay silver and gold to redeem His people. He ransomed His people by substituting His own life for them. Jesus Christ died and paid the ransom price with His own precious blood.

> For all have sinned and fall short of the glory of God, and are justified freely by his grace through the redemption that came by Christ Jesus. (Ro. 3:23-24)

> It is because of him that you are in Christ Jesus, who has become for us wisdom from God—that is, our righteousness, holiness and redemption. (1 Co. 1:30)

> Christ redeemed us from the curse of the law by becoming a curse for us, for it is written: "Cursed is everyone who is hung on a tree." (Ga. 3:13)

> In him we have redemption through his blood, the forgiveness of sins, in accordance with the riches of God's grace. (Ep. 1:7)

> In whom we have redemption, the forgiveness of sins. (Col. 1:14)

> For the grace of God that brings salvation has appeared to all men. It teaches us to say "No" to ungodliness and worldly passions, and to live self-controlled, upright and godly lives in this present age, while we wait for the blessed hope—the glorious appearing of our great God and Savior, Jesus Christ, who gave himself for us to redeem us from all wickedness and to purify for himself a people that are his very own, eager to do what is good. (Tit. 2:11-14)

> He did not enter by means of the blood of goats and calves; but he entered the Most Holy Place once for all by his own blood, having obtained eternal redemption. (He. 9:12)

> For you know that it was not with perishable things such as silver or gold that you were redeemed from the empty way of life handed down to you from your forefathers, but with the precious blood of Christ, a lamb without blemish or defect. (1 Pe. 1:18-19)

> And they sang a new song: "You are worthy to take the scroll and to open its seals, because you were slain, and with your blood you purchased men for God from every tribe and language and people and nation. You have made them to be a kingdom and priests to serve our God, and they will reign on the earth." (Re. 5:9-10)

TYPES, SYMBOLS, AND PICTURES
(Numbers 3:1-51)

Historical Term	Type or Picture (Scriptural Basis for Each)	Life Application for Today's Believer	Biblical Application
The High Priest Nu. 3:5-13; 4:1-20 (See also Le. 16:3, 6)	*The High Priest is a symbol of Jesus Christ. But keep this fact in mind: the High Priest had to approach God through the Sin Offering and Burnt Offering. He himself had to be cleansed from sin before he could make sacrifice for the sins of the people. Once his sins had been forgiven, he stood sinless and perfect before God. He was then able to represent the people before God. This is a symbol of Jesus Christ, the High Priest of God, who stood sinless and perfect before God, offering Himself as the sacrifice for sin.*	Sin has separated and alienated man from God. Sin has created a veil, a curtain, between God and man. The curtain of sin cannot be removed by man, no matter how much he tries. No matter how righteous man seeks to be, his righteousness cannot break through the curtain of sin that separates him and God. But thank God! Jesus Christ—our Great High Priest—has ripped the curtain of sin from top to bottom, opening the way into God's presence. Man now has access into the presence of God. All of us—without exception—can now enter the	*And when Jesus had cried out again in a loud voice, he gave up his spirit. At that moment the curtain of the temple was torn in two from top to bottom. The earth shook and the rocks split. (Mt. 27:50-51)* *Therefore, brothers, since we have confidence to enter the Most Holy Place by the blood of Jesus, by a new and living way opened for us through the curtain, that is, his body, and since we have a great priest over the house of God, let us draw near to God with a sincere heart in full assurance of faith, having our hearts sprinkled to cleanse us*

NUMBERS 3:1-51

Historical Term	Type or Picture (Scriptural Basis for Each)	Life Application for Today's Believer	Biblical Application
	"Appoint Aaron and his sons to serve as priests; anyone else who approaches the sanctuary must be put to death." (Nu. 3:10)	presence of God, all because of what Jesus Christ has done.	*from a guilty conscience and having our bodies washed with pure water.* (He. 10:19-22) *But your iniquities have separated you from your God; your sins have hidden his face from you, so that he will not hear.* (Is. 59:2)
Egypt Nu. 3:5-13; 9:1-14 (See also Le. 11:44-47; 19:33-34)	*Egypt is a symbol of the world. God had saved His people from the slavery of the world (Egypt), from the slavery of its sin and death. Note why:* *1. He saved them to be their God.* *2. He saved them to be set apart as His holy people.* **The LORD spoke to Moses in the Desert of Sinai in the first month of the second year after they came out of Egypt.** (Nu. 9:1) **I am the LORD who brought you up out of Egypt to be your God; therefore be holy, because I am holy.** (Le. 11:45)	The application and lesson for us is clear: 1. We must declare that God is the Savior of the world, the Savior who delivered us from the world (Egypt). We must bear testimony, strong testimony, that God is building a new race of people, a people… • who will let Him be their God • who will be set apart and live as the holy people of God To be holy means that we must learn to discern more and more between the clean and unclean, the holy and unholy. We must sharpen our power to discern, learn to distinguish between right and wrong, the just and unjust, the moral and immoral, the kind and unkind, the selfish and unselfish. 2. We must be holy because God is holy. As believers, we have no choice: the command is direct and forceful. We must be like God: consecrated—set apart—holy.	*To rescue us from the hand of our enemies, and to enable us to serve him without fear in holiness and righteousness before him all our days.* (Lu. 1:74-75) *The man without the Spirit does not accept the things that come from the Spirit of God, for they are foolishness to him, and he cannot understand them, because they are spiritually discerned.* (1 Co. 2:14) *Since we have these promises, dear friends, let us purify ourselves from everything that contaminates body and spirit, perfecting holiness out of reverence for God.* (2 Co. 7:1) *But solid food is for the mature, who by constant use have trained themselves to distinguish good from evil.* (He. 5:14) *Make every effort to live in peace with all men and to be holy; without holiness no one will see the Lord.* (He. 12:14) *But in your hearts set apart Christ as Lord. Always be prepared to give an answer to everyone who asks you to give the reason for the hope that you have. But do this with gentleness and respect.* (1 Pe. 3:15) *So give your servant a discerning heart to govern your people and to distinguish between right and wrong. For who is able to govern this great people of yours?* (1 K. 3:9)
Sunrise on the Tabernacle's Entrance Nu. 3:14-39	*The morning sun that struck the entrance of the Tabernacle symbolized the life-giving light of God that shone on His people. This symbol later became a picture of Jesus Christ, God who came in the flesh of mankind, the Light of the world.*	Jesus Christ is said to be the Light of men (Jn. 1:4) and the Light of the world (Jn. 8:12; Jn. 9:5; Jn. 12:46). It is possible for the Light, Jesus Himself, to be in men (Jn. 11:10; see also Col. 1:27), and for men to become children of Light (see POSB note—Jn. 12:34-36). Apparently, Jesus Christ	*In him was life, and that life was the light of men.* (Jn. 1:4) *When Jesus spoke again to the people, he said, "I am the light of the world. Whoever follows me will never walk in darkness, but will have the light of life."* (Jn. 8:12)

NUMBERS 3:1-51

Historical Term	Type or Picture (Scriptural Basis for Each)	Life Application for Today's Believer	Biblical Application
	Moses and Aaron and his sons were to camp to the east of the tabernacle, toward the sunrise, in front of the Tent of Meeting. They were responsible for the care of the sanctuary on behalf of the Israelites. Anyone else who approached the sanctuary was to be put to death. (Nu. 3:38)	used the word light often. John uses the word about twenty-one times. What is meant by calling Jesus the Light? 1. Jesus Christ, the Light, is light by nature. Light is what He is within Himself, within His being, His nature, His essence, His character. Scripture says... • that "God is Light" (1 Jn. 1:5); • that Jesus Christ is "the image of the invisible God" (Col. 1:15); • therefore, "Jesus Christ is Light." He is "the Light of the world." 2. Jesus Christ, the Light, tells us that He is holy, righteous, and pure. Light is the symbol of purity and holiness. Light means the absence of darkness and blindness; it has no spots of darkness or blackness, nor of sin and shame. 3. Jesus Christ, the Light, reveals. His light clearly shows the nature, the meaning, and the destiny of all things. His light shines in, spots, opens up, identifies, illuminates, and shows things as they really are. The light of Jesus Christ shows the truth about the world and man and God. The light of Jesus Christ reveals that He loves and cares for man and wants man to love and care for Him. 4. Jesus Christ, the Light, guides. His light allows a man to walk out of darkness. Man no longer has to grope, grasp, and stumble about trying to find his way through life. The path of life can now be clearly seen. 5. Jesus Christ, the Light, does away with darkness and with chaos. His light routs, wipes out, strips away and erases the darkness. The empty chaos of creation was routed by the light given by God (Ge. 1:3). Jesus	*Then Jesus told them, "You are going to have the light just a little while longer. Walk while you have the light, before darkness overtakes you. The man who walks in the dark does not know where he is going. (Jn. 12:35)* *This is the message we have heard from him and declare to you: God is light; in him there is no darkness at all. (1 Jn. 1:5)* *There will be no more night. They will not need the light of a lamp or the light of the sun, for the LORD God will give them light. And they will reign for ever and ever. (Re. 22:5)* *The Lord is my light and my salvation—whom shall I fear? The LORD is the stronghold of my life—of whom shall I be afraid? (Ps. 27:1)* *For the LORD God is a sun and shield; the LORD bestows favor and honor; no good thing does he withhold from those whose walk is blameless. (Ps. 84:11)* *The people walking in darkness have seen a great light; on those living in the land of the shadow of death a light has dawned. (Is. 9:2)* *Your sun will never set again, and your moon will wane no more; the LORD will be your everlasting light, and your days of sorrow will end. (Is. 60:20)*

NUMBERS 3:1-51

Historical Term	Type or Picture (Scriptural Basis for Each)	Life Application for Today's Believer	Biblical Application
		Christ is the Light that can save man from chaos (Jn. 14:1, 17; Jn. 12:46; Jn. 16:33).	
The Census of the Firstborn and Their Replacement by the Levites Nu. 3:40-51	*The census of the firstborn and their replacement by the Levites is a picture of redemption.* **"Take the Levites in place of all the firstborn of Israel, and the livestock of the Levites in place of their livestock. The Levites are to be mine. I am the Lord. To redeem the 273 firstborn Israelites who exceed the number of the Levites, collect five shekels for each one, according to the sanctuary shekel, which weighs twenty gerahs. (Nu. 3:45-47)**	The Levites were servants of God who redeemed the firstborn sons of Israel. As such, they are pictures of the Lord Jesus Christ who paid the redemption price for His people. But note: Jesus Christ did not pay silver and gold to redeem His people. He ransomed His people by substituting His own life for them. Jesus Christ died, paid the ransom price, with His own precious blood.	*For all have sinned and fall short of the glory of God, and are justified freely by his grace through the redemption that came by Christ Jesus. (Ro. 3:23-24)* *It is because of him that you are in Christ Jesus, who has become for us wisdom from God—that is, our righteousness, holiness and redemption. (1 Co. 1:30)* *Christ redeemed us from the curse of the law by becoming a curse for us, for it is written: "Cursed is everyone who is hung on a tree." (Ga. 3:13)* *In him we have redemption through his blood, the forgiveness of sins, in accordance with the riches of God's grace. (Ep. 1:7)* *In whom we have redemption, the forgiveness of sins. (Col. 1:14; see Tit. 2:11-14; He. 9:12; 1 Pe. 1:18-19; Re. 5:9-10).*

NUMBERS 4:1-49

C. The Organization of the Mature Levites & Their Duties—the Fourth Census: Knowing One's Job & Doing It, 4:1-49

1. **The charge to count the available workers & assign the duties to the Kohathite clans: Stresses the warning of God to respect His holiness**

   a. The charge: Must take a census, count all the men from 30 to 50 years old

   b. The work: To take care of the most holy things

   c. The critical importance of the most holy things: Can be prepared only by the priests (a symbol of Christ)
   1) The Ark
      - To cover it with the Inner Veil or Curtain
      - To then cover this with hides & with a blue cloth
      - To put the poles in place
   2) The Table of the Presence
      - To spread a blue cloth over it
      - To place all accessories & the bread upon the blue cloth
      - To cover these with a scarlet cloth & then hides of cows
      - To then put the poles in place
   3) The lampstand and all its accessories
      - To wrap in a blue cloth
      - To then wrap these in the hides of goats or sea cows
   4) The gold altar
      - To wrap the altar in a blue cloth, then with hides of goats or sea cows & put the poles in place
      - To take a blue cloth & wrap all the articles used for ministering in the sanctuary, then wrap these with hides of goats

CHAPTER 4

The LORD said to Moses and Aaron:
2 "Take a census of the Kohathite branch of the Levites by their clans and families.
3 Count all the men from thirty to fifty years of age who come to serve in the work in the Tent of Meeting.
4 "This is the work of the Kohathites in the Tent of Meeting: the care of the most holy things.
5 When the camp is to move, Aaron and his sons are to go in and take down the shielding curtain and cover the ark of the Testimony with it.
6 Then they are to cover this with hides of sea cows, spread a cloth of solid blue over that and put the poles in place.
7 "Over the table of the Presence they are to spread a blue cloth and put on it the plates, dishes and bowls, and the jars for drink offerings; the bread that is continually there is to remain on it.
8 Over these they are to spread a scarlet cloth, cover that with hides of sea cows and put its poles in place.
9 "They are to take a blue cloth and cover the lampstand that is for light, together with its lamps, its wick trimmers and trays, and all its jars for the oil used to supply it.
10 Then they are to wrap it and all its accessories in a covering of hides of sea cows and put it on a carrying frame.
11 "Over the gold altar they are to spread a blue cloth and cover that with hides of sea cows and put its poles in place.
12 "They are to take all the articles used for ministering in the sanctuary, wrap them in a blue cloth, cover that with hides of sea cows and put them on a carrying frame.
13 "They are to remove the ashes from the bronze altar and spread a purple cloth over it.
14 Then they are to place on it all the utensils used for ministering at the altar, including the firepans, meat forks, shovels and sprinkling bowls. Over it they are to spread a covering of hides of sea cows and put its poles in place.
15 "After Aaron and his sons have finished covering the holy furnishings and all the holy articles, and when the camp is ready to move, the Kohathites are to come to do the carrying. But they must not touch the holy things or they will die. The Kohathites are to carry those things that are in the Tent of Meeting.
16 "Eleazar son of Aaron, the priest, is to have charge of the oil for the light, the fragrant incense, the regular grain offering and the anointing oil. He is to be in charge of the entire tabernacle and everything in it, including its holy furnishings and articles."
17 The LORD said to Moses and Aaron,
18 "See that the Kohathite tribal clans are not cut off from the Levites.
19 So that they may live and not die when they come near the most holy things, do this for them: Aaron and his sons are to go into the sanctuary and assign to each man his work and what he is to carry.
20 But the Kohathites must not go in to look at the holy things, even for a moment, or they will die."
21 The LORD said to Moses,
22 "Take a census also of the Gershonites by their families and clans.
23 Count all the men from thirty to fifty years of age who come to serve in the work at the Tent of Meeting.
24 "This is the service of the Gershonite clans as they work and carry burdens:
25 They are to carry the curtains of the tabernacle, the

   or sea cows
   5) The bronze altar of Burnt Offering
      - To remove the ashes & put a purple cloth on it
      - To place all accessories on the purple cloth & then cover everything with hides of goats or sea cows
      - To put the poles in place for carrying

   d. The strong, emphatic warning to respect the holiness of God: Must never touch the holy things or they will be stricken dead
   1) Stricken dead if they touch when preparing for moving
   2) Stricken dead if they touch while carrying the holy things (see also 2 S. 6:6-7)

   e. The person placed in charge of the entire Tabernacle, everything in it: Eleazar the priest
   1) To personally care for the oil for the lampstand, the incense, the regular Grain Offering, & the anointing oil
   2) To oversee everything else in the Tabernacle

   f. The strong, emphatic warning restated—far more forcefully: The workers must be protected from the penalty of being cut off, stricken dead
   1) They must never be allowed to approach the holy things alone: Are to be led into the sanctuary & assigned their work by the priests

   2) The warning: Will be stricken dead if they even look at the holy things of God—must acknowledge God's holiness

2. **The charge to count the available workers & assign the duties to the Gershonite clans: Stresses the need for a willingness to do anything (general work or service)**

   a. The charge: Must know the number of workers 30 to 50 years old

   b. The service of the workers: To do general work—pack, unpack, & transport certain parts of the Tabernacle
   1) The curtains of the

NUMBERS 4:1-49

Tabernacle itself: Included the outer covering of goat or sea cow hides, & the curtain for the entrance

2) The curtains of the courtyard walls that surrounded the Tabernacle & altar: Included the curtain for the courtyard entrance, the ropes & all the altar's accessories

c. The importance of the service
  1) Was to be supervised & assigned by the priests

  2) Was to be under the general direction of Ithamar the priest, the son of Aaron

3. **The charge to count the available workers & assign the duties to the Merarite clans: Stresses the importance of each person's service**
  a. The charge: Must know the available workers 30 to 50 years old
  b. The service of the workers: To pack, unpack, & transport the frame of the Tabernacle & the surrounding courtyard
  c. The importance of each person's service
    1) Each person was to be assigned & made responsible for a particular task
    2) The service was to be under the general direction of Ithamar the priest, the son of Aaron

4. **The description & results of the census: Stresses obedience**
  a. The number of the Kohathite clans
    1) Counted all men between 30 to 50 years of age who

Tent of Meeting, its covering and the outer covering of hides of sea cows, the curtains for the entrance to the Tent of Meeting,
26 The curtains of the courtyard surrounding the tabernacle and altar, the curtain for the entrance, the ropes and all the equipment used in its service. The Gershonites are to do all that needs to be done with these things.
27 All their service, whether carrying or doing other work, is to be done under the direction of Aaron and his sons. You shall assign to them as their responsibility all they are to carry.
28 This is the service of the Gershonite clans at the Tent of Meeting. Their duties are to be under the direction of Ithamar son of Aaron, the priest.
29 "Count the Merarites by their clans and families.
30 Count all the men from thirty to fifty years of age who come to serve in the work at the Tent of Meeting.
31 This is their duty as they perform service at the Tent of Meeting: to carry the frames of the tabernacle, its crossbars, posts and bases,
32 As well as the posts of the surrounding courtyard with their bases, tent pegs, ropes, all their equipment and everything related to their use. Assign to each man the specific things he is to carry.
33 This is the service of the Merarite clans as they work at the Tent of Meeting under the direction of Ithamar son of Aaron, the priest."
34 Moses, Aaron and the leaders of the community counted the Kohathites by their clans and families.
35 All the men from thirty to fifty years of age who came

to serve in the work in the Tent of Meeting,
36 counted by clans, were 2,750.
37 This was the total of all those in the Kohathite clans who served in the Tent of Meeting. Moses and Aaron counted them according to the LORD's command through Moses.
38 The Gershonites were counted by their clans and families.
39 All the men from thirty to fifty years of age who came to serve in the work at the Tent of Meeting,
40 Counted by their clans and families, were 2,630.
41 This was the total of those in the Gershonite clans who served at the Tent of Meeting. Moses and Aaron counted them according to the LORD's command.
42 The Merarites were counted by their clans and families.
43 All the men from thirty to fifty years of age who came to serve in the work at the Tent of Meeting,
44 Counted by their clans, were 3,200.
45 This was the total of those in the Merarite clans. Moses and Aaron counted them according to the LORD's command through Moses.
46 So Moses, Aaron and the leaders of Israel counted all the Levites by their clans and families.
47 All the men from thirty to fifty years of age who came to do the work of serving and carrying the Tent of Meeting
48 Numbered 8,580.
49 At the LORD's command through Moses, each was assigned his work and told what to carry. Thus they were counted, as the LORD commanded Moses.

were eligible for service

2) Numbered 2750 men

3) The obedience of the leaders: Counted in obedience to the LORD's command

b. The number of the Gershonite clans
  1) Counted all men between 30 to 50 years of age who were eligible for service
  2) Numbered 2630 men
  3) The obedience of the leaders: Counted in obedience to the LORD's command

c. The number of the Merarite clans
  1) Counted all men between 30 to 50 years of age who were eligible for service
  2) Numbered 3200 men
  3) The obedience of the leaders: Counted in obedience to the LORD's command

d. The summary of the census
  1) Counted all the Levites by clans & families
  2) Counted all men between 30 to 50 years of age who were eligible for the work of serving & carrying the Tabernacle
  3) Totaled 8580
  4) The strong example of obedience
    • They did their work as assigned, as commanded
    • They were counted just as the LORD commanded

DIVISION I

THE PREPARATION FOR THE MARCH TO THE PROMISED LAND, 1:1–10:36

C. The Organization of the Mature Levites and Their Duties— the Fourth Census: Knowing One's Job and Doing It, 4:1-49

NUMBERS 4:1-49

(4:1-49) **Introduction—Needs, of the World, List of—Laborers, Need for—Ministering, Need for—World, Needs of—Ministry, Need for**: the world is reeling under a weight of desperate need, crying out for help. The harvest is ripe, but the laborers are few. Workers are desperately needed. Many need to step forth and commit their lives to the service of God, to meet the desperate needs of the world. Just think of the desperate needs that surround any one of us, the needs of...

- the orphans, widows, and widowers
- the brokenhearted, backslidden, and diseased
- the suffering, hungry, and thirsty
- the poor, homeless, and destitute
- the empty, lonely, and purposeless
- the blind, deaf, deformed, and handicapped
- the hospitalized, bedridden, and shut-in
- the lost, dying, and doomed

The needs are grave. People are hurting all around us. Laborers are needed, people who will step forth to do the work of the ministry. This is the challenge of the hour, the call of God Himself to every one of us: "Step forth! Accept the challenge of My call! Meet the needs of this earth! Make a commitment! Reach out to your neighbor. To your fellow worker. To your school mate. To your family. Do the work of the ministry. This is My call to you."

Knowing one's job and doing it—this is the practical subject of this passage. The Israelites knew how many Levites there were from one month old and older, but they did not know how many Levites were available to serve in the ministry of the LORD. Therefore, another census was needed to determine the number of mature Levites aged thirty to fifty. Moreover, the task of transporting the Tabernacle from campsite to campsite was the duty of the Levites. The specific task and details involved in tearing down and erecting the Tabernacle at the new campsites needed to be assigned. Every Levite needed to know his job, and he needed to do it and do it well. This is the subject of this important Scripture: *The Organization of the Mature Levites and Their Duties—the Fourth Census: Knowing One's Job and Doing It, 4:1-49.*

1. The charge to count the available workers and assign the duties to the Kohathite clans: stresses the warning of God to respect His holiness (vv.1-20).
2. The charge to count the available workers and assign the duties to the Gershonite clans: stresses the need for a willingness to do anything (general work or service) (vv.21-28).
3. The charge to count the available workers and assign the duties to the Merarite clans: stresses the importance of each person's service (vv.29-33).
4. The description and results of the census: stresses obedience (vv.34-49).

1 (4:1-20) **Holiness, of God—God, Holiness of—Laborers, Duty of—Ministers, Duty of—Kohathite, Clan of Levites—Levites, Kohathite Clan of—Levites, Duties of—Church, Care of**: there was the charge to count the available workers and assign the duties to the Kohathite clan. The work assigned stresses the warning of God, the warning to respect His holiness (vv.15-20).

a. There was the clear charge given to Moses and Aaron: they must know the number of available workers. Therefore, they were to take a census, count all the men from thirty to fifty years old (v.3). In chapter 3, the census had counted all the Levites over the age of one month (Nu.3:15). Children, of course, were not available to serve in the Tabernacle. This was the reason for this particular census, to learn the number of available workers, just how many were old enough to serve in the Tabernacle. Note that the years of service were from thirty to fifty years of age. Another Scripture mentions that the actual beginning age of service was twenty-five (Nu. 8:24). The first five years were most likely a training period, an apprenticeship for the Levite.

b. The work assigned to these clans was to take care of the most holy things (v.4). This is important to note: the primary care of the most holy things was placed into the hands of the Kohathites. How men treat the holy things of God is of critical importance to God: this is clearly seen in the restrictions placed upon the Kohathites. They themselves were not allowed to touch the holy things (v.15), nor were they allowed to even look upon the holy things (v.20). The warning and judgment were forceful: if they touched or looked upon the holy things of God, the blaze of God's holiness would flash forth like a lightning bolt and strike them dead (vv.15, 20; see 3, 4; Le. 10:1-2). In the words of *The Expositor's Bible Commentary*:

> As the holy angels who surround the throne of the Divine Presence shield their faces and feet from his presence (cf. Is.6:1-3), so the Kohathites were to shield themselves from too familiar an approach to the holiest of things (v.5); for most holy things symbolize the presence of the most holy God.[1]

c. The critical importance of the most holy things is seen in this fact: the most holy things could be prepared only by the priests. Remember that the priests stood as a symbol or picture of Christ. Only Christ can prepare the holy things and make them acceptable to God. Only the priests themselves were allowed to look upon and handle the holy things. No person could approach the holiness of God nor approach the things that represented His holiness, not without being stricken dead. The only person who is acceptable to God, who can approach God, is the perfect person, Christ Himself, or the person representing the perfect person, the priest. For this reason, the Kohathites were not allowed to touch nor look upon the holy things of God. The priests alone were allowed to enter the inner sanctuary of the Tabernacle, the symbol of the very presence of God Himself. The priests were responsible for covering and wrapping all the holy furnishing of the Tabernacle:

1) The priests covered and wrapped the Ark (vv.5-6).
2) The priests covered and wrapped the Table of the Presence or the Table of Showbread (vv.7-8).
3) The priests covered and wrapped the lampstand and all its accessories (vv.9-10).
4) The priests covered and wrapped the gold altar (vv.11-12).
5) The priests covered and wrapped the bronze altar of Burnt Offering (vv.13-14).

d. The strong, emphatic warning to respect the holiness of God is stressed: the Kohathites must never touch the holy things or they would be stricken dead (v.15). Note how strict God was:

⇒ They would be stricken dead if they touched any item while preparing it to be moved.
⇒ They would be stricken dead if they touched any item while carrying the holy things (see also 2 S. 6:6-7).

---

[1] *The Expositor's Bible Commentary*, Vol.2. Frank E. Gaebelein, Editor, p.734.

NUMBERS 4:1-49

e. The person placed in charge of the entire Tabernacle—everything in it—was Eleazar, the priest who was the son of Aaron (v.16). Note that he was personally to care for the oil for the lampstand, the incense, the regular Grain Offering, and the anointing oil. This was all he was to handle personally. He was to oversee or supervise everything else in the Tabernacle.

f. The strong, emphatic warning was restated and re-emphasized—far more forcefully: the workers must be protected from the penalty of being cut off, that is, stricken dead (vv.17-20). They absolutely must never be allowed to approach the holy things alone. They were to be led into the sanctuary and assigned their work by the priests (v.19). The warning was clear and forceful: they would be stricken dead if they even looked at the holy things of God. It was essential that they acknowledge, respect, and revere the holiness of God (v.20).

Thought 1. The stress of this point is forceful: God demands that the holiness of His presence be respected and revered. He demands that the holy things of God—the things set apart to God and His service—be respected and revered. The declaration and warning of God is clear: He is holy and the things of God are holy. Therefore, He demands that we respect and revere His holiness and the holy things committed to His service.

⇒ the church and its furnishings

> Don't you know that you yourselves [plural, the church] are God's temple and that God's Spirit lives in you? (1 Co. 3:16).

⇒ the physical body of the believer, that is, the temple of the Holy Spirit

> "Do you not know that your body is a temple of the Holy Spirit, who is in you, whom you have received from God? You are not your own; you were bought at a price. Therefore, honor God with your body. (1 Co. 6:19-20).

⇒ the gifts of money, property, and anything else that is set apart to the worship or service of God

> To those who sold doves he said, "Get these out of here! How dare you turn my Father's house into a market!" (Jn. 2:16)
>
> "Do not come any closer," God said. "Take off your sandals, for the place where you are standing is holy ground." (Ex. 3:5)
>
> Observe my Sabbaths and have reverence for my sanctuary. I am the LORD. (Le. 19:30)
>
> The commander of the LORD's army replied, "Take off your sandals, for the place where you are standing is holy." And Joshua did so. (Jos. 5:15)
>
> In your anger do not sin; when you are on your beds, search your hearts and be silent. Selah (Ps. 4:4)
>
> Send forth your light and your truth, let them guide me; let them bring me to your holy mountain, to the place where you dwell. (Ps. 43:3)
>
> In the council of the holy ones God is greatly feared; he is more awesome than all who surround him. (Ps. 89:7)
>
> Guard your steps when you go to the house of God. Go near to listen rather than to offer the sacrifice of fools, who do not know that they do wrong. (Ec. 5:1)
>
> But the LORD is in his holy temple; let all the earth be silent before him. (Hab. 2:20)

Thought 2. The Levites went through a five year training or apprenticeship (v.3). They trained for five years and served for twenty. This speaks to the church. People need to learn the Word of God before they can preach or teach the Word; they need to learn how to minister so they can be more effective in ministering; they need to learn how to reach people so more people can be won to Christ; they need to learn how to minister to the sick and poor and dying so their ministry will be more encouraging and strengthening. Far, far too often a novice—a new believer—is put into a position of leadership in a teaching or preaching ministry, and the result is catastrophic.

> "Therefore go and make disciples of all nations, baptizing them in the name of the Father and of the Son and of the Holy Spirit, and teaching them to obey everything I have commanded you. And surely I am with you always, to the very end of the age." (Mt. 28:19-20)
>
> He must not be a recent convert, or he may become conceited and fall under the same judgment as the devil. (1 Ti. 3:6)
>
> Until I come, devote yourself to the public reading of Scripture, to preaching and to teaching. Do not neglect your gift, which was given you through a prophetic message when the body of elders laid their hands on you. Be diligent in these matters; give yourself wholly to them, so that everyone may see your progress. Watch your life and doctrine closely. Persevere in them, because if you do, you will save both yourself and your hearers. (1 Ti. 4:13-16)
>
> And the things you have heard me say in the presence of many witnesses entrust to reliable men who will also be qualified to teach others. (2 Ti. 2:2)
>
> Do your best to present yourself to God as one approved, a workman who does not need to be ashamed and who correctly handles the word of truth. (2 Ti. 2:15)

2 (4:21-28) **Ministers, Duties of—Service, Dedication—Commitment, Duty to—Gershonites, a Levite Clan—Levites, Clans of:** there was the charge to count the available workers and assign the duties to the Gershonite clans. The work assigned stresses the need for a willingness to do anything, that is, to do general work and service for the LORD.

a. The charge from God was clear: the number of available workers needed to be known. Therefore, they were to count all the men in the Gershonite clans between the ages of thirty and fifty for service in the Tabernacle.

NUMBERS 4:1-49

b. The service of these workers was to do the general work of the Tabernacle: they were to pack, unpack, and transport the outer walls or curtains and hides of the Tabernacle (vv.24-26). Remember: the Kohathite workers were not allowed to touch the furnishings of the Tabernacle because of their holy nature. But now, the Gershonite workers were permitted to touch the outer curtains of the Tabernacle. They personally packed and unpacked the parts for which they were responsible.

c. The importance of this work is seen in that it was to be supervised by the priests (vv.27-28). The general superintendent of these workers was Ithamar, the priest and son of Aaron (v.28).

Thought 1. The willingness to do any task is desperately needed within the church. People need to step forth and do the general work in their service for the church. No matter what the work is, it is important to God, and it has to be done:

⇒ The small, insignificant, unknown, unrecognizable work has to be done.
⇒ The menial, manual work has to be done.
⇒ The cleaning and maintenance have to be done.
⇒ The straightening of chairs, books, tables, and podiums has to be done.
⇒ The picking up of paper and trash has to be done.
⇒ The turning on and off of lights has to be done.
⇒ The visiting of the sick, shut-ins, and dying has to be done.
⇒ The commitment of hours to study and prepare for preaching and teaching has to be done.
⇒ The witnessing and bearing of testimony to the lost at work, school, play, and home have to be done.

The point is forceful: a willingness to do any task is desperately needed within the church today. People who are willing to do anything for God—no matter how small or unseen—must step forth for God.

"And if anyone gives even a cup of cold water to one of these little ones because he is my disciple, I tell you the truth, he will certainly not lose his reward." (Mt. 10:42)

"Just as the Son of Man did not come to be served, but to serve, and to give his life as a ransom for many." (Mt. 20:28)

Not so with you. Instead, whoever wants to become great among you must be your servant, and whoever wants to be first must be slave of all. (Mk. 10:43-44)

"Which of these three do you think was a neighbor to the man who fell into the hands of robbers?" The expert in the law replied, "The one who had mercy on him." Jesus told him, "Go and do likewise." (Lu. 10:36-37)

For who is greater, the one who is at the table or the one who serves? Is it not the one who is at the table? But I am among you as one who serves. (Lu. 22:27)

So he got up from the meal, took off his outer clothing, and wrapped a towel around his waist. After that, he poured water into a basin and began to wash his disciples' feet, drying them with the towel that was wrapped around him. (Jn. 13:4-5)

Now that I, your Lord and Teacher, have washed your feet, you also should wash one another's feet. (Jn. 13:14)

Again Jesus said, "Simon son of John, do you truly love me?" He answered, "Yes, Lord, you know that I love you." Jesus said, "Take care of my sheep." (Jn. 21:16)

Therefore, my dear brothers, stand firm. Let nothing move you. Always give yourselves fully to the work of the Lord, because you know that your labor in the Lord is not in vain. (1 Co. 15:58)

Therefore, as we have opportunity, let us do good to all people, especially to those who belong to the family of believers. (Ga. 6:10)

Serve wholeheartedly, as if you were serving the Lord, not men. (Ep. 6:7)

But made himself nothing, taking the very nature of a servant, being made in human likeness. (Ph. 2:7)

And do not forget to do good and to share with others, for with such sacrifices God is pleased. (He. 13:16)

Anyone, then, who knows the good he ought to do and doesn't do it, sins. (Js. 4:17)

3 (4:29-33) **Service, Duty of—Service, Importance of—Merarites, a Major Levite Family—Levites, Families of**: there was the charge to count the available workers and assign the duties to the Merarite clans. This work stresses the need and importance of each person's service.

a. The charge was again essential: the number of available workers had to be known, those between the ages of thirty and fifty (v.30).

b. The work of these particular men was to pack, unpack, and transport the frame of the Tabernacle and the surrounding courtyard (vv.31-32). This, of course, included the crossbars, post and bases, tent pegs and ropes, and other equipment.

c. The importance of each person's service was clearly seen in this one fact: each person was to be assigned and made responsible for the specific things he was to carry (v.32). Imagine being responsible for carrying a tent peg! What was so important about carrying a tent peg? If one tent peg had been lost, then the Tabernacle wall could not have been erected and worship could not have been held, not without first making another tent peg. Each person's task was of critical importance. Nothing, absolutely nothing, could be lost or mishandled. The work had to be done, every single task, in order for the worship and ministry of God to be carried out. The importance of each person's service was also stressed by the fact that it was under the general direction of the priest, Ithamar, the son of Aaron (v.33).

Thought 1. Every believer has a duty, a role of responsibility to God. Each believer's service is important and needed—desperately needed—by God. To God, responsible service is what the work of each believer is. In the eyes of God, each believer is to be a responsible person, a person committed to fulfilling his service and fulfilling it well and faithfully. Carrying the tent pegs of the church is of critical importance to God, for the ministry cannot go forth unless the tent peg is carried. What God needs is for people

NUMBERS 4:1-49

to step forth, people who are willing to carry the tent pegs of the church...
- to wash the sinks and clean the floors
- to pay for the supplies
- to build the buildings
- to support the missionaries
- to teach
- to pray
- to visit
- to witness and bear testimony
- to spend hours in study
- to greet people
- to usher
- to keep books and records
- to turn lights on and off

On and on the list could go, for the tent pegs of the church and the ministry are innumerable. But the challenge is ever before God's people. What is needed is for people to step forth to carry the pegs of the church and the ministry. The hour is desperate: the cry of the world is for help. People are brokenhearted, backslidden, diseased, suffering, poor, empty, dying—and in many cases without Christ. The cry of God is, "Step forth! I beg you in the name of My Son, step forth! Carry this tent peg for Me! For My church! For My people who desperately need your help!"

> **Just as the Son of Man did not come to be served, but to serve, and to give his life as a ransom for many." (Mt. 20:28)**
>
> **For by the grace given me I say to every one of you: Do not think of yourself more highly than you ought, but rather think of yourself with sober judgment, in accordance with the measure of faith God has given you. Just as each of us has one body with many members, and these members do not all have the same function, so in Christ we who are many form one body, and each member belongs to all the others. We have different gifts, according to the grace given us. If a man's gift is prophesying, let him use it in proportion to his faith. If it is serving, let him serve; if it is teaching, let him teach; if it is encouraging, let him encourage; if it is contributing to the needs of others, let him give generously; if it is leadership, let him govern diligently; if it is showing mercy, let him do it cheerfully. (Ro. 12:3-8)**
>
> **Carry each other's burdens, and in this way you will fulfill the law of Christ. (Ga. 6:2)**
>
> **Let us not become weary in doing good, for at the proper time we will reap a harvest if we do not give up. (Ga. 6:9)**
>
> **When the people willingly offer themselves... (Jud. 5:2)**
>
> **If you are willing and obedient, you will eat the best from the land. (Is. 1:19)**

4 (4:34-49) **Obedience—Census, of the Levites—Levites, Census of**: there was the description and the results of the census. The point to note throughout this passage is the *obedience* of everyone involved. Obedience to the LORD's command is mentioned four times (vv.37, 41, 45, 49).

a. Note the number of the Kohathite clans: it totaled 2,750 men (vv.34-37). The obedience of the leaders is stressed: they counted in obedience to the LORD's command (v.37).

b. Note the number of the Gershonite clans: they totaled 2,630 men (vv.38-41). Again, note the obedience of the leaders: they counted in obedience to the LORD's command (v.41).

c. Note the total number of the Merarite clans: they numbered 3,200 men (vv.42-45). For the third time, the obedience of the leaders is stressed: they again counted in obedience to the LORD's command (v.45).

d. Note the summary of the census (vv.46-49):
  1) The leaders counted all Levites by clans and families (v.46).
  2) They counted all the men between the ages of thirty and fifty who were eligible for the work of serving and carrying the Tabernacle (v.47).
  3) The total number of the census was 8,580 (v.48).
  4) The strong example of obedience is stressed throughout the entire passage (v.49).
     a) The workers did the task as assigned, as commanded.
     b) The workers were counted by Moses and the leaders—just as the LORD commanded.

Thought 1. Where is the obedience today? The obedience to do the work of the ministry? The world is reeling in a state of desperate need, crying out for help. The harvest is ripe and ready to be gathered, but the laborers are few, ever so few. Many have been called and are still being called, but few are chosen. Few are making the commitment. Few are stepping forth to serve in the ministry of the Lord Jesus Christ. Few are willing to help the crying needs of the world, the needs...
- of the orphans, widows, and widowers
- of the prisoners, brokenhearted, and backslidden
- of the diseased, poor, and suffering
- of the empty, lonely, and purposeless
- of the lost, dying, and doomed—eternally

When God calls, obedience is demanded. Where are the obedient? So few can be found. Where is your obedience? Where is my obedience? The cry of the hour is for obedience.

> **"Not everyone who says to me, 'Lord, Lord,' will enter the kingdom of heaven, but only he who does the will of my Father who is in heaven." (Mt. 7:21)**
>
> **"For whoever does the will of my Father in heaven is my brother and sister and mother." (Mt. 12:50)**
>
> **Do you not say, 'Four months more and then the harvest'? I tell you, open your eyes and look at the fields! They are ripe for harvest. Even now the reaper draws his wages, even now he harvests the crop for eternal life, so that the sower and the reaper may be glad together. (Jn. 4:35-36)**
>
> **Peter and the other apostles replied: "We must obey God rather than men!" (Ac.5:29)**
>
> **Therefore, I urge you, brothers, in view of God's mercy, to offer your bodies as living sacrifices, holy and pleasing to God—**

this is your spiritual act of worship. Do not conform any longer to the pattern of this world, but be transformed by the renewing of your mind. Then you will be able to test and approve what God's will is—his good, pleasing and perfect will. (Ro. 12:1-2)

But God chose the foolish things of the world to shame the wise; God chose the weak things of the world to shame the strong. He chose the lowly things of this world and the despised things—and the things that are not—to nullify the things that are, so that no one may boast before him. (1 Co. 1:27-29)

So do not be ashamed to testify about our Lord, or ashamed of me his prisoner. But join with me in suffering for the gospel, by the power of God. (2 Ti. 1:8)

Then he said, "Here I am, I have come to do your will." He sets aside the first to establish the second. (He. 10:9)

But Samuel replied: "Does the LORD delight in burnt offerings and sacrifices as much as in obeying the voice of the LORD? To obey is better than sacrifice, and to heed is better than the fat of rams." (1 S. 15:22)

My son, give me your heart and let your eyes keep to my ways. (Pr. 23:26)

If you are willing and obedient, you will eat the best from the land. (Is. 1:19)

Then I heard the voice of the Lord saying, "Whom shall I send? And who will go for us?" And I said, "Here am I. Send me!" (Is. 6:8)

Numbers 5:1-31

CHAPTER 5

D. The Basic Laws That Keep God's People United & Pure: God's People Must Live Pure Lives, 5:1-31

1. There was the law of separation—the unclean were removed from the camp: A picture of spiritual separation
   a. The unclean identified
      1) A person with a contagious skin disease or discharge
      2) A person who came in contact with death
   b. The purpose: A picture of preventing the spread of sin
      1) To prevent the spread to others
      2) To keep from defiling the camp, the place where God is
   c. The obedience of the people: Removed the unclean

2. There was the law that controlled doing any wrong against another person
   a. The primary charge: Was counted as being unfaithful to the LORD—was guilty before God
   b. The remedy
      1) Must confess to God
      2) Must make restitution
         • To add one fifth to the property stolen
         • To give the payment of restitution to the priest if the person was dead & had no close relative
      3) Must approach God through the sacrifice of the Guilt Offering: Approach for atonement
   c. The important reminder
      1) All sacred gifts—once promised or given—belonged to the priests
      2) No gift—once promised or given—was ever to be withdrawn, neither publicly nor secretly

3. There was the law controlling the suspicion & jealousy of sexual unfaithfulness
   a. The case: A man's wife went astray & was unfaithful
      1) The immorality, impurity was undetected: There was no witness

The LORD said to Moses, 2 "Command the Israelites to send away from the camp anyone who has an infectious skin disease or a discharge of any kind, or who is ceremonially unclean because of a dead body. 3 Send away male and female alike; send them outside the camp so they will not defile their camp, where I dwell among them." 4 The Israelites did this; they sent them outside the camp. They did just as the LORD had instructed Moses.

5 The LORD said to Moses, 6 "Say to the Israelites: 'When a man or woman wrongs another in any way and so is unfaithful to the LORD, that person is guilty 7 And must confess the sin he has committed. He must make full restitution for his wrong, add one fifth to it and give it all to the person he has wronged. 8 But if that person has no close relative to whom restitution can be made for the wrong, the restitution belongs to the LORD and must be given to the priest, along with the ram with which atonement is made for him. 9 All the sacred contributions the Israelites bring to a priest will belong to him. 10 Each man's sacred gifts are his own, but what he gives to the priest will belong to the priest.'"

11 Then the LORD said to Moses, 12 "Speak to the Israelites and say to them: 'If a man's wife goes astray and is unfaithful to him 13 By sleeping with another man, and this is hidden from her husband and her impurity is undetected (since there is no witness against her and she has not been caught in the act), 14 And if feelings of jealousy come over her husband and he suspects his wife and she is impure—or if he is jealous and suspects her even though she is not impure— 15 Then he is to take his wife to the priest. He must also take an offering of a tenth of an ephah of barley flour on her behalf. He must not pour oil on it or put incense on it, because it is a grain offering for jealousy, a reminder offering to draw attention to guilt. 16 "'The priest shall bring her and have her stand before the LORD. 17 Then he shall take some holy water in a clay jar and put some dust from the tabernacle floor into the water. 18 After the priest has had the woman stand before the LORD, he shall loosen her hair and place in her hands the reminder offering, the grain offering for jealousy, while he himself holds the bitter water that brings a curse. 19 Then the priest shall put the woman under oath and say to her, "If no other man has slept with you and you have not gone astray and become impure while married to your husband, may this bitter water that brings a curse not harm you. 20 But if you have gone astray while married to your husband and you have defiled yourself by sleeping with a man other than your husband"— 21 Here the priest is to put the woman under this curse of the oath—"may the LORD cause your people to curse and denounce you when he causes your thigh to waste away and your abdomen to swell. 22 May this water that brings a curse enter your body so that your abdomen swells and your thigh wastes away." "'Then the woman is to say, "Amen. So be it." 23 "'The priest is to write these curses on a scroll and then wash them off into the

    2) The husband became suspicious, jealous: Strife, accusations, threats occurred—a broken relationship became a possibility
    3) The law was to be followed—even if the wife knew she was not guilty or defiled
  b. The couple was to seek the counsel & help of the priest (minister)
    1) To bring an offering of barley flour (two quarts) to the LORD
    2) Not to pour oil nor put incense on it: A symbol of being anointed & of one's prayers pleasing the LORD
      • Because it was not a Grain Offering of thanksgiving but an Investigative Offering to discern guilt

  c. The priest was to present the wife to the LORD
    1) The priest (minister) was to warn her of God's judgment
      • To mix some dust from the Tabernacle floor (holy dust) in some holy water
      • To loosen the woman's hair
      • To place the Investigative Offering in her hands
    2) The priest (minister) was to put the woman under oath
      • If she was not guilty of immorality, she would not suffer God's judgment or curse
      • If she was guilty of immorality—was defiled—she would suffer the judgment & curse of God: She would become infertile, unable to bear children; & if pregnant, she would suffer a miscarriage

      • The woman was forced to think through the oath & situation: She was asked to say "Amen"—to confess or to call God's curse down upon herself
    3) The priest (minister) was to write God's curses upon a leather scroll &

NUMBERS 5:1-31

then wash them off in the water: The woman then drank the water	bitter water. 24 He shall have the woman drink the bitter water that brings a curse, and this water will enter her and cause bitter suffering.	her thigh waste away, and she will become accursed among her people. 28 If, however, the woman has not defiled herself and is free from impurity, she will be cleared of guilt and will be able to have children.	being pregnant illegitimately or made infertile) & she would be accused (declared infertile, unblessed by God) • If she was innocent & pure, she would be cleared of all charges & able to bear children
4) The priest (minister) took the Grain Offering from the woman & waved it before the LORD	25 The priest is to take from her hands the grain offering for jealousy, wave it before the LORD and bring it to the altar.		d. The purpose of the law is restated: This was the law to control sexual suspicion & jealousy
5) The priest (minister) then burned a handful of the offering upon the altar 6) The priest (minister) then had the woman drink the bitter water • If she was defiled—had been sexually unfaithful—the water would cause bitter suffering: Her abdomen would swell & her thigh would waste away (a picture of	26 The priest is then to take a handful of the grain offering as a memorial offering and burn it on the altar; after that, he is to have the woman drink the water. 27 If she has defiled herself and been unfaithful to her husband, then when she is made to drink the water that brings a curse, it will go into her and cause bitter suffering; her abdomen will swell and	29 " 'This, then, is the law of jealousy when a woman goes astray and defiles herself while married to her husband, 30 Or when feelings of jealousy come over a man because he suspects his wife. The priest is to have her stand before the LORD and is to apply this entire law to her. 31 The husband will be innocent of any wrongdoing, but the woman will bear the consequences of her sin.' "	1) The entire law was to be applied to the woman 2) The husband was innocent of any wrong-doing 3) The woman would be held accountable for her sin (Le. 20:10; De. 22:22)

DIVISION I

THE PREPARATION FOR THE MARCH TO THE PROMISED LAND, 1:1–10:36

D. The Basic Laws That Keep God's People United and Pure: God's People Must Live Pure Lives, 5:1-31

(5:1-31) Introduction—Unified, Duty to Be—One, Duty to Be—Pure, Duty to Be—Holy, Duty to Be—Believers, Duty of: the human race has the greatest hope that could ever be given, the hope of the promised land. Keep in mind what the promised land means: it means…

- the promised land of conquest over all the pitfalls and enemies of life
- the promised land of heaven, of living forever in the presence of God Himself (Jehovah, Yahweh—the only living and true God)

This is the message of the great book of *Numbers*: the march of God's people to the promised land. Once a person begins to follow God, he immediately becomes a part of God's people—a member of God's family, of the church itself. God demands one basic thing of the new believer, the very thing He demands of all His people: that they be united and pure. God's people are to walk together as one, living pure and clean lives before Him. God is holy; therefore, He expects His people to be holy. The overall objective and goal of God's people is to reach the promised land; therefore, as they march, God expects them to march together, walking in formation step by step. They are to be united together as a great force of marching soldiers. Moreover, as God's people march to the promised land, God expects His people to be distinct and different from the secular world. They are soldiers of God, disciplined, following in the footsteps of their Commander-in-Chief, the Lord Jesus Christ. Christ the Commander lived a pure life before God; therefore, the army of Christ is expected to live a pure life. This is the great subject of this passage: *The Basic Laws That Keep God's People United and Pure: God's People Must Live Pure Lives,* 5:1-31.

1. There was the law of separation—the unclean were removed from the camp: a picture of spiritual separation (vv.1-4).
2. There was the law that controlled doing any wrong against another person (vv.5-10).
3. There was the law controlling the suspicion and jealousy of sexual unfaithfulness (vv.11-31).

1 (5:1-4) **Separation, Spiritual—Spiritual Separation—Church Discipline—Uncleanness, Spiritual—Uncleanness, Ceremonial—Ceremonial Uncleanness—Ritual Uncleanness—Disease, of Skin—Leprosy, Symbol of—Infectious Skin Disease, Symbol of—Death, Ceremonial Uncleanness of**: there was the law of separation: the unclean were removed from the camp. This is a picture of spiritual separation. As God's people marched to the promised land, the unclean were to be removed from the camp. The presence of the unclean among God's people was a serious situation. Note how forcefully this was stressed: the Hebrew word for *put out* or *sent away* or *remove* (salah) means just what it says, to expel the unclean person from the camp of God's people. The forcefulness of the command is seen in the fact that it is mentioned no less than four times in these four verses. Just who were the unclean who were to be expelled?

a. The unclean were identified (v.2). A person with leprosy or a contagious skin disease or discharge was counted unclean (v.2). The Hebrew word for infectious skin disease (sara`at) means all kinds of serious or contagious skin diseases or discharges. Leprosy would be an example. When a person was seen to have some kind of skin disease, he was to be removed from the community. A person who came in contact with death was also counted unclean

49

NUMBERS 5:1-31

(v.2) (see outline and notes—Le.chs.13-14 for more discussion).

b. The purpose for removing the unclean persons from the camp was twofold. One purpose was to prevent the spread of disease within the camp. Remember, the people of that day did not have the medical knowledge nor medicine to combat disease. The epidemics that have wiped out millions throughout past generations is clear demonstration of this fact. Therefore, one of the purposes of God in having the unclean removed from the camp was to prevent the spread of disease. But there was another reason, a symbolic reason why God wanted the unclean separated from His people. God Himself dwelt within the camp (v.3). His very presence dwelt within the Tabernacle. God had to teach His people that He was holy and that they must live holy, pure, and clean lives before Him. Therefore all uncleanness was to be removed from Him and from His people—lest they both become contaminated by uncleanness and impurity.

c. The obedience of the people is stressed: they removed the unclean from the camp.

Thought 1. God has called His people to spiritual separation, to be totally set apart from the sin and shame of the world. This is the point behind this Scripture. The issue is not whether God cares for the diseased and for those who hurt and suffer. God cares for the suffering and the afflicted; this has been proven throughout the generations of human history. God loves the human race, every single person upon planet earth. Moreover, He loves those who suffer and hurt with a very special love. This has been demonstrated perfectly in Christ Jesus during His walk here upon earth. As stated, God's love for the suffering and hurting is not the issue: the issue is spiritual separation from the sin and darkness of this world. God has called His people to be a distinct people, a people who are set apart totally to Him in purity of heart and behavior. God's people are to be distinct in this one fact: they do not live in the immorality, lawlessness, and violence of this world. The Israelites were not to live as the other nations who surrounded them. They were not to worship the false gods of those nations nor to engage in their lawless, violent, and immoral ways. We too are to be distinct and different in this one area: that of holiness—living pure and clean lives. Our conduct and behavior are to be moral, lawful, and peaceful—not following the ways of immorality, lawlessness, and violence. We are to be totally separated from such, living distinct and separate lives from the world.

> Be careful, or your hearts will be weighed down with dissipation, drunkenness and the anxieties of life, and that day will close on you unexpectedly like a trap. (Lu. 21:34)
>
> If you belonged to the world, it would love you as its own. As it is, you do not belong to the world, but I have chosen you out of the world. That is why the world hates you. (Jn. 15:19)
>
> With many other words he warned them; and he pleaded with them, "Save yourselves from this corrupt generation." (Ac. 2:40)
>
> Therefore, I urge you, brothers, in view of God's mercy, to offer your bodies as living sacrifices, holy and pleasing to God—this is your spiritual act of worship. Do not conform any longer to the pattern of this world, but be transformed by the renewing of your mind. Then you will be able to test and approve what God's will is—his good, pleasing and perfect will. (Ro. 12:1-2)
>
> "Therefore come out from them and be separate, says the Lord. Touch no unclean thing, and I will receive you. I will be a Father to you, and you will be my sons and daughters, says the Lord Almighty." (2 Co. 6:17-18)
>
> Have nothing to do with the fruitless deeds of darkness, but rather expose them. (Ep. 5:11)
>
> In the name of the Lord Jesus Christ, we command you, brothers, to keep away from every brother who is idle and does not live according to the teaching you received from us. (2 Th. 3:6)
>
> No one serving as a soldier gets involved in civilian affairs—he wants to please his commanding officer. (2 Ti. 2:4)
>
> Do not love the world or anything in the world. If anyone loves the world, the love of the Father is not in him. For everything in the world—the cravings of sinful man, the lust of his eyes and the boasting of what he has and does—comes not from the Father but from the world. (1 Jn. 2:15-16)
>
> Depart, depart, go out from there! Touch no unclean thing! Come out from it and be pure, you who carry the vessels of the LORD. (Is. 52:11)

Thought 2. There is a clear lesson here for the church. The church must discipline members who become engaged in serious sin. As Matthew Henry points out, "scandalous persons" must be separated from God's people, lest others become infected and defiled.[1] (See outline and notes—Mt. 18:15-20; 1 Co. 5:1-5; 1 Co. 5:6-13 for more discussion.)

> "If your brother sins against you, go and show him his fault, just between the two of you. If he listens to you, you have won your brother over. But if he will not listen, take one or two others along, so that 'every matter may be established by the testimony of two or three witnesses.' If he refuses to listen to them, tell it to the church; and if he refuses to listen even to the church, treat him as you would a pagan or a tax collector." (Mt. 18:15-17)
>
> So watch yourselves. "If your brother sins, rebuke him, and if he repents, forgive him." (Lu. 17:3)
>
> When you are assembled in the name of our Lord Jesus and I am with you in spirit, and the power of our Lord Jesus is present, hand this man over to Satan, so that the sinful nature may be destroyed and his spirit saved on the day of the Lord. Your boasting is not good. Don't you know that a little yeast works through the whole batch of dough? Get rid of the old yeast that you

---

[1] Matthew Henry. *Matthew Henry's Commentary*, Vol.1, (Old Tappan, NJ: Fleming H. Revell Co.), p.580.

may be a new batch without yeast—as you really are. For Christ, our Passover lamb, has been sacrificed. (1 Co. 5:4-7)

Holding on to faith and a good conscience. Some have rejected these and so have shipwrecked their faith. Among them are Hymenaeus and Alexander, whom I have handed over to Satan to be taught not to blaspheme. (1 Ti. 1:19-20)

Those who sin are to be rebuked publicly, so that the others may take warning. (1 Ti. 5:20)

Preach the Word; be prepared in season and out of season; correct, rebuke and encourage—with great patience and careful instruction. (2 Ti. 4:2)

And at his appointed season he brought his word to light through the preaching entrusted to me by the command of God our Savior. (Tit. 1:3)

These, then, are the things you should teach. Encourage and rebuke with all authority. Do not let anyone despise you. (Tit. 2:15)

Warn a divisive person once, and then warn him a second time. After that, have nothing to do with him. You may be sure that such a man is warped and sinful; he is self-condemned. (Tit. 3:10-11)

2 (5:5-10) **Neighbor, Sin Against—Believer, Sin Against—Believer, Wrong Committed Against—Restitution—Confession, of Sin—Law, Controlling Wrong Against Others**: there was the law that controlled doing wrong against another person. Most commentators deal with this passage as though it refers only to stolen property. Perhaps this is the correct interpretation, but the law of restitution applies to other cases as well:
⇒ A person was to pay restitution if he injured another person (Ex. 21:18-19). The restitution included the payment for all lost time and income from employment as well as all medical costs.
⇒ A person was to pay restitution if he or anything he owned damaged the property of another person (Ex. 22:5).
⇒ A person was to pay restitution f a fire started by him got out of hand, damaging another man's property (Ex. 22:6).

These are just a few examples. There are many ways that a person can do wrong against others, but this Scripture is clear: any wrong—no matter what it is—is a wrong against another person. Wrong involves injury, injury to another person. Keep in mind that a person can injure God as well as man. In fact, every time we wrong another person, we commit a wrong against God: we injure God—hurt Him, cut His heart—because we have injured a fellow human being.

a. The charge of this passage is stunning: if a person wrongs another, it is counted as being unfaithful to the LORD. The person stands guilty before God, guilty of some damaging, dreadful, lawless, or violent act—not only against another person, but against God Himself.

Among God's people, doing wrong against another person is a terrible *wrong* (maal). The word means to be unfaithful; to betray the LORD; to commit a serious, grievous transgression. It means to break faith with another person, and by breaking faith with that person, one breaks faith with God Himself. Both man and God have been violated, seriously and grievously violated. As God's people marched to the promised land, He could not allow them to break faith with one another, to do wrong against one another. Lawlessness, violence, injury—harming one another—would create social disorder. Social disorder—doing wrong against one another—would destroy God's people.

b. The remedy for doing wrong against another person involves three steps.
1) The offender must confess his sin to God. No matter what the sin is, it must be confessed to God:
⇒ some physical abuse, injury, or harm
⇒ some property damage or destruction
⇒ any harmful, lawless, or violent act against a person or his property

2) The offender was not only to confess his sin, he was to make restitution. Restitution was just as important as confession. Full restitution plus one fifth (20%) had to be paid for whatever wrong had been done. Note: if the injured person had been killed or were no longer living, or if he had no living relative, the restitution was to be paid to the priests (v.8).

3) The person who wronged others must approach God through the sacrifice of the Guilt Offering (v.8). He had to seek atonement, that is, reconciliation with God and with the offended party. Atonement was an absolute essential.

c. There is an important reminder here for God's people. All sacred gifts, once promised or given, belonged to the priests (v.9). No gift, once it had been promised or given, was ever to be withdrawn—neither publicly nor secretly (v.10). The person making the offering to the LORD could not deceive nor cheat the LORD: he could not publicly present his offering to the LORD and then secretly or quietly withdraw it when others would not know.

Thought 1. The person who wrongs other people must take the same three steps spelled out in this passage:
(1) He must confess his sin to God.

I will set out and go back to my father and say to him: Father, I have sinned against heaven and against you. (Lu. 15:18)

Repent, then, and turn to God, so that your sins may be wiped out, that times of refreshing may come from the Lord. (Ac. 3:19)

If we confess our sins, he is faithful and just and will forgive us our sins and purify us from all unrighteousness. (1 Jn. 1:9)

Now make confession to the LORD, the God of your fathers, and do his will. Separate yourselves from the peoples around you and from your foreign wives. (Ezr. 10:11)

He who conceals his sins does not prosper, but whoever confesses and renounces them finds mercy. (Pr. 28:13)

Let the wicked forsake his way and the evil man his thoughts. Let him turn to the LORD, and he will have mercy on him, and to our God, for he will freely pardon. (Is. 55:7)

NUMBERS 5:1-31

"Only acknowledge your guilt—you have rebelled against the LORD your God, you have scattered your favors to foreign gods under every spreading tree, and have not obeyed me," declares the LORD. (Je. 3:13)

(2) He must make restitution.

But Zacchaeus stood up and said to the Lord, "Look, Lord! Here and now I give half of my possessions to the poor, and if I have cheated anybody out of anything, I will pay back four times the amount." Jesus said to him, "Today salvation has come to this house, because this man, too, is a son of Abraham." (Lu. 19:8-9)

When he thus sins and becomes guilty, he must return what he has stolen or taken by extortion, or what was entrusted to him, or the lost property he found. (Le. 6:4)

The king asked the woman about it, and she told him. Then he assigned an official to her case and said to him, "Give back everything that belonged to her, including all the income from her land from the day she left the country until now." (2 K. 8:6)

"Give back to them immediately their fields, vineyards, olive groves and houses, and also the usury you are charging them—the hundredth part of the money, grain, new wine and oil." "We will give it back," they said. "And we will not demand anything more from them. We will do as you say." Then I summoned the priests and made the nobles and officials take an oath to do what they had promised. (Ne. 5:11-12)

Men do not despise a thief if he steals to satisfy his hunger when he is starving. Yet if he is caught, he must pay sevenfold, though it costs him all the wealth of his house. (Pr. 6:30-31)

But if a wicked man turns away from all the sins he has committed and keeps all my decrees and does what is just and right, he will surely live; he will not die. (Eze. 18:21)

And if I say to the wicked man, 'You will surely die,' but he then turns away from his sin and does what is just and right—if he gives back what he took in pledge for a loan, returns what he has stolen, follows the decrees that give life, and does no evil, he will surely live; he will not die. (Eze. 33:14-15)

(3) He must approach God for the atonement or reconciliation through the sacrifice of the Lord Jesus Christ. God accepts only those who approach Him through His Son, the Lord Jesus Christ. There is cleansing from sin only through Him.

And are justified freely by his grace through the redemption that came by Christ Jesus. (Ro. 3:24)

Since we have now been justified by his blood, how much more shall we be saved from God's wrath through him! (Ro. 5:9)

In him we have redemption through his blood, the forgiveness of sins, in accordance with the riches of God's grace. (Ep. 1:7)

In whom we have redemption, the forgiveness of sins. (Col. 1:14)

For the grace of God that brings salvation has appeared to all men. It teaches us to say "No" to ungodliness and worldly passions, and to live self-controlled, upright and godly lives in this present age, while we wait for the blessed hope—the glorious appearing of our great God and Savior, Jesus Christ, who gave himself for us to redeem us from all wickedness and to purify for himself a people that are his very own, eager to do what is good. (Tit. 2:11-14)

How much more, then, will the blood of Christ, who through the eternal Spirit offered himself unblemished to God, cleanse our consciences from acts that lead to death, so that we may serve the living God! (He. 9:14)

For you know that it was not with perishable things such as silver or gold that you were redeemed from the empty way of life handed down to you from your forefathers, but with the precious blood of Christ, a lamb without blemish or defect. (1 Pe. 1:18-19)

But if we walk in the light, as he is in the light, we have fellowship with one another, and the blood of Jesus, his Son, purifies us from all sin. (1 Jn. 1:7)

Thought 2. In dealing with restitution, James Philip makes a statement that needs to be heeded by the legal systems of nations today.

As to restitution, we may observe that the Mosaic law is considerably in advance of our own. Restitution has hardly figured at all in our criminal law until comparatively recently. If one's house is burgled, and valuables stolen, the thief when caught will receive a prison sentence, but we may never recover our lost property, and our courts have been very slow to help with any compensation. It is, of course, open to us to take the criminal to the civil court and sue him for damages, but the process is so cumbersome that it could take years for the case even to be heard.[2]

3 (5:11-31) **Suspicion, of Sexual Unfaithfulness—Marriage, Sexual Unfaithfulness—Jealousy, of Sexual Unfaithfulness—Israel, Laws of—Immorality—Husband, Suspicion of Unfaithfulness—Wife, Suspicion of Unfaithfulness**: there was the law controlling the suspicion and jealousy of sexual unfaithfulness. Sexual unfaithfulness is a destructive sin, very destructive. It cuts deep, ripping and tearing at the heart of the spouse. Sexual unfaithfulness damages lives and families, sometimes destroying them. Families are the foundation of society itself; therefore, sexual unfaithfulness erodes the very foundation of society. As goes the family, so goes society. If the family is strong, the society is strong. If the family is weak, society is weak. If the family is destroyed, society is destroyed. How can such a sweeping statement be made? Because this is the

---

[2] James Philip. *The Preacher's Commentary on Numbers*. (Nashville, TN: Word Publishing, 1990, 2003), pp.72-73.

NUMBERS 5:1-31

way God has made human life and society. God has established the family to be the foundation of society. Just think about the fact, about what is destroyed when sexual unfaithfulness destroys families. There is the destruction of the great values and virtues of human life, the destruction of...

- trust
- loyalty
- faithfulness
- love
- joy
- gentleness
- goodness
- control
- peace
- security
- self-esteem
- fulfillment
- satisfaction
- respect

The commandment against adultery is one of the major commandments, one of the Ten Commandments. God gave this commandment to preserve our lives, to preserve the great qualities that bring love, joy, peace, trust, and loyalty to the lives of all of us as well as to society itself. Marital faithfulness builds a healthy mind and heart and a secure, strong society. This was the reason God gave this law controlling the suspicion and jealousy of sexual unfaithfulness.

a. The case given to illustrate the law is simply stated: a man's wife went astray and was unfaithful (vv.12-14).

1) The immorality and impurity were undetected: there was no witness, and the husband was not sure about his wife, whether she had been faithful or unfaithful.
2) But the husband was suspicious (v.14). Strife, accusations, and threats occurred. A broken relationship became a live possibility. What was to be done?
3) The law was to be followed even if the wife knew that she was not guilty or defiled. She was still to obey the law in order to solve the problem, alleviating the suspicion and jealousy of her husband.

   Note how this law gave strong protection to the women among God's people. The husband could not strike out against his wife, abusing or committing some act of violence against her. This law was of critical importance in the ancient world, for women were counted as nothing more than chattel property. Among pagans, women existed for the pleasure of men, for the rearing of families, and for little else. But this was not to be so among God's people. They were to be a people of the law, controlled not by emotional outrages but by rationality and the rule of law.

b. The couple was to seek the counsel and help of the priest (a symbol of the minister) (v.15). Note that the couple was to take an offering to the LORD as well. The offering was to be two quarts of barley flour, but neither oil nor incense was to be mixed with it. This was usually done when making a Grain Offering of thanksgiving, but this was an investigative offering to discern guilt, not a thanksgiving offering. The oil and incense were a symbol of being anointed or blessed by God, of prayers being lifted up to God as a sweet aroma that pleased Him. However, in this case, God was not pleased. The issue was the possibility of sexual unfaithfulness, of suspicion and jealousy; therefore, as stated, this was an investigative offering to discern guilt. An offering was required, but not an offering that pleased the LORD.

c. The priest (minister) was to present the wife to the LORD (vv.16-28). These verses involved a ritual that the suspected wife had to undergo. Note how the ritual stressed the seriousness of sexual unfaithfulness and stood as a strong warning to all against sexual unfaithfulness.

1) The priest (minister) was to warn the suspected wife of God's judgment (vv.17-18). He was to mix some dust from the Tabernacle floor (holy dust) in some holy water, that is, water taken from inside the Tabernacle. This act was to stress the holiness of the situation, a situation that was being brought before the LORD Himself. The priest was then to loosen the woman's hair (v.18). This was probably a symbol of the woman opening up her life before the LORD and requesting that the LORD open up the truth to her husband.[3] The priest then placed the investigative offering, the Grain Offering, in her hands (v.18).

2) The priest was to put the woman under oath (vv.19-22). The priest stated these facts: if she were not guilty of immorality, she would not suffer God's judgment or curse (v.19). But if she were guilty of immorality and had defiled herself, she would suffer the judgment and curse of God. Just what this meant is unknown. Most commentators feel that the curse meant that she would become infertile, unable to bear children, and if pregnant, she would suffer a miscarriage. If she were guilty of sexual unfaithfulness, there was, of course, the possibility that she would become pregnant. Note that she was forced to think through the oath and situation: she was asked to say "Amen"; that is, to confess or to call God's curse down upon herself (v.22).

3) The priest was to write God's curses upon a piece of leather and then wash them off in the water. The woman was then to drink the water (vv.23-24).

4) The priest took the Grain Offering from the woman and waved it before the LORD (v.25).

5) The priest then burned a handful of the offering upon the altar (v.26).

6) The priest then had the woman drink the bitter water (vv.26-28). If she were defiled—had been sexually unfaithful—the water would cause bitter suffering. Note how descriptive the bitter suffering is pictured: her abdomen would swell and her thigh would waste away. This is a picture of being pregnant illegitimately or made infertile. It is also stated that she would be accursed among people; that is, declared infertile, unblessed by God. But note: if she were innocent and pure, she would be cleared of all charges and be able to bear children (v.28).

d. The purpose of the law is restated: to control sexual suspicion and jealousy (vv.29-31). Simply stated, the entire law was to be applied to the woman (v.30). The husband was innocent of any wrongdoing in this particular case (v.31). The woman was to be held accountable for her sin (Le. 20:10; De. 22:22).

Thought 1. When a man or woman goes astray or is even thought to be guilty of sexual unfaithfulness, suspicion and jealousy arise. Strife, accusations, and threats occur. Often a broken relationship results, and the couple is ripped apart. Sexual immorality always causes problems...

- guilt
- jealousy
- unwanted pregnancies
- broken marriages
- insecurity
- a false sense of security
- unhappiness

---

[3] *The Expositor's Bible Commentary*, Frank E. Gaebelein, Editor, p.746.

NUMBERS 5:1-31

- disease
- a cheapening of sex
- broken trust
- selfishness
- loss of esteem
- loss of respect for others
- loss of respect by others
- problems with children
- emotional problems
- disloyalty
- a lack of fulfillment
- loss of affection in relationships

Because of these problems and so many more, God demands faithfulness between husband and wife. The sanctity of marriage is to be kept. The health and security of God's people and of society are at stake. The foundation of the family, of children, and of society must not be undermined by sexual unfaithfulness. The family and children are to have a fundamental place in society, and the family and children are to be respected and built up, not torn down. The marriage bond is far more than just a civil contract that can be broken anytime a person wishes. The marriage bond is a contract made between two persons before God Himself. He unites the two persons into one flesh. James Philips points out what "one flesh" means: it means that a new person—a totally new person—has been brought into being by God. Therefore, it is impossible to think of a husband and wife as two individuals; they are one person created by God into "one flesh"—a totally new person. It is, therefore, against God's will for a couple to tear themselves into pieces. The picture is descriptive: the person who divorces rips and tears apart his own body.[4] The Word of God is clear:

"You have heard that it was said, 'Do not commit adultery.' But I tell you that anyone who looks at a woman lustfully has already committed adultery with her in his heart." (Mt. 5:27-28)

"It is not lawful for you to have her." (Mt. 14:4)

Do you not know that the wicked will not inherit the kingdom of God? Do not be deceived: Neither the sexually immoral nor idolaters nor adulterers nor male prostitutes nor homosexual offenders. (1 Co. 6:9)

The acts of the sinful nature are obvious: sexual immorality, impurity and debauchery; idolatry and witchcraft; hatred, discord, jealousy, fits of rage, selfish ambition, dissensions, factions and envy; drunkenness, orgies, and the like. I warn you, as I did before, that those who live like this will not inherit the kingdom of God. (Ga. 5:19-21)

With eyes full of adultery, they never stop sinning; they seduce the unstable; they are experts in greed—an accursed brood! (2 Pe. 2:14)

You shall not commit adultery. (Ex. 20:14)

If a man commits adultery with another man's wife—with the wife of his neighbor—both the adulterer and the adulteress must be put to death. (Le. 20:10)

The eye of the adulterer watches for dusk; he thinks, 'No eye will see me,' and he keeps his face concealed. (Jb. 24:15)

TYPES, SYMBOLS, AND PICTURES
(Numbers 5:1-31)

Historical Term	Type or Picture (Scriptural Basis for Each)	Life Application for Today's Believer	Biblical Application
Leprosy or Infectious Skin Disease Nu. 5:1-4; 12:13-16 (See also Le. 13:1-59)	*These contagious diseases symbolize the disease of sin, how contagious it is, and the need to prevent the spread of sin.* **When the cloud lifted from above the Tent, there stood Miriam—leprous, like snow. Aaron turned toward her and saw that she had leprosy. (Nu. 12:10)**	God gave Israel the law governing leprosy or infectious skin disease because He loves His people. God loves us and cares for us; therefore He wants us healthy—physically and spiritually. He wants us experiencing the fullness of life, worshipping and serving Him. He wants us bearing strong testimony to a world lost and reeling under the weight of desperate need. He wants all of His people throughout all generations healthy.	*On hearing this, Jesus said to them, "It is not the healthy who need a doctor, but the sick. I have not come to call the righteous, but sinners." (Mk. 2:17)* *"The Spirit of the Lord is on me, because he has anointed me to preach good news to the poor. He has sent me to proclaim freedom for the prisoners and recovery of sight for the blind, to release the oppressed. (Lu. 4:18)* *Dear friend, I pray that you may enjoy good health and that all may go well with you, even as your soul is getting along well. (3 Jn. 2)* *He said, "If you listen carefully to the voice of the*

---

4 James Philip. *The Preacher's Commentary on Numbers.* p.78.

NUMBERS 5:1-31

Historical Term	Type or Picture (Scriptural Basis for Each)	Life Application for Today's Believer	Biblical Application
			LORD your God and do what is right in his eyes, if you pay attention to his commands and keep all his decrees, I will not bring on you any of the diseases I brought on the Egyptians, for I am the LORD, who heals you." (Ex. 15:26) The LORD will keep you free from every disease. He will not inflict on you the horrible diseases you knew in Egypt, but he will inflict them on all who hate you. (De. 7:15) 'But I will restore you to health and heal your wounds,' declares the LORD, 'because you are called an outcast, Zion for whom no one cares.' (Je. 30:17) "Come, let us return to the LORD. He has torn us to pieces but he will heal us; he has injured us but he will bind up our wounds. (Ho. 6:1)
The Priest Loosening the Woman's Hair Nu. 5:11-31, esp. v.18	This was probably a symbol of the woman (suspected of unfaithfulness) opening up her life before the LORD and requesting that the LORD open up the truth to her husband. [5] The priest (minister) was to present the wife to the LORD (vv.16-28). These verses involved a ritual that the suspected wife had to undergo. Note how the ritual stressed the seriousness of sexual unfaithfulness and stood as a strong warning to all others against sexual unfaithfulness. The priest (minister) was to warn the suspected wife of God's judgment (vv.17-18). He was to mix some dust from the Tabernacle floor (holy dust) in some holy water, that is, water taken from inside the Tabernacle. This act was to stress the holiness of the situation, a situation that was being brought before the LORD Himself. The priest was then to loosen the woman's hair (v.18). The priest then placed the investigation	What is the duty of the Christian wife to her husband and of the Christian husband to his wife? If a woman wants to give her life to God, she has to give herself to her husband. Scripture says that she has to do five specific things. 1. Live in submission to her own husband (1 Pe. 3:1). 2. Live a pure life (1 Pe. 3:2). 3. Live a reverent life before God (1 Pe. 3:2). 4. Not dress to attract attention (1 Pe. 3:3). 5. Adorn her heart with a gentle and quiet spirit (1 Pe. 3:4-6).	Blessed are the pure in heart, for they will see God. (Mt. 5:8) To the married I give this command (not I, but the Lord): A wife must not separate from her husband. (1 Co. 7:10) Wives, submit to your husbands, as is fitting in the Lord. (Col. 3:18) It is God's will that you should be sanctified: that you should avoid sexual immorality. (1 Th. 4:3) The goal of this command is love, which comes from a pure heart and a good conscience and a sincere faith. (1 Ti. 1:5) In the same way, their wives are to be women worthy of respect, not malicious talkers but temperate and trustworthy in everything. (1 Ti. 3:11) Then they can train the younger women to love their husbands and children, to be self-controlled and pure, to be busy at home, to be kind, and to be subject to their husbands, so that no one will malign the word of God. (Tit. 2:4-5)

---

[5] *The Expositor's Bible Commentary,* Frank E. Gaebelein, Editor, p.746.

NUMBERS 5:1-31

Historical Term	Type or Picture (Scriptural Basis for Each)	Life Application for Today's Believer	Biblical Application
	offering, the Grain Offering, in her hands (v.18). After the priest has had the woman stand before the LORD, he shall loosen her hair and place in her hands the reminder offering, the grain offering for jealousy, while he himself holds the bitter water that brings a curse. (Nu. 5:18)		*Wives, in the same way be submissive to your husbands so that, if any of them do not believe the word, they may be won over without words by the behavior of their wives. (1 Pe. 3:1)* *These are those who did not defile themselves with women, for they kept themselves pure. They follow the Lamb wherever he goes. They were purchased from among men and offered as firstfruits to God and the Lamb. (Re. 14:4)* *She watches over the affairs of her household and does not eat the bread of idleness. (Pr. 31:27)*

NUMBERS 6:1-27

CHAPTER 6

E. The Special Provision Instituted for Drawing Closer to God—the Nazirite Vow & the Special Benediction of God: The Importance & Seriousness of Vows, 6:1-27

1. The purpose for the vow: A strong desire to draw closer to the LORD—to be separated, totally set apart to the LORD

The LORD said to Moses,
2 "Speak to the Israelites and say to them: 'If a man or woman wants to make a special vow, a vow of separation to the LORD as a Nazirite,

2. The obligations of the special vow to the LORD
   a. He must abstain from all intoxicating drink: To keep his mind clear & focused upon the LORD
      1) From wine & other fermented drinks
      2) From anything that comes from the vine: A caution to prevent temptation

3 He must abstain from wine and other fermented drink and must not drink vinegar made from wine or from other fermented drink. He must not drink grape juice or eat grapes or raisins.
4 As long as he is a Nazirite, he must not eat anything that comes from the grapevine, not even the seeds or skins.

   b. He must not cut his hair: To be the mark of his vow
      1) That he was committed to live a life of holiness & separation to God
      2) That he was committed to keep his mind focused upon God

5 " 'During the entire period of his vow of separation no razor may be used on his head. He must be holy until the period of his separation to the LORD is over; he must let the hair of his head grow long.

   c. He must not go near a dead body, not even of his family: A symbol of becoming defiled & corrupted—spiritually or ceremonially unclean
      1) The reason:
         • Being the LORD's, he was to be totally focused upon the LORD (not upon earthly things, not even the most dear things)
         • Being the LORD's, he was to have no contact with death

6 Throughout the period of his separation to the LORD he must not go near a dead body.
7 Even if his own father or mother or brother or sister dies, he must not make himself ceremonially unclean on account of them, because the symbol of his separation to God is on his head.
8 Throughout the period of his separation he is consecrated to the LORD.

      2) The provision for cleansing if a person unexpectedly died in his presence
         • Must shave his head on the 7th day, removing the mark of his vow—for it was defiled
         • Must come to God for cleansing through the sacrifice of the Sin Offering: A symbol of Christ
         • Must approach God for atonement, reconciliation through the sacrifice of the Burnt Offering: A symbol of Christ

9 " 'If someone dies suddenly in his presence, thus defiling the hair he has dedicated, he must shave his head on the day of his cleansing—the seventh day.
10 Then on the eighth day he must bring two doves or two young pigeons to the priest at the entrance to the Tent of Meeting.
11 The priest is to offer one as a sin offering and the other as a burnt offering to make atonement for him because he sinned by being in the presence of the dead body. That same day he is to consecrate his head.

         • Must rededicate himself to the LORD for the full term of his vow
         • Must seek freedom from guilt through the sacrifice of the Guilt Offering: A symbol of Christ

12 He must dedicate himself to the LORD for the period of his separation and must bring a year-old male lamb as a guilt offering. The previous days do not count, because he became defiled during his separation.

3. The worship required after the fulfillment of the vow
   a. He must approach & present his offerings to the LORD

13 " 'Now this is the law for the Nazirite when the period of his separation is over. He is to be brought to the entrance to the Tent of Meeting.

      1) The Burnt Offering: Acknowledged the atonement
      2) The Sin Offering: Acknowledged the need for cleansing
      3) The Peace or Fellowship Offering: Acknowledged the need to grow in peace & fellowship with God
      4) The Grain & Drink Offerings: A person thanked & praised the LORD, dedicating himself—pouring his life out before God

14 There he is to present his offerings to the LORD: a year-old male lamb without defect for a burnt offering, a year-old ewe lamb without defect for a sin offering, a ram without defect for a fellowship offering,
15 Together with their grain offerings and drink offerings, and a basket of bread made without yeast—cakes made of fine flour mixed with oil, and wafers spread with oil.

   b. He must have the priest make the offerings in his behalf
      1) The Sin Offering & Burnt Offering
      2) The Fellowship or Peace Offering
      3) The Grain & Drink Offering

16 " 'The priest is to present them before the LORD and make the sin offering and the burnt offering.
17 He is to present the basket of unleavened bread and is to sacrifice the ram as a fellowship offering to the LORD, together with its grain offering and drink offering.

   c. He must shave off his hair & burn it under the sacrifice of the Fellowship Offering: A symbol for a continued commitment & closer fellowship with the LORD

18 " 'Then at the entrance to the Tent of Meeting, the Nazirite must shave off the hair that he dedicated. He is to take the hair and put it in the fire that is under the sacrifice of the fellowship offering.

   d. The priest then had to place in the Nazirites' hands the boiled shoulder of the ram & one cake & wafer made without yeast
      1) The priest was to offer these as a wave offering to the LORD
      2) The priest was to receive these along with the breast & thigh pieces as the LORD's portion

19 " 'After the Nazirite has shaved off the hair of his dedication, the priest is to place in his hands a boiled shoulder of the ram, and a cake and a wafer from the basket, both made without yeast.
20 The priest shall then wave them before the LORD as a wave offering; they are holy and belong to the priest, together with the breast that was waved and the thigh that was presented. After that, the Nazirite may drink wine.

   e. The Nazirite could then drink wine

4. The seriousness & heavy weight of the vow
   a. This is a law, the law of the

21 " 'This is the law of the Nazirite who vows his offering to the LORD in accordance

57

NUMBERS 6:1-27

Nazarite vow: A complete & total separation to the LORD
b. This vow must be kept, fulfilled
5. The great priestly benediction
   a. Promised by God Himself
 	
     1) His blessing
	with his separation, in addition to whatever else he can afford. He must fulfill the vow he has made, according to the law of the Nazirite.' "
	22 The LORD said to Moses,
	23 "Tell Aaron and his sons, 'This is how you are to bless the Israelites. Say to them:
	24 " ' "The LORD bless you
		and keep you;
		25 The LORD make his face shine upon you and be gracious to you;
		26 The LORD turn his face toward you and give you peace." '
		27 "So they will put my name on the Israelites, and I will bless them."
			2) His protection, security
			3) His face, special presence
			4) His grace
			5) His acceptance, approval, pleasure (smile)
			6) His peace
			b. The result: The blessings identified the Israelites as God's people, as belonging to Him

DIVISION I

THE PREPARATION FOR THE MARCH TO THE PROMISED LAND, 1:1–10:36

E. The Special Provision Instituted for Drawing Closer to God—the Nazarite Vow and the Special Benediction of God: The Importance and Seriousness of Vows, 6:1-27

(6:1-27) **Introduction—Vow, Importance of—Nazarite Vow—Vow, Nazarite—Devotion, Desire for—Communion, Desire for—Commitment, Deeper, Desire for**: desperate circumstances often stir people to pray and make vows to God. Severe illness, accidents, marital problems, parental problems, school problems, business difficulties, threats, war, and a host of other circumstances can cause people to make vows and promises to God. Every promise and vow is important to God, and God takes the vow seriously. He expects the person to fulfill his or her vows. But there is one vow that is very, very special to God: the Nazarite vow. What is the Nazarite vow? It is a vow that seeks a deeper life with God. The person wants a closer walk with God; therefore, he sets aside a period of time to seek the LORD as never before. He seeks a closer walk with the LORD, a deeper communion and fellowship with Him. He takes more time to study the Word of God, to pray and seek the face of God. He seeks to be more conformed to the image of God. He wants to grow in holiness, to be more totally separated from the world and set apart to God. He wants to be a stronger witness and testimony for God. The passion that burns in his heart is a passion to know God more and more, to be conformed to the very image of God.

This is the great subject of this important passage of Scripture: *The Special Provision Instituted for Drawing Closer to God—the Nazarite Vow and the Special Benediction of God: The Importance and Seriousness of Vows,* 6:1-27.

1. The reason for the vow: a strong desire to draw closer to the LORD—to be separated, totally set apart to the LORD (vv.1-2).
2. The obligations of the special vow to the LORD (vv.3-12).
3. The fulfillment of and the discharge from the vow (vv.13-20).
4. The seriousness and heavy weight of the vow (v.21).
5. The great priestly benediction (vv.22-27).

1 (6:1-2) **Vow, Reason for—Separation, to the LORD—Walk, Spiritual, Duty—Walk, Spiritual, Desire for**: the purpose for the vow was a closer walk with the LORD. The Nazarite wanted to draw closer to the LORD—to be separated, totally set apart to Him. The Hebrew word for *wants to make a special vow* or *to set themselves apart* (pala) means to make a hard, difficult vow; to make a singular, distinctive, different vow; a vow that differs from the usual vows.[1] The idea is striking: the Nazarite vow was different from the common, day-to-day vow. This person had a strong, strong desire to draw closer to the LORD. He was driven to know the LORD more and more personally, to know Him intimately. He had a passionate desire to be totally devoted to the LORD, totally separated and set apart to Him. The very word *Nazarite* (nazir) means a person who has set his life apart to God. The period of dedication was usually for a specific period of time. However, a few persons apparently were set apart for the Nazarite vow for life. For example, Samson was a Nazarite from the day of his birth (Jud. 13:7), and so was Samuel (1 S. 1:11, 28).

Thought 1. The longing, the passion, the intense desire to know the LORD more and more is the point to see in the Nazarite vow. The person was driven to seek a closer walk, a deeper devotion, and more and more communion with the LORD. He craved a continued, unbroken consciousness of the LORD's presence, a moment-by-moment fellowship with Him. Moreover, he wanted to be a stronger witness and testimony for the LORD. What a dynamic, strong example for us.

> Therefore, I urge you, brothers, in view of God's mercy, to offer your bodies as living sacrifices, holy and pleasing to God—this is your spiritual act of worship. (Ro. 12:1)
> But whatever was to my profit I now consider loss for the sake of Christ. What is more, I consider everything a loss compared to the surpassing greatness of knowing Christ Jesus my Lord, for whose sake I have lost all things. I consider them rubbish, that I may gain Christ. (Ph. 3:7-8)
> I want to know Christ and the power of his resurrection and the fellowship of sharing in his sufferings, becoming like him in his death. (Ph. 3:10)
> Let us draw near to God with a sincere heart in full assurance of faith, having our

---

[1] James Strong. *Strong's Exhaustive Concordance of the Bible*. (Nashville, TN: Thomas Nelson, Inc., 1990).

hearts sprinkled to cleanse us from a guilty conscience and having our bodies washed with pure water. (He. 10:22)

Come near to God and he will come near to you. (Js. 4:8)

Here I am! I stand at the door and knock. If anyone hears my voice and opens the door, I will come in and eat with him, and he with me. (Re. 3:20)

I have set the LORD always before me. Because he is at my right hand, I will not be shaken. (Ps. 16:8)

The LORD is close to the brokenhearted and saves those who are crushed in spirit. (Ps. 34:18)

But as for me, it is good to be near God. I have made the Sovereign LORD my refuge; I will tell of all your deeds. (Ps. 73:28)

The LORD is near to all who call on him, to all who call on him in truth. (Ps. 145:18)

My son, give me your heart and let your eyes keep to my ways. (Pr. 23:26)

"You are my witnesses," declares the LORD, "and my servant whom I have chosen, so that you may know and believe me and understand that I am he. Before me no god was formed, nor will there be one after me." (Is. 43:10)

Let us acknowledge the LORD; let us press on to acknowledge him. As surely as the sun rises, he will appear; he will come to us like the winter rains, like the spring rains that water the earth. (Ho. 6:3)

2 (6:3-12) **Vow—Drunkenness—Alcohol—Wine—Dedication—Uncleanness, Ceremonial—Uncleanness, Spiritual—Ritual, Laws of Uncleanness—Laws, of Uncleanness—Nazarite, Vow of**: there were three special obligations of the Nazarite vow, three very special commitments the person made to the LORD. Note that the three commitments involved diet, appearance, and associations.[2]

a. The person was to abstain from all intoxicating drink (vv.3-4). This included any and all kinds of drugs or intoxicating drinks. In fact, anything that came from the vine or was made from the fruit of the vine such as grapes, juice, jams, seeds, or skins—all this and anything else— was prohibited. A person was to keep his mind clear, free from any intoxicating numbness or dullness. He was to focus upon the LORD with a clear, sharp mind. The person's mental faculties were needed to meditate upon the Word of God, to commune and fellowship with the LORD, to bear testimony and witness for the LORD.

b. The person must not cut his hair (v.5). Uncut hair was the *public mark* of his vow. He was declaring the awesome importance of being committed to a life of holiness and separation to God, the importance of keeping one's mind focused upon God. Uncut hair was a distinctive witness for God, a witness that a person was committed to a life of holiness, committed to keeping his mind focused upon the LORD.

c. The person must not go near a dead body, not even if it was a family member (vv.6-12). Contact with a dead body was a symbol of becoming defiled, unclean, corrupted—of becoming ceremonially, spiritually unclean. Death is the end of life: it is the corruption and decay of the human body. Death is, therefore, the symbol of corruption, decay, and defilement. The person who took the Nazarite vow was, therefore, to have nothing to do with death. He was to be an example of life, not of death. This stern restriction proclaimed the wonderful life that God gives not the death and corruption that sin brings. The person had committed himself totally to the LORD; therefore, he was to be totally set apart and focused upon the LORD, not upon the things of the earth—not even upon the most dear things to his heart.

But what happened if a person unexpectedly died in the Nazarite's presence? In such a circumstance, there was a provision for cleansing (vv.9-12).

⇒ He had to shave his head on the seventh day, removing the mark of his vow, of his holiness (devotion to God). (v.9). Because he had become defiled, corrupted, the person had to remove his hair.

⇒ He had to come to God for cleansing through the sacrifice of the Sin Offering (v.10). Remember, the sacrifice is a symbol of the sacrifice of Christ. Only Christ can forgive sins.

⇒ He had to approach God for atonement (reconciliation) through the sacrifice of the Burnt Offering (v.11). This sacrifice is also a symbol of Christ's sacrifice. We receive the atonement, reconciliation with God, through Christ and Christ alone.

⇒ He had to rededicate himself to the LORD for the full term of his vow (v.12). Why the full term? Because the period of his vow and dedication had been disrupted. Consequently, the person had to recommit himself just as he had originally done, for the full term of his vow.

⇒ He had to seek freedom from guilt through the sacrifice of the Guilt Offering (v.12). Again, the sacrifice made was a symbol of Christ's sacrifice. It is only through Christ that guilt can be removed.

Thought 1. The obligation of the Nazarite vow clearly speaks to the heart and life of the believer. The lessons are forceful:

(1) The believer must abstain from all intoxicating drinks. He must keep his mind clear and focused totally upon the LORD. The believer must not allow drugs and drink to dull or numb or damage his mind. He must keep his mind healthy, alert, and sharp to focus upon God and the promised land toward which he is marching.

Be careful, or your hearts will be weighed down with dissipation, drunkenness and the anxieties of life, and that day will close on you unexpectedly like a trap. (Lu. 21:34)

Let us behave decently, as in the daytime, not in orgies and drunkenness, not in sexual immorality and debauchery, not in dissension and jealousy. (Ro. 13:13)

The acts of the sinful nature are obvious: sexual immorality, impurity and debauchery; idolatry and witchcraft; hatred, discord, jealousy, fits of rage, selfish ambition, dissensions, factions and envy; drunkenness, orgies, and the like. I warn you, as I did before, that those who live like this will not inherit the kingdom of God. (Ga. 5:19-21)

---

[2] *The Expositor's Bible Commentary*, Frank E. Gaebelein, Editor, p.749.

Do not get drunk on wine, which leads to debauchery. Instead, be filled with the Spirit. (Ep. 5:18)

Wine is a mocker and beer a brawler; whoever is led astray by them is not wise. (Pr. 20:1)

Do not join those who drink too much wine. (Pr. 23:20)

Who has woe? Who has sorrow? Who has strife? Who has complaints? Who has needless bruises? Who has bloodshot eyes? Those who linger over wine, who go to sample bowls of mixed wine. Do not gaze at wine when it is red, when it sparkles in the cup, when it goes down smoothly! (Pr. 23:29-31)

Woe to those who rise early in the morning to run after their drinks, who stay up late at night till they are inflamed with wine. (Is. 5:11)

"Woe to him who gives drink to his neighbors, pouring it from the wineskin till they are drunk, so that he can gaze on their naked bodies." (Hab. 2:15)

(2) The believer must keep his mind clear and focused upon the LORD.

We demolish arguments and every pretension that sets itself up against the knowledge of God, and we take captive every thought to make it obedient to Christ. (2 Co. 10:5)

Finally, brothers, whatever is true, whatever is noble, whatever is right, whatever is pure, whatever is lovely, whatever is admirable—if anything is excellent or praiseworthy—think about such things. (Ph. 4:8)

Because it is consecrated by the word of God and prayer. (1 Ti. 4:5)

Do not let this Book of the Law depart from your mouth; meditate on it day everything written in it. Then you will be prosperous and successful. (Jos. 1:8)

But his delight is in the law of the LORD, and on his law he meditates day and night. (Ps. 1:2)

May the words of my mouth and the meditation of my heart be pleasing in your sight, O LORD, my Rock and my Redeemer. (Ps. 19:14)

My soul will be satisfied as with the richest of foods; with singing lips my mouth will praise you. On my bed I remember you; I think of you through the watches of the night. (Ps. 63:5-6)

May my meditation be pleasing to him, as I rejoice in the LORD. (Ps. 104:34)

My eyes stay open through the watches of the night, that I may meditate on your promises. (Ps. 119:148)

(3) The Nazarite was not allowed to shave his head because his hair was the mark of his vow to God. His hair was the mark of his holiness and separation to God. So it must be with the believer. The believer must bear the mark of holiness and separation to God. The believer must bear the mark of being totally committed to God, the mark of a holy life before God. The believer must keep his mind totally focused upon the LORD, not upon earthly things, not even upon the things that might be thought most dear. As the believer marches to the promised land, living a holy life is to be the mark of his life.

To rescue us from the hand of our enemies, and to enable us to serve him without fear in holiness and righteousness before him all our days. (Lu. 1:74-75)

Since we have these promises, dear friends, let us purify ourselves from everything that contaminates body and spirit, perfecting holiness out of reverence for God. (2 Co. 7:1)

Make every effort to live in peace with all men and to be holy; without holiness no one will see the Lord. (He. 12:14)

But just as he who called you is holy, so be holy in all you do; for it is written: "Be holy, because I am holy." (1 Pe. 1:15-16)

Since everything will be destroyed in this way, what kind of people ought you to be? You ought to live holy and godly lives as you look forward to the day of God and speed its coming. That day will bring about the destruction of the heavens by fire, and the elements will melt in the heat. But in keeping with his promise we are looking forward to a new heaven and a new earth, the home of righteousness. So then, dear friends, since you are looking forward to this, make every effort to be found spotless, blameless and at peace with him. (2 Pe. 3:11-14)

I am the LORD who brought you up out of Egypt to be your God; therefore be holy, because I am holy. (Le. 11:45)

Exalt the LORD our God and worship at his holy mountain, for the LORD our God is holy. (Ps. 99:9)

(4) The Nazarite could not touch a dead body because it symbolized corruption and decay, defilement and uncleanness. So it must be with the believer. The believer must not become corrupted and defiled by sin and shame. Sin and shame bring lawlessness, violence, and death to the earth. The believer is to symbolize life, not corruption and death. The believer is to have nothing to do with corruption and defilement. He is to be totally set apart and focused upon the LORD, not upon the things of this earth. He is to live a life that is totally separated and set apart to God.

With many other words he warned them; and he pleaded with them, "Save yourselves from this corrupt generation." (Ac. 2:40)

Therefore, I urge you, brothers, in view of God's mercy, to offer your bodies as living sacrifices, holy and pleasing to God—this is your spiritual act of worship. Do not conform any longer to the pattern of this world, but be transformed by the renewing of your mind. Then you will be able to test and approve what God's will is—his good, pleasing and perfect will. (Ro. 12:1-2)

But now I am writing you that you must not associate with anyone who calls himself a brother but is sexually immoral or greedy, an idolater or a slanderer, a drunkard or a swindler. With such a man do not even eat. (1 Co. 5:11)

Do not be yoked together with unbelievers. For what do righteousness and wickedness have in common? Or what fellowship can light have with darkness? (2 Co. 6:14)

"Therefore come out from them and be separate, says the Lord. Touch no unclean thing, and I will receive you. I will be a Father to you, and you will be my sons and daughters, says the Lord Almighty." (2 Co. 6:17-18)

Have nothing to do with the fruitless deeds of darkness, but rather expose them. (Ep. 5:11)

In the name of the Lord Jesus Christ, we command you, brothers, to keep away from every brother who is idle and does not live according to the teaching you received from us. (2 Th. 3:6)

Do not love the world or anything in the world. If anyone loves the world, the love of the Father is not in him. For everything in the world—the cravings of sinful man, the lust of his eyes and the boasting of what he has and does—comes not from the Father but from the world. (1 Jn. 2:15-16)

Blessed is the man who does not walk in the counsel of the wicked or stand in the way of sinners or sit in the seat of mockers. (Ps. 1:1)

Depart, depart, go out from there! Touch no unclean thing! Come out from it and be pure, you who carry the vessels of the LORD. (Is. 52:11)

Thought 2. There is cleansing from sin. God has made provision for cleansing. No matter what a person has done—no matter how defiled or corrupted or unclean a person is—God has made provision. What is that provision? How can a person be cleansed from sin, no matter how terrible? Through the sacrifice of the Lord Jesus Christ. Through Jesus Christ, a person...
- can be forgiven his sins
- can receive the atonement, be reconciled to God
- can have his guilt removed, be set entirely free from guilt and shame

"For God so loved the world that he gave his one and only Son, that whoever believes in him shall not perish but have eternal life." (Jn. 3:16)

You see, at just the right time, when we were still powerless, Christ died for the ungodly. (Ro. 5:6)

Since we have now been justified by his blood, how much more shall we be saved from God's wrath through him! (Ro. 5:9)

Not only is this so, but we also rejoice in God through our Lord Jesus Christ, through whom we have now received reconciliation. (Ro. 5:11)

For what I received I passed on to you as of first importance: that Christ died for our sins according to the Scriptures. (1 Co. 15:3)

In him we have redemption through his blood, the forgiveness of sins, in accordance with the riches of God's grace (Ep. 1:7)

He himself bore our sins in his body on the tree, so that we might die to sins and live for righteousness; by his wounds you have been healed. (1 Pe. 2:24)

For Christ died for sins once for all, the righteous for the unrighteous, to bring you to God. He was put to death in the body but made alive by the Spirit. (1 Pe. 3:18)

But if we walk in the light, as he is in the light, we have fellowship with one another, and the blood of Jesus, his Son, purifies us from all sin. (1 Jn. 1:7)

But he was pierced for our transgressions, he was crushed for our iniquities; the punishment that brought us peace was upon him, and by his wounds we are healed. (Is. 53:5)

3 (6:13-20) **Vow, Fulfillment of—Law, of Nazarite Vow—Nazarite, Vow of:** there was extensive worship required after the fulfillment of the vow. Naturally, the person was to continue to follow and to be totally committed to the LORD. This was the reason for this extensive worship service that marked the completion of the vow.

a. The person had to approach and present his offerings to the LORD (vv.13-15). He had to present the Burnt Offering acknowledging his continued need for the atonement (reconciliation with God). He was acknowledging that he was totally dependent upon the redemption of God (v.14).
   1) He presented the Sin Offering to God: acknowledging his need for continued cleansing (v.14).
   2) He presented the Peace or Fellowship Offering: acknowledging his need for more and more fellowship and peace with God (v.14).
   3) He presented the Grain and Drink Offerings to God (v.15). The Grain Offering was a thanksgiving offering praising God for the atonement and for forgiveness and fellowship with God. The Drink Offering was a picture of the believer pouring out his life in continued dedication to God.

b. The person had the priest make the offerings in his behalf (vv.16-17).

c. The person shaved off his hair and burned it under the sacrifice of the Fellowship Offering (v.18). Remember, his hair was the mark of his vow and devotion to God. By burning his hair under the Fellowship Offering, he was symbolizing that he wanted a continued commitment and close fellowship with the LORD.

d. The priest then placed in the Nazarite's hands the boiled shoulder of the ram and one each of a cake and wafer made without yeast from the basket (vv.19-20). These were to be offered by the priest as a wave offering to the LORD. The priest was then to receive these along with the breast and thigh pieces as the LORD's portion, that is, as a part of his livelihood.

e. Note that the Nazarite could then drink wine (v.20).

Thought 1. There are two strong lessons for the believer in this point.
   (1) The believer is totally dependent upon Christ throughout all of life. No matter how dedicated or

NUMBERS 6:1-27

holy a believer is, no matter how devoted or committed, he is still dependent upon the sacrifice of Jesus Christ—totally dependent. He must still approach God through Christ and Christ alone. He is still dependent upon Christ for atonement (reconciliation), for forgiveness of sins, and for fellowship and peace with God. His righteousness and sufficiency are and always will be in Christ, just as they always have been.

> **Jesus answered, "I am the way and the truth and the life. No one comes to the Father except through me."** (Jn. 14:6)
>
> For all have sinned and fall short of the glory of God, and are justified freely by his grace through the redemption that came by Christ Jesus. God presented him as a sacrifice of atonement, through faith in his blood. He did this to demonstrate his justice, because in his forbearance he had left the sins committed beforehand unpunished. (Ro. 3:23-25)
>
> Therefore, if anyone is in Christ, he is a new creation; the old has gone, the new has come! All this is from God, who reconciled us to himself through Christ and gave us the ministry of reconciliation: that God was reconciling the world to himself in Christ, not counting men's sins against them. And he has committed to us the message of reconciliation. We are therefore Christ's ambassadors, as though God were making his appeal through us. We implore you on Christ's behalf: Be reconciled to God. God made him who had no sin to be sin for us, so that in him we might become the righteousness of God. (2 Co. 5:17-21)
>
> For there is one God and one mediator between God and men, the man Christ Jesus, who gave himself as a ransom for all men—the testimony given in its proper time. (1 Ti. 2:5-6)
>
> He did not enter by means of the blood of goats and calves; but he entered the Most Holy Place once for all by his own blood, having obtained eternal redemption. The blood of goats and bulls and the ashes of a heifer sprinkled on those who are ceremonially unclean sanctify them so that they are outwardly clean. How much more, then, will the blood of Christ, who through the eternal Spirit offered himself unblemished to God, cleanse our consciences from acts that lead to death, so that we may serve the living God! (He. 9:12-14)
>
> For Christ did not enter a man-made sanctuary that was only a copy of the true one; he entered heaven itself, now to appear for us in God's presence. (He. 9:24)
>
> My dear children, I write this to you so that you will not sin. But if anybody does sin, we have one who speaks to the Father in our defense—Jesus Christ, the Righteous One. He is the atoning sacrifice for our sins, and not only for ours but also for the sins of the whole world. (1 Jn. 2:1-2)

(2) The believer must continue to live a life of commitment and holiness before God. The Nazarite burned his hair under the Fellowship Offering, symbolizing that he wanted a continued commitment and closer fellowship with the LORD. So it must be with the believer. No matter what the believer vows to the LORD, no matter how closely he may walk with the LORD, he must still seek a deeper commitment and fellowship with the LORD; therefore, he must never cease to grow in Christ. He cannot even come close to reaching the maturity of Christ. His journey to the promised land is an ongoing process, a seeking...

- to grow more and more into the image of Christ
- to gain more and more spiritual strength so he can overcome the pitfalls and enemies of this life

> So I say, live by the Spirit, and you will not gratify the desires of the sinful nature. (Ga. 5:16)
>
> As a prisoner for the Lord, then, I urge you to live a life worthy of the calling you have received. (Ep. 4:1)
>
> Instead, speaking the truth in love, we will in all things grow up into him who is the Head, that is, Christ. (Ep. 4:15)
>
> Be very careful, then, how you live—not as unwise but as wise. (Ep. 5:15)
>
> So then, just as you received Christ Jesus as Lord, continue to live in him, rooted and built up in him, strengthened in the faith as you were taught, and overflowing with thankfulness. (Col. 2:6-7)
>
> May the Lord make your love increase and overflow for each other and for everyone else, just as ours does for you. (1 Th. 3:12)
>
> The goal of this command is love, which comes from a pure heart and a good conscience and a sincere faith. (1 Ti. 1:5)
>
> Therefore let us leave the elementary teachings about Christ and go on to maturity, not laying again the foundation of repentance from acts that lead to death, and of faith in God. (He. 6:1)
>
> Now that you have purified yourselves by obeying the truth so that you have sincere love for your brothers, love one another deeply, from the heart. (1 Pe. 1:22)
>
> Like newborn babies, crave pure spiritual milk, so that by it you may grow up in your salvation, now that you have tasted that the Lord is good. (1 Pe. 2:2-3)
>
> For this very reason, make every effort to add to your faith goodness; and to goodness, knowledge; and to knowledge, self-control; and to self-control, perseverance; and to perseverance, godliness. (2 Pe. 1:5-6)
>
> But in keeping with his promise we are looking forward to a new heaven and a new earth, the home of righteousness. So then, dear friends, since you are looking forward to this, make every

effort to be found spotless, blameless and at peace with him. (2 Pe. 3:13-14)

But grow in the grace and knowledge of our Lord and Savior Jesus Christ. To him be glory both now and forever! Amen. (2 Pe. 3:18)

But if we walk in the light, as he is in the light, we have fellowship with one another, and the blood of Jesus, his Son, purifies us from all sin. (1 Jn. 1:7)

Whoever claims to live in him must walk as Jesus did. (1 Jn. 2:6)

4 (6:21) **Vow, Seriousness of**: note the seriousness and heavy weight of the Nazarite vow. The Nazarite vow is a law, a law established by God Himself.

The commitment of the vow is significant to God, so significant that He established a law to control the vow. The vow declared a person's desire to draw closer to the LORD, a deep desire to be separated, totally set apart to God. God accepts all vows as serious commitments, but the Nazarite vow was very special to Him. The Nazarite vow was a personal commitment to seek a closer walk with the LORD: to seek a deeper commitment, a closer fellowship and communion with the LORD. It was a commitment...

- to live increasingly in God's law or Word
- to obey God as never before
- to be totally devoted to God
- to love and worship God more and more
- to live in prayer, in an unbroken consciousness of God's presence
- to bear strong witness and testimony for God

The Nazarite vow had to be kept and fulfilled before God. The person making the vow was responsible for completing the vow. A heavy responsibility and accountability lay upon his shoulders. It was not a vow to be taken lightly. If a person made the commitment and took the time to draw closer to the LORD, the LORD accepted the commitment, the vow, and expected the person to complete it to the fullest.

Thought 1. All vows are serious to God. He accepts the commitment of any vow. But the commitment to draw closer to God—to seek a greater fellowship and communion with Him, to live more than ever before in His Word, to pray more and to bear a stronger witness and testimony for Him—has a very special meaning to God. Therefore, the person must live a holy life before God, be totally separated and set apart to God. The person must follow after God with his whole heart and life. He must be totally devoted and given over to the LORD.

Therefore, I urge you, brothers, in view of God's mercy, to offer your bodies as living sacrifices, holy and pleasing to God—this is your spiritual act of worship. Do not conform any longer to the pattern of this world, but be transformed by the renewing of your mind. Then you will be able to test and approve what God's will is—his good, pleasing and perfect will. (Ro. 12:1-2)

When a man makes a vow to the LORD or takes an oath to obligate himself by a pledge, he must not break his word but must do everything he said. (Nu. 30:2)

If you make a vow to the LORD your God, do not be slow to pay it, for the LORD your God will certainly demand it of you and you will be guilty of sin. (De. 23:21)

Keep your tongue from evil and your lips from speaking lies [a deceptive vow]. (Ps. 34:13)

When you make a vow to God, do not delay in fulfilling it. He has no pleasure in fools; fulfill your vow. (Ec. 5:4)

5 (6:22-27) **Blessing, of God—Security, Source—Protection, Source—Grace, Source—Peace, Source—Blessing, Source—Benediction, the Great Priestly—Benediction, the Aaronic**: note the great priestly benediction of God.

This prayer is sometimes called the Aaronic benediction because it was to be pronounced by Aaron the High Priest, pronounced over God's people as they marched toward the promised land. It is interesting that the benediction follows immediately after the Nazarite vow. The point of the benediction or prayer is striking: God wants to bless all His people as they march to the promised land. He wants to fulfill His covenant promise to the fullest if His people will only fulfill their part of the promise, to follow Him with all their hearts.

This is one of the most beautiful prayers in the Bible and is one of if not the most quoted benedictions of Scripture. *The Expositor's Bible Commentary* makes this statement:

> [This benediction] may be thought of as the LORD's prayer of the Old Testament (see Mt. 6:9). The priests were told how to pray for God's blessing on the people in the same way that the disciples were instructed by the Savior how to pray for God's blessing in their lives.[3]

a. The benediction was promised by God Himself (vv.23-26). God instructed Moses to instruct the priest to use this benediction on behalf of His people as they marched to the promised land. Note the points of the benediction or prayer.

1) The LORD promised His blessing: "The LORD bless you" (v.24). The idea is that God pours out His blessing upon His people. He blesses them abundantly, exceedingly. God provides all the necessities of life for His people: food, shelter, and clothing.

But seek first his kingdom and his righteousness, and all these things will be given to you as well. (Mt. 6:33)

And my God will meet all your needs according to his glorious riches in Christ Jesus. (Ph. 4:19)

Worship the LORD your God, and his blessing will be on your food and water. I will take away sickness from among you. (Ex. 23:25)

Then the LORD your God will make you most prosperous in all the work of your hands and in the fruit of your womb, the young of your livestock and the crops of your land. The LORD will

---

[3] *The Expositor's Bible Commentary*, Frank E. Gaebelein, Editor, p.754.

again delight in you and make you prosperous, just as he delighted in your fathers. (De. 30:9)

You prepare a table before me in the presence of my enemies. You anoint my head with oil; my cup overflows. (Ps. 23:5)

How great is your goodness, which you have stored up for those who fear you, which you bestow in the sight of men on those who take refuge in you. (Ps. 31:19)

You care for the land and water it; you enrich it abundantly. The streams of God are filled with water to provide the people with grain, for so you have ordained it. (Ps. 65:9)

Praise be to the LORD, to God our Savior, who daily bears our burdens. Selah (Ps. 68:19)

The LORD remembers us and will bless us: He will bless the house of Israel, he will bless the house of Aaron. (Ps. 115:12)

I will bless her with abundant provisions; her poor will I satisfy with food. (Ps. 132:15)

He will also send you rain for the seed you sow in the ground, and the food that comes from the land will be rich and plentiful. In that day your cattle will graze in broad meadows. (Is. 30:23)

"Bring the whole tithe into the storehouse, that there may be food in my house. Test me in this," says the LORD Almighty, "and see if I will not throw open the floodgates of heaven and pour out so much blessing that you will not have room enough for it." (Mal. 3:10)

2) The LORD promised His protection and security: "The LORD...keep you" (v.24). God has the power to keep His people as they march to the promised land. He has the power to deliver His people from all the pitfalls and enemies of this life.

But not a hair of your head will perish. (Lu. 21:18)

I will remain in the world no longer, but they are still in the world, and I am coming to you. Holy Father, protect them by the power of your name—the name you gave me—so that they may be one as we are one. (Jn. 17:11)

No temptation has seized you except what is common to man. And God is faithful; he will not let you be tempted beyond what you can bear. But when you are tempted, he will also provide a way out so that you can stand up under it. (1 Co. 10:13)

Being confident of this, that he who began a good work in you will carry it on to completion until the day of Christ Jesus. (Ph. 1:6)

That is why I am suffering as I am. Yet I am not ashamed, because I know whom I have believed, and am convinced that he is able to guard what I have entrusted to him for that day. (2 Ti. 1:12)

So we say with confidence, "The Lord is my helper; I will not be afraid. What can man do to me?" (He. 13:6)

Who through faith are shielded by God's power until the coming of the salvation that is ready to be revealed in the last time. (1 Pe. 1:5)

Who is going to harm you if you are eager to do good? (1 Pe. 3:13)

To him who is able to keep you from falling and to present you before his glorious presence without fault and with great joy (Jude 24)

I am with you and will watch over you wherever you go, and I will bring you back to this land. I will not leave you until I have done what I have promised you. (Ge. 28:15)

The LORD will fight for you; you need only to be still. (Ex. 14:14)

For the eyes of the LORD range throughout the earth to strengthen those whose hearts are fully committed to him. You have done a foolish thing, and from now on you will be at war. (2 Chr. 16:9)

You will be secure, because there is hope; you will look about you and take your rest in safety. (Jb. 11:18)

He will cover you with his feathers, and under his wings you will find refuge; his faithfulness will be your shield and rampart. (Ps. 91:4)

You will not fear the terror of night, nor the arrow that flies by day. (Ps. 91:5)

He will have no fear of bad news; his heart is steadfast, trusting in the LORD. (Ps. 112:7)

Indeed, he who watches over Israel will neither slumber nor sleep. (Ps. 121:4)

When you lie down, you will not be afraid; when you lie down, your sleep will be sweet. (Pr. 3:24)

3) The LORD promised that His face would shine upon His people, that His very special presence would be with them: "The LORD make his face shine upon you" (v.25). The LORD is always facing His people; His face is always shining upon them. This simply means that God's presence is always with His people. This is a beautiful, descriptive picture of God's presence with His people. The Hebrew literally means that God smiles upon His people: He is pleased with their faith and obedience in following Him.

For where two or three come together in my name, there am I with them. (Mt. 18:20)

"And teaching them to obey everything I have commanded you. And surely I am with you always, to the very end of the age." (Mt. 28:20)

I am with you and will watch over you wherever you go, and I will bring you back to this land. I will not leave you until I have done what I have promised you. (Ge. 28:15)

The LORD replied, "My Presence will go with you, and I will give you rest." (Ex. 33:14)

When you go to war against your enemies and see horses and chariots and an army greater than yours, do not be afraid of them, because the LORD your God, who brought you up out of Egypt, will be with you. (De. 20:1)

The eternal God is your refuge, and underneath are the everlasting arms. He will drive out your enemy before you, saying, 'Destroy him!' (De. 33:27)

I have set the LORD always before me. Because he is at my right hand, I will not be shaken. (Ps. 16:8)

You give me your shield of victory, and your right hand sustains me; you stoop down to make me great. (Ps. 18:35)

Yet I am poor and needy; may the LORD think of me. You are my help and my deliverer; O my God, do not delay. (Ps. 40:17)

So do not fear, for I am with you; do not be dismayed, for I am your God. I will strengthen you and help you; I will uphold you with my righteous right hand. (Is. 41:10)

When you pass through the waters, I will be with you; and when you pass through the rivers, they will not sweep over you. When you walk through the fire, you will not be burned; the flames will not set you ablaze. (Is. 43:2)

Even to your old age and gray hairs I am he, I am he who will sustain you. I have made you and I will carry you; I will sustain you and I will rescue you. (Is. 46:4)

4) The LORD promised that His grace would be showered upon His people: "The LORD...be gracious to you" (v.25). Grace means that God favors His people and strengthens them to conquer all the pitfalls and enemies of this life. Both favor and strength are included in the meaning of the word grace.

> And are justified freely by his grace through the redemption that came by Christ Jesus. (Ro. 3:24)
>
> I always thank God for you because of his grace given you in Christ Jesus. For in him you have been enriched in every way—in all your speaking and in all your knowledge. (1 Co. 1:4-5)
>
> Now this is our boast: Our conscience testifies that we have conducted ourselves in the world, and especially in our relations with you, in the holiness and sincerity that are from God. We have done so not according to worldly wisdom but according to God's grace. (2 Co. 1:12)
>
> In him we have redemption through his blood, the forgiveness of sins, in accordance with the riches of God's grace. (Ep. 1:7)
>
> In order that in the coming ages he might show the incomparable riches of his grace, expressed in his kindness to us in Christ Jesus. (Ep. 2:7)
>
> For it is by grace you have been saved, through faith—and this not from yourselves, it is the gift of God—not by works, so that no one can boast. (Ep. 2:8-9)
>
> For the grace of God that brings salvation has appeared to all men. (Tit. 2:11)
>
> So that, having been justified by his grace, we might become heirs having the hope of eternal life. (Tit. 3:7)

5) God gives His attention, His approval, His pleasure to His people: "The LORD turn his face toward you" (v.26). God never turns His face away from His people. They always have His attention. He sees everything that goes on in their lives: every threat, every temptation, every trial. The believer has the attention of God and the approval and pleasure of God. Therefore, He lifts up His countenance—turns His face—to them. He is their helper in all things.

> Indeed, the very hairs of your head are all numbered. Don't be afraid; you are worth more than many sparrows. (Lu. 12:7)
>
> You have made known to me the paths of life; you will fill me with joy in your presence. (Ac. 2:28)
>
> So we say with confidence, "The Lord is my helper; I will not be afraid. What can man do to me?" (He. 13:6)
>
> Cast all your anxiety on him because he cares for you. (1 Pe. 5:7)
>
> Surely you have granted him eternal blessings and made him glad with the joy of your presence. (Ps. 21:6)
>
> Yet I am poor and needy; may the LORD think of me. You are my help and my deliverer; O my God, do not delay. (Ps. 40:17)
>
> Have mercy on me, O God, have mercy on me, for in you my soul takes refuge. I will take refuge in the shadow of your wings until the disaster has passed. (Ps. 57:1)
>
> You have been a refuge for the poor, a refuge for the needy in his distress, a shelter from the storm and a shade from the heat. For the breath of the ruthless is like a storm driving against a wall. (Is. 25:4)
>
> So do not fear, for I am with you; do not be dismayed, for I am your God. I will strengthen you and help you; I will uphold you with my righteous right hand. (Is. 41:10)

6) The LORD gave His peace to His people: "The LORD...give you peace" (v.26). God's peace includes *peace with God* and the *peace of God*. People who reject God, who rebel against and

curse Him, need to make *peace with God*. If they fail to make *peace with God*, they are doomed eternally. However, when a person makes *peace with God*, he comes to know the *peace of God*. God's peace floods his heart and life. He has the perfect assurance that he belongs to God, that God looks after and cares for him. He knows that he has the hope of eternal life and that he is marching to the promised land of heaven. God floods him with a great sense of triumph, conquest, and victory—triumph over all the pitfalls and enemies of this life, even the enemy of death. The believer knows that when his moment comes to die, God will transport him right into His presence. He knows that he will live eternally in the promised land of heaven, in the presence of God Himself. God gives this kind of peace to His people, to those who truly trust Him. The *peace of God* floods the believer's heart and life.

> **Peace I leave with you; my peace I give you. I do not give to you as the world gives. Do not let your hearts be troubled and do not be afraid. (Jn. 14:27)**
>
> **"I have told you these things, so that in me you may have peace. In this world you will have trouble. But take heart! I have overcome the world." (Jn. 16:33)**
>
> **And the peace of God, which transcends all understanding, will guard your hearts and your minds in Christ Jesus. (Ph. 4:7)**
>
> **The LORD gives strength to his people; the LORD blesses his people with peace. (Ps. 29:11)**
>
> **Great peace have they who love your law, and nothing can make them stumble. (Ps. 119:165)**
>
> **You will keep in perfect peace him whose mind is steadfast, because he trusts in you. (Is. 26:3)**
>
> **If only you had paid attention to my commands, your peace would have been like a river, your righteousness like the waves of the sea. (Is. 48:18)**

b. Note the result of God's blessings: the blessings of God actually identify a person as belonging to God. When the blessings of God are seen upon a person's life, that person is identified as a believer. It is clearly seen that he is a follower of God. What a glorious testimony: to walk around with the blessings of God upon one's life, to be blessed so much that the blessings actually identify one as belonging to God.

> **And you also must testify, for you have been with me from the beginning. (Jn. 15:27)**
>
> **All of them were filled with the Holy Spirit and began to speak in other tongues as the Spirit enabled them. (Ac. 2:4)**
>
> **"For we cannot help speaking about what we have seen and heard." (Ac. 4:20)**
>
> **Because those who are led by the Spirit of God are sons of God. (Ro. 8:14)**
>
> **For you are a people holy to the LORD your God. Out of all the peoples on the face of the earth, the LORD has chosen you to be his treasured possession. (De. 14:2)**
>
> **"You are my witnesses," declares the LORD, "and my servant whom I have chosen, so that you may know and believe me and understand that I am he. Before me no god was formed, nor will there be one after me." (Is. 43:10)**

TYPES, SYMBOLS, AND PICTURES
(Numbers 6:1-27)

Historical Term	Type or Picture (Scriptural Basis for Each)	Life Application for Today's Believer	Biblical Application
Contact with a Dead Body Nu. 6:3-12 (See also Le. 10:4-5)	*A symbol of becoming defiled, unclean, corrupted—of becoming ceremonially or spiritually unclean.* *The person who took the Nazarite vow was to have nothing to do with death. He was to be an example of life, not of death. This stern restriction proclaimed the wonderful life that God gives, not the death and corruption that sin brings. The person had committed himself totally to the LORD; therefore, he was to be totally set apart and focused upon the LORD, not upon the things of the earth—not even upon the most dear things to his heart such as family. If a*	The Nazarite could not touch a dead body because it symbolized corruption and decay, defilement and uncleanness. So it must be with the believer. The believer must not become corrupted and defiled by sin and shame. Sin and shame bring lawlessness, violence and death to the earth. The believer is to symbolize life, not corruption and death. The believer is to have nothing to do with corruption and defilement. He is to be totally set apart and focused upon the LORD, not upon the things of this earth. He is to live a life that is totally separated and set apart to God.	*All these evils come from inside and make a man 'unclean'. (Mk. 7:23)* *Since we have these promises, dear friends, let us purify ourselves from everything that contaminates body and spirit, perfecting holiness out of reverence for God. (2 Co. 7:1)* *If a man cleanses himself from the latter, he will be an instrument for noble purposes, made holy, useful to the Master and prepared to do any good work. (2 Ti. 2:21)* *See to it that no one misses the grace of God and that no bitter root grows up to cause trouble and defile many. (He. 12:15)*

NUMBERS 6:1-27

Historical Term	Type or Picture (Scriptural Basis for Each)	Life Application for Today's Believer	Biblical Application
	family member died, he was not allowed to go near nor touch the dead body lest he become defiled by death. **Throughout the period of his separation to the LORD he must not go near a dead body. (Nu. 6:6)**		*The tongue also is a fire, a world of evil among the parts of the body. It corrupts the whole person, sets the whole course of his life on fire, and is itself set on fire by hell. (Js. 3:6)* *Come near to God and he will come near to you. Wash your hands, you sinners, and purify your hearts, you double-minded. (Js. 4:8)*
The Sin Offering Nu. 6:3-12; 28:11-15 (See also Le. 4:1-5:13. 6:24-30; 8:14-17; 9:2; 9:15; 10:17; 16:3-22)	*The Sin Offering is a type of Christ, a symbol or picture of Christ. When a person sensed the need for forgiveness of sins, he approached God through the sacrifice of the Sin Offering.* **The priest is to offer one as a sin offering and the other as a burnt offering to make atonement for him because he sinned by being in the presence of the dead body. That same day he is to consecrate his head. (Nu. 6:11)**	Jesus Christ is the Savior of the world, the One who provides the way of forgiveness for us. This He does through His sacrifice upon the cross. Through His blood we are cleansed from sin, cleansed from all unrighteousness.	*If we confess our sins, he is faithful and just and will forgive us our sins and purify us from all unrighteousness. (1 Jn. 1:9)* *He himself bore our sins in his body on the tree, so that we might die to sins and live for righteousness; by his wounds you have been healed. (1 Pe. 2:24)* *For Christ died for sins once for all, the righteous for the unrighteous, to bring you to God. He was put to death in the body but made alive by the Spirit. (1 Pe. 3:18)* *Sacrifice a bull each day as a sin offering to make atonement. Purify the altar by making atonement for it, and anoint it to consecrate it. For seven days make atonement for the altar and consecrate it. Then the altar will be most holy, and whatever touches it will be holy. (Ex. 29:36-37)* *And do with this bull just as he did with the bull for the sin offering. In this way the priest will make atonement for them, and they will be forgiven. (Le. 4:20)* *But he was pierced for our transgressions, he was crushed for our iniquities; the punishment that brought us peace was upon him, and by his wounds we are healed. (Is. 53:5)*
The Burnt Offering Nu. 6:3-12; 15:1-16; 28:11-15 (See also Le. 1:1-17; 6:8-13; 8:18-21; 16:24)	*A symbol of atonement, reconciliation with God:* *The Burnt Offering is a type of Christ, a symbol or picture of Christ dying as the substitute sacrifice for us. By dying for us:* ⇒ *Christ bore the full judgment of God against sin—paid the ransom*	Jesus Christ died for us as our substitute sacrifice. He died to secure the atonement or reconciliation with God for us. A person can now approach God and be reconciled with God; a person can now become acceptable to God. How? By approaching God through the sacrifice of Christ.	*But God demonstrates his own love for us in this: While we were still sinners, Christ died for us. Since we have now been justified by his blood, how much more shall we be saved from God's wrath through him! For if, when we were God's enemies, we were reconciled to him through the*

NUMBERS 6:1-27

Historical Term	Type or Picture (Scriptural Basis for Each)	Life Application for Today's Believer	Biblical Application
	price to deliver us from sin and death. ⇒ *Christ secured the atonement for us, reconciling us to God.* **On the first of every month, present to the LORD a burnt offering of two young bulls, one ram and seven male lambs a year old, all without defect. (Nu. 28:11)**		*death of his Son, how much more, having been reconciled, shall we be saved through his life! Not only is this so, but we also rejoice in God through our Lord Jesus Christ, through whom we have now received reconciliation. (Ro. 5:8-11)* *For this reason he had to be made like his brothers in every way, in order that he might become a merciful and faithful high priest in service to God, and that he might make atonement for the sins of the people. (He. 2:17)* *He is to lay his hand on the head of the burnt offering, and it will be accepted on his behalf to make atonement for him. (Le. 1:4)*
The Guilt Offering Nu. 6:3-12 (See also Le. 5:14-6:7)	*The Guilt Offering symbolized Jesus Christ. He is the way for a person to be set free from the weight and anguish of guilt, the pricking of conscience.* **He must dedicate himself to the LORD for the period of his separation and must bring a year-old male lamb as a guilt offering. The previous days do not count, because he became defiled during his separation. (Nu. 6:12)**	Jesus Christ bore our guilt, bore the judgment and condemnation of our sin. His sacrifice has made atonement with God, forgiving the sin and erasing the guilt of the person who comes to Him.	*God made him who had no sin to be sin for us, so that in him we might become the righteousness of God. (2 Co. 5:21)* *Who gave himself for our sins to rescue us from the present evil age, according to the will of our God and Father. (Ga. 1:4)* *Christ redeemed us from the curse of the law by becoming a curse for us, for it is written: "Cursed is everyone who is hung on a tree." (Ga. 3:13)* *Keeping a clear conscience, so that those who speak maliciously against your good behavior in Christ may be ashamed of their slander. (1 Pe. 3:16)*
The Fellowship or Peace Offering Nu. 6:13-20; 15:1-16 (See also Le. 3:1-17)	*The Fellowship or Peace Offering is a type of Christ, a symbol or picture of Christ, the One who died on the cross bearing the judgment of God for man. The sacrifice of Christ made peace between a holy God and an alienated, fallen, depraved people. The sacrifice of Christ and Christ alone brings peace and fellowship between man and God.* **There he is to present his offerings to the LORD: a year-old male lamb without defect for a burnt**	How do we grow in the fellowship and peace of God? Very simply, by seeking more of the fellowship and peace of God. We must stand upon the completed work of Christ's sacrifice on the cross. Because of Christ... • we can enjoy the fellowship of the LORD • we can experience the peace of God	*We proclaim to you what we have seen and heard, so that you also may have fellowship with us. And our fellowship is with the Father and with his Son, Jesus Christ. (1 Jn. 1:3)* *But if we walk in the light, as he is in the light, we have fellowship with one another, and the blood of Jesus, his Son, purifies us from all sin. (1 Jn. 1:7)* *Therefore, since we have been justified through faith, we have peace with God through our Lord Jesus Christ. (Ro. 5:1)*

NUMBERS 6:1-27

Historical Term	Type or Picture (Scriptural Basis for Each)	Life Application for Today's Believer	Biblical Application
	offering, a year-old ewe lamb without defect for a sin offering, a ram without defect for a fellowship offering. (Nu. 6:14)		*And through him to reconcile to himself all things, whether things on earth or things in heaven, by making peace through his blood, shed on the cross. (Col. 1:20)*
The Drink Offering Nu. 6:13-20; 15:1-16, esp. v.7	The Drink Offering is a picture of the believer pouring out his life in continued dedication to God. **Together with their grain offerings and drink offerings, and a basket of bread made without yeast—cakes made of fine flour mixed with oil, and wafers spread with oil. (Nu. 6:15)**	The application for today's believer is clear and striking: he must pour out his life in continued dedication to God.	*Therefore, I urge you, brothers, in view of God's mercy, to offer your bodies as living sacrifices, holy and pleasing to God—this is your spiritual act of worship. (Ro. 12:1)* *For we know that our old self was crucified with him so that the body of sin might be done away with, that we should no longer be slaves to sin. (Ro. 6:6)* *I have been crucified with Christ and I no longer live, but Christ lives in me. The life I live in the body, I live by faith in the Son of God, who loved me and gave himself for me. (Ga. 2:20)* *But if we walk in the light, as he is in the light, we have fellowship with one another, and the blood of Jesus, his Son, purifies us from all sin. (1 Jn. 1:7)*
The Nazarite Burning His Hair Under the Fellowship Offering Nu. 6:13-20	The Nazarite who burned his hair was symbolizing that he wanted a continued commitment and close fellowship with the LORD. **Then at the entrance to the Tent of Meeting, the Nazirite must shave off the hair that he dedicated. He is to take the hair and put it in the fire that is under the sacrifice of the fellowship offering. (Nu. 6:18)**	The believer must continue to live a life of commitment and holiness before God. The Nazarite burned his hair under the Fellowship Offering, symbolizing that he wanted a continued commitment and closer fellowship with the LORD. So it must be with the believer. No matter what the believer vows to the LORD, no matter how closely he may walk with the LORD—he must still seek a deeper commitment and fellowship with the LORD. He must never cease to grow in Christ. He cannot even come close to reaching the maturity of Christ; therefore, his journey to the promised land is an ongoing process. The believer must seek... • to grow more and more into the image of Christ • to gain more and more spiritual strength so that he can overcome the pitfalls and enemies of this life	*So I say, live by the Spirit, and you will not gratify the desires of the sinful nature. (Ga. 5:16)* *As a prisoner for the Lord, then, I urge you to live a life worthy of the calling you have received. (Ep. 4:1)* *Instead, speaking the truth in love, we will in all things grow up into him who is the Head, that is, Christ. (Ep. 4:15)* *Be very careful, then, how you live—not as unwise but as wise. (Ep. 5:15)* *So then, just as you received Christ Jesus as Lord, continue to live in him, rooted and built up in him, strengthened in the faith as you were taught, and overflowing with thankfulness. (Col. 2:6-7)* *May the Lord make your love increase and overflow for each other and for everyone else, just as ours does for you. (1 Th. 3:12)* *The goal of this command is love, which comes from a pure heart and a*

NUMBERS 6:1-27

Historical Term	Type or Picture (Scriptural Basis for Each)	Life Application for Today's Believer	Biblical Application
			good conscience and a sincere faith. (1 Ti. 1:5) *Therefore let us leave the elementary teachings about Christ and go on to maturity, not laying again the foundation of repentance from acts that lead to death, and of faith in God. (He. 6:1)*

NUMBERS 7:1-89

1. **The gifts for transporting the Tabernacle, that of carts & oxen: Demonstrated the need for joyful, spontaneous support of God's work**
   a. The gifts were given right after the dedication of the Tabernacle
      1) The gifts were given by the twelve tribal leaders

      2) The gifts were spontaneously offered to the Lord at the Tabernacle door: Six covered wagons or carts & twelve oxen

   b. The Lord instructed Moses to accept the gifts & to distribute them as needed

   c. The gifts were distributed to the Levites, the assistants responsible for transporting the Tabernacle
      1) The Gershonites received 2 carts & 4 oxen (for transporting all the curtains): Got just what they needed
      2) The Merarites received 4 carts & 8 oxen (for transporting the frame): Got just what they needed
      3) The priest Ithamar supervised the transporting of the Tabernacle
      4) The Kohathites received no carts, for they were to carry the sacred furnishings on their shoulders: They needed none of the gifts

2. **The magnificent offerings presented at the dedication of the altar—presented by each tribal leader on different days—in obedience to God's instructions: Demonstrated the need to approach God exactly as He says**

   a. The offering of the first day: Was brought by Nahshon, leader of the tribe of Judah

      1) One silver plate—

CHAPTER 7

F. The Spontaneous Offerings at the Dedication of the Tabernacle: Supporting God's Work & Approaching Him Exactly As He Says, 7:1-89

When Moses finished setting up the tabernacle, he anointed it and consecrated it and all its furnishings. He also anointed and consecrated the altar and all its utensils.
2 Then the leaders of Israel, the heads of families who were the tribal leaders in charge of those who were counted, made offerings.
3 They brought as their gifts before the LORD six covered carts and twelve oxen—an ox from each leader and a cart from every two. These they presented before the tabernacle.
4 The LORD said to Moses,
5 "Accept these from them, that they may be used in the work at the Tent of Meeting. Give them to the Levites as each man's work requires."
6 So Moses took the carts and oxen and gave them to the Levites.
7 He gave two carts and four oxen to the Gershonites, as their work required,
8 And he gave four carts and eight oxen to the Merarites, as their work required. They were all under the direction of Ithamar son of Aaron, the priest.
9 But Moses did not give any to the Kohathites, because they were to carry on their shoulders the holy things, for which they were responsible.
10 When the altar was anointed, the leaders brought their offerings for its dedication and presented them before the altar.
11 For the LORD had said to Moses, "Each day one leader is to bring his offering for the dedication of the altar."
12 The one who brought his offering on the first day was Nahshon son of Amminadab of the tribe of Judah.
13 His offering was one silver plate weighing a hundred and thirty shekels, and one silver sprinkling bowl weighing seventy shekels, both according to the sanctuary shekel, each filled with fine flour mixed with oil as a grain offering;
14 One gold dish weighing ten shekels, filled with incense;
15 One young bull, one ram and one male lamb a year old, for a burnt offering;
16 One male goat for a sin offering;
17 And two oxen, five rams, five male goats and five male lambs a year old, to be sacrificed as a fellowship offering. This was the offering of Nahshon son of Amminadab.
18 On the second day Nethanel son of Zuar, the leader of Issachar, brought his offering.
19 The offering he brought was one silver plate weighing a hundred and thirty shekels, and one silver sprinkling bowl weighing seventy shekels, both according to the sanctuary shekel, each filled with fine flour mixed with oil as a grain offering;
20 One gold dish weighing ten shekels, filled with incense;
21 One young bull, one ram and one male lamb a year old, for a burnt offering;
22 One male goat for a sin offering;
23 And two oxen, five rams, five male goats and five male lambs a year old, to be sacrificed as a fellowship offering. This was the offering of Nethanel son of Zuar.
24 On the third day, Eliab son of Helon, the leader of the people of Zebulun, brought his offering.
25 His offering was one silver plate weighing a hundred and thirty shekels, and one silver sprinkling bowl weighing seventy shekels, both according to the sanctuary shekel, each filled with fine flour mixed with oil as a grain offering;
26 One gold dish weighing ten shekels, filled with incense;
27 One young bull, one ram and one male lamb a year old,

   weighing 130 shekels (about 3¼ pounds)
   2) One silver sprinkling bowl—weighing 70 shekels (about 1¾ pounds)
   • Each was filled with fine flour mixed with oil as a Grain Offering
   3) One gold dish—weighing 10 shekels (about 4 ounces)
   • Filled with incense
   4) Animals for the offerings
   • A Burnt Offering: Acknowledging atonement
   • A Sin Offering: Seeking cleansing
   • A Fellowship or Peace Offering: Seeking more & more of the fellowship & peace of God

   b. The offering on the second day: Was brought by Nethanel, leader of the tribe of Issachar
      1) One silver plate—weighing 130 shekels (about 3¼ pounds)
      2) One silver sprinkling bowl—weighing 70 shekels (about 1¾ pounds)
      • Each was filled with fine flour mixed with oil as a Grain Offering
      3) One gold dish—weighing 10 shekels (about 4 ounces)
      • Filled with incense
      4) Animals for the offerings
      • A Burnt Offering: Seeking atonement (reconciliation)
      • A Sin Offering: Seeking cleansing
      • A Fellowship or Peace Offering: Seeking more & more of the fellowship & peace of God

   c. The offering on the third day: Was brought by Eliab, leader of the tribe of Zebulun
      1) One silver plate—weighing 130 shekels (about 3¼ pounds)
      2) One silver sprinkling bowl—weighing 70 shekels (about 1¾ pounds)
      • Each was filled with fine flour mixed with oil as a Grain Offering
      3) One gold dish—weighing 10 shekels (about 4 ounces)
      • Filled with incense
      4) Animals for the offerings
      • A Burnt Offering: Seeking

Numbers 7:1-89

      atonement (reconciliation)
- A Sin Offering: Seeking cleansing
- A Fellowship or Peace Offering: Seeking more & more of the fellowship & peace of God

d. The offering on the fourth day: Was brought by Elizur, leader of the tribe of Reuben

  1) One silver plate—weighing 130 shekels (about 3¼ pounds)
  2) One silver sprinkling bowl—weighing 70 shekels (about 1¾ pounds)
- Each was filled with fine flour mixed with oil as a Grain Offering

  3) One gold dish—weighing 10 shekels (about 4 ounces)
- Filled with incense

  4) Animals for the offerings
- A Burnt Offering: Seeking atonement (reconciliation)
- A Sin Offering: Seeking cleansing
- A Fellowship or Peace Offering: Seeking more & more of the fellowship & peace of God

e. The offering on the fifth day: Was brought by Shelumiel, leader of the tribe of Simeon

  1) One silver plate—weighing 130 shekels (about 3¼ pounds)
  2) One silver sprinkling bowl—weighing 70 shekels (about 1¾ pounds)
- Each was filled with fine flour mixed with oil as a Grain Offering

  3) One gold dish—weighing 10 shekels (about 4 ounces)
- Filled with incense

  4) Animals for the offerings
- A Burnt Offering: Seeking atonement (reconciliation)
- A Sin Offering: Seeking cleansing
- A Fellowship or Peace Offering: Seeking more & more of the fellowship & peace of God

f. The offering on the sixth day: Was brought by Eliasaph, leader of the tribe of Gad

  1) One silver plate—

---

28 One male goat for a sin offering;
29 And two oxen, five rams, five male goats and five male lambs a year old, to be sacrificed as a fellowship offering. This was the offering of Eliab son of Helon.
30 On the fourth day Elizur son of Shedeur, the leader of the people of Reuben, brought his offering.
31 His offering was one silver plate weighing a hundred and thirty shekels, and one silver sprinkling bowl weighing seventy shekels, both according to the sanctuary shekel, each filled with fine flour mixed with oil as a grain offering;
32 One gold dish weighing ten shekels, filled with incense;
33 One young bull, one ram and one male lamb a year old, for a burnt offering;
34 One male goat for a sin offering;
35 And two oxen, five rams, five male goats and five male lambs a year old, to be sacrificed as a fellowship offering. This was the offering of Elizur son of Shedeur.
36 On the fifth day Shelumiel son of Zurishaddai, the leader of the people of Simeon, brought his offering.
37 His offering was one silver plate weighing a hundred and thirty shekels, and one silver sprinkling bowl weighing seventy shekels, both according to the sanctuary shekel, each filled with fine flour mixed with oil as a grain offering;
38 One gold dish weighing ten shekels, filled with incense;
39 One young bull, one ram and one male lamb a year old, for a burnt offering;
40 One male goat for a sin offering;
41 And two oxen, five rams, five male goats and five male lambs a year old, to be sacrificed as a fellowship offering. This was the offering of Shelumiel son of Zurishaddai.
42 On the sixth day Eliasaph son of Deuel, the leader of the people of Gad, brought his offering.
43 His offering was one sil-

---

ver plate weighing a hundred and thirty shekels, and one silver sprinkling bowl weighing seventy shekels, both according to the sanctuary shekel, each filled with fine flour mixed with oil as a grain offering;
44 One gold dish weighing ten shekels, filled with incense;
45 One young bull, one ram and one male lamb a year old, for a burnt offering;
46 One male goat for a sin offering;
47 And two oxen, five rams, five male goats and five male lambs a year old, to be sacrificed as a fellowship offering. This was the offering of Eliasaph son of Deuel.
48 On the seventh day Elishama son of Ammihud, the leader of the people of Ephraim, brought his offering.
49 His offering was one silver plate weighing a hundred and thirty shekels, and one silver sprinkling bowl weighing seventy shekels, both according to the sanctuary shekel, each filled with fine flour mixed with oil as a grain offering;
50 One gold dish weighing ten shekels, filled with incense;
51 One young bull, one ram and one male lamb a year old, for a burnt offering;
52 One male goat for a sin offering;
53 And two oxen, five rams, five male goats and five male lambs a year old, to be sacrificed as a fellowship offering. This was the offering of Elishama son of Ammihud.
54 On the eighth day Gamaliel son of Pedahzur, the leader of the people of Manasseh, brought his offering.
55 His offering was one silver plate weighing a hundred and thirty shekels, and one silver sprinkling bowl weighing seventy shekels, both according to the sanctuary shekel, each filled with fine flour mixed with oil as a grain offering;
56 One gold dish weighing ten shekels, filled with incense;
57 One young bull, one ram and one male lamb a year old,

---

    weighing 130 shekels (about 3¼ pounds)
  2) One silver sprinkling bowl—weighing 70 shekels (about 1¾ pounds)
- Each was filled with fine flour mixed with oil as a Grain Offering

  3) One gold dish—weighing 10 shekels (about 4 ounces)
- Filled with incense

  4) Animals for the offerings
- A Burnt Offering: Seeking atonement (reconciliation)
- A Sin Offering: Seeking cleansing
- A Fellowship or Peace Offering: Seeking more & more of the fellowship & peace of God

g. The offering on the seventh day: Was brought by Elishama, leader of the tribe of Ephraim

  1) One silver plate—weighing 130 shekels (about 3¼ pounds)
  2) One silver sprinkling bowl—weighing 70 shekels (about 1¾ pounds)
- Each was filled with fine flour mixed with oil as a Grain Offering

  3) One gold dish—weighing 10 shekels (about 4 ounces)
- Filled with incense

  4) Animals for the offerings
- A Burnt Offering: Seeking atonement (reconciliation)
- A Sin Offering: Seeking cleansing
- A Fellowship or Peace Offering: Seeking more & more of the fellowship & peace of God

h. The offering on the eighth day: Was brought by Gamaliel, leader of the tribe of Manasseh

  1) One silver plate—weighing 130 shekels (about 3¼ pounds)
  2) One silver sprinkling bowl—weighing 70 shekels (about 1¾ pounds)
- Each was filled with fine flour mixed with oil as a Grain Offering

  3) One gold dish—weighing 10 shekels (about 4 ounces)
- Filled with incense

  4) Animals for the offerings
- A Burnt Offering: Seeking

NUMBERS 7:1-89

atonement (reconciliation)
- A Sin Offering: Seeking cleansing
- A Fellowship or Peace Offering: Seeking more & more of the fellowship & peace of God

i. The offering on the ninth day: Was brought by Abidan, leader of the tribe of Benjamin
  1) One silver plate—weighing 130 shekels (about 3¼ pounds)
  2) One silver sprinkling bowl—weighing 70 shekels (about 1¾ pounds)
     - Each was filled with fine flour mixed with oil as a Grain Offering
  3) One gold dish—weighing 10 shekels (about 4 ounces)
     - Filled with incense
  4) Animals for the offerings
     - A Burnt Offering: Seeking atonement (reconciliation)
     - A Sin Offering: Seeking cleansing
     - A Fellowship or Peace Offering: Seeking more & more of the fellowship & peace of God

j. The offering on the tenth day: Was brought by Ahiezer, leader of the tribe of Dan
  1) One silver plate—weighing 130 shekels (about 3¼ pounds)
  2) One silver sprinkling bowl—weighing 70 shekels (about 1¾ pounds)
     - Each was filled with fine flour mixed with oil as a Grain Offering
  3) One gold dish—weighing 10 shekels (about 4 ounces)
     - Filled with incense
  4) Animals for the offerings
     - A Burnt Offering: Seeking atonement (reconciliation)
     - A Sin Offering: Seeking cleansing
     - A Fellowship or Peace Offering: Seeking more & more of the fellowship & peace of God

k. The offering on the eleventh day: Was brought by Pagiel, leader of the tribe of Asher

for a burnt offering;
58 One male goat for a sin offering;
59 And two oxen, five rams, five male goats and five male lambs a year old, to be sacrificed as a fellowship offering. This was the offering of Gamaliel son of Pedahzur.
60 On the ninth day Abidan son of Gideoni, the leader of the people of Benjamin, brought his offering.
61 His offering was one silver plate weighing a hundred and thirty shekels, and one silver sprinkling bowl weighing seventy shekels, both according to the sanctuary shekel, each filled with fine flour mixed with oil as a grain offering;
62 One gold dish weighing ten shekels, filled with incense;
63 One young bull, one ram and one male lamb a year old, for a burnt offering;
64 One male goat for a sin offering;
65 And two oxen, five rams, five male goats and five male lambs a year old, to be sacrificed as a fellowship offering. This was the offering of Abidan son of Gideoni.
66 On the tenth day Ahiezer son of Ammishaddai, the leader of the people of Dan, brought his offering.
67 His offering was one silver plate weighing a hundred and thirty shekels, and one silver sprinkling bowl weighing seventy shekels, both according to the sanctuary shekel, each filled with fine flour mixed with oil as a grain offering;
68 One gold dish weighing ten shekels, filled with incense;
69 One young bull, one ram and one male lamb a year old, for a burnt offering;
70 One male goat for a sin offering;
71 And two oxen, five rams, five male goats and five male lambs a year old, to be sacrificed as a fellowship offering. This was the offering of Ahiezer son of Ammishaddai.
72 On the eleventh day Pagiel son of Ocran, the leader of the people of Asher, brought his offering.

73 His offering was one silver plate weighing a hundred and thirty shekels, and one silver sprinkling bowl weighing seventy shekels, both according to the sanctuary shekel, each filled with fine flour mixed with oil as a grain offering;
74 One gold dish weighing ten shekels, filled with incense;
75 One young bull, one ram and one male lamb a year old, for a burnt offering;
76 One male goat for a sin offering;
77 And two oxen, five rams, five male goats and five male lambs a year old, to be sacrificed as a fellowship offering. This was the offering of Pagiel son of Ocran.
78 On the twelfth day Ahira son of Enan, the leader of the people of Naphtali, brought his offering.
79 His offering was one silver plate weighing a hundred and thirty shekels, and one silver sprinkling bowl weighing seventy shekels, both according to the sanctuary shekel, each filled with fine flour mixed with oil as a grain offering;
80 One gold dish weighing ten shekels, filled with incense;
81 One young bull, one ram and one male lamb a year old, for a burnt offering;
82 One male goat for a sin offering;
83 And two oxen, five rams, five male goats and five male lambs a year old, to be sacrificed as a fellowship offering. This was the offering of Ahira son of Enan.
84 These were the offerings of the Israelite leaders for the dedication of the altar when it was anointed: twelve silver plates, twelve silver sprinkling bowls and twelve gold dishes.
85 Each silver plate weighed a hundred and thirty shekels, and each sprinkling bowl seventy shekels. Altogether, the silver dishes weighed two thousand four hundred shekels, according to the sanctuary shekel.
86 The twelve gold dishes filled with incense weighed ten shekels each, according to

1) One silver plate—weighing 130 shekels (about 3¼ pounds)
2) One silver sprinkling bowl—weighing 70 shekels (about 1¾ pounds)
   - Each was filled with fine flour mixed with oil as a Grain Offering
3) One gold dish—weighing 10 shekels (about 4 ounces)
   - Filled with incense
4) Animals for the offerings
   - A Burnt Offering: Seeking atonement (reconciliation)
   - A Sin Offering: Seeking cleansing
   - A Fellowship or Peace Offering: Seeking more & more of the fellowship & peace of God

l. The offering on the twelfth day: Was brought by Ahira, leader of the tribe of Naphtali
  1) One silver plate—weighing 130 shekels (about 3¼ pounds)
  2) One silver sprinkling bowl—weighing 70 shekels (about 1¾ pounds)
     - Each was filled with fine flour mixed with oil as a Grain Offering
  3) One gold dish—weighing 10 shekels (about 4 ounces)
     - Filled with incense
  4) Animals for the offerings
     - A Burnt Offering: Seeking atonement (reconciliation)
     - A Sin Offering: Seeking cleansing
     - A Fellowship or Peace Offering: Seeking more & more of the fellowship & peace of God

m. The totals & value of the offerings
  1) There were 12 silver plates, 12 silver bowls, & 12 gold dishes

  - The silver plates & bowls weighed about 2400 shekels (about 60 pounds)

  - The gold containers with incense weighed 120 shekels (about 3 pounds)

NUMBERS 7:1-89

2) There were a large number of animals offered • The Burnt Offering: 12 young bulls, 12 rams, 12 male lambs with their Grain Offering • The Sin Offering: 12 male goats • The Fellowship or Peace Offering: 24 oxen, 60 rams, 60 male goats, 60	the sanctuary shekel. Altogether, the gold dishes weighed a hundred and twenty shekels. 87 The total number of animals for the burnt offering came to twelve young bulls, twelve rams and twelve male lambs a year old, together with their grain offering. Twelve male goats were used for the sin offering. 88 The total number of animals for the sacrifice of the fellowship offering came to	twenty-four oxen, sixty rams, sixty male goats and sixty male lambs a year old. These were the offerings for the dedication of the altar after it was anointed. 89 When Moses entered the Tent of Meeting to speak with the LORD, he heard the voice speaking to him from between the two cherubim above the atonement cover on the ark of the Testimony. And he spoke with him.	male lambs 3. **The great assurance of God: Permanent access into His presence—His communion, guidance** a. The approach of Moses: Approached as he felt the need b. The faithfulness of God: Spoke from between the cherubim on the Ark—communed with & directed His people

DIVISION I

THE PREPARATION FOR THE MARCH TO THE PROMISED LAND, 1:1–10:36

F. The Spontaneous Offerings at the Dedication of the Tabernacle: Supporting God's Work and Approaching Him Exactly As He Says, 7:1-89

(7:1-89) **Introduction—Enemies, of Life—Victory, over Enemies of life—Stewardship, Duty of—Support, Financial, Duty of —Finances, Duty to Give—Ministry, Duty to Support**: the enemies of life are many and terrible, terrible in the sense that they can eventually capture and enslave every human being upon the earth. The attack by an enemy of life is sometimes visible and expected; at other times it is totally unexpected and shocking. Sometimes the attack is silent, lurking, slyly waiting for the opportunity to move against us. At any moment, at any time an enemy can attack and threaten our lives, an enemy such as…

- an unexpected disease or accident
- an intruder into our home or office
- a thief or swindler
- a rapist or sex offender
- a silent urge to steal or lie
- an attraction or passion for illicit sex
- adultery or unfaithfulness
- anger or abuse
- a consuming covetousness or greed
- gluttony, craving more and more
- uncontrolled passion that lusts for more and more
- addiction or drunkenness
- lawlessness or violence
- hatred or malice
- loneliness or emptiness
- lack of meaning or purpose
- lack of fulfillment or satisfaction

The enemies of life are many and varied. They repeatedly attack man until they eventually drag man into that last great enemy, the pit of death and hell—unless a person knows Christ.

What man needs is the power to conquer the enemies of life and gain the victory over them. This is exactly what God wants for the believer as he marches to the promised land: triumph and victory over all the enemies that attack him. This is the message that must be carried to the world: the enemies of life can be conquered and triumphed over. Man can be victorious throughout all of life. Man can conquer all the foes that seek to enslave and destroy him, even the last foe—death itself. This is the message of the gospel that must be carried forth: victory is in Christ Jesus our LORD.

But note this fact: money is needed to carry the message of Christ to the world. God's work needs financial support. People are needed to step forth to support God's work throughout the world: support the preachers, the evangelists, the missionaries, and the teachers of the Word. Financial support is an absolute essential, for while the gospel is free, the cost of taking it to the world is not! There is only one way to approach God: through the Lord Jesus Christ. If a person does not approach God through the sacrifice of His Son, he is doomed to an eternity of separation from God. God accepts no person except through the sacrifice of His Son. Christ Himself declared this fact. There is no alternative. Believers have no choice as they march to the promised land. They must support God's work and continue to support it until they reach the promised land of heaven. This is the subject of this great passage: *The Spontaneous Offerings at the Dedication of the Tabernacle: Supporting God's Work and Approaching Him Exactly As He Says*, 7:1-89.

1. The gifts for transporting the Tabernacle, that of carts and oxen: demonstrated the need for joyful, spontaneous support of God's work (vv.1-9).
2. The magnificent offerings presented at the dedication of the altar—presented by each tribal leader on different days—in obedience to God's instructions: demonstrated the need to approach God exactly as He says (vv.10-88).
3. The great assurance of God: permanent access into His presence—His communion, and guidance (v.89).

1 (7:1-9) **Offerings, Voluntary and Spontaneous—Giving, to the LORD—Stewardship, Duty of—Tabernacle, Dedication of—Church, Dedication of—Dedication, of Tabernacle—Gifts, Voluntary and Spontaneous—Giving, How to Give**: there were the gifts for transporting the Tabernacle, the gifts of carts and oxen.

NUMBERS 7:1-89

These gifts demonstrated the need for joyful, spontaneous support of God's work.

a. The magnificent gifts were given by the leaders right after the dedication of the Tabernacle (v.1). Exodus chapter 40 describes the completion and dedication of the Tabernacle. It was at that time that the presence of God descended upon the Tabernacle in the cloud of His glory, symbolized in the pillar of cloud (Ex. 40:34-35). This present passage (Numbers chapter 7) shows the joyful, spontaneous response of the tribal leaders right after the dedication of the Tabernacle.

Also note this fact: all the events from Exodus chapter 40 through Numbers chapter 9 describe what happened within a *one month* period. The one month stretched from the dedication of the Tabernacle (Exodus chapter 40) through all the events in Leviticus up through Numbers chapter 10. All these events took place in a period of just 1 month. How do we know this? Because the events are dated in Exodus chapter 40 to Numbers chapter 10. Note these dated events:[1]

Date	Event	Text
Day 1, first month	Completion of tabernacle	Ex.40:2
		Nu.7:1
	Laws for offerings begin	Le.1:1
	Offerings for altar begin	Nu.7:3
	Ordination of priests begins	Le.8:1
Day 8, first month	Ordination of priests completed	Le.9:1
Day 12, first month	Offerings for altar completed	Nu.7:78
	Appointment of Levites	Nu.8:5
Day 14, first month	Second Passover	Nu.9:2
Day 1, second month	Census begins	Nu.2:2
Day 14, second month	Passover for the unclean	Nu.9:11
Day 20, second month	The cloud moves, the camp begins its trek	Nu.19:11

The point to see is the glorious worship that surrounded the dedication of the Tabernacle. The leaders of the people were deeply moved, filled with joy and rejoicing, stirred to make some wonderful gifts to the LORD and His Tabernacle. Note that the leaders gave the gifts spontaneously. They offered the gifts to the LORD at the Tabernacle door itself: they gave six covered wagons or carts and twelve oxen (v.3).

b. The LORD instructed Moses to accept the gifts and to distribute them as needed (vv.4-5).

c. The gifts were distributed by Moses to the Levites, the assistants responsible for transporting the Tabernacle (vv.6-9).

    1) The Gershonites were given two carts and four oxen for transporting all the curtains: they received just what they needed for their work (v.7).

    2) The Merarites were given four carts and eight oxen for transporting the frame of the Tabernacle: they, too, received just what their work required (v.8).

    3) The priest Ithamar supervised the transporting of the Tabernacle (v.8).

    4) Note that the Kohathites were given no carts, for they were to carry the sacred furnishings on their shoulders. They needed none of the gifts that were brought by the leaders (v.9).

Thought 1. What happened to these leaders is exciting. Just think: How could the heavy curtains and the heavy framing of the Tabernacle ever be transported without wagons and oxen? There was no way. The need—a dire need—existed. A great dedication service of the Tabernacle had just taken place, a glorious and joyful celebration. There was a deep sense of the presence of God. Yet there was a dire need, a need so great that the people could not begin their march to the promised land until the need was met. The Tabernacle could not be transported without oxen and wagons, and the wagons had to be covered to protect the Tabernacle during bad weather. Obviously, at some point during the dedication service, the heart of some leader was gripped with the need, and he shared it with the other leaders. Together, they stepped forth and met the need. Joyfully and spontaneously, they supported the work of God. What a lesson for us! How desperately the needs of the church need to be met! How desperately men and women need to step forth to meet the needs of the church! To give spontaneously and joyfully to the work of the LORD!

> **Give, and it will be given to you. A good measure, pressed down, shaken together and running over, will be poured into your lap. For with the measure you use, it will be measured to you. (Lu. 6:38)**
>
> **Sell your possessions and give to the poor. Provide purses for yourselves that will not wear out, a treasure in heaven that will not be exhausted, where no thief comes near and no moth destroys. (Lu. 12:33)**
>
> **As he looked up, Jesus saw the rich putting their gifts into the temple treasury. He also saw a poor widow put in two very small copper coins. "I tell you the truth," he said, "this poor widow has put in more than all the others. All these people gave their gifts out of their wealth; but she out of her poverty put in all she had to live on." (Lu. 21:1-4)**
>
> **There were no needy persons among them. For from time to time those who owned lands or houses sold them, brought the money from the sales and put it at the apostles' feet, and it was distributed to anyone as he had need. (Ac. 4:34-35)**
>
> **"In everything I did, I showed you that by this kind of hard work we must help the weak, remembering the words the Lord Jesus himself said: 'It is more blessed to give than to receive.'" (Ac. 20:35)**
>
> **Remember this: Whoever sows sparingly will also reap sparingly, and whoever sows generously will also reap generously. (2 Co. 9:6)**
>
> **And said to Moses, "The people are bringing more than enough for doing the work the LORD commanded to be done." (Ex. 36:5)**
>
> **Besides, in my devotion to the temple of my God I now give my personal treasures of gold and silver for the temple of my**

---

[1] This chart is taken from *The Expositor's Bible Commentary*, Vol.2. Frank E. Gaebelein, Editor, p.757, which in turn is based upon Gordon J. Wenham's chart in *The Book of Numbers*, p.91. Credit is hereby given to both commentaries.

God, over and above everything I have provided for this holy temple. (1 Chr. 29:3)

All the officials and all the people brought their contributions gladly, dropping them into the chest until it was full. (2 Chr. 24:10)

A generous man will prosper; he who refreshes others will himself be refreshed. (Pr. 11:25)

A generous man will himself be blessed, for he shares his food with the poor. (Pr. 22:9)

"Bring the whole tithe into the storehouse, that there may be food in my house. Test me in this," says the LORD Almighty, "and see if I will not throw open the floodgates of heaven and pour out so much blessing that you will not have room enough for it." (Mal. 3:10)

2 (7:10-88) **Offerings, Duty to Give—Giving, Duty of—Dedication, of the Tabernacle—Church, Dedication of—Gifts, Duty to Offer—Approach, to God—Sacrifice, the Way to Approach God**: there were the magnificent offerings presented at the dedication of the altar. Note: the offerings were presented by each tribal leader on different days in obedience to God's instructions. This demonstrated the need to approach God exactly as He says. Twelve of the most majestic, meaningful worship services ever held now occurred—stretched out over 12 days. Each of the 12 leaders majestically brought his gifts on a different day for the dedication of the altar (v.11). What were the worship services like on each of the days? The fact that each leader's offering is repeated for 12 consecutive days indicates a spectacular, meaningful worship service:

⇒ a worship service of pomp and ceremony, of majesty and glory, of pageantry and celebration
⇒ a worship service of meaning, significance, and purpose
⇒ a worship service of joy and rejoicing
⇒ a worship service of deep dedication and commitment
⇒ a worship service acknowledging God's great gift of the atonement, of the forgiveness of sin, and of fellowship and peace with Him

a. Note the offering of the first day: it was brought by Nahshon, leader of the great tribe of Judah (vv.12-17).
1) He brought one silver plate, weighing about 3¼ pounds (v.13). This plate was probably for the Table of Showbread, to be used with the Bread of the Presence.
2) He brought one silver sprinkling bowl or basin that weighed about 1¾ pounds (v.13). This was probably used for the blood that was to be sprinkled upon the altar. Note that both the silver plate and the silver bowl were filled with Grain Offerings of choice flour mixed with olive oil.
3) He brought one gold dish that weighed about 4 ounces (v.13). This was filled with incense which probably means that it was used for this very purpose day by day.
4) He brought the animals necessary to approach God through the blood of the sacrifice (vv.15-17). Note:
⇒ He approached God through the Burnt Offering, acknowledging the atonement or reconciliation that God had provided for him and his tribal people.
⇒ He approached God through the Sin Offering, seeking forgiveness of sin (v.16).
⇒ He approached God through the Fellowship or Peace Offering, seeking more of the fellowship and peace of God for himself and his tribe (v.17).

Each of the 12 leaders brought the very *same gifts* as this leader from the tribe of Judah. Each tribal leader had his day before God, his day to present his gifts and offerings to the LORD. Obviously, each leader's heart was filled with joy and rejoicing, praise and honor—all lifted up to the LORD God who had saved and delivered him from the bondage of Egypt (a symbol of the world with all its enslavements). Because each of the 12 days is simply repeated with the gifts offered, the text of the other tribal leader's offerings is not being covered, nor are the Scripture and outline being repeated. The reader can easily glance back at the Scripture and outline at the beginning of this particular study.

Note the totals and great value of the offerings.
1) There were 12 silver plates, 12 silver bowls, and 12 gold dishes. The silver plates and bowls weighed about 2400 shekels or about 60 pounds. The gold containers with incense weighed 120 shekels or about 3 pounds (vv.84-86).
2) There were a large number of animals offered:
⇒ For the Burnt Offering, there were 12 young bulls, 12 rams, and 12 male lambs sacrificed with their Grain Offering (v.87).
⇒ For the Sin Offering, there were 12 male goats sacrificed (v.87).
⇒ For the Fellowship or Peace Offering, there were 24 oxen, 60 rams, 60 male goats, and 60 male lambs sacrificed (v.88).

Thought 1. The tribal leaders of Israel set a dynamic example for us.
(1) They were the leaders of the people. As leaders, they took the lead in supporting God's work. The leaders of the church must step forth to take the lead. They are in leadership positions for this very purpose: to lead God's people. Money or financial support is a part of God's work. Therefore, the leaders of the church must take the lead in meeting the financial needs of the church.

Again, it [the kingdom of heaven] will be like a man going on a journey, who called his servants and entrusted his property to them. To one he gave five talents of money, to another two talents, and to another one talent, each according to his ability. Then he went on his journey. (Mt. 25:14-15)

"But God said to him, 'You fool! This very night your life will be demanded from you. Then who will get what you have prepared for yourself?'" (Lu. 12:20)

From everyone who has been given much, much will be demanded; and from the one who has been entrusted with much, much more will be asked. (Lu. 12:48)

"In everything I did, I showed you that by this kind of hard work we must help the weak, remembering the words the Lord Jesus himself said: 'It is more blessed to give than to receive.'" (Ac. 20:35)

NUMBERS 7:1-89

Now it is required that those who have been given a trust must prove faithful. (1 Co. 4:2)

Each one should use whatever gift he has received to serve others, faithfully administering God's grace in its various forms. (1 Pe. 4:10)

All the officials and all the people brought their contributions gladly, dropping them into the chest until it was full. (2 Chr. 24:10)

(2) The tribal leaders of Israel approached God exactly as He said: through the substitute sacrifice of the offerings. This is exactly how we must approach God, exactly as He says: through the sacrifice of His Son, the Lord Jesus Christ. There is no other approach to God other than through His Son.

"For God so loved the world that he gave his one and only Son, that whoever believes in him shall not perish but have eternal life." (Jn. 3:16)

"I told you that you would die in your sins; if you do not believe that I am the one I claim to be, you will indeed die in your sins." (Jn. 8:24)

Jesus answered, "I am the way and the truth and the life. No one comes to the Father except through me." (Jn. 14:6)

Salvation is found in no one else, for there is no other name under heaven given to men by which we must be saved. (Ac. 4:12)

For no one can lay any foundation other than the one already laid, which is Jesus Christ. (1 Co. 3:11)

For there is one God and one mediator between God and men, the man Christ Jesus, who gave himself as a ransom for all men—the testimony given in its proper time. (1 Ti. 2:5-6)

But the ministry Jesus has received is as superior to theirs as the covenant of which he is mediator is superior to the old one, and it is founded on better promises. (He. 8:6)

For this reason Christ is the mediator of a new covenant, that those who are called may receive the promised eternal inheritance—now that he has died as a ransom to set them free from the sins committed under the first covenant. (He. 9:15)

For Christ did not enter a man-made sanctuary that was only a copy of the true one; he entered heaven itself, now to appear for us in God's presence. (He. 9:24)

[And] to Jesus the mediator of a new covenant, and to the sprinkled blood that speaks a better word than the blood of Abel. (He. 12:24)

My dear children, I write this to you so that you will not sin. But if anybody does sin, we have one who speaks to the Father in our defense—Jesus Christ, the Righteous One. He is the atoning sacrifice for our sins, and not only for ours but also for the sins of the whole world. (1 Jn. 2:1-2)

(3) The tribal leaders approached God for 12 consecutive days, leader after leader—all through the substitute sacrifice. Note the emphasis upon the substitute sacrifice (Nu. 7:15-17, 21-23, 27-29, 33-35, 39-41, 45-47, 51-53, 57-59, 63-65, 69-71, 75-77, 81-83, 87-88). Scripture declares that the substitute sacrifice is a symbol, a picture of the sacrifice of the Lord Jesus Christ. Jesus Christ is our substitute Sacrifice.

Who gave himself for our sins to rescue us from the present evil age, according to the will of our God and Father. (Ga. 1:4)

Christ redeemed us from the curse of the law by becoming a curse for us, for it is written: "Cursed is everyone who is hung on a tree." (Ga. 3:13)

And live a life of love, just as Christ loved us and gave himself up for us as a fragrant offering and sacrifice to God. (Ep. 5:2)

Who gave himself for us to redeem us from all wickedness and to purify for himself a people that are his very own, eager to do what is good. (Tit. 2:14)

But we see Jesus, who was made a little lower than the angels, now crowned with glory and honor because he suffered death, so that by the grace of God he might taste death for everyone. (He. 2:9)

For you know that it was not with perishable things such as silver or gold that you were redeemed from the empty way of life handed down to you from your forefathers, but with the precious blood of Christ, a lamb without blemish or defect. (1 Pe. 1:18-19)

He himself bore our sins in his body on the tree, so that we might die to sins and live for righteousness; by his wounds you have been healed. (1 Pe. 2:24)

For Christ died for sins once for all, the righteous for the unrighteous, to bring you to God. He was put to death in the body but made alive by the Spirit. (1 Pe. 3:18)

This is how we know what love is: Jesus Christ laid down his life for us. And we ought to lay down our lives for our brothers. (1 Jn. 3:16)

3 (7:89) **Assurance, of Access to God—Access, to God—Presence, of God—God, Presence of—Communion, with God—Guidance, of God**: there was the great assurance of God, the assurance of permanent access into His presence—the assurance of His communion and guidance day by day.

The twelve days of glorious worship seemed to roll in one upon another, and then it happened: Climactic! Astounding! Moses entered the Tabernacle to pray. He spoke with the LORD and, astonishingly, he actually heard the voice of God speaking to him. The voice came from between the two cherubim above the Atonement Cover on the Ark of the Testimony. God Himself actually showered His grace upon Moses and communed with him. Remember: the dedication of the Tabernacle and God's glorious presence descending upon the Tabernacle in the cloud had just taken place a few days earlier. The leaders had just made their spectacular, spontaneous offerings to the LORD on 12

NUMBERS 7:1-89

consecutive days. Then Moses entered the Tabernacle, and there God poured His presence out upon Moses, speaking to him from between the two cherubim above the Ark. God was giving great assurance of His presence—of His communion and guidance—that He was going to give His people day by day as they marched to the promised land.

Thought 1. God gave Moses two great assurances: the assurance of permanent access into God's presence and the assurance of God's guidance. The very same two assurances are given to every believer upon the earth.

(1) There is assurance of permanent access into God's presence.

> "Ask and it will be given to you; seek and you will find; knock and the door will be opened to you." (Mt. 7:7)
>
> I am the gate; whoever enters through me will be saved. He will come in and go out, and find pasture. (Jn. 10:9)
>
> Until now you have not asked for anything in my name. Ask and you will receive, and your joy will be complete. (Jn. 16:24)
>
> Therefore, since we have been justified through faith, we have peace with God through our Lord Jesus Christ, through whom we have gained access by faith into this grace in which we now stand. And we rejoice in the hope of the glory of God. (Ro. 5:1-2)
>
> For through him we both have access to the Father by one Spirit. (Ep. 2:18)
>
> In him and through faith in him we may approach God with freedom and confidence. (Ep. 3:12)
>
> (For the law made nothing perfect), and a better hope is introduced, by which we draw near to God. (He. 7:19)
>
> Let us draw near to God with a sincere heart in full assurance of faith, having our hearts sprinkled to cleanse us from a guilty conscience and having our bodies washed with pure water. (He. 10:22)
>
> Come near to God and he will come near to you. Wash your hands, you sinners, and purify your hearts, you double-minded. (Js. 4:8)
>
> Here I am! I stand at the door and knock. If anyone hears my voice and opens the door, I will come in and eat with him, and he with me. (Re. 3:20)
>
> Look to the LORD and his strength; seek his face always. (1 Chr. 16:11)
>
> Who may ascend the hill of the LORD? Who may stand in his holy place? He who has clean hands and a pure heart, who does not lift up his soul to an idol or swear by what is false. (Ps. 24:3-4)
>
> But as for me, it is good to be near God. I have made the Sovereign LORD my refuge; I will tell of all your deeds. (Ps. 73:28)
>
> You will keep in perfect peace him whose mind is steadfast, because he trusts in you. (Is. 26:3)

(2) There is the assurance of God's communion and guidance day by day.

> And surely I am with you always, to the very end of the age. (Mt. 28:20)
>
> But when he, the Spirit of truth, comes, he will guide you into all truth. He will not speak on his own; he will speak only what he hears, and he will tell you what is yet to come. (Jn. 16:13)
>
> We proclaim to you what we have seen and heard, so that you also may have fellowship with us. And our fellowship is with the Father and with his Son, Jesus Christ. (1 Jn. 1:3)
>
> Here I am! I stand at the door and knock. If anyone hears my voice and opens the door, I will come in and eat with him, and he with me. (Re. 3:20)
>
> "I am with you and will watch over you wherever you go, and I will bring you back to this land. I will not leave you until I have done what I have promised you." (Ge. 28:15)
>
> The LORD replied, "My Presence will go with you, and I will give you rest." (Ex. 33:14)
>
> When you go to war against your enemies and see horses and chariots and an army greater than yours, do not be afraid of them, because the LORD your God, who brought you up out of Egypt, will be with you. (De. 20:1)
>
> He makes me lie down in green pastures, he leads me beside quiet waters. (Ps. 23:2)
>
> He guides the humble in what is right and teaches them his way. (Ps. 25:9)
>
> For this God is our God for ever and ever; he will be our guide even to the end. (Ps. 48:14)
>
> You guide me with your counsel, and afterward you will take me into glory. (Ps. 73:24)
>
> Whether you turn to the right or to the left, your ears will hear a voice behind you, saying, "This is the way; walk in it." (Is. 30:21)
>
> I will lead the blind by ways they have not known, along unfamiliar paths I will guide them; I will turn the darkness into light before them and make the rough places smooth. These are the things I will do; I will not forsake them. (Is. 42:16)
>
> When you pass through the waters, I will be with you; and when you pass through the rivers, they will not sweep over you. When you walk through the fire, you will not be burned; the flames will not set you ablaze. (Is. 43:2)

NUMBERS 8:1-26

CHAPTER 8

G. The Placement of the Lampstand & the Setting Apart of the Levites to Serve God: Standing Forth As Lights & Servants of God, 8:1-26

1. **The placement of the Lampstand—to light the area in the Holy Place: A symbol of Christ, the Light of the world**

   The LORD said to Moses,

   a. Aaron obeyed: Set the lamps & focused the light
      1) On the 12 loaves of the bread of the Presence: Symbolized the tribes, God's people
      2) On the Altar of Incense: Symbolized prayer, access

   2 "Speak to Aaron and say to him, 'When you set up the seven lamps, they are to light the area in front of the lampstand.' "
   3 Aaron did so; he set up the lamps so that they faced forward on the lampstand, just as the LORD commanded Moses.

   b. The great value of the Lampstand
      1) Was made of hammered gold
      2) Was made exactly as God designed

   4 This is how the lampstand was made: It was made of hammered gold—from its base to its blossoms. The lampstand was made exactly like the pattern the LORD had shown Moses.

2. **The dedication of the Levites: A picture of laypersons being set apart to God**

   5 The LORD said to Moses:

   a. The Levites must be ceremonially, spiritually cleansed
      1) To be sprinkled with the water of cleansing
      2) To shave their whole heads
      3) To wash their clothes
      4) To make preparation to approach the LORD: Through the Burnt Offering, Grain Offering & Sin Offering

   6 "Take the Levites from among the other Israelites and make them ceremonially clean.
   7 To purify them, do this: Sprinkle the water of cleansing on them; then have them shave their whole bodies and wash their clothes, and so purify themselves.
   8 Have them take a young bull with its grain offering of fine flour mixed with oil; then you are to take a second young bull for a sin offering.

   b. The Levites must be presented to the LORD—at the front of the Tabernacle—& the people of God must be assembled
      1) To have the people identify with them—by laying their hands upon them

   9 Bring the Levites to the front of the Tent of Meeting and assemble the whole Israelite community.
   10 You are to bring the Levites before the LORD, and the Israelites are to lay their hands on them.

      2) To wave them (their shoulders) back & forth as a wave offering before the LORD
      3) To have the Levites identify with the sacrifice (a symbol of Christ)
      4) To then offer the sacrifice of the Sin Offering & of the Burnt Offering: To secure forgiveness & to make atonement (reconciliation)
      5) To again present them as a wave offering before the LORD

   11 Aaron is to present the Levites before the LORD as a wave offering from the Israelites, so that they may be ready to do the work of the LORD.
   12 "After the Levites lay their hands on the heads of the bulls, use the one for a sin offering to the LORD and the other for a burnt offering, to make atonement for the Levites.
   13 Have the Levites stand in front of Aaron and his sons and then present them as a wave offering to the LORD.

   c. The Levites are to be set

   14 In this way you are to set the Levites apart from the other Israelites, and the Levites will be mine.
   15 "After you have purified the Levites and presented them as a wave offering, they are to come to do their work at the Tent of Meeting.
   16 They are the Israelites who are to be given wholly to me. I have taken them as my own in place of the firstborn, the first male offspring from every Israelite woman.
   17 Every firstborn male in Israel, whether man or animal, is mine. When I struck down all the firstborn in Egypt, I set them apart for myself.
   18 And I have taken the Levites in place of all the firstborn sons in Israel.
   19 Of all the Israelites, I have given the Levites as gifts to Aaron and his sons to do the work at the Tent of Meeting on behalf of the Israelites and to make atonement for them so that no plague will strike the Israelites when they go near the sanctuary."
   20 Moses, Aaron and the whole Israelite community did with the Levites just as the LORD commanded Moses.
   21 The Levites purified themselves and washed their clothes. Then Aaron presented them as a wave offering before the LORD and made atonement for them to purify them.
   22 After that, the Levites came to do their work at the Tent of Meeting under the supervision of Aaron and his sons. They did with the Levites just as the LORD commanded Moses.
   23 The LORD said to Moses,
   24 "This applies to the Levites: Men twenty-five years old or more shall come to take part in the work at the Tent of Meeting,
   25 But at the age of fifty, they must retire from their regular service and work no longer.
   26 They may assist their brothers in performing their duties at the Tent of Meeting, but they themselves must not do the work. This, then, is how you are to assign the responsibilities of the Levites."

apart from other people, set apart to be God's people, to do a special work for God

   1) They are to be set apart only after their purification; then they are to begin their service

   2) They are the ones who are set apart by God Himself, to take the place of the firstborn son

   • Every firstborn son had been set apart by God to be His, set apart when God delivered His people from Egypt

   • Now God replaces the first-born sons with the Levites

   3) They are set apart to be the assistants to the priests
      • To do the work needed at the Tabernacle
      • To make atonement—take care of the offerings—for the people
      • To protect the people by keeping them from abusing the Tabernacle

   d. The obedience of everyone: They all set the Levites apart just as God commanded

   1) The Levites purified themselves & washed their clothes
   2) The High Priest presented them to the LORD & made atonement for them: To cleanse them spiritually
   3) The Levites began their work as assistants to the priests

   e. The Levites' length of service or retirement years

   1) They are to serve in the heavy work between the ages of 25 to 50 years old

   2) They must retire from the heavy work after 50 years of age

   3) They may assist the younger men after 50, but not do the heavy work themselves

NUMBERS 8:1-26

DIVISION I

THE PREPARATION FOR THE MARCH TO THE PROMISED LAND, 1:1–10:36

G. The Placement of the Lampstand and the Setting Apart of the Levites to Serve God: Standing Forth As Lights and Servants of God, 8:1-26

(8:1-26) **Introduction—Needy, the, List of—Laborers, Need for**: people are lost and separated from God, dying and doomed to spend eternity apart from God. But these are not the only tragedies that confront man. Tragedies attack people day after day, tragedies that cause enormous problems and difficulties. Just think of the problems and difficulties that constantly attack...

- the orphans and children of single parents
- the widows and widowers
- the brokenhearted and hurting
- the backslidden and half-hearted
- the diseased and dying
- the hungry and thirsty
- the suffering and hospitalized
- the homeless and unemployed
- the injured and handicapped
- the empty and lonely
- the lawless and prisoners
- the emotionally and mentally disturbed

All around us there are people who need help, yet the laborers are few. Few people step forth to help. There is a desperate need for people to step forth and become servants of God, a need for messengers of light and ministry who will meet the desperate needs of the world. There is a need for laborers. This is the subject of this great Scripture: *The Placement of the Lampstand and the Setting Apart of the Levites to Serve God: Standing Forth As Lights and Servants of God*, 8:1-26.

1. The placement of the Lampstand—to light the area in the Holy Place: a symbol of Christ, the Light of the world (vv.1-4).
2. The dedication of the Levites: a picture of laypersons being set apart to God (vv.5-26).

1 (8:1-4) **Lampstand, Symbol of—Jesus Christ, Symbolized by—Light, a Symbol of—Symbol, of the Lampstand**: there was the placement of the Lampstand within the Tabernacle. The Lampstand was to give light to the Holy Place within the Tabernacle. Remember, the Lampstand is a symbol of Christ, the Light of the world.

The Lampstand apparently sat close by the entrance into the Holy Place; therefore, when it was focused in front, it lit up everything in the room of the Holy Place. This meant that its beams of light focused upon both the Table of Showbread and the Altar of Incense, a significant fact. Remember that 12 loaves of bread sat upon the Table of Showbread and that the 12 loaves represented the 12 tribes of Israel. That is, the 12 loaves represented God's people. The symbolism is clear: the light of God's presence is always shining upon His people. God cares for His people and looks after them.

Remember also that the Altar of Incense was constantly burning and sending out a sweet aroma ascending up toward heaven. This was a symbol that prayer should continually ascend up to God. The incense was like a sweet aroma, very pleasing to Him. The light of the Lampstand gave focus to prayer: it emphasized prayer—that God's people should continually pray.

a. Note that Aaron obeyed: he faced the lamps forward, focusing them upon the 12 loaves of the bread of the Presence and the Altar of Incense. The message was immediately conveyed: the Light of the world—God Himself—was focusing upon His people. He was focusing His presence and love, His guidance and protection upon them. Moreover, He was focusing upon their prayers, receiving their prayers and accepting them as a sweet aroma, very pleasing to Him.

b. Note the great value of the Lampstand (v.4). It was a beautiful, exquisite furnishing, very valuable. It was made of pure hammered gold in the form of a seven-branched tree that flowered. There was, of course, a base with one major shaft. Three branches extended out on each side of the shaft. There were cups shaped like almond blossoms and buds running up and decorating the shaft and branches of the Lampstand (see outline and notes—Ex. 25:31-40 for more discussion).

Note the emphasis that the Lampstand had been made exactly as God Himself had designed it (v.4). This stresses the great value of the Lampstand: it was the Lampstand of God Himself, for God had designed and overseen the making of it through His servant Moses.

> **Thought 1**. Four clear lessons are seen in this passage.
> (1) Jesus Christ is the Light of the world. As we march toward the promised land, believers must have the light of Christ to conquer the pitfalls and enemies of this life. Again, Christ is the Light of the world.
>
> In him was life, and that life was the light of men. (Jn. 1:4)
> When Jesus spoke again to the people, he said, "I am the light of the world. Whoever follows me will never walk in darkness, but will have the light of life." (Jn. 8:12)
> Then Jesus told them, "You are going to have the light just a little while longer. Walk while you have the light, before darkness overtakes you. The man who walks in the dark does not know where he is going." (Jn. 12:35)
> I have come into the world as a light, so that no one who believes in me should stay in darkness. (Jn. 12:46)
> For God, who said, "Let light shine out of darkness," made his light shine in our hearts to give us the light of the knowledge of the glory of God in the face of Christ. (2 Co. 4:6)
> For it is light that makes everything visible. This is why it is said: "Wake up, O

sleeper, rise from the dead, and Christ will shine on you." (Ep. 5:14)

The people walking in darkness have seen a great light; on those living in the land of the shadow of death a light has dawned. (Is. 9:2)

(2) The light of the Lampstand focused upon the 12 loaves of the bread of the Presence, a symbol of the 12 tribes of Israel (God's people). The light of God's presence shines upon the true believer. God gives light to His people: His love, care, provision, direction, guidance, knowledge, and wisdom. God's light gives whatever is necessary to overcome the pitfalls and enemies of this life.

To shine on those living in darkness and in the shadow of death, to guide our feet into the path of peace. (Lu. 1:79)

We proclaim to you what we have seen and heard, so that you also may have fellowship with us. And our fellowship is with the Father and with his Son, Jesus Christ. We write this to make our joy complete. This is the message we have heard from him and declare to you: God is light; in him there is no darkness at all. (1 Jn. 1:3-5)

There will be no more night. They will not need the light of a lamp or the light of the sun, for the Lord God will give them light. And they will reign for ever and ever. (Re. 22:5)

He makes me lie down in green pastures, he leads me beside quiet waters. (Ps. 23:2)

For this God is our God for ever and ever; he will be our guide even to the end. (Ps. 48:14)

You guide me with your counsel, and afterward you will take me into glory. (Ps. 73:24)

For the LORD God is a sun and shield; the LORD bestows favor and honor; no good thing does he withhold from those whose walk is blameless. (Ps. 84:11)

Whether you turn to the right or to the left, your ears will hear a voice behind you, saying, "This is the way; walk in it." (Is. 30:21)

I will lead the blind by ways they have not known, along unfamiliar paths I will guide them; I will turn the darkness into light before them and make the rough places smooth. These are the things I will do; I will not forsake them. (Is. 42:16)

Your sun will never set again, and your moon will wane no more; the LORD will be your everlasting light, and your days of sorrow will end. (Is. 60:20)

Do not gloat over me, my enemy! Though I have fallen, I will rise. Though I sit in darkness, the LORD will be my light. (Mi. 7:8)

(3) The Lampstand focused upon the Altar of Incense, symbolizing the importance of prayer. The light of God shines upon the prayers of His people, showing us that we have access into His presence—continued, unbroken access. We can approach God anytime with anything, and He hears us.

"Ask and it will be given to you; seek and you will find; knock and the door will be opened to you." (Mt. 7:7)

If you remain in me and my words remain in you, ask whatever you wish, and it will be given you. (Jn. 15:7)

Until now you have not asked for anything in my name. Ask and you will receive, and your joy will be complete. (Jn. 16:24)

Pray continually. (1 Th. 5:17)

Is any one of you in trouble? He should pray. Is anyone happy? Let him sing songs of praise. (Js. 5:13)

Look to the LORD and his strength; seek his face always. (1 Chr. 16:11)

He will call upon me, and I will answer him; I will be with him in trouble, I will deliver him and honor him. (Ps. 91:15)

Then you will call, and the LORD will answer; you will cry for help, and he will say: Here am I. "If you do away with the yoke of oppression, with the pointing finger and malicious talk..." (Is. 58:9)

Before they call I will answer; while they are still speaking I will hear. (Is. 65:24)

Call to me and I will answer you and tell you great and unsearchable things you do not know. (Je. 33:3)

(4) The Lampstand had to be focused by Aaron. God used one of His servants to give light to the loaves (His people) and to the Altar of Incense (the importance of prayer). So it is with us. God has called His people to lift up and focus the light of the LORD Jesus Christ before the world. In fact, the Scripture declares that God's people are the light of the world. Therefore, as we march to the promised land, we must lift up the light of the LORD Jesus Christ to the surrounding people and nations of the world.

You are the light of the world. A city on a hill cannot be hidden. (Mt. 5:14)

For this is what the Lord has commanded us: " 'I have made you a light for the Gentiles, that you may bring salvation to the ends of the earth.'" (Ac.13:47)

For you were once darkness, but now you are light in the Lord. Live as children of light. (Ep. 5:8)

So that you may become blameless and pure, children of God without fault in a crooked and depraved generation, in which you shine like stars in the universe (Ph. 2:15)

2 (8:5-26) **Dedication, of the Levites—Levites, Dedication of—Ceremony, Dedication—Dedication, Ceremony of**: there was the dedication of the Levites. Remember, the Levites were laypersons set apart by God to be assistants to the priests. This passage is a picture of laypersons being set apart to God, to His service. There is a sharp distinction between the Levites and the priests, a distinction that stresses the difference between a layperson who serves as

NUMBERS 8:1-26

an assistant and the priest or minister of God. *The Expositor's Bible Commentary* points out these differences:

> *The Priests were made holy, the Levites clean; the priests were anointed and washed, the Levites sprinkled; the priests were given new garments, the Levites washed theirs; blood was applied to the priests, it was waved over the Levites.*[1]

a. The Levites had to be ceremonially, spiritually cleansed (v.6-8). They had to be sprinkled with the water of cleansing, shave their whole heads, and wash their clothes. This was a symbol of being spiritually cleansed or purified from sin. But this was not all: they were also to make preparation to approach the LORD through the Burnt Offering and the Sin Offering. Keep in mind that the Burnt Offering secured the atonement and reconciliation with God, and the Sin Offering secured the forgiveness of sin. The Grain Offering was laid upon the sacrifice burning upon the altar and symbolized the offering of thanksgiving and of one's life to God (see outline and notes—Le. 1:1-17; 2:1-16; 4:1-5:13).

b. The Levites had to be presented to the LORD at the front of the Tabernacle, and the people of God had to be assembled for the dedication service (vv.9-13).

1) The people were to identify with the Levites by laying their hands upon them (v.10). Of course, just the tribal leaders did this, as the representatives of the people. This symbolized that the Levites were to be the servants of God in behalf of the people. They were to be the people's representatives, their substitutes in serving God day by day in the Tabernacle.
2) The Levites were to be waved back and forth as a wave offering before the LORD (v.11). Obviously, Aaron took them by the shoulders and waved them back and forth or either side to side. This was a symbol that they were being offered as living sacrifices to God (Ro. 12:1-2).
3) The Levites were then to identify with the sacrifice (v.12). The sacrifice was being substituted for the Levites, bearing the judgment of God that was due the Levites and redeeming them from the wrath of God. Again, remember that the sacrifice was a symbol of Christ.
4) The Levites were then to offer the sacrifice of the Sin Offering and of the Burnt Offering (v.12). This was to secure forgiveness and to make atonement (reconciliation) for them.
5) The Levites were then to be presented a second time as a wave offering before the LORD (v.13).

c. The Levites were to be set apart from other people, set apart to be God's servants. They were to do a very special work for God (vv.14-19). Note exactly what God says: the Levites *will be His*. The Levites belonged to God, belonged to the full-time service of God.

1) But note: the Levites were to be set apart only after their purification. Once they had been cleansed and purified, they were then to begin their service (v.15).
2) Note this important fact as well: the Levites were the ones who were set apart by God Himself to take the place of the firstborn son (v.16-18; see outline and notes—Nu. 3:11-13 for more discussion). Remember, every first born son had been set apart by God to be His and to serve Him.

They were set apart when God delivered His people from Egypt (v.17). God had saved the firstborn sons of Israel when His judgment fell upon Egypt. Therefore, all the firstborn sons belonged to Him and His service. Now God replaced the firstborn sons with the Levites (v.18).
3) The Levites were set apart to be the assistants to the priests (v.19). They were to do whatever work was needed at the Tabernacle. They were to make atonement, that is, to take care of the offerings for the people. They were also to protect the people by keeping them from abusing the Tabernacle. This was essential, for if a person abused the Tabernacle—the symbol of God's holy presence—the judgment of God fell upon His people.
4) Note the obedience of everyone involved in the dedication service: Moses, Aaron, and the whole community of believers set the Levites apart just as God commanded (vv.20-22).
  a) The Levites purified themselves and washed their clothes (v.21).
  b) The High Priest presented them to the LORD and made atonement for them: to cleanse them spiritually (v.21).
  c) The Levites began their work as assistants to the priests (v.22).
5) Note the Levites' length of service or retirement years (vv.23-26). They were to serve in the heavy work of transporting the Tabernacle between the ages of 25 and 50 years old (v.24). But they had to retire from the heavy work of the Tabernacle after 50 years of age (v.25). However, they could assist the younger men in the lighter work after 50 (v.26).

Thought 1. The laborers are few. Lift up your eyes and look upon the fields, for they are ripe to harvest. Yet there are few workers reaping the harvest. Most of the harvest is going to die and decay in the fields. Most of the harvest will never fulfill the purpose for which it was planted: it will never be reaped or used. The hour is late, and the need for workers is desperate. People desperately need to step forth and join the force of workers. So much of the harvest will be lost unless thousands upon thousands step forth and join the force of God's workers. When God called and challenged the Levites, they stepped forth. God is calling and challenging you and me to step forth, challenging us as His servants to help those who are ministering the Word of Life to the world, the preachers and ministers of God.

> **"Come, follow me," Jesus said, "and I will make you fishers of men." (Mt. 4:19)**
>
> **Then he said to his disciples, "The harvest is plentiful but the workers are few. Ask the Lord of the harvest, therefore, to send out workers into his harvest field." (Mt. 9:37-38)**
>
> **Not so with you. Instead, whoever wants to become great among you must be your servant, and whoever wants to be first must be slave of all. (Mk. 10:43-44)**
>
> **The first thing Andrew did was to find his brother Simon and tell him, "We have found the Messiah" (that is, the Christ). And he brought him to Jesus. Jesus looked at him and said, "You are Simon son of**

---

[1] *The Expositor's Bible Commentary*, Frank E. Gaebelein, Editor, p.766.

John. You will be called Cephas" (which, when translated, is Peter). (Jn. 1:41-42)

Philip found Nathanael and told him, "We have found the one Moses wrote about in the Law, and about whom the prophets also wrote—Jesus of Nazareth, the son of Joseph." (Jn. 1:45)

Do you not say, 'Four months more and then the harvest'? I tell you, open your eyes and look at the fields! They are ripe for harvest. Even now the reaper draws his wages, even now he harvests the crop for eternal life, so that the sower and the reaper may be glad together. (Jn. 4:35-36)

Again Jesus said, "Simon son of John, do you truly love me?" He answered, "Yes, Lord, you know that I love you." Jesus said, "Take care of my sheep." (Jn. 21:16)

Then Barnabas went to Tarsus to look for Saul, and when he found him, he brought him to Antioch. So for a whole year Barnabas and Saul met with the church and taught great numbers of people. The disciples were called Christians first at Antioch. (Ac. 11:25-26)

Though I am free and belong to no man, I make myself a slave to everyone, to win as many as possible. To the Jews I became like a Jew, to win the Jews. To those under the law I became like one under the law (though I myself am not under the law), so as to win those under the law. (1 Co. 9:19-20)

Carry each other's burdens, and in this way you will fulfill the law of Christ. (Ga. 6:2)

Therefore, as we have opportunity, let us do good to all people, especially to those who belong to the family of believers. (Ga. 6:10)

Snatch others from the fire and save them; to others show mercy, mixed with fear—hating even the clothing stained by corrupted flesh. (Jude 23)

The fruit of the righteous is a tree of life, and he who wins souls is wise. (Pr. 11:30)

Those who are wise will shine like the brightness of the heavens, and those who lead many to righteousness, like the stars for ever and ever. (Da. 12:3)

Thought 2. One thing is absolutely essential before serving God: approaching God through the sacrifice of the Lord Jesus Christ. The Levites had to approach God through the sacrifice laid upon the altar. That sacrifice was a symbol of Christ's sacrifice. Before a person serves God, he must make sure that he has been cleansed from sin and has received the atonement or reconciliation with God. Forgiveness and atonement come only through the blood of Christ. God accepts only those who come to Him through Christ. Christ alone bore the judgment of God against sin for us—which was death. Christ died for us. Therefore, a person must accept the death of Christ as his substitute, in his place. Once he identifies with Christ, he is accepted by God. The person is then ready to step forth to serve God.

The next day John saw Jesus coming toward him and said, "Look, the Lamb of God, who takes away the sin of the world! (Jn 1:29)

Get rid of the old yeast that you may be a new batch without yeast—as you really are. For Christ, our Passover lamb, has been sacrificed. (1 Co. 5:7)

Christ redeemed us from the curse of the law by becoming a curse for us, for it is written: "Cursed is everyone who is hung on a tree." (Ga. 3:13)

And live a life of love, just as Christ loved us and gave himself up for us as a fragrant offering and sacrifice to God. (Ep. 5:2)

Since the children have flesh and blood, he too shared in their humanity so that by his death he might destroy him who holds the power of death—that is, the devil—and free those who all their lives were held in slavery by their fear of death. (He. 2:14-15)

So Christ was sacrificed once to take away the sins of many people; and he will appear a second time, not to bear sin, but to bring salvation to those who are waiting for him. (He. 9:28)

For you know that it was not with perishable things such as silver or gold that you were redeemed from the empty way of life handed down to you from your forefathers, but with the precious blood of Christ, a lamb without blemish or defect. (1 Pe. 1:18-19)

He himself bore our sins in his body on the tree, so that we might die to sins and live for righteousness; by his wounds you have been healed. (1 Pe. 2:24)

For Christ died for sins once for all, the righteous for the unrighteous, to bring you to God. He was put to death in the body but made alive by the Spirit. (1 Pe. 3:18)

But he was pierced for our transgressions, he was crushed for our iniquities; the punishment that brought us peace was upon him, and by his wounds we are healed. (Is. 53:5)

TYPES, SYMBOLS, AND PICTURES
(Numbers 8:1-26)

Historical Term	Type or Picture (Scriptural Basis for Each)	Life Application for Today's Believer	Biblical Application
The Lampstand Nu. 8:1-4 (See also Le. 24:1-4)	*The Lampstand is a symbol that the way into God's presence always shines brightly—is always open for*	The way into God's presence can be clearly seen through Jesus Christ. In fact, the brightest light ever	*In him was life, and that life was the light of men. (Jn. 1:4)* *When Jesus spoke again*

NUMBERS 8:1-26

Historical Term	Type or Picture (Scriptural Basis for Each)	Life Application for Today's Believer	Biblical Application
	people to approach God. The Lampstand is a symbol of Christ, the Light of the world. Jesus Christ gives a clear light and open access into the presence of God. "Speak to Aaron and say to him, 'When you set up the seven lamps, they are to light the area in front of the lampstand.'" (Nu. 8:2)	lived is the light of Christ that shows the way into God's presence. Through Christ, the way into God's presence has been lit so brightly that it is wide open. There is not a single barrier, not even the slightest shadow of a barrier, between man and God. Again, the most brightly lit light every created has been set ablaze by Christ Jesus, the Son of God Himself. He is the Light of the universe, giving light into God's presence.	*to the people, he said, "I am the light of the world. Whoever follows me will never walk in darkness, but will have the light of life." (Jn. 8:12)* *I have come into the world as a light, so that no one who believes in me should stay in darkness. (Jn. 12:46)* *For God, who said, "Let light shine out of darkness," made his light shine in our hearts to give us the light of the knowledge of the glory of God in the face of Christ. (2 Co. 4:6)* *The city does not need the sun or the moon to shine on it, for the glory of God gives it light, and the Lamb is its lamp. (Re. 21:23)*
12 Loaves of the Bread of the Presence Nu. 8:1-4	*The light of the Lampstand focused upon the 12 loaves of the bread of the Presence, a symbol of the 12 tribes of Israel (God's people).* "Over the table of the Presence they are to spread a blue cloth and put on it the plates, dishes and bowls, and the jars for drink offerings; the bread that is continually there is to remain on it." (Nu. 4:7)	The light of God's presence shines upon the true believer. God gives light to His people: His love, care, provision, direction, guidance, knowledge, wisdom. God's light gives whatever is necessary to overcome the pitfalls and enemies of this life.	*The LORD remembers us and will bless us: He will bless the house of Israel, he will bless the house of Aaron. (Ps. 115:12)* *So do not fear, for I am with you; do not be dismayed, for I am your God. I will strengthen you and help you; I will uphold you with my righteous right hand. (Is. 41:10)* *For the pagans run after all these things, and your heavenly Father knows that you need them. (Mt. 6:32)* *Indeed, the very hairs of your head are all numbered. Don't be afraid; you are worth more than many sparrows. (Lu. 12:7)* *Cast all your anxiety on him because he cares for you. (1 Pe. 5:7)*
The Dedication of the Levites Nu. 8:5-26	*The dedication of the Levites is a picture of laypersons being set apart to God, to His service.* *There is a sharp distinction between the Levites and the priests, a distinction that stresses the difference between a layperson who serves as an assistant and the priest or minister of God.* The Expositor's Bible Commentary *points out these differences:* *"The Priests were made holy, the Levites clean; the priests were anointed and washed, the Levites sprin-*	Each believer, each layperson, has been given the glorious privilege… • of being given a very special task upon earth. • of being given purpose and meaning and significance in life. • of being given a very special gift or gifts to fulfill his task on earth.	*And now, O Israel, what does the LORD your God ask of you but to fear the LORD your God, to walk in all his ways, to love him, to serve the LORD your God with all your heart and with all your soul. (De. 10:12)* *For we are God's fellow workers; you are God's field, God's building. (1 Co. 3:9)* *Serve wholeheartedly, as if you were serving the Lord, not men. (Ep. 6:7)* *We loved you so much that we were delighted to share with you not only the gospel of God but our lives as well, because you*

NUMBERS 8:1-26

Historical Term	Type or Picture (Scriptural Basis for Each)	Life Application for Today's Believer	Biblical Application
	kled; the priests were given new garments, the Levites washed theirs; blood was applied to the priests, it was waved over the Levites."[2] "This applies to the Levites: Men twenty-five years old or more shall come to take part in the work at the Tent of Meeting. (Nu. 8:24)		*had become so dear to us. (1 Th. 2:8)* *Therefore, since we are receiving a kingdom that cannot be shaken, let us be thankful, and so worship God acceptably with reverence and awe. (He. 12:28)*
The Levites Had to Be Sprinkled with the Water of Cleansing, Shave Their Whole Heads, and Wash Their Clothes Nu. 8:5-26	*This was a symbol of being spiritually cleansed or purified from sin.* "Take the Levites from among the other Israelites and make them ceremonially clean. To purify them, do this: Sprinkle the water of cleansing on them; then have them shave their whole bodies and wash their clothes, and so purify themselves." (Nu. 8:6-7)	No person can cleanse himself, not spiritually, not from sin. Only God's mediator, Jesus Christ, can wash and cleanse a person spiritually. This He does through the blood of His cross.	*'And now what are you waiting for? Get up, be baptized and wash your sins away, calling on his name.' (Ac. 22:16)* *In him we have redemption through his blood, the forgiveness of sins, in accordance with the riches of God's grace. (Ep. 1:7)* *How much more, then, will the blood of Christ, who through the eternal Spirit offered himself unblemished to God, cleanse our consciences from acts that lead to death, so that we may serve the living God! (He. 9:14)*

---

[2] *The Expositor's Bible Commentary,* Frank E. Gaebelein, Editor, p.766.

NUMBERS 9:1–10:10

CHAPTER 9

H. The Three Special Provisions of God: God's Great Deliverance, His Guidance, & His Call to Arise & Follow Him, 9:1-10:10

1. **The provision of the Passover: A symbol of God's great deliverance**
   a. God's command to keep the Passover: Given in the 1st month of the 2nd year
      1) To be celebrated at the appointed time: At twilight of the 1st month, the 14th day
      2) To be careful—follow all the rules governing the Passover
      3) The obedience: Moses & the people did everything exactly as the Lord commanded
   b. God's compassion & grace—a very special provision for the unclean & the traveler
      1) The problem: Some persons were unable to celebrate the Passover because they had been in touch with a dead body & were counted unclean (ceremonially, spiritually)
         • They wanted to participate, so they approached Moses
         • Moses told them to wait until he could seek the Lord's will
      2) The compassion & grace of God—a very special provision was made for the unclean & for the person away on a journey
         • They may celebrate the Passover one month later (after they are declared cleansed)
         • They must be careful to follow all the regulations: To eat the lamb with unleavened bread & bitter herbs, not leaving any of it until

1 The LORD spoke to Moses in the Desert of Sinai in the first month of the second year after they came out of Egypt. He said,
2 "Have the Israelites celebrate the Passover at the appointed time.
3 Celebrate it at the appointed time, at twilight on the fourteenth day of this month, in accordance with all its rules and regulations."
4 So Moses told the Israelites to celebrate the Passover,
5 And they did so in the Desert of Sinai at twilight on the fourteenth day of the first month. The Israelites did everything just as the LORD commanded Moses.
6 But some of them could not celebrate the Passover on that day because they were ceremonially unclean on account of a dead body. So they came to Moses and Aaron that same day
7 And said to Moses, "We have become unclean because of a dead body, but why should we be kept from presenting the LORD's offering with the other Israelites at the appointed time?"
8 Moses answered them, "Wait until I find out what the LORD commands concerning you."
9 Then the LORD said to Moses,
10 "Tell the Israelites: 'When any of you or your descendants are unclean because of a dead body or are away on a journey, they may still celebrate the LORD's Passover.
11 They are to celebrate it on the fourteenth day of the second month at twilight. They are to eat the lamb, together with unleavened bread and bitter herbs.
12 They must not leave any of it till morning or break any of its bones. When they celebrate the Passover, they must follow all the regulations.
13 But if a man who is ceremonially clean and not on a journey fails to celebrate the Passover, that person must be cut off from his people because he did not present the LORD's offering at the appointed time. That man will bear the consequences of his sin.
14 " 'An alien living among you who wants to celebrate the LORD's Passover must do so in accordance with its rules and regulations. You must have the same regulations for the alien and the native-born.' "
15 On the day the tabernacle, the Tent of the Testimony, was set up, the cloud covered it. From evening till morning the cloud above the tabernacle looked like fire.
16 That is how it continued to be; the cloud covered it, and at night it looked like fire.
17 Whenever the cloud lifted from above the Tent, the Israelites set out; wherever the cloud settled, the Israelites encamped.
18 At the LORD's command the Israelites set out, and at his command they encamped. As long as the cloud stayed over the tabernacle, they remained in camp.
19 When the cloud remained over the tabernacle a long time, the Israelites obeyed the LORD's order and did not set out.
20 Sometimes the cloud was over the tabernacle only a few days; at the LORD's command they would encamp, and then at his command they would set out.
21 Sometimes the cloud stayed only from evening till morning, and when it lifted in the morning, they set out. Whether by day or by night, whenever the cloud lifted, they set out.
22 Whether the cloud stayed over the tabernacle for two days or a month or a year, the Israelites would remain in camp and not set out; but when it lifted, they would set out.

morning nor breaking any of its bones
   c. God's strong warning: The Passover is of critical importance—a person must keep it (a picture of the importance of the Lord's Supper)
      1) The person who deliberately failed to keep it: To be cut off
      2) The person will suffer God's judgment
   d. God's open invitation to all, to the alien or foreigner
      1) The open door: Any person could observe the Passover
      2) The one restriction: He must be a believer (Ex. 12:48) & observe the Passover as instructed
2. **The provision of the fiery cloud: A symbol of God's presence & guidance**^{DS1}
   a. The cloud came down & hovered above the Tabernacle
   b. The cloud changed into a fiery cloud at night—so the people could continue to see it: Symbolized the continued, unbroken presence & guidance of God
   c. The cloud guided the Israelites
      1) If it lifted & moved, the people followed
      2) If it settled, the people camped
   d. The cloud was one of the ways the Lord commanded or spoke to His people: At His command, they would either set out or stop & camp
      1) If the cloud stayed over the Tabernacle, God was commanding His people to remain in camp
         • Sometimes for long periods of time
         • Sometimes for only a few days

         • Sometimes for only one night
      2) If the cloud lifted by day or by night, they followed

      3) If the cloud stayed above the Tabernacle for two days or one month or one year, they stayed & did not move; but if it lifted, they followed
      4) The people obeyed the

86

NUMBERS 9:1–10:10

Lord's command • Obeyed God's command to camp or travel • Obeyed God's Word—the movement of the cloud—when instructed by Moses, God's servant	23 At the LORD's command they encamped, and at the LORD's command they set out. They obeyed the LORD's order, in accordance with his command through Moses. **CHAPTER 10** The LORD said to Moses: 2 "Make two trumpets of hammered silver, and use them for calling the community together and for having the camps set out. 3 When both are sounded, the whole community is to assemble before you at the entrance to the Tent of Meeting. 4 If only one is sounded, the leaders—the heads of the clans of Israel—are to assemble before you. 5 When a trumpet blast is sounded, the tribes camping on the east are to set out. 6 At the sounding of a sec-	ond blast, the camps on the south are to set out. The blast will be the signal for setting out. 7 To gather the assembly, blow the trumpets, but not with the same signal. 8 "The sons of Aaron, the priests, are to blow the trumpets. This is to be a lasting ordinance for you and the generations to come. 9 When you go into battle in your own land against an enemy who is oppressing you, sound a blast on the trumpets. Then you will be remembered by the Lord your God and rescued from your enemies. 10 Also at your times of rejoicing—your appointed feasts and New Moon festivals—you are to sound the trumpets over your burnt offerings and fellowship offerings, and they will be a memorial for you before your God. I am the Lord your God."	• march • Another blast signaled the tribes on the south to march • The point: A different signal or blast was to be used for each purpose c. The only persons allowed to blow the trumpets—the priests, the true sons of Aaron: This was to be a permanent law for all generations d. The three very special purposes for the trumpets 1) To sound the alarm for war 2) To sound the alarm for prayer: For God to remember, rescue, & deliver His people 3) To blow in times of joy & rejoicing—at the appointed feasts & New Moon festivals • To sound over the Burnt Offerings & Fellowship or Peace Offerings • To be a memorial, a reminder of God's covenant

3. **The provision of two silver trumpets: A symbol of God's call to arise & follow Him**
   a. The command to fashion the trumpets of hammered silver
   b. The three general purposes for the trumpets
      1) To call the whole community of believers together (blew both trumpets)
      2) To call only the leaders together (blew only one trumpet)
      3) To signal the tribes when to begin marching
         • One blast signaled the tribes on the east to

DIVISION I

THE PREPARATION FOR THE MARCH TO THE PROMISED LAND, 1:1–10:36

H. The Three Special Provisions of God: like God's Great Deliverance, His Guidance, and His Call to Arise and Follow Him, 9:1–10:10

(9:1-10:10) **Introduction—Deliverance, from Enemies—Guidance, of God—Challenge, Need For:** three of the greatest needs people have are the need for deliverance, for guidance, and for a strong challenge. Why do we need deliverance? Because we are enslaved by the enemies of this life, enemies such as...

- cancer
- heart disease
- diabetes
- other diseases
- drugs
- alcohol
- immorality
- pornography
- sin
- greed
- anger
- malice
- death

In addition to deliverance, people need guidance throughout life as they confront the pitfalls and enemies of this life. Decisions often have to be made, decisions that arouse a desire for some guidance that will tell us what to do. But not only do people need deliverance and guidance, they also need a strong challenge in order to give them fulfillment throughout life. People need a sense of purpose, meaning, and significance throughout life. They need to have a sense of satisfaction and fulfillment, a sense that they are accomplishing something in life, making a contribution to loved ones and to society.

What is needed is the very special provision of God Himself. God provides deliverance. He wants to deliver us from the enslavements of this life, deliver us from sin and death to live eternally in the promised land of heaven. But this is not all: God wants to guide us in every decision and step we take day by day. God wants us to have the security and assurance that we are making the right decisions and taking the right steps throughout life. But even this is not all: God wants to challenge us, to give us the greatest challenge that could possibly be given in life. God wants to extend a call to us, a call to arise and follow Him—for He has the greatest purpose, the most meaningful and significant call in all of life. This is the subject of this great passage: *The Three Special Provisions of God: God's Great Deliverance, His Guidance, and His Call to Arise and Follow Him*, 9:1-10:10.

1. The provision of the Passover: a symbol of God's great deliverance (9:1-14).
2. The provision of the fiery cloud: a symbol of God's presence and guidance (9:15-23).
3. The provision of two silver trumpets: a symbol of God's call to arise and follow Him (10:1-10).

1 (9:1-14) **Passover—Lord's Supper, Importance of—Salvation, Celebration of—Deliverance, Celebration of:** the first provision of God focused upon deliverance, the provision of the Passover. The Passover celebrated the great exodus from Egypt, God's great deliverance of His people from Egyptian slavery. Remember that Egypt is a symbol of the world with all its bondages and enslavements. The Passover was instituted by God to stir His people to remember their great deliverance from the slavery of Egypt (the world).

NUMBERS 9:1–10:10

a. God Himself commanded His people to keep the Passover (vv.1-5). It had been one year since God's people had left Egypt, one year since they had celebrated the first Passover. At that time, back in Egypt, God had commanded His people to keep the Passover and to do so every year thereafter. He had established the feast to be a memorial, an annual celebration to remember their great deliverance from Egyptian slavery (Ex. 12:2-3, 14). Why, then, was God now having to remind His people to celebrate the Passover? Were the people going to remember—going to take the initiative on their own—to celebrate the feast? Or were the people careless? Lax? Negligent? Indifferent? Failing? Scripture does not say: it simply says that God once again commanded His people to keep the Passover, the commemoration of their great deliverance from Egyptian slavery.
   1) The people were to celebrate the Passover at the appointed time: at twilight of the first month, the fourteenth day (vv.2-3).
   2) The people were to be careful: make sure that they followed all the rules governing the Passover (v.3).
   3) Note the obedience of Moses and the people: they did everything exactly as the LORD commanded. They kept the Passover (vv.4-5).

b. God showed great compassion and grace in the Passover: He made a very special provision for the unclean and the traveler (vv.6-12).
   1) A very special problem arose at this particular Passover. Some persons were unable to celebrate the Feast because they had been in contact with a dead body and were counted unclean (ceremonially, spiritually unclean). Death is the result of sin, a symbol of corruption and decay. Therefore to illustrate this truth, a person who came in contact with death was counted spiritually unclean. The ceremonial laws of uncleanness stressed the importance of being spiritually clean, the importance of having one's sins forgiven.

   These persons wanted to participate in the Passover, so they approached Moses. Moses simply told them to wait until he could seek the Lord's will (v.8).
   2) Note the compassion and grace of God: a very special provision was made for the unclean and for the person away on a journey (vv.9-12). These persons could celebrate one month later, after they had been declared cleansed. However, they had to be careful to follow all the regulations: to eat the lamb with unleavened bread and bitter herbs, not leaving any of it until morning nor breaking any of its bones (v.12).

c. God issued a strong warning: the Passover was of critical importance. A person must keep it (v.13). This is a picture of the importance of the Lord's Supper. God declared that any person who deliberately failed to keep the Passover was to be cut off. A person will suffer God's judgment. As Gordon J. Wenham points out: "This is a threat of death by the hand of God and of eternal judgment."[1]

d. God extended an open invitation to all, to the alien or foreigner as well as to the native-born (v.14). There was an open door for any person to celebrate the Passover, as long as the person had become a true believer and member of His people. There was only one condition for any person—any foreigner or any native-born—to become a member of God's people: that condition was faith in God, believing and following God exactly as He dictated, approaching Him for the atonement (reconciliation) and forgiveness of sin through the blood of the sacrifice. This was the very purpose for the Abrahamic covenant, to bless all the people and nations of the world (Ge.12:1-3). Therefore, any person who came to God through the blood of the Passover Lamb was acceptable to God.

Thought 1. There are four significant lessons for us in this passage.
(1) Jesus Christ is the true Passover Lamb, the Lamb of God who takes away the sin of the world.

> The next day John saw Jesus coming toward him and said, "Look, the Lamb of God, who takes away the sin of the world!" (Jn. 1:29)
>
> Get rid of the old yeast that you may be a new batch without yeast—as you really are. For Christ, our Passover lamb, has been sacrificed. (1 Co. 5:7)
>
> For you know that it was not with perishable things such as silver or gold that you were redeemed from the empty way of life handed down to you from your forefathers, but with the precious blood of Christ, a lamb without blemish or defect. (1 Pe. 1:18-19)
>
> But he was pierced for our transgressions, he was crushed for our iniquities; the punishment that brought us peace was upon him, and by his wounds we are healed....He was oppressed and afflicted, yet he did not open his mouth; he was led like a lamb to the slaughter, and as a sheep before her shearers is silent, so he did not open his mouth. (Is. 53:5, 7)

(2) God commanded His people in the Old Testament to acknowledge His great deliverance through celebrating the Passover. God commands us to acknowledge His great deliverance by Christ through celebrating the Lord's Supper.

> While they were eating, Jesus took bread, gave thanks and broke it, and gave it to his disciples, saying, "Take and eat; this is my body." Then he took the cup, gave thanks and offered it to them, saying, "Drink from it, all of you. This is my blood of the covenant, which is poured out for many for the forgiveness of sins." (Mt. 26:26-28; see Mk. 14:22-24; Lu. 22:19-20)
>
> For I received from the Lord what I also passed on to you: The Lord Jesus, on the night he was betrayed, took bread, and when he had given thanks, he broke it and said, "This is my body, which is for you; do this in remembrance of me." In the same way, after supper he took the cup, saying, "This cup is the new covenant in my blood; do this, whenever you drink it, in remembrance of me." For whenever you eat this bread and drink this cup, you proclaim the Lord's death until he comes. (1 Co. 11:23-26)

---
[1] Gordon J. Wenham. *The Book of Numbers*, p.99.

NUMBERS 9:1–10:10

(3) God issues a strong warning about the Lord's Supper; the Lord's Supper is of critical importance to Him: a person must not approach nor partake of the Lord's Supper in an unworthy manner. If he does, he brings judgment upon himself. This is exactly what Scripture declares:

> For anyone who eats and drinks without recognizing the body of the Lord eats and drinks judgment on himself. That is why many among you are weak and sick, and a number of you have fallen asleep. (1 Co. 11:29-30)

(4) God extends an invitation to every person to celebrate the Lord's Supper. There is only one condition: believing God, approaching Him for the atonement (reconciliation) and forgiveness of sin through the shed blood of Christ. God opens the door into His presence for any person to be saved and delivered from sin—through the sacrifice of His Son. There is an open invitation to all.

> "Come to me, all you who are weary and burdened, and I will give you rest. (Mt. 11:28)
>
> On the last and greatest day of the Feast, Jesus stood and said in a loud voice, "If anyone is thirsty, let him come to me and drink." (Jn. 7:37)
>
> For what I received I passed on to you as of first importance: that Christ died for our sins according to the Scriptures, that he was buried, that he was raised on the third day according to the Scriptures. (1 Co. 15:3-4)
>
> Who wants all men to be saved and to come to a knowledge of the truth. For there is one God and one mediator between God and men, the man Christ Jesus, who gave himself as a ransom for all men—the testimony given in its proper time. (1 Ti. 2:4-6)
>
> But we see Jesus, who was made a little lower than the angels, now crowned with glory and honor because he suffered death, so that by the grace of God he might taste death for everyone. (He. 2:9)
>
> "Come now, let us reason together," says the LORD. "Though your sins are like scarlet, they shall be as white as snow; though they are red as crimson, they shall be like wool." (Is. 1:18)
>
> "Turn to me and be saved, all you ends of the earth; for I am God, and there is no other." (Is. 45:22)

2 (9:15-23) **Cloud, Pillar of—Guidance, of God—God, Guidance of**: there was the provision of the fiery cloud, that is, the cloud that guided God's people throughout their wilderness wanderings. The cloud was a striking symbol of God's presence and guidance.

a. The cloud came down and hovered above the Tabernacle right after the Tabernacle's dedication (see outline and note—Ex.40:34-38 for more discussion).

b. The cloud changed its appearance at night, changed into a fiery cloud so the people could continue to see it. This symbolized the continued, unbroken presence and guidance of God (vv.15-16). Hovering above the Tabernacle by day and turning into a blazing fire by night—the cloud must have been a striking, awesome sight. Obviously, it gave a great sense of assurance, confidence, comfort, and security. The people knew beyond any question that God was present with them, there to guide and protect them by day and by night.

c. The cloud guided the Israelites (v.17). If it lifted and moved, the people followed. If it settled, the people camped.

d. Note the clear statement of this point: the cloud was one of the ways the LORD commanded His people—one of the ways He spoke to His people. At His command, that is, as the cloud moved, the people would either set out or stop and camp (vv.18-23).

1) If the cloud stayed over the Tabernacle, God was commanding His people to remain in the camp (vv.18-21). Sometimes they remained in camp for long periods of time; sometimes they stayed for only a few days; and sometimes they remained for only one night. Simply stated, the cloud was one of the ways God used to speak to His people and guide them to the promised land.

2) If the cloud lifted by day or by night, they followed (v.21).

3) If the cloud stayed above the Tabernacle for two days or one month or one year, the people stayed and did not move. But if the cloud lifted, they followed it (v.22).

4) The people obeyed the LORD's command by the movement of the cloud (v.23). They obeyed God's command to camp or travel as He willed. They obeyed God's Word—the movement of the cloud—when instructed by Moses, God's servant.

Thought 1. The fiery cloud was a striking, awesome picture of God's presence and guidance.

(1) God is present with His people, always present. God never leaves the side of a person who truly believes in Him. God is always with us in an unbroken fellowship until we reach the promised land of heaven. His presence walks with us day by day.

> "For where two or three come together in my name, there am I with them." (Mt. 18:20)
>
> And surely I am with you always, to the very end of the age. (Mt. 28:20)
>
> "I am with you and will watch over you wherever you go, and I will bring you back to this land. I will not leave you until I have done what I have promised you." (Ge. 28:15)
>
> The LORD replied, "My Presence will go with you, and I will give you rest." (Ex. 33:14)
>
> When you go to war against your enemies and see horses and chariots and an army greater than yours, do not be afraid of them, because the Lord your God, who brought you up out of Egypt, will be with you. (De. 20:1)
>
> When you pass through the waters, I will be with you; and when you pass through the rivers, they will not sweep over you. When you walk through the fire, you will not be burned; the flames will not set you ablaze. (Is. 43:2)

NUMBERS 9:1–10:10

(2) God guides His people, always guides us. If a person truly believes and follows God, God guides his every step day by day. God guides us every step of the way as we march to the promised land of heaven.

> But when he, the Spirit of truth, comes, he will guide you into all truth. He will not speak on his own; he will speak only what he hears, and he will tell you what is yet to come. (Jn. 16:13)

> He makes me lie down in green pastures, he leads me beside quiet waters. (Ps. 23:2)

> He guides the humble in what is right and teaches them his way. (Ps. 25:9)

> For this God is our God for ever and ever; he will be our guide even to the end. (Ps. 48:14)

> You guide me with your counsel, and afterward you will take me into glory. (Ps. 73:24)

> Whether you turn to the right or to the left, your ears will hear a voice behind you, saying, "This is the way; walk in it." (Is. 30:21)

DEEPER STUDY #1

(9:15-23) **God, Presence of—Glory, of God—Pillar of Cloud—Cloud, Pillar of—Shekinah Glory**: the cloud of God's presence hovered, settled, rested, dwelt above the Tabernacle. The Hebrew word is shakan or sakan. This was the Shekinah Glory, the very glory of God dwelling in the midst of His people. The Shekinah Glory was the cloud that symbolized God's holy presence. It was the very cloud that had guided Israel out of Egypt and that was to rest upon the Tabernacle as long as His people remained totally obedient to Him (Ex.40:34-38). The Shekinah Glory also rested above the Mercy Seat in the Most Holy Place of the Tabernacle. Scripture describes the Shekinah Glory of the LORD as follows:

1. The glory of the LORD is like a consuming fire.

> To the Israelites the glory of the LORD looked like a consuming fire on top of the mountain. (Ex. 24:17).

2. The glory of the LORD is like a pillar of fire that radiates light.

> By day the LORD went ahead of them in a pillar of cloud to guide them on their way and by night in a pillar of fire to give them light, so that they could travel by day or night. Neither the pillar of cloud by day nor the pillar of fire by night left its place in front of the people. (Ex. 13:21-22)

3. The glory of the LORD is like a fiery furnace.

> You have not come to a mountain that can be touched and that is burning with fire; to darkness, gloom and storm....for our "God is a consuming fire." (He. 12:18, 29).

4. The glory of the LORD is like a light that radiates splendor, a light that is so full of splendor that Peter called "the Majestic Glory."

> For he received honor and glory from God the Father when the voice came to him from the Majestic Glory, saying, "This is my Son, whom I love; with him I am well pleased." (2 Pe. 1:17).

5. The glory of the LORD is a light so glorious and brilliant that there is no need for a sun.

> It shone with the glory of God, and its brilliance was like that of a very precious jewel, like a jasper, clear as crystal....The city does not need the sun or the moon to shine on it, for the glory of the God gives it light, and the Lamb is its lamp. (Re. 21:11, 23).

6. The glory of the LORD is a light so brilliant that no man approach it.

> Who alone is immortal and who lives in unapproachable light, whom no one has seen or can see. To him be honor and might forever. Amen. (1 Ti. 6:16).

3 (10:1-10) **Provision, of God—God, Provision of—Trumpets, the Two Silver**: there was the provision of two silver trumpets, a symbol of God's call to arise and follow Him. The Israelites were just about ready to begin their great march to the promised land. One final thing remained: the making of two silver trumpets to control and coordinate the people as they marched through the wilderness to the promised land. Other trumpeters were, no doubt, strategically stationed throughout the tribal camps to pass the signal along to those on the outer edges. Keep in mind that there were at least two to three million Israelites camped around the Tabernacle. It was only natural that the two main trumpets stationed at the Tabernacle, the hub of activity, would be very special trumpets.

a. God Himself gave the command to fashion the trumpets. They were to be made of hammered silver (v.2). No one knows exactly how they were shaped; but it is generally felt they were long, straight pipes, with a flared opening at the end. They could be blown to make different sounds or signals.

b. There were three *general purposes* for the trumpets (vv.3-7).

   1) The trumpets were used to call the whole community of believers for general assemblies. Note that both trumpets were blown to call the people together.

   2) The trumpets were used to call only the leaders together. Only one trumpet was used to signal the leaders (v.4).

   3) The trumpets were used to signal the tribes when to begin marching (vv.5-7). Note that one blast signaled the tribes on the east to march; another blast signaled the tribes on the south to march. That is, a different signal or blast was used for each purpose.

c. Note that the only persons allowed to blow the trumpets were the priests, the true sons of Aaron. This was to be a permanent law for all generations (v.8).

d. There were three very *special purposes* for the trumpets (vv.9-10). Keep in mind that we have already looked

at three general purposes; now, Scripture gives three very *special purposes* for the trumpets.
1) The trumpets were to sound the alarm for war (v.9). Both trumpets were to be used to sound forth the battle cry for mobilization against an enemy.
2) The trumpets were to sound the alarm for prayer: this is a picture of prayer arousing God to remember, rescue, and deliver His people.
3) The trumpets were used to blow in times of joy and rejoicing—at the appointed feasts and New Moon festival (v.10). The trumpets were to be sounded over the Burnt Offerings and the Fellowship or Peace Offerings. They were to be a memorial, a reminder of God's covenant with His people and their covenant with Him.

Note the strong declaration: "I am the LORD your God." God is declaring that He is the Sovereign, Omnipotent, Omniscient LORD God of the universe. He is the only living and true God with the power to rescue and deliver His people. Therefore they must sound the trumpet alarm for prayer: for Him to arouse Himself and act in behalf of His people—rescuing and delivering them from their enemies.

Thought 1. The trumpets were a picture of God calling His people to arise and follow Him. So it is with us. God calls us to arise and follow Him to the promised land of God, to heaven itself.

> When Jesus spoke again to the people, he said, "I am the light of the world. Whoever follows me will never walk in darkness, but will have the light of life." (Jn. 8:12)
> My sheep listen to my voice; I know them, and they follow me. (Jn. 10:27)
> Whoever serves me must follow me; and where I am, my servant also will be. My Father will honor the one who serves me. (Jn. 12:26)
> We live by faith, not by sight. (2 Co. 5:7)
> So I say, live by the Spirit, and you will not gratify the desires of the sinful nature. (Ga. 5:16)
> As a prisoner for the Lord, then, I urge you to live a life worthy of the calling you have received. (Ep. 4:1)
> And live a life of love, just as Christ loved us and gave himself up for us as a fragrant offering and sacrifice to God. (Ep. 5:2)
> Be very careful, then, how you live—not as unwise but as wise. (Ep. 5:15)
> So then, just as you received Christ Jesus as Lord, continue to live in him. (Col. 2:6)
> To this you were called, because Christ suffered for you, leaving you an example, that you should follow in his steps. (1 Pe. 2:21)
> But if we walk in the light, as he is in the light, we have fellowship with one another, and the blood of Jesus, his Son, purifies us from all sin. (1 Jn. 1:7)

Thought 2. What a strong exhortation for believers today: to sound the alarm for prayer, to cry out to God for Him to rescue and deliver us from the pitfalls and enemies of life.

> "Ask and it will be given to you; seek and you will find; knock and the door will be opened to you." (Mt. 7:7)
> "Watch and pray so that you will not fall into temptation. The spirit is willing, but the body is weak." (Mt. 26:41)
> Then Jesus told his disciples a parable to show them that they should always pray and not give up. (Lu. 18:1)
> If you remain in me and my words remain in you, ask whatever you wish, and it will be given you. (Jn. 15:7)
> And pray in the Spirit on all occasions with all kinds of prayers and requests. With this in mind, be alert and always keep on praying for all the saints. (Ep. 6:18)
> Pray continually. (1 Th. 5:17)
> But if from there you seek the LORD your God, you will find him if you look for him with all your heart and with all your soul. (De. 4:29)
> Look to the LORD and his strength; seek his face always. (1 Chr. 16:11)
> This poor man called, and the LORD heard him; he saved him out of all his troubles. (Ps. 34:6)
> From the ends of the earth I call to you, I call as my heart grows faint; lead me to the rock that is higher than I. (Ps. 61:2)
> He will call upon me, and I will answer him; I will be with him in trouble, I will deliver him and honor him. (Ps. 91:15)
> Then you will call, and the LORD will answer; you will cry for help, and he will say: Here am I. "If you do away with the yoke of oppression, with the pointing finger and malicious talk." (Is. 58:9)

NUMBERS 9:1–10:10

TYPES, SYMBOLS, AND PICTURES
(Numbers 9:10–10:10)

Historical Term	Type or Picture (Scriptural Basis for Each)	Life Application for Today's Believer	Biblical Application
The Passover Nu. 9:1-14 (See also Le. 23:5)	*The Passover is a symbol of Christ our Passover who was sacrificed for us.* *So Moses told the Israelites to celebrate the Passover, and they did so in the Desert of Sinai at twilight on the fourteenth day of the first month. The Israelites did everything just as the L*ORD *commanded Moses. (Nu. 9:4-5)*	The believer who lives and walks in Christ will be directed by God. 1. He will know God's purpose for his life (see all notes—Mt. 4:12-17). 2. He will know when to go forth to his task, when to carry out God's purpose for his life—just as Christ knew.	*The next day John saw Jesus coming toward him and said, "Look, the Lamb of God, who takes away the sin of the world" (Jn. 1:29)* *For Christ, our Passover lamb, has been sacrificed. (1 Co. 5:7)* *He was oppressed and afflicted, yet he did not open his mouth; he was led like a lamb to the slaughter, and as a sheep before her shearers is silent, so he did not open his mouth. (Is. 53:7)*
Pillar of Cloud Nu. 9:15-23	*The pillar of cloud was a symbol of God's presence and guidance.* *Sometimes the cloud stayed only from evening till morning, and when it lifted in the morning, they set out. Whether by day or by night, whenever the cloud lifted, they set out. Whether the cloud stayed over the tabernacle for two days or a month or a year, the Israelites would remain in camp and not set out; but when it lifted, they would set out. (Nu. 9:21-22)*	Jesus Christ is the perfect fulfillment of the Passover Lamb that was slain in behalf of God's people. Through the blood of Jesus Christ, a person escapes the judgment of God. God accepts the blood of His Son—the blood of the substitute sacrifice—as full payment for a person's sin and rebellion against God.	*But when he, the Spirit of truth, comes, he will guide you into all truth. He will not speak on his own; he will speak only what he hears, and he will tell you what is yet to come. (Jn. 16:13)* *Who gave himself for our sins to rescue us from the present evil age, according to the will of our God and Father. (Ga. 1:4)* *He guides the humble in what is right and teaches them his way. (Ps. 25:9)* *For this God is our God for ever and ever; he will be our guide even to the end. (Ps. 48:14)* *You guide me with your counsel, and afterward you will take me into glory. (Ps. 73:24)* *Whether you turn to the right or to the left, your ears will hear a voice behind you, saying, "This is the way; walk in it." (Is. 30:21)* *I will lead the blind by ways they have not known, along unfamiliar paths I will guide them; I will turn the darkness into light before them and make the rough places smooth. These are the things I will do; I will not forsake them. (Is. 42:16)* *This is what the L*ORD *says—your Redeemer, the Holy One of Israel: "I am the L*ORD *your God, who teaches you what is best for you, who directs you in the way you should go." (Is. 48:17)*

NUMBERS 10:11-36

CHAPTER 10

I. The Great March to the Promised Land Finally Begins: A Picture of the Believer Finally Beginning His March to the Promised Land of Heaven, 10:11-36

1. **The great day to begin the march arrived: A picture of great hope for the promised land**
   a. The date: The cloud lifted on the 20th day of the 2nd month (spent about 11 months at Mt. Sinai)
   b. The first part of the journey: Traveled from place to place until they reached the Desert of Paran
2. **The great army of God's people marched forth division by division—as commanded: A picture of obeying God as one marches to the promised land**
   a. First, the divisions of Judah led the march under their standard: Commanded by Nahshon
      1) The division of Issachar marched with Judah: Commanded by Nethanel
      2) The division of Zebulun marched with Judah: Commanded by Eliab
   b. Second, the Gershonites & the Merarites followed with the carts & oxen transporting the frame & curtains of the Tabernacle
   c. Third, the divisions of Reuben marched under their standard: Commanded by Elizur
      1) The division of Simeon marched with Reuben: Commanded by Shelumiel
      2) The division of Gad marched with Reuben: Commanded by Eliasaph
   d. Fourth, the Kohathites followed carrying the holy things of the Tabernacle: It was to be set up when they arrived
   e. Fifth, the divisions of Ephraim marched under their standard: Commanded by Elishama
      1) The division of Manasseh marched with Ephraim: Commanded by Gamaliel

11 On the twentieth day of the second month of the second year, the cloud lifted from above the tabernacle of the Testimony.
12 Then the Israelites set out from the Desert of Sinai and traveled from place to place until the cloud came to rest in the Desert of Paran.
13 They set out, this first time, at the LORD's command through Moses.
14 The divisions of the camp of Judah went first, under their standard. Nahshon son of Amminadab was in command.
15 Nethanel son of Zuar was over the division of the tribe of Issachar,
16 And Eliab son of Helon was over the division of the tribe of Zebulun.
17 Then the tabernacle was taken down, and the Gershonites and Merarites, who carried it, set out.
18 The divisions of the camp of Reuben went next, under their standard. Elizur son of Shedeur was in command.
19 Shelumiel son of Zurishaddai was over the division of the tribe of Simeon,
20 and Eliasaph son of Deuel was over the division of the tribe of Gad.
21 Then the Kohathites set out, carrying the holy things. The tabernacle was to be set up before they arrived.
22 The divisions of the camp of Ephraim went next, under their standard. Elishama son of Ammihud was in command.
23 Gamaliel son of Pedahzur was over the division of the tribe of Manasseh,
24 And Abidan son of Gideoni was over the division of the tribe of Benjamin.
25 Finally, as the rear guard for all the units, the divisions of the camp of Dan set out, under their standard. Ahiezer son of Ammishaddai was in command.
26 Pagiel son of Ocran was over the division of the tribe of Asher,
27 And Ahira son of Enan was over the division of the tribe of Naphtali.
28 This was the order of march for the Israelite divisions as they set out.
29 Now Moses said to Hobab son of Reuel the Midianite, Moses' father-in-law, "We are setting out for the place about which the LORD said, 'I will give it to you.' Come with us and we will treat you well, for the LORD has promised good things to Israel."
30 He answered, "No, I will not go; I am going back to my own land and my own people."
31 But Moses said, "Please do not leave us. You know where we should camp in the desert, and you can be our eyes.
32 If you come with us, we will share with you whatever good things the LORD gives us."
33 So they set out from the mountain of the LORD and traveled for three days. The ark of the covenant of the LORD went before them during those three days to find them a place to rest.
34 The cloud of the LORD was over them by day when they set out from the camp.
35 Whenever the ark set out, Moses said, "Rise up, O LORD! May your enemies be scattered; may your foes flee before you."
36 Whenever it came to rest, he said, "Return, O LORD, to the countless thousands of Israel."

   2) The division of Benjamin marched with Ephraim: Commanded by Abidan
   f. Finally, the divisions of Dan marched as the rear guard, under its standard: Commanded by Ahiezer
      1) The division of Asher marched with Dan: Commanded by Pagiel
      2) The division of Naphtali marched with Dan: Commanded by Ahira

3. **The appeal of Moses to his brother-in-law to join the march to the promised land: A picture of reaching out to family members to follow after the promised land of God, the promise of heaven**
   a. The brother-in-law rejected the appeal: His old life appealed to him
   b. The second appeal of Moses
      1) Challenged his brother-in-law to serve as a guide to the people of God
      2) Promised to share the good things of the LORD with him

4. **The faithfulness of God in leading His people**
   a. The first part of the journey lasted three days
   b. The ark of the covenant was carried out front, ahead of all the tribes: A symbol of the LORD's leadership step by step
   c. The fiery cloud of the LORD led them

5. **The battle cry—the great expectation & cry of Moses: Victory & rest**
   a. When the ark set out: That God would give a victorious march
   b. When the ark was set down: That God would come among His people & give them rest—both physical & spiritual rest

DIVISION I

THE PREPARATION FOR THE MARCH TO THE PROMISED LAND, 1:1–10:36

NUMBERS 10:11-36

I. The Great March to the Promised Land Finally Begins: A Picture of the Believer Finally Beginning His March to the Promised Land of Heaven, 10:11-36

(10:11-36) **Introduction—Destiny, of Man—Destiny, of the World—Promised Land, Hope For—Future, Destiny of**: What is the destiny of man? More technological and scientific and medical advances? No doubt, this will be true and will come to pass. Will there be pure air and pure water to drink? Will there be plenty of food for all the people of the earth? Some authorities say this is questionable. Pollution could contaminate the water we drink and the air we breathe. Greed and selfishness and war could, as they always have, affect the amount of food we have and whether or not everyone in the world will have enough to eat. Will there be peace and security in the world? Will lawlessness and violence continue to increase throughout the world? Will terrorist acts increase or decrease?

What is the destiny of man, of the world, out in the future? Is man's destiny bleak and dismal or hopeful? Or is it both? No person has the answer about the future, not totally. Even the most intelligent among us can only speculate and guess at what will happen. This is particularly true when the long-range future is evaluated. However, there is one destiny that awaits every human being, one terrible event that will happen to every one of us: death. It is the destiny of every man to die and then to face the judgment of God. But this is not the final word, thankfully. God declares a wonderful truth: there is the promised land of heaven lying out in the future. Moreover, every human being can enter the promised land and live eternally in God's presence. God declares that He is going to destroy the present heavens and earth, that all the elements are going to melt with fervent heat (2 Pe. 3:10-13). Moreover, God declares that He is going to make a new heavens and earth and that every genuine believer is going to be a citizen of that new world. This is the great hope and expectation of the promised land of heaven. When God speaks of heaven, He is talking about a new heavens and earth—a new world.

The point is this: God longs for every human being to live with Him in the promised land of heaven. But to do this a person has to approach God through the sacrifice of His Son, to approach Him for the atonement (reconciliation with God) and for forgiveness. God longs for every human being to join believers in their march to the promised land of heaven. God wants to guide and help every human being as he marches through this life. God wants to give triumph and victory over all the pitfalls and enemies of this life. But He can help only those who will let Him help, only those who will come to Him through Christ, and join in the great march to the promised land of heaven. This is the subject of this great passage of Scripture: *The Great March to the Promised Land Finally Begins: A Picture of the Believer Finally Beginning His March to the Promised Land of Heaven*, 10:11-36.

1. The great day to begin the march arrived: a picture of great hope for the promised land (vv.11-12).
2. The great army of God's people marched forth division by division—as commanded: a picture of obeying God as one marches to the promised land (vv.13-28).
3. The appeal of Moses to his brother-in-law to join the march to the promised land: a picture of reaching out to family members to follow after the promised land of God, the promise of heaven (vv.29-32).
4. The faithfulness of God in leading His people (vv.33-34).
5. The battle cry—the great expectation and cry of Moses: victory and rest (vv.35-36).

1 (10:11-12) **March, to the Promised Land—Land, the Promised—Promised Land, March to—Great Days—Symbol, of Salvation**: the great day to begin the march to the promised land finally arrived. At last, God's people were to move out and begin their triumphant journey to the promised land. This was a day for which the Israelites had longed with great expectation and hope, a day that would be inscribed on their minds forever. For believers of every generation, this is a picture of great expectation and hope for the promised land, the great expectation and hope of living forever with God.

a. Note the date of departure for the promised land: the cloud lifted on the 20th day of the 2nd month. This means that they had spent about 11 months at Mt. Sinai. This was a day that would never be forgotten by God's people, the day when the cloud of His presence indicated that their march to the promised land was now to begin.

b. Note the first part of the journey: they traveled from place to place until they reached the Desert of Paran (v.12). The Israelites made at least three stops on this leg of their journey: Taberah (11:3), Kibroth Hattaavah (11:35), and Hazeroth (11:35). (See Map—Nu. 33:5-49 for the location of each and the Wilderness Wanderings.)

> **Thought 1.** The Israelites had a great hope for the promised land, a great expectation of reaching the promised land of God. This is a great lesson for believers of all generations. We are to hold a great expectation and hope for the promised land of heaven, for living forever in the presence of God. With great expectation and hope, we are to look for the return of our Lord Jesus Christ.
>
> **In my Father's house are many rooms; if it were not so, I would have told you. I am going there to prepare a place for you. And if I go and prepare a place for you, I will come back and take you to be with me that you also may be where I am. (Jn. 14:2-3)**
>
> **But Stephen, full of the Holy Spirit, looked up to heaven and saw the glory of God, and Jesus standing at the right hand of God. "Look," he said, "I see heaven open and the Son of Man standing at the right hand of God." (Ac.7:55-56)**
>
> **Now we know that if the earthly tent we live in is destroyed, we have a building from God, an eternal house in heaven, not built by human hands. (2 Co. 5:1)**
>
> **But our citizenship is in heaven. And we eagerly await a Savior from there, the Lord Jesus Christ, who, by the power that enables him to bring everything under his control, will transform our lowly bodies so that they will be like his glorious body. (Ph. 3:20-21)**
>
> **It teaches us to say "No" to ungodliness and worldly passions, and to live self-controlled, upright and godly lives in this present age, while we wait for the blessed hope—the glorious appearing of our great God and Savior, Jesus Christ. (Tit. 2:12-13)**

NUMBERS 10:11-36

By faith Abraham, when called to go to a place he would later receive as his inheritance, obeyed and went, even though he did not know where he was going. By faith he made his home in the promised land like a stranger in a foreign country; he lived in tents, as did Isaac and Jacob, who were heirs with him of the same promise. For he was looking forward to the city with foundations, whose architect and builder is God. (He. 11:8-10)

All these people were still living by faith when they died. They did not receive the things promised; they only saw them and welcomed them from a distance. And they admitted that they were aliens and strangers on earth. People who say such things show that they are looking for a country of their own. If they had been thinking of the country they had left, they would have had opportunity to return. Instead, they were longing for a better country—a heavenly one. Therefore God is not ashamed to be called their God, for he has prepared a city for them. (He. 11:13-16)

Praise be to the God and Father of our Lord Jesus Christ! In his great mercy he has given us new birth into a living hope through the resurrection of Jesus Christ from the dead, and into an inheritance that can never perish, spoil or fade—kept in heaven for you. (1 Pe. 1:3-4)

But in keeping with his promise we are looking forward to a new heaven and a new earth, the home of righteousness. So then, dear friends, since you are looking forward to this, make every effort to be found spotless, blameless and at peace with him. (2 Pe. 3:13-14)

2 (10:13-28) **March, of God's People—Obedience—Land, the Promised—Army, of God's People—Believers, Title of**: the great army of God's people marched forth division by division—as commanded by God. The cloud hovering above the Tabernacle that symbolized God's presence had moved. He was now ready to guide His people to the promised land. The servant of God, Moses, had issued orders. The trumpets had sounded. The people had broken camp and taken their positions in their various divisions, tribe by tribe. Then, all of a sudden, the trumpets blasted forth the long-awaited sound for the march to begin. And the people set out. The journey had at long last begun. (See note, *Picture of the Marching Order of the Tribes*—Nu. 2:2-33.) The outline and Scripture show the marching order of the movement—division by division, tribe by tribe.

a. First, the divisions of Judah led the march under their standard: Commanded by Nashon

b. Second, the Gershonites and the Merarites followed with the carts and oxen transporting the frame and curtains of the Tabernacle.

c. Third, the divisions of Reuben marched under their standard: Commanded by Elizur.

d. Fourth, the Kohathites followed carrying the holy things of the Tabernacle: It was to be set up when they arrived.

e. Fifth, the divisions of Ephraim marched under their standard: Commanded by Elishama.

f. Finally, the divisions of Dan marched as the rear guard, under its standard: Commanded by Ahiezer.

Thought 1. The lesson in this note is obedience to God. Verse 13 makes this clear. When God commanded the people to break camp and set out for the promised land, they immediately obeyed. So it must be with us. As we march to the promised land of God, we must obey God. The only way we can conquer the pitfalls and enemies of this life is to obey God, to do exactly as He says. He alone knows the way to bypass the pitfalls and the high ground that must be taken to conquer the enemies of this life. God must be obeyed.

"Not everyone who says to me, 'Lord, Lord,' will enter the kingdom of heaven, but only he who does the will of my Father who is in heaven." (Mt. 7:21)

If you obey my commands, you will remain in my love, just as I have obeyed my Father's commands and remain in his love. (Jn. 15:10)

You are my friends if you do what I command. (Jn. 15:14)

But the man who looks intently into the perfect law that gives freedom, and continues to do this, not forgetting what he has heard, but doing it—he will be blessed in what he does. (Js. 1:25)

"Blessed are those who wash their robes, that they may have the right to the tree of life and may go through the gates into the city." (Re. 22:14)

Now if you obey me fully and keep my covenant, then out of all nations you will be my treasured possession. Although the whole earth is mine. (Ex. 19:5)

Oh, that their hearts would be inclined to fear me and keep all my commands always, so that it might go well with them and their children forever! (De. 5:29)

The LORD your God commands you this day to follow these decrees and laws; carefully observe them with all your heart and with all your soul. (De. 26:16)

Do not let this Book of the Law depart from your mouth; meditate on it day and night, so that you may be careful to do everything written in it. Then you will be prosperous and successful. (Jos. 1:8)

3 (10:29-32) **Family, Witnessing to—Witnessing, to Family Members—Testimony, to Family Members—Evangelism, to Family Members—Moses, Brother-in-Law—Hobab, Brother-in-Law to Moses—Reuel, Son of**: note that Moses appealed to his brother-in-law to join the march to the promised land.

This is a picture of reaching out to family members to seek the promised land of God, the promise of heaven. The name of the brother-in-law was Hobab, the son of Reuel or Jethro the Midianite, Moses' father-in-law (v.29). Moses had married Reuel's or Jethro's daughter. No doubt, Moses did just what any of us would do: used his personal relationship to appeal to Hobab. But notice the other appeal he used: the promised land of God itself. Moses promised his brother-in-law an inheritance in the land and the blessings of God if he would join them in the march to the promised land (v.29).

a. The brother-in-law rejected the appeal (v.30). His old life appealed to him too much. Joining the march to the promised land meant leaving the pleasures, provisions, joy, and bright lights of the world he had known. He would need to undergo a radical change of life. He would need to leave behind his old family and become a part of a new family. He would have to turn away from his religion and follow the LORD God Almighty who claimed to be the only living and true God (Jehovah, Yahweh). To his mind, this was just too much to give up.

b. Note the second appeal of Moses (vv.31-32). He challenged his brother-in-law to serve as a guide to the people of God. With strong urging, Moses challenged him to be the "eyes" for the people of God. Hobab was a Midianite from a tribe of people who lived out in the desert or wilderness. His knowledge and ability as a guide would make a significant contribution to the people of God as they marched in the wilderness. To some degree, he would know where to find water and other supplies and provisions. He might also be able to give some insight about the places to which God would be leading them and the others places they would pass through on their journey.

Note also that Moses repeated his promise to share the good things of the LORD with him: an inheritance in the promised land as well as the blessings of God (v.32). Although it is not mentioned here, Hobab did accept the appeal of Moses. He did accept the challenge to follow God and to serve as a guide for the people of God (Jud. 1:16).

> **Thought 1**. The lesson is clear: we must reach out to our family members. We must challenge them to join the march to the promised land of God, the promise of heaven. We must do all we can to bear strong witness and testimony to the saving grace of the Lord Jesus Christ. We must challenge them to approach God through the sacrifice of Christ, asking God for the atonement (reconciliation) and for forgiveness of sin. We must reach our family members for Christ. They are doomed to die in this world and be separated forever from God if we fail to reach them. This lays a heavy burden upon us, the burden to do everything we can to reach them, a burden that Moses himself must have felt for his brother-in-law. Note that Moses made two appeals, two direct attempts back-to-back to reach his brother-in-law. We, too, must make concentrated, focused efforts to reach our family for Christ.
>
> > **Jesus did not let him, but said, "Go home to your family and tell them how much the Lord has done for you, and how he has had mercy on you." (Mk. 5:19)**
> >
> > **"But you will receive power when the Holy Spirit comes on you; and you will be my witnesses in Jerusalem, and in all Judea and Samaria, and to the ends of the earth." (Ac.1:8)**
> >
> > **"For we cannot help speaking about what we have seen and heard." (Ac.4:20)**
> >
> > **Fathers, do not exasperate your children; instead, bring them up in the training and instruction of the Lord. (Ep. 6:4)**
> >
> > **I have been reminded of your sincere faith, which first lived in your grandmother Lois and in your mother Eunice and, I am persuaded, now lives in you also. (2 Ti. 1:5)**
> >
> > **And how from infancy you have known the holy Scriptures, which are able to make you wise for salvation through faith in Christ Jesus. (2 Ti. 3:15)**
> >
> > **Then they can train the younger women to love their husbands and children. (Tit. 2:4)**
> >
> > **But in your hearts set apart Christ as Lord. Always be prepared to give an answer to everyone who asks you to give the reason for the hope that you have. But do this with gentleness and respect. (1 Pe. 3:15)**
> >
> > **These commandments that I give you today are to be upon your hearts. Impress them on your children. Talk about them when you sit at home and when you walk along the road, when you lie down and when you get up. Tie them as symbols on your hands and bind them on your foreheads. Write them on the doorframes of your houses and on your gates. (De. 6:6-9)**
> >
> > **Come and listen, all you who fear God; let me tell you what he has done for me. (Ps. 66:16)**
> >
> > **Train a child in the way he should go, and when he is old he will not turn from it. (Pr. 22:6)**

4 (10:33-34) **Faithfulness, of God—God, Faithfulness of—Guidance, of God—God, Guidance of**: the faithfulness of God in leading His people is striking.

a. The first part of the journey lasted three days (v.33). This was the first organized march of God's people. When they first fled from the slavery of Egypt to Mt. Sinai, they were just a misplaced group of people who had been living as slaves for four hundred years. Then, all of a sudden, they were freed; but they were disorganized, disorderly, and fleeing for their lives from the pursuing Egyptian army. Now they were organized into a great army of military divisions, and they had been marching for three days. However, keep in mind that this was the first organized march, their very first experience in marching in military divisions.

b. The Ark of the Covenant was carried out front, ahead of all the tribes. Note that the Tabernacle and the holy furnishings within the Tabernacle were carried in the midst of the tribes as they marched, not out front (v.17, 21). However, it is stated that the Ark of the Covenant "went before them." This is interpreted differently by various commentators. Some commentators feel that the words "before them" mean "in their presence." For example, there are passages where God instructs Joshua or Moses to "go before" the people, but the meaning is clearly for them to operate from the midst of the people. They only "go before" in the sense of being visible and leading the people from "the midst of the people." Whatever the case, the Ark of the Covenant—the symbol of God's very presence, the very throne of God itself—went before the people, giving them great assurance and courage to march forward triumphantly.

c. However, the assurance and courage of the people did not come just from the Ark of the Covenant. The fiery cloud of God's holy presence led the people. The cloud of God's Shekinah Glory hovered above the people throughout the day as they marched to the promised land. God was faithful in leading His people step by step, day by day.

NUMBERS 10:11-36

Thought 1. God is faithful in leading and guiding us step by step and day by day. Moreover, God promises to be faithful through the whole journey until we reach that glorious destination, the promised land of heaven itself.

(1) God is faithful. He keeps His Word and promises.

> Heaven and earth will pass away, but my words will never pass away. (Lu. 21:33)
>
> But when he, the Spirit of truth, comes, he will guide you into all truth. He will not speak on his own; he will speak only what he hears, and he will tell you what is yet to come. (Jn. 16:13)
>
> God, who has called you into fellowship with his Son Jesus Christ our Lord, is faithful. (1 Co. 1:9)
>
> Because God wanted to make the unchanging nature of his purpose very clear to the heirs of what was promised, he confirmed it with an oath. God did this so that, by two unchangeable things in which it is impossible for God to lie, we who have fled to take hold of the hope offered to us may be greatly encouraged. We have this hope as an anchor for the soul, firm and secure. It enters the inner sanctuary behind the curtain, where Jesus, who went before us, has entered on our behalf. He has become a high priest forever, in the order of Melchizedek. (He. 6:17-20)
>
> Know therefore that the LORD your God is God; he is the faithful God, keeping his covenant of love to a thousand generations of those who love him and keep his commands. (De. 7:9)
>
> Praise be to the LORD, who has given rest to his people Israel just as he promised. Not one word has failed of all the good promises he gave through his servant Moses. (1 K. 8:56)
>
> Your love, O LORD, reaches to the heavens, your faithfulness to the skies. (Ps. 36:5)
>
> I will sing of the LORD's great love forever; with my mouth I will make your faithfulness known through all generations. (Ps. 89:1)
>
> Whether you turn to the right or to the left, your ears will hear a voice behind you, saying, "This is the way; walk in it." (Is. 30:21)
>
> I will lead the blind by ways they have not known, along unfamiliar paths I will guide them; I will turn the darkness into light before them and make the rough places smooth. These are the things I will do; I will not forsake them. (Is. 42:16)
>
> But I the LORD will speak what I will, and it shall be fulfilled without delay...declares the Sovereign LORD. (Eze. 12:25)

(2) God guides us step by step until we reach the promised land of heaven.

> To shine on those living in darkness and in the shadow of death, to guide our feet into the path of peace. (Lu. 1:79)
>
> But when he, the Spirit of truth, comes, he will guide you into all truth. He will not speak on his own; he will speak only what he hears, and he will tell you what is yet to come. (Jn. 16:13)
>
> For this God is our God for ever and ever; he will be our guide even to the end. (Ps. 48:14)
>
> You guide me with your counsel, and afterward you will take me into glory. (Ps. 73:24)
>
> Whether you turn to the right or to the left, your ears will hear a voice behind you, saying, "This is the way; walk in it." (Is. 30:21)
>
> I will lead the blind by ways they have not known, along unfamiliar paths I will guide them; I will turn the darkness into light before them and make the rough places smooth. These are the things I will do; I will not forsake them. (Is. 42:16)

5 (10:35-36) **Victory, Assurance of—Rest, Spiritual—Assurance, of Victory—Spiritual Rest**: the battle cry—the great expectation and cry of Moses—was for victory and rest.

a. This must have been a dramatic scene: there was Moses standing before the Ark of God's throne with all the tribes surrounding the Tabernacle. They were all ready to begin their march. Then it happened: Moses shouted out the great battle cry, "Rise up O LORD! Scatter your enemies! Make your foes flee before you!" (a paraphrased translation). The great battle cry was a direct appeal to God: a cry for the protection and the security of God Himself. It was declaring that God's people were totally dependent upon the strength and power of God to deliver them, to give them the triumphant victory over their enemies. They were marching in unknown terrain, a wilderness and a desert they knew absolutely nothing about. Enemies could be lurking anyplace, ready to launch a surprise attack at any time. They desperately needed the presence, guidance, and protection of God. Therefore, before Moses dared lead the people forward, he shouted out the great battle cry. God must give His people a triumphant victory as they confronted the enemies on their way to the promised land.

b. When the Ark was set down for the evening or during the day for the people to rest, Moses again shouted out: "Return, O LORD, to the many thousands, the countless thousands of Israel." He was crying for God to come among His people and give them rest throughout the night, both physical and spiritual rest. They needed to be refreshed. Their strength needed to be renewed so they could face tomorrow as they continued their march to the promised land of God.

Thought 1. God promises His people both victory and rest.

(1) God promises His people victory as they march to the promised land. He assures us: we will be triumphant, victorious over all the pitfalls and enemies of this life.

> Who shall separate us from the love of Christ? Shall trouble or hardship or persecution or famine or nakedness or danger or sword?...No, in all these things we are more than conquerors through him who

loved us. For I am convinced that neither death nor life, neither angels nor demons, neither the present nor the future, nor any powers, neither height nor depth, nor anything else in all creation, will be able to separate us from the love of God that is in Christ Jesus our Lord. (Ro. 8:35, 37-39)

No temptation has seized you except what is common to man. And God is faithful; he will not let you be tempted beyond what you can bear. But when you are tempted, he will also provide a way out so that you can stand up under it. (1 Co. 10:13)

But thanks be to God, who always leads us in triumphal procession in Christ and through us spreads everywhere the fragrance of the knowledge of him. (2 Co. 2:14)

For though we live in the world, we do not wage war as the world does. The weapons we fight with are not the weapons of the world. On the contrary, they have divine power to demolish strongholds. (2 Co. 10:3-4)

Therefore put on the full armor of God, so that when the day of evil comes, you may be able to stand your ground, and after you have done everything, to stand. (Ep. 6:13)

If this is so, then the Lord knows how to rescue godly men from trials and to hold the unrighteous for the day of judgment, while continuing their punishment. (2 Pe. 2:9)

For everyone born of God overcomes the world. This is the victory that has overcome the world, even our faith. Who is it that overcomes the world? Only he who believes that Jesus is the Son of God. (1 Jn. 5:4-5)

The LORD will fight for you; you need only to be still. (Ex. 14:14)

"I will send my terror ahead of you and throw into confusion every nation you encounter. I will make all your enemies turn their backs and run." (Ex. 23:27)

Through you we push back our enemies; through your name we trample our foes. (Ps. 44:5)

(2) God promises His people rest, both physical and spiritual rest. God promises a peaceful rest and a restful peace for the souls of His dear people as they march to the promised land.

"Come to me, all you who are weary and burdened, and I will give you rest. Take my yoke upon me and learn from me, for I am gentle and humble in heart, and you will find rest for your souls." (Mt. 11:28-29)

Peace I leave with you; my peace I give you. I do not give to you as the world gives. Do not let your hearts be troubled and do not be afraid. (Jn. 14:27)

"I have told you these things, so that in me you may have peace. In this world you will have trouble. But take heart! I have overcome the world." (Jn. 16:33)

The mind of sinful man is death, but the mind controlled by the Spirit is life and peace. (Ro. 8:6)

Do not be anxious about anything, but in everything, by prayer and petition, with thanksgiving, present your requests to God. And the peace of God, which transcends all understanding, will guard your hearts and your minds in Christ Jesus. (Ph. 4:6-7)

Whatever you have learned or received or heard from me, or seen in me—put it into practice. And the God of peace will be with you. (Ph. 4:9)

Now we who have believed enter that rest, just as God has said, "So I declared on oath in my anger, 'They shall never enter my rest.'" And yet his work has been finished since the creation of the world. (He. 4:3)

The LORD replied, "My Presence will go with you, and I will give you rest." (Ex. 33:14)

I will lie down and sleep in peace, for you alone, O LORD, make me dwell in safety. (Ps. 4:8)

The LORD is my shepherd, I shall not be in want. He makes me lie down in green pastures, he leads me beside quiet waters, he restores my soul. He guides me in paths of righteousness for his name's sake. Even though I walk through the valley of the shadow of death, I will fear no evil, for you are with me; your rod and your staff, they comfort me. You prepare a table before me in the presence of my enemies. You anoint my head with oil; my cup overflows. Surely goodness and love will follow me all the days of my life, and I will dwell in the house of the LORD forever. (Ps. 23:1-6)

The LORD gives strength to his people; the LORD blesses his people with peace. (Ps. 29:11)

Be at rest once more, O my soul, for the LORD has been good to you. (Ps. 116:7)

On the day the LORD gives you relief from suffering and turmoil and cruel bondage.... (Is. 14:3)

You will keep in perfect peace him whose mind is steadfast, because he trusts in you. (Is. 26:3)

This is what the Sovereign LORD, the Holy One of Israel, says: "In repentance and rest is your salvation, in quietness and trust is your strength, but you would have none of it." (Is. 30:15)

NUMBERS 10:11-36

TYPES, SYMBOLS, AND PICTURES
(Numbers 10:11-36)

Historical Term	Type or Picture (Scriptural Basis for Each)	Life Application for Today's Believer	Biblical Application
The Great March to the Promised Land Finally Begins Nu. 10:11-36	*The Great March to the promised land is a picture...* • *of the believer finally beginning his march to the promised land of heaven* • *of the believer's great hope for the promised land* **On the twentieth day of the second month of the second year, the cloud lifted from above the tabernacle of the Testimony. Then the Israelites set out from the Desert of Sinai and traveled from place to place until the cloud came to rest in the Desert of Paran. They set out, this first time, at the LORD's command through Moses.** (Nu.10:11-13)	Man must do two things. 1. Man must "get out" of his present surroundings and leave the world and its material comforts and corruptions. 2. Man must believe in the promise of God, that is, in the promised land of heaven.	*With many other words he warned them; and he pleaded with them, "Save yourselves from this corrupt generation."* (Ac.2:40) *"Therefore come out from them and be separate, says the Lord. Touch no unclean thing, and I will receive you. I will be a Father to you, and you will be my sons and daughters, says the Lord Almighty."* (2 Co. 6:17-18) *Have nothing to do with the fruitless deeds of darkness, but rather expose them.* (Ep. 5:11) *Do not love the world or anything in the world. If anyone loves the world, the love of the Father is not in him. For everything in the world—the cravings of sinful man, the lust of his eyes and the boasting of what he has and does—comes not from the Father but from the world.* (1 Jn. 2:15-16) *For he was looking forward to the city with foundations, whose architect and builder is God.* (He. 11:10) *Then I saw a new heaven and a new earth, for the first heaven and the first earth had passed away.* (Re. 21:1) (See also Heb. 11:13-16; 12:22; 3:14).
The Great Army of God's People Marched Forth Division by Division— as Commanded Nu. 10:13-28	*The people of God marching by divisions is a picture of obeying God as one marches to the promised land* **This was the order of march for the Israelite divisions as they set out.** (Nu. 10:28)	When God commanded the people to break camp and set out for the promised land, they immediately obeyed. So it must be with us. As we march to the promised land of God and of heaven, we must obey God. The only way we can conquer the pitfalls and enemies of this life is to obey God, to do exactly as He says. He alone knows the way to bypass the pitfalls and the high ground that must be taken to conquer the enemies of this life. God must be obeyed.	*I desire to do your will, O my God; your law is within my heart.* (Ps. 40:8) *Therefore, I urge you, brothers, in view of God's mercy, to offer your bodies as living sacrifices, holy and pleasing to God—this is your spiritual act of worship. Do not conform any longer to the pattern of this world, but be transformed by the renewing of your mind. Then you will be able to test and approve what God's will is—his good, pleasing and perfect will.* (Ro. 12:1-2) *It is God's will that you should be sanctified: that you should avoid sexual immorality.* (1 Th. 4:3)

Numbers 10:11-36

Historical Term	Type or Picture (Scriptural Basis for Each)	Life Application for Today's Believer	Biblical Application
			Give thanks in all circumstances, for this is God's will for you in Christ Jesus. (1 Th. 5:18) *For it is God's will that by doing good you should silence the ignorant talk of foolish men.* (1 Pe. 2:15) *As a result, he does not live the rest of his earthly life for evil human desires, but rather for the will of God.* (1 Pe. 4:2)
The Appeal of Moses to His Brother-In-Law to Join the March to the Promised Land Nu. 10:29-32	Moses' appeal is a picture of reaching out to family members to follow after the promised land of God, the promise of heaven. **Now Moses said to Hobab son of Reuel the Midianite, Moses' father-in-law, "We are setting out for the place about which the LORD said, 'I will give it to you.' Come with us and we will treat you well, for the LORD has promised good things to Israel."** (Nu. 10:29)	The lesson is clear: we must reach out to our family members. We must challenge them to join the march to the promised land of God, the promise of heaven. We must do all we can to bear strong witness and testimony to the saving grace of the Lord Jesus Christ. We must challenge them to approach God through the sacrifice of Christ, asking God for atonement (reconciliation) and for forgiveness of sin. We must reach our family members for Christ. They are doomed to die in this world and be separated forever from God if we fail to reach them. This lays a heavy burden upon us, a burden that Moses himself must have felt for his brother-in-law. Note that Moses made two appeals, two direct attempts back-to-back to reach his brother-in-law. We, too, must make concentrated, focused efforts to reach our family for Christ.	*Jesus did not let him, but said, "Go home to your family and tell them how much the Lord has done for you, and how he has had mercy on you."* (Mk. 5:19) *But you will receive power when the Holy Spirit comes on you; and you will be my witnesses in Jerusalem, and in all Judea and Samaria, and to the ends of the earth.* (Ac. 1:8) *For we cannot help speaking about what we have seen and heard.* (Ac. 4:20) *Fathers, do not exasperate your children; instead, bring them up in the training and instruction of the Lord.* (Ep. 6:4) *I have been reminded of your sincere faith, which first lived in your grandmother Lois and in your mother Eunice and, I am persuaded, now lives in you also.* (2 Ti. 1:5) *And how from infancy you have known the holy Scriptures, which are able to make you wise for salvation through faith in Christ Jesus.* (2 Ti. 3:15) *Then they can train the younger women to love their husbands and children.* (Tit. 2:4) *But in your hearts set apart Christ as Lord. Always be prepared to give an answer to everyone who asks you to give the reason for the hope that you have. But do this with gentleness and respect.* (1 Pe. 3:15) *Train a child in the way he should go, and when he is old he will not turn from it.* (Pr. 22:6)

NUMBERS 10:11-36

Historical Term	Type or Picture (Scriptural Basis for Each)	Life Application for Today's Believer	Biblical Application
The Ark or Chest Nu. 10:33-34 (See also Exodus 25:10-22; 40:20; 35:12; 37:1-5; 39:35; 40:3, 20-21)	*The Ark was the very special place where God's Holy presence was manifested.* 1. *The Ark was the symbol of God's presence. A very special manifestation of God's presence dwelt right above the Ark, right between the two cherubim.*	What the Ark of the Covenant taught: 1. God reveals His presence to believers in a very special way: • When people need a special sense of God's presence—when they need to feel a special closeness to God—they can go directly into the presence of God. They can worship and seek the LORD personally. How is this possible? Because of the great sacrifice of God's Son, the Lord Jesus Christ.	*The LORD replied, "My Presence will go with you, and I will give you rest."* (Ex. 33:14) *When you pass through the waters, I will be with you; and when you pass through the rivers, they will not sweep over you. When you walk through the fire, you will not be burned; the flames will not set you ablaze.* (Is. 43:2) *"Whoever has my commands and obeys them, he is the one who loves me. He who loves me will be loved by my Father, and I too will love him and show myself to him."* (Jn. 14:21)
	2. *The Mercy Seat sat on top of the Ark; therefore, the Ark was a symbol of God's mercy.*	2. God covers our lives with His mercy: • Believers are to understand that the blood shed upon the cross makes atonement for their sins, that the blood reconciles them to God. • Believers are to learn that the mercy of God is to be showered upon them because of the blood, because they believe and trust the blood of the sacrifice (Jesus Christ) to cover their sins.	*But from everlasting to everlasting the LORD's love is with those who fear him, and his righteousness with their children's children.* (Ps. 103:17) *But because of his great love for us, God, who is rich in mercy, made us alive with Christ even when we were dead in transgressions—it is by grace you have been saved. And God raised us up with Christ and seated us with him in the heavenly realms in Christ Jesus.* (Ep. 2:4-6)
	3. *The Ark was the symbol of the very throne of God. It was the place where the people sought the guidance and instruction of God.*	3. God instructs and guides His people from His heavenly throne. From that position, God speaks to His people, gives them His commandments, instructions, and guidance; therefore, when God's people need help or guidance, they are to come directly to the throne of mercy, come and find grace to help in time of need.	*He guides the humble in what is right and teaches them his way.* (Ps. 25:9) *I will instruct you and teach you in the way you should go; I will counsel you and watch over you.* (Ps. 32:8) *For we do not have a high priest who is unable to sympathize with our weaknesses, but we have one who has been tempted in every way, just as we are—yet was without sin. Let us then approach the throne of grace with confidence, so that we may receive mercy and find grace to help us in our time of need.* (He. 4:15-16)

NUMBERS 10:11-36

Historical Term	Type or Picture (Scriptural Basis for Each)	Life Application for Today's Believer	Biblical Application
	4. The Ark was the symbol of God's Law, holding the Ten Commandments.	4. God gave the Ten Commandments so we would know how to live and relate to God and to one another—so we would know how to build a just and peaceful society.	*This is love for God: to obey his commands. And his commands are not burdensome. (1 Jn. 5:3)* *Righteousness exalts a nation, but sin is a disgrace to any people. (Pr. 14:34)*
	5. The Ark was the symbol of Christ, of the very presence of Christ personally fulfilling every picture of the Ark. Remember, the word "tabernacle" means to dwell, to abide in the midst of.	5. How Christ fulfilled the symbolism of the Ark of God: ⇒ Jesus Christ promises to be with His people always	*For where two or three come together in my name, there am I with them. (Mt. 18:20)* *"And teaching them to obey everything I have commanded you. And surely I am with you always, to the very end of the age." (Mt. 28:20)*
	So they set out from the mountain of the LORD and traveled for three days. The ark of the covenant of the LORD went before them during those three days to find them a place to rest. (Nu. 10:33)	⇒ Jesus Christ shed His blood in order to have mercy upon us and to cleanse us from our sins.	*He himself bore our sins in his body on the tree, so that we might die to sins and live for righteousness; by his wounds you have been healed. (1 Pe. 2:24)* *For Christ died for sins once for all, the righteous for the unrighteous, to bring you to God. He was put to death in the body but made alive by the Spirit. (1 Pe. 3:18)* *And from Jesus Christ, who is the faithful witness, the firstborn from the dead, and the ruler of the kings of the earth. To him who loves us and has freed us from our sins by his blood. (Re. 1:5)*
		⇒ Jesus Christ is the Good Shepherd, the One who leads, protects, and guides His people.	*"And surely I am with you always, to the very end of the age." (Mt. 28:20)* *"I am the good shepherd. The good shepherd lays down his life for the sheep." (Jn. 10:11)* *Keep your lives free from the love of money and be content with what you have, because God has said, "Never will I leave you; never will I forsake you." (He. 13:5)*
		⇒ Jesus Christ kept the law of the covenant that was kept in the Ark, kept the law perfectly, without sin.	*For we do not have a high priest who is unable to sympathize with our weaknesses, but we have one who has been tempted in every way, just as we are—yet was without sin. (He. 4:15)*

DIVISION II

THE TRAGIC, DEVASTATING FAILURE OF ISRAEL: WHY PEOPLE FORFEIT THEIR RIGHT TO ENTER THE PROMISED LAND, 11:1–14:45

(11:1-14:45) **DIVISION OVERVIEW—Israel, Failure of—Israel, Privileges of—Israel, Sins of—Promised Land, March to**: totally unexpected—the heart of the first generation of believers is now exposed. They had been prepared as much as a people could be for the promised land, blessed beyond imagination, given privilege after privilege:

⇒ given the adoption: adopted by God Himself to be His holy people, His sons and daughters
⇒ given the care of God: provided for, looked after, taken care of by God Himself—never going without anything
⇒ given the law, the very Word of God Himself
⇒ given the covenant: a contract with God Himself, a contract that guarantees every good and perfect gift imaginable
⇒ given the hope of the promised land: the assurance of living a full and victorious life, conquering all the enemies of life, and the glorious promise of rest, peace, and eternal life with God
⇒ given the service of God: the wonderful privilege of serving the Creator and Sustainer of the universe, the LORD God Himself (Jehovah, Yahweh)
⇒ given the staggering hope of the promised seed: the coming Messiah and Savior of the world
⇒ given the very presence and guidance of God by day and by night: symbolized in the cloud and the Tabernacle
⇒ given all the promises of God: the perfect assurance, confidence, and conviction that all the promises would be fulfilled by God

All this had been given to the first generation. They had been prepared to march to the promised land and to conquer all the enemies of life who opposed them. Their pilgrimage, their march was to be a march of victory and triumph. But tragedy struck. The truth of their hearts was exposed. Unbelief, grumbling, and murmuring filled their hearts, not God. A spirit of selfishness and rebellion was rooted in their hearts. The first generation was not God-centered; they were self-centered: filled with all kinds of immoral, lawless passions and fleshly lusts.

As shocking as this fact is, there is even a more unbelievable fact: they rebelled within three days. Only three days—that was all it took before they exposed their true, hypocritical hearts—their hearts of unbelief. The march had barely begun and they immediately began to grumble and murmur against God and His dear servant Moses.

Now begins a series of repeated acts of unbelief and rebellion. Now begins the tragic, devastating failure that brought the judgment of God upon Israel. The first generation lost their inheritance. They were shut out—excluded—never allowed to enter the promised land. This is the stunning, bewildering story of these chapters.

THE TRAGIC, DEVASTATING FAILURE OF ISRAEL: WHY PEOPLE FORFEIT THEIR RIGHT TO ENTER THE PROMISED LAND, 11:1–14:45

A. The First Tragic Failure Seen in the People: Distrusting God—Complaining and Grumbling, Craving and Lusting, 11:1-35

B. The Second Tragic Failure Seen in Two Leaders, Miriam and Aaron: Distrusting God—Criticizing and Questioning the Call of God's Servant, Moses, 12:1-16

C. The Final Tragic Failure that Dooms the People—the Twelve Spies and Their Mixed Report: Distrusting God—Being Negative, Defeated, and Fearful, Disbelieving and Rebelling against God, 13:1–14:45

NUMBERS 11:1-35

CHAPTER 11

II. THE TRAGIC, DEVASTATING FAILURE OF ISRAEL: WHY PEOPLE FORFEIT THEIR RIGHT TO ENTER THE PROMISED LAND, 11:1–14:45

A. The First Tragic Failure Seen in the People: Distrusting God—Complaining & Grumbling, Craving & Lusting, 11:1-35

1. **Complaining & grumbling about hardships: Not trusting God & losing sight of His guidance**
   a. The LORD heard the grumbling & was angered: His judgment fell upon them; some fire burned the outskirts of the camp
   b. The people & the servant of God cried out & prayed
      1) The LORD heard the prayer
      2) The fire was extinguished
   c. The place was named Taberah, which means *burning*, a place of awful judgment
2. **Complaining & murmuring about food: Not trusting God, craving & lusting after the food & appetites of the world**
   a. The ringleaders: The rabble
   b. The complaint: Had only manna to eat
      1) Longed for the food of Egypt but exaggerated it
      2) Had lost their appetite: Were tired of "this manna"
         • It was like coriander seed
         • It looked like resin
         • It was gathered & ground in a handmill or crushed in a mortar
         • It was cooked in a pot or made into cakes
         • It tasted like something made with olive oil
         • It was miraculously given by God: Fell from the sky
   c. The terrible influence of the grumbling: Every person began to complain & murmur
   d. The response of the LORD & Moses: The LORD became angry & Moses was deeply troubled
      1) Moses questioned, poured out his heart to the LORD
         • Why had God allowed so much trouble & why was He so displeased?

Now the people complained about their hardships in the hearing of the LORD, and when he heard them his anger was aroused. Then fire from the LORD burned among them and consumed some of the outskirts of the camp. 2 When the people cried out to Moses, he prayed to the LORD and the fire died down. 3 So that place was called Taberah, because fire from the LORD had burned among them.

4 The rabble with them began to crave other food, and again the Israelites started wailing and said, "If only we had meat to eat! 5 We remember the fish we ate in Egypt at no cost—also the cucumbers, melons, leeks, onions and garlic. 6 But now we have lost our appetite; we never see anything but this manna!"

7 The manna was like coriander seed and looked like resin. 8 The people went around gathering it, and then ground it in a handmill or crushed it in a mortar. They cooked it in a pot or made it into cakes. And it tasted like something made with olive oil. 9 When the dew settled on the camp at night, the manna also came down.

10 Moses heard the people of every family wailing, each at the entrance to his tent. The LORD became exceedingly angry, and Moses was troubled. 11 He asked the LORD, "Why have you brought this trouble on your servant? What have I done to displease you that you put the burden of all these people on me? 12 Did I conceive all these people? Did I give them birth? Why do you tell me to carry them in my arms, as a nurse carries an infant, to the land you promised on oath to their forefathers? 13 Where can I get meat for all these people? They keep wailing to me, 'Give us meat to eat!' 14 I cannot carry all these people by myself; the burden is too heavy for me. 15 If this is how you are going to treat me, put me to death right now—if I have found favor in your eyes—and do not let me face my own ruin."

16 The LORD said to Moses: "Bring me seventy of Israel's elders who are known to you as leaders and officials among the people. Have them come to the Tent of Meeting, that they may stand there with you. 17 I will come down and speak with you there, and I will take of the Spirit that is on you and put the Spirit on them. They will help you carry the burden of the people so that you will not have to carry it alone.

18 "Tell the people: 'Consecrate yourselves in preparation for tomorrow, when you will eat meat. The LORD heard you when you wailed, "If only we had meat to eat! We were better off in Egypt!" Now the LORD will give you meat, and you will eat it. 19 You will not eat it for just one day, or two days, or five, ten or twenty days, 20 But for a whole month—until it comes out of your nostrils and you loathe it—because you have rejected the LORD, who is among you, and have wailed before him, saying, "Why did we ever leave Egypt?" ' "

21 But Moses said, "Here I am among six hundred thousand men on foot, and you say, 'I will give them meat to eat for a whole month!' 22 Would they have enough if flocks and herds were slaughtered for them? Would they have enough if all the

• Why had God put the burden of the people on him?
• Had he, Moses, conceived & given birth to the people?
• Why had God chosen him to carry the people—like babies—to the promised land?
• Where could he conceivably get enough meat for the people?

2) Moses cried for God to raise up others to help him: The burden was too heavy—he simply could not continue to lead them by himself
   • Cried for God to take him unless He gave him help
   • Cried for God to keep him from ruin
3) The LORD met the need of Moses
   • Instructed Moses to bring 70 elders to the Tabernacle

   • Promised to anoint the elders with God's Spirit, with the very same Spirit Moses had: They would help carry the burden of the people, help deal with their problems
e. The message of God's judgment to be given to the people
   1) To consecrate themselves: Prepare to have their complaint & grumbling answered—the complaint that they were better off in Egypt (a symbol of the world)
   2) To know that the LORD would give them meat: Not just for days, but for a whole month—so much meat they would loathe it
   3) The reason:
      • Because they had rejected the LORD
      • Because they desired to be back in Egypt (a symbol of the world)
   4) The stress & questioning of Moses
      • How could God provide meat for several million men, women, & children?
      • Would there be enough even if they slaughtered all their flocks & herds? Or if they had all the

NUMBERS 11:1-35

fish in the sea?	fish in the sea were caught for them?"	you jealous for my sake? I wish that all the LORD's people were prophets and that the LORD would put his Spirit on them!"	His desire was for the LORD's Spirit to be upon all believers & for all to be prophets
5) The LORD's rebuke to Moses: The LORD's arm (power) is not too short; He will do exactly what He says	23 The LORD answered Moses, "Is the LORD's arm too short? You will now see whether or not what I say will come true for you."	30 Then Moses and the elders of Israel returned to the camp.	3) Moses & the elders returned to the camp
f. The obedience of Moses	24 So Moses went out and told the people what the LORD had said. He brought together seventy of their elders and had them stand around the Tent.	31 Now a wind went out from the LORD and drove quail in from the sea. It brought them down all around the camp to about three feet above the ground, as far as a day's walk in any direction.	h. The judgment of God: The complaint of the people was granted
1) He declared the LORD's message to the people			
2) He summoned the 70 elders to the Tabernacle			
3) The faithfulness of the LORD	25 Then the LORD came down in the cloud and spoke with him, and he took of the Spirit that was on him and put the Spirit on the seventy elders. When the Spirit rested on them, they prophesied, but they did not do so again.		1) Three feet deep & extended a whole day's walk in every direction
• He put His Spirit on the 70 elders		32 All that day and night and all the next day the people went out and gathered quail. No one gathered less than ten homers. Then they spread them out all around the camp.	2) The people gathered quail for two days & one night: Every person gathered no less than 10 homers (50 bushels)
• They prophesied this one time, but never again			
g. The true spirit of Moses: The spirit of a humble minister, a true servant of God	26 However, two men, whose names were Eldad and Medad, had remained in the camp. They were listed among the elders, but did not go out to the Tent. Yet the Spirit also rested on them, and they prophesied in the camp.	33 But while the meat was still between their teeth and before it could be consumed, the anger of the LORD burned against the people, and he struck them with a severe plague.	3) The people acted like gluttons: Gorged themselves
1) Two elders had remained in camp & did not go to the Tabernacle: The Spirit also came upon them & they prophesied			i. The anger of the LORD: Was aroused, burned against the people
			1) He struck them with a severe plague
• A young man ran & told Moses	27 A young man ran and told Moses, "Eldad and Medad are prophesying in the camp."	34 Therefore the place was named Kibroth Hattaavah, because there they buried the people who had craved other food.	2) The place was named Kibroth Hattaavah, which means *graves of craving*
• Joshua, Moses' aide, insisted that Moses stop them	28 Joshua son of Nun, who had been Moses' aide since youth, spoke up and said, "Moses, my lord, stop them!"		
2) Moses' true servant spirit:	29 But Moses replied, "Are	35 From Kibroth Hattaavah the people traveled to Hazeroth and stayed there.	j. The march of the people: Camped at Hazeroth

DIVISION II

THE TRAGIC, DEVASTATING FAILURE OF ISRAEL: WHY PEOPLE FORFEIT THEIR RIGHT TO ENTER THE PROMISED LAND, 11:1–14:45

A. The First Tragic Failure Seen in the People: Distrusting God— Complaining and Grumbling, Craving and Lusting, 11:1-35

(11:1-35) **Introduction—Negativism, Age of—Complaining, Age of—Grumbling, Age of—Murmuring, Age of—Trials, Reaction to**: this is an age of negativism—of complaining, grumbling, and murmuring. No matter where we turn, people are being negative or complaining about something:

⇒ work
⇒ school
⇒ a wife
⇒ a husband
⇒ a parent
⇒ a child
⇒ a manager
⇒ an employer
⇒ an employee
⇒ food
⇒ clothing
⇒ shelter
⇒ personal problems
⇒ financial problems
⇒ personal hardships
⇒ accidents
⇒ unemployment
⇒ foiled plans
⇒ frustrations
⇒ failures
⇒ disappointments
⇒ sorrows
⇒ despondency
⇒ rejection
⇒ suffering
⇒ ill health
⇒ position or status

Bitter trials are the normal experience of human life. They confront us all, and they perplex and puzzle us. We often ask, "Why has God let this happen to me?" Trials are common to all people (1 Co. 10:13). When they strike us, the question is: How are we going to react? Are we going to trust God to help and strengthen us, or grumble and complain and perhaps curse God? Complaining, grumbling, and murmuring hurt and cause pain for others. But more than this, complaining and grumbling show a great distrust in God:

⇒ They show that we do not trust God to meet our needs, to provide the necessities of life.
⇒ They show that we do not trust the goodness and power of God, that He will work things out and give us victory over the pitfalls and enemies of life.

This is the subject of this important passage of Scripture. It covers the first tragic failure seen in the people of

NUMBERS 11:1-35

God as they began their march to the promised land. Within three days after beginning their march, they demonstrated tragic distrust of God. They immediately began to complain and grumble against God. Moreover, the Israelites began to crave and lust after the food and appetites of Egypt. Keep in mind that Egypt is a type or symbol of the world and its enslavements. This is: *The First Tragic Failure Seen in the People: Distrusting God—Complaining and Grumbling, Craving and Lusting,* 11:1-35.

1. Complaining and grumbling about hardships: not trusting God and losing sight of His guidance (vv.1-3).
2. Complaining and murmuring about food: not trusting God, craving and lusting after the food and appetites of the world (vv.4-35).

1 (11:1-3) **Complaining—Grumbling—Murmuring—Criti-cism, Spirit of—Discontentment, Spirit of—Hardships—Problems—Difficulties—Distrust—Unbelief—Judgment, of God—Israel, Sins of—Israel, Unbelief of—Taberah, Campsite of Israel**: there was the complaining and murmuring about hardships.

The people failed to trust God, and they lost sight of God's guidance. Shocking! Inexcusable! The people were only three days into their march. Remember, the Israelites had just left Mt. Sinai where they had been camped for eleven months. They had just begun their great march to the promised land, the day for which they had longed with great expectation. Yet within three days, they were complaining and grumbling about the hardships they were facing along the march. They were complaining to the LORD, questioning why He would allow such hardships and difficulties. Why would He not make their march to the promised land smoother and easier, with less difficulty and hardship? They were gripped by a spirit of discontentment with their lives, a critical spirit. They were complaining and grumbling about the bad things that were happening to them. Life was hard and toilsome, and they blamed God.

a. The LORD heard their grumbling and was angry. His judgment fell upon them: a fire was ignited and burned the outskirts of the camp (v.1). Note that the fire was definitely from the Lord. This probably means that God caused a bolt of lightning to strike, igniting a fire that burned some of the property and tents on the outskirts of the camp.

b. The people and Moses cried out to God for help (vv.2-3). Note that the LORD immediately heard their prayer and the fire was extinguished.

c. The place was named Taberah, which means *burning*. This was a place of awful judgment, a place that needed to stand as a warning to all people in the future. God judges those who complain, grumble, and murmur against Him because of hardships.

> **Thought 1.** The Israelites were immature believers: unspiritual, unstable, and carnal (fleshly). Their carnal hearts of unbelief took over; and they complained, grumbled, and murmured against God because of the hardships. This was a terrible sin of Israel, and it was a sin that was committed by them time and again. In fact, practically every time they faced a crisis of hardship, they complained and grumbled. Note these examples:
>
> (1) They complained and grumbled because they had no food.
>
> > **In the desert the whole community grumbled against Moses and Aaron. The Israelites said to them, "If only we had died by the LORD's hand in Egypt! There we sat around pots of meat and ate all the food we wanted, but you have brought us out into this desert to starve this entire assembly to death." (Ex. 16:2-3)**
>
> (2) They complained and grumbled because they had no water.
>
> > **But the people were thirsty for water there, and they grumbled against Moses. They said, "Why did you bring us up out of Egypt to make us and our children and livestock die of thirst?" (Ex. 17:3)**
>
> (3) They complained and grumbled because of the trials they were facing throughout their wilderness wanderings: they wished to return to Egypt.
>
> > **All the Israelites grumbled against Moses and Aaron, and the whole assembly said to them, "If only we had died in Egypt! Or in this desert! Why is the LORD bringing us to this land only to let us fall by the sword? Our wives and children will be taken as plunder. Wouldn't it be better for us to go back to Egypt?" And they said to each other, "We should choose a leader and go back to Egypt." (Nu. 14:2-4)**
>
> (4) They complained and grumbled because they became tired of their leaders, tired of Moses and Aaron's leadership.
>
> > **They came as a group to oppose Moses and Aaron and said to them, "You have gone too far! The whole community is holy, every one of them, and the LORD is with them. Why then do you set yourselves above the LORD's assembly?...It is against the LORD that you and all your followers have banded together. Who is Aaron that you should grumble against him?" (Nu. 16:3, 11)**
>
> (5) They complained and grumbled because of God's judgment, because God executed justice upon the Israelites who sinned.
>
> > **The next day the whole Israelite community grumbled against Moses and Aaron. "You have killed the LORD's people," they said. (Nu. 16:41)**
>
> **Thought 2.** Complaining and grumbling are signs of distrust, of terrible unbelief in God. When we complain and grumble, we reveal a heart of unbelief and distrust. We reveal that we do not believe God's power and goodness. We do not believe that God is in control, that He will work the situation and hardship out. A heart that trusts God will always pray, asking God to help. The trusting heart never complains nor grumbles against people and situations, especially against fellow believers—certainly not against God nor His servants. Note what Scripture declares about complaining and grumbling.
>
> (1) Complaining and grumbling are not against the hardships themselves nor against other people, but against the LORD Himself.

NUMBERS 11:1-35

Moses also said, "You will know that it was the LORD when he gives you meat to eat in the evening and all the bread you want in the morning, because he has heard your grumbling against him. Who are we? You are not grumbling against us, but against the LORD." (Ex. 16:8)

(2) Complaining and grumbling are often due to a person's lack of faith in God's Word, his refusal to listen to God's voice.

Then they despised the pleasant land; they did not believe his promise. They grumbled in their tents and did not obey the LORD. (Ps. 106:24-25)

(3) Complaining and grumbling are often due to the foolishness and sin of man.

A man's own folly ruins his life, yet his heart rages against the LORD. (Pr. 19:3)
Why should any living man complain when punished for his sins? (Lam. 3:39)

(4) Complaining and grumbling are to have no part in the believer's life.

Do everything without complaining or arguing. (Ph. 2:14)

(5) Complaining and grumbling will be severely judged by God.

And do not grumble, as some of them did—and were killed by the destroying angel. (1 Co. 10:10)
"See, the Lord is coming with thousands upon thousands of his holy ones to judge everyone, and to convict all the ungodly of all the ungodly acts they have done in the ungodly way, and of all the harsh words ungodly sinners have spoken against him." These men are grumblers and faultfinders; they follow their own evil desires; they boast about themselves and flatter others for their own advantage. (Jude 14-16)

2 (11:4-35) **Complaining—Grumbling—Murmuring—Food, Complaining about—Unbelief—Craving—Lusting**: the people complained and grumbled about their food. They did not trust God, and they craved or lusted after the food and provisions of Egypt (a symbol of the world).

How could the people conceivably be failing so soon after their rebellion and the correction of God at Taberah? Apparently, this rebellion took place at the very next campsite, although this is not clearly stated. The fact that these two passages are linked together seems to indicate this. Whatever the case, the reader is again shocked and left wondering how a people could be so carnal and unbelieving. How could the Israelites be so unbelieving and stumble so often when God had done so much for them? Is the human heart that depraved? Or were their hearts that selfish and unbelieving, hard-hearted and stubborn, resistant to God?

a. The complaining and grumbling were stirred up by certain ringleaders, the rabble among them. This is a reference to the mixed group of people (non-Israelite) who joined God's people during the exodus from Egypt (see Ex. 12:38; Le. 24:10). Note that it was the rabble who actually began to lust and crave after the food of Egypt, in particular the meat of Egypt.

b. The complaint focused upon their diet: they had only manna to eat (vv.5-9). They craved and lusted after the meat and vegetables of Egypt. In Egypt they had been able to fish in the rivers and streams and grow fresh vegetables such as cucumbers, melons, leeks, onions, and garlic (v.5). Out in the desert, they were unable to plant gardens; and, of course, there were no streams or rivers from which to catch fish. The people were, as they complained, tired of "this manna." They had lost their appetite for "this manna." Keep in mind that the manna was the provision of God, a miraculous provision of food. It was also a delicious food (see outline and notes—Ex. 16:10-26 for more discussion).

Note the people's reference to the manna as "this manna." A bitter, sarcastic complaint! This was a spirit of discontentment, of dissatisfaction with God's provision, an act of unbelief and rebellion against God. An act of unbelief and rebellion against God. Just think how they had forgotten their real condition in Egypt: they had been slaves and mistreated with brutal savagery. As slaves they had known the horrors of abuse, torture, overwork, hunger, thirst, beatings, and death. They were exaggerating the food they had in Egypt, looking back into the past with unwarranted optimism. This was tragic, for the manna was God's provision. The manna was one of the gracious provisions to keep His people alive as they marched to the promised land. Note the description of the manna, how delicious and sufficient a provision it was:

⇒ It was like coriander seed (a small spicy seed taken from a plant of the carrot family. It was used as seasoning and for medicinal purposes.)
⇒ It looked like resin from a plant or tree (v.7).
⇒ It was gathered and ground in a handmill or crushed in a mortar (v.8).
⇒ It was cooked in a pot or made into cakes.
⇒ It tasted like something made with olive oil.
⇒ It was miraculously given by God: it fell daily from the sky as the dew settled on the camp at night (v.9).

c. The grumbling had a terrible and powerful influence: it spread rapidly throughout the whole camp. Note that every family began to complain, murmur, and grumble (v.10).

d. The response of the LORD and Moses was to be expected. The LORD became very angry and Moses was deeply troubled (vv.10-17).
1) Moses questioned, poured out his heart to the LORD (vv.11-13).
⇒ Why had God allowed so much trouble?
⇒ Why was God so displeased?
⇒ Why had God put the burden of the people on him?
⇒ Was it Moses who had conceived and given birth to the people? Was it not God who had conceived and given them birth?
⇒ Why had God chosen him to carry the people in his arms—as a nurse carries a child—to the promised land?
⇒ Where could he conceivably get enough meat for the people?

2) Moses cried for God to raise up others to help him (vv.14-15). The burden was too heavy and was crushing him under its weight. He could not

NUMBERS 11:1-35

continue to lead the people by himself. At this point, Moses became intense and desperate: he asked God either to help him or take him. Why? Because he felt that he would die right there upon the spot from the intense pressure he was feeling.

    3) Note that the LORD met the need of His dear servant Moses (vv.16-17). The LORD instructed Moses to bring seventy elders to the Tabernacle. God promised to anoint the elders with His Spirit, with the very same Spirit He had given to Moses. The elders would help carry the burden of the people, help deal with the problems of the people. As always, God met the desperate need of His dear servant. God had earlier appointed some leaders to help Moses in the administrative duties of the people (Ex. 18:13f); now God was appointing seventy elders to help His dear servant in the spiritual ministry of the people (see Ex. 24:9). The intense pressure and distress of Moses were being relieved by the Lord. The enormous weight of the ministry that Moses was sensing was being lifted. As stated, God was meeting the need of His dear servant.

e. Note the message of God's judgment to be given to the people by Moses (vv.18-23).
    1) The people were to sanctify or consecrate themselves (v.18). They were to prepare to have their complaining and grumbling answered—the complaint that they were better off in Egypt.
    2) The people were to know that the LORD was going to give them meat: not just for days, but for a whole month (vv.18-20). They were going to receive just what they grumbled about: meat. In fact, they were going to receive so much meat that they would loathe it. This blessing—an overabundance of meat—was to be a judgment. The people would have all the meat they had wanted and then some! They insisted that they simply had to have meat. So God was going to give them meat. They were going to receive so much meat and be so gluttonous about it that they would spew the meat out of their nostrils—loathing and despising it.
    3) Note the reason why: because they had rejected the LORD. They had craved and desired to go back to Egypt (v.20). Keep in mind that Egypt is a symbol of the world with all of its lusts and cravings. The judgment of God was bound to fall upon these unbelievers, these complainers and grumblers who were rejecting God and rebelling against Him.
    4) Note the stressful questioning by Moses (vv.21-22); Moses was shaken:
      ⇒ How could God possibly provide meat for several million people?
      ⇒ Would there be enough meat even if they slaughtered all their flocks and herds? Or if they had all the fish in the sea?
    5) Note the Lord's rebuke to Moses: the Lord's arm (power) is not too short; He will do exactly what He says (v.23). He has the power and the knowledge to do anything. Nothing is too hard for the Lord. The promise may be staggering and seem impossible to people, but He was the Lord God Himself (Jehovah, Yahweh).

f. Note the obedience of Moses (vv.24-25). Moses declared the Lord's message to the people; then he summoned the seventy elders to the Tabernacle (v.24). As soon as Moses proved his obedience, the Lord was faithful (v.25).

The Lord came down in the cloud of His Shekinah Glory and spoke with Moses. Furthermore, He did just what He had promised: the Spirit of God came upon the seventy elders, and they prophesied. But note, this was a one-of-a-kind experience. They never again prophesied.

g. Note the true spirit of Moses, the spirit of a humble minister, of a true servant of God (vv.26-30).
    1) Two elders had remained in camp and not responded to Moses' summons to come to the Tabernacle. However, the Spirit also came upon them, and they prophesied (vv.26-28). A young man witnessed the experience and ran to tell Moses. Joshua, who was Moses' aide and standing close by, insisted that Moses stop the two elders from prophesying. Why? Perhaps Joshua felt that the two men had disobeyed by not accepting the summons of Moses; therefore, they should not be appointed as assistants to him. Or perhaps he felt the two men might be personal threats to Moses. If they had received the gift of God's Spirit outside the Tabernacle and away from Moses, this would downplay the gift of Moses. People might begin to feel that God could raise up someone else to be their leader and turn to either one of these two elders or other elders for leadership.
    2) But note the spirit of Moses, the spirit of a true servant of God. This was just what he wanted: he prayed for the LORD's Spirit to come upon all believers, for all believers to be prophets (v.29). He wanted all believers to be filled with the fullness of God, to experience the full presence and provision of God.
    3) Moses and the elders then returned to the camp (v.30).

h. Note the judgment of God: the complaint of the people was granted (vv.31-33).
    1) A wind drove quail in from the sea. Miraculously, the quail were three feet deep and extended a whole day's walk in every direction—enough quail to feed two to four million people (v.31).
    2) The people gathered quail for two days and one night. Every person gathered no less than ten homers (almost 60 bushels). A staggering amount of meat! God provided far more quail than the people could possibly eat (v.32).
    3) Note the animalistic, uncivilized, and savage behavior of the people. The people acted like gluttons: they gorged themselves (v.33). *The Expositor's Bible Commentary* describes it well:

The scene must have been similar to a riot: people screaming, birds flapping their wings, everywhere the pell-mell movement of a meat-hungry people in a sea of birds. Dare we picture people ripping at the birds, eating flesh before cooking it, bestial in behavior?[1]

i. Note the anger of the Lord (vv.33-34). His anger was aroused and burned against the people. He struck them with a severe plague. Note when: "while the meat was still between their teeth" (v.33). Obviously, a plague of choking on the meat struck the people. Before they could swallow the meat, they choked. They were choking on their craving, their lusting, their gluttony. They had cursed and

---
1 *The Expositor's Bible Commentary*. Frank E. Gaebelein, Editor, p.795.

rebelled against the name of God, craving and lusting after flesh to eat. Consequently, God gave them up to their craving and lusting (see Ro. 1:24-28). They received just what their flesh craved and lusted after: meat. Their fleshly appetite had run wild. As a result, they were given up to their fleshly appetite. And the very thing they had craved and lusted after choked them to death. They had brought the judgment of God upon themselves. Note that the place was named Kibroth Hattaavah which means "graves of craving" (v.34).

j. The people then departed and renewed their march to the promised land. But tragically, their hearts were still hard and stubborn, still filled with unbelief and grumbling. This will be seen in the next three chapters, especially chapter 14. But for now they marched on and camped at Hazeroth (v.35).

Thought 1. Note several strong lessons in this passage (vv.4-35).

(1) Seeking to fulfill one's appetites—craving and lusting after the things of the world—is wrong. Giving way to the lusts of the flesh, the desires of the sinful nature, arouses the judgment of God against us.

> Therefore God gave them over in the sinful desires of their hearts to sexual impurity for the degrading of their bodies with one another. They exchanged the truth of God for a lie, and worshiped and served created things rather than the Creator—who is forever praised. Amen. (Ro. 1:24-25)
>
> They have become filled with every kind of wickedness, evil, greed and depravity. They are full of envy, murder, strife, deceit and malice. They are gossips, slanderers, God-haters, insolent, arrogant and boastful; they invent ways of doing evil; they disobey their parents; they are senseless, faithless, heartless, ruthless. Although they know God's righteous decree that those who do such things deserve death, they not only continue to do these very things but also approve of those who practice them. (Ro. 1:29-32)
>
> The acts of the sinful nature are obvious: sexual immorality, impurity and debauchery; idolatry and witchcraft; hatred, discord, jealousy, fits of rage, selfish ambition, dissensions, factions and envy; drunkenness, orgies, and the like. I warn you, as I did before, that those who live like this will not inherit the kingdom of God. (Ga. 5:19-21)

(2) Seeking to fulfill the appetites of the flesh—lusting and craving after the world and its things—is not the call of God. The call of God is to a life of separation from the world. The believer is to live a life that is holy, righteous, and pure. He is to live a life that is totally separated to God, separated from the lusts and evil of this world.

> "Be careful, or your hearts will be weighed down with dissipation, drunkenness and the anxieties of life, and that day will close on you unexpectedly like a trap." (Lu. 21:34)
>
> Therefore, I urge you, brothers, in view of God's mercy, to offer your bodies as living sacrifices, holy and pleasing to God—this is your spiritual act of worship. Do not conform any longer to the pattern of this world, but be transformed by the renewing of your mind. Then you will be able to test and approve what God's will is—his good, pleasing and perfect will. (Ro. 12:1-2)
>
> "Therefore come out from them and be separate, says the Lord. Touch no unclean thing, and I will receive you. I will be a Father to you, and you will be my sons and daughters, says the Lord Almighty." (2 Co. 6:17-18)
>
> Have nothing to do with the fruitless deeds of darkness, but rather expose them. (Ep. 5:11)
>
> No one serving as a soldier gets involved in civilian affairs—he wants to please his commanding officer. (2 Ti. 2:4)
>
> Do not love the world or anything in the world. If anyone loves the world, the love of the Father is not in him. For everything in the world—the cravings of sinful man, the lust of his eyes and the boasting of what he has and does—comes not from the Father but from the world. (1 Jn. 2:15-16)
>
> Depart, depart, go out from there! Touch no unclean thing! Come out from it and be pure, you who carry the vessels of the LORD. (Is. 52:11)

(3) Complaining and murmuring because of food is wrong. It is sin. Why? Because God promises to meet our needs, to give us all the necessities of life. But there is one condition: we must seek first the kingdom of God and His righteousness.

> But seek first his kingdom and his righteousness, and all these things will be given to you as well. (Mt. 6:33)
>
> Now to him who is able to do immeasurably more than all we ask or imagine, according to his power that is at work within us. (Ep. 3:20)
>
> And my God will meet all your needs according to his glorious riches in Christ Jesus. (Ph. 4:19)
>
> Worship the LORD your God, and his blessing will be on your food and water. I will take away sickness from among you. (Ex. 23:25)
>
> Then the LORD your God will make you most prosperous in all the work of your hands and in the fruit of your womb, the young of your livestock and the crops of your land. The LORD will again delight in you and make you prosperous, just as he delighted in your fathers. (De. 30:9)
>
> Praise be to the Lord, to God our Savior, who daily bears our burdens. Selah (Ps. 68:19)
>
> But you would be fed with the finest of wheat; with honey from the rock I would satisfy you. (Ps. 81:16)
>
> I will bless her with abundant provisions; her poor will I satisfy with food. (Ps. 132:15)

NUMBERS 11:1-35

He will also send you rain for the seed you sow in the ground, and the food that comes from the land will be rich and plentiful. In that day your cattle will graze in broad meadows. (Is. 30:23)

"Bring the whole tithe into the storehouse, that there may be food in my house. Test me in this," says the LORD Almighty, "and see if I will not throw open the floodgates of heaven and pour out so much blessing that you will not have room enough for it." (Mal. 3:10)

(4) Seeking to fulfill the appetites of the flesh, of the sinful nature—craving and lusting after the things of the world, complaining and grumbling about food—is wrong for one clear and fundamental reason: man shall not live by bread alone. Man has to have spiritual food. He must be fed by God. He must eat, partake of the *manna* from heaven, the Word of God.

Jesus answered, "It is written: 'Man does not live on bread alone, but on every word that comes from the mouth of God.'" (Mt. 4:4)

Like newborn babies, crave pure spiritual milk, so that by it you may grow up in your salvation, now that you have tasted that the Lord is good. (1 Pe. 2:2-3)

He humbled you, causing you to hunger and then feeding you with manna, which neither you nor your fathers had known, to teach you that man does not live on bread alone but on every word that comes from the mouth of the LORD. (De. 8:3)

I have not departed from the commands of his lips; I have treasured the words of his mouth more than my daily bread. (Jb. 23:12)

How sweet are your words to my taste, sweeter than honey to my mouth! (Ps. 119:103)

When your words came, I ate them; they were my joy and my heart's delight, for I bear your name, O LORD God Almighty. (Je. 15:16)

(5) Seeking to fulfill the appetites of the flesh, of the sinful nature—craving and lusting after the things of the world, complaining and grumbling about food—is sin for one clear and obvious reason: man shall not live by bread alone. He must have and partake of the bread that God sent down out of heaven. The bread that God sent *out of* heaven is the LORD Jesus Christ Himself. He is the Bread of Life. A person must eat or partake of Him in order to have his appetites satisfied and fulfilled. Jesus Christ alone can satisfy the hunger of man.

Jesus said to them, "I tell you the truth, it is not Moses who has given you the bread from heaven, but it is my Father who gives you the true bread from heaven. For the bread of God is he who comes down from heaven and gives life to the world." "Sir," they said, "from now on give us this bread." Then Jesus declared, "I am the bread of life. He who comes to me will never go hungry, and he who believes in me will never be thirsty." (Jn. 6:32-35)

"I am the bread of life. Your forefathers ate the manna in the desert, yet they died. But here is the bread that comes down from heaven, which a man may eat and not die. I am the living bread that came down from heaven. If anyone eats of this bread, he will live forever. This bread is my flesh, which I will give for the life of the world." (Jn. 6:48-51)

"This is the bread that came down from heaven. Your forefathers ate manna and died, but he who feeds on this bread will live forever." (Jn. 6:58)

(6) Seeking to fulfill the appetites of the flesh, of the sinful nature—craving and lusting after the things of the world, doubting, complaining, grumbling, and murmuring—is the tragic failure of Israel. It has been recorded in Scripture for one undeniable purpose: to teach us not to lust after evil things as they lusted.

For I do not want you to be ignorant of the fact, brothers, that our forefathers were all under the cloud and that they all passed through the sea. They were all baptized into Moses in the cloud and in the sea. They all ate the same spiritual food and drank the same spiritual drink; for they drank from the spiritual rock that accompanied them, and that rock was Christ. Nevertheless, God was not pleased with most of them; their bodies were scattered over the desert. Now these things occurred as examples to keep us from setting our hearts on evil things as they did. Do not be idolaters, as some of them were; as it is written: "The people sat down to eat and drink and got up to indulge in pagan revelry." We should not commit sexual immorality, as some of them did—and in one day twenty-three thousand of them died. We should not test the Lord, as some of them did—and were killed by snakes. And do not grumble, as some of them did—and were killed by the destroying angel. These things happened to them as examples and were written down as warnings for us, on whom the fulfillment of the ages has come. (1 Co. 10:1-11)

Numbers 12:1-16

Outline	Scripture	Notes

CHAPTER 12
 	
B. The Second Tragic Failure Seen in Two Leaders, Miriam & Aaron: Distrusting God—Criticizing & Questioning the Call of God's Servant, 12:1-16
 	
1. The criticism & questioning of God's servant
  a. The criticizing of Moses' wife: She was of a different race
  b. The questioning of his unique call: He was not the only spokesman—God also chose & spoke through them
  c. The warning: The LORD heard them complain
  d. The response of Moses: Not reactionary nor combative but humble—he did not answer
 	
2. The chastisement & judgment of God
  a. God instructed Moses, Aaron, & Miriam to go to the Tabernacle
    1) They obeyed
    2) He descended in the pillar of cloud & stood at the entrance
    3) He summoned Aaron & Miriam to step forward
  b. God strongly rebuked them & defended His unique call to His servant
    1) God spoke to His prophets through visions & dreams
    2) God called Moses to minister to all God's house
      • Moses was faithful
	Miriam and Aaron began to talk against Moses because of his Cushite wife, for he had married a Cushite.
	2 "Has the LORD spoken only through Moses?" they asked. "Hasn't he also spoken through us?" And the LORD heard this.
	3 (Now Moses was a very humble man, more humble than anyone else on the face of the earth.)
	4 At once the LORD said to Moses, Aaron and Miriam, "Come out to the Tent of Meeting, all three of you." So the three of them came out.
	5 Then the LORD came down in a pillar of cloud; he stood at the entrance to the Tent and summoned Aaron and Miriam. When both of them stepped forward,
	6 He said, "Listen to my words: "When a prophet of the LORD is among you, I reveal myself to him in visions, I speak to him in dreams.
	7 But this is not true of my servant Moses; he is faithful in all my house.
	8 With him I speak face to face, clearly and not in riddles; he sees the form of the LORD. Why then were you not afraid to speak against my servant Moses?"
	9 The anger of the LORD burned against them, and he left them.
	10 When the cloud lifted from above the Tent, there stood Miriam—leprous, like snow. Aaron turned toward her and saw that she had leprosy;
	11 And he said to Moses, "Please, my lord, do not hold against us the sin we have so foolishly committed.
	12 Do not let her be like a stillborn infant coming from its mother's womb with its flesh half eaten away."
	13 So Moses cried out to the LORD, "O God, please heal her!"
	14 The LORD replied to Moses, "If her father had spit in her face, would she not have been in disgrace for seven days? Confine her outside the camp for seven days; after that she can be brought back."
	15 So Miriam was confined outside the camp for seven days, and the people did not move on till she was brought back.
	16 After that, the people left Hazeroth and encamped in the Desert of Paran.
		• God spoke with Moses directly, not in riddles
		• Moses actually saw the form of God
		3) God's rebuke: They should have feared questioning God's servant
		
		c. God's anger burned against Miriam & Aaron & He chastised them
		  1) God left them, lifted the cloud from the Tabernacle
		  2) Miriam was afflicted with leprosy-like skin
		  3) Aaron was stricken with terrible fear
		    • He cried to Moses for mercy, confessing their sin against him
		    • He cried for the healing of Miriam, that her flesh not be eaten away
		
		3. The great mercy & compassion of God
		  a. Moses interceded, cried out for Miriam: "Heal her!"
		  b. God healed her, but she still had to be disciplined: To undergo the waiting period of the unclean—to be cut off from God's people for seven days (see Le. 13:4-6, 21, 26-27, 31-33, etc.)
		  c. The overflowing mercy of God
		    1) God led His people to wait on Miriam until she could return & rejoin the march to the promised land
		    2) God led His people to the Desert of Paran: The staging area for entering the

DIVISION II

THE TRAGIC, DEVASTATING FAILURE OF ISRAEL: WHY PEOPLE FORFEIT THEIR RIGHT TO ENTER THE PROMISED LAND, 11:1–14:45

B. The Second Tragic Failure Seen in Two Leaders, Miriam and Aaron: Distrusting God—Criticizing and Questioning the Call of God's Servant, 12:1-16

(12:1-16) **Introduction—Criticism, Spirit of—Grumbling, Spirit of—Murmuring, Spirit of—Minister, Criticism of**: a spirit of criticism and grumbling is sweeping the earth today. Almost everyone is caught up in the spirit. A critical spirit has infiltrated the attitude and speech of most people. People are criticizing, grumbling, and murmuring about…

- employer
- employee
- neighbor
- spouse
- parent
- teachers
- school
- businesses
- friends
- money
- family members
- politicians
- government
- taxes
- health
- bad luck
- the media

The list could go on and on. But there is one person who is criticized and grumbled about as much as any other person or professional: the minister of God. True, the minister is in a high profile profession and is usually held to a higher standard than most professionals. But there is more behind the criticism than just this: there is a spiritual warfare launched against the minister because of his call to

NUMBERS 12:1-16

God and His people. In fact, one of the major strategies of the devil is to arouse criticism and complaints against the minister of God. Sometimes the criticism is even launched by a family member. This is the subject of the present passage: *The Second Tragic Failure Seen in Two Leaders, Miriam and Aaron: Distrusting God—Criticizing and Questioning the Call of God's Servant,* 12:1-16.

1. The criticism and questioning of God's servant (vv.1-3).
2. The chastisement and judgment of God (vv.4-12).
3. The great mercy and compassion of God (vv.13-16).

1 **(12:1-3) Criticism, of Ministers—Grumbling, against Ministers—Complaining, against Ministers—Miriam - Aaron, Questioned Moses' Leadership—Moses, Opposition to—Family, Criticism of—Minister, Opposition to**: there was the criticism and questioning of God's servant, Moses. What happened was heartbreaking. The very sister and brother of Moses stood against him, challenging his leadership. Keep in mind what Moses had just gone through. The people had at long last begun their march to the promised land, just within the past week. But within three days...

- the people had complained about their hardships, so much so that God was forced to chastise and judge them (Nu. 11:1-3).
- the people had complained about not having enough variety in their food—not enough meat or fresh vegetables—complained so much that God was forced for a second time to chastise them (Nu. 11:4-35).

Remember: Moses had become deeply discouraged by the people's constant criticism and complaining. The grumbling and murmuring got to Moses. He became deeply troubled, distressed to the point that he wanted God to remove him and get him out of the situation. He just wanted God to go ahead and take him home, that is, to die (Nu. 11:10-15). Now, apparently just a few days later, the very sister and brother of Moses began to criticize and attack him. Heartbreaking! Distressing! Discouraging! Cut to the core of his being, Moses was bound to be sensing deep, troubling emotions. This was his own sister and brother, and here they were attacking him immediately after his most distressing experience with the people.

a. Miriam and Aaron criticized Moses because of his wife, apparently because she was of a different race (v.1). Miriam apparently took the lead in the attack. The placement of her name first would seem to indicate this. But obviously, Aaron willingly went along with the criticism against his brother. The seriousness of this attack against God's servant is clearly seen by remembering who Miriam and Aaron were. They were both leaders among God's people. Miriam was a prophetess; in fact, she was the leader among the spirit-filled women of Israel (Ex. 15:20-22). And Aaron was the High Priest, the supreme leader of Israel next to Moses. What was happening was incomprehensible, totally irresponsible. Here they were criticizing the servant of God, interrupting and detracting him from his ministry because he had married a Cushite, a woman who was not of Israel. Who was this woman? Is this a reference to Zipporah, Moses' wife (see Ex. 2:15-22)? Moses' wife was from Midian, which is sometimes identified as Cush or Cushan (Hab. 3:7; see Ex. 2:16f). Was the skin of Zipporah different in any way from the skin of the Israelites? Or, had Zipporah died, and Moses married another woman from Cush?

The present passage seems to indicate that Moses indeed had married another woman, a Cushite. Moreover, if Miriam and Aaron were going to criticize Moses' marriage to Zipporah, they would most likely have done it years before, not now—not years later. It seems far more likely that they would be criticizing him for a recent marriage, a marriage which they opposed. The literal language of this verse seems to indicate a recent marriage to the Cushite woman. Note the literal translation of verse one: "Concerning the issue of the Cushite woman that he had married, for it was a Cushite woman whom he had married."[1]

The point to see is that Miriam and Aaron were cutting the heart of their brother Moses, the servant of God. They were distracting and interrupting his ministry, breaking his focus of thought, troubling and distressing his heart and mind. Moses was as any of us would be: heartbroken, distressed, deeply troubled emotionally and mentally, cut to the core of his being—all because his own sister and brother were now criticizing and murmuring against him.

b. Miriam and Aaron also questioned the unique call and mission of Moses (v.2). To them, Moses was not the only leader or spokesman chosen by God. God had also chosen and spoken through them. Note: they were not criticizing the right of Moses to be a leader nor grumbling against his position of leadership. They were grumbling because their call and position were not as honored or recognized as his. They wanted their position and call to be more recognized and honored among the people. They prided themselves in their abilities, in their call and position, and they felt that the people should give more respect and recognition to their service for the LORD. As stated, they did not want to replace Moses: they accepted his call and position before God. They just wanted equal respect, recognition, and honor for their call and position.

c. Note the warning: the LORD heard them complain (v.2). The implication is that the LORD hears everything. Nothing is said or done upon earth that passes His notice. He hears every criticism and attack, every grumbling and murmuring. And He saw Miriam and Moses and the primary call and ministry of His dear servant. The idea is that God stood ready to defend and execute justice on behalf of His servant.

d. Note the response of Moses (v.3): it was not reactionary nor combative, but humble. He said nothing, answered nothing to his attackers. He remained silent. Note why: he was meek and humble, more so than anyone else on the face of the earth (v.3). Remember, Moses was not eloquent; he was slow of speech and tongue. He was not fluent, not skillful with words, not expressive nor persuasive. He did not speak with ease (see outline and note—Ex.4:10-12 for more discussion). As so many who have this problem know, this probably means that Moses recoiled, withdrew as much as possible from criticism. Grumbling and murmuring upset him so much that he tried to avoid facing the situation whenever he could. He felt incapable of handling such situations because of his speech impediment. He felt that he could not adequately argue or present positions in a tense situation. Perhaps this is what was happening here: he was silent, not knowing exactly what to say to these two outstanding leaders. He knew they were wrong, but he did not know how to argue the point.

Note this fact as well: there is the possibility that Moses simply did not want to argue with his sister and brother. An argument might have severed the relationship they had with one another. Despite their obvious pride and focus upon themselves, Moses did not want to hurt them nor

---

[1] *The Expositor's Bible Commentary,* Frank E. Gaebelein, Editor, p.798.

NUMBERS 12:1-16

degrade them before one another and perhaps before other leaders who might have been present. Moses was a very meek and humble man.

Thought 1. Note two significant lessons:
(1) Criticism, grumbling, and murmuring against God's servant is forbidden by God. Attacking God's minister is a sin. They are to be honored, not attacked.

> "Do not judge, or you too will be judged." (Mt. 7:1)
>
> You, therefore, have no excuse, you who pass judgment on someone else, for at whatever point you judge the other, you are condemning yourself, because you who pass judgment do the same things. (Ro. 2:1)
>
> Who are you to judge someone else's servant [God's servant]? To his own master [God] he stands or falls. And he will stand, for the Lord is able to make him stand. (Ro. 14:4)
>
> So then, men ought to regard us as servants of Christ and as those entrusted with the secret things of God. (1 Co. 4:1)
>
> Do nothing out of selfish ambition or vain conceit, but in humility consider others better than yourselves. Each of you should look not only to your own interests, but also to the interests of others. (Ph. 2:3-4)
>
> Therefore encourage one another and build each other up, just as in fact you are doing. Now we ask you, brothers, to respect those who work hard among you, who are over you in the Lord and who admonish you. (1 Th. 5:11-12)
>
> There is only one Lawgiver and Judge, the one who is able to save and destroy. But you—who are you to judge your neighbor? (Js. 4:12)

(2) The servant of God is not to react against criticism, not to be combative. In the face of criticism, the minister is to be meek and humble—totally submissive and dependent upon God.

> Therefore, whoever humbles himself like this child is the greatest in the kingdom of heaven. (Mt. 18:4)
>
> For by the grace given me I say to every one of you: Do not think of yourself more highly than you ought, but rather think of yourself with sober judgment, in accordance with the measure of faith God has given you. (Ro. 12:3)
>
> Your attitude should be the same as that of Christ Jesus: Who, being in very nature God, did not consider equality with God something to be grasped, but made himself nothing, taking the very nature of a servant, being made in human likeness. And being found in appearance as a man, he humbled himself and became obedient to death—even death on a cross! (Ph. 2:5-8)
>
> Humble yourselves before the Lord, and he will lift you up. (Js. 4:10)
>
> Young men, in the same way be submissive to those who are older. All of you, clothe yourselves with humility toward one another, because, "God opposes the proud but gives grace to the humble." Humble yourselves, therefore, under God's mighty hand, that he may lift you up in due time. (1 Pe. 5:5-6)
>
> He has showed you, O man, what is good. And what does the LORD require of you? To act justly and to love mercy and to walk humbly with your God. (Mi. 6:8)

2 (12:4-12) **Chastisement, of God—Judgment, of God—Discipline, of God—Miriam—Aaron—Intercession—Moses, Intercession of:** there was the chastisement and judgment of God upon Miriam and Aaron. Note that God immediately took over the situation. The words *at once* (pit om) mean immediately, suddenly, unexpectedly, abruptly—the LORD spoke before anyone even had time to think about what was happening.

a. God summoned Moses, Aaron, and Miriam to go to the Tabernacle (vv.4-5). All three were obviously together, which means that Miriam and Aaron were most definitely criticizing Moses face-to-face. Note what happened when they reached the Tabernacle: the cloud of the Shekinah Glory—the very presence of God—dramatically descended, not to show mercy but wrath. God stood at the entrance of the Tabernacle to exercise judgment. Stricken with fear and terror, Miriam and Aaron were summoned to step forward toward God.

b. God strongly rebuked them and defended His unique call to His dear servant (vv.6-8). Note the first thing God said: "Listen to my words. Hear, heed what I say."

  1) God spoke to His prophets through visions and dreams, but this was not so with Moses.
  2) God had called Moses to minister to all of God's house, to all of God's people (vv.6-7). Three things in particular set Moses apart from all other prophets:

    ⇒ First, Moses was extremely faithful to the LORD and the ministry to which God called him (v.7).
    ⇒ Second, God spoke with Moses directly, not in riddles (v.8).
    ⇒ Third, Moses actually saw the form of God (v.8).

  What does this mean, Moses saw the *form* (tmonah) of God? It does not mean that he saw the *unveiled* presence of God. It means that Moses saw a form, a shape, a cloudy image of God, not the very being of God.

  3) Note God's rebuke of Miriam and Aaron. They should have feared questioning the mission of God's servant: "Why were you not afraid to speak against my servant?"

c. God's anger burned against Miriam and Aaron, and He chastised them (vv.9-12).

  1) God left them: the cloud of His presence abruptly lifted from the Tabernacle (v.10). The confrontation had taken place. The judgment had been pronounced.
  2) Miriam—because she was apparently the instigator of the attack upon God's servant—was immediately afflicted with leprosy-like skin (v.10). She had committed a terrible sin; consequently, she was afflicted with the very disease that symbolized the sinful nature of man.

3) Aaron was stricken with terrible fear (vv.10-12). When he turned, he saw the ghastly disease that had suddenly covered Miriam's body. Stricken with horror, he cried out to Moses for mercy, confessing his and Miriam's sin against him (v.11). He cried for the healing of Miriam, that her flesh not be eaten away (v.12).

Thought 1. God judges or chastises His people. When we sin, God disciplines and corrects us.

> He cuts off every branch in me that bears no fruit, while every branch that does bear fruit he prunes so that it will be even more fruitful. (Jn. 15:2)
> When we are judged by the Lord, we are being disciplined so that we will not be condemned with the world. (1 Co. 11:32)
> And you have forgotten that word of encouragement that addresses you as sons: "My son, do not make light of the Lord's discipline, and do not lose heart when he rebukes you, because the Lord disciplines those he loves, and he punishes everyone he accepts as a son." (He. 12:5-6)
> Know then in your heart that as a man disciplines his son, so the LORD your God disciplines you. (De. 8:5)
> Blessed is the man you discipline, O LORD, the man you teach from your law. (Ps. 94:12)
> My son, do not despise the LORD's discipline and do not resent his rebuke, because the LORD disciplines those he loves, as a father the son he delights in. (Pr. 3:11-12)

Thought 2. Aaron feared the anger and judgment of God. We, too, must fear the anger and judgment of God. God is going to judge us, judge everything that we do—all our works. No matter what people think or say, this is the strong declaration of Scripture.

> For the Son of Man is going to come in his Father's glory with his angels, and then he will reward each person according to what he has done. (Mt. 16:27)
> For we must all appear before the judgment seat of Christ, that each one may receive what is due him for the things done while in the body, whether good or bad. (2 Co. 5:10)
> Since you call on a Father who judges each man's work impartially, live your lives as strangers here in reverent fear. (1 Pe. 1:17)
> "Behold, I am coming soon! My reward is with me, and I will give to everyone according to what he has done." (Re. 22:12)
> And that you, O Lord, are loving. Surely you will reward each person according to what he has done. (Ps. 62:12)
> "I the LORD search the heart and examine the mind, to reward a man according to his conduct, according to what his deeds deserve." (Je. 17:10)

Thought 3. God calls and gifts believers differently. Every believer is called to a distinct, specific service. Moses was called to his particular ministry; Miriam and Aaron to theirs. So it is with all believers. God calls every one of us to serve Him and to serve Him faithfully in the ministry given us.

> We have different gifts, according to the grace given us. If a man's gift is prophesying, let him use it in proportion to his faith. If it is serving, let him serve; if it is teaching, let him teach; if it is encouraging, let him encourage; if it is contributing to the needs of others, let him give generously; if it is leadership, let him govern diligently; if it is showing mercy, let him do it cheerfully. (Ro. 12:6-8)
> Now it is required that those who have been given a trust must prove faithful. (1 Co. 4:2)
> There are different kinds of gifts, but the same Spirit. There are different kinds of service, but the same Lord. There are different kinds of working, but the same God works all of them in all men. Now to each one the manifestation of the Spirit is given for the common good. To one there is given through the Spirit the message of wisdom, to another the message of knowledge by means of the same Spirit, to another faith by the same Spirit, to another gifts of healing by that one Spirit, to another miraculous powers, to another prophecy, to another distinguishing between spirits, to another speaking in different kinds of tongues, and to still another the interpretation of tongues. All these are the work of one and the same Spirit, and he gives them to each one, just as he determines. (1 Co. 12:4-11)
> But to each one of us grace has been given as Christ apportioned it. (Ep. 4:7)
> It was he who gave some to be apostles, some to be prophets, some to be evangelists, and some to be pastors and teachers, to prepare God's people for works of service, so that the body of Christ may be built up until we all reach unity in the faith and in the knowledge of the Son of God and become mature, attaining to the whole measure of the fullness of Christ. (Ep. 4:11-13)

3 (12:13-16) **Mercy, of God—Compassion, of God—Prayer, Intercession—Intercession**: there was the great mercy and compassion of God.

a. Moses interceded, cried out from the depths of his heart, cried out to God for his sister Miriam: "O God, please heal her!" (v.3). The chastisement or the affliction had immediately stricken Miriam. The need was desperate. Miriam was suffering, apparently doomed to a life of alienation and death unless God immediately had mercy on her. Moses was helpless except for prayer. He and Aaron both knew this. Therefore, Moses cried out, "O God, please heal her!"

b. God acted: He healed her. But she was still to be disciplined (v.14). She had committed a serious offense; therefore, she needed to learn that a person reaps what he sows, that she must not be critical and prideful, but instead meek and humble. Thus, God insisted that she undergo the waiting period for the ceremonially unclean. For seven days, she had to be put out of the camp, cut off from God's people (see Le. 13:4-6, 21, 26-27, 31-33). Remember, leprosy or serious skin disease was a symbol of sin. Therefore, the discipline of Miriam—being removed from God's people—is a picture of the church exercising discipline when members commit serious sin.

  c. Note the overflowing mercy of God (vv.15-16).
    1) God led His people to wait on her until she returned and could rejoin the march to the promised land. (v.15).
    2) God led His people to the Desert of Paran which was to be the staging area for entering the promised land (v.16).

Thought 1. Note two strong lessons for every generation of people.

(1) God hears prayer. If a believer cries out to the LORD—cries out from the depths of his heart—God hears and answers. Oh, how believers must cry out for their families, their brothers and sisters, their parents and children.

"Ask and it will be given to you; seek and you will find; knock and the door will be opened to you." (Mt. 7:7)

"Watch and pray so that you will not fall into temptation. The spirit is willing, but the body is weak." (Mt. 26:41)

So I say to you: Ask and it will be given to you; seek and you will find; knock and the door will be opened to you. (Lu. 11:9)

If you remain in me and my words remain in you, ask whatever you wish, and it will be given you. (Jn. 15:7)

Until now you have not asked for anything in my name. Ask and you will receive, and your joy will be complete. (Jn. 16:24)

This is the confidence we have in approaching God: that if we ask anything according to his will, he hears us. And if we know that he hears us—whatever we ask—we know that we have what we asked of him. (1 Jn. 5:14-15)

He will call upon me, and I will answer him; I will be with him in trouble, I will deliver him and honor him. (Ps. 91:15)

Then you will call, and the LORD will answer; you will cry for help, and he will say: Here am I. "If you do away with the yoke of oppression, with the pointing finger and malicious talk..." (Is. 58:9)

Before they call I will answer; while they are still speaking I will hear. (Is. 65:24)

(2) God is merciful and compassionate. He forgave Miriam's sin and met her need. He will forgive our sins and cleanse us—if only we will call out to Him.

In him we have redemption through his blood, the forgiveness of sins, in accordance with the riches of God's grace. (Ep. 1:7)

If we confess our sins, he is faithful and just and will forgive us our sins and purify us from all unrighteousness. (1 Jn. 1:9)

My dear children, I write this to you so that you will not sin. But if anybody does sin, we have one who speaks to the Father in our defense—Jesus Christ, the Righteous One. He is the atoning sacrifice for our sins, and not only for ours but also for the sins of the whole world. (1 Jn. 2:1-2)

Yet he was merciful; he forgave their iniquities and did not destroy them. Time after time he restrained his anger and did not stir up his full wrath. (Ps. 78:38)

But you, O Lord, are a compassionate and gracious God, slow to anger, abounding in love and faithfulness. (Ps. 86:15)

But after I uproot them, I will again have compassion and will bring each of them back to his own inheritance and his own country. (Je. 12:15)

Because of the LORD's great love we are not consumed, for his compassions never fail. (Lam. 3:22)

Though he brings grief, he will show compassion, so great is his unfailing love. (Lam. 3:32)

I led them with cords of human kindness, with ties of love; I lifted the yoke from their neck and bent down to feed them. (Ho.11:4)

Rend your heart and not your garments. Return to the LORD your God, for he is gracious and compassionate, slow to anger and abounding in love, and he relents from sending calamity. (Joel 2:13)

Who is a God like you, who pardons sin and forgives the transgression of the remnant of his inheritance? You do not stay angry forever but delight to show mercy. You will again have compassion on us; you will tread our sins underfoot and hurl all our iniquities into the depths of the sea. (Mi. 7:18-19)

Numbers 13:1–14:45

CHAPTER 13

C. The Final Tragic Failure That Dooms the People—the Twelve Spies & Their Mixed Report: Distrusting God—Being Negative, Fearful, & Defeated, Disbelieving & Rebelling against God, 13:1–14:45

1. **The command to send 12 men to spy out the land of Canaan**
   a. The men selected were to be leaders, one from each tribe
      1) The spies were sent out from the Desert of Paran
      2) The spies were different leaders than the tribal chiefs
         - From the tribe of Reuben: Shammua
         - From the tribe of Simeon: Shaphat
         - From the tribe of Judah: Caleb
         - From the tribe of Issachar: Igal
         - From the tribe of Ephraim: Hoshea (Joshua)
         - From the tribe of Benjamin: Palti
         - From the tribe of Zebulun: Gaddiel
         - From the tribe of Manasseh: Gaddi
         - From the tribe of Dan: Ammiel
         - From the tribe of Asher: Sethur
         - From the tribe of Naphtali: Nahbi
         - From the tribe of Gad: Geuel
      3) The name of the personal assistant to Moses was changed from Hoshea to Joshua
         - Hoshea means *salvation*
         - Joshua means *God saves*
   b. The mission given to the spies: To spy out the most southern part of Canaan, the Negev, & then move north through the hill country
      1) To see if the people were strong or weak, few or many
      2) To see what the land was like, good or bad
      3) To see if the towns were fortified or unwalled reports
      4) To check the soil to see if it was fertile or poor, barren or full of trees
      5) To bring back samples of the fruit (it was grape season)
   c. The mission carried out: Began at the Desert of Zin & spied as far as Rehob^{DS1} near Lebo Hamath^{DS2} (see 34:8)
      1) The first city they spied out: Hebron^{DS3}
         - Was inhabited by the Anakites (giants, a tall people, see v.28, 33)
         - Had been built seven years before Zoan^{DS4} in Egypt
      2) The Valley of Eshcol was very fruitful
         - A single cluster of grapes was so large that it had to be carried on a pole by two men, along with other fruit
         - The valley was given the name Eshcol by the Israelites because of the large grapes: "The Valley of the Cluster"
      3) The spies returned after a 40-day mission

2. **The report & different conclusion of the spies**
   a. The report was given to Moses, Aaron, & the whole community; then the fruit was shown to them
   b. The report of the spies
      1) The positive factors: The land flowed with milk & honey; the fruit was proof
      2) The negative factors
         - The people were powerful & the cities fortified
         - The descendants of Anak (giants) lived there
         - The Amalekites were in the Negev
         - The Hittites, Jebusites, & Amorites in the hill country
         - The Canaanites along the sea & the Jordan River
   c. The different conclusions
      1) The conclusion of Caleb
         - Silenced the people
         - Declared that they should go up & take the land
      2) The conclusion of ten spies (not Joshua)—declared that they could not attack, for the nations were stronger: Began to spread unbelief & exaggerated,

---

The LORD said to Moses, 2 "Send some men to explore the land of Canaan, which I am giving to the Israelites. From each ancestral tribe send one of its leaders." 3 So at the LORD's command Moses sent them out from the Desert of Paran. All of them were leaders of the Israelites. 4 These are their names: from the tribe of Reuben, Shammua son of Zaccur; 5 From the tribe of Simeon, Shaphat son of Hori; 6 From the tribe of Judah, Caleb son of Jephunneh; 7 From the tribe of Issachar, Igal son of Joseph; 8 From the tribe of Ephraim, Hoshea son of Nun; 9 From the tribe of Benjamin, Palti son of Raphu; 10 From the tribe of Zebulun, Gaddiel son of Sodi; 11 From the tribe of Manasseh (a tribe of Joseph), Gaddi son of Susi; 12 From the tribe of Dan, Ammiel son of Gemalli; 13 From the tribe of Asher, Sethur son of Michael; 14 From the tribe of Naphtali, Nahbi son of Vophsi; 15 From the tribe of Gad, Geuel son of Maki. 16 These are the names of the men Moses sent to explore the land. (Moses gave Hoshea son of Nun the name Joshua.)

17 When Moses sent them to explore Canaan, he said, "Go up through the Negev and on into the hill country. 18 See what the land is like and whether the people who live there are strong or weak, few or many. 19 What kind of land do they live in? Is it good or bad? What kind of towns do they live in? Are they unwalled or fortified? 20 How is the soil? Is it fertile or poor? Are there trees on it or not? Do your best to bring back some of the fruit of the land." (It was the season for the first ripe grapes.)

21 So they went up and explored the land from the Desert of Zin as far as Rehob, toward Lebo Hamath. 22 They went up through the Negev and came to Hebron, where Ahiman, Sheshai and Talmai, the descendants of Anak, lived. (Hebron had been built seven years before Zoan in Egypt.) 23 When they reached the Valley of Eshcol, they cut off a branch bearing a single cluster of grapes. Two of them carried it on a pole between them, along with some pomegranates and figs. 24 That place was called the Valley of Eshcol because of the cluster of grapes the Israelites cut off there. 25 At the end of forty days they returned from exploring the land.

26 They came back to Moses and Aaron and the whole Israelite community at Kadesh in the Desert of Paran. There they reported to them and to the whole assembly and showed them the fruit of the land. 27 They gave Moses this account: "We went into the land to which you sent us, and it does flow with milk and honey! Here is its fruit. 28 But the people who live there are powerful, and the cities are fortified and very large. We even saw descendants of Anak there. 29 The Amalekites live in the Negev; the Hittites, Jebusites and Amorites live in the hill country; and the Canaanites live near the sea and along the Jordan."

30 Then Caleb silenced the people before Moses and said, "We should go up and take possession of the land, for we can certainly do it."

31 But the men who had gone up with him said, "We can't attack those people; they are stronger than we are."

32 And they spread among

116

NUMBERS 13:1–14:45

discouraging
- The land—its harsh environment—consumed its inhabitants
- The people—all of them—were huge, gigantic
- The Nephilim—descendants of Anak (the giants)—were there: The Israelites were like grasshoppers before them

3. The fatal response of the people: Grumbling, fear, unbelief, & rebellion
   a. The grumbling unbelief emphasized: "All the people," "all the Israelites," "the whole assembly"
      1) Were against the leaders
      2) Felt death in Egypt or the desert would have been better
      3) Accused the LORD of forsaking them & their families
      4) Questioned if it would not be better to return to Egypt
      5) Suggested that a new leader be chosen who would lead them back to Egypt (see Ne. 9:17, he was actually chosen)
   b. The response of Moses & Aaron: Fell face down before the people—helpless, submissive before God
   c. The response of Joshua & Caleb: Tore their clothes & declared the truthful facts about the land they had spied out
      1) The land was exceedingly good (would not consume them as the other spies had claimed)
      2) The LORD would lead & give them the land

      3) The people must not rebel against the LORD nor be afraid of the inhabitants
         - They would swallow up the inhabitants
         - The LORD was with them
   d. The fatal rejection: They plotted to stone the godly leaders
4. The anger & fierce judgment of the LORD & the intercession of Moses
   a. The glory of the LORD burst

the Israelites a bad report about the land they had explored. They said, "The land we explored devours those living in it. All the people we saw there are of great size. 33 We saw the Nephilim there (the descendants of Anak come from the Nephilim). We seemed like grasshoppers in our own eyes, and we looked the same to them."

CHAPTER 14

That night all the people of the community raised their voices and wept aloud. 2 All the Israelites grumbled against Moses and Aaron, and the whole assembly said to them, "If only we had died in Egypt! Or in this desert! 3 Why is the LORD bringing us to this land only to let us fall by the sword? Our wives and children will be taken as plunder. Wouldn't it be better for us to go back to Egypt?" 4 And they said to each other, "We should choose a leader and go back to Egypt." 5 Then Moses and Aaron fell facedown in front of the whole Israelite assembly gathered there. 6 Joshua son of Nun and Caleb son of Jephunneh, who were among those who had explored the land, tore their clothes 7 And said to the entire Israelite assembly, "The land we passed through and explored is exceedingly good. 8 If the LORD is pleased with us, he will lead us into that land, a land flowing with milk and honey, and will give it to us. 9 Only do not rebel against the LORD. And do not be afraid of the people of the land, because we will swallow them up. Their protection is gone, but the LORD is with us. Do not be afraid of them." 10 But the whole assembly talked about stoning them. Then the glory of the LORD appeared at the Tent of Meeting to all the Israelites. 11 The LORD said to Moses,

"How long will these people treat me with contempt? How long will they refuse to believe in me, in spite of all the miraculous signs I have performed among them? 12 I will strike them down with a plague and destroy them, but I will make you into a nation greater and stronger than they." 13 Moses said to the LORD, "Then the Egyptians will hear about it! By your power you brought these people up from among them. 14 And they will tell the inhabitants of this land about it. They have already heard that you, O LORD, are with these people and that you, O LORD, have been seen face to face, that your cloud stays over them, and that you go before them in a pillar of cloud by day and a pillar of fire by night. 15 If you put these people to death all at one time, the nations who have heard this report about you will say, 16 'The LORD was not able to bring these people into the land he promised them on oath; so he slaughtered them in the desert.' 17 "Now may the Lord's strength be displayed, just as you have declared: 18 'The LORD is slow to anger, abounding in love and forgiving sin and rebellion. Yet he does not leave the guilty unpunished; he punishes the children for the sin of the fathers to the third and fourth generation.' 19 In accordance with your great love, forgive the sin of these people, just as you have pardoned them from the time they left Egypt until now." 20 The LORD replied, "I have forgiven them, as you asked. 21 Nevertheless, as surely as I live and as surely as the glory of the LORD fills the whole earth, 22 Not one of the men who saw my glory and the miraculous signs I performed in Egypt and in the desert but who disobeyed me and tested me ten times— 23 Not one of them will ever see the land I promised

forth at the Tabernacle before all
1) Questioned how long the people would treat God with contempt: Refuse to believe in Him & the miracles He had performed
2) Threatened to destroy them with a plague: To use Moses to build a new race of people, greater & stronger
b. The intercession, the pleading of Moses
1) The reputation of God was at stake: The Egyptians would hear about Israel's destruction & tell the Canaanites about it
   - The Canaanites had already heard that the God of the Israelites guided & protected them

   - The Canaanites would question the power & promises of God to His people

   - The strength of God must be demonstrated, His Word kept
2) The love & forgiveness of God were at stake, as well as the discipline or chastisement of God: Moses understood this (God was both loving & just)
3) The cry of Moses for God to forgive the sin of the people: Just as He had since their deliverance from Egyptian slavery
c. The astounding forgiveness of the LORD
d. The sure judgment—discipline, chastisement—of the LORD: Was carried out without reservation upon every adult who disobeyed & tested God time and again (note: ten times)[DS5]

1) The first discipline, chastisement: Not one of

117

NUMBERS 13:1–14:45

the adults would see the promised land—were to die in the wilderness or desert

2) The one exception, Caleb (& Joshua, v.38): Because they were loyal, followed the LORD wholeheartedly

3) The second discipline, chastisement: To turn back toward the Red Sea, to wander about in the wilderness or desert

5. **The declaration of God's charge & judgment (discipline, chastisement)**
  a. God's charge against the people: Unbelief—grumbling, complaining against Him
  b. God's judgment against the people: To reap the very things they had said (the just or judicial judgment of God)
    1) Their bodies would die in the wilderness or desert
      • Every adult 20 years old or older—everyone who grumbled
      • Not a person would ever enter the promised land: Except Caleb & Joshua

    2) Their children would be brought into the land & enjoy it: Not enslaved (their false charge against God letting this happen, v.3)
      • The parents would die in the desert
      • The children would be shepherds, having to suffer & wander about in the desert for 40 years: Because of the parents' unfaithfulness
    3) Their judgment would cover a 40 year span: One year for each of the 40 days they spied out the land of Canaan
      • Because they had sinned
      • Because God had to discipline & chastise them

on oath to their forefathers. No one who has treated me with contempt will ever see it.
24 But because my servant Caleb has a different spirit and follows me wholeheartedly, I will bring him into the land he went to, and his descendants will inherit it.
25 Since the Amalekites and Canaanites are living in the valleys, turn back tomorrow and set out toward the desert along the route to the Red Sea."
26 The LORD said to Moses and Aaron:
27 "How long will this wicked community grumble against me? I have heard the complaints of these grumbling Israelites.
28 So tell them, 'As surely as I live, declares the LORD, I will do to you the very things I heard you say:
29 In this desert your bodies will fall—every one of you twenty years old or more who was counted in the census and who has grumbled against me.
30 Not one of you will enter the land I swore with uplifted hand to make your home, except Caleb son of Jephunneh and Joshua son of Nun.
31 As for your children that you said would be taken as plunder, I will bring them in to enjoy the land you have rejected.
32 But you—your bodies will fall in this desert.
33 Your children will be shepherds here for forty years, suffering for your unfaithfulness, until the last of your bodies lies in the desert.
34 For forty years—one year for each of the forty days you explored the land—you will suffer for your sins and know what it is like to have me against you.'

35 I, the LORD, have spoken, and I will surely do these things to this whole wicked community, which has banded together against me. They will meet their end in this desert; here they will die."
36 So the men Moses had sent to explore the land, who returned and made the whole community grumble against him by spreading a bad report about it—
37 These men responsible for spreading the bad report about the land were struck down and died of a plague before the LORD.
38 Of the men who went to explore the land, only Joshua son of Nun and Caleb son of Jephunneh survived.
39 When Moses reported this to all the Israelites, they mourned bitterly.
40 Early the next morning they went up toward the high hill country. "We have sinned," they said. "We will go up to the place the LORD promised."
41 But Moses said, "Why are you disobeying the LORD's command? This will not succeed!
42 Do not go up, because the LORD is not with you. You will be defeated by your enemies,
43 For the Amalekites and Canaanites will face you there. Because you have turned away from the LORD, he will not be with you and you will fall by the sword."
44 Nevertheless, in their presumption they went up toward the high hill country, though neither Moses nor the ark of the LORD's covenant moved from the camp.
45 Then the Amalekites and Canaanites who lived in that hill country came down and attacked them and beat them down all the way to Hormah.

  4) Their fate was sealed, set in the concrete of God's Word—all because they had banded together against God: They were to meet their end in the desert; they were to die there

  c. God's judgment against the ten unbelieving spies
    1) The reason
      • Because they misled the people to distrust & grumble against God
      • Because they spread disbelief, an exaggerated report
    2) The judgment: Stricken with a plague & died
    3) The judgment of God spared Joshua & Caleb: Among the spies, they alone survived

  d. The response of the people to the declaration of God's judgment: Sorrow, bitter mourning

6. **The incomplete confession & defeat of Israel,**
  a. The incomplete confession: No repentance
  b. The disobedience:
    1) Refusing to turn around & march toward the Red Sea (v.25)
    2) Planning to march into the promised land
  c. The clear, strong warning of Moses: Would not succeed, but would be defeated by the inhabitants of Canaan

    1) Because they had turned away from the LORD
    2) Because He would not be with them
  d. The people disobeyed: Marched toward the hill country without Moses or the Ark of the Covenant (a symbol of God's presence & power)
  e. The result: The Amalekites & Canaanites attacked them & sent them fleeing as far as Hormah^{DS6}

DIVISION II

THE TRAGIC, DEVASTATING FAILURE OF ISRAEL: WHY PEOPLE FORFEIT THEIR RIGHT TO ENTER THE PROMISED LAND, 11:1–14:45

NUMBERS 13:1–14:45

C. The Final Tragic Failure That Dooms the People—the Twelve Spies and Their Mixed Report: Distrusting God—Being Negative, Fearful, and Defeated, Disbelieving and Rebelling against God, 13:1–14:45

(13:1-14:45) **Introduction—Negativism, Attitude of—Defeatism, Attitude of—Unbelief, Attitude of—Israel, Failure of**: there is an attitude that will defeat and sometimes destroy a person—that of negativism. There are several words that describe a negative attitude:

⇒ defeated   ⇒ cynical
⇒ fearful   ⇒ pessimistic
⇒ unbelieving   ⇒ despairing

A negative attitude is often unwilling to face the facts, to face the truth of a situation. In fact, a negative attitude that is deeply rooted will often lead to rebellion, an unwillingness to listen and follow the truth.

This was the fundamental problem with Israel: a negative, defeatist, fearful, unbelieving attitude. The result was tragic: rebellion against God and His dear servant Moses.

This present passage is the climax to the history of the first generation of Israelites. This rebellion was the final blow, the tenth rebellion of unbelief and grumbling within two years. However, in this rebellion, God knew their hearts would never change, never trust Him and His Word—not fully, not completely, not like they should. God had no choice. God had to judge His people and judge them permanently. Negativism, defeatism, unbelief, fear, and rebellion were all embedded too deeply within their hearts. They were self-willed, stubborn, and stiff-necked, grounded as hard as concrete in their refusal to follow God. They simply refused to enter the promised land as God demanded: through sheer faith in His Word, believing the promises of God—in particular the promises of the promised land and the promised seed (a symbol of the coming Savior of the world, Christ Jesus Himself).

Again, this is the climactic passage that dooms the first generation of Israelites from ever entering the promised land. This is: *The Final Tragic Failure That Dooms the People—the Twelve Spies and Their Mixed Report: Distrusting God—Being Negative and Defeated, Fearful and Unbelieving—Rejecting and Rebelling against God, 13:1–14:45*

1. The command to send 12 men to spy out the land of Canaan (vv.1-25).
2. The report and different conclusion of the spies (vv. 26-33).
3. The fatal response of the people: grumbling, fear, unbelief, and rebellion (vv.1-10).
4. The anger and fierce judgment of the LORD and the intercession of Moses (vv.10-25).
5. The declaration of God's charge and judgment (discipline, chastisement) (vv.26-39).
6. The incomplete confession and defeat of Israel (vv.40-45).

1 (13:1-25) **Joshua, Name of—Spies, the Twelve—Israel, Leaders of, Weak—Canaan, Land of**: there was the command to send twelve men to spy out the land of Canaan. At last, the Israelites had reached the Desert of Paran that was to be the launching point for entering the promised land. The journey had been long and difficult, primarily because of the unbelief—the grumbling and complaining of the people. So many of them had caused problem after problem with their complaints and divisiveness, arousing the chastisement of God against them. But now—at long last—here they stood ready to enter the promised land, ready to experience the fulfillment of all their hopes and dreams. But before they entered, they needed to spy out the land. They needed to gather all the tactical information they could about the land and the people living there, to learn all they could about what pitfalls and enemies might lie ahead.

a. The men selected as spies were to be leaders, one from each of the twelve tribes (vv.2-15). They were sent out from their present position, the Desert of Paran (v.3). Note that the spies were selected from the leadership of each tribe. They were obviously outstanding young men, men of courage with spirits of adventure. Such traits within these young men had apparently caught the eye of Moses and the tribal leaders. They were:

⇒ from the tribe of Reuben: Shammua (v.4)
⇒ from the tribe of Simeon: Shaphat (v.5)
⇒ from the tribe of Judah: Caleb (v.6)
⇒ from the tribe of Issachar: Igal v.7)
⇒ from the tribe of Ephraim: Hoshea (Joshua) (v.8)
⇒ from the tribe of Benjamin: Palti (v.9)
⇒ from the tribe of Zebulun: Gaddiel (v.10)
⇒ from the tribe of Manasseh: Gaddi (v.11)
⇒ from the tribe of Dan: Ammiel (v.12)
⇒ from the tribe of Asher: Sethur (v.13)
⇒ from the tribe of Naphtali: Nahbi (v.14)
⇒ from the tribe of Gad: Geuel (v.15)

Note that the name of Joshua, the assistant to Moses, was changed from Hoshea to Joshua (v.16). There is tenderness and destiny in this fact. Tenderness is seen in that it was Moses who actually changed Joshua's name. This points to a close, father-like relationship between Moses and Joshua. The destiny is also seen in the fact that Moses changed Joshua's name. By changing his name, Moses was pointing the people to Joshua as a future leader. Note the two names of Joshua: Hoshea means *salvation*; Joshua means *God saves*. His very name pictured the great salvation God was going to provide for His people in the promised land.

b. The mission of the spies was clear and thorough: they were to spy out the most southern part of Canaan, the Negev, and then move north through the hill country (vv.17-20). Their mission involved spying out most of the land of Canaan. Gordon J. Wenham says that Canaan would include modern-day Israel, Lebanon, and much of southern Syria.[1] (See outline and note—Nu. 34:1-15, *Map*.) The spies were...

- to see if the people were strong or weak, few or many (v.18)
- to see what the land was like, good or bad (v.19)
- to see if the towns were fortified or unwalled (v.19)
- to check the soil to see if it was fertile or poor, barren or full of trees (v.20)
- to bring back samples of the fruit (it was grape season) (v.20)

c. The mission was carried out. The spies launched their mission from the southern border at the Desert of Zin. This was just northeast of Kadesh (see Nu. 20:1; Jos.15:1). They spied as far north as Rehob near Lebo

---
[1] Gordon J. Wenham. *The Book of Numbers*, p.117.

NUMBERS 13:1–14:45

Hamath which was at the northern frontier (see Nu. 34:8) (vv.21-25). The distance from south to north was about 250 miles, a total of about 500 miles, so the mission took them 40 days.[2]

1) The first city they spied out was Hebron (v.22). What they found shocked them:
   ⇒ The Amalekites lived there, that is, the giants of the land, the huge, towering people.
   ⇒ The city of Hebron had been built seven years before Zoan in Egypt. This emphasis probably means that the city was a large, well-fortified city with large buildings.[3]

   Note the report on Hebron: the spies said nothing about the part the city and area had played in the history of Abraham and the great promises God had made to him:[4]
   ⇒ God made His promise to Abraham near Hebron, that he would inherit the promised land (Ge. 13:14-18).
   ⇒ Abraham camped in the area of Hebron. It became his base of operations in rescuing Lot and defeating the coalition of kings who had conquered Sodom and Gomorrah and other surrounding areas (Ge. 14:13f).
   ⇒ Abraham purchased some land in Hebron and buried his wife Sara there. Moreover, other patriarchs were later buried there—all believing in the great hope of the promised land (Ge. 23:1f; 25:9; 35:27f; 50:13).

2) The spies explored the unusually fruitful Valley of Eshcol (vv.23-24). This valley was so productive, so fruitful that it was almost unbelievable. A single cluster of grapes was so large that it had to be carried, along with other fruit, on a pole by two men. The valley was given the name Eshcol by the Israelites because of the large grapes. The word Eshcol means "the valley of the cluster" (v.24).

3) The spies returned after a 40 day mission (v.25).

Thought 1. God does not show favoritism. God is no respecter of persons. However, God does choose some persons to be leaders. He sees the human heart—and He knows who has the courage, strength, humility, and willingness to lead. This is the person whom God chooses and equips to lead.

(1) God does not show favoritism. God is no respecter of persons.

> Then Peter began to speak: "I now realize how true it is that God does not show favoritism but accepts men from every nation who fear him and do what is right." (Ac.10:34-35)
> For there is no difference between Jew and Gentile—the same Lord is Lord of all and richly blesses all who call on him. (Ro. 10:12)

(2) God calls some to be leaders.[5]
   (a) God called Abraham to be a leader.

> The LORD had said to Abram, "Leave your country, your people and your father's household and go to the land I will show you." (Ge. 12:1)

   (b) God called Moses to be a leader.

> So now, go. I am sending you to Pharaoh to bring my people the Israelites out of Egypt. (Ex. 3:10)

   (c) God called Gideon to be a leader.

> The Lord turned to him and said, "Go in the strength you have and save Israel out of Midian's hand. Am I not sending you?" (Jud. 6:14)

   (d) God called Elisha to be a leader.

> So Elijah went from there and found Elisha son of Shaphat. He was plowing with twelve yoke of oxen, and he himself was driving the twelfth pair. Elijah went up to him and threw his cloak around him. (1 K. 19:19)

   (e) God called Isaiah to be a leader.

> Then I heard the voice of the LORD saying, "Whom shall I send? And who will go for us?" And I said, "Here am I. Send me!" (Is. 6:8)

   (f) God called Paul to be a leader.

> Now get up and stand on your feet. I have appeared to you to appoint you as a servant and as a witness of what you have seen of me and what I will show you. (Ac.26:16)

   (g) God calls many today to be leaders.

> You did not choose me, but I chose you and appointed you to go and bear fruit—fruit that will last. Then the Father will give you whatever you ask in my name. (Jn. 15:16)
> For by the grace given me I say to every one of you: Do not think of yourself more highly than you ought, but rather think of yourself with sober judgment, in accordance with the measure of faith God has given you. Just as each of us has one body with many members, and these members do not all have the same function, so in Christ we who are many form one body, and each member belongs to all the others. We have different gifts, according to the grace given us. If a man's gift is prophesying, let him use it in proportion to

---

2 Gordon J. Wenham. *The Book of Numbers,* p.118.
3 *The Expositor's Bible Commentary,* Vol.2. Frank E. Gaebelein, Editor, p.810.
4 Gordon J. Wenham. *The Book of Numbers,* pp.118-119.
5 *The New Thompson Chain Reference Bible,* Condensed Cyclopedia. (Indianapolis, IN: B.B. Kirkbride Bible Co., Inc., 1964), #1790.

his faith. If it is serving, let him serve; if it is teaching, let him teach; if it is encouraging, let him encourage; if it is contributing to the needs of others, let him give generously; if it is leadership, let him govern diligently; if it is showing mercy, let him do it cheerfully. (Ro.12:3-8)

It was he who gave some to be apostles, some to be prophets, some to be evangelists, and some to be pastors and teachers, to prepare God's people for works of service, so that the body of Christ may be built up until we all reach unity in the faith and in the knowledge of the Son of God and become mature, attaining to the whole measure of the fullness of Christ. (Ep. 4:11-13)

Thought 2. There is a need for unbelievers to do just what the spies did: spy out and investigate the promised land of God. Unbelievers need to know that the promised land...
- is a land that flows with milk and honey, with all the provisions of God, all that man ever needs or could want
- is a land that assures conquest over all the pitfalls and enemies of life
- is a land that brings rest, both physical and spiritual rest, to the body and soul
- is a land that guarantees eternal life with God Himself

(1) This is the land that the unbeliever needs to explore and investigate. This is heaven itself, the new heavens and earth promised by God.

But the day of the Lord will come like a thief. The heavens will disappear with a roar; the elements will be destroyed by fire, and the earth and everything in it will be laid bare. Since everything will be destroyed in this way, what kind of people ought you to be? You ought to live holy and godly lives as you look forward to the day of God and speed its coming. That day will bring about the destruction of the heavens by fire, and the elements will melt in the heat. But in keeping with his promise we are looking forward to a new heaven and a new earth, the home of righteousness. (2 Pe. 3:10-13)

Then I saw a new heaven and a new earth, for the first heaven and the first earth had passed away, and there was no longer any sea. (Re. 21:1)

Behold, I will create new heavens and a new earth. The former things will not be remembered, nor will they come to mind. (Is. 65:17)

"As the new heavens and the new earth that I make will endure before me," declares the LORD, "so will your name and descendants endure." (Is. 66:22)

(2) The unbeliever needs to investigate and seek out the promised land of God.

Come to me, all you who are weary and burdened, and I will give you rest. (Mt. 11:28)

Then he sent some more servants and said, 'Tell those who have been invited that I have prepared my dinner: My oxen and fattened cattle have been butchered, and everything is ready. Come to the wedding banquet.' (Mt. 22:4)

But if from there you seek the LORD your God, you will find him if you look for him with all your heart and with all your soul. (De. 4:29)

"Come now, let us reason together," says the LORD. "Though your sins are like scarlet, they shall be as white as snow; though they are red as crimson, they shall be like wool." (Is. 1:18)

Come, all you who are thirsty, come to the waters; and you who have no money, come, buy and eat! Come, buy wine and milk without money and without cost. (Is. 55:1)

Seek the LORD while he may be found; call on him while he is near. (Is. 55:6)

You will seek me and find me when you seek me with all your heart. (Je. 29:13)

Thought 3. Moses changed Hosea's name to Joshua because Joshua was the appointed leader to lead God's people into the promised land (v.16). The Greek name for Joshua is *Jesus*. Both Joshua and Jesus mean *God saves*. Joshua is a type of Christ. Jesus Christ is the person who saves us and leads us into the promised land of heaven.

Today in the town of David a Savior has been born to you; he is Christ the Lord. (Lu. 2:11)

For the Son of Man came to seek and to save what was lost. (Lu. 19:10)

For God did not send his Son into the world to condemn the world, but to save the world through him. (Jn. 3:17)

I am the gate; whoever enters through me will be saved. He will come in and go out, and find pasture. (Jn. 10:9)

Jesus answered, "I am the way and the truth and the life. No one comes to the Father except through me." (Jn. 14:6)

Salvation is found in no one else, for there is no other name under heaven given to men by which we must be saved. (Ac.4:12)

Here is a trustworthy saying that deserves full acceptance: Christ Jesus came into the world to save sinners—of whom I am the worst. (1 Ti. 1:15)

Therefore he is able to save completely those who come to God through him, because he always lives to intercede for them. (He. 7:25)

NUMBERS 13:1–14:45

DEEPER STUDY # 1
(Nu. 13:21) **Rehob, City of**: it was located in upper Galilee and was the farthest point of the twelve spies' mission. The Hebrew meaning of Rehob is "broad or open place." Rehob was assigned to the Levites (Jos. 12:31; 1 Chr. 6:75)
See other Scripture references for study:
> Jos. 19:28; Jos. 19:30; Jud. 1:31; Jud. 18:28; Nu. 13:21; Jos. 19:28; Jos. 19:30; Jos. 21:31; Jud. 1:31; Jud. 18:28; 2 S. 8:3; 2 S. 8:12: 2 S. 10:6: 2 S. 10:8: 1 Chr. 6:75

DEEPER STUDY # 2
(Nu. 13:21) **Lebo-Hamath, City of**: it was located on the northern boundary of Canaan, the promised land. (See Map—Nu. 34:1-29, end of commentary.) The Hebrew meaning of Lebo-Hamath is "entrance to or to come to Hamath." See other Scripture references for study:
> Nu. 13:21; Nu. 34:7-8; Jos. 13:5; Jud. 3:3; 1 K. 8:65; 2 K. 14:25; 1 Chr. 13:5; 2 Chr. 7:8; Eze. 47:15; Eze. 47:20; Eze. 48:1; Am. 6:14

DEEPER STUDY # 3
(Nu. 13:22) **Hebron, City of**: it was located in the hill country of Judah about nineteen miles south of Jerusalem and fifteen miles west of the Dead Sea. (See Map—Nu. 34:11-29 end of commentary.) The Hebrew meaning of Hebron is *association* or *league*. Hebron possessed plenty of water and fertile soil. It was inhabited by the tribe of Anak. Hebron was built seven years prior to the building of the Egyptian city of Tanis (Nu. 13:22). See other Scripture references for study:
> Ge. 13:18; Ge. 23:2; Ge. 23:19; Ge. 35:27; Ge. 37:14; Jos. 10:3; Jos. 10:5; Jos. 10:23; Jos. 10:36; Jos. 10:39; Jos. 11:21; Jos. 12:10; Jos. 14:13-15; Jos. 15:13; Jos. 15:54; Jos. 19:28; Jos. 20:7; Jos. 21:11; Jos. 21:13; Jud. 1:10; Jud. 1:20; Jud. 16:3; 1 S. 30:31; 2 S. 2:1; 2 S. 2:3; 2 S. 2:11; 2 S. 2:32; 2 S. 3:2; 2 S. 3:5; 2 S. 3:19-20; 2 S. 3:22; 2 S. 3:27; 2 S. 3:32; 2 S. 4:1; 2 S. 4:8; 2 S. 4:12-5:1; 2 S. 5:3; 2 S. 5:5; 2 S. 5:13; 2 S. 15:7; 2 S. 15:9-10; 1 K. 2:11; 1 Chr. 2:42-43; 1 Chr. 3:1; 1 Chr. 3:4; 1 Chr. 6:55; 1 Chr. 6:57; 1 Chr. 11:1; 1 Chr. 11:3; 1 Chr. 12:23; 1 Chr. 12:38; 1 Chr. 29:27; 2 Chr. 11:10

DEEPER STUDY # 4
(Nu. 13:22) **Zoan, City of**: it was located in Egypt on a Tanitic branch of the Nile River. See Map—Nu. 33:5-49, end of commentary.) Zoan was the Hebrew name for the Egyptian city of Tanis. It was also the setting for several miracles (see Ps.78:12; Ps.78:43). Zoan was a royal city of storage. It was a point of reference that the Old Testament prophets used to speak against the Egyptian government and its actions (see Is.19:11; Is.19:13; Is. 30:4; Eze. 30:14) See other Scripture references for study:
> Ps. 78:12; Ps. 78:43; Is.19:11; Is.19:13; Is.30:4; Eze.30:14

2 (13:26-33) **Spies, the Twelve—Joshua—Caleb—Unbelief—Canaan, Described—Promised Land, Described**: there was the spirit and the different conclusions of the spies. The spy mission had been a success: not a single soldier had been lost, and a complete surveillance of the promised land had been made. The spies had carried out their mission and returned after 40 exhausting days in enemy territory. Now, the people were anxiously waiting on their report, filled with excitement and great expectation. They were soon to begin their march into the promised land of God. But unknown to them, a crushing and horrible shock was coming. Some of the spies were gripped with unbelief and were to give a negative report, a defeatist report.

a. The report was given to Moses, Aaron, and the entire community; then the fruit was shown to them (vv.26-29).

b. Note that the report given by the spies was mixed (vv.27-29). There was one strong, positive factor about the land: the land flowed with milk and honey. The proof was seen in the fruit they brought back (v.27). The land was fertile, very productive and fruitful. It would abundantly feed the people and their livestock, giving them all they could ever need or desire.

But note what then happened: some of the spies were gripped with an attitude of *defeat*. They stressed the shocking, negative factors and then embellished the facts. Of course, they should report the truth about the land, but we know from the response to their report that they gave the account in a negative, pessimistic way. Note how they continually stressed the negative:

⇒ The people who lived there were powerful and
⇒ the cities fortified (be surot) and very large (v.28). The idea of the Hebrew is that the cities were fortresses, impregnable—that they could not be taken.
⇒ The descendants of Anak, the giants, lived there (v.28).
⇒ The Amalekites lived in the Negev (v.29).
⇒ The Hittites, Jebusites, and Amorites occupied the hill country.
⇒ The Canaanites occupied land along the seacoast (Mediterranean) and along the Jordan River (v.29).

c. The conclusions reached by the spies were very divisive (vv.30-33). In fact, the negative, defeatist attitude of ten spies was so distrusting of God that their report is called a *bad, evil report* (v.32).

1) The conclusion of one spy—Caleb—was that of courage and strong faith. Note that he had to silence the leaders who stood around Moses before he could speak. As would be the case with any group of leaders who had heard such a negative, defeatist report, they had begun to murmur and discuss the issues among themselves. Boldly, forcefully—Caleb declared...

• that they should go up and take possession of the promised land
• that they could defeat the enemies of the promised land

2) But the conclusion of the ten spies prevailed (vv.31-33). They continued to hold to their negative, unbelieving, defeatist position. They could not attack the enemies of the promised land, for they were stronger.
Then the unimaginable happened: a terrible, evil spirit of divisiveness took over the ten spies.

They began to spread their bad, evil report (dibbah) among the people (v.32). Note how they stressed, exaggerated, and distorted the negative factors:

⇒ The land—its hostile environment—consumed, swallowed up the people living there. The environment was hostile: it took a high toll upon human life (v.32).
⇒ The people—all of them—were gigantic, absolutely huge: a complete distortion to arouse and win people to their defeatist, unbelieving position (v.32).
⇒ The Nephilim, the descendants of Anak the giant, were there: the Israelites were like grasshoppers before them (v.33).

This negative, defeatist attitude and this exaggerated, distorted report of the ten spies were to doom both the spies and the people. Imagine how Moses' heart was cut standing there before the spies, listening to their negativism and their unbelief and then hearing about them spreading their evil report among the people. Imagine how the heart of God was cut as He witnessed such irresponsible behavior and unbelief. The ten spies were declaring that God could not fulfill His promise to give them the promised land, that the power of God was not great enough to conquer the enemies of the promised land.

Thought 1. Three strong lessons are seen in this point.
(1) The ten spies spread an evil report among the people. They exaggerated and distorted the truth. They became stumblingblocks to Israel. Scripture is clear: we are not to be stumblingblocks, not to cause people to stumble and fall.

Woe to you, teachers of the law and Pharisees, you hypocrites! You shut the kingdom of heaven in men's faces. You yourselves do not enter, nor will you let those enter who are trying to. (Mt. 23:13)

Therefore let us stop passing judgment on one another. Instead, make up your mind not to put any stumbling block or obstacle in your brother's way. (Ro. 14:13)

If your brother is distressed because of what you eat, you are no longer acting in love. Do not by your eating destroy your brother for whom Christ died. (Ro. 14:15)

Be careful, however, that the exercise of your freedom does not become a stumbling block to the weak. (1 Co. 8:9)

Therefore, if what I eat causes my brother to fall into sin, I will never eat meat again, so that I will not cause him to fall. (1 Co. 8:13)

You were running a good race. Who cut in on you and kept you from obeying the truth? That kind of persuasion does not come from the one who calls you. "A little yeast works through the whole batch of dough." (Ga. 5:7-9)

And it will be said: "Build up, build up, prepare the road! Remove the obstacles out of the way of my people." (Is. 57:14)

"For the lips of a priest ought to preserve knowledge, and from his mouth men should seek instruction—because he is the messenger of the LORD Almighty. But you have turned from the way and by your teaching have caused many to stumble; you have violated the covenant with Levi," says the LORD Almighty. (Mal. 2:7-8)

(2) The ten spies were gripped with fear and cowardice. Scripture is clear: believers are not to fear.

So don't be afraid; you are worth more than many sparrows. (Mt. 10:31)

Yet at the same time many even among the leaders believed in him. But because of the Pharisees they would not confess their faith for fear they would be put out of the synagogue. (Jn. 12:42)

For God did not give us a spirit of timidity, but a spirit of power, of love and of self-discipline. (2 Ti. 1:7)

That night the LORD appeared to him and said, "I am the God of your father Abraham. Do not be afraid, for I am with you; I will bless you and will increase the number of your descendants for the sake of my servant Abraham." (Ge. 26:24)

Then the officers shall add, "Is any man afraid or fainthearted? Let him go home so that his brothers will not become disheartened too." (De. 20:8)

Fear of man will prove to be a snare, but whoever trusts in the LORD is kept safe. (Pr. 29:25)

So do not fear, for I am with you; do not be dismayed, for I am your God. I will strengthen you and help you; I will uphold you with my righteous right hand. (Is. 41:10)

But now, this is what the LORD says—he who created you, O Jacob, he who formed you, O Israel: "Fear not, for I have redeemed you; I have summoned you by name; you are mine." (Is. 43:1)

When you pass through the waters, I will be with you; and when you pass through the rivers, they will not sweep over you. When you walk through the fire, you will not be burned; the flames will not set you ablaze. (Is. 43:2)

I, even I, am he who comforts you. Who are you that you fear mortal men, the sons of men, who are but grass. (Is. 51:12)

(3) The testimony of Caleb was that of strength and courage. Believers are to be strong and courageous.

Be on your guard; stand firm in the faith; be men of courage; be strong. (1 Co. 16:13)

Finally, be strong in the Lord and in his mighty power. (Ep. 6:10)

You then, my son, be strong in the grace that is in Christ Jesus. (2 Ti. 2:1)

Endure hardship with us like a good soldier of Christ Jesus. No one serving as a soldier gets involved in civilian affairs—he wants to please his commanding officer. (2 Ti. 2:3-4)

Be strong and courageous. Do not be afraid or terrified because of them, for the

NUMBERS 13:1–14:45

LORD your God goes with you; he will never leave you nor forsake you. (De. 31:6)

"I am about to go the way of all the earth," he said. "So be strong, show yourself a man" (1 K. 2:2)

I will not fear the tens of thousands drawn up against me on every side. (Ps. 3:6)

The LORD is my light and my salvation—whom shall I fear? The LORD is the stronghold of my life—of whom shall I be afraid? When evil men advance against me to devour my flesh, when my enemies and my foes attack me, they will stumble and fall. Though an army besiege me, my heart will not fear; though war break out against me, even then will I be confident. (Ps. 27:1-3)

You will not fear the terror of night, nor the arrow that flies by day. (Ps. 91:5)

The LORD is with me; I will not be afraid. What can man do to me? (Ps. 118:6)

Do not withhold good from those who deserve it, when it is in your power to act. (Pr. 3:27)

Surely God is my salvation; I will trust and not be afraid. The LORD, the LORD, is my strength and my song; he has become my salvation. (Is. 12:2)

I looked for a man among them who would build up the wall and stand before me in the gap on behalf of the land so I would not have to destroy it, but I found none. (Eze. 22:30)

3 (14:1-10) **Unbelief—Grumbling—Murmuring—Complaining—Rebellion, Against God—Israel, Failure - Errors of**: there was the fatal response of the people. They grumbled, doubted, and feared. They failed to believe God and rebelled against Him. The negative, unbelieving, and defeatist report of the ten spies spread among the people like wildfire on a rampage, consuming everything in its path. What happened then was the fatal climax to a whole generation of people. *The Expositor's Bible Commentary* gives a descriptive picture of the scene that is well worth quoting in full:

The malicious report of the ten spies (13:26-33) spread throughout the populace like a vicious virus on rampage. The words of Caleb and Joshua were not heard. Everywhere people heard of walled cities, strong men, giants, and the fabled Nephilim. The giant clusters of grapes were a portent of doom. If clusters of grapes were as great as these, imagine what the people would be like! No one talked about God's grace. None recited his miracles. Forgotten was the act of God where the most powerful nation of their world was stymied at the rushing of waters back to their beds. The thunder of Sinai, the fire of God, that he had spoken and delivered and graced his people beyond imagination—all these things were forgotten in their...fear. Fear unchecked becomes its own fuel, a self-propelling force that expands as it expends. The words of a mid-twentieth-century American president, 'The only thing we have to fear is fear itself,' have their outworking in the self-consumptive absorption with terror that raged through the camps that night.[6]

a. The grumbling unbelief of the people is emphasized: "all the people," "all the Israelites," "the whole assembly"—every adult was grumbling in unbelief. Not a single person was trusting God, believing that He could lead them into the promised land (vv.1-4). Note that they raised their voices and wept aloud (v.1). The entire community was "wailing, as only people in the east can do....We are to imagine the worst sort of rage, a picture of screaming, rending, throwing, cursing anger—an intoxication of grief."[7]

1) The people railed against Moses and Aaron.
2) The people felt that death in Egypt or the desert would have been better.
3) The people accused the LORD of forsaking them and their families (v.3). They accused the LORD of bringing them up to the promised land only to let them be destroyed or enslaved by their enemies (v.3).
4) The people questioned if it would not be better to return to Egypt.
5) The people, in fact, suggested that a new leader be chosen who would lead them back to Egypt (v.4). We know from Nehemiah that the people actually chose a leader to stand opposed to Moses (Ne. 9:17). This shows that a riot was taking place. The people had made their decision: they wanted nothing else to do with Moses or God. They were in total rebellion against God and His appointed leader. They were on a rampage, storming about and making preparation to return back to Egypt. Since an opposition leader had already been chosen, the lives of Moses and Aaron were threatened. Again, *The Expositor's Bible Commentary* gives an excellent picture of the scene:

The more the people wailed, the more excessive their words. The more the people cried, the more they outreached one another in protests of rage. This is the crowd psychology that leads to riots, lynchings, stormings, and rampages. Now they begin to aim their anger more directly at Yahweh himself. Moses and Aaron were the fall guys, but the LORD was the one really to blame; he had delivered them from Egypt. He had brought Pharaoh to his knees, had cast horse and rider into the sea, had led them through a barren land, and had provided bread from heaven and water from a gushing rock. He had spoken, revealing grace and wonder, power and gentleness, direction and Torah [law]. God was the one at fault! And they began to curse him, to contemn his goodness, to reject his grace.

Forgetful of God's power against Egypt...the people worked themselves into such a frenzy of fear that they wished that God had not brought them here at all. Why had he not just left them alone? Slavery began to look good to them. The hovels in Egypt became home again. The memory of a variety of food made the memory of oppressive taskmasters less fearsome.

So it was that the frightening words of the faithless spies led to the mourning of the entire

---

[6] *The Expositor's Bible Commentary*, Vol. 2. Frank E. Gaebelein, p.813.
[7] Ibid., p.813.

NUMBERS 13:1–14:45

community and to their great rebellion against the LORD. They forgot all the miracles that the LORD had done for them; they contemned his mercies and spurned his might. In their ingratitude they preferred death (v.2). Unfortunately, it was death they deserved and death they were to get. The most reprehensible charge against the grace of God was that concerning their children (see vv.31-33). Only their children would survive. All the rest would die in the desert they had chosen over the Land of Promise.[8]

b. Moses and Aaron did all they could: they fell face down before the people, helpless and submissive before God (v.5). No doubt they did just what any committed believers would do under such circumstances: they prayed, seeking deliverance through the power of God.

c. The response of Joshua and Caleb was different (vv.6-9). These two young men tore their clothes in a symbol of ritual mourning. Then they declared the truthful facts about the land they had spied out: the land was exceedingly good. It would not consume the people as the other spies had claimed (v.7).

⇒ The LORD would lead His people into the promised land if they would only obey and please Him. God would give the land—a land that flowed with milk and honey (v.8).

⇒ The people must not rebel against the LORD nor be afraid of the inhabitants of the land (v.9). God's people would swallow the inhabitants up, for the LORD was with His people.

d. But note what happened: the fatal rejection. The people plotted to assassinate, to stone the four godly leaders (v.10).

Thought 1. Unbelief and rebellion are very serious offenses against God, very serious. God will not tolerate unbelief and rebellion from any person.

(1) Scripture is clear: unbelief is condemned.

> Whoever believes in the Son has eternal life, but whoever rejects the Son will not see life, for God's wrath remains on him. (Jn. 3:36)
> I told you that you would die in your sins; if you do not believe that I am the one I claim to be, you will indeed die in your sins. (Jn. 8:24)
> See to it, brothers, that none of you has a sinful, unbelieving heart that turns away from the living God. (He. 3:12)
> Let us, therefore, make every effort to enter that rest, so that no one will fall by following their example of disobedience [Israel's unbelief]. (He. 4:11)
> Though you already know all this, I want to remind you that the Lord delivered his people out of Egypt, but later destroyed those who did not believe. (Jude 5)

(2) Scripture is clear: rebellion against God is condemned.

> Let no one deceive you with empty words, for because of such things God's wrath comes on those who are disobedient [rebellious]. (Ep. 5:6)
> He will punish those who do not know God and do not obey the gospel of our Lord Jesus. (2 Th. 1:8)
> For if the message spoken by angels was binding, and every violation and disobedience [rebellion] received its just punishment, how shall we escape if we ignore such a great salvation? This salvation, which was first announced by the Lord, was confirmed to us by those who heard him. (He. 2:2-3)
> You have been rebellious against the LORD ever since I have known you. (De. 9:24)
> For rebellion is like the sin of divination, and arrogance like the evil of idolatry. Because you have rejected the word of the LORD, he has rejected you as king. (1 S. 15:23)
> "Woe to the obstinate children," declares the LORD, "to those who carry out plans that are not mine, forming an alliance, but not by my Spirit, heaping sin upon sin." (Is. 30:1)
> All day long I have held out my hands to an obstinate people, who walk in ways not good, pursuing their own imaginations. (Is. 65:2)
> He said: "Son of man, I am sending you to the Israelites, to a rebellious nation that has rebelled against me; they and their fathers have been in revolt against me to this very day." (Eze. 2:3)
> Son of man, you are living among a rebellious people. They have eyes to see but do not see and ears to hear but do not hear, for they are a rebellious people. (Eze. 12:2)

4 (14:10-25) **Judgment, of God—Judgment, Mitigated—Anger, of God—Intercession—Moses, Intercession of—Chastisement, of God— Discipline, of Believers—Israel, Judgment of:** there was the anger and fierce judgment of the LORD and the intercession of Moses.

a. The glory of the LORD burst forth—right at the peak of the people's rage and threatened assault against God's four servants. God's glory burst forth at the Tabernacle in the sight of all the people (vv.11-12).

1) God questioned Moses: How long would the people treat the LORD with contempt? How long would they refuse to believe in Him and the miraculous signs He had performed? The word for *contempt* (na'ats) means to spurn, despise, revile, reject; to treat with utter disregard—to the point of provoking God.

2) God threatened to destroy the people with a plague. Moreover, He threatened to use Moses to build a new race of people, a greater and stronger race. The anger of God against rebellion and unbelief had reached a fevered pitch: it was time for the justice of God to fall and judgment to be executed.

b. Note the intercession, the pleading of Moses for the people of God who had committed such gross sins (vv.13-19). He cried out for God to consider three critical points:

---
[8] Ibid., p.814.

NUMBERS 13:1–14:45

1) God must remember that His own reputation and character were at stake: the Egyptians would hear about Israel's destruction and tell the Canaanites about it (vv.13-17). God must not let this happen! God's character and reputation were worth more than Moses and the people themselves. They were not worth the destruction of God's character in the eyes of the Egyptians and Canaanites.
   ⇒ The Canaanites had already heard that the LORD had delivered His people from Egyptian slavery, guiding and protecting them up to the present moment (v.14).
   ⇒ The Canaanites would question the power and promises of God to His people if God now destroyed His people (vv.15-16). The strength of God must be demonstrated, His Word kept (v.17).

2) God must show love and forgiveness (for both were at stake) as well as the discipline (chastisement) of God. Note how Moses understood that God was both loving and just, and he declared both in appealing for the lives of God's people (v.18). God is both loving and just.

3) God must forgive the sin of His people, just as He had been forgiving them since their deliverance from Egyptian slavery (v.19).

c. The forgiveness of the LORD was astounding (v.20). God declared a marvelous truth: God forgave their sins, as awful and terrible as they were. Note why: because Moses had prayed, interceded for the people, asking God to forgive them. And God heard the prayer for forgiveness.

d. The judgment (discipline) and chastisement of the LORD were sure, certain (vv.21-25). Note that the judgment was carried out without reservation upon every adult who had disobeyed and tested God time and again. In fact, God stated that the people had tested Him ten different times (see DEEPER STUDY # 1—Nu. 14:22 for more discussion). Because of the people's continued disobedience and rebellion, God executed His perfect justice and judgment:

1) The first judgment was to be a tragic chastisement: none of the adults—not a single one—would ever see the promised land. They were to die in the wilderness or desert (v.23). Note: this is a picture of *mitigated judgment*; that is, God put a 'check' on His judgment, diminished or softened His judgment because of His dear servant's prayer and intercession. This is an excellent picture of the power of intercessory prayer. Abraham's prayer and intercession for Sodom needs to be compared with this passage (Ge. 18:16-33).

2) There was to be one exception to God's discipline and chastisement, that of Caleb and Joshua (v.24, see with v.38). These two dear servants were to enter the promised land because they had been loyal and followed the LORD wholeheartedly, believing in Him totally. Note what God says: the *seed* or descendants of Caleb will inherit the promised land. This is one step in the fulfillment of God's wonderful promise concerning *the Promised Seed*, a symbol of the coming Savior of the world, Christ Jesus Himself.

3) The second discipline or chastisement was a move by God to protect His people from the enemies of the promised land (v.25). God told Moses to turn the people back toward the Red Sea, to wander about in the wilderness or desert. This was a necessary step because the Amalekites and Canaanites were living in the valleys right below where the Israelites were camped. The people had marched right up to the border of the promised land. They were so close and yet so far away. Their unbelief and rebellion against God had placed an impassable gulf between them and God. Their unbelief and rebellion had separated them from God. Instead of entering the promised land, they were to wander about in the wilderness for a total of 40 years. The desert was to be the gravesite of these unbelieving, rebellious people.

Thought 1. There are two clear and forceful lessons in this point for us:

(1) God judges and chastises (disciplines) His people when they sin—when they fail to believe and follow Him.

> **For the Son of Man is going to come in his Father's glory with his angels, and then he will reward each person according to what he has done. (Mt. 16:27)**
>
> **He cuts off every branch in me that bears no fruit, while every branch that does bear fruit he prunes so that it will be even more fruitful. (Jn. 15:2)**
>
> **When we are judged by the Lord, we are being disciplined so that we will not be condemned with the world. (1 Co. 11:32)**
>
> **For we must all appear before the judgment seat of Christ, that each one may receive what is due him for the things done while in the body, whether good or bad. (2 Co. 5:10)**
>
> **And you have forgotten that word of encouragement that addresses you as sons: "My son, do not make light of the Lord's discipline, and do not lose heart when he rebukes you, because the Lord disciplines those he loves, and he punishes everyone he accepts as a son." (He. 12:5-6)**
>
> **Since you call on a Father who judges each man's work impartially, live your lives as strangers here in reverent fear. (1 Pe. 1:17)**
>
> **Behold, I am coming soon! My reward is with me, and I will give to everyone according to what he has done. (Re. 22:12)**
>
> **And that you, O LORD, are loving. Surely you will reward each person according to what he has done. (Ps. 62:12)**
>
> **My son, do not despise the LORD's discipline and do not resent his rebuke, because the LORD disciplines those he loves, as a father the son he delights in. (Pr. 3:11-12)**
>
> **"I the LORD search the heart and examine the mind, to reward a man according to his conduct, according to what his deeds deserve." (Je. 17:10)**

(2) God hears the prayers of His people in behalf of others. Intercessory prayer is like sweet incense ascending up and pleasing God. God loves, accepts, and answers intercessory prayer.

> **Ask and it will be given to you; seek and you will find; knock and the door will be opened to you. (Mt. 7:7)**

NUMBERS 13:1–14:45

If you remain in me and my words remain in you, ask whatever you wish, and it will be given you. (Jn. 15:7)

God exalted him to his own right hand as Prince and Savior that he might give repentance and forgiveness of sins to Israel. (Ac.5:31)

And pray in the Spirit on all occasions with all kinds of prayers and requests. With this in mind, be alert and always keep on praying for all the saints. (Ep. 6:18)

If we confess our sins, he is faithful and just and will forgive us our sins and purify us from all unrighteousness. (1 Jn. 1:9)

My dear children, I write this to you so that you will not sin. But if anybody does sin, we have one who speaks to the Father in our defense—Jesus Christ, the Righteous One. He is the atoning sacrifice for our sins, and not only for ours but also for the sins of the whole world. (1 Jn. 2:1-2)

Before they call I will answer; while they are still speaking I will hear. (Is. 65:24)

DEEPER STUDY # 5
(14:22) **Israel, Failure of, Ten Failures—Israel, Sins of**: the Israelites failed God, continually failed Him. Here God says that they tested and provoked Him, failed to believe Him, grumbling and murmuring ten different times. The ten times are probably as follows:

1. At the Red Sea, the people complained, grumbled, and murmured instead of trusting God.

As Pharaoh approached, the Israelites looked up, and there were the Egyptians, marching after them. They were terrified and cried out to the LORD. They said to Moses, "Was it because there were no graves in Egypt that you brought us to the desert to die? What have you done to us by bringing us out of Egypt? Didn't we say to you in Egypt, 'Leave us alone; let us serve the Egyptians'? It would have been better for us to serve the Egyptians than to die in the desert!" (Ex. 14:10-12)

2. At Marah, the people complained because the water was bitter and they had no water. They failed to trust God.

When they came to Marah, they could not drink its water because it was bitter. (That is why the place is called Marah.) So the people grumbled against Moses, saying, "What are we to drink?" (Ex. 15:23-24)

3. In the wilderness or Desert of Sin, the people complained because of no food instead of crying out to God and trusting Him.

The whole Israelite community set out from Elim and came to the Desert of Sin, which is between Elim and Sinai, on the fifteenth day of the second month after they had come out of Egypt. In the desert the whole community grumbled against Moses and Aaron. The Israelites said to them, "If only we had died by the LORD's hand in Egypt! There we sat around pots of meat and ate all the food we wanted, but you have brought us out into this desert to starve this entire assembly to death." (Ex. 16:1-3)

4. In the wilderness or Desert of Sin, the people tragically disobeyed God.

Then Moses said to them, "No one is to keep any of it until morning." However, some of them paid no attention to Moses; they kept part of it until morning, but it was full of maggots and began to smell. So Moses was angry with them. (Ex. 16:19-20)

5. In the wilderness or Desert of Sin, the people disobeyed God for a second time.

"Six days you are to gather it, but on the seventh day, the Sabbath, there will not be any." Nevertheless, some of the people went out on the seventh day to gather it, but they found none. Then the LORD said to Moses, "How long will you refuse to keep my commands and my instructions?" (Ex. 16:26-28)

6. At Rephidim, the people complained and quarreled with Moses and God because they had no water.

The whole Israelite community set out from the Desert of Sin, traveling from place to place as the LORD commanded. They camped at Rephidim, but there was no water for the people to drink. So they quarreled with Moses and said, "Give us water to drink." Moses replied, "Why do you quarrel with me? Why do you put the LORD to the test?" But the people were thirsty for water there, and they grumbled against Moses. They said, "Why did you bring us up out of Egypt to make us and our children and livestock die of thirst?" Then Moses cried out to the LORD, "What am I to do with these people? They are almost ready to stone me." (Ex. 17:1-4)

7. At the foot of Mt. Sinai, the people turned to idolatry, the worship of the golden calf.

When the people saw that Moses was so long in coming down from the mountain, they gathered around Aaron and said, "Come, make us gods who will go before us. As for this fellow Moses who brought us up out of Egypt, we don't know what has happened to him." Aaron answered them, "Take off the gold earrings that your wives, your sons and your daughters are wearing, and bring them to me." So all the people took off their earrings and brought them to Aaron. He took what they handed him and made it into an idol

NUMBERS 13:1–14:45

cast in the shape of a calf, fashioning it with a tool. Then they said, "These are your gods, O Israel, who brought you up out of Egypt." (Ex. 32:1-4)

8. Within three days after leaving Sinai and beginning their march to the promised land—at Taberah—the people complained and grumbled because of their hardships.

> Now the people complained about their hardships in the hearing of the LORD, and when he heard them his anger was aroused. Then fire from the LORD burned among them and consumed some of the outskirts of the camp. When the people cried out to Moses, he prayed to the LORD and the fire died down. So that place was called Taberah, because fire from the LORD had burned among them. (Nu. 11:1-3)

9. Soon after the above event—at Kibroth Hattaavah—the people complained and grumbled about food, grumbled about having enough variety, grumbled against the heavenly manna.

> The rabble with them began to crave other food, and again the Israelites started wailing and said, "If only we had meat to eat! We remember the fish we ate in Egypt at no cost—also the cucumbers, melons, leeks, onions and garlic. But now we have lost our appetite; we never see anything but this manna!" (Nu. 11:4-6)

10. At Kadesh (the present passage) the report of the ten spies threw the people into a raging frenzy of unbelief and rebellion.

> That night all the people of the community raised their voices and wept aloud. All the Israelites grumbled against Moses and Aaron, and the whole assembly said to them, "If only we had died in Egypt! Or in this desert! Why is the LORD bringing us to this land only to let us fall by the sword? Our wives and children will be taken as plunder. Wouldn't it be better for us to go back to Egypt?" And they said to each other, "We should choose a leader and go back to Egypt." (Nu. 14:1-4)

In addition to the above ten episodes of unbelief and rebellion by the people, there was the opposition against Moses by his very own sister and brother, Miriam and Aaron.

> Miriam and Aaron began to talk against Moses because of his Cushite wife, for he had married a Cushite. "Has the LORD spoken only through Moses?" they asked. "Hasn't he also spoken through us?" And the LORD heard this. (Nu. 12:1-2)

5 (14:26-39) **Judgment, of God—Discipline, of God—Chastisement, of God—Judgment, Judicial—Wilderness Wanderings, the—Spies, the Ten**: there was the declaration of God's charge and judgment (His discipline or chastisement). For the most part, this point elaborates on the judgment just passed upon the people.

a. God's charge against the people was clear: they were guilty of unbelief—of grumbling and complaining against Him (v.27). God clearly says that He hears the complaints of His grumbling people.

b. God's judgment against the people was also clear: they were to reap the very things they had said (v.28). This is the just or judicial judgment of God: what a person sows, that shall he also reap (Ga. 6:7) (see outline and DEEPER STUDY # 1—Jn. 12:39-41 for more discussion).

  1) Their bodies would die in the wilderness or desert (vv.29-30). They had complained and grumbled that they would rather die in the desert than to have to face the enemies of the promised land. God executed perfect justice: this was exactly the discipline or chastisement pronounced by God. Every adult twenty years old or older—everyone who had grumbled against God—would die in the desert. Not a single person who had ever grumbled or complained against God would ever enter the promised land, except Caleb and Joshua (v.30).

  2) However, the children of the Israelites would be brought into the promised land and enjoy it (vv.31-33). Not a single child would ever be enslaved. Remember, the people had made this false charge against God, that He was going to let their children become slaves of their enemies (Nu. 14:3). But God again executed perfect justice: the parents would be the one's who died in the desert and the children would enter the promised land. However, the children would have to live like shepherds, having to suffer and wander about in the desert with their parents for 40 years—all because of the parents' unfaithfulness (v.33). God would use this time to strengthen, toughen, discipline, and teach the children to follow Him with their whole hearts. For 40 long years, this people—these unbelievers and rebellious sinners—would be forced to remember their terrible sin against their LORD who had done so much for them.

  3) Note that their judgment would cover a 40 year span. The people were to wander about in the wilderness for 40 long, hard years—one year for each of the 40 days the unbelieving spies had explored the land of Canaan (v.34). The people—the unbelieving and rebellious sinners—were to suffer through the wilderness wanderings because they had tragically sinned, rebelling against God. It must never be forgotten by any people: God has to discipline and chastise those who sin and rebel against His love and goodness, against the great promise of the promised land.

  4) The people's fate was sealed, set in the concrete of God's Holy Word—all because they had banded together against God. They were to meet their end in the desert: they were to die there (v.35). Only the younger generation twenty years old or younger would be allowed to enter the promised land.

c. Note God's judgment against the ten unbelieving spies (vv.36-38): the people had received a lighter judgment, but

NUMBERS 13:1–14:45

not the ten unbelieving spies. The spies had misled the people, become a stumblingblock to them. Through exaggeration and distortion of the facts, they had misled the people to distrust and grumble against God. They had spread unbelief and a frenzy of fear among the people, causing them to go into a fit of rage and rioting, even threatening the very lives of God's servants. The ten unbelieving spies were totally irresponsible. Obviously, there was no other alternative: they had to be severely judged. Perfect justice had to be executed; therefore, God's judgment fell, and they were stricken with a plague and died (v.37). But note: the judgment of God spared Joshua and Caleb, for they believed God, believed in His gift of the promised land. Among the twelve spies, they alone survived.

d. Note what happened when Moses declared the judgment of God to the people: they were gripped with sorrow and bitter mourning (v.39). But it was too late. The people had gone too long and too far in sin. Within just two years, the people had committed ten grievous sins of unbelief and rebellion against God, ten grievous episodes of complaining, grumbling, and murmuring against God and His dear servant Moses—an astounding episode of rebellion against God about every two months.

> **Thought 1.** There is to be a day of judgment out in the future, a day when God will judge every human being who has ever lived.
>
> **Just as man is destined to die once, and after that to face judgment. (He. 9:27)**
>
> **When the Son of Man comes in his glory, and all the angels with him, he will sit on his throne in heavenly glory. All the nations will be gathered before him, and he will separate the people one from another as a shepherd separates the sheep from the goats. He will put the sheep on his right and the goats on his left. (Mt. 25:31-33)**
>
> **And give relief to you who are troubled, and to us as well. This will happen when the Lord Jesus is revealed from heaven in blazing fire with his powerful angels. He will punish those who do not know God and do not obey the gospel of our Lord Jesus. (2 Th. 1:7-8)**
>
> **If this is so, then the Lord knows how to rescue godly men from trials and to hold the unrighteous for the day of judgment, while continuing their punishment. (2 Pe. 2:9)**
>
> **By the same word the present heavens and earth are reserved for fire, being kept for the day of judgment and destruction of ungodly men. (2 Pe. 3:7)**
>
> **See, the Lord is coming with thousands upon thousands of his holy ones to judge everyone, and to convict all the ungodly of all the ungodly acts they have done in the ungodly way, and of all the harsh words ungodly sinners have spoken against him. (Jude 14-15)**
>
> **Look, he is coming with the clouds, and every eye will see him, even those who pierced him; and all the peoples of the earth will mourn because of him. So shall it be! Amen. (Re. 1:7)**
>
> **They will sing before the Lord, for he comes, he comes to judge the earth. He will judge the world in righteousness and the peoples in his truth. (Ps. 96:13)**
>
> **I thought in my heart, "God will bring to judgment both the righteous and the wicked, for there will be a time for every activity, a time for every deed." (Ec. 3:17)**

6 (14:40-45) **Confession—Israel, Defeat of—Rebellion, Against God—Repentance, False—Confession, False**: there was the incomplete confession of the Israelites and their defeat because they had acted without God. What happened was tragic: the people continued in their unbelief and rebellion. They heard what Moses said about the judgment of God, that they were to die and only their children would be allowed to enter the promised land. But they did not really believe the judgment of God.

a. They made an incomplete, partial, false confession; that is, they confessed their sin, but they did not repent. They did not turn to God and accept or trust what He had said (v.40). Obviously, they were sensing deep sorrow for their sin. But the sorrow they felt was a worldly sorrow, not a godly sorrow that leads to repentance. They were sorry that they were missing out on the promised land, not that they had sinned and cut the heart of God. This was a selfish, self-centered people, totally focused upon themselves and their own fleshly desires.

b. Note the tragic disobedience, an astonishing disobedience in light of what had just happened (v.40): the people refused to turn around and march into the wilderness toward the Red Sea (v.25). Instead, they planned to march into the promised land. A foolish, rash, totally disobedient action! A deliberate act of unbelief and rebellion against God!

c. The clear, strong warning of Moses was forceful: the people would not succeed. They would be defeated by the enemies of Canaan. The Amalekites and Canaanites would face them in the valleys and defeat them. Note why: because they had turned away from the LORD, and the LORD would not be with them (v.43).

d. The warning fell upon deaf ears: the people were caught up in a spirit of disobedience and rebellion against God. They marched in the arm of the flesh—marched toward the hill country without Moses or the Ark of the Covenant, the symbol of the presence and power of God (v.44).

e. The result was predictable: just as God through Moses had declared, the Amalekites and Canaanites attacked them. The enemies of the promised land sent them fleeing as far as Hormah (v.45).

> **Thought 1.** True confession always involves repentance, a turning away from sin to God. A person who repents and turns to God follows God. He obeys God. He does not disobey God and turn away from what God has instructed. True repentance listens to God's Word and does exactly what God's Word says. As stated, true repentance obeys God—explicitly obeys. This is the only confession that receives the forgiveness of sin.
>
> **Peter replied, "Repent and be baptized, every one of you, in the name of Jesus Christ for the forgiveness of your sins. And you will receive the gift of the Holy Spirit." (Ac. 2:38)**
>
> **Repent, then, and turn to God, so that your sins may be wiped out, that times of refreshing may come from the Lord. (Ac. 3:19)**

NUMBERS 13:1–14:45

Repent of this wickedness and pray to the Lord. Perhaps he will forgive you for having such a thought in your heart. (Ac. 8:22)

If we confess our sins, he is faithful and just and will forgive us our sins and purify us from all unrighteousness. (1 Jn. 1:9)

If my people, who are called by my name, will humble themselves and pray and seek my face and turn from their wicked ways, then will I hear from heaven and will forgive their sin and will heal their land. (2 Chr. 7:14)

Let the wicked forsake his way and the evil man his thoughts. Let him turn to the LORD, and he will have mercy on him, and to our God, for he will freely pardon. (Is. 55:7)

But if a wicked man turns away from all the sins he has committed and keeps all my decrees and does what is just and right, he will surely live; he will not die. (Eze. 18:21)

Rid yourselves of all the offenses you have committed, and get a new heart and a new spirit. Why will you die, O house of Israel? (Eze. 18:31)

DEEPER STUDY # 6
(Nu. 14:45) **Hormah, City of**: it was located in the territory assigned to the tribe of Simeon (Joshua 19:4). The Hebrew meaning of Hormah is *split rock* or *cursed for destruction*. The city of Hormah marked the limits to which the Canaanites had driven the Israelites.
See other Scripture references for study:
    De. 1:44; Jos. 12:14; Jos. 15:30; Jos. 19:4; Jud. 1:17; 1 S. 30:30; 1 Chr. 4:30

TYPES, SYMBOLS, AND PICTURES
(Numbers 13:1–14:45)

Historical Term	Type or Picture (Scriptural Basis for Each)	Life Application for Today's Believer	Biblical Application
Joshua Nu. 13:1-25; 27:18	*Joshua is a type or picture of Christ, the Person who saves us and leads us into the promised land forever. His very name pictured the great salvation that God was going to provide for His dear people in the promised land.* **So the LORD said to Moses, "Take Joshua son of Nun, a man in whom is the spirit, and lay your hand on him. (Nu. 27:18).**	The Greek name for Joshua is *Jesus*. Both Joshua and Jesus mean *God saves*. Moses changed "Hosea's" name to *Joshua* because Joshua was the appointed leader to lead God's people into the promised land (v.16). Joshua is a type of Christ. Jesus Christ is the Person who saves us and leads us into the promised land of heaven.	*Today in the town of David a Savior has been born to you; he is Christ the Lord. (Lu. 2:11)* *For the Son of Man came to seek and to save what was lost. (Lu. 19:10)* *For God did not send his Son into the world to condemn the world, but to save the world through him. (Jn. 3:17)* *I am the gate; whoever enters through me will be saved. He will come in and go out, and find pasture. (Jn. 10:9)* *Jesus answered, "I am the way and the truth and the life. No one comes to the Father except through me." (Jn. 14:6)* *Salvation is found in no one else, for there is no other name under heaven given to men by which we must be saved. (Ac. 4:12)* *Here is a trustworthy saying that deserves full acceptance: Christ Jesus came into the world to save sinners—of whom I am the worst. (1 Ti. 1:15)* *Therefore he is able to save completely those who come to God through him, because he always lives to intercede for them. (He. 7:25)*
Tearing of Clothes Nu. 14:1-10, esp. v.6	*The tearing of clothes was a symbol of ritual mourning.* **Joshua son of Nun and Caleb son of Jephunneh, who were among those**	Who is it that mourns? Who is it so full of grief that he cries and weeps and utters groanings deep from within? There are three persons who mourn and utter such	*But the tax collector stood at a distance. He would not even look up to heaven, but beat his breast and said, 'God, have mercy on me, a sinner.' (Lu. 18:13)*

NUMBERS 13:1–14:45

Historical Term	Type or Picture (Scriptural Basis for Each)	Life Application for Today's Believer	Biblical Application
	had explored the land, tore their clothes (Nu. 14:6).	groanings. 1. The person who is desperately sorry for his sins and feels ever so unworthy before the Lord. He has such a sense of sin that his heart is just broken. (Lu. 18:13) 2. The person who really feels the desperate plight and terrible suffering of others. The tragedies, the problems, the sinful behavior of others—the state, the condition, the lostness of the world—all weigh ever so heavily upon the heart of the mourner. 3. The person who experiences personal tragedy and intense trauma.	*When he saw the crowds, he had compassion on them, because they were harassed and helpless, like sheep without a shepherd. (Mt. 9:36)* *When Jesus landed and saw a large crowd, he had compassion on them and healed their sick. (Mt. 14:14)* *As a father has compassion on his children, so the Lord has compassion on those who fear him. (Ps. 103:13)* *In all their distress he too was distressed, and the angel of his presence saved them. In his love and mercy he redeemed them; he lifted them up and carried them all the days of old. (Is. 63:9)*

DIVISION III

THE FORTY LONG YEARS OF WILDERNESS WANDERINGS: A PICTURE OF THE BELIEVER'S PILGRIMAGE THROUGH THIS WORLD AS HE PREPARES TO ENTER THE PROMISED LAND, 15:1–25:18

(15:1–25:18) **DIVISION OVERVIEW—Wilderness Wanderings—Desert Journeys—Israel, Wilderness Wanderings of—Israel, Second Generation, Preparation of**: "the Wilderness Wanderings"—"the Desert Journeys": this is the all-important subject of this division of Numbers. One of the most fascinating, captivating, and intriguing subjects in all of Scripture. The first generation of Israelites have just committed the final, tragic rebellion that dooms them to wander about in the desert wilderness until they die (chapters 13-14). Now, chapter 15 begins as though nothing has happened. Why? One reason: the second generation—the children twenty years old or younger—now have to be prepared to conquer and claim the inheritance of the promised land. They have to be taught the laws of the land, strengthened, disciplined, and toughened. They must become the best soldiers possible: strong enough to endure the march and to defeat and conquer all the enemies who will oppose them.

God takes the forty years of *wilderness wanderings* and uses them for good. He takes these years of chastisement against the first generation and uses them to prepare their children to claim the inheritance the parents had forfeited by their evil unbelief and rebellion.

Immediately after the final, tragic failure of the first generation, God gave the laws covered in chapter 15. The laws were to help govern the second generation of believers after they entered the promised land. This is surprising; most of these laws would not be needed for about forty years. Why give the laws now, forty years ahead of time? To encourage the parents—who had just failed so miserably—and the children who were the hope of the future. God was encouraging them all, declaring that the promised land was real, so real that He was going to begin training the children in the laws of the land now—immediately. The parents were not to live defeated lives, spending the rest of their days depressed, angry, and discouraged. They were to place their hope in their children. About forty years from then, the children would march into the promised land. Here were laws they would need to govern them during those days. This is exactly what God says in 15:2: "After you come into the land I am giving you," you are to do this and that.

As one reads through the *wilderness wanderings*, a surprising fact emerges: little is really said about the long, hard years of suffering. A few events are shared, but only a few. Considering that the time frame of the *wilderness wanderings* covers about thirty-eight years, we are left wondering what happened during all the silent, unrecorded time.

The point that must be kept in mind during the reading of the *wilderness wanderings* is this: the events that were recorded are for us. They stand as a warning to us: that we must escape the evil of the Israelites. We must not wallow around in unbelief, grumbling, and complaining against God. We must not curse God nor rebel against Him. This fact is the clear declaration of Scripture:

> For everything that was written in the past was written to teach us, so that through endurance and the encouragement of the Scriptures we might have hope. (Ro. 15:4)
>
> Now these things occurred as examples to keep us from setting our hearts on evil things as they did. Do not be idolaters, as some of them were; as it is written: "The people sat down to eat and drink and got up to indulge in pagan revelry." We should not commit sexual immorality, as some of them did—and in one day twenty-three thousand of them died. We should not test the Lord, as some of them did—and were killed by snakes. And do not grumble, as some of them did—and were killed by the destroying angel. These things happened to them as examples and were written down as warnings for us, on whom the fulfillment of the ages has come. (1 Co. 10:6-11)

THE FORTY LONG YEARS OF WILDERNESS WANDERINGS: A PICTURE OF THE BELIEVER'S PILGRIMAGE THROUGH THIS WORLD AS HE PREPARES TO ENTER THE PROMISED LAND, 15:1–25:18

A. Event 1—God Gave Various Laws to Help Govern His People: Being Reassured and Prepared for the Promised Land, 15:1-41

DIVISION III
15:1–25:18

B. Event 2—a Dangerous Rebellion by Korah and His Allies: God Judges All Grumbling and Unbelief, All Rebellion and Unauthorized Approaches, 16:1-50

C. Event 3—the Budding of Aaron's Staff: The Test to Vindicate God's Priest and His Ministry (a Symbol of Christ or of the Minister), 17:1-13

D. Event 4—God Spelled Out the Service of the Priests and Levites: The Duties, Support, and Tithing of God's Ministers, 18:1-32

E. Event 5—God Gave the Law to Govern the Offering of the Red Heifer and the Cleansing Water: A Symbol of Christ, His Sacrifice and Cleansing Power, 19:1-22

F. Event 6—the Last Year of Israel in the Wilderness: Five Sad Events, 20:1-29

G. Event 7—the First Military Victories and the Bronze Snake: A Picture of Desperate Vows, of Christ the Savior, and of God's Protection and Victory, 21:1-35

H. Event 8—the Story of Balaam, His Donkey, and His Three Encounters with God: A Picture of the Unseen, Unknown Attempts by the Powers of Darkness to Defeat God's People, 22:1-41

I. Event 9—the Story of Balaam and the Seven Startling Oracles or Prophecies Pronounced by Him: The Blessings of God and a Glimpse into the Future, 23:1–24:25

J. Event 10—the Ultimate Rebellion of God's People and the End of the Forty Years of Wilderness Wanderings: Apostasy—Turning to Worldliness, to the Worship of Sex and Other Gods, 25:1-18

Numbers 15:1-41

CHAPTER 15

III. THE FORTY LONG YEARS OF WILDERNESS WANDERINGS: A PICTURE OF THE BELIEVER'S PILGRIMAGE THROUGH THIS WORLD AS HE PREPARES TO ENTER THE PROMISED LAND, 15:1-25:18

A. Event 1—God Gave Various Laws to Help Govern His People: Being Reassured & Prepared for the Promised Land, 15:1-41

1. **The law governing special Grain & Drink Offerings: A symbol of dedication & of thanksgiving**
   a. When to present the offerings
      1) After entering promised land
      2) When offering sacrifices made by fire (the Burnt & the Peace Offerings)
         - Because they pleased the LORD
         - Because they involved vows & freewill or festival occasions
   b. The amount to offer
      1) When sacrificing a lamb: A symbol of Christ's sacrifice
         - The Grain Offering: 2 qts. of flour mixed with 1 qt. of oil (a symbol of dedication & of thanking God)
         - The Drink Offering: 1 qt. of wine (a symbol of pouring out one's life to God)
      2) When sacrificing a ram: A symbol of Christ's sacrifice
         - The Grain Offering: 3 qts. of flour mixed with 2½ pints of oil
         - The Drink Offering: 2½ pints of wine (a symbol of Christ's sacrifice)
         - The result: An aroma that pleases the LORD
      3) When sacrificing a young bull: A symbol of Christ's sacrifice
         - The Grain Offering: 5 qts. of flour mixed with 2 qts. of oil (a symbol of giving thanks for the sacrifice)
         - The Drink Offering: 2 qts. of wine (a symbol of pouring out one's life to God)
         - The result: An aroma that pleases the LORD
   c. The absolute necessity for obedience: Must be strictly followed with each sacrifice

The LORD said to Moses,
2 "Speak to the Israelites and say to them: 'After you enter the land I am giving you as a home
3 And you present to the LORD offerings made by fire, from the herd or the flock, as an aroma pleasing to the LORD—whether burnt offerings or sacrifices, for special vows or freewill offerings or festival offerings—
4 Then the one who brings his offering shall present to the LORD a grain offering of a tenth of an ephah of fine flour mixed with a quarter of a hin of oil.
5 With each lamb for the burnt offering or the sacrifice, prepare a quarter of a hin of wine as a drink offering.
6 " 'With a ram prepare a grain offering of two-tenths of an ephah of fine flour mixed with a third of a hin of oil,
7 And a third of a hin of wine as a drink offering. Offer it as an aroma pleasing to the LORD.
8 " 'When you prepare a young bull as a burnt offering or sacrifice, for a special vow or a fellowship offering to the LORD,
9 Bring with the bull a grain offering of three-tenths of an ephah of fine flour mixed with half a hin of oil.
10 Also bring half a hin of wine as a drink offering. It will be an offering made by fire, an aroma pleasing to the LORD.
11 Each bull or ram, each lamb or young goat, is to be prepared in this manner.
12 Do this for each one, for as many as you prepare.
13 " 'Everyone who is native-born must do these things in this way when he brings an offering made by fire as an aroma pleasing to the LORD.
14 For the generations to come, whenever an alien or anyone else living among you presents an offering made by fire as an aroma pleasing to the LORD, he must do exactly as you do.
15 The community is to have the same rules for you and for the alien living among you; this is a lasting ordinance for the generations to come. You and the alien shall be the same before the LORD:
16 The same laws and regulations will apply both to you and to the alien living among you.' "
17 The LORD said to Moses,
18 "Speak to the Israelites and say to them: 'When you enter the land to which I am taking you
19 And you eat the food of the land, present a portion as an offering to the LORD.
20 Present a cake from the first of your ground meal and present it as an offering from the threshing floor.
21 Throughout the generations to come you are to give this offering to the LORD from the first of your ground meal.
22 " 'Now if you unintentionally fail to keep any of these commands the LORD gave Moses—
23 Any of the LORD's commands to you through him, from the day the LORD gave them and continuing through the generations to come—
24 And if this is done unintentionally without the community being aware of it, then the whole community is to offer a young bull for a burnt offering as an aroma pleasing to the LORD, along with its prescribed grain offering and drink offering, and a male goat for a sin offering.
25 The priest is to make atonement for the whole Israelite community, and they will be forgiven, for it was

   d. The persons who must obey
      1) The native-born: Must dedicate himself & present praise to God when approaching God through the sacrifice (a symbol of Christ)
      2) The alien or anyone else: Must dedicate himself & offer praise to God when approaching God through the sacrifice (a symbol of Christ)
      3) The point stressed: The same rules apply to everyone
      4) The law is to be a permanent law
      5) The love of God declared:
         - Everyone is the same, equal before the LORD
         - The same law & regulation applies to everyone, native-born & foreigner

2. **The law governing the firstfruits: A picture of tithes & offerings**
   a. When to present the offering: After entering the promised land & eating the food of the land
   b. What to present
      1) A portion of what one eats
      2) A cake made from the first of the ground meal—made from the grain harvest
   c. The importance of the law stressed
      1) To be a permanent law
      2) To be presented from the very first of the ground meal

3. **The law governing forgiveness for unintentional sin**
   a. The whole community of believers can be forgiven
      1) The two conditions for forgiveness:
         - First, the sin must be unintentional—committed in ignorance, being unaware of the sin
         - Second, the community must approach God for forgiveness through the sacrificing of the Burnt Offering & the Sin Offering (a symbol of approaching God through Christ, our sacrifice)
      2) The promise of God:
         - He will accept the sacrifice as atonement (reconciliation) & forgive the

NUMBERS 15:1-41

community (a symbol of accepting Christ as the basis for atonement & forgiveness)
• He will forgive the entire community, native-born & foreigner: Because the sin was unintentional
b. The individual can be forgiven
  1) The 2 conditions:
    • The sin must be unintentional
    • The person must come to God thru the sacrifice of the Sin Offering (a symbol of Christ's sacrifice)
  2) The promise of God:
    • He accepts the sacrifice as atonement & forgives
    • He forgives any person who approaches Him as stipulated by this law, whether native-born or foreigner
4. The law governing deliberate, defiant, or brazen sin—sin that dares to presume upon God
a. The nature of defiant sin
  1) Blasphemes the LORD
  2) Despises God's Word
  3) Deliberately breaks God's commandments
b. The judgment: Must be cut off—completely, eternally
c. The example of deliberate, defiant sin: A man gathered wood on the Sabbath—defiantly broke the law of the Sabbath
	not intentional and they have brought to the LORD for their wrong an offering made by fire and a sin offering.
	26 The whole Israelite community and the aliens living among them will be forgiven, because all the people were involved in the unintentional wrong.
	27 " 'But if just one person sins unintentionally, he must bring a year-old female goat for a sin offering.
	28 The priest is to make atonement before the LORD for the one who erred by sinning unintentionally, and when atonement has been made for him, he will be forgiven.
	29 One and the same law applies to everyone who sins unintentionally, whether he is a native-born Israelite or an alien.
	30 " 'But anyone who sins defiantly, whether native-born or alien, blasphemes the LORD, and that person must be cut off from his people.
	31 Because he has despised the LORD's word and broken his commands, that person must surely be cut off; his guilt remains on him.' "
	32 While the Israelites were in the desert, a man was found gathering wood on the
		Sabbath day.
		33 Those who found him gathering wood brought him to Moses and Aaron and the whole assembly,
		34 And they kept him in custody, because it was not clear what should be done to him.
		35 Then the LORD said to Moses, "The man must die. The whole assembly must stone him outside the camp."
		36 So the assembly took him outside the camp and stoned him to death, as the LORD commanded Moses.
		37 The LORD said to Moses,
		38 "Speak to the Israelites and say to them: 'Throughout the generations to come you are to make tassels on the corners of your garments, with a blue cord on each tassel.
		39 You will have these tassels to look at and so you will remember all the commands of the LORD, that you may obey them and not prostitute yourselves by going after the lusts of your own hearts and eyes.
		40 Then you will remember to obey all my commands and will be consecrated to your God.
		41 I am the LORD your God, who brought you out of Egypt to be your God. I am the LORD your God.' "
			1) He was arrested & brought to the authorities, Moses & Aaron, & before all the people
			2) He was held in custody until Moses could seek the LORD about what should be done
			3) He was sentenced to death by the LORD: To be stoned in the presence of the entire assembly—outside the camp
			4) He was executed as the LORD commanded
			5. The law instructing the believer to wear tassels on the hem of his clothing, attached with a blue cord: Pictures the need to live a holy, godly life
			a. The importance of the law: To be a permanent law
			b. The purpose:
			  1) To stir the believer to remember God's commandments
			  2) To stir the believer to live a life of separation from the world: Not to prostitute himself through fleshly lusts
			  3) To stir the believer to obey all God's commands: To be totally committed to God
			c. The authority behind the laws
			  1) The LORD: The only living & true God
			  2) The LORD *your* God
			  3) The LORD who saved you

DIVISION III

THE FORTY LONG YEARS OF WILDERNESS WANDERINGS: A PICTURE OF THE BELIEVER'S PILGRIMAGE THROUGH THIS WORLD AS HE PREPARES TO ENTER THE PROMISED LAND, 15:1–25:18

A. Event 1—God Gave Various Laws to Help Govern His People: Being Reassured and Prepared for the Promised Land, 15:1-41

(15:1-41) **Introduction—Assurance, Importance of—Confidence, Importance of**: assurance is a wonderful thing. If a person feels assured, he walks with confidence throughout life, conquering the problems and difficulties, the trials and temptations of life. He is victorious over all the pitfalls and enemies of life. This is what makes assurance so important. Assurance makes us confident, confident that we can conquer all.

But note: this kind of assurance—this confidence—comes only from God. Without God, we know that no matter how strong we are, disease or accident and eventually death will take us to the grave. Only God can conquer death, and only God can give us the perfect assurance to conquer all the pitfalls and enemies of life. Once a person genuinely comes to God through Jesus Christ, God saves that person and places His precious Holy Spirit within the new believer. The Holy Spirit gives the believer whatever assurance and confidence is needed to walk triumphantly throughout life. Moreover, the Spirit of God assures the believer of the promised land, of living forever in the presence of God.

This is the subject of the present passage. The Israelites had just committed the gross, terrible sin of unbelief and apostasy against God. (See outlines and notes—Nu. 13:1-14:45 for more discussion.) They even elected a new leader to replace God's servant Moses and were about to kill the four godly leaders: Moses, Aaron, Joshua, and Caleb. The people had gone too far, beyond repentance, beyond ever following God with a heart of true belief and righteousness. God knew this; consequently, He had to step in and judge the Israelites. This He did: the people were barred from entering the promised land. They were to die out in the desert or wilderness—wandering about for a total of 40 years until all the adults twenty years old or older had died. Only the children under twenty years old would be allowed to enter the promised land. The people were, of course, discouraged. They sensed defeat, failure, and some sorrow for their sin.

But into the midst of their discouragement and loss of heart God came. God filled their hearts with His grace, assuring them that their children would enter the promised land. The land would be their inheritance, the inheritance of the children.

How could God take a people so gripped with a spirit of despondency and raise their spirits, lifting them as high as the eagle soars? How could God place a deep-seated assurance within the hearts of His people, an assurance so strong that they could go on living and rearing their children—in order that their children might have a better life than the poor life they were having to live? God did one simple but powerful thing: He gave them several major laws that were to govern the children after they entered the land. It was to be about 40 years before the children would ever need some of these laws. But the day was coming when they would be needed, the day when the children would enter the promised land. Therefore, the adults were to teach these laws to their children. Hereafter, their task as adults was to focus almost entirely upon their children: to prepare their children to enter the promised land.

This is the subject of this passage of Scripture: *Event 1— God Gave Various Laws to Help Govern His People: Being Reassured and Prepared for the Promised Land*, 15:1-41.

1. The law governing special Grain and Drink Offerings: a symbol of dedication and of thanking God for Christ's sacrifice (vv.1-16).
2. The law governing the firstfruits: a picture of tithes and offerings (vv.17-21).
3. The law governing forgiveness for unintentional sin (vv.22-29).
4. The law governing deliberate, defiant, brazen sin—sin that dares to presume upon God (vv.30-36).
5. The law instructing the believer to wear tassels on the hem of his clothing—attached with a blue cord: pictures the need to live a holy, godly life (vv.37-41).

1 (15:1-16) **Dedication, to God—Submission, to God—Thanksgiving, to God—Praise, to God—Offerings, When to Present—Grain Offering—Drink Offering—Symbol, of Dedication—Symbol, of Submission**: God gave a law that governed special Grain and Drink Offerings. These offerings were a symbol of dedication and submission to God. They were also a symbol of thanking God for the atonement or reconciliation made through the substitute sacrifice.

⇒ Remember this about the Grain Offering: when a person laid his Grain Offering upon the burning sacrifice, he was offering his grain to God as a symbol of himself—of all he had and was. This was a picture of dedication, of laying all he had upon God. But dedication was not the only picture seen in his offering: by laying his grain upon the substitute sacrifice, he was thanking God for the sacrifice, that the sacrifice made atonement for him, reconciling him to God. Thus, the Grain Offering was an offering of dedication and thanksgiving to God, especially for the atonement (see outline and notes—Le. 2:1-16 for more discussion).

⇒ Remember this about the Drink Offering: when the wine was poured out upon the altar, the person was symbolizing that he was pouring out the best he had to offer before God, pouring out his life before God—submitting himself totally to God.

A quick glance back at the Scripture and outline will show the points covered by the law. Keep in mind that the Grain Offerings were important to God, very important, for they exposed the human heart of a person. The offerings revealed the true response of the person's heart to the sacrifice being made in his behalf. The sacrifice was a symbol of God's dear Son, the Lord Jesus Christ, who was to sacrifice His life for us all. It was this—the person's response to the sacrifice, a symbol of God's Son—that made the Grain and Drink Offerings so important to God. God gave His Son, the Lord Jesus Christ, to die for the sins of the world so that man would respond to Him, respond in love and obedience.

a. Note when the offerings were to be presented (vv.2-3).
  1) They were to present the Grain and Drink Offerings after entering the promised land. This was a glorious promise: the people were going to enter the promised land. Remember, the people had just committed gross sins against God, rebelling against Him and threatening to kill Moses, Aaron, Joshua, and Caleb (Nu. 13:1-14:45). The result was catastrophic: the judgment of God had fallen and the older generation—twenty years old and older—was condemned never to enter the promised land. Only their children would inherit the land. But God was giving assurance here: the children—the second generation of God's people—would inherit the land. The day would come, and when it came, they were to present the Grain and Drink Offerings to God. Even in the midst of judgment, the grace of God flows out to His people: great assurance is given to them. Their children will enter the promised land. The Word of God guarantees it.

  Note this fact: the people were unable to offer the Grain and Drink Offerings out in the desert or wilderness. They would not have the fields of grain nor the vines of grapes until they settled down in the promised land. This fact reinforces the grace and encouragement of God to His people. There was no apparent need to give this law to His people at this time. God could easily have waited and given it to them when they were going to need the law—some 38 years later, right before they were to enter the promised land. But here God was showering His grace upon His people, using the law as a clear means to encourage them. They could rest assured: their children would enter the promised land. Here was a law they would need when they settled in the land, a law they would need some 38 years in the future. Giving this law then gave assurance—absolute assurance—that God was going to lead the children, the second generation, into the promised land of God.

  2) They were to present the Grain and Drink Offerings with every sacrifice made by fire (v.3). This term *made by fire* refers to the Burnt Offering and the Peace or Fellowship Offering (see vv.3, 8). (See outlines and notes—Lev. 1:1-17; 3:1-17 for more discussion.) The whole sacrifice of the Burnt Offering was burned on the altar, but just a part of the sacrifice was burned in the Peace or Fellowship Offering. The rest of the animal was shared between the priest and the

worshippers. This is the first mention in Scripture that the wine offerings were to be offered with all Burnt Offerings and Peace or Fellowship Offerings. The picture was this:

⇒ When a person wanted to seek atonement or reconciliation with God, he approached God through the sacrifice of the Burnt Offering (a symbol of Christ's sacrifice). The sacrifice bore the penalty for sin that was due the person: the sacrifice paid the ransom, redeemed the person. The sacrifice made atonement, reconciled the person to God. Therefore, in thanksgiving for the atoning sacrifice, the person offered himself—all he was and had—to God. This act of dedication was symbolized by laying the Grain Offering upon the burning sacrifice (a picture of dying with the sacrifice, dying to self). Moreover, the person poured wine out upon the altar to symbolize that he was pouring out his life as an offering to God, submitting himself to God—all he was and had.

⇒ When a person wanted to grow in the peace and fellowship of God, he approached God through the sacrifice of the Peace or Fellowship Offering. The peace and fellowship of God came through the sacrifice. By bringing the sacrifice, a person's mind stayed focused upon seeking more and more of the peace and fellowship of God. Once again, the person was to offer the Grain and Drink Offerings...
- to express both thanksgiving and dedication
- to seek more and more of the peace and fellowship of God

Now, note why a person was to offer the Grain and Drink Offerings with these two particular sacrifices: because these two sacrifices pleased the LORD in a very special way. The sacrifice of the Burnt Offering secured atonement and reconciliation for His dear people, and the sacrifice of the Peace or Fellowship Offering enabled His people to experience and grow in peace and fellowship with Him.

But this was not all: these two sacrifices were offered during meaningful occasions. They were offered when making special vows, or freewill or festival offerings—times that involved special periods of dedication and thanksgiving. It was, therefore, only natural to offer Grain and Drink Offerings along with the sacrifices made during these occasions.

b. Note the amount of grain and drink that was to be offered with each sacrifice (vv.4-10). The Scripture and outline above gives the amount, making it unnecessary to repeat here. Note this one fact about the flour in the Grain Offering (vv.4, 6, 9): the flour was not to be the regular, ordinary flour used day by day. It was to be *fine, choice flour* (solet), the very best flour that could be made. A person was to give his very best to God, the best he had.

c. Note the absolute necessity for obedience: each sacrifice had to be prepared in this way—without exception (vv.11-12). The sacrifice was of critical importance to God, for the sacrifice was a symbol, a type of the sacrifice of His dear Son, the Lord Jesus Christ. Therefore, everything about the sacrifice—every single preparation—had to be carried out exactly as God dictated. Everything had to be done in the order and way He prescribed. Nothing else was acceptable.

d. Note that persons must approach God in this way: through the substitute sacrifice and the Grain and Drink Offerings (vv.13-14). Both the native-born Israelite and the foreigner or anyone else living among God's people had to approach God in this way. Atonement or reconciliation with God came only through the substitute sacrifice of the Burnt Offering. Peace and fellowship with God comes only through the substitute sacrifice of the Peace or Fellowship Offering. There was no other approach to God other than through the substitute sacrifice, no other approach that was acceptable to God. This was the way approaching God had to be, for the sacrifice represented the sacrifice of His dear Son who was to die for the world as the Lamb of God, die in order to take away the sin of the world.

Moreover, when a person approached God through the substitute sacrifice, he had to be genuine—completely sincere: he had to dedicate himself to God and be thankful for what God was doing for him through the substitute sacrifice. No matter who the person was—native-born or foreigner or anyone else—this was the only way he could approach God. This and this alone was the way he had to approach God if he wanted to be acceptable to Him.

The point is stressed and reemphasized: the same rules apply to everyone, no matter who he is—native-born or foreigner (v.15). No person—no matter who he is—is ever acceptable to God unless he follows these rules. He must approach God through the substitute sacrifice and be sincere enough to dedicate his life to God, offering thanksgiving for the atonement (reconciliation).

This law was established as a permanent law (v.15). It even applies to us and to all future generations. To be acceptable to God, we have to approach Him through the substitute sacrifice of His dear Son, the Lord Jesus Christ. Moreover, common sense tells us we must be sincere in our approach. We must be sincere enough to dedicate our lives to God, offering thanksgiving and praise to Him for what He does for us through Christ (atonement, reconciliation).

Note the great love of God declared by God Himself (vv.15-16): everyone is the same in approaching God. All are equal before the LORD: there are no favorites with God, no partiality shown by God. The same law and regulation applies to everyone. Each person must approach God through the substitute sacrifice. Each person must dedicate himself to God, offering thanksgiving and praise to Him for what He does for His people.

> **Thought 1.** Scripture makes it perfectly clear: there is only one approach to God, only one way to become acceptable to Him—through the substitute sacrifice of Jesus Christ. This is the very reason Christ died upon the cross; this is the meaning of the cross.
> (1) Jesus Christ died as our substitute sacrifice to secure atonement for us. Through His sacrificial death, we are ransomed, redeemed, reconciled to God.
>
> **You see, at just the right time, when we were still powerless, Christ died for the ungodly. (Ro. 5:6)**
>
> **For if, when we were God's enemies, we were reconciled to him through the death of his Son, how much more, having been reconciled, shall we be saved through his life! Not only is this so, but we also rejoice in God through our Lord Jesus Christ, through whom we have now received reconciliation. (Ro. 5:10-11)**

NUMBERS 15:1-41

Get rid of the old yeast that you may be a new batch without yeast—as you really are. For Christ, our Passover lamb, has been sacrificed. (1 Co. 5:7)

Christ redeemed us from the curse of the law by becoming a curse for us, for it is written: "Cursed is everyone who is hung on a tree." (Ga. 3:13)

And live a life of love, just as Christ loved us and gave himself up for us as a fragrant offering and sacrifice to God. (Ep. 5:2)

Who gave himself for us to redeem us from all wickedness and to purify for himself a people that are his very own, eager to do what is good. (Tit. 2:14)

For you know that it was not with perishable things such as silver or gold that you were redeemed from the empty way of life handed down to you from your forefathers, but with the precious blood of Christ, a lamb without blemish or defect. (1 Pe. 1:18-19)

For Christ died for sins once for all, the righteous for the unrighteous, to bring you to God. He was put to death in the body but made alive by the Spirit. (1 Pe. 3:18)

This is how we know what love is: Jesus Christ laid down his life for us. And we ought to lay down our lives for our brothers. (1 Jn. 3:16)

(2) Jesus Christ died as our substitute to secure peace and fellowship with God for us.

For God so loved the world that he gave his one and only Son, that whoever believes in him shall not perish but have eternal life. (Jn. 3:16)

You know the message God sent to the people of Israel, telling the good news of peace through Jesus Christ, who is Lord of all. (Ac. 10:36)

Therefore, since we have been justified through faith, we have peace with God through our Lord Jesus Christ. (Ro. 5:1)

But God demonstrates his own love for us in this: While we were still sinners, Christ died for us. (Ro. 5:8)

For he himself is our peace, who has made the two one and has destroyed the barrier, the dividing wall of hostility. (Ep. 2:14)

And through him to reconcile to himself all things, whether things on earth or things in heaven, by making peace through his blood, shed on the cross. (Col. 1:20)

We proclaim to you what we have seen and heard, so that you also may have fellowship with us. And our fellowship is with the Father and with his Son, Jesus Christ. (1 Jn. 1:3)

But he was pierced for our transgressions, he was crushed for our iniquities; the punishment that brought us peace was upon him, and by his wounds we are healed. (Is. 53:5)

Thought 2. The only approach to God is through the sacrifice of His dear Son, the Lord Jesus Christ. God accepts no other approach.

Jesus replied, "I tell you the truth, everyone who sins is a slave to sin." (Jn. 8:34)

Jesus answered, "I am the way and the truth and the life. No one comes to the Father except through me." (Jn. 14:6)

Salvation is found in no one else, for there is no other name under heaven given to men by which we must be saved. (Ac. 4:12)

For no one can lay any foundation other than the one already laid, which is Jesus Christ. (1 Co. 3:11)

For there is one God and one mediator between God and men, the man Christ Jesus, who gave himself as a ransom for all men—the testimony given in its proper time. (1 Ti. 2:5-6)

My dear children, I write this to you so that you will not sin. But if anybody does sin, we have one who speaks to the Father in our defense—Jesus Christ, the Righteous One. He is the atoning sacrifice for our sins, and not only for ours but also for the sins of the whole world. (1 Jn. 2:1-2)

Thought 3. When we approach God, we must be sincere, genuinely sincere. We must be willing to give our lives totally to Him:

(1) We must be willing to dedicate ourselves to Him just as the Old Testament believers symbolized in the Grain Offering. We must give our whole hearts to God.

Therefore, I urge you, brothers, in view of God's mercy, to offer your bodies as living sacrifices, holy and pleasing to God—this is your spiritual act of worship. Do not conform any longer to the pattern of this world, but be transformed by the renewing of your mind. Then you will be able to test and approve what God's will is—his good, pleasing and perfect will. (Ro. 12:1-2)

Love the LORD your God with all your heart and with all your soul and with all your strength. (De. 6:5)

Trust in the LORD with all your heart and lean not on your own understanding. (Pr. 3:5)

My son, give me your heart and let your eyes keep to my ways. (Pr. 23:26)

You will seek me and find me when you seek me with all your heart. (Je. 29:13)

"Even now," declares the LORD, "return to me with all your heart, with fasting and weeping and mourning." (Joel 2:12)

(2) We must be willing to pour out our lives to God, totally surrender and submit ourselves to Him. This is perhaps the same as being totally dedicated to God. However, being totally surrendered and submissive to God is another way to see exactly what God demands. Therefore, to help the reader see both pictures of God's demand, surrender to God is being treated as a different subject from dedication.

Do not offer the parts of your body to sin, as instruments of wickedness, but rather offer yourselves to God, as those who have been brought from death to life; and offer the parts of your body to him as instruments of righteousness. (Ro. 6:13)

Therefore, I urge you, brothers, in view of God's mercy, to offer your bodies as living sacrifices, holy and pleasing to God—this is your spiritual act of worship. Do not conform any longer to the pattern of this world, but be transformed by the renewing of your mind. Then you will be able to test and approve what God's will is—his good, pleasing and perfect will. (Ro. 12:1-2)

Submit yourselves, then, to God. Resist the devil, and he will flee from you. (Js. 4:7)

(3) We must thank God for the sacrifice of His dear Son, Christ Jesus the LORD. We must thank God for all He does for us through Christ, for the atonement (reconciliation) and for the peace and fellowship with God that Christ has brought about.

Always giving thanks to God the Father for everything, in the name of our Lord Jesus Christ. (Ep. 5:20)

Do not be anxious about anything, but in everything, by prayer and petition, with thanksgiving, present your requests to God. And the peace of God, which transcends all understanding, will guard your hearts and your minds in Christ Jesus. (Ph. 4:6-7)

Giving thanks to the Father, who has qualified you to share in the inheritance of the saints in the kingdom of light. (Col. 1:12)

And whatever you do, whether in word or deed, do it all in the name of the Lord Jesus, giving thanks to God the Father through him. (Col. 3:17)

Give thanks in all circumstances, for this is God's will for you in Christ Jesus. (1 Th. 5:18)

Enter his gates with thanksgiving and his courts with praise; give thanks to him and praise his name. (Ps. 100:4)

Let them sacrifice thank offerings and tell of his works with songs of joy. (Ps. 107:22)

2 (15:17-21) **Tithing—Offerings, to God—Firstfruits, Offering of:** God gave the law to govern the offering of the firstfruits. This was a picture of tithing one's income to the LORD as well as giving other offerings to the LORD. Whatever a person received, it was a gift from God. Therefore, the firstfruit—the first part—of whatever one received was to be given to God.

a. Note when the offering was to be presented to God (v.18). The firstfruit offering was to begin after the people entered and settled in the promised land, after they reaped their first crops and were ready to begin eating the food.

Again, God's wonderful grace just flows out upon His dear people. For the second time in these laws, He is giving them great assurance, encouraging and shoring up their hearts: their children would enter the promised land. It is a guaranteed fact: they will come to the day when they must begin offering the firstfruit of their crops to the LORD. They will be settled in the promised land and able to eat the food from their own fields. How merciful God is! How gracious and encouraging! The adults had hard, stubborn, immovable, and unyielding hearts—hearts of unbelief and rebellion against God. God knew they would never repent and follow Him—not completely, not in full dedication and surrender. Consequently, He had to judge them by keeping them out of the promised land. But not their precious children. The children would enter the promised land. Note how this would give some encouragement to the adults as well as the older children. The adults at least knew that their children would have a much better life than they.

b. God spelled out exactly what was to be presented as the firstfruit offering (vv.19-20). The people were actually to offer a portion of what they ate, that is, a cake from the very first of their flour or dough.

c. Note the importance of the law: it was to be a permanent offering (v.21). The very first of their ground meal was to be given to the LORD.

Thought 1. The lesson is clear: we are to give tithes and offerings to God. In fact, we are to give the firstfruit, the very first of our income and the very first of whatever we receive to God. Why? Because all things come from God. Everything we have—much or little—comes from God. He is the Source of every good and perfect gift.

Every good and perfect gift is from above, coming down from the Father of the heavenly lights, who does not change like shifting shadows. (Js. 1:17)

The disciples, each according to his ability, decided to provide help for the brothers living in Judea. (Ac.11:29)

On the first day of every week, each one of you should set aside a sum of money in keeping with his income, saving it up, so that when I come no collections will have to be made. (1 Co. 16:2)

For if the willingness is there, the gift is acceptable according to what one has, not according to what he does not have. (2 Co. 8:12)

Each man should give what he has decided in his heart to give, not reluctantly or under compulsion, for God loves a cheerful giver. (2 Co. 9:7)

A tithe of everything from the land, whether grain from the soil or fruit from the trees, belongs to the LORD; it is holy to the LORD. (Le. 27:30)

Each of you must bring a gift in proportion to the way the LORD your God has blessed you. (De. 16:17)

According to their ability they gave to the treasury for this work. (Ezr. 2:69)

Honor the LORD with your wealth, with the firstfruits of all your crops. (Pr. 3:9)

"Bring the whole tithe into the storehouse, that there may be food in my house. Test me in this," says the LORD Almighty, "and see if I will not throw open the floodgates of heaven and pour out so much blessing that you will not have room enough for it." (Mal. 3:10)

NUMBERS 15:1-41

3 (15:22-29) **Forgiveness, of Sin—Sin, Forgiveness of—Sin, Unintentional—Sin, in Ignorance—Sin, Unknown**: God gave the law that controlled forgiveness for the sins of ignorance or unintentional sins. A whole community of believers can sin unintentionally and need forgiveness as well as individuals. God covers both cases in this point:

a. The whole community of believers could be forgiven if they broke the law of God. Note exactly what is said: if the community of believers failed to keep any of God's commandments, they could be forgiven (vv.22-26). There were two conditions for forgiveness. First, the sin must be unintentional—committed in ignorance. The people had to be totally unaware that they were sinning. The sin had to be inadvertent: accidental, not on purpose, unmindful, unthinking, unthoughtful. If the sin was unintentional—committed in ignorance—God would forgive the whole community of believers.

Second, the community must approach God for forgiveness through the substitute sacrifice—the sacrifice of the Grain Offering and the Sin Offering (v.24). Remember, the substitute sacrifice is a symbol or type of the sacrifice of the Lord Jesus Christ.

b. The promise of God was and still is wonderful (vv.25-26). God promised two marvelous things:

⇒ God would accept the substitute sacrifice as atonement or reconciliation and would forgive the community. Note how this is a clear picture of our need to accept Christ as the basis for atonement and forgiveness of sin.

⇒ God would forgive the entire community, both native-born and foreigner—all because the sin was unintentional, done in ignorance, not knowing that it was sin (v.26).

c. The individual believer could be forgiven if he broke the law of God (vv.27-29).

1) But note: the same two conditions applied to the individual.

First, the sin had to be unintentional—committed in ignorance. The individual believer had to be totally unaware that he was sinning (v.27).

Second, the believer had to come to God for forgiveness—had to come through the substitute sacrifice of the sin offering (vv.27-28). Again, the substitute sacrifice is a symbol of the sacrifice of Jesus Christ for the sins of the world. When we sin, we must come to God for forgiveness, come through the substitute sacrifice of Christ.

2) The promises of God to the individual believer were most wonderful (vv.27-28). Any believer who had sinned unintentionally could be forgiven. God accepted the substitute sacrifice as atonement or reconciliation and forgave the sinning believer. No matter who the believer was—native-born or foreigner—he was forgiven if he came to God as stipulated by this law (v.29).

Thought 1. We often sin. In fact, we cannot keep from sinning. Why? Because we are "short of God's glory"—flawed, imperfect beings. We are defective and blemished, both morally and righteously. Consequently, we sin: fail and come short of God's glory, short of what God demands. Usually we are not even aware of the sins we commit. We sin unintentionally and in ignorance. But note: God forgives unintentional sins, sins that we know nothing about—if we will do one thing: come to Him through the substitute sacrifice of Jesus Christ and confess our sin, repenting and turning to Him in renewed dedication. This is the strong declaration of Scripture:

> The next day John saw Jesus coming toward him and said, "Look, the Lamb of God, who takes away the sin of the world!" (Jn. 1:29)

> Repent, then, and turn to God, so that your sins may be wiped out, that times of refreshing may come from the Lord. (Ac.3:19)

> God exalted him to his own right hand as Prince and Savior that he might give repentance and forgiveness of sins to Israel. (Ac.5:31)

> Therefore, my brothers, I want you to know that through Jesus the forgiveness of sins is proclaimed to you. (Ac.13:38)

> In him we have redemption through his blood, the forgiveness of sins, in accordance with the riches of God's grace. (Ep. 1:7)

> If we confess our sins, he is faithful and just and will forgive us our sins and purify us from all unrighteousness. (1 Jn. 1:9)

> He who conceals his sins does not prosper, but whoever confesses and renounces them finds mercy. (Pr. 28:13)

4 (15:30-36) **Sin, Defiant—Sin, Deliberate—Sin, Brazen—Sin, Presumptuous—Sin, Blasphemy—Sin, Presuming upon God—Sin, Despising God's Word**: God gave the law that controlled defiant, deliberate, brazen sin—sin that dares or presumes upon God or thinks that God will not judge or condemn. This law stands as a severe warning to every person within every generation. The word for *defiant* (yad) means with a high hand. Therefore, the person who commits this sin does so with a *high hand*, a hand lifted up in the face of God. This is...

- defiant sin
- deliberate sin
- brazen sin
- presumptuous sin (sin that assumes or thinks God will not judge, that dares God)

God has a strong warning to the defiant sinner, to the person who goes out and deliberately sins, knowing full well that he is sinning. Note the Scripture and outline:

a. Note the nature of defiant, deliberate sin (vv.30-31). In very simple terms, God spells out exactly what He means. Defiant, deliberate, presumptuous sin means...

- to blaspheme the LORD (v.30)
- to despise God's Word (v.31)
- to deliberately break God's commandments (v.31)

b. Severe judgment is to fall upon the defiant sinner (v.31). God's warning is clear: the defiant sinner must be completely cut off. The idea is eternal separation from God and His people. The person will join all defiant sinners and unbelievers someplace totally apart from God, out of God's presence forever. The defiant sinner wanted nothing to do with God during this earthly life. Therefore, God will give him his wish: the defiant sinner will have nothing to do with God throughout eternity. The sinner has condemned himself to be cut off—to be separated from God eternally.

NUMBERS 15:1-41

"At that time the sign of the Son of Man will appear in the sky, and all the nations of the earth will mourn. They will see the Son of Man coming on the clouds of the sky, with power and great glory." (Mt. 24:30)

When the Son of Man comes in his glory, and all the angels with him, he will sit on his throne in heavenly glory. All the nations will be gathered before him, and he will separate the people one from another as a shepherd separates the sheep from the goats. He will put the sheep on his right and the goats on his left. (Mt. 25:31-33)

If anyone is ashamed of me and my words in this adulterous and sinful generation, the Son of Man will be ashamed of him when he comes in his Father's glory with the holy angels. (Mk. 8:38)

And give relief to you who are troubled, and to us as well. This will happen when the Lord Jesus is revealed from heaven in blazing fire with his powerful angels. He will punish those who do not know God and do not obey the gospel of our Lord Jesus. (2 Th. 1:7-8)

Just as man is destined to die once, and after that to face judgment. (He. 9:27)

If this is so, then the Lord knows how to rescue godly men from trials and to hold the unrighteous for the day of judgment, while continuing their punishment. (2 Pe. 2:9)

By the same word the present heavens and earth are reserved for fire, being kept for the day of judgment and destruction of ungodly men. (2 Pe. 3:7)

"See, the Lord is coming with thousands upon thousands of his holy ones to judge everyone, and to convict all the ungodly of all the ungodly acts they have done in the ungodly way, and of all the harsh words ungodly sinners have spoken against him." (Jude 14-15)

Look, he is coming with the clouds, and every eye will see him, even those who pierced him; and all the peoples of the earth will mourn because of him. So shall it be! Amen. (Re. 1:7)

Then I saw a great white throne and him who was seated on it. Earth and sky fled from his presence, and there was no place for them. And I saw the dead, great and small, standing before the throne, and books were opened. Another book was opened, which is the book of life. The dead were judged according to what they had done as recorded in the books. The sea gave up the dead that were in it, and death and Hades gave up the dead that were in them, and each person was judged according to what he had done. Then death and Hades were thrown into the lake of fire. The lake of fire is the second death. If anyone's name was not found written in the book of life, he was thrown into the lake of fire. (Re. 20:11-15)

c. A clear example of deliberate, defiant sin is given (vv.32-36). The picture is that of a man who defiantly raised his fist in the face of God, who deliberately broke the Sabbath law of God. Remember this fact: the Sabbath law was of critical importance to God's people. Resting and meeting together for worship were essential to hold the community of believers together and for carrying out their mission assigned by God. Therefore, for this man to defiantly and deliberately break the Sabbath law was a gross, terrible offense against God and His people. Note what happened:
  1) The sinner was arrested and brought to the authorities, Moses and Aaron, and before all the people.
  2) The sinner was held in custody until Moses could seek the LORD about what should be done.
  3) The sinner was sentenced to death by the LORD: to be stoned in the presence of the entire assembly—outside the camp.
  4) The sinner was executed as the LORD commanded.

Thought 1. The Sabbath or Sunday is of critical importance to God and His people. Preserving a day for rest and worship is an absolute essential. The day is so important that it is one of the Ten Commandments. Why is it so important?
⇒ Because the human body needs one day of every seven for rest, relaxation, and recreation. The human body breaks down without a period of rest. (See outline and notes—Ex. 20:11 for more discussion.)
⇒ Because God's people need to worship together and carry out the ministry of the LORD together. Simply stated, the task cannot be done by individual believers acting alone. The task requires the church—all of God's people—worshipping and reaching out together.

This was the reason God established the Sabbath, the reason why He set aside one day for rest and worship. For this reason, the day of rest and worship must be preserved and respected.

How much more valuable is a man than a sheep! Therefore it is lawful to do good on the Sabbath. (Mt. 12:12)

He went to Nazareth, where he had been brought up, and on the Sabbath day he went into the synagogue, as was his custom. And he stood up to read. (Lu. 4:16)

Now the day on which Jesus had made the mud and opened the man's eyes was a Sabbath. (Jn. 9:14)

On the Sabbath we went outside the city gate to the river, where we expected to find a place of prayer. We sat down and began to speak to the women who had gathered there. (Ac. 16:13)

As his custom was, Paul went into the synagogue, and on three Sabbath days he reasoned with them from the Scriptures. (Ac. 17:2)

On the first day of the week we came together to break bread. Paul spoke to the people and, because he intended to leave the next day, kept on talking until midnight. (Ac. 20:7)

Let us not give up meeting together, as some are in the habit of doing, but let us encourage one another—and all the more as you see the Day approaching. (He. 10:25)

Remember the Sabbath day by keeping it holy. (Ex. 20:8)

Observe the Sabbath, because it is holy to you. Anyone who desecrates it must be put to death; whoever does any work on that day must be cut off from his people. (Ex. 31:14)

Six days you shall labor, but on the seventh day you shall rest; even during the plowing season and harvest you must rest. (Ex. 34:21)

When the neighboring peoples bring merchandise or grain to sell on the Sabbath, we will not buy from them on the Sabbath or on any holy day. (Ne. 10:31)

In those days I saw men in Judah treading winepresses on the Sabbath and bringing in grain and loading it on donkeys, together with wine, grapes, figs and all other kinds of loads. And they were bringing all this into Jerusalem on the Sabbath. Therefore I warned them against selling food on that day. (Ne. 13:15)

Blessed is the man who does this, the man who holds it fast, who keeps the Sabbath without desecrating it, and keeps his hand from doing any evil. (Is. 56:2)

"If you keep your feet from breaking the Sabbath and from doing as you please on my holy day, if you call the Sabbath a delight and the LORD's holy day honorable, and if you honor it by not going your own way and not doing as you please or speaking idle words, then you will find your joy in the LORD, and I will cause you to ride on the heights of the land and to feast on the inheritance of your father Jacob." The mouth of the LORD has spoken. (Is. 58:13-14)

Yet the people of Israel rebelled against me in the desert. They did not follow my decrees but rejected my laws—although the man who obeys them will live by them—and they utterly desecrated my Sabbaths. So I said I would pour out my wrath on them and destroy them in the desert. (Eze. 20:13)

5 (15:37-41) **Holiness, of Life—Holy, Duty to Be—Mind, Duty to Protect—Thoughts, Duty to Protect—Mind, Duty to Concentrate—Concentration, Duty to—Commandments, Duty to Remember—Separation, Spiritual**: God gave the law that instructed the believer to wear tassels on the hem of his clothing—attached with a blue cord. Note that this pictured the need for all believers to live a holy, godly life. *The Expositor's Bible Commentary* points out that this law is the basis for wearing the traditional prayer shawl of Israel, and that the prayer shawl is the pattern for the flag of the state of Israel today.

a. The importance of the law is seen in that it was established as a permanent law (v.38).

b. The purpose was threefold:
⇒ to stir the believer to remember God's commandments (v.39)
⇒ to stir the believer to live a life of separation from the world: not to prostitute himself through fleshly lusts (v.39)
⇒ to stir the believer to obey all God's commands: to be totally committed to God (v.40)

As a believer moved through the day, the tassels would be flapping about, occasionally attracting his attention. At that point he was to focus—for just a moment—upon the fact that he was to obey God's commandments and live a life of separation from the world. He was to live a holy life, not going after the lusts of his own selfish, fleshly heart and eyes. Note how this is described: the believer was not to live a life of spiritual prostitution, not to turn away from his devotion to God, not to turn to the world with all its fleshly lusts and false gods.

c. The authority behind the laws given in this passage is the LORD Himself (v.41).
1) The person who gave the laws is "the LORD": the only living and true God.
2) The person who gave the laws is "the LORD *your* God": He is personal—has established a personal relationship with the believer.
3) He is "the Lord who [saved] you"—"who brought you out of Egypt" [a symbol of the world]: the only living God who has the power to truly save His people from the world and all its enslavements.

Thought 1. Note several significant lessons:
(1) We must control our minds and think of God throughout the day. We must train our minds to think of Him at set times throughout the day—after every so many minutes—to focus upon Him for just a moment.

We demolish arguments and every pretension that sets itself up against the knowledge of God, and we take captive every thought to make it obedient to Christ. (2 Co. 10:5)

The mind of sinful man is death, but the mind controlled by the Spirit is life and peace. (Ro. 8:6)

Your attitude should be the same as that of Christ Jesus. (Ph. 2:5)

Be diligent in these matters; give yourself wholly to them, so that everyone may see your progress. (1 Ti. 4:15)

This is the covenant I will make with the house of Israel after that time, declares the Lord. I will put my laws in their minds and write them on their hearts. I will be their God, and they will be my people. (He. 8:10; see He. 10:16)

Do not let this Book of the Law depart from your mouth; meditate on it day and night, so that you may be careful to do everything written in it. Then you will be prosperous and successful. (Jos. 1:8)

But his delight is in the law of the LORD, and on his law he meditates day and night. (Ps. 1:2)

In your anger do not sin; when you are on your beds, search your hearts and be silent. Selah. (Ps. 4:4)

May the words of my mouth and the meditation of my heart be pleasing in your sight, O LORD, my Rock and my Redeemer. (Ps. 19:14)

How can a young man keep his way pure? By living according to your word. (Ps. 119:9)

I have hidden your word in my heart that I might not sin against you. (Ps. 119:11)

(2) We must remember and obey God's commandments throughout the day.

"Not everyone who says to me, 'Lord, Lord,' will enter the kingdom of heaven, but only he who does the will of my Father who is in heaven." (Mt. 7:21)

Jesus replied, "If anyone loves me, he will obey my teaching. My Father will love him, and we will come to him and make our home with him." (Jn. 14:23)

If you obey my commands, you will remain in my love, just as I have obeyed my Father's commands and remain in his love. (Jn. 15:10)

You are my friends if you do what I command. (Jn. 15:14)

Blessed are those who wash their robes, that they may have the right to the tree of life and may go through the gates into the city. (Re. 22:14)

Love the Lord your God with all your heart and with all your soul and with all your strength. These commandments that I give you today are to be upon your hearts. Impress them on your children. Talk about them when you sit at home and when you walk along the road, when you lie down and when you get up. Tie them as symbols on your hands and bind them on your foreheads. Write them on the doorframes of your houses and on your gates. (De. 6:5-9)

The Lord your God commands you this day to follow these decrees and laws; carefully observe them with all your heart and with all your soul. (De. 26:16)

Be very strong; be careful to obey all that is written in the Book of the Law of Moses, without turning aside to the right or to the left. (Jos. 23:6)

But Samuel replied: "Does the Lord delight in burnt offerings and sacrifices as much as in obeying the voice of the Lord? To obey is better than sacrifice, and to heed is better than the fat of rams." (1 S. 15:22)

(3) We must keep our minds focused upon living a holy life throughout the day—a life of separation from the world.

With many other words he warned them; and he pleaded with them, "Save yourselves from this corrupt generation." (Ac. 2:40)

Do not conform any longer to the pattern of this world, but be transformed by the renewing of your mind. Then you will be able to test and approve what God's will is—his good, pleasing and perfect will. (Ro. 12:2)

But now I am writing you that you must not associate with anyone who calls himself a brother but is sexually immoral or greedy, an idolater or a slanderer, a drunkard or a swindler. With such a man do not even eat. (1 Co. 5:11)

Do not be yoked together with unbelievers. For what do righteousness and wickedness have in common? Or what fellowship can light have with darkness? (2 Co. 6:14)

"Therefore come out from them and be separate, says the Lord. Touch no unclean thing, and I will receive you. I will be a Father to you, and you will be my sons and daughters, says the Lord Almighty." (2 Co. 6:17-18)

Have nothing to do with the fruitless deeds of darkness, but rather expose them. (Ep. 5:11)

In the name of the Lord Jesus Christ, we command you, brothers, to keep away from every brother who is idle and does not live according to the teaching you received from us. (2 Th. 3:6)

Do not follow the crowd in doing wrong. When you give testimony in a lawsuit, do not pervert justice by siding with the crowd. (Ex. 23:2)

Be careful not to make a treaty with those who live in the land where you are going, or they will be a snare among you. (Ex. 34:12)

I meditate on your precepts and consider your ways. (Ps. 119:15)

Do not set foot on the path of the wicked or walk in the way of evil men. (Pr. 4:14)

Depart, depart, go out from there! Touch no unclean thing! Come out from it and be pure, you who carry the vessels of the Lord. (Is. 52:11)

TYPES, SYMBOLS, AND PICTURES
(Numbers 15:1-41)

Historical Term	Type or Picture (Scriptural Basis for Each)	Life Application for Today's Believer	Biblical Application
Grain Offering Nu. 15:1-16 (See also Le. 2:3)	*The Grain Offering is a symbol of three things:* 1. *A symbol of joy and thanksgiving to God...* • *for the joy of atonement: salvation, redemption, reconciliation*	The symbol of the Grain Offering teaches us three things: 1. We are to offer the joy and thanksgiving of our hearts to God for everything: a. For the joy of atonement: salvation, redemption, reconciliation	*While they were eating, Jesus took bread, gave thanks and broke it, and gave it to his disciples, saying, "Take it; this is my body." (Mk. 14:22) For the bread of God is he who comes down from heaven and gives life to the world."*

NUMBERS 15:1-41

Historical Term	Type or Picture (Scriptural Basis for Each)	Life Application for Today's Believer	Biblical Application
	• for one's livelihood: the harvest, crops, rain, sunshine, housing, clothing *2. A symbol of an act of dedication and dependence upon God* *3. A symbol of Christ, the Bread of Life.* **With a ram prepare a grain offering of two-tenths of an ephah of fine flour mixed with a third of a hin of oil. (Nu. 15:6)**	b. For our livelihood: the harvest food, crops, rain, sunshine, housing, clothing 2. It is God who has given us life: air, water, sun, moon, stars, crops, food, clothing, housing—all the necessities of life. God created the materials of the universe, everything that sustains our lives and keeps us going. We owe God everything we are and have: we must, therefore, give the offering of dedication to God and declare our dependence upon Him. 3. Jesus Christ is the Bread of Life... • who feeds us • who nourishes us • who sustains us with Himself	*"Sir," they said, "from now on give us this bread." Then Jesus declared, "I am the bread of life. He who comes to me will never go hungry, and he who believes in me will never be thirsty." (Jn. 6:33-35)* *I tell you the truth, he who believes has everlasting life. I am the bread of life. (Jn. 6:47-48)* *"I am the living bread that came down from heaven. If anyone eats of this bread, he will live forever. This bread is my flesh, which I will give for the life of the world." (Jn. 6:51)* *"This is the bread that came down from heaven. Your forefathers ate manna and died, but he who feeds on this bread will live forever." (Jn. 6:58)*
Firstfruits Nu. 15:17-21	*The firstfruits is a picture of tithing one's income as well as other offerings to the* LORD. *Whatever a person received, it was a gift from God. Therefore, the firstfruit—the first part—of whatever one received was to be given to God.* **Present a cake from the first of your ground meal and present it as an offering from the threshing floor. Throughout the generations to come you are to give this offering to the** LORD **from the first of your ground meal. (Nu. 15:20-21)**	The lesson is clear: we are to give tithes and offerings to God. In fact, we are to give the firstfruit, the very first of our income and the very first of whatever we receive to God. Why? Because all things come from God. Everything we have—much or little—comes from God. He is the Source of every good and perfect gift.	*Every good and perfect gift is from above, coming down from the Father of the heavenly lights, who does not change like shifting shadows. (Js. 1:17)* *The disciples, each according to his ability, decided to provide help for the brothers living in Judea. (Ac. 11:29)* *On the first day of every week, each one of you should set aside a sum of money in keeping with his income, saving it up, so that when I come no collections will have to be made. (1 Co. 16:2)* *For if the willingness is there, the gift is acceptable according to what one has, not according to what he does not have. (2 Co. 8:12)* *Each man should give what he has decided in his heart to give, not reluctantly or under compulsion, for God loves a cheerful giver. (2 Co. 9:7; see also De. 16:17; Le. 27:30; Ezr. 2:69; Pr. 3:9; Mal. 3:10).*

NUMBERS 16:1-50

CHAPTER 16

B. Event 2—A Dangerous Rebellion by Korah & His Allies: God Judges All Grumbling & Unbelief, All Rebellion & Unauthorized Approaches, 16:1-50

1. **The revolt & the issues at stake**
   a. The rebels or conspirators
      1) Korah: A Levite & a cousin to Moses—their fathers were brothers
      2) Dathan, Abiram & On: Reubenites
      3) 250 well-known leaders, official representatives of the nation: Some were Levites, religious workers (see vv.8-11)
   b. The issue or protest: Opposition to Moses & Aaron
      1) Their charge: Assumed too much authority—had gone too far by turning from the promised land.
      2) Their desire: The power of leadership & the priesthood (v.7-14)
   c. The reaction of Moses: He fell face down—seeking God
      1) He arose & challenged Korah & his allies: To let the LORD choose His own leader—show who really belonged to God & who could approach Him for leadership in guiding God's people
         • To prove themselves by taking censers & burning incense before the LORD
         • To prove themselves by letting the LORD choose His leader, the one who was truly holy, set apart
      2) He rebuked, warned the Levites
         • They were the ones who had gone too far (v.7)
         • They were guilty of abusing & trampling underfoot God's call to them: To serve as Levites, the privilege of being set apart to serve God & His people
         • They were guilty of seeking the priesthood itself—seeking position that should come only from God
         • They were revolting

Korah son of Izhar, the son of Kohath, the son of Levi, and certain Reubenites—Dathan and Abiram, sons of Eliab, and On son of Peleth—became insolent
2 And rose up against Moses. With them were 250 Israelite men, well-known community leaders who had been appointed members of the council.
3 They came as a group to oppose Moses and Aaron and said to them, "You have gone too far! The whole community is holy, every one of them, and the LORD is with them. Why then do you set yourselves above the LORD's assembly?"
4 When Moses heard this, he fell facedown.
5 Then he said to Korah and all his followers: "In the morning the LORD will show who belongs to him and who is holy, and he will have that person come near him. The man he chooses he will cause to come near him.
6 You, Korah, and all your followers are to do this: Take censers
7 And tomorrow put fire and incense in them before the LORD. The man the LORD chooses will be the one who is holy. You Levites have gone too far!"
8 Moses also said to Korah, "Now listen, you Levites!
9 Isn't it enough for you that the God of Israel has separated you from the rest of the Israelite community and brought you near himself to do the work at the LORD's tabernacle and to stand before the community and minister to them?
10 He has brought you and all your fellow Levites near himself, but now you are trying to get the priesthood too.
11 It is against the LORD that you and all your followers have banded together. Who is Aaron that you should grumble against him?"
12 Then Moses summoned Dathan and Abiram, the sons of Eliab. But they said, "We will not come!
13 Isn't it enough that you have brought us up out of a land flowing with milk and honey to kill us in the desert? And now you also want to lord it over us?
14 Moreover, you haven't brought us into a land flowing with milk and honey or given us an inheritance of fields and vineyards. Will you gouge out the eyes of these men? No, we will not come!"
15 Then Moses became very angry and said to the LORD, "Do not accept their offering. I have not taken so much as a donkey from them, nor have I wronged any of them."
16 Moses said to Korah, "You and all your followers are to appear before the LORD tomorrow—you and they and Aaron.
17 Each man is to take his censer and put incense in it—250 censers in all—and present it before the LORD. You and Aaron are to present your censers also."
18 So each man took his censer, put fire and incense in it, and stood with Moses and Aaron at the entrance to the Tent of Meeting.
19 When Korah had gathered all his followers in opposition to them at the entrance to the Tent of Meeting, the glory of the LORD appeared to the entire assembly.
20 The LORD said to Moses and Aaron,
21 "Separate yourselves from this assembly so I can put an end to them at once."
22 But Moses and Aaron fell facedown and cried out, "O God, God of the spirits of all mankind, will you be angry with the entire assembly when only one man sins?"
23 Then the LORD said to Moses,
24 "Say to the assembly, 'Move away from the tents of Korah, Dathan and

against the LORD not against Aaron

d. The confrontation, contempt, & defiance of Dathan & Abiram
   1) They rejected the summons, refused to meet with Moses
   2) They exaggerated their former life & provision in Egypt
   3) They blamed Moses for their plight in the wilderness
   4) They accused him of lording it over them
   5) They blamed him for failing to enter the promised land
   6) They charged him with abuse of power—with deception, ulterior motives
   7) They repeated their outrage, their contempt & defiance: would not meet with Moses
e. The angry reaction of Moses
   1) Cried out for God not to accept the incense offering of the rebels
   2) Declared he was innocent: Had not misused his office for gain nor wronged anyone

2. **The showdown & the judgment of the rebels**
   a. The challenge to Korah & his allies repeated
      1) To approach the LORD tomorrow
      2) To have each man take his censer & present incense before the LORD—all 250 of the rebels
      3) To include Korah & Aaron
   b. The arrogant, defiant stand of the rebels against Moses & Aaron: At the entrance to the Tabernacle
      1) The response of the LORD
         • Suddenly, immediately—the glory of the LORD flashed & burst forth, visible to everyone
         • The LORD threatened to destroy the nation—at once, immediately
      2) The response of Moses & Aaron: They fell down before God, crying out
         • To the Creator: "God of the spirits of all mankind"
         • Begged God not to destroy all because of one man's sins
      3) The warning of the LORD: Charge the people to move away from the tents of the rebel ringleaders—Korah, Dathan, & Abiram

145

Numbers 16:1-50

c. The catastrophic judgment upon Dathan, Abiram, & Korah: The ringleaders were confronted by the true servants of God, Moses & the elders of Israel
1) The people were warned to move back, out of the presence of these wicked men
- They must separate themselves totally from the wicked: Not touch anything of theirs
- They obeyed the warning

2) The two ringleaders had come out with their families to confront & stand against God's leaders, Moses & the elders

3) The judgment of God would validate or prove that Moses was God's servant: He proposed a test
- If God's judgment did not fall upon the rebels—that would prove that Moses was not God's choice for a leader
- If God's judgment fell in some spectacular way, that would validate Moses as God's servant

4) The judgment of God would fall in a spectacular way
- The earth would open up & swallow the rebels & all their belongings
- The rebels would go down alive into the grave

5) The catastrophic judgment fell—suddenly, immediately
- The ground split open
- The earth swallowed all the rebels, their households, their followers & their possessions
- The rebels fell alive into the grave: The earth closed over them & they perished

6) The fear of the people: They fled as they heard the screams & commotion of the earthquake

d. The terrifying judgment upon the 250 men offering incense: Fire blazed forth from God's presence & burned them up

3. **The step taken to stir the memory of this judgment**
   a. The command of the LORD
   1) To save the censers of the 250 wicked men who were judged: The censers

Abiram.'"
25 Moses got up and went to Dathan and Abiram, and the elders of Israel followed him.
26 He warned the assembly, "Move back from the tents of these wicked men! Do not touch anything belonging to them, or you will be swept away because of all their sins."
27 So they moved away from the tents of Korah, Dathan and Abiram. Dathan and Abiram had come out and were standing with their wives, children and little ones at the entrances to their tents.
28 Then Moses said, "This is how you will know that the LORD has sent me to do all these things and that it was not my idea:
29 If these men die a natural death and experience only what usually happens to men, then the LORD has not sent me.
30 But if the LORD brings about something totally new, and the earth opens its mouth and swallows them, with everything that belongs to them, and they go down alive into the grave, then you will know that these men have treated the LORD with contempt."
31 As soon as he finished saying all this, the ground under them split apart
32 And the earth opened its mouth and swallowed them, with their households and all Korah's men and all their possessions.
33 They went down alive into the grave, with everything they owned; the earth closed over them, and they perished and were gone from the community.
34 At their cries, all the Israelites around them fled, shouting, "The earth is going to swallow us too!"
35 And fire came out from the LORD and consumed the 250 men who were offering the incense.
36 The LORD said to Moses,
37 "Tell Eleazar son of Aaron, the priest, to take the censers out of the smoldering remains and scatter the coals some distance away, for the censers are holy—
38 The censers of the men who sinned at the cost of their lives. Hammer the censers into sheets to overlay the altar, for they were presented before the LORD and have become holy. Let them be a sign to the Israelites."
39 So Eleazar the priest collected the bronze censers brought by those who had been burned up, and he had them hammered out to overlay the altar,
40 As the LORD directed him through Moses. This was to remind the Israelites that no one except a descendant of Aaron should come to burn incense before the LORD, or he would become like Korah and his followers.
41 The next day the whole Israelite community grumbled against Moses and Aaron. "You have killed the LORD's people," they said.
42 But when the assembly gathered in opposition to Moses and Aaron and turned toward the Tent of Meeting, suddenly the cloud covered it and the glory of the LORD appeared.
43 Then Moses and Aaron went to the front of the Tent of Meeting,
44 And the LORD said to Moses,
45 "Get away from this assembly so I can put an end to them at once." And they fell facedown.
46 Then Moses said to Aaron, "Take your censer and put incense in it, along with fire from the altar, and hurry to the assembly to make atonement for them. Wrath has come out from the LORD; the plague has started."
47 So Aaron did as Moses said, and ran into the midst of the assembly. The plague had already started among the people, but Aaron offered the incense and made atonement for them.
48 He stood between the living and the dead, and the plague stopped.
49 But 14,700 people died from the plague, in addition

were holy, had been set apart to God

2) To hammer the censers into sheets of metal & use them to overlay the altar

3) The purpose: To be a warning of God's judgment

b. The obedience of Eleazar the priest, the son of Aaron
1) He collected the censers & had them hammered out to overlay the altar

2) The purpose: To remind the people...
- that no unauthorized person could approach God
- that an unauthorized approach to God would be judged—just as Korah & his allies had been

4. **The staggering unbelief of the people: Murmured & grumbled the very next day**
   a. The false charge: Accused them of causing the rebels' deaths—gathered to oppose them
   b. The intervention of God: The cloud covered the Tabernacle & the glory of the LORD burst forth—giving the appearance & threat of judgment

   1) The servants of God approached God's presence
   2) The threat of God: He was instantly going to destroy the people

   c. The response of Moses & Aaron: Fell down in prayer

   d. The judgment of God: A plague
   1) Moses gave quick instructions to Aaron
   - To take his censer with incense & burning coals from the altar
   - To rush among the people, make atonement
   - The reason: To stop God's judgment, plague
   2) Aaron obeyed
   - Rushed to the people
   - Offered incense & made atonement for them

   - Stood between the living & the dead: The judgment (plague) was stopped
   3) The result of God's judgment
   - 14,700 people died plus

NUMBERS 16:1-50

Korah & his allies • Aaron returned to Moses at the Tabernacle (no doubt, to thank God for delivering them & sparing the people)	to those who had died because of Korah. 50 Then Aaron returned to Moses at the entrance to the Tent of Meeting, for the plague had stopped.

DIVISION III

THE FORTY LONG YEARS OF WILDERNESS WANDERINGS: A PICTURE OF THE BELIEVER'S PILGRIMAGE THROUGH THIS WORLD AS HE PREPARES TO ENTER THE PROMISED LAND, 15:1–25:18

B. Event 2—A Dangerous Rebellion by Korah and His Allies: God Judges All Grumbling and Unbelief, All Rebellion and Unauthorized Approaches, 16:1-50

(16:1-50) **Introduction—Power, Seeking—Position, Seeking—Self-seeking, Example of**: seeking power and authority, position and rule, honor and recognition—all these are sought by people and sought often. But in seeking these things, the motive is often wrong. The motive must always be to serve people, not to rule and lord authority over people. The motive must be to help and to make a contribution to society, not to hold positions in order to receive more money or the esteem and honor of men. It is wrong to covet positions for selfish purposes. Selfishness leads to strife and division, disintegration and destruction. Seeking position, authority, or rule for selfish purposes can destroy lives, corrupt organizations and cause revolt and rebellion within nations. Selfishness and self-seeking lie at the root of so many of the problems we see throughout society.

What happens now to Israel paints a clear picture of what selfishness and self-seeking can do to disrupt the lives of people. Because of their terrible unbelief and rebellion against God, the people were forced to turn back from the promised land and wander about in the desert wilderness. Because of this drastic change of plans, a group of leaders banded together to lead a revolt against God's dear servants, Moses and Aaron. This passage covers this dangerous rebellion, a rebellion that suffered a horrible, terrifying judgment. This is: *Event 2—a Dangerous Rebellion by Korah and His Allies: God Judges All Grumbling and Unbelief, All Rebellion and Unauthorized Approaches*, 16:1-50.

1. The revolt and the issues at stake (vv.1-15).
2. The showdown and the judgment of the rebels (vv.16-35).
3. The step taken to stir the memory of this judgment (vv.36-40).
4. The staggering unbelief of the people: murmured and grumbled against God's servants—the very next day (vv.41-50).

1 (16:1-15) **Unbelief, Example of—Grumbling, Against the Minister—Complaining, Against the Minister—Rebellion, Against God—Approach, To God, Wrong—Conspiracy, Against the Minister—Korah—Opposition, to the Minister—Moses, Opposition to**: there was the revolt and the issues at stake. In all revolts or rebellions there are critical issues at stake, strong differences that lead to division and usually to injury, slaughter, and death. Revolts are caused by such things as...

- broken promises
- injustice
- greed
- a true heart for service
- lust for power
- selfishness
- dissatisfaction with leadership or policies
- a belief that one can actually do a better job than the present leader

In the present situation, Korah and his allies were disgusted with the leadership of Moses and Aaron. Remember: under God's direction, Moses had just turned Israel around from the promised land back into the desert wilderness. The adults twenty years old or older were condemned to wander about and die in the wilderness over the next 38 years—all because of their terrible sin (see outline and notes—Nu. 13:1-14:45 for more discussion). Korah and his allies were ready to take action, and take action they did. They conspired and incited a coup against Moses and Aaron. Rebellion, revolt, and insurrection against God and His leaders were actually taking place. Korah and his allies were fed up, filled with anger and wrath, fire and fury against Moses and Aaron. They blamed Moses and Aaron for not fulfilling the promise to take the Israelites into the promised land. If Moses would not take the leadership reins, then they would. By force they would take over the leadership role and lead the people into the promised land.

The charges against Moses and Aaron are scattered throughout the chapter. For this reason, they are being listed here in one place for a quicker, better understanding. Korah and his allies...

- opposed the leadership of Moses, wanting to replace him—craving the power of the national leader (vv.3, 13-14)
- wanted the Levites promoted as priests (vv.3, 7)
- craved the priesthood, the power of the High Priest (v.10)
- blamed Moses for failing to enter the promised land (v.14)

a. Note that the rebels are conspirators (vv.1-2). Korah was the ringleader of the coup. He was a Levite and, interestingly, a cousin to Moses. Their fathers were brothers. Three other brothers of the tribe of Reuben were also ringleaders: Dathan, Abiram, and On. Korah was from the Kohathite clan. The Kohathites and the tribe of Reuben camped on the south side of the Tabernacle, camped side by side. Living close together and being friends and co-leaders gave them ample opportunity to sit around in the evenings grumbling, murmuring, and sharing their complaints and disappointments. About what? About having turned away from the promised land to wander about in the

NUMBERS 16:1-50

desert, a journey that Moses had said would be a 40 year wilderness wandering. Somehow, some way, at some point in time, the four ringleaders shared their complaints and grumbling and began to plot a revolt against the leaders of God, Moses and Aaron. At some point in time, 250 well-known leaders were incited to join the revolt. Note that these were official representatives, appointed members of the council of rulers. Some were even Levites, the religious leaders of the nation who worked under Aaron the priest (see vv.8-11).

b. Note that the issue of protest was opposition to the leadership of Moses and Aaron (v.3). Their charge was a pointed attack against the authority of Moses and Aaron. The charge was direct and sharp: the two leaders had assumed too much authority—had gone too far this time by turning them away from the promised land. The Israelites were a holy people, not unholy, and certainly not so unholy and sinful that they could be kept from entering the promised land. The LORD was among them and with them. Why then did Moses set himself above the assembly as having the authority to turn them away from the promised land, dashing their hopes upon the rocks of despair?

This was the thrust of the rebel attack against Moses and Aaron. Simply stated, Korah and his allies lusted after the power and authority of leadership. They were after the position and power of Moses (vv.7, 12-14) and the position and power of the priesthood (vv.3, 9-10). Note that the whole group stood face to face against Moses and Aaron, full of fire and fury, ready to take over the reins of government and rule over the people.

c. Note the reaction of Moses: he fell face down, seeking God (vv.4-11). How long he stayed upon his face seeking the LORD is not stated. But falling prostrate apparently so startled the rebels that they temporarily held their peace, somewhat backing off until he arose from the ground. Note that Moses did not lash out nor retaliate against the rebels. When they first confronted him face to face, he simply fell prostrate to the ground—in great meekness and humility—and took the matter to the LORD.

1) When Moses arose, he posed a challenge to Korah and his allies (vv.5-7). He suggested a test by fire: to let the LORD choose His own leader—to show who really belonged to God and who could really approach Him for leadership in guiding God's people (v.5). The test by fire was simple: they would all prove themselves by taking censers and burning incense before the LORD (v.6). Only the priests were allowed to burn incense before the LORD, so this would give God a dramatic opportunity to show just who He wanted in the leadership positions. Remember that two priests, Nadab and Abihu, had offered "unauthorized fire" in burning incense and been stricken dead because of their false approach to God (see outline and note—Le. 10:1-2 for more discussion). Obviously, what Moses was suggesting here was a dramatic demonstration of God's will. God would show exactly whom He wanted to serve as leaders of His people. If Korah and his allies survived *the trial by fire,* then the leadership positions would be theirs. They would immediately become the leaders of God's people. Moses declared that the result would be final: the LORD would definitely show His leader by this *test by fire.* The LORD would choose the one who was truly holy (set apart by God) to be the leader of His people (v.7).

2) Moses rebuked and warned the Levites, Korah, and the other Levites among the 250 rebels (vv.7-11). Note that Moses was hot, fiery hot. He shouted:

⇒ They were the ones who had gone too far. He used their own charge against them (v.7, see v.3). They were guilty of abusing and trampling underfoot God's call to them to serve as Levites (vv.8-9). They had personally been given the privilege of being set apart to serve God and His people. This should have been enough: they were already leaders and servants of God, appointed to lead God's people as directed by Him.

⇒ They were guilty of seeking the priesthood itself—seeking a much higher position that should come only from God, never from selfish effort (v.10).

⇒ They were revolting against the LORD Himself, banding together against Him not against Aaron (v.11).

d. Note the confrontation, contempt, and defiance of Dathan and Abiram (vv.12-14). Obviously someone had mentioned to Moses that Dathan and Abiram were also part of the conspiracy. Therefore, Moses summoned them to meet with him.

1) They rejected the summons, refusing to meet with Moses (v.12). Note their outrage: "We will not come!" Anger, wrath, fury, contempt—all the emotions of a rebellious heart flooded their souls. Two times they expressed their contempt and defiance, declaring that they absolutely would not come! (vv.12-14).

2) They exaggerated their former life and provision in Egypt (v.13). With hearts full of contempt, they described Egypt as the true land that flows with milk and honey.

3) They blamed Moses for their plight in the wilderness (v.13).

4) They accused Moses of lording it over them (v.13).

5) They blamed Moses for failing to lead them into the promised land as he had promised (v.14).

6) They charged him with abuse of power—with ulterior motives, with deceiving the people (v.14).

7) They repeated their outrage, their contempt and disdain: they would not meet with Moses (v.14).

e. Note the angry reaction of Moses (v.15). He cried out to God not to accept the incense offering of the rebels. He declared that he was innocent: he had not misused his office for any gain nor had he wronged anyone.

Thought 1. There are several important lessons for us in this point:

(1) Seeking to be great or seeking positions of power is wrong. A person must seek to serve people, not to hold positions of power. A person after position demonstrates selfish motives and will be severely judged by God.

> "What is it you want?" he asked. She said, "Grant that one of these two sons of mine may sit at your right and the other at your left in your kingdom." (Mt. 20:21)
> For whoever exalts himself will be humbled, and whoever humbles himself will be exalted. (Mt. 23:12)
> Also a dispute arose among them as to which of them was considered to be greatest. (Lu. 22:24)

How can you believe if you accept praise from one another, yet make no effort to obtain the praise that comes from the only God? (Jn. 5:44)

For everything in the world—the cravings of sinful man, the lust of his eyes and the boasting of what he has and does—comes not from the Father but from the world. (1 Jn. 2:16)

He [Absalom] would get up early and stand by the side of the road leading to the city gate. Whenever anyone came with a complaint to be placed before the king for a decision, Absalom would call out to him, "What town are you from?" He would answer, "Your servant is from one of the tribes of Israel." ...And Absalom would add, "If only I were appointed judge in the land! Then everyone who has a complaint or case could come to me and I would see that he gets justice." (2 S. 15:2, 4)

Now Adonijah, whose mother was Haggith, put himself forward and said, "I will be king." So he got chariots and horses ready, with fifty men to run ahead of him. (1 K. 1:5)

Therefore pride is their necklace; they clothe themselves with violence. (Ps. 73:6)

When pride comes, then comes disgrace, but with humility comes wisdom. (Pr. 11:2)

Pride goes before destruction, a haughty spirit before a fall. (Pr. 16:18)

Do not exalt yourself in the king's presence, and do not claim a place among great men; it is better for him to say to you, "Come up here," than for him to humiliate you before a nobleman. (Pr. 25:6-7)

A greedy man stirs up dissension, but he who trusts in the LORD will prosper. (Pr. 28:25)

You said in your heart, "I will ascend to heaven; I will raise my throne above the stars of God; I will sit enthroned on the mount of assembly, on the utmost heights of the sacred mountain. I will ascend above the tops of the clouds; I will make myself like the Most High." (Is. 14:13-14)

"Son of man, say to the ruler of Tyre, 'This is what the Sovereign LORD says: 'In the pride of your heart you say, "I am a god; I sit on the throne of a god in the heart of the seas." But you are a man and not a god, though you think you are as wise as a god....Therefore this is what the Sovereign LORD says: 'Because you think you are wise, as wise as a god, I am going to bring foreigners against you, the most ruthless of nations; they will draw their swords against your beauty and wisdom and pierce your shining splendor. They will bring you down to the pit, and you will die a violent death in the heart of the seas." (Eze. 28:2, 6-8)

"Though you soar like the eagle and make your nest among the stars, from there I will bring you down," declares the LORD. (Ob. 4)

(2) When opposition arises, a godly leader must not strike back nor attack the opposition. He must first go before the LORD and do two things:

(a) He must seek the LORD to make sure his leadership has been pure and just, to make sure he has worked hard and fulfilled his service before the LORD and the people.

> Never be lacking in zeal, but keep your spiritual fervor, serving the Lord. (Ro. 12:11)
>
> Now it is required that those who have been given a trust must prove faithful. (1 Co. 4:2)
>
> Therefore, my dear brothers, stand firm. Let nothing move you. Always give yourselves fully to the work of the Lord, because you know that your labor in the Lord is not in vain. (1 Co. 15:58)
>
> And whatever you do, whether in word or deed, do it all in the name of the Lord Jesus, giving thanks to God the Father through him. (Col. 3:17)
>
> Whatever you do, work at it with all your heart, as working for the Lord, not for men. (Col. 3:23)
>
> Each one should use whatever gift he has received to serve others, faithfully administering God's grace in its various forms. (1 Pe. 4:10)
>
> So then, dear friends, since you are looking forward to this, make every effort to be found spotless, blameless and at peace with him. (2 Pe. 3:14)
>
> Do you see a man skilled in his work? He will serve before kings; he will not serve before obscure men. (Pr. 22:29)
>
> Whatever your hand finds to do, do it with all your might, for in the grave, where you are going, there is neither working nor planning nor knowledge nor wisdom. (Ec. 9:10)

(b) The leader must seek the LORD and handle the opposition in a humble, loving, and just way.

> For everyone who asks receives; he who seeks finds; and to him who knocks, the door will be opened. (Lu. 11:10)
>
> If you remain in me and my words remain in you, ask whatever you wish, and it will be given you. (Jn. 15:7)
>
> Look to the LORD and his strength; seek his face always. (1 Chr. 16:11)
>
> He will call upon me, and I will answer him; I will be with him in trouble, I will deliver him and honor him. (Ps. 91:15)
>
> Look to the LORD and his strength; seek his face always. (Ps. 105:4)
>
> Before they call I will answer; while they are still speaking I will hear. (Is. 65:24)
>
>> This third I will bring into the fire; I will refine them like silver and test them like gold. They will call on my name and I will answer them; I will say, 'They are my people,' and they

NUMBERS 16:1-50

will say, 'The LORD is our God.' (Zec. 13:9)

(3) Godly leaders must live meek, humble lives, seeking to serve others.

> But when you are invited, take the lowest place, so that when your host comes, he will say to you, 'Friend, move up to a better place.' Then you will be honored in the presence of all your fellow guests. (Lu. 14:10)
>
> But you are not to be like that. Instead, the greatest among you should be like the youngest, and the one who rules like the one who serves. (Lu. 22:26)
>
> For by the grace given me I say to every one of you: Do not think of yourself more highly than you ought, but rather think of yourself with sober judgment, in accordance with the measure of faith God has given you. (Ro. 12:3)
>
> Do nothing out of selfish ambition or vain conceit, but in humility consider others better than yourselves. (Ph. 2:3)
>
> Humble yourselves before the Lord, and he will lift you up. (Js. 4:10)
>
> Young men, in the same way be submissive to those who are older. All of you, clothe yourselves with humility toward one another, because, "God opposes the proud but gives grace to the humble." (1 Pe. 5:5)
>
> He has showed you, O man, what is good. And what does the LORD require of you? To act justly and to love mercy and to walk humbly with your God. (Mi. 6:8)

(4) Believers must not complain, grumble, or murmur against their leaders. Scripture is clear: grumbling, murmuring, and causing strife is forbidden.

> And do not grumble, as some of them did—and were killed [the Israelites] by the destroying angel. (1 Co. 10:10)
>
> Do nothing out of selfish ambition or vain conceit, but in humility consider others better than yourselves. (Ph. 2:3)
>
> Do everything without complaining or arguing. (Ph. 2:14)
>
> Keep reminding them of these things. Warn them before God against quarreling about words; it is of no value, and only ruins those who listen. (2 Ti. 2:14)
>
> And the Lord's servant must not quarrel; instead, he must be kind to everyone, able to teach, not resentful. (2 Ti. 2:24)
>
> A hot-tempered man stirs up dissension, but a patient man calms a quarrel. (Pr. 15:18)
>
> He who loves a quarrel loves sin; he who builds a high gate invites destruction. (Pr. 17:19)
>
> A fool's lips bring him strife, and his mouth invites a beating. (Pr. 18:6)
>
> As charcoal to embers and as wood to fire, so is a quarrelsome man for kindling strife. (Pr. 26:21)

2 (16:16-35) **Rebellion—Strife—Contention—Judgment, Of God—Korah, Judgment of—Unbelief, Judgment of—Approach, To God—Judgment, Of False Approaches to God**: there was the showdown and the judgment of the rebels. The *trial by fire* was set. Korah and his allies had accepted the challenge. Now the LORD would dramatically show who His leaders were to be.

a. The challenge to Korah and his allies was repeated (vv.16-17). They were all to approach the LORD the next day. Note that each individual was stressed: "each man" was to take his censer and put incense in it—all 250 of the rebels (v.17). Note also that both Korah and Aaron, were to take their censers.

b. The most arrogant, defiant stand was taken by the rebels against Moses and Aaron (vv.18-24). Note that the "test by fire" would take place at the entrance of the Tabernacle. It was there that God would choose which men were to be His leaders.

1) The response of the LORD was sudden, immediate: the glory of the LORD flashed or burst forth, visible to everyone (vv.19-20). The LORD addressed Moses and Aaron and His message was clear, spelling out doom for all the people. Note this fact: the LORD threatened to destroy the entire nation—at once, immediately (vv.20-21). Not only were the rebels to be destroyed, but the whole nation of people as well. This fact indicates that multitudes supported the cause of the rebels. Remember that the rebels were official representatives of the nation, community leaders who had been members of the ruling council of the nation. Obviously, they had been sent to Moses by the vast, vast majority of the people. Again, most of the people obviously supported the cause of the rebel leadership. The rebels were representing the people in their attempt to overthrow the leadership of Moses and Aaron.

2) The response of Moses and Aaron demonstrated godly character: they fell face down before God, crying out in prayer (v.22). Note how they addressed God: as the Creator, the "God of the spirits of all mankind." They begged God not to destroy all the people because of one man's sins. Note that Moses lay most of the blame for the revolt on Korah. But there is the possibility that this was a rhetorical question as well; that is, that the words "one man" referred to the four ringleaders of the revolt (Korah, Dathan, Abiram, and On).

3) The LORD answered the prayer but warned Moses that judgment was still going to fall. He charged Moses to move the people away from the tents of the rebel ringleaders (vv.23-24).

c. The catastrophic judgment fell upon Dathan, Abiram, and Korah. Korah, with some of his men, had obviously joined this rebellious group (v.25; see v.32; 26:10-11). The ringleaders were confronted by the true servants of God, Moses and the elders of Israel.

1) The people were warned to move back, out of the presence of these wicked men (vv.26-27). The instructions were strong: they must separate themselves totally from the wicked, not touch anything of theirs. Hearing these words, the people obeyed the warning.

2) Note that the two ringleaders had come out of their tents. They were standing with their families to confront and stand against God's leaders (v.27).

NUMBERS 16:1-50

3) But Moses was courageous and bold: he declared that the judgment of God would validate or prove that he was God's servant (vv.28-30). Then Moses proposed a test:
⇒ If God's judgment did not fall upon the rebels, that would prove that Moses was not God's choice for leader (v.29).
⇒ If God's judgment fell in some spectacular way, that would validate Moses as God's servant (v.30).

4) The declaration by Moses was bold: he declared that the judgment of God would fall in a spectacular way (v.30). He even spelled out exactly what the judgment was going to be: the earth would open up, swallowing the rebels and all their belongings. They would go down alive into the grave (Sheol).

5) The catastrophic judgment fell—suddenly, immediately (vv.31-33). Just as soon as Moses had finished speaking, the most horrible and frightening thing happened. The ground split open and the earth swallowed the rebels, their households, the followers standing with them, and all their possessions. Miraculously, a great earthquake opened the jaws of the earth, and these rebels fell alive into the grave. The earth closed over them, and they perished and were gone forever from the community of God's believers (v.33).

6) Note the fear of the people: they fled as they heard the screams of the rebels and commotion of the earthquake (v.44).

d. Immediately, the terrifying judgment also fell upon the 250 men offering incense at the Tabernacle: fire blazed forth from God's presence and burned them up (v.35). A lightning bolt from God's glory flashed forth and scorched them alive.

Note this fact: some of Korah's family survived the judgment (Nu. 26:10-11). Obviously, they were not involved in the revolt nor did they support it or else God's judgment would have fallen upon them as well. It is interesting to note that some of Korah's descendants composed several of the Psalms (see the headings to Psalm 42; 44-49; 84-85; 87-88; see Ex. 6:21, 24; 1 Chr. 6:22-31).[1]

Thought 1. God's judgment is just, perfectly just. Only unbelievers are to suffer the eternal judgment of God. Children and spouses do not have to follow in the footsteps of ungodly, wicked mothers and fathers. God will judge all unbelief and rebellion against Him and His appointed leaders. Believers must pray for and support their leaders, not criticize and attack them. The leaders of both the church and the government need our prayers and support, not the complaints of a selfish heart.

(1) The judgment of God against unbelief and rebellion is sure. All unbelievers and rebellious hearts will suffer the judgment of God.

Whoever believes in him is not condemned, but whoever does not believe stands condemned already because he has not believed in the name of God's one and only Son. (Jn. 3:18)

Whoever believes in the Son has eternal life, but whoever rejects the Son will not see life, for God's wrath remains on him. (Jn. 3:36)

I told you that you would die in your sins; if you do not believe that I am the one I claim to be, you will indeed die in your sins. (Jn. 8:24)

For he has set a day when he will judge the world with justice by the man he has appointed. He has given proof of this to all men by raising him from the dead. (Ac.17:31)

And give relief to you who are troubled, and to us as well. This will happen when the Lord Jesus is revealed from heaven in blazing fire with his powerful angels. He will punish those who do not know God and do not obey the gospel of our Lord Jesus. (2 Th. 1:7-8)

See to it, brothers, that none of you has a sinful, unbelieving heart that turns away from the living God. (He. 3:12)

If this is so, then the Lord knows how to rescue godly men from trials and to hold the unrighteous for the day of judgment, while continuing their punishment. (2 Pe. 2:9)

By the same word the present heavens and earth are reserved for fire, being kept for the day of judgment and destruction of ungodly men. (2 Pe. 3:7)

"See, the Lord is coming with thousands upon thousands of his holy ones to judge everyone, and to convict all the ungodly of all the ungodly acts they have done in the ungodly way, and of all the harsh words ungodly sinners have spoken against him." (Jude 14-15)

They will sing before the LORD, for he comes, he comes to judge the earth. He will judge the world in righteousness and the peoples in his truth. (Ps. 96:13)

I thought in my heart, "God will bring to judgment both the righteous and the wicked, for there will be a time for every activity, a time for every deed." (Ec. 3:17)

(2) We must pray for and support all leaders, both church and government leaders. Scripture is clear about this:

Paul replied, "Brothers, I did not realize that he was the high priest; for it is written: 'Do not speak evil about the ruler of your people.' " (Ac. 23:5)

Everyone must submit himself to the governing authorities, for there is no authority except that which God has established. The authorities that exist have been established by God. (Ro. 13:1)

I urge, then, first of all, that requests, prayers, intercession and thanksgiving be made for everyone— for kings and all those in authority, that we may live peaceful and quiet lives in all godliness and holiness. This is good, and pleases God our Savior, who wants all men to be saved and to come to a knowledge of the truth. (1 Ti. 2:1-4)

---

[1] *The Expositor's Bible Commentary.* Frank E. Gaebelein, Editor, p.841.

NUMBERS 16:1-50

Remind the people to be subject to rulers and authorities, to be obedient, to be ready to do whatever is good. (Tit. 3:1)

Show proper respect to everyone: Love the brotherhood of believers, fear God, honor the king. (1 Pe. 2:17)

Do not...curse the ruler of your people. (Ex. 22:28)

3 (16:36-40) **Judgment, Duty to Remember—Censers, the Incense—Rebellion, Judgment Of—Warning, Of Judgment**: there was the step to stir the memory of this judgment.

a. The LORD gave a command that was to serve as a warning to the people (vv.37-38). Eleazar, the son of Aaron the priest, was to save the censers of the 250 men who were judged. Note that the censers are said to have been holy, that is, set apart to God for special service. For this reason, they had to be saved. All holy things have to be treated as holy—always. Therefore, Eleazar was to walk among the charred bodies of the rebels and save the censers. But note what he was to do with the burning coals: he was to take them some distance away and dispose of them. These burning coals were "unauthorized fire" (see outline and notes—Le.10:1-2 for more discussion). The censers were to be hammered into sheets of metal and used to overlay the altar (v.38). They were to be a sign, a warning to the people of God's judgment.

b. The obedience of Eleazar is stressed: he did exactly what God had instructed (vv.39-40). He collected the censers and had them hammered to overlay the altar. The purpose is clearly stated: the censers were to remind the people...

- that no unauthorized person could approach God
- that an unauthorized approach would be judged, just as Korah's and his allies' approach was judged

In mercy, God wanted to prevent any future unbelief and rebellion against Him. He wanted to keep people from approaching Him in a false, unauthorized way. No person could approach God with the burning incense other than the priest. Keep in mind that the priest is a symbol of the Lord Jesus Christ, and that the incense is a symbol of prayers being offered up to God. All this is a symbol that only Jesus Christ can make prayer acceptable to God. The believer must approach God through Christ and Christ alone for his prayers to be answered.

Thought 1. The judgment of God must be remembered. God warns all people: He judges all false and unauthorized approaches to Him. There is only one approach that is acceptable: the approach that comes through Jesus Christ. Christ is the only Mediator who stands between God and man. Christ alone is the way into God's presence.

I am the gate; whoever enters through me will be saved. He will come in and go out, and find pasture. (Jn. 10:9)

Jesus answered, "I am the way and the truth and the life. No one comes to the Father except through me." (Jn. 14:6)

Salvation is found in no one else, for there is no other name under heaven given to men by which we must be saved. (Ac.4:12)

Through whom we have gained access by faith into this grace in which we now stand. And we rejoice in the hope of the glory of God. (Ro. 5:2)

Who is he that condemns? Christ Jesus, who died—more than that, who was raised to life—is at the right hand of God and is also interceding for us. (Ro. 8:34)

For through him we both have access to the Father by one Spirit. (Ep. 2:18)

In him and through faith in him we may approach God with freedom and confidence. (Ep. 3:12)

For there is one God and one mediator between God and men, the man Christ Jesus, who gave himself as a ransom for all men—the testimony given in its proper time. (1 Ti. 2:5-6)

For this reason he had to be made like his brothers in every way, in order that he might become a merciful and faithful high priest in service to God, and that he might make atonement for the sins of the people. (He. 2:17)

Therefore, since we have a great high priest who has gone through the heavens, Jesus the Son of God, let us hold firmly to the faith we profess. For we do not have a high priest who is unable to sympathize with our weaknesses, but we have one who has been tempted in every way, just as we are—yet was without sin. (He. 4:14-15)

Therefore he is able to save completely those who come to God through him, because he always lives to intercede for them. (He. 7:25)

Such a high priest meets our need—one who is holy, blameless, pure, set apart from sinners, exalted above the heavens. (He. 7:26)

The point of what we are saying is this: We do have such a high priest, who sat down at the right hand of the throne of the Majesty in heaven. (He. 8:1)

4 (16:41-50) **Unbelief, Of Israel—Israel, Unbelief of—Complaining, against God's Servants—Murmuring, against God's Servants—Minister, Grumbling against**: the staggering unbelief of the people shows just how hard the human heart can become. Overnight the people began to murmur and grumble against Moses and Aaron again. Note that Scripture says it was the very next day (v.41).

a. Note the false charge: they accused Moses and Aaron of causing the death of the rebels (v.41). The people still did not interpret the judgment of God correctly. They still did not understand unbelief, that unbelief was the rejection of God's Word and refusing to follow Him, failing to do exactly what He says. They still did not understand that grumbling and murmuring against God's leaders and servants were wrong. They still did not understand that they must not stand in opposition to God's leader. Their minds were blinded to the truth of God's Word, blinded to obedience, blinded against following God in a spirit of love and service as He demanded. Consequently, the very next day the whole community grumbled against Moses and Aaron—not just some of the people, but all of the people. They had actually gathered in opposition to these two dear servants of God.

NUMBERS 16:1-50

b. The intervention of God was quick and dramatic: the cloud of God's presence covered the Tabernacle and the Glory of the LORD burst forth. This gave the appearance and threat of judgment about to fall (vv.42-45). But again, note the character of Moses and Aaron: instead of striking back in anger at the people, these two dear servants approached God's presence in front of the Tabernacle (v.43). It was then that God spoke, threatening the people: He was instantly going to destroy them (vv.44-45). He told Moses and Aaron to move away, to leave the people so He could put an end to them immediately.

c. As stated, the response of Moses and Aaron revealed a true character of ministry: they fell down upon their faces in prayer (vv.45-50). The bursting forth of God's glory had obviously stricken fear and terror among the people, stopping them dead in their tracks and keeping them from attacking the two servants of God.

d. Nevertheless, the judgment of God fell. Without warning, a plague instantly struck the people (vv.46-50).

1) Moses knew immediately what was happening and gave quick instructions to Aaron (v.46). He instructed Aaron to do the work of the *atoning priest:*
   ⇒ He was to take his censer with incense and place burning coals on it from the altar.
   ⇒ He was to rush among the people and make atonement for them.

   This was necessary because God's judgment had already started. A severe plague—a rapidly spreading plague—had already broken out among the people and they were dropping like flies.

2) Aaron immediately obeyed and rushed to the people, offering incense and making atonement for them (vv.47-48). Remember that Aaron was most likely eighty-plus years old at this time; nevertheless, he ran among the people as the High Priest who alone could make atonement for the people, as the High Priest who alone could deliver the people from disease and death. Scripture is clear: the High Priest appointed by God stood between the living and the dead, and the judgment of God was stopped (v.48).

3) Note the result of God's judgment, the result of the rapidly spreading plague: 14,700 people died in addition to Korah and his allies (v.49). After Aaron completed his atoning work, he returned to Moses at the Tabernacle. No doubt he and Moses thanked God for delivering them and sparing some of the people (v.50).

Thought 1. The staggering unbelief of so many people is difficult to understand. God has given evidence after evidence of His existence. Only a fool says, "There is no God" (Ps. 14:1; 53:1). Moreover, God has given His Word to reveal the truth to us and to give us the commandments to live by (2 Ti. 3:16). But far more than this, God has sent His Son, the Lord Jesus Christ, to reveal the truth of life to man. God has given us far more than just written words to understand the truth; He has given us His very own Son to live the truth out before us. With so much evidence of God's existence and will for man, it is most difficult to understand the hardness of heart, the stubborn will of man that causes him to stand in unbelief and rebellion. Just as God warned the people of Israel, He warns us in the Holy Scripture:

Whoever believes in the Son has eternal life, but whoever rejects the Son will not see life, for God's wrath remains on him. (Jn. 3:36)

I told you that you would die in your sins; if you do not believe that I am the one I claim to be, you will indeed die in your sins. (Jn. 8:24)

For this people's heart has become calloused; they hardly hear with their ears, and they have closed their eyes. Otherwise they might see with their eyes, hear with their ears, understand with their hearts and turn, and I would heal them. (Ac. 28:27)

But because of your stubbornness and your unrepentant heart, you are storing up wrath against yourself for the day of God's wrath, when his righteous judgment will be revealed. (Ro. 2:5)

Having lost all sensitivity, they have given themselves over to sensuality so as to indulge in every kind of impurity, with a continual lust for more. (Ep. 4:19)

See to it, brothers, that none of you has a sinful, unbelieving heart that turns away from the living God. But encourage one another daily, as long as it is called Today, so that none of you may be hardened by sin's deceitfulness. (He. 3:12-13)

The fool says in his heart, "There is no God." They are corrupt, their deeds are vile; there is no one who does good. The LORD looks down from heaven on the sons of men to see if there are any who understand, any who seek God. All have turned aside, they have together become corrupt; there is no one who does good, not even one. (Ps. 14:1-3)

Do not be like the horse or the mule, which have no understanding but must be controlled by bit and bridle or they will not come to you. Many are the woes of the wicked, but the LORD's unfailing love surrounds the man who trusts in him. (Ps. 32:9-10)

The fool says in his heart, "There is no God." They are corrupt, and their ways are vile; there is no one who does good. God looks down from heaven on the sons of men to see if there are any who understand, any who seek God. Everyone has turned away, they have together become corrupt; there is no one who does good, not even one. (Ps. 53:1-3)

They would not be like their forefathers—a stubborn and rebellious generation, whose hearts were not loyal to God, whose spirits were not faithful to him. (Ps. 78:8)

Do not harden your hearts as you did at Meribah, as you did that day at Massah in the desert, where your fathers tested and tried me, though they had seen what I did. For forty years I was angry with that generation; I said, "They are a people whose hearts go astray, and they have not known my ways." So I declared on oath in my

NUMBERS 16:1-50

anger, "They shall never enter my rest." (Ps. 95:8-11)

A man who remains stiff-necked after many rebukes will suddenly be destroyed—without remedy. (Pr. 29:1)

Listen to me, you stubborn-hearted, you who are far from righteousness. (Is. 46:12)

"If you do not listen, and if you do not set your heart to honor my name," says the LORD Almighty, "I will send a curse upon you, and I will curse your blessings. Yes, I have already cursed them, because you have not set your heart to honor me." (Mal. 2:2)

TYPES, SYMBOLS, AND PICTURES
(Numbers 16:1-50)

Historical Term	Type or Picture (Scriptural Basis for Each)	Life Application for Today's Believer	Biblical Application
Censers Nu. 16:36-40	*The censers are a picture of acceptable prayer to God: only Christ can make prayer acceptable to God.* *So Eleazar the priest collected the bronze censers brought by those who had been burned up, and he had them hammered out to overlay the altar, as the LORD directed him through Moses. This was to remind the Israelites that no one except a descendant of Aaron should come to burn incense before the LORD, or he would become like Korah and his followers. (Nu. 16:39-40)*	Keep in mind that the priest is a symbol of the Lord Jesus Christ, and that the incense is a symbol of prayers being offered up to God. All this is a symbol that Jesus Christ alone can make prayer acceptable to God. The believer must approach God through Christ and Christ alone for his prayers to be answered.	*And I will do whatever you ask in my name, so that the Son may bring glory to the Father. (Jn. 14:13)* *You did not choose me, but I chose you and appointed you to go and bear fruit—fruit that will last. Then the Father will give you whatever you ask in my name. (Jn. 15:16)* *In that day you will ask in my name. I am not saying that I will ask the Father on your behalf. (Jn. 16:26)* *She kept this up for many days. Finally Paul became so troubled that he turned around and said to the spirit, "In the name of Jesus Christ I command you to come out of her!" At that moment the spirit left her. (Ac. 16:18)* *Always giving thanks to God the Father for everything, in the name of our Lord Jesus Christ. (Ep. 5:20)*

NUMBERS 17:1-13

1. The test was set up by God
2. The test was to vindicate the priest, to prove that he was God's choice (a symbol of Christ or of the minister)
  a. To secure 12 staffs, one from the leader of each tribe
  b. To put their names on the staffs
  c. To write Aaron's name on the staff of Levi: He was the head of the priestly tribe (a symbol of Christ)
  d. To place the 12 staffs in the Tabernacle, in front of the Ark of the Covenant
  e. The purpose
    1) To cause the staff of God's servant to sprout (produce life, fruit)
    2) To stop all opposition
3. The test was carried out: Moses obeyed God
  a. The 12 staffs were secured, one from each tribal leader
	CHAPTER 17
	
	C. Event 3—the Budding of Aaron's Staff: The Test to Vindicate God's Priest & His Ministry (a Symbol of Christ or of the Minister), 17:1-13
	
	The LORD said to Moses, 2 "Speak to the Israelites and get twelve staffs from them, one from the leader of each of their ancestral tribes. Write the name of each man on his staff. 3 On the staff of Levi write Aaron's name, for there must be one staff for the head of each ancestral tribe. 4 Place them in the Tent of Meeting in front of the Testimony, where I meet with you. 5 The staff belonging to the man I choose will sprout, and I will rid myself of this constant grumbling against you by the Israelites." 6 So Moses spoke to the Israelites, and their leaders gave him twelve staffs, one for the leader of each of their ancestral tribes, and Aaron's
		staff was among them. 7 Moses placed the staffs before the LORD in the Tent of the Testimony. 8 The next day Moses entered the Tent of the Testimony and saw that Aaron's staff, which represented the house of Levi, had not only sprouted but had budded, blossomed and produced almonds. 9 Then Moses brought out all the staffs from the LORD's presence to all the Israelites. They looked at them, and each man took his own staff. 10 The LORD said to Moses, "Put back Aaron's staff in front of the Testimony, to be kept as a sign to the rebellious. This will put an end to their grumbling against me, so that they will not die." 11 Moses did just as the LORD commanded him. 12 The Israelites said to Moses, "We will die! We are lost, we are all lost! 13 Anyone who even comes near the tabernacle of the LORD will die. Are we all going to die?"	b. The 12 staffs were placed before the LORD (the Ark) in the Tabernacle
			c. The next day, the staff of God's true priest had been given life—sprouted, budded, blossomed, & produced almonds (a symbol of Christ or the minister bearing fruit & life by God's miraculous power)
			d. The result: The leaders knew that Aaron was the true priest or servant of God (a symbol of Christ or of the minister): Knew by the life & fruit produced—through God's power
			4. **The staff of Aaron was kept as a permanent sign & warning of God's power**
			  a. Power to vindicate His name & His servant (Christ or the minister)
			  b. Power to judge—stop & wipe out rebellion & grumbling
			  c. The response of the grumbling, rebellious people
			    1) Sensed deep guilt & failure
			    2) Sensed a deep fear of God's judgment & power

DIVISION III

THE FORTY LONG YEARS OF WILDERNESS WANDERINGS: A PICTURE OF THE BELIEVER'S PILGRIMAGE THROUGH THIS WORLD AS HE PREPARES TO ENTER THE PROMISED LAND, 15:1–25:18

C. Event 3—the Budding of Aaron's Staff: The Test to Vindicate God's Priest and His Ministry (a Symbol of Christ or of the Minister), 17:1-13

(17:1-13) **Introduction—Minister, Opposition to—Grumbling, against Ministers—Criticism, of Ministers—Ministers, Criticism of**: grumbling and murmuring against God's minister are constant occurrences throughout society, and far too often within the church itself. Many people frankly feel they have a right to grumble against their minister and sometimes even to oppose and rebel against him. But seldom if ever is the will of God sought by these same people: little time is spent in prayer to seek God's will in the issue or difference.

Grumbling against and attacking the minister of God s a critical issue to God. The minister is God's servant, appointed by God. He serves under God, being totally responsible to God. Because of His appointment and responsibility, he is held to a much higher accountability by God. God is able to take care of His minister, whether to discipline and chastise or approve him. However, when His minister is criticized and attacked, God wants His people to know one thing: He has the power to vindicate His minister, the power to protect him and deliver him through the grumbling and the opposition. But He also has the power to judge—to stop and wipe out all grumbling and rebellion against His dear servant. This is the subject of this great passage of Scripture. Aaron, God's dear servant, had just been attacked. Some of God's people had banded together to stand in opposition to Aaron and his priesthood. They had attempted to remove Aaron from the ministry and to place their own man in the priesthood. The judgment of God had fallen upon the grumbling, rebellious opposition. Now God wanted to warn His people and to give them an eternal warning: He is able to vindicate and protect His chosen servant, and He will do just that. This is: *Event 3—the Budding of Aaron's Staff: The Test to Vindicate God's Priest and His Ministry (a Symbol of Christ or of the Minister), 17:1-13.*

1. The test was set up by God (v.1).
2. The test was to vindicate the priest, to prove that he was God's choice (a symbol of Christ or of the minister) (vv.2-5).
3. The test was carried out: Moses obeyed God (vv.6-9).
4. The staff of Aaron was kept as a permanent sign and warning of God's power (vv.10-13).

Numbers 17:1-13

1 (17:1) **Test, of Minister—Minister, Proof of—Vindication, of Minister—Proof, of Minister's Call—Israel, Priesthood of—Priesthood, Vindication of**: the test was set up by God Himself. God loved the priest (minister) with a very special love because He had called the priest to a very special ministry.

Remember that the priest was a symbol or type of Christ. God had called the priest to be His representative upon the earth, to be the mediator between man and God. The priest was called to share the Word of God and to minister to God's people. How people treated the priest (minister) was, therefore, of critical concern to God. There had just been two attempts to remove Aaron from the priesthood, one by Korah and his allies and the other by the people themselves (Nu. 16:1-35; 16:36-50). God was determined to stop the opposition against His dear servant, stop their grumbling and murmuring against him. Aaron was His minister, appointed by Him to stand as the High Priest between God and man. Aaron was a type of the perfect High Priest who was yet to come, and who alone could secure eternal salvation for God's people. Therefore, the High Priesthood had to be protected as God had established, for it was to give man a picture of the High Priesthood of His dear Son, the Lord Jesus Christ, who was to be the perfect Representative, the great Mediator who stands between God and man.

The Israelites had attacked the High Priesthood of His dear servant Aaron too many times. Therefore, God set up a test to prove forever that Aaron and his descendants were His appointed priests. They and they alone were the line of descendants who were to serve as priests until the Perfect Priest came, the Lord Jesus Christ Himself. Only the Perfect Priest could represent man perfectly before God.

Thought 1. Jesus Christ is the Perfect Priest. He and He alone stands in perfection, perfectly representing God to man and man to God. Jesus Christ alone has established the perfect priesthood:

⇒ the perfect approach to God
⇒ the perfect way to reveal God
⇒ the perfect way to make people acceptable to God
⇒ the perfect way to share the Word of God
⇒ the perfect way to minister and to help people
⇒ the perfect way to pray and make intercession for people
⇒ the perfect way to conquer sin and death
⇒ the perfect way to live victoriously over the pitfalls and enemies of this life
⇒ the perfect way to experience the abundance of life, life now and life eternally

Who is he that condemns? Christ Jesus, who died—more than that, who was raised to life—is at the right hand of God and is also interceding for us. (Ro. 8:34)

For this reason he had to be made like his brothers in every way, in order that he might become a merciful and faithful high priest in service to God, and that he might make atonement for the sins of the people (He. 2:17)

Therefore, since we have a great high priest who has gone through the heavens, Jesus the Son of God, let us hold firmly to the faith we profess. For we do not have a high priest who is unable to sympathize with our weaknesses, but we have one who has been tempted in every way, just as we are—yet was without sin. (He. 4:14-15)

Every high priest is selected from among men and is appointed to represent them in matters related to God, to offer gifts and sacrifices for sins. He is able to deal gently with those who are ignorant and are going astray, since he himself is subject to weakness. This is why he has to offer sacrifices for his own sins, as well as for the sins of the people. No one takes this honor upon himself; he must be called by God, just as Aaron was. So Christ also did not take upon himself the glory of becoming a high priest. But God said to him, "You are my Son; today I have become your Father." (He. 5:1-5)

God did this so that...we who have fled to take hold of the hope offered to us may be greatly encouraged. We have this hope as an anchor for the soul, firm and secure. It enters the inner sanctuary behind the curtain, where Jesus, who went before us, has entered on our behalf. He has become a high priest forever, in the order of Melchizedek. (He. 6:18-20)

Therefore he is able to save completely those who come to God through him, because he always lives to intercede for them. Such a high priest meets our need—one who is holy, blameless, pure, set apart from sinners, exalted above the heavens. Unlike the other high priests, he does not need to offer sacrifices day after day, first for his own sins, and then for the sins of the people. He sacrificed for their sins once for all when he offered himself. For the law appoints as high priests men who are weak; but the oath, which came after the law, appointed the Son, who has been made perfect forever. (He. 7:25-28)

The point of what we are saying is this: We do have such a high priest, who sat down at the right hand of the throne of the Majesty in heaven. (He. 8:1)

2 (17:2-5) **Vindication, of the Minister—Priest, Vindication of—Ministry, Vindication of—Aaron, Vindication of—High Priesthood, Vindication of—Proof, of the Minister**: the test was to vindicate the priest, to prove that he was God's choice to serve the people. Remember that the priest was a symbol of Christ or of the minister. The test needed to be strong, so strong that it would settle the issue forever in the minds of the people. Aaron and his descendants were God's choice to fill the position of High Priest, standing between God and man. The people needed to learn this fact once and for all: there was to be no grumbling or murmuring, no opposition to His dear servant, the High Priest (a symbol of Christ or of the minister).

Far too often people grumble and murmur against the minister, even attacking him. Sometimes the attack is...

- against him as a person
- against his family
- against his preaching or teaching ability
- against some idea or program he is trying to get started
- against some position he has taken

NUMBERS 17:1-13

On and on the list could go. All grumbling against and opposition to God's dear servant are troubling concerns to God. The opposition to Aaron concerned God deeply, just as any attack against a minister of God concerns Him. This was the reason God was setting up this test: to stop the irrational, demonic grumbling and attacks against His dear servant, to stop the opposition once and for all. The test was a simple one, but it would prove once and for all that Aaron was God's dear servant. The outline lays out the test explicitly:

⇒ Moses was to secure twelve staffs, one from the leader of each tribe (v.2).
⇒ Moses was to write the names of each leader on the staffs (v.3).
⇒ Moses was to write Aaron's name on the staff of Levi: Aaron was the head of the priestly tribe that was always to fill the position of High Priest. Therefore, Aaron was not standing alone but, rather, standing for the whole tribe of Levi (v.3).
⇒ Moses was to place the twelve staffs in the Tabernacle, right in front of the Ark of the Covenant (v.4).
⇒ The purpose is clearly stated: the staff that belonged to the man whom God chose would sprout. It would produce fruit (v.5). But note, this was not the only purpose God had for the test. God clearly stated that one purpose for the test was to stop the grumbling, the opposition against His dear servant. God was out to establish forever the Aaronic priesthood. The line or descendants of Aaron were to be a type of the Perfect Priesthood of the Lord Jesus Christ.

Thought 1. Grumbling and murmuring against God's servant must be stopped, in fact, must never be allowed. The person truly chosen and appointed by God is God's dear servant. He stands totally accountable *to* God, and he will be held accountable *by* God. In fact, his judgment will be far more severe than that of others. This is the clear teaching of Scripture. He will be held accountable by God not man. There is a clear reason for this: no man sees perfectly nor understands perfectly. The minister sometimes fails and comes short, just as all men do. We all stumble as we seek to do the best we can before our LORD. This is the reason God forbids His people to grumble and murmur—not just against the minister but against one another as well. God is against all grumbling and murmuring against any person. Complaining and strife are not of God; they are of self and of the world, even of the evil one, Satan himself. For this reason, all grumbling and murmuring must be stopped.

> When the Pharisees saw this, they asked his disciples, "Why does your teacher eat with tax collectors and 'sinners'?" On hearing this, Jesus said, "It is not the healthy who need a doctor, but the sick. But go and learn what this means: 'I desire mercy, not sacrifice.' For I have not come to call the righteous, but sinners." (Mt. 9:11-13)

> When the Pharisees saw this, they said to him, "Look! Your disciples are doing what is unlawful on the Sabbath." He answered, "Haven't you read what David did when he and his companions were hungry? He entered the house of God, and he and his companions ate the consecrated bread—which was not lawful for them to do, but only for the priests." (Mt. 12:2-4)

> "Why do your disciples break the tradition of the elders? They don't wash their hands before they eat!" (Mt. 15:2)

> "Why does this fellow talk like that? He's blaspheming! Who can forgive sins but God alone?" Immediately Jesus knew in his spirit that this was what they were thinking in their hearts, and he said to them, "Why are you thinking these things? Which is easier: to say to the paralytic, 'Your sins are forgiven,' or to say, 'Get up, take your mat and walk'? But that you may know that the Son of Man has authority on earth to forgive sins. . ." He said to the paralytic, "I tell you, get up, take your mat and go home." (Mk. 2:7-11)

> When the teachers of the law who were Pharisees saw him eating with the "sinners" and tax collectors, they asked his disciples: "Why does he eat with tax collectors and 'sinners'?" On hearing this, Jesus said to them, "It is not the healthy who need a doctor, but the sick. I have not come to call the righteous, but sinners." (Mk. 2:16-17)

> Saw some of his disciples eating food with hands that were "unclean," that is, unwashed. (Mk. 7:2)

> But the Pharisees and the teachers of the law muttered, "This man welcomes sinners and eats with them." (Lu. 15:2)

> All the people saw this and began to mutter, "He has gone to be the guest of a 'sinner.' " (Lu. 19:7)

> At this the Jews began to grumble about him because he said, "I am the bread that came down from heaven." They said, "Is this not Jesus, the son of Joseph, whose father and mother we know? How can he now say, 'I came down from heaven'?" "Stop grumbling among yourselves," Jesus answered. "No one can come to me unless the Father who sent me draws him, and I will raise him up at the last day." (Jn. 6:41-44)

> And do not grumble, as some of them did—and were killed by the destroying angel. These things happened to them as examples and were written down as warnings for us, on whom the fulfillment of the ages has come. So, if you think you are standing firm, be careful that you don't fall! (1 Co. 10:10-12)

> Do everything without complaining or arguing, so that you may become blameless and pure, children of God without fault in a crooked and depraved generation, in which you shine like stars in the universe. (Ph. 2:14-15)

> A man's own folly ruins his life, yet his heart rages against the LORD. (Pr. 19:3)

Thought 2. The minister of God is God's chosen instrument. He has been chosen by God to declare the Word of God to God's people. Moreover, he has been called to minister to God's people, encouraging

NUMBERS 17:1-13

and strengthening them in the faith and doing all he can to conform them to the image of Christ. But this is not all: he has been called to lead God's people to reach out to the lost of the world. But even this is not all: he has been called to bear the authority and weight of all the duties of the church itself, both the spiritual and the administrative duties. The weight of the dear minister is heavy with responsibility and accountability before God. Nevertheless, he has to minister because he is the chosen instrument of God. God wants His people to know, respect, and honor this.

> **The kingdom of heaven is like a king who prepared a wedding banquet for his son. He sent his servants to those who had been invited to the banquet to tell them to come, but they refused to come. (Mt. 22:2-3)**
>
> **You did not choose me, but I chose you and appointed you to go and bear fruit—fruit that will last. Then the Father will give you whatever you ask in my name. (Jn. 15:16)**
>
> **But the Lord said to Ananias, "Go! This man is my chosen instrument to carry my name before the Gentiles and their kings and before the people of Israel." (Ac. 9:15)**
>
> **'Now get up and stand on your feet. I have appeared to you to appoint you as a servant and as a witness of what you have seen of me and what I will show you. (Ac. 26:16)**
>
> **But God chose the foolish things of the world to shame the wise; God chose the weak things of the world to shame the strong. He chose the lowly things of this world and the despised things—and the things that are not—to nullify the things that are, so that no one may boast before him. (1 Co. 1:27-29)**
>
> **We are therefore Christ's ambassadors, as though God were making his appeal through us. We implore you on Christ's behalf: Be reconciled to God. God made him who had no sin to be sin for us, so that in him we might become the righteousness of God. (2 Co. 5:20-21)**
>
> **It was he who gave some to be apostles, some to be prophets, some to be evangelists, and some to be pastors and teachers, to prepare God's people for works of service, so that the body of Christ may be built up. (Ep. 4:11-12)**
>
> **Obey your leaders and submit to their authority. They keep watch over you as men who must give an account. Obey them so that their work will be a joy, not a burden, for that would be of no advantage to you. (He. 13:17)**
>
> **Then I heard the voice of the Lord saying, "Whom shall I send? And who will go for us?" And I said, "Here am I. Send me!" (Is. 6:8)**
>
> **Again and again I sent all my servants the prophets to you. They said, "Each of you must turn from your wicked ways and reform your actions; do not follow other gods to serve them. Then you will live in the land I have given to you and your fathers." But you have not paid attention or listened to me. (Je. 35:15)**
>
> **"Son of man, I have made you a watchman for the house of Israel; so hear the word I speak and give them warning from me." (Eze. 3:17)**

3 (17:6-9) **Ministry, Fruit of—Fruit, of Ministry—Ministry, Proof of—Minister, Proof of—Vindication, of Minister—Israel, Priesthood of, Established—Priesthood, of Aaron, Established—Aaron, Staff of—Staff, of Aaron**: Moses obeyed God explicitly, without reservation. What happened then gave unequivocal proof, convincing evidence that Aaron was God's man. Aaron was God's choice to be the priest, the minister who was to stand in the gap between God and man.

Note that something happened to Aaron's staff that did not happen to the staffs of the other tribal leaders. Aaron's staff sprouted, budded, blossomed, and produced almonds (v.8). It is impossible for a dead piece of wood in the shape of a staff to sprout and produce fruit—an absolute impossibility. This was the miraculous power of God, a convincing, indisputable demonstration of God's power. James Philips points out two things about the staff:

First, the staff was a symbol of God's power and authority. By giving life to the staff, God was showing that His authority to serve as the priest or minister of His people was being given to Aaron. The very authority and power of God Himself was being placed upon Aaron.

Second, the staff bore fruit by the hand of God. It sprouted, budded, blossomed, and produced almonds—all by the hand and blessing of God Himself. This was a sign that the ministry of Aaron (his priesthood) would be a life-giving ministry, a ministry that would bear fruit and bring life to the people he served.[1]

The budding of Aaron's staff was a symbol of Christ or of the minister bearing fruit and bringing life to people—all through God's miraculous power! The budding of the staff was not by chance; it was by the miraculous power of God. The budding of the staff produced life and fruit: it was a clear symbol that Aaron was to produce life and fruit in his ministry by the hand of God. An astonishing miracle! An indisputable sign that Aaron was a true servant and minister of God, the man who was to stand as the High Priest between God and His people.

Note the result of the miracle: the leaders knew beyond question that Aaron was the true priest or servant of God (v.9). They knew by the life and fruit produced through the power of God. Never again could any of the tribal leaders legitimately question the choice of Aaron as God's minister. Note that Moses brought all the staffs out from the presence of the LORD and returned them to each of the tribal leaders. Scripture says that each man looked at his staff and saw that it was *dead,* that it bore no fruit. Each man knew that he was not God's choice to bear the fruit of God's Word among God's people. Aaron was. Note that each man took his own staff back home with him. All tribal leaders knew with finality—clearly and unequivocally—that Aaron was God's choice to be the priest and minister of God to the people.

> **Thought 1.** The budding staff of Aaron bore fruit and gave life. This was the proof of Aaron's ministry and priesthood. By the authority and power of God, Aaron's ministry was appointed to give life and bear fruit among God's people. The power of God is to

---

[1] James Philip. *The Preacher's Commentary on Numbers*, p. 200.

rest upon every minister and servant of God. Every minister and servant is to share the Word of life and bear fruit among God's people. What does it mean to say that a minister must bear fruit?

(1) Bearing fruit means to bear converts.

> "Come, follow me," Jesus said, "and I will make you fishers of men." (Mt. 4:19)
>
> Then he said to his disciples, "The harvest is plentiful but the workers are few. Ask the Lord of the harvest, therefore, to send out workers into his harvest field." (Mt. 9:37-38)
>
> As soon as the grain is ripe, he puts the sickle to it, because the harvest has come. (Mk. 4:29)
>
> He told them, "The harvest is plentiful, but the workers are few. Ask the Lord of the harvest, therefore, to send out workers into his harvest field." (Lu. 10:2)
>
> Do you not say, 'Four months more and then the harvest'? I tell you, open your eyes and look at the fields! They are ripe for harvest. Even now the reaper draws his wages, even now he harvests the crop for eternal life, so that the sower and the reaper may be glad together. (Jn. 4:35-36)
>
> I do not want you to be unaware, brothers, that I planned many times to come to you (but have been prevented from doing so until now) in order that I might have a harvest among you, just as I have had among the other Gentiles. (Ro. 1:13)
>
> Let us not become weary in doing good, for at the proper time we will reap a harvest if we do not give up. (Ga. 6:9)
>
> The fruit of the righteous is a tree of life, and he who wins souls is wise. (Pr. 11:30)

(2) Bearing fruit means to bear righteousness, to bear a holy life.

> For I tell you that unless your righteousness surpasses that of the Pharisees and the teachers of the law, you will certainly not enter the kingdom of heaven. (Mt. 5:20)
>
> To rescue us from the hand of our enemies, and to enable us to serve him without fear in holiness and righteousness before him all our days. (Lu. 1:74-75)
>
> What benefit did you reap at that time from the things you are now ashamed of? Those things result in death! But now that you have been set free from sin and have become slaves to God, the benefit you reap leads to holiness, and the result is eternal life. For the wages of sin is death, but the gift of God is eternal life in Christ Jesus our Lord. (Ro. 6:21-23)
>
> Come back to your senses as you ought, and stop sinning; for there are some who are ignorant of God—I say this to your shame. (1 Co. 15:34)
>
> Filled with the fruit of righteousness that comes through Jesus Christ—to the glory and praise of God. (Ph. 1:11)
>
> Make every effort to live in peace with all men and to be holy; without holiness no one will see the Lord. (He. 12:14)
>
> But just as he who called you is holy, so be holy in all you do; for it is written: "Be holy, because I am holy." (1 Pe. 1:15-16)
>
> Since everything will be destroyed in this way, what kind of people ought you to be? You ought to live holy and godly lives as you look forward to the day of God and speed its coming. That day will bring about the destruction of the heavens by fire, and the elements will melt in the heat. But in keeping with his promise we are looking forward to a new heaven and a new earth, the home of righteousness. So then, dear friends, since you are looking forward to this, make every effort to be found spotless, blameless and at peace with him. (2 Pe. 3:11-14)

(3) Bearing fruit means to bear the Christian character or the fruit of the Spirit.

> But the fruit of the Spirit is love, joy, peace, patience, kindness, goodness, faithfulness, gentleness and self-control. Against such things there is no law. (Ga. 5:22-23)
>
> For you were once darkness, but now you are light in the Lord. Live as children of light (for the fruit of the light consists in all goodness, righteousness and truth) and find out what pleases the Lord. Have nothing to do with the fruitless deeds of darkness, but rather expose them. For it is shameful even to mention what the disobedient do in secret. (Ep. 5:8-12)
>
> But the wisdom that comes from heaven is first of all pure; then peace-loving, considerate, submissive, full of mercy and good fruit, impartial and sincere. (Js. 3:17)

4 (17:10-13) **Warning, of God's Power—Warning, against Grumbling and Rebellion—Grumbling, Warning against—Rebellion, Warning against—Staff of Aaron—Aaron, Staff of—Signs, to Prove God's Ministry**: the staff of Aaron was kept as a permanent sign and warning of God's power. The staffs of the tribal leaders were returned to them, but not Aaron's. Aaron was not allowed to keep his staff. It was to be placed in the Tabernacle, in the Ark of the Covenant itself. Remember that the Ten Commandments (the tables of law) had already been placed into the Ark of the Covenant and so had a jar of manna (Ex. 25:16; 16:33-34). Now Aaron's staff was to be the third item placed into the Ark of the Covenant. All three were to serve as a memorial, a reminder of three great and significant events in the lives of God's people. God's people were always to remember the Ten Commandments and the great provision of God, that He continually feeds His people both physically (manna, bread) and spiritually (the Word of God). Now they were never to forget that God did the choosing of His priests, His ministers. Man did not choose God's servants: God did.

a. The staff of Aaron was a sign of God's power to vindicate His name and His servant (v.10). Remember that the priest was a symbol of Christ or of the minister. The grumblers, unbelievers, and rebellious of the world—both within and without the church—must heed the warning:

NUMBERS 17:1-13

God has the power to vindicate His own name and the name of His servant.

b. The staff of Aaron was a sign of God's power to judge all who grumble against Him and His dear servant. God has the power to stop and wipe out all rebellion and grumbling. The budding staff of Aaron stands as a warning to all who grumble and rebel: they need not die. They can live if they will only stop their grumbling and rebellion against Him and His servant. This was the very reason the budding staff was being placed as a memorial in the Ark of the Covenant.

c. Note the response of the Israelites, the grumbling and rebellious people (vv.12-13). They sensed deep guilt and failure, and they feared God's judgment and power. They began to cry out, fearing that they were going to die under the hand of God's judgment. God could strike out against them in the fury of His holiness just as He had done against the rebellion launched by Korah. They felt what they should have felt: that they were alienated, cut off from the Tabernacle, from the very presence of God Himself. Their sin had, in fact, alienated and separated them from God's presence, and they were sensing the alienation and separation. As with us, this would lead to genuine repentance. At long last, it seemed as though they grasped the glorious truth...

- that God is the Preeminent, Holy One
- that God can be approached only as He dictates
- that there is only one appointed High Priest who can stand in God's presence on behalf of people
- that no person can approach God except through the High Priest

The High Priesthood was established forever in the minds of God's people: there was only one man appointed to be the High Priest, and only one man through whom a person could approach God. No person must ever dare to grumble or rebel against the priest or minister appointed by God. To grumble and rebel against God's appointed servant would arouse the judgment of God.

Thought 1. Note two clear and strong lessons:

(1) The staff of Aaron is a memorial to God's power to protect His name and His servant. Any who grumble or rebel against God or His servant will face the judgment of God.

> And if any place will not welcome you or listen to you, shake the dust off your feet when you leave, as a testimony against them. (Mk. 6:11)
> If anyone is ashamed of me and my words in this adulterous and sinful generation, the Son of Man will be ashamed of him when he comes in his Father's glory with the holy angels. (Mk. 8:38)
> For he has set a day when he will judge the world with justice by the man he has appointed. He has given proof of this to all men by raising him from the dead. (Ac. 17:31)
> This will take place on the day when God will judge men's secrets through Jesus Christ, as my gospel declares. (Ro. 2:16)
> And give relief to you who are troubled, and to us as well. This will happen when the Lord Jesus is revealed from heaven in blazing fire with his powerful angels. He will punish those who do not know God and do not obey the gospel of our Lord Jesus. (2 Th. 1:7-8)
> Just as man is destined to die once, and after that to face judgment. (He. 9:27)
> If this is so, then the Lord knows how to rescue godly men from trials and to hold the unrighteous for the day of judgment, while continuing their punishment. (2 Pe. 2:9)
> By the same word the present heavens and earth are reserved for fire, being kept for the day of judgment and destruction of ungodly men. (2 Pe. 3:7)
> "See, the Lord is coming with thousands upon thousands of his holy ones to judge everyone, and to convict all the ungodly of all the ungodly acts they have done in the ungodly way, and of all the harsh words ungodly sinners have spoken against him." (Jude 14-15)
> And I saw the dead, great and small, standing before the throne, and books were opened. Another book was opened, which is the book of life. The dead were judged according to what they had done as recorded in the books. (Re. 20:12)
> They will sing before the LORD, for he comes, he comes to judge the earth. He will judge the world in righteousness and the peoples in his truth. (Ps. 96:13)
> There will be a time for every activity, a time for every deed. (Ec. 3:17)
> "I the LORD search the heart and examine the mind, to reward a man according to his conduct, according to what his deeds deserve." (Je. 17:10)

(2) Any person who has grumbled and rebelled against God or His minister must confess and repent of his sin. He must turn back to God—totally and wholly—doing all he can to help the minister in the work of the church. The grumbling and rebellious person must sense deep guilt and failure, sense a deep fear of God's judgment and power. God is going to judge all grumbling and murmuring and rebellion. We must, therefore, repent, turning totally and wholly to God. We must support the ministers of God who proclaim the Word of God to us and bear the enormous responsibility of leading us as we carry out the mission of the church.

> Repent of this wickedness and pray to the Lord. Perhaps he will forgive you for having such a thought in your heart. (Ac. 8:22)
> I urge you, brothers, by our Lord Jesus Christ and by the love of the Spirit, to join me in my struggle by praying to God for me. (Ro. 15:30)
> To submit to such as these and to everyone who joins in the work, and labors at it. (1 Co. 16:16)
> But when the time had fully come, God sent his Son, born of a woman, born under law. (Ga. 4:4)
> Welcome him in the Lord with great joy, and honor men like him. (Ph. 2:29)

NUMBERS 17:1-13

Now we ask you, brothers, to respect those who work hard among you, who are over you in the Lord and who admonish you. Hold them in the highest regard in love because of their work. Live in peace with each other. (1 Th. 5:12-13)

Remember your leaders, who spoke the word of God to you. Consider the outcome of their way of life and imitate their faith. (He. 13:7)

If we confess our sins, he is faithful and just and will forgive us our sins and purify us from all unrighteousness. (1 Jn. 1:9)

If my people, who are called by my name, will humble themselves and pray and seek my face and turn from their wicked ways, then will I hear from heaven and will forgive their sin and will heal their land. (2 Chr. 7:14)

Let the wicked forsake his way and the evil man his thoughts. Let him turn to the LORD, and he will have mercy on him, and to our God, for he will freely pardon. (Is. 55:7)

But if a wicked man turns away from all the sins he has committed and keeps all my decrees and does what is just and right, he will surely live; he will not die. (Eze. 18:21)

Rid yourselves of all the offenses you have committed, and get a new heart and a new spirit. Why will you die, O house of Israel? (Eze. 18:31)

TYPES, SYMBOLS, AND PICTURES
(Numbers 17:1-13)

Historical Term	Type or Picture (Scriptural Basis for Each)	Life Application for Today's Believer	Biblical Application
The Test to Vindicate the Priest, to Prove That He Was God's Choice Nu. 17:2-5	*The priest was a symbol of Christ or the minister. The test to prove Aaron's call and ministry needed to be strong, so strong that it would settle the issue forever in the minds of the people. Aaron and his descendants were God's choice to fill the position of High Priest, standing between God and man. The people needed to learn this fact once and for all: there was to be no grumbling or murmuring, no opposition to His dear servant, the High Priest (a symbol of Christ or of the minister).* **The staff belonging to the man I choose will sprout, and I will rid myself of this constant grumbling against you by the Israelites. (Nu. 17:5)**	The minister of God is God's chosen instrument. He has been chosen by God to declare the Word of God to God's people. Moreover, he has been called to minister to God's people, encouraging and strengthening them in the faith and doing all he can to conform them to the image of Christ. But this is not all: he has been called to reach out and to lead God's people to reach out to the lost of the world. But even this is not all: he has been called to bear the authority and weight of all the duties of the church itself, both the spiritual and administrative duties. The weight of the dear minister is heavy, weighed down with responsibility and accountability before God. Nevertheless, he has to minister because he is the chosen instrument of God. This God wants His people to know, respect, and honor.	*But the Lord said to Ananias, "Go! This man is my chosen instrument to carry my name before the Gentiles and their kings and before the people of Israel." (Ac. 9:15)* *Now get up and stand on your feet. I have appeared to you to appoint you as a servant and as a witness of what you have seen of me and what I will show you. (Ac. 26:16)* *But God chose the foolish things of the world to shame the wise; God chose the weak things of the world to shame the strong. He chose the lowly things of this world and the despised things—and the things that are not—to nullify the things that are, so that no one may boast before him. (1 Co. 1:27-29)* *And he has committed to us the message of reconciliation. We are therefore Christ's ambassadors, as though God were making his appeal through us. We implore you on Christ's behalf: Be reconciled to God. (2 Co. 5:19-20)* *It was he who gave some to be apostles, some to be prophets, some to be evangelists, and some to be pastors and teachers, to prepare God's people for works of service, so that the body of Christ may be built up. (Ep. 4:11-12; see also He. 13:17; Is. 6:8; Je. 35:15; Eze. 3:17).*

NUMBERS 17:1-13

Historical Term	Type or Picture (Scriptural Basis for Each)	Life Application for Today's Believer	Biblical Application
Aaron's Staff Nu. 17:6-9	*Aaron's staff or rod is a symbol of God's power & authority; of the authority of Christ or the minister to bear fruit and bring life to people. The budding of the rod was not by chance; it was by the miraculous power of God. The budding of the rod produced life and fruit: it was a clear symbol that Aaron was to produce life and fruit in his ministry by the hand of God. An astonishing miracle! An indisputable sign that Aaron was a true servant and minister of God, the man who was to stand as the High Priest between God and His people.* **The next day Moses entered the Tent of the Testimony and saw that Aaron's staff, which represented the house of Levi, had not only sprouted but had budded, blossomed and produced almonds. (Nu. 17:8)**	The budding staff of Aaron bore fruit and gave life. This was the proof of Aaron's ministry and priesthood. By the authority and power of God, Aaron's ministry was appointed to give life and bear fruit among God's people. The power of God is to rest upon every minister and servant of God. Every minister and servant is to share the Word of life and bear fruit among God's people. What does it mean to say that a minister must bear fruit? 1. Bearing fruit means to bear converts. 2. Bearing fruit means to bear righteousness, to bear a holy life. 3. Bearing fruit means to bear the Christian character or the fruit of the Spirit.	*"Come, follow me," Jesus said, "and I will make you fishers of men." (Mt. 4:19)* *As soon as the grain is ripe, he puts the sickle to it, because the harvest has come. (Mk. 4:29)* *Do you not say, 'Four months more and then the harvest'? I tell you, open your eyes and look at the fields! They are ripe for harvest. Even now the reaper draws his wages, even now he harvests the crop for eternal life, so that the sower and the reaper may be glad together. (Jn. 4:35-36; see also Ro. 1:13; Ga. 6:9; Pr. 11:30)* *What benefit did you reap at that time from the things you are now ashamed of? Those things result in death! But now that you have been set free from sin and have become slaves to God, the benefit you reap leads to holiness, and the result is eternal life. For the wages of sin is death, but the gift of God is eternal life in Christ Jesus our Lord. (Ro. 6:21-23)* *But the fruit of the Spirit is love, joy, peace, patience, kindness, goodness, faithfulness, gentleness and self-control. Against such things there is no law. (Ga. 5:22-23)*

NUMBERS 18:1-32

CHAPTER 18

D. Event 4—God Spelled Out the Service of the Priests & Levites: The Duties, Support, & Tithing of God's Ministers, 18:1-32

1. **The duties of the priests & Levites (a picture of ministers)**
   a. Duty 1: To be responsible along with their assistants (the Levites) for any offense against the sanctuary
   b. Duty 2: To be personally responsible for any offense against the priesthood
   c. Duty 3: To be responsible for supervising or overseeing their assistants, the Levites

   1) The assistants were to perform all the manual work
   2) The assistants were never to go near the sacred objects or altar
   3) The warning: If the sacred objects were violated, God's judgment fell (death)

   d. Duty 4: To be responsible, along with their assistants, for the care & protection of the Tabernacle
   1) Must make absolutely sure no one ever violates its precincts
   2) The reason: To prevent the judgment of God—His anger & wrath—from falling upon the violators

   e. Duty 5: To accept their fellow assistants (the Levites) as a gift from God: They were dedicated to the LORD & His service

   f. Duty 6: To accept the priesthood (God's call & ministry) as a gift from God
   1) Must personally handle all the sacred service: Anything associated with the altar & inside the inner curtain
   2) The reason: God's judgment death for any violator

2. **The support or income of the priests & Levites (ministers)**
   a. The priests (God's ministers) were to receive support or income, a share of the holy offerings given by the people

The LORD said to Aaron, "You, your sons and your father's family are to bear the responsibility for offenses against the sanctuary, and you and your sons alone are to bear the responsibility for offenses against the priesthood.
2 Bring your fellow Levites from your ancestral tribe to join you and assist you when you and your sons minister before the Tent of the Testimony.
3 They are to be responsible to you and are to perform all the duties of the Tent, but they must not go near the furnishings of the sanctuary or the altar, or both they and you will die.
4 They are to join you and be responsible for the care of the Tent of Meeting—all the work at the Tent—and no one else may come near where you are.
5 "You are to be responsible for the care of the sanctuary and the altar, so that wrath will not fall on the Israelites again.
6 I myself have selected your fellow Levites from among the Israelites as a gift to you, dedicated to the LORD to do the work at the Tent of Meeting.
7 But only you and your sons may serve as priests in connection with everything at the altar and inside the curtain. I am giving you the service of the priesthood as a gift. Anyone else who comes near the sanctuary must be put to death."
8 Then the LORD said to Aaron, "I myself have put you in charge of the offerings presented to me; all the holy offerings the Israelites give me I give to you and your sons as your portion and regular share.
9 You are to have the part of the most holy offerings that is kept from the fire. From all the gifts they bring me as most holy offerings, whether grain or sin or guilt offerings, that part belongs to you and your sons.
10 Eat it as something most holy; every male shall eat it. You must regard it as holy.
11 "This also is yours: whatever is set aside from the gifts of all the wave offerings of the Israelites. I give this to you and your sons and daughters as your regular share. Everyone in your household who is ceremonially clean may eat it.
12 "I give you all the finest olive oil and all the finest new wine and grain they give the LORD as the firstfruits of their harvest.
13 All the land's firstfruits that they bring to the LORD will be yours. Everyone in your household who is ceremonially clean may eat it.
14 "Everything in Israel that is devoted to the LORD is yours.
15 The first offspring of every womb, both man and animal, that is offered to the LORD is yours. But you must redeem every firstborn son and every firstborn male of unclean animals.
16 When they are a month old, you must redeem them at the redemption price set at five shekels of silver, according to the sanctuary shekel, which weighs twenty gerahs.
17 "But you must not redeem the firstborn of an ox, a sheep or a goat; they are holy. Sprinkle their blood on the altar and burn their fat as an offering made by fire, an aroma pleasing to the LORD.
18 Their meat is to be yours, just as the breast of the wave offering and the right thigh are yours.
19 Whatever is set aside from the holy offerings the Israelites present to the LORD I give to you and your sons and daughters as your regular share. It is an everlasting covenant of salt before the LORD for both you and your offspring."
20 The LORD said to Aaron,

   1) The portion that was not used or burned in the sacrifices
      • This included portions from the Grain, Sin, & Guilt Offerings
      • This food (income) was to be treated & eaten as something most holy: Because it had been given to God for His service
   2) The wave offerings (offerings of thanksgiving)
      • This provision (income) was for the entire family
      • It was to be used or eaten only by the ceremonially clean (again, because it was a holy offering, given to God for His service)
   3) The firstfruit offering—all of the first harvest that was given to God
      • The finest olive oil, new wine, & grain
      • The one restriction: Only the ceremonially clean could use or eat what had been presented to the LORD
   4) The gifts that were devoted or set apart to God
   5) The firstborn male of every human or animal that was offered to the LORD
      • The firstborn sons & the firstborn males of unclean animals were to be redeemed: The redemption price was five pieces of silver

      • The firstborn of clean animals such as oxen, sheep, or goats was not to be redeemed: It was holy & was to be sacrificed as instructed, & a portion of its meat was to be given to the priests

   b. The importance of the priest (minister) receiving support & income
      1) The law of support was laid down by God Himself
      2) The law of support was established by God as a covenant of salt (an unbreakable covenant)
      3) The priests were not to

NUMBERS 18:1-32

inherit or own any of the land of Canaan because they were to receive a very special share & inheritance: The LORD Himself
c. The Levites (assistant ministers) were to receive support or income: All the tithes
  1) Because they deserved to be paid for their work
  2) Because they guarded the Tabernacle & shielded the people from the blazing judgment of God's holiness
  3) Because they bore heavy responsibility: They were accountable for any offenses against the sanctuary
  4) Because the law of support was established by God as a permanent law
  5) Because they were not to receive any share or inheritance of the land
  6) Because the law of daily support & income replaces the inheritance of the land they would otherwise be receiving
3. The contributions or tithes of the Levites (assistant ministers)
  a. They must tithe one tenth of
	"You will have no inheritance in their land, nor will you have any share among them; I am your share and your inheritance among the Israelites.
	21 "I give to the Levites all the tithes in Israel as their inheritance in return for the work they do while serving at the Tent of Meeting.
	22 From now on the Israelites must not go near the Tent of Meeting, or they will bear the consequences of their sin and will die.
	23 It is the Levites who are to do the work at the Tent of Meeting and bear the responsibility for offenses against it. This is a lasting ordinance for the generations to come. They will receive no inheritance among the Israelites.
	24 Instead, I give to the Levites as their inheritance the tithes that the Israelites present as an offering to the LORD. That is why I said concerning them: 'They will have no inheritance among the Israelites.' "
	25 The LORD said to Moses,
	26 "Speak to the Levites and say to them: 'When you receive from the Israelites the
		tithe I give you as your inheritance, you must present a tenth of that tithe as the LORD's offering.
		27 Your offering will be reckoned to you as grain from the threshing floor or juice from the winepress.
		28 In this way you also will present an offering to the LORD from all the tithes you receive from the Israelites. From these tithes you must give the LORD's portion to Aaron the priest.
		29 You must present as the LORD's portion the best and holiest part of everything given to you.'
		30 "Say to the Levites: 'When you present the best part, it will be reckoned to you as the product of the threshing floor or the winepress.
		31 You and your households may eat the rest of it anywhere, for it is your wages for your work at the Tent of Meeting.
		32 By presenting the best part of it you will not be guilty in this matter; then you will not defile the holy offerings of the Israelites, and you will not die.' "
			their income, the support they received from the people
			
			  1) Would be counted as their Grain Offering from the harvest
			
			  2) Would be counted as their gift or offering to the LORD
			b. They must give the tithe to the LORD's representative, the priest (minister)
			
			c. They must give the best portion of the tithe to the LORD
			
			  1) The spirit of giving the best was counted as the offering of the firstfruit: Accepted, blessed by God
			
			  2) The rest of the support or income was counted as the person's wages
			
			d. They must heed the warning: They must tithe the best or stand guilty of defiling the holy offerings & face the eternal judgment of God

DIVISION III

THE FORTY LONG YEARS OF WILDERNESS WANDERINGS: A PICTURE OF THE BELIEVER'S PILGRIMAGE THROUGH THIS WORLD AS HE PREPARES TO ENTER THE PROMISED LAND, 15:1–25:18

D. Event 4—God Spelled Out the Service of the Priests and Levites: The Duties, Support, and Tithing of God's Ministers, 18:1-32

(18:1-32) **Introduction—Support, of Ministers—Stewardship, Support of Ministers**: it is absolutely essential to support the ministers of God. God demands that His people support them, give them an income for their labor. Why? Because the minister of God serves the people of God. He is to spend as much time as possible in the ministry, every conceivable hour possible. The minister is called by God to proclaim the Word of God. Hour after hour of prayer and preparation is required. But in addition to these long hours, the minister is called to serve people…

- visiting in their homes
- motivating support for missions and outreach
- visiting the shut-ins
- counseling those with problems
- visiting the church members
- visiting the hospitals
- marrying the young
- visiting the grief-stricken and bereaved
- nurturing, nourishing, and growing people
- visiting the leadership
- overseeing the finances and distribution of money
- reaching out to the lost
- burying the dead
- overseeing all the committees and administrative work of the church

On and on the list could go: the work of the ministry never ends. It is a constant battle for the minister to merely stay afloat, for the work is constant, hard, and long. On top of all the work, he has to spend hour after hour in prayer and Bible study in order to victoriously lead the people of God on their march to the promised land of God. The pastor earns his keep, his income. He is to be compensated as well as possible for his ministry to God's people. This is the subject of this great passage of Scripture: *Event 4—God Spelled Out the Service of the Priests and Levites: The Duties, Support, and Tithing of God's Ministers*, 18:1-32.

NUMBERS 18:1-32

1. The duties of the priests and Levites (a picture of ministers) (vv.1-7).
2. The support or income of the priests and Levites (ministers) (vv.8-24).
3. The contributions or tithes of the Levites (assistant ministers) (vv.25-32).

1 (18:1-7) **Ministers, Duties Of—Priests, Duties Of—Levites, Duties Of—Layman, Service Of—Church, Protection Of—Ministry, A Gift or Privilege From God**: the duties of the priests and the Levites are spelled out. Note that God is speaking only to Aaron throughout this passage. As the leader and High Priest, it was his duty to teach and supervise the other priests in the work of the ministry.

Remember: within the past two days, the people had seen the judgment of God fall upon a revolt against Aaron's priesthood. Moreover, they had witnessed the power of God in causing the staff of Aaron to bud and bear fruit, indicating his call and ministry. These two events had stricken a terrifying fear in the hearts of the people, a fear that kept them from approaching the sanctuary or presence of God. They feared, for they saw no way to be reconciled to God, no way to approach God. This is part of what God is doing in this passage. God is declaring that He has provided exactly what the people are crying out for. He has provided a High Priest who stands between God and man, a High Priest who can approach God on their behalf, a High Priest who can protect them from the holiness and judgment of God, a High Priest who can save them and give them life. But there is more in this passage: the duties and responsibilities of the priests and Levites (ministers) are also being spelled out. Note the six duties spelled out.

a. First, the priests were responsible, along with their assistants (the Levites), for any offense against the sanctuary (v.1). Note the word *offenses* (avown): it means fault, mischief, sin. It is a general word that applies to all kinds of sin or offenses against the sanctuary of God. The primary duty to protect the sanctuary, God's very presence, was the responsibility of the priests along with the Levites. No person was to make a wrong approach into God's presence: it was the priests' duty to teach the people how to approach God and to prevent them from approaching Him in their own self-righteous ways. No person was to be allowed to defile, damage, or destroy the sanctuary.

b. Second, the priests were personally responsible for any offense against the priesthood (v.1). No person was to be allowed to destroy the priesthood that had been established by God. No grumbling, no attack, and no opposition were to be allowed. The call and ministry of the priest was to be protected at all costs, for it had been established by God. The priest had been called and appointed by God. He was the minister of God to the people of God:

⇒ to represent God before the people and the people before God
⇒ to declare the Word of God to the people
⇒ to counsel and give guidance to the people
⇒ to minister to the needs of people

No person was to attack the priesthood; no person was to seek to destroy the priest or his ministry. It was the duty of the priest to prevent this. He was personally responsible to protect his call and ministry before God.

c. Third, the priests were responsible for supervising their assistants, the Levites (vv.2-3). The Levite assistants were to perform all the manual work around the Tabernacle. But note: they were never to go near the sacred objects or altar. If they ever violated the sacred objects, God's judgment would fall upon them (v.3). The Levite assistants were never to usurp the call or ministry of the priests. They themselves were not the priests; this was not their call. They had their own call: a different and distinctive service to do for God. They were to be faithful to their call, never trying to replace the priest. If they did, the warning was clear: the judgment of God would fall and they would die.

d. Fourth, the priests were responsible, along with the Levite assistants, for the care and protection of the Tabernacle (vv.4-5). They were to make absolutely sure that no one ever violated its precincts. Note the reason: to prevent the judgment of God, His anger and wrath, from falling upon the violators (v.5). If a person approached God's holy presence in a wrong way—in his own self-righteous way—the fire of God's holiness would flash out and strike him in judgment. There was only one way to approach God: through the ministry of the priest (a symbol of the ministry of Jesus Christ).

e. Fifth, the priests were to accept their fellow assistants (the Levites) as a gift from God. The Levites were given by God to be their assistants. The Levites were dedicated to the LORD and His service just as the priests were. Each had his own service, his own work to do for the LORD; therefore, the priests were to respect and honor the Levite assistants. They were never to downplay the assistants nor their work for God, never degrade them in any way. They were a very special gift from God to carry on the work and service of God, assisting the priests.

f. Sixth, the priests were responsible for accepting the priesthood as a gift from God (v.7). It was God who had called and given them the ministry of the priesthood; therefore, they were to honor the ministry. They had been highly privileged by God, given the privilege to serve God and God's people. No greater call or ministry could ever be endowed upon a person. The priests and all others were to know this fact: God loves His people; therefore, He wants them cared for and looked after with all diligence.

There is a strong lesson here that points to Christ. Of all people, Aaron alone could approach God. He alone stood between God and man, representing God to man and man to God. He and he alone had been appointed to stand between God and man. This is a clear and descriptive picture of Jesus Christ and His High Priesthood. Note that the priest personally had to handle all the sacred service. The sacred service included anything that was associated with the altar and that was inside the inner curtain. The privilege of entering inside the Holy of Holies and of approaching God through the sacrifice laid upon the altar was a priceless gift. The priest was to accept this priceless gift as coming from God and from Him alone. Note that anyone else who came near the sanctuary was to be put to death. The judgment of God was to fall upon him.

Thought 1. There are at least five strong lessons in this point for the minister of God.

(1) The minister of God is ultimately responsible for the church and its care. Just as the priest was responsible for any offense against the sanctuary, so the minister is responsible for any sin committed against Christ and His church. It is the duty of the minister to teach people to respect Christ and the church. Christ is not to be dishonored and the church is not to be disturbed or abused, neither verbally or physically. The lives of God's people are not to be destroyed, neither is the property of God's church to be abused or destroyed. The minister is to protect and care for the church,

NUMBERS 18:1-32

including the people of God and the property of God's church.

For we are God's fellow workers; you are God's field, God's building. By the grace God has given me, I laid a foundation as an expert builder, and someone else is building on it. But each one should be careful how he builds. For no one can lay any foundation other than the one already laid, which is Jesus Christ. If any man builds on this foundation using gold, silver, costly stones, wood, hay or straw, his work will be shown for what it is, because the Day will bring it to light. It will be revealed with fire, and the fire will test the quality of each man's work. If what he has built survives, he will receive his reward. If it is burned up, he will suffer loss; he himself will be saved, but only as one escaping through the flames. (1 Co. 3:9-15)

Don't you know that you [plural, the church] yourselves are God's temple and that God's Spirit lives in you? If anyone destroys God's temple, God will destroy him; for God's temple is sacred, and you are that temple. (1 Co. 3:16-17)

Consequently, you are no longer foreigners and aliens, but fellow citizens with God's people and members of God's household, built on the foundation of the apostles and prophets, with Christ Jesus himself as the chief cornerstone. In him the whole building is joined together and rises to become a holy temple in the Lord. And in him you too are being built together to become a dwelling in which God lives by his Spirit. (Ep. 2:19-22)

You also, like living stones, are being built into a spiritual house to be a holy priesthood, offering spiritual sacrifices acceptable to God through Jesus Christ. (1 Pe. 2:5)

(2) The minister of God is to be diligent in performing his duties. He is to be very responsible. He is to work hard, be steadfast and persevering, working his fingers to the bone to get the work of the ministry done.

Now it is required that those who have been given a trust must prove faithful. (1 Co. 4:2)

Therefore, my dear brothers, stand firm. Let nothing move you. Always give yourselves fully to the work of the Lord, because you know that your labor in the Lord is not in vain. (1 Co. 15:58)

And whatever you do, whether in word or deed, do it all in the name of the Lord Jesus, giving thanks to God the Father through him. (Col. 3:17)

Whatever you do, work at it with all your heart, as working for the Lord, not for men. (Col. 3:23)

This is a trustworthy saying that deserves full acceptance (and for this we labor and strive), that we have put our hope in the living God, who is the Savior of all men, and especially of those who believe. Command and teach these things. Don't let anyone look down on you because you are young, but set an example for the believers in speech, in life, in love, in faith and in purity. Until I come, devote yourself to the public reading of Scripture, to preaching and to teaching. Do not neglect your gift, which was given you through a prophetic message when the body of elders laid their hands on you. Be diligent in these matters; give yourself wholly to them, so that everyone may see your progress. Watch your life and doctrine closely. Persevere in them, because if you do, you will save both yourself and your hearers. (1 Ti. 4:9-16)

Preach the Word; be prepared in season and out of season; correct, rebuke and encourage—with great patience and careful instruction. For the time will come when men will not put up with sound doctrine. Instead, to suit their own desires, they will gather around them a great number of teachers to say what their itching ears want to hear. They will turn their ears away from the truth and turn aside to myths. But you, keep your head in all situations, endure hardship, do the work of an evangelist, discharge all the duties of your ministry. For I am already being poured out like a drink offering, and the time has come for my departure. I have fought the good fight, I have finished the race, I have kept the faith. Now there is in store for me the crown of righteousness, which the Lord, the righteous Judge, will award to me on that day—and not only to me, but also to all who have longed for his appearing. (2 Ti. 4:2-8)

So then, dear friends, since you are looking forward to this, make every effort to be found spotless, blameless and at peace with him. (2 Pe. 3:14)

(3) The minister is to point people to the Lord Jesus Christ as the Perfect Priest. Jesus Christ is the One who stands between God and man, stands in perfection as the Perfect Intercessor and Mediator. Jesus Christ is the only person who can eternally and perfectly satisfy the holiness of God. He is the only One who is perfectly acceptable to God. The minister must point to Jesus Christ as the Perfect Priest who stands before God, representing God to man and man to God. Jesus Christ is the only person who can bring us to God and make us acceptable to Him.

For this reason he had to be made like his brothers in every way, in order that he might become a merciful and faithful high priest in service to God, and that he might make atonement for the sins of the people. (He. 2:17)

Therefore, since we have a great high priest who has gone through the heavens, Jesus the Son of God, let us hold firmly to the faith we profess. For we do not have a high priest who is unable to sympathize with our weaknesses, but we have one who has been tempted in every way, just as we are—yet was without sin. (He. 4:14-15)

Every high priest is selected from among men and is appointed to represent them in matters related to God, to offer gifts and sacrifices for sins. He is able to deal gently with those who are ignorant and are going astray, since he himself is subject to weakness. This is why he has to offer sacrifices for his own sins, as well as for the sins of the people. No one takes this honor upon himself; he must be called by God, just as Aaron was. So Christ also did not take upon himself the glory of becoming a high priest. But God said to him, "You are my Son; today I have become your Father." (He. 5:1-5)

We have this hope as an anchor for the soul, firm and secure. It enters the inner sanctuary behind the curtain, where Jesus, who went before us, has entered on our behalf. He has become a high priest forever, in the order of Melchizedek. (He. 6:19-20)

Therefore he is able to save completely those who come to God through him, because he always lives to intercede for them. Such a high priest meets our need—one who is holy, blameless, pure, set apart from sinners, exalted above the heavens. Unlike the other high priests, he does not need to offer sacrifices day after day, first for his own sins, and then for the sins of the people. He sacrificed for their sins once for all when he offered himself. (He. 7:25-27)

The point of what we are saying is this: We do have such a high priest, who sat down at the right hand of the throne of the Majesty in heaven. (He. 8:1)

(4) The minister must know that he represents Christ before the people of the world. He himself must, therefore, live a holy and pure life before God. He must guard himself day by day, making absolutely sure that he walks righteously and godly before people.

For I tell you that unless your righteousness surpasses that of the Pharisees and the teachers of the law, you will certainly not enter the kingdom of heaven. (Mt. 5:20)

To rescue us from the hand of our enemies, and to enable us to serve him without fear in holiness and righteousness before him all our days. (Lu. 1:74-75)

Come back to your senses as you ought, and stop sinning; for there are some who are ignorant of God—I say this to your shame. (1 Co. 15:34)

Since we have these promises, dear friends, let us purify ourselves from everything that contaminates body and spirit, perfecting holiness out of reverence for God. (2 Co. 7:1)

Stand firm then, with the belt of truth buckled around your waist, with the breastplate of righteousness in place. (Ep. 6:14)

Filled with the fruit of righteousness that comes through Jesus Christ—to the glory and praise of God. (Ph. 1:11)

The goal of this command is love, which comes from a pure heart and a good conscience and a sincere faith. (1 Ti. 1:5)

But you, man of God, flee from all this, and pursue righteousness, godliness, faith, love, endurance and gentleness. (1 Ti. 6:11)

For the grace of God that brings salvation has appeared to all men. It teaches us to say "No" to ungodliness and worldly passions, and to live self-controlled, upright and godly lives in this present age. (Tit. 2:11-12)

Make every effort to live in peace with all men and to be holy; without holiness no one will see the Lord. (He. 12:14)

Religion that God our Father accepts as pure and faultless is this: to look after orphans and widows in their distress and to keep oneself from being polluted by the world. (Js. 1:27)

But just as he who called you is holy, so be holy in all you do; for it is written: "Be holy, because I am holy." (1 Pe. 1:15-16)

Since everything will be destroyed in this way, what kind of people ought you to be? You ought to live holy and godly lives as you look forward to the day of God and speed its coming. That day will bring about the destruction of the heavens by fire, and the elements will melt in the heat. But in keeping with his promise we are looking forward to a new heaven and a new earth, the home of righteousness. So then, dear friends, since you are looking forward to this, make every effort to be found spotless, blameless and at peace with him. (2 Pe. 3:11-14)

I am the LORD who brought you up out of Egypt to be your God; therefore be holy, because I am holy. (Le. 11:45)

(5) The minister of God must accept his call and ministry as a gift from God. He must know that he is called by God and that his ministry has been given by God. Therefore, he must honor and highly esteem his call and ministry. He must recognize that he has been highly privileged, but even more than this, he must know that he has been given an awesome responsibility and will be held more accountable than any other individual. He has been entrusted with the awesome responsibility of God's Holy Word—to proclaim it—and the care and nurturing of God's people. God loves His people above and beyond anything we can possibly imagine. He gave His very own Son to die in their behalf. He allowed His own Son to bear the judgment of God that was due His people, allowed His Son to bear their sin in order to save them. God loves His dear people so much that He has appointed a profession of people—the ministers of God—to look after and care for them. No person dare fail in the call and ministry of God. To fail will be to face the awesome, terrifying judgment of God. No greater call could be extended to a person than to be called to the ministry of God. It is a privilege, but it is also an awesome

responsibility. The ministry and its call is the gift of God. This the minister is to honor.

> Now it is required that those who have been given a trust must prove faithful. (1 Co. 4:2)
>
> That God was reconciling the world to himself in Christ, not counting men's sins against them. And he has committed to us the message of reconciliation. We are therefore Christ's ambassadors, as though God were making his appeal through us. We implore you on Christ's behalf: Be reconciled to God. God made him who had no sin to be sin for us, so that in him we might become the righteousness of God. (2 Co. 5:19-21)
>
> I became a servant of this gospel by the gift of God's grace given me through the working of his power. Although I am less than the least of all God's people, this grace was given me: to preach to the Gentiles the unsearchable riches of Christ. (Ep. 3:7-8)
>
> I have become its servant by the commission God gave me to present to you the word of God in its fullness. (Col. 1:25)
>
> I thank Christ Jesus our Lord, who has given me strength, that he considered me faithful, appointing me to his service. (1 Ti. 1:12)
>
> And of this gospel I was appointed a herald and an apostle and a teacher. That is why I am suffering as I am. Yet I am not ashamed, because I know whom I have believed, and am convinced that he is able to guard what I have entrusted to him for that day. (2 Ti. 1:11-12)

2 (18:8-24) **Support, of Ministers—Ministers, Support of—Priests, Support of—Levites, Support of**: there was the support or income of the priests and Levites that was spelled out in detail. Keep in mind that the priests and Levites were a symbol of the minister of God. God's people are to support the servants of God around the world. This is a strong message to the priests and Levites, a strong message to the ministers of God: they were to earn their living. They were to work and work hard for their livelihood. In honor of their service and ministry, the people were to support them. The provision of their support is clearly and fully spelled out in this passage.

   a. The priests (God's ministers) were to receive support or income from the holy offerings given by the people (vv.8-18).

      1) The portion of meat that was not used in the sacrifices offered upon the altar was to be the priest's (vv.9-10). This included portions from the Grain, Sin, and Guilt Offerings. Note that this food or income was to be treated as something most holy. Keep in mind that anything offered and given to God is considered holy, that is, set apart for His service. When the holy food or income was transferred to the priest, it remained holy. It did not lose its holiness. The priest was, therefore, to count his food or income as holy; and he was to use it only for holy purposes. He was never to allow the food or income to be used in some worldly occasion or endeavor.

      2) The wave offerings were part of the support and income of the priest (v.11). Note that this provision was for the entire family of the priest. However, if a family member was ceremonially or spiritually unclean, he could not eat the food or use the income. Why? Because it was a holy offering, given to God only for His service. Again, the food or income must not be used for any unclean or worldly purpose (see outline and notes—Le. 22:1-9, for God's provision for cleansing).

      3) The firstfruit offering—all of the harvest that was given to God—became part of the food or income of the priest (vv.12-13). This included the finest olive oil, new wine, and grain. But again note the one restriction: only the family member who was ceremonially or spiritually clean could eat what had been presented to the LORD.

      Note the word *finest*: only the finest of the firstfruit was to be offered to God. This meant that both God and the priest received the best of the first.[1] The first and the best of the harvest were given to God, which meant that the first and best became part of the support or income of the priest. God's dear minister was to be cared for and looked after, highly honored and supported by the people.

      4) The gifts that were *devoted* (herem) or set apart to God were to be a part of the income of the priest. The Hebrew word has the idea of being under a ban, prohibited from being used for anything else. The gift was given to God and it was to remain in the possession of God. As the representative of God, the priest had the right to use the gift. But no one else had that right. It was under the ban, consecrated totally to the service of God and to be used only by the minister of God.

      5) The firstborn male of every human or animal that was offered to the LORD became part of the income of the priest (vv.15-18). (Also see outline and note—Ex. 13:1-16 for more discussion.)

        a) Note that the firstborn sons and the firstborn males of unclean animals were to be redeemed. God never has and never will accept the human sacrifice of a person or the sacrifice of an unclean animal. The very idea of a human being sacrificed in order to appease God's wrath and judgment has always been repulsive to God. The only approach that God accepts is through the substitute sacrifice of His dear Son. Prior to the coming of Christ, God did establish the sacrifice of clean animals to be a picture of the true approach to God, that of a person approaching Him through His Son, the Promised Seed and Savior of the world. But note: only a clean animal could be offered, an animal with no defect whatsoever. No unclean animal was ever accepted as a substitute sacrifice for the sins of man. This is the reason that both the firstborn sons and the firstborn males of unclean animals were to be redeemed. The redemption price was five pieces of silver. This, too, became part of the income of the priest.

        b) The firstborn of clean animals such as an ox, sheep, or goat was not to be redeemed. Why? Because they were already counted holy and were to be sacrificed as instructed, and a portion of their meat was to be given to the priest (vv.17-18).

---

[1] *The Expositor's Bible Commentary,* Frank E. Gaebelein, Editor, p.853.

b. Note the importance of the priest receiving support and income from the people of God (vv.19-20). God is clear: the law of supporting the minister has been laid down by God Himself. God has established the law of support as strongly as a covenant of salt. A covenant of salt simply means an unbreakable, indestructible covenant. It is established forever; God's people are to support the priests and ministers of God. This is an absolute essential. Note why: because the priests were not to inherit any of the land within the promised land (v.20). However, the priest or minister shares an inheritance: the LORD Himself. The priest was given a very special relationship with God, a relationship of love and intimacy, of deep communion and fellowship. The priest or minister was to devote his time to nurturing this relationship not to looking after property and material things.

c. Note that the Levites (assistant ministers) were also to receive support or income from the people. In fact, they were to receive all the *tithes* given to the work of God. The financial support of the Levites or assistant ministers was a new law being established by God. Note why the assistant ministers were to be supported by God's people.

1) The assistant ministers were to be supported because they deserved to be paid for their work (v.21). They served and ministered to God's people within the Tabernacle. Because they worked within the worship center of God, they were to be compensated for their work.
2) The assistant ministers were to be supported because they protected the Tabernacle and shielded the people from the blazing judgment of God's holiness (v.22). It was their duty to keep people from approaching God in their own self-righteous ways, to make sure the people approached God only through the priest. They kept people from coming near the Tabernacle lest the fury of God's holiness strike them dead.
3) The assistant ministers were to receive support because they bore heavy responsibility. They were personally accountable for any offenses against the sanctuary (v.23). This would include any abuse or destruction of the sanctuary.
4) The assistant ministers were to be supported because the law of support was established by God as a permanent law. It was to last for all generations to come. God's people were always to support the assistant ministers serving in His worship center.
5) The assistant ministers were to be supported because they were not to receive any share or inheritance in the promised land (v.23).
6) The assistant ministers were to be supported because the law of daily support and income replaced the inheritance of the land they would otherwise have been receiving (v.24). Simply stated, the assistant ministers had no income apart from the support of God's people. When they arrived in the promised land, they would own no land to farm or produce food. They were totally dependent upon the tithes of the people.

Thought 1. Financial support for the minister of God is an absolute essential. The people of God are the ones responsible for supporting the minister. The minister serves the people of God, proclaiming the Word of God to them and ministering to their needs:

⇒ nurturing and nourishing the people
⇒ caring for the sick and dying
⇒ looking after the hospitalized
⇒ marrying the young
⇒ visiting the membership and the lost of the world
⇒ giving oversight to the finances of the church
⇒ motivating commitment to the mission work of the church
⇒ overseeing and giving direction to all the committees and administrative work of the church.

On and on the list could go, for the work of the ministry never ends. But no matter how much work is involved, the minister of God still has to spend hour after hour in prayer and in the study of God's Word. He has to preach and teach, instructing and rooting the people in the Holy Word of God. Above all else, he must proclaim the unsearchable riches of Christ, rooting people in the righteousness of God Himself. It is this that pleases God first and foremost.

The minister of God earns his income. If he is really committed to the LORD and to the ministry, he more than earns it. In fact, he could never be compensated anywhere close to what he deserves. The truth is this: he is not in the ministry for money or gain, but for God and for the people of God whom he loves with all his heart. It is the love of people in particular that causes him to devote his life to them. The love of Christ compels him to love the people of God, making sure that he proclaims the unsearchable riches of Christ to them and ministers to their needs.

The point is this: the people of God are to support the minister of God financially. God has established this law forever: financial support is to be given to the minister of God.

> **Do not take along any gold or silver or copper in your belts; take no bag for the journey, or extra tunic, or sandals or a staff; for the worker is worth his keep. (Mt. 10:9-10)**
>
> **Don't you know that those who work in the temple get their food from the temple, and those who serve at the altar share in what is offered on the altar? In the same way, the Lord has commanded that those who preach the gospel should receive their living from the gospel. (1 Co. 9:13-14)**
>
> **On the first day of every week, each one of you should set aside a sum of money in keeping with his income, saving it up, so that when I come no collections will have to be made. (1 Co. 16:2)**
>
> **Anyone who receives instruction in the word must share all good things with his instructor. (Ga. 6:6)**
>
> **Yet it was good of you to share in my troubles. (Ph. 4:14)**
>
> **The elders who direct the affairs of the church well are worthy of double honor, especially those whose work is preaching and teaching. For the Scripture says, "Do not muzzle the ox while it is treading out the grain," and "The worker deserves his wages." (1 Ti. 5:17-18)**

3 (18:25-32) **Ministers, Duty to Tithe—Tithing, Of Ministers—Assistant Ministers, Duty to Tithe**: there were the contributions or tithes of the Levites (assistant ministers) (vv.25-32). The minister of God is to tithe his

NUMBERS 18:1-32

income just as everyone else does. *The Expositor's Bible Commentary* makes an excellent comment that speaks to the heart of the minister:

> There is a tendency, then and now, for persons to believe that if their lives are spent in the LORD's work, then they are exempt from contributing to that work. This leads to a concept, lamentably, more and more observed in our own day, that payment for ministry is something deserved and is something to be demanded.[2]

This is a direct commandment from God to the Levites or assistant ministers: "you must tithe" (v.26). This is a direct commandment that speaks to all the ministers of God down through all generations: you must tithe just as everyone else is required to tithe.

   a. The Levites (assistant ministers) were to tithe one tenth of their support or income (vv.26-28). Note an interesting statement: God would accept their tithe as their Grain Offering from the harvest. But God would accept or count their tithe as a Grain Offering from the harvest.

   b. The Levites (assistant ministers) must give the tithe to the LORD's representatives, that is, the priests (v.28). The priest was God's representative upon the earth, overseeing the operation of the Tabernacle or worship center. He was responsible to see that the tithes of everyone were used for the work of God. Therefore, the assistant ministers were to make their tithe to the LORD's representative, the priest.

   c. The Levites (assistant ministers) must give the best portion of the tithe to the LORD (vv.29-31). The People were going to be giving the best possessions as tithes to the LORD, which in turn were to be given to the Levites or assistant ministers. Therefore the assistant ministers must give the best portion of their income to the LORD. Note that the spirit of giving the best was counted as the offering of the firstfruit: it was accepted and blessed by God (v.30). Keep in mind that the Levite would have no land or crops to give a firstfruit offering to God. But God would accept the best portion of his income as a firstfruit offering. Note the clear statement of God: the rest of the income of the Levite or assistant minister was counted as his wages. He could keep and use the food or income as he wished.

   d. The Levites (assistant ministers) must heed the warning: they must tithe the best or stand guilty of defiling the holy offerings and be forced to face the eternal judgment of God (v.32). Under no circumstances could the leftovers or the last fruits be given to God. God was to be given the first and the best.

> **Thought 1.** The minister of God is to tithe just as everyone else tithes. He is more responsible to tithe and support God's work than the average person. Why? Because he has been appointed by God to be the minister of God, to get the Word of God out and to meet the desperate needs of people both within and without the church.
>
> Now a man came up to Jesus and asked, "Teacher, what good thing must I do to get eternal life?".....Jesus answered, "If you want to be perfect, go, sell your possessions and give to the poor, and you will have treasure in heaven. Then come, follow me." (Mt. 19:16, 21)
>
> He went to him and bandaged his wounds, pouring on oil and wine. Then he put the man on his own donkey, took him to an inn and took care of him. The next day he took out two silver coins and gave them to the innkeeper. 'Look after him,' he said, 'and when I return, I will reimburse you for any extra expense you may have.' (Lu. 10:34-35)
>
> Sell your possessions and give to the poor. Provide purses for yourselves that will not wear out, a treasure in heaven that will not be exhausted, where no thief comes near and no moth destroys. (Lu. 12:33)
>
> As he looked up, Jesus saw the rich putting their gifts into the temple treasury. He also saw a poor widow put in two very small copper coins. "I tell you the truth," he said, "this poor widow has put in more than all the others. All these people gave their gifts out of their wealth; but she out of her poverty put in all she had to live on." (Lu. 21:1-4)
>
> There were no needy persons among them. For from time to time those who owned lands or houses sold them, brought the money from the sales and put it at the apostles' feet, and it was distributed to anyone as he had need. (Ac. 4:34-35)
>
> In everything I did, I showed you that by this kind of hard work we must help the weak, remembering the words the Lord Jesus himself said: 'It is more blessed to give than to receive.' " (Ac. 20:35)
>
> Share with God's people who are in need. Practice hospitality. (Ro. 12:13)
>
> On the first day of every week, each one of you should set aside a sum of money in keeping with his income, saving it up, so that when I come no collections will have to be made. (1 Co. 16:2)
>
> Therefore, as we have opportunity, let us do good to all people, especially to those who belong to the family of believers. (Ga. 6:10)
>
> And this stone that I have set up as a pillar will be God's house, and of all that you give me I will give you a tenth." (Ge. 28:22)
>
> " 'A tithe of everything from the land, whether grain from the soil or fruit from the trees, belongs to the LORD; it is holy to the LORD. (Le. 27:30)
>
> As soon as the order went out, the Israelites generously gave the firstfruits of their grain, new wine, oil and honey and all that the fields produced. They brought a great amount, a tithe of everything. (2 Chr. 31:5)
>
> Bring the whole tithe into the storehouse, that there may be food in my house. Test me in this," says the LORD Almighty, "and see if I will not throw open the floodgates of heaven and pour out so much blessing that you will not have room enough for it. (Mal. 3:10)

---

[2] *The Expositor's Bible Commentary*, Frank E. Gaebelein, Editor, p.857.

NUMBERS 19:1-22

CHAPTER 19

E. Event 5—God Gave the Law to Govern the Offering of the Red Heifer & the Cleansing Water: A Symbol of Christ, His Sacrifice & Cleansing Power, 19:1-22

1. The offering of the red heifer (female cow): A symbol of the sacrifice of Christ cleansing a person defiled by death

The LORD said to Moses and Aaron:
2 "This is a requirement of the law that the LORD has commanded: Tell the Israelites to bring you a red heifer without defect or blemish and that has never been under a yoke.

   a. To have no defect: A symbol of Christ's perfection
   b. To be unused (never under a yoke): A symbol of freedom, the voluntary sacrifice of Christ
   c. To be put to death outside the camp: A symbol of Christ dying outside the city gate (He.13:12)

3 Give it to Eleazar the priest; it is to be taken outside the camp and slaughtered in his presence.

   d. To sprinkle some blood seven times toward the front of the Tabernacle: A symbol that Christ's sacrifice was being offered to God as full satisfaction for sin

4 Then Eleazar the priest is to take some of its blood on his finger and sprinkle it seven times toward the front of the Tent of Meeting.

   e. To wholly burn the heifer, all its parts: A symbol of the extreme sufferings of Christ

5 While he watches, the heifer is to be burned—its hide, flesh, blood and offal.

   f. To burn some cedar wood, hyssop, & scarlet wool with the heifer: A picture of using everything to intensify the *purifying power* of the offering

6 The priest is to take some cedar wood, hyssop and scarlet wool and throw them onto the burning heifer.

   g. To have every person involved in the sacrifice cleanse himself & his clothes: A symbol that all, even priests, stood guilty & needed cleansing
      1) The priest had to be cleansed

7 After that, the priest must wash his clothes and bathe himself with water. He may then come into the camp, but he will be ceremonially unclean till evening.

      2) The person who burned the sacrifice needed to be cleansed

8 The man who burns it must also wash his clothes and bathe with water, and he too will be unclean till evening.

   h. To have a clean person gather up the ashes of the sacrifice & keep them in a clean place outside the camp
      1) The ashes were kept for mixing in the *water of cleansing*—for the purification from sin: A symbol of Christ cleansing man from sin
      2) The man who gathered up the ashes was counted unclean, guilty: He had to wash himself & his clothes
   i. To establish this as a permanent law for Israel & for all foreigners among them: A picture of the eternal sacrifice & cleansing power of Christ

9 "A man who is clean shall gather up the ashes of the heifer and put them in a ceremonially clean place outside the camp. They shall be kept by the Israelite community for use in the water of cleansing; it is for purification from sin.
10 The man who gathers up the ashes of the heifer must also wash his clothes, and he too will be unclean till evening. This will be a lasting ordinance both for the Israelites and for the aliens living among them.

11 "Whoever touches the dead body of anyone will be unclean for seven days.
12 He must purify himself with the water on the third day and on the seventh day; then he will be clean. But if he does not purify himself on the third and seventh days, he will not be clean.
13 Whoever touches the dead body of anyone and fails to purify himself defiles the LORD's tabernacle. That person must be cut off from Israel. Because the water of cleansing has not been sprinkled on him, he is unclean; his uncleanness remains on him.

2. The basic cause of uncleanness—being defiled by death: A symbol of sin that causes death
   a. The one strict essential: Had to be purified with the cleansing water twice, on the 3rd & 7th days (a symbol of being totally defiled and of the power of Christ to fully & completely cleanse a person)
   b. The strong warning: A person who had been in contact with death defiled the LORD's Tabernacle, the very presence of God, & was cut off (a symbol of eternal judgment if one refuses to be cleansed by Christ)

   c. The caution against day-to-day uncleanness
      1) Must guard against being defiled by death within the tent

14 "This is the law that applies when a person dies in a tent: Anyone who enters the tent and anyone who is in it will be unclean for seven days,
15 And every open container without a lid fastened on it will be unclean.

      2) Must guard against being defiled by death out in the open

16 "Anyone out in the open who touches someone who has been killed with a sword or someone who has died a natural death, or anyone who touches a human bone or a grave, will be unclean for seven days.

3. The way to secure cleansing
   a. To have the unclean person mix some ashes from the sacrificed heifer in a jar of water
   b. To have a clean person take some hyssop & sprinkle the *cleansing water* upon all that was defiled by death
      1) All that was defiled with a tent
      2) All that was defiled out in the open

17 "For the unclean person, put some ashes from the burned purification offering into a jar and pour fresh water over them.
18 Then a man who is ceremonially clean is to take some hyssop, dip it in the water and sprinkle the tent and all the furnishings and the people who were there. He must also sprinkle anyone who has touched a human bone or a grave or someone who has been killed or someone who has died a natural death.

   c. To have the clean person sprinkle the unclean person on the 3rd & 7th days; also to have the unclean person wash himself & his clothes on the 7th day: A symbol of full & complete cleansing through the sacrifice & power of Christ

19 The man who is clean is to sprinkle the unclean person on the third and seventh days, and on the seventh day he is to purify him. The person being cleansed must wash his clothes and bathe with water, and that evening he will be clean.

4. The strong warning reemphasized
   a. The person who was unclean & refused to be cleansed:

20 But if a person who is unclean does not purify himself, he must be cut off from the community, because

NUMBERS 19:1-22

Was to be cut off 1) Because he defiled the sanctuary 2) Because he had not been cleansed b. The law of cleansing is a permanent law: A symbol that all need to be cleansed c. The people involved in han-	he has defiled the sanctuary of the LORD. The water of cleansing has not been sprinkled on him, and he is unclean. 21 This is a lasting ordinance for them. "The man who sprinkles the water of cleansing must also wash his	clothes, and anyone who touches the water of cleansing will be unclean till evening. 22 Anything that an unclean person touches becomes unclean, and anyone who touches it becomes unclean till evening."	dling the water: All were unclean & needed cleansing 1) The person who sprinkled it 2) Any person who touched it 3) Anyone & anything who became unclean by touching a defiled person or object

DIVISION III

THE FORTY LONG YEARS OF WILDERNESS WANDERINGS: A PICTURE OF THE BELIEVER'S PILGRIMAGE THROUGH THIS WORLD AS HE PREPARES TO ENTER THE PROMISED LAND, 15:1–25:18

E. Event 5—God Gave the Law to Govern the Offering of the Red Heifer and the Cleansing Water: A Symbol of Christ, His Sacrifice and Cleansing Power, 19:1-22

(19:1-22) **Introduction—Death, Caused by—Death, Results of—Death, Defilement of—Death, Corruption of—Defilement, of Death**: death is the ultimate defilement, the ultimate defilement or corruption of man. Man was never created to die but rather to live eternally in all the abundance of life. Man was created to worship and serve God, living in perfect communion and fellowship with Him. But selfishness and sin changed man. Selfishness and sin corrupted man, planting the seed of deterioration and decay, of death itself, within man. The result of selfishness and sin is death: corruption, deterioration, and decay. Nothing defiles a man like death. Death is the ultimate defilement. Death is contrary to God's purpose for man, totally contrary to man's reason for existing. This is the great concern of the present Scripture: how to be cleansed from the defilement of death. God wants man to live eternally with him, fulfilling his purpose to the fullest. God wants man living in all the abundance of life, being victorious and triumphant over all the enemies of life that drag him down into the pit of corruption and decay. God wants man to conquer death and to live eternally with Him.

The glorious news is just this: God has provided a way for man to be cleansed from defilement, even from the defilement of death. Cleansing from defilement was pictured or symbolized in the offering of the red heifer (a red female cow). The red heifer symbolized the cleansing power of Jesus Christ, the power of His sacrifice to cleanse from the defilement of sin and death. This is the great subject of this passage: *Event 5—God Gave the Law to Govern the Offering of the Red Heifer and the Cleansing Water: A Symbol of Christ, His Sacrifice and Cleansing Power, 19:1-22.*

1. The offering of the red heifer (female cow): a symbol of the sacrifice of Christ cleansing a person defiled by death (vv.11-10).
2. The basic cause of uncleanness—being defiled by death: a symbol of sin that causes death (vv.11-16).
3. The way to secure cleansing (vv.17-19).
4. The strong warning reemphasized (vv.20-22).

1 (19:1-10) **Red Heifer—Sacrifice, of Red Heifer—Cleansing, from Sin—Sin, Cleansing from—Symbol, of Christ's Sacrifice—Sacrifice, of Christ, Symbol of—Forgiveness, of Sin—Defilement, by Death—Death, Causes Defilement**: there was the offering of the red heifer (a red female cow). The offering of the red heifer was instituted by God for a good reason: it met a dire need of the people. If a person sinned while the Israelites were marching along, Moses could not stop the march in its tracks, put up the Tabernacle, then go through the ritual of approaching God for forgiveness through the substitute sacrifice. What, then, was a person to do if he sinned while marching along the way? The answer lay in the offering of the red heifer: the priest would take a small amount of ashes from the red heifer and mix those ashes with fresh water. Then the priest would take some hyssop, dip it in the mixed water, and sprinkle the person who had sinned. Keep in mind that this is a picture of the cleansing, purifying power of Christ's sacrifice.

a. The red heifer was to have no defect or blemish: it was to be a perfect offering. This was a symbol of the perfection of Jesus Christ. He was the sinless, perfect sacrifice offered up to God (v.2).

> **God made him who had no sin to be sin for us, so that in him we might become the righteousness of God. (2 Co. 5:21)**
>
> **In bringing many sons to glory, it was fitting that God, for whom and through whom everything exists, should make the author of their salvation perfect through suffering. (He. 2:10)**
>
> **For we do not have a high priest who is unable to sympathize with our weaknesses, but we have one who has been tempted in every way, just as we are—yet was without sin. (He. 4:15)**
>
> **And, once made perfect, he became the source of eternal salvation for all who obey him. (He. 5:9)**
>
> **Such a high priest meets our need—one who is holy, blameless, pure, set apart from sinners, exalted above the heavens. (He. 7:26)**
>
> **For the law appoints as high priests men who are weak; but the oath, which came after the law, appointed the Son, who has been made perfect forever. (He. 7:28)**

b. The red heifer was to be unused, that is, an animal that had never been worked with a yoke around its neck. It had always been a free animal. This was a symbol of Christ being free to choose or voluntarily sacrifice Himself for the sins of the human race (v.2).

> For the Son of Man came to seek and to save what was lost. (Lu. 19:10)
> Here is a trustworthy saying that deserves full acceptance: Christ Jesus came into the world to save sinners—of whom I am the worst. (1 Ti. 1:15)
> Therefore, when Christ came into the world, he said: "Sacrifice and offering you did not desire, but a body you prepared for me; with burnt offerings and sin offerings you were not pleased. Then I said, 'Here I am—it is written about me in the scroll—I have come to do your will, O God.' First he said, "Sacrifices and offerings, burnt offerings and sin offerings you did not desire, nor were you pleased with them" (although the law required them to be made). Then he said, "Here I am, I have come to do your will." He sets aside the first to establish the second. And by that will, we have been made holy through the sacrifice of the body of Jesus Christ once for all. (He. 10:5-10)
> For zeal for your house consumes me, and the insults of those who insult you fall on me. (Ps. 69:9)

c. The red heifer was to be put to death outside the camp. This was a symbol of Christ being put to death outside the city gate.

> And so Jesus also suffered outside the city gate to make the people holy through his own blood. (He. 13:12).

d. Some blood of the red heifer was to be sprinkled seven times toward the front of the Tabernacle. Remember that the number seven was a symbol of full and complete acceptance. The blood of the red heifer was being accepted by God as full and complete satisfaction for sin. Of course, this was a symbol that Christ's sacrifice was being offered to God as complete satisfaction for sin. God accepts the sacrifice of Christ fully and completely. Our sins are fully and completely forgiven—all through Christ (v.4).

> God exalted him to his own right hand as Prince and Savior that he might give repentance and forgiveness of sins to Israel. (Ac.5:31)
> And live a life of love, just as Christ loved us and gave himself up for us as a fragrant [pleasing] offering and sacrifice to God. (Ep. 5:2)

e. The red heifer was to be wholly burned, all its parts. The burning of the entire heifer was a symbol of the extreme sufferings of Christ (v.5).

> And at the ninth hour Jesus cried out in a loud voice, "Eloi, Eloi, lama sabachthani?"—which means, "My God, my God, why have you forsaken me?" (Mk. 15:34)
> And being in anguish, he prayed more earnestly, and his sweat was like drops of blood falling to the ground. (Lu. 22:44)
> I offered my back to those who beat me, my cheeks to those who pulled out my beard; I did not hide my face from mocking and spitting. (Is. 50:6)

f. The priest was to burn some cedar wood, hyssop, and scarlet wool with the red heifer. All these materials were considered to have some cleansing elements or properties (see Le.14:4). This was a picture of using everything to intensify the purifying power of the offering (v.6).

> In him we have redemption through his blood, the forgiveness of sins, in accordance with the riches of God's grace. (Ep. 1:7)
> Wash away all my iniquity and cleanse me from my sin....Cleanse me with hyssop, and I will be clean; wash me, and I will be whiter than snow. (Ps. 51:2, 7)
> "Come now, let us reason together," says the LORD. "Though your sins are like scarlet, they shall be as white as snow; though they are red as crimson, they shall be like wool." (Is. 1:18)

g. Note that everyone who had anything to do with the sacrifice had to cleanse himself and his clothes. This is a symbol that everyone, including priests, stands guilty before God and must be cleansed (vv.7-8).

> As it is written: "There is no one righteous, not even one; there is no one who understands, no one who seeks God. All have turned away, they have together become worthless; there is no one who does good, not even one." (Ro. 3:10-12)
> For all have sinned and fall short of the glory of God. (Ro. 3:23)

h. Note that a clean person was to gather up the ashes of the sacrifice and keep them in a clean place outside the camp (vv.9-10). The ashes were to be kept for future use, for mixing in the water of cleansing. The mixture was to be used in the ritual of purification. This is a symbol of Christ cleansing us from sin (v.9). Note that the man who gathered up the ashes was counted unclean, guilty. He, too, had to wash himself and his clothes (v.10).

i. The offering of the red heifer was established as a permanent law for Israel and for all foreigners among them. By being established as a permanent law, this was a picture of the permanent, eternal sacrifice and cleansing power of Christ (v.10).

> For we know that since Christ was raised from the dead, he cannot die again; death no longer has mastery over him. The death he died, he died to sin once for all; but the life he lives, he lives to God. (Ro. 6:9-10)
> He did not enter by means of the blood of goats and calves; but he entered the Most Holy Place once for all by his own blood, having obtained eternal redemption. The blood of goats and bulls and the ashes of a heifer sprinkled on those who are ceremonially unclean sanctify them so that they are outwardly clean. How much more, then, will the blood of Christ, who through the eternal Spirit offered himself unblemished

NUMBERS 19:1-22

to God, cleanse our consciences from acts that lead to death, so that we may serve the living God! (He. 9:12-14)

> So Christ was sacrificed once to take away the sins of many people; and he will appear a second time, not to bear sin, but to bring salvation to those who are waiting for him. (He. 9:28)

> For Christ died for sins once for all, the righteous for the unrighteous, to bring you to God. He was put to death in the body but made alive by the Spirit. (1 Pe. 3:18)

2 (19:11-16) **Uncleanness, Cause of—Defilement, Caused by—Death, Caused by**: the basic cause of uncleanness or defilement is death. Man is unclean just by being born and living in a corruptible world. Positionally—standing in the world as a human being—man is defiled. This is what is known as *positional defilement*. *Positionally* man sins; *positionally* man dies. Furthermore, man becomes even more defiled as he walks throughout life. Every time man sins, he defiles himself. But the basic cause of defilement is death itself. Death is the ultimate defilement, the ultimate enemy of life. Death takes man down into the grave to waste away and decay. Again, death is the ultimate, final defilement. This was the major focus of the red heifer offering: to cleanse man from all defilement, but in particular from the ultimate defilement of death. All this was pictured in the ritual of the red heifer. Any person who came in contact with death by any means was to be cleansed through the ritual of the red heifer. Keep in mind that this ritual was a symbol of man's need to be cleansed, a symbol of the power of Christ's sacrifice to cleanse him.

a. There was one strict essential in order to be cleansed: the unclean person had to be purified with the cleansing water on the third and seventh days (v.12). He was counted unclean for the full seven days, but he had to be sprinkled with the cleansing water on two different occasions. This was a symbol of the person's being totally defiled and of the power of Christ to completely cleanse him.

b. Note the strong warning: a person who had been in contact with death defiled the LORD's Tabernacle. He defiled the very presence of God Himself. Consequently, he was to be cut off (v.13). He was to be removed from the people, put outside the camp. He was unclean, defiled, and could not approach God nor fellowship with the people of God until he had been cleansed. This is a symbol of eternal judgment, of being cut off and separated from God eternally if a person refuses to be cleansed by Christ.

c. Note the caution against day-to-day uncleanness (vv.14-16). A person was to guard against becoming defiled by death within his home or tent. Sometimes this could not be prevented, for family members did die. However, family members or close friends who came in contact with the dead relative were still counted unclean for seven days. In addition, any container or coffin that was left open was counted as defiled. The people also had to guard against being defiled by death out in the open, outside the home (v.16). If a person touched someone who had been killed by any means or had died a natural death, or if he touched a human bone or grave—he himself would be unclean for seven days.

Death is the ultimate defilement of man, so God gave His people a picture, a strong caution to fight against sin and death. Man is to do all he can to struggle, to conquer, to triumph, to gain the victory over sin and death. This is what God was picturing through these cautions.

Thought 1. There are two strong lessons in this point:

(1) We must understand that people are totally defiled. We are all sinful, short of God's glory, standing in need of cleansing.

> As it is written: "There is no one righteous, not even one; there is no one who understands, no one who seeks God. All have turned away, they have together become worthless; there is no one who does good, not even one. Their throats are open graves; their tongues practice deceit. The poison of vipers is on their lips. Their mouths are full of cursing and bitterness. Their feet are swift to shed blood; ruin and misery mark their ways, and the way of peace they do not know. There is no fear of God before their eyes." (Ro. 3:10-18)

> For all have sinned and fall short of the glory of God. (Ro. 3:23)

> If we claim to be without sin, we deceive ourselves and the truth is not in us. (1 Jn. 1:8)

> The LORD saw how great man's wickedness on the earth had become, and that every inclination of the thoughts of his heart was only evil all the time. (Ge. 6:5)

> For there is no one who does not sin. (1 K. 8:46)

> Who can say, "I have kept my heart pure; I am clean and without sin"? (Pr. 20:9)

> We all, like sheep, have gone astray, each of us has turned to his own way; and the LORD has laid on him the iniquity of us all. (Is. 53:6)

> All of us have become like one who is unclean, and all our righteous acts are like filthy rags; we all shrivel up like a leaf, and like the wind our sins sweep us away. (Is. 64:6)

(2) We must guard against defilement and uncleanness. We must seek cleansing through the Lord Jesus Christ and seek to stay clean and undefiled.

> This is my blood of the covenant, which is poured out for many for the forgiveness of sins. (Mt. 26:28)

> And now what are you waiting for? Get up, be baptized and wash your sins away, calling on his name. (Ac.22:16)

> Since we have these promises, dear friends, let us purify ourselves from everything that contaminates body and spirit, perfecting holiness out of reverence for God. (2 Co. 7:1)

> In him we have redemption through his blood, the forgiveness of sins, in accordance with the riches of God's grace. (Ep. 1:7)

> Come near to God and he will come near to you. Wash your hands, you sinners, and purify your hearts, you double-minded. (Js. 4:8)

> And from Jesus Christ, who is the faithful witness, the firstborn from the dead, and the ruler of the kings of the earth. To

him who loves us and has freed us from our sins by his blood. (Re. 1:5)

Wash and make yourselves clean. Take your evil deeds out of my sight! Stop doing wrong. (Is. 1:16)

O Jerusalem, wash the evil from your heart and be saved. How long will you harbor wicked thoughts? (Je. 4:14)

3 (19:17-19) **Cleansing, How to Secure—Forgiveness, How to Secure**: the way to secure cleansing was spelled out explicitly. These verses explain the actual ritual involving the red heifer, the ritual that a person went through to secure cleansing. Keep this fact in mind: the ritual or symbol was being used just like all rituals or symbols are used by men, to picture some truth. For example, the flag of nations symbolizes loyalty and devotion; the wine and bread symbolize the blood and body of Jesus Christ; the waters of baptism symbolize identification with Christ—all these symbols are pictures of some truth. So it is with the ritual or symbol of the red heifer. The red heifer symbolized the way to secure cleansing from defilement, in particular how to be cleansed from the ultimate defilement, death itself.

a. The unclean person was to mix some ashes from this heifer in a jar of water (v.17).

b. The unclean person was to secure the help of a friend who was clean (ceremonially, spiritually clean). The clean person was to take some hyssop and sprinkle the *cleansing water* upon anyone who had been defiled by coming in contact with death (vv.18-19). Note that all who had been defiled by death, either within or without their homes, were to be cleansed.

c. The clean person was to sprinkle the unclean person on the third and seventh days. Then the unclean person was to wash himself and his clothes on the seventh day (v.19). The number seven was a symbol of full and complete cleansing through the sacrifice of Christ.

> **Thought 1.** The only way to secure cleansing is through the sacrifice and power of Christ. No person can make himself acceptable to God. No person can sacrifice enough to cleanse himself, no matter what he does. Man can picture every sacrifice he knows and come to only one conclusion: there is no perfect sacrifice known to man. There is no perfect sacrifice any place in this world. Consequently, man is confronted with the most serious problem imaginable: his sacrifice can never be acceptable to a perfect God. The reason: man is imperfect and therefore cannot provide a perfect sacrifice to stand in his place before the perfect, holy God. Man's only hope is for God Himself to provide the perfect sacrifice who can stand as man's substitute, making him acceptable to God. This perfect sacrifice is Christ, who died for the sins of man. The only way to secure cleansing from sin is through the sacrifice of Christ. To become acceptable to God, a person must approach God through Christ and Christ alone. It is His sacrifice that atones for the sins of man, that satisfies the justice and judgment of God against sin.
>
> This is my blood of the covenant, which is poured out for many for the forgiveness of sins. (Mt. 26:28)
>
> Who gave himself for our sins to rescue us from the present evil age, according to the will of our God and Father. (Ga. 1:4)
>
> Christ redeemed us from the curse of the law by becoming a curse for us, for it is written: "Cursed is everyone who is hung on a tree." (Ga. 3:13)
>
> In him we have redemption through his blood, the forgiveness of sins, in accordance with the riches of God's grace. (Ep. 1:7)
>
> Who gave himself for us to redeem us from all wickedness and to purify for himself a people that are his very own, eager to do what is good. (Tit. 2:14)
>
> So Christ was sacrificed once to take away the sins of many people; and he will appear a second time, not to bear sin, but to bring salvation to those who are waiting for him. (He. 9:28)
>
> He himself bore our sins in his body on the tree, so that we might die to sins and live for righteousness; by his wounds you have been healed. (1 Pe. 2:24)
>
> For Christ died for sins once for all, the righteous for the unrighteous, to bring you to God. He was put to death in the body but made alive by the Spirit. (1 Pe. 3:18)
>
> But if we walk in the light, as he is in the light, we have fellowship with one another, and the blood of Jesus, his Son, purifies us from all sin. (1 Jn. 1:7)
>
> But you know that he appeared so that he might take away our sins. And in him is no sin. (1 Jn. 3:5)

4 (19:20-22) **Warning, against Rejection—Defilement, Warning against—Uncleanness, Warning against—Rejection, Warning against—Rebellion, Warning against—Sin, Warning against**: the strong warning is re-emphasized, stressed even more forcefully. The failure to be cleansed from defilement causes man to face the most serious consequences.

a. The person who was unclean and refused to be cleansed was to be cut off from the community of believers (v.20). There was a clear reason for this judgment:

⇒ because the person defiled the sanctuary of God's presence. His uncleanness contaminated or polluted the ground and atmosphere of God's presence. This could not be allowed, for God is holy, dwelling in perfect righteousness and purity. The ground of the sanctuary was holy ground, ground that had been set apart for the service and worship of God. No defiled person was ever to be allowed in the presence of the holy and perfect God.

⇒ because the person had not been cleansed by the "cleansing water." The person had deliberately chosen to remain defiled and unclean. Through carelessness, neglect, hardness of heart, or deliberate decision, the defiled person failed to be cleansed.

b. There was no other choice. The defiled and unclean person was to be condemned, cut off from the presence of God and from the community of believers. He was to be put *outside the camp*, not allowed to worship God nor to fellowship with God's people. He was "cut off," ostracized, separated, alienated from God and God's people. Note what else is reemphasized: the law of cleansing was

NUMBERS 19:1-22

to be a permanent law. Remember this was a symbol that every person needed to be cleansed by Christ (v.21).

c. All the people involved in handling the ritual were counted unclean and needed to be cleansed (vv.21-22). This included...
- the person who sprinkled the cleansing water
- the person who touched the water of cleansing
- anyone and anything that became unclean by touching a defiled person (v.22)

Thought 1. The judgment of God is going to fall upon every unclean and defiled person. God is going to execute justice against all defilement and uncleanness. There will be no escape. The holiness of God will not be violated; the presence of God will not be contaminated. God could never allow this to happen. God will not allow pollution in His presence, no injustice or immorality, no defilement or uncleanness whatsoever. The defiled person will be judged if he refuses to be cleansed. This is the warning of God to every person who is unclean or defiled.

> For the Son of Man is going to come in his Father's glory with his angels, and then he will reward each person according to what he has done. (Mt. 16:27)
> For he has set a day when he will judge the world with justice by the man [Christ] he has appointed. He has given proof of this to all men by raising him from the dead. (Ac.17:31)
> Just as man is destined to die once, and after that to face judgment. (He. 9:27)
> If this is so, then the Lord knows how to rescue godly men from trials and to hold the unrighteous for the day of judgment, while continuing their punishment. (2 Pe. 2:9)
> By the same word the present heavens and earth are reserved for fire, being kept for the day of judgment and destruction of ungodly men. (2 Pe. 3:7)
> See, the Lord is coming with thousands upon thousands of his holy ones to judge everyone, and to convict all the ungodly of all the ungodly acts they have done in the ungodly way, and of all the harsh words ungodly sinners have spoken against him." (Jude 1:14-15)
> And I saw the dead, great and small, standing before the throne, and books were opened. Another book was opened, which is the book of life. The dead were judged according to what they had done as recorded in the books. (Re. 20:12)
> They will sing before the LORD, for he comes, he comes to judge the earth. He will judge the world in righteousness and the peoples in his truth. (Ps. 96:13)

TYPES, SYMBOLS, AND PICTURES
(Numbers 19:1-22)

Historical Term	Type or Picture (Scriptural Basis for Each)	Life Application for Today's Believer	Biblical Application
Offering of the Red Heifer (A Red Female Cow) Nu. 19:1-22	*The red heifer symbolized the cleansing power of Jesus Christ, the power of His sacrifice to cleanse from the defilement of sin and death.* *The offering of the red heifer was instituted by God for a good reason: it met a dire need of the people. If a person sinned while the Israelites were marching along, Moses could not stop the march in its tracks, put up the Tabernacle, then go through the ritual of approaching God for forgiveness through the substitute sacrifice. What then was a person to do if he sinned while marching along the way? The answer lay in the offering of the red heifer: they would take a small amount of ashes from the red heifer and mix those ashes with fresh water. Then they would take some hyssop, dip it in the mixed water, and sprinkle the person who had sinned. Keep in mind that this is a picture of the cleansing, purifying*	As the believer walks throughout life—marching to the promised land of God—he becomes contaminated by the pollutions of this world. He must be cleansed from the pollution of sin. Cleansing is through the sacrifice of Jesus Christ. Jesus Christ cleanses us from all sin.	*In him we have redemption through his blood, the forgiveness of sins, in accordance with the riches of God's grace. (Ep. 1:7)* *And that is what some of you were. But you were washed, you were sanctified, you were justified in the name of the Lord Jesus Christ and by the Spirit of our God. (1 Co. 6:11)* *If we confess our sins, he is faithful and just and will forgive us our sins and purify us from all unrighteousness. (1 Jn. 1:9)*

NUMBERS 19:1-22

Historical Term	Type or Picture (Scriptural Basis for Each)	Life Application for Today's Believer	Biblical Application
	power of Christ's sacrifice This is a requirement of the law that the LORD has commanded: Tell the Israelites to bring you a red heifer without defect or blemish and that has never been under a yoke. (Nu. 19:2)		
The Red Heifer Was to Have No Defect or Blemish Nu. 19:1-10, esp. v.2	*The perfect red heifer was a symbol of the perfection of Jesus Christ.* This is a requirement of the law that the LORD has commanded: Tell the Israelites to bring you a red heifer without defect or blemish and that has never been under a yoke. (Nu. 19:2)	Jesus Christ was the sinless, perfect sacrifice offered up to God.	*God made him who had no sin to be sin for us, so that in him we might become the righteousness of God. (2 Co. 5:21)* *In bringing many sons to glory, it was fitting that God, for whom and through whom everything exists, should make the author of their salvation perfect through suffering. (He. 2:10)* *For we do not have a high priest who is unable to sympathize with our weaknesses, but we have one who has been tempted in every way, just as we are—yet was without sin. (He. 4:15)* *And, once made perfect, he became the source of eternal salvation for all who obey him (He. 5:9)* *Such a high priest meets our need—one who is holy, blameless, pure, set apart from sinners, exalted above the heavens. (He. 7:26)* *For the law appoints as high priests men who are weak; but the oath, which came after the law, appointed the Son, who has been made perfect forever. (He. 7:28)*
An Unused Red Heifer Nu. 19:1-10, esp. v.2	*This was a symbol of Christ being free to choose or voluntarily sacrifice Himself for the sins of the human race. The red heifer was to be unused, that is, an animal that had never been worked with a yoke around its neck. it had always been a free animal.* This is a requirement of the law that the LORD has commanded: Tell the Israelites to bring you a red heifer without defect or blemish and that has never been under a yoke. (Nu. 19:2)	Jesus Christ willingly, voluntarily died for us. This He did in obedience to God. He obeyed God perfectly. He ignored and despised the shame of the cross in order to finish the race of perfect obedience to God. And because He was perfectly obedient, He has blazed the path of perfect righteousness, of the very faith that makes us acceptable to God. The Christian race exists because Jesus Christ disciplined Himself; He obeyed God perfectly, even to the extent of dying for us. This He willingly did, and because He did,	*For the Son of Man came to seek and to save what was lost. (Lu. 19:10)* *Here is a trustworthy saying that deserves full acceptance: Christ Jesus came into the world to save sinners—of whom I am the worst. (1 Ti. 1:15)* *Therefore, when Christ came into the world, he said: "Sacrifice and offering you did not desire, but a body you prepared for me; with burnt offerings and sin offerings you were not pleased. Then I said, 'Here I am—it is written about me in the scroll—I have come to do your will,*

NUMBERS 19:1-22

Historical Term	Type or Picture (Scriptural Basis for Each)	Life Application for Today's Believer	Biblical Application
		He is the supreme example for us. We should endure in our belief and obedience to God no matter the cost or price we have to pay, even if it means martyrdom.	*O God.' " First he said, "Sacrifices and offerings, burnt offerings and sin offerings you did not desire, nor were you pleased with them" (although the law required them to be made). Then he said, "Here I am, I have come to do your will." He sets aside the first to establish the second. And by that will, we have been made holy through the sacrifice of the body of Jesus Christ once for all. (He. 10:5-10)* *But you know that he appeared so that he might take away our sins. And in him is no sin. (1 Jn. 3:5)* *For zeal for your house consumes me, and the insults of those who insult you fall on me. (Ps. 69:9)*
The Red Heifer Was to Be Put to Death Outside the Camp Nu. 19:1-10, esp. v.3	*This was a symbol of Christ being put to death outside the city gate.* **Give it to Eleazar the priest; it is to be taken outside the camp and slaughtered in his presence. (Nu. 19:3)**	Under the Old Testament or covenant, the sacrificial animals were burned outside and away from the camp. This shows how perfectly Jesus Christ fulfilled the type and symbol of the Lamb of God. Jesus Christ was crucified outside the city of Jerusalem and away from the temple just as the animals suffered outside the camp. Jesus Christ was the Perfect Sacrifice, fulfilling the sacrificial type perfectly.	*And so Jesus also suffered outside the city gate to make the people holy through his own blood. (He. 13:12)* *For what I received I passed on to you as of first importance: that Christ died for our sins according to the Scriptures. (1 Co. 15:3)* *And he died for all, that those who live should no longer live for themselves but for him who died for them and was raised again. (2 Co. 5:15)* *Who gave himself for our sins to rescue us from the present evil age, according to the will of our God and Father. (Ga. 1:4)* *And live a life of love, just as Christ loved us and gave himself up for us as a fragrant offering and sacrifice to God. (Ep. 5:2)* *Who gave himself for us to redeem us from all wickedness and to purify for himself a people that are his very own, eager to do what is good. (Tit. 2:14)*
Some Blood of the Red Heifer Was to Be Sprinkled Seven Times at the Front of the Tabernacle Nu. 19:1-10, esp. v.4	*The number seven is a symbol of full and complete acceptance. The blood of the red heifer was being accepted by God as full and complete satisfaction for sin. Of course, this was a symbol that Christ's sacrifice was*	God accepts the sacrifice of Christ fully and completely. Our sins are fully and completely forgiven—all through Christ.	*God exalted him to his own right hand as Prince and Savior that he might give repentance and forgiveness of sins to Israel. (Ac. 5:31)*

NUMBERS 19:1-22

Historical Term	Type or Picture (Scriptural Basis for Each)	Life Application for Today's Believer	Biblical Application
	being offered to God as complete satisfaction for sin. **Then Eleazar the priest is to take some of its blood on his finger and sprinkle it seven times toward the front of the Tent of Meeting. (Nu. 19:4)**		*And live a life of love, just as Christ loved us and gave himself up for us as a fragrant [pleasing] offering and sacrifice to God. (Ep. 5:2)* *For God so loved the world that he gave his one and only Son, that whoever believes in him shall not perish but have eternal life. (Jn. 3:16)*
The Red Heifer Was to Be Wholly Burned, All Its Parts Nu. 19:1-10, esp. v.5	*The burning of the entire heifer was a symbol of the extreme sufferings of Christ.* **While he watches, the heifer is to be burned—its hide, flesh, blood and offal. (Nu. 19:5)**	Words could never express what Christ experienced. Words are just totally inadequate. Using all the descriptive words in the world would be insufficient in describing the sufferings of Christ as using a syringe to drain an ocean. 1. There was the *mental and emotional agony*: the weight, pressure, anguish, sorrow, and excessive strain such as no man has ever experienced. 2. There was the *physical experience of death while being the Son of God.* 3. There was *the spiritual experience of death* while being the Son of Man (see note—Mt. 5:17-18; DEEPER STUDY #3—Mt. 8:20; note—Ro. 8:2-4).	*And at the ninth hour Jesus cried out in a loud voice, "Eloi, Eloi, lama sabachthani?"—which means, "My God, my God, why have you forsaken me?" (Mk. 15:34)* *And being in anguish, he prayed more earnestly, and his sweat was like drops of blood falling to the ground. (Lu. 22:44)* *You see, at just the right time, when we were still powerless, Christ died for the ungodly. (Ro. 5:6)* *Although he was a son, he learned obedience from what he suffered and, once made perfect, he became the source of eternal salvation for all who obey him. (He. 5:8-9)* *I offered my back to those who beat me, my cheeks to those who pulled out my beard; I did not hide my face from mocking and spitting. (Is. 50:6)* *But he was pierced for our transgressions, he was crushed for our iniquities; the punishment that brought us peace was upon him, and by his wounds we are healed. (Is. 53:5)*
The Priest Was to Burn Some Cedar Wood, Hyssop and Scarlet Wool with the Red Heifer Nu. 19:1-10, esp. v.6	*This was a picture of using everything [cedar wood, hyssop and scarlet wool] to intensify the purifying power of the offering. Note: All these materials were considered to have some cleansing elements or properties (see Le.14:4).* **The priest is to take some cedar wood, hyssop and scarlet wool and throw them onto the burning heifer. (Nu. 19:6)**	A person is cleansed or made pure by the blood of Jesus Christ. The cleansing, purifying power to forgive sins is found in Him and Him alone.	*In him we have redemption through his blood, the forgiveness of sins, in accordance with the riches of God's grace. (Ep. 1:7)* *Wash away all my iniquity and cleanse me from my sin....Cleanse me with hyssop, and I will be clean; wash me, and I will be whiter than snow. (Ps. 51:2, 7)* *"Come now, let us reason together," says the LORD. "Though your sins are like scarlet, they shall be as white as snow; though they are red as crimson, they shall be like wool." (Is. 1:18)*

NUMBERS 19:1-22

Historical Term	Type or Picture (Scriptural Basis for Each)	Life Application for Today's Believer	Biblical Application
Everyone Who Had Anything to Do with the Sacrifice Had to Cleanse Himself and His Clothes Nu. 19:1-10, esp. vv.7-8	*This is a symbol that everyone, including priests, stands guilty before God and must be cleansed.* **After that, the priest must wash his clothes and bathe himself with water. He may then come into the camp, but he will be ceremonially unclean till evening. The man who burns it must also wash his clothes and bathe with water, and he too will be unclean till evening. (Nu. 19:7-8)**	The only way to secure cleansing is through the sacrifice and power of Christ. No person can make himself acceptable to God. No person can sacrifice enough to cleanse himself, no matter what he does. Man can picture every sacrifice he knows and come to only one conclusion: there is no perfect sacrifice known to man. There is no perfect sacrifice anyplace in this world. Consequently, man is confronted with the most serious problem imaginable: his sacrifice can never be acceptable to a perfect God. The reason: man is imperfect and therefore cannot provide a perfect sacrifice to stand in his place before the perfect, holy God. Man's only hope is for God Himself to provide the perfect sacrifice, a perfect sacrifice that can stand as man's substitute, making him acceptable to God. This perfect sacrifice is Christ, who died for the sins of man.	*As it is written: "There is no one righteous, not even one; there is no one who understands, no one who seeks God. All have turned away, they have together become worthless; there is no one who does good, not even one." (Ro. 3:10-12)* *For all have sinned and fall short of the glory of God. (Ro. 3:23)* *This is my blood of the covenant, which is poured out for many for the forgiveness of sins. (Mt. 26:28)* *Who gave himself for our sins to rescue us from the present evil age, according to the will of our God and Father. (Ga. 1:4)* *Christ redeemed us from the curse of the law by becoming a curse for us, for it is written: "Cursed is everyone who is hung on a tree." (Ga. 3:13)* *In him we have redemption through his blood, the forgiveness of sins, in accordance with the riches of God's grace. (Ep. 1:7)*
A Clean Person Was to Gather Up the Ashes of the Sacrifice and Keep Them in a Clean Place Outside the Camp Nu. 19:1-10, esp. vv.9-10	*This is a symbol of Christ cleansing us from sin (v.9). The ashes were to be kept for future use, for mixing in the water of cleansing. Note that the man who gathered up the ashes was counted unclean, guilty. He, too, had to wash himself and his clothes (v.10).* **A man who is clean shall gather up the ashes of the heifer and put them in a ceremonially clean place outside the camp. They shall be kept by the Israelite community for use in the water of cleans-ing; it is for purification from sin. (Nu. 19:9)**	The only way to secure cleansing from sin is through the sacrifice of Christ. To become acceptable to God a person must approach God through Christ and Christ alone. It is His sacrifice that atones for the sins of man, that satisfies the justice and judgment of God against sin.	*So Christ was sacrificed once to take away the sins of many people; and he will appear a second time, not to bear sin, but to bring salvation to those who are waiting for him. (He. 9:28)* *Who gave himself for us to redeem us from all wickedness and to purify for himself a people that are his very own, eager to do what is good. (Tit. 2:14)* *He himself bore our sins in his body on the tree, so that we might die to sins and live for righteousness; by his wounds you have been healed. (1 Pe. 2:24)* *For Christ died for sins once for all, the righteous for the unrighteous, to bring you to God. He was put to death in the body but made alive by the Spirit. (1 Pe. 3:18)*
The Offering of the Red Heifer Was Established As a Permanent Law for Israel and for All Foreigners Among Them Nu. 19:1-10, esp. v.10	*By being established as a permanent law, this was a picture of the permanent, eternal sacrifice and cleansing power of Christ (v.10).*	Christ was once offered to bear the sins and judgment of many. Christ has taken our sins upon Himself. He has sacrificed Himself for our sins and borne our judgment for us. We no longer have to bear the	*For we know that since Christ was raised from the dead, he cannot die again; death no longer has mastery over him. The death he died, he died to sin once for all; but the life he lives, he lives to God. (Ro. 6:9-10)*

NUMBERS 19:1-22

Historical Term	Type or Picture (Scriptural Basis for Each)	Life Application for Today's Believer	Biblical Application
	The man who gathers up the ashes of the heifer must also wash his clothes, and he too will be unclean till evening. This will be a lasting ordinance both for the Israelites and for the aliens living among them. (Nu. 19:10)	judgment for our sins and imperfections. If we believe—truly trust Jesus Christ to bear our sins and judgment—then God counts our sins as having been borne by Christ. God counts us as being free from sin—as being perfect and acceptable to Him. Therefore, we never have to be judged and condemned for sin. But note: this glorious salvation is not brought about in the lives of all people. A person has to believe and trust in the sacrifice of Jesus Christ. This is only reasonable: if a person does not believe in something, he does not allow it to work *for* him. But if he does believe, he does allow it to work *for* him. When we believe—really believe—then the sacrifice of Jesus Christ works *for* us. His sacrifice covers our sins and we become acceptable to God. We never have to face the judgment and condemnation for our sins.	*He did not enter by means of the blood of goats and calves; but he entered the Most Holy Place once for all by his own blood, having obtained eternal redemption. The blood of goats and bulls and the ashes of a heifer sprinkled on those who are ceremonially unclean sanctify them so that they are outwardly clean. How much more, then, will the blood of Christ, who through the eternal Spirit offered himself unblemished to God, cleanse our consciences from acts that lead to death, so that we may serve the living God! (He. 9:12-14)* *So Christ was sacrificed once to take away the sins of many people; and he will appear a second time, not to bear sin, but to bring salvation to those who are waiting for him. (He. 9:28)* *For Christ died for sins once for all, the righteous for the unrighteous, to bring you to God. He was put to death in the body but made alive by the Spirit. (1 Pe. 3:18)*
Death Nu. 19:11-16	*Death is a type or symbol of uncleanness.* *Man is unclean just by being born and living in a corruptible world. Positionally—standing in the world as a human being—man is defiled. This is what is known as positional defilement. Positionally man sins; positionally man dies. Furthermore, man becomes even more defiled as he walks throughout life. Every time man sins, he defiles himself. But the basic cause of defilement is death itself. Death is the ultimate defilement, the ultimate enemy of life. Death takes man down into the grave to waste away and decay. Again, death is the ultimate, final defilement. This was the major focus of the red heifer offering: to cleanse man from all defilement, but in particular from the ultimate defilement of death.*	There are two strong lessons in this point: 1. We must understand that people are totally defiled. We are all sinful, short of God's glory, standing in need of cleansing. 2. We must guard against defilement and uncleanness. We must seek to stay clean and undefiled, seeking cleansing through the Lord Jesus Christ.	*This is my blood of the covenant, which is poured out for many for the forgiveness of sins. (Mt. 26:28)* *As it is written: "There is no one righteous, not even one; there is no one who understands, no one who seeks God. All have turned away, they have together become worthless; there is no one who does good, not even one. Their throats are open graves; their tongues practice deceit. The poison of vipers is on their lips. Their mouths are full of cursing and bitterness. Their feet are swift to shed blood; ruin and misery mark their ways, and the way of peace they do not know. There is no fear of God before their eyes." (Ro. 3:10-18)* *For all have sinned and fall short of the glory of God. (Ro. 3:23)* *In him we have redemption through his blood, the forgiveness of*

NUMBERS 19:1-22

Historical Term	Type or Picture (Scriptural Basis for Each)	Life Application for Today's Believer	Biblical Application
	Whoever touches the dead body of anyone and fails to purify himself defiles the LORD's tabernacle. That person must be cut off from Israel. Because the water of cleans-ing has not been sprinkled on him, he is unclean; his uncleanness remains on him. (Nu. 19:13)		*sins, in accordance with the riches of God's grace. (Ep. 1:7)* *If we claim to be without sin, we deceive ourselves and the truth is not in us. (1 Jn. 1:8)* *And from Jesus Christ, who is the faithful witness, the firstborn from the dead, and the ruler of the kings of the earth. To him who loves us and has freed us from our sins by his blood. (Re. 1:5)*
The Unclean Person Had to Be Purified With the Cleansing Water *On the Third and Seventh Days* Nu. 19:11-16, esp. v.12	*This was a picture of the person being totally defiled and of the power of Christ to completely cleanse him. The unclean person was counted unclean for the full seven days, but he had to be sprinkled with the cleansing water on two different occasions.* He must purify himself with the water on the third day and on the seventh day; then he will be clean. But if he does not purify himself on the third and seventh days, he will not be clean. (Nu. 19:12)	There are two strong lessons in this point: 1. We must understand that people are totally defiled. We are all sinful, short of God's glory, standing in need of cleansing (Ro. 3:23). 2. We must guard against defilement and uncleanness. We must seek cleansing through the Lord Jesus Christ and seek to stay clean and undefiled.	*As it is written: "There is no one righteous, not even one; there is no one who understands, no one who seeks God. All have turned away, they have together become worthless; there is no one who does good, not even one. Their throats are open graves; their tongues practice deceit. The poison of vipers is on their lips. Their mouths are full of cursing and bitterness. Their feet are swift to shed blood; ruin and misery mark their ways, and the way of peace they do not know. There is no fear of God before their eyes." (Ro. 3:10-18)* *For all have sinned and fall short of the glory of God. (Ro. 3:23)* *In him we have redemption through his blood, the forgiveness of sins, in accordance with the riches of God's grace. (Ep. 1:7)* *And from Jesus Christ, who is the faithful witness, the firstborn from the dead, and the ruler of the kings of the earth. To him who loves us and has freed us from our sins by his blood. (Re. 1:5)*
A Person Who Had Been In Contact With Death Defiled the Lord's Tabernacle: He Was to Be Cut Off Nu. 19:11-16, esp. v.13	*This is a picture of eternal judgment, of being cut off and separated from God eternally if a person refuses to be cleansed by Christ. He was to be removed from the people, put outside the camp. He was unclean, defiled, and could not approach God nor fellowship with the people of God until he had been cleansed.*	It is critical to note the words of Christ: "These shall go away into everlasting punishment" (Mt. 25:46). The judgment is for eternity. There is no second chance; judgment is unchangeable.	*Then the king told the attendants, 'Tie him hand and foot, and throw him outside, into the darkness, where there will be weeping and gnashing of teeth.' (Mt. 22:13; see Mt. 25:30)* *And throw that worthless servant outside, into the darkness, where there will be weeping and gnashing of teeth. (Mt. 25:30)* *Then he will say to those on his left, 'Depart from*

NUMBERS 19:1-22

Historical Term	Type or Picture (Scriptural Basis for Each)	Life Application for Today's Believer	Biblical Application
	Whoever touches the dead body of anyone and fails to purify himself defiles the LORD's tabernacle. That person must be cut off from Israel. Because the water of cleansing has not been sprinkled on him, he is unclean; his uncleanness remains on him. (Nu. 19:13)		*me, you who are cursed, into the eternal fire prepared for the devil and his angels.' (Mt. 25:41)* *And the devil, who deceived them, was thrown into the lake of burning sulfur, where the beast and the false prophet had been thrown. They will be tormented day and night for ever and ever. Then I saw a great white throne and him who was seated on it. Earth and sky fled from his presence, and there was no place for them. And I saw the dead, great and small, standing before the throne, and books were opened. Another book was opened, which is the book of life. The dead were judged according to what they had done as recorded in the books. The sea gave up the dead that were in it, and death and Hades gave up the dead that were in them, and each person was judged according to what he had done. Then death and Hades were thrown into the lake of fire. The lake of fire is the second death. If anyone's name was not found written in the book of life, he was thrown into the lake of fire. (Re. 20:10-15; see Mt. 25:44)*

NUMBERS 20:1-29

F. Event 6—the Last Year of Israel in the Wilderness: Five Sad Events, 20:1-29

1. **The sad death of Miriam**
   a. In the first month (early spring)
   b. In the Desert of Zin, at Kadesh

2. **The sad, continued grumbling of the people over having no food & no water**
   a. The confrontation: Gathered to oppose Moses & Aaron
      1) Blamed God: Shouted they would have preferred to die with their brothers under God's judgment than suffer in the wilderness
      2) Rioted & blamed Moses
         • For bringing them into this wilderness where they & their livestock were facing death from no water
         • For leading them out of Egypt, away from the land of plenty—taking them to this terrible place with no affluence & no water
   b. The response of Moses & Aaron
      1) They went to the Tabernacle & fell face down
      2) The glory of the LORD appeared to them

3. **The sad, tragic failure & sin of Moses**
   a. The clear instructions of the LORD
      1) To take the staff & gather the people together
      2) To speak to the rock that God identified as being the source of water
      3) The result: Water would flow
   b. The response of Moses
      1) Obeyed God: Took the staff & gathered the people together in front of the rock
      2) Disobeyed God:
         • By speaking to the people & not the rock
         • By not giving God the full credit & honor: "Must we bring you water?"
         • By striking the rock (twice) instead of speaking to it as commanded: He failed to trust God's Word
   c. The response of the LORD
      1) He gave water from the rock
      2) He charged Moses & Aaron
         • With failing to trust Him

CHAPTER 20

In the first month the whole Israelite community arrived at the Desert of Zin, and they stayed at Kadesh. There Miriam died and was buried.
2 Now there was no water for the community, and the people gathered in opposition to Moses and Aaron.
3 They quarreled with Moses and said, "If only we had died when our brothers fell dead before the LORD!
4 Why did you bring the LORD's community into this desert, that we and our livestock should die here?
5 Why did you bring us up out of Egypt to this terrible place? It has no grain or figs, grapevines or pomegranates. And there is no water to drink!"
6 Moses and Aaron went from the assembly to the entrance to the Tent of Meeting and fell facedown, and the glory of the LORD appeared to them.
7 The LORD said to Moses,
8 "Take the staff, and you and your brother Aaron gather the assembly together. Speak to that rock before their eyes and it will pour out its water. You will bring water out of the rock for the community so they and their livestock can drink."
9 So Moses took the staff from the LORD's presence, just as he commanded him.
10 He and Aaron gathered the assembly together in front of the rock and Moses said to them, "Listen, you rebels, must we bring you water out of this rock?"
11 Then Moses raised his arm and struck the rock twice with his staff. Water gushed out, and the community and their livestock drank.
12 But the LORD said to Moses and Aaron, "Because you did not trust in me enough to honor me as holy in the sight of the Israelites, you will not bring this community into the land I give them."
13 These were the waters of Meribah, where the Israelites quarreled with the LORD and where he showed himself holy among them.
14 Moses sent messengers from Kadesh to the king of Edom, saying: "This is what your brother Israel says: You know about all the hardships that have come upon us.
15 Our forefathers went down into Egypt, and we lived there many years. The Egyptians mistreated us and our fathers,
16 But when we cried out to the LORD, he heard our cry and sent an angel and brought us out of Egypt. "Now we are here at Kadesh, a town on the edge of your territory.
17 Please let us pass through your country. We will not go through any field or vineyard, or drink water from any well. We will travel along the king's highway and not turn to the right or to the left until we have passed through your territory."
18 But Edom answered: "You may not pass through here; if you try, we will march out and attack you with the sword."
19 The Israelites replied: "We will go along the main road, and if we or our livestock drink any of your water, we will pay for it. We only want to pass through on foot—nothing else."
20 Again they answered: "You may not pass through." Then Edom came out against them with a large and powerful army.
21 Since Edom refused to let them go through their territory, Israel turned away from them.
22 The whole Israelite community set out from Kadesh and came to Mount Hor.
23 At Mount Hor, near the border of Edom, the LORD said to Moses and Aaron,
24 "Aaron will be gathered to his people. He will not enter the land I give the Israelites, because both of

• With not honoring Him as holy before the people
      3) He chastised Moses: Would not be allowed to enter the promised land
   d. The naming of the place: Meribah, meaning a place of strife, arguing, or grumbling

4. **The sad, arrogant resistance of Edom**
   a. The appeal to the king of Edom for safe passage through his land
      1) Addressed Edom as Israel's brother (through Esau)
      2) Mentioned the predicament & hardships that Israel had suffered under Egyptian slavery
      3) Acknowledged that the LORD had delivered Israel
      4) Stated their present location

      5) Requested permission to pass through his country
      6) Promised & gave assurance
         • That they would not damage any of the land nor forage any of the crops
         • That they would travel only along the king's highway, that they would not veer off any whatsoever
   b. The answer or response of the king: Rejection—a hostile, blunt refusal & a rash threat of war

   c. The counter-request & assurances
      1) Would travel only the main road
      2) Would pay for any water used
      3) Had no hidden motive: No plan to conquer Edom
   d. The absolute rejection of Edom & the abrupt show of force

   e. The backing off of Israel & the march to Mount Hor

5. **The sad, touching death of Aaron**
   a. The LORD Himself revealed Aaron's impending death
      1) He was to be "gathered to his people": A picture of joining former believers

NUMBERS 20:1-29

in the presence of God
   2) He would not enter the promised land: Because he & Moses had disobeyed God
   3) He & his son Eleazar & Moses were to climb Mt. Hor
   4) Moses was to transfer the power of the High Priest from Aaron to Eleazar: Symbolized by putting Aaron's garments on Eleazar
  b. The obedience of Moses
   1) He led the two priests up Mt. Hor
	you rebelled against my command at the waters of Meribah.
	25 Get Aaron and his son Eleazar and take them up Mount Hor.
	26 Remove Aaron's garments and put them on his son Eleazar, for Aaron will be gathered to his people; he will die there."
	27 Moses did as the LORD commanded: They went up Mount Hor in
		the sight of the whole community.
		28 Moses removed Aaron's garments and put them on his son Eleazar. And Aaron died there on top of the mountain. Then Moses and Eleazar came down from the mountain,
		29 And when the whole community learned that Aaron had died, the entire house of Israel mourned for him thirty days.
			2) He transferred the power of the High Priest from Aaron to Eleazar
			  c. The death of Aaron on top of Mt. Hor: Obviously buried by Moses & Eleazar
			
			  d. The mourning of Israel for Aaron: Thirty days

DIVISION III

THE FORTY LONG YEARS OF WILDERNESS WANDERINGS: A PICTURE OF THE BELIEVER'S PILGRIMAGE THROUGH THIS WORLD AS HE PREPARES TO ENTER THE PROMISED LAND, 15:1–25:18

F. Event 6—the Last Year of Israel in the Wilderness: Five Sad Events, 20:1-29

(20:1-29) **Introduction—Unhappiness, Caused by—Sadness, Caused by**: unhappy, sad events are a common occurrence. The daily news media are filled with such reports. If the truth were known, many people are so depressed, downcast, and heartsick that the pain is almost unbearable. They are hurting due to the grief of some sad, unhappy experience—an experience so intense—they can hardly go on. The unfortunate experience may be caused...

- by the death of a loved one
- by unfaithfulness or adultery
- by being abandoned or forsaken
- by the news of some serious disease
- by suffering a critical accident
- by losing one's job
- by having one's money stolen or lost
- by going bankrupt
- by losing one's closest and dearest friend
- by sensing no purpose, significance, or meaning in life
- by suffering some deep depression or discouragement
- by not securing an expected promotion or raise
- by suffering some catastrophic holocaust

It is impossible to walk through life without suffering sad, unhappy experiences. We all suffer the most sad experiences known to man: severe diseases and sicknesses and then eventually death. None of these are escaped by any of us. But there is glorious news: in the midst of the deepest moments of sadness and unhappiness, God promises deliverance. There is victory and triumph over all the enemies that attempt to sap the life out of us. This is the thrust of this particular chapter of Holy Scripture. Five sad, unhappy events take place in the life of Israel. And note: all five unhappy events take place within the span of one year. This is Israel's fortieth year in the wilderness. During the last year, five of the saddest experiences that could happen to a nation of people took place in the life of the Israelites. This is the subject of this present Scripture. *Event 6—the Last Year of Israel in the Wilderness: Five Sad Events*, 20:1-29.

1. The sad death of Miriam (v.1).
2. The sad, continued grumbling of the people over having no food and no water (vv.2-6).
3. The sad, tragic failure and sin of Moses (vv.7-13).
4. The sad, arrogant resistance of Edom (vv.14-22).
5. The sad, touching death of Aaron (vv.23-29).

1 (20:1) **Death, of Miriam—Miriam, Death of**: there was the sad death of Miriam. Remember, Miriam was the sister of Moses and Aaron. She was the leader among the women of the nation. Three facts show us this:

⇒ First, Miriam was the person who led all the women in singing praise to God after their great deliverance from Egyptian slavery.

> Then Miriam the prophetess, Aaron's sister, took a tambourine in her hand, and all the women followed her, with tambourines and dancing. Miriam sang to them: "Sing to the Lord, for he is highly exalted. The horse and its rider he has hurled into the sea." (Ex. 15:20-21)

⇒ The LORD Himself identifies Miriam as being a leader right alongside Moses and Aaron.

> I brought you up out of Egypt and redeemed you from the land of slavery. I sent Moses to lead you, also Aaron and Miriam. (Mi. 6:4)

⇒ Miriam took the lead in challenging the leadership and authority of Moses, attempting to secure some of the authority for herself and her older brother Aaron.

> Miriam and Aaron began to talk against Moses because of his Cushite wife, for he had married a Cushite. "Has the LORD spoken only through Moses?" they asked. "Hasn't he also spoken through us?" And the LORD heard this. (Nu. 12:1-2)

It was this rebellion against God and His appointed minister that kept Miriam from ever entering the promised land. This is the reason she was now dying

Numbers 20:1-29

out in the wilderness or desert. She died in the wilderness and was buried in the wilderness, not in the promised land of God. Note when she died: in the first month, which was early spring out in the desert of Zin, at Kadesh. The year is not given in this verse, but we know from other passages that it was in the fortieth year after the Exodus (see Nu. 20:22-29 with Nu. 33:38). Remember that the wilderness wanderings or desert journeys lasted for forty years. This means that most of the first generation of Israelites had already died off, as dictated by God's judgment (see outline and note—Nu. 14:26-39 for more discussion). The new generation was on the verge of being ready to enter the promised land. But not Miriam. Because of her rebellion against God and His dear servant, she died and was buried in the sands of the desert wilderness. She was not allowed to enter the promised land.

Thought 1. The enemies of life conquered Miriam, instead of her conquering them. She gave in to the enemy of grumbling and unbelief to the point of actually rebelling against God's dear servant. Because of unbelief and rebellion, she never entered the spiritual rest and conquest of the promised land. She never received the inheritance of God's rest and victory over the enemies of life. She never received an inheritance in the promised land.

Grumbling, unbelief, and rebellion will keep any of us out of the promised land. Only God can give us victory over the enemies of life, for only He has the power to conquer and triumph. If we allow the enemy of unbelief and rebellion to take hold of our hearts, then we will be as Miriam: dying out in the wilderness and desert of this world. We will be doomed, never allowed to enter the promised land of spiritual rest and victory.

> See to it, brothers, that none of you has a sinful, unbelieving heart that turns away from the living God. But encourage one another daily, as long as it is called Today, so that none of you may be hardened by sin's deceitfulness. (He. 3:12-13)
>
> Therefore, since the promise of entering his rest still stands, let us be careful that none of you be found to have fallen short of it. For we also have had the gospel preached to us, just as they did; but the message they heard was of no value to them, because those who heard did not combine it with faith. Now we who have believed enter that rest, just as God has said, "So I declared on oath in my anger, 'They shall never enter my rest.'" (He. 4:1-3)
>
> Let us, therefore, make every effort to enter that rest, so that no one will fall by following their example of disobedience. (He. 4:11)
>
> Though you already know all this, I want to remind you that the Lord delivered his people out of Egypt, but later destroyed those who did not believe. (Jude 5)
>
> Be at rest once more, O my soul, for the LORD has been good to you. (Ps. 116:7)
>
> To whom he said, "This is the resting place, let the weary rest"; and, "This is the place of repose"—but they would not listen. (Is. 28:12)
>
> This is what the Sovereign LORD, the Holy One of Israel, says: "In repentance and rest is your salvation, in quietness and trust is your strength, but you would have none of it." (Is. 30:15)

2 (20:2-6) **Complaining—Grumbling—Opposition, Against God's Servant—Unbelief—Israel, Sins of, Complaining and Grumbling—Water, Grumbling Over**: there was the sad, continued grumbling of the people over no food and no water. This was a clear picture of how children follow in the footsteps of their parents. On several occasions the parents had grumbled over inadequate food and water supplies (see outline and notes Ex. 15:22-27; Ex. 16:1-36; Ex. 17:1-7; Nu. 11:1-35; Nu. 21:4-9). They had demonstrated little faith in God and His gracious provision. Their unbelief cut the heart of God, causing great pain for Him, for He loved them dearly. They allowed a seed of unbelief, stubbornness, resistance, and hardness of heart to take root against God. It was this unbelief that kept the first generation—the parents—out of the promised land. It was this unbelief that doomed them to die out in the desert wilderness. Now the same threat of unbelief was seen in the children. They were walking in the footsteps of their parents, failing to trust the promise of God—that He would provide the necessities of life as they marched to the promised land.

a. Note the confrontation: the people gathered in opposition to Moses and Aaron, arguing against Moses (vv.2-5). The younger generation of believers blamed God for not having adequate water and food supplies. They shouted out against God, they would have preferred to die with their brothers under God's judgment than to suffer in the wilderness (v.3). But they were not only accusing God of failing them; they also attacked Moses. They blamed Moses for bringing them into the wilderness where they and their livestock were facing death from lack of water. They blamed him for taking them out of Egypt, the land of plenty, where they had all the delicious luxuries they ever wanted. They blamed Moses for taking them out of the wonderful land of Egypt to this terrible place with no luxuries and no water (vv.4-5).

b. Note the response of Moses and Aaron (v.6): they went to the Tabernacle and fell face down before the LORD. As always, the LORD met their need. The glory of the LORD appeared to them.

Thought 1. Grumbling against God and against His dear servant is a terrible sin. Grumbling reveals a heart of unbelief, a distrust of God. Grumbling stands up in the face of God and declares: "I do not like what is happening to me in life. Not enough good things are happening. I am not getting enough good breaks nor enough of the good things in life. God's provision to me is too meager, His supplies too few. I do not have enough money, food, clothing, housing, property, recognition, esteem, honor, or position."

Not trusting God and His provision and care for us arouses grumbling and unbelief. It was grumbling and unbelief that kept God's people from entering the promised land. A believer never learns to walk victoriously through life as long as he grumbles and fails to trust God. He never conquers the pitfalls and enemies of this life. He never learns to rest and trust in the provision of God. He never has fellowship and communion with God, never knows God personally and intimately, never knows what it is to be carried along and sustained by God day by day. Unbelief and grumbling keep a person out of the promised land.

> "Stop grumbling among yourselves," Jesus answered. (Jn. 6:43)
> And do not grumble, as some of them did—and were killed by the destroying angel. (1 Co. 10:10)
> Do everything without complaining or arguing. (Ph. 2:14)
> See to it, brothers, that none of you has a sinful, unbelieving heart that turns away from the living God. (He. 3:12)
> Let us, therefore, make every effort to enter that rest, so that no one will fall by following their example of disobedience. (He. 4:11)
> Though you already know all this, I want to remind you that the Lord delivered his people out of Egypt, but later destroyed those who did not believe. (Jude 5)
> A man's own folly ruins his life, yet his heart rages against the LORD. (Pr. 19:3)

3 (20:7-13) **Moses, Sin of—Believers, Failure of—Sin, Example of, Moses**: there was the sad, tragic failure and sin of Moses. What happened next breaks the heart of the reader who has truly followed the life of Moses through Exodus, Leviticus, and now Numbers. This dear servant of God finally exploded. In utter frustration and anger, he struck out against the people. For the first time in his ministry, he committed a terrible, serious offense against God. He disobeyed God, failing to trust Him. He did not honor God before the people, did not give God the full credit and honor for meeting their needs. For this failure, the heart of this dear servant was crushed. He had failed to follow the LORD who had loved and cared for him through all the years, looking after his every need. Consequently, he lost that which he most wanted and for which he had so long sought: the promised land. He lost the privilege of entering the promised land, of leading the people to victory over the enemies of life. He lost the privilege of experiencing the spiritual rest and conquest of the promised land, the spiritual rest that the promised land brings to the human soul. A crushing blow to the soul of one of the dearest servants of God who has ever lived! He would live with God eternally, but he had lost one of the privileges of ministry, the privilege of leading the people in their conquest of the promised land. He had lost the privilege of leading the people to victory over the enemies of life.

a. The instructions of the LORD were clear, perfectly clear: Moses was to take his staff and gather the people together. He was then to speak to the rock that God identified as being the source of water, the source of living water—the water that would keep them alive. Note how this is a clear symbol of Jesus Christ, the source of living water. The Scripture also declares that Jesus Christ was that rock (Jn. 7:38; 1 Co. 10:4). God made a phenomenal promise to Moses, a glorious event would happen: water would miraculously flow from the rock (v.8)

b. The response of Moses began in obedience: he took the staff from the LORD's presence in the Tabernacle and gathered the people just as God had commanded (vv.9-10). But then the tragedy happened; he exploded and burst out against the people. He committed three gross errors of disobedience:

⇒ He spoke to the people and not to the rock (v.10). Remember that God had given clear instructions: Moses was to address the rock.
⇒ He did not give God the full credit and honor (v.10). He charged the people with being rebels and asked them, "Must 'we bring' you water out of this rock?" Note that he puts himself on a level with God, suggesting that it was he and God who were going to provide water for them. Standing there before the people, he failed to honor God as the only one who can meet man's need, in particular man's need for *living water*. Moses exalted himself, accepting some of the credit for the miracle that was about to happen.
⇒ He struck the rock (in anger) instead of merely speaking to it as commanded by God. And note: he struck the rock not once but twice. His anger and frustration had taken complete control of his spirit. This dear servant of God had lost control of his behavior (v.11).

c. The response of the LORD was immediate. Moreover, in light of God's love and justice, His response was to be expected (vv.11-12). In love God caused water to gush out of the rock. But in justice and chastisement, God made two charges against Moses and Aaron:

⇒ That they had not trusted God, had not obeyed Him as He commanded. Instead of speaking to the rock, Moses had spoken to the people and had reacted in utter frustration and anger.
⇒ That they had not honored God as holy before the people, as the only person who was to be revered as the provision to meet man's needs.

God had no choice: His dear servant had to be chastised. Moses would not be allowed to enter the promised land (v.12). His rash behavior barred him from the glorious privilege of leading the people to victory and rest in the promised land of God.

d. Note that the place was given a name so that it would never be forgotten: Meribah, which means a place of strife, arguing, or grumbling (v.13).

Thought 1. There are two important lessons in this point.
(1) God will not share His glory with any person.

> "Hallowed be your name....Give us today our daily bread." (Mt. 6:9, 11)
> Ascribe to the LORD the glory due his name; worship the LORD in the splendor of his holiness. (Ps. 29:2)
> Glorify the LORD with me; let us exalt his name together. (Ps. 34:3)
> Let them exalt him in the assembly of the people and praise him in the council of the elders. (Ps. 107:32)
> O LORD, you are my God; I will exalt you and praise your name, for in perfect faithfulness you have done marvelous things, things planned long ago. (Is. 25:1)
> "I am the LORD; that is my name! I will not give my glory to another or my praise to idols." (Is. 42:8)

(2) God chastises the disobedient believer and servant of God. God never allows His dear people to continue in sin without correcting them. To do so would lead to disastrous results:

NUMBERS 20:1-29

⇒ the growth of more and more sin
⇒ the misleading of others
⇒ the putting of stumbling blocks in the way of others
⇒ the damaging of our bodies through such things as overeating, drugs, accidents, and reckless living
⇒ the destruction of marriages and homes
⇒ the acts of lawlessness such as stealing and cheating
⇒ the more serious acts such as abuse and violence

On and on the list could go, but the point is well made: if a child of God is allowed to continue in sin without being corrected by God, then sin abounds. Sin grows and grows until it overflows, damaging people well beyond anything ever thought. God chastises the disobedient believer because God loves him. God wants to prevent him from harming himself and others.

> He cuts off every branch in me that bears no fruit, while every branch that does bear fruit he prunes so that it will be even more fruitful. (Jn. 15:2)
> And you have forgotten that word of encouragement that addresses you as sons: "My son, do not make light of the Lord's discipline, and do not lose heart when he rebukes you, because the Lord disciplines those he loves, and he punishes everyone he accepts as a son." (He. 12:5-6)
> No discipline seems pleasant at the time, but painful. Later on, however, it produces a harvest of righteousness and peace for those who have been trained by it. Therefore, strengthen your feeble arms and weak knees. "Make level paths for your feet," so that the lame may not be disabled, but rather healed. Make every effort to live in peace with all men and to be holy; without holiness no one will see the Lord. See to it that no one misses the grace of God and that no bitter root grows up to cause trouble and defile many. (He. 12:11-15)
> Know then in your heart that as a man disciplines his son, so the LORD your God disciplines you. (De. 8:5)
> Blessed is the man you discipline, O LORD, the man you teach from your law. (Ps. 94:12)
> My son, do not despise the LORD's discipline and do not resent his rebuke, because the LORD disciplines those he loves, as a father the son he delights in. (Pr. 3:11-12)

4 (20:14-22) **Arrogance, Against God's People—Resistance, Against God's People—Edom**: there was the sad, arrogant resistance of Edom against God's people. The events that bring sadness and grief to the human heart continue through this Scripture. God's people were marching to the promised land. As they marched, they approached the border of one of the nations that surrounded the land of Canaan. That nation was the land of Edom. If Edom granted permission to pass through its land, the march to the promised land would be much shorter. Receiving the inheritance of the promised land—that for which the Israelites had hoped so long—would be fulfilled much quicker. God's people could enter the promised land much sooner if Edom would just grant the right of *safe passage* through their land. To secure this permission, Moses sent a diplomatic letter to the king of Edom.

a. Note the appeal to the king of Edom for *safe passage* through his land (vv.14-17). Moses referred to Edom as Israel's brother. This was because Edom was a descendant of Esau, a brother of Jacob (Ge. 27:30; 32:28; 36:1). Moses then mentioned the predicament and hardships that Israel had suffered under Egyptian slavery, acknowledging that the LORD Himself had been the One who delivered Israel (vv.15-16). Note that Moses then gave the present location where the Israelites were camped (v.16). Finally Moses came to the heart of the matter: he requested permission to pass safely through the country of Edom (v.17). Moses did a wise thing: he promised and gave assurance...

- that Israel would not damage any of the land nor forage any of the crops
- that Israel would travel only along the king's highway, that they would not veer off the main highway any whatsoever (v.17)

b. The answer or response of the king was rejection: a hostile, blunt refusal and a rash threat of war (v.18).

c. However, Moses made the counter-request and did all he could to reassure Edom: Israel would travel only along the main road, and they would pay for any water used. He assured the king that the Israelites had no hidden motive, no plan to conquer Edom (v.19).

d. Note the absolute rejection of Edom and the abrupt show of force. The king mobilized his army and actually marched out against Israel. Scripture says that the army was large and powerful, a dangerous threat to God's people.

e. Israel immediately backed off and marched in order to escape the threat of Edom. God's people marched to Mount Hor (vv.21-22).

Thought 1. God protects His people. We may have to go through trials and sufferings, threats and dangers throughout life, but God protects us and looks after us. He delivers us from all evil, even saving us from the most terrible evil, that of death. God will protect us and deliver us from every evil until we reach the promised land of heaven.

> No temptation has seized you except what is common to man. And God is aithful; he will not let you be tempted beyond what you can bear. But when you are tempted, he will also provide a way out so that you can stand up under it. (1 Co. 10:13)
> He has delivered us from such a deadly peril, and he will deliver us. On him we have set our hope that he will continue to deliver us. (2 Co. 1:10)
> The Lord will rescue me from every evil attack and will bring me safely to his heavenly kingdom. To him be glory for ever and ever. Amen. (2 Ti. 4:18)
> Since the children have flesh and blood, he too shared in their humanity so that by his death he might destroy him who holds the power of death—that is, the devil— and free those who all their lives were held in slavery by their fear of death. (He. 2:14-15)
> If this is so, then the Lord knows how to rescue godly men from trials and to hold

the unrighteous for the day of judgment, while continuing their punishment. (2 Pe. 2:9)

He said: "The LORD is my rock, my fortress and my deliverer." (2 S. 22:2)

Surely he will save you from the fowler's snare and from the deadly pestilence. (Ps. 91:3)

Even to your old age and gray hairs I am he, I am he who will sustain you. I have made you and I will carry you; I will sustain you and I will rescue you. (Is. 46:4)

"Do not be afraid of them, for I am with you and will rescue you," declares the LORD. (Je. 1:8)

Thought 2. James Philip has an excellent application dealing with God's protection of the Israelites. Although long, the quotation is well worth quoting in full:

> *He who touches God's people touches the apple of His eye. God could chastise His people, judge them or discipline them, but woe betide any one else who did them harm and ill....This also is the grace of God: He would buffet and bruise them, sending judgment after judgment upon them, but He cared for them. He would never let them go, and He would allow no other to touch them with impunity. This is a phenomenon that has remained true throughout history to the present time. In our own day any nation that has done despite to God's covenant people has fallen into trouble.*
>
> *The following quotation serves to underline the miraculous preservation of God's people, against all the attempts of their enemies to destroy them:*
>
> *Four hundred years in Egypt; forty in the wilderness; a long dark and terrible period of warfare, backsliding and idolatry; a brief gleam of sunshine in the reigns of David and Solomon, a rapid downward career of apostacy, discord and sin, to the time of the Babylonian captivity; seventy years' exile, a long interval of darkness and oppression; the great rejection of the Lord of glory, the frightful sufferings and downfall of Jerusalem, and nineteen centuries of shame, oppression, dispersion, and above all, unbelief, blindness, hatred to God's dear Son, the only Saviour....*
>
> *Why do they exist after all the persecutions that they have endured? Pharaoh tried to drown them, but they could not be drowned; Nebuchadnezzar tried to burn them, but they could not be burned; Haman tried to hang them, but it was of no avail. All the nations of the earth have persecuted them, but here they are, and more numerous at the present day than ever before. Why? Because God calls them an everlasting nation."*[1]

And we could well add to these words the horrors of the Holocaust and Nazi Germany's "final solution," to which the answer of God has been the establishment of modern Israel as a nation, after so many centuries of dispersion.[2]

5 (20:23-29) **Aaron, Death of—Priesthood, of Eleazar—Eleazar, Priesthood of—High Priest, Transferring Power of—Heaven, Hope of—"Gathered to His People," Meaning—Hope, for Heaven**: there was the sad, touching death of Aaron. Despite the sadness and grief of this experience, there is a preciousness and tenderness about what happened. Aaron did not die suddenly, with no indication that death was pending. To the contrary, the LORD Himself prepared His dear servant for departing this world. In tenderness and love, compassion and mercy, God reached down and strengthened His dear servant for the experience of death. Note exactly what happened:

a. The LORD Himself informed both Moses and Aaron of Aaron's impending death (vv.23-26). The scene is tender, and God is handling His two dear servants with the care of a father for his child. By this time Aaron was elderly, 123 years old (Nu. 33:39). He had walked with the LORD many years, sometimes failing rather seriously; nevertheless, he had remained true to the faith, persevered to the end. Despite his enormous failures, God still loved His dear servant, loved him deeply. The journey had been long and difficult and would have taken its toll upon anyone. This was proven by the fact that not a single adult who had started out on the journey from the slavery of Egypt was allowed to enter the promised land, not even Moses. Even he had committed a serious act of disobedience. Only two men who started out on the journey would enter the promised land: Caleb and Joshua. The point is this: Aaron had failed God and failed Him miserably on several occasions. But in every instance, Aaron had repented—genuinely repented—and God had forgiven him his sins. God had restored him and used him more mightily than ever before, using his position as High Priest to be the prime symbol of God's dear Son who was yet to come into the world. Because Aaron kept the faith and persevered to the end, God held him ever so dear to His heart. Therefore, when it came time to depart this world, his departure was to be a very special occasion between God and Aaron and his dear brother, Moses. Words are really inadequate to express the tenderness of the occasion, the face-to-face meeting between God and His dear servant Aaron. The first man ever chosen to fill the position of High Priest, the symbol of God's own beloved Son, was coming home. God reached out with all the tenderness, compassion, and mercy that filled His heart and prepared His dear servant for the glorious occasion.

1) Note what God said: Aaron was to be "gathered to his people." This is a picture of Aaron joining former believers in the presence of God (see outline and notes, point 3—Ge. 25:7-10 for more discussion).

2) However, Aaron would not be allowed to enter the promised land because he and Moses had disobeyed God (v.24).

3). Aaron, his son Eleazar, and Moses were to climb Mount Hor (v.25). The purpose for this is seen in the next point.

4) Moses was to transfer the power of the High Priest from Aaron to Eleazar (v.26). The transfer of power was to be symbolized by putting Aaron's garments on Eleazar.

---

[1] Adolph Saphir. *Christ and Israel.* (Grand Rapids, MI: Kregel Publications), p.165.

[2] James Philip. *The Preacher's Commentary on Numbers*, pp.226-227.

b. Note the obedience of Moses (vv.27-28). Moses led the two priests up Mount Hor and did exactly what God had said: he transferred the power of the High Priest from Aaron to Eleazar. Remember that it was the special clothing that identified the High Priest. The clothing was the symbol of the official position of the High Priest (see outline and notes—Vol.2, Ex. 29:29-30 for more discussion).

c. Aaron then died on top of Mount Hor and was obviously buried there by Moses and Eleazar the new High Priest, the son of Aaron (v.28).

d. Note that Israel mourned for Aaron for thirty days (v.29).

Thought 1. The death of God's dear people is very precious to God. The death of any believer is a tender moment to the LORD, for one of God's dear servants is coming home to be with Him. The believer must always remember this fact about death: to be absent from the body is to be present with the LORD. When a believer's moment comes to leave this earth, quicker than the eye can blink God transfers the believer right into His presence. Suddenly, immediately, the believer is face-to-face with the Father and His dear Son, the Lord Jesus Christ. The believer is perfected, living in perfect fellowship and communion with God, ready to begin his eternal worship and service for God. Eternal life—living face-to-face with God in heaven—is a living reality. This is the strong declaration of Scripture.

> For God so loved the world that he gave his one and only Son, that whoever believes in him shall not perish but have eternal life. (Jn. 3:16)
>
> However, do not rejoice that the spirits submit to you, but rejoice that your names are written in heaven. (Lu. 10:20)
>
> Whoever believes in the Son has eternal life. (Jn. 3:36)
>
> In my Father's house are many rooms; if it were not so, I would have told you. I am going there to prepare a place for you. And if I go and prepare a place for you, I will come back and take you to be with me that you also may be where I am. (Jn. 14:2-3)
>
> Now this is eternal life: that they may know you, the only true God, and Jesus Christ, whom you have sent. (Jn. 17:3)
>
> Now we know that if the earthly tent we live in is destroyed, we have a building from God, an eternal house in heaven, not built by human hands. (2 Co. 5:1)
>
> But our citizenship is in heaven. And we eagerly await a Savior from there, the Lord Jesus Christ, who, by the power that enables him to bring everything under his control, will transform our lowly bodies so that they will be like his glorious body. (Ph. 3:20-21)
>
> By faith Abraham, when called to go to a place he would later receive as his inheritance, obeyed and went, even though he did not know where he was going. By faith he made his home in the promised land like a stranger in a foreign country; he lived in tents, as did Isaac and Jacob, who were heirs with him of the same promise. For he was looking forward to the city with foundations, whose architect and builder is God. (He. 11:8-10)
>
> All these people were still living by faith when they died. They did not receive the things promised; they only saw them and welcomed them from a distance. And they admitted that they were aliens and strangers on earth. People who say such things show that they are looking for a country of their own....Instead, they were longing for a better country—a heavenly one. Therefore God is not ashamed to be called their God, for he has prepared a city for them. (He. 11:13-14, 16)
>
> Praise be to the God and Father of our Lord Jesus Christ! In his great mercy he has given us new birth into a living hope through the resurrection of Jesus Christ from the dead, and into an inheritance that can never perish, spoil or fade—kept in heaven for you. (1 Pe. 1:3-4)
>
> Therefore, my brothers, be all the more eager to make your calling and election sure. For if you do these things, you will never fall, and you will receive a rich welcome into the eternal kingdom of our Lord and Savior Jesus Christ. (2 Pe. 1:10-11)
>
> But the day of the Lord will come like a thief. The heavens will disappear with a roar; the elements will be destroyed by fire, and the earth and everything in it will be laid bare. Since everything will be destroyed in this way, what kind of people ought you to be? You ought to live holy and godly lives as you look forward to the day of God and speed its coming. That day will bring about the destruction of the heavens by fire, and the elements will melt in the heat. But in keeping with his promise we are looking forward to a new heaven and a new earth, the home of righteousness. (2 Pe. 3:10-13)

TYPES, SYMBOLS, AND PICTURES
(Numbers 20:1-29)

Historical Term	Type or Picture (Scriptural Basis for Each)	Life Application for Today's Believer	Biblical Application
Gathered to His People Nu. 20:23-29	*A picture of joining former believers in the presence of God.*	The death of God's dear people is very precious to God. The death of any believer is a tender moment to the Lord, for one of God's	*Precious in the sight of the Lord is the death of his saints. (Ps. 116:15) For God so loved the world that he gave his one and*
	Aaron will be gathered to his people. He will not	dear servants is coming home to be with Him. The	*only Son, that whoever believes in him shall not*

NUMBERS 20:1-29

Historical Term	Type or Picture (Scriptural Basis for Each)	Life Application for Today's Believer	Biblical Application
	enter the land I give the Israelites, because both of you rebelled against my command at the waters of Meribah. (Nu. 20:24)	believer must always remember this fact about death: to be absent from the body is to be present with the Lord. When a believer's moment comes to leave this earth, quicker than the eye can blink God transfers the believer right into His presence. Suddenly, immediately, the believer is face to face with the Father and His dear Son, the Lord Jesus Christ. The believer is perfected, living in perfect fellowship and communion with God, ready to begin his eternal worship and service for God. Eternal life—living face to face with God in heaven—is a living reality. This is the strong declaration of Scripture.	*perish but have eternal life. (Jn. 3:16)* *However, do not rejoice that the spirits submit to you, but rejoice that your names are written in heaven. (Lu. 10:20)* *Whoever believes in the Son has eternal life. (Jn. 3:36)* *In my Father's house are many rooms; if it were not so, I would have told you. I am going there to prepare a place for you. And if I go and prepare a place for you, I will come back and take you to be with me that you also may be where I am. (Jn. 14:2-3)*
Putting Aaron's Garments on Eleazar Nu. 20:23-29	*A symbol of transferring the power of the High Priest.* **Moses removed Aaron's garments and put them on his son Eleazar. And Aaron died there on top of the mountain. Then Moses and Eleazar came down from the mountain. (Nu. 20:28)**	Remember that it was the special clothing that identified the High Priest. The symbol of the High Priest's special call was his clothing. The purpose of his clothing was to stir dignity and honor for God's call and for the Priestly office. When the High Priest put on these holy garments, it lent dignity to his work. In the same sense, when the believer puts on holy garments it also lends dignity to his work for the Lord. ⇒ The believer is to put on Christ (Ga. 3:27). ⇒ The believer is to put on the new man (Ep. 4:24; Col. 3:10). ⇒ The believer is to put on the armor of God, the whole armor (Ep. 6:11). ⇒ The believer is to put on the armor of light (Ro. 13:12). ⇒ The believer is to put on love (Col. 3:14). ⇒ The believer is to put on compassion, kindness, humility, gentleness, and patience (Col. 3:12). ⇒ The believer is to put on incorruption and immortality (1 Co. 15:53-54).	*The night is nearly over; the day is almost here. So let us put aside the deeds of darkness and put on the armor of light. (Ro. 13:12)* *For the perishable must clothe itself with the imperishable, and the mortal with immortality. When the perishable has been clothed with the imperishable, and the mortal with immortality, then the saying that is written will come true: "Death has been swallowed up in victory." (1 Co. 15:53-54)* *For all of you who were baptized into Christ have clothed yourselves with Christ. (Ga. 3:27)* *And to put on the new self, created to be like God in true righteousness and holiness. (Ep. 4:24)* *Put on the full armor of God so that you can take your stand against the devil's schemes. (Ep. 6:11)* *And have put on the new self, which is being renewed in knowledge in the image of its Creator. (Col. 3:10)* *Therefore, as God's chosen people, holy and dearly loved, clothe yourselves with compassion, kindness, humility, gentleness and patience. (Col. 3:12)* *And over all these virtues put on love, which binds them all together in perfect unity. (Col. 3:14)*

NUMBERS 20:1-29

Historical Term	Type or Picture (Scriptural Basis for Each)	Life Application for Today's Believer	Biblical Application
			Praise be to the God and Father of our Lord Jesus Christ! In his great mercy he has given us new birth into a living hope through the resurrection of Jesus Christ from the dead, and into an inheritance that can never perish, spoil or fade—kept in heaven for you. (1 Pe. 1:3-4)

NUMBERS 21:1-35

CHAPTER 21

G. Event 7—the First Military Victories & the Bronze Snake: A Picture of Desperate Vows, of Christ the Savior, & of God's Protection & Victory, 21:1-35

1. **The first military victory: A picture of making & fulfilling vows**
   a. The secret attack & capture of some Israelites: By Arad's Canaanite king[DS1]
   b. The reaction of Israel: A courageous determination & faith
      1) They made a vow: If God would give victory, they would destroy them
      2) They were heard by the LORD: He gave them victory
      3) They fulfilled their vow: Completely destroyed the savage, evil attackers (see Ge. 15:16)[DS2]

2. **The bronze snake: A picture of unbelief & of Christ the Savior**
   a. The tragic situation
      1) Had to bypass Edom, a long distance out of the way
      2) Grew impatient & grumbled against God & Moses
         • Asked why they had led them out of Egypt into the desert to die: Had no bread & no water
         • Stated they detested the *worthless manna*
   b. The judgment, chastisement of the LORD
      1) He sent snakes among them
      2) Many died
   c. The confession & repentance of the people
      1) They confessed their sin
      2) They asked Moses, their mediator, to pray for God to take away the snakes
      3) Moses prayed for them
   d. The answer of the LORD
      1) To make a replica of a snake & hang it on a high pole
      2) The condition for deliverance: Must look at it to live
   e. The obedience of Moses: Hung a bronze snake on a pole
   f. The deliverance: Some looked, believed, & lived (a picture of deliverance by looking at Christ, Jn.3:14-15)

3. **The march around Moab: A picture of progress—marching forth from place to place in a spirit of strong assurance**
   a. They camped at Oboth (v.10)
   b. They camped at Iye Abarim
   c. They camped at the Zered Valley
   d. They camped alongside the Arnon River
      1) It flowed into Amorite territory
      2) It was the border between Moab & the Amorites
      3) It was a famous river: A place where significant battles had been fought
   e. They camped at the well Beer
      1) The well was dug in obedience to the LORD's instructions
      2) The gift of water led God's people to compose a song of joy, the *Song of the Well*
   f. They camped at Mattanah
   g. They camped at Nahaliel
   h. They camped at Bamoth
   i. They camped in Moab in the valley below Pisgah Peak—an excellent lookout to spy out the land

4. **The military victory over Sihon, the king of the Amorites: A picture of God's protection when attacked by enemies**
   a. The diplomatic, non-threatening request by Israel for safe passage
   b. The hostile attack against Israel at Jahaz[DS3]
   c. The great victory of Israel
      1) Conquered all the Amorite territory
      2) Stopped at the Ammonite border: Because the border was fortified
      3) Captured & occupied all the cities of the Amorites: Included Heshbon[DS4] & its surrounding villages

---

When the Canaanite king of Arad, who lived in the Negev, heard that Israel was coming along the road to Atharim, he attacked the Israelites and captured some of them. 2 Then Israel made this vow to the LORD: "If you will deliver these people into our hands, we will totally destroy their cities." 3 The LORD listened to Israel's plea and gave the Canaanites over to them. They completely destroyed them and their towns; so the place was named Hormah.
4 They traveled from Mount Hor along the route to the Red Sea, to go around Edom. But the people grew impatient on the way; 5 They spoke against God and against Moses, and said, "Why have you brought us up out of Egypt to die in the desert? There is no bread! There is no water! And we detest this miserable food!"
6 Then the LORD sent venomous snakes among them; they bit the people and many Israelites died.
7 The people came to Moses and said, "We sinned when we spoke against the LORD and against you. Pray that the LORD will take the snakes away from us." So Moses prayed for the people.
8 The LORD said to Moses, "Make a snake and put it up on a pole; anyone who is bitten can look at it and live."
9 So Moses made a bronze snake and put it up on a pole. Then when anyone was bitten by a snake and looked at the bronze snake, he lived.
10 The Israelites moved on and camped at Oboth.
11 Then they set out from Oboth and camped in Iye Abarim, in the desert that faces Moab toward the sunrise.
12 From there they moved on and camped in the Zered Valley.
13 They set out from there and camped alongside the Arnon, which is in the desert extending into Amorite territory. The Arnon is the border of Moab, between Moab and the Amorites.
14 That is why the Book of the Wars of the LORD says:
"... Waheb in Suphah and the ravines, the Arnon
15 And the slopes of the ravines that lead to the site of Ar and lie along the border of Moab."
16 From there they continued on to Beer, the well where the LORD said to Moses, "Gather the people together and I will give them water."
17 Then Israel sang this song: "Spring up, O well! Sing about it,
18 About the well that the princes dug, that the nobles of the people sank— the nobles with scepters and staffs." Then they went from the desert to Mattanah,
19 From Mattanah to Nahaliel, from Nahaliel to Bamoth,
20 And from Bamoth to the valley in Moab where the top of Pisgah overlooks the wasteland.
21 Israel sent messengers to say to Sihon king of the Amorites:
22 "Let us pass through your country. We will not turn aside into any field or vineyard, or drink water from any well. We will travel along the king's highway until we have passed through your territory."
23 But Sihon would not let Israel pass through his territory. He mustered his entire army and marched out into the desert against Israel. When he reached Jahaz, he fought with Israel.
24 Israel, however, put him to the sword and took over his land from the Arnon to the Jabbok, but only as far as the Ammonites, because their border was fortified.
25 Israel captured all the cities of the Amorites and occupied them, including Heshbon and all its surrounding

NUMBERS 21:1-35

d. The significance of the victory: A great victory over a celebrated king & army had been achieved 1) This is seen in the conquest of the great city of Heshbon: It was the capital of the Amorites 2) This is seen in the great King Sihon: He had formerly conquered Moab, a conquest so great that it had been celebrated by ancient poets	settlements. 26 Heshbon was the city of Sihon king of the Amorites, who had fought against the former king of Moab and had taken from him all his land as far as the Arnon. 27 That is why the poets say: "Come to Heshbon and let it be rebuilt; let Sihon's city be restored. 28 "Fire went out from Heshbon, a blaze from the city of Sihon. It consumed Ar of Moab, the citizens of Arnon's heights. 29 Woe to you, O Moab! You are destroyed, O people of Chemosh! He has given up his sons as fugitives and his daughters as captives to Sihon king of the Amorites. 30 "But we have overthrown them; Heshbon is destroyed all the way to Dibon. We have demolished them as far as Nophah, which extends to Medeba."	31 So Israel settled in the land of the Amorites. 32 After Moses had sent spies to Jazer, the Israelites captured its surrounding settlements and drove out the Amorites who were there. 33 Then they turned and went up along the road toward Bashan, and Og king of Bashan and his whole army marched out to meet them in battle at Edrei. 34 The LORD said to Moses, "Do not be afraid of him, for I have handed him over to you, with his whole army and his land. Do to him what you did to Sihon king of the Amorites, who reigned in Heshbon." 35 So they struck him down, together with his sons and his whole army, leaving them no survivors. And they took possession of his land.	3) Now Israel had proven stronger than the Amorites e. The victory was even extended: Sent spies to Jazer & captured the towns, driving out the Amorite citizens 5. **The military victory over Og, the king of Bashan: A picture of victory through the power of God (Ge. 15:16; Ps. 136:19)** a. The attack of Og: Marched his whole army against Israel at Edrei^{DS5} b. The strong assurance of victory from the LORD 1) God's people were not to fear their enemy: Total & complete victory was assured 2) God's people were to use the same pattern as before: Pursuit & total conquest c. The obedience & victory 1) They struck down all the wicked: Their cup was full of sin, had "reached its full measure" (Ge. 15:16) 2) They occupied the land

DIVISION III

THE FORTY LONG YEARS OF WILDERNESS WANDERINGS: A PICTURE OF THE BELIEVER'S PILGRIMAGE THROUGH THIS WORLD AS HE PREPARES TO ENTER THE PROMISED LAND, 15:1–25:18

G. Event 7—the First Military Victories and the Bronze Snake: A Picture of Desperate Vows, of Christ the Savior, and of God's Protection and Victory, 21:1-35

(21:1-35) **Introduction—Vows, Reasons for Making—Crises, List of**: when facing a desperate crisis, people often make vows. They promise to do certain things if God will only deliver them through the crisis. The crisis may be created by...

- war
- abuse
- financial problems
- disease
- accident
- unfaithfulness
- family problems
- unemployment
- unwanted pregnancy
- mismanagement by self or others
- drugs
- alcohol

Crises are serious matters to God. God expects us to fulfill the vows and promises we make during crises. But making vows is only one picture seen in the events of this Scripture. There are two others:

⇒ the picture of Christ the Savior
⇒ the picture of God's protection and victory against the enemies that attack His dear people as they march to the promised land

This is a passage that speaks to the deepest needs of man, a passage that needs to be heeded by us all. This is: *Event 7—the First Military Victories and the Bronze Snake: A Picture of Desperate Vows, of Christ the Savior, and of God's Protection and Victory*, 21:1-35.

1. The first military victory: a picture of making and fulfilling vows (vv.1-3).
2. The bronze snake: a picture of unbelief and of Christ the Savior (vv.4-9).
3. The march around Moab: a picture of progress—marching forth from place to place in a spirit of strong assurance (vv.10-20).
4. The military victory over Sihon, the king of the Amorites: a picture of God's protection when attacked by enemies (vv.21-32).
5. The military victory over Og, the king of Bashan: a picture of victory through the power of God (Ge. 15:16; Ps. 136:19) (vv.33-35).

1 (21:1-3) **Victory, Over Enemies—Faith, Courageous—Triumph, Over Enemies—Conquest, of Enemies—Israel, Conquest of Enemies—Canaanites, Conquest of—Arad, Conquered by Israel**: there was the first military victory of Israel, a victory over the Canaanite king of Arad. This is a clear picture of making vows to God and fulfilling the vows. This was the launch of a new day in the history of Israel. After wandering about in the wilderness for forty years, they experienced their very first military victory, a victory over one of the Canaanite nations. Remember, the Canaanite nations were so savage, evil, and corrupt that they were beyond repair or repentance (see

NUMBERS 21:1-35

Ge. 15:16; see outline and note, pt.4, d—Ge. 15:7-21 for more discussion). Forty years earlier, from this same area, Israel had attempted to enter the promised land. This was right after the spies had returned from their mission of spying out the land. But as we have seen, because of the terrible unbelief of the spies and the people, the march into the promised land had to be aborted. The people were condemned to spend forty years wandering about in the wilderness until the entire first generation of faithless believers had died. For forty years the people of God had been wandering about in the wilderness of this world. They were defeated, disappointed, frustrated, beaten down—all because of unbelief, grumbling, and murmuring against God and His dear servant Moses. They had failed to lay hold of the promises of God, that He would give them victory over the pitfalls and enemies of this life. As a result, they were unable to enter the promised land. But now their children, the second generation, were about ready to enter. The new day was dawning; here they were on the threshold of claiming the great promise of God, the hope of the promised land. Here is the very first military victory, a victory over a formidable enemy, an enemy that was set on destroying them.

a. The Canaanite king of Arad heard that Israel was traveling close by (v.1). For some reason, he launched a savage, secret attack against the Israelites. He apparently attacked some of the Israelites on the outskirts of the campsite. His armed forces were apparently not large enough to launch an all out attack against the military of Israel. Whatever the case, he captured some of the Israelites and took them back to the capital of Arad.

b. Note the reaction of Israel: a courageous determination and faith (vv.2-3). They made a *vow* to the Lord that if God would give them victory, they would totally destroy the Arads. God heard the prayer of their *vow* and He gave them victory. Note the total obedience of the people in fulfilling their vow: they completely destroyed the savage, evil Canaanites (v.3) (see DEEPER STUDY # 1—Nu. 21:2-3 for more discussion).

> **Thought 1.** Making vows is a serious matter. When we make a vow, God expects us to keep the vow. He expects us to fulfill what we promise. This was true with Israelites, and it is true with us. We must fulfill our vows, the promises we make to the LORD.
>
> **When a man makes a vow to the LORD or takes an oath to obligate himself by a pledge, he must not break his word but must do everything he said. (Nu. 30:2)**
>
> **If you make a vow to the LORD your God, do not be slow to pay it, for the LORD your God will certainly demand it of you and you will be guilty of sin. But if you refrain from making a vow, you will not be guilty. Whatever your lips utter you must be sure to do, because you made your vow freely to the LORD your God with your own mouth. (De. 23:21-23)**
>
> **You will pray to him, and he will hear you, and you will fulfill your vows. (Jb. 22:27)**
>
> **Sacrifice thank offerings to God, fulfill your vows to the Most High. (Ps. 50:14)**
>
> **Make vows to the LORD your God and fulfill them; let all the neighboring lands bring gifts to the One to be feared. (Ps. 76:11)**
>
> **When you make a vow to God, do not delay in fulfilling it. He has no pleasure in fools; fulfill your vow. It is better not to vow than to make a vow and not fulfill it. Do not let your mouth lead you into sin. And do not protest to the temple messenger, "My vow was a mistake." Why should God be angry at what you say and destroy the work of your hands? (Ec. 5:4-6)**

DEEPER STUDY # 1
(Nu. 21:1) **Arad, City of**: it was located in the Negev in the southern extreme of Judah's territory. (See Map—Nu. 33:5-49, end of commentary.) Arad was a Canaanite city about eleven miles west southwest of Beersheba. It was also the headquarters of the Canaanite king of Arad and the scene of Israel's first military victory.

See other Scripture references for study:
Nu. 33:40; Jos. 12:14; Jud. 1:16

DEEPER STUDY # 2
(21:2-3) **Sin, Full Measure of—Iniquity, Cup of—Nations, Destruction of—Nations, Savage and Evil—Nations, Judgment of—Canaanites, Destruction of**: the words *totally destroy* (harami or charam) mean to annihilate, exterminate, eliminate, or abolish. The word is related to the Hebrew *herem* which means "to devote to the ban."[1] Once something had been promised or devoted to God, it was placed under the ban: it could not be removed. If it was a gift, it had to be given to God. If it was the promise to do something, then it had to be done. If it was a vow to devote something to destruction, then it had to be destroyed or exterminated. In ancient days, this was known as the herem principal or law. Once a person or thing had been devoted to the LORD, it could not be removed. It went to the LORD.

In the present case, Israel made a promise to God: if God would give them victory over the savage Canaanites, they would totally destroy the Canaanite cities. (See note, pt.4, d—Ge. 15:7-21 for more discussion.)

The very idea that God and moral people would be set on the total destruction of a people is offensive to some persons. How could God and moral people possibly endorse such an act? In looking at this, certain factors need to be kept in mind:

1. People can become so savage, evil, and corrupt that they are beyond repair or repentance, beyond hope or correction. This is what is known as the *cup of sin reaching its full measure* (Ge. 15:16)—filled to the point that it overflows and continues to overflow with...

- savagery
- violence
- brutality
- slavery
- ruthlessness
- lawlessness
- abuse
- cruelty
- atrocities
- barbarism
- corruption
- evil
- immorality
- injustice

History has shown that such behavior can be true of both individuals and nations. A person's or a nation's *cup of iniquity* can become full—well beyond repair or repentance, well beyond hope or correction. God declares this fact time and again as the Scriptures below show (Ge. 15:16).

---

[1] *The Expositor's Bible Commentary*. Frank E. Gaebelein, Editor, p.874.

NUMBERS 21:1-35

God wants justice executed against these people. Scripture is clear about this fact: this is the very purpose for the judgment of God.

> In the fourth generation your descendants will come back here, for the sin of the Amorites has not yet reached its full measure. (Ge. 15:16)
>
> Do not defile yourselves in any of these ways, because this is how the nations that I am going to drive out before you became defiled. Even the land was defiled; so I punished it for its sin, and the land vomited out its inhabitants. (Le. 18:24-25)
>
> You must not live according to the customs of the nations I am going to drive out before you. Because they did all these things, I abhorred them. (Le. 20:23)
>
> After the LORD your God has driven them out before you, do not say to yourself, "The LORD has brought me here to take possession of this land because of my righteousness." No, it is on account of the wickedness of these nations that the LORD is going to drive them out before you. It is not because of your righteousness or your integrity that you are going in to take possession of their land; but on account of the wickedness of these nations, the LORD your God will drive them out before you, to accomplish what he swore to your fathers, to Abraham, Isaac and Jacob. (De. 9:4-5)
>
> He did evil in the eyes of the LORD, following the detestable practices of the nations the LORD had driven out before the Israelites. (2 K. 21:2)
>
> He burned sacrifices in the Valley of Ben Hinnom and sacrificed his sons in the fire, following the detestable ways of the nations the LORD had driven out before the Israelites. (2 Chr. 28:3)
>
> He did evil in the eyes of the LORD, following the detestable practices of the nations the LORD had driven out before the Israelites. (2 Chr. 33:2)
>
> They shed innocent blood, the blood of their sons and daughters, whom they sacrificed to the idols of Canaan, and the land was desecrated by their blood. (Ps. 106:38)
>
> The earth is defiled by its people; they have disobeyed the laws, violated the statutes and broken the everlasting covenant. (Is. 24:5)
>
> You have defiled the land with your prostitution and wickedness. (Je. 3:2)
>
> I will repay them double for their wickedness and their sin, because they have defiled my land with the lifeless forms of their vile images and have filled my inheritance with their detestable idols. (Je. 16:18)

2. God is a just God as well as a God of love. God loves all people—every individual and all the people of every nation upon earth. His love continually flows out to everyone. But God is also a just God, the Sovereign Lord who executes justice upon the earth. God is not an *indulgent grandfather* type of person who pampers the evil and savage of this world. To allow injustice to go unpunished, He would be a God of evil, a God who showed partiality and favoritism. He would be favoring the evil of the earth by allowing them to go unpunished and showing injustice to the moral of the earth by allowing them to continue to suffer under the injustices of evil people.

When the "cup of sin reaches its full measure"—well beyond repair or repentance, well beyond hope or correction—that person or people are to be judged. Justice is to be executed upon them. God wants justice executed against such persons. This is the reason He has appointed a day in which He will judge the world.

> For the Son of Man is going to come in his Father's glory with his angels, and then he will reward each person according to what he has done. (Mt. 16:27)
>
> When the Son of Man comes in his glory, and all the angels with him, he will sit on his throne in heavenly glory. All the nations will be gathered before him, and he will separate the people one from another as a shepherd separates the sheep from the goats. He will put the sheep on his right and the goats on his left. (Mt. 25:31-33)
>
> For he has set a day when he will judge the world with justice by the man he has appointed. He has given proof of this to all men by raising him from the dead. (Ac. 17:31)
>
> This will take place on the day when God will judge men's secrets through Jesus Christ, as my gospel declares. (Ro. 2:16)
>
> In the presence of God and of Christ Jesus, who will judge the living and the dead, and in view of his appearing and his kingdom, I give you this charge. (2 Ti. 4:1)
>
> Just as man is destined to die once, and after that to face judgment. (He. 9:27)
>
> If this is so, then the Lord knows how to rescue godly men from trials and to hold the unrighteous for the day of judgment, while continuing their punishment. (2 Pe. 2:9)
>
> The Lord is not slow in keeping his promise, as some understand slowness. He is patient with you, not wanting anyone to perish, but everyone to come to repentance. (2 Pe. 3:9)
>
> Enoch, the seventh from Adam, prophesied about these men: "See, the Lord is coming with thousands upon thousands of his holy ones to judge everyone, and to convict all the ungodly of all the ungodly acts they have done in the ungodly way, and of all the harsh words ungodly sinners have spoken against him." (Jude 1:14-15)

And I saw the dead, great and small, standing before the throne, and books were opened. Another book was opened, which is the book of life. The dead were judged according to what they had done as recorded in the books. (Re. 20:12)

3. Israel was used by God as His instrument of justice and judgment against the nations of Canaan. The Israelites did not receive the promised land of Canaan because of some merit or value within themselves nor because of their own strength or power. In justice and judgment, God Himself destroyed the Canaanites, and it was because of their wickedness that He destroyed them.

Again, it is critical to note this fact: Israel as a people did not receive the promised land because of their merit or value nor because of some righteousness they possessed. The Canaanites were destroyed because they were evil and their "cup of iniquity" had been filled to the brim. They reached the point of no repentance; they were beyond correction. Moses himself declared to the Israelites:

a. "It is not because of any personal righteousness within you, not because you have pure hearts, that you inherit the promised land (De. 9:5). The enemies of the land are to be conquered and destroyed for two reasons:
⇒ Because of their wickedness and because they are an evil people; their 'cup of sin' has reached its full measure.
⇒ Because God is faithful; He fulfills His promise to the forefathers, to Abraham, Isaac, and Jacob. God has promised to give the promised land to their descendants, to all those down through the centuries who believe His Word, His promises."

b. "Understand this warning: it is not because of your righteousness that God gives you the promised land. On the contrary, you are a stiff-necked, stubborn people (De. 9:6). You are a sinful people. You have no righteousness within yourselves that merits God's favor. Your hearts are not upright nor pure enough to make God accept you and give you the victory over the enemies of the promised land. You are a stiff-necked, stubborn people."

It is not because of your righteousness or your integrity that you are going in to take possession of their land; but on account of the wickedness of these nations, the LORD your God will drive them out before you, to accomplish what he swore to your fathers, to Abraham, Isaac and Jacob. Understand, then, that it is not because of your righteousness that the LORD your God is giving you this good land to possess, for you are a stiff-necked people. (De. 9:5-6)

Thought 1. James Philip makes an excellent statement on the justice and judgment of God that is well worth quoting in full.

God was using His people as the rod of His anger against peoples whose cup of iniquity was full to overflowing. They were being judged for their sins and their depravities. This is, of course, stated explicitly more than once in the Old Testament itself (cf. Ge. 15:16 and Le. 18:24-30). The time of their destruction was ripe. This is why they were thus dealt with, and it was no arbitrary act of injustice that drove them out of their land. They had forfeited the right to live as nations in Canaan by the extremes of their debauchery and depravity, just as Sodom and Gomorrah had done (Ge. 19), and just as the Cainite civilization as a whole had done, bringing upon itself the judgment of the Flood (Ge. 6). Furthermore, it should be remembered that God dealt with His own people in similar fashion when they proved themselves unworthy to life in the land of promise, and He brought them into the captivity of Babylon in 586 B.C. To understand God's burning passion for righteousness in His creatures is to understand the basic reason for these judgments upon men and nations that refused to be righteous, and who rendered themselves incapable of being so by their continued sin.[1]

2 (21:4-9) **Bronze Snake:** the bronze snake is a picture of unbelief and of Christ the Savior. Marching out in the wilderness was hard and difficult. At the end of each day, the people were bound to be tired, exhausted, and bone-weary. This passage shows how fatigue and exhaustion got to the people, how they had become so bone-weary that they lapsed back into their grumbling and unbelief. They began once again to attack God and His dear servant.

a. Note the tragic situation: the people had to bypass or detour around Edom. This was a long distance out of the way (vv.4-5). Remember, Moses had sent two diplomatic letters to the king of Edom asking permission to pass through their land. The king had rejected the appeal and had even gone so far as to threaten attack against the Israelites. Therefore, Moses had to lead the people on a detour around the land of Edom. As stated, this was a long distance out of the way for the people to travel. Fatigue and exhaustion set in, and they grew impatient. They began to grumble and murmur against God and against Moses:
⇒ They asked why they had been led out of Egypt into the desert wilderness to die: there was no bread and no water in the desert wilderness.
⇒ They stated that they detested the *worthless manna*. Remember that the manna was the bread from heaven, the bread that God Himself had provided to feed the people through their wilderness wanderings. The word the people used to describe the *manna* was ballehem haqqeloqel. This means *contemptible, worthless bread*; it means miserable, wretched, despicable, cheap bread. It even has the idea of cursing the heavenly bread, the bread that had been provided by God Himself.[3] The people had constantly grumbled about God's gracious provision during their 40 year wilderness wandering, but this time it was different. They actually stated that they detested the *manna*, and they cursed it. It was despicable, worthless, at best *junk food*. This time,

---
2 *The Expositor's Bible Commentary.* Frank E. Gaebelein, Editor, p.874.
3 James Philip. *The Preacher's Commentary on Numbers*, p.311.

the people had gone too far. God had no choice but to judge and chastise them and to do so severely.

b. Note the judgment, the chastisement of the LORD: He sent snakes among them, and many of them died (v.6). They were "venomous snakes," that is, *poisonous snakes*. The poison was obviously strong, very potent—the kind of venom that causes a horrible, agonizing death. This is indicated by the fact that many of the people subsequently died.

c. Note the confession and repentance of the people: they confessed their sin and asked Moses to pray for them, asking God to take away the snakes (v.7). This Moses did. He was the servant of God, so he once again forgave them for their attacks against him and the Lord. As their minister, he loved them, so he again became their intercessor and mediator before God. No doubt, he begged God to forgive the sin of the people and to have mercy upon them.

d. Note the surprising answer of the Lord (v.8): the Lord told Moses to make a replica of a snake and hang it on a high pole. Then God spelled out a condition for deliverance and healing: a person had to look at the snake hanging upon the pole. If he looked, he would be healed and would live.

This is one of the great symbols of Jesus Christ in the Scripture—His being hung upon the cross for the sins of the world. This is exactly what Christ Himself said:

> Just as Moses lifted up the snake in the desert, so the Son of Man must be lifted up, that everyone who believes in him may have eternal life. For God so loved the world that he gave his one and only Son, that whoever believes in him shall not perish but have eternal life. (Jn. 3:14-16)

e. Now, note the obedience of Moses: he hung a bronze snake on a pole just as instructed by God (v.9).

f. The people were delivered, but only some. Only those who looked at the snake and believed the promise of God lived (v.9). Keep in mind, this is a picture of deliverance by looking at (believing in) the cross of Jesus Christ (Jn. 3:14-15).

Thought 1. There are three significant lessons in this point for us.

(1) Jesus Christ is the manna, the bread from heaven. God has given Jesus Christ to feed the souls of people. People hunger and crave for the food of purpose, meaning, and significance in life. Christ and Christ alone can meet the hunger of the human soul. Jesus Christ is the Bread of Life.

> But seek first his kingdom and his righteousness, and all these things will be given to you as well. (Mt. 6:33)

> Jesus said to them, "I tell you the truth, it is not Moses who has given you the bread from heaven, but it is my Father who gives you the true bread from heaven. For the bread of God is he who comes down from heaven and gives life to the world." "Sir," they said, "from now on give us this bread." Then Jesus declared, "I am the bread of life. He who comes to me will never go hungry, and he who believes in me will never be thirsty." (Jn. 6:32-35)

> "I am the bread of life. Your forefathers ate the manna in the desert, yet they died. But here is the bread that comes down from heaven, which a man may eat and not die. I am the living bread that came down from heaven. If anyone eats of this bread, he will live forever. This bread is my flesh, which I will give for the life of the world." (Jn. 6:48-51)

> "This is the bread that came down from heaven. Your forefathers ate manna and died, but he who feeds on this bread will live forever." (Jn. 6:58)

> He who has an ear, let him hear what the Spirit says to the churches. To him who overcomes, I will give the right to eat from the tree of life, which is in the paradise of God. (Re. 2:7)

> Why spend money on what is not bread, and your labor on what does not satisfy? Listen, listen to me, and eat what is good, and your soul will delight in the richest of fare. (Is. 55:2)

(2) The Israelites cursed the bread of God which was a symbol of Jesus Christ. Any person who curses Jesus Christ will be judged by God, severely judged. Any person who looks upon Jesus Christ as contemptible, worthless, wretched—as being useless—is going to face the wrath of God, a judgment beyond comprehension.

> Whoever believes in the Son has eternal life, but whoever rejects the Son will not see life, for God's wrath remains on him. (Jn. 3:36)

> The wrath of God is being revealed from heaven against all the godlessness and wickedness of men who suppress the truth by their wickedness. (Ro. 1:18)

> But for those who are self-seeking and who reject the truth and follow evil, there will be wrath and anger. (Ro. 2:8)

> Be imitators of God, therefore, as dearly loved children and live a life of love, just as Christ loved us and gave himself up for us as a fragrant offering and sacrifice to God. But among you there must not be even a hint of sexual immorality, or of any kind of impurity, or of greed, because these are improper for God's holy people. Nor should there be obscenity, foolish talk or coarse joking, which are out of place, but rather thanksgiving. For of this you can be sure: No immoral, impure or greedy person—such a man is an idolater—has any inheritance in the kingdom of Christ and of God. Let no one deceive you with empty words, for because of such things God's wrath comes on those who are disobedient. (Ep. 5:1-6)

> And give relief to you who are troubled, and to us as well. This will happen when the Lord Jesus is revealed from heaven in blazing fire with his powerful angels. He will punish those who do not know God and do not obey the gospel of our Lord Jesus. (2 Th. 1:7-8)

If this is so, then the Lord knows how to rescue godly men from trials and to hold the unrighteous for the day of judgment, while continuing their punishment. (2 Pe. 2:9)

By the same word the present heavens and earth are reserved for fire, being kept for the day of judgment and destruction of ungodly men. (2 Pe. 3:7)

See, the Lord is coming with thousands upon thousands of his holy ones to judge everyone, and to convict all the ungodly of all the ungodly acts they have done in the ungodly way, and of all the harsh words ungodly sinners have spoken against him. (Jude 14-15)

Look, he is coming with the clouds, and every eye will see him, even those who pierced him; and all the peoples of the earth will mourn because of him. So shall it be! Amen. (Re. 1:7)

Kiss the Son, lest he be angry and you be destroyed in your way, for his wrath can flare up in a moment. Blessed are all who take refuge in him. (Ps. 2:12)

(3) Jesus Christ has been lifted up as the Savior of the world. God lifted up Christ just as the snake was lifted up, as a symbol of deliverance. Any person who looks upon Christ and believes in Him will be delivered, that is, saved.

Just as Moses lifted up the snake in the desert, so the Son of Man must be lifted up, that everyone who believes in him may have eternal life. "For God so loved the world that he gave his one and only Son, that whoever believes in him shall not perish but have eternal life." (Jn. 3:14-16)

I tell you the truth, whoever hears my word and believes him who sent me has eternal life and will not be condemned; he has crossed over from death to life. (Jn. 5:24)

Jesus said to her, "I am the resurrection and the life. He who believes in me will live, even though he dies." (Jn. 11:25)

I have come into the world as a light, so that no one who believes in me should stay in darkness. (Jn. 12:46)

But these are written that you may believe that Jesus is the Christ, the Son of God, and that by believing you may have life in his name. (Jn. 20:31)

That if you confess with your mouth, "Jesus is Lord," and believe in your heart that God raised him from the dead, you will be saved. For it is with your heart that you believe and are justified, and it is with your mouth that you confess and are saved. (Ro. 10:9-10)

3 (21:10-20) **March, the Believer's—Walk, the Believer's—Confidence—Assurance:** there was the march around Moab. This is a picture of progress, of marching forth from place to place in a spirit of strong assurance. Now the people were ready for their final march right up to the border of the promised land. At last, they were on the verge of reaching their destination. As they marched along, the excitement of their hearts could be seen in a faster pace: the tempo of their steps increased as they marched day by day. Note how Scripture paints the scene with a graphic fast-paced stroke.

   a. The Israelites camped at Oboth (v.10).
   b. The Israelites camped at Iye Abarim (v.11).
   c. The Israelites camped at the Zered Valley (v.12).
   d. The Israelites camped alongside the Arnon River (vv.13-15). This was one of the famous rivers of ancient history, a river that flowed into Amorite territory. The river was actually the border between Moab and the Amorite territory. A large number of significant battles had been fought in the area around the river (vv.14-15). Note the reference to the "Book of the Wars of the Lord." This is actually the only mention of this book, the only thing we know about it. Obviously, it was a book of songs about famous battles and wars that had been fought in those days.
   e. The Israelites camped at the well Beer (vv.16-17). The people again were apparently without water, but the Lord stepped into the situation and told them where they could dig a well and hit water. Note that the gift of water led God's people to compose a song of joy, the "Song of the Well."
   f. The Israelites camped at Mattanah (v.18).
   g. The Israelites camped at Nahaliel (v.19).
   h. The Israelites camped at Bamoth (v.19).
   i. The Israelites camped in Moab in the valley below Pisgah peak, an excellent location to spy out the land of Canaan (v.20).

Thought 1. This is a different picture of God's people than seen before. Up until now, the picture painted has been that of an unbelieving people, a grumbling people, a people who lacked assurance and confidence in the Lord. They just did not believe He had the power to carry them into the promised land. But this scene of Scripture is entirely different: it is a picture of a quick pace, an excitement to reach their destination. The picture painted is that of breaking camp, marching, stopping, and setting up camp; then again breaking camp, marching, stopping, and setting up camp; then again breaking camp, marching, stopping, and setting up camp; and on and on. The idea is that of a fast pace, of purpose and motivation, of enthusiasm and excitement. This has not been seen before, but now the people are rapidly approaching the promised land. They seem to be trusting God more than ever before. Therefore, God pours out His grace upon them, providing for them and meeting their need for water and all else.

The lesson for us is this: we must be diligent as we march to the promised land of God. We need a quick, fast pace in trusting and obeying God, in following the leadership of God as He leads us to the promised land.

By faith Abraham, when called to go to a place he would later receive as his inheritance, obeyed and went, even though he did not know where he was going. By faith he made his home in the promised land like a stranger in a foreign country; he lived in tents, as did Isaac and Jacob, who were heirs with him of the same promise. For he was looking forward to the city with foundations, whose architect and builder is God. (He. 11:8-10)

All these people were still living by faith when they died. They did not receive the things promised; they only saw them and welcomed them from a distance. And they admitted that they were aliens and strangers on earth. People who say such things show that they are looking for a country of their own. (He. 11:13-14)

But the day of the Lord will come like a thief. The heavens will disappear with a roar; the elements will be destroyed by fire, and the earth and everything in it will be laid bare. Since everything will be destroyed in this way, what kind of people ought you to be? You ought to live holy and godly lives as you look forward to the day of God and speed its coming. That day will bring about the destruction of the heavens by fire, and the elements will melt in the heat. But in keeping with his promise we are looking forward to a new heaven and a new earth, the home of righteousness. So then, dear friends, since you are looking forward to this, make every effort to be found spotless, blameless and at peace with him. (2 Pe. 3:10-14)

Blessed are those who wash their robes, that they may have the right to the tree of life and may go through the gates into the city. (Re. 22:14)

But if from there you seek the LORD your God, you will find him if you look for him with all your heart and with all your soul. (De. 4:29)

Seek the LORD while he may be found; call on him while he is near. (Is. 55:6)

You will seek me and find me when you seek me with all your heart. (Je. 29:13)

DEEPER STUDY # 3

(Nu.21:23) **Jahaz, City of (See other spellings—Jahaza, Jahazah)**: the exact location is unknown. Jahaz became part of the tribal territory of Reuben (Jos. 13:18). Sihon the Amorite was defeated there after attacking Israel. It became a city of the Levites (Jos. 21:36).

See other Scripture references for study: De. 2:32; Jos. 13:18; Jos. 21:36; Jud. 11:20; Is. 15:4; Je. 48:21; Je. 48:34

DEEPER STUDY # 4

(Nu. 21:25-30; Nu. 32:37-38) **Heshbon, City of**: it was located east of the Dead Sea and north of the Arnon River in Moab. (See Map—Nu. 33:5-49, end of commentary.) The Hebrew meaning of Heshbon is *reckoning*. It was assigned to the tribe of Reuben and later chosen to be a Levitical city (Joshua 13:27-28; Joshua 21:38-39).

See other Scripture references for study: Nu. 21:25-28; Nu. 21:30; Nu. 21:34; Nu. 32:3; Nu. 32:37; De. 1:4; De. 2:24; De. 2:26; De. 2:30; De. 3:2; De. 3:6; De. 4:46; De. 29:7; Jos. 9:10; Jos. 12:2; Jos. 12:5; Jos. 13:10; Jos. 13:17; Jos. 13:21; Jos. 13:26-27; Jos. 21:39; Jud. 11:19; Jud. 11:26; 1 Chr. 6:81; Ne. 9:22; Song 7:4; Is. 15:4; Is. 16:8-9; Je. 48:2; Je. 48:34; Je. 48:45; Je. 49:3

---

4 (21:21-32) **Victory, Military—Victory, over Enemies—Enemies, Victory over—Justice, of God—Faithfulness, of God—Amorites, Conquered by Israel—Israel, Conquest of Amorites—Sihon**: there was the military victory over Sihon, the king of the Amorites. This is a picture of God's protection when attacked by enemies (Ge. 15:16; Ps. 136:19). As the Israelites marched to the promised land, they came to the border of the Amorite nation. The land of the Amorites stood between them and the promised land. God's people had no choice: if they were going to continue their journey to the promised land, they had to pass through the land of the Amorites. What happened is most interesting:

a. Note the diplomatic, non-threatening request of Israel for safe passage (v.22). Moses promised that the Israelites would not do any damage to the fields or crops or water as they marched through Amorite territory. He promised to stay strictly on the king's highway until they had passed completely through the territory.

b. Note the surprise, hostile attack against Israel (v.23). King Sihon rejected the request of Israel for safe passage. Instead, the king and his officials mobilized their entire army and marched out against Israel. When the Amorites reached Jahaz, they attacked.

c. Despite the surprise attack, Israel was victorious (vv.24-25). They routed the Amorite army and pursued them all over Amorite territory, conquering the entire nation. But they stopped at the Amorite border because of the fortifications. However, they did capture and occupy all the cities of the Amorites including the capital of Heshbon and its surrounding villages (v.25).

d. Note the significance of the victory: a great victory over a celebrated king and army had been achieved (vv.26-31).

 1) The great victory is seen in the conquest of the great city of Heshbon: as stated, it was the capital of the Amorites' king, Sihon (v.26).

 2) The great victory is also seen in the defeat of the great king Sihon: he had formerly conquered Moab, a conquest so great that it had been celebrated by ancient poets (vv.27-31). The thrust of the poem is this: King Sihon had been so powerful that he was able to conquer Moab. Therefore, the people of God must be even more powerful, for they had conquered the great King Sihon. The message was clear: Israel was the super-power of the area, stronger than either the Amorites or the Moabites.

e. The victory was even extended to the major city of Jazer (v.32). Moses sent spies to Jazer and captured the towns surrounding it. He also drove out all the Amorite citizens of that area.

> **Thought 1.** The king of the Amorites launched a surprise, hostile attack against God's people. This is a picture of the world and the enemies of life attacking us as we walk through life. As we march to the promised land of heaven, enemy after enemy will attack us, enemies such as...
>
> - disease
> - accident
> - immorality
> - greed
> - covetousness
> - anger
> - discouragement
> - depression
>
> - failure
> - financial difficulty
> - unemployment
> - lack of purpose
> - loneliness
> - emptiness
> - death

Some enemies are small and weak, amounting to nothing more than minor problems or difficulties. Such enemies are easy to conquer, even by the arm of the flesh. But there are other enemies that are far more powerful and brutal in their attack. These enemies can never be defeated by man, such enemies as a terminal disease, a paralyzing accident, or even death. Such enemies as these can be conquered only by the power of God Himself. Note this: God says that He will protect His people when they are attacked by enemies. No matter the size or power of an enemy, God promises to protect His dear people from their attack and onslaught.

> But not a hair of your head will perish. (Lu. 21:18)
>
> So we say with confidence, "The Lord is my helper; I will not be afraid. What can man do to me?" (He. 13:6)
>
> The LORD will fight for you; you need only to be still. (Ex. 14:14)
>
> I will send my terror ahead of you and throw into confusion every nation you encounter. I will make all your enemies turn their backs and run. (Ex. 23:27)
>
> For the eyes of the LORD range throughout the earth to strengthen those whose hearts are fully committed to him. You have done a foolish thing, and from now on you will be at war. (2 Chr. 16:9)
>
> With him is only the arm of flesh, but with us is the LORD our God to help us and to fight our battles. (2 Chr. 32:8)
>
> For in the day of trouble he will keep me safe in his dwelling; he will hide me in the shelter of his tabernacle and set me high upon a rock. (Ps. 27:5)
>
> The LORD is my strength and my shield; my heart trusts in him, and I am helped. My heart leaps for joy and I will give thanks to him in song. (Ps. 28:7)
>
> In the shelter of your presence you hide them from the intrigues of men; in your dwelling you keep them safe from accusing tongues. (Ps. 31:20)
>
> The angel of the LORD encamps around those who fear him, and he delivers them. (Ps. 34:7)
>
> He will cover you with his feathers, and under his wings you will find refuge; his faithfulness will be your shield and rampart. (Ps. 91:4)
>
> So do not fear, for I am with you; do not be dismayed, for I am your God. I will strengthen you and help you; I will uphold you with my righteous right hand. (Is. 41:10)

5 (21:33-35) **Victory, over Enemies—Military, Victory of—Israel, Military Victory of—Triumph, over Enemies—Og, King of Bashan**: there was the military victory over Og, the king of Bashan. This is a clear picture of victory through the power of God. As the Israelites marched to the promised land, their journey took them along the road toward Bashan. Obviously, the king and his officials felt threatened and feared being overthrown just like the Amorite king Sihon. The picture is dramatic:

a. The king of Og marched his whole army out to attack Israel at Edrei (v.33).

b. But God gave His people strong assurance of victory (v.34). Moses and the people were not to fear their enemy. Total and complete victory was assured. Moreover, God's people were to use the same pattern as before: pursuit and total conquest, just as they had done with Sihon, king of the Amorites. The whole nation of Bashan was to be conquered and the cities destroyed.

c. Note the obedience of God's people and the victory given (v.35). They struck down all the wicked whose *cup was full of sin*—all whose sin had "reached its full measure" (Ge. 15:16; see DEEPER STUDY # 1—Nu. 21:2-3 for more discussion). Once the victory had been achieved, the Israelites occupied the land.

Thought 1. Note verse 34: God told His people not to fear, for He had handed their enemies over to them. He guaranteed total and complete victory over the enemies of His dear people. God promises us victory over the enemies of this life. Total and complete victory is assured. As we march to the promised land of heaven, the enemies of life can be conquered, triumphed over—through the power of God Himself.

> Through you we push back our enemies; through your name we trample our foes. (Ps. 44:5)
>
> Who shall separate us from the love of Christ? Shall trouble or hardship or persecution or famine or nakedness or danger or sword?...No, in all these things we are more than conquerors through him who loved us. For I am convinced that neither death nor life, neither angels nor demons, neither the present nor the future, nor any powers, neither height nor depth, nor anything else in all creation, will be able to separate us from the love of God that is in Christ Jesus our Lord. (Ro. 8:35, 37-39)
>
> No temptation has seized you except what is common to man. And God is faithful; he will not let you be tempted beyond what you can bear. But when you are tempted, he will also provide a way out so that you can stand up under it. (1 Co. 10:13)
>
> Put on the full armor of God so that you can take your stand against the devil's schemes. For our struggle is not against flesh and blood, but against the rulers, against the authorities, against the powers of this dark world and against the spiritual forces of evil in the heavenly realms. Therefore put on the full armor of God, so that when the day of evil comes, you may be able to stand your ground, and after you have done everything, to stand. (Ep. 6:11-13)
>
> For everyone born of God overcomes the world. This is the victory that has overcome the world, even our faith. Who is it that overcomes the world? Only he who believes that Jesus is the Son of God. (1 Jn. 5:4-5)

NUMBERS 21:1-35

DEEPER STUDY # 5 (Nu. 21:33-35) **Edrei, City of**: it was located in the tribal territory of Naphtali, near Kedesh and Hazor (Jos. 19:37). (See Map—Nu. 33:5-49, end of commentary.) The Hebrew meaning of Edrei is *mighty*. Edrei	was a fortified city. It was the place where Israel won the victory over Og, king of Bashan. **See other Scripture references for study:** **De. 1:4; De. 3:1; De. 3:10; Jos. 12:4; Jos. 13:12; Jos. 13:31; Jos. 19:37**

TYPES, SYMBOLS, AND PICTURES
(Numbers 21:1-31)

Historical Term	Type or Picture (Scriptural Basis for Each)	Life Application for Today's Believer	Biblical Application
Bronze Snake Nu. 21:4-9	*The Bronze snake is a type of Christ the Savior who delivers us from perishing.* **The LORD said to Moses, "Make a snake and put it up on a pole; anyone who is bitten can look at it and live." (Nu. 21:8)**	This is one of the great symbols of Jesus Christ in the Scripture, of His being hung upon the cross in order to deliver His people from perishing. This is exactly what Christ Himself said (Jn. 3:14-16). Jesus Christ has been lifted up as the Savior of the world. God lifted up Christ just as the snake was lifted up, as a symbol of deliverance. Any person who looks upon Christ and believes in Him will be delivered—saved.	*Just as Moses lifted up the snake in the desert, so the Son of Man must be lifted up, that everyone who believes in him may have eternal life. For God so loved the world that he gave his one and only Son, that whoever believes in him shall not perish but have eternal life. (Jn. 3:14-16)* *I tell you the truth, whoever hears my word and believes him who sent me has eternal life and will not be condemned; he has crossed over from death to life. (Jn. 5:24)* *Jesus said to her, "I am the resurrection and the life. He who believes in me will live, even though he dies." (Jn. 11:25)* *I have come into the world as a light, so that no one who believes in me should stay in darkness. (Jn. 12:46)* *But these are written that you may believe that Jesus is the Christ, the Son of God, and that by believing you may have life in his name. (Jn. 20:31)* *That if you confess with your mouth, "Jesus is Lord," and believe in your heart that God raised him from the dead, you will be saved. For it is with your heart that you believe and are justified, and it is with your mouth that you confess and are saved. (Ro. 10:9-10)*
Attack upon Israel *(by the Amorites)* Nu. 21:21-32	*An attack upon Israel [by the Amorites] is a picture of the world and the enemies of life attacking as we walk through this life.* **But Sihon would not let Israel pass through his territory. He mustered his entire army and marched out into**	Some enemies are small and weak, amounting to nothing more than minor problems or difficulties. Such enemies are easy to conquer, even by the arm of the flesh. But there are other enemies that are far more powerful and brutal in their attack. These enemies can never be defeated by man,	*But not a hair of your head will perish. (Lu. 21:18)* *So we say with confidence, "The Lord is my helper; I will not be afraid. What can man do to me?" (He. 13:6)* *The Lord will fight for you; you need only to be still. (Ex. 14:14)*

Numbers 21:1-35

Historical Term	Type or Picture (Scriptural Basis for Each)	Life Application for Today's Believer	Biblical Application
	the desert against Israel. When he reached Jahaz, he fought with Israel. Israel, however, put him to the sword and took over his land from the Arnon to the Jabbok, but only as far as the Ammonites, because their border was fortified. (Nu. 21:23-24)	such enemies as a terminal disease, a paralyzing accident, or even death. Such enemies as these can be conquered only by the power of God Himself. Note this: God says that He will protect His people when they are attacked by enemies. No matter the size or power of an enemy, God promises to protect His dear people from their attack and onslaught.	*I will send my terror ahead of you and throw into confusion every nation you encounter. I will make all your enemies turn their backs and run. (Ex. 23:27)* *For the eyes of the Lord range throughout the earth to strengthen those whose hearts are fully committed to him. You have done a foolish thing, and from now on you will be at war. (2 Chr. 16:9)* *With him is only the arm of flesh, but with us is the Lord our God to help us and to fight our battles." And the people gained confidence from what Hezekiah the king of Judah said. (2 Chr. 32:8)* *For in the day of trouble he will keep me safe in his dwelling; he will hide me in the shelter of his tabernacle and set me high upon a rock. (Ps. 27:5)* *The Lord is my strength and my shield; my heart trusts in him, and I am helped. My heart leaps for joy and I will give thanks to him in song. (Ps. 28:7)*

NUMBERS 22:1-41

CHAPTER 22

H. Event 8—the Story of Balaam, His Donkey, & His Three Encounters with God: A Picture of the Unseen, Unknown Attempts by the Powers of Darkness to Defeat God's People, 22:1-41

1. **The dramatic background to the encounters with God: A false belief in divination**
   a. The Israelites were poised to enter the promised land^{DS1}
   b. The king of Moab heard about Israel
      1) Heard they were nearby & about their military exploits
      2) Was terrified, filled with dread because of the Israelites
   c. The king formed an alliance with the leaders of Midian: Feared Israel would devour everything just like an ox devours grass
   d. The king sought to curse & defeat Israel by pagan divination: He sent for Balaam, a famous diviner with an international reputation^{DS2}
      1) Related how a horde of people had arrived from Egypt & settled next to him
      2) Wanted Balaam to put a curse on them so he could defeat them in battle
      3) Stated that he believed strongly in the divination powers of Balaam: The people Balaam blessed were blessed, & those he cursed were cursed

2. **The 1st encounter of Balaam with God: A man who earned money dishonestly (2 Pe. 2:15)**
   a. The officials from both Moab & Midian traveled to see Balaam with the fee for divination
   b. The response of Balaam was immediate: He invited the officials to spend the night while he sought God's will
   c. The 1st encounter with God
      1) God asked who the men were visiting him
      2) Balaam identified them as officials from Balak, the king of Edom, & related their request for a curse to be put upon Israel

Then the Israelites traveled to the plains of Moab and camped along the Jordan across from Jericho.
2 Now Balak son of Zippor saw all that Israel had done to the Amorites,
3 And Moab was terrified because there were so many people. Indeed, Moab was filled with dread because of the Israelites.
4 The Moabites said to the elders of Midian, "This horde is going to lick up everything around us, as an ox licks up the grass of the field." So Balak son of Zippor, who was king of Moab at that time,
5 Sent messengers to summon Balaam son of Beor, who was at Pethor, near the River, in his native land. Balak said: "A people has come out of Egypt; they cover the face of the land and have settled next to me.
6 Now come and put a curse on these people, because they are too powerful for me. Perhaps then I will be able to defeat them and drive them out of the country. For I know that those you bless are blessed, and those you curse are cursed."
7 The elders of Moab and Midian left, taking with them the fee for divination. When they came to Balaam, they told him what Balak had said.
8 "Spend the night here," Balaam said to them, "and I will bring you back the answer the LORD gives me." So the Moabite princes stayed with him.
9 God came to Balaam and asked, "Who are these men with you?"
10 Balaam said to God, "Balak son of Zippor, king of Moab, sent me this message:
11 'A people that has come out of Egypt covers the face of the land. Now come and put a curse on them for me. Perhaps then I will be able to fight them and drive them away.' "
12 But God said to Balaam, "Do not go with them. You must not put a curse on those people, because they are blessed."
13 The next morning Balaam got up and said to Balak's princes, "Go back to your own country, for the LORD has refused to let me go with you."
14 So the Moabite princes returned to Balak and said, "Balaam refused to come with us."
15 Then Balak sent other princes, more numerous and more distinguished than the first.
16 They came to Balaam and said: "This is what Balak son of Zippor says: Do not let anything keep you from coming to me,
17 Because I will reward you handsomely and do whatever you say. Come and put a curse on these people for me."
18 But Balaam answered them, "Even if Balak gave me his palace filled with silver and gold, I could not do anything great or small to go beyond the command of the LORD my God.
19 Now stay here tonight as the others did, and I will find out what else the LORD will tell me."
20 That night God came to Balaam and said, "Since these men have come to summon you, go with them, but do only what I tell you."
21 Balaam got up in the morning, saddled his donkey, and went with the princes of Moab.
22 But God was very angry when he went, and the angel of the LORD stood in the road to oppose him. Balaam was riding on his donkey, and his two servants were with him.
23 When the donkey saw the angel of the LORD standing in the road with a drawn sword in his hand, she turned off the road into a field. Balaam beat

      3) God's warning to Balaam
         • Was not to go with them
         • Was not to curse Israel
         • The reason: They were God's people—blessed
   d. The clear-cut response of Balaam to the confrontation with God
      1) He refused to go with the officials
      2) The officials returned & related Balaam's refusal to the king

3. **The 2nd encounter of Balaam with God: A man who would do anything for money (Jude 11)**
   a. The king tried a more urgent request: He sent other officials—a larger number & more distinguished—with a far more appealing offer to Balaam
      1) He would reward him well
      2) He would do anything
      3) He was desperate: Begged Balaam to come & put a curse on Israel
   b. The response of Balaam: Revealed a spirit enslaved by greed
      1) He declared that nothing could change his mind, not to go against God's will (not even for a palace filled with silver & gold)
      2) He invited the officials to spend the night while he sought God (just in case God would let him go)
   c. The 2nd encounter with God: Gave Balaam over to his greed (Ro. 1:28-32)
      1) Gave permission to go
      2) But warned him: Had better do only what God told him
   d. The response of Balaam to the confrontation: He went with the officials (let greed consume him, v.12)

4. **The 3rd encounter of Balaam with God (the story of the donkey): The anger of God over greed & the signs of His anger**
   a. The angel of the Lord stood in the road to block Balaam's way
      1) The donkey saw the angel of the LORD blocking the road with a drawn sword: Turned off the road into a field

NUMBERS 22:1-41

2) Balaam beat her to get her back on the road
b. The angel of the LORD blocked the path again, a narrow path with walls on both sides
  1) The donkey again saw the angel of the LORD: Tried to squeeze by & crushed Balaam's foot
  2) Balaam again beat the animal
c. The angel of the LORD then moved ahead to a place so narrow that the donkey could not get by
  1) The donkey saw the angel of the LORD & just lay down under Balaam
  2) Balaam, in anger, beat her with his staff
d. The LORD opened the donkey's mouth & the animal miraculously, shockingly spoke to Balaam (see 2 Pe. 2:16)
  1) The donkey complained of Balaam's cruelty
  2) Balaam—in a fit of rage—wished he had a sword to kill the animal: Because it had made a fool of him
  3) The donkey reasoned with Balaam
    • That she was Balaam's property
    • That she had always served Balaam well
    • That she had never behaved like this before
  4) Balaam agreed
e. The LORD opened Balaam's eyes
  1) Balaam saw the angel of the LORD standing with his sword drawn (a symbol of God's anger, a strong warning): He fell face down on the ground
  2) The angel of the LORD confronted Balaam
	her to get her back on the road.
	24 Then the angel of the LORD stood in a narrow path between two vineyards, with walls on both sides.
	25 When the donkey saw the angel of the LORD, she pressed close to the wall, crushing Balaam's foot against it. So he beat her again.
	26 Then the angel of the LORD moved on ahead and stood in a narrow place where there was no room to turn, either to the right or to the left.
	27 When the donkey saw the angel of the LORD, she lay down under Balaam, and he was angry and beat her with his staff.
	28 Then the LORD opened the donkey's mouth, and she said to Balaam, "What have I done to you to make you beat me these three times?"
	29 Balaam answered the donkey, "You have made a fool of me! If I had a sword in my hand, I would kill you right now."
	30 The donkey said to Balaam, "Am I not your own donkey, which you have always ridden, to this day? Have I been in the habit of doing this to you?" "No," he said.
	31 Then the LORD opened Balaam's eyes, and he saw the angel of the LORD standing in the road with his sword drawn. So he bowed low and fell facedown.
	32 The angel of the LORD asked him, "Why have you beaten your donkey these
		three times? I have come here to oppose you because your path is a reckless one before me.
		33 The donkey saw me and turned away from me these three times. If she had not turned away, I would certainly have killed you by now, but I would have spared her."
		34 Balaam said to the angel of the LORD, "I have sinned. I did not realize you were standing in the road to oppose me. Now if you are displeased, I will go back."
		35 The angel of the LORD said to Balaam, "Go with the men, but speak only what I tell you." So Balaam went with the princes of Balak.
		36 When Balak heard that Balaam was coming, he went out to meet him at the Moabite town on the Arnon border, at the edge of his territory.
		37 Balak said to Balaam, "Did I not send you an urgent summons? Why didn't you come to me? Am I really not able to reward you?"
		38 "Well, I have come to you now," Balaam replied. "But can I say just anything? I must speak only what God puts in my mouth."
		39 Then Balaam went with Balak to Kiriath Huzoth.
		40 Balak sacrificed cattle and sheep, and gave some to Balaam and the princes who were with him.
		41 The next morning Balak took Balaam up to Bamoth Baal, and from there he saw part of the people.
			• Rebuked him for mistreatment of an animal
			• Condemned him because of his reckless, stubborn heart & resistance to God
			• Warned him that God would have taken his life by now because of his resistance if the donkey had not stopped
			
			3) Balaam confessed his sin & offered to return (but did not repent)
			
			4) The response of the angel of the LORD: Gave Balaam over to his greed—he could go, but he must speak only what God said
			5. The effect of the encounters & warnings upon Balaam
			a. The excitement of king Balak at Balaam's coming
			  1) He traveled all the way to the border to meet Balaam
			  2) He expressed disappointment at Balaam's refusal of the first request—especially in light of the offer to be so well rewarded
			b. The effect of the encounters with the LORD & His warnings: Balaam replied that He had now come, but he could speak only the message God gave him
			c. The king celebrated Balaam's coming
			  1) He offered pagan sacrifices to his gods: Balaam participated with Balak
			  2) He took Balaam up to Bamoth Baal, some hill or high place where Baal was worshipped: To scan the camp of Israel

DIVISION III

THE FORTY LONG YEARS OF WILDERNESS WANDERINGS: A PICTURE OF THE BELIEVER'S PILGRIMAGE THROUGH THIS WORLD AS HE PREPARES TO ENTER THE PROMISED LAND, 15:1–25:18

H. Event 8—the Story of Balaam, His Donkey, and His Three Encounters with God: A Picture of the Unseen, Unknown Attempts by the Powers of Darkness to Defeat God's People, 22:1-41

(22:1-41) **Introduction—Spiritual World, Warfare of—Evil Spirits, Work of—Occult, World of—Sorcery, Evil of—Psychics, Evil of—Diviners, Evil of—Darkness, Powers of, Described**: there is an unseen warfare going on behind the events of world history. This warfare is conducted by the evil spirits of darkness, evil spirits who serve under a supreme power that is identified in the Holy Scripture as Satan or the devil. In deep malice and wrath against

God, these evil forces try their best, when possible, to frustrate the plan of God for this world. Evil spirits seek to cut the heart of God because of God's judgment against their arrogance and rejection of Him. The way they seek to hurt God is by taking over the normal desires and the obsessive passions of men, using them to destroy people. They use the passions that enslave people, passions such as...

- greed
- drugs
- alcohol
- gluttony
- lust
- cravings
- vulgarity
- profanity
- pornography
- immorality
- abuse
- killing
- bestiality

If the curtain were rolled back between earth and heaven, man would easily see what lies behind all the sin and evil, all the conflicts and struggles of this world. He would clearly see a horde of evil spirits seeking to cut the heart of God by deceiving people, by turning them away from God (see outline and notes—Lu. 8:26-39 for more discussion). One of the ways used by these evil spirits is the world of the occult, the world of the false prophet, the diviner, the sorcerer, the psychic, the palm-reader, the fortune-teller, the astrologer, and a host of others. The leaders of the occult advertise and cry out for the attention of people, claiming that they know the future, can meet needs, and can bring blessings into the lives of people. Some even go so far as to claim that they can control and alter the future, that they can bring blessings upon those whom they bless and cursings upon those whom they curse. Under the power of darkness and spiritual wickedness in high places, they mislead people and cause them to turn away from the only living and true God, the LORD God Himself (Jehovah, Yahweh). The world of the occult is a world controlled by evil spirits who are set upon destroying the lives of people and cutting the heart of God. (See outline and notes—Ac. 16:16-17; Re. 12:3-4; 12:9 for more discussion.)

> **For our struggle is not against flesh and blood, but against the rulers, against the authorities, against the powers of this dark world and against the spiritual forces of evil in the heavenly realms. (Ep. 6:12)**

Remember, Israel is camped in the plains of Moab by the Jordan River across from the great city of Jericho. The present Scripture is an event that takes place totally unknown to the Israelites. It is a picture of the unseen, unknown attempts by the powers of darkness and spiritual wickedness in high places—an attempt to destroy the people of God in order to break the heart of God. Keep in mind that Israel is totally unaware of what is happening. But not God. God knows, and God protects His people. He will not allow any person to touch His people, to call a curse of judgment and destruction down upon them. Judgment and destruction are in His hands and no one else's. To curse His people with judgment and destruction will never happen, never be allowed. This is the story of this Scripture: *Event 8—the Story of Balaam, His Donkey, and His Three Encounters with God: A Picture of the Unseen, Unknown Attempts by the Powers of Darkness to Defeat God's People*, 22:1-41.

1. The dramatic background to the encounters with God: a false belief in divination (vv.1-6).
2. The 1st encounter of Balaam with God: a man who earned money dishonestly (vv.7-14).
3. The 2nd encounter of Balaam with God: a man who would do anything for money (vv.15-21).
4. The 3rd encounter of Balaam with God (the story of the donkey): the anger of God over greed and the signs of His anger (vv.22-35).
5. The effect of the encounters and warnings upon Balaam (vv.36-41).

1 (22:1-6) **Divination—Sorcery—Occult—Balaam—Balak**: the background to Balaam's encounters with God was dramatic. A false belief in the world of divination, sorcery, and the occult is seen.

a. The Israelites were poised to enter the promised land (v.1). At long last, the Israelites had reached the plains of Moab and camped along the Jordan River right across from the great city of Jericho. From this vantage point, the promised land was in plain view and God's people would soon lay claim to the wonderful inheritance God had promised them. Picture the excitement of the people as they sat around their campfires by night: the children playing, running, and dancing around; the adults sharing their joys and plans for the land they are soon to inherit and the homes they are to build. Excitement, joy, anticipation, great expectation—all the hopes and dreams of a people who had been freed from slavery and were about to return home—were wrapped up in the moment of these days. But behind this scene of great excitement and joy, another dramatic plot was being played out. The unseen, unknown powers of darkness were scheming to destroy God's people.

b. The king of Moab had heard about Israel, that they were camped nearby in the plains of Moab (vv.2-3). He of course had also heard about the military exploits of Israel against the Amorites and the kingdom of Bashan. This news struck fear in king Balak and his people. Note what Scripture says: they were terrified, greatly distressed, and filled with dread because of the Israelites. The word *terrified* (gur) means a dreadful, horrifying fear. It has the idea of being frightened or terrified out of one's mind. But even this does not fully describe the depth of fear they were experiencing. Note the word *dread* (qus): this means a sickening, nauseating, debilitating, incapacitating, hopeless, and helpless fear. The king and his officials saw no way to stop the march of the Israelites. If he launched a military operation against the Israelites, he would be defeated and his nation utterly destroyed. A surprise military action was therefore out of the question. Some other way had to be devised to defeat God's people. No doubt after days of consultation and consideration of contingency plans, the king and his official came up with a devious plot. To modern ears within industrial societies, their devious plot may sound strange, but divination, sorcery, and the world of the occult were a part of everyday society among pagan people in the ancient world. To be honest, the world of the occult—diviners, psychics, witch doctors, astrologers, and many others—is just as active today as ever.

c. The king and his advisors formed an alliance with the leaders of Midian (v.4). Note how Balak described the strength of Israel to the Midianites: Israel was so strong and powerful that she was just like an ox that devours grass. It should be noted that this particular plot against God's people by these two nations would fail. However, a later plot by Moab and Midian would succeed, and Balaam—this false prophet—would again be right in the middle of the plot. In fact, he would actually devise the plan and scheme that would overthrow the children of God (Nu. 25:1-18). Now note the devious and strange sounding plot.

d. The king (in alliance with the Midianites) sought to curse and defeat Israel by pagan divination or sorcery (vv.4-6). The king sent messengers to secure the help of Balaam, a famous diviner or sorcerer with an international reputation. The summons sent to the false prophet spelled out exactly what the king wanted:

⇒ He related how a horde of people had arrived from Egypt and settled next to him (v.5).

⇒ He wanted Balaam to come and put a curse on them so he could defeat them in battle (v.6).

⇒ He stated that he believed strongly in the divination or sorcery powers of Balaam; that is, the people Balaam blessed were blessed, and those he cursed were cursed (v.6).

The king was desperate: the Israelites were too powerful for him to fight without the help of the "gods." There was no hope for victory unless the gods helped him by cursing the Israelites and blessing his own military forces. Consequently, he summoned one of the famous diviners or psychics of that day and time. Along with so many others down through history and even up until this day, he believed that the gods had gifted some persons who could pronounce cursings or blessings upon people. He believed if Balaam could just pronounce a curse upon the Israelites, either some supernatural event would wipe them out or else he would be able to defeat them in battle.

Thought 1. Psychics, fortune-tellers, palm-readers, sorcerers, diviners, psychics, self-proclaimed prophets of new-age movements or of the zodiac—the whole world of the occult—have all been sought by people down through the centuries of human history. People want to know their destiny, what the future holds. They want the blessings of the gods that be, or else they want some enemy cursed. They want only good things to happen to them, not bad things. They want good experiences, not bad experiences. They want plenty, not the bare necessities. They want more, not less. They want acceptance, not rejection. They want to be highly esteemed, not put down. They want position and power, not servitude and enslavement.

For these reasons and for so many more, people seek the leaders of the occult. They seek the help of any person who claims to have the power of astrology, the power to read the stars, the zodiac, or any other medium. If a person claims to have the answer to the future or to people's problems, they flock to him. But Scripture is clear: the world of the occult is a world of sin and evil. Man is to have nothing—absolutely nothing—to do with the world of the occult.

> Once when we were going to the place of prayer, we were met by a slave girl who had a spirit by which she predicted the future. She earned a great deal of money for her owners by fortune-telling. This girl followed Paul and the rest of us, shouting, "These men are servants of the Most High God, who are telling you the way to be saved." She kept this up for many days. Finally Paul became so troubled that he turned around and said to the spirit, "In the name of Jesus Christ I command you to come out of her!" At that moment the spirit left her. When the owners of the slave girl realized that their hope of making money was gone, they seized Paul and Silas and dragged them into the marketplace to face the authorities. (Ac. 16:16-19)

> The acts of the sinful nature are obvious: sexual immorality, impurity and debauchery; idolatry and witchcraft; hatred, discord, jealousy, fits of rage, selfish ambition, dissensions, factions and envy; drunkenness, orgies, and the like. I warn you, as I did before, that those who live like this will not inherit the kingdom of God. (Ga. 5:19-21)

> But the cowardly, the unbelieving, the vile, the murderers, the sexually immoral, those who practice magic arts, the idolaters and all liars—their place will be in the fiery lake of burning sulfur. This is the second death. (Re. 21:8)

> When you enter the land the LORD your God is giving you, do not learn to imitate the detestable ways of the nations there. Let no one be found among you who sacrifices his son or daughter in the fire, who practices divination or sorcery, interprets omens, engages in witchcraft, or casts spells, or who is a medium or spiritist or who consults the dead. Anyone who does these things is detestable to the LORD, and because of these detestable practices the LORD your God will drive out those nations before you. You must be blameless before the LORD your God. (De. 18:9-13)

> They sacrificed their sons and daughters in the fire. They practiced divination and sorcery and sold themselves to do evil in the eyes of the LORD, provoking him to anger. (2 K. 17:17)

> He [King Manasseh] sacrificed his own son in the fire, practiced sorcery and divination, and consulted mediums and spiritists. He did much evil in the eyes of the LORD, provoking him to anger. (2 K. 21:6)

> Both of these will overtake you in a moment, on a single day: loss of children and widowhood. They will come upon you in full measure, in spite of your many sorceries and all your potent spells. (Is. 47:9)

> Now, son of man, set your face against the daughters of your people who prophesy out of their own imagination. Prophesy against them and say, 'This is what the Sovereign LORD says: Woe to the women who sew magic charms on all their wrists and make veils of various lengths for their heads in order to ensnare people. Will you ensnare the lives of my people but preserve your own?...Because you disheartened the righteous with your lies, when I had brought them no grief, and because you encouraged the wicked not to turn from their evil ways and so save their lives, therefore you will no longer see false visions or practice divination. I will save my people from your hands. And then you will know that I am the LORD. (Eze. 13:17-18, 22-23)

> I will destroy your witchcraft and you will no longer cast spells. (Mi. 5:12)

> The idols speak deceit, diviners see visions that lie; they tell dreams that are

false, they give comfort in vain. Therefore the people wander like sheep oppressed for lack of a shepherd. (Zec. 10:2)

But now we call the arrogant blessed. Certainly the evildoers prosper, and even those who challenge God escape. (Mal. 3:15)

2 (22:7-14) **Encounter, with God—Confrontation, with God—Warning, of God—Balaam, Warned by God—Money, Earned Dishonestly—Divination, Evil of—Sorcery, Evil of**: the first encounter of Balaam with God was a warning. This false prophet, this diviner, needed a severe warning. He was a man who earned money the wrong way, by dishonesty.

> They have left the straight way and wandered off to follow the way of Balaam son of Beor, who loved the wages of wickedness [by divination, sorcery]. (2 Pe. 2:15)

He earned a living by playing off the fears, sufferings, and hopes of people—claiming to have the answer to whatever they wanted or needed. He could bless and a person would be blessed, or he could curse and a person would be cursed. He could help people, give them exactly what they needed. But for his help he was to receive a fee, obviously a large fee because of his international reputation. God condemns diviners, sorcerers, mystics, or anyone else who preys upon people seeking direction or help.

a. The officials from both Moab and Midian traveled to see Balaam. Special attention is called to the fact that they took with them a large *fee for divination* (v.7). This fact suggests that Balaam had a heart consumed with greed, the desire for money and possessions—the things of this world (1 Jn. 2:15-16).

b. The response of Balaam was immediate: he invited the officials to spend the night while he sought God's will (v.8). Note that he was going to seek God during the night, while the others were asleep.

c. Note the first confrontation with God. Balaam got the surprise of his life: shockingly, astoundingly, the LORD Himself (Jehovah, Yahweh) confronted this false prophet, this seer, this diviner, this psychic, this sorcerer.

1) God asked who the men were visiting Balaam (v.9).
2) No doubt in shock, Balaam identified them as officials from Balak, the king of Edom. He related their request for a curse to be put upon Israel so that the king might fight and drive them out of his land (vv.10-11).
3) Upon hearing the word "curse," God immediately issued a strong warning to Balaam:
   ⇒ He was not to go with the messengers to the king.
   ⇒ He was not under any circumstance to "curse" Israel.
   ⇒ The reason was clearly stated: they were God's people, especially blessed by God Himself (v.12).

God loves His dear people, for they bear His name and stand as a strong testimony to His name. They live righteous and godly lives before God, proclaiming the absolute necessity for man to live righteously and godly. God loves His dear people because they are the heirs of the Abrahamic covenant, the great covenant God made with His people through Abraham:
⇒ the promise of the promised seed
⇒ the promise of the promised land (see outline and notes—Ge. 12:1-3 for more discussion)

d. The response of Balaam to the confrontation with God was decisive, clear-cut: he refused to go with the officials, and the officials returned to relate the refusal to the king (vv.13-14).

Thought 1. God's people are very special to Him, a very special treasure (Ex. 19:5). What makes them so special is God's call: the fact that He has called and set them apart to be His followers. Simply stated, genuine believers live holy and righteous lives before God. They seek with all their hearts to live lives...

- of morality and purity
- of honesty and fairness
- of truthfulness and integrity
- of giving and sharing
- of service and ministry
- of healing and helping
- of encouragement and consolation
- of strengthening and equipping
- of generosity and good will
- of supporting and building up
- of preaching and teaching
- of witnessing and sharing Christ

For these reasons and for many others, God loves His dear people. He has called and appointed them to be His witnesses upon this earth, just as He had the Israelites. No person can call upon God to curse His people. Once God has called a person and set that person apart to become a member of His people, that person cannot be cursed. He is destined to live eternally—some day out in the future—with God Himself, face-to-face. The believer is God's heritage, God's treasure, God's chosen, God's elect, God's heir, God's adopted son or daughter—very, very special to God!

> You did not choose me, but I chose you and appointed you to go and bear fruit—fruit that will last. Then the Father will give you whatever you ask in my name. (Jn. 15:16)

> Who will bring any charge against those whom God has chosen? It is God who justifies. Who is he that condemns? Christ Jesus, who died—more than that, who was raised to life—is at the right hand of God and is also interceding for us. (Ro. 8:33-34)

> But when the time had fully come, God sent his Son, born of a woman, born under law, to redeem those under law, that we might receive the full rights of sons. Because you are sons, God sent the Spirit of his Son into our hearts, the Spirit who calls out, "Abba, Father." (Ga. 4:4-6)

> For he chose us in him before the creation of the world to be holy and blameless in his sight. In love (Ep. 1:4)

> Blessed is the man who perseveres under trial, because when he has stood the test, he will receive the crown of life that God

has promised to those who love him. (Js. 1:12)

How great is the love the Father has lavished on us, that we should be called children of God! And that is what we are! The reason the world does not know us is that it did not know him. (1 Jn. 3:1)

Now if you obey me fully and keep my covenant, then out of all nations you will be my treasured possession. Although the whole earth is mine. (Ex. 19:5)

3 (22:15-21) **Encounter, with God—Greed—Money, Lust for—Judgment, Judicial—Judicial Judgment—Balaam**: the second encounter of Balaam with God was stunning and revealing: it revealed a double-minded, hypocritical, and greedy heart. This encounter with God exposed a man who would do anything for money.

Woe to them! They have taken the way of Cain; they have rushed for profit into Balaam's error; they have been destroyed in Korah's rebellion. (Jude 11).

a. The king was not going to give up, for he was desperate. He tried a more urgent request with Balaam: he sent other officials, a larger number and more distinguished. Note that he also sent a far more appealing offer:
⇒ The king would pay him well, in essence, pay Balaam whatever he desired.
⇒ The king would do anything, bestow whatever honor Balaam desired.
⇒ The king was desperate: he begged Balaam to come and put a curse on Israel (v.17).

Note how the king appealed to the greed and covetousness of the human heart. He offered this false prophet, this diviner, this sorcerer, this psychic anything he wanted—any amount of money and any honor. He appealed to his greed, his pride, and his ambition. The king was desperate: this diviner must come and put a curse on God's people so that he could defeat them and drive them out of his country (see v.6).

b. The response of Balaam revealed a spirit that was totally enslaved by greed (vv.18-19). Note how Balaam's actions were for appearance only. He only seemed to be resisting the summons and offer of the king.
1) Balaam declared that nothing could change his mind, not to go against God's will. He would not even go against God's will for a palace filled with silver and gold (v.18). Remember, God had already revealed His will: the false prophet was not to go (v.12). He knew exactly what God wanted him to do: he was not to curse Israel. They were God's people, followers of the only living and true God. Therefore, there was no chance that God was going to curse His people nor allow anyone else to put a true curse upon them. No one would ever be allowed to defeat His people nor to curse His people to the judgment of death. Only the LORD God Himself (Jehovah, Yahweh) had the power to curse and judge people to death. No one else had this power. Consequently, there was no chance that God was going to judge His own people, those who sought to follow after Him. Moreover, there was no chance that He was going to allow Balaam or anyone else to curse His dear people. All this Balaam already knew. God had revealed it to him, forbidding him from going and attempting to curse God's people. But note how wavering, double-minded, and hypocritical Balaam was.
2) He told the officials to stay and spend the night while he sought God, just in case God would give him another message and allow him to go (v.19). This shows a strong, strong urge and intention to accept the offer. This was a terrible reflection upon God, as though God were double-minded and would change His mind, allowing him to go and put a curse upon the people of God. The heart and mind of this man were so corrupt and twisted that he played the role of a hypocrite, of a double-minded man himself. Deceiving and misleading the officials were nothing to him. He would not go against God's will even for a palace filled with silver and gold, but he would take the night to seek God just in case God would let him go. He was play-acting with the name of God, preying upon the needs, the hopes, and the dreams of people—all for money and profit. Obviously to him, God was little higher than man himself who wavered back and forth, changing his mind day by day. Simply stated, he already knew God's will. He knew that he was not to go, for God had already told him that he was not to go nor to put a curse upon the precious people of God.

c. Note the second encounter with God: God gave Balaam over to his greed, gave him up to the lusts of his own heart (Ro. 1:28-32). Balaam's heart was set on going. He lusted to go, craved after the wealth and honors offered by the king. The lust and greed had enslaved his heart. His mind had already made the decision: he was going. But note what happened when he got alone that night: God came to Balaam and gave him a severe warning: "Since these men had come to summon him—since he had determined to go with them—he could go. But he had better do only what God told him" (v.20). The decision to rebel against God by going was made by Balaam. The permission to allow Balaam to follow through was given by God. Balaam was permitted to go, but he was warned and warned severely: he must do only what God told him to do.

d. The response of Balaam to the confrontation with God was just what would be expected from a greedy heart: he got up in the morning and went with the officials. He still had the freedom to obey God, the ability to choose not to go, not to put a curse upon God's people. But the choice was made, driven by the consuming passion of greed, the lust after money and honor.

Thought 1. Greed and covetousness are wrong; they are sin before God and man. A covetous, greedy person violates the very commandment of God Himself. Moreover, the covetous, greedy person causes suffering by not sharing and distributing to those who are in need. And sometimes, by stealing from the needy and poor, covetousness and greed consume a person, eating away at his spirit and life. A greedy, covetous person actually falls into many foolish and hurtful passions, doing many foolish and hurtful things. Greed and covetousness actually plunge men into destruction and doom.

So Judas threw the money into the temple and left. Then he went away and hanged himself. (Mt. 27:5)

NUMBERS 22:1-41

Then he said to them, "Watch out! Be on your guard against all kinds of greed; a man's life does not consist in the abundance of his possessions." (Lu. 12:15)

Put to death, therefore, whatever belongs to your earthly nature: sexual immorality, impurity, lust, evil desires and greed, which is idolatry. (Col. 3:5)

People who want to get rich fall into temptation and a trap and into many foolish and harmful desires that plunge men into ruin and destruction. For the love of money is a root of all kinds of evil. Some people, eager for money, have wandered from the faith and pierced themselves with many griefs. (1 Ti. 6:9-10)

Your gold and silver are corroded. Their corrosion will testify against you and eat your flesh like fire. You have hoarded wealth in the last days. Look! The wages you failed to pay the workmen who mowed your fields are crying out against you. The cries of the harvesters have reached the ears of the Lord Almighty. (Jas. 5:3-4)

"You shall not covet your neighbor's house. You shall not covet your neighbor's wife, or his manservant or maidservant, his ox or donkey, or anything that belongs to your neighbor." (Ex. 20:17)

A greedy man brings trouble to his family, but he who hates bribes will live. (Pr. 15:27)

Better a little with righteousness than much gain with injustice. (Pr. 16:8)

A fortune made by a lying tongue is a fleeting vapor and a deadly snare. (Pr. 21:6)

He who oppresses the poor to increase his wealth and he who gives gifts to the rich—both come to poverty. (Pr. 22:16)

Whoever loves money never has money enough; whoever loves wealth is never satisfied with his income. This too is meaningless. (Ec. 5:10)

Like a partridge that hatches eggs it did not lay is the man who gains riches by unjust means. When his life is half gone, they will desert him, and in the end he will prove to be a fool. (Je. 17:11)

"Woe to him who builds his palace by unrighteousness, his upper rooms by injustice, making his countrymen work for nothing, not paying them for their labor." (Je. 22:13)

My people come to you, as they usually do, and sit before you to listen to your words, but they do not put them into practice. With their mouths they express devotion, but their hearts are greedy for unjust gain. (Eze. 33:31)

They covet fields and seize them, and houses, and take them. They defraud a man of his home, a fellowman of his inheritance. (Mi. 2:2)

"Woe to him who builds his realm by unjust gain to set his nest on high, to escape the clutches of ruin! You have plotted the ruin of many peoples, shaming your own house and forfeiting your life." (Hab. 2:9-10)

4 (22:22-35) **Greed, Results—Anger, of God—God, Anger of—Balaam, Story of the Donkey—Encounter, with God—Money, Love of**: the third encounter of Balaam with God aroused the anger of God. This is the story of Balaam and the donkey, a story that reveals the anger of God over greed. Simply stated, God used the donkey as a sign of His anger against the greed of this false prophet. God used the donkey as a warning of judgment if the false prophet did not do exactly what God instructed. This is a dramatic lesson that shows God's anger and displeasure with the world of the occult. God stands opposed to any false prophet, diviner, sorcerer, psychic, palm-reader, fortune-teller, or astrologer. God is angry with any person who uses the fears and hopes of people to gain profit or money. The leaders of the occult world are stumblingblocks to people: they lead people into a false belief, away from the only living and true LORD (Jehovah, Yahweh). But even more terrible than this, they doom people to an eternity of separation from God in the judgment to come. This is the reason God is angry with the world of the occult, the reason He is going to severely judge the world of the occult. This was certainly part of the reason God spoke through the donkey to Balaam. In this dramatic event of the donkey speaking, God was warning Balaam, giving him a severe warning: he must do exactly what God says. This dramatic experience emphasized the point to Balaam, gave him an experience that he could not ignore. Note exactly what Scripture says: God's anger was aroused because Balaam went (v.22). Balaam had known exactly what God's will was; nevertheless, he ignored God and went anyway. But this one thing God determined: this false prophet was not going to curse the dear people of God.

a. In anger, the angel of the LORD stood in the road to block Balaam's way (vv.22-23). This blind, false prophet was so blinded by his covetousness and greed that he could not see the angel of the LORD. But the donkey saw the angel standing with a drawn sword in the middle of the road. Frightened, the donkey turned off the road into a field. Balaam beat the donkey to get her back on the road.

b. But again, the angel of the LORD blocked the path, a narrow path with walls on both sides (vv.24-25). The result was the same: the donkey saw the angel with his sword drawn and tried to squeeze by, crushing Balaam's foot against one of the walls. Balaam again beat the animal.

c. The angel of the LORD then moved ahead to a place so narrow that the donkey simply could not get by (vv.26-27). This time the donkey saw the angel of the LORD and simply lay down under Balaam. In anger, Balaam struck the donkey, beating her with his staff.

d. Then it was that the drama began: in dramatic fashion God opened the donkey's mouth. The animal miraculously, shockingly spoke to Balaam (see 2 Pt. 2:16). The reader must keep this fact in mind: the donkey did not speak by its own power; it spoke by the power of God. This was a miracle, a miracle brought about by the hand of God Himself. Note what the donkey did:

1) The donkey did what any living creature would do if it could speak: it complained of Balaam's cruelty (v.28).
2) Balaam flew into a fit of rage, stating that he wished he had a sword to kill the animal. The animal had made a fool out of him (v.29).
3) But note how the donkey miraculously reasoned with Balaam (v.30). She argued that she was Balaam's property and that she had always served

Balaam well. Moreover, she had never behaved like this before (v.30).

4) Balaam, obviously stunned and amazed at the dumb animal speaking to him, could only agree.

e. At this point, the LORD opened Balaam's eyes (vv.31-35).

1) Balaam immediately saw the angel of the LORD standing with his sword drawn. The drawn sword was a symbol of God's anger, a strong warning to Balaam. Stricken with fear, he fell face down on the ground.

2) The angel of the LORD then confronted this obstinate, hard-hearted false prophet who was so consumed with greed (vv.32-33). The LORD immediately rebuked him for mistreating an animal. Then it happened: God condemned him because of his reckless, stubborn heart, because of his resistance to God. Balaam had chosen to follow the sinful way of greed, the stubborn, reckless way that stands in opposition to God. God warned Balaam in no uncertain terms: God would have taken his life by now because of his stubborn, disobedient resistance if the donkey had not stopped (v.33). (See DEEPER STUDY # 1—Nu. 22:15-21 for more discussion.)

3) Balaam confessed his sin and offered to return (v.34). But note: he did not repent. This was only a partial confession, for true confession involves repentance. Repentance is the turning back to God, obeying God totally, fully, and completely—doing exactly what God commands. If Balaam had been sincere, he would have truly repented, returned home, and given his life to God, becoming a follower of the only living and true God. But this Balaam did not do. With one eye on the sword in the hand of the angel and with a heart filled with greed, he half-heartedly said that he would return if he had displeased the LORD. Of this, there was no question. The LORD had already told him never to leave to go to king Balak. Balaam had disobeyed the instructions of the LORD, and he was continuing to disobey them: all because his heart was full of greed and covetousness.

4) Note the response of the angel of the LORD: he gave Balaam over to his greed (Ro. 1:28-32). He could go, but he must speak only what God told him (v.35).

Thought 1. There are two clear lessons for us in this point:

(1) God had the power to speak through the donkey of Balaam. God has the power to perform miracles in order to achieve His purposes upon this earth. One of His purposes is the same purpose that He was working out through Balaam: the purpose of protecting His dear people. God has the power to protect His precious people and protect them He will. God's power is unlimited, and He will use whatever amount of power is needed to protect and take care of His dear people.

> Jesus looked at them and said, "With man this is impossible, but with God all things are possible." (Mt. 19:26)
>
> For nothing is impossible with God. (Lu. 1:37)
>
> Now to him who is able to establish you by my gospel and the proclamation of Jesus Christ, according to the revelation of the mystery hidden for long ages past. (Ro. 16:25)
>
> Now to him who is able to do immeasurably more than all we ask or imagine, according to his power that is at work within us. (Ep. 3:20)
>
> Being confident of this, that he who began a good work in you will carry it on to completion until the day of Christ Jesus. (Ph. 1:6)
>
> But our citizenship is in heaven. And we eagerly await a Savior from there, the Lord Jesus Christ, who, by the power that enables him to bring everything under his control, will transform our lowly bodies so that they will be like his glorious body. (Ph. 3:20-21)
>
> The Lord will rescue me from every evil attack and will bring me safely to his heavenly kingdom. To him be glory for ever and ever. Amen. (2 Ti. 4:18)
>
> So we say with confidence, "The Lord is my helper; I will not be afraid. What can man do to me?" (He. 13:6)
>
> To him who is able to keep you from falling and to present you before his glorious presence without fault and with great joy. (Jude 24)
>
> He said: "The LORD is my rock, my fortress and my deliverer." (2 S. 22:2)
>
> I know that you can do all things; no plan of yours can be thwarted. (Jb. 42:2)
>
> Yet I am poor and needy; may the Lord think of me. You are my help and my deliverer; O my God, do not delay. (Ps. 40:17)
>
> Our God is in heaven; he does whatever pleases him. (Ps. 115:3)
>
> So do not fear, for I am with you; do not be dismayed, for I am your God. I will strengthen you and help you; I will uphold you with my righteous right hand. (Is. 41:10)
>
> Yes, and from ancient days I am he. No one can deliver out of my hand. When I act, who can reverse it? (Is. 43:13)
>
> "Do not be afraid of them, for I am with you and will rescue you," declares the LORD. (Je. 1:8)

(2) The heart of Balaam was reckless, stubborn, and resistant to God. He was a hard-hearted person whose mind was set on the things of this world, its money and possessions. He was possessed by greed and covetousness. As a result, his heart was hard and stubborn against God. Scripture declares in no uncertain terms: a stubborn, hard heart is condemned by God. A hard-hearted, stubborn person will face the judgment of God and be eternally separated from God—tragically, all because the person resists the salvation of God provided through Christ Jesus. Hardness of heart condemns a person.

> But because of your stubbornness and your unrepentant heart, you are storing up wrath against yourself for the day of God's wrath, when his righteous judgment will be revealed. (Ro. 2:5)

But encourage one another daily, as long as it is called Today, so that none of you may be hardened by sin's deceitfulness. (He. 3:13)

For rebellion is like the sin of divination, and arrogance like the evil of idolatry. Because you have rejected the word of the LORD, he has rejected you as king. (1 S. 15:23)

Blessed is the man who always fears the LORD, but he who hardens his heart falls into trouble. (Pr. 28:14)

A man who remains stiff-necked after many rebukes will suddenly be destroyed—without remedy. (Pr. 29:1)

If you do not listen, and if you do not set your heart to honor my name," says the LORD Almighty, "I will send a curse upon you, and I will curse your blessings. Yes, I have already cursed them, because you have not set your heart to honor me. (Mal. 2:2)

5 (22:36-41) **Encounter, with God—Warning, of God—Sacrifices, Pagan**: the effect of God's encounters and warnings upon Balaam was a lesson that was going to be heeded. Remember what God had just told Balaam along the journey: He had considered striking Balaam dead (v.33). This threat and the experience with the donkey had gotten across to Balaam. Balaam was to be an instrument, a mouth-piece for God to share some very special messages with the world. Balaam did not yet know this, but he soon would. This false prophet was ready to share with the king only what God Himself revealed.

a. Note the excitement and expectation of king Balak at the coming of Balaam (vv.36-37). He traveled all the way to the border to meet Balaam. After their greetings, the king expressed disappointment in Balaam's refusal of his first request. He could not understand the refusal in light of the rich rewards he had so willingly offered Balaam.

b. Note the effect of Balaam's encounters with the LORD, the effect of God's warnings to him (v.38). Balaam replied to the king that he had now come despite his earlier reluctance. But Balaam added that he still could speak only the message that God gave him. No doubt, the image of the drawn sword in the hand of the angel dominated the thoughts of Balaam. Stricken with the fear of the angel and the threat of God, Balaam was determined to share only the message God wanted shared.

c. Note how the king celebrated Balaam's coming (vv.39-41). The king offered pagan sacrifices of sheep and goats to his "gods." Note that Balaam participated with Balak, eating the meat that was sacrificed. The king then took Balaam up to Bamoth Baal, that is, some hill or high place where Baal was worshipped. He did this so that they could scan the camp of Israel together.

Thought 1. God is sovereign, in total control of the universe and of all that happens within the universe. This does not mean that God overrides the free will of people; rather it means that God works all things out for good...

- in order to achieve His eternal purpose
- in order to look after His people and conform them to the image of His dear Son

God takes all the events throughout the universe, twisting and turning and working them out for the good of those who love Him, those who have been called according to His eternal purpose. This is exactly what God was doing with Balaam: twisting and turning and using the experiences of Balaam to protect His dear people. Moreover, He was going to use Balaam to proclaim some glorious messages to the world. God is God; that is, He is Sovereign, Almighty, able to do exactly what He wills. Therefore, God overrode Balaam's greed and covetousness, determining to use him to bless God's dear people instead of cursing them.

The point to see is this: God is sovereign, in control of all things. Therefore, God works all things out for the good of His dear people, for the good of all those who love Him and are called by Him.

And we know that in all things God works for the good of those who love him, who have been called according to his purpose. (Ro. 8:28)

For our light and momentary troubles are achieving for us an eternal glory that far outweighs them all. (2 Co. 4:17)

But he said to me, "My grace is sufficient for you, for my power is made perfect in weakness." Therefore I will boast all the more gladly about my weaknesses, so that Christ's power may rest on me. (2 Co. 12:9)

Dear friends, do not be surprised at the painful trial you are suffering, as though something strange were happening to you. But rejoice that you participate in the sufferings of Christ, so that you may be overjoyed when his glory is revealed. (1 Pe. 4:12-13)

For his anger lasts only a moment, but his favor lasts a lifetime; weeping may remain for a night, but rejoicing comes in the morning. (Ps. 30:5)

A righteous man may have many troubles, but the LORD delivers him from them all. (Ps. 34:19)

The LORD will sustain him on his sickbed and restore him from his bed of illness. (Ps. 41:3)

You are God my stronghold. Why have you rejected me? Why must I go about mourning, oppressed by the enemy? (Ps. 43:2)

And call upon me in the day of trouble; I will deliver you, and you will honor me. (Ps. 50:15)

Though I walk in the midst of trouble, you preserve my life; you stretch out your hand against the anger of my foes, with your right hand you save me. (Ps. 138:7)

NUMBERS 22:1-41

TYPES, SYMBOLS, AND PICTURES
(Numbers 22:1-41)

Historical Term	Type or Picture (Scriptural Basis for Each)	Life Application for Today's Believer	Biblical Application
The Sword of the Angel of the LORD Nu. 22:22-35	*A type or symbol of God's anger and warning. Balaam immediately saw the angel of the* LORD *standing with his sword drawn. The sword was a strong warning to Balaam.* *When the donkey saw the angel of the* LORD *standing in the road with a drawn sword in his hand, she turned off the road into a field. Balaam beat her to get her back on the road.* (Nu. 22:23)	God is angry with men... • who are ungodly, who do not love and obey God. • who are unrighteous, who do not love and treat others as they should. • who hold the truth to themselves while they live ungodly and unrighteous lives	"But when he saw many of the Pharisees and Sadducees coming to where he was baptizing, he said to them: "You brood of vipers! Who warned you to flee from the coming wrath?" (Mt.3:7) "The wrath of God is being revealed from heaven against all the godlessness and wickedness of men who suppress the truth by their wickedness" (Ro. 1:18) "But for those who are self-seeking and who reject the truth and follow evil, there will be wrath and anger. There will be trouble and distress for every human being who does evil: first for the Jew, then for the Gentile;" (Ro. 2:8-9) "All of us also lived among them at one time, gratifying the cravings of our sinful nature and following its desires and thoughts. Like the rest, we were by nature objects of wrath." (Ep. 2:3) "Let no one deceive you with empty words, for because of such things God's wrath comes on those who are disobedient." (Ep. 5:6; see Col. 3:6) "So I declared on oath in my anger, 'They shall never enter my rest.' " (He. 3:11) "Kiss the Son, lest he be angry and you be destroyed in your way, for his wrath can flare up in a moment. Blessed are all who take refuge in him." (Ps. 2:12)

NUMBERS 23:1–24:25

I. Event 9—the Story of Balaam & the Seven Startling Oracles or Prophecies Pronounced by Him: The Blessings of God & a Glimpse into the Future[1], 23:1-24:25

1. **The 1st prophecy: The blessings of God's people**
   a. The preparation for the prophecy
      1) Balaam requested that seven altars be built for sacrifice
      2) Balaam & the king offered pagan sacrifice: To secure the favor of their gods (24:1)
      3) Balaam then climbed a high hill to be alone, hoping the Lord would meet him
         • Instructed the king to wait beside his offering
         • Promised to tell the king whatever the Lord revealed
      4) God met with Balaam
         • Balaam immediately sought God's favor: Told God that he had offered seven sacrifices
         • God ignored the sacrifices
         • God did, however, give Balaam a message for king Balak
      5) Balaam returned to the king: Found him still standing by his offering with all the officials of Moab
   b. The prophecy Balaam declared: The blessings of Israel (a symbol of God's people)
      1) They were an innocent, secure people (a justified people): God had not cursed nor denounced them; therefore, he could not do so
      2) They were a new, separated, distinctive people
      3) They were a numerous people
      4) They were a righteous people with eternal hope: He wished to share in their destiny
   c. The result of the prophecy
      1) Balak was enraged, furi-ous: Reproached Balaam
      2) Balaam defended himself: As a diviner, he could speak only what God revealed

2. **The 2nd prophecy: The source of the blessings, God Himself**
   a. The preparation for the prophecy
      1) Balak tried a different tactic: Suggested cursing Israel from a site where only a small number could be seen
         • Took Balaam to the top of Mt. Pisgah
         • Built seven altars & offered pagan sacrifices: Sought to secure the favor of the gods
      2) Balaam then walked some distance to seek God: Hoping that God would again meet him
      3) God met with Balaam: Gave him a message for King Balak
      4) Balaam returned: Found King Balak standing beside his offerings with the officials of Moab
   b. The prophecy: The source that guarantees the blessings of God's people
      1) God's truthfulness & unchangableness: He does not lie nor change His mind
      2) God's faithfulness: He speaks & acts; He promises & fulfills
      3) God's promises: His promises & blessings are irrevocable—they cannot be changed
         • No misfortune is seen
         • No misery or trouble is in store
      4) God's presence: His presence assures the blessing of His people
      5) God's power: His power assures the protection & deliverance of His people
         • Assures deliverance from all sorcery & divination
         • Assures a strong testimony for God
         • Assures victory over all enemies

CHAPTER 23

Balaam said, "Build me seven altars here, and prepare seven bulls and seven rams for me."
2 Balak did as Balaam said, and the two of them offered a bull and a ram on each altar.
3 Then Balaam said to Balak, "Stay here beside your offering while I go aside. Perhaps the LORD will come to meet with me. Whatever he reveals to me I will tell you." Then he went off to a barren height.
4 God met with him, and Balaam said, "I have prepared seven altars, and on each altar I have offered a bull and a ram."
5 The LORD put a message in Balaam's mouth and said, "Go back to Balak and give him this message."
6 So he went back to him and found him standing beside his offering, with all the princes of Moab.
7 Then Balaam uttered his oracle: "Balak brought me from Aram, the king of Moab from the eastern mountains. 'Come,' he said, 'curse Jacob for me; come, denounce Israel.'
8 How can I curse those whom God has not cursed? How can I denounce those whom the LORD has not denounced?
9 From the rocky peaks I see them, from the heights I view them. I see a people who live apart and do not consider themselves one of the nations.
10 Who can count the dust of Jacob or number the fourth part of Israel? Let me die the death of the righteous, and may my end be like theirs!"
11 Balak said to Balaam, "What have you done to me? I brought you to curse my enemies, but you have done nothing but bless them!"
12 He answered, "Must I not speak what the LORD puts in my mouth?"
13 Then Balak said to him, "Come with me to another place where you can see them; you will see only a part but not all of them. And from there, curse them for me."
14 So he took him to the field of Zophim on the top of Pisgah, and there he built seven altars and offered a bull and a ram on each altar.
15 Balaam said to Balak, "Stay here beside your offering while I meet with him over there."
16 The LORD met with Balaam and put a message in his mouth and said, "Go back to Balak and give him this message."
17 So he went to him and found him standing beside his offering, with the princes of Moab. Balak asked him, "What did the LORD say?"
18 Then he uttered his oracle: "Arise, Balak, and listen; hear me, son of Zippor.
19 God is not a man, that he should lie, nor a son of man, that he should change his mind. Does he speak and then not act? Does he promise and not fulfill?
20 I have received a command to bless; he has blessed, and I cannot change it.
21 "No misfortune is seen in Jacob, no misery observed in Israel. The LORD their God is with them; the shout of the King is among them.
22 God brought them out of Egypt; they have the strength of a wild ox.
23 There is no sorcery against Jacob, no divination against Israel. It will now be said of Jacob and of Israel, 'See what God has done!'
24 The people rise like a lioness; they rouse themselves like a lion that does not rest till he devours his prey and drinks the blood of his

---

[1] Some thoughts and statements for this outline were gleaned from *The Expositor's Bible Commentary*. Frank E. Gaebelein, Editor, pp.895-913.

NUMBERS 23:1–24:25

c. The result of the prophecy
  1) Balak was desperate: He commanded "Stop! Say nothing! Neither curse nor bless them!"
  2) Balaam insisted upon his rights as sorcerer (see 24:1)

3. **The 3rd prophecy: A picture of how God blesses His people**
  a. The preparation for the prophecy
   1) Balak suggested a third site
     • He was desperate—Israel must be cursed
     • He took Balaam to the top of Mt. Peor
   2) Balaam requested that seven altars be built

   3) Balaam offered pagan sacrifices upon the altar

   4) Balaam made a significant change: He did not resort to sorcery (chants, spells, charms, magic)

   5) Balaam looked out over the camp of Israel tribe by tribe & was stricken by the sight: Suddenly, the Spirit of God came upon him & Balaam declared...
     • That his eyes saw clearly
     • That he heard the Word of God
     • That he saw a vision from the Almighty
     • That his eyes were opened
  b. The prophecy: A picture of how God blesses His people
   1) Their dwelling place—homes & land will be beautiful
   2) Their homes & lands will be fruitful before the Lord
   3) Their resources will be sufficient & even overflow
   4) Their leaders & kingdom will be powerful & exalted
   5) Their Deliverer is God Himself
   6) Their strength is as an ox
   7) Their victory is assured over all hostile enemies
   8) Their courage & security are assured

victims."
25 Then Balak said to Balaam, "Neither curse them at all nor bless them at all!"
26 Balaam answered, "Did I not tell you I must do whatever the LORD says?"
27 Then Balak said to Balaam, "Come, let me take you to another place. Perhaps it will please God to let you curse them for me from there."
28 And Balak took Balaam to the top of Peor, overlooking the wasteland.
29 Balaam said, "Build me seven altars here, and prepare seven bulls and seven rams for me."
30 Balak did as Balaam had said, and offered a bull and a ram on each altar.

CHAPTER 24

Now when Balaam saw that it pleased the LORD to bless Israel, he did not resort to sorcery as at other times, but turned his face toward the desert.
2 When Balaam looked out and saw Israel encamped tribe by tribe, the Spirit of God came upon him
3 And he uttered his oracle: "The oracle of Balaam son of Beor, the oracle of one whose eye sees clearly,
4 The oracle of one who hears the words of God, who sees a vision from the Almighty, who falls prostrate, and whose eyes are opened:
5 "How beautiful are your tents, O Jacob, your dwelling places, O Israel!
6 "Like valleys they spread out, like gardens beside a river, like aloes planted by the LORD, like cedars beside the waters.
7 Water will flow from their buckets; their seed will have abundant water. "Their king will be greater than Agag; their kingdom will be exalted.
8 "God brought them out of Egypt; they have the strength of a wild ox. They devour hostile nations and break their bones in pieces; with their arrows they pierce them.
9 Like a lion they crouch and lie down, like a lioness—

who dares to rouse them? "May those who bless you be blessed and those who curse you be cursed!"
10 Then Balak's anger burned against Balaam. He struck his hands together and said to him, "I summoned you to curse my enemies, but you have blessed them these three times.
11 Now leave at once and go home! I said I would reward you handsomely, but the LORD has kept you from being rewarded."
12 Balaam answered Balak, "Did I not tell the messengers you sent me,
13 'Even if Balak gave me his palace filled with silver and gold, I could not do anything of my own accord, good or bad, to go beyond the command of the LORD—and I must say only what the LORD says'?
14 Now I am going back to my people, but come, let me warn you of what this people will do to your people in days to come."
15 Then he uttered his oracle: "The oracle of Balaam son of Beor, the oracle of one whose eye sees clearly,
16 The oracle of one who hears the words of God, who has knowledge from the Most High, who sees a vision from the Almighty, who falls prostrate, and whose eyes are opened:
17 "I see him, but not now; I behold him, but not near. A star will come out of Jacob; a scepter will rise out of Israel. He will crush the foreheads of Moab, the skulls of all the sons of Sheth.
18 Edom will be conquered; Seir, his enemy, will be conquered, but Israel will grow strong.
19 A ruler will come out of Jacob and destroy the survivors of the city."
20 Then Balaam saw Amalek and uttered his oracle: "Amalek was first among the nations, but he will come to ruin at last."
21 Then he saw the Kenites and uttered his oracle: "Your dwelling place is

   9) Their blessings are guaranteed by the promise of God Himself (see Ge. 12:2-3)
  c. The result of the prophecy
   1) Balak flew into a rage
     • Charged Balaam with breaking their agreement: Was summoned to curse Israel; instead, he had blessed them three times
     • Charged Balaam to leave immediately—go home!
     • Dismissed him without pay: The ultimate insult to his greed (2 Pe. 2:15)
   2) Balaam attempted to excuse himself (in his professional pride as a sorcerer): Reminded Balak of the terms laid down with his officials
     • He could only speak what the LORD said
     • He was powerless to do anything against the LORD—no matter how much the king paid him

4. **The 4th prophecy: A picture of the coming Deliverer**
  a. The preparation for the prophecy
   1) Balaam started to leave, but he was suddenly constrained by God to prophesy: About the days to come
   2) Balaam declared...
     • That his eyes saw clearly
     • That he heard the Words of God
     • That he had knowledge from the Most High
     • That he saw a vision from the Almighty
     • That his eyes were opened
  b. The prophecy: A picture of the coming Deliverer
   1) He will come in the future
   2) He will be a star & a scepter (have dominion)
   3) He will be victorious over all enemies, including Moab & Edom
   4) He will guarantee the growing strength of His people (Israel)

   5) He will guarantee the triumph & dominion of God's people

5. **The 5th prophecy: A picture of victory over the greatest enemies**
  a. Balaam saw Amalek & prophesied
  b. Amalek, the greatest of nations, would be destroyed

6. **The 6th prophecy: A picture of the greatest fortresses of the enemy being destroyed**

a. Balaam saw the Kenites & prophesied b. The Kenites & their impregnable fortress would be destroyed by Assyria 7. **The 7th prophecy: A picture of God's judgment against all whose *cup is full of sin* (has reached the**	secure, your nest is set in a rock; 22 Yet you Kenites will be destroyed when Asshur takes you captive." 23 Then he uttered his oracle: "Ah, who can live when God does this?	24 Ships will come from the shores of Kittim; they will subdue Asshur and Eber, but they too will come to ruin." 25 Then Balaam got up and returned home and Balak went his own way.	full measure that God allows) a. Balaam again prophesied the future b. Assyria & Eber would be destroyed: By an invading force coming across the sea c. Balaam & Balak separated & returned home

DIVISION III

THE FORTY LONG YEARS OF WILDERNESS WANDERINGS: A PICTURE OF THE BELIEVER'S PILGRIMAGE THROUGH THIS WORLD AS HE PREPARES TO ENTER THE PROMISED LAND, 15:1–25:18

I. Event 9—the Story of Balaam and the Seven Startling Oracles or Prophecies Pronounced by Him: The Blessings of God and a Glimpse into the Future, 23:1–24:25

(23:1–24:25) Introduction—Future, Question About: a glimpse into the future—what would a person give to have such a revelation, to be able to see into the future? Would it even be wise to know the future? Would knowing the future bring joy? Sorrow? Pain? Suffering? Anger? Frustration? Loneliness? Unemployment? Divorce? Death? What does lie out in the future? A glimpse into the future is the subject of this passage of Scripture.

Remember what had happened: the king of Moab and his people had become terrified of the Israelites who were camped nearby. They felt hopeless and helpless, so the king sent for a diviner, a sorcerer or false prophet named Balaam who had an international reputation. He wanted Balaam to call upon the "gods" to put a curse upon the Israelites. He felt the curse would help him defeat the Israelites in battle (Nu. 22:6). This chapter focuses upon Balaam trying to curse Israel, God's people. However, God stops Balaam in his tracks. God refuses to let Balaam curse His people. Instead, God takes control of Balaam's tongue and makes seven astounding prophecies about His people, prophecies that speak to all of God's people down through human history. This is: *Event 9—the Story of Balaam and the Seven Startling Oracles or Prophecies Pronounced by Him: The Blessings of God and a Glimpse into the Future,* 23:1-24:25.

1. The 1st prophecy: the blessings of God's people (vv.1-12).
2. The 2nd prophecy: the source of the blessings, God Himself (vv.13-26).
3. The 3rd prophecy: a picture of how God blesses His people (ch. 23:27-24:13).
4. The 4th prophecy: a picture of the coming Deliverer (vv.14-19).
5. The 5th prophecy: a picture of victory over the greatest enemies (v.20).
6. The 6th prophecy: a picture of the greatest fortresses of the enemy being destroyed (vv.21-22).
7. The 7th prophecy: a picture of God's judgment against all whose *cup is full of sin* (has reached the full measure that God allows) (vv.23-25).

1 **(23:1-12) Blessings, of God's People—Believers, Blessings of—Israel, Blessings of—Prophecy, Concerning God's People**: the first prophecy focuses upon the blessings of God's people. Remember why the king and this false prophet were together: to curse God's people, to call down upon them the judgment and destruction of God.

The Israelites were camped in the plain of Moab nearby the Jordan River, camped right across from the great city of Jericho. As stated, king Balak and his people feared the Israelites: a sense of helplessness and hopelessness had swept over the king and his people. To the king, the only hope he and his people had lay in the hands of their gods. In desperation, the king hoped that this diviner could put a curse upon the Israelites, a curse that would allow him to defeat them in battle (Nu. 22:6). Now, here stood the king and the false prophet on a hill that overlooked the campsites of the Israelites, a high place that was dedicated to the worship of the false god Baal (Nu. 22:41). The scene is dramatic, for a false prophet of international reputation is ready to call down a terrifying, destructive curse upon the people of God. Note what happened:

a. Note the preparation for the prophecy (vv.1-6).
  1) Balaam requested that the king build seven altars for sacrifice (v.1).
  2) Balaam and the king offered pagan sacrifice. This is a pagan sacrifice not the true sacrifice of the Lord God, the only living and true God (Jehovah, Yahweh). They attempted to secure the favor of their gods to curse Israel. This was clearly an act of sorcery (24:1).
  3) Balaam then climbed a high hill, seeking to be alone and hoping that the Lord would meet him (v.3). He instructed the king to wait beside his offering, obviously praying to his gods. He then promised to tell the king whatever the Lord revealed to him up on the mountain.
  4) Note that God met with Balaam (vv.4-5). Balaam immediately sought to secure God's favor, to bribe Him. He told God that he had offered seven sacrifices in His name. Keep in mind that this false prophet did not know who God was, not personally. To him, God was only one among many gods. In his mind, this particular god was only the 'god of the Israelites.' Therefore, in order to secure the favor of the Israelite God, he had offered the sacrifices in His name. But note what God did: He completely ignored the sacrifices (v.5). However, He did give this false prophet Balaam a message for the king.
  5) After receiving the message, Balaam returned to the king and found him still standing by his offering with all the other officials of Moab (v.6).

b. Balaam immediately declared the prophecy. Note that the prophecy focused upon the blessings of Israel, but

NUMBERS 23:1–24:25

these blessings are also blessings that God has given to all His people down through the ages (vv.7-10). Most likely the Lord had taken over the tongue of Balaam just as He had with the donkey. God was speaking through Balaam the message He wanted conveyed to the king and to all succeeding generations. It is most unlikely that Balaam—of his own free will—would dare proclaim these prophecies for fear of the king. Obviously, his tongue was under God's control. Note the blessings of God's people:

1) God's people are an innocent, secure people (v.8). God had not cursed the people, for they were an innocent, justified people before Him. Since they were innocent or justified, He could not denounce or curse them.
2) God's people are a new, separated, and distinctive people (v.9). They are distinctive in that they live holy lives, lives that are totally set apart to the Lord God (Jehovah, Yahweh). They live lives that are separated from the people of the world. They are a totally new people, a new race of people. (See outline and note—Ep. 4:17-19 for more discussion.)
3) God's people are a numerous people (v.10). One of the amazing promises of God concerns this very point: by the end of the world they will number as the stars of the sky and as the sands by the seashore. As Balaam asked: "Who can count the dust of Jacob or number even the fourth part of Israel?"
4) God's people are a righteous people with an eternal hope. Note what Balaam cried out: that he too could wish to die the death of the righteous and to have an end just like theirs (v.10). This is a clear reference to heaven, to living eternally with God.

c. The result of the prophecy is to be expected: Balak was enraged, furious (vv.11-12). He severely rebuked and reproached Balaam. But Balaam defended himself: as a diviner, he could only speak what God revealed to him. No doubt, Balaam was fearful of the reaction of Balak and was counting on the king's fear of the gods to protect him.

Thought 1. The blessings of God given in this passage are gifts of God to all His people. Note the blessings one by one.

(1) God's people are an innocent, secure people—a people who are justified, eternally secure before God. God has forgiven our sins and justified us, counted us innocent before Him. Moreover, He has given us the greatest security that could be given: the inner witness of His Spirit who assures us of eternal life, of living with Him face to face throughout all of eternity. The person who believes—who truly trusts the Lord Jesus Christ as his Savior—is justified before God, that is, counted innocent and secure forever and ever. God's Spirit guarantees our security.

> I give them eternal life, and they shall never perish; no one can snatch them out of my hand. (Jn. 10:28)
> Therefore, since we have been justified through faith, we have peace with God through our Lord Jesus Christ. (Ro. 5:1)
> The Spirit himself testifies with our spirit that we are God's children. Now if we are children, then we are heirs—heirs of God and co-heirs with Christ, if indeed we share in his sufferings in order that we may also share in his glory. (Ro. 8:16-17)
> Who will bring any charge against those whom God has chosen? It is God who justifies. (Ro. 8:33)
> And that is what some of you were. But you were washed, you were sanctified, you were justified in the name of the Lord Jesus Christ and by the Spirit of our God. (1 Co. 6:11)
> Consider Abraham: "He believed God, and it was credited to him as righteousness." (Ga. 3:6)
> Because you are sons, God sent the Spirit of his Son into our hearts, the Spirit who calls out, "Abba, Father." (Ga. 4:6)
> Praise be to the God and Father of our Lord Jesus Christ! In his great mercy he has given us new birth into a living hope through the resurrection of Jesus Christ from the dead, and into an inheritance that can never perish, spoil or fade—kept in heaven for you, who through faith are shielded by God's power until the coming of the salvation that is ready to be revealed in the last time. (1 Pe. 1:3-5)
> Those who obey his commands live in him, and he in them. And this is how we know that he lives in us: We know it by the Spirit he gave us. (1 Jn. 3:24)
> We know that we live in him and he in us, because he has given us of his Spirit. (1 Jn. 4:13)
> To him who is able to keep you from falling and to present you before his glorious presence without fault and with great joy—to the only God our Savior be glory, majesty, power and authority, through Jesus Christ our Lord, before all ages, now and forevermore! Amen. (Jude 24-25)
> Abram believed the Lord, and he credited it to him as righteousness. (Ge. 15:6)

(2) God's people are a separated and distinctive people. The genuine believer lives a holy life before God, a life that is pure and righteous, moral and clean, just and fair. The believer lives a life of separation from the world, a life that has nothing to do with...

- stealing
- lying
- cheating
- greed
- covetousness
- sorcery
- divination
- illicit sex
- pornography
- abuse
- revenge
- anger
- the occult

A life of separation—the life that is totally different from the immoral, unjust, and violent of this earth, a life that is totally distinct and different from neighbors and communities who live in disobedience to God—is the call of God to us. We are to be a separated people, a distinctive people in this one fact: we are to live holy, pure, and righteous lives. We are to be strong witnesses for the lost of the world, that they too are to live pure and righteous lives before God. This is the life of separation to which God calls us.

> If you belonged to the world, it would love you as its own. As it is, you do not

belong to the world, but I have chosen you out of the world. That is why the world hates you. (Jn. 15:19)

But now I am writing you that you must not associate with anyone who calls himself a brother but is sexually immoral or greedy, an idolater or a slanderer, a drunkard or a swindler. With such a man do not even eat. (1 Co. 5:11)

Therefore, if anyone is in Christ, he is a new creation; the old has gone, the new has come! (2 Co. 5:17)

Do not be yoked together with unbelievers. For what do righteousness and wickedness have in common? Or what fellowship can light have with darkness? (2 Co. 6:14)

"Therefore come out from them and be separate, says the Lord. Touch no unclean thing, and I will receive you. I will be a Father to you, and you will be my sons and daughters, says the Lord Almighty." (2 Co. 6:17-18)

Have nothing to do with the fruitless deeds of darkness, but rather expose them. (Ep. 5:11)

In the name of the Lord Jesus Christ, we command you, brothers, to keep away from every brother who is idle and does not live according to the teaching you received from us. (2 Th. 3:6)

Do not love the world or anything in the world. If anyone loves the world, the love of the Father is not in him. For everything in the world—the cravings of sinful man, the lust of his eyes and the boasting of what he has and does—comes not from the Father but from the world. (1 Jn. 2:15-16)

Do not follow the crowd in doing wrong. When you give testimony in a lawsuit, do not pervert justice by siding with the crowd. (Ex. 23:2)

Be careful not to make a treaty with those who live in the land where you are going, or they will be a snare among you. (Ex. 34:12)

Blessed is the man who does not walk in the counsel of the wicked or stand in the way of sinners or sit in the seat of mockers. (Ps. 1:1)

Do not set foot on the path of the wicked or walk in the way of evil men. (Pr. 4:14)

Do not envy wicked men, do not desire their company. (Pr. 24:1)

Depart, depart, go out from there! Touch no unclean thing! Come out from it and be pure, you who carry the vessels of the LORD. (Is. 52:11)

(3) God's people are eventually to be a numerous people. This was the promise made to Abraham and his descendants, that is, all the succeeding generations of believers down through the ages. Believers are eventually to number as the stars of the sky and as the sands by the seashore.

I will surely bless you and make your descendants as numerous as the stars in the sky and as the sand on the seashore. Your descendants will take possession of the cities of their enemies. (Ge. 22:17)

But you have said, 'I will surely make you prosper and will make your descendants like the sand of the sea, which cannot be counted.' (Ge. 32:12)

(4) God's people are a righteous people with eternal hope. A genuine believer is counted righteous through the righteousness of Jesus Christ. Jesus Christ is the believer's only approach to God. A person can approach God only through Christ, only through His righteousness. When a person comes to God through Christ's righteousness, God accepts that person; God counts that person justified, righteous. Once the person has been justified—counted righteous—he is given the wonderful hope of living eternally with God.

Just as Moses lifted up the snake in the desert, so the Son of Man must be lifted up, that everyone who believes in him may have eternal life. (Jn. 3:14-15)

For God so loved the world that he gave his one and only Son, that whoever believes in him shall not perish but have eternal life. (Jn. 3:16)

Whoever believes in the Son has eternal life, but whoever rejects the Son will not see life, for God's wrath remains on him. (Jn. 3:36)

I tell you the truth, if anyone keeps my word, he will never see death. (Jn. 8:51)

Whoever lives and believes in me will never die. Do you believe this? (Jn. 11:26)

For the perishable must clothe itself with the imperishable, and the mortal with immortality. When the perishable has been clothed with the imperishable, and the mortal with immortality, then the saying that is written will come true: "Death has been swallowed up in victory." (1 Co. 15:53-54)

Now we know that if the earthly tent we live in is destroyed, we have a building from God, an eternal house in heaven, not built by human hands. (2 Co. 5:1)

For the Lord himself will come down from heaven, with a loud command, with the voice of the archangel and with the trumpet call of God, and the dead in Christ will rise first. After that, we who are still alive and are left will be caught up together with them in the clouds to meet the Lord in the air. And so we will be with the Lord forever. (1 Th. 4:16-17)

2 (23:13-26) **Blessings, Source of—God, Blessings of—Assurance, of God's Faithfulness—Faithfulness, of God**: the second prophecy focused upon the source of the blessings, God Himself. The first attempt to curse God's people backfired. Instead of cursing, the false prophet had declared the blessings of God's people. The power of God had taken control of his tongue and stopped him from cursing Israel. When the king heard the blessings prophesied, he became enraged, furious. Now, note what happened:

a. The preparation for the prophecy was the same as for the first prophecy (vv.14-17).

NUMBERS 23:1–24:25

1) King Balak tried a different tactic: he suggested cursing Israel from a site where only a small number of the people could be seen. By reducing the number that could be seen, he obviously hoped to reduce the impact they might make upon Balaam. Seeing the enormous number of Israelites earlier had, perhaps, aroused a fear within Balaam, a fear that kept him from cursing the king's enemies. Therefore, he took him to the top of Mt. Pisgah, where only a few of the king's enemies could be seen. Note that he again built seven altars and offered pagan sacrifices, seeking to bribe the gods and to secure their favor to curse Israel. Keep in mind that these are pagan offerings not the true worship of God. In fact, Gordon J. Wenham tells us that a Babylonian tablet actually describes a similar pagan offering that was offered up to three Babylonian gods and offered upon seven altars. The pagan offering also made use of seven incense burners and poured out the blood of seven sheep.[2]
2) Balaam then walked some distance away to seek God, hoping that God would again meet him (v.15). No doubt, Balaam was somewhat concerned for his life, unless God actually allowed him to curse the enemies of the king.
3) God did meet with Balaam and gave him a message for King Balak (v.16). Note exactly what this verse says: God "put the word, the message, the oracle" in the mouth of the prophet. God was controlling the tongue of the false prophet to speak exactly what God wanted proclaimed.
4) Balaam then returned and found King Balak standing beside his offerings with the officials of Moab (v.17).

b. The prophecy focused upon the source of the blessings, God Himself (vv.18-24). The people of God are blessed because of God not because of man. Kings and advisors, nations and armies are not the source of the blessings that come upon God's people; God is the source of the blessings. Consequently, the blessings can never be removed; the people of God can never be cursed. The people of God are conquerors over all the enemies who stand against them and attempt to curse them. They are victorious and triumphant throughout all of life—all because their source is God Himself. He is the source of all their blessings. This is the prophecy—the word and oracle—now being proclaimed by the false prophet.

1) God's truthfulness and unchangeableness guarantee the blessings of God's people. God does not lie nor change His mind (v.19). God is not like man who sometimes does lie and change his mind.
2) God's faithfulness guarantees the promises to His people. God speaks and acts; He promises and fulfills. When God says something He carries it through. He acts and does exactly what He says.
3) God's promises are the guarantee of His blessings. God's promises and blessings are irrevocable: they cannot be changed (vv.20-21). God has promised to bless His people; therefore, when trials and problems arise, God strengthens His people to conquer the trials. This is His promise. No misfortune will conquer His people, and no misery or trouble will overcome them. Again, God's promises are irrevocable; therefore, the blessings that are promised to His people are irrevocable.
4) God's presence guarantees the blessings of His people. The LORD their God is with the Israelites. He is proclaimed to be their King. Moreover, the shout of their King defends them against all enemies. His shout is mighty and powerful, striking fear in the heart of the enemy, routing and defeating them—all on behalf of His people.
5) God's power guarantees the blessings of Israel. His power assures their protection and deliverance. This was perfectly demonstrated in their deliverance from Egyptian slavery: it was the power of God Himself that brought them out of Egypt. The power of God is like the strength of a wild ox (v.22). Note the great assurance that God's power gives to His people:
    ⇒ the assurance of deliverance from all sorcery and divination (v.23)
    ⇒ the assurance of a strong testimony for God (v.23)
    ⇒ the assurance of victory over all enemies (v.24)

c. Note the result, what happened as soon as Balaam completed the prophecy (vv.25-26). In desperation, king Balak cried out: "Stop! Say nothing more! Neither curse nor bless them!" Once again Balaam tried to protect himself by insisting on his rights as a sorcerer (see Nu. 24:1).

Thought 1. Great and wonderful blessings have been promised to God's people, blessings that explode the human imagination. But what guarantee do we have, we who live in this day and time? That we will receive the blessings of God? That the blessings will actually be given to us? As we march to the promised land of heaven, what assurance do we have that God is going to bless us? How can we know that good things are going to happen to us, that we are going to be blessed? We can know because of God, because of who God is. God guarantees His blessings for all generations of believers. If a person truly follows God, God promises to bless him. It is God Himself who guarantees that He will bless the believer. God gives five guarantees to the believer:

(1) God's truthfulness and unchangeableness guarantee that He will bless His people.

> **Not at all! Let God be true, and every man a liar. As it is written: "So that you may be proved right when you speak and prevail when you judge." (Ro. 3:4)**
>
> **God did this so that, by two unchangeable things in which it is impossible for God to lie, we who have fled to take hold of the hope offered to us may be greatly encouraged. (He. 6:18)**
>
> **Every good and perfect gift is from above, coming down from the Father of the heavenly lights, who does not change like shifting shadows. (Js. 1:17)**
>
> **O Sovereign LORD, you are God! Your words are trustworthy, and you have promised these good things to your servant. (2 S. 7:28)**
>
> **The Maker of heaven and earth, the sea, and everything in them—the LORD, who remains faithful forever. (Ps. 146:6)**
>
> **I the LORD do not change. (Mal. 3:6)**

---

[2] Gordon J. Wenham. *The Book of Numbers*, p.172.

Numbers 23:1–24:25

(2) God's faithfulness guarantees that He will bless His people.

> God, who has called you into fellowship with his Son Jesus Christ our Lord, is faithful. (1 Co. 1:9)
>
> So then, those who suffer according to God's will should commit themselves to their faithful Creator and continue to do good. (1 Pe. 4:19)
>
> Know therefore that the LORD your God is God; he is the faithful God, keeping his covenant of love to a thousand generations of those who love him and keep his commands. (De. 7:9)
>
> I will sing of the LORD's great love forever; with my mouth I will make your faithfulness known through all generations. (Ps. 89:1)

(3) God's promises guarantee that He will bless His people.

> Yet he did not waver through unbelief regarding the promise of God, but was strengthened in his faith and gave glory to God, being fully persuaded that God had power to do what he had promised. (Ro. 4:20-21)
>
> For no matter how many promises God has made, they are "Yes" in Christ. And so through him the "Amen" is spoken by us to the glory of God. (2 Co. 1:20)
>
> Through these he has given us his very great and precious promises, so that through them you may participate in the divine nature and escape the corruption in the world caused by evil desires. (2 Pe. 1:4)
>
> And this is what he promised us—even eternal life. (1 Jn. 2:25)
>
> Praise be to the LORD, who has given rest to his people Israel just as he promised. Not one word has failed of all the good promises he gave through his servant Moses. (1 K. 8:56)

(4) God's presence guarantees and assures the blessings of His people.

> And surely I am with you always, to the very end of the age. (Mt. 28:20)
>
> I am with you and will watch over you wherever you go, and I will bring you back to this land. I will not leave you until I have done what I have promised you. (Ge. 28:15)
>
> The LORD replied, "My Presence will go with you, and I will give you rest." (Ex. 33:14)
>
> When you go to war against your enemies and see horses and chariots and an army greater than yours, do not be afraid of them, because the LORD your God, who brought you up out of Egypt, will be with you. (De. 20:1)
>
> When you pass through the waters, I will be with you; and when you pass through the rivers, they will not sweep over you. When you walk through the fire, you will not be burned; the flames will not set you ablaze. (Is. 43:2)

(5) God's power guarantees that He will bless His people, that He will protect and deliver them.

> Jesus looked at them and said, "With man this is impossible, but with God all things are possible." (Mt. 19:26)
>
> For nothing is impossible with God. (Lu. 1:37)
>
> But not a hair of your head will perish. (Lu. 21:18)
>
> Now to him who is able to establish you by my gospel and the proclamation of Jesus Christ, according to the revelation of the mystery hidden for long ages past....to the only wise God be glory forever through Jesus Christ! Amen. (Ro. 16:25, 27)
>
> No temptation has seized you except what is common to man. And God is faithful; he will not let you be tempted beyond what you can bear. But when you are tempted, he will also provide a way out so that you can stand up under it. (1 Co. 10:13)
>
> But he said to me, "My grace is sufficient for you, for my power is made perfect in weakness." Therefore I will boast all the more gladly about my weaknesses, so that Christ's power may rest on me. That is why, for Christ's sake, I delight in weaknesses, in insults, in hardships, in persecutions, in difficulties. For when I am weak, then I am strong. (2 Co. 12:9-10)
>
> Now to him who is able to do immeasurably more than all we ask or imagine, according to his power that is at work within us. (Ep. 3:20)
>
> The Lord will rescue me from every evil attack and will bring me safely to his heavenly kingdom. To him be glory for ever and ever. Amen. (2 Ti. 4:18)
>
> If this is so, then the Lord knows how to rescue godly men from trials and to hold the unrighteous for the day of judgment, while continuing their punishment. (2 Pe. 2:9)
>
> Wealth and honor come from you; you are the ruler of all things. In your hands are strength and power to exalt and give strength to all. (1 Chr. 29:12)
>
> For the eyes of the LORD range throughout the earth to strengthen those whose hearts are fully committed to him. (2 Chr. 16:9)
>
> I know that you can do all things; no plan of yours can be thwarted. (Jb. 42:2)
>
> The angel of the LORD encamps around those who fear him, and he delivers them. (Ps. 34:7)
>
> Surely he will save you from the fowler's snare and from the deadly pestilence. (Ps. 91:3)
>
> He will cover you with his feathers, and under his wings you will find refuge; his faithfulness will be your shield and rampart. (Ps. 91:4)

Our God is in heaven; he does whatever pleases him. (Ps. 115:3)

Yes, and from ancient days I am he. No one can deliver out of my hand. When I act, who can reverse it? (Is. 43:13)

3 (23:27-24:13) **Blessings, of God's People—Prophecy, of God's Blessings**: the third prophecy focused upon how God blesses His people. The king was desperate, so he could not give up. Somehow, some way, the Israelites had to be cursed. It was the only hope he had of defeating them in battle; therefore he must continue to seek the face of the gods, hoping that they would curse Israel. In desperation, he again appealed to the false prophet Balaam, the diviner who claimed to have the ear of the gods.

  a. Note the preparation for the prophecy (23:27-24:4).
    1) King Balak suggested a third site, hoping that a change of location would make a difference to the gods. He was desperate: a curse must be called down upon Israel. It was the only way his people and nation could be saved from the threat of invasion by the Israelites. Note that he took Balaam to the top of Mt. Peor. This was apparently the center of Baal worship in Moab (Nu. 25:3).
    2) Balaam again requested that seven altars be built (v.29).
    3) Once again, the false prophet offered pagan sacrifices upon the altar (v.30).
    4) At this point, Balaam made a significant change from what he had been doing: he did not resort to sorcery. He did not begin the usual chants, spells, charms, or magic tricks that were used to deceive the people (24:1).
    5) Instead, Balaam looked out over the camp of Israel tribe by tribe. Obviously, the sight struck him with a deep sense of God's presence among His people, that God was truly protecting them and blessing them beyond all imagination (vv.2-4). Suddenly, the Spirit of God came upon the false prophet in some kind of ecstatic trance or control. Under the control of God's Spirit, Balaam declared...
- that his eyes saw clearly
- that he heard the Word of God
- that he saw a vision from the Almighty
- that his eyes were opened

  b. Balaam then proclaimed the prophecy, a prophecy that shows exactly how God blesses His people (vv.5-9). Standing there on top of the mountain and looking down upon the campsites of Israel, this false prophet was stricken with the beauty of the sight. What he saw was immediately transferred over into the future. He began to predict what the future blessings of God would be upon His dear people.
    1) God would bless their dwelling places: their homes and lands would be beautiful (v.5).
    2) God would bless the fruitfulness of their homes and lands. Both the people and the land would be very productive and fruitful.
    3) God would bless the resources of the people. There would always be sufficient, overflowing water to take care of the crops and production (v.7). This was a clear promise of God taking care of the necessities of life.
    4) God would bless the leaders and the kingdom of His people. Both the leaders and the kingdom of God's people would be powerful and exalted, far greater than any ruler or kingdom surrounding them (v.7).
    5) God would bless their deliverance, for He Himself was their Deliverer. He would always deliver them from the attacks of their enemies (v.8).
    6) God would bless their strength and make them personally as strong as oxen (v.8).
    7) God would bless their struggle against all enemies. They were assured of complete and total victory (v.8). All enemies would be defeated by His people (v.8).
    8) God would bless their courage and security. They would always be courageous and secure under His watch (v.9). They would be as courageous and secure as a lion who lies down in the deep grass knowing that he is perfectly secure.
    9) God guaranteed the blessings of His people. The guarantee was the promise of God Himself (v.9). Any who blessed His people would be blessed, and any who cursed His people would be cursed. This was the very promise of the Abrahamic covenant (see Ge. 12:2-3).

  c. Note the result of the prophecy: the message could not be missed, neither by the king nor by his officials (vv.10-13).
    1) King Balak flew into a rage of anger, clapped his hands and shouted out at Balaam:
    ⇒ He charged Balaam with breaking their agreement. The false prophet had been summoned to curse Israel; instead, he had blessed them three times. He shouted out at Balaam to leave immediately and go home.
    ⇒ He dismissed Balaam without pay. This was the ultimate insult to the greed of this false prophet, this sorcerer who loved to make money through the unrighteous profession of sorcery (2 Pe. 2:15).

    2) Balaam attempted to excuse the disappointment of the king in his ability as a diviner or sorcerer. No doubt, Balaam was somewhat concerned about his reputation as a diviner with other leaders and nations. He reminded the king of the terms laid down with his officials when they first summoned him. He had made it perfectly clear that he could speak only what the LORD had said, that he was powerless to do anything against the LORD—even if the king gave him a palace filled with gold and silver (Nu. 22:18).

Thought 1. The blessings given to Israel are applicable to the believer. God promises to bless the believer with great and wonderful blessings.
(1) God blesses the believer with all the necessities of life: with shelter, food, and clothing.

So do not worry, saying, 'What shall we eat?' or 'What shall we drink?' or 'What shall we wear?' For the pagans run after all these things, and your heavenly Father knows that you need them. But seek first his kingdom and his righteousness, and all these things will be given to you as well. (Mt. 6:31-33)

And my God will meet all your needs according to his glorious riches in Christ Jesus. (Ph. 4:19)

NUMBERS 23:1–24:25

(2) God blesses His people with a fruitful, overflowing life.

> Worship the LORD your God, and his blessing will be on your food and water. I will take away sickness from among you. (Ex. 23:25)
>
> You prepare a table before me in the presence of my enemies. You anoint my head with oil; my cup overflows. (Ps. 23:5)
>
> How great is your goodness, which you have stored up for those who fear you, which you bestow in the sight of men on those who take refuge in you. (Ps. 31:19)
>
> "The days are coming," declares the LORD, "when the reaper will be overtaken by the plowman and the planter by the one treading grapes. New wine will drip from the mountains and flow from all the hills." (Am. 9:13)
>
> "Bring the whole tithe into the storehouse, that there may be food in my house. Test me in this," says the LORD Almighty, "and see if I will not throw open the floodgates of heaven and pour out so much blessing that you will not have room enough for it." (Mal. 3:10)

(3) God blesses His people with outstanding leaders and strong church fellowships.

> Keep watch over yourselves and all the flock of which the Holy Spirit has made you overseers. Be shepherds of the church of God, which he bought with his own blood. (Ac. 20:28)
>
> It was he who gave some to be apostles, some to be prophets, some to be evangelists, and some to be pastors and teachers, to prepare God's people for works of service, so that the body of Christ may be built up. (Ep. 4:11-12)
>
> Be shepherds of God's flock that is under your care, serving as overseers—not because you must, but because you are willing, as God wants you to be; not greedy for money, but eager to serve. (1 Pe. 5:2)
>
> Then I will give you shepherds after my own heart, who will lead you with knowledge and understanding. (Je. 3:15)
>
> "I will place shepherds over them who will tend them, and they will no longer be afraid or terrified, nor will any be missing," declares the LORD. (Je. 23:4)

(4) God blesses the believer with deliverance through all the trials and temptations of life.

> No temptation has seized you except what is common to man. And God is faithful; he will not let you be tempted beyond what you can bear. But when you are tempted, he will also provide a way out so that you can stand up under it. (1 Co. 10:13)
>
> The Lord will rescue me from every evil attack and will bring me safely to his heavenly kingdom. To him be glory for ever and ever. Amen. (2 Ti. 4:18)
>
> If this is so, then the Lord knows how to rescue godly men from trials and to hold the unrighteous for the day of judgment, while continuing their punishment. (2 Pe. 2:9)
>
> Surely he will save you from the fowler's snare and from the deadly pestilence. (Ps. 91:3)

(5) God blesses the believer with strength, both physical and spiritual.

> But he said to me, "My grace is sufficient for you, for my power is made perfect in weakness." Therefore I will boast all the more gladly about my weaknesses, so that Christ's power may rest on me. That is why, for Christ's sake, I delight in weaknesses, in insults, in hardships, in persecutions, in difficulties. For when I am weak, then I am strong. (2 Co. 12:9-10)
>
> I pray that out of his glorious riches he may strengthen you with power through his Spirit in your inner being. (Ep. 3:16)
>
> Who through faith conquered kingdoms, administered justice, and gained what was promised; who shut the mouths of lions, quenched the fury of the flames, and escaped the edge of the sword; whose weakness was turned to strength; and who became powerful in battle and routed foreign armies. (He. 11:33-34)
>
> But those who hope in the LORD will renew their strength. They will soar on wings like eagles; they will run and not grow weary, they will walk and not be faint. (Is. 40:31)
>
> So do not fear, for I am with you; do not be dismayed, for I am your God. I will strengthen you and help you; I will uphold you with my righteous right hand. (Is. 41:10)

(6) God blesses His people with victory over all the pitfalls and enemies of this life.

> Who shall separate us from the love of Christ? Shall trouble or hardship or persecution or famine or nakedness or danger or sword? (Ro. 8:35)
>
> No, in all these things we are more than conquerors through him who loved us. For I am convinced that neither death nor life, neither angels nor demons, neither the present nor the future, nor any powers, neither height nor depth, nor anything else in all creation, will be able to separate us from the love of God that is in Christ Jesus our Lord. (Ro. 8:37-39)
>
> For everyone born of God overcomes the world. This is the victory that has overcome the world, even our faith. Who is it that overcomes the world? Only he who believes that Jesus is the Son of God. (1 Jn. 5:4-5)
>
> Through you we push back our enemies; through your name we trample our foes. (Ps. 44:5)

(7) God blesses His people with courage and security throughout life.

> So we say with confidence, "The Lord is my helper; I will not be afraid. What can man do to me?" (He. 13:6)
> The LORD is my light and my salvation—whom shall I fear? The LORD is the stronghold of my life—of whom shall I be afraid? When evil men advance against me to devour my flesh, when my enemies and my foes attack me, they will stumble and fall. Though an army besiege me, my heart will not fear; though war break out against me, even then will I be confident. (Ps. 27:1-3)
> I will say of the LORD, "He is my refuge and my fortress, my God, in whom I trust." Surely he will save you from the fowler's snare and from the deadly pestilence. He will cover you with his feathers, and under his wings you will find refuge; his faithfulness will be your shield and rampart. You will not fear the terror of night, nor the arrow that flies by day, nor the pestilence that stalks in the darkness, nor the plague that destroys at midday. (Ps. 91:2-6)
> The LORD is with me; I will not be afraid. What can man do to me? (Ps. 118:6)
> When you lie down, you will not be afraid; when you lie down, your sleep will be sweet. (Pr. 3:24)
> Surely God is my salvation; I will trust and not be afraid. The LORD, the LORD, is my strength and my song; he has become my salvation. (Is. 12:2)

(8) God guarantees that the believer will be blessed by Him. God will keep His promises to His people and fulfill every promise.

> Yet he did not waver through unbelief regarding the promise of God, but was strengthened in his faith and gave glory to God, being fully persuaded that God had power to do what he had promised. (Ro. 4:20-21)
> For no matter how many promises God has made, they are "Yes" in Christ. And so through him the "Amen" is spoken by us to the glory of God. (2 Co. 1:20)
> Through these he has given us his very great and precious promises, so that through them you may participate in the divine nature and escape the corruption in the world caused by evil desires. (2 Pe. 1:4)
> Praise be to the LORD, who has given rest to his people Israel just as he promised. Not one word has failed of all the good promises he gave through his servant Moses. (1 K. 8:56)

4 (24:14-19) **Prophecy, Concerning the Coming Deliverer—Deliverance, Prophecy Concerning—Jesus Christ, Prophecy Concerning—Prophecy, of Jesus Christ**: the fourth prophecy focused upon the coming Deliverer. This was a picture of the coming of the Lord Jesus Christ as the Messianic Ruler over all the universe.

a. There was the preparation for the prophecy (vv.14-16). Just as Balaam turned to leave, suddenly he was constrained by the power of God to begin prophesying. The subject of this prophecy concerned the latter days, the days yet to come. Of course, this is a reference to the future.

Balaam declared...
- that his eyes saw the future clearly
- that he actually heard the words of God
- that he had knowledge from the Most High
- that he saw a vision from the Almighty
- that his eyes were opened to see into the future

b. The prophecy focused upon the coming Deliverer, the coming Messiah who was to reign as the Sovereign Lord over all (vv.17-19). Note exactly what was said:
1) He would come in the future. The false prophet saw Him but His coming was not yet near (v.17).
2) He would be a star and a scepter that would come out of Jacob and rise out of Israel. This is a reference to the rule and reign of Jesus Christ during the Messianic Kingdom and throughout all eternity (v.17).
3) He would be victorious. He would crush both Moab and Edom (v.17). Imagine the impact of these words upon the king of Edom standing right there listening to this prophecy as it was being proclaimed.
4) He would guarantee the growing strength of His people, Israel. They would grow stronger and stronger (v.18).
5) He would guarantee the triumph and dominion of God's people. He would lead God's people to destroy all their enemies (v.19).

Thought 1. Jesus Christ is the promised Deliverer, the Messiah and Messianic King who was to come and rule over all the universe. He is the Sovereign Lord and King of the universe.

> And I confer on you a kingdom, just as my Father conferred one on me, so that you may eat and drink at my table in my kingdom and sit on thrones, judging the twelve tribes of Israel. (Lu. 22:29-30)
> Then he said, "Jesus, remember me when you come into your kingdom." (Lu. 23:42)
> Then Nathanael declared, "Rabbi, you are the Son of God; you are the King of Israel." (Jn. 1:49)
> "I have told you these things, so that in me you may have peace. In this world you will have trouble. But take heart! I have overcome the world." (Jn. 16:33)
> Jesus said, "My kingdom is not of this world. If it were, my servants would fight to prevent my arrest by the Jews. But now my kingdom is from another place." "You are a king, then!" said Pilate. Jesus answered, "You are right in saying I am a king. In fact, for this reason I was born, and for this I came into the world, to testify to the truth. Everyone on the side of truth listens to me." (Jn. 18:36-37)
> For as in Adam all die, so in Christ all will be made alive. But each in his own turn: Christ, the firstfruits; then, when he

comes, those who belong to him. Then the end will come, when he hands over the kingdom to God the Father after he has destroyed all dominion, authority and power. For he must reign until he has put all his enemies under his feet. (1 Co. 15:22-25)

To him who overcomes, I will give the right to sit with me on my throne, just as I overcame and sat down with my Father on his throne. (Re. 3:21)

They will make war against the Lamb, but the Lamb will overcome them because he is Lord of lords and King of kings—and with him will be his called, chosen and faithful followers. (Re. 17:14)

Of the increase of his government and peace there will be no end. He will reign on David's throne and over his kingdom, establishing and upholding it with justice and righteousness from that time on and forever. The zeal of the LORD Almighty will accomplish this. (Is. 9:7)

Therefore I will give him a portion among the great, and he will divide the spoils with the strong, because he poured out his life unto death, and was numbered with the transgressors. For he bore the sin of many, and made intercession for the transgressors. (Is. 53:12)

"The days are coming," declares the LORD, "when I will raise up to David a righteous Branch, a King who will reign wisely and do what is just and right in the land. (Je. 23:5)

He was given authority, glory and sovereign power; all peoples, nations and men of every language worshiped him. His dominion is an everlasting dominion that will not pass away, and his kingdom is one that will never be destroyed. (Da. 7:14)

5 (24:20) **Victory, over Enemies—Enemies, Victory over—Prophecy, Concerning Victory over Enemies—Amalek, Prophecy Concerning Destruction—Israel, Prophecy of Victories**: the fifth prophecy focused upon the victory of Israel over the greatest of enemies. This prophecy and the final two are brief predictions concerning the enemies of God's people. These prophecies must have shaken the king to the core of his being. His purpose had been to bring a curse upon the Israelites; but instead he was being cursed and, not only him, but all the other enemies who stood opposed to the people of God. They were having the curse or judgment of God cast upon them as well. One thing was sure: it was not wise to oppose God's people. The prophecy was very simple: the false prophet saw Amalek and prophesied that this greatest of nations would be destroyed.

Thought 1. There is one strong lesson in this prophecy: victory is assured to God's people, even over the greatest of enemies. No matter how strong the enemy, no matter how great the assault, no matter how often the attack—victory belongs to God's people. The believer will conquer and triumph over all enemies, even the greatest of enemies.

(1) God gives victory over death.

For God so loved the world that he gave his one and only Son, that whoever believes in him shall not perish but have eternal life. (Jn. 3:16)

Do not let your hearts be troubled. Trust in God; trust also in me. In my Father's house are many rooms; if it were not so, I would have told you. I am going there to prepare a place for you. (Jn. 14:1-2)

Since the children have flesh and blood, he too shared in their humanity so that by his death he might destroy him who holds the power of death—that is, the devil—and free those who all their lives were held in slavery by their fear of death. (He. 2:14-15)

(2) God gives victory over the world with all its enslavements and bondages.

Then you will know the truth, and the truth will set you free. (Jn. 8:32)

In the same way, count yourselves dead to sin but alive to God in Christ Jesus. Therefore do not let sin reign in your mortal body so that you obey its evil desires. Do not offer the parts of your body to sin, as instruments of wickedness, but rather offer yourselves to God, as those who have been brought from death to life; and offer the parts of your body to him as instruments of righteousness. For sin shall not be your master, because you are not under law, but under grace. (Ro. 6:11-14)

So I find this law at work: When I want to do good, evil is right there with me. For in my inner being I delight in God's law; but I see another law at work in the members of my body, waging war against the law of my mind and making me a prisoner of the law of sin at work within my members. What a wretched man I am! Who will rescue me from this body of death? Thanks be to God—through Jesus Christ our Lord! So then, I myself in my mind am a slave to God's law, but in the sinful nature a slave to the law of sin. (Ro. 7:21-25)

Because through Christ Jesus the law of the Spirit of life set me free from the law of sin and death. (Ro. 8:2)

For everyone born of God overcomes the world. This is the victory that has overcome the world, even our faith. Who is it that overcomes the world? Only he who believes that Jesus is the Son of God. (1 Jn. 5:4-5)

(3) God gives victory over the evil of men, over all who oppose us and stand as enemies against us.

The Lord will rescue me from every evil attack and will bring me safely to his heavenly kingdom. To him be glory for ever and ever. Amen. (2 Ti. 4:18)

The LORD will fight for you; you need only to be still. (Ex. 14:14)

I will send my terror ahead of you and throw into confusion every nation you encounter. I will make all your enemies turn their backs and run. (Ex. 23:27)

Through you we push back our enemies; through your name we trample our foes. (Ps. 44:5)

(4) God gives victory over the temptations and trials of life.

No temptation has seized you except what is common to man. And God is faithful; he will not let you be tempted beyond what you can bear. But when you are tempted, he will also provide a way out so that you can stand up under it. (1 Co. 10:13)

A righteous man may have many troubles, but the LORD delivers him from them all. (Ps. 34:19)

The LORD will sustain him on his sickbed and restore him from his bed of illness. (Ps. 41:3)

When you pass through the waters, I will be with you; and when you pass through the rivers, they will not sweep over you. When you walk through the fire, you will not be burned; the flames will not set you ablaze. (Is. 43:2)

(5) God gives victory over all the evil powers and rulers of darkness, over all the spiritual wickedness that attacks us.

Finally, be strong in the Lord and in his mighty power. Put on the full armor of God so that you can take your stand against the devil's schemes. For our struggle is not against flesh and blood, but against the rulers, against the authorities, against the powers of this dark world and against the spiritual forces of evil in the heavenly realms. Therefore put on the full armor of God, so that when the day of evil comes, you may be able to stand your ground, and after you have done everything, to stand. (Ep. 6:10-13)

Submit yourselves, then, to God. Resist the devil, and he will flee from you. (Js. 4:7)

Be self-controlled and alert. Your enemy the devil prowls around like a roaring lion looking for someone to devour. (1 Pe. 5:8)

They overcame him by the blood of the Lamb and by the word of their testimony; they did not love their lives so much as to shrink from death. (Re. 12:11)

(6) God gives victory over any person or any thing, in this world and in the spiritual world.

Who shall separate us from the love of Christ? Shall trouble or hardship or persecution or famine or nakedness or danger or sword?...No, in all these things we are more than conquerors through him who loved us. For I am convinced that neither death nor life, neither angels nor demons, neither the present nor the future, nor any powers, neither height nor depth, nor anything else in all creation, will be able to separate us from the love of God that is in Christ Jesus our Lord. (Ro. 8:35, 37-39)

(7) God gives us victory over persecution.

For our light and momentary troubles are achieving for us an eternal glory that far outweighs them all. (2 Co. 4:17)

Dear friends, do not be surprised at the painful trial you are suffering, as though something strange were happening to you. But rejoice that you participate in the sufferings of Christ, so that you may be overjoyed when his glory is revealed. (1 Pe. 4:12-13)

6 (24:21-22) **Victory, over Enemies—Triumph, over Enemies—Prophecy, Victory over Enemies—Israel, Prophecies Concerning—Kenites, Prophecy Concerning—Prophecy, Concerning the Kenites—Assyria, Prophecy Concerning**: the sixth prophecy focused upon the greatest fortresses of the enemy being destroyed. Note that the Kenites were said to be secure, living behind an impregnable fortress. But they would be destroyed.

Someday out in the future, the great nation of Assyria would conquer the Kenites and take them captive. This is a prophecy that was looking ahead to the future, several centuries ahead. Assyria was not yet a powerful nation, not the powerful nation that was to be moving across the face of the earth seeking world domination. It should be noted that some commentators say that Asshur mentioned here was actually a small tribe that lived in northern Sinai (Ge. 25:3, 18; 2 S. 2:9; Ps. 83:8). If this is accurate, it means that the Kenites were conquered by a small tribe of people who lived close by. However, this position is most unlikely.

Thought 1. Every believer has certain enemies that seem impregnable, immovable. Certain temptations and trials seem to afflict him time and again. Temptation after temptation and trial after trial seem to lurk behind fortresses that just cannot be torn down. The believer tries to get rid of the temptations or trials, but they seem to be secure, settled in as though behind concrete fortresses—immovable, impregnable. The barrage of temptations and trials seems relentless. At times they attack the mind: the believer tries his best to get rid of the thoughts continually assaulting him. Foul words, lustful thoughts, cravings for food, drugs, or alcohol; seeking recognition or position; coveting more money, possessions, or property—a shower of tempting thoughts assault the believer all throughout the day. No matter how hard he tries, the temptations or trials seem to be impregnable; they cannot be cast down. But note the strong proclamation of Scripture: the greatest fortresses of the enemy can be destroyed. This is the promise of God.

Who shall separate us from the love of Christ? Shall trouble or hardship or persecution or famine or nakedness or danger or sword?...No, in all these things we are more than conquerors through him who loved us. For I am convinced that neither death nor life, neither angels nor demons, neither the present nor the future, nor any powers, neither height nor depth, nor anything else in all creation, will be able to separate us from the love of God that is in Christ Jesus our Lord. (Ro. 8:35, 37-39)

The weapons we fight with are not the weapons of the world. On the contrary, they have divine power to demolish strongholds. We demolish arguments and every pretension that sets itself up against the knowledge of God, and we take captive every thought to make it obedient to Christ. (2 Co. 10:4-5)

Finally, be strong in the Lord and in his mighty power. Put on the full armor of God so that you can take your stand against the devil's schemes. For our struggle is not against flesh and blood, but against the rulers, against the authorities, against the powers of this dark world and against the spiritual forces of evil in the heavenly realms. Therefore put on the full armor of God, so that when the day of evil comes, you may be able to stand your ground, and after you have done everything, to stand. (Ep. 6:10-13)

For the word of God is living and active. Sharper than any double-edged sword, it penetrates even to dividing soul and spirit, joints and marrow; it judges the thoughts and attitudes of the heart. (He. 4:12)

Be self-controlled and alert. Your enemy the devil prowls around like a roaring lion looking for someone to devour. Resist him, standing firm in the faith, because you know that your brothers throughout the world are undergoing the same kind of sufferings. And the God of all grace, who called you to his eternal glory in Christ, after you have suffered a little while, will himself restore you and make you strong, firm and steadfast. (1 Pe. 5:8-10)

Through you we push back our enemies; through your name we trample our foes. (Ps. 44:5)

7 (24:23-25) **Judgment, Against All Enemies—Prophecy, of Judgment—Judicial Judgment, of God—Nations, Cup Full of Iniquity—Cup, Full of Sin—Judgment, Full Measure of**: the seventh prophecy focused upon God's judgment against all enemies whose *cup was full of sin* This simply means that a nation had reached the full measure of evil that God allows. They would not be allowed to go any further, not allowed to continue committing one atrocity after another. They would be judged and destroyed as a nation.

Note that Balaam again prophesied the future. Assyria and Eber would be destroyed by an invading force coming from across the sea. After this prophecy, Balaam and Balak separated and returned home.

Thought 1. The judgment of God will fall upon the wicked and evil, the lawless and immoral of this earth. There will be no escape. When the "cup of sin" is full, when the full measure of sin has been committed by a person—that person will leave this earth and face the judgment of God. But note: this is not only true of individuals, it is also true of nations. When the "cup of sin," the full measure of evil and brutality, has been filled to overflowing by nations—that nation will be destroyed by the terrifying hand of God's judgment. This is the record of human history, as any objective and honest historian can testify.

(1) God will judge the nations of this earth.

When the Son of Man comes in his glory, and all the angels with him, he will sit on his throne in heavenly glory. All the nations will be gathered before him, and he will separate the people one from another as a shepherd separates the sheep from the goats. He will put the sheep on his right and the goats on his left....Then he will say to those on his left, 'Depart from me, you who are cursed, into the eternal fire prepared for the devil and his angels.'...Then they will go away to eternal punishment, but the righteous to eternal life. (Mt. 25:31-33, 41, 46)

For he has set a day when he will judge the world with justice by the man he has appointed. He has given proof of this to all men by raising him from the dead. (Ac. 17:31)

(2) God will judge the people of this earth, individual by individual—every one of us.

This will take place on the day when God will judge men's secrets through Jesus Christ, as my gospel declares. (Ro. 2:16)

So then, each of us will give an account of himself to God. (Ro. 14:12)

Just as man is destined to die once, and after that to face judgment. (He. 9:27)

If this is so, then the Lord knows how to rescue godly men from trials and to hold the unrighteous for the day of judgment, while continuing their punishment. (2 Pe. 2:9)

By the same word the present heavens and earth are reserved for fire, being kept for the day of judgment and destruction of ungodly men. (2 Pe. 3:7)

Enoch, the seventh from Adam, prophesied about these men: "See, the Lord is coming with thousands upon thousands of his holy ones to judge everyone, and to convict all the ungodly of all the ungodly acts they have done in the ungodly way, and of all the harsh words ungodly sinners have spoken against him." (Jude 14-15)

NUMBERS 23:1–24:25

TYPES, SYMBOLS, AND PICTURES
(Numbers 23:1–24:25)

Historical Term	Type or Picture (Scriptural Basis for Each)	Life Application for Today's Believer	Biblical Application
Israel Nu. 23:1-12	*Israel is a type or symbol of God's people.* **Then Balaam uttered his oracle: "Balak brought me from Aram, the king of Moab from the eastern mountains. 'Come,' he said, 'curse Jacob for me; come, denounce Israel.' How can I curse those whom God has not cursed? How can I denounce those whom the Lord has not denounced? From the rocky peaks I see them, from the heights I view them. I see a people who live apart and do not consider themselves one of the nations. Who can count the dust of Jacob or number the fourth part of Israel? Let me die the death of the righteous, and may my end be like theirs!" (Nu. 23:7-10)**	The blessings of God given in this passage are gifts of God to all His people (Nu. 23:1-12). Note the blessings one by one. 1. God's people are an innocent, secure people—a people who are justified, eternally secure before God. God has forgiven our sins and justified us, counted us innocent before Him.	*I give them eternal life, and they shall never perish; no one can snatch them out of my hand. (Jn. 10:28)*
		2. God's people are a separated and distinctive people. The genuine believer lives a holy life before God, a life that is pure and righteous, moral and clean, just and fair. The believer lives a life of separation from the world.	*If you belonged to the world, it would love you as its own. As it is, you do not belong to the world, but I have chosen you out of the world. That is why the world hates you. (Jn. 15:19)* *Have nothing to do with the fruitless deeds of darkness, but rather expose them. (Ep. 5:11)*
		3. God's people are eventually to be a numerous people. This was the promise made to Abraham and his descendants, that is, all the succeeding generations of believers down through the ages. Believers are eventually to number as the stars of the sky and as the sands by the seashore.	*I will surely bless you and make your descendants as numerous as the stars in the sky and as the sand on the seashore. Your descendants will take possession of the cities of their enemies. (Ge. 22:17)*
		4. God's people are a righteous people with eternal hope. A genuine believer is counted righteous through the righteousness of Jesus Christ. Jesus Christ is the believer's only approach to God. A person can approach God only through Christ, only through His righteousness. When a person comes to God through Christ's righteousness, God accepts that person; God counts that person justified, righteous. Once the person has been justified—counted righteous—he is given the wonderful hope of living eternally with God.	*Christ is the end of the law so that there may be righteousness for everyone who believes. (Ro. 10:4)* *It is because of him that you are in Christ Jesus, who has become for us wisdom from God—that is, our righteousness, holiness and redemption. (1 Co. 1:30)* *And be found in him, not having a righteousness of my own that comes from the law, but that which is through faith in Christ—the righteousness that comes from God and is by faith. (Ph. 3:9)*

NUMBERS 23:1–24:25

Historical Term	Type or Picture (Scriptural Basis for Each)	Life Application for Today's Believer	Biblical Application
The Third Prophecy of Balaam Nu. 23:27-24:14	*The third prophecy of Balaam is a picture of how God blesses His people.* *Balaam began to predict what the future blessings of God would be upon His dear people.* 1. *God would bless their dwelling places: their homes and lands would be beautiful (v.5).* 2. *God would bless the fruitfulness of their homes and lands. Both the people and the land would be very productive and fruitful.* 3. *God would bless the resources of the people. There would always be sufficient, overflowing water to take care of the crops and production (v.7). This was a clear promise of God taking care of the necessities of life.* 4. *God would bless the leaders and the kingdom of His people. Both the leaders and the kingdom of God's people would be powerful and exalted, far greater than any ruler or kingdom surrounding them (v.7).* 5. *God would bless their deliverance, for He Himself was their Deliverer. He would always deliver them from the attacks of their enemies (v.8).* 6. *God would bless their strength and make them personally as strong as oxen (v.8).* 7. *God would bless their struggle against all enemies. He assured them of complete and total victory (v.8). All enemies would be defeated by His people (v.8).* 8. *God would bless their courage and security. They were assured that they would always be courageous and secure under His watch (v.9). They would be as courageous and secure as a lion who lies down in the deep grass knowing that he is perfectly secure.* 9. *God guaranteed the blessings of His people.*	The blessings given to Israel are applicable to the believer. God promises to bless the believer with great and wonderful blessings. ⇒ God blesses the believer with all the necessities of life: with shelter, food, and clothing. ⇒ God blesses His people with a fruitful, overflowing life. ⇒ God blesses His people with outstanding leaders and strong church fellowships. ⇒ God blesses the believer with deliverance through all the trials and temptations of life. ⇒ God blesses the believer with strength, both physical and spiritual. ⇒ God blesses His people with victory over all the pitfalls and enemies of this life. ⇒ God blesses His people with courage and security throughout life. ⇒ God guarantees that the believer will be blessed by Him. God will keep His promises to His people and fulfill every promise.	*So do not worry, saying, 'What shall we eat?' or 'What shall we drink?' or 'What shall we wear?' For the pagans run after all these things, and your heavenly Father knows that you need them. But seek first his kingdom and his righteousness, and all these things will be given to you as well. (Mt. 6:31-33)* *Keep watch over yourselves and all the flock of which the Holy Spirit has made you overseers. Be shepherds of the church of God, which he bought with his own blood. (Ac. 20:28)* *Yet he did not waver through unbelief regarding the promise of God, but was strengthened in his faith and gave glory to God, being fully persuaded that God had power to do what he had promised. (Ro. 4:20-21)* *Who shall separate us from the love of Christ? Shall trouble or hardship or persecution or famine or nakedness or danger or sword? (Ro. 8:35)* *No temptation has seized you except what is common to man. And God is faithful; he will not let you be tempted beyond what you can bear. But when you are tempted, he will also provide a way out so that you can stand up under it. (1 Co. 10:13)* *I pray that out of his glorious riches he may strengthen you with power through his Spirit in your inner being. (Ep. 3:16)* *So we say with confidence, "The Lord is my helper; I will not be afraid. What can man do to me?" (He. 13:6)* *Worship the Lord your God, and his blessing will be on your food and water. I will take away sickness from among you. (Ex. 23:25)*

NUMBERS 23:1–24:25

Historical Term	Type or Picture (Scriptural Basis for Each)	Life Application for Today's Believer	Biblical Application
	The guarantee was the promise of God Himself (v.9). Any who blessed His people would be blessed, and any who cursed His people would be cursed. This was the very promise of the Abrahamic covenant (see Ge. 12:2-3).		
	"How beautiful are your tents, O Jacob, your dwelling places, O Israel! Like valleys they spread out, like gardens beside a river, like aloes planted by the Lord, like cedars beside the waters. Water will flow from their buckets; their seed will have abundant water. Their king will be greater than Agag; their kingdom will be exalted." (Nu. 24:5-7)		
The Coming Deliverer Nu. 24:14-19	*The coming Deliverer is a symbol of the coming of the Lord Jesus Christ as the Messianic Ruler over all the universe.* *The prophecy focused upon the coming Deliverer, the coming Messiah who was to reign as the Sovereign Lord over all (vv.17-19). Note exactly what was said:* 1. *He would come in the future. The false prophet saw Him, but His coming was not yet near (v.17).* 2. *He would be a star and a scepter that would come out of Jacob and rise out of Israel. This is a reference to the rule and reign of Jesus Christ during the Messianic Kingdom and throughout all eternity (v.17).* 3. *He would be victorious. He would crush both Moab and Edom (v.17). Imagine the impact of these words upon the king of Edom standing right there listening to this prophecy as it was being proclaimed.* 4. *He would guarantee the growing strength of His people, Israel. They would grow stronger and stronger (v.18).* 5. *He would guarantee the triumph and dominion of*	Jesus Christ is the promised Deliverer, the Messiah and Messianic King who was to come and rule over all the universe. He is the Sovereign Lord and King of the universe.	And I confer on you a kingdom, just as my Father conferred one on me, so that you may eat and drink at my table in my kingdom and sit on thrones, judging the twelve tribes of Israel. (Lu. 22:29-30) Then Nathanael declared, "Rabbi, you are the Son of God; you are the King of Israel." (Jn. 1:49) "I have told you these things, so that in me you may have peace. In this world you will have trouble. But take heart! I have overcome the world." (Jn. 16:33) Jesus said, "My kingdom is not of this world. If it were, my servants would fight to prevent my arrest by the Jews. But now my kingdom is from another place." (Jn. 18:36) "You are a king, then!" said Pilate. Jesus answered, "You are right in saying I am a king. In fact, for this reason I was born, and for this I came into the world, to testify to the truth. Everyone on the side of truth listens to me." (Jn. 18:37) For as in Adam all die, so in Christ all will be made alive. But each in his own turn: Christ, the firstfruits; then, when he comes, those who belong to him. Then the end will come, when he

NUMBERS 23:1–24:25

Historical Term	Type or Picture (Scriptural Basis for Each)	Life Application for Today's Believer	Biblical Application
	God's people. He would lead God's people to destroy all their enemies (v.19). "I see him, but not now; I behold him, but not near. A star will come out of Jacob; a scepter will rise out of Israel. He will crush the foreheads of Moab, the skulls of all the sons of Sheth. (Nu. 24:17)		*hands over the kingdom to God the Father after he has destroyed all dominion, authority and power. (1 Co. 15:22-24) For he must reign until he has put all his enemies under his feet. (1 Co. 15:25) To him who overcomes, I will give the right to sit with me on my throne, just as I overcame and sat down with my Father on his throne. (Re. 3:21)*
Assyria Destroying the Kenites Nu. 24:21-22	*Assyria Destroying the Kenites is a picture of the greatest fortress of the enemy being defeated. Note that the Kenites were said to be secure, living behind an impregnable fortress. But they would be destroyed.* **Then he saw the Kenites and uttered his oracle: "Your dwelling place is secure, your nest is set in a rock; yet you Kenites will be destroyed when Asshur takes you captive." (Nu. 24:21-22)**	Every believer has challenges or problems that feel insurmountable. Certain temptations and trials bombard him repeatedly, as though on a fixed, immovable schedule. Whatever the weakness—foul language, lustful images, unhealthy cravings for food, drugs, or alcohol, recognition or position, more money, possessions, or property—a shower of enticing thoughts assault the believer throughout the day. Indeed, the attacks seem endless. No matter how hard he tries, the believer cannot cast down the temptations and trials on his own. But note the wonderful proclamation of Scripture: the mighty power of God can destroy the greatest strongholds or fortresses of the enemy. This is the surefire promise of God.	*Who shall separate us from the love of Christ? Shall trouble or hardship or persecution or famine or nakedness or danger or sword?...No, in all these things we are more than conquerors through him who loved us. For I am convinced that neither death nor life, neither angels nor demons, neither the present nor the future, nor any powers, neither height nor depth, nor anything else in all creation, will be able to separate us from the love of God that is in Christ Jesus our Lord. (Ro. 8:35, 37-39) The weapons we fight with are not the weapons of the world. On the contrary, they have divine power to demolish strongholds. We demolish arguments and every pretension that sets itself up against the knowledge of God, and we take captive every thought to make it obedient to Christ. (2 Co. 10:4-5) Finally, be strong in the Lord and in his mighty power. Put on the full armor of God so that you can take your stand against the devil's schemes. For our struggle is not against flesh and blood, but against the rulers, against the authorities, against the powers of this dark world and against the spiritual forces of evil in the heavenly realms. Therefore put on the full armor of God, so that when the day of evil comes, you may be able to stand your ground, and after you have done everything, to stand. (Ep. 6:10-13)*

NUMBERS 25:1-18

CHAPTER 25

J. Event 10—the Ultimate Rebellion of God's People & the End of the Forty Years of Wilderness Wanderings: Apostasy—Turning to Worldliness, to the Worship of Sex & Other Gods, 25:1-18

1. **The cause of the apostasy**
   a. Sexual immorality: The men began to have sex with their neighbors, the Moabite women
   b. Worshipping other gods
      1) The Moabite women seduced the men to join them in their festivals of worship
      2) The men—before long—yielded & joined in their false worship
2. **The judgment of God**
   a. He was angry: Sent a plague, v.8
   b. He commanded Moses to execute the ringleaders
      1) In broad daylight, publicly, as a strong warning
      2) In obedience to the law (Le. 18:24-30; 20:10)
   c. Moses obeyed: Charged the judges to execute all who had worshipped & turned to the false god Baal of Peor
3. **The way the judgment was stopped**
   a. The zeal of a priest, Phinehas, stopped the judgment
      1) An outrageous sin: A man & a pagan woman showed public, sexual affection before Moses & the people
      2) The righteous zeal of the priest Phinehas
         • He jumped up & left the prayer assembly, taking a spear

While Israel was staying in Shittim, the men began to indulge in sexual immorality with Moabite women,
2 Who invited them to the sacrifices to their gods. The people ate and bowed down before these gods.
3 So Israel joined in worshiping the Baal of Peor. And the LORD's anger burned against them.
4 The LORD said to Moses, "Take all the leaders of these people, kill them and expose them in broad daylight before the LORD, so that the LORD's fierce anger may turn away from Israel."
5 So Moses said to Israel's judges, "Each of you must put to death those of your men who have joined in worshiping the Baal of Peor."
6 Then an Israelite man brought to his family a Midianite woman right before the eyes of Moses and the whole assembly of Israel while they were weeping at the entrance to the Tent of Meeting.
7 When Phinehas son of Eleazar, the son of Aaron, the priest, saw this, he left the assembly, took a spear in his hand
8 And followed the Israelite into the tent. He drove the spear through both of them—through the Israelite and into the woman's body. Then the plague against the Israelites was stopped;
9 But those who died in the plague numbered 24,000.
10 The LORD said to Moses,
11 "Phinehas son of Eleazar, the son of Aaron, the priest, has turned my anger away from the Israelites; for he was as zealous as I am for my honor among them, so that in my zeal I did not put an end to them.
12 Therefore tell him I am making my covenant of peace with him.
13 He and his descendants will have a covenant of a lasting priesthood, because he was zealous for the honor of his God and made atonement for the Israelites."
14 The name of the Israelite who was killed with the Midianite woman was Zimri son of Salu, the leader of a Simeonite family.
15 And the name of the Midianite woman who was put to death was Cozbi daughter of Zur, a tribal chief of a Midianite family.
16 The LORD said to Moses,
17 "Treat the Midianites as enemies and kill them,
18 Because they treated you as enemies when they deceived you in the affair of Peor and their sister Cozbi, the daughter of a Midianite leader, the woman who was killed when the plague came as a result of Peor."

   • He followed the couple who showed such outrageous contempt against God & the people
   • He went into the tent & executed the couple
   3) The judgment stopped: The plague ended, but 24,000 people had died
   b. The result of the priest's zeal
      1) God stopped the judgment
      2) God acknowledged the greatness of his zeal: He was zealous for God's honor
      3) God made His covenant of peace with Phinehas: His kind of zeal made peace between God & man
      4) God established that the High Priest would come from his descendants
      5) God accepted his act of zeal as atonement (reconciliation) for the people
4. **The dangerous threat of apostasy & immorality**
   a. The man & woman would have influenced many to sin
      1) He was the son of a prominent leader, the leader of the great tribe of Simeon
      2) She was the daughter of a Midianite (1 K. 31:8)
   b. The strategy of the Midianites would have destroyed Israel
      1) The clear fact: They were enemies & had to be executed
      2) The reason: Because their strategy was clearly seen
         • They seduced through illicit sex & the false worship of Baal Peor
         • They had contempt for God & His people: Seen in the outrageous sin of Cozbi, v.6

DIVISION III

THE FORTY LONG YEARS OF WILDERNESS WANDERINGS: A PICTURE OF THE BELIEVER'S PILGRIMAGE THROUGH THIS WORLD AS HE PREPARES TO ENTER THE PROMISED LAND, 15:1–25:18

J. Event 10—The Ultimate Rebellion of God's People and the End of the Forty Years of Wilderness Wanderings: Apostasy—Turning to Worldliness, to the Worship of Sex and Other Gods, 25:1-18

(25:1-18) **Introduction—Sex, Age of—Society, Facts, Bombarded with Sex—Society, Problems of, False Worship—Immorality, Age of**: this is an age that worships sex. It has even been called "the age of the sexual revolution." It is an age when sex is used to advertise practically every product that is sold, certainly most of the products.

NUMBERS 25:1-18

Newspapers, magazines, films, television, radio, videos—little can be read or seen for more than a few brief moments before some sexual image or insinuation has bombarded the human mind. Society is being taught that all forms of sexual behavior are acceptable:

⇒ adultery
⇒ living together outside of marriage
⇒ premarital sex
⇒ spouse-swapping
⇒ homosexuality
⇒ pornography
⇒ sex with children
⇒ masochism
⇒ sadism bestiality

All forms of sexual abnormalities and deviancies are being hurled at society today. There seems to be a deliberate attempt to destroy common decency and the control of fleshly lusts and passions. But this is not the only problem faced today: our society also faces the problem of false worship. Scripture is clear: there is only one true and living God, the Lord God Himself (Jehovah, Yahweh). Therefore, there is only one true worship, the worship of Him and Him alone. Any other worship is false. This is the subject of this passage of Scripture, a passage that clearly speaks to all of us: *Event 10: The Ultimate Rebellion of God's People and the End of the Forty Years of Wilderness Wanderings: Apostasy—Turning to Worldliness, to the Worship of Sex and Other Gods,* 25:1-18.

1. The cause of the apostasy (vv.1-3).
2. The judgment of God (vv.4-5).
3. The way the judgment was stopped (vv.6-13).
4. The dangerous threat of apostasy and immorality (vv.14-18).

1 (25:1-3) **Apostasy, Cause of—Immorality—Israel, Apostasy of—Apostasy, of Israel—Israel, Sins of—Baal of Peor**: the cause of the apostasy was twofold: sexual immorality and false worship. This was the ultimate rebellion of God's people against Him and the end of the forty years of wilderness wanderings. With this rebellion, the last of the first generation died. Tragically, they had all died because of sin and the inevitable judgment of God against sin. It is important to note this fact: all the first generation of Israel had now died; only their children—the second generation—survived. Only the second generation would enter the promised land of God. The first generation that had left Egypt—that had experienced the saving power of God from slavery—had all died in the desert wilderness. Terrible unbelief and grumbling against God and His dear servant had brought the judgment of God upon them. They would never enter the promised land: never know the conquering, victorious power of God over the pitfalls and enemies of this life. They would never know the spiritual rest—the peace, love, and joy—that God gives to the human soul who trusts Him. The first generation of Israelites failed God, miserably failed Him, and they failed to lay hold of the fullness of life. Now, the last of them died, died just as the first of them had—under the hand of God's judgment. However, there is one difference between the two sins they were committing in this current passage and the sins they had committed before: the sins now committed would be the very sins that would eventually bring about the downfall of Israel as a nation—the sins of sexual immorality and apostasy, the worship of false gods. Incomprehensible! Unbelievable! But it did happen. This is seen later on in the Old Testament. But for now, note that some Israelite men began to participate in the false worship of their neighbors—all for sex.

a. The first terrible cause of apostasy was sexual immorality (v.1). Remember, Israel was camped in the plains of Moab along the Jordan River right across from the great city of Jericho. The area was also called Shittim. What then happened to Israel was a satanic plot devised by the false prophet—the diviner and sorcerer—Balaam. Remember, he had been unable to call down a curse upon God's people. But he came up with another idea, a satanic plot and scheme. He suggested to the king of Moab the following: that Moabite women seduce the Israelite men to have sex. Once they were enslaved to sex, the women could invite them to their festivals of worship, encouraging them to join in the worship of their gods. Obviously, he suggested that this perhaps would arouse the anger of God against the Israelites, causing God to judge and curse them. This satanic plot and scheme was followed through with: the Moabite women became stumblingblocks to the men of Israel. They seduced the men into immorality and no doubt even some of the husbands into committing adultery against their dear wives. As history and human nature show, men have strong sexual urges. The king and the Moabite women used these basic urges to seduce the men, and in the weakness of the flesh the men caved in. They were not focused upon God enough. They were not spiritually strong in their day-to-day walk with God; consequently, they fell into the gross sin of immorality.

As the great book of Proverbs says: they were attracted...

- by the lips and the kisses of the strange woman (Pr.7:13)
- by the beauty of her face and the shape of her body (Pr.7:15)
- by the coverings and the perfume of her bed (Pr.7:16-17)
- by making love with her until the morning (Pr.7:18)
- by her sweet voice and flattering words (Pr.7:21)

Because of the weakness of their flesh, the men crumbled and fell. They were not walking closely enough with God, not day by day. They failed to withstand the seductive, enticing appeal for pleasure. In utter weakness of the flesh, the men forgot God. They ignored and broke the seventh commandment, "You shall not commit adultery" (Ex.20:14).

b. Before long, the men yielded and joined in the false worship of their neighbors (vv.2-3). Once the seductive women had the men enslaved to sex, they invited the men to join them at their festival occasions which were centered around their worship. The men soon accepted the invitations and joined the women at the festivals. Once there, it was not long before the men were joining in the worship of their gods, in particular the god known as *Baal of Peor. Peor* was a mountain in Moab that was close to where the Israelites were camped. Most likely because of its high elevation, it had been chosen to be the major site for the worship of the false god Baal. (See DEEPER STUDY # 1—Nu.25:3 for more discussion.) Note the word *joined* (tsamad, Strong's; samad, NIV). The word means to be linked together, fastened, framed, joined together. It means to be harnessed, strapped, yoked together. The men had actually attached or joined themselves to the false worship of the people, to the worship of this false god. The women of Moab had been the tempters and conquerors of the men. At first, the men had yielded to the temptations of sex, but now they were yielding to the seductions of *false worship*. In unbelief and disobedience to God, they had slipped back into the world, seduced by the fleshly lusts and false worship of the world.

Thought 1. The lessons for us are clear, and they speak loudly.
(1) We must not break the seventh commandment. Scripture is clear: we must not commit adultery.

> But I tell you that anyone who looks at a woman lustfully has already committed adultery with her in his heart. (Mt. 5:28)

> Therefore God gave them over in the sinful desires of their hearts to sexual impurity for the degrading of their bodies with one another....Because of this, God gave them over to shameful lusts. Even their women exchanged natural relations for unnatural ones. In the same way the men also abandoned natural relations with women and were inflamed with lust for one another. Men committed indecent acts with other men, and received in themselves the due penalty for their perversion. Furthermore, since they did not think it worthwhile to retain the knowledge of God, he gave them over to a depraved mind, to do what ought not to be done. (Ro. 1:24, 26-28)

> Do you not know that the wicked will not inherit the kingdom of God? Do not be deceived: Neither the sexually immoral nor idolaters nor adulterers nor male prostitutes nor homosexual offenders nor thieves nor the greedy nor drunkards nor slanderers nor swindlers will inherit the kingdom of God. And that is what some of you were. But you were washed, you were sanctified, you were justified in the name of the Lord Jesus Christ and by the Spirit of our God. (1 Co. 6:9-11)

> Flee from sexual immorality. All other sins a man commits are outside his body, but he who sins sexually sins against his own body. (1 Co. 6:18)

> But among you there must not be even a hint of sexual immorality, or of any kind of impurity, or of greed, because these are improper for God's holy people. Nor should there be obscenity, foolish talk or coarse joking, which are out of place, but rather thanksgiving. (Ep. 5:3-4)

> It is God's will that you should be sanctified: that you should avoid sexual immorality; that each of you should learn to control his own body in a way that is holy and honorable, not in passionate lust like the heathen, who do not know God. (1 Th. 4:3-5)

> Avoid every kind of evil. (1 Th. 5:22)

> Marriage should be honored by all, and the marriage bed kept pure, for God will judge the adulterer and all the sexually immoral. (He. 13:4)

> Dear friends, I urge you, as aliens and strangers in the world, to abstain from sinful desires, which war against your soul. (1 Pe. 2:11)

> But the cowardly, the unbelieving, the vile, the murderers, the sexually immoral, those who practice magic arts, the idolaters and all liars—their place will be in the fiery lake of burning sulfur. This is the second death. (Re. 21:8)

> You shall not commit adultery. (Ex. 20:14)

> If a man commits adultery with another man's wife—with the wife of his neighbor—both the adulterer and the adulteress must be put to death. (Le. 20:10)

> Do not lust in your heart after her beauty or let her captivate you with her eyes. (Pr. 6:25)

> But a man who commits adultery lacks judgment; whoever does so destroys himself. (Pr. 6:32)

(2) We must not join in the false worship of the world. We must not worship the false gods of this world. There is only one true and living God, the Lord God Himself (Jehovah, Yahweh). There is only one true approach to God, only one approach that is acceptable to God: the approach through the Lord Jesus Christ, the very Son of God Himself. We must never attempt to approach God through anyone other than the Lord Jesus Christ. Any other approach or any other worship is false. There is only one God and one mediator between God and man, the Lord Jesus Christ.

The Israelite men made a fatal mistake: they joined the false worship of the world. They worshipped the false gods that had been created and formed by the imaginations of men. The people of that day did just what the people of today do: they used the highest, most elevated thoughts they could think, the greatest ideas they could conceive, and they imagined what God was like. They created a god they wanted to follow, a god who would allow them to behave and do the things they wanted. They formed their god around their own morality and ideas of justice. Man is corrupt, filled with immoral, selfish, and unjust thoughts; therefore, when he creates a god to match his behavior and desires—his god is no higher than himself. His god is a man-made god.

This is what the Moabites had done in creating Baal. This was part of the reason the Israelite men gave themselves over to follow the false worship and gods of their neighbors. The false worship allowed them to live immoral lives, to enjoy the bright lights and pleasures of their society. They were able to fulfill the lusts of the flesh, the eyes, and the pride of life. But Scripture is clear: "You shall have no other gods before me" (Ex. 20:3). You shall not engage in false worship—the false worship and religions of this world—the false worship created by the imaginations and ideas of men.

> I told you that you would die in your sins; if you do not believe that I am the one I claim to be, you will indeed die in your sins. (Jn. 8:24)

> The wrath of God is being revealed from heaven against all the godlessness and wickedness of men who suppress the truth by their wickedness, since what may be known about God is plain to them, because God has made it plain to them. For since the creation of the world God's invisible qualities—his eternal power and divine

NUMBERS 25:1-18

nature—have been clearly seen, being understood from what has been made, so that men are without excuse. For although they knew God, they neither glorified him as God nor gave thanks to him, but their thinking became futile and their foolish hearts were darkened. Although they claimed to be wise, they became fools and exchanged the glory of the immortal God for images made to look like mortal man and birds and animals and reptiles. (Ro. 1:18-23)

For even if there are so-called gods, whether in heaven or on earth (as indeed there are many "gods" and many "lords"), yet for us there is but one God, the Father, from whom all things came and for whom we live; and there is but one Lord, Jesus Christ, through whom all things came and through whom we live. (1 Co. 8:5-6)

You know that when you were pagans, somehow or other you were influenced and led astray to mute idols. (1 Co. 12:2)

For this reason God sends them a powerful delusion so that they will believe the lie and so that all will be condemned who have not believed the truth but have delighted in wickedness. (2 Th. 2:11-12)

But the cowardly, the unbelieving, the vile, the murderers, the sexually immoral, those who practice magic arts, the idolaters and all liars—their place will be in the fiery lake of burning sulfur. This is the second death. (Re. 21:8)

The fool says in his heart, "There is no God." They are corrupt, their deeds are vile; there is no one who does good. (Ps. 14:1)

But their idols are silver and gold, made by the hands of men. They have mouths, but cannot speak, eyes, but they cannot see; they have ears, but cannot hear, noses, but they cannot smell; they have hands, but cannot feel, feet, but they cannot walk; nor can they utter a sound with their throats. Those who make them will be like them, and so will all who trust in them. (Ps. 115:4-8)

To whom, then, will you compare God? What image will you compare him to? As for an idol, a craftsman casts it, and a goldsmith overlays it with gold and fashions silver chains for it. A man too poor to present such an offering selects wood that will not rot. He looks for a skilled craftsman to set up an idol that will not topple. (Is. 40:18-20)

"I am the Lord; that is my name! I will not give my glory to another or my praise to idols." (Is. 42:8)

Gather together and come; assemble, you fugitives from the nations. Ignorant are those who carry about idols of wood, who pray to gods that cannot save. (Is. 45:20)

Has a nation ever changed its gods? (Yet they are not gods at all.) But my people have exchanged their Glory for worthless idols. (Je. 2:11)

This is what the LORD says: "Do not learn the ways of the nations or be terrified by signs in the sky, though the nations are terrified by them. For the customs of the peoples are worthless; they cut a tree out of the forest, and a craftsman shapes it with his chisel. They adorn it with silver and gold; they fasten it with hammer and nails so it will not totter. Like a scarecrow in a melon patch, their idols cannot speak; they must be carried because they cannot walk. Do not fear them; they can do no harm nor can they do any good." (Je. 10:2-5)

Do men make their own gods? Yes, but they are not gods! (Je. 16:20)

2 (25:4-5) **Judgment, of God—Immorality, Judgment of—Idolatry, Judgment of—Worship, False, Judgment of**: the judgment of God was quick and sure. The immoral and the false worshippers were immediately judged. They had broken two of the major commandments of God, two of the Ten Commandments. By their terrible sins, they had aroused the anger of God. Both the holiness and justice of God had been violated. His commandment was ignored and abused. His holy, pure, and righteous nature had to be satisfied. His justice had to be executed. Judgment upon the immoral and false worshippers was carried out:

a. God was greatly angered because the people had committed sexual immorality and joined in false worship (v.3). His justice against sin had to be executed; consequently, He sent a plague among them (see v.8). There were obviously thousands of people involved in this gross sin, for twenty-four thousand people died in the plague.

b. God commanded Moses to execute the ringleaders (v.4). They were to be executed in broad daylight—publicly—so they would stand as a strong warning to the whole community. Because of the strong sexual drive of many, there was the danger that many others would fall into sexual immorality. Remember, there was a deliberate plot to destroy Israel through the lure of illicit sex and the worship of the false gods of their neighbors—a deliberate plot devised by the false prophet Balaam and the king of Moab. By publicly executing the ringleaders, the people would be warned: they must not cave in to the seduction of sexual immorality nor join in the worship of the false gods of their neighbors. Some commentators think that the execution even involved hanging the ringleaders up on a pole in full sight of all who passed by. However, Scripture seems to indicate elsewhere that a public execution and display of the dead bodies were probably what happened (2 S. 21:6-13). The penalty for adultery and for false worship or idolatry was death (Le. 18:24-30; 20:10).

c. Moses obeyed God: he charged the judges to execute all who had worshipped and turned to the false god Baal of Peor (v.5).

Thought 1. The focus of this point is the judgment of God, the fact that God judges sin. God is holy, righteous, pure, perfect. The fact that God is holy means that He will someday judge the world. God cannot allow His holy presence to become contaminated, polluted, unclean, or defiled. To allow any sin in His presence would defile the very atmosphere around God. This God must never allow. But God is not only holy; He is just. God dwells in perfect justice. He cannot allow a single act of injustice to exist in His presence. To do so would mean that injustices dwell and defile the very presence and atmosphere surrounding God. This God must never allow.

There is only one solution to the problem created by the sin, the immoralities, and the injustices of the world: that solution is the judgment of God. All the sin and injustices, and all the people who have committed these, must be removed from God's holy and just presence. This is the reason the judgment of God fell upon those who committed sexual immorality and joined in the false worship of their neighbors. Some day every human being who has ever lived will face the judgment of God. God will judge the world in righteousness. The judgment of God is coming just as it came upon the Israelites.

> "When the Son of Man comes in his glory, and all the angels with him, he will sit on his throne in heavenly glory. All the nations will be gathered before him, and he will separate the people one from another as a shepherd separates the sheep from the goats. He will put the sheep on his right and the goats on his left....Then he will say to those on his left, 'Depart from me, you who are cursed, into the eternal fire prepared for the devil and his angels.'...Then they will go away to eternal punishment, but the righteous to eternal life." (Mt. 25:31-33, 41, 46)
>
> The wrath of God is being revealed from heaven against all the godlessness and wickedness of men who suppress the truth by their wickedness. (Ro. 1:18)
>
> But for those who are self-seeking and who reject the truth and follow evil, there will be wrath and anger. (Ro. 2:8)
>
> But among you there must not be even a hint of sexual immorality, or of any kind of impurity, or of greed, because these are improper for God's holy people. Nor should there be obscenity, foolish talk or coarse joking, which are out of place, but rather thanksgiving. For of this you can be sure: No immoral, impure or greedy person—such a man is an idolater—has any inheritance in the kingdom of Christ and of God. Let no one deceive you with empty words, for because of such things God's wrath comes on those who are disobedient. (Ep. 5:3-6)
>
> Just as man is destined to die once, and after that to face judgment. (He. 9:27)
>
> If this is so, then the Lord knows how to rescue godly men from trials and to hold the unrighteous for the day of judgment, while continuing their punishment. (2 Pe. 2:9)
>
> By the same word the present heavens and earth are reserved for fire, being kept for the day of judgment and destruction of ungodly men. (2 Pe. 3:7)
>
> Enoch, the seventh from Adam, prophesied about these men: "See, the Lord is coming with thousands upon thousands of his holy ones to judge everyone, and to convict all the ungodly of all the ungodly acts they have done in the ungodly way, and of all the harsh words ungodly sinners have spoken against him." (Jude 14-15)

3 (25:6-13) **Immorality, Example of—Affection, Public Display of—Immorality, Public Display of—Disrespect, Example of—Irreverence, Example of—Sin, Irreverence—Zeal, Example of—Phinehas, the Priest**: the judgment was stopped in a dramatic way. The scene needs to be grasped by the mind's eye. While Moses and the people were weeping in prayer, seeking the Lord to stop the plague from among the people, a shocking and outrageous event happened. A shameful sin took place between a man who professed to be a believer and a pagan woman.

a. The zeal of a priest, Phinehas, stopped the judgment.
   1) The man and woman showed public, sexual affection before the very eyes of Moses and the people while they were weeping in prayer. The people were praying at the entrance to the Tabernacle, so this meant that the sexual affection and stimulating pleasure took place right there at the Tabernacle. Note what happened: the Israelite man brought the immoral woman to meet his parents in the midst of the prayer meeting. Obviously his parents were involved in the prayer meeting. This young man had no more reverence for the things of God than to show public, sexual affection in the presence of God's people. These two immoral young people...
   • had a contempt for the holy things of God
   • cared nothing for the Word of the Lord
   • scorned the holiness of God
   • showed outrageous, incomprehensible, and unspeakable behavior
   • disgraced the holiness and majesty of God
   • demonstrated the depth of disrespect and irreverence for the people of God

   2) Note the righteous zeal of the priest Phinehas (vv.7-8). Obviously, the young couple had left the Tabernacle to go to the young man's tent or home. After thinking for a few minutes about what had happened, Phinehas jumped up and left the prayer meeting, grabbing a spear or javelin as he left. He followed the couple who had shown such outrageous contempt for God and His people. He found them in the man's tent and executed them both (v.8).
   3) Immediately the judgment stopped and the plague ended. But note: twenty-four thousand people had died in the plague. Most likely, the plague had been some sexually transmitted disease that vindicated the warning of God's Holy Word: "A man reaps what he sows" (Ga. 6:7).

b. Note the result of the priest's zeal (vv.10-13).
   1) God stopped the judgment, stopped it immediately. God turned His anger away from the sinful and guilty Israelites (v.11).
   2) God acknowledged the great zeal of the young priest: he was zealous for God's honor and had dramatically demonstrated his respect for God and His righteousness (v.11). He stood up for righteousness when no one else would. All the judges and leaders of Israel were most likely in the prayer meeting, certainly most of them. Yet not one jumped to his feet to stand up for the holiness and righteousness of God, only Phinehas. The others were either too embarrassed or afraid to stand up for righteousness. But not this young priest; he had a zeal for God, a very special zeal. As a priest, he represented God before men and men before God. He knew that he was to be a testimony of righteousness before God and the

people. He knew that the plague—the hand of God's judgment against the sin—could not be stopped as long as the sin continued to be committed by the people. The sin was the very cause for the judgment of the plague; therefore, the plague could not be stopped until the sin was removed. With holy zeal, this young man, this young priest, stood up for righteousness when others would not. In fact, Scripture declares that God took this act of zeal and counted it to Phinehas for righteousness. Moreover, his zeal for righteousness stands as an example of righteousness forever.

But Phinehas stood up and intervened, and the plague was checked. This was credited to him as righteousness for endless generations to come. (Ps. 106:30-31)

3) God made His covenant of peace with Phinehas: that is, his kind of zeal made peace between God and man (v.12). It was his zeal that had stopped the plague, the hand of God's judgment against the sin. The sin of the people had alienated and separated them from God. The sin had created a great gulf, a chasm of unrighteousness and ungodliness between God and the people. The people were alienated from God and God from the people. But the zeal of this young man to remove the sin brought peace and reconciliation between God and the people. Because of his zeal, God made an eternal covenant of peace with Phinehas; that is, his kind of zeal for righteousness would always bring peace between God and people. What God wants is for people to stand up for righteousness, removing sin from their presence. When a person does this—removes sin from among a group of people—God will take that person's zeal and make peace with the people. Once the sin has been removed, God reconciles the people to Himself.

4) God established that the High Priest would come from the descendants of this young priest (v.13). Phinehas was the son of Eleazar and the grandson of Aaron himself. Remember that the High Priest is a type of Christ and His priesthood. What God was doing was bestowing one of the highest privileges upon this young priest. Phinehas was to stand forth forever as a type of Christ.

5) God accepted the act of this young man's zeal as atonement for the people (v.13). Note this fact: there was *corporate guilt and responsibility* for this sin. All the people stood guilty before God, corporately. They were either guilty of engaging in the sins themselves or else guilty of not stepping in and preventing the sin. Both the sins of *commission* and *omission were committed*. The people—in particular the leadership of the nation—all stood guilty of not having stopped those who were engaging in the sin. The sin should never have been allowed to get a grip on the people. Yet it did. It took control because those who knew about the seduction going on did nothing.

⇒ Silence ruled the day.
⇒ Silence allowed the sin.
⇒ Silence encouraged the sin.
⇒ Silence supported the sin.
⇒ Silence promoted the sin.
⇒ Silence validated the sin.
⇒ Silence affirmed the sin.
⇒ Silence granted the sin.
⇒ Silenced endorsed the sin.
⇒ Silence gave permission for the sin.
⇒ Silence sanctioned the sin.
⇒ Silence tolerated the sin.

All the people were guilty; therefore, all the people stood corporately responsible before God. This was the reason that atonement (reconciliation) had to be made for all the people. The people had to be reconciled as a corporate body. Because of their guilt, all the people were guilty; therefore, all the people had to be reconciled to God. But note: the zeal of this young priest for God and His righteousness was counted as atonement for the people. God accepted his *zeal for righteousness* as atonement, as the act of reconciliation for the people.

Thought 1. Note several lessons for us.
(1) The zeal of this young man, this young priest, is a dynamic example for us. We, too, need a strong zeal for God and His righteousness. God calls us to righteousness and He demands righteousness. We must have a zeal for living holy, pure, and righteous lives before God.

For I tell you that unless your righteousness surpasses that of the Pharisees and the teachers of the law, you will certainly not enter the kingdom of heaven. (Mt. 5:20)

His disciples remembered that it is written: "Zeal for your house will consume me." (Jn. 2:17)

"My food," said Jesus, "is to do the will of him who sent me and to finish his work." (Jn. 4:34)

As long as it is day, we must do the work of him who sent me. Night is coming, when no one can work. (Jn. 9:4)

He had been instructed in the way of the Lord, and he spoke with great fervor and taught about Jesus accurately, though he knew only the baptism of John. (Ac.18:25)

Brothers, my heart's desire and prayer to God for the Israelites is that they may be saved. (Ro. 10:1)

Come back to your senses as you ought, and stop sinning; for there are some who are ignorant of God—I say this to your shame. (1 Co. 15:34)

Those whom I love I rebuke and discipline. So be earnest, and repent. (Re. 3:19)

My zeal wears me out, for my enemies ignore your words. (Ps. 119:139)

For Zion's sake I will not keep silent, for Jerusalem's sake I will not remain quiet, till her righteousness shines out like the dawn, her salvation like a blazing torch. (Is. 62:1)

"Therefore, O king, be pleased to accept my advice: Renounce your sins by doing what is right, and your wickedness by being kind to the oppressed. It may be that then your prosperity will continue." (Da. 4:27)

(2) This young priest was chosen by God to be the next High Priest. He was given the glorious privilege of being a symbol or type of the coming Messiah and His Priesthood. For all generations

down through human history, this young man stands forth as a type of the Lord Jesus Christ, the perfect High Priest.

For this reason he had to be made like his brothers in every way, in order that he might become a merciful and faithful high priest in service to God, and that he might make atonement for the sins of the people. (He. 2:17)

Therefore, since we have a great high priest who has gone through the heavens, Jesus the Son of God, let us hold firmly to the faith we profess. For we do not have a high priest who is unable to sympathize with our weaknesses, but we have one who has been tempted in every way, just as we are—yet was without sin. (He. 4:14-15)

Every high priest is selected from among men and is appointed to represent them in matters related to God, to offer gifts and sacrifices for sins. He is able to deal gently with those who are ignorant and are going astray, since he himself is subject to weakness. This is why he has to offer sacrifices for his own sins, as well as for the sins of the people. No one takes this honor upon himself; he must be called by God, just as Aaron was. So Christ also did not take upon himself the glory of becoming a high priest. But God said to him, "You are my Son; today I have become your Father." (He. 5:1-5)

We have this hope as an anchor for the soul, firm and secure. It enters the inner sanctuary behind the curtain, where Jesus, who went before us, has entered on our behalf. He has become a high priest forever, in the order of Melchizedek. (He. 6:19-20)

Therefore he is able to save completely those who come to God through him, because he always lives to intercede for them. Such a high priest meets our need—one who is holy, blameless, pure, set apart from sinners, exalted above the heavens. Unlike the other high priests, he does not need to offer sacrifices day after day, first for his own sins, and then for the sins of the people. He sacrificed for their sins once for all when he offered himself. (He. 7:25-27)

The point of what we are saying is this: We do have such a high priest, who sat down at the right hand of the throne of the Majesty in heaven. (He. 8:1)

(3) The zeal of this young man, this priest, made atonement or reconciliation for the people. The atonement made by him is a picture of the atonement and reconciliation made by the Lord Jesus Christ. Atonement has been made for us: we are reconciled to God by the zeal of Christ to provide righteousness for us. He provided righteousness for us by living a perfect life, the ideal life of righteousness. As the ideal, His righteousness can stand for us and cover us. Therefore, when God looks at us, He sees us covered, standing in the perfect righteousness of Jesus Christ. God is able to accept us in the ideal righteousness of Christ, able to count us as righteous—all because we stand in His perfect, ideal righteousness.

But this is not all: Jesus Christ secured righteousness for us by dying for us. He took our sin and the punishment due our sin upon Himself. He died for our sin, as our substitute, in our place. His death is the ideal, perfect death in the eyes of God. Therefore, God accepts His death, His substitute sacrifice as our death. When we place our faith in Christ, God counts the death of Christ in our place. Therefore, we do not have to suffer or bear the condemnation and judgment of God. As stated above, we are accepted by God through the righteousness of Jesus Christ. Moreover, we are freed from ever having to suffer the judgment of God through the sacrifice of Jesus Christ.

The zeal for righteousness that the young priest Phinehas had stood as a type of the righteous zeal of Christ. Jesus Christ secured righteousness for man and bore the judgment of God for man. By this zeal, Christ secured atonement and reconciled man to God. Jesus Christ is our atonement, the way we are reconciled to God.

Therefore, since we have been justified through faith, we have peace with God through our Lord Jesus Christ. (Ro. 5:1)

Since we have now been justified by his blood, how much more shall we be saved from God's wrath through him! For if, when we were God's enemies, we were reconciled to him through the death of his Son, how much more, having been reconciled, shall we be saved through his life! Not only is this so, but we also rejoice in God through our Lord Jesus Christ, through whom we have now received reconciliation. (Ro. 5:9-11)

God made him who had no sin to be sin for us, so that in him we might become the righteousness of God. (2 Co. 5:21)

Who gave himself for our sins to rescue us from the present evil age, according to the will of our God and Father. (Ga. 1:4)

Consider Abraham: "He believed God, and it was credited to him as righteousness." (Ga. 3:6)

He himself bore our sins in his body on the tree, so that we might die to sins and live for righteousness; by his wounds you have been healed. (1 Pe. 2:24)

For Christ died for sins once for all, the righteous for the unrighteous, to bring you to God. He was put to death in the body but made alive by the Spirit. (1 Pe. 3:18)

4 (25:14-18) **Apostasy, Danger of—Immorality, Danger of—Israel, Failure of, Caused by—Zimri—Cozbi**: the dangerous threat of apostasy and immorality was real. A cesspool of immorality and apostasy had been dug by the people. The corruption had become so pervasive that it threatened to destroy the people. Tragically, many of the leaders themselves had engaged in the sexual immorality and false worship (v.4). When leaders become involved in sin, a much greater threat to survival is created because of the leaders' influence. This is clearly seen in these points.

a. The man and woman who showed public, sexual affection would have influenced and led many to sin (vv.14-15). They were young leaders within their respective communities. Note that his name was Zimri, the son of the leader of the great tribe of Simeon. The young lady was named Cozbi, the daughter of Zur, who was a king of the Midianites (v.15; see 31:8). Being from prominent families meant that their influence would have been far and wide. They would have led many into sin. This is just one example of influential leaders who had obviously been involved in sexual immorality and false worship. But this was not the only dangerous threat to the survival of the Israelites.

b. The strategy of the Midianites would also have destroyed Israel. This is the reason God commanded that the Midianites be treated as enemies and be executed once they had been conquered in battle (vv.16-17). Note that the reason is clearly spelled out: because their strategy was to seduce God's people through illicit sex and the false worship of Baal Peor (v.18). They had shown contempt for God and His people. Therefore, they were to be destroyed for their outrageous sin.

Thought 1. Every believer influences other people. Eyes are always watching our behavior:
⇒ Children watch parents.
⇒ Parents watch children.
⇒ Spouses watch each other.
⇒ Employers watch employees.
⇒ Employees watch employers as well as their co-workers.
⇒ Neighbors watch neighbors.
⇒ Fans watch athletes.
⇒ Athletes watch fellow athletes.

On and on the list could go. How we live influences other people. If we live holy, righteous, and pure lives, we influence people to live lives of holiness, righteousness, and purity. If we live sinful and evil lives, we influence people to live sinful and evil lives. If we break the law, we encourage people to break the law. If we are violent and abusive, we encourage people to be violent and abusive. Our lives influence people either to be good or to be bad. It is that simple. Our lives either build people up or tear people down, either teach people to live for God or to live for the world (against God). We either live for good or for bad, and we influence people to live for good or for bad. If we live sinful lives—engaging in sexual immorality and false worship—we are a threat to other people and to society. We are a danger to other people and to society in that we add more corruption and defilement to the world. And our corruption and defilement in turn multiply and influence at least several others, and through them even more are influenced. It is this, the multiplying effect of sin, that makes the influence of sin such a threat and danger to us all. This is the reason we must guard and protect our testimony for God. We must make sure that we are living holy, righteous, and pure lives before God and the community in which we live. We must never become a dangerous threat, a bad and evil influence, leading others into sin and the condemnation of God's judgment.

You are the salt of the earth. But if the salt loses its saltiness, how can it be made salty again? It is no longer good for anything, except to be thrown out and trampled by men. (Mt. 5:13)

Woe to you, teachers of the law and Pharisees, you hypocrites! You give a tenth of your spices—mint, dill and cummin. But you have neglected the more important matters of the law—justice, mercy and faithfulness. You should have practiced the latter, without neglecting the former. (Mt. 23:23)

Therefore let us stop passing judgment on one another. Instead, make up your mind not to put any stumbling block or obstacle in your brother's way. (Ro. 14:13)

If your brother is distressed because of what you eat, you are no longer acting in love. Do not by your eating destroy your brother for whom Christ died. Do not allow what you consider good to be spoken of as evil. (Ro. 14:15-16)

Your boasting is not good. Don't you know that a little yeast works through the whole batch of dough? Get rid of the old yeast that you may be a new batch without yeast—as you really are. For Christ, our Passover lamb, has been sacrificed. (1 Co. 5:6-7)

For if anyone with a weak conscience sees you who have this knowledge eating in an idol's temple, won't he be emboldened to eat what has been sacrificed to idols? So this weak brother, for whom Christ died, is destroyed by your knowledge. When you sin against your brothers in this way and wound their weak conscience, you sin against Christ. Therefore, if what I eat causes my brother to fall into sin, I will never eat meat again, so that I will not cause him to fall. (1 Co. 8:10-13)

You were running a good race. Who cut in on you and kept you from obeying the truth? That kind of persuasion does not come from the one who calls you. "A little yeast works through the whole batch of dough." (Ga. 5:7-9)

Whoever loves his brother lives in the light, and there is nothing in him to make him stumble. (1 Jn. 2:10)

And it will be said: "Build up, build up, prepare the road! Remove the obstacles out of the way of my people." (Is. 57:14)

"For the lips of a priest ought to preserve knowledge, and from his mouth men should seek instruction—because he is the messenger of the LORD Almighty. But you have turned from the way and by your teaching have caused many to stumble; you have violated the covenant with Levi," says the LORD Almighty. (Mal. 2:7-8)

NUMBERS 25:1-18

TYPES, SYMBOLS, AND PICTURES
(Numbers 1:1–2:34)

Historical Term	Type or Picture (Scriptural Basis for Each)	Life Application for Today's Believer	Biblical Application
Phinehas Nu. 25:6-13	*Phinehas as High Priest is a type or symbol of Christ.* God established that the High Priest would come from the descendants of this young priest (v.13). Phinehas was the son of Eleazar and the grandson of Aaron himself. Remember that the High Priest is a type of Christ and His priesthood. What God was doing was bestowing one of the highest privileges upon this young priest. Phinehas was to stand forth forever as a type of Christ. "Phinehas son of Eleazar, the son of Aaron, the priest, has turned my anger away from the Israelites; for he was as zealous as I am for my honor among them, so that in my zeal I did not put an end to them. Therefore tell him I am making my covenant of peace with him. He and his descendants will have a covenant of a lasting priesthood, because he was zealous for the honor of his God and made atonement for the Israelites." (Nu. 25:11-13)	This young priest was chosen by God to be the next High Priest. He was given the glorious privilege of being a type of the coming Messiah and His Priesthood. For all generations down through human history, this young man stands forth as a type of the Lord Jesus Christ as the perfect High Priest.	For this reason he had to be made like his brothers in every way, in order that he might become a merciful and faithful high priest in service to God, and that he might make atonement for the sins of the people. (He. 2:17) Therefore, since we have a great high priest who has gone through the heavens, Jesus the Son of God, let us hold firmly to the faith we profess. For we do not have a high priest who is unable to sympathize with our weaknesses, but we have one who has been tempted in every way, just as we are—yet was without sin. (He. 4:14-15) Every high priest is selected from among men and is appointed to represent them in matters related to God, to offer gifts and sacrifices for sins. He is able to deal gently with those who are ignorant and are going astray, since he himself is subject to weakness. This is why he has to offer sacrifices for his own sins, as well as for the sins of the people. No one takes this honor upon himself; he must be called by God, just as Aaron was. So Christ also did not take upon himself the glory of becoming a high priest. But God said to him, "You are my Son; today I have become your Father." (He. 5:1-5) We have this hope as an anchor for the soul, firm and secure. It enters the inner sanctuary behind the curtain, where Jesus, who went before us, has entered on our behalf. He has become a high priest forever, in the order of Melchizedek. (He. 6:19-20; see also Heb. 7:25-27) The point of what we are saying is this: We do have such a high priest, who sat down at the right hand of the throne of the Majesty in heaven. (He. 8:1)

NUMBERS 25:1-18

Historical Term	Type or Picture (Scriptural Basis for Each)	Life Application for Today's Believer	Biblical Application
The Zeal of Phinehas that Made Atonement or Reconciliation for the People Nu. 25:6-13	*The atonement made by Phinehas is a picture of the atonement and reconciliation made by the Lord Jesus Christ.* **He and his descendants will have a covenant of a lasting priesthood, because he was zealous for the honor of his God and made atonement for the Israelites. (Nu. 25:13)**	Atonement has been made for us: we are reconciled to God by the zeal of Christ to provide righteousness for us. He provided righteousness for us by living a perfect life, the ideal life of righteousness. As the ideal, His righteousness can stand for us and cover us. Therefore, when God looks at us, He sees us covered, standing in the perfect righteousness of Jesus Christ. God is able to accept us in the ideal righteousness of Christ, able to count us as righteous—all because we stand in His perfect, ideal righteousness. But this is not all: Jesus Christ secured righteousness for us by dying for us. He took our sin and the punishment due our sin upon Himself. He died for our sin, as our substitute, in our place. His death is the ideal, perfect death in the eyes of God. Therefore, God accepts His death, His substitute sacrifice as our death. When we place our faith in Christ, God counts the death of Christ in our place. Therefore, we do not have to suffer or bear the condemnation and judgment of God. As stated above, we are accepted by God through the righteousness of Jesus Christ. Moreover, we are freed from ever having to suffer the judgment of God through the sacrifice of Jesus Christ.	*Since we have now been justified by his blood, how much more shall we be saved from God's wrath through him! For if, when we were God's enemies, we were reconciled to him through the death of his Son, how much more, having been reconciled, shall we be saved through his life! Not only is this so, but we also rejoice in God through our Lord Jesus Christ, through whom we have now received reconciliation. (Ro. 5:9-11)* *God made him who had no sin to be sin for us, so that in him we might become the righteousness of God. (2 Co. 5:21)* *He himself bore our sins in his body on the tree, so that we might die to sins and live for righteousness; by his wounds you have been healed. (1 Pe. 2:24)*
Phinehas' Zeal for Righteousness Nu. 25:6-13	*The zeal for righteousness that the young priest Phinehas had stood as a type of the righteous zeal of Christ.* **He and his descendants will have a covenant of a lasting priesthood, because he was zealous for the honor of his God and made atonement for the Israelites. (Nu. 25:13)**	Jesus Christ secured righteousness for man and bore the judgment of God for man. By this zeal, Christ secured atonement and reconciled man to God. Jesus Christ is our atonement, the way we are reconciled to God.	*Therefore, since we have been justified through faith, we have peace with God through our Lord Jesus Christ. (Ro. 5:1)* *Who gave himself for our sins to rescue us from the present evil age, according to the will of our God and Father. (Ga. 1:4)* *Consider Abraham: "He believed God, and it was credited to him as righteousness." (Ga. 3:6)*

DIVISION IV

THE PREPARATION FOR THE MARCH INTO THE PROMISED LAND, 26:1–36:13

(26:1-36:13) **DIVISION OVERVIEW—Wilderness Wan-derings—Desert Journeys—Israel, Second Generation, Preparation of**: the forty years of the wilderness wanderings had now ended. The first generation of Israelites had died off. Tragically, their journey with God had ended just as it had begun: in unbelief and rebellion. They had committed the ultimate rebellion against God, apostasy—turning to worldliness, to the worship of sex and false gods. The result: death. A plague swept through the camp and killed thousands of them. Among the dead were the last of the first generation of Israelites, those whose lives had been so tragic—so marked by unbelief and grumbling.

Now, God is ready to make final preparations for the second generation of believers to enter the promised land and receive their glorious inheritance. As *The Expositor's Bible Commentary* says:

> *The expression "after the plague" [26:2] is...the turning point from the first generation to the second, the shift from the fathers and mothers to sons and daughters. God was about to begin a new work with a new people. The younger generation would begin to have their day....*
>
> *So [we face]...a great, haunting question: What will the children be like? Will they be like their parents? Or will they be like Moses and Aaron, like Joshua and Caleb, like Miriam and others faithful to God? Will they believe in him, obey his commands, and take up their weapons as they march in victory song?*[1]

THE PREPARATION FOR THE MARCH INTO THE PROMISED LAND, 26:1–36:13

A. The Organization of the Second Generation—the Second Nationwide Census: Mobilizing God's People to Enter and Inherit the Promised Land, 26:1-65
B. The Basic Law That Gave Women an Inheritance in the Promised Land: Five Women of Enormous Courage, Faith, and Hope, 27:1-11
C. The Appointment of Joshua as the Successor to Moses: A Strong Picture of God Preparing the Believer for Death, 27:12-23
D. The Offerings and Sacrifices Commanded by the Lord: A Picture of Man's Need to Continually Approach and Worship God through the Atonement Secured by the Sacrifice (a Symbol of God's Dear Son, the Lord Jesus Christ), 28:1–29:40
E. The Laws that Govern Vows: The Obligation to Keep Vows and to Consider Others in Making Vows, 30:1-16
F. The Conquest of the Most Dangerous and Threatening of Enemies, the Midianites: A Picture of Conquering the Seductive, Immoral Enemies of the World, 31:1-54

---

1 *The Expositor's Bible Commentary.* Frank E. Gaebelein, Editor, pp.924-925.

DIVISION IV
26:1–36:13

G. The Settlement East of the Jordan River: A Picture of Compromise, Selfishness, Covetousness, Disloyalty, and Half-Hearted Commitment, 32:1-42

H. The Review of the Wilderness Wanderings and a Strong Charge to Take Possession of the Promised Land: A Picture of God's Faithfulness and Man's Failure, 33:1-56

I. The Boundaries of Canaan, the Promised Land: The Great Gift and Assurance of God—His People Will Inherit the Promised Land, 34:1-29

J. The Inheritance of the Levites and the Cities of Refuge: The Provision of God for His Ministers and for All Who Need Refuge from the Storms and Threats of Life, 35:1-34

K. The Women Who Inherited Property: A Picture of Strong Faith in the Promised Land of God, 37:1-13

NUMBERS 26:1-65

1. **The strong emphasis: "The Lord spoke": A picture of God guiding His people**
2. **The 1st purpose of the census—military: A picture of the people of God preparing for warfare**
   a. To count all men able to serve 20 years old or older
   b. To count while camped by the Jordan across from Jericho

3. **The number counted, division by division—counted just as they came out of Egypt: A picture of the faithfulness of God & a strong warning to man**
   a. The division & tribe of Reuben
      1) The tribal clans
         - The Hanochite clan
         - The Pallu clan
         - The Hezron clan
         - The Carmite clan

      2) The total number: 43,730

      3) The tragic record of Korah's rebellion & the descendants of Reuben who rebelled with Korah (see Jude 11)
         - The son of the clan leader Pallu was Eliab
         - Two of the sons of Eliab rebelled with Korah

         - They were severely judged by God along with 250 other rebels (see 16:35)
         - They are a warning to all who reject & rebel against God
         - The line of Korah did not die out completely
   b. The division & tribe of Simeon

CHAPTER 26

IV. THE PREPARATION FOR THE MARCH INTO THE PROMISED LAND, 26:1–36:13

A. The Organization of the Second Generation—the Second Nationwide Census: Mobilizing God's People to Enter & Inherit the Promised Land, 26:1-65

After the plague the LORD said to Moses and Eleazar son of Aaron, the priest,
2 "Take a census of the whole Israelite community by families—all those twenty years old or more who are able to serve in the army of Israel."
3 So on the plains of Moab by the Jordan across from Jericho, Moses and Eleazar the priest spoke with them and said,
4 "Take a census of the men twenty years old or more, as the LORD commanded Moses." These were the Israelites who came out of Egypt:
5 The descendants of Reuben, the firstborn son of Israel, were: through Hanoch, the Hanochite clan; through Pallu, the Palluite clan;
6 through Hezron, the Hezronite clan; through Carmi, the Carmite clan.
7 These were the clans of Reuben; those numbered were 43,730.
8 The son of Pallu was Eliab,
9 And the sons of Eliab were Nemuel, Dathan and Abiram. The same Dathan and Abiram were the community officials who rebelled against Moses and Aaron and were among Korah's followers when they rebelled against the LORD.
10 The earth opened its mouth and swallowed them along with Korah, whose followers died when the fire devoured the 250 men. And they served as a warning sign.
11 The line of Korah, however, did not die out.
12 The descendants of Simeon by their clans were: through Nemuel, the Nemuelite clan; through Jamin, the Jaminite clan; through Jakin, the Jakinite clan;
13 Through Zerah, the Zerahite clan; through Shaul, the Shaulite clan.
14 These were the clans of Simeon; there were 22,200 men.
15 The descendants of Gad by their clans were: through Zephon, the Zephonite clan; through Haggi, the Haggite clan; through Shuni, the Shunite clan;
16 Through Ozni, the Oznite clan; through Eri, the Erite clan;
17 Through Arodi, the Arodite clan; through Areli, the Arelite clan.
18 These were the clans of Gad; those numbered were 40,500.
19 Er and Onan were sons of Judah, but they died in Canaan.
20 The descendants of Judah by their clans were: through Shelah, the Shelanite clan; through Perez, the Perezite clan; through Zerah, the Zerahite clan.
21 The descendants of Perez were: through Hezron, the Hezronite clan; through Hamul, the Hamulite clan.
22 These were the clans of Judah; those numbered were 76,500.
23 The descendants of Issachar by their clans were: through Tola, the Tolaite clan; through Puah, the Puite clan;
24 Through Jashub, the Jashubite clan; through Shimron, the Shimronite clan.
25 These were the clans of Issachar; those numbered were 64,300.
26 The descendants of Zebulun by their clans were: through Sered, the Seredite clan; through Elon, the Elonite clan; through Jahleel, the Jahleelite clan.
27 These were the clans of Zebulun; those numbered were 60,500.
28 The descendants of Joseph by their clans through Manasseh and Ephraim were:
29 The descendants of Manasseh: through Makir, the Makirite clan (Makir was

1) The tribal clans
   - The Nemuelite clan
   - The Jaminite clan
   - The Jakinite clan
   - The Zerahite clan
   - The Shaulite clan

2) The total number: 22,200

c. The division & tribe of Gad
   1) The tribal clans
      - The Zephonite clan
      - The Haggite clan
      - The Shunite clan

      - The Oznite clan
      - The Erite clan

      - The Arodite clan
      - The Arelite clan

   2) The total number: 40,500

d. The division & tribe of Judah
   1) The two sons of Judah who died in Canaan: Er & Onan
   2) The tribal clans through Judah
      - The Shelanite clan
      - The Perezite clan
      - The Zerahite clan

   3) The tribal clan through Perez
      - The Hezronite clan
      - The Hamulite clan

   4) The total number: 76,500

e. The division & tribe of Issachar
   1) The tribal clans
      - The Tolaite clan
      - The Puite clan
      - The Jashubite clan
      - The Shimronite clan

   2) The total number: 64,300

f. The division & tribe of Zebulun
   1) The tribal clans
      - The Seredite clan
      - The Elonite clan
      - The Jahleelite clan

   2) The total number: 60,500

g. The division & tribes of Joseph: He was granted a double honor, two major divisions or tribes (see Ge. 48:1-6)
h. The division & tribe of Manasseh
   1) The tribal clan

NUMBERS 26:1-65

- The Makirite clan: The father of Gilead
- The Gileadite clan
2) The tribal clans through Gilead
  - The Iezerite clan
  - The Helekite clan
  - The Asrielite clan
  - The Shechemite clan
  - The Shemidaite clan
  - The Hepherite clan
3) The son of Hepher, Zelophehad, had only daughters
4) The total number: 52,700

i. The divisions & tribes of Ephraim
1) The tribal clans
  - The Shuthelahite clan
  - The Bekerite clan
  - The Tahanite clan
2) The tribal clans through Shuthelah: The Eranite tribe
3) The total number: 32,500

j. The divisions & tribes of Benjamin
1) The tribal clans
  - The Belaite clan
  - The Ashbelite clan
  - The Ahiramite clan
  - The Shuphamite clan
  - The Huphamite clan
2) The tribal clans of Bela
  - Through Ard, the Ardite clan
  - Through Naaman, the Naamite clan
3) The total number: 45,600

k. The divisions & tribes of Dan
1) The tribal clan numbered just one: The Shuhamite clan
2) The total number: 64,400

l. The division & tribes of Asher
1) The tribal clans
  - The Imnite clan
  - The Ishvite clan
  - The Beriite clan

the father of Gilead); through Gilead, the Gileadite clan.
30 These were the descendants of Gilead: through Iezer, the Iezerite clan; through Helek, the Helekite clan;
31 Through Asriel, the Asrielite clan; through Shechem, the Shechemite clan;
32 Through Shemida, the Shemidaite clan; through Hepher, the Hepherite clan.
33 (Zelophehad son of Hepher had no sons; he had only daughters, whose names were Mahlah, Noah, Hoglah, Milcah and Tirzah.)
34 These were the clans of Manasseh; those numbered were 52,700.
35 These were the descendants of Ephraim by their clans: through Shuthelah, the Shuthelahite clan; through Beker, the Bekerite clan; through Tahan, the Tahanite clan.
36 These were the descendants of Shuthelah: through Eran, the Eranite clan.
37 These were the clans of Ephraim; those numbered were 32,500. These were the descendants of Joseph by their clans.
38 The descendants of Benjamin by their clans were: through Bela, the Belaite clan; through Ashbel, the Ashbelite clan; through Ahiram, the Ahiramite clan;
39 Through Shupham, the Shuphamite clan; through Hupham, the Huphamite clan.
40 The descendants of Bela through Ard and Naaman were: through Ard, the Ardite clan; through Naaman, the Naamite clan.
41 These were the clans of Benjamin; those numbered were 45,600.
42 These were the descendants of Dan by their clans: through Shuham, the Shuhamite clan. These were the clans of Dan:
43 All of them were Shuhamite clans; and those numbered were 64,400.
44 The descendants of Asher by their clans were: through Imnah, the Imnite clan; through Ishvi, the Ishvite clan; through Beriah, the Beriite clan;

45 And through the descendants of Beriah: through Heber, the Heberite clan; through Malkiel, the Malkielite clan.
46 (Asher had a daughter named Serah.)
47 These were the clans of Asher; those numbered were 53,400.
48 The descendants of Naphtali by their clans were: through Jahzeel, the Jahzeelite clan; through Guni, the Gunite clan;
49 Through Jezer, the Jezerite clan; through Shillem, the Shillemite clan.
50 These were the clans of Naphtali; those numbered were 45,400.
51 The total number of the men of Israel was 601,730.
52 The LORD said to Moses,
53 "The land is to be allotted to them as an inheritance based on the number of names.
54 To a larger group give a larger inheritance, and to a smaller group a smaller one; each is to receive its inheritance according to the number of those listed.
55 Be sure that the land is distributed by lot. What each group inherits will be according to the names for its ancestral tribe.
56 Each inheritance is to be distributed by lot among the larger and smaller groups."
57 These were the Levites who were counted by their clans: through Gershon, the Gershonite clan; through Kohath, the Kohathite clan; through Merari, the Merarite clan.
58 These also were Levite clans: the Libnite clan, the Hebronite clan, the Mahlite clan, the Mushite clan, the Korahite clan. (Kohath was the forefather of Amram;
59 The name of Amram's wife was Jochebed, a descendant of Levi, who was born to the Levites in Egypt. To Amram she bore Aaron, Moses and their sister Miriam.
60 Aaron was the father of Nadab and Abihu, Eleazar and Ithamar.
61 But Nadab and Abihu died when they made an offering before the LORD with

2) The tribal clans through Beriah
  - The Heberite clan
  - The Malkielite clan
3) The daughter of Asher: Serah
4) The total number: 53,400

m. The divisions & tribes of Naphtali
1) The tribal clans
  - The Jahzeelite clan
  - The Gunite clan
  - The Jezerite clan
  - The Shillemite clan
2) The total number: 45,400

n. The total number of all divisions or tribes: 601,730

4. **The 2nd purpose of the census—to divide the inheritance of the promised land: A picture of the believer's assurance of the promised land**
a. The size of a tribe determined the amount of land it inherited
  1) If large, the tribe received a large inheritance
  2) If small, the tribe received a small inheritance
b. The land was to be divided by lot
c. The importance of these two regulations reemphasized
  1) The inheritance of each tribe was to be based on the size of each tribe
  2) The land was to be distributed by lot

5. **The census of the Levites: A picture of being totally dedicated to God & His service**
a. The major clans
  1) The Gershonite clan
  2) The Kohathite clan
  3) The Merarite clan
b. The sub-clans
  1) The Libnite clan
  2) The Hebronite clan
  3) The Mahlite clan
  4) The Mushite clan
  5) The Korahite clan
c. The lineage of Moses, Aaron, & Miriam
  1) Kohath was the forefather of Amram
  2) Amram & Jochebed were the parents
d. The descendants of Aaron:
  1) His sons: Nadab, Abihu, Eleazar, & Ithamar
  2) The tragic record of Aaron's family: Nadab & Abihu died under the

Numbers 26:1-65

judgment of God
e. The total number of Levites: 23,000
  1) The number was based upon one month old or older
  2) They were counted separately because they received no inheritance of land
6. The tragic record of the second census: A picture of the sure judgment of God
  a. The people were counted right before they were to en-
	unauthorized fire.)
	62 All the male Levites a month old or more numbered 23,000. They were not counted along with the other Israelites because they received no inheritance among them.
	63 These are the ones counted by Moses and Eleazar the priest when they counted the Israelites on the plains of Moab by the Jordan
		across from Jericho.
		64 Not one of them was among those counted by Moses and Aaron the priest when they counted the Israelites in the Desert of Sinai.
		65 For the LORD had told those Israelites they would surely die in the desert, and not one of them was left except Caleb son of Jephunneh and Joshua son of Nun.
			ter the promised land
			  b. The tragic fact: Not a single person from the first census was listed
			
			    1) They had all died in the desert wilderness, died because of their unbelief & sin (see Nu. 11:1-14:45)
			    2) They had all died except Caleb & Joshua

DIVISION IV

THE PREPARATION FOR THE MARCH INTO THE PROMISED LAND, 26:1–36:13

A. The Organization of the Second Generation—the Second Nationwide Census: Mobilizing God's People to Enter and Inherit the Promised Land, 26:1-65

(26:1-65) Introduction—Israel, Judgment of, Death of First Generation—Promised Land, How to Enter: heaven is real. God has given the great hope of the promised land of heaven. The person who has trusted Jesus Christ as his Savior and truly follows after Him will inherit the promised land of God—heaven itself. This is the great promise of God. But note: it is not the person who *professes* to believe in God and Christ who will inherit the promised land of heaven. It is the person who *follows* after and *obeys* God who will inherit heaven. This is the clear message of this passage.

Note the very first three words of verse one: "After the plague." This is a reference to the plague of the former chapter, the plague that had wiped out the last of the first generation of believers. The people had given themselves over to immorality and false worship; consequently, the judgment of God had fallen. When the plague of God's judgment had ended, the last of the first generation of believers had died out in the desert wilderness—died "outside" the promised land. From this point on, the focus will be upon the second generation of believers, the children of the parents who had failed so miserably in life. In the words of *The Expositor's Bible Commentary*:

> *(This is) the turning point from the first generation to the second, the shift from the fathers and mothers to sons and daughters. God was about to begin a new work with a new people. The younger generation would begin to have their day.*[1]

God now begins to mobilize the children, the second generation of believers, to actually enter and inherit the promised land. This is the subject of this passage of Scripture: *The Organization of the Second Generation—the Second Census: Mobilizing God's People to Enter and Inherit the Promised Land*, 26:1-65.

1. The strong emphasis: "the Lord spoke": a picture of God guiding His people (v.1).
2. The 1st purpose of the census—military: a picture of the people of God preparing for warfare (vv.2-3).
3. The number counted, division by division—counted just as they came out of Egypt: a picture of the faithfulness of God and a strong warning to man (vv.4-51).
4. The 2nd purpose of the census—to divide the inheritance of the promised land: a picture of the believer's assurance of the promised land (vv.52-56).
5. The census of the Levites: a picture of being totally dedicated to God and His service (vv.57-62).
6. The tragic record of the second census: a picture of the sure judgment of God (vv.63-65).

1 (26:1) Word of God, Purpose—Guidance, of God—Leadership, of God: there was the strong emphasis, "The Lord spoke." This is a picture of God guiding His people—the believers of all generations—as they prepare to march into the promised land.

The first generation had died off, every one of them except Joshua and Caleb. They had lived carnal, fleshly lives. Unbelief and grumbling had gripped their lives. They were constantly grumbling about the hardships, the problems, and the difficulties in life. Moreover, they were continually murmuring against and opposing Moses, the servant of God. They never learned to trust God, to believe and rest in Him. Unbelief and grumbling were the dominant traits of their lives. Consequently, they never were able to enter the promised land. Instead they were doomed to wander about in the desert wilderness for forty years until they had all died away. Now they had all gone: the forty years had passed. Only the children—the second generation—survived. It was now time to prepare this second generation of believers to enter the promised land. Therefore, "God spoke." God spoke to Moses and to the new High Priest Eleazar, the son of Aaron. God spoke, giving instructions for preparation, telling His people how to prepare for their entrance into the promised land. The point is this: God guided His people by His Word. Remember, God's guiding His people by *His Word* is one of the strongest emphases of the book of *Numbers*. "The LORD spoke"—guided His people—is used over one hundred and fifty times in twenty plus ways in this great book. God guides His people by speaking to them through His precious Word. The second generation of believers had to be prepared to enter the promised land. They had to learn to trust God, learn the *spiritual rest* that God brings to the souls of those who trust Him. If they were to conquer the

---

[1] *The Expositor's Bible Commentary*. Frank E. Gaebelein, Editor, p.924.

NUMBERS 26:1-65

pitfalls and enemies of the promised land, they had to learn to trust he conquering power of God. Therefore, God spoke in order to begin preparing them to trust Him more and more. God spoke in order to give them all the guidance they needed for preparation.

Thought 1. God guides His people through His precious Holy Word. God has spoken in His precious Holy Word. It is in the Holy Scriptures that we are guided throughout life. In the Holy Scriptures we find out...
- how to live and how not to live
- where to go and where not to go
- what to do and what not to do
- how to speak and how not to speak
- how to approach God and how not to approach God
- how to worship God and how not to worship God

God has spoken to us through the Holy Scriptures. God has given us the Holy Scriptures to guide us throughout life. It is His Word that tells us how to prepare and how to enter the promised land of heaven.

> All Scripture is God-breathed and is useful for teaching, rebuking, correcting and training in righteousness. (2 Ti. 3:16)
> Do your best to present yourself to God as one approved, a workman who does not need to be ashamed and who correctly handles the word of truth. (2 Ti. 2:15)
> Jesus answered, "It is written: 'Man does not live on bread alone, but on every word that comes from the mouth of God.'" (Mt. 4:4)
> I tell you the truth, until heaven and earth disappear, not the smallest letter, not the least stroke of a pen, will by any means disappear from the Law until everything is accomplished. (Mt. 5:18)
> Heaven and earth will pass away, but my words will never pass away. (Mt. 24:35)
> You are already clean because of the word I have spoken to you. (Jn. 15:3)
> But these are written that you may believe that Jesus is the Christ, the Son of God, and that by believing you may have life in his name. (Jn. 20:31)
> For everything that was written in the past was written to teach us, so that through endurance and the encouragement of the Scriptures we might have hope. (Ro. 15:4)
> These things happened to them as examples and were written down as warnings for us, on whom the fulfillment of the ages has come. (1 Co. 10:11)
> For the word of God is living and active. Sharper than any double-edged sword, it penetrates even to dividing soul and spirit, joints and marrow; it judges the thoughts and attitudes of the heart. (He. 4:12)
> "But the word of the Lord stands forever." And this is the word that was preached to you. (1 Pe. 1:25)
> Like newborn babies, crave pure spiritual milk, so that by it you may grow up in your salvation, now that you have tasted that the Lord is good. (1 Pe. 2:2-3)
> And we have the word of the prophets [the Word of God] made more certain, and you will do well to pay attention to it, as to a light shining in a dark place, until the day dawns and the morning star rises in your hearts....For prophecy never had its origin in the will of man, but men spoke from God as they were carried along by the Holy Spirit. (2 Pe. 1:19, 21)
> I write these things to you who believe in the name of the Son of God so that you may know that you have eternal life. (1 Jn. 5:13)
> He humbled you, causing you to hunger and then feeding you with manna, which neither you nor your fathers had known, to teach you that man does not live on bread alone but on every word that comes from the mouth of the LORD. (De. 8:3)
> I have not departed from the commands of his lips; I have treasured the words of his mouth more than my daily bread. (Jb. 23:12)
> How can a young man keep his way pure? By living according to your word. (Ps. 119:9)
> Your word is a lamp to my feet and a light for my path. (Ps. 119:105)
> The unfolding of your words gives light; it gives understanding to the simple. (Ps. 119:130)
> For these commands are a lamp, this teaching is a light, and the corrections of discipline are the way to life. (Pr. 6:23)

2 (26:2-3) **Israel, Census of—Military, Census of—Warfare, Spiritual—Spiritual Warfare—Census, of Israel**: there was the first purpose of the census, that of taking a military count. This was a picture of God's people preparing for warfare. Keep this fact in mind: this is a census of the second generation of believers. The first census had been taken by the first generation over thirty-eight years earlier. All that generation had died out in the desert wilderness. Now it was time for their children, the second generation, to prepare to enter and inherit the promised land. But before they could, the leadership needed to know how many men were available to fight. Entering the promised land was to be a hard and difficult struggle. There were pitfalls—traps and snares—that had to be bypassed and guarded against as God's people marched into the promised land. Moreover, there were strong enemies that had to be conquered. How strong was Israel? How many fighting men were available? This fact had to be known before they could even think about entering the promised land. Therefore, the people were to count all the men able to serve in the military who were twenty years old or older. Note: they took the census while they were camped by the Jordan River across from the great city of Jericho.

Thought 1. The military census is a picture of the people of God preparing for warfare. This is a strong lesson for us: we are engaged in a spiritual warfare. There are pitfalls throughout life—traps and snares—that will trip us up and ruin our lives. Furthermore, there are strong enemies that oppose us, trying to keep us out of the promised land of heaven. There are enemies in this life that strongly oppose God and us, enemies such as...

- humanism
- secularism
- atheism
- agnosticism
- covetousness
- greed
- immorality
- drugs
- alcohol
- peer pressure
- selfishness
- self-centeredness
- pride
- anger
- hostility
- revenge
- adultery
- divorce
- disease
- sorcery
- witchcraft
- psychics
- the world of the occult

The list of pitfalls and enemies that oppose the promised land of heaven is innumerable. These pitfalls and enemies are all around us, confronting us every day of our lives. To conquer, to triumph, to be victorious, we must prepare. We must be prepared for spiritual warfare, prepared to stand by the power of God Himself.

> We demolish arguments and every pretension that sets itself up against the knowledge of God, and we take captive every thought to make it obedient to Christ. (2 Co. 10:5)
>
> Finally, be strong in the Lord and in his mighty power. Put on the full armor of God so that you can take your stand against the devil's schemes. For our struggle is not against flesh and blood, but against the rulers, against the authorities, against the powers of this dark world and against the spiritual forces of evil in the heavenly realms. Therefore put on the full armor of God, so that when the day of evil comes, you may be able to stand your ground, and after you have done everything, to stand. (Ep. 6:10-13; see also vv. 14-18)
>
> But since we belong to the day, let us be self-controlled, putting on faith and love as a breastplate, and the hope of salvation as a helmet. For God did not appoint us to suffer wrath but to receive salvation through our Lord Jesus Christ. (1 Th. 5:8-9)
>
> Timothy, my son, I give you this instruction in keeping with the prophecies once made about you, so that by following them you may fight the good fight. (1 Ti. 1:18)
>
> But you, man of God, flee from all this, and pursue righteousness, godliness, faith, love, endurance and gentleness. Fight the good fight of the faith. Take hold of the eternal life to which you were called when you made your good confession in the presence of many witnesses. (1 Ti. 6:11-12)
>
> Endure hardship with us like a good soldier of Christ Jesus. No one serving as a soldier gets involved in civilian affairs—he wants to please his commanding officer. (2 Ti. 2:3-4)
>
> Be self-controlled and alert. Your enemy the devil prowls around like a roaring lion looking for someone to devour. Resist him, standing firm in the faith, because you know that your brothers throughout the world are undergoing the same kind of sufferings. And the God of all grace, who called you to his eternal glory in Christ, after you have suffered a little while, will himself restore you and make you strong, firm and steadfast. (1 Pe. 5:8-10)
>
> For everyone born of God overcomes the world. This is the victory that has overcome the world, even our faith. Who is it that overcomes the world? Only he who believes that Jesus is the Son of God. (1 Jn. 5:4-5)
>
> For the eyes of the LORD range throughout the earth to strengthen those whose hearts are fully committed to him. You have done a foolish thing, and from now on you will be at war. (2 Chr. 16:9)
>
> The angel of the LORD encamps around those who fear him, and he delivers them. (Ps. 34:7)
>
> He will cover you with his feathers, and under his wings you will find refuge; his faithfulness will be your shield and rampart. (Ps. 91:4)

3 (26:4-51) **Census, of Israel—Israel, Census of—Army, of God—Military, of God—Faithfulness, of God—Promises, of God—Power, of God**: there was the number counted, division by division—counted just as they came out of Egypt. This census is a picture of the faithfulness of God, and it stands as a strong warning to man. Note three significant facts about this census. First, the clans within each tribe are of Korah's rebellion is recorded for all succeeding generations. Even we today are reading about it. It stands as a strong warning against disbelieving God, against rejecting and rebelling against Him. Thirdly, the total number of people listed in this census is almost the same total counted in the first census: 601,730 compared to 603,550, a difference of only 820 (v.51, see 1:46).

This is a strong picture of God's faithfulness. God had promised Abraham that his descendants would become a great nation of people (see outline and notes—Ge. 12:1-3 for more discussion). When his grandson Jacob went down into Egypt with his twelve sons, the descendants of Abraham numbered less than one hundred persons. But four hundred years later when God delivered His people out of Egypt, they obviously numbered somewhere between two to four million persons. This is indicated by the military census that numbers over six hundred thousand men alone, men who were of military fighting age—twenty years old or older. An astounding miracle by God! A clear demonstration of God's faithfulness! He was fulfilling His promise given to His dear servant Abraham.

Thought 1. Note two clear lessons for us.
(1) God is faithful, never failing to keep His promises. What God has promised, He will do, do everything He says. Failure is not in the vocabulary of God: the one thing God cannot do is fail to keep His Word. Once God has spoken, He will fulfill His promises to us just as He did to Abraham and to the Israelites. God is faithful, always faithful to His Word, always faithful to do exactly what He promises us.

God, who has called you into fellowship with his Son Jesus Christ our Lord, is faithful. (1 Co. 1:9)

Because God wanted to make the unchanging nature of his purpose very clear to the heirs of what was promised, he confirmed it with an oath. God did this so that, by two unchangeable things in which it is impossible for God to lie, we who have fled to take hold of the hope offered to us may be greatly encouraged. (He. 6:17-18)

So then, those who suffer according to God's will should commit themselves to their faithful Creator and continue to do good. (1 Pe. 4:19)

Know therefore that the LORD your God is God; he is the faithful God, keeping his covenant of love to a thousand generations of those who love him and keep his commands. (De. 7:9)

Praise be to the LORD, who has given rest to his people Israel just as he promised. Not one word has failed of all the good promises he gave through his servant Moses. (1 K. 8:56)

Your love, O LORD, reaches to the heavens, your faithfulness to the skies. (Ps. 36:5)

Praise be to the Lord, to God our Savior, who daily bears our burdens. Selah (Ps. 68:19)

I will sing of the LORD's great love forever; with my mouth I will make your faithfulness known through all generations. (Ps. 89:1)

(2) Two facts about this census stand as a strong warning to us. First, this is a census of the second generation of believers. The parents failed to believe and follow after God. Consequently, they were disallowed and barred from ever entering the promised land. Second, the rebellion of Korah is recorded in this census. He led an uprising against the servant of God, rejecting and refusing to follow God and His dear servant.

This census stands as a strong warning to us all: being listed in the army of God—having one's name written on the roll—does not guarantee entrance into the promised land.

⇒ A person must believe and follow God.
⇒ A person must believe and obey God.
⇒ A person must possess Christ as well as profess Christ.
⇒ A person must live for God and not live for the world.
⇒ A person must walk in Christ and not walk in the lust of the flesh.
⇒ A person must keep his mind upon spiritual things and not upon carnal things.
⇒ A person must live a life of faith and not a life of unbelief.

Because of these things, the first generation of believers never entered the promised land of God. They died out in the desert wilderness. This census declares this fact to all succeeding generations: we can miss out on the promised land of God. What we profess is not what matters to God. What matters is what we do, how we live. Do we follow Christ? Are we living holy, righteous, and pure lives? Are we a testimony to God and His saving grace?

God warns us: just because our names are listed in the army of God does not mean that we will enter the promised land of God. We must live out what we profess. To believe means to obey God.

"Not everyone who says to me, 'Lord, Lord,' will enter the kingdom of heaven, but only he who does the will of my Father who is in heaven." (Mt. 7:21)

He replied, "Isaiah was right when he prophesied about you hypocrites; as it is written: 'These people honor me with their lips, but their hearts are far from me.'" (Mk. 7:6)

Do not be deceived: God cannot be mocked. A man reaps what he sows. (Ga. 6:7)

They claim to know God, but by their actions they deny him. They are detestable, disobedient and unfit for doing anything good. (Tit. 1:16)

Dear children, let us not love with words or tongue but with actions and in truth. (1 Jn. 3:18)

They remembered that God was their Rock, that God Most High was their Redeemer. But then they would flatter him with their mouths, lying to him with their tongues. (Ps. 78:35-36)

My people come to you, as they usually do, and sit before you to listen to your words, but they do not put them into practice. With their mouths they express devotion, but their hearts are greedy for unjust gain. (Eze. 33:31)

4 (26:52-56) **Inheritance, of the Believer—Inheritance, of Israel—Land, the Promised, Inheritance of**: there was the second purpose of the census—to divide the inheritance of the promised land. This is a picture of the believer's assurance of the promised land. This census had two major purposes: to determine the size of the tribes for military purposes and to serve as the basis for dividing up the promised land of God.

a. As would be expected, the size of a tribe determined the amount of land it was to inherit. If the tribe was large, it was to receive a large inheritance. A smaller tribe received a smaller inheritance.

b. As would be expected, the land was to be divided and distributed by lot (v.55). This was to prevent any favoritism from being shown when the land was distributed and to prevent any charge of favoritism.

c. As would be expected, the importance of these two regulations was repeated for reemphasis (vv.55-56). The inheritance of each tribe was to be based on the size of each tribe, and the land was to be distributed by lot. Inheriting the promised land of God was the longing of God's people, the beat of their hearts. With great expectation, they were waiting for that glorious day when they would receive their inheritance. It was of critical importance that the land be distributed fairly, without partiality or favoritism. The people had to have confidence in the distribution

NUMBERS 26:1-65

of the land. This was the reason for the census: to give every believer full assurance, complete confidence that he would receive his inheritance in the promised land.

Thought 1. The believer can rest assured: he will receive his inheritance in the promised land of heaven. This glorious fact has been settled by God once and for all: the person who truly believes and follows God will live eternally with God. He will enter the promised land of heaven and serve God forever and ever. This is the assurance, the confidence that God gives the genuine believer.

> For God so loved the world that he gave his one and only Son, that whoever believes in him shall not perish but have eternal life. (Jn. 3:16)
> I give them eternal life, and they shall never perish; no one can snatch them out of my hand. (Jn. 10:28)
> Now I commit you to God and to the word of his grace, which can build you up and give you an inheritance among all those who are sanctified. (Ac.20:32)
> To open their eyes and turn them from darkness to light, and from the power of Satan to God, so that they may receive forgiveness of sins and a place among those who are sanctified by faith in me. (Ac.26:18)
> To those who by persistence in doing good seek glory, honor and immortality, he will give eternal life. (Ro. 2:7)
> But now that you have been set free from sin and have become slaves to God, the benefit you reap leads to holiness, and the result is eternal life. (Ro. 6:22)
> The Spirit himself testifies with our spirit that we are God's children. Now if we are children, then we are heirs—heirs of God and co-heirs with Christ, if indeed we share in his sufferings in order that we may also share in his glory. (Ro. 8:16-17)
> You are all sons of God through faith in Christ Jesus, for all of you who were baptized into Christ have clothed yourselves with Christ. There is neither Jew nor Greek, slave nor free, male nor female, for you are all one in Christ Jesus. If you belong to Christ, then you are Abraham's seed, and heirs according to the promise. (Ga. 3:26-29)
> Giving thanks to the Father, who has qualified you to share in the inheritance of the saints in the kingdom of light. (Col. 1:12)
> Since you know that you will receive an inheritance from the Lord as a reward. It is the Lord Christ you are serving. (Col. 3:24)
> In this way they will lay up treasure for themselves as a firm foundation for the coming age, so that they may take hold of the life that is truly life. (1 Ti. 6:19)
> A faith and knowledge resting on the hope of eternal life, which God, who does not lie, promised before the beginning of time. (Tit. 1:2)
> So that, having been justified by his grace, we might become heirs having the hope of eternal life. (Tit. 3:7)
> Praise be to the God and Father of our Lord Jesus Christ! In his great mercy he has given us new birth into a living hope through the resurrection of Jesus Christ from the dead, and into an inheritance that can never perish, spoil or fade—kept in heaven for you. (1 Pe. 1:3-4)
> But the day of the Lord will come like a thief. The heavens will disappear with a roar; the elements will be destroyed by fire, and the earth and everything in it will be laid bare. Since everything will be destroyed in this way, what kind of people ought you to be? You ought to live holy and godly lives as you look forward to the day of God and speed its coming. That day will bring about the destruction of the heavens by fire, and the elements will melt in the heat. But in keeping with his promise we are looking forward to a new heaven and a new earth, the home of righteousness. (2 Pe. 3:10-13)
> And this is what he promised us—even eternal life. (1 Jn. 2:25)
> Keep yourselves in God's love as you wait for the mercy of our Lord Jesus Christ to bring you to eternal life. (Jude 21)
> Then I saw a new heaven and a new earth, for the first heaven and the first earth had passed away, and there was no longer any sea....He will wipe every tear from their eyes. There will be no more death or mourning or crying or pain, for the old order of things has passed away. (Re. 21:1, 4)
> Multitudes who sleep in the dust of the earth will awake: some to everlasting life, others to shame and everlasting contempt. (Da. 12:2)

5 (26:57-62) **Ministers, Appointed—Ministers, Dedication of—Census, of Levites**: there was the census of the Levites. This is a picture of being totally dedicated to God and His service. A new census of the Levites was necessary to determine how many were available to serve in the ministry of the Lord. It was necessary to know this fact because the Levites were going to be scattered throughout the nation as ministers to the people. Forty-eight towns were going to be assigned to the Levites, a certain number within each tribe. This would put the ministers out among the people so they could better minister to them and help them in their moments of need (see outline and notes—Nu.35:1-8 for more discussion).

Thought 1. The minister of God is to be totally dedicated to God, totally dedicated to the call God has given him. His call is to minister to people. In fact, the ministry is people. Without people there would be no ministry. Therefore, the minister is to reach out to those people, helping them and meeting their needs. He is to be totally dedicated to God and to people.

Just as the Son of Man did not come to be served, but to serve, and to give his life as a ransom for many. (Mt. 20:28)

Therefore go and make disciples of all nations, baptizing them in the name of the Father and of the Son and of the Holy Spirit, and teaching them to obey everything I have commanded you. And surely I am with you always, to the very end of the age. (Mt. 28:19-20)

You did not choose me, but I chose you and appointed you to go and bear fruit—fruit that will last. Then the Father will give you whatever you ask in my name. (Jn. 15:16)

The third time he said to him, "Simon son of John, do you love me?" Peter was hurt because Jesus asked him the third time, "Do you love me?" He said, "Lord, you know all things; you know that I love you." Jesus said, "Feed my sheep." (Jn. 21:17)

But the Lord said to Ananias, "Go! This man is my chosen instrument to carry my name before the Gentiles and their kings and before the people of Israel." (Ac. 9:15)

Those who oppose him he must gently instruct, in the hope that God will grant them repentance leading them to a knowledge of the truth. (2 Ti. 2:25)

Be shepherds of God's flock that is under your care, serving as overseers—not because you must, but because you are willing, as God wants you to be; not greedy for money, but eager to serve. (1 Pe. 5:2)

"I will place shepherds over them who will tend them, and they will no longer be afraid or terrified, nor will any be missing," declares the LORD. (Je. 23:4)

Son of man, I have made you a watchman for the house of Israel; so hear the word I speak and give them warning from me. (Eze. 3:17)

But if the watchman sees the sword coming and does not blow the trumpet to warn the people and the sword comes and takes the life of one of them, that man will be taken away because of his sin, but I will hold the watchman accountable for his blood. (Eze. 33:6)

6 (26:63-65) **Judgment, of God—Israel, Failure of—Census**: there was the tragic record of the second census. This record is a picture of the sure judgment of God.

a. Note that the census was taken right before the people were to enter the promised land. Remember, they were camped on the plains of Moab by the Jordan River, right across from the great city of Jericho (v.63).

b. The tragic record of the second census is this: not a single person from the first census was listed (v.64). Note that this is the clear statement of Scripture, the subject of these two verses. Not a single person from the first generation of believers was allowed to enter the promised land. They had all died in the desert wilderness, died because of their unbelief and sin. (See outline and notes—Nu. 11:1-14:45.) They had all died except Caleb and Joshua. Only these two had believed in the promises of God, that He would lead them into the promised land. Therefore, they had escaped the judgment of God and were to receive a glorious inheritance in the promised land.

Thought 1. The judgment of God against unbelief and sin is sure. Judgment will fall upon every unbeliever and sinner in this world. We will all—every one of us—stand before God and give an account for what we have done. Both believer and unbeliever are going to stand before God. Believers will be judged for the work they have done for God or failed to do. Unbelievers will be judged because they failed to approach God through His Son Jesus Christ, failed to trust the Savior of the world who could have forgiven their sins and made them acceptable to God. Every one of us will stand before God and give an account.

Just as man is destined to die once, and after that to face judgment. (He. 9:27)

For the Son of Man is going to come in his Father's glory with his angels, and then he will reward each person according to what he has done. (Mt. 16:27)

When the Son of Man comes in his glory, and all the angels with him, he will sit on his throne in heavenly glory. All the nations will be gathered before him, and he will separate the people one from another as a shepherd separates the sheep from the goats. He will put the sheep on his right and the goats on his left. (Mt. 25:31-33)

This will take place on the day when God will judge men's secrets through Jesus Christ, as my gospel declares. (Ro. 2:16)

For we must all appear before the judgment seat of Christ, that each one may receive what is due him for the things done while in the body, whether good or bad. (2 Co. 5:10)

And give relief to you who are troubled, and to us as well. This will happen when the Lord Jesus is revealed from heaven in blazing fire with his powerful angels. He will punish those who do not know God and do not obey the gospel of our Lord Jesus. (2 Th. 1:7-8)

Since you call on a Father who judges each man's work impartially, live your lives as strangers here in reverent fear. (1 Pe. 1:17)

If this is so, then the Lord knows how to rescue godly men from trials and to hold the unrighteous for the day of judgment, while continuing their punishment. (2 Pe. 2:9)

By the same word the present heavens and earth are reserved for fire, being kept for the day of judgment and destruction of ungodly men. (2 Pe. 3:7)

See, the Lord is coming with thousands upon thousands of his holy ones to judge everyone, and to convict all the ungodly of all the ungodly acts they have done in the ungodly way, and of all the harsh words ungodly sinners have spoken against him. (Jude 14-15)

And I saw the dead, great and small, standing before the throne, and books were opened. Another book was opened, which is the book of life. The dead were judged according to what they had done as recorded in the books. (Re. 20:12)

"Behold, I am coming soon! My reward is with me, and I will give to everyone according to what he has done." (Re. 22:12)

And that you, O Lord, are loving. Surely you will reward each person according to what he has done. (Ps. 62:12)

I the LORD search the heart and examine the mind, to reward a man according to his conduct, according to what his deeds deserve. (Je. 17:10)

TYPES, SYMBOLS, AND PICTURES
(Numbers 26:1-65)

Historical Term	Type or Picture (Scriptural Basis for Each)	Life Application for Today's Believer	Biblical Application
Dividing the Inheritance of the Promised Land Nu. 26:53-56	*The division of the inheritance is a picture of the believer's assurance of the promised land.* **The land is to be allotted to them as an inheritance based on the number of names. (Nu. 26:53)**	The believer can rest assured: he will receive his inheritance in the promised land of heaven. This glorious fact has been settled by God once and for all: the person who truly believes and follows God will live eternally with God. He will enter the promised land of heaven and serve God forever and ever. This is the assurance, the confidence that God gives the genuine believer.	*For God so loved the world that he gave his one and only Son, that whoever believes in him shall not perish but have eternal life. (Jn. 3:16)* *I give them eternal life, and they shall never perish; no one can snatch them out of my hand. (Jn. 10:28)* *Now I commit you to God and to the word of his grace, which can build you up and give you an inheritance among all those who are sanctified. (Ac.20:32)* *But now that you have been set free from sin and have become slaves to God, the benefit you reap leads to holiness, and the result is eternal life. (Ro. 6:22)*
"The Lord Spoke (said)" Nu. 26:1	*This is a picture of God's Word guiding His people—the believers, all generations—as they prepare to march into the promised land.* **After the plague the Lord said to Moses and Eleazar son of Aaron, the priest. (Nu. 26:1)**	God guides His people through His Holy Word. God has spoken in His precious Word. It is in the Holy Scriptures that we are guided throughout life. In the Holy Scriptures we find out... • how to live and how not to live • where to go and where not to go • what to do and what not to do • how to speak and how not to speak • how to approach God and how not to approach God • how to worship God and how not to worship God God has spoken to us through the Holy Scriptures. God has given us the Holy Scriptures to guide us throughout life. It is His Word that tells us how to prepare and how to enter the promised land of heaven.	*All Scripture is God-breathed and is useful for teaching, rebuking, correcting and training in righteousness. (2 Ti. 3:16)* *Do your best to present yourself to God as one approved, a workman who does not need to be ashamed and who correctly handles the word of truth. (2 Ti. 2:15)* *Jesus answered, "It is written: 'Man does not live on bread alone, but on every word that comes from the mouth of God.'" (Mt. 4:4)* *Heaven and earth will pass away, but my words will never pass away. (Mt. 24:35)* *You are already clean because of the word I have spoken to you. (Jn. 15:3)* *But these are written that you may believe that Jesus is the Christ, the Son of God, and that by believing you may have life in his name. (Jn. 20:31)* *For everything that was written in the past was written to teach us, so that*

NUMBERS 26:1-65

Historical Term	Type or Picture (Scriptural Basis for Each)	Life Application for Today's Believer	Biblical Application
			through endurance and the encouragement of the Scriptures we might have hope. (Ro. 15:4)
			These things happened to them as examples and were written down as warnings for us, on whom the fulfillment of the ages has come. (1 Co. 10:11)
			For the word of God is living and active. Sharper than any double-edged sword, it penetrates even to dividing soul and spirit, joints and marrow; it judges the thoughts and attitudes of the heart. (He. 4:12)
			But the word of the Lord stands forever. And this is the word that was preached to you. (1 Pe. 1:25)

NUMBERS 27:1-11

Outline	Scripture	Outline (cont.)
	CHAPTER 27 **B. The Basic Law That Gave Women an Inheritance in the Promised Land: Five Women of Enormous Courage, Faith, & Hope, 27:1-11**	

1. The godly heritage & the names of the women
a. Their heritage: Belonged to the tribe of Manasseh, son of Joseph (one of the most godly persons in Scripture, Ge.39:1f)
b. Their names
 	
2. The courage of the women
a. They approached the Tabernacle
b. They approached the highest legal body of the nation, Israel's supreme court
 	
3. The concern, the great faith, & the hope of the women
a. Their father had died with no sons: Died believing in the promised land, not in Korah's rebellion against God's promises
b. Their faith in the promised land
	The daughters of Zelophehad son of Hepher, the son of Gilead, the son of Makir, the son of Manasseh, belonged to the clans of Manasseh son of Joseph. The names of the daughters were Mahlah, Noah, Hoglah, Milcah and Tirzah. They approached 2 The entrance to the Tent of Meeting and stood before Moses, Eleazar the priest, the leaders and the whole assembly, and said, 3 "Our father died in the desert. He was not among Korah's followers, who banded together against the LORD, but he died for his own sin and left no sons. 4 Why should our father's name disappear from his clan because he had no son? Give us property among our father's relatives." 5 So Moses brought their case before the LORD 6 And the LORD said to him, 7 "What Zelophehad's daughters are saying is right. You must certainly give them property as an inheritance among their father's relatives and turn their father's inheritance over to them. 8 "Say to the Israelites, 'If a man dies and leaves no son, turn his inheritance over to his daughter. 9 If he has no daughter, give his inheritance to his brothers. 10 If he has no brothers, give his inheritance to his father's brothers. 11 If his father had no brothers, give his inheritance to the nearest relative in his clan, that he may possess it. This is to be a legal requirement for the Israelites, as the LORD commanded Moses.' "	1) Wanted their father's name—the testimony of his faith—preserved
		2) Requested his inheritance
		
		4. The case was taken to the Lord by Moses: A picture of seeking God for help in solving problems
		a. He granted the request:
		  1) Gave them their father's inheritance
		  2) Honored the faith & hope of the women in the promised land
		
		b. He established the case as a legal precedent for other cases
		  1) If a man had no son, his inheritance went to his daughter
		  2) If he had no daughter, it went to his brothers
		  3) If he had no brothers, it went to his father's brothers
		  4) If his father had no brothers, it went to the nearest relative in his clan
		  5) The point: To keep the inheritance as close as possible to the family line

DIVISION IV

THE PREPARATION FOR THE MARCH INTO THE PROMISED LAND, 26:1–36:13

B. The Basic Law That Gave Women an Inheritance in the Promised Land: Five Women of Enormous Courage, Faith, and Hope, 27:1-11

(27:1-11) Introduction—Rights Equal—Non-Discrimination, Need for—Impartiality, Need for—Prejudice, Trait of Nations—Unbiased, Need for Being—Treatment, Fair, Need for: throughout history, the rights of minorities have been neglected, ignored, and abused. Even in the twentieth century, most nations and communities still do not give equal rights to minorities. Mistreatment of people still takes place, the abuse of different races, nationalities, religions, and positions. The handicapped or physically deformed are seldom given equal rights within any society. Sometimes unequal rights are deliberately fostered by communities and nations; at other times equal rights are deprived out of ignorance—people simply are not aware that a person is not experiencing equal rights. But there is one person who is aware of mistreatment and abuse: God. Concern for the mistreated is the beat of God's heart. God cares for the helpless and the needy, for the abused and unprotected, for the underprivileged and the people who do not have adequate provision. God cares for every need we have, for the lack of any provision in our lives. This is the subject that is now to be studied: *The Basic Law That Gave Women an Inheritance in the Promised Land: Five Women of Enormous Courage, Faith, and Hope*, 27:1-11.

1. The godly heritage and the names of the women (v.1).
2. The courage of the women (v.2).
3. The concern, the great faith, and the hope of the women (vv.3-4).
4. The case was taken to the LORD by Moses: a picture of seeking God for help in solving problems (vv.5-11).

1 **(27:1) Heritage, Godly, Importance of—Parents, Godly, Importance of**: there was the godly heritage and the names of the women. They belonged to the tribe of Manasseh who was one of the two sons of Joseph. Remember: one of the most godly persons in Scripture was Joseph (Ge. 39:1f). His godly and moral character soared to the highest degree imaginable, just as an eagle soars above the clouds of the earth. Because of his godly character, his son Manasseh lived a godly life; and because Manasseh lived a godly life, his grandson Makir lived a godly life. Because Makir lived a godly life, his son Gilead lived a godly life; and because Gilead lived a godly life, his son Hepher lived a godly life. And because Hepher lived a godly life, Zelophehad lived a godly life. As Zelophehad was the father of these five godly daughters, the godly heritage was carried through the entire line of Manasseh, who had a godly father, Joseph himself. This is the first fact to note about these five women of enormous courage, faith, and hope: they had a godly heritage.

The need for a godly heritage cannot be over-emphasized. Parents need to live godly lives before their children. Children need parents...
- who believe and trust the LORD
- who will love them, nurture and nourish them
- who will take care of them and look after them.
- who will teach and instruct them in the ways of the LORD
- who will encourage them and see that they receive an education
- who will discipline and correct them when they are wrong

Parents need to live holy, pure, and righteous lives for the sake of their children, yes. But this is not all. Society desperately needs the example of a godly heritage. The cry of society is for godly parents, parents who will leave a godly heritage to the world. Lawlessness, violence, immorality, abuse, greed—all the evils of society—will be corrected only through the example of godly parents. A godly heritage cannot be over-emphasized.

> Now I commit you to God and to the word of his grace, which can build you up and give you an inheritance among all those who are sanctified. (Ac. 20:32)
>
> Fathers, do not exasperate your children; instead, bring them up in the training and instruction of the Lord. (Ep. 6:4)
>
> I have been reminded of your sincere faith, which first lived in your grandmother Lois and in your mother Eunice and, I am persuaded, now lives in you also. (2 Ti. 1:5)
>
> And how from infancy you have known the holy Scriptures, which are able to make you wise for salvation through faith in Christ Jesus. (2 Ti. 3:15)
>
> Then they can train the younger women to love their husbands and children. (Tit. 2:4)
>
> Impress them on your children. Talk about them when you sit at home and when you walk along the road, when you lie down and when you get up. (De. 6:7)
>
> For you have heard my vows, O God; you have given me the heritage of those who fear your name. (Ps. 61:5)
>
> Train a child in the way he should go, and when he is old he will not turn from it. (Pr. 22:6)

2 (27:2) **Courage, Example of—Women, Courage of**: there was the unusual courage of the women. First, their remarkable courage is seen in two facts. First, they approached the Tabernacle, the very place that symbolized God's holy presence. As they approached, they obviously had complete confidence that they were not displeasing God at all. They were well aware that God's holiness struck out and consumed any who violated God's presence, who approached God with hypocritical motives. Obviously, within their hearts, they had prayed and entrusted their case into the hands of God. Second, they approached the highest legal body of the nation, Israel's supreme court. There they stood before Moses himself, Eleazar the priest, and all the other leaders of the whole nation. What enormous courage!

Thought 1. These dear women—all sisters—stand as a dynamic example of courage for all believers of all generations. They felt that an injustice was being done, not only to them, but to so many other of the women throughout the nation. The injustice will be seen in the next point. For now, the point to see is their courage—their great courage. Just as these women stood up against injustice, so we must stand up against injustice, so we must stand up and be courageous. We need courage to stand against the injustices, lawlessness, violence, immorality, and sins of society. Courageous people—people who will stand staunchly, with hearts filled with courage—are desperately needed. Fearlessness is needed to combat the evils of this world. Brave, bold, valiant people are needed, people with courage, people who are lionhearted.

> Be on your guard; stand firm in the faith; be men of courage; be strong. (1 Co. 16:13)
>
> Finally, be strong in the Lord and in his mighty power. (Ep. 6:10)
>
> Therefore put on the full armor of God, so that when the day of evil comes, you may be able to stand your ground, and after you have done everything, to stand. (Ep. 6:13)
>
> Whatever happens, conduct yourselves in a manner worthy of the gospel of Christ. Then, whether I come and see you or only hear about you in my absence, I will know that you stand firm in one spirit, contending as one man for the faith of the gospel without being frightened in any way by those who oppose you. This is a sign to them that they will be destroyed, but that you will be saved—and that by God. (Ph. 1:27-28)
>
> For God did not give us a spirit of timidity, but a spirit of power, of love and of self-discipline. So do not be ashamed to testify about our Lord, or ashamed of me his prisoner. But join with me in suffering for the gospel, by the power of God. (2 Ti. 1:7-8)
>
> You then, my son, be strong in the grace that is in Christ Jesus. (2 Ti. 2:1)
>
> Endure hardship with us like a good soldier of Christ Jesus. (2 Ti. 2:3)
>
> Let us then approach the throne of grace with confidence, so that we may receive mercy and find grace to help us in our time of need. (He. 4:16)
>
> Be strong and courageous. Do not be afraid or terrified because of them, for the LORD your God goes with you; he will never leave you nor forsake you. (De. 31:6)
>
> The LORD is my light and my salvation—whom shall I fear? The LORD is the stronghold of my life—of whom shall I be afraid? When evil men advance against me to devour my flesh, when my enemies and my foes attack me, they will stumble and fall. Though an army besiege me, my heart will not fear; though war break out against me, even then will I be confident. (Ps. 27:1-3)

I will say of the LORD, "He is my refuge and my fortress, my God, in whom I trust." Surely he will save you from the fowler's snare and from the deadly pestilence. He will cover you with his feathers, and under his wings you will find refuge; his faithfulness will be your shield and rampart. You will not fear the terror of night, nor the arrow that flies by day, nor the pestilence that stalks in the darkness, nor the plague that destroys at midday. (Ps. 91:2-6)

The LORD is with me; I will not be afraid. What can man do to me? (Ps. 118:6)

When you lie down, you will not be afraid; when you lie down, your sleep will be sweet. (Pr. 3:24)

Surely God is my salvation; I will trust and not be afraid. The LORD, the LORD, is my strength and my song; he has become my salvation. (Is. 12:2)

3 **(27:3-4) Faith, Great—Hope, Great—Land, the Promised, Faith in—Faith, in the Promised Land**: there was the concern, the great faith, and the hope of the women. In the ancient world, a father's property was divided among his sons. The oldest son received twice as much as the younger sons (De. 21:15-17; see DEEPER STUDY # 1, *Birthright*—Ge. 25:31 for more discussion). Daughters did not receive property. Rather, when they were married, they received a dowry or a wedding present from their father. Of course, what they received depended upon the wealth of the father. Wealthy fathers were known to give large dowries such as expensive clothing, jewelry, perfumes, money, furniture, slave-help, and sometimes even houses and entire cities (Ge. 29:24, 29; Jud. 1:13-15; 1 K. 9:16). Once the daughter had married, the father had no more responsibility for her, and she received no inheritance of land or property upon his death. By law she became a full-fledged member of the family into which she married.1 This was the deep concern that had gripped the hearts of these five dear sisters. The Scripture and outline state in very simple terms the injustice they were feeling, no doubt an injustice that existed with other women throughout the nation.

a. The father of these dear sisters had died with no sons, leaving only them as the surviving members of the family. Note that he had died believing in the promised land, not in Korah's rebellion that sought to replace Moses and to lead the Israelites back to Egypt. Their father had been a true believer in God's promises: he had not been a seeker after the pleasures of Egypt nor of this world. (See outline and notes—Nu. 16:1-50 for more discussion.)

b. Their faith in the promised land was strong. No doubt their testimony touched the hearts of the judges who sat on the supreme court hearing their case. Note what they wanted: their father's name—the testimony of his faith—preserved. Therefore, they were requesting his inheritance (v.4). Note what they asked the supreme court: Why should the name of their father disappear from history, lose its identity—just because he had no sons? The point to see is the great faith and hope of the women in the promised land. Keep in mind that Israel had not yet entered the promised land, yet these dear women had faith in God. They knew that God was going to lead the Israelites into the promised land and give them their inheritance. Entering and inheriting the promised land was not a question to them. They knew that God was going to fulfill His prom-

ise. They were women of deep conviction, faith, and hope in the great inheritance promised by God. Their faith was strong, so strong that they did something that had never been done in the history of the world. They appeared before the supreme court of the land to change one of the most basic and ancient laws in all of history, a history that had been dominated by men. That law was the law of inheritance or of the birthright, a law that gave the inheritance of land only to the sons of a family. But these dear women believed God's promise, believed in the promised land so much that they were willing to risk everything in order to secure their inheritance. They wanted the godly heritage and inheritance of their family's name to be carried on through succeeding generations. They wanted their inheritance in the promised land of God.

Thought 1. The only person who will ever enter the promised land of heaven will be the person who follows in the steps of these five dear sisters. Murderers will never enter the promised land of heaven. Neither will the violent, the lawless, the abuser, the drunk, the drug addict, the greedy, the immoral, the hater, the liar, the thief, nor the person who uses profanity and takes God's name in vain—no person who walks or lives in sin will ever enter the promised land of God. As stated, the only person who will ever enter heaven is the person who follows in the steps of these five dear sisters. They believed with all their hearts in God and in the promised land. Their faith in the inheritance promised by God was strong, very strong. Our faith in God and the promised land of heaven must be strong. God promises us an inheritance in the new heavens and earth. By faith, we must lay hold of our inheritance, lay hold of the promised land of heaven.

But store up for yourselves treasures in heaven, where moth and rust do not destroy, and where thieves do not break in and steal. (Mt. 6:20)

"Do not let your hearts be troubled. Trust in God; trust also in me. In my Father's house are many rooms; if it were not so, I would have told you. I am going there to prepare a place for you. And if I go and prepare a place for you, I will come back and take you to be with me that you also may be where I am." (Jn. 14:1-3)

Now we know that if the earthly tent we live in is destroyed, we have a building from God, an eternal house in heaven, not built by human hands. (2 Co. 5:1)

But our citizenship is in heaven. And we eagerly await a Savior from there, the Lord Jesus Christ, who, by the power that enables him to bring everything under his control, will transform our lowly bodies so that they will be like his glorious body. (Ph. 3:20-21)

By faith Abraham, when called to go to a place he would later receive as his inheritance, obeyed and went, even though he did not know where he was going. By faith he made his home in the promised land like a stranger in a foreign country; he lived in tents, as did Isaac and Jacob, who were heirs with him of the same promise. For he was looking forward to the city with foundations, whose architect and builder is God. (He. 11:8-10)

All these people [believers] were still living by faith when they died. They did not receive the things promised; they only saw them and welcomed them from a distance. And they admitted that they were aliens and strangers on earth. People who say such things show that they are looking for a country of their own. If they had been thinking of the country they had left, they would have had opportunity to return. Instead, they were longing for a better country—a heavenly one. Therefore God is not ashamed to be called their God, for he has prepared a city for them. (He. 11:13-16)

Praise be to the God and Father of our Lord Jesus Christ! In his great mercy he has given us new birth into a living hope through the resurrection of Jesus Christ from the dead, and into an inheritance that can never perish, spoil or fade—kept in heaven for you. (1 Pe. 1:3-4)

But the day of the Lord will come like a thief. The heavens will disappear with a roar; the elements will be destroyed by fire, and the earth and everything in it will be laid bare. Since everything will be destroyed in this way, what kind of people ought you to be? You ought to live holy and godly lives as you look forward to the day of God and speed its coming. That day will bring about the destruction of the heavens by fire, and the elements will melt in the heat. But in keeping with his promise we are looking forward to a new heaven and a new earth, the home of righteousness. (2 Pe. 3:10-13)

Nothing impure will ever enter it [heaven], nor will anyone who does what is shameful or deceitful, but only those whose names are written in the Lamb's book of life. (Re. 21:27)

4 (27:5-11) **Seeking, of God—God, Seeking for—Problems, Seeking Answer to—Prayer, Seeking Answers to:** the case was taken to the LORD by Moses. This is a picture of seeking God for help in solving problems. Keep in mind the earth-shattering case of these dear women, a request to change a law that was commonly known and had been practiced by all civilizations down through human history. At the very least, the judges sitting on the supreme court of the nation were bound to be surprised if not shocked by the request of the women. Most rulers and courts of that day would have reacted against such a request. But note the spiritual sensitivity of God's servant Moses. Obviously, he sensed the deep faith and sincerity of these dear women. Therefore he did not react but, rather, responded. He took their case before the LORD. The Scripture and outline demonstrate a wonderful fact: the love and grace of God are as open to women as they are to men. With God there is no partiality or favoritism, no discrimination whatsoever. There are no minorities: not women or men, not black, red, yellow, or white. There is no race or nationality or sex that stands as a favorite with God. There is no discrimination with God whatsoever. This is the clear teaching of Scripture.

a. Note that God granted the request of these dear sisters (vv.6-7). He gave them their father's inheritance, honored their faith and hope in the promised land.

b. God established the case as a legal precedent for other cases (vv.8-11). Simply stated, if a man had no son, his inheritance went to his daughter(s) (v.8). If he had no daughter, then the land passed to his nearest male relative (vv.9-11). The point of the law was to keep the inheritance as close as possible to the family line.

Thought 1. This was an earth-shattering case, a case that created a serious problem for Moses. In seeking God, Moses sets a dynamic example for us. When problems confront us, we should seek the face of the LORD. The LORD will help us if only we will seek Him. Too often we attempt to handle problems and circumstances alone, in our own strength. In so doing, we often dig ditches so deep that it is difficult to claw our way out of them. We merely create more and more problems for ourselves. The answer to problems is the Divine Helper, God Himself. God wants to help us. But He wants us first to seek Him, to draw near Him, to fellowship and commune with Him. This was the very purpose for which He created us; therefore, we must first seek Him. When we seek Him, He steps in and helps us conquer the problems of this life. Seeking the LORD is the answer to a victorious life. We triumph over the pitfalls of this life, over the problems and circumstances of this life when we seek the face of the LORD God Himself.

For everyone who asks receives; he who seeks finds; and to him who knocks, the door will be opened. (Lu. 11:10)

Until now you have not asked for anything in my name. Ask and you will receive, and your joy will be complete. (Jn. 16:24)

Do not be anxious about anything, but in everything, by prayer and petition, with thanksgiving, present your requests to God. And the peace of God, which transcends all understanding, will guard your hearts and your minds in Christ Jesus. (Ph. 4:6-7)

Devote yourselves to prayer, being watchful and thankful. And pray for us, too, that God may open a door for our message, so that we may proclaim the mystery of Christ, for which I am in chains. (Col. 4:2-3)

Is any one of you in trouble? He should pray. Is anyone happy? Let him sing songs of praise. Is any one of you sick? He should call the elders of the church to pray over him and anoint him with oil in the name of the Lord. (Jas. 5:13-14)

But if from there you seek the LORD your God, you will find him if you look for him with all your heart and with all your soul. (De. 4:29)

Look to the LORD and his strength; seek his face always. (1 Chr. 16:11)

He will call upon me, and I will answer him; I will be with him in trouble, I will deliver him and honor him. (Ps. 91:15)

Look to the LORD and his strength; seek his face always. (Ps. 105:4)

Numbers 27:1-11

Seek the LORD while he may be found; call on him while he is near. (Is. 55:6)

Then you will call, and the LORD will answer; you will cry for help, and he will say: Here am I. "If you do away with the yoke of oppression, with the pointing finger and malicious talk…" (Is. 58:9)

Before they call I will answer; while they are still speaking I will hear. (Is. 65:24)

You will seek me and find me when you seek me with all your heart. (Je. 29:13)

This is what the LORD says to the house of Israel: "Seek me and live." (Am. 5:4)

Seek the LORD, all you humble of the land, you who do what he commands. Seek righteousness, seek humility; perhaps you will be sheltered on the day of the LORD's anger. (Zep. 2:3)

NUMBERS 27:12-23

	C. The Appointment of Joshua As the Successor to Moses: A Strong Picture of God Preparing the Believer for Death, 27:12-23	not be like sheep without a shepherd." 18 So the LORD said to Moses, "Take Joshua son of Nun, a man in whom is the spirit, and lay your hand on him.	with no shepherd 3. God instructed Moses to appoint Joshua: A picture of God providing a leader for His people a. To know God's Spirit is in Joshua
1. God told Moses to prepare for death: A picture of God preparing the believer for death a. God granted Moses a glimpse of the promised land b. God assured Moses that he would "be gathered to his people": Live with them eternally in the promised land of heaven 2. God reminded Moses why he could not enter the promised land: A picture of the holiness & justice of God against sin a. Moses had disobeyed God b. Moses had failed to honor God & failed to demonstrate His holiness c. Moses responded with broken humility & deep concern 1) Accepted the judgment 2) Prayed for the Sovereign LORD to appoint a successor • To lead the people • To be a shepherd to them—to keep them from being like sheep	12 Then the LORD said to Moses, "Go up this mountain in the Abarim range and see the land I have given the Israelites. 13 After you have seen it, you too will be gathered to your people, as your brother Aaron was, 14 For when the community rebelled at the waters in the Desert of Zin, both of you disobeyed my command to honor me as holy before their eyes." (These were the waters of Meribah Kadesh, in the Desert of Zin.) 15 Moses said to the LORD, 16 "May the LORD, the God of the spirits of all mankind, appoint a man over this community 17 To go out and come in before them, one who will lead them out and bring them in, so the LORD's people will	19 Have him stand before Eleazar the priest and the entire assembly and commission him in their presence. 20 Give him some of your authority so the whole Israelite community will obey him. 21 He is to stand before Eleazar the priest, who will obtain decisions for him by inquiring of the Urim before the LORD. At his command he and the entire community of the Israelites will go out, and at his command they will come in." 22 Moses did as the LORD commanded him. He took Joshua and had him stand before Eleazar the priest and the whole assembly. 23 Then he laid his hands on him and commissioned him, as the LORD instructed through Moses.	b. To identify him as the new leader c. To commission him in the presence of everyone: Standing before the High Priest & the entire assembly d. To assign some day-to-day authority to him: Gradually transferring authority so the people would follow him e. To have him approach God for major decisions through the High Priest: The High Priest was to seek God's will through the Urim (sacred lots) f. To have him take over immediate command of the marching divisions g. The obedience of Moses 1) He had Joshua stand before the High Priest, Eleazar, & the entire assembly 2) He laid his hands on him: Identified him as the new leader 3) They were commissioned by God

DIVISION IV

THE PREPARATION FOR THE MARCH INTO THE PROMISED LAND, 26:1–36:13

C. The Appointment of Joshua As the Successor to Moses: A Strong Picture of God Preparing the Believer for Death, 27:12-23

(27:12-23) **Introduction—Death, Experience of—Death, Hope of—Death, of Moses**: death is inevitable. Every person dies—some sooner some later, but the grim hand of death eventually comes. Scripture declares that death is a horrifying experience for any person who has not followed Jesus Christ. But Scripture also declares that death is a glorious experience for the believer, for the person who has truly followed Christ. This glorious experience is seen in the life of Moses. It was time for Moses to leave this earth and go to live with God eternally. God was ready to welcome him and give him a triumphant entrance into the kingdom of heaven. But before God could take him home, a successor had to be appointed to lead God's people into the promised land. This is the subject of this great passage of Scripture: *The Appointment of Joshua As the Successor to Moses: A Strong Picture of God's Grace, Holiness, and Sovereignty,* 27:12-23.

1. God told Moses to prepare for death: a picture of God preparing the believer for death (vv.12-13).
2. God reminded Moses why he could not enter the promised land: a picture of the holiness and justice of God against sin (vv.14-17).
3. God instructed Moses to appoint Joshua: a picture of God providing a leader for His people (vv.18-23).

1 (27:12-13) **Death, of Moses—Death, Preparation for—Grace, of God—Love, of God—Death, of Believer, Preparation for**: God told Moses to prepare for death. This was a strong picture of God preparing the believer for death. Moses was an old man now, almost one hundred and twenty years old. This dear servant of God had served the people for almost forty years, serving them faithfully and well. He had persevered to the end, and now it was about time for him to leave this earth and go home to God. Moses had committed a terrible sin at Kadesh, a sin so terrible that he was disallowed or barred from entering the promised land. This will be seen in point two below. For now, the point to see is God's preparation of Moses for death. Because of his sin, Moses was heartsick, brokenhearted. His heart was heavy, feeling deep pain, hurt, and regret. He was crushed, disappointed, sorrowful, humbled, and subdued. He was a bruised man, hurt and shamed, marked for life by his sin. His sin never left him: it was always before his face and upon his mind. This dear servant had been so faithful through the forty years in leading God's people through the desert wilderness, through some of the most difficult problems and hardships imaginable. By the grace and appointment of God he had taken over two million slaves and led them to freedom. He had molded them into a very distinctive nation of people who were set apart to be the followers of the only living and true God. But there came a day when he failed to control the passions of his flesh, committing a terrible sin before God and the people. Because of his sin, he had forfeited his right to enter the promised land. He was not allowed to lead the people to their spiritual rest, not allowed to lead them through the victorious conquest of their enemies. He would live eternally with God, but his ultimate reward was affected. He had lost the privilege of seeing his dear people receive their inheritance in the promised land, lost the privilege of seeing them enter their spiritual rest. This crushing blow never left Moses: it marked him every day for the rest of his life. As he walked through each day, he felt the pain, hurt, and regret with a heart that was broken, a heart that sensed his failure ever so deeply.

God knew the feelings of Moses, knew exactly how he felt. God's heart went out to His dear servant, a servant who had been so faithful to his call except in this one instance. Therefore when it was time for God to take Moses home, God wanted to make his death a very special occasion, a precious time of communion and intimacy between Him and His dear servant. God determined to do a very special thing for Moses: to give him a glimpse of the promised land.

a. In mercy, God granted Moses a glimpse of the promised land (v.12). Note that God told Moses to climb to the top of a particular mountain and survey the land which He was giving to the Israelites. Despite the terrible sin of Moses, God poured out His mercy and goodness upon Moses. God showed him great love and compassion. This dear servant was about ready to go home to heaven, and God wanted to be there for him. But before God took His dear servant home, God wanted to reassure and encourage him: his faith in the promised land was a living reality. God gave him a glimpse of the land. Just imagine the assurance that flowed through Moses' heart as he stood on top of the mountain, stood there surveying the promised land lying out before him. Tears, perhaps even a brokenness, poured out from his soul—for there lay before him the inheritance of the promised land given by God to His dear people. Most likely, Moses fell to his knees with a heart filled with mixed emotions: yes, sorrow and regret for his sin that was keeping him from leading the dear people of God into the land. But he also felt joy and rejoicing at the promise of God that was soon becoming a living reality in their hearts and lives. Other Scriptures tell us that Moses begged God to let him cross over the Jordan and survey the promised land before God took him home. But God said, "No." Moses had sinned; therefore the justice and judgment of God had to be executed. His dear servant could not enter the promised land.

b. However, God assured Moses that he would "be gathered to his people." This means that Moses would join all the believers who had gone before him and live with them eternally in the promised land of heaven, face to face with God. God was preparing His dear servant for the moment of death, the moment when He would transfer him from this earth into heaven. In that moment, God wanted to be there for His dear servant. God's heart went out to him and embraced him with feelings of warmth, tenderness, and gentleness. God reached out to prepare His dear servant for the fast-approaching day of his death, reached out to comfort and console him, to give him perfect assurance and confidence.

Thought 1. The death of a believer is a warm, tender, gentle, and touching experience. This is because of Jesus Christ and His death upon the cross. Christ died for us. Because He died for us, we are to live forever, never dying. When we come to that moment that is commonly called *death*—quicker than the eye can blink—God transfers us from this world into His presence. We never taste or experience death. In one moment of time we are on this earth; in the next moment of time we are face to face with God in heaven. In one moment we are in this world, in the physical dimension of being; in the next moment of time we are in the spiritual world, in the spiritual dimension of being. Just as God prepared Moses for heaven, giving him perfect assurance and confidence, so God prepares us. When that moment comes, God will infuse within our beings the greatest assurance and confidence imaginable, yea, perfect assurance and confidence. We will live forever face to face with God in heaven.

I give them eternal life, and they shall never perish; no one can snatch them out of my hand. (Jn. 10:28)

"Do not let your hearts be troubled. Trust in God; trust also in me. In my Father's house are many rooms; if it were not so, I would have told you. I am going there to prepare a place for you. And if I go and prepare a place for you, I will come back and take you to be with me that you also may be where I am." (Jn. 14:1-3)

To those who by persistence in doing good seek glory, honor and immortality, he will give eternal life. (Ro. 2:7)

For none of us lives to himself alone and none of us dies to himself alone. If we live, we live to the Lord; and if we die, we die to the Lord. So, whether we live or die, we belong to the Lord. For this very reason, Christ died and returned to life so that he might be the Lord of both the dead and the living. (Ro. 14:7-9)

Now we know that if the earthly tent we live in is destroyed, we have a building from God, an eternal house in heaven, not built by human hands. (2 Co. 5:1)

We are confident, I say, and would prefer to be away from the body and at home with the Lord. (2 Co. 5:8)

For to me, to live is Christ and to die is gain. (Ph. 1:21)

I am torn between the two: I desire to depart and be with Christ, which is better by far. (Ph. 1:23)

But our citizenship is in heaven. And we eagerly await a Savior from there, the Lord Jesus Christ, who, by the power that enables him to bring everything under his control, will transform our lowly bodies so that they will be like his glorious body. (Ph. 3:20-21)

A faith and knowledge resting on the hope of eternal life, which God, who does not lie, promised before the beginning of time. (Tit. 1:2)

All these people [believers] were still living by faith when they died. They did not receive the things promised; they only saw them and welcomed them from a distance. And they admitted that they were aliens and strangers on earth. People who say

such things show that they are looking for a country of their own. (He. 11:13-14)

Praise be to the God and Father of our Lord Jesus Christ! In his great mercy he has given us new birth into a living hope through the resurrection of Jesus Christ from the dead, and into an inheritance that can never perish, spoil or fade—kept in heaven for you. (1 Pe. 1:3-4)

And this is what he promised us—even eternal life. (1 Jn. 2:25)

Then I heard a voice from heaven say, "Write: Blessed are the dead who die in the Lord from now on." "Yes," says the Spirit, "they will rest from their labor, for their deeds will follow them." (Re. 14:13)

And I saw an angel coming down out of heaven, having the key to the Abyss and holding in his hand a great chain....I saw thrones on which were seated those who had been given authority to judge. And I saw the souls of those who had been beheaded because of their testimony for Jesus and because of the word of God. They had not worshiped the beast or his image and had not received his mark on their foreheads or their hands. They came to life and reigned with Christ a thousand years. (The rest of the dead did not come to life until the thousand years were ended.) This is the first resurrection. Blessed and holy are those who have part in the first resurrection. The second death has no power over them, but they will be priests of God and of Christ and will reign with him for a thousand years. When the thousand years are over, Satan will be released from his prison. (Re. 20:1, 4-7)

Let me die the death of the righteous, and may my end be like theirs! (Nu. 23:10)

Even though I walk through the valley of the shadow of death, I will fear no evil, for you are with me; your rod and your staff, they comfort me. (Ps. 23:4)

Precious in the sight of the LORD is the death of his saints. (Ps. 116:15)

2 (27:14-17) **Moses, Sin of—Holiness, of God—Justice, of God—Minister, Heart of—Moses, Heart of—Minister, Described as, Shepherd**: God reminded Moses why he could not enter the promised land. This is a strong picture of the holiness and justice of God against sin. Moses and Aaron were both guilty of the sins that are covered in this passage. The Scripture clearly spells out the sins.

a. The first sin was disobedience. Moses disobeyed God's command (v.14). Remember, the people needed water. God told Moses to walk over to a particular rock and call for water to gush out. The result would be a wonderful miracle: water would pour out from the rock. Another important command involved the people: Moses was to call the people together so they could be eyewitnesses of the event. They were to know beyond any question that it was God who was meeting their need. God Himself was providing for them. But Moses had disobeyed God. Moses had done the exact opposite of what God had instructed.

b. Moses had failed to honor God and failed to demonstrate His holiness before the people (v.14). Moses had disobeyed God in three ways:
⇒ Moses had spoken to the people in anger instead of addressing the rock as commanded by God. In fact he had lashed out at the people, calling them "rebels."
⇒ Moses had not given God the full credit and honor for providing the water. He took some of the credit himself. In anger, he lashed out at the people, shouting "Must 'we' bring you water?" By saying "we," Moses was assuming some of the credit himself. This was a serious offense to God, for God will not share His glory with any man.
⇒ Moses struck the rock with his staff instead of speaking to it as God had commanded. In fact, he was so angry that he struck the rock twice.

Note what God then told Moses in this passage: the dear servant had failed to honor God as holy before the eyes of the people (v.14). Moses had failed to acknowledge God as the sole provider for His people. Moses had lost complete control of his emotions, becoming violently angry. He was acting ungodly, unrighteously, and completely out of control before the people. He was doing anything but bringing honor and glory to God. He was demonstrating the very opposite of God's holiness. He had degraded and torn down the image of God in the people's minds, desecrating the holiness of God. Moses had committed the terrible sin of disobedience. This was the reason Moses was disallowed or barred from entering the promised land. The holiness and justice of God against sin had to be executed. The servant of God had gone too far in violating the holiness of God in the eyes of the people. Consequently, he had to be judged, chastised.

c. Moses responded with a broken humility and deep concern for the people of God (vv.15-17). Moses accepted the judgment of God and accepted the fact that he was now "to be gathered to his people." The real character and heart of this dear servant of God is clearly seen in what happened next. He immediately began to pray for the Sovereign LORD to appoint a successor. Note how he addressed the LORD: "the LORD, the God of the spirits of all mankind." He was acknowledging that God...
- was the only living and true God
- was the great Creator and Sustainer of all mankind
- was the Giver of all life
- was sovereign over all people
- was the only God who could provide for His people

If Moses was leaving the scene, another leader had to be raised up, another successor had to be appointed. The people would desperately need a leader, a successor to replace Moses. Without a leader, the people would be like sheep with no shepherd. Without a shepherd, they would be wandering about, lost and scattered abroad. God must give a shepherd to continue leading His dear people to the promised land. This was the primary concern that gripped the heart of Moses.

Thought 1. There are two clear lessons for us in this point.
(1) God judges sin. His holiness and justice demand that He judge and chastise His people when they sin. This is the clear declaration of Scripture:

He cuts off every branch in me that bears no fruit, while every branch that does bear fruit he prunes so that it will be even more fruitful. (Jn. 15:2)

That is why many among you are weak and sick, and a number of you [believers] have fallen asleep. But if we judged ourselves, we would not come under judgment. When we are judged by the Lord, we are being disciplined so that we will not be condemned with the world. (1 Co. 11:30-32)

And you have forgotten that word of encouragement that addresses you as sons: "My son, do not make light of the Lord's discipline, and do not lose heart when he rebukes you, because the Lord disciplines those he loves, and he punishes everyone he accepts as a son." (He. 12:5-6)

Those whom I love I rebuke and discipline. So be earnest, and repent. (Re. 3:19)

Know then in your heart that as a man disciplines his son, so the LORD your God disciplines you. (De. 8:5)

Blessed is the man you discipline, O LORD, the man you teach from your law. (Ps. 94:12)

My son, do not despise the LORD's discipline and do not resent his rebuke, because the LORD disciplines those he loves, as a father the son he delights in. (Pr. 3:11-12)

(2) Believers must pray for God to raise up leaders, strong leaders who will serve God's people faithfully. This was the concern of Moses, and it was the concern of the Lord Jesus Christ. In fact, Christ used the very comparison that Moses used in describing the minister as a shepherd. He said that people are as sheep without a shepherd (Mt. 9:1, 36-38).

God answers prayer. He moves when His people pray. The challenge of the hour is for leaders, godly leaders. People who are sold out to Jesus Christ and to meeting the needs of people are desperately needed. God will raise up leaders if we pray. The church will have faithful shepherds who will lead and feed the people if we will pray.

Ask and it will be given to you; seek and you will find; knock and the door will be opened to you. (Mt. 7:7)

When he saw the crowds, he had compassion on them, because they were harassed and helpless, like sheep without a shepherd. Then he said to his disciples, "The harvest is plentiful but the workers are few. Ask the Lord of the harvest, therefore, to send out workers into his harvest field." (Mt. 9:36-38)

Before they call I will answer; while they are still speaking I will hear. (Is. 65:24)

Then I will give you shepherds after my own heart, who will lead you with knowledge and understanding. (Je. 3:15)

"I will place shepherds over them who will tend them, and they will no longer be afraid or terrified, nor will any be missing," declares the LORD. (Je. 23:4)

My sheep wandered over all the mountains and on every high hill. They were scattered over the whole earth, and no one searched or looked for them. (Eze. 34:6)

3 (27:18-23) **Ministers, Appointed by God—Call, of God—Joshua, Appointed by God—Israel, Leaders of—Leaders, Appointment of—Leaders, Example of, Joshua**: God instructed Moses to appoint Joshua as his successor. This is a strong picture of God providing a leader for His people. Remember, Joshua had been the assistant to Moses for many years, probably from his earliest youth (Nu. 11:28; Ex. 17:9f; 24:13; 32:17). Joshua had also been one of the twelve spies who years earlier had spied out the land of Canaan. Along with Caleb, he had stood staunchly against the other ten spies, declaring that Israel could march in and conquer the enemies of the promised land. He had proven to be a strong believer in the great promises of God, a man of strong courage and faith, a leader who soared head and shoulders above other leaders. He was a man after God's own heart. He was, therefore, the choice of God to follow in the footsteps of Moses. He was to be the leader who would take God's dear people into the promised land and give them their inheritance. Remember that Joshua is the Hebrew name *Jesus* in the Greek. He was to be the deliverer of God's people, a type of the coming Deliverer who was to save the whole world, the LORD Jesus Christ Himself. God gave clear instructions to Moses concerning Joshua:

a. Moses was to know that God's Spirit was in Joshua (v.18). No man could lead God's people apart from the Spirit of God. For this reason, God had already placed His Spirit in Joshua. The Holy Spirit was now controlling Joshua's life and preparing him to lead God's people.

b. Moses was to identify Joshua as the new leader of God's people. This was to be done publicly by laying hands on him (v.18).

c. Moses was to commission Joshua in the presence of the people. He was to call the people together and stand Joshua before the High Priest in the sight of everyone. Then he was to commission him *publicly* (v.19).

d. Moses was to assign some day-to-day authority to Joshua. Authority was to be transferred to him gradually so the people would learn to follow him (v.20). This was essential so the people could learn to trust his leadership. They needed to see that he was capable of leading day by day; thereby, they would learn to trust him more and more. Being without Moses, God's great leader for so many years, was going to be a traumatic experience for the people. Following in his footsteps would be difficult for any leader. The gradual transfer of power to Joshua would give the people time to gain confidence in his leadership.

e. Moses was to have Joshua approach God for major decisions through the High Priest. Joshua did not have the same privilege that Moses had, that of approaching God in the Tabernacle. Joshua had to approach God the same as everyone else, through the appointed mediator, Eleazar the priest (a symbol of Christ our High Priest). When Joshua had a decision to make, he was to go to the priest and the priest was to seek God's will in his behalf. Note that he was to use the Urim, which was a sacred lot utilized in seeking God's will. (See note, pt.3, b—Ex. 28:15-30 for more discussion.)

f. Moses was to have Joshua take over immediate command of the marching divisions (v.21).

g. Note the obedience of Moses (vv.22-23). He had Joshua stand before Eleazar the High Priest and the entire assembly. Then he laid his hands on him, identifying him as the new leader. He commissioned this young man who was to take over the leadership reins of God's dear people.

Thought 1. This is a grave hour, an hour when leaders are desperately needed. Christ Himself said that the fields were ripe, ready for harvest, but the laborers were few. We need laborers, leaders who will step forth and make themselves available to God and His service. Where are such laborers? Where are the people who will step forth? To a large degree, the plight of the world is due to a lack of godly leadership. God's eyes search the earth to find people who will love and obey Him, stepping forth to serve His dear people (2 Chr. 16:9). God calls many, but few are chosen (Mt. 20:16). Few accept the call and step forth to meet the desperate needs of the world. In searching the earth, who is available? Where are the persons who will make the commitment to serve? Who has rejected the call? God longs to choose, to appoint those who are called to serve Him and His dear people. God wants men and women to make themselves available. God wants to choose and appoint leaders to go and meet the desperate needs of the world.

"So the last will be first, and the first will be last." (Mt. 20:16; see Mt. 22:14)

Just as the Son of Man did not come to be served, but to serve, and to give his life as a ransom for many. (Mt. 20:28)

Therefore go and make disciples of all nations, baptizing them in the name of the Father and of the Son and of the Holy Spirit, and teaching them to obey everything I have commanded you. And surely I am with you always, to the very end of the age. (Mt. 28:19-20)

He said to them, "Go into all the world and preach the good news to all creation." (Mk. 16:15)

You did not choose me, but I chose you and appointed you to go and bear fruit—fruit that will last. Then the Father will give you whatever you ask in my name. (Jn. 15:16)

Again Jesus said, "Peace be with you! As the Father has sent me, I am sending you." (Jn. 20:21)

The third time he said to him, "Simon son of John, do you love me?" Peter was hurt because Jesus asked him the third time, "Do you love me?" He said, "Lord, you know all things; you know that I love you." Jesus said, "Feed my sheep." (Jn. 21:17)

But the Lord said to Ananias, "Go! This man is my chosen instrument to carry my name before the Gentiles and their kings and before the people of Israel." (Ac. 9:15)

Then I will give you shepherds after my own heart, who will lead you with knowledge and understanding. (Je. 3:15)

"I will place shepherds over them who will tend them, and they will no longer be afraid or terrified, nor will any be missing," declares the LORD. (Je. 23:4)

NUMBERS 28:1–29:40

CHAPTER 28

D. The Offerings & Sacrifices Commanded by the LORD: A Picture of Man's Need to Continually Approach & Worship God Through the Atonement Secured by the Sacrifice (a Symbol of God's Dear Son, the Lord Jesus Christ), 28:1–29:40

1. The importance of the offerings or sacrifices
   a. Were a clear command of God
   b. Were to be presented exactly at the appointed time
   c. Were an aroma that pleased God
2. The daily sacrifices of the Burnt Offering: A symbol of Christ's sacrifice that secured atonement or reconciliation for man
   a. To sacrifice two lambs: A year old without defect (a symbol of the perfection of Christ)
   b. To sacrifice one in the morning & one in the evening
   c. To offer a Grain Offering with each sacrifice (a symbol of thanking God for the atonement & all else): Two qts. of choice flour mixed with one qt. oil
   d. The result: A pleasing aroma to the LORD (a symbol that God is pleased with the sacrifice of Christ & with a person's faith in Christ)
   e. To offer the Drink Offering (a symbol of dedication, of pouring out one's life to God)^{DS1}
      1) One qt. of fermented drink with each sacrifice
      2) To be poured out to God
   f. To prepare the 2nd lamb at twilight
      1) To offer the same Grain Offering & Drink Offering
      2) The result: An aroma pleasing to the LORD
3. The Sabbath Day sacrifices: A symbol of Christ, our Sabbath rest (He. 3:10–4:16)
   a. To sacrifice two lambs: One year old without defect
   b. To offer the Drink Offering
   c. To offer a Grain Offering: Three qts. of flour with oil
   d. To be known as the Sabbath Burnt Offering: An additional offering to the regular Burnt Offering
4. The monthly sacrifices: A symbol of Christ's sacrifice
   a. To present a Burnt Offering on the 1st day of every month: Two bulls, one ram, seven male lambs one year old without defect
   b. To offer a Grain Offering of choice flour mixed with oil for each sacrifice (a symbol of thanking God for the atonement & for all else)
      1) Five qts. with each bull
      2) Three qts. with the ram
      3) Two qts. with each lamb
   c. The result: A Burnt Offering that pleased the Lord (a symbol of God's pleasure with Christ's sacrifice & with one's faith in Christ)
   d. To give a Drink Offering of wine with each sacrifice (a symbol of dedication)
      1) Two qts. with each bull
      2) Two & one half pints with the ram
      3) One qt. with each lamb
   e. To strictly observe the Burnt Offering sacrifice each month (a symbol of the atonement)
   f. To also sacrifice one male goat as a Sin Offering (a symbol of Christ's sacrifice, His dying for sin)
5. The Passover: A symbol of Christ the Lamb of God
   a. The date: 1st month, 14th day
   b. To observe the festival of unleavened bread for seven days (a symbol of rushing to be free from the slavery of this world)
      1) On the 15th day
      2) Eat no bread with yeast
   c. To call a sacred assembly on the 1st day: Do no work
   d. To present a Burnt Offering on the sacred assembly day: Two bulls, one ram, seven male lambs a year old, without defect (a symbol of Christ's sacrifice)
   e. To offer a Grain Offering with each sacrifice (a symbol of thanking God for the atonement & for all else)
      1) Five qts. with each bull
      2) Three qts. with the ram
      3) Two qts. with each lamb
   f. To also sacrifice a male goat as a Sin Offering: To make atonement (reconciliation)
   g. To be additional sacrifices to the regular morning sacrifice
   h. To offer these Burnt Offerings on each of the seven days (a symbol of the atonement secured by Christ's

---

CHAPTER 28

The LORD said to Moses, 2 "Give this command to the Israelites and say to them: 'See that you present to me at the appointed time the food for my offerings made by fire, as an aroma pleasing to me.'
3 Say to them: 'This is the offering made by fire that you are to present to the LORD: two lambs a year old without defect, as a regular burnt offering each day. 4 Prepare one lamb in the morning and the other at twilight, 5 Together with a grain offering of a tenth of an ephah of fine flour mixed with a quarter of a hin of oil from pressed olives. 6 This is the regular burnt offering instituted at Mount Sinai as a pleasing aroma, an offering made to the LORD by fire. 7 The accompanying drink offering is to be a quarter of a hin of fermented drink with each lamb. Pour out the drink offering to the LORD at the sanctuary. 8 Prepare the second lamb at twilight, along with the same kind of grain offering and drink offering that you prepare in the morning. This is an offering made by fire, an aroma pleasing to the LORD.
9 " 'On the Sabbath day, make an offering of two lambs a year old without defect, together with its drink offering and a grain offering of two-tenths of an ephah of fine flour mixed with oil. 10 This is the burnt offering for every Sabbath, in addition to the regular burnt offering and its drink offering.
11 " 'On the first of every month, present to the LORD a burnt offering of two young bulls, one ram and seven male lambs a year old, all without defect. 12 With each bull there is to be a grain offering of three-tenths of an ephah of fine flour mixed with oil; with the ram, a grain offering of two-tenths of an ephah of fine flour mixed with oil; 13 And with each lamb, a grain offering of a tenth of an ephah of fine flour mixed with oil. This is for a burnt offering, a pleasing aroma, an offering made to the LORD by fire. 14 With each bull there is to be a drink offering of half a hin of wine; with the ram, a third of a hin; and with each lamb, a quarter of a hin. This is the monthly burnt offering to be made at each new moon during the year. 15 Besides the regular burnt offering with its drink offering, one male goat is to be presented to the LORD as a sin offering.
16 " 'On the fourteenth day of the first month the LORD's Passover is to be held. 17 On the fifteenth day of this month there is to be a festival; for seven days eat bread made without yeast. 18 On the first day hold a sacred assembly and do no regular work. 19 Present to the LORD an offering made by fire, a burnt offering of two young bulls, one ram and seven male lambs a year old, all without defect. 20 With each bull prepare a grain offering of three-tenths of an ephah of fine flour mixed with oil; with the ram, two-tenths; 21 And with each of the seven lambs, one-tenth. 22 Include one male goat as a sin offering to make atonement for you. 23 Prepare these in addition to the regular morning burnt offering. 24 In this way prepare the food for the offering made by fire every day for seven days as an aroma pleasing to the

263

NUMBERS 28:1–29:40

sacrifice)
    1) Was an aroma pleasing to the LORD
    2) Was in addition to the regular Burnt Offering
  i. To call a sacred assembly day on the 7th day: Do no work
6. **The Feast of Weeks or Firstfruits: To thank God for the harvest & dedicate one's life anew (a symbol of Pentecost, the great harvest of souls)**
  a. To call a sacred assembly & do no work
  b. To present a Burnt Offering
    1) Two bulls, one ram, seven male lambs a year old
    2) Would be an aroma that pleased the LORD
  c. To offer a Grain Offering of choice flour mixed with oil (a symbol of giving thanks to God for the atonement & for all else)
    1) Five qts. with each bull
    2) Three qts. with the ram
    3) Two qts. with each lamb
  d. To sacrifice one male goat as a Sin Offering (a symbol of atonement made by Christ)
  e. To be in addition to the regular Burnt Offering
  f. To diligently guard one requirement: The sacrifices must be without defect (a symbol of the perfection of Christ)

7. **The Feast of Trumpets: To arouse all to trust God more & more (a symbol of salvation & the Rapture—Christ's return)**
  a. The date: 7th month, 1st day
  b. To offer a Burnt Offering (a symbol of Christ's sacrifice)
    1) One bull, one ram, seven male lambs with no defect
    2) Result: Pleased the LORD
  c. To offer a Grain Offering of choice flour mixed with oil (a symbol of giving thanks to God for the atonement & for all else)
    1) Five qts. with the bull
    2) Three qts. with the ram
    3) Two qts. with each lamb
  d. To sacrifice one male goat as a Sin Offering (a symbol of atonement made by Christ)
  e. To be in addition to the monthly & daily Burnt Offerings
  f. Result: All the offerings pleased the Lord (a symbol of pleasure with the sacrifice of Christ & one's faith in Christ)

LORD; it is to be prepared in addition to the regular burnt offering and its drink offering.

25 On the seventh day hold a sacred assembly and do no regular work.

26 "'On the day of firstfruits, when you present to the LORD an offering of new grain during the Feast of Weeks, hold a sacred assembly and do no regular work.

27 Present a burnt offering of two young bulls, one ram and seven male lambs a year old as an aroma pleasing to the LORD.

28 With each bull there is to be a grain offering of three-tenths of an ephah of fine flour mixed with oil; with the ram, two-tenths;

29 And with each of the seven lambs, one-tenth.

30 Include one male goat to make atonement for you.

31 Prepare these together with their drink offerings, in addition to the regular burnt offering and its grain offering. Be sure the animals are without defect.

CHAPTER 29

"'On the first day of the seventh month hold a sacred assembly and do no regular work. It is a day for you to sound the trumpets.

2 As an aroma pleasing to the LORD, prepare a burnt offering of one young bull, one ram and seven male lambs a year old, all without defect.

3 With the bull prepare a grain offering of three-tenths of an ephah of fine flour mixed with oil; with the ram, two-tenths;

4 And with each of the seven lambs, one-tenth.

5 Include one male goat as a sin offering to make atonement for you.

6 These are in addition to the monthly and daily burnt offerings with their grain offerings and drink offerings as specified. They are offerings made to the LORD by fire—a pleasing aroma.

7 "'On the tenth day of this seventh month hold a sacred assembly. You must deny yourselves and do no work.

8 Present as an aroma pleasing to the LORD a burnt offering of one young bull, one ram and seven male lambs a year old, all without defect.

9 With the bull prepare a grain offering of three-tenths of an ephah of fine flour mixed with oil; with the ram, two-tenths;

10 And with each of the seven lambs, one-tenth.

11 Include one male goat as a sin offering, in addition to the sin offering for atonement and the regular burnt offering with its grain offering, and their drink offerings.

12 "'On the fifteenth day of the seventh month, hold a sacred assembly and do no regular work. Celebrate a festival to the LORD for seven days.

13 Present an offering made by fire as an aroma pleasing to the LORD, a burnt offering of thirteen young bulls, two rams and fourteen male lambs a year old, all without defect.

14 With each of the thirteen bulls prepare a grain offering of three-tenths of an ephah of fine flour mixed with oil; with each of the two rams, two-tenths;

15 And with each of the fourteen lambs, one-tenth.

16 Include one male goat as a sin offering, in addition to the regular burnt offering with its grain offering and drink offering.

17 "'On the second day prepare twelve young bulls, two rams and fourteen male lambs a year old, all without defect.

18 With the bulls, rams and lambs, prepare their grain offerings and drink offerings according to the number specified.

19 Include one male goat as a sin offering, in addition to the regular burnt offering with its grain offering, and their drink offerings.

20 "'On the third day prepare eleven bulls, two rams

8. **The Day of Atonement or Yom Kippur: Symbolized the only way to approach God—through the shed blood of Christ**
  a. The date: 7th month, 10th day
  b. To offer a Burnt Offering (a symbol of Christ's sacrifice)
    1) One bull, one ram, seven male lambs with no defect
    2) Result: Pleased the LORD
  c. To offer a Grain Offering of choice flour mixed with oil (a symbol of giving thanks to God for the atonement & for all else)
    1) Five qts. with the bull
    2) Three qts. with the ram
    3) Two qts. with each lamb
  d. To sacrifice one male goat as a Sin Offering (a symbol of atonement made by Christ)
  e. To be in addition to the other Sin Offering for the atonement & the regular Burnt Offering

9. **The Feast of Tabernacles: To thank God for deliverance & for the harvest (a symbol of the believer's march through this world)**
  a. The date: 7th month, 15th day
  b. To offer a Burnt Offering (a symbol of Christ's sacrifice securing atonement [reconciliation] for us)
    1) Thirteen bulls, two rams, fourteen lambs with no defect
    2) Result: Pleased the LORD
  c. To offer a Grain Offering of choice flour mixed with oil (a symbol of giving thanks to God for the atonement & for all else)
    1) Five qts. with the bull
    2) Three qts. with the ram
    3) Two qts. with each lamb
  d. To sacrifice a male goat as a Sin Offering (a symbol of Christ dying for sin)
  e. To be in addition to the regular Burnt Offering
  f. To offer a Burnt Offering on the 2nd day of this festival but reduce the bulls by one: Sacrifice only 12 bulls (a symbol of Christ's atoning sacrifice)
    1) Offer the Grain Offering & Drink Offerings as specified (a symbol of thanking God & pouring one's life out in dedication to God)
    2) Sacrifice one male goat as a Sin Offering (a symbol of Christ dying for sin)
    3) Was to be in addition to the regular Burnt Offering
  g. To offer a Burnt Offering on the 3rd day but reduce the

NUMBERS 28:1–29:40

bulls by one: Sacrifice 11 bulls (a symbol of Christ's atoning sacrifice)
  1) Offer the Grain & the Drink Offerings as specified (a symbol of thanking God & pouring one's life out)
  2) Sacrifice one male goat as a Sin Offering (a symbol of Christ dying for sin)
  3) Was to be in addition to the regular Burnt Offering
h. To offer a Burnt Offering on the 4th day but reduce the bulls by one: Sacrifice 10 bulls (a symbol of Christ's sacrifice)
  1) Offer the Grain & the Drink Offerings as specified (a symbol of thanking God & pouring one's life out in dedication to God)
  2) Sacrifice one male goat as a Sin Offering (a symbol of Christ dying for sin)
  3) Was to be in addition to the regular Burnt Offering
i. To offer a Burnt Offering on the 5th day but reduce the bulls by one: Sacrifice 9 bulls (a symbol of Christ's sacrifice)
  1) Offer the Grain & the Drink Offerings as specified (a symbol of thanking God & pouring one's life out in dedication to God)
  2) Sacrifice one male goat as a Sin Offering (a symbol of Christ dying for sin)
  3) Was to be in addition to the regular Burnt Offering
j. To offer a Burnt Offering on the 6th day but reduce the bulls by one: Sacrifice 8 bulls (a symbol of Christ's sacrifice)
  1) Offer the Grain & the Drink Offerings as specified (a symbol of thanking God & pouring one's life out in dedication to God)

and fourteen male lambs a year old, all without defect. 21 With the bulls, rams and lambs, prepare their grain offerings and drink offerings according to the number specified. 22 Include one male goat as a sin offering, in addition to the regular burnt offering with its grain offering and drink offering. 23 " 'On the fourth day prepare ten bulls, two rams and fourteen male lambs a year old, all without defect. 24 With the bulls, rams and lambs, prepare their grain offerings and drink offerings according to the number specified. 25 Include one male goat as a sin offering, in addition to the regular burnt offering with its grain offering and drink offering. 26 " 'On the fifth day prepare nine bulls, two rams and fourteen male lambs a year old, all without defect. 27 With the bulls, rams and lambs, prepare their grain offerings and drink offerings according to the number specified. 28 Include one male goat as a sin offering, in addition to the regular burnt offering with its grain offering and drink offering. 29 " 'On the sixth day prepare eight bulls, two rams and fourteen male lambs a year old, all without defect. 30 With the bulls, rams and lambs, prepare their grain offerings and drink offerings according to the number specified.

31 Include one male goat as a sin offering, in addition to the regular burnt offering with its grain offering and drink offering. 32 " 'On the seventh day prepare seven bulls, two rams and fourteen male lambs a year old, all without defect. 33 With the bulls, rams and lambs, prepare their grain offerings and drink offerings according to the number specified. 34 Include one male goat as a sin offering, in addition to the regular burnt offering with its grain offering and drink offering. 35 " 'On the eighth day hold an assembly and do no regular work. 36 Present an offering made by fire as an aroma pleasing to the LORD, a burnt offering of one bull, one ram and seven male lambs a year old, all without defect. 37 With the bull, the ram and the lambs, prepare their grain offerings and drink offerings according to the number specified. 38 Include one male goat as a sin offering, in addition to the regular burnt offering with its grain offering and drink offering. 39 " 'In addition to what you vow and your freewill offerings, prepare these for the LORD at your appointed feasts: your burnt offerings, grain offerings, drink offerings and fellowship offerings.' " 40 Moses told the Israelites all that the LORD commanded him.

  2) Sacrifice one male goat as a Sin Offering (a symbol of Christ dying for sin)
  3) Was to be in addition to the regular Burnt Offering
k. To offer a Burnt Offering on the 7th day but reduce the bulls by one: Sacrifice 7 bulls (a symbol of Christ's sacrifice)
  1) Offer the Grain & the Drink Offerings as specified (a symbol of thanking God & pouring one's life out in dedication to God)
  2) Sacrifice one male goat as a Sin Offering (a symbol of Christ dying for sin)
  3) Was to be in addition to the regular Burnt Offering
l. To call an assembly on the 8th day: Were to do no work
  1) Present a Burnt Offering (a symbol of Christ's sacrifice)
     • One bull, one ram, seven male lambs: With no defect (a symbol of Christ's perfection)
     • Result: Pleased the LORD
  2) Offer the Grain & the Drink Offerings as specified (a symbol of thanking God & pouring one's life out in dedication to God)
  3) Sacrifice one male goat as a Sin Offering (a symbol of Christ dying for sin)
  4) Was to be in addition to the regular Burnt Offering
10. The awesome importance of the offerings
  a. They were additional sacrifices
  b. They symbolized Christ
    1) Burnt Offering: His sacrifice
    2) Grain Offering: Giving thanks
    3) Drink Offering: Pouring out, sacrificing one's life to Him
    4) Fellowship Offering: Seeking more fellowship, v.39
  c. They were commanded by God

DIVISION IV

THE PREPARATION FOR THE MARCH INTO THE PROMISED LAND, 26:1–36:13

D. The Offerings and Sacrifices Commanded by the LORD: A Picture of Man's Need to Continually Approach and Worship God Through the Atonement Secured by the Sacrifice (a Symbol of God's Dear Son, the Lord Jesus Christ), 28:1–29:40

(28:1–29:40) **Introduction—Approach, to God—Way, Only One—Access, to God**: there is only one way to approach God, only one way that He accepts. There are not many ways—no matter what people may say. No matter how much people may despise the fact or deny and object to the fact—there is only one way to approach God. This is the clear declaration of Scripture from beginning to end. In fact, this is one of the major lessons taught by the offerings and sacrifices of the Old Testament.

Remember, the first generation of Israelites had died out during the forty years of wandering about in the desert wilderness. Now the second generation of believers was about to enter the promised land and receive its inheritance. It had been almost forty years since God had last covered the laws governing the sacrifices and offerings with His

265

people. Before the new generation of believers could ever enter the promised land, He had to teach them this one absolute essential that they must never forget: there is only one approach to God that is acceptable to Him. How was God going to teach this essential truth to them? Through the offerings and sacrifices that He had commanded forty years earlier. Therefore, it was necessary for God to cover the offerings and sacrifices with the new generation of believers. This is the subject of this all-important passage of Scripture: *The Offerings and Sacrifices Commanded by the LORD: A Picture of Man's Need to Continually Approach and Worship God Through the Atonement Secured by the Sacrifice (a Symbol of God's Dear Son, the Lord Jesus Christ),* 28:1–29:40.

1. The importance of the offerings or sacrifices (vv.1-2).
2. The daily sacrifices of the Burnt Offering: a symbol of Christ's sacrifice that secured atonement or reconciliation for man (vv.3-8).
3. The Sabbath Day sacrifices: a symbol of Christ, our Sabbath rest (He. 3:10-4:16) (vv.9-10).
4. The monthly sacrifices: a symbol of Christ's sacrifice (vv.11-15).
5. The Passover: a symbol of Christ the Lamb of God (vv.16-25).
6. The Feast of Weeks or Firstfruits: to thank God for the harvest and dedicate one's life anew (a symbol of Pentecost, the great harvest of souls) (vv.26-31).
7. The Feast of Trumpets: to arouse all to trust God more and more, (a symbol of salvation and the Rapture—Christ's return) (ch.29:1-6).
8. The Day of Atonement or Yom Kippur: symbolized the only way to approach God—through the shed blood of Christ (vv.7-11).
9. The Feast of Tabernacles: to thank God for deliverance through the wilderness wanderings and for the harvest (a symbol of the believer's march through this world) (vv.12-38).
10. The awesome importance of the offerings (vv.39-40).

1 (28:1-2) **Sacrifices, Importance of—Offerings, Importance of—Animal Sacrifices, Importance of**: God Himself spelled out the importance of the offerings or sacrifices. Three clear reasons are given for presenting the offerings or sacrifices to God.

a. The offerings and sacrifices were a clear command of God Himself. God had established them to teach men how to approach and worship Him. Each offering or sacrifice taught a different truth about how to approach God. Each symbolized a different feature or attitude needed in worship. When God gave the offerings or sacrifices to man, He knew what He was doing. He knew that man needed to learn how to approach and worship Him. Therefore, God established the sacrifices and offerings as a commandment, a commandment that man was to obey.

b. The offerings or sacrifices were to be presented exactly at the appointed time. This was of critical importance for one central reason: to teach man that certain events had to take place before he could approach God. The approach to God is exact, precise, and very specific. In fact, there is only one acceptable way to approach God: through the substitute sacrifice. Therefore the sacrifice first had to be offered before man could approach God and make any other offering he wished to present to God. There was a specific order in which the offerings or sacrifices were to be made. There was a set time, an appointed time, a "fullness of time" for the substitute sacrifice to be offered and for all the other offerings to be presented. Each had its set time in order to teach man when and how to approach and worship God.

c. The offerings or sacrifices were an aroma that pleased God. The aroma that ascended up was a symbol that God was pleased with the offering. He accepted the offering or sacrifice presented by the person.

Thought 1. The offerings or sacrifices symbolized Christ, the coming Savior and Messiah of the world. It was this fact that gave the offerings or sacrifices such importance. Each taught a different truth about Christ, a truth that man had to understand in order to approach God and become acceptable to God. Without grasping the truth of Christ as the Savior of the world, man could never become acceptable to God. He would perish, be doomed to an eternity of separation from God.

> For God so loved the world that he gave his one and only Son, that whoever believes in him shall not perish but have eternal life.
> (Jn. 3:16)
> I told you that you would die in your sins; if you do not believe that I am the one I claim to be, you will indeed die in your sins.
> (Jn. 8:24)
> Salvation is found in no one else, for there is no other name under heaven given to men by which we must be saved.
> (Ac.4:12)

2 (28:3-8) **Sacrifice, of Christ—Atonement—Reconcilia-tion—Sacrifice, of the Burnt Offering—Offering, the Burnt—Burnt Offering—Animal Sacrifice, In the Burnt Offering**: the daily sacrifice of the Burnt Offering was the basic offering to be presented by the people. This was a symbol of Christ's sacrifice that secured atonement or reconciliation for man. (See outline and notes—Le. 1:1-17 for more discussion.) The Burnt Offering taught man one essential truth: there is only one way to approach God and become acceptable to Him—through the *substitute sacrifice*. It was the Burnt Offering that made atonement or reconciliation between God and man. Man was reconciled to God through the substitute sacrifice and it alone. Keep in mind that the substitute sacrifice is a symbol of the sacrifice of the Lord Jesus Christ. It was Christ and Christ alone who secured atonement or reconciled man to God. Christ and Christ alone is the only way into the presence of God, the only approach that is acceptable to God.

a. The daily sacrifice of the Burnt Offering required two lambs that were one year old. They were to be without blemish, without any defect whatsoever. This was the significant fact about the lambs, for they symbolized the perfection of Jesus Christ. The only sacrifice acceptable to God was the perfect sacrifice. The perfection of the sacrifice was an absolute essential, for the sacrifice had to be the ideal sacrifice, the pattern of all sacrifices. The sacrifice of Jesus Christ had to be the ideal sacrifice, the pattern that could stand for and represent every human who was ever to be born. As the ideal and the pattern, His sacrifice could cover the sins of every human being. His sacrifice could represent every human being before God, making atonement and reconciling every person to God. This was the reason the lambs of the Burnt Offering had to be without blemish or defect: they were a symbol, a type of coming Savior of the world who was going to be sacrificed as man's substitute. The Savior was going to make atonement and reconciliation for the people.

> God made him who had no sin to be sin for us, so that in him we might become the righteousness of God. (2 Co. 5:21)
> For you know that it was not with perishable things such as silver or gold that you were redeemed from the empty way of life handed down to you from your forefathers, but with the precious blood of Christ, a lamb without blemish or defect. (1 Pe. 1:18-19)

b. The Burnt Offering was to be offered in the morning and again in the evening. One lamb was to be sacrificed each time (v.4).

c. A Grain Offering was to be made with both the morning and the evening sacrifices. The Grain Offering was simply two quarts of choice flour mixed with one quart of oil taken from pressed olives. The person simply took the Grain Offering and placed it upon the burning sacrifice lying upon the altar. The Grain Offering was...

- a declaration of thanksgiving to God for the atonement (reconciliation) and for all else God had done
- a declaration of laying one's life upon God—all one was and had—and committing oneself totally to God

When the priests made the sacrifices on behalf of the nation, they were doing two things: offering thanksgiving to God and declaring that the people were dedicating their lives to God. All this was being done on behalf of every Israelite. The Burnt Offering...

- included the atoning sacrifice that made reconciliation with God
- included the Grain Offering that presented thanksgiving to God for the atoning sacrifice and reconciliation

Moreover, by laying the Grain Offering upon the substitute sacrifice, the people were declaring that they owed their lives in dedication to God because of the sacrifice that was being substituted for them.

> Who gave himself for us to redeem us from all wickedness and to purify for himself a people that are his very own, eager to do what is good. (Tit. 2:14)
> This is how we know what love is: Jesus Christ laid down his life for us. And we ought to lay down our lives for our brothers. (1 Jn. 3:16)

d. Note the result of the sacrifice in the Burnt Offering: the sacrifice was a pleasing aroma to the LORD. This was a symbol that God is pleased with the sacrifice of Christ and with a person's faith and dedication to Christ.

> And live a life of love, just as Christ loved us and gave himself up for us as a fragrant offering and sacrifice to God. (Ep. 5:2)

e. A Drink Offering was also to be presented to the LORD with each sacrifice of the Burnt Offering. The Drink Offering was either poured out upon the altar or, more likely, at the foot of the altar. The Drink Offering...

- was a symbol of the blood of Christ that is pictured in the Lord's Supper
- was a symbol of a person's dedication, of his life being poured out to God

> Therefore, I urge you, brothers, in view of God's mercy, to offer your bodies as living sacrifices, holy and pleasing to God—this is your spiritual act of worship. (Ro. 12:1)
> But even if I am being poured out like a drink offering on the sacrifice and service coming from your faith, I am glad and rejoice with all of you. (Ph. 2:17)

DEEPER STUDY # 1
(28:7) **Drink Offering**: the Drink Offering was first mentioned in Exodus (see Ex. 29:40; 30:9. see Le. 23:13, 18, 37; Nu. 6:15; De. 32:38.) Note these facts.

1. The Drink Offering was usually wine or oil. It was sometimes drunk (De. 32:38) and sometimes poured out on the altar as a sacrifice (Ge. 35:14). However, Scripture seems to indicate that it was to be poured and not drunk (Ex. 30:9).
2. The Drink Offering was usually used in connection with other offerings. However, Jacob apparently used it by itself as an independent offering.
3. The Drink Offering was one of the offerings used by Israel (Nu. 15:5-7), but it was not included in the Levitical offerings (Le. 1-7).
4. The Drink Offering was a type of Christ in that Christ "poured out His life unto death" (Is. 53:12; see Ps. 22:14).
5. The Drink Offering symbolized the dedication, the giving, the pouring out of one's heart and life to God. It symbolized that a person was offering, sacrificing, and pouring out his whole being in dedication to God and His service.

---

f. The second lamb was to be prepared and offered in the evening, at twilight (v.8). During the evening sacrifice, the same Grain Offering and Drink Offering were to be offered. Once offered, the result was the same: the aroma—the sacrifice—pleased the LORD.

Thought 1. The sacrifice of the Burnt Offering is a symbol of Christ's sacrifice which secured atonement or reconciliation for us. Through the sacrifice of Christ, we received the atonement: we are reconciled to God. Remember: our sins have separated us from God, and we stand condemned before God to an eternity of separation from Him. But Jesus Christ took the judgment of God that was due us and bore that judgment—the judgment of death. Jesus Christ paid the ransom price to deliver us from sin and its penalty. All this He did to make atonement for us, that is, to reconcile us to God.

> For if, when we were God's enemies, we were reconciled to him through the death of his Son, how much more, having been reconciled, shall we be saved through his life! Not only is this so, but we also rejoice in God through our Lord Jesus Christ, through whom we have now received reconciliation. (Ro. 5:10-11)
> For Christ died for sins once for all, the righteous for the unrighteous, to bring you to God. He was put to death in the body but made alive by the Spirit. (1 Pe. 3:18)

But he was pierced for our transgressions, he was crushed for our iniquities; the punishment that brought us peace was upon him, and by his wounds we are healed. (Is. 53:5)

3 (28:9-10) **Sabbath Day, Sacrifices on—Sacrifices, on Sabbath Day—Jesus Christ, Our Sabbath Rest—Spiritual Rest, Symbol of—Symbol, of Christ Our Spiritual Rest**: there were the Sabbath day sacrifices. These sacrifices were a symbol of Christ, our Sabbath rest (He.3:10-4:16). The people rested on the Sabbath day, but not the priest. While the people rested, the priest made a very special Burnt Offering to God. Again, this Burnt Offering included the sacrifice of two lambs, the Drink Offering, and a Grain Offering. But note: this was an additional offering to the regular two Burnt Offerings. This means that the Sabbath day was marked off as a special day of holiness, a day when a very special third Burnt Offering was presented to the LORD. The body and blood of the sacrifice were offered up to God as a special offering on every Sabbath day. This is a strong message, a strong symbol to the people of God: His people are to celebrate their redemption every Sabbath or Sunday.

Thought 1. There are two lessons for us in this point:
(1) We must do just what the Israelites did: celebrate our redemption on the Sabbath. As commanded in other Scriptures, we must worship the LORD on the Sabbath.
(2) Jesus Christ is our Sabbath rest. He gives us rest from all the storms of life; He and He alone brings spiritual rest to the human soul: peace, assurance, confidence, purpose, meaning, significance, security, fulfillment and satisfaction.

Blessed are those who hunger and thirst for righteousness, for they will be filled. (Mt. 5:6)
Take my yoke upon you and learn from me, for I am gentle and humble in heart, and you will find rest for your souls. (Mt. 11:29)
Peace I leave with you; my peace I give you. I do not give to you as the world gives. Do not let your hearts be troubled and do not be afraid. (Jn. 14:27)
"I have told you these things, so that in me you may have peace. In this world you will have trouble. But take heart! I have overcome the world." (Jn. 16:33)
Now we who have believed enter that rest, just as God has said, "So I declared on oath in my anger, 'They shall never enter my rest.'" And yet his work has been finished since the creation of the world. (He. 4:3)
For if Joshua had given them rest, God would not have spoken later about another day. There remains, then, a Sabbath-rest for the people of God; for anyone who enters God's rest also rests from his own work, just as God did from his. (He. 4:8-10)
Then I heard a voice from heaven say, "Write: Blessed are the dead who die in the Lord from now on." "Yes," says the Spirit, "they will rest from their labor, for their deeds will follow them." (Re. 14:13)
The LORD replied, "My Presence will go with you, and I will give you rest." (Ex. 33:14)
I will lie down and sleep in peace, for you alone, O LORD, make me dwell in safety. (Ps. 4:8)
And I—in righteousness I will see your face; when I awake, I will be satisfied with seeing your likeness. (Ps. 17:15)
For he satisfies the thirsty and fills the hungry with good things. (Ps. 107:9)
Be at rest once more, O my soul, for the LORD has been good to you. (Ps. 116:7)
To whom he said, "This is the resting place, let the weary rest"; and, "This is the place of repose"—but they would not listen. (Is. 28:12)
This is what the Sovereign LORD, the Holy One of Israel, says: "In repentance and rest is your salvation, in quietness and trust is your strength, but you would have none of it." (Is. 30:15)

4 (28:11-15) **Monthly Sacrifices—Sacrifices, the Monthly—Animal Sacrifice, In the Monthly Offerings—Offerings, the Monthly—Symbol, of Christ's Sacrifice—Sacrifice, of Christ, Symbol of**: there were the monthly sacrifices that were to be made. These were sometimes referred to as the new moon offerings; that is, they were to be presented to the LORD at every new or full moon. These sacrifices were a clear symbol of the sacrifice of Christ. Note that a much larger number of animals were to be offered at the monthly sacrifice. This meant that a larger Grain Offering and Drink Offering were also to be presented to the LORD. Note also that a Sin Offering was to be presented to God during the monthly sacrifices (v.15). Later in the history of Israel, the new moon festivals were abused. They apparently became festivals for partying, drinking, and immoral behavior (Is. 1:13-14).[1]

Thought 1. The sacrifice of the Burnt Offering symbolized the death of Jesus Christ, but so did the Sin Offering. The Sin Offering was a symbol of Christ's sacrifice for the sins of the world. He died to provide forgiveness of sins for us. Through the blood of Christ, we are forgiven for all sin. But note: there is a condition for forgiveness. We must confess and repent of our sins. We must turn away from sin and turn to follow after Christ. Both confession and repentance are essential for forgiveness of sins.

This is my blood of the covenant, which is poured out for many for the forgiveness of sins. (Mt. 26:28)
Peter replied, "Repent and be baptized, every one of you, in the name of Jesus Christ for the forgiveness of your sins. And you will receive the gift of the Holy Spirit." (Ac.2:38)
Repent, then, and turn to God, so that your sins may be wiped out, that times of

---

[1] *The Expositor's Bible Commentary.* Frank E. Gaebelein, Editor, p.951.

refreshing may come from the Lord. (Ac. 3:19)

Repent of this wickedness and pray to the Lord. Perhaps he will forgive you for having such a thought in your heart. (Ac. 8:22)

In him we have redemption through his blood, the forgiveness of sins, in accordance with the riches of God's grace. (Ep. 1:7)

But if we walk in the light, as he is in the light, we have fellowship with one another, and the blood of Jesus, his Son, purifies us from all sin. (1 Jn. 1:7)

If we confess our sins, he is faithful and just and will forgive us our sins and purify us from all unrighteousness. (1 Jn. 1:9)

To him who loves us and has freed us from our sins by his blood. (Re. 1:5)

Let the wicked forsake his way and the evil man his thoughts. Let him turn to the LORD, and he will have mercy on him, and to our God, for he will freely pardon. (Is. 55:7)

But if a wicked man turns away from all the sins he has committed and keeps all my decrees and does what is just and right, he will surely live; he will not die. (Eze. 18:21)

5 (28:16-25) **Passover—Lamb of God, Symbol of Christ—Christ, the Lamb of God**: there was the Passover, a symbol of Christ the Lamb of God who takes away the sins of the world. The Passover celebrated the great deliverance of God from Egyptian slavery. God freed His people from the world so that they could live life to the fullest in the promised land of God. They were freed to live life to the fullest, freed to worship and serve God fully. They were to live lives that...

- were holy, righteous, and pure
- would be dynamic witnesses to the surrounding nations of unbelievers

This was the very purpose for which God had delivered and given freedom to His people. This was the reason for celebrating the Passover. God's people were never to forget the great deliverance of God: their freedom and liberty to live life to the fullest and the great hope of the promised land were gifts from God.

Note that the Passover was tied to the festival of unleavened bread (v.17f). This was the first of the great national festival that were held each year. It was celebrated in the first month of the year, Nisan, which was somewhere around March or April on our calendar.

Thought 1. The Passover was a symbol of Christ and His sacrifice. Note these facts:

(1) Jesus Christ referred to His death as an exodus or departure from this world. The word *exodus* actually means death, decease, or departing.

[Moses and Elijah] appeared in glorious splendor, talking with Jesus. They spoke about his departure, which he was about to bring to fulfillment at Jerusalem. (Lu. 9:31)

(2) One of the requirements of the Passover lamb was that no bone was ever to be broken. This was a picture that pointed to Christ, none of whose bones were ever broken.

These things happened so that the scripture would be fulfilled: "Not one of his bones will be broken." (Jn. 19:36)

(3) Yeast was a type "or symbol" of sin; therefore all yeast had to be thrown out of a person's house prior to the Passover. Scripture declares that believers must be ruthless in purging out the old yeast, the sins of their lives.[2]

Get rid of the old yeast that you may be a new batch without yeast—as you really are. For Christ, our Passover lamb, has been sacrificed. Therefore let us keep the Festival, not with the old yeast, the yeast of malice and wickedness, but with bread without yeast, the bread of sincerity and truth. (1 Co. 5:7-8)

(4) Jesus Christ is the Passover Lamb, the lamb who takes away the sin of the world.

The next day John saw Jesus coming toward him and said, "Look, the Lamb of God, who takes away the sin of the world!" (Jn. 1:29)

Get rid of the old yeast that you may be a new batch without yeast—as you really are. For Christ, our Passover lamb, has been sacrificed. (1 Co. 5:7)

For you know that it was not with perishable things such as silver or gold that you were redeemed from the empty way of life handed down to you from your forefathers, but with the precious blood of Christ, a lamb without blemish or defect. (1 Pe. 1:18-19)

Then I saw a Lamb, looking as if it had been slain, standing in the center of the throne, encircled by the four living creatures and the elders. He had seven horns and seven eyes, which are the seven spirits of God sent out into all the earth. He came and took the scroll from the right hand of him who sat on the throne. And when he had taken it, the four living creatures and the twenty-four elders fell down before the Lamb. Each one had a harp and they were holding golden bowls full of incense, which are the prayers of the saints. And they sang a new song: "You are worthy to take the scroll and to open its seals, because you were slain, and with your blood you purchased men for God from every tribe and language and people and nation. You have made them to be a kingdom and priests to serve our God, and they will reign on the earth." (Re. 5:6-10)

After this I looked and there before me was a great multitude that no one could count, from every nation, tribe, people and language, standing before the throne and in front of the Lamb. They were wearing

---

2 The idea for these first three applications comes from Gordon J. Wenham. *The Book of Numbers*, p.201.

white robes and were holding palm branches in their hands. (Re. 7:9)

And sang the song of Moses the servant of God and the song of the Lamb: "Great and marvelous are your deeds, Lord God Almighty. Just and true are your ways, King of the ages." (Re. 15:3)

I did not see a temple in the city, because the Lord God Almighty and the Lamb are its temple. (Re. 21:22)

He was oppressed and afflicted, yet he did not open his mouth; he was led like a lamb to the slaughter, and as a sheep before her shearers is silent, so he did not open his mouth. (Is. 53:7)

6 (28:26-31) **Feast, of Weeks—Feast, of Firstfruits—Firstfruits, Feast of—Weeks, Feast of**: there was the Feast of Weeks or Firstfruits. This was a festival to give thanks to God for the harvest and to dedicate one's life anew to God. This was a symbol of Pentecost, the great harvest of souls and of people giving their lives to God. The festival of firstfruits was held exactly fifty days after the feast of unleavened bread (see outline and notes—Le. 23:15-22 for more discussion). Pentecost took place fifty days after the resurrection of Christ, the great day when the Holy Spirit came upon the disciples and gave a great harvest of souls (Ac.2:1, 4). The very same number of sacrifices was required at this festival as was required at the feast of unleavened bread and at the monthly or new moon offerings.

> **Thought 1.** The lesson for the believer is clear: as we march to the promised land, we are constantly to be giving our lives anew to God and bearing strong testimony for Him. We are constantly to be seeking a great harvest of souls.

> When the day of Pentecost came, they were all together in one place....All of them were filled with the Holy Spirit and began to speak in other tongues as the Spirit enabled them. (Ac.2:1, 4)

> "Come, follow me," Jesus said, "and I will make you fishers of men." (Mt. 4:19)

> Therefore go and make disciples of all nations, baptizing them in the name of the Father and of the Son and of the Holy Spirit, and teaching them to obey everything I have commanded you. And surely I am with you always, to the very end of the age. (Mt. 28:19-20)

> He said to them, "Go into all the world and preach the good news to all creation." (Mk. 16:15)

> But you will receive power when the Holy Spirit comes on you; and you will be my witnesses in Jerusalem, and in all Judea and Samaria, and to the ends of the earth. (Ac. 1:8)

> For we cannot help speaking about what we have seen and heard. (Ac. 4:20)

> Therefore, I urge you, brothers, in view of God's mercy, to offer your bodies as living sacrifices, holy and pleasing to God—this is your spiritual act of worship. (Ro. 12:1)

> Though I am free and belong to no man, I make myself a slave to everyone, to win as many as possible. To the Jews I became like a Jew, to win the Jews. To those under the law I became like one under the law (though I myself am not under the law), so as to win those under the law. (1 Co. 9:19-20)

> Snatch others from the fire and save them; to others show mercy, mixed with fear—hating even the clothing stained by corrupted flesh. (Jude 23)

> Love the LORD your God with all your heart and with all your soul and with all your strength. (De. 6:5)

> Trust in the LORD with all your heart and lean not on your own understanding. (Pr. 3:5)

> The fruit of the righteous is a tree of life, and he who wins souls is wise. (Pr. 11:30)

> My son, give me your heart and let your eyes keep to my ways. (Pr. 23:26)

> Those who are wise will shine like the brightness of the heavens, and those who lead many to righteousness, like the stars for ever and ever. (Da. 12:3)

7 (29:1-6) **Trumpets, Feast of—Festivals, Trumpets of—Commitment—Dedication—Witnessing, to Christ**: there was the Feast of Trumpets which had a twofold purpose: to arouse the people to trust God more and more, and to proclaim the message of joy for the atonement or reconciliation with God. This feast was held on the first day of the seventh month, which was to be a great month of worship for the people. The Feast of Trumpets is a symbol of salvation and of the Rapture, the glorious day when Christ will return and take believers to be with Him forever. There were actually three major festivals held during this month:

⇒ The Feast of Trumpets was held on the first day of the seventh month (v.1).
⇒ The Day of Atonement was held on the tenth day of the seventh month (v.7).
⇒ The Feast of Tabernacles was held for eight consecutive days beginning on the fifteenth day of the seventh month (vv.12, 35).

The Feast of Trumpets eventually became known as Rosh Hashanah, which became the beginning of the new year for the Jewish people. The trumpets are still blown in the synagogue worship on this particular day.

> **Thought 1.** The Feast of Trumpets is a clear symbol of salvation and of the Rapture. The glorious day is coming when Christ will return and take believers to be with Him forever. As we march to the promised land of heaven, we are to grow in our trust and joy; we are to be ever maturing, learning to focus and to bear a stronger witness to the atoning sacrifice of Christ. We are to focus upon the LORD and His glorious return.

> For as lightning that comes from the east is visible even in the west, so will be the coming of the Son of Man....No one knows about that day or hour, not even the

angels in heaven, nor the Son, but only the Father. (Mt. 24:27, 36)

"Yes, it is as you say," Jesus replied. "But I say to all of you: In the future you will see the Son of Man sitting at the right hand of the Mighty One and coming on the clouds of heaven." (Mt. 26:64)

It will be good for those servants whose master finds them watching when he comes. I tell you the truth, he will dress himself to serve, will have them recline at the table and will come and wait on them. (Lu. 12:37)

You also must be ready, because the Son of Man will come at an hour when you do not expect him. (Lu. 12:40)

At that time they will see the Son of Man coming in a cloud with power and great glory. (Lu. 21:27)

In my Father's house are many rooms; if it were not so, I would have told you. I am going there to prepare a place for you. And if I go and prepare a place for you, I will come back and take you to be with me that you also may be where I am. (Jn. 14:2-3)

"Men of Galilee," they said, "why do you stand here looking into the sky? This same Jesus, who has been taken from you into heaven, will come back in the same way you have seen him go into heaven." (Ac.1:11)

But our citizenship is in heaven. And we eagerly await a Savior from there, the Lord Jesus Christ, who, by the power that enables him to bring everything under his control, will transform our lowly bodies wo that they will be like his glorious body. (Ph. 3:20-21)

When Christ, who is your life, appears, then you also will appear with him in glory. (Col. 3:4)

For the Lord himself will come down from heaven, with a loud command, with the voice of the archangel and with the trumpet call of God, and the dead in Christ will rise first. After that, we who are still alive and are left will be caught up together with them in the clouds to meet the Lord in the air. And so we will be with the Lord forever. (1 Th. 4:16-17)

For you know very well that the day of the Lord will come like a thief in the night. (1 Th. 5:2)

So Christ was sacrificed once to take away the sins of many people; and he will appear a second time, not to bear sin, but to bring salvation to those who are waiting for him. (He. 9:28)

And when the Chief Shepherd appears, you will receive the crown of glory that will never fade away. (1 Pe. 5:4)

Dear friends, now we are children of God, and what we will be has not yet been made known. But we know that when he appears, we shall be like him, for we shall see him as he is. (1 Jn. 3:2)

"Behold, I come like a thief! Blessed is he who stays awake and keeps his clothes with him, so that he may not go naked and be shamefully exposed." (Re. 16:15)

8 (29:7-11) **Atonement, Day of—Feast, Day of Atonement—Yom Kippur, Festival of—Approach, to God—Symbol, of Christ's Atonement**: there was the Day of Atonement or Yom Kippur. This feast symbolized the only way to approach God, through the shed blood of the substitute sacrifice. The substitute sacrifice was a clear symbol of Christ, our substitute sacrifice (see outline and notes—Le. 23:26-32). Note the words "afflict your souls" (KJV) or "deny yourselves" (NIV) or "humble yourselves" (NASB) or "go without food" (NLT). The Day of Atonement was not to be a day of festivities but rather of denial and fasting. It was to be devoted totally to worship, focusing upon the atonement or reconciliation with God that had been brought about through the *substitute sacrifice*. A Day of Atonement was established to teach people that there was only one way to become acceptable to God: through the atonement and reconciliation made by the substitute sacrifice. The Day of Atonement was the most sacred, holy day of the year. Keep in mind that the Day of Atonement was held only one day of the year: the tenth day of the seventh month.

> **Thought 1.** Jesus Christ has secured the atonement or reconciliation with God for us. We are to keep our minds upon the atoning sacrifice of the Lord Jesus Christ. We must never forget that there is only one way to become acceptable to God: through the sacrifice of God's dear Son, the Lord Jesus Christ Himself. It is He who cleanses us from sin and delivers us from the penalty of death.
>
> You see, at just the right time, when we were still powerless, Christ died for the ungodly. (Ro. 5:6)
> But God demonstrates his own love for us in this: While we were still sinners, Christ died for us. (Ro. 5:8)
> Since we have now been justified by his blood, how much more shall we be saved from God's wrath through him! For if, when we were God's enemies, we were reconciled to him through the death of his Son, how much more, having been reconciled, shall we be saved through his life! Not only is this so, but we also rejoice in God through our Lord Jesus Christ, through whom we have now received reconciliation. (Ro. 5:9-11)
> For what I received I passed on to you as of first importance: that Christ died for our sins according to the Scriptures, that
> he was buried, that he was raised on the third day according to the Scriptures. (1 Co. 15:3-4)
> Who gave himself for our sins to rescue us from the present evil age, according to the will of our God and Father. (Ga. 1:4)
> Christ redeemed us from the curse of the law by becoming a curse for us, for it is written: "Cursed is everyone who is hung on a tree." (Ga. 3:13)
> But we see Jesus, who was made a little lower than the angels, now crowned with glory and honor because he suffered death,

so that by the grace of God he might taste death for everyone. (He. 2:9)

He did not enter by means of the blood of goats and calves; but he entered the Most Holy Place once for all by his own blood, having obtained eternal redemption. The blood of goats and bulls and the ashes of a heifer sprinkled on those who are ceremonially unclean sanctify them so that they are outwardly clean. How much more, then, will the blood of Christ, who through the eternal Spirit offered himself unblemished to God, cleanse our consciences from acts that lead to death, so that we may serve the living God! (He. 9:12-14)

He himself bore our sins in his body on the tree, so that we might die to sins and live for righteousness; by his wounds you have been healed. (1 Pe. 2:24)

For Christ died for sins once for all, the righteous for the unrighteous, to bring you to God. He was put to death in the body but made alive by the Spirit. (1 Pe. 3:18)

9 (29:12-38) **Feast, of Tabernacles—Tabernacles, Festival of—Wilderness Wanderings—Journeys, Wilderness—Heaven, Journey to**: there was the Feast of Tabernacles. This was a festival to thank God for deliverance through the wilderness wanderings and for the harvest. This feast symbolized the believer's march through this world to heaven, a symbol of how temporary the believer's march through the world is (see outline and notes—Le. 23:33-44 for more discussion). This feast was to celebrate the wanderings, when the people lived in tents on their way to the promised land, and to thank God for the harvest. During this period of time, the people lived in temporary tents or booths. Despite the harsh conditions of their lives, they were to be ever thankful to God and to keep their minds focused upon the promised land.

Note this fact: there were far more animals sacrificed during the Festival of Tabernacles than any other festival. In fact, there were more bulls and rams sacrificed than during all the other festivals combined. This festival lasted for a full eight days. Note that thirteen bulls, two rams, and fourteen lambs were sacrificed on the first day (v.13). But the number of bulls was decreased by one each day thereafter. The same number of rams and lambs were sacrificed, but there was a change in the number of bulls offered to the LORD. Scripture does not say why. Perhaps it was because of the extreme cost of a bull. Whatever the reason, this fact needs to be noted. Note one other fact: all these sacrifices were in addition to the regular Burnt Offering (v.38). The importance of the sacrifice of the daily Burnt Offerings—both morning and evening—cannot be over-emphasized. There is only one way to approach God that is acceptable to God: through the *substitute sacrifice*. This one fact must always be kept in mind by believers throughout all generations: there is only one approach to God that is acceptable; that approach is through the atoning sacrifice of the Lord Jesus Christ.

Thought 1. The Festival of Tabernacles celebrated the wilderness wanderings when the people lived in tents on their way to the promised land. This is a clear symbol of the believer's march through this world to heaven, a symbol of how short-lived the believer's march through this world is. As the believer marches to heaven, his dwelling upon this earth is only temporary. No matter what kind of house we live in, it is only temporary. It is made out of decaying, corruptible materials. It will waste away and some day, perhaps decades or even a few centuries away, it will cease to be. Earthly homes are only transient structures. Moreover, we are living in mortal bodies, bodies that the Bible describes as a temporary tent or tabernacle. The body is corruptible and will decay and cease to exist. Our journey through this world is only a short-lived pilgrimage. We are marching to our permanent and eternal home in heaven, marching forth to live forever in the presence of God.

But store up for yourselves treasures in heaven, where moth and rust do not destroy, and where thieves do not break in and steal. (Mt. 6:20)

Now we know that if the earthly tent we live in is destroyed, we have a building from God, an eternal house in heaven, not built by human hands. (2 Co. 5:1)

But our citizenship is in heaven. And we eagerly await a Savior from there, the Lord Jesus Christ, who, by the power that enables him to bring everything under his control, will transform our lowly bodies so that they will be like his glorious body. (Ph. 3:20-21)

So that, having been justified by his grace, we might become heirs having the hope of eternal life. (Tit. 3:7)

For he [Abraham] was looking forward to the city with foundations, whose architect and builder is God. (He. 11:10)

Praise be to the God and Father of our Lord Jesus Christ! In his great mercy he has given us new birth into a living hope through the resurrection of Jesus Christ from the dead, and into an inheritance that can never perish, spoil or fade—kept in heaven for you. (1 Pe. 1:3-4)

Blessed are those who wash their robes, that they may have the right to the tree of life and may go through the gates into the city. (Re. 22:14)

10 (29:39-40) **Offerings, Importance of—Sacrifices, Importance of—Symbol, of Christ, Importance of**: there was the awesome importance of the offerings.

a. Note that these offerings were to be additional sacrifices to any other offerings that a person might bring. People who were seeking God often brought offerings, but the offerings spelled out in this chapter were to be additional sacrifices. A constant presentation of sacrifices to God was to be conducted in the Tabernacle. The offering of the *substitute sacrifice* was to be continually upon the minds of the people. They were to know one fact beyond any question: there is only one approach to God—through the *substitute sacrifice*. This one truth was to be driven into their hearts and minds. For this reason, God established all these offerings and sacrifices. Presenting the substitute sacrifices to God was a constant ministry conducted on behalf of the people. When one considers all these offerings and all the voluntary offerings that were brought to the Tabernacle by the people, presenting the substitute sacrifice to God was most likely a continuous, unbroken offering that was being offered up to God. Again, the purpose was to keep this one essential fact before the people: they must approach God through the *substitute sacrifice*. No other approach was acceptable to God. The only way they could ever secure the approval of God was to approach Him through the *substitute sacrifice*.

   b. The sacrifice symbolized Christ. Note exactly how:
- ⇒ The Burnt Offering symbolized the atonement or reconciliation secured by the sacrifice of Christ.
- ⇒ The Grain Offering symbolized the giving of thanks for the atoning sacrifice and the dedication of one's life because of the atoning sacrifice.
- ⇒ The Drink Offering symbolized the pouring out, the sacrificing of a person's life in thanksgiving for the substitute sacrifice.
- ⇒ The Fellowship Offering symbolized the believer seeking to grow in the fellowship and peace of God—all because of the substitute sacrifice that brought about the atonement or reconciliation with God.

   c. Note that the offerings and sacrifices were commanded by God.

     Thought 1. The offering of the substitute sacrifice was a symbol of the coming Savior of the world. God sent His Son into the world to save us.

     Today in the town of David a Savior has been born to you; he is Christ the Lord. (Lu. 2:11)

     For the Son of Man came to seek and to save what was lost. (Lu. 19:10)

     For God so loved the world that he gave his one and only Son, that whoever believes in him shall not perish but have eternal life. For God did not send his Son into the world to condemn the world, but to save the world through him. (Jn. 3:16-17)

     I am the gate; whoever enters through me will be saved. He will come in and go out, and find pasture. (Jn. 10:9)

     God exalted him to his own right hand as Prince and Savior that he might give repentance and forgiveness of sins to Israel. (Ac. 5:31)

     But God demonstrates his own love for us in this: While we were still sinners, Christ died for us. Since we have now been justified by his blood, how much more shall we be saved from God's wrath through him! For if, when we were God's enemies, we were reconciled to him through the death of his Son, how much more, having been reconciled, shall we be saved through his life! Not only is this so, but we also rejoice in God through our Lord Jesus Christ, through whom we have now received reconciliation. (Ro. 5:8-11)

     Here is a trustworthy saying that deserves full acceptance: Christ Jesus came into the world to save sinners—of whom I am the worst. (1 Ti. 1:15)

     Although he was a son, he learned obedience from what he suffered and, once made perfect, he became the source of eternal salvation for all who obey him. (He. 5:8-9)

     Therefore he is able to save completely those who come to God through him, because he always lives to intercede for them. (He. 7:25)

     So Christ was sacrificed once to take the sins of many people; and he will appear a second time, not to bear sin, but to bring salvation to those who are waiting for him. (He. 9:28)

TYPES, SYMBOLS, AND PICTURES
(Numbers 25:1-18)

Historical Term	Type or Picture (Scriptural Basis for Each)	Life Application for Today's Believer	Biblical Application
The Sweet Aroma Nu. 28:1-2; 28:3-8 (See also Le. 1:9; 8:21; 16:27-28)	*The aroma ascending up is...* • *a symbol of the person's faith (obedience) in the sacrifice ascending up like a sweet aroma to the Lord* • *a picture of faith and obedience: the sweet aroma of the sacrifice pleased the Lord.* • *a symbol that God was pleased with the offering. He accepted the offering or sacrifice presented by the person.* **Give this command to the Israelites and say to them: 'See that you present to me at the appointed time the**	What can we do to please the Lord? We must have faith in the sacrifice of Christ. We must obey God, do exactly what God says: approach Him through the sacrifice of Christ. When we approach God through the sacrifice of Christ, God is pleased and He accepts us. God reconciles us to Him.	*And live a life of love, just as Christ loved us and gave himself up for us as a fragrant offering and sacrifice to God. (Ep. 5:2)* *For if, when we were God's enemies, we were reconciled to him through the death of his Son, how much more, having been reconciled, shall we be saved through his life! Not only is this so, but we also rejoice in God through our Lord Jesus Christ, through whom we have now received reconciliation. (Ro. 5:10-11)* *For God so loved the world that he gave his one and only Son, that whoever*

Numbers 28:1–29:40

Historical Term	Type or Picture (Scriptural Basis for Each)	Life Application for Today's Believer	Biblical Application
	food for my offerings made by fire, as an aroma pleasing to me.' (Nu. 28:2)		believes in him shall not perish but have eternal life. (Jn. 3:16)
Rest, Spiritual Nu. 28:9-10	Spiritual rest is a type or symbol of Christ, our spiritual rest. On the Sabbath day, make an offering of two lambs a year old without defect, together with its drink offering and a grain offering of two-tenths of an ephah of fine flour mixed with oil. This is the burnt offering for every Sabbath, in addition to the regular burnt offering and its drink offering. (Nu. 28:9-10)	Jesus Christ is our Sabbath rest. He and He alone brings spiritual rest to the human soul: peace, assurance, confidence, purpose, meaning, significance, security, fulfillment, and satisfaction.	Blessed are those who hunger and thirst for righteousness, for they will be filled. (Mt. 5:6) Take my yoke upon you and learn from me, for I am gentle and humble in heart, and you will find rest for your souls. (Mt. 11:29) Peace I leave with you; my peace I give you. I do not give to you as the world gives. Do not let your hearts be troubled and do not be afraid. (Jn. 14:27) "I have told you these things, so that in me you may have peace. In this world you will have trouble. But take heart! I have overcome the world." (Jn. 16:33) Now we who have believed enter that rest, just as God has said, "So I declared on oath in my anger, 'They shall never enter my rest.'" And yet his work has been finished since the creation of the world. (He. 4:3) For if Joshua had given them rest, God would not have spoken later about another day. There remains, then, a Sabbath-rest for the people of God; for anyone who enters God's rest also rests from his own work, just as God did from his. (He. 4:8-10) Then I heard a voice from heaven say, "Write: Blessed are the dead who die in the Lord from now on." "Yes," says the Spirit, "they will rest from their labor, for their deeds will follow them." (Re. 14:13) The LORD replied, "My Presence will go with you, and I will give you rest." (Ex. 33:14) I will lie down and sleep in peace, for you alone, O LORD, make me dwell in safety. (Ps. 4:8)
Monthly Offerings of Animal Sacrifices Nu. 28:11-15	A picture of Christ's sacrifice: these were sometimes referred to as the new moon offerings; that is, they were to be presented to the	The sacrifice of the Burnt Offering symbolized the death of Jesus Christ, but so did the Sin Offering. The Sin Offering was a symbol	This is my blood of the covenant, which is poured out for many for the forgiveness of sins. (Mt. 26:28)

NUMBERS 28:1–29:40

Historical Term	Type or Picture (Scriptural Basis for Each)	Life Application for Today's Believer	Biblical Application
	*Lord at every new or full moon. These sacrifices were a clear symbol of the sacrifice of Christ. Note that a much larger number of animals were to be offered at the monthly sacrifice. This meant that a larger Grain Offering and Drink Offering were also to be presented to the Lord. Note also that a Sin Offering was to be presented to God during the monthly sacrifices (v.15). Later in the history of Israel, the new moon festivals were abused. They apparently became festivals for partying involving drink and occasions for immoral behavior (Is.1:13-14).*³ **On the first of every month, present to the LORD a burnt offering of two young bulls, one ram and seven male lambs a year old, all without defect. (Nu. 28:11)**	of Christ's sacrifice for the sins of the world. He died to provide forgiveness of sins for us. Through the blood of Christ, we are forgiven for all sin. But note: there is a condition for forgiveness. We must confess and repent of our sins. We must turn away from sin and turn to follow after Christ. Both confession and repentance are essential for forgiveness of sins.	*Peter replied, "Repent and be baptized, every one of you, in the name of Jesus Christ for the forgiveness of your sins. And you will receive the gift of the Holy Spirit." (Ac.2:38)* *Repent, then, and turn to God, so that your sins may be wiped out, that times of refreshing may come from the Lord. (Ac.3:19)* *Repent of this wickedness and pray to the Lord. Perhaps he will forgive you for having such a thought in your heart. (Ac.8:22)* *In him we have redemption through his blood, the forgiveness of sins, in accordance with the riches of God's grace. (Ep. 1:7)* *If we confess our sins, he is faithful and just and will forgive us our sins and purify us from all unrighteousness. (1 Jn. 1:9)*
The Passover Nu. 28:16-25 (See also Le. 23:5)	*The Passover is a symbol of Christ our Passover who was sacrificed for us.* **Present to the LORD an offering made by fire, a burnt offering of two young bulls, one ram and seven male lambs a year old, all without defect. (Nu. 28:19)**	Jesus Christ is the perfect fulfillment of the Passover Lamb that was slain in behalf of God's people. Through the blood of Jesus Christ, a person escapes the judgment of God. God accepts the blood of His Son—the blood of the substitute sacrifice—as full payment for a person's sin and rebellion against God.	*The next day John saw Jesus coming toward him and said, "Look, the Lamb of God, who takes away the sin of the world!" (Jn. 1:29)* *For Christ, our Passover lamb, has been sacrificed. (1 Co. 5:7)* *Who gave himself for our sins to rescue us from the present evil age, according to the will of our God and Father. (Ga. 1:4)* *He was oppressed and afflicted, yet he did not open his mouth; he was led like a lamb to the slaughter, and as a sheep before her shearers is silent, so he did not open his mouth. (Is. 53:7)*
The Festival of Firstfruits Nu. 28:26-31 (See also Le. 23:9-14)	*The Festival of Firstfruits is a symbol of Christ's resurrection: He is the first of the harvest, the first to arise from the dead.* *The Festival of Firstfruits is also a symbol of Pentecost, the great harvest of souls and of people giving their lives to God.* **On the day of first-fruits, when you present to the LORD an offering of**	Christ is the first of the harvest, the first to arise from the dead. It is Jesus Christ and His resurrection that gives the believer hope of arising from the dead and living eternally with God. The prophetic picture of salvation is this: the Passover symbolized the believer's deliverance or redemption from the world; the Festival of Unleavened Bread symbolized the urgency	*That the Christ would suffer and, as the first to rise from the dead, would proclaim light to his own people and to the Gentiles. (Ac. 26:23)* *But Christ has indeed been raised from the dead, the firstfruits of those who have fallen asleep. For since death came through a man, the resurrection of the dead comes also through a man. For as in Adam all*

---

³ *The Expositor's Bible Commentary.* Frank E. Gaebelein, Editor, p.951.

NUMBERS 28:1–29:40

Historical Term	Type or Picture (Scriptural Basis for Each)	Life Application for Today's Believer	Biblical Application
	new grain during the Feast of Weeks, hold a sacred assembly and do no regular work. (Nu. 28:26)	of the believer to leave the world and begin his march to the promised land; and now, the Festival of Firstfruits symbolizes the glorious hope the believer has as he marches toward the promised land, the hope of being raised from the dead and living eternally with God—all because of the resurrection of Christ.	*die, so in Christ all will be made alive. But each in his own turn: Christ, the firstfruits; then, when he comes, those who belong to him. (1 Co. 15:20-23)* *Because we know that the one who raised the Lord Jesus from the dead will also raise us with Jesus and present us with you in his presence. (2 Co. 4:14)* *Praise be to the God and Father of our Lord Jesus Christ! In his great mercy he has given us new birth into a living hope through the resurrection of Jesus Christ from the dead, and into an inheritance that can never perish, spoil or fade—kept in heaven for you. (1 Pe. 1:3-4)*
The Festival of Trumpets Nu. 29:1-6 (See also Le. 23:23-25)	*The Festival of Trumpets is a picture of salvation and of the Rapture, the glorious day when Christ will return and take believers—both the living and the dead—to live with Him forever.* **On the first day of the seventh month hold a sacred assembly and do no regular work. It is a day for you to sound the trumpets. (Nu. 29:1)**	As the believer marches to the promised land, he is to focus upon God, learning to trust God more and more and to heed the message of joy over the atonement or reconciliation with God. God has saved him; consequently, the believer is to joy in his salvation, joy in the atonement and reconciliation with God. Moreover, he is to focus upon God increasingly, learning to trust God more and more. Simply stated, the believer is to grow in his trust and joy; he is to be ever maturing, learning to focus upon the Lord.	*Brothers, we do not want you to be ignorant about those who fall asleep, or to grieve like the rest of men, who have no hope. We believe that Jesus died and rose again and so we believe that God will bring with Jesus those who have fallen asleep in him. According to the Lord's own word, we tell you that we who are still alive, who are left till the coming of the Lord, will certainly not precede those who have fallen asleep. For the Lord himself will come down from heaven, with a loud command, with the voice of the archangel and with the trumpet call of God, and the dead in Christ will rise first. After that, we who are still alive and are left will be caught up together with them in the clouds to meet the Lord in the air. And so we will be with the Lord forever. Therefore encourage each other with these words. (1 Th. 4:13-18)*
The Day of Atonement Nu. 29:7-11 (See also Le. 16:1-34; Le. 23:27)	*The Day of Atonement symbolizes the only way to approach God: through the shed blood of the atoning sacrifice of the Lord Jesus Christ. A person is forgiven his sins and reconciled to God only through the atoning sacrifice of Christ.*	The penalty for sin has been paid. How? By Jesus Christ. Jesus Christ died as our atoning sacrifice, reconciling us to God. Hanging upon the cross, Jesus Christ... • bore our sins, taking them away • allowed the justice and judgment of God	*Therefore, brothers, since we have confidence to enter the Most Holy Place by the blood of Jesus, by a new and living way opened for us through the curtain, that is, his body, and since we have a great priest over the house of God, let us draw near to God with a sincere heart in full assurance of*

NUMBERS 28:1–29:40

Historical Term	Type or Picture (Scriptural Basis for Each)	Life Application for Today's Believer	Biblical Application
	On the tenth day of this seventh month hold a sacred assembly. You must deny yourselves and do no work. (Nu. 29:7)	to be executed against Him, suffering the punishment due us • paid the penalty of sin and death, bearing the alienation and separation from God for us	*faith, having our hearts sprinkled to cleanse us from a guilty conscience and having our bodies washed with pure water. (He. 10:19-22)* *Therefore, since we have been justified through faith, we have peace with God through our Lord Jesus Christ, through whom we have gained access by faith into this grace in which we now stand. And we rejoice in the hope of the glory of God. (Ro. 5:1-2)*
The Festival of Tabernacles or Booths or Shelters Nu. 29:12-38 (See also Le. 23:33-34)	*The Festival of Tabernacles is a symbol of the believer's short, temporary life and march through this world to the promised land of heaven.* On the fifteenth day of the seventh month, hold a sacred assembly and do no regular work. Celebrate a festival to the LORD for seven days. (Nu. 29:12)	As the believer marches through this world to the promised land of heaven, his dwelling is only temporary. No matter what kind of house he lives in, it is temporary. It is made out of decaying, corruptible materials. It will waste away and some day, perhaps decades or even centuries away, it will cease to be. Earthly homes are only temporary structures. Moreover, the believer is living in a temporary body, a body that the Bible describes as a temporary tent or tabernacle. The body is corruptible and will decay and cease to exist. The believer's journey or pilgrimage through this world is only temporary. He is marching to his permanent and eternal home in heaven where he will live forever in the presence of God.	*Now we know that if the earthly tent we live in is destroyed, we have a building from God, an eternal house in heaven, not built by human hands. (2 Co. 5:1)* *Those who use the things of the world, as if not engrossed in them. For this world in its present form is passing away. (1 Co. 7:31)* *So we fix our eyes not on what is seen, but on what is unseen. For what is seen is temporary, but what is unseen is eternal. (2 Co. 4:18; see Pe. 3:10; Re. 21:1)* *In the beginning you laid the foundations of the earth, and the heavens are the work of your hands. They will perish, but you remain; they will all wear out like a garment. Like clothing you will change them and they will be discarded. (Ps. 102:25-26)*

NUMBERS 30:1-16

	CHAPTER 30 E. The Laws That Govern Vows: The Obligation to Keep Vows & to Consider Others in Making Vows, 30:1-16	gates her or the rash promise by which she obligates herself, and the LORD will release her. 9 "Any vow or obligation taken by a widow or divorced woman will be binding on her.	3) The point: Spouses are to be considered in vows (because of finances, hardships, health, etc.) 4. The vows or pledges of a widow or divorced woman: Are binding—must still be fulfilled
1. The importance of vows or pledges a. Vows or pledges concern the LORD Himself & are governed by the LORD b. Vows or pledges must not be broken	Moses said to the heads of the tribes of Israel: "This is what the LORD commands: 2 When a man makes a vow to the LORD or takes an oath to obligate himself by a pledge, he must not break his word but must do everything he said.	10 "If a woman living with her husband makes a vow or obligates herself by a pledge under oath 11 And her husband hears about it but says nothing to her and does not forbid her, then all her vows or the pledges by which she obligated herself will stand.	5. The vows or pledges of a married woman a. The obligation: She must keep her vow or pledge b. The one exception: The husband's authority 1) If her husband approves, the vow or pledge stands
2. The vows or pledges of a young woman still living with her parents a. The obligation: She must keep her vow or pledge b. The one exception: The parents' authority must be respected & followed 1) If her father approves, the vow stands 2) If her father objects, the vow is released 3) The point: The parent must be considered (because of finances, hardship, health—whatever the vow involved)	3 "When a young woman still living in her father's house makes a vow to the LORD or obligates herself by a pledge 4 And her father hears about her vow or pledge but says nothing to her, then all her vows and every pledge by which she obligated herself will stand. 5 But if her father forbids her when he hears about it, none of her vows or the pledges by which she obligated herself will stand; the LORD will release her because her father has forbidden her.	12 But if her husband nullifies them when he hears about them, then none of the vows or pledges that came from her lips will stand. Her husband has nullified them, and the LORD will release her. 13 Her husband may confirm or nullify any vow she makes or any sworn pledge to deny herself. 14 But if her husband says nothing to her about it from day to day, then he confirms all her vows or the pledges binding on her. He confirms them by saying nothing to her when he hears about them.	2) If her husband disapproves, the vow or pledge is nullified: The LORD releases her c. The point: Consideration must be given to the husband (spouse) when making vows or pledges 1) He (as family head) has the right to confirm or disallow 2) He confirms by saying nothing on the day he hears about the vow or pledge
3. The vows or pledges of a woman who marries while her commitment is still in force a. The obligation: Must keep her vow, even rash promises b. The one exception: The husband's authority 1) If her husband approves, the vow or pledge stands 2) If her husband objects, the vow or pledge is nullified: The LORD releases her	6 "If she marries after she makes a vow or after her lips utter a rash promise by which she obligates herself 7 and her husband hears about it but says nothing to her, then her vows or the pledges by which she obligated herself will stand. 8 But if her husband forbids her when he hears about it, he nullifies the vow that obli-	15 If, however, he nullifies them some time after he hears about them, then he is responsible for her guilt." 16 These are the regulations the LORD gave Moses concerning relationships between a man and his wife, and between a father and his young daughter still living in his house.	3) He personally stands guilty before God if he nullifies them some time after hearing about them 6. The concern of God for order in families a. These laws build the relationship between man & wife b. These laws build the relationship between father & daughter

DIVISION IV

THE PREPARATION FOR THE MARCH INTO THE PROMISED LAND, 26:1–36:13

E. The Laws That Govern Vows: The Obligation to Keep Vows and to Consider Others in Making Vows, 30:1-16

(30:1-16) **Introduction—Non-Profit Organizations—Organizations, Non-Profit—Support, of Non-Profit Organizations—Pledges, to Support Ministries—Church, Support of—Vows, Discussed**: thousands of institutions and non-profit organizations depend upon the vows or pledges of people. If people stopped giving to these organizations, their doors would close. Some of these organizations are meeting desperate needs within their own community while others are meeting desperate needs around the world. They are legitimate organizations that should be supported, even supported to the point of sacrifice. Because they are meeting desperate needs, many of these organizations are very dear to the hearts of people. People pour their hard-earned dollars into meeting the needs of their communities and of the world. They even make pledges and commitments to give something on a regular basis in order to have a part in meeting the continued need that cries out so desperately for help. The point is this: once a vow or pledge has been made, the commitment is to be kept. This is the law of God. This is the discussion

NUMBERS 30:1-16

of this important passage of Scripture: *The Laws That Govern Vows: The Obligation to Keep Vows and to Consider Others in Making Vows*, 30:1-16.

1. The importance of vows or pledges (vv.1-2).
2. The vows or pledges of a young woman still living with her parents (vv.3-5).
3. The vows or pledges of a woman who marries while her commitment is still in force (vv.6-8).
4. The vows or pledges of a widow or divorced woman: are binding—must still be fulfilled (v.9).
5. The vows or pledges of a married woman (vv.10-15).
6. The concern of God for order in families (v.16).

1 (30:1-2) **Vows, Importance of—Pledges, Importance of—Vows, Duty of**: the importance of vows or pledges can be seen in two facts.

First, vows or pledges concern the LORD Himself and are governed by the LORD (v.1). Anything that concerns God is of critical importance, for the destiny of human life is in His hands. Both blessings and judgment are determined by God. If a person approaches God as he should, he is blessed. But if he approaches God in a wrong or false way, he is condemned and to be judged by God. This is one reason vows or pledges are so important. They involve and concern the LORD; they are offered up to God Himself. This is the reason God gave certain laws to govern vows or pledges. In love, God wants man to understand exactly how vows or pledges are to be made. God loves man and does not want him to come under condemnation. He wants a perfect understanding between Himself and man. He wants man to be blessed, not cursed to face judgment.

The second fact that makes vows or pledges important is this: vows or pledges must not be broken (v.2). A person must be conscientious; he must not break his word when he makes a promise to God. God has declared that a person can make a vow or pledge to Him, but once made, the promise must be kept—absolutely kept. Hypocrisy—a hypocritical approach to God—profanes and defiles God's holy name. It is far better not to make a vow than to break a vow (Ec.5:5). Man must not deceive himself. Scripture is clear: "God is not mocked: for whatsoever a man soweth, that shall he also reap" (Ga.6:9). A person must keep his vows once they are made. He must not break his word, his promise to God. He must do everything he vowed or pledged.

> **Thought 1.** A person must keep the vows or pledges made to God. Failing to keep his promises, his word, makes a person a liar. But this is not the worst offense: his broken promise profanes and defiles the holy name of God. This God will never tolerate. Once a vow or pledge has been made, it must be kept. This is the strong declaration of Scripture:
>
> **When a man makes a vow to the LORD or takes an oath to obligate himself by a pledge, he must not break his word but must do everything he said. (Nu. 30:2)**
>
> **If you make a vow to the LORD your God, do not be slow to pay it, for the LORD your God will certainly demand it of you and you will be guilty of sin. But if you refrain from making a vow, you will not be guilty. Whatever your lips utter you must be sure to do, because you made your vow freely to the LORD your God with your own mouth. (De. 23:21-23)**
>
> **It is a trap for a man to dedicate something rashly and only later to consider his vows. (Pr. 20:25)**
>
> **When you make a vow to God, do not delay in fulfilling it. He has no pleasure in fools; fulfill your vow. It is better not to vow than to make a vow and not fulfill it. Do not let your mouth lead you into sin. And do not protest to the temple messenger, "My vow was a mistake." Why should God be angry at what you say and destroy the work of your hands? (Ec. 5:4-6)**

2 (30:3-5) **Vows, of Children—Pledges, of Children—Vows, of Single Women—Parents, Duties to Children**: there was the law governing the vows or pledges of a daughter who still lived with her parents. The hearts of young people are tender and sensitive, subject to following whatever examples or influences surround them. Hopefully, the example and influence around a young person are godly. When a young person has a godly example, the child often makes vows or pledges to God. This was definitely true with the children of the Israelites. The parents stressed the importance of following God, of learning His commandments and obeying them. Because of this strong instruction in righteousness, children often made vows or pledges to God. The point to see is this: sometimes a child's pledge could cause a serious problem for the family, in particular if the pledge involved an expensive gift or a large quantity of some item. For example, a young daughter might pledge food or clothing to the poor, or a large sum of money that she had saved, or jewelry that was of great value and offered security to the family, or some animal that provided necessary security for her and her family, or any other property or expensive possession she held under her care. There was the possibility that her vow could damage or bring hardship to the family. Since parents usually try to protect their children from crises situations, they seldom discuss crises or genuine hardships with their children. A father could be facing severe loss, even bankruptcy involving the loss of business, house, or property. A young daughter still living at home would likely have no way of knowing this. God knew that situations like this would arise; therefore, with a heart full of grace and love for young children who love Him so much that they would make vows in order to draw closer to Him, He made provision for their safeguard and such dire circumstances.

a. Note the obligation of the young woman who had made a vow or pledge: she must keep the promise she made to God. If a vow or pledge was made, there was no excuse: she had to keep her word.

b. But as stated, with a heart full of love for the young daughter, God made one exception: the parents' authority must be respected and followed. The parents knew whether or not her vow would cause problems or hardships for the family. Therefore, the child was to obey the instructions of her parents. If the father approved, the vow stood. If her father objected, the vow was released from the young woman. She would not face the condemnation and judgment of God. But note: the father had to object to the vow immediately after hearing about it. Once he had heard about the vow, if he said nothing, the vow was to stand. He was not to allow the vow to stand unopposed and then one day object to the vow and disallow it. If the father first allowed the vow and then stepped in and stopped the vow at a later date, he personally became obligated to fulfill the vow himself (see v.15).

NUMBERS 30:1-16

The point is this: a young daughter must consider her parents when she makes a vow, and she must obey her parents if her parents object to the vow. This is because of finances, hardships, health reasons, or any other factor that might damage the family and its welfare.

> **Thought 1**. Children must obey parents. This is particularly true when making vows or pledges. Only the parent knows the full situation within the family, what problems the family may be facing such as...
> - financial difficulty
> - loss of employment
> - change of employment
> - health problems
> - relocation
> - marital problems
> - financial commitments and obligations
>
> The child simply has no way to know the overall picture of the family. Therefore, the child must always obey the parent, in particular when making vows or pledges to the LORD.
>
> > For God said, 'Honor your father and mother' and 'Anyone who curses his father or mother must be put to death.' (Mt. 15:4)
> > Children, obey your parents in the Lord, for this is right. "Honor your father and mother"—which is the first commandment with a promise—"that it may go well with you and that you may enjoy long life on the earth." (Ep. 6:1-3)
> > Children, obey your parents in everything, for this pleases the Lord. (Col. 3:20)
> > But if a widow has children or grandchildren, these should learn first of all to put their religion into practice by caring for their own family and so repaying their parents and grandparents, for this is pleasing to God. (1 Ti. 5:4)
> > Honor your father and your mother, so that you may live long in the land the LORD your God is giving you. (Ex. 20:12)
> > Each of you must respect his mother and father, and you must observe my Sabbaths. I am the LORD your God. (Le. 19:3)
> > "Cursed is the man who dishonors his father or his mother." Then all the people shall say, "Amen!" (De. 27:16)
> > Listen, my son, to your father's instruction and do not forsake your mother's teaching. (Pr. 1:8)
> > My son, keep your father's commands and do not forsake your mother's teaching. (Pr. 6:20)
> > The eye that mocks a father, that scorns obedience to a mother, will be pecked out by the ravens of the valley, will be eaten by the vultures. (Pr. 30:17)

3 (30:6-8) **Vows, Law Governing—Pledges, Law Governing—Women, Duties of, to Keep Vows**: there was the law governing the vows or pledges of a woman who married while her commitment was still in force.

a. The young woman was obligated to keep her vow (v.6). She had made the vow or pledge in good faith; therefore, she was to keep the promise. She was to fulfill her word, do exactly what she had said. Even if the vow was a rash promise, uttered in an impulsive moment, she was still to keep her promise. Note this is exactly what Scripture says (v.6).

But what happens if her vow creates a hardship for her and her husband? After all, she had made the vow before their marriage, and she had no idea that it would create a hardship upon them. But it had. So what was she to do? God knew the problem this would create for His dear people; therefore, He instituted a law that would release her from her vow.

b. Note the law: this is one exception that is based upon the husband's authority within the family (v.7-8). In ancient society, the husband always managed the property, looked after the finances, and handled the business dealings for the family. Within the family, the husband was the one who knew the overall financial situation. Therefore, if a young woman made a vow before she was married, the husband had the authority either to approve or disapprove the vow after the marriage. If her husband approved the vow, the vow or pledge stood. She could fulfill her promise, keep her word. But if her husband objected, the vow or pledge was nullified. The LORD released her (v.8). The point is this: spouses were to consider one another when evaluating vows or pledges. This was an absolute essential because of finances, business dealings, employment, and a host of other factors that might create hardship upon young people who had just been married.

> **Thought 1**. God cares about young married couples. He wants them to have a full and rich life, establishing godly families upon this earth. He knows that young people have tender hearts and can be challenged to step out in great faith, step out in making strong vows and commitments to follow after Him. The vows or pledges may involve the giving of a certain amount of money, the commitment of a life to missionary service, the commitment of so much time or of certain possessions or a host of other commitments. In facing marriage, sometimes the young person will have to decide between keeping the vow made to God or marriage. A choice will have to be made. For example, a choice may have to be made between missionary service and marriage. But before the marriage is the time for the decision to be made. However, after marriage, if the vow creates a hardship for the young married couple, the young woman is released from her vow. Her first obligation is to her husband. She will not be held guilty by God.
>
> The point to see in this law is God's love and care for His dear people. God knows that we get ourselves into difficult situations sometimes, situations that create hardships. God does not want this. With tenderness and care, He releases a young person from a vow that creates a hardship after marriage. God does not want a young couple suffering under hardship nor any other pressure or strain. He wants young people free from difficult circumstances so they can focus upon building a strong, godly love and family. God is mindful of their needs and He wants to provide for all of them. This is the reason God frees a young person from a vow or pledge after marriage. He loves and He cares for His dear people. This is the strong declaration of Scripture.
>
> > But seek first his kingdom and his righteousness, and all these things will be given to you as well. (Mt. 6:33)
> > Indeed, the very hairs of your head are all numbered. Don't be afraid; you are

worth more than many sparrows. (Lu. 12:7)

Cast all your anxiety on him because he cares for you. (1 Pe. 5:7)

The eternal God is your refuge, and underneath are the everlasting arms. He will drive out your enemy before you, saying, 'Destroy him!' (De. 33:27)

The LORD is my strength and my shield; my heart trusts in him, and I am helped. My heart leaps for joy and I will give thanks to him in song. (Ps. 28:7)

The LORD remembers us and will bless us: He will bless the house of Israel, he will bless the house of Aaron. (Ps. 115:12)

So do not fear, for I am with you; do not be dismayed, for I am your God. I will strengthen you and help you; I will uphold you with my righteous right hand. (Is. 41:10)

4 (30:9) **Vows, of the Divorced—Pledges, of the Divorced—Widows, Vows or Pledges of**: the vows or pledges of a widow or divorced woman are binding. They must still be fulfilled even after divorce or after becoming a widow.

Sometimes a recently widowed or divorced woman would return home to her parents or go live with a child, at least temporarily. In such situations, the woman was still considered to be the sole authority of her own affairs. Neither her father nor son could insist that she break her vow. The divorced or widowed woman was still obligated to fulfill her promise, to make her pledge. She was to be faithful to her word, to do exactly what she had promised.

> When a man makes a vow to the LORD or takes an oath to obligate himself by a pledge, he must not break his word but must do everything he said. (Nu. 30:2)
>
> If you make a vow to the LORD your God, do not be slow to pay it, for the LORD your God will certainly demand it of you and you will be guilty of sin. (De. 23:21)
>
> When you make a vow to God, do not delay in fulfilling it. He has no pleasure in fools; fulfill your vow. (Ec. 5:4)

5 (30:10-15) **Vows, of Married Women—Women, Married, Pledges of**: there was the law governing the vows or pledges of a married woman. A woman who follows after the LORD often makes pledges or vows. Seeing and hearing about needs touches her heart, needs such as...

- suffering people
- poor families
- disaster-stricken areas
- disease-stricken children or adults
- the appeals of mission organizations
- opportunities to get the gospel out
- the hungry and homeless
- the poor and destitute
- the suffering and dying
- fire victims

By their very nature, women are nurturing; therefore, they are tenderhearted and often reach out to meet the needs of others. Sometimes the meeting of these needs requires making commitments on a regular basis. If a woman made a vow or pledge without the knowledge of her husband, what was to be done? This law governed the situation:

a. The wife was obligated to keep the vow or pledge. She had made the commitment; therefore she was to fulfill her commitment. She was to keep her vow, do exactly what she had said and promised.

b. But note, there was one exception: the husband's authority (vv.11-12). If the husband heard about the vow and said nothing, the vow or pledge stood. But if the husband disapproved, the vow or pledge was nullified. The LORD released the wife from her vow. Remember, the husband managed the finances, looked after the property, and took care of business matters for the family. He was the only family member who saw the overall financial situation of the family. Therefore, he knew whether or not the vow would bring hardship upon the family. He must have a voice in the vow or pledge being made by the wife. If she made the vow on her own, without considering her husband, she had made an unwise decision, a decision that could bankrupt or create extreme hardship for the family. God knew this and He cared, not wanting the family to live under the strain of hardship or financial difficulty. Therefore, God made provision for the wife to be released from the vow or pledge she made. She would not stand guilty before God if she broke her vow. She was free to listen and follow the request or demand of her husband that the vow be annulled.

c. Note the point: consideration must be given to the husband when making vows or pledges (vv.13-15). As stated, in ancient Israel, the husband was the person who managed the finances, property, and business dealings of the family. Therefore, he had the right to confirm or disallow all vows or pledges. He confirmed a vow by saying nothing when he heard about it. The wife was free to fulfill her vow or pledge. But note: if he nullified the vow sometime after having heard about it, he personally stood guilty before God. The guilt for having broken the vow was not counted against the wife but against him. In God's eyes, he was the guilty party; therefore, he was to stand accountable to God in the day of judgment.

> **Thought 1.** Wives and husbands are to consider one another when making vows or pledges to God. No pledge or vow should be made by either party without discussing it first with the other spouse. Once married, a couple is a unit, bound together as one body in the eyes of God. Therefore, whatever one spouse does affects the other spouse, even if the one making the pledge or vow manages the finances and business affairs of the family. Consideration must always be given to the other spouse before making vows or pledges. The other spouse may know something that would create a hardship upon the family, some upcoming misfortune such as...
>
> - health problems
> - financial difficulties
> - unemployment
> - bankruptcy
> - loss of property
> - dropping stock prices
> - lower interest income
> - possible relocation
>
> For these and a host of other reasons, spouses must always consider one another when making vows or pledges. God does not want a family going through hardships or financial difficulties. He wants a husband and wife focused upon building a godly

family, not focused upon hardships and difficulties that put undue strain upon them. God wants His dear people experiencing the spiritual rest of the promised land, not suffering under the strain and hardships of life. He wants them bound together in love, focused upon Him, one another, and the rest of their family. God wants strong, godly families who know the fullness of life in all of the love and joy of His Spirit. He wants them marching together to the promised land, being victorious over all the hardships and enemies of this life, conquering and triumphing over all. If a couple is living separately and making decisions alone without considering the other spouse, the fullness of life can never be experienced by the family. Therefore, no spouse is to make a vow without considering the other spouse. In making vows or pledges, consideration of the other spouse is always a necessity.

> **Wives, submit to your husbands as to the Lord. (Ep. 5:22)**
>
> **Husbands, love your wives, just as Christ loved the church and gave himself up for her. (Ep. 5:25)**
>
> **However, each one of you also must love his wife as he loves himself, and the wife must respect her husband. (Ep. 5:33)**
>
> **In the same way, their wives are to be women worthy of respect, not malicious talkers but temperate and trustworthy in everything. (1 Ti. 3:11)**
>
> **Husbands, in the same way be considerate as you live with your wives, and treat them with respect as the weaker partner and as heirs with you of the gracious gift of life, so that nothing will hinder your prayers. (1 Pe. 3:7)**
>
> **For this reason a man will leave his father and mother and be united to his wife, and they will become one flesh. (Ge. 2:24)**
>
> **May your fountain be blessed, and may you rejoice in the wife of your youth. (Pr. 5:18)**

6 (30:16) **Families, Order Within—Organization, of Families—Relationships, Between Man and Wife—Relationships, Between Father and Children**: there was the concern of God for order and organization within families. One of the very first institutions ever created was that of the family. Adam was the first man and Eve the first woman upon earth. When they came together to have a child, the first family was instituted. This was the very purpose of God for putting man and woman upon earth, to share together as husband and wife and as the parental heads of the family. God cares about the family, about how it functions, wanting the family to experience the richness and fullness of life. This is the very reason for this present law governing vows made by various family members. As has been seen, these laws built the relationship between man and wife and between father and daughter or children.

Thought 1. This fact is true of the human body: without a head, there is no living body. So it is within any body of people. There has to be a head who has ultimate authority for any organization to function properly. Without a head, without someone in charge, there is chaos. There is no accountability, no one to make sure that the functions of an organization or project are adequately carried out. Within the family, the head is one of the parents. If the family is a one-parent family, then the one parent is the head. If the family is a two-parent family, then the ultimate responsibility for the love, care, and protection of the family is the father's. He is to love the family to the point of sacrificing himself totally if necessary, just as Christ sacrificed and gave Himself for the church (Ep. 5:25). The point to see is this: God is concerned about order in the family; therefore, He gave these laws to build a strong relationship between man and wife and between father and daughter or children. God wants the strongest relationships possible to exist among all family members. This is the clear declaration of Scripture:

> **Submit to one another out of reverence for Christ. Wives, submit to your husbands as to the Lord. For the husband is the head of the wife as Christ is the head of the church, his body, of which he is the Savior. Now as the church submits to Christ, so also wives should submit to their husbands in everything. Husbands, love your wives, just as Christ loved the church and gave himself up for her. (Ep. 5:21-25)**
>
> **In this same way, husbands ought to love their wives as their own bodies. He who loves his wife loves himself. After all, no one ever hated his own body, but he feeds and cares for it, just as Christ does the church— for we are members of his body. "For this reason a man will leave his father and mother and be united to his wife, and the two will become one flesh." (Ep. 5:28-31)**
>
> **Fathers, do not exasperate your children; instead, bring them up in the training and instruction of the Lord. (Ep. 6:4)**
>
> **In the same way, their wives are to be women worthy of respect, not malicious talkers but temperate and trustworthy in everything. (1 Ti. 3:11)**
>
> **Then they can train the younger women to love their husbands and children. (Tit. 2:4)**
>
> **Husbands, in the same way be considerate as you live with your wives, and treat them with respect as the weaker partner and as heirs with you of the gracious gift of life, so that nothing will hinder your prayers. (1 Pe. 3:7)**
>
> **Impress them on your children. Talk about them when you sit at home and when you walk along the road, when you lie down and when you get up. (De. 6:7)**
>
> **Train a child in the way he should go, and when he is old he will not turn from it. (Pr. 22:6)**

NUMBERS 31:1-54

CHAPTER 31

F. The Conquest of the Most Dangerous & Threatening Enemies, the Midianites: A Picture of Conquering the Seductive, Immoral Enemies of the World, 31:1-54

1. The order to launch the campaign: God judges the evil of this world
   a. The reason: God's justice
      1) The Midianites[DS1] had seduced & tried to destroy God's people
      2) Moses was soon to die
   b. The call to arms by Moses: He charged the people to prepare for war against the Midianites
      1) To carry out God's vengeance on the seductive, immoral enemies
      2) To arm 1000 soldiers from each tribe: A total of 12,000 armed soldiers
      3) To take the priest Phinehas with them
         • With the holy objects of the sanctuary
         • With the trumpets for sounding the charge

2. The victorious campaign: A picture of victory over the evil, seductive, & immoral enemies of life
   a. They triumphed over Midian
      1) The five kings of Midian were killed
      2) The wicked advisor of the evil, seductive plan, Balaam, was killed (22:1—25:18)
   b. They captured the women, children, animals, & possessions—even the women who had seduced & sought to destroy them
   c. They burned all the cities & camps
   d. They triumphantly marched back to their camp with the captives, spoils, & plunder
      1) They expected a triumphant celebration with Moses, Eleazar, & the people
      2) Moses, Eleazar, & all the leaders went to meet the

The LORD said to Moses, 2 "Take vengeance on the Midianites for the Israelites. After that, you will be gathered to your people." 3 So Moses said to the people, "Arm some of your men to go to war against the Midianites and to carry out the LORD's vengeance on them. 4 Send into battle a thousand men from each of the tribes of Israel." 5 So twelve thousand men armed for battle, a thousand from each tribe, were supplied from the clans of Israel. 6 Moses sent them into battle, a thousand from each tribe, along with Phinehas son of Eleazar, the priest, who took with him articles from the sanctuary and the trumpets for signaling. 7 They fought against Midian, as the LORD commanded Moses, and killed every man. 8 Among their victims were Evi, Rekem, Zur, Hur and Reba—the five kings of Midian. They also killed Balaam son of Beor with the sword. 9 The Israelites captured the Midianite women and children and took all the Midianite herds, flocks and goods as plunder. 10 They burned all the towns where the Midianites had settled, as well as all their camps. 11 They took all the plunder and spoils, including the people and animals, 12 And brought the captives, spoils and plunder to Moses and Eleazar the priest and the Israelite assembly at their camp on the plains of Moab, by the Jordan across from Jericho. 13 Moses, Eleazar the priest and all the leaders of the community went to meet them outside the camp. 14 Moses was angry with the officers of the army—the commanders of thousands and commanders of hundreds—who returned from the battle. 15 "Have you allowed all the women to live?" he asked them. 16 "They were the ones who followed Balaam's advice and were the means of turning the Israelites away from the LORD in what happened at Peor, so that a plague struck the LORD's people. 17 Now kill all the boys. And kill every woman who has slept with a man, 18 But save for yourselves every girl who has never slept with a man. 19 "All of you who have killed anyone or touched anyone who was killed must stay outside the camp seven days. On the third and seventh days you must purify yourselves and your captives. 20 Purify every garment as well as everything made of leather, goat hair or wood." 21 Then Eleazar the priest said to the soldiers who had gone into battle, "This is the requirement of the law that the LORD gave Moses: 22 Gold, silver, bronze, iron, tin, lead 23 And anything else that can withstand fire must be put through the fire, and then it will be clean. But it must also be purified with the water of cleansing. And whatever cannot withstand fire must be put through that water. 24 On the seventh day wash your clothes and you will be clean. Then you may come into the camp." 25 The LORD said to Moses, 26 "You and Eleazar the priest and the family heads of the community are to count all the people and animals that were captured. 27 Divide the spoils between the soldiers who took part in the battle and the rest of the community. 28 From the soldiers who

victorious army outside the camp

3. The shocking military error: A picture of failing to fully destroy the evil, seductive & immoral enemies of life
   a. The anger of Moses with the officers of the army
      1) They had spared some of the most dangerous enemies, the women
      2) The women had seduced them into immoral behavior & false worship in an attempt to destroy them
      3) The women had caused the judgment of God to fall: A plague that killed 21,000 Israelites
   b. The enemies—all who sought or could seek to destroy Israel—had to be destroyed: Women & boys
   c. The innocent & non-threatening girls were saved

4. The purification of the soldiers & the spoils: A reminder that death is the ultimate corruption
   a. They were unclean: Had been in contact with death
      1) Could not go in the camp
      2) Had to cleanse themselves & the captives
      3) Had to cleanse every garment & all else made of leather & cloth
   b. They had to fully obey the law of cleansing in detail: It was God's command

      1) All metal objects had to be cleansed by fire & water: Gold, silver, bronze, iron, tin, & lead objects
      2) All other objects had to be cleansed by water

      3) All personal clothing had to be washed
      4) The result: Could enter camp—be reconciled

5. The division of the spoils: A picture of rewards & of giving thanks to God
   a. The command of the LORD
      1) The leaders were to count all the spoils
      2) The leaders were to divide the spoils between the soldiers & the people
      3) The soldiers were to

contribute a portion to the LORD • To give one out of every 500 of everything • To give the LORD's part to the priest: The LORD's representative—His minister to the people 4) The people were to contribute a portion to the LORD • To give one out of every 50 of everything • To give to the Levites: The LORD's servants who cared for the Tabernacle b. The obedience of Moses & Eleazar, the High Priest 1) They counted the plunder • The sheep: 675,000 • The cattle: 72,000 • The donkeys: 61,000 • The innocent women: 32,000 2) They distributed the soldiers' share • The sheep: 337,500 with 675 given to the LORD • The cattle: 36,000 with 72 given to the LORD • The donkeys: 30,500 with 61 given to the LORD • The people: 16,000 with 32 given to the LORD • The strong picture of faithfulness: Gave the LORD's share to the High Priest—just as God commanded 3) They distributed the people's share: One half of the spoils	fought in the battle, set apart as tribute for the LORD one out of every five hundred, whether persons, cattle, donkeys, sheep or goats. 29 Take this tribute from their half share and give it to Eleazar the priest as the LORD's part. 30 From the Israelites' half, select one out of every fifty, whether persons, cattle, donkeys, sheep, goats or other animals. Give them to the Levites, who are responsible for the care of the LORD's tabernacle." 31 So Moses and Eleazar the priest did as the LORD commanded Moses. 32 The plunder remaining from the spoils that the soldiers took was 675,000 sheep, 33 72,000 cattle, 34 61,000 donkeys 35 And 32,000 women who had never slept with a man. 36 The half share of those who fought in the battle was: 337,500 sheep, 37 Of which the tribute for the LORD was 675; 38 36,000 cattle, of which the tribute for the LORD was 72; 39 30,500 donkeys, of which the tribute for the LORD was 61; 40 16,000 people, of which the tribute for the LORD was 32. 41 Moses gave the tribute to Eleazar the priest as the LORD's part, as the LORD commanded Moses. 42 The half belonging to the Israelites, which Moses set apart from that of the fighting men—	43 The community's half—was 337,500 sheep, 44 36,000 cattle, 45 30,500 donkeys 46 And 16,000 people. 47 From the Israelites' half, Moses selected one out of every fifty persons and animals, as the LORD commanded him, and gave them to the Levites, who were responsible for the care of the LORD's tabernacle. 48 Then the officers who were over the units of the army—the commanders of thousands and commanders of hundreds—went to Moses 49 And said to him, "Your servants have counted the soldiers under our command, and not one is missing. 50 So we have brought as an offering to the LORD the gold articles each of us acquired—armlets, bracelets, signet rings, earrings and necklaces—to make atonement for ourselves before the LORD." 51 Moses and Eleazar the priest accepted from them the gold—all the crafted articles. 52 All the gold from the commanders of thousands and commanders of hundreds that Moses and Eleazar presented as a gift to the LORD weighed 16,750 shekels. 53 Each soldier had taken plunder for himself. 54 Moses and Eleazar the priest accepted the gold from the commanders of thousands and commanders of hundreds and brought it into the Tent of Meeting as a memorial for the Israelites before the LORD.	• The sheep: 337,500 • The cattle 36,000 • The donkeys: 30,500 • The people: 16,000 • The strong picture of faithfulness: Gave the LORD's share to the Levites for the care of the Tabernacle—just as God commanded c. The very special, spontaneous gifts of the officers & commanders 1) The astounding, miraculous fact that stirred them to make the very special gift: Had no casualties, not one 2) The gift of thanksgiving: All the gold articles they had acquired 3) Their purpose: To make atonement before God—to pay Him for the lives that would have been lost but were saved, all due to Him 4) The acceptance of the gift by Moses & the High Priest, Eleazar • The gold weighed 420 pounds • The gold came from the plunder of the officers • The gift was taken into the Tabernacle as a memorial: Was a reminder of the great victory God had given over the evil, seductive & immoral enemies who sought to destroy them

DIVISION IV

THE PREPARATION FOR THE MARCH INTO THE PROMISED LAND, 26:1–36:13

F. The Conquest of the Most Dangerous and Threatening Enemies, the Midianites: A Picture of Conquering the Seductive, Immoral Enemies of the World, 31:1-54

(31:1-54) **Introduction—Enemies, Kinds of—Enemies, Evil and Seductive**: There are enemies in the world who are evil, seductive, and immoral. These enemies seek to tempt and lead people astray, to lead them down the road of defilement and uncleanness, of corruption and death. If a person does not stand guard against these enemies, he will be corrupted and enslaved and led down the path of destruction. Just think of the evil, seductive, and immoral enemies that stand opposed to people:

⇒ drunkenness and drug addiction
⇒ adultery and immorality
⇒ pornography and sexual deviancy
⇒ gluttony and other enslaving habits
⇒ false religion and idolatry
⇒ lawlessness and violence
⇒ greed and covetousness
⇒ lusts and enslavements

NUMBERS 31:1-54

These are just a few of the evil, seductive, and immoral enemies of the world that can easily destroy the lives of people. This is the discussion of this important passage: *The Conquest of the Most Dangerous and Threatening Enemies, the Midianites: A Picture of Conquering the Seductive, Immoral Enemies of the World*, 31:1-54.

1. The order to launch the campaign: God judges the evil of this world (vv.1-6).
2. The victorious campaign: a picture of victory over the evil, seductive, and immoral enemies of life (vv.7-13).
3. The shocking military error: a picture of failing to fully destroy the evil, seductive, and immoral enemies of life (vv.14-18).
4. The purification of the soldiers and the spoils: a reminder that death is the ultimate corruption (vv.19-24).
5. The division of the spoils: a picture of rewards and of giving thanks to God (vv.25-54).

1 (31:1-6) **Justice, of God—Vengeance, of God—Israel, Conquest of Midianites—Midianites, Conquered By Israel—Wars, of Israel—Nations, Evil, Judged by God—Evil, Judged by God**: there was the order to launch the campaign against the Midianites. This is a picture of God's judgment against the evil of this world.

a. God Himself gave the command for Israel to go to war against the Midianites (vv.1-2). God's justice was to be executed against this evil, seductive, and immoral people. Remember, the Midianites had seduced and attempted to destroy God's people. But they were unable to defeat Israel in battle, so they devised a devious scheme to corrupt them. They, along with the Moabites, sent their women and their temple prostitutes to seduce the men of Israel. Once the men were seduced and hooked, they invited them to their festivals of nites were beyond repair or repentance as a nation of people, beyond hope or correction. Their cup of iniquity or evil was full—filled to the point that it overflowed and would continue to overflow against God's people and the other peoples of the world (see DEEPER STUDY #1—Nu. 21:2-3 for more discussion). It was time for the justice of God against the Midianites to be executed, time for the judgment of God to fall upon them. Consequently, God gave the orders for the Midianite nation to be destroyed. Note: the Midianites were to be conquered before Moses died, before he was "gathered to his people." This enemy had attempted to destroy God's people during Moses' leadership: therefore, they were to be conquered during his administration.

b. Note the call to arms by Moses: he charged the people to prepare for war against the Midianites (vv.3-6). They were to carry out God's vengeance, His justice upon the evil, seductive, and immoral enemies of God's people. But all they needed was a strike force not the entire army. A small strike force of twelve thousand well-equipped men was all that was needed. The officers were to select one thousand soldiers from each tribe (vv.4-5). The evil, seductive, and immoral enemy had threatened the very existence of each tribe; therefore, each tribe was to have a part in the destruction of the evil Midianites.

Note that the priest Phinehas was to go with them. He was to take the holy objects of the sanctuary and the trumpets for sounding the battle charge (v.6, see 10:9).

Thought 1. The judgment of God is coming. All the evil, seductive, and immoral people and nations of this earth will face the judgment of God. God is going to judge the world in righteousness, judge every human being for all the evil, seductive, and immoral deeds they have done. This is the strong declaration of Holy Scripture:

> Just as man is destined to die once, and after that to face judgment. (He. 9:27)
>
> For the Son of Man is going to come in his Father's glory with his angels, and then he will reward each person according to what he has done. (Mt. 16:27)
>
> When the Son of Man comes in his glory, and all the angels with him, he will sit on his throne in heavenly glory. All the nations will be gathered before him, and he will separate the people one from another as a shepherd separates the sheep from the goats. He will put the sheep on his right and the goats on his left. (Mt. 25:31-33)
>
> Do not be amazed at this, for a time is coming when all who are in their graves will hear his voice and come out—those who have done good will rise to live, and those who have done evil will rise to be condemned. (Jn. 5:28-29)
>
> If this is so, then the Lord knows how to rescue godly men from trials and to hold the unrighteous for the day of judgment, while continuing their punishment. (2 Pe. 2:9)
>
> By the same word the present heavens and earth are reserved for fire, being kept for the day of judgment and destruction of ungodly men. (2 Pe. 3:7)
>
> See, the Lord is coming with thousands upon thousands of his holy ones to judge everyone, and to convict all the ungodly of all the ungodly acts they have done in the ungodly way, and of all the harsh words ungodly sinners have spoken against him. (Jude 14-15)
>
> And I saw the dead, great and small, standing before the throne, and books were opened. Another book was opened, which is the book of life. The dead were judged according to what they had done as recorded in the books. (Re. 20:12)

DEEPER STUDY # 1
(31:1-3) **The Midianites**: these people were a large confederation of tribes who were mainly nomads roaming throughout the Sinai Desert and south of Moab throughout the Negev and East Jordan. They did not merge with the other people of Palestine, but rather formed alliances with them, for example with...

- the Moabites (Nu. 22:4f)
- the Amalekites (Jud. 6:3, 33; 7:12)
- the Ishmaelites (Ge. 37:28; Jud. 8:22-24)
- Ephah (Ge. 25:4; Is. 66)

Midian was a son of Abraham and Keturah. When Moses fled from Egypt, he stayed with a Midianite shepherd, Jethro or Reuel. He later married Jethro's daughter, Zipporah (Ex. 2:15-3:1). The Midianites are sometimes referred to as the Ishmaelites (Jud. 8:24). There was a group of merchants from the tribe of Ishmael who purchased Joseph when he was sold as a slave by his brothers (Ge. 37:25f). In confederation with other tribes, the Midianites were to be a constant thorn in Israel's side

(Judges, Chapters 6-8). The kings of the Midianites were known for wearing gold rings, earrings, gold chains and the purple clothing so often worn by kings (Jud. 8:26).

The Midianites defeated by Moses were those who had formed an alliance with Moab, not the whole confederation of tribes.[1]

2 (31:7-13) **Victory, Over Enemies of This Life—Israel, Victories of, Over the Midianites—Midianites, Conquered by Israel—Balaam, Death of—Judgment, of God**: there was the victorious campaign against the Midianites. This is a picture of a believer's victory over the evil, seductive, and immoral enemies of life. The strike force was successful against the Midianites and a decisive victory was carried out.

a. The Israelites triumphed over the evil, seductive, and immoral Midianites (vv.7-8). The reference here to killing every man does not mean that every Midianite male citizen was killed, for we find that the Midianites fought against Israel in the days of Gideon (Jud. 6:3). Note that five kings of the Midianites were killed as well as Balaam, the wicked adviser who had worked out the evil, seductive plan to destroy God's people (v.16; see outline and notes—Nu. 22:1-25:18 for more discussion).

b. The Israelites captured the women, children, animals, and possessions (v.9). Among the women would be those who had seduced and sought to destroy them through sexual immorality and false worship.

c. The Israelites burned all the cities and camps of the Midianites (v.10).

d. The Israelites triumphantly marched back to their camp with the captives, spoils, and plunder (vv.11-12). The strike force expected a triumphant celebration when they returned with the news of their glorious victory and with the spoils of their conquest. With excitement, Moses, Eleazar the High Priest, and all the leaders went outside the camp to meet the victorious army.

> **Thought 1**. God gives victory over the evil, seductive, and immoral enemies of this life. Some of the most powerful enemies that confront and attack us are...
> - adultery
> - premarital sex
> - homosexuality
> - pedophilia
> - sexual deviancy
> - bestiality
> - pornography
> - drunkenness
> - drug addiction
> - gluttony
> - false worship
> - idolatry
> - witchcraft
> - sorcery
> - astrology
> - psychic readings
> - divination
> - lawless acts
> - greed
> - covetousness
> - lusts
> - enslavements
>
> The temptations and attacks of the enemies of this life are innumerable. But victory is assured, victory by the power of God.
>
> "Simon, Simon, Satan has asked to sift you as wheat. But I have prayed for you, Simon, that your faith may not fail. And when you have turned back, strengthen your brothers." (Lu. 22:31-32)
>
> No, in all these things we are more than conquerors through him who loved us. (Ro. 8:37)
>
> The God of peace will soon crush Satan under your feet. The grace of our Lord Jesus be with you. (Ro. 16:20)
>
> No temptation has seized you except what is common to man. And God is faithful; he will not let you be tempted beyond what you can bear. But when you are tempted, he will also provide a way out so that you can stand up under it. (1 Co. 10:13)
>
> Therefore put on the full armor of God, so that when the day of evil comes, you may be able to stand your ground, and after you have done everything, to stand. (Ep. 6:13)
>
> For this reason he had to be made like his brothers in every way, in order that he might become a merciful and faithful high priest in service to God, and that he might make atonement for the sins of the people. Because he himself suffered when he was tempted, he is able to help those who are being tempted. (He. 2:17-18)
>
> For we do not have a high priest who is unable to sympathize with our weaknesses, but we have one who has been tempted in every way, just as we are—yet was without sin. Let us then approach the throne of grace with confidence, so that we may receive mercy and find grace to help us in our time of need. (He. 4:15-16)
>
> Consider it pure joy, my brothers, whenever you face trials of many kinds, because you know that the testing of your faith develops perseverance. Perseverance must finish its work so that you may be mature and complete, not lacking anything. If any of you lacks wisdom, he should ask God, who gives generously to all without finding fault, and it will be given to him. (Js. 1:2-5)
>
> Submit yourselves, then, to God. Resist the devil, and he will flee from you. (Js. 4:7)
>
> If this is so, then the Lord knows how to rescue godly men from trials and to hold the unrighteous for the day of judgment, while continuing their punishment. (2 Pe. 2:9)
>
> For everyone born of God overcomes the world. This is the victory that has overcome the world, even our faith. Who is it that overcomes the world? Only he who believes that Jesus is the Son of God. (1 Jn. 5:4-5)
>
> The LORD will fight for you; you need only to be still. (Ex. 14:14)
>
> Through you we push back our enemies; through your name we trample our foes. (Ps. 44:5)

3 (31:14-18) **Military, Error of—Enemies, Failing to Destroy—Judgment, of God—Iniquity, Cup of, Filled—Nations, Savage and Evil—Nations, Destruction of, Total**: there was the shocking military error by the strike force of the Israelites. This is a picture of failing to totally

---

[1] Gordon J. Wenham. *The Book of Numbers*, p.209.

destroy the evil, seductive, and immoral enemies of life. The strike force was expecting a triumphant reception and celebration upon their return. But what they received was an utter shock.

a. Note the anger of Moses with the officers and commanders of the armies (vv.14-16). Moses was furious, for the officers had obviously disobeyed orders. They had spared some of the most dangerous of the enemies—the women who had seduced the Israelites into immoral behavior and false worship in an attempt to destroy them. It was these very women who had caused the judgment of God to fall upon the Israelites, a plague that had killed 21,000 people.

b. The enemies of God's people had to be destroyed—all who had sought or could seek in the future to destroy Israel. Note that this included all the women who had slept with an Israelite man and all the boys, for they were potential future enemies of Israel. It was dangerous to let the women live, for they would still be tempting the Israelites to uncleanness and to false worship which would eventually destroy the nation. In fact, we know from future Scripture that it was the evil, seductive immorality of surrounding nations and their false worship that eventually led to the loss of the promised land by the Israelites.

Why was it necessary to execute all the male children? James Philip says this:

> *But little children? Could God have ordained this? Some things need to be said in this connection. We must insist that it was not mere wanton brutality, for the slaughter was not indiscriminate. Not all the children were slain, only the males. They were the future "Midian," a potential danger and peril for Israel if allowed to grow up. What we must realize is that there are such things as national character and national traits and propensities. We speak of such and such a people being a military people, and as such liable to be war-like and belligerent. So it was with the Midianites.*
>
> *That is the first thing, and the second is this: we have to remember something much closer to our own time, the extirpation and destruction of whole cities during World War II by huge bombing raids on Germany. We estimated, rightly or wrongly, that the only way for the Nazi menace to be destroyed was to have done this, when doing it involved innocent civilians, children included.*[2]

c. The innocent and unthreatening girls and young women were saved (v.18). They were adopted by the Israelite families and obviously taught about the only living and true God (Jehovah, Yahweh). They became a part of the great nation of God's people.

> **Thought 1.** The believer must fully—completely and wholly—destroy the evil, seductive, and immoral enemies of life. He must put these enemies to death:
> ⇒ all forms of immorality and illicit sex
> ⇒ all pornography: films, audio, music, and reading material
> ⇒ all drunkenness and drug addictions
> ⇒ all gluttony and other enslaving habits
> ⇒ all forms of lusts and enslavements
> ⇒ all greed and lawlessness

The believer must never play around with such sins, allowing them to entice him. The believer must combat cravings of sinful man (the lust of the flesh) and the lust of the eyes and boasting of what he has and does (the pride of life) (1 Jn. 2:15-16). He must not refuse to put these sins to death. By the power of Christ, he must strike a fatal blow against the evil, seductive, and immoral sins that constantly bombard him.

> **You have heard that it was said, 'Do not commit adultery.' But I tell you that anyone who looks at a woman lustfully has already committed adultery with her in his heart. If your right eye causes you to sin, gouge it out and throw it away. It is better for you to lose one part of your body than for your whole body to be thrown into hell. And if your right hand causes you to sin, cut it off and throw it away. It is better for you to lose one part of your body than for your whole body to go into hell. (Mt. 5:27-30)**
>
> **Be careful, or your hearts will be weighed down with dissipation, drunkenness and the anxieties of life, and that day will close on you unexpectedly like a trap. (Lu. 21:34)**
>
> **In the same way, count yourselves dead to sin but alive to God in Christ Jesus. Therefore do not let sin reign in your mortal body so that you obey its evil desires. Do not offer the parts of your body to sin, as instruments of wickedness, but rather offer yourselves to God, as those who have been brought from death to life; and offer the parts of your body to him as instruments of righteousness. (Ro. 6:11-13)**
>
> **For if you live according to the sinful nature, you will die; but if by the Spirit you put to death the misdeeds of the body, you will live. (Ro. 8:13)**
>
> **Rather, clothe yourselves with the Lord Jesus Christ, and do not think about how to gratify the desires of the sinful nature. (Ro. 13:14)**
>
> **So I say, live by the Spirit, and you will not gratify the desires of the sinful nature. For the sinful nature desires what is contrary to the Spirit, and the Spirit what is contrary to the sinful nature. They are in conflict with each other, so that you do not do what you want. But if you are led by the Spirit, you are not under law. The acts of the sinful nature are obvious: sexual immorality, impurity and debauchery; idolatry and witchcraft; hatred, discord, jealousy, fits of rage, selfish ambition, dissensions, factions and envy; drunkenness, orgies, and the like. I warn you, as I did before, that those who live like this will not inherit the kingdom of God. (Ga. 5:16-21)**
>
> **Put to death, therefore, whatever belongs to your earthly nature: sexual immorality, impurity, lust, evil desires and greed, which is idolatry. (Col. 3:5)**
>
> **Dear friends, I urge you, as aliens and strangers in the world, to abstain from sinful desires, which war against your soul. (1 Pe. 2:11)**

---

[2] James Philip. *The Preacher's Commentary on Numbers*, p.313.

As a result, he does not live the rest of his earthly life for evil human desires, but rather for the will of God. (1 Pe. 4:2)

Do not love the world or anything in the world. If anyone loves the world, the love of the Father is not in him. For everything in the world—the cravings of sinful man, the lust of his eyes and the boasting of what he has and does—comes not from the Father but from the world. (1 Jn. 2:15-16)

4 (31:19-24) **Purification, From Sin—Forgiveness, of Sin—Cleansing, From Sin—Death, Symbol of Corruption—Killing, Result of, Defiled a Person—Warfare, Results of, Defiled a Soldier**: there was the purification of the soldiers and the spoils. This is a reminder that death is the ultimate symbol of defilement and uncleanness, of corruption and decay.

a. The soldiers were unclean, for they had been in contact with death (vv.19-20). They could not, therefore, go into the camp until they had cleansed themselves and the captives they had taken in battle. They also had to cleanse every garment and all else that had been made out of leather and cloth. Death takes the life out of a person: it is the "catastrophic destruction of God's creation."[3] Death destroys the physical life of a person. Therefore, it is the ultimate defilement and uncleanness, corruption and decay. God wants this fact to stick in the minds of His dear people. For this reason, the soldiers had to be cleansed before they could go into the camp. Uncleanness and defilement, corruption and decay were not to coexist with God's people. The soldiers had to be cleansed before they could be reunited with the society of God's people.

b. The soldiers had to fully obey the law of cleansing in every detail. This was the command of God (vv.22-24). All possessions had to be cleansed, for possessions could contaminate and corrupt God's people. Note the command of God:

1) All metal objects had to be cleansed both by fire and by water: all the gold, silver, bronze, iron, tin, and lead objects (v.22).
2) All other objects had to be cleansed by water (v.23).
3) All personal clothing had to be washed (v.24).
4) Note the result: once all this had been done, the soldiers could enter camp and be reconciled with their families and the rest of God's people (v.24).

Thought 1. There is a lesson in this for the church and for individual believers.

(1) A person must be cleansed from all defilement and uncleanness, corruption and decay before he is allowed in the camp or membership of God's people. The purity and righteousness of the camp or church body must be protected. The church membership is for genuine believers, those who live holy lives before God, those who have been set apart to live righteous and pure lives. The church membership is a body of believers who have been set apart by God to worship and serve Him and to go out into the world as strong witnesses of His saving grace. The church must make sure that its members have been cleansed from all defilement and uncleanness, corruption and decay.

And now what are you waiting for? Get up, be baptized and wash your sins away, calling on his name. (Ac.22:16)

Do you not know that the wicked will not inherit the kingdom of God? Do not be deceived: Neither the sexually immoral nor idolaters nor adulterers nor male prostitutes nor homosexual offenders nor thieves nor the greedy nor drunkards nor slanderers nor swindlers will inherit the kingdom of God. And that is what some of you were. But you were washed, you were sanctified, you were justified in the name of the Lord Jesus Christ and by the Spirit of our God. (1 Co. 6:9-11)

Husbands, love your wives, just as Christ loved the church and gave himself up for her to make her holy, cleansing her by the washing with water through the word. (Ep. 5:25-26)

How much more, then, will the blood of Christ, who through the eternal Spirit offered himself unblemished to God, cleanse our consciences from acts that lead to death, so that we may serve the living God! (He. 9:14)

Come near to God and he will come near to you. Wash your hands, you sinners, and purify your hearts, you double-minded. (Js. 4:8)

But if we walk in the light, as he is in the light, we have fellowship with one another, and the blood of Jesus, his Son, purifies us from all sin. (1 Jn. 1:7)

"Come now, let us reason together," says the LORD. "Though your sins are like scarlet, they shall be as white as snow; though they are red as crimson, they shall be like wool." (Is. 1:18)

(2) The possessions and things of this world can defile and make a person unclean. Possessions can take hold of a person and enslave him. Things can arouse greed and covetousness within a person, arouse a passion for more and more. This is the reason our possessions must be dedicated, set apart to God and His service. As the root of all evil, money and possessions can consume the human heart and destroy our lives. Possessions and money must be cleansed, purified, set apart, dedicated, and given over to God. If not, they will consume and destroy us.

Jesus answered, "If you want to be perfect, go, sell your possessions and give to the poor, and you will have treasure in heaven. Then come, follow me." When the young man heard this, he went away sad, because he had great wealth. Then Jesus said to his disciples, "I tell you the truth, it is hard for a rich man to enter the kingdom of heaven. Again I tell you, it is easier for a camel to go through the eye of a needle than for a rich man to enter the kingdom of God." (Mt. 19:21-24)

But the worries of this life, the deceitfulness of wealth and the desires for other things come in and choke the word, making it unfruitful. (Mk. 4:19)

---

[3] Gordon J. Wenham. *The Book of Numbers*, p.212.

"Therefore come out from them and be separate, says the Lord. Touch no unclean thing, and I will receive you. I will be a Father to you, and you will be my sons and daughters, says the Lord Almighty." (2 Co. 6:17-18)

Put to death, therefore, whatever belongs to your earthly nature: sexual immorality, impurity, lust, evil desires and greed, which is idolatry. (Col. 3:5)

People who want to get rich fall into temptation and a trap and into many foolish and harmful desires that plunge men into ruin and destruction. For the love of money is a root of all kinds of evil. Some people, eager for money, have wandered from the faith and pierced themselves with many griefs. (1 Ti. 6:9-10)

Keep your lives free from the love of money and be content with what you have, because God has said, "Never will I leave you; never will I forsake you." (He. 13:5)

And when your herds and flocks grow large and your silver and gold increase and all you have is multiplied, then your heart will become proud and you will forget the LORD your God, who brought you out of Egypt, out of the land of slavery. (De. 8:13-14)

Do not trust in extortion or take pride in stolen goods; though your riches increase, do not set your heart on them. (Ps. 62:10)

5 (31:25-54) **Spoils, of Warfare—Offerings, Voluntary—Stewardship, of Income—Rewards, For Fighting a Good Warfare—Thanksgiving, to God**: there was the division of the spoils, of the plunder taken from the defeated enemy. This is a picture of the rewards for fighting a good warfare and a picture of giving thanks to God.

Note three significant facts about the division of the spoils.

a. First, the rewards of battle were divided equally between the soldiers and the people; that is, half went to the soldiers and half went to the people. Of course, this meant far more rewards for the 12,000 soldiers than for the people, who most likely numbered between two to four million persons. But this was a fair distribution since the soldiers had actually done the fighting, putting their lives at risk for the sake of the nation. A summary of the rewards of battle is given in the following chart:

**The Rewards of Battle—
For Fighting a Good Warfare**

	Total	Soldiers' Share	People's Share	Lord's Tithe	Levites' Share
Sheep (inc. goats)	675,000	337,500	337,500	675	6750
Cattle	72,000	36,000	36,000	72	720
Donkeys	61,000	30,500	30,500	61	610
Women (virgins)	32,000	16,000	16,000	32	320

b. The faithfulness of the people in stewardship should be noted. They gave exactly what had been commanded by the LORD: a strong, strong picture of faithfulness in stewardship (vv.41-47).

c. The very special and spontaneous gifts of the officers and commanders should also be noted (vv.48-54).
1) There was an astounding, miraculous fact that stirred them to make the very special gift: they had suffered no casualties; not a single soldier had lost his life in the battle against the Midianites (vv.48-49). A deep spirit of gratitude swelled up in their hearts for what God had done in protecting them and the strike force of the soldiers under their command.
2) Note the gift of thanksgiving: they gave all the gold articles they had acquired (v.50).
3) Their purpose was to make atonement before God, to pay Him for the lives that would have been lost but were saved. The miracle was totally due to Him; therefore, the officers and commanders wanted to make payment—to pay a ransom—in return for all the soldiers that would ordinarily have lost their lives in battle. However, in this case, God had delivered them all and given them back into the hands of His dear people. Therefore they owed Him a ransom, an atonement for His great gift of life.
4) Note the acceptance of the gift by Moses and the High Priest Eleazar (vv.51-53). The gold itself weighed over four hundred and twenty pounds. An enormous gift of gratitude from these officers!
5) The gift of gold was taken into the Tabernacle by Moses and Eleazar as a memorial. This was a reminder of the great victory God had given over the evil, seductive, and immoral enemies who had sought to destroy God's people (v.54).

Thought 1. There are two strong lessons for us in this point:
(1) There are rewards in heaven. Faithful believers are to be rewarded if they fight a good warfare while on this earth. We must, therefore, keep our eyes on the reward that lies out ahead of us, that awaits us when we arrive in heaven. Even Jesus Christ endured the cross and its shame because of the joy of the reward that was set before Him (He. 12:2). God promises to reward us abundantly if we are faithful. We must, then, follow in the steps of Christ, fix our eyes upon Him: stand fast and persevere to the end—all for the joy of the reward that awaits us in heaven. (See notes—Lu. 16:10-12; 1 Co. 13-15; Tit. 3:6; 1 Pe. 1:4 for more discussion.)

And if anyone gives even a cup of cold water to one of these little ones because he is my disciple, I tell you the truth, he will certainly not lose his reward. (Mt. 10:42)

His master replied, 'Well done, good and faithful servant! You have been faithful with a few things; I will put you in charge of many things. Come and share your master's happiness!' (Mt. 25:23)

But love your enemies, do good to them, and lend to them without expecting to get anything back. Then your reward will be great, and you will be sons of the Most High, because he is kind to the ungrateful and wicked. (Lu. 6:35)

But glory, honor and peace for everyone who does good: first for the Jew, then for the Gentile. (Ro. 2:10)

Numbers 31:1-54

Everyone who competes in the games goes into strict training. They do it to get a crown that will not last; but we do it to get a crown that will last forever. (1 Co. 9:25)

Therefore, my dear brothers, stand firm. Let nothing move you. Always give yourselves fully to the work of the Lord, because you know that your labor in the Lord is not in vain. (1 Co. 15:58)

Because you know that the Lord will reward everyone for whatever good he does, whether he is slave or free. (Ep. 6:8)

Now there is in store for me the crown of righteousness, which the Lord, the righteous Judge, will award to me on that day—and not only to me, but also to all who have longed for his appearing. (2 Ti. 4:8)

Therefore, since we are surrounded by such a great cloud of witnesses, let us throw off everything that hinders and the sin that so easily entangles, and let us run with perseverance the race marked out for us. Let us fix our eyes on Jesus, the author and perfecter of our faith, who for the joy set before him endured the cross, scorning its shame, and sat down at the right hand of the throne of God. Consider him who endured such opposition from sinful men, so that you will not grow weary and lose heart. In your struggle against sin, you have not yet resisted to the point of shedding your blood. (He. 12:1-4)

Blessed is the man who perseveres under trial, because when he has stood the test, he will receive the crown of life that God has promised to those who love him. (Js. 1:12)

And when the Chief Shepherd appears, you will receive the crown of glory that will never fade away. (1 Pe. 5:4)

I am coming soon. Hold on to what you have, so that no one will take your crown. (Re. 3:11)

The twenty-four elders fall down before him who sits on the throne, and worship him who lives for ever and ever. They lay their crowns before the throne and say: (Re. 4:10)

Behold, I am coming soon! My reward is with me, and I will give to everyone according to what he has done. (Re. 22:12)

(2) The commanders and officers were deeply grateful to God for the miracle He had performed for His dear people. Miraculously, not a single soldier had lost his life in the battle. When God does a marvelous thing for us, we should make an offering of thanksgiving to Him. Whatever God gives us, we must do exactly what Scripture teaches: give God His share of the gift He has given us. Whatever God does for us, we must make a gift of thanksgiving to Him for having acted in our behalf. Not only tithes should be given, but additional offerings should be made to God—all in appreciation to God for the very special things He does for us as we march to the promised land of heaven.

Sell your possessions and give to the poor. Provide purses for yourselves that will not wear out, a treasure in heaven that will not be exhausted, where no thief comes near and no moth destroys. (Lu. 12:33)

For where your treasure is, there your heart will be also. Be dressed ready for service and keep your lamps burning. (Lu. 12:34-35)

As he looked up, Jesus saw the rich putting their gifts into the temple treasury. He also saw a poor widow put in two very small copper coins. "I tell you the truth," he said, "this poor widow has put in more than all the others. All these people gave their gifts out of their wealth; but she out of her poverty put in all she had to live on." (Lu. 21:1-4)

There were no needy persons among them. For from time to time those who owned lands or houses sold them, brought the money from the sales and put it at the apostles' feet, and it was distributed to anyone as he had need. (Ac.4:34-35)

In everything I did, I showed you that by this kind of hard work we must help the weak, remembering the words the Lord Jesus himself said: 'It is more blessed to give than to receive.' (Ac. 20:35)

Always giving thanks to God the Father for everything, in the name of our Lord Jesus Christ. (Ep. 5:20)

Giving thanks to the Father, who has qualified you to share in the inheritance of the saints in the kingdom of light. (Col. 1:12)

And blessed be God Most High, who delivered your enemies into your hand. Then Abram gave him a tenth of everything. (Ge. 14:20)

All who were willing, men and women alike, came and brought gold jewelry of all kinds: brooches, earrings, rings and ornaments. They all presented their gold as a wave offering to the LORD. (Ex. 35:22)

And said to Moses, "The people are bringing more than enough for doing the work the LORD commanded to be done." (Ex. 36:5)

They brought as their gifts before the LORD six covered carts and twelve oxen—an ox from each leader and a cart from every two. These they presented before the tabernacle. (Nu. 7:3)

But remember the LORD your God, for it is he who gives you the ability to produce wealth, and so confirms his covenant, which he swore to your forefathers, as it is today. (De. 8:18)

Besides, in my devotion to the temple of my God I now give my personal treasures of gold and silver for the temple of my God, over and above everything I have provided for this holy temple: three thousand talents of gold (gold of Ophir) and seven thousand talents of refined silver, for the overlaying of the walls of the buildings. (1 Chr. 29:3-4)

All the officials and all the people brought their contributions gladly, dropping them into the chest until it was full. (2 Chr. 24:10)

All their neighbors assisted them with articles of silver and gold, with goods and livestock, and with valuable gifts, in addition to all the freewill offerings. (Ezr. 1:6)

Let them sacrifice thank offerings and tell of his works with songs of joy. (Ps. 107:22)

TYPES, SYMBOLS, AND PICTURES
(Numbers 31:1-54)

Historical Term	Type or Picture (Scriptural Basis for Each)	Life Application for Today's Believer	Biblical Application
Conquest of the Midianites Nu.31:1-54	The conquest of the Midianites is a picture of conquering the seductive, immoral enemies of the world. They fought against Midian, as the LORD commanded Moses; and killed every man" (Nu. 31:7).	There are enemies in the world who are evil, seductive, and immoral. These enemies seek to tempt and lead people astray, to lead them down the road of defilement and uncleanness, of corruption and death. If a person does not stand guard against these enemies, he will be corrupted and enslaved and led down the path of destruction. Just think of the evil, seductive, and immoral enemies that stand opposed to people: ⇒ drunkenness and drug addiction ⇒ adultery and immorality ⇒ pornography and sexual deviancy ⇒ gluttony and other enslaving habits ⇒ false religion and idolatry ⇒ lawlessness and violence ⇒ greed and covetous ⇒ lust and enslavements These are just a few of the evil, seductive, and immoral enemies of the world that can easily destroy the lives of people.	When the woman saw that the fruit of the tree was good for food and pleasing to the eye, and also desirable for gaining wisdom, she took some and ate it. She also gave some to her husband, who was with her, and he ate it. (Ge.3:6) "Stolen water is sweet; food eaten in secret is delicious!" (Pr.9:17) There is a way that seems right to a man, but in the end it leads to death. (Pr.14:12) For they mouth empty, boastful words and, by appealing to the lustful desires of sinful human nature, they entice people who are just escaping from those who live in error. (2 Pe.2:18) But each one is tempted when, by his own evil desire, he is dragged away and enticed. (Js.1:14) My son, if sinners entice you, do not give in to them. (Pr.1:10) Do not set foot on the path of the wicked or walk in the way of evil men. (Pr.4:14) Do not offer the parts of your body to sin, as instruments of wickedness, but rather offer yourselves to God, as those who have been brought from death to life; and offer the parts of your body to him as instruments of righteousness. (Ro.6:13) Therefore put on the full armor of God, so that when the day of evil comes, you may be able to stand your ground, and after you have done everything, to stand. (Ep.6:13)
Israel's Shocking Military Error against Midian Nu.31:14-18	Israel's failure to completely destroy Midian is a picture of failing to fully destroy the	The believer must fully—completely and totally—destroy the evil, seductive,	"You have heard that it was said, 'Do not commit adultery.' But I tell you

Numbers 31:1-54

Historical Term	Type or Picture (Scriptural Basis for Each)	Life Application for Today's Believer	Biblical Application
	evil, seductive, and immoral enemies of life. Moses was angry with the officers of the army--the commanders of thousands and commanders of hundreds--who returned from the battle. "Have you allowed all the women to live?" he asked them. "They were the ones who followed Balaam's advice and were the means of turning the Israelites away from the LORD in what happened at Peor, so that a plague struck the LORD's people. Now kill all the boys. And kill every woman who has slept with a man, (Nu. 31:14-17).	and immoral enemies of life. He must put these enemies to death: ⇒ all forms of immorality and illicit sex ⇒ all pornography: films, audio, music, and reading material ⇒ all drunkenness and drug addictions ⇒ all gluttony and other enslaving habits ⇒ all forms of lust and covetousness ⇒ all acts of greed and lawlessness The believer must never play around with such sins, allowing them to entice him. The believer must combat the lust of the flesh and the lust of the eyes and the pride of life (1 Jn.2:15-16). He must not refuse to put these sins to death. By the power of Christ, he must strike a fatal blow against the evil, seductive, and immoral sins that constantly bombard him.	*that anyone who looks at a woman lustfully has already committed adultery with her in his heart. If your right eye causes you to sin, gouge it out and throw it away. It is better for you to lose one part of your body than for your whole body to be thrown into hell. And if your right hand causes you to sin, cut it off and throw it away. It is better for you to lose one part of your body than for your whole body to go into hell. (Mt.5:27-30).* *"Be careful, or your hearts will be weighed down with dissipation, drunkenness and the anxieties of life, and that day will close on you unexpectedly like a trap. (Lu.21:34).* *In the same way, count yourselves dead to sin but alive to God in Christ Jesus. Therefore do not let sin reign in your mortal body so that you obey its evil desires. Do not offer the parts of your body to sin, as instruments of wickedness, but rather offer yourselves to God, as those who have been brought from death to life; and offer the parts of your body to him as instruments of righteousness. (Ro.6:11-13; see also 8:13; 13:14; Ga.5:16-21; Col.3:5).*
Spoils Taken from the Defeated Enemy Nu.31:25-54	*The spoils taken from a defeated enemy are a picture of rewards for fighting a good warfare and a picture of giving thanks to God.* The LORD said to Moses, "You and Eleazar the priest and the family heads of the community are to count all the people and animals that were captured. Divide the spoils between the soldiers who took part in the battle and the rest of the community. From the soldiers who fought in the battle, set apart as tribute for the LORD one out of every five hundred, whether persons, cattle, donkeys, sheep or goats. (Nu. 31:25-28).	There are two strong lessons for us in this point: 1. There are rewards in heaven. Faithful believers are to be rewarded if they fight a good warfare while on this earth. We must therefore keep our eyes on the reward that lies out ahead of us, awaiting us when we arrive in heaven. Even Jesus Christ endured the cross and its shame because of the joy of the reward that was set before Him (He.12:2). God promises to reward us abundantly if we are faithful. We must, then, follow in the steps of Christ, fix our eyes upon Him: stand fast and persevere to the end—all for the joy	*And if anyone gives even a cup of cold water to one of these little ones because he is my disciple, I tell you the truth, he will certainly not lose his reward." (Mt.10:42).* *"His master replied, 'Well done, good and faithful servant! You have been faithful with a few things; I will put you in charge of many things. Come and share your master's happiness!' (Mt.25:23).* *But love your enemies, do good to them, and lend to them without expecting to get anything back. Then your reward will be great, and you will be sons of the Most High, because he is kind to the ungrateful and wicked. (Lu.6:35).*

Numbers 31:1-54

Historical Term	Type or Picture (Scriptural Basis for Each)	Life Application for Today's Believer	Biblical Application
		of the reward that awaits us in heaven. (See notes—Lu. 16:10-12; 1 Co.13-15; Tit.3:6; 1 Pe.1:4 for more discussion.) 2. The commanders and officers were deeply grateful to God for the incomprehensible miracle He had performed for His dear people. Miraculously, not a single soldier had lost his life in the battle. When God does a marvelous thing for us, we should make an offering of thanksgiving to Him. Whatever God gives us, we must do exactly what Scripture teaches: give God His share of the gift He has given us. Whatever God does for us, we must make a gift of thanksgiving to Him for having acted in our behalf. Not only tithes should be given, but additional offerings should be made to God—all in appreciation to God for the very special things He does for us as we march to the promised land of heaven.	*But glory, honor and peace for everyone who does good: first for the Jew, then for the Gentile. (Ro.2:10).* *Everyone who competes in the games goes into strict training. They do it to get a crown that will not last; but we do it to get a crown that will last forever. (1 Co.9:25).* *Giving thanks to the Father, who has qualified you to share in the inheritance of the saints in the kingdom of light. (Col.1:12).* *But remember the LORD your God, for it is he who gives you the ability to produce wealth, and so confirms his covenant, which he swore to your forefathers, as it is today. (De.8:18).* *Let them sacrifice thank offerings and tell of his works with songs of joy. (Ps.107:22).*

NUMBERS 32:1-42

CHAPTER 32

G. The Settlement East of the Jordan River: A Picture of Compromise, Selfishness, Covetousness, Disloyalty & Half-Hearted Commitment, 32:1-42

1. **The compromise of two tribes: A picture of selfishness, covetousness, disloyalty—half-hearted commitment**
   a. Saw & coveted the fertile land
   b. Considered only their livestock
   c. Went to Moses & the leaders: Stated three points
      1) That the East Jordan land was a gift of God by conquest (21:1-35, 31:1-54)
      2) That the conquered land was fertile, good pastureland for their livestock
      3) That they wanted this land as their possession: They did not want to cross over the Jordan with the other tribes to fight for the promised land

2. **The angry reaction of Moses: A charge of disloyalty & half-hearted commitment**
   a. Their disloyalty: Wanted to sit while the others fought—this would discourage the others from crossing over into the promised land
   b. Their guilt: Guilty of the same sins committed by the 10 spies at Kadesh Barnea: The sins of unbelief, disloyalty—half-hearted commitment (13:1–14:45)
      1) The spies discouraged the former generation from entering the promised land
      2) The spies aroused the LORD's anger
         • God accused them of a half-hearted commitment: They were not following Him wholeheartedly
         • God judged the people: Not one person 20 years old or older was ever allowed to enter the promised land
         • God was going to allow only two exceptions—Caleb & Joshua: Because they followed the LORD with their whole hearts

1 The Reubenites and Gadites, who had very large herds and flocks, saw that the lands of Jazer and Gilead were suitable for livestock.
2 So they came to Moses and Eleazar the priest and to the leaders of the community, and said,
3 "Ataroth, Dibon, Jazer, Nimrah, Heshbon, Elealeh, Sebam, Nebo and Beon—
4 the land the LORD subdued before the people of Israel—are suitable for livestock, and your servants have livestock.
5 If we have found favor in your eyes," they said, "let this land be given to your servants as our possession. Do not make us cross the Jordan."
6 Moses said to the Gadites and Reubenites, "Shall your countrymen go to war while you sit here?
7 Why do you discourage the Israelites from going over into the land the LORD has given them?
8 This is what your fathers did when I sent them from Kadesh Barnea to look over the land.
9 After they went up to the Valley of Eshcol and viewed the land, they discouraged the Israelites from entering the land the LORD had given them.
10 The LORD's anger was aroused that day and he swore this oath:
11 'Because they have not followed me wholeheartedly, not one of the men twenty years old or more who came up out of Egypt will see the land I promised on oath to Abraham, Isaac and Jacob—
12 Not one except Caleb son of Jephunneh the Kenizzite and Joshua son of Nun, for they followed the LORD wholeheartedly.'
13 The LORD's anger burned against Israel and he made them wander in the desert forty years, until the whole generation of those who had done evil in his sight was gone.
14 "And here you are, a brood of sinners, standing in the place of your fathers and making the LORD even more angry with Israel.
15 If you turn away from following him, he will again leave all this people in the desert, and you will be the cause of their destruction."
16 Then they came up to him and said, "We would like to build pens here for our livestock and cities for our women and children.
17 But we are ready to arm ourselves and go ahead of the Israelites until we have brought them to their place. Meanwhile our women and children will live in fortified cities, for protection from the inhabitants of the land.
18 We will not return to our homes until every Israelite has received his inheritance.
19 We will not receive any inheritance with them on the other side of the Jordan, because our inheritance has come to us on the east side of the Jordan."
20 Then Moses said to them, "If you will do this—if you will arm yourselves before the LORD for battle,
21 And if all of you will go armed over the Jordan before the LORD until he has driven his enemies out before him—
22 Then when the land is subdued before the LORD, you may return and be free from your obligation to the LORD and to Israel. And this land will be your possession before the LORD.
23 "But if you fail to do this, you will be sinning against the LORD; and you may be sure that your sin will find you out.
24 Build cities for your women and children, and pens for your flocks, but do

• God's anger burned against the half-hearted—all who sinned—& He chastised them: They had to wander in the wilderness for 40 years until all died
   c. Their sin & its consequences
      1) They were a *brood of sinners*
      2) They were arousing the LORD's anger—even more than their fathers
      3) If they turned away from following God into the promised land...
         • The disunity would cause God to chastise the people
         • They would be responsible

3. **The selfish insistence of the two tribes & the forced compromise permitted**
   a. The insistence: The right to build pens for their livestock & fortified cities for their families
   b. The promises
      1) They would fight with the other tribes: Actually take the lead in battle until they secured their inheritance (see Jos. 4:12f; 22:1f)
         • They wanted their families protected in fortified cities while they were off fighting
         • They would not return until all the people had received their inheritance
      2) They would not lay claim to any inheritance on the other side of the Jordan (the boundaries of the promised land: see v.20-22, 30, 32; 34:1-12)
   c. The forced compromise by Moses
      1) Moses granted their request: To maintain the unity of the people
         • They must, however, fulfill their promise:
         • They must join the others in fighting until the LORD had defeated His enemies
         • They could then return & claim the East Jordan as their land of the possession
      2) Moses issued a strong warning to the two compromising tribes: If they failed, their sin would find them out (1 Chr. 5:18-26)
      3) Moses then gave two charges
         • To go & build cities & pens

294

NUMBERS 32:1-42

- To fulfill their promise
4) The two compromising tribes repeated the conditions of the agreement
  - Their women & children would remain in the cities of Gilead with their livestock
  - They—every soldier—would cross over Jordan & fight

4. **The agreement with the two compromising tribes publicly declared & the territory assigned**
  a. The agreement declared by Moses to all the leadership
    1) If the two compromising tribes crossed over the Jordan & joined the other tribes in subduing the promised land, they were to be given the land of Gilead as their inheritance
    2) If the two compromising tribes did not help fight, they had to accept an inheritance inside the promised land
  b. The public declaration by the two compromising tribes
    1) They would obey the LORD
    2) They would cross over & fight for the promised land
    3) Their inheritance would be on the east side of the Jordan

what you have promised."
25 The Gadites and Reubenites said to Moses, "We your servants will do as our lord commands.
26 Our children and wives, our flocks and herds will remain here in the cities of Gilead.
27 But your servants, every man armed for battle, will cross over to fight before the LORD, just as our lord says."
28 Then Moses gave orders about them to Eleazar the priest and Joshua son of Nun and to the family heads of the Israelite tribes.
29 He said to them, "If the Gadites and Reubenites, every man armed for battle, cross over the Jordan with you before the LORD, then when the land is subdued before you, give them the land of Gilead as their possession.
30 But if they do not cross over with you armed, they must accept their possession with you in Canaan."
31 The Gadites and Reubenites answered, "Your servants will do what the LORD has said.
32 We will cross over before the LORD into Canaan armed, but the property we inherit will be on this side of the Jordan."
33 Then Moses gave to the Gadites, the Reubenites and the half-tribe of Manasseh son of Joseph the kingdom of Sihon king of the Amorites and the kingdom of Og king of Bashan—the whole land with its cities and the territory around them.
34 The Gadites built up Dibon, Ataroth, Aroer,
35 Atroth Shophan, Jazer, Jogbehah,
36 Beth Nimrah and Beth Haran as fortified cities, and built pens for their flocks.
37 And the Reubenites rebuilt Heshbon, Elealeh and Kiriathaim,
38 As well as Nebo and Baal Meon (these names were changed) and Sibmah. They gave names to the cities they rebuilt.
39 The descendants of Makir son of Manasseh went to Gilead, captured it and drove out the Amorites who were there.
40 So Moses gave Gilead to the Makirites, the descendants of Manasseh, and they settled there.
41 Jair, a descendant of Manasseh, captured their settlements and called them Havvoth Jair.
42 And Nobah captured Kenath and its surrounding settlements and called it Nobah after himself.

c. The territory was assigned to the two compromising tribes & to the half-tribe of Manasseh
  1) The territory included the lands of King Sihon of the Amorites & of King Og of Bashan
  2) The Gadites rebuilt nine cities, fortified them, & built pens for their livestock[DS1-8]
  3) The Reubenites rebuilt & renamed six cities[DS9-13]
  4) The descendants of Makir of the tribe of Manasseh conquered Gilead
  5) The people of Jair—a clan of Manasseh—conquered many of the cities: Called them Havvoth Jair[DS14]
  6) A man named Nobah captured Kenath[DS15] & the surrounding villages: Named them after himself[DS16]

DIVISION IV

THE PREPARATION FOR THE MARCH INTO THE PROMISED LAND, 26:1–36:13

G. The Settlement, East of the Jordan River: A Picture of Compromise, Selfishness, Covetousness, Disloyalty, and Half-Hearted Commitment, 32:1-42

(32:1-42) **Introduction**: compromising with worldliness can destroy a person. Compromise can put us in jeopardy and endanger us. Compromise can discredit us and put us under suspicion. Compromise can ruin, weaken, and destroy us. The things of the world attract us, appealing to the lust of the eyes, the lust of the flesh, and the pride of life. If we compromise with the things of this world, they will often enslave us, putting us in bondage to them. This is always true with the things of the world, things such as…

- drugs
- alcohol
- illicit sex
- gluttony
- pornography
- lust
- covetousness
- greed
- power
- fame
- false worship
- profanity
- indulgence
- a spirit of disrespect

Compromise with worldliness always weakens us, leading to disloyalty and half-hearted commitments. This is what happened in the present passage of Scripture. The Israelites were camped by the Jordan River right across from the great city of Jericho. They were poised, almost ready to cross the Jordan into the promised land, when two tribes declared their desire to stay behind. Their proposal was a devastating compromise, a compromise to accept an inheritance in the world instead of the inheritance of the promised land. This is the important subject of the Scripture.

The Settlement East of the Jordan River: A Picture of Compromise, Selfishness, Covetousness, Disloyalty, and Half-Hearted Commitment, 32:1-42.

1. The compromise of two tribes: a picture of selfishness, covetousness, disloyalty—half-hearted commitment (vv.1-5).
2. The angry reaction of Moses: a charge of disloyalty and half-hearted commitment (vv.6-15).

NUMBERS 32:1-42

3. The selfish insistence of the two tribes and the forced compromise permitted (vv.16-27).
4. The agreement with the two compromising tribes publicly declared and the territory assigned (vv.28-42).

1 (32:1-5) **Selfishness, Example of—Covetousness, Example of—Compromise, Example of—Disloyalty, Example of—Disunity, Example of—Tribe of Reuben, Location of—Tribe of Gad, Location of—Israel, Tribes of, Location of**: there was the compromise of the two tribes. This is a picture of selfishness, covetousness, disloyalty—a half-hearted commitment to the LORD and to the other tribes of Israel. Remember, the Israelites had been camped for some months in the plains of Moab by the River Jordan, right across from the great city of Jericho. They had conquered much of the land east of the Jordan River, including the land of the Amorites, the land of Bashan, and the land of the Midianites. They were sitting there in the comfort and security of conquerors. They and their livestock were enjoying the beauty, tranquility and fruitfulness of the roaming pasture lands and the production of fertile soil. Then it happened: the value and potential of this land began to prey upon the minds of several tribes, the tribes of Reuben, Gad, and half of the tribe of Manasseh.

a. These tribes saw and coveted the fertile land of the nations they had conquered. The fertility of the land was obviously as rich as a person could ever desire. The tribes of Reuben and Gad had large herds and flocks of livestock. At some point some of the leaders began to covet the surrounding land. They knew that East Jordan—the land they coveted—was outside Canaan, was not a part of the promised land of God. The south boundary of the promised land began at the Sea of Galilee and stretched northward along the Jordan River. The Jordan River was the eastern frontier of the promised land of Canaan (v.34:3, 12; see outline and note—Nu. 34:2-15 for more discussion). However, this fact did not stop these two tribes from desiring the land as their own.

⇒ Selfishly, they saw the land, that it was very fertile and suitable for livestock (v.1).
⇒ Selfishly, they focused their eyes upon the land, and converted it.
⇒ Selfishly, they were willing to compromise in order to secure the land.

After some time these two tribes sent representatives to Moses and the other leaders, requesting that the land of East Jordan be given them as their inheritance (v.2-5). They stated that it was God who had led them to conquer the land of the East Jordan. They pointed out that the conquered land was fertile, that it would make good pastureland for their livestock; therefore they wanted this land as their possession. They then made a statement that exposed hearts of disloyalty to God and to the other tribes, hearts that exposed half-hearted commitment to the call of God and to the promised land: they did not want to cross over the Jordan with the other tribes to fight for the promised land (v.5). These two tribes were not only guilty of compromise by their desire for an inheritance outside the promised land. They were also guilty of disloyalty and of half-hearted commitment. They did not want to help the other tribes as the tribes struggled to gain their inheritance, as they fought to conquer the enemies of the promised land. These two tribes were guilty of compromise: they had been gripped by selfishness, covetousness, and disloyalty. They had only a half-hearted commitment to God and to the other tribes, only a half-hearted commitment to the promised land.

Thought 1. God warns a person against compromise. Compromising with the world is sin. Far too many of us lose sight of the promised land of heaven and begin to focus upon the world. We look at the world and see what it has to offer and we begin to covet...
• the pleasures and bright lights of the world
• the stimulations and excitements of the world
• the comforts and recreations of the world
• the properties and land of the world
• the money and wealth of the world
• the possessions and provisions of the world

Covetousness and greed set in and begin consuming our hearts. We want more and more and soon, we lose sight of the promised land of heaven. By focusing upon the things of the world instead of the things of God, we compromise with the world. We accept a lesser inheritance, far fewer riches than what the promised land of heaven has to offer. We become entangled with the things of the world. We compromise and become selfish, covetous, and disloyal to God and to other believers, all because of our attraction to the world and its things. Worldliness stands opposed to God and to the kingdom of heaven. This is the reason God warns us against worldliness.

> **What good will it be for a man if he gains the whole world, yet forfeits his soul? Or what can a man give in exchange for his soul? (Mt. 16:26)**
> **Be careful, or your hearts will be weighed down with dissipation, drunkenness and the anxieties of life, and that day will close on you unexpectedly like a trap. (Lu. 21:34)**
> **Do not conform any longer to the pattern of this world, but be transformed by the renewing of your mind. Then you will be able to test and approve what God's will is—his good, pleasing and perfect will. (Ro. 12:2)**
> **Those who use the things of the world, as if not engrossed in them. For this world in its present form is passing away. (1 Co. 7:31)**
> **As for you, you were dead in your transgressions and sins, in which you used to live when you followed the ways of this world and of the ruler of the kingdom of the air, the spirit who is now at work in those who are disobedient. All of us also lived among them at one time, gratifying the cravings of our sinful nature and following its desires and thoughts. Like the rest, we were by nature objects of wrath. (Ep. 2:1-3)**
> **Set your minds on things above, not on earthly things. (Col. 3:2)**
> **No one serving as a soldier gets involved in civilian affairs—he wants to please his commanding officer. (2 Ti. 2:4)**
> **For Demas, because he loved this world, has deserted me and has gone to Thessalonica. Crescens has gone to Galatia, and Titus to Dalmatia. (2 Ti. 4:10)**
> **It teaches us to say "No" to ungodliness and worldly passions, and to live self-controlled,**

upright and godly lives in this present age, while we wait for the blessed hope—the glorious appearing of our great God and Savior, Jesus Christ. (Tit. 2:12-13)

By faith Moses, when he had grown up, refused to be known as the son of Pharaoh's daughter. He chose to be mistreated along with the people of God rather than to enjoy the pleasures of sin for a short time. (He. 11:24-25)

You adulterous people, don't you know that friendship with the world is hatred toward God? Anyone who chooses to be a friend of the world becomes an enemy of God. (Js. 4:4)

Do not love the world or anything in the world. If anyone loves the world, the love of the Father is not in him. For everything in the world—the cravings of sinful man, the lust of his eyes and the boasting of what he has and does—comes not from the Father but from the world. (1 Jn. 2:15-16)

They rejected his decrees and the covenant he had made with their fathers and the warnings he had given them. They followed worthless idols and themselves became worthless. They imitated the nations around them although the LORD had ordered them, "Do not do as they do," and they did the things the LORD had forbidden them to do. (2 K. 17:15)

2 (32:6-15) **Disunity, Example of—Half-hearted, Example of—Commitment, Half-hearted, Example of**: there was the angry reaction of Moses against the representatives of Gad and Reuben. He charged them with a spirit of disunity, with having a half-hearted commitment to God and to the other tribes. This was a severe rebuke of the two tribes. Moses was burning with anger because of their willingness to compromise and their unwillingness to cross over the Jordan with the other tribes to fight for the promised land. In a rage of anger, he charged them with disloyalty and issued a strong warning to them: they were as guilty of disloyalty as their fathers were at Kadesh Barnea and were on the verge of arousing God's anger and judgment even as their fathers had.

a. Note the charge of disloyalty against the tribe of Reuben and Gad: they wanted to sit while the others fought to conquer the promised land. Their sitting would discourage the people of God from crossing over into the promised land. Their desire for comfort and ease was going to influence the lives of many others, discouraging them from continuing on and persevering until they secured their inheritance. This act of disloyalty was dangerous, a threat to the very survival of God's people. They all might begin to desire the ease and comfort of the land outside the promised land of God. They all might begin to compromise and give up the struggle against the enemies of the promised land. It would be far easier to accept the ease and comfort outside the promised land than to cross over the Jordan and have to fight for one's inheritance. This was the threat of this dangerous proposal being made by the two tribes.

b. Note their guilt: they were guilty of the same sins committed by the ten spies at Kadesh Barnea, that is, the sins of unbelief, disloyalty, and half-hearted commitment (vv.8-13). By reviewing the story of the ten unfaithful spies, Moses was issuing a strong warning to these two tribes.

1) The ten spies had discouraged the former generation from entering the promised land. This was exactly what these two tribes were in danger of doing: discouraging the other tribes from entering the promised land (v.9).
2) The spies aroused the LORD's anger against them and against the people (vv.10-13). God judged the people, not allowing one person twenty years old or older to enter the promised land. There were only two exceptions to this judgment: Caleb and Joshua. God's anger had burned against the ten spies and the people because of their disloyalty and half-hearted commitment.

c. The sins of these two tribes were about to bring the very same consequences upon the people of God (vv.14-15). Note what Moses called them: they were a *brood of sinners* who were arousing the LORD's anger even more than their fathers. If they turned away from following God into the promised land, they would cause disunity, cause the people to be disloyal to the LORD. This disunity and disloyalty would cause God to chastise the people and they would personally be responsible.

Thought 1. God warns us against comfort and ease. He has called us to a life of commitment, wholehearted commitment. We are engaged in a spiritual warfare, struggling against the enemies of this life, enemies that keep us out of the promised land:

⇒ compromise ⇒ neglect
⇒ covetousness ⇒ ignorance
⇒ disloyalty ⇒ comfort and ease
⇒ selfishness ⇒ worldliness
⇒ half-hearted commitment ⇒ lust of the eyes
⇒ unbelief ⇒ worldly desires
⇒ indifference ⇒ indulgence
  ⇒ self-gratification

The enemies of life and of the promised land are many and varied. God warns us: we must conquer these enemies and press on to the promised land. We must not seek the comfort and ease of this world, not compromise with worldliness. We must press on to secure the great inheritance God has promised us.

But everyone who hears these words of mine and does not put them into practice is like a foolish man who built his house on sand. The rain came down, the streams rose, and the winds blew and beat against that house, and it fell with a great crash. (Mt. 7:26-27)

Because of the increase of wickedness, the love of most will grow cold, but he who stands firm to the end will be saved. (Mt. 24:12-13)

That servant who knows his master's will and does not get ready or does not do what his master wants will be beaten with many blows. (Lu. 12:47)

What good is it, my brothers, if a man claims to have faith but has no deeds? Can such faith save him? (Js. 2:14)

Anyone, then, who knows the good he ought to do and doesn't do it, sins. (Js. 4:17)

So Joshua said to the Israelites: "How long will you wait before you begin to take possession of the land that the LORD, the

God of your fathers, has given you?" (Jos. 18:3)

He did what was right in the eyes of the LORD, but not wholeheartedly. (2 Chr. 25:2)

We have endured much ridicule from the proud, much contempt from the arrogant. (Ps. 123:4)

You women who are so complacent, rise up and listen to me; you daughters who feel secure, hear what I have to say! In little more than a year you who feel secure will tremble; the grape harvest will fail, and the harvest of fruit will not come. Tremble, you complacent women; shudder, you daughters who feel secure! Strip off your clothes, put sackcloth around your waists. (Is. 32:9-11)

A curse on him who is lax in doing the LORD's work! A curse on him who keeps his sword from bloodshed! (Je. 48:10)

Woe to you who are complacent in Zion, and to you who feel secure on Mount Samaria, you notable men of the foremost nation, to whom the people of Israel come! (Am. 6:1)

3 (32:16-27) **Compromise—Half-hearted—Commitment, Half-hearted**: there was the selfish insistence of the two tribes and the forced compromise permitted. The representatives from the compromising tribes were most likely shaken at the angry reaction and the severe charge of disloyalty by Moses. Apparently, the two tribes requested permission to withdraw and reconsider their proposal. They just were not willing to lose out on the property: a passion, a covetousness had gripped their hearts for the land of the East Jordan. Within their own minds, they had to figure out some way, some modification to their proposal that Moses would accept. They had to work out a compromise and insist upon it. This was exactly what they did. At some point they returned and made the following modified promises to Moses, a compromised proposal.

a. The compromising tribes insisted on the right to inherit the land, to build pens for their livestock and fortified cities for their families (v.16).

b. In return for the right to inherit the land, they would make two strong promises to Moses and the rest of the tribes.

  1) They would fight with the other tribes. They would actually take the lead in battle until the other tribes secured their inheritance. They just wanted their families protected and their cities fortified while they were fighting off then they would not return until all the people of Israel had received their inheritance. They knew that they were just as accountable as the other tribes for fighting against the enemies of the promised land. In no way would they shirk their duty until all the enemies of the promised land had been defeated and conquered. Later history shows that these two tribes did exactly what they had promised (Jos. 4:12-13; 22:1f).

  3) They personally would not lay claim to any inheritance on the other side of the Jordan. Their inheritance would be on the east side of the Jordan River, not on the west side, not in the promised land of God (see 34:1-12).

c. Moses was forced to accept the compromise proposal. What more could he do? The two compromising tribes were insisting that their modified promises, their compromised proposal be accepted (vv.20-27).

  1) Moses therefore granted their request in order to maintain the unity of the people (vv.20-22). However the two compromising tribes must fulfill their promise: they must join the others in fighting until the LORD had defeated His enemies, the enemies who would oppose His people entering the promised land. The two compromising tribes could then return and claim the East Jordan as their possession.

  2) But note that Moses issued a strong warning to the two compromising tribes: if they failed to keep their promises, they could rest assured: "Your sin will find you out." The sin of these two compromising tribes did eventually find them out and brought terrible judgment upon them time and time again. By choosing to remain outside the promised land, they were tempted more and more to compromise with the surrounding nations. Moreover, it was far easier for them to be attacked by the enemies of God's people. This is seen time and again in the later history of these compromising tribes (Jud. 10:6-9; 10:17-18; 1 K. 22:3; 2 K. 10:32-33; 15:27-29; 1 Chr. 5:18-26).

  3) Moses then gave two charges to these compromising tribes: they were to go build cities and pens for their families and livestock, but they were to make absolutely sure that they fulfilled their promises.

  4) The two compromising tribes repeated their promises and the conditions of the agreement. They would do just what they had said: their women and children would remain in the cities of Gilead with their livestock while they every soldier among them—would cross over Jordan and fight the enemies of the promised land. This would do for the LORD, just as He had commanded (vv.25-27).

Thought 1. The compromising tribes were determined to go their own way. They wanted the inheritance on the east side of the Jordan. They did not want to cross over the Jordan into the promised land. They liked what they saw where they were, and they wanted what they saw.

This is just like so many people today: they are determined to go their own way instead of God's way. They like what they see out in the world, and they compromise with the world. But God warns us all: "Your sin will find you out." Compromise and sin will be exposed. It cannot be hidden. What we sow, we will reap. This happened to the compromising tribes and it will happen to any of us who compromise with the world and its sin.

There is nothing concealed that will not be disclosed, or hidden that will not be made known. (Lu. 12:2)

Therefore judge nothing before the appointed time; wait till the Lord comes. He will bring to light what is hidden in darkness and will expose the motives of men's hearts. At that time each will receive his praise from God. (1 Co. 4:5)

Do not be deceived: God cannot be mocked. A man reaps what he sows. (Ga. 6:7)

But if you fail to do this, you will be sinning against the LORD; and you may be sure that your sin will find you out. (Nu. 32:23)

If I sinned, you would be watching me and would not let my offense go unpunished. (Jb. 10:14)

Surely then you will count my steps but not keep track of my sin. (Jb. 14:16)

The heavens will expose his guilt; the earth will rise up against him. (Jb. 20:27)

His malice may be concealed by deception, but his wickedness will be exposed in the assembly. (Pr. 26:26)

For God will bring every deed into judgment, including every hidden thing, whether it is good or evil. (Ec. 12:14)

"Although you wash yourself with soda and use an abundance of soap, the stain of your guilt is still before me," declares the Sovereign LORD. (Je. 2:22)

My eyes are on all their ways; they are not hidden from me, nor is their sin concealed from my eyes. (Je. 16:17)

But I know what is going through your mind. (Eze. 11:5)

But they do not realize that I remember all their evil deeds. Their sins engulf them; they are always before me. (Ho. 7:2)

4 (32:28-42) **Reuben, Territory of—Gad, Territory of—Manasseh, Half-tribe of, Territory of**: the agreement with the two compromising tribes was publicly declared and the territory was assigned to them. What then happened was a legal and binding contract between the two compromising tribes and the rest of Israel.

a. The agreement was declared by Moses to all the leadership of Israel. This included Eleazar the priest, Joshua the son of Nun, and all the tribal leaders of Israel (vv.28-30). If the two compromising tribes crossed over the Jordan and joined the other tribes in subduing the promised land, they were to be given the land of Gilead as their inheritance. But the two compromising tribes were strongly warned: if they did not cross over the Jordan to fight the enemies of God's people, they had to accept an inheritance inside the promised land.

b. The two compromising tribes then made a public declaration to all the leadership (vv.31-32): they would obey the LORD and cross over to fight against the enemies of the promised land. Their inheritance would be on the east side of the Jordan.

c. The territory was then assigned to the two compromising tribes and to the half-tribe of Manasseh (vv.33-42). This is the first time the half-tribe of Manasseh has been mentioned as being a part of the compromise proposal. Most likely they initially feared approaching Moses with the other two tribes, so they waited until the compromise proposal had been accepted before they joined in the contract agreement.

1) The territory included the lands that had been conquered from Sihon King of the Amorites and from King Og of Bashan (v.33).
2) The Gadites rebuilt nine cities, fortified them, and built pens for their livestock (vv.34-36). Obviously these were exciting and joyful days even for these compromising tribes. Individuals and families are usually most happy when they are working together on projects such as building their own homes. The people of Israel had not owned land nor had homes for generations. Now for the first time they possessed land and were in the process of constructing their homes. What an exciting and joyful occasion this must have been for them.
3) The Reubenites rebuilt and renamed six cities (vv.37-38). In some cases the old names of the cities had been named after false gods such as Baal; therefore the people of God felt compelled to change their names.
4) The descendants of Makir of the tribe of Manasseh conquered Gilead (vv.39-40).
5) The people of Jair—a clan of Manasseh—conquered many of the cities and settlements of Gilead. These they called Havvoth Jair (v.41).
6) A man named Nobah captured Kenath and the surrounding villages. These he named Nobah, after himself (v.42).

Thought 1. The lesson to see in this point is the promise of the compromising tribes: they would obey the LORD (v.31). They promised that they would cross over and fight with the other tribes against the enemies of the promised land.

The one thing God demands of every believer is obedience. To obey is the supreme demand of God. Obeying God means more to Him than sacrifice, even the sacrifice of one's life to Him. When we declare that we are sacrificing our lives to God, this promise is only profession—only words. If we are sincere in the sacrifice of our lives, we prove our sincerity by obedience. It is the obedience that matters to God, not our words of promise. Our promise is proven by our obedience. It is the obedience that God is after. This was true with these compromising tribes, and it is also true with us. They clearly stated that they would obey the LORD when they were not obeying the LORD in the first place. They were choosing to compromise with the world, to accept an inheritance outside the promised land. It is not our words that matter to God: it is our obedience. First and foremost, God demands that we obey Him.

But Samuel replied: "Does the LORD delight in burnt offerings and sacrifices as much as in obeying the voice of the LORD? To obey is better than sacrifice, and to heed is better than the fat of rams." (1 S. 15:22)

Not everyone who says to me, 'Lord, Lord,' will enter the kingdom of heaven, but only he who does the will of my Father who is in heaven. (Mt. 7:21)

Jesus replied, "If anyone loves me, he will obey my teaching. My Father will love him, and we will come to him and make our home with him." (Jn. 14:23)

If you obey my commands, you will remain in my love, just as I have obeyed my Father's commands and remain in his love. (Jn. 15:10)

You are my friends if you do what I command. (Jn. 15:14)

Blessed are those who wash their robes, that they may have the right to the tree of life and may go through the gates into the city. (Re. 22:14)

The LORD your God commands you this day to follow these decrees and laws; carefully observe them with all your heart and with all your soul. (De. 26:16)

Numbers 32:1-42

But if you do not obey the LORD, and if you rebel against his commands, his hand will be against you, as it was against your fathers. (1 S. 12:15)

DEEPER STUDY # 1
(Nu. 32:34-36) **Dibon, City of** (See also Dibon-Gad; Dimonah): it was located east of the Jordan River, about thirteen miles east of the Dead Sea. The Hebrew meaning of Dibon is *pining away* or *fence of tubes*. Dibon was the capital city of the Moabites (Nu. 21:21-31). It was rebuilt by the tribe of Gad and was later named Dibon-Gad.
See other Scripture references for study:
Nu. 21:30; Nu. 32:3; Nu. 33:45-46; Jos. 13:9; Jos. 13:17; Jos. 15:22; Ne. 11:25; Is. 15:2; Is. 15:9; Je. 48:18; Je. 48:22

DEEPER STUDY # 2
(Nu. 32:34-36) **Ataroth, City of**: it was located eight miles northwest of Dibon and eight miles east of the Dead Sea. The Hebrew meaning of Ataroth is *crowns*. It was rebuilt by the tribe of Gad (Nu. 32:3; Nu. 32:34). There is a different town on the border of Benjamin and Ephraim called Ataroth-addar (Jos. 16:2; Jos. 16:7). Also note that there is a different town called *Ataroth of the house of Joab* in the tribe of Judah, a city founded by the descendants of Salma (1 Chr. 2:54. See also Atroth-Beth-Joab.)
See other Scripture references for study:
Nu. 32:3; Jos. 16:2-3; Jos. 16:5; Jos. 16:7; Jos. 18:13; 1 Chr. 2:54

DEEPER STUDY # 3
(Nu. 32:34-36) **Aroer, City of**: it was located on the northern bank of the Arnon River, the southernmost town of Israel east of the Jordan River (Jos. 13:9). The Hebrew meaning of Aroer is *juniper* or *nudity*. It was the capital city of Shion, king of the Amorites (Jos. 12:2). Aroer was rebuilt by the tribe of Gad (Nu. 32:34).
See other Scripture references for study:
De. 2:36; De. 3:12; De. 4:48; Jos. 12:2; Jos. 13:9; Jos. 13:16; Jos. 13:25; Jud. 11:26; Jud. 11:33; 1 S. 30:28; 2 S. 24:5; 2 K. 10:33; 1 Chr. 5:8; Is. 17:2; Je. 48:19

DEEPER STUDY # 4
(Nu. 32:34-36) **Atroth Shophan, City of**: the location is unknown. It was rebuilt by the tribe of Gad.
See other Scripture references for study:
Nu. 32:35 (Only reference in Scripture)

DEEPER STUDY # 5
(Nu. 32:34-36) **Jazer, City of**: it was located east of the Jordan River, in or near Gilead, between Dibon and Nimrah. (See Map—Nu. 33:5-49, end of commentary.) The Hebrew meaning of Jazer is *may He help* or *helpful*. It was a former Amorite city state conquered by Israel on its march to the promised land. Jazer was rebuilt by the tribe of Gad (Nu. 32:35). It was later chosen to be a Levitical city (Jos. 21:39).
See other Scripture references for study:
Nu. 32:1; Nu. 32:3; Jos. 13:25; Jos. 21:39; 2 S. 24:5; 1 Chr. 6:81; 1 Chr. 26:31; Is. 16:8-9; Je. 48:32

DEEPER STUDY # 6
(Nu. 32:34-36) **Jogbehah, City of**: it was located east of the Jordan River. The Hebrew meaning of Jogbehah is *height, little hill* or *hillock*. It was rebuilt and settled by the tribe of Gad (Nu. 32:35). Gideon defeated the kings of Midian at Jogbehah (Jud. 8:11).
See other Scripture references for study:
Nu. 32:35; Jud. 8:11

DEEPER STUDY # 7
(Nu. 32:34-36) **Beth Nimrah, City of**: it was located east, about ten miles from the mouth of the Jordan River. The Hebrew meaning of Beth Nimrah is *house of the panther* or *house of the leopard*. Beth Nimrah was a fenced or fortified city (Nu. 32:36) It was rebuilt and settled by the tribe of Gad (Nu. 32:36).
See other Scripture references for study:
Nu. 32:3; Jos. 13:27

DEEPER STUDY # 8
(Nu. 32:34-36) **Beth Haran, City of** (See also Bethharam): it was located east of the Jordan River. The Hebrew meaning of Beth Haran is *house of height* or *built*. It was rebuilt and settled by the tribe of Gad (Nu. 32:36). Beth Haran was a fenced or fortified city (Nu. 32:36).
See other Scripture reference for study:
Jos. 13:27

DEEPER STUDY # 9
(Nu. 32:37-38) **Elealeh, City of**: it was located east of the Jordan River, a former town of the Amorites. The Hebrew meaning of Elealeh is *God has ascended*, *God went up*, or *high ground*. The tribe of Reuben asked Moses for this town. It was rebuilt, strengthened by the tribe of Reuben.
See other Scripture references for study:
Nu. 32:3; Is. 15:4; Is. 16:9; Je. 48:34

DEEPER STUDY # 10
(Nu. 32:37-38) **Kiriathaim, City of** (See also Kirjathaim; Kartan): it was located in the tribal territory of Naphtali (1 Chr. 6:76). The Hebrew meaning of Kiriathaim is *double city* or *two cities*. It was taken from the Amorites and assigned to the tribe of Reuben (Nu. 32:37; Jos. 13:9). Kiriathaim became a Levitical city and a city of refuge.
See other Scripture references for study:
Ge. 14:5; Nu. 32:37; Jos. 13:19; Jos. 21:32; 1 Chr. 6:76; Je. 48:1; Je. 48:23; Eze. 25:9

DEEPER STUDY # 11
(Nu. 32:37-38) **Nebo, City of**: it was located east of the Jordan River, southwest of Heshbon. The Hebrew meaning of Nebo is *height*. It was a Moabite city assigned to the tribe of Reuben.
See other Scripture references for study:
Nu. 32:3; 1 Chr. 5:8; Is. 15:2; Is.46:1; Je. 48:1; Je. 48:22

DEEPER STUDY # 12
(Nu. 32:37-38) Baal Meon, City of: it was located east of the Jordan River, toward the northern border of the tribe of Reuben, about nine miles east of the Dead Sea. The

Hebrew meaning of Baal Meon is *lord of the residence, dwelling* or *Baal of the residence*. It was rebuilt by the tribe of Reuben and renamed (Nu. 32:38).
See other Scripture references for study:
Jos. 13:17; 1 Chr. 5:8; Eze. 25:9

DEEPER STUDY # 13
(Nu. 32:37-38) **Sibmah, City of (See also Sebam; Shibmah)**: it was located east of the Jordan River. The Hebrew meaning of Sibmah is *cold, coolness* or *high*. It was assigned to the tribe of Reuben and rebuilt by the tribe of Reuben.
See other Scripture references for study:
Nu. 32:3; Jos. 13:19; Is. 16:8-9; Je. 48:32

DEEPER STUDY # 14
(Nu. 32:41) **Havvoth Jair, City of (See also Havoth Jair)**: it was located in Bashan, east of the Jordan River.

The Hebrew meaning of Havvoth Jair is *hut, hamlets, tents of Jair*. There was a district of villages which Jair, the son of Manasseh, captured and called by his name (Nu. 32:41).
See other Scripture references for study:
De. 3:14; Jud. 10:4; 1 Chr. 2:23

DEEPER STUDY # 15
(Nu. 32:42) **Kenath, City of**: it was located in eastern Gilead. The Hebrew meaning of Kenath is uncertain.
See other Scripture reference for study:
1 Chr. 2:23

DEEPER STUDY # 16
(Nu. 32:42) **Nobah, City of**: it was located in eastern Gilead. The Hebrew meaning of Nobah is *barking* or *howling*. It was Nobah, the leader of the tribe of Manasseh, who conquered Keneth and renamed it after himself.
See other Scripture reference for study:
Jud. 8:11

TYPES, SYMBOLS, AND PICTURES
(Numbers 32:1-42)

Historical Term	Type or Picture (Scriptural Basis for Each)	Life Application for Today's Believer	Biblical Application
The Compromise of Gad and Reuben Nu. 32:1-42	The compromise of Gad and Reuben is a picture of selfishness, covetousness, disloyalty and half-hearted commitment. Compromise with worldliness always weakens us, leading to disloyalty and half-hearted commitments. This is what happened in the present passage of Scripture. The Israelites were camped by the Jordan River right across from the great city of Jericho. They were poised, almost ready to cross the Jordan into the promised land, when two tribes declared their desire to stay behind. Their proposal was a devastating compromise, a compromise to accept an inheritance in East Jordan, an inheritance in the world instead of the inheritance of the promised land. "If we have found favor in your eyes," they said, "let this land be given to your servants as our possession. Do not make us cross the Jordan." (Nu. 32:5)	Compromising with worldliness can destroy a person. Compromise can put us in jeopardy and endanger us. Compromise can discredit us and put us under suspicion. Compromise can ruin, weaken, and destroy us. The things of the world attract us, appealing to the lust of the eyes, the lust of the flesh, and the pride of life. If we compromise with the things of this world, they will often enslave us, putting us in bondage to them.	*What good will it be for a man if he gains the whole world, yet forfeits his soul? Or what can a man give in exchange for his soul?* (Mt. 16:26) *Be careful, or your hearts will be weighed down with dissipation, drunkenness and the anxieties of life, and that day will close on you unexpectedly like a trap.* (Lu. 21:34) *Set your minds on things above, not on earthly things.* (Col. 3:2) *For Demas, because he loved this world, has deserted me and has gone to Thessalonica. Crescens has gone to Galatia, and Titus to Dalmatia.* (2 Ti. 4:10) *It teaches us to say "No" to ungodliness and worldly passions, and to live self-controlled, upright and godly lives in this present age.* (Tit. 2:12) *You adulterous people, don't you know that friendship with the world is hatred toward God? Anyone who chooses to be a friend of the world becomes an enemy of God.* (Js. 4:4)

NUMBERS 33:1-56

CHAPTER 33

H. The Review of the Wilderness Wanderings & a Strong Charge to Take Possession of the Promised Land: A Picture of God's Faithfulness & Man's Failure, 33:1-56

1. **The faithfulness of God in leading & guiding His people**
   a. God led His people out of Egypt (a symbol of the world)
      1) Led orderly by divisions
      2) Led by Moses & Aaron
   b. God led Moses to record the stages or camps of the march to the promised land
   c. God led His people to march out triumphantly—as a great nation of people
      1) On the 15th of the first month
      2) In full view of all Egyptians
         - As they were burying their firstborn
         - God had judged them

2. **The wilderness wanderings: A picture of man's failure—40 years of no progress**[1]
   a. The camps from Rameses to Mt. Sinai: Left Rameses—Egypt
      1) Succoth (Ex. 13:20)
      2) Etham (Ex. 13:20): First reference to the cloud
      3) Pi Hahiroth (Ex. 14:2, 9): The campsite from which they crossed the Red Sea (Ex. 14:1f)
      4) Marah (Ex. 15:23) Bitter waters sweetened by God
      5) Elim (Ex. 15:27): An oasis in the desert
      6) The Red Sea: Not mentioned as a camp
      7) Desert of Sin (Ex. 16:1)
      8) Dophkah: No reference in Exodus
      9) Alush: No reference in Exodus
      10) Rephidim (Ex. 17:1): No water to drink

Here are the stages in the journey of the Israelites when they came out of Egypt by divisions under the leadership of Moses and Aaron.
2 At the LORD's command Moses recorded the stages in their journey. This is their journey by stages:
3 The Israelites set out from Rameses on the fifteenth day of the first month, the day after the Passover. They marched out boldly in full view of all the Egyptians,
4 Who were burying all their firstborn, whom the LORD had struck down among them; for the LORD had brought judgment on their gods.
5 The Israelites left Rameses and camped at Succoth.
6 They left Succoth and camped at Etham, on the edge of the desert.
7 They left Etham, turned back to Pi Hahiroth, to the east of Baal Zephon, and camped near Migdol.
8 They left Pi Hahiroth and passed through the sea into the desert, and when they had traveled for three days in the Desert of Etham, they camped at Marah.
9 They left Marah and went to Elim, where there were twelve springs and seventy palm trees, and they camped there.
10 They left Elim and camped by the Red Sea.
11 They left the Red Sea and camped in the Desert of Sin.
12 They left the Desert of Sin and camped at Dophkah.
13 They left Dophkah and camped at Alush.
14 They left Alush and camped at Rephidim, where there was no water for the people to drink.
15 They left Rephidim and camped in the Desert of Sinai.
16 They left the Desert of Sinai and camped at Kibroth Hattaavah.
17 They left Kibroth Hattaavah and camped at Hazeroth.
18 They left Hazeroth and camped at Rithmah.
19 They left Rithmah and camped at Rimmon Perez.
20 They left Rimmon Perez and camped at Libnah.
21 They left Libnah and camped at Rissah.
22 They left Rissah and camped at Kehelathah.
23 They left Kehelathah and camped at Mount Shepher.
24 They left Mount Shepher and camped at Haradah.
25 They left Haradah and camped at Makheloth.
26 They left Makheloth and camped at Tahath.
27 They left Tahath and camped at Terah.
28 They left Terah and camped at Mithcah.
29 They left Mithcah and camped at Hashmonah.
30 They left Hashmonah and camped at Moseroth.
31 They left Moseroth and camped at Bene Jaakan.
32 They left Bene Jaakan and camped at Hor Haggidgad.
33 They left Hor Haggidgad and camped at Jotbathah.
34 They left Jotbathah and camped at Abronah.
35 They left Abronah and camped at Ezion Geber.
36 They left Ezion Geber and camped at Kadesh, in the Desert of Zin.
37 They left Kadesh and camped at Mount Hor, on the border of Edom.
38 At the LORD's command Aaron the priest went up Mount Hor, where he died on the first day of the fifth month of the fortieth year after the Israelites came out of Egypt.
39 Aaron was a hundred and twenty-three years old when he died on Mount Hor.
40 The Canaanite king of Arad, who lived in the Negev of Canaan, heard that the Israelites were coming.
41 They left Mount Hor and

11) Desert of Sinai (Ex. 19:2): The law was given
   b. The camps from Mt. Sinai to Mt. Hor
      1) Kibroth Hattaavah (Nu. 11:34): Was 3 days from Sinai
      2) Hazeroth (Nu. 11:35; 12:16; De. 1:1)
      3) Rithmah: No other reference
      4) Rimmon Perez: No other reference
      5) Libnah: No other reference
      6) Rissah: No other reference
      7) Kehelathah: No other reference
      8) Mount Shepher: No other reference
      9) Haradah: No other reference
      10) Makheloth: No other reference
      11) Tahath: No other reference
      12) Terah: No other reference
      13) Mithcah: No other reference
      14) Hashmonah: No other reference
      15) Moseroth (De. 10:6): Place of Aaron's death (see v.38)
      16) Bene Jaakan (Ge. 36:27; De. 10:6; 1 Chr. 1:42)
      17) Hor-Hagidgad (De. 10:7)
      18) Jotbathah (De. 10:7)
      19) Abronah: No other reference
      20) Ezion Geber (De. 2:8; 1 K. 9:26): A well-known oasis
      21) Kadesh (Nu. 13:21): Place where 12 spies were sent out & 10 rebelled
   c. The campsite at Mt. Hor
      1) God took Aaron home to heaven while on Mt. Hor: Died on the 1st day of the 5th month, 40 years after Israel's deliverance (Nu. 20:23-29)
      2) God gave Aaron a long, fruitful life: 123 years
      3) God was faithful & gave His people their first military victory at Mt. Hor (Nu. 21:1-3)
   d. The camps from Mt. Hor to

---

[1] The brief notes and Scripture cross-references for the campsites were gleaned from *The Expositor's Bible Commentary*, pp. 987-990.

NUMBERS 33:1-56

Outline	Scripture	Scripture (cont.)	Commentary
the Jordan River across from Jericho 1) Zalmonah: No other reference 2) Punon (Ge. 36:41; 1 Chr. 1:52) 3) Oboth (Nu. 21:10-11) 4) Iye Abarim (Nu. 21:11): A place on the border of Moab 5) Dibon Gad (Nu. 21:30; 32:3): Was in Moab 6) Almon Diblathaim (Je. 48:22) 7) Mountains of Abarim, near Nebo (Nu. 27:12): A range of mountains in NW Moab just NE of the Dead Sea 8) The plains of Moab by the Jordan across from Jericho: • The final staging point for marching into the promised land • The camp stretched from Beth Jeshimoth to Abel Shittim: Over five miles 3. The charge & warning of God to take possession of the promised land: A picture of spiritual conquest & rest a. The strong charge: Five strong commands are given	camped at Zalmonah. 42 They left Zalmonah and camped at Punon. 43 They left Punon and camped at Oboth. 44 They left Oboth and camped at Iye Abarim, on the border of Moab. 45 They left Iyim and camped at Dibon Gad. 46 They left Dibon Gad and camped at Almon Diblathaim. 47 They left Almon Diblathaim and camped in the mountains of Abarim, near Nebo. 48 They left the mountains of Abarim and camped on the plains of Moab by the Jordan across from Jericho. 49 There on the plains of Moab they camped along the Jordan from Beth Jeshimoth to Abel Shittim. 50 On the plains of Moab by the Jordan across from Jericho the LORD said to Moses, 51 "Speak to the Israelites and say to them: 'When you	cross the Jordan into Canaan, 52 Drive out all the inhabitants of the land before you. Destroy all their carved images and their cast idols, and demolish all their high places. 53 Take possession of the land and settle in it, for I have given you the land to possess. 54 Distribute the land by lot, according to your clans. To a larger group give a larger inheritance, and to a smaller group a smaller one. Whatever falls to them by lot will be theirs. Distribute it according to your ancestral tribes. 55 " 'But if you do not drive out the inhabitants of the land, those you allow to remain will become barbs in your eyes and thorns in your sides. They will give you trouble in the land where you will live. 56 And then I will do to you what I plan to do to them.' "	1) To drive out all the enemies who opposed their entering the promised land 2) To destroy all their idols 3) To demolish all the false worship sites 4) To take possession of the promised land & settle it: It was the gift of God, their inheritance 5) To distribute the land by sacred lot • Give a larger inheritance to the larger tribes • Give a smaller inheritance to the smaller tribes b. The strong warning: A failure to drive out the enemies of the land would result in severe judgment 1) The enemies would be constant trouble: Like splinters in one's eye & thorns in one's side 2) The LORD would dispossess & remove His people from the promised land

DIVISION IV

THE PREPARATION FOR THE MARCH INTO THE PROMISED LAND, 26:1–36:13

H. The Review of the Wilderness Wanderings and a Strong Charge to Take Possession of the Promised Land: A Picture of God's Faithfulness and Man's Failure, 33:1-56

(33:1-56) **Introduction—Sin, Enslavement to—Death, Enslavement to—Man, Unbelief of**: man is enslaved to sin and death. In fact, two things are certain in this life: man sins and man dies. But God is faithful: the provision to be delivered from sin and death has been offered to man. No longer do we have to be gripped by sin; neither do we have to die. There is strong deliverance from sin and triumphant, victorious deliverance from death. This is one message in the present Scripture, but there is also another message: man's failure. God has been faithful in making every provision necessary to save man and to give him an abundant life. A life that overflows with love, joy, and peace is now available to man. But man does not believe God. Man curses God, doing the unimaginable, the incomprehensible—taking God's name in vain. But this is not all: man questions and even denies the very existence of God. But even this is not all: the vast majority of people reject God, ignoring and neglecting Him, following after the false worship of gods created by their own imaginations. Man wallows around in unbelief, closing his eyes and refusing to believe the only living and true God, the LORD God Himself (Jehovah, Yahweh). And, tragically, man takes pride in his unbelief, sometimes even boasting and freely discussing his unbelief with others. Unbelief dooms a person to wander about in the wilderness of this world without the help of the only living and true God. An unbeliever does not have God's care, provision, protection, security, nor the indwelling assurance of living eternally with God face to face. Unbelief dooms a person to wander about in the wilderness of this world without the help and support of God. The person has only the help and support that other people can give him. Unbelief shuts God out of a person's life. This is the subject of this passage of Scripture: *The Review of the Wilderness Wanderings and a Strong Charge to Take Possession of the Promised Land: a Picture of God's Faithfulness and Man's Failure*, 33:1-56.

1. The faithfulness of God in leading and guiding His people (vv.1-4).
2. The wilderness wanderings: a picture of man's failure—40 years of no progress (vv.5-49).
3. The charge and warning of God to take possession of the promised land: a picture of spiritual conquest and rest (vv.50-56).

1 (33:1-4) **Faithfulness, of God—Wilderness Wanderings—Campsites, of Israel—Israel, Date of Deliverance**: there was the faithfulness of God in leading and guiding His people from Egyptian slavery. God delivered His people so they could begin their march to the promised land of God. The point of these few verses is clear: if God had the power to lead His people from Egyptian slavery, then He had the power to lead them *into* the promised land. God's guidance and leadership are clearly seen.

a. God led His people out of Egypt (a symbol of the world). He lead them to march out of Egypt like a mighty

NUMBERS 33:1-56

army, division by division, marching under the leadership of Moses and Aaron (v.1).

b. God led Moses to record the stages or campsites along the journey. They were marching to the promised land of God; therefore, it was important to have an accurate record of the events that took place along the journey.

c. God led His people to march out triumphantly—as a great nation of people (vv.3-4). The exact date that they marched out of Egypt is recorded: the fifteenth of the first month. Note the spirit in which they marched out: they marched out with a bold, courageous, and defiant spirit; not with a fearful, cowering, slavish spirit.

Thought 1. One of the strongest messages of Scripture is this: God is faithful. Day and night, night and day—God is faithful. God is faithful to save us from the enslavements of this world just as He saved Israel from the enslavement of Egypt. We are enslaved to sin and death. No person can keep from sinning nor from dying. We all sin and we all die. We are enslaved to sin and death. But God is faithful: He saves us from sin and death. But this is not all: just as God was faithful to lead and guide the Israelites, so He will lead and guide us to the promised land of heaven. This is the strong declaration of Scripture: God will not fail us. He will lead and guide us every step of the way as we march to the promised land of heaven.

> To shine on those living in darkness and in the shadow of death, to guide our feet into the path of peace. (Lu. 1:79)
>
> But when he, the Spirit of truth, comes, he will guide you into all truth. He will not speak on his own; he will speak only what he hears, and he will tell you what is yet to come. (Jn. 16:13)
>
> God, who has called you into fellowship with his Son Jesus Christ our Lord, is faithful. (1 Co. 1:9)
>
> Know therefore that the LORD your God is God; he is the faithful God, keeping his covenant of love to a thousand generations of those who love him and keep his commands. (De. 7:9)
>
> Remember how the LORD your God led you all the way in the desert these forty years, to humble you and to test you in order to know what was in your heart, whether or not you would keep his commands. (De. 8:2)
>
> Like an eagle that stirs up its nest and hovers over its young, that spreads its wings to catch them and carries them on its pinions. The LORD alone led him; no foreign god was with him. (De. 32:11-12)
>
> Praise be to the LORD, who has given rest to his people Israel just as he promised. Not one word has failed of all the good promises he gave through his servant Moses. (1 K. 8:56)
>
> He guides the humble in what is right and teaches them his way. (Ps. 25:9)
>
> Teach me your way, O LORD; lead me in a straight path because of my oppressors. (Ps. 27:11)
>
> For this God is our God for ever and ever; he will be our guide even to the end. (Ps. 48:14)
>
> You guide me with your counsel, and afterward you will take me into glory. (Ps. 73:24)
>
> You led your people like a flock by the hand of Moses and Aaron. (Ps. 77:20)
>
> If I rise on the wings of the dawn, if I settle on the far side of the sea, even there your hand will guide me, your right hand will hold me fast. (Ps. 139:9-10)
>
> Whether you turn to the right or to the left, your ears will hear a voice behind you, saying, "This is the way; walk in it." (Is. 30:21)
>
> I will lead the blind by ways they have not known, along unfamiliar paths I will guide them; I will turn the darkness into light before them and make the rough places smooth. These are the things I will do; I will not forsake them. (Is. 42:16)

2 (33:5-49) **Wilderness Wanderings, Failure During—Israel, Failure of—Unbelief, of Believers, Example of**: there was the wilderness wanderings of the Israelites. This is a picture of man's failure, of following after God for *forty long years* and making no progress. Remember, the Israelites had committed the terrible sin of unbelief against God. They had failed to trust the faithfulness of God in leading and guiding them. They had complained, grumbled, and murmured against God time and time again—all because of the hardships of life that confronted them as they marched to the promised land. They grumbled about the things that happened to them, complained because of the bad breaks they received. They felt not enough good things happened to them, that they did not receive enough of the good things of life. They blamed God for the bad and complained because the good was not good enough. Tragically, they refused to believe and trust God; they rebelled against God. They refused to follow His leadership and guidance. Consequently, they were condemned to wander about in the wilderness until the last of the first generation had died.

The following list of campsites covers the desert experience of the Israelites as they wandered about in the wilderness. As the campsites are studied, several difficulties arise. For example, some of the places are not recorded elsewhere in *Exodus* and *Numbers* (see v.19-29). However, other places that are mentioned in Numbers are not included here (for example, Taberah, 11:3; see 21:19). Other places given here are mentioned in *Deuteronomy*, but they are spelled differently (v.30-34 see De. 10:6-7).[2] It is difficult to know the exact location of some of the cities and campsites listed in the Scripture because some of the places no longer exist and others have changed names. Even if the name of a particular city has survived to the present day, it is actually attached to a different city or location.[3] Despite these problems, a map is being included to help the reader as he attempts to grasp the wilderness wanderings of the Israelites (see map of *The Desert or Wilderness Wanderings of Israel*—Nu. 33:5-49, p.332).

Thought 1. The wilderness wanderings would never have taken place but for one thing: unbelief. A spirit of unbelief gripped the hearts of the Israelites. They refused to believe and trust God. Unbelief is a

---
[2] *The Expositor's Bible Commentary.* Frank E. Gaebelein, Editor, p. 984.
[3] Gordon J. Wenham. *The Book of Numbers*, p.220.

terrible sin. It is an insult to God: an outrage, an abuse, a slap in the face of God. God promises to save His people, to lead and guide them to the promised land of heaven. He promises to give us victory, a conquering power over all the pitfalls and enemies of this life. Moreover, God promises to give us an abundant life, a life that overflows with love, joy, and peace—a life that is beyond comprehension. Every good thing and every gift that we ever experience come from the hand of God (Js. 1:17). All this is what makes unbelief such a terrible insult against God. Unbelief will keep us in the wilderness of this world, keep us out of the promised land of heaven. Unbelief means that the enemies of life will eventually conquer and gain the victory over us. Unbelief means that we will be enslaved by sin and someday be led into the grave of death. Unbelief means that we will face the terrifying judgment of God and be doomed to an eternity separated from God. Unbelief is the most devastating, destructive position a man can take. Unbelief doomed the Israelites to the wilderness wanderings for over forty years, doomed them to death in the wilderness. Not a single one escaped except Caleb and Joshua who believed and trusted God. All the unbelievers perished in the desert never knowing the victory of God over the enemies of this life. Again, not one of the unbelievers escaped. Unbelief will doom us to perish in the wilderness of this world and doom us to suffer the eternal judgment of God.

> **Whoever believes in him is not condemned, but whoever does not believe stands condemned already because he has not believed in the name of God's one and only Son. (Jn. 3:18)**
>
> **Whoever believes in the Son has eternal life, but whoever rejects the Son will not see life, for God's wrath remains on him. (Jn. 3:36)**
>
> **I told you that you would die in your sins; if you do not believe that I am the one I claim to be, you will indeed die in your sins. (Jn. 8:24)**
>
> **And so that all will be condemned who have not believed the truth but have delighted in wickedness. (2 Th. 2:12)**
>
> **See to it, brothers, that none of you has a sinful, unbelieving heart that turns away from the living God. (He. 3:12)**
>
> **Let us, therefore, make every effort to enter that rest, so that no one will fall by following their example of disobedience. (He. 4:11)**
>
> **Though you already know all this, I want to remind you that the Lord delivered his people out of Egypt, but later destroyed those who did not believe. (Jude 5)**

3 (33:50-56) **Warning, of God—Land, the Promised, Duty Toward—Spiritual Victory—Victory, Spiritual—Rest, Spiritual**: there was the charge and warning of God to take possession of the promised land. This was a picture of spiritual conquest and rest. Behind the Israelites lay the terrible tragedy of the wilderness wanderings, but now they sat on the plains of Moab by the Jordan River, directly across from the great city of Jericho. They sat there poised to enter the promised land. But before they could enter, a strong charge and warning had to be given to them.

a. Note the charge: five strong commands were given (vv.51-54).

1) The Israelites were to drive out all the enemies who opposed their entering the promised land (v.52). No unbeliever was to be allowed to live in the promised land. All the enemies who stood opposed to God were to be rejected. God's people were to build a new nation, a nation of people who lived holy lives, lives that were set apart to serve God. They were to live pure and righteous lives and be witnesses to the surrounding nations who lived around them. But the enemies who stood opposed to them and sought to keep God's people out of the promised land were to be destroyed. The promised land was to be the inheritance of God's people; therefore, the Israelites were to drive out all the enemies who opposed God and His people.

2) The Israelites were to destroy all the idols and false worship that were in the promised land (v.52). Any image and any false worship were to be destroyed. There is only one true and living God, the LORD God Himself (Jehovah, Yahweh). He and He alone is to be worshipped. False gods and false worship are nothing more than the creation of the imaginations of men. They have no life and can hear no prayer; neither can they help any person in time of need. Therefore, the images and idols of all false gods were to be destroyed as well as all false worship.

3) The Israelites were to demolish all the false worship sites in the promised land (v.52). No false worship whatsoever was to be allowed. So long as worship sites remained, there would be a tendency for the weak and wicked person to seek false worship in order to ease his conscience. For this reason, all the false worship sites were to be demolished.

4) The Israelites were to take possession of the promised land and settle it. It was the gift of God, their inheritance; therefore, they were not to fear the enemies who would confront them. They were to be courageous and march forth to conquer any who opposed God and their possession of the promised land (v.53).

5) The Israelites were to distribute the land by sacred lot. Remember, God controlled the roll of the sacred lots. By throwing the lots, there would be no partiality or favoritism shown in the distribution of the land; neither could there be a charge of favoritism or partiality. The larger tribes were to receive a larger inheritance, and the smaller tribes were to receive a smaller inheritance—all based upon population.

b. God issued a strong, strong warning: a failure to drive out the enemies of the land would result in severe judgment (vv.55-56). If the people of God failed to drive out the enemies, the enemies would be constant trouble for them. Note the descriptive picture given: the enemies would be like splinters in one's eye and thorns in one's side. They would be constant trouble, causing a constant flow of tears and flowing blood. But this was not all: the LORD Himself would dispossess and remove His people from the promised land (v.56). God would do to His people exactly what He planned to do to the enemies who stood opposed to Him. Severe judgment would fall upon His people: they would be expelled from the promised land of God.

NUMBERS 33:1-56

Thought 1. God's people are to live lives of separation. They are to live holy lives, lives that are totally set apart to God. They are to live righteous and pure lives, seeking to be conformed to the very image of Jesus Christ. This was the reason the Israelites were to drive out all the enemies of the promised land. And this is the reason the believer is to be separated to God, to live a life that is different and distinct from the immoral, lawless, and violent ways of the world. The believer is to be moral, not immoral; to be lawful, not lawless; to make peace, not violence. As the believer marches to the promised land of heaven, he is not to embrace the evil of the unbelievers of this world; rather, he is to be a witness to them. The holiness of God, His demand for righteousness and purity, is to be proclaimed. In all this the believer is to live a life of separation to God, not a life of worldliness. He is not to walk in the lies and deceit of this world but in the light and truth of God. His life is to be given over—totally separated and set apart—to the only living and true God, the LORD God Himself (Jehovah, Yahweh).

> To rescue us from the hand of our enemies, and to enable us to serve him without fear in holiness and righteousness before him all our days. (Lu. 1:74-75)
>
> If you belonged to the world, it would love you as its own. As it is, you do not belong to the world, but I have chosen you out of the world. That is why the world hates you. (Jn. 15:19)
>
> With many other words he warned them; and he pleaded with them, "Save yourselves from this corrupt generation." (Ac.2:40)
>
> But now I am writing you that you must not associate with anyone who calls himself a brother but is sexually immoral or greedy, an idolater or a slanderer, a drunkard or a swindler. With such a man do not even eat. (1 Co. 5:11)
>
> Do not be yoked together with unbelievers. For what do righteousness and wickedness have in common? Or what fellowship can light have with darkness? (2 Co. 6:14)
>
> "Therefore come out from them and be separate, says the Lord. Touch no unclean thing, and I will receive you. I will be a Father to you, and you will be my sons and daughters, says the Lord Almighty." (2 Co. 6:17-18)
>
> Since we have these promises, dear friends, let us purify ourselves from everything that contaminates body and spirit, perfecting holiness out of reverence for God. (2 Co. 7:1)
>
> Have nothing to do with the fruitless deeds of darkness, but rather expose them. (Ep. 5:11)
>
> In the name of the Lord Jesus Christ, we command you, brothers, to keep away from every brother who is idle and does not live according to the teaching you received from us. (2 Th. 3:6)
>
> Make every effort to live in peace with all men and to be holy; without holiness no one will see the Lord. (He. 12:14)
>
> But just as he who called you is holy, so be holy in all you do; for it is written: "Be holy, because I am holy." (1 Pe. 1:15-16)
>
> Since everything will be destroyed in this way, what kind of people ought you to be? You ought to live holy and godly lives as you look forward to the day of God and speed its coming. That day will bring about the destruction of the heavens by fire, and the elements will melt in the heat. But in keeping with his promise we are looking forward to a new heaven and a new earth, the home of righteousness. So then, dear friends, since you are looking forward to this, make every effort to be found spotless, blameless and at peace with him. (2 Pe. 3:11-14)
>
> Who will not fear you, O Lord, and bring glory to your name? For you alone are holy. All nations will come and worship before you, for your righteous acts have been revealed. (Re. 15:4)
>
> Do not follow the crowd in doing wrong. When you give testimony in a lawsuit, do not pervert justice by siding with the crowd. (Ex. 23:2)
>
> Be careful not to make a treaty with those who live in the land where you are going, or they will be a snare among you. (Ex. 34:12)
>
> I am the LORD who brought you up out of Egypt to be your God; therefore be holy, because I am holy. (Le. 11:45)
>
> Blessed is the man who does not walk in the counsel of the wicked or stand in the way of sinners or sit in the seat of mockers. (Ps. 1:1)
>
> Do not set foot on the path of the wicked or walk in the way of evil men. (Pr. 4:14)
>
> Do not envy wicked men, do not desire their company. (Pr. 24:1)
>
> Depart, depart, go out from there! Touch no unclean thing! Come out from it and be pure, you who carry the vessels of the LORD. (Is. 52:11)

NUMBERS 34:1-29

CHAPTER 34

I. The Boundaries of Canaan, the Promised Land: The Great Gift & Assurance of God—His People Will Inherit the Promised Land, 34:1-29

1. **The great gift of God: The gift of the promised land (a symbol of spiritual conquest & rest) (Ex. 23:31)**[DS1]

   a. The southern border
   1) Included some of the Desert of Zin near Edom
   2) Started at the Salt Sea

   3) Crossed south of Scorpion Pass & ran to Zin & south of Kadesh Barnea
   4) Went to Hazar Adar & Azmon
   5) Joined the brooks of Egypt
   6) Ended at the Mediterranean Sea

   b. The western border: Ran up the coast of the Mediterranean Sea

   c. The northern border
   1) Ran along the Great Sea over to Mount Hor
   2) Went to Lebo Hamath then to Zedad

   3) Ran to Ziphron
   4) Ended at Hazar Enan

   d. The eastern border
   1) Started at Hazar Enan
   2) Ran to Shepham
   3) Went to Riblah, on the east side of Ain
   4) Ran along the eastern edge of the Sea of Galilee (Kinnereth)
   5) Continued along the Jordan River
   6) Ended at the Dead Sea

   e. The land was to be assigned

The LORD said to Moses, 2 "Command the Israelites and say to them: 'When you enter Canaan, the land that will be allotted to you as an inheritance will have these boundaries:
3 " 'Your southern side will include some of the Desert of Zin along the border of Edom. On the east, your southern boundary will start from the end of the Salt Sea,
4 Cross south of Scorpion Pass, continue on to Zin and go south of Kadesh Barnea. Then it will go to Hazar Addar and over to Azmon,
5 Where it will turn, join the Wadi of Egypt and end at the Sea.
6 " 'Your western boundary will be the coast of the Great Sea. This will be your boundary on the west.
7 " 'For your northern boundary, run a line from the Great Sea to Mount Hor
8 And from Mount Hor to Lebo Hamath. Then the boundary will go to Zedad,
9 Continue to Ziphron and end at Hazar Enan. This will be your boundary on the north.
10 " 'For your eastern boundary, run a line from Hazar Enan to Shepham.
11 The boundary will go down from Shepham to Riblah on the east side of Ain and continue along the slopes east of the Sea of Kinnereth.
12 Then the boundary will go down along the Jordan and end at the Salt Sea. " 'This will be your land, with its boundaries on every side.' "
13 Moses commanded the Israelites: "Assign this land by lot as an inheritance. The LORD has ordered that it be given to the nine and a half tribes,
14 Because the families of the tribe of Reuben, the tribe of Gad and the half-tribe of Manasseh have received their inheritance.
15 These two and a half tribes have received their inheritance on the east side of the Jordan of Jericho, toward the sunrise."
16 The LORD said to Moses,
17 "These are the names of the men who are to assign the land for you as an inheritance: Eleazar the priest and Joshua son of Nun.
18 And appoint one leader from each tribe to help assign the land.
19 These are their names: Caleb son of Jephunneh, from the tribe of Judah;
20 Shemuel son of Ammihud, from the tribe of Simeon;
21 Elidad son of Kislon, from the tribe of Benjamin;
22 Bukki son of Jogli, the leader from the tribe of Dan;
23 Hanniel son of Ephod, the leader from the tribe of Manasseh son of Joseph;
24 Kemuel son of Shiphtan, the leader from the tribe of Ephraim son of Joseph;
25 Elizaphan son of Parnach, the leader from the tribe of Zebulun;
26 Paltiel son of Azzan, the leader from the tribe of Issachar;
27 Ahihud son of Shelomi, the leader from the tribe of Asher;
28 Pedahel son of Ammihud, the leader from the tribe of Naphtali."
29 These are the men the LORD commanded to assign the inheritance to the Israelites in the land of Canaan.

by lot to the 9½ tribes

1) The tribes of Reuben, Gad, & the half tribe of Manasseh had received their inheritance (32:1-42)

2) Their inheritance was on the east side of the Jordan across from Jericho: They settled outside of the promised land because of their compromise (32:1-42)

2. **The great assurance of God: The leaders who were to assign the land were appointed ahead of time (a picture of the great assurance of God)**
   a. The supervisors: Eleazar the priest & Joshua
   b. The leaders from each tribe: Some must be willing to lead, handling difficult tasks
   1) Tribe of Judah: Caleb

   2) Tribe of Simeon: Shemuel

   3) Tribe of Benjamin: Elidad

   4) Tribe of Dan: Bukki

   5) Tribe of Manasseh: Hanniel

   6) Tribe of Ephraim: Kemuel

   7) Tribe of Zebulun: Elizaphan

   8) Tribe of Issachar: Paltiel

   9) Tribe of Asher: Ahihud

   10) Tribe of Naphtali: Pedahel

   c. The difficult task of dividing land among heirs: These were the willing leaders appointed to the task

DIVISION IV

THE PREPARATION FOR THE MARCH INTO THE PROMISED LAND, 26:1–36:13

I. The Boundaries of Canaan, the Promised Land: The Great Gift and Assurance of God—His People Will Inherit the Promised Land, 34:1-29

NUMBERS 34:1-29

(34:1-29) Introduction—Eternal Life—Promised Land: How can a person know that he is going to live forever? Beyond doubt, can we know that there is life eternal? That heaven is real? That the good news is true? That we can live face to face with God forever and ever? Is there such absolute assurance and conviction for the human soul? Scripture declares a resounding "Yes!"

This is the subject of this passage of Scripture. The Israelites were camped on the plains of Moab by the Jordan River across from the great city of Jericho. They were poised, ready to cross over the Jordan into the promised land, but note: they had not yet crossed over nor entered. Yet in this Scripture, God outlines the boundaries of the promised land and appoints the leaders who were to assign the inheritance to each tribe. God outlined the boundaries and appointed the leaders ahead of time, before His people ever entered the land. He was giving them assurance and confidence in the promised land. The promised land was as good as theirs: this was the oath, the promise that God was swearing to His people. He had made a covenant, a contract between Himself and His people: if they would follow Him, He would give them the promised land. Here they were camped right across from the land, poised and ready to walk in. Therefore, God was ready to fulfill His promise: they would inherit and possess the land. He flooded their spirits with assurance and conviction: the promised land was real. The inheritance was to be theirs. This is the great subject of this encouraging passage: *The Boundaries of Canaan, the Promised Land: The Great Gift and Assurance of God—His People Will Inherit the Promised Land,* 34:1-29.

1. The great gift of God: the gift of the promised land (a symbol of spiritual conquest and rest) (Ex. 23:31) (vv.1-15).
2. The great assurance of God: the leaders who were to assign the land were appointed ahead of time (a picture of the great assurance of God) (vv.16-29).

1 **(34:1-15) Land, the Promised—Gift, of God, the Promised Land—Spiritual Conquest—Spiritual Rest—Symbol, of Spiritual Conquest and Rest:** the glorious gift of God was the promised land. God's people were to inherit the land of Canaan. The promised land was a symbol of heaven, but also of spiritual conquest and rest. It was a symbol of God's people conquering the enemies of life and finding rest for their souls. (See DEEPER STUDY # 1—Nu. 34:1-15 for more discussion.) The four boundaries of the promised land are actually spelled out in this passage:

⇒ the southern border (vv.3-5)
⇒ the western border (v.6)
⇒ the northern border (vv.7-9)
⇒ the eastern border (vv.10-12)

The promised land was the glorious gift of God to His people. Years before, God had made this great covenant with Abraham, the covenant of the promised land. If Abraham would follow God with all of his heart, he would receive the great gifts of God, the gift of the promised land and the gift of the promised seed (the Savior and Messiah of the world). The present passage concerns the great gift of the promised land. It is now hundreds of years later, and finally the descendants of Abraham are poised to enter the promised land. Once again, God is spelling out the borders of the land that the Israelites were to inherit. Note several points about the great gift of God, the promised land.

a. First, some of the boundary cities cannot be accurately located because they do not presently exist. However, enough is known about the location of most of the boundary markers to give a fairly accurate map of the promised land (see Map—Nu. 34:1-15 at the end of this commentary).

b. Second Israel never did claim all of the promised land outlined in this passage. King David did control most of Canaan and most of Transjordan. However, even he failed to conquer and lay claim to the outer reaches of the promised land.[1]

c. Third, God Himself is the One who outlines the boundaries of the promised land (vv.1-12). These boundaries are not drawn by a man, nor were they determined by the nation Israel. God Himself had given the promise of the promised land to Abraham and his descendants who truly followed Him. The very existence and idea of the promised land was created in God's mind, not man's. The location, fertility, richness, fruitfulness, environment, quality of life, and everything else about the promised land was conceived in the mind of God, created and controlled by the hand of God. It was God who gave the hope of the promised land to His dear people, the hope of a land that would bring fullness of life, peace, and rest to their bodies and souls (He. 11:13-16).

d. Fourth, the promise of the promised land is based upon a covenant between God and His people. The gift of God is a contract established by Him, a contract that requires obedience in order to inherit the promised land. (See DEEPER STUDY # 1—Nu. 34:1-15 for more discussion.)

DEEPER STUDY # 1

(34:1-15) The Promised Land—Promises of God: the promise of the *promised land* is based upon a covenant. The covenant or contract between God and man is conditional: a person must obey God in order to enter and inherit the promised land. Scripture has made this clear from the beginning when God initially approached Abraham with the covenant. Note the major references to the covenant, the contract involving the promised land of God:

⇒ Abraham had to obey God, had to leave his old life and follow God in order to inherit the promised land.

> The LORD had said to Abram, "Leave your country, your people and your father's household and go to the land I will show you. I will make you into a great nation and I will bless you; I will make your name great, and you will be a blessing. I will bless those who bless you, and whoever curses you I will curse; and all peoples on earth will be blessed through you." (Ge. 12:1-3)

⇒ Abraham obeyed God; therefore, God reconfirmed His covenant time and again with His dear servant.

> The LORD said to Abram after Lot had parted from him, "Lift up your eyes from where you are and look north and south, east and west. All the land that you see I will give to you and your offspring forever. I will make your offspring like the dust of the earth, so that if anyone could count the dust, then your offspring could be counted. Go, walk through the length and breadth of the land, for I am giving it to you." (Ge. 13:14-17)

---

[1] Gordon J. Wenham. *The Book of Numbers,* p.232. Also *The Expositor's Bible Commentary.* Frank E. Gaebelein, Editor, p.996.

On that day the LORD made a covenant with Abram and said, "To your descendants I give this land, from the river of Egypt to the great river, the Euphrates—the land of the Kenites, Kenizzites, Kadmonites, Hittites, Perizzites, Rephaites, Amorites, Canaanites, Girgashites and Jebusites." (Ge. 15:18-21)

"The whole land of Canaan, where you are now an alien, I will give as an everlasting possession to you and your descendants after you; and I will be their God." (Ge. 17:8)

⇒ Joseph and his eleven brothers, the sons of Jacob, believed God and followed after God during their lives; therefore, God established His promise with them.

Then Joseph said to his brothers, "I am about to die. But God will surely come to your aid and take you up out of this land to the land he promised on oath to Abraham, Isaac and Jacob." (Ge. 50:24)

⇒ Moses obeyed and followed after God; therefore, God established the covenant of the promised land with him.

And I will bring you to the land I swore with uplifted hand to give to Abraham, to Isaac and to Jacob. I will give it to you as a possession. I am the LORD. (Ex. 6:8)

⇒ God gave the promise of the promised land to the people of Israel; however, they had to cleave to Him. They had to diligently keep His commandments and love God—with their whole hearts. Then and only then would He strengthen them to defeat the enemies of the promised land.

"I will send my terror ahead of you and throw into confusion every nation you encounter. I will make all your enemies turn their backs and run. I will send the hornet ahead of you to drive the Hivites, Canaanites and Hittites out of your way. But I will not drive them out in a single year, because the land would become desolate and the wild animals too numerous for you. Little by little I will drive them out before you, until you have increased enough to take possession of the land. "I will establish your borders from the Red Sea to the Sea of the Philistines, and from the desert to the River. I will hand over to you the people who live in the land and you will drive them out before you. Do not make a covenant with them or with their gods. Do not let them live in your land, or they will cause you to sin against me, because the worship of their gods will certainly be a snare to you." (Ex. 23:27-33)

Keep all my decrees and laws and follow them, so that the land where I am bringing you to live may not vomit you out. You must not live according to the customs of the nations I am going to drive out before you. Because they did all these things, I abhorred them. But I said to you, "You will possess their land; I will give it to you as an inheritance, a land flowing with milk and honey." I am the LORD your God, who has set you apart from the nations. (Le. 20:22-24)

If the LORD is pleased with us, he will lead us into that land, a land flowing with milk and honey, and will give it to us. (Nu. 14:8)

If you carefully observe all these commands I am giving you to follow—to love the LORD your God, to walk in all his ways and to hold fast to him— then the LORD will drive out all these nations before you, and you will dispossess nations larger and stronger than you. Every place where you set your foot will be yours: Your territory will extend from the desert to Lebanon, and from the Euphrates River to the western sea. No man will be able to stand against you. The LORD your God, as he promised you, will put the terror and fear of you on the whole land, wherever you go. (De. 11:22-25)

"Now write down for yourselves this song and teach it to the Israelites and have them sing it, so that it may be a witness for me against them. When I have brought them into the land flowing with milk and honey, the land I promised on oath to their forefathers, and when they eat their fill and thrive, they will turn to other gods and worship them, rejecting me and breaking my covenant. And when many disasters and difficulties come upon them, this song will testify against them, because it will not be forgotten by their descendants. I know what they are disposed to do, even before I bring them into the land I promised them on oath." (De. 31:19-21)

The Israelites had moved about in the desert forty years until all the men who were of military age when they left Egypt had died, since they had not obeyed the LORD. For the LORD had sworn to them that they would not see the land that he had solemnly promised their fathers to give us, a land flowing with milk and honey. (Jos. 5:6)

The angel of the LORD went up from Gilgal to Bokim and said, "I brought you up out of Egypt and led you into the land that I swore to give to your forefathers. I said, 'I will never break my covenant with you, and you shall not make a covenant with the people of this land, but you shall break down their altars.' Yet you have disobeyed me. Why have you done this? Now therefore I tell you that I will not drive them out before you; they will be thorns in your sides and their gods will be a snare to you." (Jud. 2:1-3)

NUMBERS 34:1-29

Thought 1. There are several lessons for us in this point.

(1) The great gift of God is the promised land. To the believer, the promised land means several things:

  (a) The promised land means heaven itself, the new heavens and new earth that God is going to create for His dear people someday out in the future.

> In my Father's house are many rooms; if it were not so, I would have told you. I am going there to prepare a place for you. And if I go and prepare a place for you, I will come back and take you to be with me that you also may be where I am. (Jn. 14:2-3)

> Now we know that if the earthly tent we live in is destroyed, we have a building from God, an eternal house in heaven, not built by human hands. (2 Co. 5:1)

> But the day of the Lord will come like a thief. The heavens will disappear with a roar; the elements will be destroyed by fire, and the earth and everything in it will be laid bare. Since everything will be destroyed in this way, what kind of people ought you to be? You ought to live holy and godly lives as you look forward to the day of God and speed its coming. That day will bring about the destruction of the heavens by fire, and the elements will melt in the heat. But in keeping with his promise we are looking forward to a new heaven and a new earth, the home of righteousness. (2 Pe. 3:10-13)

> Then I saw a new heaven and a new earth, for the first heaven and the first earth had passed away, and there was no longer any sea. I saw the Holy City, the new Jerusalem, coming down out of heaven from God, prepared as a bride beautifully dressed for her husband. And I heard a loud voice from the throne saying, "Now the dwelling of God is with men, and he will live with them. They will be his people, and God himself will be with them and be their God. He will wipe every tear from their eyes. There will be no more death or mourning or crying or pain, for the old order of things has passed away." (Re. 21:1-4)

> Behold, I will create new heavens and a new earth. The former things will not be remembered, nor will they come to mind. (Is. 65:17)

  (b) The promised land means spiritual conquest and rest. It means that God's people conquer the enemies of life and find rest for their souls.

> Take my yoke upon you and learn from me, for I am gentle and humble in heart, and you will find rest for your souls. (Mt. 11:29)

> Who shall separate us from the love of Christ? Shall trouble or hardship or persecution or famine or nakedness or danger or sword?...No, in all these things we are more than conquerors through him who loved us. For I am convinced that neither death nor life, neither angels nor demons, neither the present nor the future, nor any powers, neither height nor depth, nor anything else in all creation, will be able to separate us from the love of God that is in Christ Jesus our Lord. (Ro. 8:35, 37-39)

> Therefore, since the promise of entering his rest still stands, let us be careful that none of you be found to have fallen short of it. For we also have had the gospel preached to us, just as they did; but the message they heard was of no value to them, because those who heard did not combine it with faith. Now we who have believed enter that rest, just as God has said, "So I declared on oath in my anger, 'They shall never enter my rest.'" And yet his work has been finished since the creation of the world. (He. 4:1-3)

> Let us, therefore, make every effort to enter that rest, so that no one will fall by following their example of disobedience. (He. 4:11)

> For everyone born of God overcomes the world. This is the victory that has overcome the world, even our faith. Who is it that overcomes the world? Only he who believes that Jesus is the Son of God. (1 Jn. 5:4-5)

> Then I heard a voice from heaven say, "Write: Blessed are the dead who die in the Lord from now on." "Yes," says the Spirit, "they will rest from their labor, for their deeds will follow them." (Re. 14:13)

> The LORD replied, "My Presence will go with you, and I will give you rest." (Ex. 33:14)

> Through you we push back our enemies; through your name we trample our foes. (Ps. 44:5)

> Be at rest once more, O my soul, for the LORD has been good to you. (Ps. 116:7)

> To whom he said, "This is the resting place, let the weary rest"; and, "This is the place of repose"—but they would not listen. (Is. 28:12)

(2) Entrance into the promised land is conditional. A person has to believe God and obey Him in order to enter the promised land of heaven. If a person is covetous, immoral, wicked, lawless, violent, or ungodly, he cannot inherit the kingdom of God, the promised land of heaven. A person has to believe God—trust His dear Son—if he is to inherit the promised land of heaven.

> And this is his command: to believe in the name of his Son, Jesus Christ, and to love one another as he commanded us. (1 Jn. 3:23)

But store up for yourselves treasures in heaven, where moth and rust do not destroy, and where thieves do not break in and steal. (Mt. 6:20)

For God so loved the world that he gave his one and only Son, that whoever believes in him shall not perish but have eternal life. (Jn. 3:16)

The acts of the sinful nature are obvious: sexual immorality, impurity and debauchery; idolatry and witchcraft; hatred, discord, jealousy, fits of rage, selfish ambition, dissensions, factions and envy; drunkenness, orgies, and the like. I warn you, as I did before, that those who live like this will not inherit the kingdom of God. (Ga. 5:19-21)

For of this you can be sure: No immoral, impure or greedy person—such a man is an idolater—has any inheritance in the kingdom of Christ and of God. (Ep. 5:5)

Nothing impure will ever enter it, nor will anyone who does what is shameful or deceitful, but only those whose names are written in the Lamb's book of life. (Re. 21:27)

2 (34:16-29) **Assurance, of God—Leaders, of Israel—Israel, Leadership of—Land, the Promised, Assignment of**: the great assurance of God was seen in one clear fact: God appointed the leaders to assign the land before Israel ever entered the land. The day was coming when their inheritance would be assigned to them, and it was coming soon—during their lifetime—for the leaders were being appointed now. What excitement must have filled the hearts of God's people. They were being assured by God that they were on the verge of receiving their inheritance. A sense of full knowledge flooded their souls, the knowledge that they were definitely going to receive their inheritance. No doubt God was flooding their souls with assurance and confidence in the promised land.

Thought 1. Assurance, confidence, and conviction in the promised land have been given by God. The person who approaches God through Christ is given the assurance of living forever with God. When a person receives Christ as his Savior, the Holy Spirit of God enters his life. God places His Spirit within the person, and the Spirit of God becomes the guarantee of living forever within the promised land of heaven. The Holy Spirit within a person is the guarantee, the surety of heaven.

The Spirit himself testifies with our spirit that we are God's children. Now if we are children, then we are heirs—heirs of God and co-heirs with Christ, if indeed we share in his sufferings in order that we may also share in his glory. (Ro. 8:16-17)

Because you are sons, God sent the Spirit of his Son into our hearts, the Spirit who calls out, "Abba, Father." (Ga. 4:6)

And you also were included in Christ when you heard the word of truth, the gospel of your salvation. Having believed, you were marked in him with a seal, the promised Holy Spirit, who is a deposit guaranteeing our inheritance until the redemption of those who are God's possession—to the praise of his glory. (Ep. 1:13-14)

That is why I am suffering as I am. Yet I am not ashamed, because I know whom I have believed, and am convinced that he is able to guard what I have entrusted to him for that day. (2 Ti. 1:12)

Let us draw near to God with a sincere heart in full assurance of faith, having our hearts sprinkled to cleanse us from a guilty conscience and having our bodies washed with pure water. (He. 10:22)

Those who obey his commands live in him, and he in them. And this is how we know that he lives in us: We know it by the Spirit he gave us. (1 Jn. 3:24)

We know that we live in him and he in us, because he has given us of his Spirit. (1 Jn. 4:13)

Anyone who believes in the Son of God has this testimony in his heart. Anyone who does not believe God has made him out to be a liar, because he has not believed the testimony God has given about his Son. (1 Jn. 5:10)

And this is the testimony: God has given us eternal life, and this life is in his Son. He who has the Son has life; he who does not have the Son of God does not have life. (1 Jn. 5:11-12)

NUMBERS 35:1-34

1. **God's provision for the Levites: A picture of ministry & of God's provision of necessities for His servants**
   a. The people were to give towns & pastureland to support God's servants, the Levites (see also 18:1-32)
      1) The purpose
         - To spread them out in the community among the people—for ministry
         - To give them a home & pastureland for their livestock
      2) The size of the pastureland
         - To extend out 1500' from the wall of the town
         - To measure about 3000' on each side with the town in the center (the footage was no doubt enlarged as the town & population grew)

   b. The people were to give six towns as cities of refuge: A place of safety for a person guilty of accidental manslaughter
   c. The people were to give 48 towns total
      1) Forty-two homesites
      2) Six cities of refuge
   d. The people were to be fair in selecting the towns & land to be given
      1) Fair to God's servants: An understood fact
      2) Fair to each tribe: To give in proportion to the size of the tribe

2. **God's provision of refuge—establishing the cities of refuge: A picture of Christ our Refuge—a refuge from the threats & storms of life**
   a. The basic purpose of the cities of refuge
      1) To be a refuge, an asylum for persons guilty of accidental murder
      2) To be a place to flee from the avenger
      3) To be a place of safety until a trial could be set by community courts

   b. The location of the cities of refuge
      1) Three in Transjordan
      2) Three in Canaan

   c. The open access of the cities of refuge: Any person—native born, foreigner, or traveling merchant—could flee for refuge in the cities (picture that any person can flee to Christ)

   d. The cases of willful murder excluded a person from the cities of refuge
      1) The person who picks up an iron object does so willfully; he is a murderer & is to be executed
      2) The person who picks up a stone does so willfully: He is a murderer & is to be executed
      3) The person who picks up a wooden object does so willfully: He is a murderer & is to be executed

      4) The victim's nearest relative (the avenger of blood) is responsible for the execution
      5) The person who murders someone with premeditated malice by shoving or throwing something is a murderer
      6) The person who angrily kills anyone with his fists is a murderer: He is to be executed by the victim's avenger or nearest relative (5:8; Le. 25:25-26)

   e. The cases of murder that allowed a person to flee to a city of refuge: Cases without hostility, that were unintentional, such as accidentally shoving or throwing something or by dropping an object

      1) The courts must decide between the slayer & the avenger or nearest relative
      2) The courts must protect

CHAPTER 35

J. The Inheritance of the Levites & the Cities of Refuge: The Provision of God for His Ministers & for All Who Need Refuge from the Storms & Threats of Life, 35:1-34

On the plains of Moab by the Jordan across from Jericho, the LORD said to Moses, 2 "Command the Israelites to give the Levites towns to live in from the inheritance the Israelites will possess. And give them pasturelands around the towns. 3 Then they will have towns to live in and pasturelands for their cattle, flocks and all their other livestock.

4 "The pasturelands around the towns that you give the Levites will extend out fifteen hundred feet from the town wall. 5 Outside the town, measure three thousand feet on the east side, three thousand on the south side, three thousand on the west and three thousand on the north, with the town in the center. They will have this area as pastureland for the towns.

6 "Six of the towns you give the Levites will be cities of refuge, to which a person who has killed someone may flee. In addition, give them forty-two other towns. 7 In all you must give the Levites forty-eight towns, together with their pasturelands.

8 The towns you give the Levites from the land the Israelites possess are to be given in proportion to each tribe: Take many towns from a tribe that has many, but few from one that has few."

9 Then the LORD said to Moses: 10 "Speak to the Israelites and say to them: 'When you cross the Jordan into Canaan, 11 Select some towns to be your cities of refuge, to which a person who has killed someone accidentally may flee. 12 They will be places of refuge from the avenger, so that a person accused of murder may not die before he stands trial before the assembly. 13 These six towns you give will be your cities of refuge. 14 Give three on this side of the Jordan and three in Canaan as cities of refuge. 15 These six towns will be a place of refuge for Israelites, aliens and any other people living among them, so that anyone who has killed another accidentally can flee there.

16 "'If a man strikes someone with an iron object so that he dies, he is a murderer; the murderer shall be put to death. 17 Or if anyone has a stone in his hand that could kill, and he strikes someone so that he dies, he is a murderer; the murderer shall be put to death. 18 Or if anyone has a wooden object in his hand that could kill, and he hits someone so that he dies, he is a murderer; the murderer shall be put to death. 19 The avenger of blood shall put the murderer to death; when he meets him, he shall put him to death. 20 If anyone with malice aforethought shoves another or throws something at him intentionally so that he dies 21 Or if in hostility he hits him with his fist so that he dies, that person shall be put to death; he is a murderer. The avenger of blood shall put the murderer to death when he meets him.

22 "'But if without hostility someone suddenly shoves another or throws something at him unintentionally 23 Or, without seeing him, drops a stone on him that could kill him, and he dies, then since he was not his enemy and he did not intend to harm him, 24 The assembly must judge between him and the avenger of blood according to these regulations. 25 The assembly must protect

NUMBERS 35:1-34

Outline	Scripture	Scripture (cont.)	Outline (cont.)
the accused by sending him to a city of refuge 3) The accused must stay in the city of refuge until the death of the High Priest: A picture of deliverance by the death of Christ f. The strong warning to the accused (a picture of God's warning to the accused sinner) 1) The avenger could execute the accused if the accused ever left the city of refuge 2) The accused must stay in the city of refuge until the death of the High Priest (a symbol of Christ our Refuge, the Deliverer from the avenger of death) g. The laws governing the cities of refuge were established as permanent laws 3. God's provision of mercy in	the one accused of murder from the avenger of blood and send him back to the city of refuge to which he fled. He must stay there until the death of the high priest, who was anointed with the holy oil. 26 " 'But if the accused ever goes outside the limits of the city of refuge to which he has fled 27 And the avenger of blood finds him outside the city, the avenger of blood may kill the accused without being guilty of murder. 28 The accused must stay in his city of refuge until the death of the high priest; only after the death of the high priest may he return to his own property. 29 " 'These are to be legal requirements for you throughout the generations to come, wherever you live. 30 " 'Anyone who kills a	person is to be put to death as a murderer only on the testimony of witnesses. But no one is to be put to death on the testimony of only one witness. 31 " 'Do not accept a ransom for the life of a murderer, who deserves to die. He must surely be put to death. 32 " 'Do not accept a ransom for anyone who has fled to a city of refuge and so allow him to go back and live on his own land before the death of the high priest. 33 " 'Do not pollute the land where you are. Bloodshed pollutes the land, and atonement cannot be made for the land on which blood has been shed, except by the blood of the one who shed it. 34 Do not defile the land where you live and where I dwell, for I, the LORD, dwell among the Israelites.' "	dealing with murder a. Two or more witnesses are required to execute a person b. No unequal justice is to be allowed; no ransom is ever to be accepted from a rich murderer: He is to be executed c. No ransom is to be accepted from a rich person in a city of refuge: No person is to be allowed to buy his freedom d. No land is to be polluted by murder 1) Bloodshed—murder—pollutes the land 2) Atonement can be made only by the blood or execution of the murderer, the one who shed blood e. God demands justice, demands that the land not be defiled: The reason—He lives there, lives among His people

DIVISION IV

THE PREPARATION FOR THE MARCH INTO THE PROMISED LAND, 26:1–36:13

J. The Inheritance of the Levites and the Cities of Refuge: The Provision of God for His Ministers and for All Who Need Refuge from the Storms and Threats of Life, 35:1-34

(35:1-34) **Introduction**: water, food, clothing, and housing—all are necessities that every human being must have in order to survive and sustain life. But physical and material items are not the only things necessary to sustain life. Meaning, significance, purpose, satisfaction, and fulfillment—all these are necessary to live a full and free life upon this earth. The necessities of life are provisions that we absolutely must have in order to live and experience the fullness of life.

When dealing with the necessities of life, there is wonderful, glorious news. God promises to meet every need of human life. There is no need that God does not promise to meet. Provision to meet the needs of every human being is in the hands of God. This is the loud and clear declaration of Scripture: *The Inheritance of the Levites and the Cities of Refuge: the Provision of God for His Ministers and for All Who Need Refuge from the Storms and Threats of Life*, 35:1-34.

1. God's provision for the Levites: a picture of ministry and of God's provision of necessities for His servants (vv.1-8).
2. God's provision of refuge—establishing the cities of refuge: a picture of Christ our Refuge—a refuge from the threats and storms of life (vv.9-29).
3. God's provision of mercy in dealing with murder (vv.30-34).

1 (35:1-8) **Provision, For God's Ministers—Ministers, Provision For—Levites, Provision For—Necessities, Provision of—Provision, of God—Ministers, Ministry of**: there was God's provision for the Levites. This is a picture of ministry and of God's provision for His servants. The Levites were not to inherit any land in Canaan in order that they might focus entirely upon the ministry to the people. If they owned land, they would have to be involved in the business affairs of their property. This was not their call: they were called to serve and minister to the people. This was to be their sole focus. God Himself—His worship and His ministry—was to be their inheritance (Nu. 18:20-24). However, the Levites and their families needed a place to live and their livestock needed good pastureland. These needs were now met by God:

a. The people were to give town's and pastureland to support God's servants, the Levites (vv.2-5). Keep in mind that the Levites were supported by God's people; therefore they did not need land for a garden nor for farming (see outline and notes—Nu. 18:8-24 for more discussion).

1) The gift of towns and pastureland was an absolute essential for two purposes. First, there was a need for the Levites to live out among the people within their very communities so that they could minister to them. When the people needed help, the ministers of God needed to be available to help. They were the representatives of God's love and care; therefore they were to be living within the communities of the people and demonstrating God's love and care. They were to be teaching the truth and instructing people in the law of God.

NUMBERS 35:1-34

And you [Levites, ministers] must teach the Israelites all the decrees the LORD has given them through Moses. (Le. 10:11)

So Moses wrote down this law and gave it to the priests, the sons of Levi, who carried the ark of the covenant of the LORD, and to all the elders of Israel. Then Moses commanded them: "At the end of every seven years, in the year for canceling debts, during the Feast of Tabernacles, when all Israel comes to appear before the LORD your God at the place he will choose, you shall read this law before them in their hearing. Assemble the people—men, women and children, and the aliens living in your towns—so they can listen and learn to fear the LORD your God and follow carefully all the words of this law. Their children, who do not know this law, must hear it and learn to fear the LORD your God as long as you live in the land you are crossing the Jordan to possess." (De. 31:9-13)

He teaches your precepts to Jacob and your law to Israel. He offers incense before you and whole burnt offerings on your altar. (De. 33:10)

The second purpose for giving towns and pastureland to the Levites was to provide a home for them, their families and their livestock. Very simply, they needed a place to live. There are several other major passages that deal with the cities and pasturelands of the Levites (Le. 25:32-34; Jos. 14:4; 1 Chr. 13:2; 2 Chr. 11:14; 31:15, 19). There are also other passages that refer to the Levite cities (Ezr. 2:70; Ne. 7:73; 11:3, 20, 36. Also see Eze. 48:8-14.)[1]

2) Note that the amount of land to be given was dictated by God (v.4-5). The pastureland was to extend out 1500 feet from the wall of the town. The surveyor was then to measure about 3000 feet on each side with the town in the center. The footage was no doubt enlarged as the town and population grew. A diagram of the city would look like the drawing below:[2]

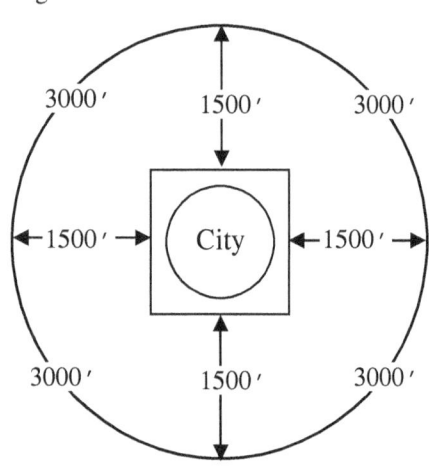

---

[1] *The Expositor's Bible Commentary*, Frank E. Gaebelein, Editor, p.999.
[2] This diagram is suggested by Gordon J. Wenham. *The Book of Numbers*, p.234.

b. The people were also to give six towns as cities of refuge. These cities were a place of safety for a person guilty of accidental manslaughter (v.6). Three cities of refuge were to be located in the promised land of Canaan and three among the two and a half tribes that settled in East Jordan. Joshua tells us that these cities were strategically located throughout the land (Jos. 20:1-9). These cities will be discussed in detail in note two (vv.9-29).

c. The people were to give a total of forty-eight towns: forty-two home sites for the Levites and six cities of refuge (vv.6-7).

d. The people were to be fair in selecting the towns and land to be given. They were to give in proportion to the size of the inheritance of the tribe (v.8).

Thought 1. The minister of God is to be out among people, ministering to them. He is to be available to help in times of need. Moreover, he is to be teaching and instructing God's people in the truth of God's Holy Word, and he is to be reaching out to the lost of the world.

(1) The minister of God is to be available to help in times of need, seeking to do good at every opportunity possible.

> Just as the Son of Man did not come to be served, but to serve, and to give his life as a ransom for many. (Mt. 20:28)
>
> And whoever wants to be first must be slave of all. (Mk. 10:44)
>
> For who is greater, the one who is at the table or the one who serves? Is it not the one who is at the table? But I am among you as one who serves. (Lu. 22:27)
>
> Now that I, your Lord and Teacher, have washed your feet, you also should wash one another's feet. (Jn. 13:14)
>
> Carry each other's burdens, and in this way you will fulfill the law of Christ. (Ga. 6:2)
>
> Therefore, as we have opportunity, let us do good to all people, especially to those who belong to the family of believers. (Ga. 6:10)

(2) The minister is to teach and instruct God's people in the truth of God's Word.

> And teaching them to obey everything I have commanded you. And surely I am with you always, to the very end of the age. (Mt. 28:20)
>
> The third time he said to him, "Simon son of John, do you love me?" Peter was hurt because Jesus asked him the third time, "Do you love me?" He said, "Lord, you know all things; you know that I love you." Jesus said, "Feed my sheep." (Jn. 21:17)
>
> Keep watch over yourselves and all the flock of which the Holy Spirit has made you overseers. Be shepherds of the church of God, which he bought with his own blood. (Ac. 20:28)
>
> Now the overseer must be above reproach, the husband of but one wife, temperate, self-controlled, respectable, hospitable, able to teach. (1 Ti. 3:2)

NUMBERS 35:1-34

Command and teach these things. (1 Ti. 4:11)

Those who oppose him he must gently instruct, in the hope that God will grant them repentance leading them to a knowledge of the truth. (2 Ti. 2:25)

Be shepherds of God's flock that is under your care, serving as overseers—not because you must, but because you are willing, as God wants you to be; not greedy for money, but eager to serve. (1 Pe. 5:2)

Then I will give you shepherds after my own heart, who will lead you with knowledge and understanding. (Je. 3:15)

"I will place shepherds over them who will tend them, and they will no longer be afraid or terrified, nor will any be missing," declares the LORD. (Je. 23:4)

(3) The minister of God is to reach out and bear testimony and witness for Christ.

Therefore go and make disciples of all nations, baptizing them in the name of the Father and of the Son and of the Holy Spirit, and teaching them to obey everything I have commanded you. And surely I am with you always, to the very end of the age. (Mt. 28:19-20)

He said to them, "Go into all the world and preach the good news to all creation." (Mk. 16:15)

But you will receive power when the Holy Spirit comes on you; and you will be my witnesses in Jerusalem, and in all Judea and Samaria, and to the ends of the earth. (Ac.1:8)

To the one we are the smell of death; to the other, the fragrance of life. And who is equal to such a task? (2 Co. 2:16)

That God was reconciling the world to himself in Christ, not counting men's sins against them. And he has committed to us the message of reconciliation. We are therefore Christ's ambassadors, as though God were making his appeal through us. We implore you on Christ's behalf: Be reconciled to God. God made him who had no sin to be sin for us, so that in him we might become the righteousness of God. (2 Co. 5:19-21)

But you, keep your head in all situations, endure hardship, do the work of an evangelist, discharge all the duties of your ministry. (2 Ti. 4:5)

"You are my witnesses," declares the LORD, "and my servant whom I have chosen, so that you may know and believe me and understand that I am he. Before me no god was formed, nor will there be one after me." (Is. 43:10)

I have posted watchmen on your walls, O Jerusalem; they will never be silent day or night. You who call on the LORD, give yourselves no rest. (Is. 62:6)

But if the watchman sees the sword coming and does not blow the trumpet to warn the people and the sword comes and takes the life of one of them, that man will be taken away because of his sin, but I will hold the watchman accountable for his blood. (Eze. 33:6)

Thought 2. God promises to provide all the necessities of life for His dear people. The person who truly follows God will be looked after by God. God will take care of him, meeting his every need, and often giving him an overflowing provision.

But seek first his kingdom and his righteousness, and all these things will be given to you as well. (Mt. 6:33)

The thief comes only to steal and kill and destroy; I have come that they may have life, and have it to the full. (Jn. 10:10)

And God is able to make all grace abound to you, so that in all things at all times, having all that you need, you will abound in every good work. (2 Co. 9:8)

Now to him who is able to do immeasurably more than all we ask or imagine, according to his power that is at work within us. (Ep. 3:20)

And my God will meet all your needs according to his glorious riches in Christ Jesus. (Ph. 4:19)

And you will receive a rich welcome into the eternal kingdom of our Lord and Savior Jesus Christ. (2 Pe. 1:11)

Worship the LORD your God, and his blessing will be on your food and water. I will take away sickness from among you. (Ex. 23:25)

Praise be to the Lord, to God our Savior, who daily bears our burdens. Selah (Ps. 68:19)

"Bring the whole tithe into the storehouse, that there may be food in my house. Test me in this," says the LORD Almighty, "and see if I will not throw open the floodgates of heaven and pour out so much blessing that you will not have room enough for it." (Mal. 3:10)

2 (35:9-29) **Refuge, Cities of—Cities of Refuge—Christ, Our Refuge—Symbol, of Christ, Our Refuge**: there was God's provision of refuge, that of establishing the cities of refuge for persons who were guilty of accidental manslaughter. This is a clear picture of Christ, our Refuge from the threats and storms of life. This passage deals with the law governing cases of murder and manslaughter. The grace and mercy of God is clearly seen in setting up the cities of refuge for the murderer.

a. Note the basic purpose for the cities of refuge: the cities were to be a refuge, an asylum for persons guilty of accidental murder. They were to provide a place for the murderer to flee from the avenger, a place of safety until a trial could be set by community courts (vv.11-12). In ancient days it was the responsibility of the nearest relative to protect the family rights of the victim. The nearest relative was known as the *redeemer* or *kinsman* (goel). The nearest relative or *kinsman* was responsible by law to save his relative from any trouble he faced. Moreover, if the relative had been killed, the *kinsman* became his avenger or the avenger of blood (vv.12, 19, 21, 24-25, 27. See also Nu.

NUMBERS 35:1-34

5:8; Le. 25:25-26; Ru. 3:12f; 4:1, 6, 8; Jb. 19:25; Is. 59:20.)³

b. The location of the cities of refuge was given: three were to be located in Transjordan and three in Canaan proper or the promised land itself (v.14). These, of course, were to be strategically located so that the people would have equal access to the cities of refuge.

c. Note the open access to the cities of refuge: any person—native-born, foreigner, or traveling merchant—could flee for refuge to the cities (v.15). This is a picture of the wonderful grace of God and a picture that any person can flee to Christ for refuge.

d. Note that the cases of willful murder were excluded from the cities of refuge (vv.16-21). Several examples are given to serve as precedence to cover any cases that might arise. The idea behind the six cases given has to do with willful intent, premeditation, or deliberate murder. The six cases are clearly seen by glancing up at the Scripture and outline (vv.16-21).

e. Note the cases of murder that allowed a person to flee to a city of refuge (vv.22-25).

1) Persons who had committed murder without hostility—unintentionally or involuntarily—could flee to the city of refuge. For example, if a person accidentally shoved or threw something or dropped an object on a person that killed the victim, he could flee to a city of refuge (vv.22-23).

2) In these cases, the courts had to decide between the slayer and the avenger or nearest relative (v.24). If the courts decided that the person had committed deliberate or premeditated murder, he was turned over to the avenger and executed.

3) However, if the courts found the person innocent, the courts sent him to a city of refuge where he would be protected (v.25).

4) But note: the accused had to stay in the city of refuge until the current High Priest had died (v.25). The death of the High Priest was a picture of atonement, of the atoning death of the coming Savior Jesus Christ. Therefore when the High Priest died, the person who had committed accidental, unintentional murder was set free. This was a clear picture of deliverance from sin and death through the sacrifice and death of Jesus Christ. When Jesus Christ died as our High Priest, we were set free from the condemnation of death.

f. Note the strong warning to the accused (vv.26-28): the avenger could execute him if he ever left the city of refuge. Therefore, the accused must stay in the city of refuge until the death of the High Priest. Again note the symbolism: this is a clear symbol of Christ our Refuge, the Deliverer from the avenger of death.

g. The laws governing the cities of refuge were established as permanent laws (v.29).

Thought 1. The LORD is our Refuge from the threats and storms of life. Scripture declares four wonderful truths about the protection the LORD gives us.

(1) The LORD is our Refuge.

The eternal God is your refuge, and underneath are the everlasting arms. He will drive out your enemy before you, saying, 'Destroy him!' (De. 33:27)

God is our refuge and strength, an ever-present help in trouble. (Ps. 46:1)

Be my rock of refuge, to which I can always go; give the command to save me, for you are my rock and my fortress. (Ps. 71:3)

The name of the LORD is a strong tower; the righteous run to it and are safe. (Pr. 18:10)

You have been a refuge for the poor, a refuge for the needy in his distress, a shelter from the storm and a shade from the heat. For the breath of the ruthless is like a storm driving against a wall. (Is. 25:4)

Return to your fortress, O prisoners of hope. (Zec. 9:12)

(2) The LORD is our Hiding Place.

Keep me as the apple of your eye; hide me in the shadow of your wings. (Ps. 17:8)

For in the day of trouble he will keep me safe in his dwelling; he will hide me in the shelter of his tabernacle and set me high upon a rock. (Ps. 27:5)

In the shelter of your presence you hide them from the intrigues of men; in your dwelling you keep them safe from accusing tongues. (Ps. 31:20)

You are my hiding place; you will protect me from trouble and surround me with songs of deliverance. *Selah* **(Ps. 32:7)**

Hide me from the conspiracy of the wicked, from that noisy crowd of evildoers. (Ps. 64:2)

You are my refuge and my shield; I have put my hope in your word. (Ps. 119:114)

Rescue me from my enemies, O LORD, for I hide myself in you. (Ps. 143:9)

Each man will be like a shelter from the wind and a refuge from the storm, like streams of water in the desert and the shadow of a great rock in a thirsty land. (Is. 32:2)

(3) The LORD is our Shield in protecting us.

After this, the word of the LORD came to Abram in a vision: "Do not be afraid, Abram. I am your shield, your very great reward." (Ge. 15:1)

We wait in hope for the LORD; he is our help and our shield. (Ps. 33:20)

For the LORD God is a sun and shield; the LORD bestows favor and honor; no good thing does he withhold from those whose walk is blameless. (Ps. 84:11)

O house of Israel, trust in the LORD—he is their help and shield. (Ps. 115:9)

(4) The LORD is our Atoning Sacrifice who delivers us from the avenger of death.

For God so loved the world that he gave his one and only Son, that whoever believes in him shall not perish but have eternal life. (Jn. 3:16)

And whoever lives and believes in me will never die. Do you believe this? (Jn. 11:26)

---

³ Gordon J. Wenham. *The Book of Numbers*, p.236.

NUMBERS 35:1-34

The last enemy to be destroyed is death. (1 Co. 15:26)

For the perishable must clothe itself with the imperishable, and the mortal with immortality. When the perishable has been clothed with the imperishable, and the mortal with immortality, then the saying that is written will come true: "Death has been swallowed up in victory." (1 Co. 15:53-54)

Now we know that if the earthly tent we live in is destroyed, we have a building from God, an eternal house in heaven, not built by human hands. (2 Co. 5:1)

For the Lord himself will come down from heaven, with a loud command, with the voice of the archangel and with the trumpet call of God, and the dead in Christ will rise first. After that, we who are still alive and are left will be caught up together with them in the clouds to meet the Lord in the air. And so we will be with the Lord forever. (1 Th. 4:16-17)

But it has now been revealed through the appearing of our Savior, Christ Jesus, who has destroyed death and has brought life and immortality to light through the gospel. (2 Ti. 1:10)

But we see Jesus, who was made a little lower than the angels, now crowned with glory and honor because he suffered death, so that by the grace of God he might taste death for everyone. (He. 2:9)

Since the children have flesh and blood, he too shared in their humanity so that by his death he might destroy him who holds the power of death—that is, the devil—and free those who all their lives were held in slavery by their fear of death. (He. 2:14-15)

He will wipe every tear from their eyes. There will be no more death or mourning or crying or pain, for the old order of things has passed away. (Re. 21:4)

He will swallow up death forever. The Sovereign LORD will wipe away the tears from all faces; he will remove the disgrace of his people from all the earth. The LORD has spoken. (Is. 25:8)

3 (35:30-34) **Mercy, of God—Murder, Laws Governing—Provision, For Murderers**: there is God's provision of mercy in dealing with murder.

a. Two or more witnesses were required to execute a person. This law was established by God to protect a person from execution based on insufficient evidence. Tragically, down through the centuries, some persons have been condemned and executed on insufficient evidence. Note the Scripture: no person was to be put to death on the testimony of only one witness. At least two witnesses were always necessary.

b. No unequal justice was to be allowed: no ransom was ever to be accepted from a rich murderer (v.31). Justice was to be impartial, showing no favoritism whatsoever to the wealthy. If there were sufficient evidence and the wealthy person was sentenced to death, he was to be executed.

c. Even if a rich person was in a city of refuge and had been temporarily protected, a ransom was not to be accepted from him. No person was ever to be allowed to buy his freedom, not if there was sufficient evidence against him (v.32).

d. No land was to be polluted by murder. Note that bloodshed or murder pollutes the land. Blood pollutes the land because the land belongs to God, and God lives in the land just as His people live in the land. God is holy; therefore He demands that the land be holy. God's very holiness demands that justice be executed against any who commit murder and shed blood. The murderer pollutes the land; consequently, he must be executed. Note that atonement can be made only by the blood or execution of the murderer, the execution of the one who shed blood. Man is made in the image of God; therefore murder is one of the most serious crimes against the sanctity of life (Ge. 9:5-6; Ex. 21:12-14, 28-32; De. 19:1-13; 21:1-9).

e. God demands justice, demands that the land not be defiled because He lives in the land, lives among His people (v.34).

Thought 1. God forgives sin. No matter what the sin is—no matter how serious, how unlawful, violent, or abusive—God forgives the sin. But there is a condition for forgiveness: confession and repentance, turning away from the sin and turning to God. A person has to turn his life completely and totally over to God, to live a holy and righteous life. With all his heart, mind, body, and soul, a person must follow God. A person must begin to love and obey God, seeking to be conformed to the very image of Jesus Christ. This is the only way a person can be forgiven: by confessing and repenting, turning his life completely over to the Lord Jesus Christ. This is the great provision of mercy that God has made for murderers and for all other sinners upon this earth: the provision of confession and repentance. Through confession and repentance, we are forgiven our sins.

And saying, "Repent, for the kingdom of heaven is near." (Mt. 3:2)

I tell you, no! But unless you repent, you too will all perish. (Lu. 13:3)

Peter replied, "Repent and be baptized, every one of you, in the name of Jesus Christ for the forgiveness of your sins. And you will receive the gift of the Holy Spirit." (Ac. 2:38)

Repent, then, and turn to God, so that your sins may be wiped out, that times of refreshing may come from the Lord. (Ac. 3:19)

Repent of this wickedness and pray to the Lord. Perhaps he will forgive you for having such a thought in your heart. (Ac. 8:22)

If we confess our sins, he is faithful and just and will forgive us our sins and purify us from all unrighteousness. (1 Jn. 1:9)

Now make confession to the LORD, the God of your fathers, and do his will. Separate yourselves from the peoples around you and from your foreign wives. (Ezr. 10:11)

He who conceals his sins does not prosper, but whoever confesses and renounces them finds mercy. (Pr. 28:13)

NUMBERS 35:1-34

Let the wicked forsake his way and the evil man his thoughts. Let him turn to the LORD, and he will have mercy on him, and to our God, for he will freely pardon. (Is. 55:7)

"Only acknowledge your guilt—you have rebelled against the LORD your God, you have scattered your favors to foreign gods under every spreading tree, and have not obeyed me," declares the LORD. (Je. 3:13)

But if a wicked man turns away from all the sins he has committed and keeps all my decrees and does what is just and right, he will surely live; he will not die. (Eze. 18:21)

TYPES, SYMBOLS, AND PICTURES
(Numbers 35:1-34)

Historical Term	Type or Picture (Scriptural Basis for Each)	Life Application for Today's Believer	Biblical Application
Cities of Refuge Nu. 35:9-29	*The cities of refuge are a picture of Christ, our refuge from the threats and storms of life.* **Select some towns to be your cities of refuge, to which a person who has killed someone accidentally may flee. (Nu. 35:11)**	The LORD is our Refuge from the threats and storms of life. Scripture declares four wonderful truths about the protection the LORD gives us. 1. The LORD is our Refuge.	*The eternal God is your refuge, and underneath are the everlasting arms. He will drive out your enemy before you, saying, 'Destroy him!' (De. 33:27) My God is my rock, in whom I take refuge, my shield and the horn of my salvation. He is my stronghold, my refuge and my savior—from violent men you save me. (2 S. 22:3) The LORD is a refuge for the oppressed, a stronghold in times of trouble. (Ps. 9:9) God is our refuge and strength, an ever-present help in trouble. (Ps. 46:1) My salvation and my honor depend on God; he is my mighty rock, my refuge. (Ps. 62:7) If you make the Most High your dwelling—even the LORD, who is my refuge. (Ps. 91:9)*
		2. The LORD is our Hiding Place.	*You are my hiding place; you will protect me from trouble and surround me with songs of deliverance. Selah (Ps. 32:7) You are my refuge and my shield; I have put my hope in your word. (Ps. 119:114)*
		3. The LORD is our Shield in protecting us.	*After this, the word of the LORD came to Abram in a vision: "Do not be afraid, Abram. I am your shield, your very great reward." (Ge. 15:1) Blessed are you, O Israel! Who is like you, a people saved by the LORD?*

NUMBERS 35:1-34

Historical Term	Type or Picture (Scriptural Basis for Each)	Life Application for Today's Believer	Biblical Application
			He is your shield and helper and your glorious sword. Your enemies will cower before you, and you will trample down their high places. (De. 33:29) *My God is my rock, in whom I take refuge, my shield and the horn of my salvation. He is my stronghold, my refuge and my savior—from violent men you save me.* (2 S. 22:3) *You give me your shield of victory; you stoop down to make me great.* (2 S. 22:36) *But you are a shield around me, O LORD; you bestow glory on me and lift up my head.* (Ps. 3:3) *For surely, O LORD, you bless the righteous; you surround them with your favor as with a shield.* (Ps. 5:12) *You give me your shield of victory, and your right hand sustains me; you stoop down to make me great.* (Ps. 18:35) *The LORD is my strength and my shield; my heart trusts in him, and I am helped. My heart leaps for joy and I will give thanks to him in song.* (Ps. 28:7) *He is my loving God and my fortress, my stronghold and my deliverer, my shield, in whom I take refuge, who subdues peoples under me.* (Ps. 144:2) *Every word of God is flawless; he is a shield to those who take refuge in him.* (Pr. 30:5)
		4. The LORD is our Atoning Sacrifice who delivers us from the avenger of death.	*For God so loved the world that he gave his one and only Son, that whoever believes in him shall not perish but have eternal life.* (Jn. 3:16) *And whoever lives and believes in me will never die. Do you believe this?* (Jn. 11:26) *To those who by persistence in doing good seek glory, honor and immortality, he will give eternal life.* (Ro. 2:7) *The last enemy to be destroyed is death.* (1 Co. 15:26)

NUMBERS 36:1-13

	CHAPTER 36		
	K. The Women Who Inherited Property: A Picture of Strong Faith in the Promised Land of God, 36:1-13		
1. The legal question: What happened to an inheritance if a woman married outside her tribe? (a picture of great humility & faith)	The family heads of the clan of Gilead son of Makir, the son of Manasseh, who were from the clans of the descendants of Joseph, came and spoke before Moses and the leaders, the heads of the Israelite families.	tribe of the descendants of Joseph is saying is right.	**common interests & true faith in the promised land)**
a. The humble approach to Moses & the leaders		6 This is what the LORD commands for Zelophehad's daughters: They may marry anyone they please as long as they marry within the tribal clan of their father.	a. The law was expanded
1) Did not complain against the law (27:1-11)			1) The women could marry any man they desired, but the men had to be from their own tribal clan (of common interests & faith)
2) Were not anti-feminists: Not against the daughters inheriting their brothers' land	2 They said, "When the LORD commanded my lord to give the land as an inheritance to the Israelites by lot, he ordered you to give the inheritance of our brother Zelophehad to his daughters.	7 No inheritance in Israel is to pass from tribe to tribe, for every Israelite shall keep the tribal land inherited from his forefathers.	2) The promised land was not to pass from tribe to tribe
		8 Every daughter who inherits land in any Israelite tribe must marry someone in her father's tribal clan, so that every Israelite will possess the inheritance of his fathers.	3) The land of every person must be kept in the tribe that inherited the land
b. The humble & legitimate question: What happened to the land if a daughter married a man from another tribe	3 Now suppose they marry men from other Israelite tribes; then their inheritance will be taken from our ancestral inheritance and added to that of the tribe they marry into. And so part of the inheritance allotted to us will be taken away.		b. The law was set as a precedent
1) The inherited land would go with the daughters			1) The law applied to all women inheriting land
2) The total area of tribal land would decrease		9 No inheritance may pass from tribe to tribe, for each Israelite tribe is to keep the land it inherits."	2) Each family was to retain its inheritance in the promised land
3) The Year of Jubilee would cause the land to be permanently added to the other tribe—lost forever to the ancestral tribe	4 When the Year of Jubilee for the Israelites comes, their inheritance will be added to that of the tribe into which they marry, and their property will be taken from the tribal inheritance of our forefathers."	10 So Zelophehad's daughters did as the LORD commanded Moses.	**3. The faith of the five daughters (a picture of obedience) (Nu. 27:1-11)**
		11 Zelophehad's daughters—Mahlah, Tirzah, Hoglah, Milcah and Noah—married their cousins on their father's side.	a. They married their distant cousins: Men of common interests & true spiritual commitment
c. The great faith in the promised land: Believed—but had not yet entered the land		12 They married within the clans of the descendants of Manasseh son of Joseph, and their inheritance remained in their father's clan and tribe.	b. They kept their inheritance in the promised land in their father's clan & tribe: A picture of protecting one's inheritance in the promised land by obeying God
2. The legal solution: Marrying within one's tribe (a picture of marrying a person with	5 Then at the LORD's command Moses gave this order to the Israelites: "What the	13 These are the commands and regulations the LORD gave through Moses to the Israelites on the plains of Moab by the Jordan across from Jericho.	**4. The commands of God**
			a. Given to the people thru Moses the mediator (a symbol of Christ the perfect Mediator)
			b. Given to guide the believer's march to the promised land

DIVISION IV

THE PREPARATION FOR THE MARCH INTO THE PROMISED LAND, 26:1–36:13

K. The Women Who Inherited Property: A Picture of Strong Faith in the Promised Land of God Heaven, 36:1-13

(36:1-13) **Introduction—Society, Foundation of—Law, Basis of Society**: legal matters or laws govern everything about us. Buying and selling, driving and walking, food and drink, words and behavior—there are laws to govern practically every act and everything that concerns human life. The laws and regulations that govern society, the way we relate to one another, are important. Without the law, society would disintegrate and every person would go his or her own way. Lawlessness and violence would reign supreme. There would be no respect of property and very little if any reverence for life. Utter chaos would be the way of life. The laws or regulations to control human behavior are absolute essentials for society to exist.

The present Scripture concerns the expansion of a particular law that had just recently been established in the law books of Israel. The problem that arose and the legal solution to the problem are the topics of discussion in this passage. It is a passage that focuses upon the inheritance of women in the promised land, a passage that speaks against anti-feminism and against being anti-any person. This is a passage that is desperately needed by society today: *The Women Who Inherited Property: A Picture of Strong Faith in the Promised Land of God, 36:1-13.*

1. The legal question: What happened to an inheritance if a woman married outside her tribe? (a picture of great humility and faith) (vv.1-4).
2. The legal solution: marrying within one's tribe (a picture of marrying a person with common interests and true faith in the promised land) (vv. 5-9).

NUMBERS 36:1-13

3. The faith of the five daughters (a picture of obedience) (Nu. 27:1-11), (vv.10-12).
4. The commands of God (v.13).

1 (36:1-4) **Humility, Example of—Faith, Example of—Law, Governing Women's Inheritance—Land, the Promised, Law Governing—Inheritance, of Women, Law Governing**: there was the legal question: What happened to an inheritance if a woman married outside her tribe? This event is a picture of great humility and faith. Remember, a law had already been established that allowed women to inherit their father's land if he had no sons (see outline and notes—Nu. 27:1-11 for more discussion). But there was another problem that arose: if the daughter married outside her family line, the property would pass to her husband's side of the family. This meant that all property like it would be split up all across the nation, that there would be an unequal ownership of the property among the tribal families. God's plan for each tribe to inherit a just and fair amount of land would be upset.

a. Note the humble approach to Moses and the leaders of the nation (vv.1-2). Some leaders from the clan of Gilead foresaw the problem created by the newly established law. They did not react by complaining against the law—grumbling and murmuring that it was unfair and unjust. Neither were they anti-feminists, against daughters inheriting their brothers' land. On the contrary, they were humble and considerate, men of great faith in the promised land. This was clearly seen by their humble approach to Moses and the leaders, the supreme court of the nation.

b. Note the humble and legitimate question they asked: What happened to the land if a daughter married a man from another tribe (vv.3-4)? They pointed out that the inherited land would go with the daughters, and that the total area of their tribal land would decrease. In the Year of Jubilee, the land would be permanently added to the other tribe, lost forever to the ancestral or family tribe. This was a legitimate problem brought to the attention of the supreme court in a most humble way. But humility is not the only lesson of importance.

c. Note the faith of the family heads of Gilead: they had strong faith in the promised land. They had not yet entered into the promised land, yet they believed this problem would arise. They were going to have to deal with the problem. They believed they were going to enter the promised land and be facing this problem. They had great faith in the promise of God, that they were going to inherit the promised land of God.

Thought 1. There are several lessons in this point for us.
(1) Equality before God is a right that is to be given to every human being. These men were not anti-feminists; neither are we to be. Scripture declares that we are not to be anti-*any person*. Every person upon this earth is created equal before God. Of course, there are differences between us. For example, some are short, others are tall; some are good looking, others are not so good looking; some are very intelligent, others are not so intelligent; some are handicapped, others are not. Women are able to bear children, and men are not. Some are born with the genes and brain cells that allow them to progress and achieve far beyond what the rest of us are able to accomplish. Some are driven to work far harder than others; therefore they achieve and secure far more. These persons usually hold positions of wealth and leadership in our communities and nation, just as these leaders from Gilead did and the leaders who sat upon the supreme court of Israel. But Scripture declares this one strong fact: the same spirit of humility and faith that was in the leaders of Gilead is to be within our hearts. There is to be no inequality, no anti-feminism nor anti-any person. There are to be equal opportunities and equal rights for every human being.

> There is neither Jew nor Greek, slave nor free, male nor female, for you are all one in Christ Jesus. (Ga. 3:28)
> But you are not to be called 'Rabbi,' for you have only one Master and you are all brothers. (Mt. 23:8)
> He said to them: "You are well aware that it is against our law for a Jew to associate with a Gentile or visit him. But God has shown me that I should not call any man impure or unclean." (Ac.10:28)
> Then Peter began to speak: "I now realize how true it is that God does not show favoritism but accepts men from every nation who fear him and do what is right." (Ac.10:34-35)
> For there is no difference between Jew and Gentile—the same Lord is Lord of all and richly blesses all who call on him. (Ro. 10:12)
> I charge you, in the sight of God and Christ Jesus and the elect angels, to keep these instructions without partiality, and to do nothing out of favoritism. (1 Ti. 5:21)
> My brothers, as believers in our glorious Lord Jesus Christ, don't show favoritism. Suppose a man comes into your meeting wearing a gold ring and fine clothes, and a poor man in shabby clothes also comes in. If you show special attention to the man wearing fine clothes and say, "Here's a good seat for you," but say to the poor man, "You stand there" or "Sit on the floor by my feet," have you not discriminated among yourselves and become judges with evil thoughts? Listen, my dear brothers: Has not God chosen those who are poor in the eyes of the world to be rich in faith and to inherit the kingdom he promised those who love him? (Js. 2:1-5)
> Do not pervert justice; do not show partiality to the poor or favoritism to the great, but judge your neighbor fairly. (Le. 19:15)
> He would surely rebuke you if you secretly showed partiality. (Jb. 13:10)
> Rich and poor have this in common: The LORD is the Maker of them all. (Pr. 22:2)

(2) Humility is the demand of God. We are to walk humbly before one another, demonstrating humility in dealing with one another.

> Therefore, whoever humbles himself like this child is the greatest in the kingdom of heaven. (Mt. 18:4)
> But when you are invited, take the lowest place, so that when your host comes, he

will say to you, 'Friend, move up to a better place.' Then you will be honored in the presence of all your fellow guests. (Lu. 14:10)

But you are not to be like that. Instead, the greatest among you should be like the youngest, and the one who rules like the one who serves. (Lu. 22:26)

For by the grace given me I say to every one of you: Do not think of yourself more highly than you ought, but rather think of yourself with sober judgment, in accordance with the measure of faith God has given you. (Ro. 12:3)

Humble yourselves before the Lord, and he will lift you up. (Js. 4:10)

Young men, in the same way be submissive to those who are older. All of you, clothe yourselves with humility toward one another, because, "God opposes the proud but gives grace to the humble." Humble yourselves, therefore, under God's mighty hand, that he may lift you up in due time. (1 Pe. 5:5-6)

Better to be lowly in spirit and among the oppressed than to share plunder with the proud. (Pr. 16:19)

Humility and the fear of the LORD bring wealth and honor and life. (Pr. 22:4)

A man's pride brings him low, but a man of lowly spirit gains honor. (Pr. 29:23)

For this is what the high and lofty One says—he who lives forever, whose name is holy: "I live in a high and holy place, but also with him who is contrite and lowly in spirit, to revive the spirit of the lowly and to revive the heart of the contrite." (Is. 57:15)

He has showed you, O man, what is good. And what does the LORD require of you? To act justly and to love mercy and to walk humbly with your God. (Mi. 6:8)

(3) There is only one way to enter the promised land of heaven: a person must believe in God and His promises. The men from Gilead believed in God and in the inheritance of the promised land of God. They were just as we are, standing there not yet having entered the promised land. Yet they believed and trusted the promise of God. So it is to be with us: we must believe God and His promises, believe in the promised land of heaven. Faith in God and in His promises is an absolute essential. This is the clear declaration of Scripture:

For God so loved the world that he gave his one and only Son, that whoever believes in him shall not perish but have eternal life. (Jn. 3:16)

I tell you the truth, whoever hears my word and believes him who sent me has eternal life and will not be condemned; he has crossed over from death to life. (Jn. 5:24)

Then they asked him, "What must we do to do the works God requires?" Jesus answered, "The work of God is this: to believe in the one he has sent." (Jn. 6:28-29)

Jesus said to her, "I am the resurrection and the life. He who believes in me will live, even though he dies." (Jn. 11:25)

But these are written that you may believe that Jesus is the Christ, the Son of God, and that by believing you may have life in his name. (Jn. 20:31)

And without faith it is impossible to please God, because anyone who comes to him must believe that he exists and that he rewards those who earnestly seek him. (He. 11:6)

By faith Noah, when warned about things not yet seen, in holy fear built an ark to save his family. By his faith he condemned the world and became heir of the righteousness that comes by faith. By faith Abraham, when called to go to a place he would later receive as his inheritance, obeyed and went, even though he did not know where he was going. By faith he made his home in the promised land like a stranger in a foreign country; he lived in tents, as did Isaac and Jacob, who were heirs with him of the same promise. For he was looking forward to the city with foundations, whose architect and builder is God. (He. 11:7-10)

All these people were still living by faith when they died. They did not receive the things promised; they only saw them and welcomed them from a distance. And they admitted that they were aliens and strangers on earth. People who say such things show that they are looking for a country of their own. If they had been thinking of the country they had left, they would have had opportunity to return. Instead, they were longing for a better country—a heavenly one. Therefore God is not ashamed to be called their God, for he has prepared a city for them. (He. 11:13-16)

And this is his command: to believe in the name of his Son, Jesus Christ, and to love one another as he commanded us. (1 Jn. 3:23)

Early in the morning they left for the Desert of Tekoa. As they set out, Jehoshaphat stood and said, "Listen to me, Judah and people of Jerusalem! Have faith in the LORD your God and you will be upheld; have faith in his prophets and you will be successful." (2 Chr. 20:20)

2 (36:5-9) **Marriage, Duties of—Inheritance, Laws Governing—Laws, of Inheritance—Women, Inheritance of**: there was the legal solution governing the inheritance of women. This is a picture of marrying a person with common interests and true faith in the promised land.

a. The law was expanded by the Lord and related to the people by Moses (vv.5-7). The woman could marry any man she desired, but the man had to be from her own tribal or family clan. Note how this is a picture of a young couple considering common interest in faith before marrying. The promised land—the land of inheritance—was not to pass from tribe to tribe. The land of every person was to be kept within the tribe that inherited the land.

NUMBERS 36:1-13

b. The law was established as a precedent (vv.8-9). The law applied to all women inheriting land. Each family was to retain its inheritance in the promised land, and each tribe was to preserve the land it inherited. Just as a man was to cleave to his wife, so a person was to cleave to the land he or she inherited (Ge. 2:24).¹

Thought 1. Marriage was not to jeopardize the inheritance of a person nor take the inheritance away from the family or out of the tribe. Again, if a woman wished to marry out of her tribe, she could. But she was not able to transfer the property of her inheritance over to the family of her husband.

This is a strong lesson for marriage, a strong lesson for young couples who are considering marriage. A person should never marry anyone who does not believe in the inheritance of God, in the promised land of heaven. But something else is just as important: common interests, purpose, culture, emotional compatibility. All these factors must be considered in order to have a loving and successful marriage. Husband and wife have to be fitted for one another in all these ways in order to adjust and experience the fullness of life together.

Consider this fact: many, many people make a mistake in marrying. A large percentage of marriages end in divorce. But this is not all: a great number of spouses stay together who are not happy. Combine the divorces and the unhappy spouses who remain together and only one conclusion can be reached: the vast majority of marriages are unhappy. Believers must always do what this law pictures: marry within the tribe or family of faith. Both spouses must believe in God and His promises, believe in the promised land of heaven. Two persons cannot walk through life divided, one marching to the promised land of heaven and the other marching to a life of separation from God. Both must have their eyes and lives focused upon the inheritance of God, upon His great gift of the promised land of heaven. A divided family equals unhappiness. Division causes discord—trouble, dissension, arguments, conflict, hurt, pain, and regret. Far better to solve this issue while dating than after marriage. This is the important lesson of this point: a person must marry someone with common interests and a true faith in God and the promised land of heaven.

> But seek first his kingdom and his righteousness, and all these things will be given to you as well. (Mt. 6:33)
> But now I am writing you that you must not associate with anyone who calls himself a brother but is sexually immoral or greedy, an idolater or a slanderer, a drunkard or a swindler. With such a man do not even eat. (1 Co. 5:11)
> Do not be yoked together with unbelievers. For what do righteousness and wickedness have in common? Or what fellowship can light have with darkness? (2 Co. 6:14)
> "Therefore come out from them and be separate, says the Lord. Touch no unclean thing, and I will receive you. I will be a Father to you, and you will be my sons and daughters, says the Lord Almighty." (2 Co. 6:17-18)
> Wives, submit to your husbands as to the Lord. (Ep. 5:22)
> Husbands, love your wives, just as Christ loved the church and gave himself up for her. (Ep. 5:25)
> So I counsel younger widows to marry, to have children, to manage their homes and to give the enemy no opportunity for slander. (1 Ti. 5:14)
> For this reason a man will leave his father and mother and be united to his wife, and they will become one flesh. (Ge. 2:24)
> I am a friend to all who fear you, to all who follow your precepts. (Ps. 119:63)
> Thus you will walk in the ways of good men and keep to the paths of the righteous. (Pr. 2:20)
> He who walks with the wise grows wise, but a companion of fools suffers harm. (Pr. 13:20)

3 (36:10-12) **Obedience—Inheritance, Spiritual—Land, the Promised, Protecting One's Inheritance**: there was the obedience of the five daughters of faith. These were the daughters of Zelophehad who had died without sons. Because of this problem, these five daughters had become concerned about their father's inheritance in the promised land. It was their problem that had led to the original law, the law that granted the inheritance of land to daughters who had no brothers. The point to note is the strong faith of these daughters, all five of them. They believed in the promised land, so much so that they were going to obey the new law that had just been established. No matter the cost, they were going to cling to the inheritance promised by God.

a. The five daughters of faith married within their tribal families, married distant cousins. They married men of common family or tribal interests and men of true spiritual faith and commitment (v.11).

b. These five daughters kept their inheritance in the promised land, kept it in their father's clan and family tribe.

Thought 1. This is a clear picture of a person protecting his inheritance in the promised land by obeying God. Obedience is absolutely necessary in order to receive one's inheritance. This fact cannot be stressed enough in modern society, a society of 'cheap faith.' The meaning of faith is not really understood by many people today; faith is often distorted, twisted, and watered down. It is thought to mean mental *ascent*, simply believing that something is true, that it is historically true. It is thought that faith does not necessarily have a bearing upon a person's behavior, that it makes no difference how a person lives just so he believes. Of course, this is absurd. This is nothing more than the *emptying* of faith, taking faith and *emptying* it of all meaning. It is profession *only*, a false profession. It is, quite frankly, only empty, meaningless words. A person who truly believes, obeys. To believe is to obey and to obey is to believe. If a person genuinely believes something, he will act upon it. He will do exactly what his faith says. Obedience is the great lesson taught us by these five women of faith. If we believe in the promised

---
¹ *The Expositor's Bible Commentary*. Frank E. Gaebelein, Editor, p. 1007.

land of heaven, then we will obey God and follow after Him. We will seek after—actively pursue—the righteousness of heaven. We will do all we can to enter the promised land of heaven. We will actively obey God so that He will accept us in that glorious day.

> "Not everyone who says to me, 'Lord, Lord,' will enter the kingdom of heaven, but only he who does the will of my Father who is in heaven." (Mt. 7:21)
>
> He replied, "Isaiah was right when he prophesied about you hypocrites; as it is written: 'These people honor me with their lips, but their hearts are far from me.'" (Mk. 7:6)
>
> Whoever has my commands and obeys them, he is the one who loves me. He who loves me will be loved by my Father, and I too will love him and show myself to him. (Jn. 14:21)
>
> Jesus replied, "If anyone loves me, he will obey my teaching. My Father will love him, and we will come to him and make our home with him." (Jn. 14:23)
>
> If you obey my commands, you will remain in my love, just as I have obeyed my Father's commands and remain in his love. (Jn. 15:10)
>
> They claim to know God, but by their actions they deny him. They are detestable, disobedient and unfit for doing anything good. (Tit. 1:16)
>
> Blessed are those who wash their robes, that they may have the right to the tree of life and may go through the gates into the city. (Re. 22:14)
>
> The LORD your God commands you this day to follow these decrees and laws; carefully observe them with all your heart and with all your soul. (De. 26:16)
>
> Do not let this Book of the Law depart from your mouth; meditate on it day and night, so that you may be careful to do everything written in it. Then you will be prosperous and successful. (Jos. 1:8)

4 (36:13) **Numbers, Conclusion of—Commandments, of God, Purpose for—Pilgrimage, of the Believer—March, of the Believer—Believers, Pilgrimage of—Believers, March of**: there were the commands and regulations of God. This is the conclusion to the great book of Numbers. Remember, the Israelites were camped in the plains of Moab beside the Jordan River, right across from the great city of Jericho. They were poised to "cross over" the Jordan and enter the promised land to claim their inheritance. But keep this fact in mind: this was the second generation of believers, the sons and daughters of the generation that had marched out of Egypt. The march or pilgrimage of the first generation was a miserable failure. Unbelief and rebellion, grumbling and murmuring against God and His dear servant Moses—all the terrible sins that can be imagined—had been the traits, characteristics, and character flaws of the first generation. They had forced the hand of God, forced Him to chastise them. Consequently, they had been condemned to die in the desert wilderness. They were barred, never allowed to enter the promised land of God. The wilderness wanderings—the forty years of wandering about in the desert wilderness—were now over. The new generation of believers now stood poised to "cross over" the Jordan River and claim the inheritance promised by God, to lay hold of the promised land. The tragic pilgrimage of the first generation of believers and the raising up of the second generation of believers has been the story of the great book of Numbers. The first generation has passed from the scene, having been doomed to die in the desert wilderness of this world; now the second generation stands poised to "cross over" the Jordan to claim its inheritance in the promised land of God. Laying hold of the promise of God by this new generation of believers will be the story of the great book of *Joshua*.

In closing the great book of *Numbers*, Scripture declares two significant facts:

a. First, the commandments and regulations of God have been given to the people through Moses, the mediator between God and man.

b. Second, the commandments and regulations of God have been given to guide the believer's march or pilgrimage to the promised land.

Thought 1. Two significant lessons are seen in this point.

(1) As mediator, Moses was appointed by God to be a type of Christ. Jesus Christ is the Perfect Mediator who stands between God and man. He is the Perfect Intercessor, the Advocate who stands and pleads our case before God. Jesus Christ is the only Mediator who bridges the great gulf between God and man. No person can approach God apart from Christ and be accepted. God accepts only those who come to Him through His dear Son, the Lord Jesus Christ. Christ and Christ alone is the Mediator who can reconcile people to God.

> Jesus answered, "I am the way and the truth and the life. No one comes to the Father except through me." (Jn. 14:6)
>
> Salvation is found in no one else, for there is no other name under heaven given to men by which we must be saved. (Ac. 4:12)
>
> Who is he that condemns? Christ Jesus, who died—more than that, who was raised to life—is at the right hand of God and is also interceding for us. (Ro. 8:34)
>
> For there is one God and one mediator between God and men, the man Christ Jesus, who gave himself as a ransom for all men—the testimony given in its proper time. (1 Ti. 2:5-6)
>
> For this reason he had to be made like his brothers in every way, in order that he might become a merciful and faithful high priest in service to God, and that he might make atonement for the sins of the people. (He. 2:17)
>
> Therefore, since we have a great high priest who has gone through the heavens, Jesus the Son of God, let us hold firmly to the faith we profess. For we do not have a high priest who is unable to sympathize with our weaknesses, but we have one who has been tempted in every way, just as we are—yet was without sin. (He. 4:14-15)
>
> Every high priest is selected from among men and is appointed to represent them in matters related to God, to offer gifts and

sacrifices for sins. He is able to deal gently with those who are ignorant and are going astray, since he himself is subject to weakness. This is why he has to offer sacrifices for his own sins, as well as for the sins of the people. No one takes this honor upon himself; he must be called by God, just as Aaron was. So Christ also did not take upon himself the glory of becoming a high priest. But God said to him, "You are my Son; today I have become your Father." (He. 5:1-5)

We have this hope as an anchor for the soul, firm and secure. It enters the inner sanctuary behind the curtain, where Jesus, who went before us, has entered on our behalf. He has become a high priest forever, in the order of Melchizedek. (He. 6:19-20)

Therefore he is able to save completely those who come to God through him, because he always lives to intercede for them. Such a high priest meets our need—one who is holy, blameless, pure, set apart from sinners, exalted above the heavens. Unlike the other high priests, he does not need to offer sacrifices day after day, first for his own sins, and then for the sins of the people. He sacrificed for their sins once for all when he offered himself. (He. 7:25-27)

But the ministry Jesus has received is as superior to theirs as the covenant of which he is mediator is superior to the old one, and it is founded on better promises. (He. 8:6)

For this reason Christ is the mediator of a new covenant, that those who are called may receive the promised eternal inheritance—now that he has died as a ransom to set them free from the sins committed under the first covenant. (He. 9:15)

For Christ did not enter a man-made sanctuary that was only a copy of the true one; he entered heaven itself, now to appear for us in God's presence. Nor did he enter heaven to offer himself again and again, the way the high priest enters the Most Holy Place every year with blood that is not his own. Then Christ would have had to suffer many times since the creation of the world. But now he has appeared once for all at the end of the ages to do away with sin by the sacrifice of himself. Just as man is destined to die once, and after that to face judgment, so Christ was sacrificed once to take away the sins of many people; and he will appear a second time, not to bear sin, but to bring salvation to those who are waiting for him. (He. 9:24-28)

My dear children, I write this to you so that you will not sin. But if anybody does sin, we have one who speaks to the Father in our defense—Jesus Christ, the Righteous One. He is the atoning sacrifice for our sins, and not only for ours but also for the sins of the whole world. (1 Jn. 2:1-2)

(2) The Word of God—His commandments and regulations—guide the believer's pilgrimage as he marches to the promised land of heaven. There are pitfalls and enemies that stand opposed to the promised land of God. As we march throughout life, we need to know how to bypass the pitfalls and how to conquer the enemies who oppose us. There are pitfalls and enemies such as...

- disease
- accident
- failure
- unemployment
- immorality
- greed
- covetousness
- anger
- discouragement
- emptiness
- financial difficulty
- loneliness
- depression
- death
- lack of fulfillment
- lack of purpose

The pitfalls and enemies of life are innumerable. Any one of them can attack us at any time. This is the reason we need the Word of God to guide us.

As we march to the promised land of God, the only way to finish our pilgrimage is to listen to God. We must study, learn, and teach the commandments and regulations of God. We must live in His Word and obey His Word. Above all the lessons in the great book of Numbers, this is the one lesson that has been demonstrated before our very eyes, the one lesson that we ourselves must learn: we must obey God's Holy Word. This is the declaration of this last concluding verse of *Numbers*: these are the commandments and regulations given by God to His people as they were poised to "cross over" into the promised land. These are the commandments, the Word of God given to guide the believer's pilgrimage or march to the promised land of heaven.

You are already clean because of the word I have spoken to you. (Jn. 15:3)

Sanctify them by the truth; your word is truth. (Jn. 17:17)

But these are written that you may believe that Jesus is the Christ, the Son of God, and that by believing you may have life in his name. (Jn. 20:31)

To make her [the church] holy, cleansing her by the washing with water through the word. (Ep. 5:26)

Let the word of Christ dwell in you richly as you teach and admonish one another with all wisdom, and as you sing psalms, hymns and spiritual songs with gratitude in your hearts to God. (Col. 3:16)

Do your best to present yourself to God as one approved, a workman who does not need to be ashamed and who correctly handles the word of truth. (2 Ti. 2:15)

All Scripture is God-breathed and is useful for teaching, rebuking, correcting and training in righteousness. (2 Ti. 3:16)

For the word of God is living and active. Sharper than any double-edged sword, it penetrates even to dividing soul and spirit, joints and marrow; it judges the thoughts and attitudes of the heart. (He. 4:12)

I write these things to you who believe in the name of the Son of God so that you may know that you have eternal life. (1 Jn. 5:13)

How can a young man keep his way pure? By living according to your word. (Ps. 119:9)
I have hidden your word in my heart that I might not sin against you. (Ps. 119:11)
Your word is a lamp to my feet and a light for my path. (Ps. 119:105)
The unfolding of your words gives light; it gives understanding to the simple. (Ps. 119:130)

Thought 2. The great book of *Numbers* has been written to teach us, so that we might grow in endurance, encouragement, and hope. But this is not the only purpose for the great book of *Numbers*: it was also written to serve as a warning. The tragic failure of the first generation of believers stands as an example, as a strong warning to us upon whom the end of the world and the fulfillment of the ages has come.

For everything that was written in the past was written to teach us, so that through endurance and the encouragement of the Scriptures we might have hope. (Ro. 15:4)
These things happened to them as examples and were written down as warnings for us, on whom the fulfillment of the ages has come. (1 Co. 10:11)

TYPES, SYMBOLS, AND PICTURES
(Numbers 36:1-13)

Historical Term	Type or Picture (Scriptural Basis for Each)	Life Application for Today's Believer	Biblical Application
Moses Nu. 36:13 (See also Le. 1:1; 8:1-5)	*A clear type of Jesus Christ, the appointed Mediator, who stood between man and God. As the mediator, he revealed and declared the way to God.* *These are the commands and regulations the* LORD *gave through Moses to the Israelites on the plains of Moab by the Jordan across from Jericho. (Nu. 36:13)*	It is Jesus Christ who is the appointed Mediator. It is Christ, and Christ alone... • who stands in the gap between God and man. Through believing on Jesus Christ (the Mediator) a person believes on God. Through seeing Jesus Christ (the Mediator) a person sees God. • who proclaims the way to God • who opens the way into God's presence	*For there is one God and one mediator between God and men, the man Christ Jesus. (1 Ti. 2:5)* *In the past God spoke to our forefathers through the prophets at many times and in various ways, but in these last days he has spoken to us by his Son, whom he appointed heir of all things, and through whom he made the universe. The Son is the radiance of God's glory and the exact representation of his being, sustaining all things by his powerful word. After he had provided purification for sins, he sat down at the right hand of the Majesty in heaven. (He. 1:1-3)* *My dear children, I write this to you so that you will not sin. But if anybody does sin, we have one who speaks to the Father in our defense—Jesus Christ, the Righteous One. (1 Jn. 2:1; see Jn. 14:6)*

RESOURCES

NUMBERS

	PAGE
PRACTICAL BIBLE HELPS AND RESOURCES	
CHART 1: The Tabernacle in the Wilderness	329
CHART 2: The Tabernacle Interior	330
CHART 3: The Encampment of the Tribes	331
CHART 4: The Marching Positions of the Tribes	331
MAP 1: The Desert or Wilderness Wanderings of Israel	332
MAP 2: The Borders of the Promised Land of Canaan and the Mission of the Twelve Spies	333
TYPES, SYMBOLS, AND PICTURES	
➢ Alphabetical Outline	334
➢ Chronological Outline	339
OUTLINE AND SUBJECT INDEX	343

The Tabernacle in the Wilderness

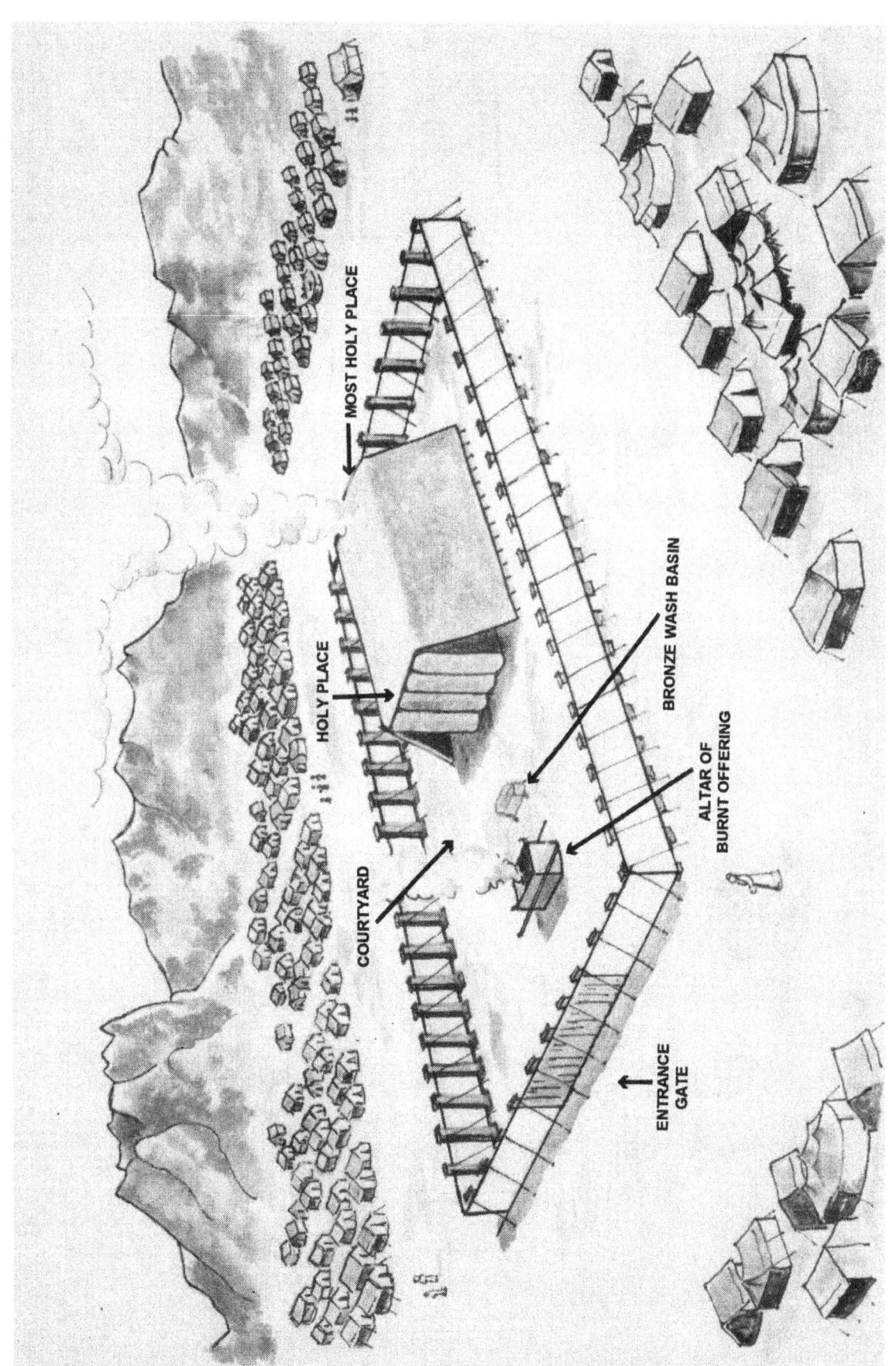

THE TABERNACLE (INTERIOR)

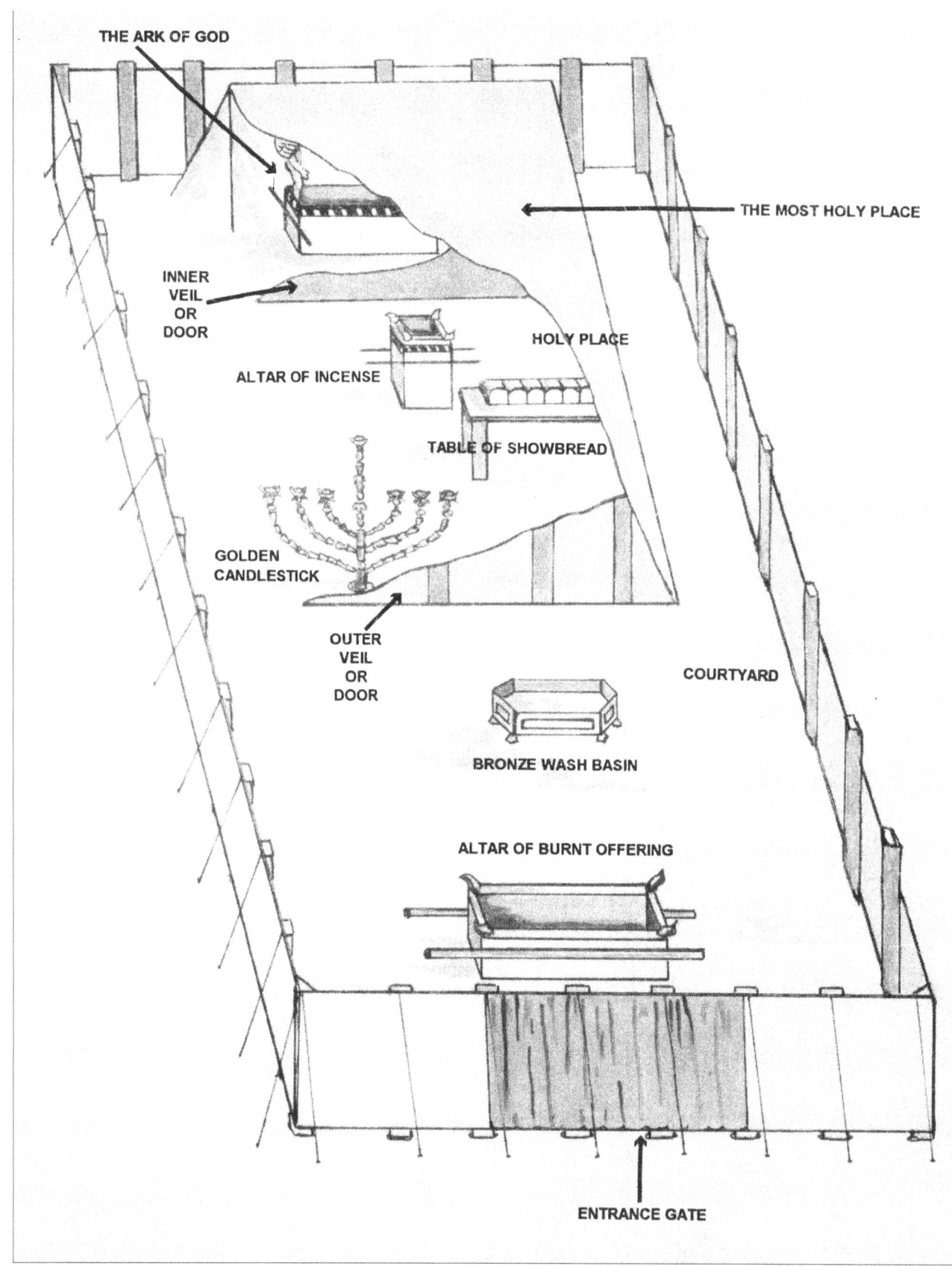

THE ENCAMPMENT OF THE TRIBES

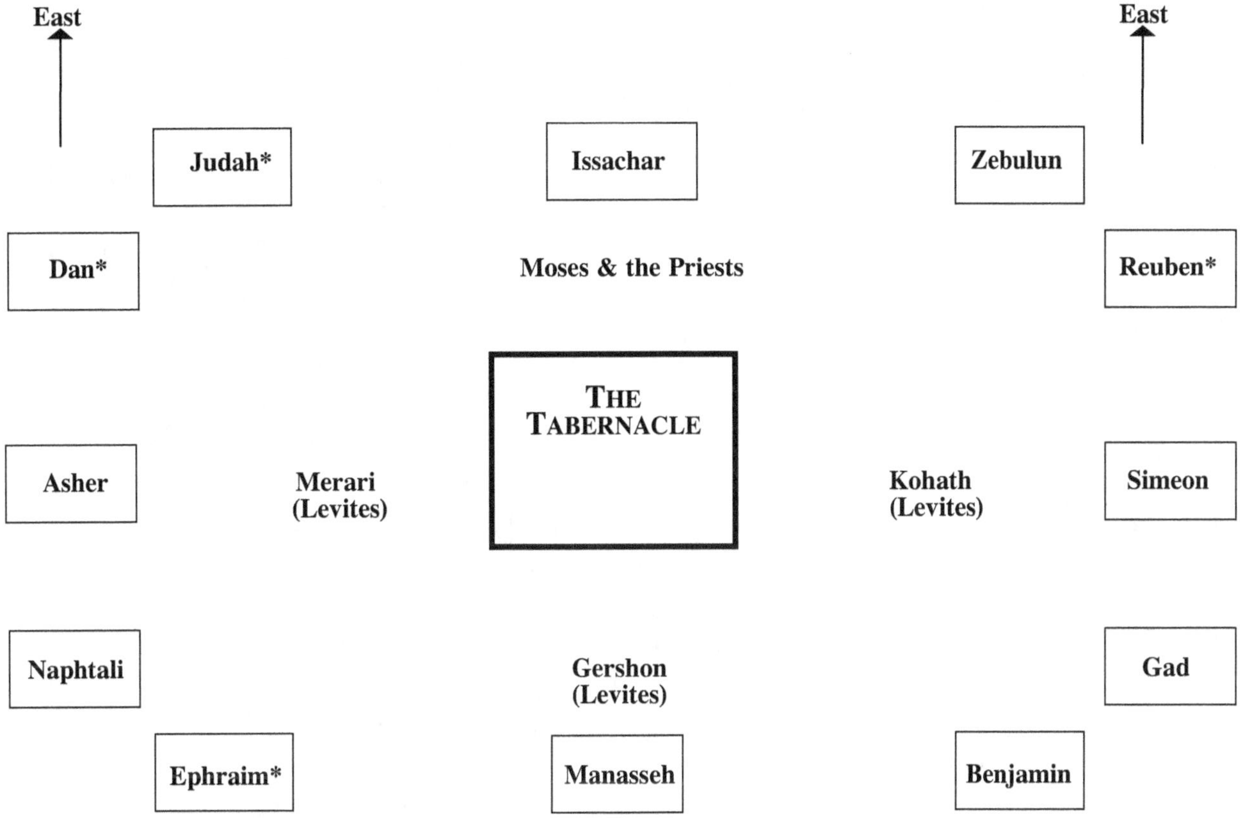

East
East
Judah*
Issachar
Zebulun
Dan*
Moses & the Priests
Reuben*
THE TABERNACLE
Asher
Merari (Levites)
Kohath (Levites)
Simeon
Naphtali
Gershon (Levites)
Gad
Ephraim*
Manasseh
Benjamin

(* *The leading tribe of the group*)

THE MARCHING POSITIONS OF THE TRIBES[1]

DAN
EPHRAIM
REUBEN
JUDAH
ASHER
Kohathites carry the Tabernacle furnishings
MANASSEH
Gershonites & Merarites carry the Tabernacle
SIMEON
Levites carry the ark
ISSACHAR
NAPHTALI
BENJAMIN
GAD
ZEBULUN

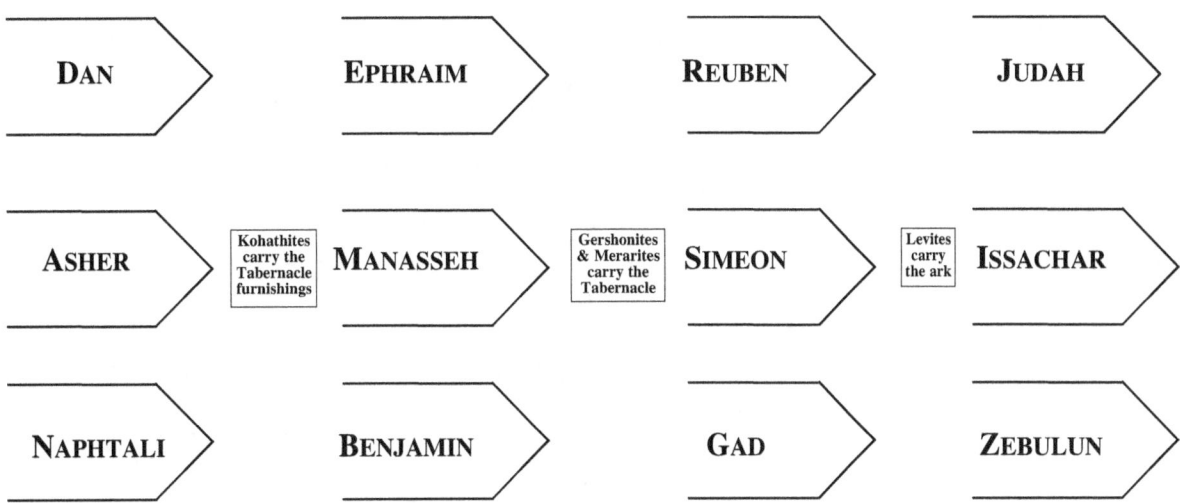

1 The idea for the Marching Positions of the Tribes is taken from the *New International Version Study Bible*. (Grand Rapids, MI: Zondervan Bible Publishers, 1985), p.192.

THE DESERT OR WILDERNESS WANDERINGS OF ISRAEL

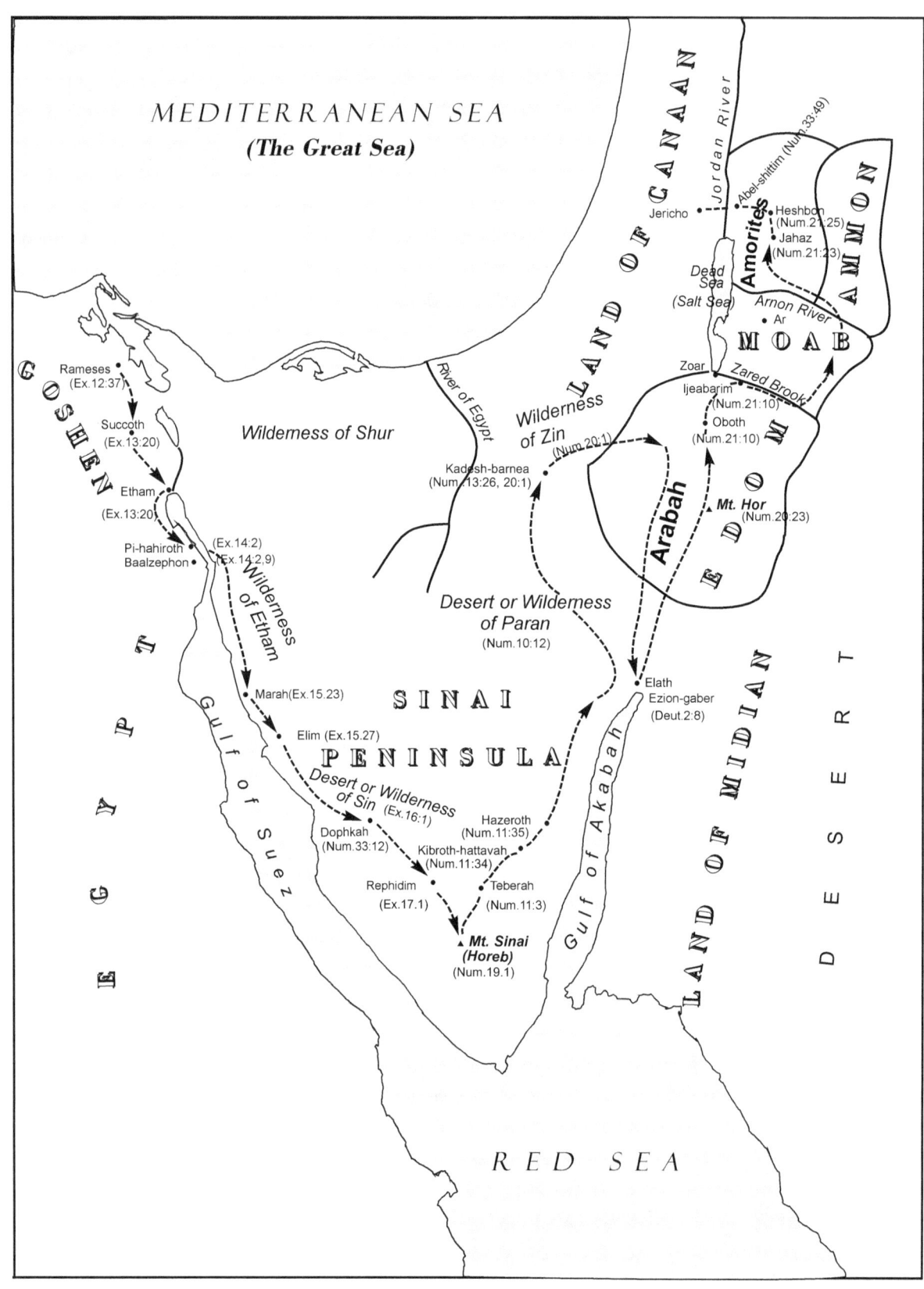

THE BORDERS OF THE PROMISED LAND OF CANAAN

AND

THE MISSION OF THE TWELVE SPIES

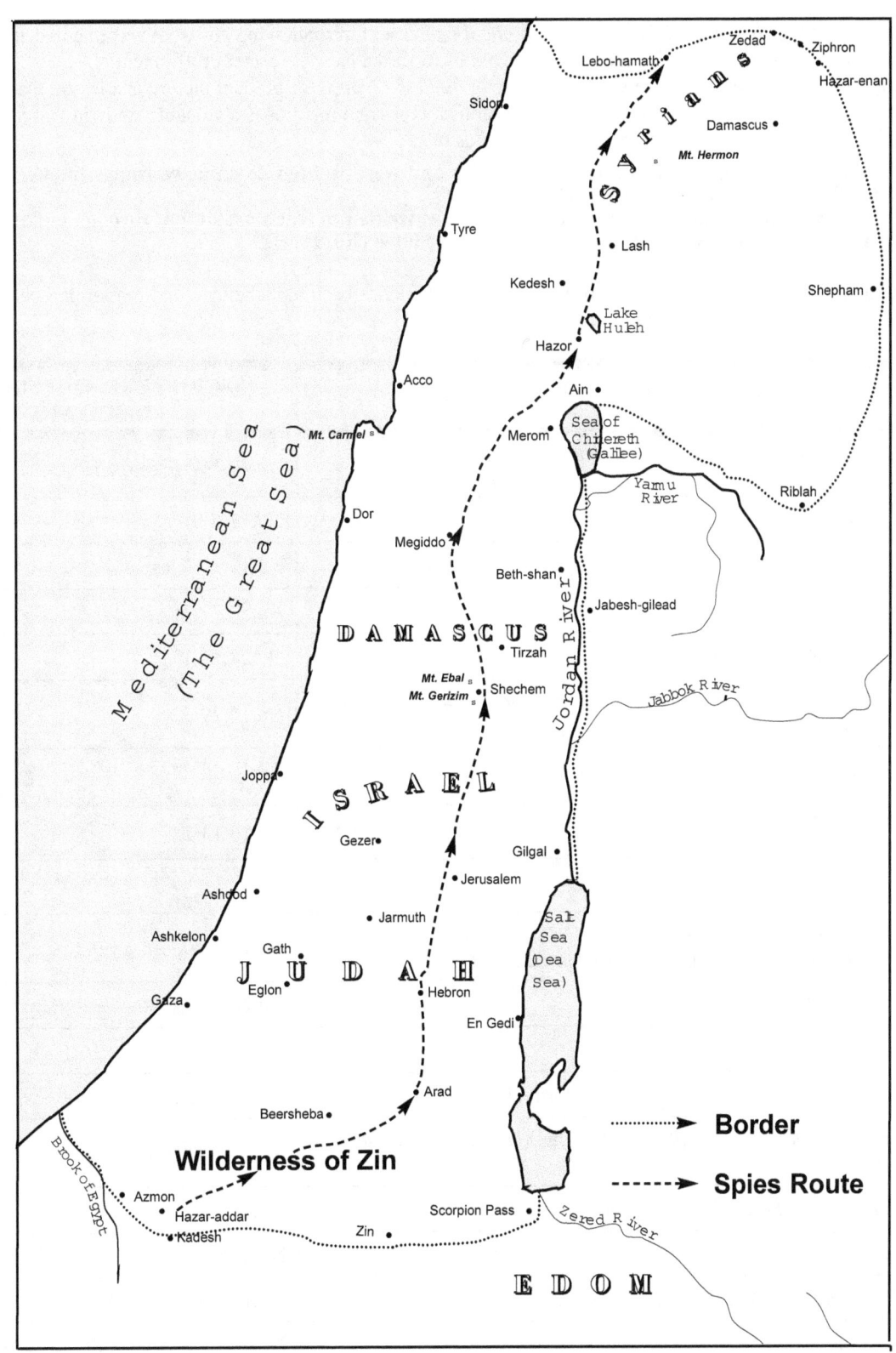

TYPES, SYMBOLS, AND PICTURES
THE BOOK OF NUMBERS

ALPHABETICAL OUTLINE

What is a biblical type or symbol? Simply put, a *biblical type* is a "foreshadowing" of what was to come at a later time in history. Through a person, place or thing a biblical type points toward a New Testament fulfillment.

In addition to biblical types, there are what we may call *biblical pictures*. A biblical picture is a lesson that we can see in the Scriptures *without distorting the truth*. The study of biblical types and pictures is a valuable study in that it helps us apply the truth of the Scriptures in our lives. Scripture itself tells us this:

> **These things happened to them as examples and were written down as warnings for us, on whom the fulfillment of the ages has come (1 Co. 10:11).**
> **For everything that was written in the past was written to teach us, so that through endurance and the encouragement of the Scriptures we might have hope (Ro. 15:4).**

For quick and easy reference, every type or picture in *Numbers* has been alphabetized and cross-referenced with similar subjects. Scripture references are also included.

PERSON/PLACE/THING	SCRIPTURE, OUTLINE AND DISCUSSION
A Person Who Had Been In Contact with Death Defiled the LORD's Tabernacle: He Was to Be Cut Off (See Death, Contact with...)	Nu.19:11-16, esp. v.13
Aaron's Staff (See Staff...)	Nu.17:6-9
An Unused Red Heifer (See Red Heifer...)	Nu.19:1-10, esp. v.2
Angel of the LORD, the Sword of the	Nu.22:22-35
Animal Sacrifices, Monthly Offerings of	Nu.28:11-15
Appeal of Moses to His Brother-In-Law to Join the March to the Promised Land (See Moses...)	Nu.10:29-32
Ark or Chest, the	Nu.10:33-34 (see Ex.25:10-22; 40:20; 35:12; 37:1-5; 39:35; 40:3, 20-21)
Army of God's People Marched Forth Division by Division— as Commanded	Nu.10:13-28
Aroma, the Sweet	Nu.28:1-2; 28:3-8 (see Le.1:9; 8:21; 16:27-28)
Ashes of the Sacrifice: A Clean Person Was to Gather Up the Ashes of the Sacrifice And Keep Them In A Clean Place Outside the Camp	Nu.19:1-10, esp. vv.9-10
Assyria Destroying the Kenites.	Nu.24:21-22
Atonement, Day of (See Day of Atonement...)	Nu.29:7-11 (see Le.16:1-34; Le.23:27)
Attack upon Israel [by the Amorites] (See Israel, Attack Upon...)	Nu.21:21-32
Blood (of the Red Heifer) Was Sprinkled Seven Times at the Front of the Tabernacle.	Nu.19:1-10, esp. v.4
Bread of the Presence, the Twelve Loaves of	Nu.8:1-4
Bronze Snake	Nu.21:4-9
Burned, Wholly: the Red Heifer Was to Be Wholly Burned, All Its Parts	Nu.19:1-10, esp. v.5
Burnt Offering, the	Nu.6:3-12; 15:1-16; 28:11-15 (see Le.1:1-17; 6:8-13; 8:18-21; 16:24)

TYPES, SYMBOLS, AND PICTURES
Alphabetical Outline

PERSON/PLACE/THING	SCRIPTURE, OUTLINE AND DISCUSSION
Camp, Outside the: Red Heifer Was to Be Put to Death	Nu.19:1-10, esp. v.3
Censers	Nu.16:36-40
Census of the Firstborn and Their Replacement by the Levites, the (See Firstborn, Census of...)	Nu.3:40-51
Cities of Refuge (See Refuge...)	Nu.35:9-29
Clean Person Was to Gather Up the Ashes of the Sacrifice And Keep Them In A Clean Place Outside the Camp (See Ashes of the Sacrifice...)	Nu.19:1-10, esp. vv.9-10
Cleansing of Everyone Who Had Anything to Do with the Sacrifice Had to Cleanse Himself And His Clothes	Nu.19:1-10, esp. vv.7-8
Cleansing of the Levites	Nu.8:5-26
Cleansing Water: Unclean Person Had to Be Purified with the Cleansing Water On the Third And Seventh Days	Nu.19:11-16, esp. v.12
Clothes, Tearing of	Nu.14:1-10, esp. v.6
Clothes, Washing of the Levites'	Nu.8:5-26
Cloud, Pillar of	Nu.9:15-23
Coming Deliverer, the (See Deliverer...)	Nu.24:14-19
Compromise of Gad and Reuben	Nu.32:1-42
Conquest of the Midianites (See Midianites...)	Nu.31:1-54
Contact with a Dead Body (See Dead Body...)	Nu.6:3-12 (see Le.10:4-5)
Day of Atonement, the	Nu.29:7-11 (see Le.16:1-34; Le.23:27)
Dead Body, Contact with	Nu.6:3-12 (see Le.10:4-5)
Death	Nu.19:11-16
Death, Contact with: A Person Who Had Been In Contact with Death Defiled the LORD's Tabernacle: He Was to Be Cut Off	Nu.19:11-16, esp. v.13
Dedication of the Levites (See Levites....)	Nu.8:5-26
Deliverer, Coming the	Nu.24:14-19
Dividing the Inheritance of the Promised Land (See Promised Land, Inheritance of...)	Nu.26:53-56
Drink Offering, the	Nu.6:13-20; 15:1-16, esp. v.7
Egypt	Nu.3:5-13; 9:1-14 (see Le.11:44-47; 19:33-34)
Everyone Who Had Anything to Do with the Sacrifice Had to Cleanse Himself And His Clothes. (See Cleansing of...)	Nu.19:1-10, esp. vv.7-8
Fellowship Offering, the Nazarite Burning His Hair (See Nazarite Burning...)	Nu.6:13-20
Fellowship or Peace Offering, the (See Peace Offering...)	Nu.6:13-20; 15:1-16 (see Le.3:1-17)
Festival of Firstfruits, the (See Firstfruits...)	Nu.28:26-31 (see Le.23:9-14)

TYPES, SYMBOLS, AND PICTURES
ALPHABETICAL OUTLINE

PERSON/PLACE/THING	SCRIPTURE, OUTLINE AND DISCUSSION
Festival of Tabernacles or Booths or Shelters, the (See Tabernacles...)	Nu.29:12-38 (see Le.23:33-34)
Festival of Trumpets, the (See Trumpets...)	Nu.29:1-6 (see Le.23:23-25)
Firstborn, Census of (See Census of the Firstborn...)	Nu.3:40-51
Firstfruits	Nu.15:17-21
Firstfruits, Festival of	Nu.28:26-31 (see Le.23:9-14)
Garments of Aaron: Putting Aaron's Garments on Eleazar	Nu.20:23-29
Gathered to His People	Nu.20:23-29
Grain Offering	Nu.15:1-16 (see Le.2:3)
Great Army of God's People Marched Forth Division by Division—as Commanded (See Army of God...)	Nu.10:13-28
Great March to the Promised Land Finally Begins (See March...)	Nu.10:11-36
Guilt Offering, the	Nu.6:3-12 (see Le.5:14-6:7)
Hair, the Nazarite Burning His (See Nazarite Burning...)	Nu.6:13-20
High Priest, the	Nu.3:5-13; 4:1-20 (see Le.16:3, 6)
Israel	Nu.23:1-12
Israel's Shocking Military Error against Midian.(See Israel, Error against...)	Nu.31:14-18
Israel, Attack Upon [by the Amorites]	Nu.21:21-32
Israel, Error against Midian	Nu.31:14-18
Joshua	Nu.13:1-25; 27:18
Lampstand, the	Nu.8:1-4 (see Le.24:1-4)
Leprosy or Infectious Skin Disease (See Skin Disease...)	Nu.5:1-4; 12:13-16 (see Le.13:1-59)
Levites Had to be Sprinkled with the Water of Cleansing, Shave Their Whole Heads, and Wash Their Clothes (See Cleansing...; see Shaving;...see Clothes...)	Nu.8:5-26
Levites, Dedication of	Nu.8:5-26
LORD Spoke (Said), The	Nu.26:1
March to the Promised Land Finally Begins	Nu.10:11-36
Midianites, Conquest of	Nu.31:1-54
Monthly Offerings of Animal Sacrifices (See Animal Sacrifices...)	Nu.28:11-15
Moses	Nu.36:13 (see Le.1:1; 8:1-5)
Moses' Appeal to His Brother-In-Law to Join the March to the Promised Land	Nu.10:29-32
Nazarite Burning His Hair under the Fellowship Offering (See Hair...; see Fellowship Offering...)	Nu.6:13-20

TYPES, SYMBOLS, AND PICTURES
ALPHABETICAL OUTLINE

PERSON/PLACE/THING	SCRIPTURE, OUTLINE AND DISCUSSION
Offering of the Red Heifer (A Red Female Cow). (See Red Heifer...)	Nu.19:1-22
Offering of the Red Heifer Was Established As A Permanent Law For Israel And For All Foreigners Among Them. (See Red Heifer, Offering of...)	Nu.19:1-10, esp. v.10
Passover, the	Nu.9:1-14; Nu.28:16-25 (see also Le.23:5)
Peace Offering or Fellowship, the (See Fellowship Offering...)	Nu.6:13-20; 15:1-16 (see Le.3:1-17)
Perfection of the Red Heifer Was to Have No Defect or Blemish	Nu.19:1-10, esp. v.2
Phinehas	Nu.25:6-13
Phinehas' Zeal for Righteousness	Nu.25:6-13
Phinehas, Zeal of: To Make Atonement or Reconciliation for the People.	Nu.25:6-13
Pillar of Cloud. (See Cloud...)	Nu.9:15-23
Priest (the) Was to Burn Some Cedar Wood, Hyssop And Scarlet Wool with the Red Heifer.	Nu.19:1-10, esp. v.6
Priest Loosening the Woman's Hair, the (See Woman's Hair...)	Nu.5:11-31, esp. v.18
Priest. The Test to Vindicate the Priest, to Prove That He Was God's Choice	Nu.17:2-5
Promised Land, Inheritance of	Nu.26:53-56
Promised Land, the	Nu.1:1-2:34; 5:1-31; 34:1-15
Putting Aaron's Garments on Eleazar (See Garments of Aaron...)	Nu.20:23-29
Red Heifer Was to Be Put to Death Outside the Camp. (See Camp, Outside the...)	Nu.19:1-10, esp. v.3
Red Heifer Was to Be Wholly Burned, All Its Parts. (See Burned, Wholly...)	Nu.19:1-10, esp. v.5
Red Heifer Was to Have No Defect or Blemish (See Perfection of...)	Nu.19:1-10, esp. v.2
Red Heifer, an Unused	Nu.19:1-10, esp. v.2
Red Heifer, Offering of the	Nu.19:1-22
Red Heifer, Offering of: Was Established As A Permanent Law For Israel And For All Foreigners Among Them.	Nu.19:1-10, esp. v.10
Red Heifer: Some Blood of the Red Heifer Was to Be Sprinkled Seven Times at the Front of the Tabernacle. (See Blood Sprinkled Seven Times...)	Nu.19:1-10, esp. v.4
Refuge, Cities of	Nu.35:9-29
Rest, Spiritual	Nu.28:9-10
Shaving of the Levites' Heads	Nu.8:5-26
Sin Offering, the	Nu.6:3-12; 28:11-15 (see Le.4:1-5:13. 6:24-30; 8:14-17; 9:2; 9:15; 10:17; 16:3-22)
Skin Disease (See Leprosy...)	Nu.5:1-4; 12:13-16 (see Le.13:1-59)
Spoils Taken from the Defeated Enemy	Nu.31:25-54

TYPES, SYMBOLS, AND PICTURES
ALPHABETICAL OUTLINE

PERSON/PLACE/THING	SCRIPTURE, OUTLINE AND DISCUSSION
Staff of Aaron	Nu.17:6-9
Sunrise on the Tabernacle's Entrance (See Tabernacle, Sunrise on...)	Nu.3:14-39
Sweet Aroma, the (See Aroma...)	Nu.28:1-2; 28:3-8 (see Le.1:9; 8:21; 16:27-28)
Sword (the) of the Angel of the LORD (See Angel of the LORD...)	Nu.22:22-35
Tabernacle, Sunrise on Entrance (See Sunrise on the Tabernacle...)	Nu.3:14-39
Tabernacle, the	Nu.1:47-54; 4:1-20 (see Le.17:3-9)
Tabernacles, Festival of	Nu.29:12-38 (see Le.23:33-34)
Tearing of Clothes. (See Clothes...)	Nu.14:1-10, esp. v.6
Test to Vindicate the Priest, to Prove That He Was God's Choice (See Priest...)	Nu.17:2-5
Third Prophecy of Balaam	Nu.23:27-24:14
Trumpets, Festival of	Nu.29:1-6 (see Le.23:23-25)
Twelve Loaves of Bread of the Presence (See Bread of the Presence...)	Nu.8:1-4
Unclean Person Had to Be Purified with the Cleansing Water On the Third And Seventh Days (See Cleansing Water...)	Nu.19:11-16, esp. v.12
Wilderness Wanderings	Nu.33:5-49
Woman's Hair, the Priest Loosening the	Nu.5:11-31, esp. v.18
Zeal of Phinehas that Made Atonement or Reconciliation For the People (See Phinehas, Zeal of...)	Nu.25:6-13

TYPES, SYMBOLS, AND PICTURES
THE BOOK OF NUMBERS

Chronological Outline

What is a biblical type or symbol? Simply put, a *biblical type* is a "foreshadowing" of what was to come at a later time in history. Through a person, place or thing a biblical type points toward a New Testament fulfillment.

In addition to biblical types, there are what we may call *biblical pictures*. A biblical picture is a lesson that we can see in the Scriptures *without distorting the truth*. The study of biblical types and pictures is a valuable study in that it helps us apply the truth of the Scriptures in our lives. Scripture itself tells us this:

> **These things happened to them as examples and were written down as warnings for us, on whom the fulfillment of the ages has come (1 Co.10:11).**
> **For everything that was written in the past was written to teach us, so that through endurance and the encouragement of the Scriptures we might have hope (Ro.15:4).**

PERSON/PLACE/THING	SCRIPTURE, OUTLINE, & DISCUSSION
Promised Land, the	Nu.1:1-2:34; 5:1-31; 34:1-15
Tabernacle, the	Nu.1:47-54; 4:1-20 (see Le.17:3-9)
Egypt	Nu.3:5-13; 9:1-14 (see Le.11:44-47; 19:33-34)
High Priest, the	Nu.3:5-13; 4:1-20 (see Le.16:3, 6)
Sunrise on the Tabernacle's Entrance	Nu.3:14-39
Census of the Firstborn and Their Replacement by the Levites, the	Nu.3:40-51
Leprosy or Infectious Skin Disease	Nu.5:1-4; 12:13-16 (see Le.13:1-59)
Priest Loosening the Woman's Hair, the	Nu.5:11-31, esp. v.18
Contact with a Dead Body	Nu.6:3-12 (see Le.10:4-5)
Sin Offering, the	Nu.6:3-12; 28:11-15 (see Le.4:1-5:13. 6:24-30; 8:14-17; 9:2; 9:15; 10:17; 16:3-22)
Burnt Offering, the	Nu.6:3-12; 15:1-16; 28:11-15 (see Le.1:1-17; 6:8-13; 8:18-21; 16:24)
Guilt Offering, the	Nu.6:3-12 (see Le.5:14-6:7)
Nazarite Burning His Hair under the Fellowship Offering	Nu.6:13-20
Drink Offering, the	Nu.6:13-20; 15:1-16, esp. v.7
Fellowship Offering, the Nazarite Burning His Hair	Nu.6:13-20
Fellowship or Peace Offering, the	Nu.6:13-20; 15:1-16 (see Le.3:1-17)
Twelve Loaves of Bread of the Presence	Nu.8:1-4
Lampstand, the	Nu.8:1-4 (see Le.24:1-4)
Shaving of the Levites' Heads	Nu.8:5-26
Levites Had to be Sprinkled with the Water of Cleansing, Shave Their Whole Heads, and Wash Their Clothes	Nu.8:5-26
Cleansing of the Levites	Nu.8:5-26
Dedication of the Levites	Nu.8:5-26

TYPES, SYMBOLS, AND PICTURES
CHRONOLOGICAL OUTLINE

PERSON/PLACE/THING	SCRIPTURE, OUTLINE, & DISCUSSION
Passover, the	Nu.9:1-14; 28:16-25 (see also Le.23:5)
Pillar of Cloud.	Nu.9:15-23
Great March to the Promised Land Finally Begins	Nu.10:11-36
Great Army of God's People Marched Forth Division by Division—as Commanded	Nu.10:13-28
Appeal of Moses to His Brother-In-Law to Join the March to the Promised Land	Nu.10:29-32
Ark or Chest, the	Nu.10:33-34 (see Ex.25:10-22; 40:20; 35:12; 37:1-5; 39:35; 40:3, 20-21)
Joshua	Nu.13:1-25; 27:18
Tearing of Clothes.	Nu.14:1-10, esp. v.6
Grain Offering	Nu.15:1-16 (see Le.2:3)
Firstfruits	Nu.15:17-21
Censers	Nu.16:36-40
Test to Vindicate the Priest, to Prove That He Was God's Choice	Nu.17:2-5
Aaron's Staff	Nu.17:6-9
An Unused Red Heifer	Nu.19:1-10, esp. v.2
Red Heifer Was to Have No Defect or Blemish	Nu.19:1-10, esp. v.2
Red Heifer Was to Be Put to Death Outside the Camp.	Nu.19:1-10, esp. v.3
Blood (of the Red Heifer) Was Sprinkled Seven Times at the Front of the Tabernacle.	Nu.19:1-10, esp. v.4
Red Heifer Was to Be Wholly Burned, All Its Parts.	Nu.19:1-10, esp. v.5
Priest (the) Was to Burn Some Cedar Wood, Hyssop And Scarlet Wool with the Red Heifer.	Nu.19:1-10, esp. v.6
Everyone Who Had Anything to Do with the Sacrifice Had to Cleanse Himself And His Clothes.	Nu.19:1-10, esp. v.7-8
Clean Person Was to Gather Up the Ashes of the Sacrifice And Keep Them In A Clean Place Outside the Camp	Nu.19:1-10, esp. v.9-10
Offering of the Red Heifer Was Established As A Permanent Law For Israel And For All Foreigners Among Them.	Nu.19:1-10, esp. v.10
Offering of the Red Heifer (A Red Female Cow).	Nu.19:1-22
Unclean Person Had to Be Purified with the Cleansing Water On the Third And Seventh Days	Nu.19:11-16, esp. v.12
A Person Who Had Been In Contact with Death Defiled the Lord's Tabernacle: He Was to Be Cut Off	Nu.19:11-16, esp. v.13
Death	Nu.19:11-16
Garments of Aaron: Putting Aaron's Garments on Eleazar	Nu.20:23-29

TYPES, SYMBOLS, AND PICTURES
CHRONOLOGICAL OUTLINE

PERSON/PLACE/THING	SCRIPTURE, OUTLINE, & DISCUSSION
Gathered to His People	Nu.20:23-29
Bronze Snake	Nu.21:4-9
Attack upon Israel [by the Amorites]	Nu.21:21-32
Sword (the) of the Angel of the Lord	Nu.22:22-35
Israel	Nu.23:1-12
Third Prophecy of Balaam	Nu.23:27-24:14
Coming Deliverer, the	Nu.24:14-19
Assyria Destroying the Kenites.	Nu.24:21-22
Phinehas	Nu.25:6-13
Phinehas' Zeal For Righteousness	Nu.25:6-13
Zeal of Phinehas that Made Atonement or Reconciliation For the People	Nu.25:6-13
LORD Spoke (Said), The	Nu.26:1
Dividing the Inheritance of the Promised Land	Nu.26:53-56
Sweet Aroma, the	Nu.28:1-2; 28:3-8 (see Le.1:9; 8:21; 16:27-28)
Rest, Spiritual	Nu.28:9-10
Monthly Offerings of Animal Sacrifices	Nu.28:11-15
Passover, the	Nu.28:16-25 (see Le.23:5)
Festival of Firstfruits, the	Nu.28:26-31 (see Le.23:9-14)
Festival of Trumpets, the	Nu.29:1-6 (see Le.23:23-25)
Day of Atonement, the	Nu.29:7-11 (see Le.16:1-34; Le.23:27)
Festival of Tabernacles or Booths or Shelters, the	Nu.29:12-38 (see Le.23:33-34)
Conquest of the Midianites	Nu.31:1-54
Israel's Shocking Military Error against Midian.	Nu.31:14-18
Spoils Taken from the Defeated Enemy	Nu.31:25-54
Compromise of Gad and Reuben	Nu.32:1-42
Wilderness Wanderings	Nu.33:5-49
Cities of Refuge	Nu.35:9-29
Moses	Nu.36:13 (see Le.1:1; 8:1-5)

THE OUTLINE & SUBJECT INDEX

NUMBERS

REMEMBER: When you look up a subject and turn to the Scripture reference, you have not just the Scripture but also an outline and a discussion (commentary) of the Scripture and subject.

This is one of the GREAT FEATURES of *The Preacher's Outline & Sermon Bible*®. Once you have all the volumes, you will not only have what all other Bible indexes give you, that is, a list of all the subjects and their Scripture references, BUT in addition you will have...
- an outline of every Scripture and subject in the Bible
- a discussion (commentary) on every Scripture and subject
- every subject supported by other Scripture, already written out or cross referenced

DISCOVER THE UNIQUE VALUE for yourself. Quickly glance below to the first subject of the Index.

AARON
Benediction of. 6:22-27
Clothing of the High Priest. Symbol of the official position of the High Priest. 20:23-29
Death of. 20:23-29; 33:30-31

Turn to the first reference. Glance at the Scripture and outline of the Scripture, then read the commentary. You will immediately see the TREMENDOUS BENEFIT of the INDEX of *The Preacher's Outline & Sermon Bible*®.

OUTLINE AND SUBJECT INDEX

A

AARON
Benediction of. 6:22-27
Clothing of the High Priest. Symbol of the official position of the High Priest. 20:23-29
Death of. 20:23-29; 33:30-31
Discussed.
  Aroused God's anger. Burned against him. 12:4-12, esp. vv.9-12
  Criticized & questioned God's servant, Moses. 12:1-3
  Did the work of the atoning priest. 16:41-50
  Feared the anger & judgment of God. 12:4-12, Thgt.2
  Lost the privilege of entering into the promised land. 20:23-29, esp. v.24
Facts.
  Death was mourned by Israel for thirty days. 20:23-29, esp. v.29
  Four sons anointed & ordained to serve God. 3:1-4
  The High Priest, the supreme leader of Israel, next to Moses. 12:1-3
Family line of. 3:1-4
Intercession of. Petitioned Moses on Miriam's behalf. 12:4-12, esp. vv.11-12
Sons of. Stand as a stark warning to the ministers of God. 3:1-4, Thgt.2
Staff of.
  Budding of. 17:1-13; 17:6-9
  Placed in Ark. Reason why. 17:10-13
Type - Symbol of.
  Christ or the minister bearing fruit & bringing life to people. 17:6-9
  God's power & authority. 17:6-9
Pride of. Questioned the unique call & mission of Moses. 12:1-3, esp. v.2
Priesthood of.
  Established. 17:6-9
  Vindication of. 17:2-5

ABEL SHITTIM
Campsite of Israel. 33:48-49; See RESOURCE Section

ABIDAN
Leader of tribe of Benjamin. 1:4-16; esp. v.11

ABIHU
Family of. Son of Aaron. 3:1-4
Ministry of. 3:1-4
Warning. His death stands as a stark warning to the ministers of God. 3:1-4, Thgt.2

ABIRAM
Discussed.
  Conspiracy of. 16:1-15, esp. v.1
  Defiance of. 16:1-15, esp. vv.12-14

ABRAHAM
Call of. God called Abraham to be a leader. 13:1-25, Thgt.1

ABRAIM, MOUNTAINS OF
Campsite of Israel. 33:47-48, See RESOURCE Section
Discussed. Place where Moses got a glimpse of the promised land. 27:12-13, esp. v.12

ABRONAH
Campsite of Israel. 33:47-48; See RESOURCE Section

ACCEPTANCE
Discussed.
  Only Jesus Christ can make prayer acceptable to God. 16:36-40
  The offerings or sacrifices pleased God. 28:1-2

ACCESS (See **APPROACH - APPROACHABLE**)
To God. 7:89; 15:1-16, Thgt.1

ADULTERY (See **SEX**)
Seriousness of. God gave the commandment against a. to preserve society. 5:11-31
Warning. The penalty for **a.** & for false worship or idolatry was death. 25:4-5 (see Le.18:24-30; Le.20:10)

AFFECTION
Problem with. Public display of. 25:6-13

AHIEZER
Leader of tribe of Dan. 1:4-16; esp. v.12

AHIHUD
Appointed by Moses as a supervisor of the promised land. 34:16-29
Led the tribe of Asher into the promised land. 34:16-29

AHIRA
Leader of tribe of Naphtali. 1:4-16; esp. v.15

ALCOHOL
Duty. Must abstain from all intoxicating drink. 6:3-12; esp. v.3-4

ALIEN (See **FOREIGNER**)
Fact. Was invited to participate in the Passover. 9:1-14

ALMON DIBLATHAIM
Campsite of Israel. 33:46-47; See RESOURCE Section

ALTAR OF BURNT OFFERING (See **BURNT OFFERING**)
Reason for. Need for atonement. 6:13-20; 28:3-8
Type - Symbol of. Christ's sacrifice that secured atonement or reconciliation for man. 28:3-8

ALTAR OF INCENSE
Type - Symbol of. The importance of prayer. 8:1-4, Thgt.1

343

INDEX – NUMBERS

ALUSH
Campsite of Israel. 33:13-14; See RESOURCE Section

AMALEK
Discussed. Prophecy concerning destruction of. 24:20

AMALEKITES
Inhabitants of the promised land. 13:26-33, esp. v.29
Lived in the Negev. 13:26-33, esp. v.29
Warfare of. Defeated the Israelites. 14:40-45

AMMIEL
Spy from the tribe of Dan. 13:1-25; esp. v.12

AMORITES
Conquered by Israel. 21:21-32
Inhabitants of the promised land. 13:26-33, esp. v.29
Picture of. Attack upon Israel is a picture of the world & the enemies of life attacking as we walk through this life. 21:21-32, Thgt.1

AMRAMITES
Of the Kohathite clan. 3:14-39; esp. v.27

ANAK
Descendants (the Nephilim) inhabited the promised land. 13:26-33, esp. v.33

ANGEL OF THE LORD
Discussed. Blocked Balaam's way. 22:22-35

ANGER
Of the LORD. 11:1-3; 11:4-35, esp. v.33; 12:4-12; 14:10-25; 22:22-35

ANIMALS
Discussed.
  Passover Lamb. 28:16-25
  Sacrifice of. 28:3-8
Kinds of.
  Bulls. 28:11-15; 28:16-25
  Goat. 28:11-15
  Lambs. 28:3-8; 28:16-25
  Rams. 28:11-15; 28:16-25
  Red heifer. 19:1-10
Type - Symbol of.
  Christ the Lamb of God who takes away the sins of the world. 28:16-25
  Christ's sacrifice, His dying for sin: male goat as a Sin Offering. 28:11-15
  The perfection of Jesus Christ: lambs without blemish or defect. 28:3-8

ANIMAL SACRIFICE (See **SACRIFICE, ANIMAL**)
Discussed.
  Importance of. 28:1-2
  In the burnt offering. 28:3-8
  In the monthly offerings. 28:11-15
  Passover Lamb. 28:16-25
  Red heifer. 19:1-10

Type - Symbol of.
  Christ's sacrifice, His dying for sin: male goat as a Sin Offering. 28:11-15
  Christ the Lamb of God who takes away the sins of the world. 28:16-25
  The perfection of Jesus Christ: lambs without blemish or defect. 28:3-8

ANOINT - ANOINTING
Fact. Some persons are anointed & ordained to serve God. 3:1-4, Thgt.1
Of ministers. 3:1-4, Thgt.1

APOSTASY
Cause of. 25:1-3
Danger of. 25:14-18
Of Israel. 25:1-3
Warning. The ultimate rebellion of God's people against Him. 25:1-3

APPETITE - APPETITES
Warning. Seeking to fulfill one's appetite for the world is wrong. 11:4-35, Thgt.1

APPRENTICESHIP
Fact. The Levites went through a five year training or a. 4:1-20; esp. v.3

APPROACH—APPROACHABLE
Discussed. Approaching God exactly as He says. 7:1-89
Duty.
  Must a. God through the sacrifice of Jesus Christ. 8:5-26, Thgt.2; 15:1-16, Thgt.2
  Must be genuinely sincere when we a. God 15:1-16, Thgt.3
To God.
  Judgment of false a. to God. 16:16-35
  Must a. God exactly as He says. 7:10-88
  Only one way to a. God. 28:1-29:40, Intro.
  Wrong a. 16:1-15
Typed - Symbolized - Pictured. Day of Atonement: the only way to a. God, through the shed blood of the substitute sacrifice (Christ). 29:7-11
Warning. God judges all rebellion & unauthorized a. 16:1-50

APPROVAL
List of Scriptures. God giving His attention, approval, pleasure to His people. 6:22-27; esp. v.26
Of God. 6:22-27; esp. v.26

ARAD
Discussed.
  Canaanite king of **A**. 21:1-3
  First military victory of Israel. 21:1-3
  Was completely destroyed by the Israelites. 21:1-3
Location of. 21:1; D.S. #1

ARK OF THE COVENANT
Discussed.
  A. went before the tribes. 10:33-34
  Israel marched toward the hill country without Moses or the Ark. 14:40-45, esp. v.44
Type - Symbol of.
  The LORD's leadership step by step. 10:33-34
  The presence & power of God. 14:40-45, esp. v.44

ARMY
Of God. 1:17-46; 26:4-51
Of God's people. 10:13-28

ARNON RIVER
Israel camped here on their way to the promised land. 21:10-20, esp. v.13-15

AROER
Location of. 32:34-36; D.S. #3
Territory of. The tribe of Gad.
  Cities rebuilt.
    Dibon, Ataroth, Aroer, Atroth Shophan, Jazer, Jogbehah, Beth Nimrah & Beth Haran. 32:28-42, esp. vv.34-36

AROMA
Discussed. The offerings or sacrifices were an **a**. that pleased God. 28:1-2
Type - Symbol of. God being pleased with the offering. 28:1-2; 28:3-8

ARROGANCE
Discussed. Against God's people. 20:14-22

ASHER, TRIBE OF
Census of.
  1st census. 41,500 fighting men. 1:17-46; esp. v.41
  2nd census. 53,400 fighting men. 26:4-51, esp. v.47
Leaders of:
  Ahihud.
    Appointed by Moses as a supervisor of the promised land. 34:16-29
    Led the tribe of Asher into the promised land. 34:16-29
  Pagiel. Helped with the first census. 1:4-16; esp. v.13
  Spy. Sethur. One of the twelve spies. 13:1-25; esp. v.13

ASSASSINATION
Of leaders. 14:1-10, esp. v.10

ASSISTANT MINISTERS
Discussed.
  Duty to tithe. 18:25-32
  Treatment of. 18:8-24, esp. v.21-24
Duty.
  Must give one tenth of their support or income. 18:25-32
  Must give the best portion of the tithe to the LORD. 18:25-32
  Must give the tithe to the LORD's representative, that is, the priests. 18:25-32
  Must heed the warning: must tithe the best or face eternal judgment. 18:25-33

ASSISTANTS
Duties of. 3:14-39
Fact. Some are set apart to be a. 3:5-13

ASSURANCE
Of what.
  Of access to God. 7:89
  Of God's faithfulness. 23:13-26
  Of marching forth from place to place in a spirit of strong assurance. 21:10-20
  Of two great assurances. 7:89, Thgt.1
  Of victory. 10:35-36, Thgt.1

INDEX – NUMBERS

Picture of. The great assurance of God. Leaders who were assigned to the land were appointed ahead of time. 34:16-29

ASSYRIA
Prophecy concerning. 24:21-22

ATAROTH
Location of. 32:34-36; D.S. #2
Territory of. The tribe of Gad.
  Cities rebuilt.
    Dibon, Ataroth, Aroer, Atroth Shophan, Jazer, Jogbehah, Beth Nimrah & Beth Haran. 32:28-42, esp. vv.34-36

ATHARIM
Some Israelites attacked & captured by the king of Arad on the road to **A**. 21:1-3

ATONEMENT (See **RECONCILIATION**)
Day of. 29:1-6, esp. v.7; 29:7-11
Discussed. Christ secured atonement or reconciliation for man. 28:3-8; 29:7-11, Thgt.1
Typed - Symbolized - Pictured. By the Burnt Offering. Christ's sacrifice that secured atonement or reconciliation for man. 28:3-8

ATONEMENT, DAY OF (See **DAY OF ATONEMENT**)

ATONING SACRIFICE
Discussed. Christ's sacrifice that secured atonement or reconciliation for man. 28:3-8

ATROTH SHOPHAN
Location of. 32:34-36; D.S. #4
Territory of. The tribe of Gad.
  Cities rebuilt.
    Dibon, Ataroth, Aroer, Atroth Shophan, Jazer, Jogbehah, Beth Nimrah & Beth Haran. 32:28-42, esp. vv.34-36

ATTENTION
List of Scriptures. God giving His attention, approval, pleasure to His people. 6:22-27, esp. v.26
Of God. 6:22-27, esp. v.26

AWE (See **HOLINESS, OF GOD; REVERENCE; FEAR, OF GOD**)

B

BAAL MEON
Fact. Name changed. 32:38
Location of. 32:37-38; D.S. #12
Territory of. The tribe of Reuben.
  Cities rebuilt & renamed.
    Heshbon, Elealeh, Kiriathaim, Nebo, Baal Meon, Sibmah. 32:28-42, esp. vv.37-38

BAAL OF PEOR
The men of Israel worshipped this false god of the Moabites. 25:1-3

BAD REPORT
Character of. A double-minded, hypocritical & greedy heart. 22:15-21
Source of. From the twelve spies. 13:26-33

Results of. Spread among the people. 13:26-33, esp. v.32

BALAAM
Death of. 31:7-13
Discussed.
  A satanic plot devised by **B**. 25:1-3
  Story of the donkey. 22:22-35
  The story of **B**., his donkey, & his three encounters with God. 22:1-41
  Warned by God. 22:7-14
False belief of. **B**. false belief in divination. 22:1-6
Warning. God gave **B**. over to his greed. 22:15-21

BALAK
King of Moab. 22:1-6
Son of Zippor. 22:1-6, esp. v.2

BAMOTH
Place where Israel camped on its way to the promised land. 21:10-20, esp. v.19

BAMOTH BAAL
Place where Balak took Balaam to spy out the camp of Israel. 22:36-41; esp. vv.39-41

BASHAN
King of **B**. Og. 21:33-35

BATTLE CRY
The great expectation & cry of Moses: victory & rest. 10:35-36

BEARING FRUIT
Meaning of.
  To bear converts. 17:6-9, Thgt.1
  To bear righteousness; to bear a holy life. 17:6-9, Thgt.1
  To bear the Christian character or the fruit of the Spirit. 17:6-9, Thgt.1

BEER, THE WELL
Place where Israel camped on its way to the promised land. 21:10-20, esp. vv.16-17

BELIEVE -BELIEVING
Meaning of. To obey God. 26:4-51, Thgt.1

BELIEVER -BELIEVERS
Blessings of.
  A fruitful, overflowing life. 23:27-23:13, Thgt.1
  A new, separated & distinctive people. 23:1-12, esp. v.9
  A numerous people. 23:1-12, esp. v.10
  A righteous people with an eternal hope. 23:1-12, esp. v.10
  All the necessities of life: shelter, food, & clothing. 23:27-23:13, Thgt.1
  An innocent, secure people. 23:1-12, esp. v.8
  Courage & security throughout life. 23:27-23:13, Thgt.1
  Deliverance through all the trials & temptations of life. 23:27-23:13, Thgt.1
  Outstanding leaders & strong church fellowships. 23:27-23:13, Thgt.1
  Strength, both physical & spiritual. 23:27-23:13, Thgt.1
  Victory over all the pitfalls of life. 23:27-23:13, Thgt.1
  Will be blessed by God. 23:27-23:13, Thgt.1
Call of.
  God calls & gifts believers differently. 12:4-12, Thgt.3
  God calls many today to be leaders. 13:1-25, Thgt.1
  To step forth & be assistants, helpers in the ministry. 3:5-13
  When God calls, obedience is demanded. 4:34-49, Thgt.1
Death of.
  Is a warm, tender, gentle & touching experience. 27:12-13, Thgt.1
  Preparation for. 27:12-13
Discussed.
  Blessings of. 23:1-12
  Five guarantees to the believer:
    God's faithfulness. 23:13-26, Thgt.1
    God's power. 23:13-26, Thgt.1
    God's presence. 23:13-26, Thgt.1
    God's promises. 23:13-26, Thgt.1
    God's truthfulness & unchangeableness. 23:13-26, Thgt.1
  God's people are very special to Him, a very special treasure. 22:7-14, Thgt.1
  Wrong committed against. 5:5-10
Discipline of. 14:10-25
Duty.
  Must abstain from all intoxicating drinks. 6:3-12, Thgt.1
  Must accept the challenge of special ministries. 1:47-54, Thgt.1
  Must arise & follow Him to the promised land of God, even to heaven itself. 10:1-10, Thgt.1
  Must be constantly seeking a great harvest of souls. 28:26-31, Thgt.1
  Must be diligent as we march to the promised land of God. 21:10-20, Thgt.1
  Must be genuinely sincere when we approach God 15:1-16, Thgt.3
  Must be holy. 15:37-41
  Must be meek & humble—totally submissive & dependent upon God. 12:1-3, Thgt.1
  Must be prepared for spiritual warfare. 26:2-3, Thgt.1
  Must be prepared for warfare as we march to the promised land. 1:2-3
  Must be strong & courageous. 13:26-33, Thgt.1
  Must be totally set apart from the sin & shame of the world. 5:1-4, Thgt.1
  Must be willing to do any work or service. 4:21-28
  Must be willing to pour out our lives to God, surrendering ourselves to Him. 15:1-16, Thgt.3
  Must bear the mark of being totally committed to God. 6:3-12, Thgt.1
  Must bear the mark of holiness & separation to God. 6:3-12, Thgt.1
  Must believe God & serve in the army of God. 1:17-46
  Must celebrate God's deliverance by Christ through the Lord's Supper. 9:1-14, Thgt.1
  Must celebrate our redemption every Sabbath or Sunday. 28:9-10
  Must continue to live a life of commitment & holiness before God. 6:13-20, Thgt.1

INDEX – NUMBERS

Must control our minds & think of God throughout the day. 15:37-41, Thgt.1
Must do everything God commands. 2:34
Must fear the anger & judgment of God. 12:4-12, Thgt.2
Must fulfill our vows, the promises we make to the LORD. 21:1-3
Must fully destroy the evil, seductive, & immoral enemies of life. 31:14-18, Thgt.1
Must give our tithes & offerings to God. 15:17-21, Thgt.1
Must give to the LORD's work. 7:1-89, Intro.
Must guard against defilement & uncleanness. 19:11-16, Thgt.1
Must have a zeal for living holy, pure, & righteous lives before God. 25:6-13, Thgt.1
Must hold a great expectation & hope for the promised land of heaven. 10:11-12, Thgt.1
Must keep his mind clear & focused totally upon the LORD. 6:3-12, Thgt.1
Must keep his mind healthy, alert, & sharp to focus upon God & the promised land toward which he is marching. 6:3-12, Thgt.1
Must keep our minds focused upon living a holy life throughout the day. 15:37-41, Thgt.1
Must know that God dwells in the midst of His people. 2:1-2
Must know that God guides him as he marches to the promised land. 2:1-2
Must know that people are totally defiled. 19:11-16, Thgt.1
Must make concentrated, focused efforts to reach our family for Christ. 10:29-32, Thgt.1
Must obey God as we march to the promised land. 10:13-28, Thgt.1
Must pray for & support all leaders, both church & government leaders. 16:16-36, Thgt.1
Must pray for God to raise up strong leaders who will serve God's people faithfully. 27:14-17, Thgt.1
Must reach out to our family members. 10:29-32, Thgt.1
Must remember & keep God's commandments throughout the day. 15:37-41, Thgt.1
Must remember & keep the Sabbath. 15:30-36, Thgt.1
Must respect & revere God's holiness & the holy things committed to His service. 4:1-20, Thgt.1
Must seek to serve people not to hold positions of power. 16:1-15, Thgt.1
Must sound the alarm for prayer. 10:1-10, Thgt.1
Must stand fast under the banner of God's family. 2:2-33
Must support the ministers of God who proclaim the Word of God to us. 17:10-13, Thgt.1
Must take one's place under the standard of Christ. 2:2-33
Must thank God for the sacrifice of His dear Son, Christ Jesus the LORD. 15:1-16, Thgt.3
Must walk together. 5:1-31, Intro.
Facts.
    First generation of believers never entered the promised land of God. 26:4-51, Thgt.1
    God gives five guarantees to the believer. 23:13-26, Thgt.1
    The Holy Spirit dwells within the body of every individual **b**. 2:2-33, Thgt.3
    The peace of God floods the believer's heart & life. 6:22-27; esp. v.26
    True confession always involves repentance, a turning away from sin to God. 14:40-45, Thgt.1
    We can approach God anytime with anything, & He hears us. 8:1-4, Thgt.1
Failure of. 20:7-13
Life & Walk.
    A believer has certain enemies that seem impregnable, immovable. 24:21-22, Thgt.1
    A believer has his part to play for God. 4:29-33, Thgt.1
    A believer influences other people. 25:14-18, Thgt.1
    A believer is like a pilgrim walking through the desert & wilderness of this world. 2:2-33, Thgt.1
    A believer is like a soldier in the desert & wilderness of this world. 2:2-33, Thgt.1
    A believer is to live a life of separation. 33:50-56, Thgt.1
    A believer is to make an offering of thanksgiving to God. 31:25-54, Thgt.1
    A believer is totally dependent upon Christ throughout all of life. 6:13-20, Thgt.1
    A believer's goal is to have a closer walk with the LORD. 6:1-2
    A believer's life is filled with pitfalls & enemies. 1:1-2:34, Intro.
List.
    Blessings of God's people. 23:1-12
    Of enemies. 1:1-2:34, Intro.
March of. 36:16
Pilgrimage of. 36:13
Prayers of. God hears the prayers of His people in behalf of others. 14:10-25, Thgt.1
Rewards. God blesses & guides only those who listen to Him, who obey His instructions. 2:1-2, Thgt.2
Sin against. 5:5-10
Spiritual separation. Purpose of.
    To stir the believer to live a life of separation from the world. 15:37-41, esp. v.39
    To stir the believer to obey all God's commands. 15:37-41, esp. v.40
    To stir the believer to remember God's commandments. 15:37-41, esp. v.39
    To the believer, the promised land means several things. 34:1-15, D.S. #1, Thgt.1
Title of. Army of God. 10:13-28
Warning.
    God chastises the disobedient believer & servant of God. 20:7-13, Thgt.1
    God judges or chastises His people when they sin. 12:4-12, Thgt.1; 14:10-25, Thgt.1
    Must not allow drugs & drink to dull, numb, or damage his mind. 6:3-12, Thgt.1
    Must not approach nor partake of the LORD's Supper unworthily. 9:1-14, Thgt.1
    Must not be stumblingblocks to others. 13:26-33, Thgt.1
    Must not become corrupted & defiled by sin & shame. 6:3-12, Thgt.1
    Must not break the seventh commandment (adultery). 25:1-3, Thgt.1
    Must not complain, grumble, & murmur against their leaders. 16:1-15, Thgt.1
    Must not fear. 13:26-33, Thgt.1
    Must not have nothing to do with corruption & defilement. 6:3-12, Thgt.1
    Must not join in the false worship of the world. 25:1-3, Thgt.1

BENEDICTION
Blessings of. God's blessing, protection, grace, acceptance, peace. 6:22-27
Discussed.
    Aaronic. 6:22-27
    Great priestly benediction. 6:22-27
    LORD's prayer of the O.T. 6:22-27
Source of. God Himself. 6:22-27; esp. vv.23-26

BENE JAAKAN
Campsite of Israel. 33:31-32; See RESOURCE Section

BENJAMIN, TRIBE OF
Census of.
    1st census. 35,400 fighting men. 1:17-46; esp. v.37
    2nd census. 45,600 fighting men. 26:4-51, esp. v.41
Leaders of.
    Abidan. Helped with the first census. 1:4-16; esp. v.11
    Appointed by Moses as a supervisor of the promised land. 34:16-29
    Elidad. Led the tribe of Benjamin into the promised land. 34:16-29
Spy. Palti. One of the twelve spies. 13:1-25; esp. v.9

BETH HARAN
Fact. Fortified city. 32:28-42, esp. v.36
Location of. 32:34-36; D.S. #8
Territory of. The tribe of Gad.
    Cities rebuilt.
        Dibon, Ataroth, Aroer, Atroth Shophan, Jazer, Jogbehah, Beth Nimrah & Beth Haran. 32:28-42, esp. vv.34-36

BETH JESHIMOTH
Campsite of Israel. 33:48-49; See RESOURCE Section

BETH NIMRAH
Fact. Fortified city. 32:28-42, esp. v.36
Location of. 32:34-36; D.S. #7
Territory of. The tribe of Gad.
    Cities rebuilt.
        Dibon, Ataroth, Aroer, Atroth Shophan, Jazer, Jogbehah, Beth

INDEX – NUMBERS

Nimrah & Beth Haran. 32:28-42, esp. vv.34-36

BIRDS
Discussed.
Amount of quail. Three feet deep, a whole day's walk in every direction. 11:4-35
Judgment of an overabundance of meat. 11:4-35
Plague of. 11:4-35

BITTER WATER
Judgment of. Its use in the law to control the suspicion & jealousy of sexual unfaithfulness. 5:11-31; esp.vv.26-28

BLASPHEMY (See **CURSE - CURSING**)

BLESS - BLESSING - BLESSINGS
Of the believer. The blessing of.
Of being a new, separated & distinctive people. 23:1-12, esp. v.9
Of being a numerous people. 23:1-12, esp. v.10
Of being a righteous people with an eternal hope. 23:1-12, esp. v.10
Of being an innocent, secure people. 23:1-12, esp. v.8
Of being blessed by God. 23:27-23:13, Thgt.1
Of having a fruitful, overflowing life. 23:27-23:13, Thgt.1
Of having all the necessities of life: shelter, food, & clothing. 23:27-23:13, Thgt.1
Of having courage & security throughout life. 23:27-23:13, Thgt.1
Of having deliverance through all the trials & temptations of life. 23:27-23:13, Thgt.1
Of having outstanding leaders & strong church fellowships. 23:27-23:13, Thgt.1
Of having strength, both physical & spiritual. 23:27-23:13, Thgt.1
Of having victory over all the pitfalls of life. 23:27-23:13, Thgt.1
Discussed.
God provides all the necessities of life for His people. 6:22-27
Of God's people. 23:1-12; 23:27–24:13
The blessings of God & a glimpse into the future. 23:1-24:25
The promise of God's **b**. 6:22-27
Kinds of. Of God: blessing, protection, grace, acceptance, peace. 6:22-27
List of Scriptures. Of blessing. 6:22-27
Results of. The **b**. identified the Israelites as God's people, as belonging to Him. 6:22-27; esp. v.27
Source. God. 6:22-27; 23:13-26

BLOOD
Typed - Pictured - Symbolized. By the Drink Offering: a symbol of the blood of Christ that is pictured in the LORD's Supper. 28:3-8

BONDAGE
Deliverance from. By God. God gives victory over the world with all its enslavements & bondages. 24:20, Thgt.1

BOOK OF LIFE
Fact. God keeps a register in which the name of every true believer is written. 1:17-46, Thgt.1

BOOK OF THE WARS OF THE LORD
Contents of. 21:10-20, esp. v.14

BREAD, HOLY (See **SHOWBREAD**)

BREAD OF THE PRESENCE (See **SHOWBREAD**)

BRONZE SNAKE
Discussed. Purpose of. 21:4-9
Type - Symbol of.
Christ the Savior. 21:4-9
Unbelief. 21:4-9

BUKKI
Appointed by Moses as a supervisor of the promised land. 34:16-29
Led the tribe of Dan into the promised land. 34:16-29

BULL
Sacrifice of. As a sacrifice in the burnt offering. 28:11-15; 28:16-25

BURNT OFFERING
Discussed. The worship required after the fulfillment of the Nazarite vow. 6:13-20
Facts.
Was the basic offering to be presented by the people. 28:3-8
Was to be offered in the morning & again in the evening. 28:3-8, esp. v.4
Meaning of. 28:3-8
Purpose.
Was part of the Levites' ceremonial, spiritual cleansing. 9:5-26
Was when a person wanted to seek atonement or reconciliation with God. 15:1-16
Results of.
Atonement, reconciliation with God. 6:13-20, esp. v.14
Cleansing. 6:3-12, esp. v.11
Type - Symbol of. Christ's sacrifice (His death) which secured atonement or reconciliation for us. 6:3-12, esp. v.11; 15:1-16; 28:3-8; 28:11-15, Thgt.1; 29:12-38

C

CALEB
Appointed by Moses as a supervisor of the promised land. 34:16-29
Report of. 13:26-33
Spy from the tribe of Judah. 13:1-25; esp. v.6

CALL - CALLED
Of God.
God called Abraham to be a leader. 13:1-25, Thgt.1
God called Elisha to be a leader. 13:1-25, Thgt.1
God called Gideon to be a leader. 13:1-25, Thgt.1
God called Isaiah to be leader. 13:1-25, Thgt.1
God called Joshua to succeed Moses as leader. 27:18-23
God called Moses to be a leader. 13:1-25, Thgt.1
God called Paul to be a leader. 13:1-25, Thgt.1
God calls & gifts believers differently. 12:4-12, Thgt.3

God calls many today to be leaders. 13:1-25, Thgt.1
Proof of. Minister's **c**. 17:1

CAMPSITES (See **CITIES - AREAS**)
Chart of. See RESOURCE Section
Fact. Difficult to know the exact location of some **c**. 33:5-49
Of Israel.
Abel Shittim. A camp located between Mt. Hor & the Jordan River across from Jericho. 33:48-49
Abraim, mountains of. A camp located between Mt. Hor & the Jordan River across from Jericho. 33:47-48
Abronah. A camp located between Mt. Sinai & Mt. Hor. 33:34-35
Almon Diblathaim. A camp located between Mt. Hor & the Jordan River across from Jericho. 33:46-47
Alush. A camp located between Rameses & Mt. Sinai. 33:13-14
Bene Jaakan. A camp located between Mt. Sinai & Mt. Hor. 33:31-32
Beth Jeshimoth. A camp located between Mt. Hor & the Jordan River across from Jericho. 33:48-49
Desert of Sin. A camp located between Rameses & Mt. Sinai. 33:11-12
Desert of Sinai. A camp located between Rameses & Mt. Sinai. Discussed. The law was given. 33:15-16
Dibon Gad. A camp located between Mt. Hor & the Jordan River across from Jericho. 33:45-46; 33:1-56, D.S. #1
Discussed. Was in Moab. 33:45-46
Dophkah. A camp located between Rameses & Mt. Sinai. 33:12-13
Elim. A camp located between Rameses & Mt. Sinai. Discussed. An oasis in the desert. 33:9-10
Etham. A camp located between Rameses & Mt. Sinai. Discussed. First ref. to the cloud. 33:6-7
Ezion-Gaber. A camp located between Mt. Sinai & Mt. Hor. Discussed. A well-known oasis. 33:35-36
Haradah. A camp located between Mt. Sinai & Mt. Hor. 33:24-25
Hashmonah. A camp located between Mt. Sinai & Mt. Hor. 33:29-30
Hazeroth. A camp located between Mt. Sinai & Mt. Hor. 33:17-18
Hor Haggidgad. A camp located between Mt. Sinai & Mt. Hor. 33:32-33
Iye Abarim. A camp located between Mt. Hor & the Jordan River across from Jericho. Discussed. On the border of Moab. 33:44-45
Jotbathah. A camp located between Mt. Sinai & Mt. Hor. 33:33-34
Kadesh. A camp located between Mt. Sinai & Mt. Hor. Discussed. Place where 12 spies were sent out & 10 rebelled. 33:36-37
Kehelathah. A camp located between Mt. Sinai & Mt. Hor. 33:22-23
Kibroth Hattaavah. A camp located between Mt. Sinai & Mt. Hor. Discussed. Was three days from Sinai. 33:16-17

INDEX – NUMBERS

Libnah. A camp located between Mt. Sinai & Mt. Hor. 33:20-21
Makheloth. A camp located between Mt. Sinai & Mt. Hor. 33:25-26
Marah. A camp located between Rameses & Mt. Sinai. Discussed. Bitter waters sweetened by God. 33:8-9
Mithcah. A camp located between Mt. Sinai & Mt. Hor. 33:28-29
Moab, plains of. A camp located between Mt. Hor & the Jordan River across from Jericho.
   Camp stretched from Beth Jeshimoth & Abel Shittim (over five miles). 33:48-49
   Discussed. By the Jordan, across from Jericho. 33:48-49
   Final staging point for marching into the promised land. 33:48-49
Moseroth. A camp located between Mt. Sinai & Mt. Hor. Discussed. Place of Aaron's death. 33:30-31
Mt. Hor. A camp located between Mt. Sinai & Mt. Hor.
   Discussed. Place of Israel's first military victory. 33:40
   Where Aaron died. 33:37-39
Mt. Shepher. A camp located between Mt. Sinai & Mt. Hor. 33:23-24
Oboth. A camp located between Mt. Hor & the Jordan River across from Jericho. 33:43-44
Pi Hahiroth. A camp located between Rameses & Mt. Sinai. Discussed. C. from which they crossed the Red Sea. 33:7-8
Punon. A camp located between Mt. Hor & the Jordan River across from Jericho. 33:42-43
Rameses. A camp located between Rameses & Mt. Sinai. Discussed. Departed from Egypt from this place. 33:5
Rephidim. A camp located between Rameses & Mt. Sinai. Discussed. No water to drink. 33:14-15
Rimmon Perez. A camp located between Mt. Sinai & Mt. Hor. 33:19-20
Rissah. A camp located between Mt. Sinai & Mt. Hor. 33:21-22
Rithmah. A camp located between Mt. Sinai & Mt. Hor. 33:18-19
Succoth. A camp located between Rameses & Mt. Sinai. Discussed. First c. 33:5-6
Tahath. A camp located between Mt. Sinai & Mt. Hor. 33:26-27
Terah. A camp located between Mt. Sinai & Mt. Hor. 33:27-28
Zalmonah. A camp located between Mt. Hor & the Jordan River across from Jericho. 33:41-42
Map of. 33:5-49
Record of. 33:1-4

CANAAN, LAND OF
Description of. 13:26-33
Discussed. The spying out of the land. 13:1-25
Inhabitants of.
   Amalekites. 13:26-33, esp. v.29
   Amorites. 13:26-33, esp. v.29
   Canaanites. 13:26-33, esp. v.29
   Hittites. 13:26-33, esp. v.29
   Jebusites. 13:26-33, esp. v.29
   Nephilim, the descendants of Anak, the giant. 13:26-33, esp. v.33

Location of. Modern-day Israel, Lebanon, & much of southern Syria. 13:1-25

CANAANITES
Destruction of. 21:2-3, D.S. #1
Inhabitants of the promised land. 13:26-33, esp. v.29
Warfare of. Defeated the Israelites. 14:40-45

CENSERS
Discussed. Hammered into sheets of metal & used to overlay the altar. Reason for. 16:36-40
Incense of. 16:36-40
Typed - Symbolized - Pictured. A symbol of prayer acceptable to God. (Only Christ can make prayer acceptable to God.) 16:36-40

CENSUS
Discussed. The tragic record of the second c. 26:63-65
Of Israel. 1:2-3; 1:17-46; 26:4-51
Of the firstborn. 3:40-51
Of the Gershonites. 4:21-28
Of the Kohathites. 4:1-20
Of the Levites. 3:14-39; 26:57-62
Of the Merarites. 4:29-33
Of the second generation. 26:1-65
   Discussed. The numerical growth of Israel. 26:4-51
   Facts.
     Not a single person from the first census was listed. 26:63-65, esp. v.64
     Total number counted. 603,550. 26:4-51, esp. v.51
   Picture of.
     Being totally dedicated to God & His service: The Levites. 26:57-62
     God guiding His people: The LORD spoke. 26:1
     The believer's assurance of the promised land: Dividing the inheritance of the promised land. 26:53-56
     The faithfulness of God & a strong warning to man: Number counted, division by division. 26:4-52
     The people of God preparing for warfare. 26:2-3
     The sure judgment of God. 26:63-65
   Purpose of.
     Military. 26:2-3
     To divide the inheritance of the promised land. 26:53-56
Warning. Having one's name written on the roll does not guarantee entrance into the promised land. 26:4-51, Thgt.1

CEREMONIAL UNCLEANNESS
Discussed. Who were the unclean who were to be expelled from the camp? 5:1-4

CEREMONY
Dedication of. 8:5-26

CHALLENGE
Discussed. Need for. 9:1-10:10, Intro.

CHARACTER OF GOD
Discussed. At stake. 14:10-25, esp. vv.13-17

CHARTS
Of dated events. From *Exodus* 40 to *Numbers* 10. 7:1-9
Of Israel's campsites. Of the Tabernacle. See RESOURCE Section
Of the Tabernacle.
   Marching position of the tribes. 2:2-33, note 10
   Placement of. 2:2-33, note 10

CHASTISEMENT
Of God. 12:4-12; 14:10-25; 14:26-39

CHILDREN
Duty. Must obey parents. 30:3-5, Thgt.1

CHRISTIAN LIFE (See **BELIEVER**)

CHRIST, JESUS (See **JESUS CHRIST**)

CHURCH
Care of.
   The church & its furnishings. 4:1-20, Thgt.1
   The gifts of money, property, & anything that is set apart to the worship or service of God. 4:1-20, Thgt.1
   The physical body of the believer, that is, the temple of the Holy Spirit. 4:1-20, Thgt.1
Dedication of. 7:1-9; 7:10-88
Duty.
   Must be willing to do any work or service. 4:21-28
   Must stand fast under the banner of God's family. 2:2-33
   Must take one's place under the standard of Christ. 2:2-33
Leadership of.
   Discussed. Appointment of. 1:4-16
   Duty.
     Must be willing to serve. 1:4-16
     Must learn the Word of God before they can preach or teach the Word. 4:1-20, Thgt.2
     Must take the lead in meeting the financial needs of the church. 7:10-88, Thgt.1
Need of. 1:4-16; 4:29-33, Thgt.1
Protection of. 18:1-7
Rewards of. A c. that follows God's Word. 2:1-2, Thgt.2

CHURCH DISCIPLINE
Discussed. A person must be cleansed from all defilement & uncleanness, corruption & decay before he or she is allowed in the camp of God's people. 31:19-24, Thgt.1
Duty. Must discipline members who become engaged in serious sin. 5:1-4, Thgt.1
Typed - Symbolized - Pictured. By Leprosy: a symbol of sin, of a member who commits serious sin being removed from God's people. 12:13-16

CITIES - AREAS (See **CAMPSITES**)
Arad.
   Discussed. First military victory of Israel. 21:1-3
   Canaanite king of A. 21:1-3
   Location of. 21:1; D.S. #1
   Was completely destroyed by the Israelites. 21:1-3
Arnon River. Place where Israel camped on its way to the promised land. 21:10-20, esp. v.13-15

INDEX – NUMBERS

Aroer.
    City of. The tribe of Gad. 32:28-42, esp. vv.34-36
    Location of. 32:34-36; D.S. #3
Assyria. Discussed. Prophecy concerning. 24:21-22
Ataroth.
    City of. The tribe of Gad. 32:28-42, esp. v.34-36
    Location of. 32:34-36; D.S. #2
Atroth Shophan.
    City of. The tribe of Gad. 32:28-42, esp. vv.34-36
    Location of. 32:34-36; D.S. #4
Baal Meon.
    City of. The tribe of Reuben. 32:28-42, esp. vv.37-38
    Fact. Name changed. 32:38
    Location of. 32:37-38; D.S. #12
Bamoth. Place where Israel camped on its way to the promised land. 21:10-20, esp. v.19
Bashan. Discussed. Og. king of **B**. 21:33-35
Beer, The Well. Place where Israel camped on its way to the promised land. 21:10-20, esp. v.16-17
Beth Haran.
    City of. The tribe of Gad. 32:28-42, esp. vv.34-36
    Location of. 32:34-36; D.S. #8
Beth Nimrah.
    City of. The tribe of Gad. 32:28-42, esp. vv.34-36
    Location of. 32:34-36; D.S. #7
Dibon.
    City of. The tribe of Gad. 32:28-42, esp. v.34-36
    Location of. 32:34-36; D.S. #1
Edom. Land of. 20:14-22
Edrei.
    Discussed. The place where Israel won the victory over Og, the king of Bashan. 21:33-35
    Location of. 21:33-35; D.S. #5
Elealeh.
    City of. The tribe of Reuben. 32:28-42, esp. v.37-38
    Location of. 32:37-38; D.S. #9
Gilead. Territory of. The tribe of Manasseh, descendants of Makir. 32:28-42, esp. vv.39-40
Havvoth Jair.
    City of. The tribe of Manasseh, people of Jair. 32:28-42, esp. v.41
    Location of. 32:41; D.S. #14
Hazeroth.
    Campsite of Israel.11:35; 33:17-18; See RESOURCE Section
    Israel waited here until Miriam's confinement was over. 12:16
Hebron.
    Location of. About nineteen miles south of Jerusalem & fifteen miles west of the Dead Sea. 13:22; D.S. #3
    Meaning of. "Association" or "league." 13:22
    The first city spied out. 13:22
Heshbon.
    Location of. 21:25-30; D.S. #4
    Territory of. The tribe of Reuben. 32:28-42, esp. vv.37-38
    The capital of the Amorites. 21:21-32, esp. v.26

Hor, Mount.
    Place where Aaron died & was buried. 20:23-29; esp. v.28
    Transfer of power of the High Priest. 20:23-29, esp. vv.27-28
Hormah.
    Discussed. Israel fled to this place after being attacked. 14:45
    Israel destroyed the kingdom of Arad. Named it H. 21:1-3, esp. v.3
    Location of. Uncertain, but in the territory given to Simeon. 14:45; D.S. #6
    Meaning of. "Split rock" or "cursed for destruction." 14:45
Iye Abarim. Place where Israel camped on its way to the promised land. 21:10-20, esp. v.11
Jahaz. The place where the Amorites attacked Israel. 21:21-32, esp. v.23; D.S. #3
Jazer.
    City of. The tribe of Gad. 32:28-42, esp. v.34-36
    Location of. 32:34-36; D.S. #5
Jericho.
    City of. Israel camped in the plains of Moab by the Jordan River across from **J**. 22:1-41, esp. v.1
    Location of. 22:1; D.S. #1
Jogbehah.
    City of. The tribe of Gad. 32:28-42, esp. vv.34-36
    Location of. 32:34-36; D.S. #6
Kadesh.
    Campsite of Israel. 33:36-37; See RESOURCE Section
    In the desert of Zin. Where Miriam died & was buried. 20:1
    Place where 12 spies were sent out & 10 rebelled. 33:36-37
Kenath (See Nobah).
    Discussed.
        Nobah captured the city of K. & its surrounding villages. 32:42
        Nobah named the city of K. after himself. 32:42
    Location of. 32:42; D.S. #15
Kibroth Hattaavah. 11:35
    Meaning of. "Graves of craving." 11:35
    Place of quail judgment. 11:35
Kiriathaim. City of. The tribe of Reuben. 32:28-42, esp. v.37-38
Lebo-Hamath.
    Discussed. The 12 spies spied as far as Lebo-Hamath. 13:21
    Location of. The northern boundary of Canaan promised to Israel. 13:21; D.S. #2
    Meaning of. "Entrance to Hamath" or "to come to Hamath." 13:21
Mattanah. Place where Israel camped on its way to the promised land. 21:10-20, esp. v.18
Moab. Place where Israel camped on its way to the promised land. 21:10-20, esp. v.20
Nahaliel. Place where Israel camped on its way to the promised land. 21:10-20, esp. v.19

Nebo.
    City of. The tribe of Reuben. 32:28-42, esp. v.37-38
    Fact. Name changed. 32:38
    Location of. 32:37-38; D.S. # 11
Nobah (See Kenath).
    City of.
        N. captured the city of Kenath & its surrounding villages. 32:42
        N. named the city of Kenath after himself. 32:42
    Location of. 32:42; D.S. #16
Oboth. Place where Israel camped on its way to the promised land. 21:10-20, esp. v.10
Peor, Mount. The center of Baal worship in Moab. 23:27-24:13; 25:1-3
Pethor.
    Home of Balaam. 22:1-6, esp. v.5
    Location of. 22:5; D.S. #2
Pisgah Peak.
    An excellent place to spy out the promised land. 21:10-20, esp. v.20
    Balak took Balaam here to curse Israel. 23:13-26, esp. vv.14-17
    Place where Israel camped on its way to the promised land. 21:10-20, esp. v.20
Rehob.
    Discussed. The furthest point where the 12 spies went. 13:21
    Location of. Town in the vicinity of Laish in upper Galilee. 13:21; D.S. #1
    Meaning of. "Broad or open place." 13:21
Shittim. Location of. The plains of Moab, right across from the great city of Jericho. 25:1-3, esp. v.1
Sibmah.
    City of. The tribe of Reuben. 32:28-42, esp. v.37-38
    Location of. 32:37-38; D.S. #13
Taberah. 11:3
    Campsite of Israel. 11:1-3; esp. v.3;
    Meaning of. "Burning," a place of awful judgment. 11:1-3, esp. v.3; See RESOURCE Section
Zered Valley, The. Place where Israel camped on its way to the promised land. 21:10-20, esp. v.12
Zin, Desert Of.
    Southern border of the promised land. 34:3
    The place where the mission of the 12 spies began. 13:21
    Where Miriam died. 20:1
    Where the community rebelled at the waters. 27:14
Zoan.
    Hebron was built seven years before Zoan. 13:22
    Location of. In Egypt. 13:22; D.S. #4

CITIES OF REFUGE (See **REFUGE, CITIES OF**)

CLEANSING
Discussed. The only way to secure c. is through the sacrifice & power of Christ. 19:17-19, Thgt.1
From sin. 31:19-24
How to secure **c**. 19:17-19

CLEANSING, CEREMONIAL
Example of the Levites. 8:1-26

INDEX – NUMBERS

CLEANSING, SPIRITUAL
  Discussed. The only way to secure c. is through the sacrifice & power of Christ. 19:17-19, Thgt.1
  From sin. 19:1-10
  How to secure. 19:17-19
  Typed - Symbolized - Pictured. By the cleansing of the Levites. 8:5-26

CLOTHES - CLOTHING
  Of the High Priest. Symbol of the official position of the High Priest. 20:23-29
  Of the Levites. Levites had to wash their clothes. 8:5-26
  Of the priests. Priests were given new, clean garments. 8:5-26
  Typed - Pictured - Symbolized. By tearing of clothes. A symbol of ritual mourning. 14:1-10, esp. v.7

CLOUD, PILLAR OF (See **PILLAR OF CLOUD**)
  Facts.
    God guides His people, always guides them. 9:15-23, Thgt.1
    God is present with His people, always present. 9:15-23, Thgt.1
  Qualities of.
    Changed its appearance at night: a fiery cloud. 9:15-23; esp. v.15-16
    Contained the glory of God. 7:1-9; esp. v.1; 9:15-23
    Guided the Israelites. 9:15-23; esp. v.17
    One of the ways God spoke to His people. 9:15-23; esp. v.18-23
  The Shekinah Glory. 9:15-23, D.S. #1
  Type - Symbol of. God's presence & guidance. 9:15-23

COMFORT
  Warning. God warns us against comfort & ease. 32:6-15, Thgt.1

COMMANDS - COMMANDMENTS
  Duty.
    Must not break the seventh commandment (adultery). 25:1-3, Thgt.1
    Must not join in the false worship of the world. 25:1-3, Thgt.1
    Must remember & keep God's commandments throughout the day. 15:37-41, Thgt.1
    To remember. 15:37-41
  Of God. Duty. Must do everything God commands. 2:34; 36:13
  Of Israel. Five strong commands given to Israel.
    To demolish all the false worship sites in the promised land. 33:50-56, esp. v.52
    To destroy all the idols that were in the promised land. 33:50-56, esp. v.52
    To distribute the land by sacred lot. 33:50-56, esp. v.52
    To drive out all the enemies who opposed their entering the promised land. 33:50-56, esp. v.52
    To take possession of the promised land & settle it. 33:50-56, esp. v.52
  Purpose of. 36:13

COMMANDMENTS, THE TEN
  Warning. The penalty for adultery & for false worship or idolatry was death. 25:4-5 (see Le.18:24-30; Le.20:10)

COMMIT - COMMITMENT (See **DEDICATION**)
  Discussed. Festival of Trumpets. 29:1-6
  Duty to. Must be willing to do any work or service. 4:21-28
  Half-hearted. Example of. 32:6-15; 32:16-27

COMMITMENT, DEEPER
  Discussed. Desire for. 6:1-27, Intro.

COMMUNE - COMMUNION
  Discussed. Desire for. 6:1-27, Intro.
  With God. 7:89

COMPASSION
  Discussed. God is merciful & compassionate. 12:13-16, Thgt.1
  Of God. 12:13-16

COMPLAIN - COMPLAINING - COMPLAINT
  Against ministers.
    One of the major strategies of the devil is to arouse criticism against ministers. 12:1-16, Intro.
    The rebellion of Korah & his allies. 16:1-15
  Discussed.
    Against God's servants. 16:41-50
    Complaining & grumbling are signs of distrust, of terrible unbelief in God. 11:1-3, Thgt.2
    How children follow in the footsteps of their parents. 20:2-6
    Israel's hardships led to c. 11:1-3
    List. What Scripture declares about c. & grumbling. 11:1-3, Thgt.2
    Of Israel. Fatal response of Israel. 14:1-10
  Reasons for. Israel's c.
    God's judgment upon sin. 11:1-3, Thgt.1
    No food. 11:1-3, Thgt.1; 11:4-35
    No water. 11:1-3, Thgt.1
    Tired of leadership. 11:1-3, Thgt.1
    Trials in the wilderness wanderings. 11:1-3, Thgt.1
  Warning. God hears everything. 11:1-3, esp. v.2

COMPROMISE - COMPROMISING
  Example of. Tribes of Gad & Reuben. 32:16-27
  Warning.
    C. with worldliness can destroy a person. 32:1-42, Intro.
    God warns a person against compromise. 32:1-5, Thgt.1

CONFESS - CONFESSION
  Discussed. Israel's incomplete c. 14:40-45
  Duty. Of the sinner. Must confess his sins to God. 5:5-10
  False c.
    Balaam's partial confession. 22:22-35, esp. v.34
    Incomplete confession. 14:40-45
  Qualities of. True confession always involves repentance, a turning away from sin to God. 14:40-45, Thgt.1; 22:22-35, esp. v.34

CONFIDENCE
  Picture of. Marching forth from place to place in a spirit of strong assurance. 21:10-20

CONFRONTATION
  With God. 22:7-14

CONQUEST
  Of enemies. 21:1-3

CONSECRATE - CONSECRATION
  Of the Levites. Service for God. Example of. 8:1-26
  Typed - Symbolized - Pictured. The dedication ceremony of the Levites: A picture of laypersons being set apart to God. 8:5-26

CONSPIRACY
  Against the minister. 16:1-15

CONTEMPT
  Meaning of. 14:1-25, esp. v.11

CONTENTION
  Judgment of. The showdown & judgment of Korah & his allies. 16:16-35

CORRUPTION
  Results of. Death causes defilement, corruption. 19:1-10

COURAGE
  Example of. The five daughters of Zelophehad. 27:1-2

COVENANT
  Between God & His people. The promise of the promised land. 34:1-15, D.S. #1
  Of salt. meaning. 18:8-24, esp. vv.19-20

COVET - COVETOUSNESS
  Warning. Greed & covetousness actually plunge men into destruction & doom. 22:15-22, Thgt.1

COW (See **BULL**)

COZBI
  Daughter of Zur, king of the Midianites. 25:14-18
  Executed. Reason for. 25:14-18

CRAVE - CRAVING
  Of Israel. 11:4-35

CRISIS
  List of. 21:1-35, Intro.

CRITICISM
  Of ministers.
    A constant occurrence throughout society. 17:1-13, Intro.
    One of the major strategies of the devil is to arouse criticism against ministers. 12:1-16, Intro.
  Reasons for. Israel's c.
    Of being tired of leadership. 11:1-3, Thgt.1
    Of God's judgment upon sin. 11:1-3, Thgt.1
    Of no food. 11:1-3, Thgt.1; 11:4-35
    Of no water. 11:1-3, Thgt.1
    Of trials in the wilderness wanderings. 11:1-3, Thgt.1

INDEX – NUMBERS

Spirit of. 11:1-3
Warning. Complaining & grumbling are signs of distrust, of terrible unbelief in God. 11:1-3, Thgt.2

CROSS, THE
Meaning of. 15:1-16, Thgt.1

CUP OF INIQUITY - CUP FULL OF INIQUITY
Meaning of. 21:2-3, D.S. #1
Warning. God's judgment against all enemies whose "cup was full of iniquity." 24:23-35

CURSE - CURSING
Example of. Balak sought to curse & defeat Israel by pagan divination or sorcery. 22:1-6, esp. v.4-6
Purpose of. To defeat Israel in battle. 22:1-6, esp. v.6

D

DAN, TRIBE OF
Census of.
  1st census. 62,700 fighting men. 1:17-46; esp. v.39
  2nd census. 64,400 fighting men. 26:4-51, esp. v.43
Leaders of:
  Ahiezer. Helped with the first census. 1:4-16; esp. v.12
  Bukki.
    Appointed by Moses as a supervisor of the promised land. 34:16-29
    Led the tribe of Dan into the promised land. 34:16-29
Spy. Ammiel. One of the twelve spies. 13:1-25; esp. v.12

DARKNESS
Power of. Described. 22:1-41, Intro.

DATHAN
Conspiracy of. 16:1-15, esp. v.1
Defiance of. 16:1-15, esp. vv.12-14

DAUGHTERS
Courage of. Five d. of Zelophehad. 27:1-2

DAY OF ATONEMENT
Discussed.
  Was established to teach people that there was only one way to become acceptable to God. 29:7-11
  Was held on the tenth day of the seventh month. 29:7
  Was the most sacred, holy day of the year. 29:7-11
Type - Symbol of. The only way to approach God, through the shed blood of the substitute sacrifice (Christ). 29:7-11

DEATH
Caused by. 19:11-16
Discussed.
  Causes defilement. 19:1-10
  Is the ultimate defilement, corruption of man. 19:1-22, Intro.
  The ceremonial uncleanness of. 5:1-4
  The death of God's dear people is very precious to God. 20:23-29, Thgt.1
Experience of. 27:12-23, Intro.
Facts.
  God gives victory over death. 24:20, Thgt.1
  The death of a believer is a warm, tender, gentle & touching experience. 27:12-13, Thgt.1
  To be absent from the body is to be present with the Lord. 20:23-29, Thgt.1
Hope of. 27:12-23, Intro.
Of Aaron. 20:23-29
Of Balaam. 31:7-13
Of believer. 27:12-13
Of Miriam. 20:1
  Leader of the women of Israel. Three facts. 20:1
Of Moses. 27:12-23, Intro.; 27:12-13
Picture of. God preparing the believer for death: God told Moses to prepare for d. 27:12-13
Preparation for.
  Death of believer. 27:12-13
  Death of Moses. 27:12-13
Type - Symbol of.
  Corruption. 31:19-24
  Uncleanness. 19:11-16

DEDICATION - DEDICATE
Ceremony of. 8:5-26
Discussed.
  Festival of Trumpets. 29:1-6
  Three special obligations of the Nazarite vow. 6:3-12
Of Tabernacle. 7:1-9; 7:10-88
Of the Levites. 8:5-26
To God. 15:1-16

DEFIANT SIN
Example of. A picture of a man who defiantly raised his fist in the face of God. 15:30-36
Judgment of. Severe j. 15:30-36
Meaning of. 15:30-36

DEFILE - DEFILEMENT
Caused by. 19:11-16
Discussed. By death. 19:1-10
Duty.
  Must guard against defilement & uncleanness. 19:11-16, Thgt.1
  Must know that people are totally defiled. 19:11-16, Thgt.1
Kind of. Positional d. 19:11-16
Typed - Symbolized - Pictured. By the Red Heifer Offering. A symbol of cleansing a person defiled by death. 19:1-10
Warning.
  The judgment of God is going to fall upon every unclean & defiled person. 19:20-22, Thgt.1
  The possessions & things of this world can defile & make a person unclean. 31:19-24, Thgt.1

DELIVER - DELIVERANCE
Discussed.
  Celebration of. 9:1-14
  From the enemies of life. 9:1-10:10, Intro.
Prophecy concerning. 24:14-19
Type - Symbol of. The coming Deliverer. The coming of the Lord Jesus Christ as the Messianic Ruler over all the universe. 24:14-19

DESERT OF SIN
Campsite of Israel. 33:11-12; See RESOURCE Section

DESERT OF SINAI
Campsite of Israel.33:15-16; See RESOURCE Section
Fact. Place where the law was given. 33:15-16

DESERT OF ZIN (See **ZIN, DESERT OF**)
Location of. Southern border of the promised land. 34:3
Place where Miriam died. 20:1
Place where the community rebelled at the waters. 27:14
Place where the mission of the 12 spies began. 13:21

DESERTS
Of Paran.
  Encamped here after Israel left Hazeroth. 12:16
  Spies sent out from P. 13:1-25
  The cloud came to rest in the desert of P. 10:11-12
Of Sin. Christ's sacrifice that secured atonement or reconciliation for man. 28:3-8. 33:11-12:,33:1-56, D.S. #1
Of Sinai. The Israelites set out from the desert of S. on their march to the promised land. 10:11-12
Of Zin. The place where the mission of the 12 spies began. 13:21

DESTINY
Of man. 10:11-36, Intro.
Of the world. 10:11-36, Intro.

DEVOTION TO GOD
Discussed. Desire for. 6:1-27, Intro.

DIBON
Location of. 32:37-38; D.S. #1
Territory of. The tribe of Gad.
  Cities rebuilt.
    Dibon, Ataroth, Aroer, Atroth Shophan, Jazer, Jogbehah, Beth Nimrah & Beth Haran. 32:28-42, esp. vv.34-36

DIBON GAD
Campsite of Israel. 33:45-46; See RESOURCE Section

DIET (See **FOOD**)

DIFFICULTIES
Of Israel. 11:1-3

DISCIPLINE
Of believers. 14:10-25
Of God. 12:4-12; 14:26-39

DISCONTENTMENT
Discussed. Dissatisfaction with God's provision. 11:4-35
Reasons for. Israel's d.
  Being tired of leadership. 11:1-3, Thgt.1
  God's judgment upon sin. 11:1-3, Thgt.1
  No food. 11:1-3, Thgt.1; 11:4-35
  No water. 11:1-3, Thgt.1
  Trials in the wilderness wanderings. 11:1-3, Thgt.1
Spirit of. 11:1-3
Warning. Complaining & grumbling are signs of distrust, of terrible unbelief in God. 11:1-3, Thgt.2

INDEX – NUMBERS

DISEASE
Kinds. Of skin. Leprosy. 5:1-4

DISOBEY - DISOBEDIENCE
Warning. Leads to serious consequences. 20:7-13, Thgt.1

DISRESPECT
Example of. 25:6-13

DISTRUST
Of Israel. 11:1-3

DISUNITY
Example of. 32:6-15

DIVINATION
Discussed.
Balaam's false belief in d. 22:1-6
Balak sought to curse & defeat Israel by pagan divination or sorcery. 22:1-6, esp. v.4-6
Fee for. 22:7-14, esp. v.7
Evil of. 22:7-14

DIVINERS
Evil of. 22:1-41, Intro.
Warning. God condemns diviners, sorcerers, mystics, or anyone else who preys upon people seeking direction or help. 22:7-14

DIVISION (See **HOST**)
Meaning of. 2:2-33; esp. v.4, 6, 8, etc.

DIVORCE - DIVORCED
Vows of. 30:9

DOCUMENTARY HYPOTHESIS
Discussed. History of. Introduction to *Numbers*: Author

DONKEY
Discussed. Story of the d. 22:22-35
Fact. Did not speak by its own power; it spoke by the power of God. 22:22-35

DOPHKAH
Campsite of Israel. 33:12-13, See RESOURCE Section

DRINK OFFERING
Discussed.
A picture of the believer pouring out his life in continued devotion to God. 6:13-20, esp. v.15
Law governing special grain & drink offerings. 15:1-16
Type - Symbol of.
Christ's sacrifice. 15:1-16, esp. v.7
Pouring out one's life to God. 15:1-16, esp. v.5, 10; 28:3-8; 29:12-38
The blood of Christ that is pictured in the Lord's Supper. 28:3-8

DRUNK - DRUNKENNESS
Duty: Must abstain from all intoxicating drink. 6:3-12; esp. v.3-4

F

FAILURE
Of Israel. Ten failures of. 14:22, D.S.#1
Picture of. Man's **f.**, of following after God for forty years & making no progress: Wilderness Wanderings. 33:5-49

FAITH
Discussed.
Courageous **f.** 21:1-3
Great **f.** 27:3-4
In the promised land. 27:3-4
Example of. 36:1-4
Picture of. Strong faith in the promised land of God: women who inherited property. 36:1-13

FAITHFULNESS
Of God. 10:33-34; 21:21-32; 23:13-26; 26:4-51; 33:1-4
Picture of. God's faithfulness & man's failure: Review of the wilderness wanderings & a strong charge to take possession of the promised land. 33:1-56

FALSE WORSHIPPERS
Example of. The men of Israel worshipped Baal Peor, the false god of the Moabites. 25:1-3
Judgment of. Were immediately judged. 25:4-5
Warning.
Must not join in the false worship of the world. 25:1-3, Thgt.1
The penalty for adultery & for false worship or idolatry was death. 25:4-5 (see Le.18:24-30; Le.20:10)

FAMILY
Authority of. There has to be a head who has ultimate authority for any organization or body of people to function properly. 30:16, Thgt.1
Criticism of. 12:1-3
Discussed. Sexual unfaithfulness damages & destroys families. 5:11-31
Duty.
Must make concentrated, focused efforts to reach our family for Christ. 10:29-32, Thgt.1
Must reach out to our family members. 10:29-32, Thgt.1
List. Of what is destroyed when sexual unfaithfulness plagues a family. 5:11-31
Witnessing to. 10:29-32

FAMILY OF GOD
Duty.
Must stand fast under the banner of God's family. 2:2-33
Must take one's place under the standard of Christ. 2:2-33

FELLOWSHIP OFFERING (See **PEACE OFFERING**)
Discussed.
Christ died as our substitute to secure peace & fellowship with God for us. 15:1-16, Thgt.1
The Nazarite burned his hair under the sacrifice of the Fellowship Offering. 6:13-20; esp. v.18
Results of. More & more fellowship & peace with God. 6:13-20; esp. v.14
Type - Symbol of. Fellowship & peace with God. 6:13-20; esp. v.14

FESTIVAL OF FIRSTFRUITS (See **FIRSTFRUITS, FESTIVAL OF**)

FESTIVAL OF HARVEST (See **HARVEST, FESTIVAL OF**)

FESTIVAL OF TABERNACLES (See **TABERNACLES, FESTIVAL OF**)

FESTIVAL OF TRUMPETS (See **TRUMPETS, FESTIVAL OF**)

FESTIVAL OF UNLEAVENED BREAD (See **UNLEAVENED BREAD, FESTIVAL OF**)

FINANCIAL SUPPORT
Duty. To give to the LORD's work. 7:1-89, Intro.
Of God's work. Money is needed to support God's work throughout the world. 7:1-89, Intro.

FIRE
Discussed.
Test by **f.** 16:1-15
Unauthorized **f.** 3:1-4, pt.2
Of judgment. 11:1-3; 16:16-35, esp. v.35

FIRSTBORN
Census of. 3:40-51
Discussed. Male of every human or animal offered to the LORD. Became part of the income of the priest. 18:8-24, esp. v.15-18
Type - Symbolized - Pictured. By firstborn's replacement by the Levites. A picture of redemption. 3:40-51

FIRSTFRUITS, FESTIVAL OF
Type - Symbol of. Pentecost, the great harvest of souls & of people giving their lives to God. 28:26-31

FIRSTFRUITS, OFFERING OF
Discussed.
A permanent offering. 15:17-21
Became part of the food or income of the priest. 18:8-24, esp. vv.12-13
When to begin. 15:17-21
Duty. Must give our tithes & offerings to God. 15:17-21, Thgt.1
Picture of. Tithing one's income to the LORD as well as other offerings. 15:17-21
Type - Symbol of. Tithes & offerings. 15:17-21

FOOD
Discussed.
Complaining about. 11:4-35
For the Levites. 18:1-32
Land compared to milk & honey. 13:26-39, esp. v.27
Kinds of.
Figs. 13:1-25, esp. v.23
Grapes. 13:1-25, esp. v.23
Manna. 11:4-35, esp. vv.7-9; 21:4-9
Pomegranates. 13:1-25, esp. v.23
Quail. 11:4-35, esp. v.31

FOREIGNER, THE
Fact. Was invited to participate in the Passover. 9:1-14

FORGIVE - FORGIVENESS
How to secure. 19:17-19
Of God. Why God forgave Israel's sins. Prayers of Moses. 14:10-25, esp. vv.13-17
Of sin. 15:22-29; 19:1-10; 31:19-24

FORTUNE TELLING (See **OCCULT**)

FRUIT
Discussed. Bearing **f.** 17:6-9
Of ministry. 17:6-9
Of the promised land.

INDEX – NUMBERS

Figs. 13:1-25, esp. v.23
Grapes. 13:1-25, esp. v.23
Pomegranates. 13:1-25, esp. v.23

FUTURE
Discussed.
  Destiny of. 10:11-36, Intro.
  Question about. 23:1-24:25, Intro.
  The blessings of God & a glimpse into the future. 23:1–24:25

G

GAD, TRIBE OF
Census of.
  1st census. 45,650 fighting men. 1:17-46; esp. v.25
  2nd census. 40,500 fighting men. 26:4-51, esp. v.18
Leader of: Eliasaph. Helped with the first census. 1:4-16; esp. v.14
Settlement, east of the Jordan River. 32:1-42
Sins of.
  Unbelief, disloyalty, & half-hearted commitment. 32:6-15, esp. v.8-13
  Wanted to sit while others fought to conquer the promised land. 32:6-15
Spy. Geuel. One of the twelve spies 13:1-25; esp. v.15
Territory of.
  Cities rebuilt.
    Dibon, Ataroth, Aroer, Atroth Shophan, Jazer, Jogbehah, Beth Nimrah & Beth Haran. 32:28-42, esp. vv.34-36
Typed - Pictured - Symbolized. A picture of selfishness, covetousness, disloyalty: the compromise of Gad & Reuben. 32:1-42

GADDI
Spy from the tribe of Manasseh. 13:1-25; esp. v.11

GADDIEL
Spy from the tribe of Zebulun. 13:1-25; esp. v.10

GAMALIEL
Leader of tribe of Manasseh. 1:4-16; esp. v.10

GATHERED TO HIS PEOPLE
Discussed.
  Aaron. 20:23-29
  Moses. 27:12-13
Meaning of. 20:23-29; 27:12-13
Type - Symbol of. A picture of joining former believers in the presence of God. 20:23-29

GERSHON - GERSHONITES
Campsite: to the west behind the Tabernacle. 3:14-39, esp. v.23
Census of.
  2,630 in number. 4:34-49
  All men from thirty to fifty years old. 4:21-28, esp. v.23
  Reason: to learn the number of available workers. 4:21-28, esp. v.23
Clans of.
  7,500 in number. 3:14-39, esp. v.22
  Libnites & Shimeites. 3:14-39, esp. v.21
Duty of. To take care of the tent of the Tabernacle. 3:14-39, esp. vv.21-26; 10:13-28, esp. v.17
Leader of: Eliasaph, son of Lael. 3:14-39, esp. v.24

GEUEL
Spy from the tribe of Gad. 13:1-25; esp. v.15

GIDEON
Call of. God called Gideon to be a leader. 13:1-25, Thgt.1

GIFT - GIFTS
Duty. To offer to the LORD. 7:10-88
Fact. All sacred **g.**, once promised or given, belonged to the priests. 5:5-10
Kind. Voluntary & spontaneous **g**. 7:1-9
Of God.
  God calls & gifts believers differently. 12:4-12, Thgt.3;
  The promised land. 34:1-15

GILEAD
Territory of. Captured by the tribe of Manasseh. Gilead. Descendants of Makir. 32:28-42, esp. vv.39-40

GIVE - GIVING
Discussed. How to give. 7:1-9
Duty. To the LORD. 7:1-9; 7:10-88
Kind. Voluntary & spontaneous **g**. 7:1-9

GLORY OF GOD
Typed - Pictured - Symbolized. By the pillar cloud. 7:1-9; esp. v.1; 9:15-23, D.S. #1

GOAT
Type - Symbol of. Christ's sacrifice, His dying for sin: male goat as a Sin Offering. 28:11-15

GOD
Access to. 15:1-16, Thgt.1
Anger of. 11:1-3; Nu.11:4-35, esp. v.33; 12:4-12; 14:10-25; 22:22-35
Approach to. 15:1-16, Thgt.1
Approval of. 6:22-27; esp. v.26
Attention of. 6:22-27; esp. v.26
Blessings of.
  Five guarantees to the believer:
    God's faithfulness. 23:13-26,Thgt.1
    God's power. 23:13-26, Thgt.1
    God's presence. 23:13-26, Thgt.1
    God's promises. 23:13-26, Thgt.1
    God's truthfulness & unchangeableness. 23:13-26, Thgt.1
Call of.
  God called Abraham to be a leader. 13:1-25, Thgt.1
  God called Elisha to be a leader. 13:1-25, Thgt.1
  God called Gideon to be a leader. 13:1-25, Thgt.1
  God called Isaiah to be leader. 13:1-25, Thgt.1
  God called Moses to be a leader. 13:1-25, Thgt.1
  God called Paul to be a leader. 13:1-25, Thgt.1
  God calls many today to be leaders. 13:1-25, Thgt.1
Care of. 6:13-20, Thgt.1
Character of. 14:10-25, esp. v.13-17
Chastisement of. 14:10-25; 14:26-39
Compassion of God. 12:13-16
Discipline of. 12:4-12; 14:10-25; 14:26-39
Duty to. (Man's duty to.)
  Must acknowledge God & acknowledge Him as holy.
  Must approach God in the right way. 7:1-89; 8:5-26, Thgt.2; 15:1-16, Thgt.2
  Must be holy. 6:3-12, Thgt.1
  Must not turn to idols or false gods. 25:4-5
  Must respect God's appointed order within the family. 30:16, Thgt.1
  Must seek God. 27:5-11
  Must worship on the Sabbath. 15:30-36, Thgt.1
Face of. 6:22-27; esp. v.25
Facts.
  God does choose some persons to be leaders. 13:1-25, Thgt.1
  God dwells in the midst of His people. 2:1-2
  God forgives sin. 35:30-34, Thgt.1
  God gives five guarantees to the believer. 23:13-26, Thgt.1
  God guides His people as they march to the promised land. 2:1-2
  God hears everything (criticism). 11:1-3, esp. v.2
  God hears prayer. 12:13-16, Thgt.1
  God is faithful in leading & guiding us step by step & day by day. 10:33-34, Thgt.1
  God is merciful & compassionate. 12:13-16, Thgt.1
  God is no respecter of persons. 13:1-25, Thgt.1
  God is the Great Communicator. 1:1
  God judges or chastises His people when they sin. 12:4-12, Thgt.1
  God's judgment against unbelief & rebellion is sure. 16:16-35, Thgt.1
  God promises to provide all the necessities of life for His dear people. 35:1-8, Thgt.2
  God protects His people. 20:14-22
  God speaks to us. 1:1
  God will judge the world in righteousness. 25:4-5, Thgt.1
  Source of Laws. 15:41
Faithfulness of. 10:33-34; 33:1-4
Forgiveness of God. 14:10-25, esp. vv.13-17
Glory of. 9:15-23, D.S. #1
Grace of. 6:22-27; esp. v.25; 27:12-13
Guidance of. 2:1-2; Nu.10:33-34; 26:1
Help of. 2:1-2
Holiness of. 4:1-20
Judgment of. 11:1-3; Nu.12:4-12; 14:10-25; 14:26-39; 16:16-35; 31:1-6
Justice of. 21:21-32
Leadership of. 26:1
Love of God. 14:10-25, esp. vv.13-17; 27:12-13
Mercy of. 12:13-16; 35:30-34
Peace of. 6:22-27; esp. v.26
Pleasure of. 6:22-27; esp. v.26
Presence of. 2:2-33, Thgt.3; 6:22-27; esp. v.25; 7:89; 9:15-23, D.S. #1
Promises of. (See **PROMISES**)
  God gives us victory over persecution. 24:20, Thgt.1
  God gives victory over all the evil powers & rulers of darkness, over all

INDEX – NUMBERS

the spiritual wickedness that attacks us. 24:20, Thgt.1
God gives victory over any person or any thing in this world & in the spiritual world. 24:20, Thgt.1
God gives victory over death. 24:20, Thgt.1
God gives victory over the evil of men, over evil men who oppose us & stand as enemies against us. 24:20, Thgt.1
God gives victory over the temptations & trials of life. 24:20, Thgt.1
God gives victory over the world with all its enslavements & bondages. 24:20, Thgt.1
Protection of. 20:14-22
Provision of. 9:1-10:10
Sovereignty of. 22:36-41, Thgt.1
Tenderness of. 20:23-29, Thgt.1
Vengeance of. 31:1-6
Warning.
God demands justice. 35:30-34, esp. v.34
God judges all grumbling & unbelief. 16:1-50
God judges all rebellion & unauthorized approaches. 16:1-50
God judges & chastises His people when they sin. 14:10-25, Thgt.1
God judges sin. 27:14-17, Thgt.1
God warns us against comfort & ease. 32:6-15, Thgt.1
God will judge every human being who has ever lived. 14:26-39, Thgt.1
God will judge the nations of this earth. 24:23-35, Thgt.1
God will judge the people of this earth, individual by individual. 24:23-35
God will not share His glory with any person. 20:7-13, Thgt.1
God will not tolerate unbelief & rebellion from any person. 14:1-10, Thgt.1

GOLD
Gift of. 31:25-54

GRACE
Discussed. The promise of God's g. 6:22-27
List of Scriptures. Of grace. 6:22-27; esp. v.25
Of God. 27:12-13
Source. God. 6:22-27; esp. v.25

GRAIN OFFERING (See **MEAL OFFERING**)
Discussed.
Law governing special grain & drink offerings. 15:1-16
Made with both the morning & the evening sacrifices. 28:3-8
Purpose of.
Was a thanksgiving offering praising God for the atonement & for forgiveness & fellowship with God. 6:13-20; esp. v.15
Was part of the Levites' ceremonial, spiritual cleansing. 9:5-26
Type - Symbol of.
Dedication & thanking God for Christ's sacrifice. 15:1-16; 29:12-38
Thanking God for the atonement or reconciliation made through the substitute sacrifice. 15:1-16

GRAPES
Discussed. Size of **g**. in the promised land. 13:1-25, esp. v.23

GRASSHOPPERS
Discussed. How the Israelites saw themselves before the Nephilim. 13:26-33, esp. v.33

GREAT DAYS
Fact. The day the march to the promised land began. 10:11-12

GREED
Of Balaam. 22:15-21
Results of. 22:22-35
Warning.
God gave Balaam over to his greed. 22:15-21
Greed & covetousness actually plunge men into destruction & doom. 22:15-22, Thgt.1

GRUMBLE - GRUMBLING
Against ministers.
A constant occurrence throughout society. 17:1-13, Intro.
One of the major strategies of the devil is to arouse criticism against ministers. 12:1-16, Intro.
The rebellion of Korah & his allies. 16:1-15
Discussed.
Against God's servants. 16:41-50
How children follow in the footsteps of their parents. 20:2-6
Is a terrible sin. 20:2-6, Thgt.1
Israel's hardships led to **g**. 11:1-3
Over water & food. 20:2-6
Duty.
Must be stopped against God's servant, never allowed. 17:2-5, Thgt.1
Must confess & repent of his sins. 17:10-13, Thgt.1
Fact. Reveals a heart of unbelief, a distrust of God. 20:2-6, Thgt.1
List. What Scripture declares about complaining & **g**. 11:1-3, Thgt.2
Of Israel. Fatal response of. 14:1-10
Reasons for. Israel's **g**.
Of being tired of leadership. 11:1-3, Thgt.1
Of God's judgment upon sin. 11:1-3, Thgt.1
Of no food. 11:1-3, Thgt.1; 11:4-35
Of no water. 11:1-3, Thgt.1
Of trials in the wilderness wanderings. 11:1-3, Thgt.1
Results of. Spreads rapidly throughout the whole camp. 11:4-35, esp. v.10
Warning.
Any who grumble or rebel against God or His servant will face judgment. 17:10-13, Thgt.1
Complaining & grumbling are signs of distrust, of terrible unbelief in God. 11:1-3, Thgt.2
God judges all grumbling & unbelief. 16:1-50; 17:10-13
Will keep any of us out of the promised land. 20:1, Thgt.1

GUIDANCE
Of God. 2:1-2; 7:89; 9:1-10:10, Intro.; Nu.10:33-34; 26:1
Promise of.
God guides His people, always guides us. 9:15-23, Thgt.1
God guides His people through His precious Holy Word. 26:1, Thgt.1
God is faithful in leading & guiding us step by step & day by day. 10:33-34, Thgt.1
God is present with His people, always present. 9:15-23, Thgt.1
Typed - Symbolized - Pictured. By the pillar of cloud. a symbol of God's presence & guidance. 9:15-23

GUILT OFFERING
Purpose of. The worship required after the fulfillment of the Nazarite vow. 6:13-20
Results of. Cleansing. 6:3-12; esp. v.12
Type - Symbol of. Christ's sacrifice. 6:3-12; esp. v.12

H

HAIR
Discussed.
Cutting **h**.: provision for cleansing. 6:3-12; esp. vv.9-12
Nazarite must not cut his hair. 6:3-12; esp. v.5
Meaning of.
Burning **h**. under the sacrifice of the Fellowship Offering. 6:13-20; esp. v.18
Uncut **h**. 6:3-12; esp. v.5

HALF-HEARTED
Example of. 32:6-15; 32:16-27

HANNIEL
Appointed by Moses as a supervisor of the promised land. 34:16-29
Led the tribe of Manasseh into the promised land. 34:16-29

HARADAH
Campsite of Israel. 33:24-25; See RESOURCE Section

HARDNESS OF HEART
Warning. Condemns a person. 22:22-35, Thgt.1

HARDSHIP - HARDSHIPS
Of Israel. 11:1-3

HARVEST
Discussed. The fields are ripe, ready for harvest, but the laborers are few. 27:18-23, Thgt.1

HARVEST, FESTIVAL OF
Type - Symbol of. Pentecost, the great harvest of souls & of people giving their lives to God. 28:26-31

HASHMONAH
Campsite of Israel. 33:29-30; See RESOURCE Section

HAVVOTH JAIR
Location of. 32:41; D.S. #14
Territory of. Cities captured by the tribe of Manasseh. Havvoth Jair. A clan of Manasseh. 32:28-42, esp. v.41

HAZEROTH
Campsite of Israel. 11:35; 33:17-18; See RESOURCE Section
Israel waited here until Miriam's confinement was over. 12:16

INDEX – NUMBERS

HEART
Hardness of. Difficult to understand. 16:41-50, Thgt.1
Warning. Hardness of heart condemns a person. 22:22-35, Thgt.1

HEAVEN
Hope of. 20:23-29
Inheritance of. It is the person who follows after God who will inherit heaven. 26:1-65, Thgt.1
Journey to. 29:12-38

HEBRON
Discussed.
  Built seven years before Zoan in Egypt. 13:22
  Inhabited by the Anakites (giants, a tall people). 13:22
  Spies said nothing about Abraham's relationship to **H**. 13:1-25
  The first city spied out. 13:22
Location of.
  About 19 miles south of Jerusalem & 15 miles west of the Dead Sea. 13:22; D.S. #3
  Location of. 32:42; D.S. #16
  Meaning of. "Association" or "league." 13:22

HEBRONITES
Of the Kohathite clan. 3:14-39; esp. v.27

HELP - HELPER
Source of. God is our **H**. 2:1-2

HERITAGE
Godly. Importance of. 27:1

HESHBON
Capital of the Amorites. 21:21-32, esp. v.26
Location of. 21:25-30; D.S. #4
Territory of. The tribe of Reuben.
  Cities rebuilt.
    Heshbon, Elealeh, Kiriathaim, Nebo, Baal Meon, Sibmah 32:28-42, esp. v.37-38

HIGH PRIEST
Anointing of. Eleazar. 20:23-29
Clothing of. The symbol of the official position of the High Priest. 20:23-29, esp. v.26
Transferring power of. Symbolized by putting Aaron's garments on Eleazar. 20:23-29
Type - Symbol of. Jesus Christ. 20:23-29
Of righteousness. The clothing of the High Priest. 20:23-29, esp. v.26

HIGH PRIESTHOOD
Established. 17:6-9
Transfer of power of the High Priest. 20:23-29, esp. v.27
Vindication of. 17:2-5

HITTITES
Inhabitants of the promised land. 13:26-33, esp. v.29

HOBAB
Evangelism of. Moses witnessed to H., appealing him to join the march to the promised land. 10:29-32
Family of.
  Brother-in-law of Moses. 10:29-32
  Son of Reuel. 10:29-32, esp. v.29

HOLY - HOLINESS
Duty. To be holy. 15:37-41
Of God. 4:1-20; 27:14-17
Of life. 15:37-41
Warning. How men treat the holy things of God is of critical importance to God. 4:1-20; esp. v.4

HOLY SPIRIT
Dwelling of.
  Dwells within the body of every individual believer. 2:2-33, Thgt.3
  Dwells within the church. 2:2-33, Thgt.3

HONEY
Discussed. Promised land compared to milk & honey. 13:26-39, esp. v.27

HOPE
Discussed.
  For heaven. 20:23-29
  Great **h**. 27:3-4

HOR HAGGIDGAD
Campsite of Israel. 33:32-33; See RESOURCE Section

HOR, MOUNT
Campsite of Israel. 33:37-39; See RESOURCE Section
Discussed.
  Transfer of power of the High Priest. 20:23-29, esp. v.27-28
  Where Aaron died & was buried. (See **MOSEROTH**) 20:23-29; esp. v.28; 33:30-31

HORMAH
Discussed.
  Israel destroyed the kingdom of Arad. Named it **H**. 21:1-3, esp. v.3
  Israel fled to this place after being attacked. 14:45
Location of. Uncertain, but in the territory given to Simeon. 14:45; D.S. #6
Meaning of. "Split rock" or "cursed for destruction." 14:45

HOSHEA (See also **JOSHUA**)
Discussed. Name of. 13:1-25
Meaning of. Salvation. 13:1-25

HOST (See **DIVISION**)
Meaning of. 2:2-33; esp. vv.4, 6, 8, etc.

HUMILITY
Character of. Moses.
  Not reactionary nor combative but humble. 12:1-3, esp. v.3
  The spirit of a humble minister, of a true servant of God. 11:4-35, esp. vv.26-30
Duty.
  To be meek & humble—totally submissive & dependent upon God. 12:1-3, Thgt.1
  To walk humbly before one another. 36:1-4, Thgt.1
Example of. 36:1-4

HUSBAND
Laws concerning. Law controlling suspicion of unfaithfulness. 5:11-31

IDOLS - IDOLATRY
Warnings against.
  Judgment of. 25:4-5
  The penalty for adultery & for false worship or idolatry was death. 25:4-5 (see Le.18:24-30; Le.20:10)

I

IGAL
Spy from the tribe of Issachar. 13:1-25; esp. v.7

IMMORAL - IMMORALITY
Danger of. 25:14-18
Discussed.
  Age of. 25:1-18, Intro.
  Causes apostasy. 25:1-3
  Law controlling suspicion of unfaithfulness. 5:11-31
  Public display of. 25:6-13
Example of. 25:6-13
Judgment of. 25:4-5

IMPARTIALITY
Discussed. Need for. 27:1-11, Intro.
Fact. With God there is no partiality or favoritism, no discrimination whatsoever. 27:5-11

INCENSE
Type - Symbol of. Prayers being offered up to God. 16:36-40

INFECTIOUS SKIN DISEASE
Type - Symbol of. The spread of sin. 5:1-4

INHERITANCE
Laws governing. 36:5-9
Of Israel. 26:52-56
Of the believer. 26:52-56
Of women. Law governing. 36:1-4
Spiritual **I**. 36:10-12

INIQUITY
Discussed.
  Cup of. 21:2-3, D.S. #1
  Cup of. Filled. 31:14-18

INTERCESSION
Discussion.
  God hears prayer. 12:13-16, Thgt.1
  God hears the prayers of His people in behalf of others. 14:10-25, Thgt.1
  Three critical points. 14:10-25
Of Moses. 12:4-12; 12:13-16; 14:10-25; 16:16-35

INTOXICATING DRINK (See **ALCOHOL**)

INTOXICATION OF GRIEF
Results of. Unbelief & rebellion. 14:1-10

IRREVERENCE
Example of. 25:6-13

ISAIAH
Call of. God called Isaiah to be leader. 13:1-25, Thgt.1

ISRAEL
Apostasy of. 25:1-3
Blessings of.
  A new, separated, & distinctive people. 23:1-12, esp. v.9
  A numerous people. 23:1-12, esp. v.10
  A righteous people with an eternal hope. 23:1-12, esp. v.10
  An innocent, secure people. 23:1-12, esp. v.8
  Type - Symbol of. God's people. 23:1-12
Census of. 1:2-3; 1:17-46; 26:2-3; 26:4-51

INDEX – NUMBERS

Defeat of. 14:40-45
Discussed.
  Date of deliverance. 33:1-4
  Death of first generation. 26:1-65, Intro.
  Five strong commands given to Israel.
    To demolish all the false worship sites in the promised land. 33:50-56, esp. v.52
    To destroy all the idols that were in the promised land. 33:50-56, esp. v.52
    To distribute the land by sacred lot. 33:50-56, esp. v.52
    To drive out all the enemies who opposed their entering the promised land. 33:50-56, esp. v.52
    To take possession of the promised land & settle it. 33:50-56, esp. v.52
  Prophecies of victories. 24:20
  Rebelled within three days of the march. 11:1-14:45, Division Overview
Campsites of. (See **CAMPSITES**)
Errors of. 14:1-10
Example of.
  Immature believers. 11:1-3, Thgt.1
  To teach us not to lust after evil things as they lusted. 11:4-35, Thgt.1
Failure of. 11:1-14:45; 14:1-10; 25:14-18; 26:63-65; 33:5-49
Ten failures of. 14:22, D.S.#1
Judgment of. 14:10-25; 14:26-39; 26:1-65, Intro.
Laws of.
  Basic l. that keep God's people united & pure. 5:1-31
  Basic l. that gave women an inheritance in the promised land. 27:1-11
  Controlling wrong against others. 5:5-10
  Inheritance. 36:5-9
  Instructing the believer to wear tassels on the hem of his clothing. 15:37-41
  L. governing deliberate, defiant, brazen sin. 15:30-36
  L. governing forgiveness for unintentional sin. 15:22-29
  L. governing restitution. 5:5-10
  L. governing special Grain & Drink offerings. 15:1-16
  L. governing the firstfruits. 15:17-21
  L. governing the Nazarite vow. 6:13-20
  L. governing uncleanness. 6:3-12
  L. governing women's inheritance. 36:1-4
  The law controlling the suspicion & jealousy of sexual unfaithfulness. 5:11-31
  Various l. to help govern God's people. 15:1-41
Leaders of.
  God instructed Moses to appoint Joshua as his successor. 27:18-23
  One man from each tribe made up the twelve spies. 13:1-25
  Weakness of leaders. 13:1-25
  Were appointed to the promised land ahead of time. 34:16-29
Picture of. Failing to fully destroy the evil, seductive, & immoral enemies of life: Israel's conquest of Midian. 31:14-18
Priesthood established. 17:6-9
Priesthood of. 17:1; 17:6-9
Prophecies concerning.
  A picture of the greatest fortresses of the enemy being defeated. 24:21-22
  Prophecies of victories. 24:20
Sins of.
  Apostasy. 25:1-3
  Complaints & grumbling of. 20:2-6
  Failure to fully destroy the evil, seductive & immoral enemies of life. 31:14-18
  Incomplete confession. 14:40-45
  Not trusting God & losing sight of His guidance. 11:1-3
  Ten failures of. 14:22, D.S.#1
  Unbelief. 11:1-3; 16:41-50
Warfare of.
  Conquest of Amorites. 21:21-32; 21:33-35
  Conquest of enemies. 21:1-3
  Conquests of Midianites. 31:1-6; 31:7-13
  Were defeated by the Amalekites & Canaanites. 14:40-45

ISSACHAR, TRIBE OF
Census of.
  1st census. 54,400 fighting men. 1:17-46; esp. v.29
  2nd census. 64,300 fighting men. 26:4-51, esp. v.25
Leaders of: Nethanel. Helped with the first census. 1:4-16, esp. v.8
Paltiel.
  Appointment by Moses as a supervisor of the promised land. 34:16-29
  Led the tribe of Issachar into the promised land. 34:16-29
Spy. Igal. One of the twelve spies. 13:1-25, esp. v.7

ITHAMAR
Family of. Son of Aaron. 3:1-4
Ministry of.
  Anointed & ordained to serve as a priest. 3:1-4
  Placed in charge of the Gershonites. 4:21-28

IYE ABARIM
Campsite of Israel. 21:10-20, esp. v.11; 33:44-45; See RESOURCE Section

IZHORITES
Of the Kohathite clan. 3:14-39; esp. v.27

J

JAHAZ
Location of. 21:23; D.S. #3
zIsrael. 21:21-32, esp. v.23

JAZER
Location of. 32:34-36; D.S. #5
Territory of. The tribe of Gad.
  Cities rebuilt.
    Dibon, Ataroth, Aroer, Atroth Shophan, Jazer, Jogbehah, Beth Nimrah & Beth Haran. 32:28-42, esp. vv.34-36

JEALOUS – JEALOUSY
Discussed. Of sexual unfaithfulness. 5:11-31

JEBUSITES
Inhabitants of the promised land. 13:26-33, esp. v.29

JERICHO
Israel camped in the plains of Moab by the Jordan River across from J. 22:1-41, esp. v.1
Location of. 22:1; D.S. #1

JESUS CHRIST
Blood of. Typed - Pictured - Symbolized. By the Drink Offering: a symbol of the blood of Christ that is pictured in the Lord's Supper. 28:3-8
Death of. Referred to His death as an exodus or departure from this world. 28:16-25, Thgt.1
Discussed.
  Is the Light of the world. 8:1-4
  Is the promised Deliverer, Messiah, & Messianic King. 24:14-19, Thgt.1
  Our Sabbath Rest. 28:9-10, Thgt.1
Fact. Has been lifted up as the Savior of the world. 21:4-9, Thgt.1
Incarnation of. Became flesh & dwelt among us. 2:2-33, Thgt.3
Mediation of. Is the perfect Mediator who stands between God & man. 36:13, Thgt.1
Protection of.
  Our hiding place. 35:9-29, Thgt.1
  Our refuge. 35:9-29
  Our shield in protecting us. 35:9-29, Thgt.1
Sacrifice of.
  Is the sinless, perfect sacrifice offered up to God. 19:1-10, esp. v.2
  Our Atoning Sacrifice who delivers us from the avenger of death. 35:9-29, Thgt.1
Sovereignty of. Is the Sovereign LORD & King of the universe. 24:14-19, Thgt.1
Priesthood of. Is the Perfect Priest. 17:1, Thgt.1
Prophecy concerning. 24:14-19
Protection of. 35:9-29, Thgt.1
Sacrifice of.
  Died as our substitute sacrifice to secure atonement for us. 15:1-16, Thgt.1
  Died as our substitute to secure peace & fellowship with God for us. 15:1-16, Thgt.1
  Voluntarily sacrificed Himself for the sins of the human race. 19:1-10, esp. v.2
Typed - Symbolized - Pictured.
  By Joshua: Christ is the person who saves us & leads us into the promised land forever. 13:1-25, Thgt.3
  By manna: Christ is the bread from heaven. 21:4-9, Thgt.1
  By the bronze serpent: Christ being hung on the cross for the world's sins. 21:4-9
  By the hammered censers laid upon the altar: Christ, the Mediator. 16:36-40, Thgt.1
  By the lampstand: Christ, the Light of the world. 8:1-4
  By the Passover Lamb: Christ the Lamb of God who takes away the sins of the world. 28:16-25
  By the red heifer: Christ, the One who cleanses us from defilement & death. 19:1-10
Type - Symbol of.

INDEX – NUMBERS

Righteousness. The clothing of the High Priest. 20:23-29, esp. v.26
The High Priest. 20:23-29
The Lamb of God who takes away the sins of the world. 28:16-25
The perfect Priest. 17:1, Thgt.1
The Rock, the source of living water. 20:7-13
Warning. Any person who curses Jesus Christ will be judged by God. 21:4-9, Thgt.1

JOGBEHAH
Location of. 32:34-36; D.S. #6
Territory of. The tribe of Gad.
Cities rebuilt.
Dibon, Ataroth, Aroer, Atroth Shophan, Jazer, Jogbehah, Beth Nimrah & Beth Haran. 32:28-42, esp. vv.34-36

JOSHUA
Appointed by God. 27:18-23
Appointed by Moses as a supervisor of the promised land. 34:16-29
Character of. A man after God's own heart. 27:18-23
Fact. Had to approach God the same as everyone else, through the High Priest. 27:18-23
Meaning of. God saves. 13:1-25; 27:18-23
Name of. 13:1-25
Report of. 13:26-33
Spy from the tribe of Ephraim. 13:1-25; esp. v.8
Type - Symbol of. Christ, the person who saves us & leads us into the promised land forever. 13:1-25, Thgt.3

JOTBATHAH
Campsite of Israel. 33:33-34; See RESOURCE Section

JOURNEYS, WILDERNESS (See **WILDERNESS WANDERING**)

JUDAH, TRIBE OF
Census of.
1st census. 74,600 fighting men. 1:17-46; esp. v.27
2nd census. 76,500 fighting men. 26:4-51, esp. v.22
Leader of: Nahshon. Helped with the first census. 1:4-16, esp. v.7
Led the march to the promised land. 10:13-28, esp. v.14

JUDGMENT
Discussed.
Full measure of. 24:23-35
God will judge the world in righteousness. 25:4-5, Thgt.1
Of an overabundance of meat. 11:4-35, esp. vv.18-20
Upon the ten unbelieving spies. 14:26-39, esp. v.36-38
Duty. To remember. 16:36-40
Kind of.
Against all enemies. 24:23-35
False approach to God. 16:16-35
Judicial. 14:26-39; 22:15-21
Of God. 11:1-3; Nu.12:4-12; 14:10-25; 14:26-39; 16:16-35; 25:4-5; 26:63-65; 31:7-13; 31:14-18
Of Israel.
Had to wander about in the wilderness or desert. 14:10-25, esp. v.25
No adult over the age of 20 would ever see the promised land. 14:10-25, esp. v.23
Of the fiery snakes, poisonous snakes. 21:4-9
Warning.
God judges & chastises His people when they sin. 14:10-25, Thgt.1
God will judge the nations of this earth. 24:23-35, Thgt.1
God will judge the people of this earth, individual by individual. 24:23-35
The judgment of God is going to fall upon every unclean & defiled person. 19:20-22, Thgt.1
The penalty for adultery & for false worship or idolatry was death. 25:4-5 (see Le.18:24-30; Le.20:10)
There will be a day of judgment out in the future, a day when God will judge every human being who has ever lived. 14:26-39, Thgt.1

JUDICIAL JUDGMENT
Discussed.
Example of. Balaam. 22:15-21
Will fall upon the wicked & evil, the lawless & immoral of this earth. 24:23-35

JUSTICE
Of God. 21:21-32; 27:14-17; 31:1-6

K

KADESH
Campsite of Israel. 33:36-37; See RESOURCE Section
In the desert of Zin. Where Miriam died & was buried. 20:1
Place where 12 spies were sent out & 10 rebelled. 33:36-37

KEHELATHAH
Campsite of Israel. 33:22-33; See RESOURCE Section

KEMUEL
Appointed by Moses as a supervisor of the promised land. 34:16-29
Led the tribe of Ephraim into the promised land. 34:16-29

KENATH (See **NOBAH**)
Discussed.
Location of. 32:42; D.S. #15
Nobah captured the city of Kenath & its surrounding villages. 32:42
Nobah named the city of Kenath after himself. 32:42

KIBROTH HATTAAVAH
Campsite of Israel. 33:16-17; See RESOURCE Section
Discussed. Place of quail judgment. 11:35
Meaning of. "Graves of craving." 11:35

KILL - KILLING
Result of. Defiled a person. 31:19-24

KINITES
Prophecy concerning. 24:21-22

KINSMAN REDEEMER
Meaning of kinsman or redeemer. 35:9-29

KIRIATHAIM
Location of. 32:37-38; D.S. #10
Territory of. The tribe of Reuben.
Cities rebuilt.
Heshbon, Elealeh, Kiriathaim, Nebo, Baal Meon, Sibmah 32:28-42, esp. vv.37-38

KOHATH - KOHATHITES
Campsite: to the south side of the Tabernacle. 3:14-39, esp. v.29
Census of.
2,700 in number. 4:34-49, esp. vv.34-37
All men from thirty to fifty years old. 4:1-20, esp. v.3
Reason: to learn the number of available workers. 4:1-20, esp. v.3
Clans of.
8,600 in number. 3:14-39, esp. v.28
Amramites, Izhorites, Hebronites, Uzzielites. 3:14-39, esp. v.27
Duty of.
To respect God's holiness. 4;1-20, esp. v.15-20
To take care of the furnishings of the Tabernacle. 3:14-39, esp. v.27-32; 4:1-20; 10:13-28, esp. v.21
Leader of: Elizaphan, son of Uzziel. 3:14-39, esp. v.30
Warning to.
Would be stricken dead if they touched the holy things. 4:1-20, esp. v.15

KORAH
Discussed.
Charges of K. & his allies. 16:1-15
Disgust with the leadership of Moses & Aaron. 16:1-15
Rebellion by K. & his allies. 16:1-50
Family of.
A cousin of Moses. 16:1-15, esp. vv.1-2
A Levite. 16:1-15, esp. v.1
Some of Korah's descendants composed several of the Psalms. 16:16-35
Some of Korah's family survived the judgment (Nu. 26:10-11). 16:16-35
Judgment of. 16:16-35
Rebellion of.
Blamed Moses for failing to enter the promised land. 16:1-15, esp. v.14
Craved the priesthood, the power of the High Priest. 16:1-15, esp. v.10
Opposed the leadership of Moses, wanting to replace him. 16:1-15, esp. vv.3, 13-14
Wanted the Levites promoted as priests. 16:1-15, esp. vv.3, 7

L

LABORERS
Discussed. Need for. 8:1-26, Intro.
Duty of.
Must acknowledge God's holiness. 4:1-20; esp. v.20
Must take care of the most holy things. 4:1-20
Fact. L. are few. 8:5-26, Thgt.1

INDEX – NUMBERS

LAMB OF GOD
  Type - Symbol of. Christ the Lamb of God who takes away the sins of the world. 28:16-25

LAMB, PERFECT
  Type - Symbol of.
    Christ, the Lamb of God. 28:3-8
    The perfection of Jesus Christ. 28:3-8

LAMPSTAND
  Discussed.
    Description of. 8:1-4
    The placement of the l. 8:1-4
    Purpose of. To light the area in front of the Tabernacle. 8:1-4
  Type - Symbol of.
    Christ, the Light of the world. 8:1-4
    The way into God's presence must always shine brightly.

LAND (See **PROMISED LAND, THE**)
  Boundaries of. Promised land. 34:1-29
  Discussed.
    Charge: to take the promised land. 33:50-56
    Compared to milk & honey. 13:26-39, esp. v.27
    Faith in the promised land. 27:3-4
    Five daughters of Zelophehad hope for their inheritance of the promised land. 27:3-4
    Leaders were appointed to the promised land ahead of time. 34:16-29
    No land was to be polluted by murder. 35:30-34
    The promised. 10:11-12; 10:13-28
  Inheritance of.
    Protecting one's inheritance. 36:10-12
    The promised land. 26:52-56
  Laws governing. Women's inheritance. 36:1-4

LAW - LAWS
  Discussed.
    Basic l. that gave women an inheritance in the promised land. 27:1-11
    Basic l. that keep God's people united & pure. 5:1-31
    Controlling wrong against others. 5:5-10
    Instructing the believer to wear tassels on the hem of his clothing. 15:37-41
    L. of Nazarite vow. 6:13-20
    L. of uncleanness. 6:3-12
    Various l. to help govern God's people. 15:1-41
  Kinds of.
    L. governing deliberate, defiant, brazen sin. 15:30-36
    L. governing forgiveness for unintentional sin. 15:22-29
    L. governing special Grain & Drink offerings. 15:1-16
    L. governing the Firstfruits. 15:17-21
    L. governing women's inheritance. 36:1-4
  Meaning of. Law of restitution. 5:5-10
  Of inheritance. 36:5-9
  Source of. God. 15:41

LAW-GIVER (THE LORD)
  Discussed. Authority behind the laws. 15:41

LAYMEN - LAYPERSONS
  Call of. To step forth & be assistants, helpers in the ministry. 3:5-13
  Discussed. Service of. 18:1-7
  Duties of. Must accept the challenge of special ministries. 1:47-54, Thgt.1

LEADER - LEADERSHIP
  Appointment of. 1:4-16; 27:18-23
  Assassination of leaders. 14:1-10, esp. v.10
  Duty.
    Of believers. Must pray for God to raise up strong leaders who will serve God's people faithfully. 27:14-17, Thgt.1
    Of leaders.
      Must be willing to serve. 1:4-16
      Must learn the Word of God before they can preach or teach the Word. 4:1-20, Thgt.2
      Must live meek, humble lives, seeking to serve others. 16:1-15, Thgt.1
      Must not strike back nor attack the opposition when it arises. 16:1-15, Thgt.1
      Must seek the LORD & handle the opposition in a humble, loving, & just way. 16:1-15, Thgt.1
      Must seek the LORD to make sure one's leadership has been pure & just. 16:1-15, Thgt.1
      Must seek to serve people, not to hold positions of power. 16:1-15, Thgt.1
      Must take the lead in meeting the financial needs of the church. 7:10-88, Thgt.1
  Example of. Joshua. 27:18-23
  Of God. God guides His people through His precious Holy Word. 26:1, Thgt.1
  Of Israel. Were appointed to the promised land ahead of time. 34:16-29

LEAVEN (See **YEAST**)
  Type - Symbol of. Sin. 28:16-25, Thgt.1

LEBO-HAMATH
  Discussed. The 12 spies spied as far as Lebo-Hamath. 13:21
  Location of. The northern boundary of Canaan promised to Israel. 13:21; D.S. #2
  Meaning of. "Entrance to or to come to Hamath." 13:21

LEPROSY
  Type - Symbol of. The spread of sin. 5:1-4; 12:13-16

LEVI
  Sons of. Gershon, Kohath, & Merari. 3:14-39

LEVITES
  Call of. To step forth & be assistants, helpers in the ministry. 3:5-13
  Census of. 3:14-39; 26:57-62
  Cities of. Purpose of giving the Levites towns. 35:1-8
  Clan of L.
    The Gershonites. 4:21-28
    The Kohathites. 4:1-20
    The Merarites (a major Levite family). 4:29-33
  Dedication of. 8:5-26

  Discussed.
    A sharp distinction between the L. & the priests. 8:5-26
    Food for the Levites. 18:1-32
    Length of service. 8:5-26; esp. vv.23-26
    Set apart to be assistants to the High Priest. 3:5-13
    Six duties of the priests & Levites. 18:1-7
    Support of. 18:8-24
    Were to receive all the tithes given to the work of God. 18:8-24
  Duty of.
    Must give one tenth of their support or income. 18:25-32
    Must give the best portion of the tithe to the LORD. 18:25-32
    Must give the tithe to the LORD's representative, that is, the priests. 18:25-32
    Must heed the warning: must tithe the best or face eternal judgment. 18:25-33
    Must respect God's holiness. 4:1-20; esp. vv.15-20
    Must take charge of the Tabernacle. 1:47-54; 3:14-39
  Facts.
    Belonged to God, to the full-time service of God. 8:5-26; esp. vv.14-19
    Forty-eight towns were assigned to the Levites. 26:57-62
    The Levites went through a five year training or apprenticeship. 4:1-20; esp. v.3
  Inheritance of. 35:1-34
  Placement of. 3:14-39
  Provision for. 35:1-8
  Typed - Symbolized - Pictured. By the dedication ceremony of the Levites: A picture of laypersons being set apart to God. 8:5-26

LIBNAH
  Campsite of Israel. 33:20-21, See RESOURCE Section

LIBNITES
  Of the Gershonite clan. 3:14-39; esp. v.21

LIFE
  Discussed. How a person can know that he is going to live forever. 34:1-29, Intro.

LIGHT
  Typed - Pictured - Symbolized. By the Lampstand: Christ, the Light of the world. 8:1-4

LORD'S SUPPER
  Discussed.
    Importance of. 9:1-14, Thgt.1
    Invitation to. 9:1-14, Thgt.1
  Duty. Must celebrate God's deliverance by Christ through the Lord's Supper. 9:1-14, Thgt.1
  Warning. Must not approach nor partake of the Lord's Supper unworthily. 9:1-14, Thgt.1

LOVE
  Of God. 27:12-13

LUST - LUSTING
  Of Israel. 11:4-35

INDEX – NUMBERS

M

MAHLITES
Of the Merarite clan. 3:14-39; esp. v.33

MAKHELOTH
Campsite of Israel. 33:25-26; See RESOURCE Section

MAN
Bondages of. Is enslaved to sin & death. 33:1-56, Intro.
Deliverance from evil men. God gives victory over the evil of men, over evil men who oppose us & stand as enemies against us. 24:20, Thgt.1
Discussed. What is the destiny of **M**.? 10:11-36, Intro.
Picture of. God's faithfulness & man's failure: Review of the wilderness wanderings & a strong charge to take possession of the promised land. 33:1-56
Sin of. Is unclean just by being born & living in a corruptible world. 19:11-16

MANASSEH, TRIBE OF
Census of.
   1st census. 32,200 fighting men. 1:17-46; esp. v.35
   2nd census. 52,700 fighting men. 26:4-51, esp. v.34
Leaders of.
   Gamaliel. Helped with the first census. 1:4-16; esp. v.10
   Hanniel.
     Appointed by Moses as a supervisor of the promised land. 34:16-29
     Led the tribe of Manasseh into the promised land. 34:16-29
Settlement, east of the Jordan River. 32:1-42
Spy. Gaddi. One of the twelve spies. 13:1-25; esp. v.11
Territory of. Half-tribe of. Cities captured by the tribe of Manasseh.
   Gilead. Descendants of Makir. 32:28-42, esp. v.39-40
   Havvoth Jair. A clan of Manasseh. 32:28-42, esp. v.41
Typed - Pictured - Symbolized. By a picture of selfishness, covetousness, disloyalty: the compromise of Gad & Reuben. 32:1-42

MANKIND
Discussed. What is the destiny of **M**.? 10:11-36, Intro.

MANNA
Description of. 11:4-35, esp. v.7-9
Discussed. Israel detested the "worthless manna." 21:4-9

MAPS
The Borders of the Promised Land of Canaan & the Mission of the Twelve Spies. 34:1-29
The Desert or Wilderness Wanderings of Israel. 33:1-56

MARAH
Campsite of Israel. 33:8-9; See RESOURCE Section
Discussed. Bitter waters sweetened by God. 33:8-9

MARCH
Discussed.
   First organized march, marching in military divisions. 10:33-34
   One of the greatest spiritual journeys ever taken by a body of believers. 1:1-10:36, Division Overview
   The believer's m. 21:10-20; 36:13
   To the promised land. 10:11-12
List. Of the order of the tribes. 10:13-28
Of God's people. 10:13-28
Picture of the marching order of the tribes. 2:2-33

MARRIAGE
Authority of. There has to be a head who has ultimate authority for any organization or body of people to function properly. 30:16, Thgt.1
Discussed. God cares about young married couples. 30:6-8, Thgt.1
Duty of (spouses).
   Must consider one another in making vows & pledges. 30:6-8; 30:10-15
   Must marry someone with common interests & true faith in God & the promised land of heaven. 36:5-9, Thgt.1
Picture of. Marrying a person with common interests & true faith in the promised land: the legal solution governing the inheritance of women. 36:5-9
Sexual relationships in. Sexual unfaithfulness in **m**. 5:11-31

MATTANAH
Place where Israel camped on its way to the promised land. 21:10-20, esp. v.18

MEAL OFFERING (See **GRAIN OFFERING**)
Purpose of. A thanksgiving offering praising God for the atonement & for forgiveness & fellowship with God. 6:13-20; esp. v.15

MEAT
Judgment of. An overabundance of meat. 11:4-35, esp. v.18-20

MEDIATOR
Of Israel. Moses was the **m**. 21:4-9
Type - Symbol of. Christ, the perfect Mediator who stands between God & man. 36:13, Thgt.1

MEDIUMS (See **PSYCHICS**)

MERARI - MERARITES
Campsite: to the north side of the Tabernacle. 3:14-39; esp. v.35
Census of.
   3,200 in number. 4:34-49; esp. vv.42-45
   All men from thirty to fifty years old. 4:29-33
   Reason: to learn the number of available workers. 4:29-33
Clans of.
   6,200 in number. 3:14-39; esp. v.34
   Mahlites & the Mushites. 3:14-39; esp. v.33
Duty of. To take care of the support structures of the Tabernacle. 3:14-39; esp. v.33-37; 10:13-28, esp. v.17
Leader of: Zuriel, son of Abihail. 3:14-39; esp. v.35

MERCY
Discussed. God is merciful & compassionate. 12:13-16, Thgt.1
Of God. 12:13-16; 35:30-34

MERIBAH
Location of. Where Moses struck the rock, disobeying God. 20:7-13
Meaning of. A place of strife, arguing, or grumbling. 20:7-13, esp. v.13

MIDIAN - MIDIANITES
Discussed.
   Conquered by Israel. 31:1-6; 31:7-13
   Defeated by Moses. 31:1-3, D.S.#1
   Sometimes referred to as the Ishmaelites. 31:1-3, D.S.#1
   Were beyond repentance as a nation of people, beyond hope or correction. 31:1-6
   Zur, King of the Midianites. 25:14-18
Facts.
   Midian was a son of Abraham & Keturah. 31:1-3, D.S.#1
   The strategy of the Midianites would have destroyed Israel. 25:14-18
Picture of. Conquest of the M.: Conquering the seductive, immoral enemies of the world. 31:1-54

MILITARY
Army of God. 1:17-46; 26:4-51
Census of. 1:2-3; 26:2-3
Chart. Of the total number of fighting men within each tribe. 1:17-46
Error of. 31:14-18
Fact. The total number of men listed to fight, twenty years & older: 603,550 1:17-46; esp. v.46
Victory of. 21:33-35

MILK
Discussed. Promised land compared to milk & honey. 13:26-39, esp. v.27

MIND
Duty.
   Must concentrate. 15:37-41
   Must control our minds & think of God throughout the day. 15:37-41, Thgt.1
   Must keep our minds focused upon living a holy life throughout the day. 15:37-41, Thgt.1
   Must protect. 15:37-41

MINISTERS (See **PRIESTS**)
Appointed. 26:57-62; 27:18-23
Assistant ministers. 18:8-24, esp. vv.21-24
Assistants to. 3:14-39
Called. 3:1-4
Dedication of. 26:57-62
Described as. Shepherd. 27:14-17
Discussed.
   Often criticized & grumbled about. 12:1-16, Intro.
   One of the major strategies of the devil is to arouse criticism against m. 12:1-16, Intro.
   People of God are responsible for supporting the **m**. financially. 18:8-24, Thgt.1
   Six duties of the priests & Levites. 18:1-7

INDEX – NUMBERS

Duty of.
    Must accept his call & ministry as a gift from God. 18:1-7, Thgt.1
    Must acknowledge God's holiness. 4:1-20, esp. v.20
    Must approach God exactly as God says. 3:1-4, Thgt.2
    Must be available to help in times of need. 35:1-8, Thgt.1
    Must be diligent in performing his duties. 18:1-7, Thgt.1
    Must be humble, not to react against criticism, not to be combative. 12:1-3, Thgt.1
    Must be out among people, ministering to them. 35:1-8, Thgt.1
    Must be totally dedicated to God, totally dedicated to the call God has given him. 26:57-62, Thgt.1
    Must be willing to do any work or service. 4:21-28
    Must know that he represents Christ before the people of the world. 18:1-7, Thgt.1
    Must point people to the Lord Jesus Christ as the Perfect Priest. 18:1-7
    Must reach out & bear testimony & witness for Christ. 35:1-8, Thgt.1
    Must teach & instruct God's people in the truth & in the Word of God. 35:1-8, Thgt.1
    Must teach the people to respect Christ & the church. 18:1-7, Thgt.1
    Must take care of the most holy things. 4:1-20
    Must tithe to the work of the LORD. 18:25-32
Grumbling against. 16:41-50
Heart of. 27:14-17
Judgment of. **M.** responded with a broken humility & deep concern for God's people. 27:14-17
Ministry of. 35:1-8
Opposition to.
    Aaron. 17:1-13
    Criticism, grumbling, & murmuring against **m**. forbidden by God. 12:1-3, Thgt.1
Proof of. 17:1
Qualification of. Is God's chosen instrument. 17:2-5, Thgt.2
Support of. 18:1-32, Intro.; 18:8-24
Vindication of. 17:1
Warning to. Example of the death of Aaron's sons. 3:1-4, Thgt.2

MINISTRY
Discussed.
    A gift or privilege from God. 18:1-7
    Distinctives between priests & Levites. 8:5-26
Duty of.
    Must believe God & serve in the army of God. 1:17-46
    Must give to the LORD's work. 7:1-89, Intro.
    Must help with the enormous weight of ministry. 11:4-35, esp. v.16-17
Fruit of. 17:6-9
Proof of. 17:2-5
Support of. Money is needed to support God's work throughout the world. 7:1-89, Intro.
Vindication of. 17:2-5

MIRACLES
Discussed. God has the power to perform **m**. in order to achieve His purposes upon this earth. 22:22-35, Thgt.1
Example of. Story of the donkey. 22:22-35

MIRIAM
Death of. 20:1
Judgment of.
    God's anger burned against her. 12:4-12, esp. vv.9-12
    Struck with leprosy. 12:4-12, esp. v.10
    Was not allowed to enter the promised land. 20:1
Leadership of. A prophetess, the leader among the spirit-filled women of Israel. 12:1-3
Pride of.
    Criticized & questioned God's servant, Moses. 12:1-3
    Questioned the unique call & mission of Moses. 12:1-3, esp. v.2

MITHCAH
Campsite of Israel. 33:28-29, See RESOURCE Section

MOAB - MOABITES
Balak. King of Moab. 22:1-6
Fact. Were afraid of the Israelites. 22:1-6
Place where Israel camped on its way to the promised land. 21:10-20, esp. v.20

MOAB, PLAINS OF
Campsite of Israel. 33:48-49; See RESOURCE Section
Discussed.
    Final staging point for marching into the promised land. 33:48-49
    March stretched from Beth Jeshimoth to Abel Shittim (over five miles). 33:48-49
Location of. By the Jordan, across from Jericho. 33:48-49

MONEY
Discussed. Earned dishonestly. 22:7-14
Love of. 22:22-35
Lust for. 22:15-21
Purpose of. Money is needed to support God's work throughout the world. 7:1-89, Intro.
Warning. God gave Balaam over to his greed. 22:15-21

MONTHLY SACRIFICES
Discussed. Also referred to as the new moon offerings. 28:11-15

MORNING SUN (See **SUNRISE ON THE TABERNACLE'S ENTRANCE**)

MOSEROTH
Campsite of Israel. 33:30-31; See RESOURCE Section
Discussed. Place of Aaron's death. (See **HOR, MOUNT**) 33:30-31

MOSES
Authorship of *Numbers* Introduction to *Numbers*: Author
Call of. God called Moses to be a leader. 13:1-25, Thgt.1

Character of.
    Not reactionary nor combative but humble. 12:1-3, esp. v.3
    The spirit of a humble minister, of a true servant of God. 11:4-35, esp. vv.26-30
Discussed.
    Charges of Korah & his allies. 16:1-15
    God granted Moses a glimpse of the promised land. 27:12-13, esp. v.12
    God made two charges against Moses & Aaron. 20:7-13, esp. vv.11-12
    Hobab, his brother-in-law. 10:29-32
    Questioned, poured out his heart to the LORD. 11:4-35, esp. vv.11-13
Family line of. 3:1-4
Heart of. 27:14-17
Intercession of.
    Aaron petitioned Moses on Miriam's behalf. 12:4-12, esp. v.11-12
    Moses for Miriam. 12:13-16
    Pled for Israel's sake. 14:10-25
Ministry of.
    Actually saw the form of God. 12:4-12, esp. v.8
    Cried out for God to raise up others to help him. 11:4-35, esp. vv.14-15
    God spoke with Moses directly, not in riddles. 12:4-12, esp. v.8
    Helpless except for prayer. 12:13-16, esp. v.3
    Served as God's mediator.
    Was extremely faithful to the LORD & to his ministry. 12:4-12, esp. v.7
    Witnessed to Hobab, appealing to him to join the march to the promised land. 10:29-32
Opposition to.
    Aaron & Miriam questioned his leadership. 12:1-3
    Korah & his allies rebelled against **M**. 16:1-15
Sin of.
    Disobedience. 27:14-17
    Failed to honor God & failed to demonstrate God's holiness before the people. 27:14-17
    Lost the privilege of entering into the promised land. 20:7-13
    Three gross errors of disobedience. 20:7-13
Type - Symbol of. Christ, the perfect Mediator who stands between God & man. 36:13, Thgt.1
Wife of **M**.: a Cushite. 12:1-3, esp. v.1

MOUNT PISGAH (See **PISGAH PEAK**)
An excellent place to spy out the promised land. 21:10-20, esp. v.20
Balak took Balaam there to curse Israel. 23:13-26, esp. v.14-17
Place where Israel camped on its way to the promised land. 21:10-20, esp. v.20

MURDER
Discussed.
    No land was to be polluted by murder. 35:30-34
    Two or more witnesses were required to execute a person. 35:30-34
Kinds of. 35:9-29, esp. v.16-21
Laws governing. 35:30-34

INDEX – NUMBERS

MURMUR - MURMURING
Discussed.
    Against God's servants. 16:41-50
    Israel's hardships led to **m**. 11:1-3
Duty. Must be stopped against God's servant, never allowed. 17:2-5, Thgt.1
Reasons for. Israel's complaining.
    Of being tired of leadership. 11:1-3, Thgt.1
    Of God's judgment upon sin. 11:1-3, Thgt.1
    Of no food. 11:1-3, Thgt.1; 11:4-35
    Of no water. 11:1-3, Thgt.1
    Of trials in the wilderness wanderings. 11:1-3, Thgt.1

MUSHITES
Of the Merarite clan. 3:14-39; esp. v.33

MYSTIC - MYSTICS
Warning. God condemns diviners, sorcerers, mystics, or anyone else who preys upon people seeking direction or help. 22:7-14

N

NADAB
Family of. Son of Aaron. .3:1-4
Ministry of. 3:1-4
Warning. His death stands as a stark warning to the ministers of God. 3:1-4, Thgt.2

NAHALIEL
Place where Israel camped on its way to the promised land. 21:10-20, esp. v.19

NAHBI
Spy from the tribe of Naphtali. 13:1-25; esp. v.14

NAHSHON
Leader of the great tribe of Judah. 1:4-16; esp. v.7; 7:10-88; esp. v.12-17

NAPHTALI, TRIBE OF
Census of.
    1st census. 53,400 fighting men. 1:17-46; esp. v.43
    2nd census. 45,400 fighting men. 26:4-51, esp. v.50
Leaders of: Ahira. Helped with the first census. 1:4-16; esp. v.15
Pedahel.
    Appointed by Moses as a supervisor of the promised land. 34:16-29
    Led the tribe of Naphtali into the promised land. 34:16-29
Spy. Nahbi. One of the twelve spies. 13:1-25; esp. v.14

NATION - NATIONS (See **SOCIETY**)
Assyria.
    Discussed. Prophecy concerning. 24:21-22
    Location of. 32:42; D.S. #16
Destruction of. 21:2-3, D.S. #1;
Discussed.
    Cup full of iniquity. 24:23-35; 31:14-18
    Judgment of. 21:2-3, D.S. #1; 31:1-6
Inhabitants of. Promised land.
    Amalekites. 13:26-33, esp. v.29
    Amorites. 13:26-33, esp. v.29
    Canaanites. 13:26-33, esp. v.29
    Hittites. 13:26-33, esp. v.29
    Jebusites. 13:26-33, esp. v.29
    Nephilim, the descendants of Anak, the giant. 13:26-33, esp. v.33
Judgment of. Evil. Judged by God. 31:1-6
Kind of. Savage & evil. 21:2-3, D.S. #1; 31:14-18
Kinites. Discussed. Prophecy concerning. 24:21-22
Warning. God will judge the nations of this earth. 24:23-35, Thgt.1

NAZARITE VOW
Discussed.
    Hair: the mark of his vow to God. 6:3-12
    Period of dedication. 6:1-2
    Provision for spiritual cleansing. 6:3-12; esp. vv.9-12
    Seriousness & heavy weight of the vow. 6:21
    The great priestly benediction. 6:22-27
    When the Nazarite could drink wine. 6:13-20; esp. v.20
Duty.
    To be kept & fulfilled before God. 6:21
    To the obligations of a special vow to the LORD. 6:3-12
    To the worship required after the fulfillment of a vow. 6:13-20
Importance of. 6:1-27, Intro.
Meaning of. A vow that seeks a deeper life with God. 6:1-27, Intro.
Obligations of.
    Appearance: must not cut his hair. 6:3-12; esp. v.5
    Associations: must not go near a dead body. 6:3-12; esp. v.6
    Diet: must abstain from all intoxicating drink. 6:3-12; esp. v.3-4
    Three special obligations of the Nazarite vow. 6:3-12
Purpose of. 6:1-2
Reason for. 6:1-2

NEBO
Fact. Name changed. 32:38
Location of. 32:37-38; D.S. #11
Territory of. The tribe of Reuben.
    Cities rebuilt & renamed.
        Heshbon, Elealeh, Kiriathaim, Nebo, Baal Meon, Sibmah 32:28-42, esp. vv.37-38

NECESSITIES
Provision for. 35:1-8

NEEDS
Discussed. Three of the greatest needs people have. 9:1-10:10, Intro.
Fact. Are grave. 4:1-49, Intro.
Of every community. List. 1:17-46, Thgt.1
Of the church. List. 4:29-33, Thgt.1

NEEDY, THE
List of. 8:1-26, Intro.

NEGATIVISM
Discussed.
    Age of **n**. 11:1-35
    An attitude of **n**. 13:1-14:45, Intro.

NEGEV, THE
The Amalekites were in the **N**. 13:29

NEIGHBOR
Sin against. 5:5-10

NEPHILIM
Descendants of Anak, the giant. 13:26-33, esp. v.33
Inhabited the promised land. 13:26-33, esp. v.33

NETHANEL
Leader of tribe of Issachar. 1:4-16; esp. v.8

NEW AGE MOVEMENT (See **OCCULT**)
Warning. Must have nothing to do with the world of the occult. 22:1-6, Thgt.1

NEW MOON FESTIVALS
Discussed. Abuse of by Israel. 28:11-15

NOBAH
Captured the city of Kenath & its surrounding villages. 32:42
Location of. 32:42; D.S. #16
Named the city of Kenath after himself. 32:42

NON-DISCRIMINATION
Discussed. Need for. 27:1-11, Intro.

NOVICE
Warning. Dangers of having a **n**. placed into a position of leadership. 4:1-20; Thgt.2

NUMBERS, THE BOOK OF
Discussed.
    Authorship of. Introduction to *Numbers*: Author
    Conclusion of. 36:13
    Date of Introduction to *Numbers*: Date
    Purpose of. 36:13, Thgt.2; Introduction to *Numbers*: Purpose
    Special features of. Introduction to *Numbers*: Special features
    This statement, "The LORD spoke," is used over 150 times in twenty-plus ways in the book of *Numbers* alone. 1:1
    Written to. Introduction to *Numbers*: To Whom Written (Audience)

O

OBEY - OBEDIENCE
Discussed. Where is **o**. today? 4:34-49, Thgt.1
Duty.
    Must do everything God commands. 2:34
    Must obey God as we march to the promised land. 10:13-28, Thgt.1
Example of.
    Five daughters of faith. 36:10-12
    God's people marched forth division by division. 10:13-28
Picture of. Obedience: the **o**. of the five daughters of faith. 36:10-12
Rewards. Of a church that follows God's Word. 2:1-2, Thgt.2

OBOTH
Campsite of Israel. 33:43-44; See RESOURCE Section
Place where Israel camped on its way to the promised land. 21:10-20, esp. v.10

INDEX – NUMBERS

OCCULT
  Discussed.
    Balak sought to curse & defeat Israel by pagan divination or sorcery. 22:1-6, esp. vv.4-6
    Balaam's false belief in **o**. 22:1-6
  Warning.
    A world controlled by evil spirits who are set upon destroying the lives of people & cutting the heart of God. 22:1-41
    Is just as active today as ever. 22:1-6
    Leaders of the **o**. doom people to an eternity of separation from God in the judgment to come. 22:22-35
    Must have nothing to do with the world of the occult. 22:1-6, Thgt.1
  World of. 22:1-41, Intro.

OFFERINGS
  Discussed.
    Importance of the offerings or sacrifices. 28:1-2; 29:39-40
    The people were unable to offer the Grain & Drink Offerings out in the desert or wilderness. 15:1-16, esp. vv.2-3
    Voluntary & spontaneous **o**. 7:1-9
    When to present. 15:1-16
  Duty.
    Must give our tithes & offerings to God. 15:17-21, Thgt.1
    To be presented at the appointed time. 28:1-2
    To give. 7:10-88
  List of.
    Burnt **O**. 6:13-20; 23:3-8
    Drink **O**. 15:1-16; 28:3-8
    Firstfruits **O**. 15:17-21; 18:8-24, esp. vv.12-13
    Fellowship or Peace **O**. 6:13-20, esp. v.14
    Freewill **O**.
    Grain or Meal **O**. 6:13-20, esp. v.15; 15:1-16; 28:3-8
    Guilt **O**. 6:13-20
    Monthly **o**. 28:11-15
    Red Heifer **O**. 19:1-10
    Sin **O**. 6:13-20
    Spontaneous **o**. 7:1-9
    Voluntary **o**. 7:1-9; 31:25-54
    Wave **o**. 18:8-24, esp. v.11
    Wine **O**. 15:1-16
  Of God. A picture of tithing one's income to the LORD as well as other offerings. 15:17-21

OG
  King of Bashan. 21:33-35

ON
  Discussed. Conspiracy of. 16:1-15, esp. v.1

ONE FLESH
  Meaning of. 5:11-31, Thgt.1

ONENESS
  Duty. Must walk together. 5:1-31, Intro.

OPPOSITION
  Discussed.
    Against God's servant. 20:2-6
    To the minister. 16:1-15

ORDINATION
  Fact. Some persons are anointed & ordained to serve God. 3:1-4, Thgt.1
  Of ministers. 3:1-4, Thgt.1

ORGANIZATION
  Of families. 30:16

P

PAGAN - PAGANISM
  An act of sorcery. 23:1-12; 24:1

PAGIEL
  Leader of tribe of Asher. 1:4-16; esp. v.13

PALTI
  Spy from the tribe of Benjamin. 13:1-25; esp. v.9

PALTIEL
  Appointed by Moses as a supervisor of the promised land. 34:16-29
  Led the tribe of Issachar into the promised land. 34:16-29

PARAN, DESERT OF (See **DESERTS**)
  Place where Israel encamped after they left Hazeroth. 12:16
  Spies sent out from **P**. 13:1-25
  The cloud came to rest in the desert of **P**. 10:11-12

PARENTS
  Authority of. There has to be a head who has ultimate authority for any organization or body of people to function properly. 30:16, Thgt.1
  Discussed.
    Duties to children. 30:3-5
    Godly. Importance of. 27:1
  Duty. Must live godly lives before their children. 27:1

PARTIALITY (See **EQUAL; JUSTICE**)
  Discussed. Need for impartiality. 27:1-11, Intro.
  Fact. With God there is no **p**. or favoritism, no discrimination whatsoever. 27:5-11

PASSOVER, THE
  Discussed.
    Four significant lessons. 9:1-14, Thgt.1
    P. Lamb. No bone was ever to be broken. a picture of Christ. 28:16-25, Thgt.1
  Duty. Must celebrate God's deliverance by Christ through the Lord's Supper. 9:1-14, Thgt.1
  Facts.
    God showed great compassion & grace in the **P**. 9:1-14
    Jesus Christ is the true Passover Lamb. 9:1-14, Thgt.1
    Was tied in to the Festival of Unleavened Bread. 28:16-25
  Purpose of. To remember God's great deliverance. 9:1-14
  Type - Symbol of. Christ the Lamb of God who takes away the sins of the world. 28:16-25
  Warning. The **P**. was of critical importance. 9:1-14

PAUL, THE APOSTLE
  Call of. God called Paul to be a leader. 13:1-25, Thgt.1

PEACE
  Discussed. The promise of God's **p**. 6:22-27
  Fact. The peace of God floods the believer's heart & life. 6:22-27; esp. v.26
  List of Scriptures. Of God's peace. 6:22-27; esp. v.26
  Source. God. 6:22-27

PEACE OFFERING (See **FELLOWSHIP OFFERING**)
  Discussed. Christ died as our substitute to secure peace & fellowship with God for us. 15:1-16, Thgt.1
  Results of. More & more fellowship & peace with God. 6:13-20; esp. v.14
  Type - Symbol of. Fellowship & peace with God. 6:13-20; esp. v.14

PEDAHEL
  Appointed by Moses as a supervisor of the promised land. 34:16-29
  Led the tribe of Naphtali into the promised land. 34:16-29

PENTECOST (See **HARVEST, FESTIVAL OF**)

PEOR, MOUNT
  The center of Baal worship in Moab. 23:27-24:13; 25:1-3

PERSECUTE - PERSECUTION
  Victory over. God gives us victory over persecution. 24:20, Thgt.1

PERSEVERANCE
  Duty.
    Must take one's place under the standard of Christ. 2:2-33
    Must stand fast under the banner of God's family. 2:2-33

PETHOR
  Home of Balaam. 22:1-6, esp. v.5
  Location of. 22:5; D.S. #2

PHINEHAS
  Discussed.
    God's covenant of peace with **P**. 25:6-13, esp. v.12
    Went into battle against the Midianites. 31:1-6
    Zeal of. For righteousness. 25:6-13
  Family of. Son of Eleazar. 25:6-13, esp. v.7
  Ministry of. Atonement for the people. 25:6-13
  Office of. The High Priest. 25:6-13
  Type - Symbol of. Christ. 25:6-13

PI HAHIROTH
  Campsite of Israel. 33:7-8; See **RESOURCE** Section
  Place from which Israel crossed the Red Sea. 33:7-8

PILGRIMAGE
  Of the believer. 36:13

PILGRIMS
  Life & walk. Believers are like **p**. walking through the desert & wilderness of this world. 2:2-33, Thgt.1

INDEX – NUMBERS

PILLAR OF CLOUD (See **CLOUD, PILLAR OF**)
  Characteristics of.
    Changed its appearance at night: a fiery cloud. 9:15-23; esp. vv.15-16
    Contained the glory of God. 7:1-9; esp. v.1; 9:15-23
    Guided the Israelites. 9:15-23; esp. v.17
    One of the ways God spoke to His people. 9:15-23; esp. v.18-23
  Facts.
    God guides His people, always guides them. 9:15-23, Thgt.1
    God is always present with His people. 9:15-23, Thgt.1
  The Shekinah Glory. 9:15-23, D.S. #1
  Type - Symbol of. God's presence & guidance. 9:15-23

PISGAH PEAK (See **MOUNT PISGAH**)
  An excellent place to spy out the promised land. 21:10-20, esp. v.20
  Balak took Balaam here to curse Israel. 23:13-26, esp. v.14-17
  Place where Israel camped on its way to the promised land. 21:10-20, esp. v.20

PITFALLS
  List of. 1:1-2:34, Intro.
  Warning. Life is filled with **p.** & enemies. 1:1-2:34, Intro.

PLAGUE - PLAGUES
  Of quails. 11:4-35, esp. v.31-34

PLEDGE
  Discussed.
    Law governing. 30:6-8
    Spouses must consider one another in making vows & pledges. 30:6-8; 30:10-15
  Importance of. 30:1-2
  Kinds of.
    By children. 30:3-5
    By married women. 30:10-15
    By single women. 30:3-5
    By the divorced. 30:9
    By widows. 30:9

PRAISE
  To God. 15:1-16

PRAY - PRAYER - PRAYING
  Discussed.
    God hears prayer. 12:13-16, Thgt.1
    God hears the prayers of His people on behalf of others. 14:10-25, Thgt.1
    Only Jesus Christ can make prayer acceptable to God. 16:36-40
    Two silver trumpets. Purpose of. To sound the alarm for prayer. 10:1-10, esp. v.9
    When problems confront us, we should seek the face of the LORD. 27:5-11, Thgt.1
  Duty.
    Must pray for & support all leaders, both church & government leaders. 16:16-36, Thgt.1
    Must sound the alarm for prayer. 10:1-10, Thgt.1
  Of Moses.
    His intercession for Miriam. 12:13-16
    His intercession for God to spare the people after the rebellion by Korah. 16:16-35, esp. v.22
  Seeking answers to. 27:5-11

PREJUDICE
  Discussed. Trait of nations. 27:1-11, Intro.

PRESENCE
  Of God. 2:2-33, Thgt.3; 6:22-27; esp. v.25; 7:89

PRIEST (See **MINISTER**)
  Discussed.
    Only the priests were allowed to enter the inner sanctuary of the Tabernacle. 4:1-20
    Only the priests were allowed to wrap & cover the holy furnishings. 4:1-20
    The people rested on the Sabbath day, but not the priest. 28:9-10
  Duties - Responsibilities.
    Six duties of the priests & Levites. 18:1-7
    To cover & wrap the Ark. 4:1-20; esp. vv.5-6
    To cover & wrap the bronze altar of Burnt Offering. 4:1-20; esp. vv.13-14
    To cover & wrap the gold altar. 4:1-20; esp. v.11-12
    To cover & wrap the lampstand & all its accessories. 4:1-20; esp. v.9-10
    To cover & wrap the Table of the Presence or Table of Showbread. 4:1-20; esp. vv.7-8
  Facts.
    Jesus Christ is the Perfect Priest. 17:1, Thgt.1
    The most holy things could be prepared only by the priests. 4:1-20; esp. v.5
  Support of. 18:8-24
  Type - Symbol of.
    Christ. 3:5-13, pt.1; 4:1-20; esp. v.5; 17:1, Thgt.1; 17:2-5
    The minister. 17:2-5
  Vindication of. 17:2-5

PRIEST, HIGH (See **HIGH PRIEST**)

PRIESTHOOD
  Established. 17:6-9
  Of Aaron. 17:6-9
  Of Eleazar. 20:23-29
  Of Phinehas. 25:6-13
  Vindication of. 17:1

PROBLEMS
  Discussed. Seeking answers to. 27:5-11
  Of Israel. 11:1-3
  Response to. When problems confront us, we should seek the face of the LORD. 27:5-11, Thgt.1

PROMISED LAND, THE
  Boundaries of. 34:1-29
    Eastern border. 34:10-12
    Northern border. 34:7-9
    Southern border. 34:3-5
    Western border. 34:6
  Description of. 13:26-33
  Discussed. Introduction to *Numbers*, Special Feature # 26
  Based upon a covenant between God & His people. 34:1-15; 34:1-15, D.S. #1
  Charge: to take the promised land. 33:50-56
  Compared to milk & honey. 13:26-39, esp. v.27
  Date of departure for. 10:11-12
  Faith in the promised land. 27:3-4
  God granted Moses a glimpse of the promised land. 27:12-13, esp. v.12
  Leaders were appointed to the promised land ahead of time. 34:16-29
  No land was to be polluted by murder. 35:30-34
  Duty.
    Must hold a great expectation & hope for the promised land of heaven. 10:11-12, Thgt.1
    To take possession of. 33:50-56
  Facts.
    Israel never did claim all of the promised land. 34:1-15
    There is only one way to enter the promised land of heaven. 36:1-4, Thgt.1
  Hope for. 10:11-36, Intro.
  Inhabitants of.
    Amalekites. 13:26-33, esp. v.29
    Amorites. 13:26-33, esp. v.29
    Canaanites. 13:26-33, esp. v.29
    Hittites. 13:26-33, esp. v.29
    Jebusites. 13:26-33, esp. v.29
    Nephilim, the descendants of Anak, the giant. 13:26-33, esp. v.33
  Inheritance of. 26:52-56
  Map of. 34:1-15
  March to. 10:11-12
  Meaning of. 1:1-2:34, Intro.; 5:1-31, Intro.
  Supervisors of. 34:16-29
  Type - Symbol of. Heaven, of spiritual conquest & rest. 34:1-15

PROMISED SEED
  Type - Symbol of. The coming Savior of the world, Christ Jesus Himself. 13:1-14:45, Intro.

PROMISES
  Of God.
    God is faithful, never failing to keep His **p.** 26:4-51, Thgt.1
    God promises to provide all the necessities of life for His dear people. 35:1-8, Thgt.2
    The promise of the promised land. 34:1-15, D.S. #1

PROOF
  Of minister's call. 17:1
  Of the minister. 17:2-5; 17:6-9

PROPERTY (See **LAND**)

PROPHECY
  Concerning Assyria. 24:21-22
  Concerning God's people. 23:1-12
  Concerning the coming Deliverer. 24:14-19
  Concerning the Kenites. 24:21-22
  Concerning victory over enemies. 24:20
  Discussed. Victory over enemies. 24:21-22
  Of God's blessings. 23:27-24:13
  Of Jesus Christ. 24:14-19
  Of judgment. 24:23-35

INDEX – NUMBERS

PROTECT - PROTECTION
Discussed. The promise of God's **p**.
6:22-27; 20:14-22, Thgt.1, Thgt.2
List of Scriptures. Of protection.
6:22-27
Source. God. 6:22-27

PROVERBS, THE BOOK OF
Discussed. Acts of sexual immorality.
25:1-3

PROVISION
Discussed.
    For God's ministers. 35:1-8
    For Levites. 35:1-8
    For murderers. 35:30-34
    Of God.
        Fiery cloud. 9:15-23
        Life's necessities. 35:1-8
        Passover. 9:1-14
        Two silver trumpets. 10:1-10
Picture of. Ministry & of God's provision of necessities for His servants (the Levites). 35:1-8

PSYCHICS
Discussed. Evil of. 22:1-41, Intro.

PUNISH - PUNISHMENT (See **JUDGMENT**)

PUNON
Campsite of Israel. 33:42-43; See RESOURCE Section

PURE - PURITY
Duty. Must live a pure life before God.
5:1-31, Intro.

PURIFICATION
From sin. 31:19-24

Q

QUAIL
Discussed. Amount of **q**. Three feet deep, a whole day's walk in every direction. 11:4-35, esp. v.31
Plague of. 11:4-35, esp. vv.33-34

R

RABBLE, THE
Discussed.
    Stirred up complaining & grumbling.
    11:4-35, esp. v.4
    Who were the **r**.? 11:4-35, esp. v.4

RAM
Sacrifice of. 28:11-15; 28:16-25

RAMESES
Campsite of Israel. 33:5; See RESOURCE Section
Place where Israel departed from Egypt.
33:5

REAPING & SOWING
Example of. Israel's unbelief. 14:26-39

REBEL - REBELLION
Against God.
    Incomplete confession. 14:40-45
    Is condemned. 14:1-10, Thgt.1
    Fatal response of Israel. 14:1-10
    The rebellion of Korah & his allies.
    16:1-15
    Warning against. 19:20-22
Against leaders. Assassination of leaders.
14:1-10, esp. v.10
Against Moses.
    Rebellion of. Korah.
        Blamed Moses for failing to enter the promised land. 16:1-15, esp. v.14
        Craved the priesthood, the power of the High Priest. 16:1-15, esp. v.10
        Opposed the leadership of Moses, wanting to replace him. 16:1-15, esp. vv.3, 13-14
        Wanted the Levites promoted as priests. 16:1-15, esp. vv.3, 7
Discussed. The showdown & judgment of Korah & his allies. 16:16-35
Duty (of believer). Must confess & repent of his sins. 17:10-13, Thgt.1
Judgment of. Purpose of. 16:36-40
Warning.
    Any who grumble or rebel against God or His servant will face judgment.
    17:10-13, Thgt.1
    God judges all rebellion & unauthorized approaches. 16:1-50
    God will not tolerate unbelief & rebellion from any person. 14:1-10, Thgt.1; 17:10-13
    God's judgment against unbelief & rebellion is sure. 16:16-35, Thgt.1
    Will keep any of us out of the promised land. 20:1, Thgt.1

RECONCILE - RECONCILIATION (See **ATONEMENT**)
Source of. Christ secured atonement or reconciliation for man. 28:3-8

RED HEIFER (FEMALE COW)
Instructions for.
    A clean person was to gather up the ashes of the sacrifice & keep them in a clean place outside the camp. 19:1-10, esp. vv.9-10
    Everyone who had anything to do with the sacrifice had to cleanse himself & his clothes. 19:1-10, esp. vv.7-8
    Some blood of the red heifer was to be sprinkled seven times toward the front of the Tabernacle. 19:1-10, esp. v.4
    The priest was to burn some cedar wood, hyssop & scarlet wool with the red heifer. 19:1-10, esp. v.6
    Was to be put to death outside the camp. 19:1-10, esp. v.3
    Was to be unused, that is, an animal that had never been worked with a yoke around it's neck. 19:1-10, esp. v.2
    Was to be wholly burned, all its parts. 19:1-10, esp. v.5
    Was to have no defect or blemish. 19:1-10, esp. v.2
Offering of. 19:1-10
Purpose of. Was established as a permanent law for Israel & for all foreigners among them. 19:1-10, esp. v.10
Sacrifice of. 19:1-10
Type - Symbol of.
    Of cleansing a person defiled by death. 19:1-10
    The cleansing power of Jesus Christ, the power of His sacrifice to cleanse from the defilement of sin & death. 19:1-22, Intro.; 19:1-10

REDEEM - REDEMPTION
Picture of. **R**. Census of the firstborn & their replacement by the Levites. 3:40-51
Price of. 3:40-51

REDEEMER
Meaning of kinsman or **r**. 35:9-29

REFUGE, CITIES OF
Discussed. Provision for all who need refuge from the storms & threats of life. 35:1-34
Location of. 35:9-29
Picture of. Christ, our refuge from the threats & storms of life. 35:9-29
Purpose of. 35:9-29

REHOB
Discussed. The furthest point where the 12 spies went. 13:21
Location of. Town in the vicinity of Laish in upper Galilee. 13:21; D.S. #1
Meaning of. "Broad or open place." 13:21

REJECTION
Against God.
    Fatal response of Israel. 14:1-10
    Warning against. 19:20-22
Against leaders. Assassination of leaders. 14:1-10, esp. v.10

RELATIONSHIPS
Authority of. There has to be a head who has ultimate authority for any organization or body of people to function properly. 30:16, Thgt.1
Between father & children. 30:16
Between man & wife. 30:16
Duty.
    Must stand fast under the banner of God's family. 2:2-33
    Must take one's place under the standard of Christ. 2:2-33

REPENT - REPENTANCE
False **r**.
    Incomplete confession. 14:40-45
Result of. True confession always involves repentance, a turning away from sin to God. 14:40-45, Thgt.1

REPHIDIM
Campsite of Israel. 33:14-15; See RESOURCE Section
Discussed. No water to drink. 33:14-15

RESIST - RESISTANCE
Discussed. Against God's people. 20:14-22

REST, PHYSICAL
Discussed. God promises His people rest, both physical & spiritual **r**. 10:35-36, Thgt.1

REST, SPIRITUAL
Discussed.
    God promises His people rest, both physical & spiritual **r**. 10:35-36, Thgt.1
    The gift of the promised land. 34:1-29
Picture of. Spiritual conquest & rest: taking possession of the promised land. 33:50-56
Type - Symbol of. Christ, our spiritual rest. 28:9-10

INDEX – NUMBERS

RESTITUTION
Discussed.
Law of **r**. 5:5-10
Superiority of **r**. compared to modern criminal law. 5:5-10, Thgt.2
Duty. Must make **r**. 5:5-10, Thgt.1

REUBEN, TRIBE OF
Census of.
1st census. 46,500 fighting men. 1:7-46, esp. v.21
2nd census. 43,730 fighting men. 26:4-51, esp. v.6
Leaders of.
Dathan, Abiram, & On. Co-conspirators with Korah. 16:1-15, esp. v.1
Elizur. Helped with the first census. 1:4-16, esp. v.5
Settlement, east of the Jordan River. 32:1-42
Sins of.
Unbelief, disloyalty, & half-hearted commitment. 32:6-15, esp. vv.8-13
Wanted to sit while others fought to conquer the promised land. 32:6-15
Spy. Shammua. One of the twelve spies. 13:1-25, esp. v.4
Territory of.
Cities rebuilt.
Heshbon, Elealeh, Kiriathaim, Nebo, Baal Meon, Sibmah. 32:28-42, esp. vv.37-38
Lands that had been conquered from Shion, king of the Amorites, & from king Og of Bashan. 32:28-42, esp. v.33
Typed - Pictured - Symbolized. A picture of selfishness, coveteousness, disloyalty: the compromise of Gad & Reuben. 32:1-42

REUEL, SON OF
Family of.
Hobab: brother-in-law of Moses. 10:29-32
Hobab: son of Reuel. 10:29-32, esp. v.29

REVOLT - REVOLTS
Discussed. Caused by. 16:1-15

REWARD - REWARDS
Discussed. For fighting a good warfare. 31:25-54
Example of. A church that follows God's Word. 2:1-2, Thgt.2
Of battle. 31:25-54
Results of. There are rewards in heaven. 31:25-54, Thgt.1

RIGHTEOUSNESS
Typed - Symbolized - Pictured. By the clothing of the High Priest: a symbol of righteousness. 20:23-29

RIGHTS
Discussed. Equal. 27:1-11, Intro.

RIMMON PEREZ
Campsite of Israel. 33:19-20; See RESOURCE Section

RISSAH
Campsite of Israel. 33:21-22; See RESOURCE Section

RITHMAH
Campsite of Israel. 33:18-19

RITUAL UNCLEANNESS (See **CEREMONIAL UNCLEANNESS**)

ROCK
Type - Symbol of. Christ, the source of living water. 20:7-13

ROSH HASHANAH (See **TRUMPETS, FEAST OF**)
Discussed. The beginning of the new year for the Jewish people. 29:1-6

S

SABBATH
Discussed.
Day. Sacrifices on. 28:9-10
The people rested on the Sabbath day, but not the priest. 28:9-10
Duty. Must celebrate our redemption every Sabbath or Sunday. 28:9-10
Importance of. 15:30-36, Thgt.1
Judgment of. Breaking the **S**. Severe judgment. 15:30-36

SACRIFICE - SACRIFICES (See **OFFERINGS**)
Discussed.
A clear command of God. 28:1-2
Importance of the offerings or sacrifices. 28:1-2
S. on the Sabbath Day. 28:9-10
The way to approach God. 7:10-88
Duty. To be presented at the appointed time. 28:1-2
Kinds of.
Animal. 28:1-2; 28:11-15
Burnt Offering. 6:13-20; 28:3-8
Evening **s**. 28:3-8
Grain Offering. 6:13-20; esp. v.15
Guilt Offering. 6:3-12; esp. v.12
Monthly. 28:11-15
Pagan. 22:36-41
Peace or Fellowship Offering. 6:13-20; esp. v.14
Red Heifer. 19:1-10
Sin Offering. 6:3-12
Of Christ.
Cleanses a person defiled by death. 19:1-10
Died as our substitute sacrifice to secure atonement for us. 15:1-16, Thgt.1
Secured atonement or reconciliation for man. 28:3-8
List. Examples of the substitute sacrifice. 7:10-88, Thgt.1
Type - Symbol of.
Christ, the coming Savior & Messiah of the world. 28:1-2, Thgt.1
God's dear Son, the Lord Jesus Christ. 28:1-29:40
Typed - Symbolized - Pictured.
By monthly offerings: A symbol of Christ's sacrifice. 28:11-15
By Red Heifer Offering. Cleansing a person defiled by death. 19:1-10

SAD - SADNESS
Causes of. 20:1-29, Intro.

SALT
Covenant of **s**. 18:8-24, esp. v.19-20

SALVATION
Celebration of. 9:1-14

SATAN
Strategy of. One of the major strategies of **S**. is to arouse criticism against the minister. 12:1-16, Intro.

SECURE - SECURITY
Discussed. The promise of God's **s**. 6:22-27
List of Scriptures. Of security. 6:22-27
Source. God. 6:22-27

SEEK - SEEKING
Of God. 27:5-11

SEPARATION, SPIRITUAL
Discussed.
Purpose for removing the unclean from the camp. 5:1-4
To the LORD. 6:1-2
Duty. Must be totally set apart from the sin & shame of the world. 5:1-4, Thgt.1; 15:37-41
Purpose of.
To stir the believer to live a life of separation from the world. 15:37-41, esp. v.39
To stir the believer to obey all God's commands. 15:37-41, esp. v.40
To stir the believer to remember God's commandments. 15:37-41, esp. v.39

SERVE - SERVANT
Duty.
Must accept the challenge of special ministries. 1:47-54, Thgt.1
Must be constantly seeking a great harvest of souls. 28:26-31, Thgt.1
Must be meek & humble—totally submissive & dependent upon God. 12:1-3, Thgt.1
Must be prepared for spiritual warfare. 26:2-3, Thgt.1
Must be strong & courageous. 13:26-33, Thgt.1
Must be totally set apart from the sin & shame of the world. 5:1-4, Thgt.1
Must be willing to do any work or service. 4:21-28
Must be willing to pour out our lives to God, surrendering ourselves to Him. 15:1-16, Thgt.3
Must bear the mark of being totally committed to God. 6:3-12, Thgt.1
Must bear the mark of holiness & separation to God. 6:3-12, Thgt.1
Must believe God & serve in the army of God. 1:17-46
Must continue to live a life of commitment & holiness before God. 6:13-20, Thgt.1
Must control our minds & think of God throughout the day. 15:37-41, Thgt.1
Must do everything God commands. 2:34
Must fulfill our vows, the promises we make to the LORD. 21:1-3
Must fully destroy the evil, seductive, & immoral enemies of life. 31:14-18, Thgt.1
Must give our tithes & offerings to God. 15:17-21, Thgt.1
Must give to the LORD's work. 7:1-89, Intro.
Must guard against defilement & uncleanness. 19:11-16, Thgt.1
Must have a zeal for living holy, pure, & righteous lives before God. 25:6-13, Thgt.1

Must keep his mind clear & focused totally upon the LORD. 6:3-12, Thgt.1
Must keep our minds focused upon living a holy life throughout the day. 15:37-41, Thgt.1
Must know that God dwells in the midst of His people. 2:1-2
Must know that people are totally defiled. 19:11-16, Thgt.1
Must make concentrated, focused efforts to reach our family for Christ. 10:29-32, Thgt.1
Must pray for & support all leaders, both church & government leaders. 16:16-36, Thgt.1
Must pray for God to raise up leaders, strong leaders who will serve God's people faithfully. 27:14-17, Thgt.1
Must reach out to our family members. 10:29-32, Thgt.1
Must remember & keep God's commandments throughout the day. 15:37-41, Thgt.1
Must seek to serve people, not to hold positions of power. 16:1-15, Thgt.1
Must sound the alarm for prayer. 10:1-10, Thgt.1
Must stand fast under the banner of God's family. 2:2-33
Must support the ministers of God who proclaim the Word of God to us! 17:10-13, Thgt.1
Must take one's place under the standard of Christ. 2:2-33
Must walk together. 5:1-31, Intro.

SERVICE
Dedication. Must be willing to do any work or service. 4:21-28; 4:29-33
Duty of. Must believe God & serve in the army of God. 1:17-46
Importance of. Every believer has his part to play for God. 4:29-33, Thgt.1

SETHUR
Spy from the tribe of Asher. 13:1-25; esp. v.13

SEVEN, THE NUMBER
Type - Symbol of. Full & complete acceptance. 19:1-10, esp. v.4

SEX
Discussed. Age of. 25:1-18, Intro.

SEXUAL IMMORALITY
Discussed. A satanic plot devised by Balaam. 25:1-3
Warning of.
Always causes problems. 5:11-31, Thgt.1
Causes apostasy. 25:1-3

SEXUAL UNFAITHFULNESS
Warning against. A destructive sin. 5:11-31

SHAMMUA
Spy from the tribe of Reuben. 13:1-25; esp. v.4

SHAPHAT
Spy from the tribe of Simeon. 13:1-25; esp. v.5

SHEKINAH GLORY
Discussed.

Is a light so brilliant that no man can approach it. 9:15-23, D.S. #1
Is a light so glorious that there is no need for a sun. 9:15-23, D.S. #1
Is like a consuming fire. 9:15-23, D.S. #1
Is like a light that radiates splendor. 9:15-23, D.S. #1
Is like a pillar that radiates light. 9:15-23, D.S. #1

SHELUMIEL
Leader of tribe of Simeon. 1:4-16; esp. v.6

SHEMUEL
Appointed by Moses as a supervisor of the promised land. 34:16-29
Led the tribe of Simeon into the promised land. 34:16-29

SHEPHER, MOUNT
Campsite of Israel. 33:23-24; See RESOURCE Section

SHIMEITES
Of the Gershonite clan. 3:14-39; esp. v.21

SHITTIM
The plains of Moab, right across from the great city of Jericho. 25:1-3, esp. v.1

SHOWBREAD (See **BREAD, HOLY**)
Type - Symbol of. A symbol of the 12 tribes of Israel or of God's people. 8:1-4, Thgt.1

SIBMAH
Location of. 32:37-38; D.S. #13
Territory of. The tribe of Reuben.
Cities rebuilt.
Heshbon, Elealeh, Kiriathaim, Nebo, Baal Meon, Sibmah 32:28-42, esp. v.37-38

SIHON
King of Amorites. 21:21-32, esp. v.23

SIMEON, TRIBE OF
Census of.
1st census. 59,300 fighting men. 1:17-46; esp. v.23
2nd census. 22,200 fighting men. 26:4-51, esp. v.14
Leaders of. Shelumiel. Helped with the first census. 1:4-16; esp. v.6
Shemuel.
Appointed by Moses as a supervisor of the promised land. 34:16-29
Led the tribe of Simeon into the promised land. 34:16-29
Spy. Shaphat. One of the twelve spies. 13:1-25; esp. v.5

SINAI, DESERT OF (See **DESERTS**)
Place where the Israelites set out on their march to the promised land. 10:11-12

SIN - SINS
Discussed. In ignorance. 15:22-29
Duty. Must be totally set apart from the sin & shame of the world. 5:1-4, Thgt.1
Example of. Moses. 20:7-13

Facts.
Man is enslaved to sin & death. 33:1-56, Intro.
The whole community of believers could be forgiven if they broke the law of God. 15:22-29
We often sin; we cannot keep from sinning. 15:22-29, Thgt.1
Forgiveness of. 15:22-29
Kinds of.
Against one's neighbor. 5:5-10
Attacking God's minister. 12:1-3, Thgt.1
Blasphemy. 15:30-36
Brazen **s**. 15:30-36
Breaking the commandments of God. 25:4-5
Defiant **s**. 15:30-36
Deliberate **s**. 15:30-36
Despising God's Word. 15:30-36
Ignorance. 15:22-29
Irreverence. 25:6-13
National **s**. 15:30-36
Presumptuous **s**. 15:30-36
Sexual. 25:4-5
S. through ignorance. 15:22-29
Unintentional **s**. 15:22-29
Unknown **s**. 15:22-29
Of Israel.
Not trusting God & losing sight of His guidance. 11:1-3
Why God forgave Israel's sins. Prayers of Moses. 14:10-25, esp. vv.13-17
Remedy for.
God forgives sin. 35:30-34, Thgt.1
There is cleansing from sin. 6:3-12, Thgt.2; 19:1-10
True confession always involves repentance, a turning away from sin to God. 14:40-45, Thgt.1
Seriousness of.
God judges sin. 27:14-17, Thgt.1
Must discipline church members who become engaged in serious sin. 5:1-4, Thgt.1
Warning against. 19:20-22

SIN OFFERING, THE
Purpose of.
Was part of the Levites' ceremonial, spiritual cleansing. 9:5-26
Was the worship required after the fulfillment of the Nazarite vow. 6:13-20
Results of.
Cleansing. 6:3-12; esp. v.10
Continual cleansing. 6:13-20; esp. v.14
Type - Symbol of. Christ's sacrifice for the sins of the world. 6:3-12; esp. v.10; 28:11-15, Thgt.1

SMILE
Of God. 6:22-27; esp. v.25

SOCIETY
Problems of.
Bombarded with sex. 25:1-18, Intro.
False worship. 25:1-18, Intro.
Is being taught that all forms of sexual behavior are acceptable. 25:1-18, Intro.

SOLDIERS
Life & walk. Believers are like **s**. walking through the desert & wilderness of this world. 2:2-33, Thgt.1

INDEX – NUMBERS

SORCERY (See **FORTUNE TELLING**)
  Evil of. 22:1-41, Intro.; 22:7-14
  Example of.
    Balaam's false belief in s. 22:1-6
    Balak sought to curse & defeat Israel by pagan divination or sorcery. 22:1-6, esp. vv.4-6
  Warning. God condemns diviners, sorcerers, mystics, or anyone else who preys upon people seeking direction or help. 22:7-14

SOVEREIGN - SOVEREIGNTY
  Of God. God is s., in total control of the universe & all that happens within the universe. 22:36-41, Thgt.1

SPIES, THE TWELVE
  Duty of.
    To bring back samples of the fruit. 13:1-25, esp. v.20
    To check the soil to see if it was fertile or poor, barren or full of trees. 13:1-25, esp. v.20
    To see if the people were strong or weak, few or many. 13:1-25, esp. v.18
    To see if the towns were fortified or unwalled. 13:1-25, esp. v.19
    To see what the land was like, good or bad. 13:1-25, esp. v.19
  Judgment of. Upon the ten unbelieving spies. 14:26-39, esp. vv.36-38
  List of. One man from each tribe. 13:1-25
  Mission of.
    Distance of total mission. About 500 miles. 13:1-25
    Length of mission in days: 40. 13:1-25, esp. v.25
    Spies said nothing about Abraham's relationship to Hebron. 13:1-25
  Report of. 13:26-33

SPIRITISTS (See **PSYCHICS**)

SPIRITUAL CONQUEST
  Discussed. The gift of the promised land. 34:1-29

SPIRITUAL REST (See **REST, SPIRITUAL**)

SPIRITUAL SEPARATION (See **SEPARATION, SPIRITUAL**)

SPIRITUAL VICTORY
  Picture of. Spiritual conquest & rest: taking possession of the promised land. 33:50-56

SPIRITUAL WARFARE
  Warning. Believers must be prepared for w. as they march to the promised land. 1:2-3

SPIRITUAL WORLD
  Warfare of. 22:1-41, Intro.

SPOILS
  Of warfare. 31:25-54
  Picture of.
    Giving thanks to God: Division of the spoils taken from the defeated enemy. 31:25-54
    Rewards for fighting a good warfare: Division of the spoils taken from the defeated enemy. 31:25-54

SPOKE, THE LORD
  Examples of.
    In the desert or wilderness. 1:1
    In the Tent of Meeting. 1:1
  Fact. This phrase is used over 150 times in 20 plus ways in the book of *Numbers*. 1:1

STAFF, AARON'S
  Discussed.
    Placed in Ark. Reason why. 17:10-13
    Sprouted, budded, blossomed, & produced almonds. 17:6-9
  Typed - Symbolized - Pictured.
    By Christ or the minister bearing fruit & bringing life to people. 17:6-9
    By God's power & authority. 17:6-9

STANDING FAST
  Duty.
    Must stand fast under the banner of God's family. 2:2-33
    Must take one's place under the standard of Christ. 2:2-33

STEWARD - STEWARDSHIP
  Duty. To the LORD. 7:1-9
  Of income. 31:25-54

STRANGER
  Meaning of. 3:5-13

STRIFE
  Discussed. The showdown & judgment of Korah & his allies. 16:16-35

SUBMISSION
  Duty. Must be willing to pour out our lives to God, surrendering ourselves to Him. 15:1-16, Thgt.3
  To God. 15:1-16

SUCCOTH
  Campsite of Israel. 33:5-6; See RESOURCE Section
  Place of Israel's first campsite after leaving Egypt. 33:5-6

SUNRISE ON THE TABERNACLE'S ENTRANCE
  Typed - Symbolized - Pictured. By the morning sun rising & shining on the entrance of the Tabernacle, symbolizing the life-giving light of God that shone on His people. 3:14-39

SUPPORT
  Of ministers. 18:8-24

SURRENDER
  Duty. Must be willing to pour out our lives to God, surrendering ourselves to Him. 15:1-16, Thgt.3
  To God. 15:1-16

SUSPICION
  Of sexual unfaithfulness. 5:11-31

SWORD
  Discussed. Balaam immediately saw the angel of the LORD standing with his sword drawn. 22:22-35
  Type - Symbol of. God's anger. 22:22-35

SYMBOL
  Assyria destroying the Kenites: A picture of the greatest fortress of the enemy being defeated. 24:21-22
  Drawn sword: God's anger. 22:22-35

List of. Types, Symbols, & Pictures in the book of *Numbers*. Introductory Material: Alphabetical & Chronological Indexes
  Of Christ, our Refuge. 35:9-29
  Of Christ's sacrifice: Monthly Offerings. 28:11-15
  Of Christ's sacrifice: Red Heifer. 19:1-10
  Of dedication. Grain Offering. 15:1-16
  Of salvation. The day the march to the promised land began. 10:11-12
  Of submission. Drink Offering. 15:1-16
  Of spiritual conquest & rest. 34:1-29
  Of the lampstand: Christ, the Light of the world. 8:1-4
  The promised land. 1:1-2:34, Intro.; 10:11-36
  The promised seed. The coming Savior of the world, Christ Jesus Himself. 13:1-14:45, Intro.
  The third prophecy of Balaam: a picture of how God blesses His people. 23:27-24:14

T

TABERAH
  Campsite of Israel. 11:1-3; esp. v.3
  Meaning of. Burning, a place of awful judgment. 11:1-3, esp. v.3

TABERNACLE
  Chart.
    Marching position of the tribes. 2:2-33, note 10
    Placement of. 2:2-33, note 10
  Dedication of. 7:1-9
  Meaning of the word **T**. 1:1
  Picture of. 1-2, note 9
  Placement of. 2:2-33
  Protection of. The Levites: to take charge of the Tabernacle. 1:47-54
  Type - Symbol of. The church. 1:47-54

TABERNACLES, FEAST OF (See **TABERNACLES, FESTIVAL OF**)
  Discussed.
    Eventually became known as Rosh Hashanah, the beginning of the new year for the Jewish people. 29:1-6
    Was held for eight consecutive days beginning on the fifteenth day of the seventh month. 29:12, 35

TABERNACLES, FESTIVAL OF (See **TABERNACLES, FEAST OF**)
  Discussed. Was held for eight consecutive days beginning on the fifteenth day of the seventh month. 29:12, 35

TAHATH
  Campsite of Israel. 33:26-27; See RESOURCE Section

TEMPT - TEMPTATION
  Victory over. God gives victory over the temptations & trials of life. 24:20, Thgt.1

TENDER - TENDERNESS
  Of God. 20:23-29, Thgt.1

TENT PEG
  Discussed. Importance of. 4:29-33

INDEX – NUMBERS

TERAH
  Campsite of Israel. 33:27-28; See RESOURCE Section
TEST
  Of minister. 17:1
TESTIFY - TESTIMONY
  To family members. 10:29-32
THANKS - THANKSGIVING
  Duty. Must make an offering of thanksgiving to God. 31:25-54, Thgt.1
  To God. 15:1-16; 31:25-54
THOUGHTS - THOUGHT LIFE
  Duty.
    Must concentrate. 15:37-41
    Must control our minds & think of God throughout the day. 15:37-41, Thgt.1
    Must keep our minds focused upon living a holy life throughout the day. 15:37-41, Thgt.1
    Must protect. 15:37-41
TITHE - TITHING
  Discussed. Levites were to receive all the tithes given to the work of God. 18:8-24
  Duty. Must give our tithes & offerings to God. 15:17-21, Thgt.1
  Of ministers. 18:25-32
  Picture of. Tithing one's income to the LORD as well as other offerings. 15:17-21
TREATMENT
  Discussed. Fair. Need for. 27:1-11, Intro.
TRESPASS
  Meaning of. 5:5-10
TRIALS
  Fact. God gives victory over the temptations & trials of life. 24:20, Thgt.1
TRIBES OF ISRAEL
  Leaders of. Leaders chosen from the **T**. 1:4-16
TRIUMPH
  Fact. God gives victory over the temptations & trials of life. 24:20, Thgt.1
  Over enemies. 21:1-3; 21:33-35; 24:21-22
TRUMPETS, FEAST OF
  Discussed. Was held on the first day of the seventh month. 29:1-6, esp. v.1
  Purpose of.
    To arouse the people to trust God more & more. 29:1-6
    To proclaim the message of joy for the atonement or reconciliation with God. 29:1-6
  Type - Symbol of. Salvation & of the rapture. 29:1-6
TRUMPETS, FESTIVAL OF
  Discussed. Was held on the first day of the seventh month. 29:1-6, esp. v.1
  Purpose of.
    To arouse the people to trust God more & more. 29:1-6
    To proclaim the message of joy for the atonement or reconciliation with God. 29:1-6
  Type - Symbol of. Salvation & of the rapture. 29:1-6
TRUMPETS, TWO SILVER
  Discussed.
    Made of hammered silver. 10:1-10, esp. v.2
    Three general purposes for the trumpets. 10:1-10, esp. v.3-7
    Three very special purposes for the trumpets. 10:1-10, esp. v.9-10
  Fact. Only the priests, the true sons of Aaron, were allowed to blow the trumpets. 10:1-10, esp. v.8
  Purpose of.
    To blow in times of joy & rejoicing. 10:1-10, esp. v.10
    To call general assemblies together. 10:1-10, esp. v.3
    To call only the leaders together. 10:1-10, esp. v.4
    To signal the tribes when to begin marching. 10:1-10, esp. v.5-7
    To sound the alarm for prayer. 10:1-10, esp. v.9
    To sound the alarm for war. 10:1-10, esp. v.9
  Type - Symbol of. God's call to arise & follow Him. 10:1-10

U

UNAUTHORIZED FIRE (See **FIRE**)
UNBELIEF
  Discussed.
    Difficult to understand. 16:41-50, Thgt.1
    How children follow in the footsteps of their parents. 20:2-6
  Example of.
    Report of the twelve spies. 13:26-33
    The rebellion of Korah & his allies. 16:1-15
  Judgment of. 16:16-35
  Of believers. Example of. 33:5-49
  Of Israel. 11:1-3; 11:4-35; 14:1-10; 16:41-50
  Warning.
    God judges all grumbling & unbelief. 16:1-50
    God will not tolerate unbelief & rebellion from any person. 14:1-10, Thgt.1
    God's judgment against unbelief & rebellion is sure. 16:16-35, Thgt.1
    Will keep any of us out of the promised land. 20:1, Thgt.1
UNBELIEVER - UNBELIEVERS
  Duty. Must investigate the promised land. 13:1-25, Thgt.2
UNBIASED
  Discussed. Need for being. 27:1-11, Intro.
UNCLEAN - UNCLEANNESS
  Cause of. 19:11-16
  Ceremonial **u**. 5:1-4; Nu. 6:3-12
  Discussed.
    Ritual **u**. 5:1-4; Nu. 6:3-12
    Spiritual **u**. 5:1-4; Nu. 6:3-12
    Warning against. 19:20-22
    Why an unclean person was removed from the camp. 5:1-4; esp. v.3
  Facts.
    Man is unclean just by being born & living in a corruptible world. 19:11-16
    There is cleansing from sin. 6:3-12, Thgt.2
  Meaning of. A person with leprosy or a contagious skin disease or discharge. 5:1-4; esp. v.2
  Warning.
    The judgment of God is going to fall upon every unclean & defiled person. 19:20-22, Thgt.1
    The possessions & things of this world can defile & make a person unclean. 31:19-24, Thgt.1
UNINTENTIONAL SIN (See **SIN**)
UNITY
  Discussed. How God's people stay united & pure. 5:1-31, Intro.
  Duty. Must walk together. 5:1-31, Intro.
UNIVERSE
  Discussed. God is sovereign, in total control of the **u**. & all that happens within the **u**. 22:36-41, Thgt.1
UNLEAVENED BREAD, FESTIVAL OF
  Discussed. Passover was tied in to the Festival of Unleavened Bread. 28:16-25
URIM
  Purpose of. A sacred lot that was to be utilized in seeking God's will. 27:18-23, esp. v.21
  Type - Symbol of. The High Priest seeking the will of God for the people.
UZZIELITES
  Of the Kohathite clan. 3:14-39, esp. v.27

V

VENGEANCE
  Of God. 31:1-6
VICTORY
  Assurance of. 10:35-36
  Discussed.
    God gives us the victory over the evil, seductive, & immoral enemies of this life. 31:7-13, Thgt.1
    God gives us victory over persecution. 24:20, Thgt.1
    God gives victory over all the evil powers & rulers of darkness, over all the spiritual wickedness that attacks us. 24:20, Thgt.1
    God gives victory over any person or any thing in this world & in the spiritual world. 24:20, Thgt.1
    God gives victory over death. 24:20, Thgt.1
    God gives victory over the evil of men, over evil men who oppose us & stand as enemies against us. 24:20, Thgt.1
    God gives victory over the temptations & trials of life. 24:20, Thgt.1
    God gives victory over the world with all its enslavements & bondages. 24:20, Thgt.1
  Kind of.
    Military. 21:21-32
    Over enemies of life. 7:1-89, Intro.; 21:1-3; 21:21-32; 21:33-35; 24:20; 24:21-22; 31:7-13
    Spiritual. 33:50-56

INDEX – NUMBERS

VINDICATE - VINDICATION
Of the minister. 17:1; 17:2-5; 17:6-9

VOW - VOWS (See **COMMIT - COMMITMENTS**)
Discussed.
  Laws that govern vows. 30:1-16; 30:6-8
  Reasons for making. 21:1-35, Intro.
  Spouses must consider one another in making vows & pledges. 30:6-8; 30:10-15
  Three special obligations of the Nazarite vow. 6:3-12
Duty.
  Must fulfill our vows, the promises we make to the LORD. 21:1-3
  Must keep our commitments. 30:1-16, Intro.
  Must not be broken. 30:1-2
Fulfillment of. 6:13-20
Importance of. 30:1-2
Kind of.
  By children. 30:3-5
  By married women. 30:10-15
  By single women. 30:3-5
  By the divorced. 30:9
  By widows. 30:9
  Nazarite v. 6:1-27, Intro
Seriousness of. All vows are serious to God. 6:21, Thgt.1

W

WALK, SPIRITUAL
Duty. To have a closer walk with the Lord. 6:1-2
Life & walk. The believer's walk. 21:10-20

WAR - WARS
Of the Israelites.
  Conquest of the Midianites. 31:1-6
  Were defeated by the Amalekites & Canaanites. 14:40-45

WARFARE
Results of. Defiled a soldier. 31:19-24

WARFARE, SPIRITUAL
Duty. Must be prepared for spiritual warfare. 26:2-3, Thgt.1
Fact. Believers must be prepared for w. as they march to the promised land. 1:2-3
Picture of. The military census. The people of God preparing for warfare. 26:2-3, Thgt.1

WARN - WARNING
Discussed.
  Against grumbling & rebellion. 17:10-13
  Against having a hard heart, a stubborn will. 16:41-50, Thgt.1
  Against rejection. 19:20-22
  Every one of us will stand before God & give an account. 26:63-65, Thgt.1
  Example of the death of Aaron's sons. 3:1-4, Thgt.2
  Greed & covetousness actually plunge men into destruction & doom. 22:15-22, Thgt.1
  Hardness of heart condemns a person. 22:22-35, Thgt.1
  Having one's name written on the roll does not guarantee entrance into the promised land. 26:4-51, Thgt.1
  Leaders of the occult doom people to an eternity of separation from God in the judgment to come. 22:22-35
Duty. Must escape the evil of the Israelites. 15:1-25:18, Division Overview
Of God. 22:7-14; 22:36-41; 33:50-56
Of God's power. 17:10-13
Of judgment.
  Purpose of. 16:36-40
  The judgment of God is coming. 31:1-6, Thgt.1
Warning.
  God condemns diviners, sorcerers, mystics, or anyone else who preys upon people seeking direction or help. 22:7-14
  God hears everything. 11:1-3, esp. v.2
  God judges all grumbling & unbelief. 16:1-50
  God judges all rebellion & unauthorized approaches. 16:1-50
  God judges & chastises His people when they sin. 14:10-25, Thgt.1
  God warns a person against compromise. 32:1-5, Thgt.1
  God warns us against comfort & ease. 32:6-15, Thgt.1
  God will judge every human being who has ever lived. 14:26-39, Thgt.1
  God will judge the nations of this earth. 24:23-35, Thgt.1
  God will judge the people of this earth, individual by individual. 24:23-35
  God will not tolerate unbelief & rebellion from any person. 14:1-10, Thgt.1

WASH - WASHING
Type - Symbol of. Being spiritually, ceremonially cleansed. 8:5-26

WATER
Discussed. Grumbling over. 20:2-6

WAVE OFFERING
Purpose of. Was a part of the support & income of the priest. 18:8-24, esp. v.11

WEEKS, FEAST OF (See **HARVEST, FESTIVAL OF**)

WIDOWS
Vows or pledges of. 30:9

WIFE
Discussed. Law controlling suspicion of unfaithfulness. 5:11-31

WILDERNESS WANDERINGS, THE
Discussed. Feast or festival of Tabernacles. 29:12-38
Fact. Would never have taken place but for one thing: unbelief. 33:5-49, Thgt.1
Failure during. 33:5-49
Judgment of. To spend 40 years in the desert. 14:26-39
Review of. 33:1-4

WINE
Duty: Must abstain from all intoxicating drink. 6:3-12; esp. v.3-4
When the Nazarite could drink wine. 6:13-20; esp. v.20

WINE OFFERINGS
Discussed. The first mention in Scripture that wine o. were to be offered with all Burnt Offerings & Peace or Fellowship Offerings. 15:1-16

WITCHCRAFT (See **FORTUNE TELLING**)

WITNESS - WITNESSING
Duty.
  Must make concentrated, focused efforts to reach our family for Christ. 10:29-32, Thgt.1
  Must reach out to our family members. 10:29-32, Thgt.1
To Christ. 29:1-6
To family members. 10:29-32

WOMEN
Discussed.
  Courage of. The five daughters of Zelophehad. 27:1-2
  W. who inherited property. 36:1-13; 36:5-9
Duties of. To keep vows. 30:6-8
Married. Pledges of. 30:10-15

WORD OF GOD
Provision of. God guides His people through His precious Holy Word. 26:1, Thgt.1; 36:13, Thgt.1
Purpose. 26:1

WORK
Kinds of. God's w. 7:1-88

WORLD, THE
Discussed. What is the destiny of the w.? 10:11-36, Intro.

WORLDLINESS (See **CORRUPTION**)
Warning. Compromising with worldliness can destroy a person. 32:1-42, Intro.

WORSHIP
Discussed. Question: what were the w. services like? 7:1-88
False w. The immoral & false worshippers were immediately judged. 25:4-5
List. A worship service:
  Of acknowledging God's great gift of the atonement, of the forgiveness of sin & of fellowship & peace with Him. 7:1-88
  Of deep dedication & commitment. 7:1-88
  Of joy & rejoicing. 7:1-88
  Of meaning, significance, & purpose. 7:1-88
  Of pomp & ceremony, of majesty & glory, of pageantry & celebration. 7:1-88
Type - Symbol of. The Tabernacle & its w. symbolized the coming of the Savior of the world & His great sacrifice upon the cross.

WORSHIP, FALSE (See **FALSE WORSHIPPERS**)

Y

YEAST
Type - Symbol of. Sin, corruption, or worldliness. 28:16-25, Thgt.1

YOM KIPPUR (See **DAY OF ATONEMENT**)
Discussed. Festival of. 29:7-11

OUTLINE BIBLE RESOURCES

This material, like similar works, has come from imperfect man and is thus susceptible to human error. We are nevertheless grateful to God for both calling us and empowering us through His Holy Spirit to undertake this task. Because of His goodness and grace, *The Preacher's Outline & Sermon Bible*® New Testament is complete and the Old Testament volumes are releasing periodically.

The Minister's Personal Handbook and other helpful **Outline Bible Resources** are available in printed form as well as releasing electronically on WORDsearch software.

God has given the strength and stamina to bring us this far. Our confidence is that as we keep our eyes on Him and grounded in the undeniable truths of the Word, we will continue working through the Old Testament volumes. The future includes other helpful Outline Bible Resources for God's dear servants to use in their Bible Study and discipleship.

We offer this material first to Him in whose Name we labor and serve and for whose glory it has been produced and, second, to everyone everywhere who preaches and teaches the Word.

Our daily prayer is that each volume will lead thousands, millions, yes even billions, into a better understanding of the Holy Scriptures and a fuller knowledge of Jesus Christ the Incarnate Word, of whom the Scriptures so faithfully testify.

> You will be pleased to know that Leadership Ministries Worldwide partners with Christian organizations, printers, and mission groups around the world to make Outline Bible Resources available and affordable in many countries and foreign languages. It is our goal that *every* leader around the world, both clergy and lay, will be able to understand God's Holy Word and present God's message with more clarity, authority, and understanding—all beyond his or her own power.

LEADERSHIP MINISTRIES WORLDWIDE
PO Box 21310 • Chattanooga, TN 37424-0310
423) 855-2181 • FAX (423) 855-8616
info@outlinebible.org
www.outlinebible.org - FREE Download materials

LEADERSHIP MINISTRIES WORLDWIDE
Publishers of Outline Bible Resources

Currently Available Materials, with New Volumes Releasing Regularly

- **THE PREACHER'S OUTLINE & SERMON BIBLE® (POSB)**

NEW TESTAMENT

Matthew I (chapters 1–15)	1 & 2 Corinthians
Matthew II (chapters 16–28)	Galatians, Ephesians, Philippians, Colossians
Mark	1 & 2 Thessalonians, 1 & 2 Timothy, Titus, Philemon
Luke	Hebrews, James
John	1 & 2 Peter, 1, 2, & 3 John, Jude
Acts	Revelation
Romans	Master Outline & Subject Index

OLD TESTAMENT

Genesis I (chapters 1–11)	1 Kings	Isaiah 2 (chapters 36-66)
Genesis II (chapters 12–50)	2 Kings	Jeremiah 1 (chapters 1-29)
Exodus I (chapters 1–18)	1 Chronicles	Jeremiah 2 (chapters 30-52),
Exodus II (chapters 19–40)	2 Chronicles	Lamentations
Leviticus	Ezra, Nehemiah, Esther	Ezekiel
Numbers	Job	Daniel, Hosea
Deuteronomy	Psalms 1 (chapters 1-41)	Joel, Amos, Obadiah, Jonah,
Joshua	Psalms 2 (chapters 42-106)	Micah, Nahum
Judges, Ruth	Proverbs	Habakkuk, Zephaniah, Haggai,
1 Samuel	Ecclesiastes, Song of Solomon	Zechariah, Malachi
2 Samuel	Isaiah 1 (chapters 1-35)	*New volumes release periodically*

KJV Available in Deluxe 3-Ring Binders or Softbound Edition • NIV Available in Softbound Only

- **The Preacher's Outline & Sermon Bible New Testament — 3 Vol. Hardcover • KJV – NIV**

- ***What the Bible Says to the Believer* — The Believer's Personal Handbook**
  11 Chs. – Over 500 Subjects, 300 Promises, & 400 Verses Expounded - Italian Imitation Leather or Paperback

- ***What the Bible Says to the Minister* — The Minister's Personal Handbook**
  12 Chs. - 127 Subjects - 400 Verses Expounded - Italian Imitation Leather or Paperback

- **Practical Word Studies In the New Testament — 2 Vol. Hardcover Set**

- **The Teacher's Outline & Study Bible™ - Various New Testament Books**
  Complete 30 - 45 minute lessons – with illustrations and discussion questions

- **Practical Illustrations — Companion to the POSB**
  Arranged by topic and Scripture reference

- **What the Bible Says Series – Various Subjects**
  Prayer • The Passion • The Ten Commandments • The Tabernacle

- **Software – Various products powered by WORDsearch**
  New Testament • Pentateuch • History • Prophets • Practical Word Studies • Various Poetry/Wisdom

- **Topical Sermons Series – Available online only**
  7 sermons per series • Sermons are from The Preacher's Outline & Sermon Bible

- **Non-English Translations of various books**
  Included languages are: Russian – Spanish – Korean – Hindi – Chinese – Bulgarian – Romanian – Malayalam – Nepali – Italian – Arabic
  - Future: French, Portuguese

— *Contact LMW for Specific Language Availability and Prices* —

For quantity orders and information, please contact:
LEADERSHIP MINISTRIES WORLDWIDE or Your Local Christian Bookstore
PO Box 21310 • Chattanooga, TN 37424-0310
(423) 855-2181 (9am – 5pm Eastern) • FAX (423) 855-8616
E-mail - info@outlinebible.org Order online at www.outlinebible.org

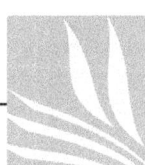# LEADERSHIP MINISTRIES WORLDWIDE

PURPOSE STATEMENT

LEADERSHIP MINISTRIES WORLDWIDE exists to equip ministers, teachers, and laymen in their understanding, preaching, and teaching of God's Word by publishing and distributing worldwide *The Preacher's Outline & Sermon Bible®* and related **Outline Bible Resources**; to reach & disciple men, women, boys and girls for Jesus Christ.

MISSION STATEMENT

1. To make the Bible so understandable – its truth so clear and plain – that men and women everywhere, whether teacher or student, preacher or hearer, can grasp its message and receive Jesus Christ as Savior, and…

2. To place the Bible in the hands of all who will preach and teach God's Holy Word, verse by verse, precept by precept, regardless of the individual's ability to purchase it.

The **Outline Bible Resources** have been given to LMW for printing and especially distribution worldwide at/below cost, by those who remain anonymous. One fact, however, is as true today as it was in the time of Christ:

THE GOSPEL IS FREE, BUT THE COST OF TAKING IT IS NOT

LMW depends on the generous gifts of believers with a heart for Him and a love for the lost. They help pay for the printing, translating, and distributing of **Outline Bible Resources** into the hands of God's servants worldwide, who will present the Gospel message with clarity, authority, and understanding beyond their own.

LMW was incorporated in the state of Tennessee in July 1992 and received IRS 501 (c)(3) nonprofit status in March 1994. LMW is an international, nondenominational mission organization. All proceeds from USA sales, along with donations from donor partners, go directly to underwrite our translation and distribution projects of **Outline Bible Resources** to preachers, church and lay leaders, and Bible students around the world.

www.ingramcontent.com/pod-product-compliance
Lightning Source LLC
Chambersburg PA
CBHW080723300426
44114CB00019B/2476